T5-CCL-500

THE OFFICIAL®
1996 PRICE GUIDE TO

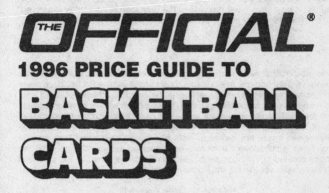

BASKETBALL CARDS

BY
DR. JAMES BECKETT

FIFTH EDITION

HOUSE OF COLLECTIBLES • NEW YORK

Important Notice: All of the information, including valuations, in this book has
been compiled from the most reliable sources, and every effort has been made
to eliminate errors and questionable data. Nevertheless, the possibility of error
in a work of such scope always exists. The publisher will not be held responsible for losses which may occur in the purchase, sale or other transaction of
items because of information contained herein. Readers who feel they have
discovered errors are invited to write and inform us, so that they may be
corrected in subsequent editions. Those seeking further information on the
topics covered in this book are advised to refer to the complete line of *Official
Price Guides* published by the House of Collectibles.

© 1995 by James Beckett III

All rights reserved under International
and Pan-American Copyright Conventions.

H This is a registered trademark of Random House, Inc.

Published by:
House of Collectibles
201 East 50th Street
New York, New York 10022

Distributed by Ballantine Books, a division of Random House, Inc.,
New York, and simultaneously in Canada by
Random House of Canada Limited, Toronto

Manufactured in the United States of America

ISSN: 1062-6980

ISBN: 0-876-37970-6

Fifth Edition: December 1995

10 9 8 7 6 5 4 3 2 1

Table of Contents

About the Author

Jim Beckett, the leading authority on sport card values in the United States, maintains a wide range of activities in the world of sports. He possesses one of the finest collections of sports cards and autographs in the world, has made numerous appearances on radio and television, and has been frequently cited in many national publications. He was awarded the first "Special Achievement Award" for Contributions to the Hobby by the National Sports Collectors Convention in 1980, the "Jock-Jaspersen Award" for Hobby Dedication in 1983, and the "Buck Barker, Spirit of the Hobby Award" in 1991.

Dr. Beckett is the author of *Beckett Baseball Card Price Guide, The Official Price Guide to Baseball Cards, The Sport Americana Price Guide to Baseball Collectibles, The Sport Americana Baseball Memorabilia and Autograph Price Guide, Beckett Football Card Price Guide, The Official Price Guide to Football Cards, Beckett Hockey Card Price Guide, The Official Price Guide to Hockey Cards, Beckett Basketball Card Price Guide, The Official Price Guide to Basketball Cards,* and *The Sport Americana Baseball Card Alphabetical Checklist.* In addition, he is the founder, publisher, and editor of *Beckett Baseball Card Monthly, Beckett Basketball Monthly, Beckett Football Card Monthly, Beckett Hockey Monthly, Beckett Future Stars, Beckett Tribute,* and *Beckett Racing Monthly* magazines.

Jim Beckett received his Ph.D. in Statistics from Southern Methodist University in 1975. Prior to starting Beckett Publications in 1984, Dr. Beckett served as an Associate Professor of Statistics at Bowling Green State University and as a Vice President of a consulting firm in Dallas, Texas. He currently resides in Dallas with his wife, Patti, and their daughters, Christina, Rebecca, and Melissa.

How to Use This Book

Isn't it great? Every year this book gets bigger and bigger with all the new sets coming out. But even more exciting is that every year there are more attractive choices and, subsequently, more interest in the cards we love so much. This edition has been enhanced and expanded from the previous edition. The cards you collect — who appears on them, what they look like, where they are from, and (most important to most of you) what their current values are — are enumerated within. Many of the features contained in the other *Beckett Price Guides* have been incorporated into this volume since condition grading, terminology, and many other aspects of collecting are common to the card hobby in general. We hope you find the book both interesting and useful in your collecting pursuits.

The Beckett Guide has been successful where other attempts have failed because it is complete, current, and valid. This Price Guide contains not just one, but three prices by condition for all the basketball cards listed. These account for most of the basketball cards in existence. The prices were added to the card lists just prior to printing and reflect not the author's opinions or desires but the going retail prices for each card, based on the marketplace (sports memorabilia conventions and shows, sports card shops, hobby papers, current mail-order catalogs, local club meetings, auction results, and other firsthand reportings of actually realized prices).

What is the best price guide available on the market today? Of course card sellers will prefer the price guide with the highest prices, while card buyers will naturally prefer the one with the lowest prices. Accuracy, however, is the true test. Use the price guide used by more collectors and dealers than all the others combined. Look for the Beckett name. I won't put my name on anything I won't stake my reputation on. Not the lowest and not the highest — but the most accurate, with integrity.

To facilitate your use of this book, read the complete introductory section on the following pages before going to the pricing pages. Every collectible field has its own terminology; we've tried to capture most of these terms and definitions in our glossary. Please read carefully the section on grading and the condition of your cards, as you will not be able to determine which price column is appropriate for a given card without first knowing its condition.

Introduction

Welcome to the exciting world of sports card collecting, one of America's most popular avocations. You have made a good choice in buying this book, since it will open up to you the entire panorama of this field in the simplest, most concise way.

The growth of *Beckett Baseball Card Monthly, Beckett Basketball Monthly, Beckett Football Card Monthly, Beckett Hockey Monthly, Beckett Future Stars,* and *Beckett Racing Monthly* is another indication of the unprecedented popularity of sports cards. Founded in 1984 by Dr. James Beckett, the author of this Price Guide, *Beckett Baseball Card Monthly* contains the most extensive and accepted monthly Price Guide, collectible glossy superstar covers, colorful feature articles, "Hot List," Convention Calendar, tips for beginners, "Readers Write" letters to and responses from the editor, information on errors and varieties, autograph collecting tips and profiles of the sport's Hottest stars. Published every month, *BBCM* is the hobby's largest paid circulation periodical. The other five magazines were built on the success of *BBCM*.

So collecting sports cards — while still pursued as a hobby with youthful exuberance by kids in the neighborhood — has also taken on the trappings of an industry, with thousands of full- and part-time card dealers, as well as vendors of supplies, clubs and conventions. In fact, each year since 1980 thousands of hobbyists have assembled for a National Sports Collectors Convention, at which hundreds of dealers have displayed their wares, seminars have been conducted, autographs penned by sports notables, and millions of cards changed hands.

The Beckett Guide is the best annual guide available to the exciting world of basketball cards. Read it and use it. May your enjoyment and your card collection increase in the coming months and years.

How to Collect

Each collection is personal and reflects the individuality of its owner. There are no set rules on how to collect cards. Since card collecting is a hobby or leisure pastime, what you collect, how much you collect, and how much time and money you spend collecting are entirely up to you. The funds you have available for collecting and your own personal taste should determine how you collect. The information and ideas presented here are intended to help you get the most enjoyment from this hobby.

It is impossible to collect every card ever produced. Therefore, beginners as well as intermediate and advanced collectors usually specialize in some way. One of the reasons this hobby is popular is that individual collectors can define and tailor their collecting methods to match their own tastes. To give you some ideas of the various approaches to collecting, we will list some of the more popular areas of specialization.

Many collectors select complete sets from particular years. For example, they may concentrate on assembling complete sets from all the years since their birth or since they became avid sports fans. They may try to collect a card for every player during that specified period of time. Many others wish to acquire only certain players. Usually such players are the superstars of the sport, but occasionally collectors will specialize in all the cards of players who attended a particular college or came from a certain town. Some collectors are only interested in the first cards or Rookie Cards of certain players.

Another fun way to collect cards is by team. Most fans have a favorite team, and it is natural for that loyalty to be translated into a desire for cards of the players on that favorite team. For most of the recent years, team sets (all the cards from a given team for that year) are readily available at a reasonable price. *The Sport Americana Team Football* and *Basketball Card Checklist* will open up this field to the collector.

Obtaining Cards

Several avenues are open to card collectors. Cards still can be purchased in the traditional way: by the pack at the local discount, grocery or convenience stores. But there are also thousands of card shops across the country that specialize in selling cards individually or by the pack, box, or set. Another alternative is the thousands of card shows held each month around the country, which feature anywhere from five to 800 tables of sports cards and memorabilia for sale.

For many years, it has been possible to purchase complete sets of cards through mail-order advertisers found in traditional sports media publications, such as *The Sporting News, Football Digest, Street & Smith* yearbooks, and others. These sets also are advertised in the card collecting periodicals. Many collectors will begin by subscribing to at least one of the hobby periodicals, all with good up-to-date information. In fact, subscription offers can be found in the advertising section of this book.

Most serious card collectors obtain old (and new) cards from one or more of several main sources: (1) trading or buying from other collectors or dealers; (2) responding to sale or auction ads in the hobby publications; (3) buying at a local hobby store; and/or (4) attending sports collectibles shows or conventions.

We advise that you try all four methods since each has its own distinct advantages: (1) trading is a great way to make new friends; (2) hobby periodicals help you keep up with what's going on in the hobby (including when and where the conventions are happening); (3) stores provide the opportunity to enjoy personalized service and consider a great diversity of material in a relaxed sports-oriented atmosphere; and (4) shows allow you to choose from multiple dealers and thousands of cards under one roof in a competitive situation.

Preserving Your Cards

Cards are fragile. They must be handled properly in order to retain their value. Careless handling can easily result in creased or bent cards. It is, however, not recommended that tweezers or tongs be used to pick up your cards since such utensils might mar or indent card surfaces and thus reduce those cards' conditions and values. In general, your cards should be handled directly as little as possible. This is sometimes easier to say than to do.

Although there are still many who use custom boxes, storage trays, or even shoe boxes, plastic sheets are the preferred method of many collectors for storing cards. A collection stored in plastic pages in a three-ring album allows you to view your collection at any time without the need to touch the card itself. Cards can also be kept in single holders (of various types and thickness) designed for the enjoyment of each card individually. For a large collection, some collectors may use a combination of the above methods. When purchasing plastic sheets for your cards, be sure that you find the pocket size that fits the cards snugly. Don't put your 1969-70 Topps in a sheet designed to fit 1992-93 Topps.

Most hobby and collectibles shops and virtually all collectors' conventions will have these plastic pages available in quantity for the various sizes offered, or you can purchase them directly from the advertisers in this book. Also, remember that pocket size isn't the only factor to consider when looking for plastic sheets. Other factors such as safety, economy, appearance, availability, or personal preference also may indicate which types of sheets a collector may want to buy.

Damp, sunny and/or hot conditions — no, this is not a weather forecast — are three elements to avoid in extremes if you are interested in preserving your collection. Too much (or too little) humidity can cause gradual deterioration of a card. Direct, bright sun (or fluorescent light) over time will bleach out the color of a card. Extreme heat accelerates the decomposition of the card. On the other hand, many cards have lasted more than 50 years without much scientific intervention. So be cautious, even if the above factors typically present a problem only when present in the extreme. It never hurts to be prudent.

Collecting vs. Investing

Collecting individual players and collecting complete sets are both popular vehicles for investment and speculation. Most investors and speculators stock up on complete sets or on quantities of players they think have good investment potential.

There is obviously no guarantee in this book, or anywhere else for that matter, that cards will outperform the stock market or other investment alternatives in the future. After all, basketball cards do not pay quarterly dividends and cards cannot be sold at their "current values" as easily as stocks or bonds.

Nevertheless, investors have noticed a favorable long-term trend in the past performance of sports collectibles, and certain cards and sets have outperformed just about any other investment in some years. Many hobbyists maintain that the best investment is and always will be the building of a collection, which traditionally has held up better than outright speculation.

Some of the obvious questions are: Which cards? When to buy? When to sell? The best investment you can make is in your own education. The more you know about your collection and the hobby, the more informed the decisions you will be able to make. We're not selling investment tips. We're selling information about the current value of basketball cards. It's up to you to use that information to your best advantage.

Glossary/Legend

Our glossary defines terms frequently used in the card collecting hobby. Many of these terms are also common to other types of sports memorabilia collecting. Some terms may have several meanings depending on use and context.

ABA - American Basketball Association.

ACC - Accomplishment.

ACO - Assistant Coach Card.

AL - Active Leader.

ART - All-Rookie Team.

AS - All-Star.

ASA - All-Star Advice.

ASW - All-Star Weekend.

AUTO - Autograph.

AW - Award Winner.

BC - Bonus Card.

BRICK - A group or "lot" or cards, usually 50 or more having common characteristics, that is intended to be bought, sold, or traded as a unit.

BT - Beam Team or Breakaway Threats.

CBA - Continental Basketball Association.

CL - Checklist card. A card that lists in order the cards and players in the set or series. Older checklist cards in Mint condition that have not been checked off are very desirable and command large premiums.

CO - Coach card.

COIN - A small disc of metal or plastic portraying a player in its center.

COLLECTOR - A person who engages in the hobby of collecting cards primarily for his own enjoyment, with any profit motive being secondary.

COMBINATION CARD - A single card depicting two or more players (not including team cards).

COMMON CARD - The typical card of any set; it has no premium value accruing from subject matter, numerical scarcity, popular demand, or anomaly.

CONVENTION ISSUE - A set produced in conjunction with a sports collectibles convention to commemorate or promote the show. Most recent convention issues could also be classified as promo sets.

COR - Corrected card. A version of an error card that was fixed by the manufacturer.

COUPON - See Tab.

DEALER - A person who engages in buying, selling, and trading sports collectibles or supplies. A dealer may also be a collector, but as a dealer, he anticipates a profit.

DIE-CUT - A card with part of its stock partially cut for ornamental reasons.

DISC - A circular-shaped card.

DISPLAY SHEET - A clear, plastic page that is punched for insertion into a binder (with standard three-ring spacing) containing pockets for displaying cards. Many different styles of sheets exist with pockets of varying sizes to hold the many differing card formats. The vast majority of current cards measure 2 1/2 by 3 1/2 inches and fit in nine-pocket sheets.

DP - Double Print. A card that was printed in approximately double the quantity compared to other cards in the same series, or draft pick card.

ERR - Error card. A card with erroneous information, spelling, or depiction on either side of the card. Most errors are never corrected by the producing card company.

FIN - Finals.

FLB - Flashback.

FPM - Future Playoff MVP's.

FSL - Future Scoring Leaders.

FULL SHEET - A complete sheet of cards that has not been cut into individual cards by the manufacturer. Also called an uncut sheet.

GQ - Gentleman's Quarterly.

HL - Highlight card.

HOF - Hall of Fame, or Hall of Famer (also abbreviated HOFer).

HOR - Horizontal pose on a card as opposed to the standard vertical orientation found on most cards.

IA - In Action card. A special type of card depicting a player in an action photo, such as the 1982 Topps cards.

INSERT - A card of a different type, e.g., a poster, or any other sports collectible contained and sold in the same package along with a card or cards of a major set.

IS - Inside Stuff.

ISSUE - Synonymous with set, but usually used in conjunction with a manufacturer, e.g., a Topps issue.

JWA - John Wooden Award.

KID - Kid Picture card.

LEGITIMATE ISSUE - A set produced to promote or boost sales of a product or service, e.g., bubble gum, cereal, cigarettes, etc. Most collector issues are not legitimate issues in this sense.

LID - A circular-shaped card (possibly with tab) that forms the top of the container for the product being promoted.

MAG - Magic of SkyBox cards.

MAJOR SET - A set produced by a national manufacturer of cards, containing a large number of cards: Usually 100 or more different cards comprise a major set.

MC - Members Choice.

MEM - Memorial.

MO - McDonald's Open.

MINI - A small card or stamp (the 1991-92 SkyBox Canadian set, for example).

MVP - Most Valuable Player.

NNO - No number on back.

NY - New York.

OBVERSE - The front, face, or pictured side of the card.

OLY - Olympic card.

PANEL - An extended card that is composed of multiple individual cards.

PC - Poster card.

PERIPHERAL SET - A loosely defined term that applies to any non-regular issue set. This term most often is used to describe food issue, giveaway, regional or sendaway sets that contain a fairly small number of cards and are not accepted by the hobby as major sets.

PF - Pacific Finest.

POY - Player of the Year.

PREMIUM - A card, sometimes on photographic stock, that is purchased or obtained in conjunction with (or redeemed for) another card or product. This term applies mainly to older products, as newer cards distributed in this manner are generally lumped together as peripheral sets.

PREMIUM CARDS - A class of products introduced recently, intended to have higher quality card stock and photography than regular cards, but more limited production and higher cost. Defining what is and isn't a premium card is somewhat subjective.

PROMOTIONAL SET - A set, usually containing a small number of cards, issued by a national card producer and distributed in limited quantities or to a select group of people, such as major show attendees or dealers with wholesale accounts. Presumably, the purpose of a promo set is to stir up demand for an upcoming set. Also called a preview, prototype or test set.

RARE - A card or series of cards of very limited availability. Unfortunately, "rare" is a subjective term sometimes used indiscriminately. Using the strict definitions, rare cards are harder to obtain than scarce cards.

RC - Rookie Card. A player's first appearance on a regular issue card from one of the major card companies. Each company has only one regular issue set per season, and that is the widely available traditional set. With a few exceptions, each player has only one RC in any given set. A Rookie Card cannot be an All-Star, Highlight, In Action, League Leader, Super Action or Team Leader card. It can, however, be a coach card or draft pick card.

REGIONAL - A card issued and distributed only in a limited geographical area of the country. The producer may or may not be a major, national producer of trading cards. The key is whether the set was distributed nationally in any form or not.

REVERSE - The back or narrative side of the card.

REV NEG - Reversed or flopped photo side of the card. This is a major type of error card, but only some are corrected.

RIS - Rising Star.

ROY - Rookie of the Year.

SA - Super Action card. Similar to an In Action card.

SAL - SkyBox Salutes.

SASE - Self-addressed, stamped envelope.

SCARCE - A card or series of cards of limited availability. This subjective term is sometimes used indiscriminately to promote or hype value. Using strict definitions, scarce cards are easier to obtain than rare cards.

SERIES - The entire set of cards issued by a particular producer in a particular year, e.g., the 1978-79 Topps series. Also, within a particular set, series can refer to a group of (consecutively numbered) cards printed at the same time, e.g., the first series of the 1972-73 Topps set (#1 through #132).

SET - One each of an entire run of cards of the same type, produced by a particular manufacturer during a single season. In other words, if you have a complete set of 1989-90 Fleer cards, then you have every card from #1 up to and including #132; i.e., all the different cards that were produced.

SHOOT - Shooting Star.

SHOW - A large gathering of dealers and collectors at a single location for the purpose of buying, selling, and trading sorts cards and memorabilia. Conventions are open to the public and sometimes also feature autograph guests, door prizes, films, contests, etc.

SKED - Schedules.

SP - Single or Short Print. A card which was printed in lesser quantity compared to the other cards in the same series (also see DP). This term only can be used in a relative sense and in reference to one particular set. For instance, the 1989-90 Hoops Pistons Championship card (#353A) is less common than the other cards in that set, but it isn't necessarily scarcer than regular cards of any other set.

SPECIAL CARD - A card that portrays something other than a single player or team.

SS - Star Stats.

STANDARD SIZE - The standard size for sports cards is 2 1/2 by 3 1/2 inches. All exceptions, such as 1969-70 Topps, are noted in card descriptions.

STAR CARD - A card that portrays a player of some repute, usually determined by his ability, but sometimes referring to sheer popularity.

STAY - Stay in School.

STICKER - A card-like item with a removable layer that can be affixed to another surface. Example: 1986-87 through 1989-90 Fleer bonus cards.

STOCK - The cardboard or paper on which the card is printed.

SUPERSTAR CARD - A card that portrays a superstar, e.g., a Hall of Fame member or a player whose current performance may eventually warrant serious Hall of Fame consideration.

SY - Schoolyard Stars.

TC - Team card or team checklist card.

TD - Triple Double. A term used for having double digit totals in three categories.

TEAM CARD - A card that depicts an entire team, notably the 1989-90 and 1990-91 NBA Hoops Detroit Pistons championship cards and the 1991-92 NBA Hoops subset.

TEST SET - A set, usually containing a small number of cards, issued by a national producer and distributed in a limited section of the country or to a select group of people. Presumably, the purpose of a test set is to measure market appeal for a particular type of card. Also called a promo or prototype set.

TFC - Team Fact card.

TL - Team Leader.

TO - Tip-off.

TR - Traded card.

TRIB - Tribune.

TRV - Trivia.

TT - Team Tickets card.

UER - Uncorrected Error card.

USA - Team USA.

VAR - Variation card. One of two or more cards from the same series, with the same card number (or player with identical pose, if the series is unnumbered) differing from one another in some aspect, from the printing, stock or other feature of the card. This is often caused when the manufacturer of the cards notices an error in a particular card, corrects the error and then resumes the print run. In this case there will be two versions or variations of the same card. Sometimes one of the variations is relatively scarce. Variations also can result from accidental or deliberate design changes, information updates, photo substitutions, etc.

VERT - Vertical pose on a card.

XRC - Extended Rookie Card. A player's first appearance on a card, but issued in a set that was not distributed nationally nor in packs. In basketball sets, this term only refers to the 1983, '84 and '85 Star Company sets.

YB - Yearbook.

20A - Twenty assist club.

50P - Fifty point club.

6M - Sixth Man.

! - Condition sensitive card or set *(see Grading Your Cards)*.

* - Multi-sport set.

Understanding Card Values

Determining Value

Why are some cards more valuable than others? Obviously, the economic laws of supply and demand are applicable to card collecting just as they are to any other field where a commodity is bought, sold or traded in a free, unregulated market.

Supply (the number of cards available on the market) is less than the total number of cards originally produced since attrition diminishes that original quantity. Each year a percentage of cards is typically thrown away, destroyed or otherwise lost to collectors. This percentage is much, much smaller today than it was in the past because more and more people have become increasingly aware of the value of their cards.

For those who collect only Mint condition cards, the supply of older cards can be quite small indeed. Until recently, collectors were not so conscious of the need to preserve the condition of their cards. For this reason, it is difficult to know exactly how many 1957-58 Topps are currently available, Mint or otherwise. It is generally accepted that there are fewer 1957-58 Topps available than 1969-70, 1979-80 or 1992-93 Topps cards. If demand were equal for each of these sets, the law of supply and demand would increase the price for the least available sets.

Demand, however, is never equal for all sets, so price correlations can be complicated. The demand for a card is influenced by many factors. These include: (1) the age of the card; (2) the number of cards printed; (3) the player(s) portrayed on the card; (4) the attractiveness and popularity of the set; and (5) the physical condition of the card.

In general, (1) the older the card, (2) the fewer the number of the cards printed, (3) the more famous, popular and talented the player, (4) the more attractive and popular the set, and (5) the better the condition of the card, the higher the value of the card will be. There are exceptions to all but one of these factors: the condition of the card. Given two cards similar in all respects except condition, the one in the best condition will always be valued higher.

While those guidelines help to establish the value of a card, the countless exceptions and peculiarities make any simple, direct mathematical formula to determine card values impossible.

Regional Variation

Since the market varies from region to region, card prices of local players may be higher. This is known as a regional premium. How significant the premium is — and if there is any premium at all — depends on the local popularity of the team and the player.

The largest regional premiums usually do not apply to superstars, who often are so well known nationwide that the prices of their key cards are too high for local dealers to realize a premium.

Lesser stars often command the strongest premiums. Their popularity is concentrated in their home region, creating local demand that greatly exceeds overall demand.

Regional premiums can apply to popular retired players and sometimes can be found in the areas where the players grew up or starred in college.

A regional discount is the converse of a regional premium. Regional discounts occur when a player has been so popular in his region for so long that local collectors and dealers have accumulated quantities of his cards. The abundant supply may make the cards available in that area at the lowest prices anywhere.

Set Prices

A somewhat paradoxical situation exists in the price of a complete set vs. the combined cost of the individual cards in the set. In nearly every case, the sum of the prices for the individual cards is higher than the cost for the complete set. This is prevalent especially in the cards of the past few years. The reasons for this apparent anomaly stem from the habits of collectors and from the carrying costs to dealers. Today, each card in a set normally is produced in the same quantity as all others in its set.

Many collectors pick up only stars, superstars and particular teams. As a result, the dealer is left with a shortage of certain player cards and an abundance of others. He therefore incurs an expense in simply "carrying" these less desirable cards in stock. On the other hand, if he sells a complete set, he gets rid of large numbers of cards at one time. For this reason, he generally is willing to receive less money for a complete set. By doing this, he recovers all of his costs and also makes a profit.

Set prices do not include rare card varieties, unless specifically stated. Of course, the prices for sets do include one example of each type for the given set, but this is the least expensive variety.

Scarce Series

Only a select few basketball sets contain scarce series: 1948 Bowman, 1970-71 and 1972-73 Topps, 1983-84, 1984-85 and 1985-86 Star. The 1948 Bowman set was printed on two 36-card sheets, the second of which was issued in significantly lower quantities. The two Topps scarce series are only marginally tougher than the set as a whole. The Star Company scarcities relate to particular team sets that, to different extents, were less widely distributed.

We are always looking for information or photographs of printing sheets of cards for research. Each year, we try to update the hobby's knowledge of distribution anomalies. Please let us know at the address in this book if you have first-hand knowledge that would be helpful in this pursuit.

Grading Your Cards

Each hobby has its own grading terminology — stamps, coins, comic books, record collecting, etc. Collectors of sports cards are no exception. The one invariable criterion for determining the value of a card is its condition: the better the condition of the card, the more valuable it is. Condition grading, however, is subjective. Individual card dealers and collectors differ in the strictness of their grading, but the stated condition of a card should be determined without regard to whether it is being bought or sold.

No allowance is made for age. A 1961-62 Fleer card is judged by the same standards as a 1991-92 Fleer card. But there are specific sets and cards that are condition sensitive (marked with "!" in the Price Guide) because of their border color, consistently poor centering, etc. Such cards and sets sometimes command premiums above the listed percentages in Mint condition.

Centering

Current centering terminology uses numbers representing the percentage of border on either side of the main design. Obviously, centering is diminished in importance for borderless cards such as Stadium Club.

Slightly Off-Center (60/40): A slightly off-center card is one that upon close inspection is found to have one border bigger than the opposite border. This degree once was offensive to only purists, but now some hobbyists try to avoid cards that are anything other than perfectly centered.

Off-Center (70/30): An off-center card has one border that is noticeably more than twice as wide as the opposite border.

Badly Off-Center (80/20 or worse): A badly off-center card has virtually no border on one side of the card.

Miscut: A miscut card actually shows part of the adjacent card in its larger

Centering

Well-centered

Slightly off-centered

Off-centered

Badly off-centered

Miscut

border and consequently a corresponding amount of its card is cut off.

Corner Wear

Corner wear is the most scrutinized grading criteria in the hobby. These are the major categories of corner wear:

Corner with a slight touch of wear: The corner still is sharp, but there is a slight touch of wear showing. On a dark-bordered card, this shows as a dot of white.

Fuzzy corner: The corner still comes to a point, but the point has just begun to fray. A slightly "dinged" corner is considered the same as a fuzzy corner.

Slightly rounded corner: The fraying of the corner has increased to where there is only a hint of a point. Mild layering may be evident. A "dinged" corner is considered the same as a slightly rounded corner.

Rounded corner: The point is completely gone. Some layering is noticeable.

Badly rounded corner: The corner is completely round and rough. Severe layering is evident.

Creases

A third common defect is the crease. The degree of creasing in a card is difficult to show in a drawing or picture. On giving the specific condition of an expensive card for sale, the seller should note any creases additionally. Creases can be categorized as to severity according to the following scale.

Light Crease: A light crease is a crease that is barely noticeable upon close inspection. In fact, when cards are in plastic sheets or holders, a light crease may not be seen (until the card is taken out of the holder). A light crease on the front is much more serious than a light crease on the card back only.

Medium Crease: A medium crease is noticeable when held and studied at arm's length by the naked eye, but does not overly detract from the appearance of the card. It is an obvious crease, but not one that breaks the picture surface of the card.

Heavy Crease: A heavy crease is one that has torn or broken through the card's picture surface, e.g., puts a tear in the photo surface.

Alterations

Deceptive Trimming: This occurs when someone alters the card in order (1) to shave off edge wear, (2) to improve the sharpness of the corners, or (3) to improve centering — obviously their objective is to falsely increase the perceived value of the card to an unsuspecting buyer. The shrinkage usually is evident only if the trimmed card is compared to an adjacent full-sized card or if the trimmed card is itself measured.

Obvious Trimming: Obvious trimming is noticeable and unfortunate. It is usually performed by non-collectors who give no thought to the present or future value of their cards.

Deceptively Retouched Borders: This occurs when the borders (especially on those cards with dark borders) are touched up on the edges and corners with magic marker or crayons of appropriate color in order to make the card appear to be Mint.

Categorization of Defects

Miscellaneous Flaws

The following are common minor flaws that, depending on severity, lower a card's condition by one to four grades and often render it no better than Excellent-Mint: bubbles (lumps in surface), gum and wax stains, diamond cutting (slanted borders), notching, off-centered backs, paper wrinkles, scratched-off cartoons or puzzles on back, rubber band marks, scratches, surface

Corner Wear

The partial cards here have been photographed at 300%. This was done in order to magnify each card's corner wear to such a degree that differences could be shown on a printed page.

This 1986-87 Fleer Mark Aguirre card has a touch of wear. Notice the extremely slight fraying on the corner.

This 1986-87 Fleer Isiah Thomas card has a fuzzy corner. Notice that there is no longer a sharp corner.

This 1986-87 Fleer Wayman Tisdale card has a slightly rounded corner evident by the lack of a sharp point and heavy wear on both edges.

This 1986-87 Fleer Herb Williams card displays a badly rounded corner. Notice a large portion of missing cardboard accompanied by heavy wear and excessive fraying.

This 1986-87 Fleer Maurice Cheeks card displays several creases of varying degrees. Light creases (middle of the card) may not break the card's surface, while heavy creases (right side) will.

impressions and warping.

The following are common serious flaws that, depending on severity, lower a card's condition at least four grades and often render it no better than Good: chemical or sun fading, erasure marks, mildew, miscutting (severe off-centering), holes, bleached or retouched borders, tape marks, tears, trimming, water or coffee stains and writing.

Condition Guide

Grades

Mint (Mt) - A card with no flaws or wear. The card has four perfect corners, 60/40 or better centering from top to bottom and from left to right, original gloss, smooth edges and original color borders. A Mint card does not have print spots, color or focus imperfections.

Near Mint-Mint (NrMt-Mt) - A card with one minor flaw. Any one of the following would lower a Mint card to Near Mint-Mint: one corner with a slight touch of wear, barely noticeable print spots, color or focus imperfections. The card must have 60/40 or better centering in both directions, original gloss, smooth edges and original color borders.

Near Mint (NrMt) - A card with one minor flaw. Any one of the following would lower a Mint card to Near Mint: one fuzzy corner or two to four corners with slight touches of wear, 70/30 to 60/40 centering, slightly rough edges, minor print spots, color or focus imperfections. The card must have original gloss and original color borders.

Excellent-Mint (ExMt) - A card with two or three fuzzy, but not rounded, corners and centering no worse than 80/20. The card may have no more than two of the following: slightly rough edges, very slightly discolored borders, minor print spots, color or focus imperfections. The card must have original gloss.

Excellent (Ex) - A card with four fuzzy but definitely not rounded corners and centering no worse than 80/20. The card may have a small amount of original gloss lost, rough edges, slightly discolored borders and minor print spots, color or focus imperfections.

Very Good (Vg) - A card that has been handled but not abused: slightly rounded corners with slight layering, slight notching on edges, a significant amount of gloss lost from the surface but no scuffing and moderate discoloration of borders. The card may have a few light creases.

Good (G), Fair (F), Poor (P) - A well-worn, mishandled or abused card: badly rounded and layered corners, scuffing, most or all original gloss missing, seriously discolored borders, moderate or heavy creases, and one or more serious flaws. The grade of Good, Fair or Poor depends on the severity of wear and flaws. Good, Fair and Poor cards generally are used only as fillers.

The most widely used grades are defined above. Obviously, many cards will not perfectly fit one of the definitions.

Therefore, categories between the major grades known as in-between grades are used, such as Good to Very Good (G-Vg), Very Good to Excellent (VgEx), and Excellent-Mint to Near Mint (ExMt-NrMt). Such grades indicate a card with all qualities of the lower category but with at least a few qualities of the higher category.

This Price Guide book lists each card and set in three grades, with the middle grade valued at about 40-45% of the top grade, and the bottom grade valued at about 10-15% of the top grade.

The value of cards that fall between the listed columns can also be calculated using a percentage of the top grade. For example, a card that falls between the top and middle grades (Ex, ExMt or NrMt in most cases) will generally be valued at anywhere from 50% to 90% of the top grade.

Similarly, a card that falls between the middle and bottom grades (G-Vg, Vg or VgEx in most cases) will generally be valued at anywhere from 20% to 40% of the top grade.

There are also cases where cards are in better condition than the top grade or worse than the bottom grade. Cards that grade worse than the lowest grade are generally valued at 5-10% of the top grade.

When a card exceeds the top grade by one — such as NrMt-Mt when the top grade is NrMt, or Mint when the top grade is NrMt-Mt — a premium of up to 50% is possible, with 10-20% the usual norm.

When a card exceeds the top grade by two — such as Mint when the top grade is NrMt, or NrMt-Mt when the top grade is ExMt — a premium of 25-50% is the usual norm. But certain condition sensitive cards or sets, particularly those from the pre-war era, can bring premiums of up to 100% or even more.

Unopened packs, boxes and factory-collated sets are considered Mint in their unknown (and presumed perfect) state. Once opened, however, each card can be graded (and valued) in its own right by taking into account any defects that may be present in spite of the fact that the card has never been handled.

Selling Your Cards

Just about every collector sells cards or will sell cards eventually. Someday you may be interested in selling your duplicates or maybe even your whole collection. You may sell to other collectors, friends or dealers. You may even sell cards you purchased from a certain dealer back to that same dealer. In any event, it helps to know some of the mechanics of the typical transaction between buyer and seller.

Dealers will buy cards in order to resell them to other collectors who are interested in the cards. Dealers will always pay a higher percentage for items that (in their opinion) can be resold quickly, and a much lower percentage for those items that are perceived as having low demand and hence are slow moving. In either case, dealers must buy at a price that allows for the expense of doing business and a margin for profit.

If you have cards for sale, the best advice we can give is that you get several offers for your cards — either from card shops or at a card show — and take the best offer, all things considered. Note, the "best" offer may not be the one for the highest amount. And remember, if a dealer really wants your cards, he won't let you get away without making his best competitive offer. Another alternative is to place your cards in an auction as one or several lots.

Many people think nothing of going into a department store and paying $15 for an item of clothing for which the store paid $5. But if you were selling your $15 card to a dealer and he offered you $5 for it, you might think his mark-up unreasonable. To complete the analogy: most department stores (and card dealers) that consistently pay $10 for $15 items eventually go out of business. An exception is when the dealer has lined up a willing buyer for the item(s) you are attempting to sell, or if the cards are so Hot that it's likely he'll have to hold the cards for only a short period of time.

In those cases, an offer of up to 75 percent of book value still will allow the dealer to make a reasonable profit considering the short time he will need to hold the merchandise. In general, however, most cards and collections will bring offers in the range of 25 to 50 percent of retail price. Also consider that most material from the past five to 10 years is plentiful. If that's what you're selling, don't be surprised if your best offer is well below that range.

Interesting Notes

The first card numerically of an issue is the single card most likely to obtain excessive wear. Consequently, you typically will find the price on the #1 card (in NrMt or Mint condition) somewhat higher than might otherwise be the case. Similarly, but to a lesser extent (because normally the less important, reverse side of the card is the one exposed), the last card numerically in an issue also is prone to abnormal wear. This extra wear and tear occurs because the first and last cards are exposed to the elements (human element included) more than any other cards. They are generally end cards in any brick formations, rubber bandings, stackings on wet surfaces, and like activities.

Sports cards have no intrinsic value. The value of a card, like the value of other collectibles, can be determined only by you and your enjoyment in viewing and possessing these cardboard treasures.

Remember, the buyer ultimately determines the price of each card. You are the determining price factor because you have the ability to say "No" to the price of any card by not exchanging your hard-earned money for a given card. When the cost of a trading card exceeds the enjoyment you will receive from it, your answer should be "No." We assess and report the prices. You set them!

We are always interested in receiving the price input of collectors and dealers from around the country. We happily credit all contributors. We welcome your opinions, since your contributions assist us in ensuring a better guide each year. If you would like to join our survey list for the next editions of this book and others authored by Dr. Beckett, please send your name and address to Dr. James Beckett, 15850 Dallas Parkway, Dallas, Texas 75248.

History of Basketball Cards

The earliest basketball collectibles known are team postcards issued at the turn of the 20th century. Many of these postcards feature collegiate or high school teams of that day. Postcards were intermittently issued throughout the first half of the 20th century, with the bulk of them coming out in the 1920s and '30s. Unfortunately, the cataloging of these collectibles is sporadic at best. In addition, many collectors consider these postcards as memorabilia more so than trading cards, thus their exclusion from this book.

In 1910, College Athlete Felts (catalog number B-33) made their debut. Of a total of 270 felts, 20 featured basketball plays.

The first true basketball trading cards were issued by Murad cigarettes in 1911. The "College Series" cards depict a number of various sports and colleges, including four basketball cards (Luther, Northwestern, Williams and Xavier). In addition to these small (2-by-3 inch) cards, Murad issued a large (8-by-5 inch) basketball card featuring Williams college (catalog number T-6) as part of another multisport set.

The first basketball cards ever to be issued in gum packs were distributed in 1933 by Goudey in its multisport Sport Kings set, which was the first issue to list individual and professional players. Four cards from the complete 48-card set feature Boston Celtics basketball players Nat Holman, Ed Wachter, Joe Lapchick and Eddie Burke.

The period of growth that the NBA experienced from 1948 to 1951 marked the first initial boom, both for that sport and the cards that chronicle it. In 1948, Bowman created the first trading card set exclusively devoted to basketball cards, ushering in the modern era of hoops collectibles. The 72-card Bowman set contains the Rookie Card of HOFer George Mikan, one of the most valuable, and important, basketball cards in the hobby. Mikan, pro basketball's first dominant big man, set the stage for Bill Russell, Wilt Chamberlain and all the other legendary centers who have played the game since.

In addition to the Bowman release, Topps included 11 basketball cards in its 252-card multisport 1948 Magic Photo set. Five of the cards feature individual players (including collegiate great "Easy" Ed Macauley), another five feature colleges, and one additional card highlights a Manhattan-Dartmouth game. These 11 cards represent Topps first effort to produce basketball trading cards. Kellogg's also created an 18-card multisport set of trading cards in 1948 that were inserted into boxes of Pep cereal. The only basketball card in the set features Mikan. Throughout 1948 and 1949, the Exhibit Supply Company of Chicago issued oversized thick-stock multisport trading cards in conjunction with the 1948 Olympic games. Six basketball players were featured, including HOFers Mikan and Joe Fulks, among others. The cards were distributed through penny arcade machines.

In 1950-51, Scott's Chips issued a 13-card set featuring the Minneapolis Lakers. The cards were issued in Scott's Potato and Cheese Potato Chip boxes. The cards are extremely scarce today due to the fact that many were redeemed back in 1950-51 in exchange for game tickets and signed team pictures. This set contains possibly the scarcest Mikan issue in existence. In 1951, a Philadelphia-based meat company called Berk Ross issued a four-series, 72-card multisport set. The set contains five different basketball players, including the first cards of HOFers Bob Cousy and Bill Sharman.

Wheaties issued an oversized six-card multisport set on the backs of its cereal boxes in 1951. The only basketball player featured in the set is Mikan.

In 1952, Wheaties expanded the cereal box set to 30 cards, including six issues featuring basketball players of that day. Of these six cards, two feature Mikan (a portrait and an action shot). The 1952 cards are significantly smaller than the previous year's issue. That same year, the 32-card Bread for Health set was issued. The set was one of the few trading card issues of that decade exclusively devoted to the sport of basketball. The cards are actually bread end labels and were probably meant to be housed in an album. To date, the only companies known to have issued this set are Fisher's Bread in the New Jersey, New York and Pennsylvania areas and NBC Bread in the Michigan area.

One must skip ahead to 1957-58 to find the next major basketball issue, again produced by Topps. Its 80-card basketball set from that year is recognized within the hobby as the second major modern basketball issue, including Rookie Cards of all-time greats such as Bill Russell, Bob Cousy and Bob Pettit.

In 1960, Post cereal created a nine-card multisport set by devoting most of the back of the actual cereal boxes to full color picture frames of the athletes. HOFers Cousy and Pettit are the two featured basketball players.

In 1961-62, Fleer issued the third major modern basketball set. The 66-card set contains the Rookie Cards of all-time greats such as Wilt Chamberlain, Oscar Robertson and Jerry West. That same year, Bell Brand Potato Chips inserted trading cards (one per bag) featuring the L.A. Lakers team of that year and including scarce, early issues of HOFers West and Elgin Baylor.

From 1963 to 1968 no major companies manufactured basketball cards. Kahn's (an Ohio-based meat company) issued small regional basketball sets from 1957-58 through 1965-66 (including the first cards of Jerry West and

Oscar Robertson in its 1960-61 set). All the Kahn's sets feature members of the Cincinnati Royals, except for the few issues featuring the Lakers' West.

In 1968, Topps printed a very limited quantity of standard-size black-and-white test issue cards, preluding its 1969-70 nationwide return to the basketball card market.

The 1969-70 Topps set began a 13-year run of producing nationally distributed basketball card sets which ended in 1981-82. This was about the time the league's popularity bottomed out and was about to begin its ascent to the lofty level it's at today.

Topps' run included several sets that are troublesome for today's collectors. The 1969-70, 1970-71 and 1976-77 sets are larger than standard size, thus making them hard to store and preserve. The 1980-81 set consists of standard-size panels containing three cards each. Completing and cataloging the 1980-81 set (which features the classic Larry Bird RC/Magic Johnson RC/Julius Erving panel) is challenging, to say the least.

In 1983, this basketball card void was filled by the Star Company, a small company which issued three attractive sets of basketball cards, along with a plethora of peripheral sets. Star's 1983-84 premiere offering was issued in four groups, with the first series (cards 1-100) very difficult to obtain, as many of the early team subsets were miscut and destroyed before release. The 1984-85 and 1985-86 sets were more widely and evenly distributed. Even so, players' initial appearances on any of the three Star Company sets are considered Extended Rookie Cards, not regular Rookie Cards, because of the relatively limited distribution. Chief among these is Michael Jordan's 1984-85 Star XRC, the most valuable sports card issued in a 1980s major set.

Then, in 1986, Fleer took over the rights to produce cards for the NBA. Their 1986-87, 1987-88 and 1988-89 sets each contain 132 attractive, colorful cards depicting mostly stars and superstars. They were sold in the familiar wax pack format (12 cards and one sticker per pack). Fleer increased its set size to 168 in 1989-90, and was joined by NBA Hoops, which produced a 300-card first series (containing David Robinson's only Rookie Card) and a 52-card second series. The demand for all three Star Company sets, along with the first four Fleer sets and the premiere NBA Hoops set, skyrocketed during the early part of 1990.

The basketball card market stabilized somewhat in 1990-91, with both Fleer and Hoops stepping up production tremendously. A new major set, SkyBox, also made a splash in the market with its unique "high-tech" cards featuring computer-generated backgrounds. Because of overproduction, none of the three major 1990-91 sets have experienced significant price growth, although the increased competition has led to higher quality and more innovative products.

Another milestone in 1990-91 was the first-time inclusion of current rookies in update sets (NBA Hoops and SkyBox Series II, Fleer Update). The NBA Hoops and SkyBox issues contain just the 11 lottery picks, while Fleer's 100-card boxed set includes all rookies of any significance. A small company called "Star Pics" (not to be confused with Star Company) tried to fill this niche by printing a 70-card set in late 1990, but because the set was not licensed by the NBA, it is not considered a major set by the majority of collectors. It does, however, contain the first nationally distributed cards of 1990-91 rookies such as Derrick Coleman and Kendall Gill, among others.

In 1991-92, the draft pick set market that Star Pics opened in 1990-91 expanded to include several competitors. More significantly, that season brought with it the three established NBA card brands plus Upper Deck, known throughout the hobby for its high quality card stock and photography in other sports. Upper Deck's first basketball set probably captured NBA action better than any previous set. But its value — like all other major 1990-91 and 1991-92 NBA sets — declined because of overproduction.

On the bright side, the historic entrance of NBA players to Olympic competition kept interest in basketball cards going long after the Chicago Bulls won their second straight NBA championship. So for at least one year, the basketball card market — probably the most seasonal of the four major team sports — remained in the spotlight for an extended period of time.

The 1992-93 season will be remembered as the year of Shaq — the debut campaign of the most heralded rookie in many years. Shaquille O'Neal headlined the most promising rookie class in NBA history, sparking unprecedented interest in basketball cards. Among O'Neal's many talented rookie companions were Alonzo Mourning, Jim Jackson and Latrell Sprewell.

Classic Games, known primarily for producing draft picks and minor league baseball cards, signed O'Neal to an exclusive contract through 1992, thus postponing the appearances of O'Neal's NBA-licensed cards.

Shaquille's Classic and NBA cards, particularly the inserts, became some of the most sought-after collectibles in years. As a direct result of O'Neal and his fellow rookie standouts, the basketball card market achieved a new level of popularity in 1993.

The hobby rode that crest of popularity throughout the 1993-94 season. Michael Jordan may have retired, but his absence only spurred interest in some of his tougher inserts. Another strong rookie class followed Shaq, and Reggie Miller elevated his collectibility to a superstar level. Hakeem Olajuwon, by leading the Rockets to an NBA title, boosted his early cards to levels surpassed only by Jordan.

No new cardmakers came on board, but super premium Topps Finest raised the stakes, and the parallel set came into its own.

In 1994-95, the return of Michael Jordan, coupled with the high impact splash of Detroit Pistons rookie Grant Hill, kept collector interest high. In addition, the NBA granted all the licensed manufacturers the opportunity to create a fourth brand of basketball cards that year, allowing each company to create a selection of clearly defined niche products at different price points. The manufacturers also expanded the calendar release dates with 1994-95 cards being released on a consistent basis from August, 1994 all the way through June, 1995. The super-premium card market expanded greatly as the battle for the best selling five dollar (or more) pack reached epic levels by season's end. The key new super premium products included the premier of Upper Deck SP, Topps Embossed and SkyBox Emotion.

Additional Reading

Each year Beckett Publications produces comprehensive annual price guides for each of the four major sports: *Beckett Baseball Card Price Guide*, *Beckett Football Card Price Guide*, *Beckett Basketball Card Price Guide*, and *Beckett Hockey Card Price Guide*. The aim of these annual guides is to provide information and accurate pricing on a wide array of sports cards, ranging from main issues by the major card manufacturers to various regional, promotional, and food issues. Also alphabetical checklists, such as *Sport Americana Baseball Card Alphabetical Checklist #6*, are published to assist the collector in identifying all the cards of a particular player. The seasoned collector will find these tools valuable sources of information that will enable him to pursue his hobby interests.

In addition, abridged editions of the Beckett Price Guides have been published for each of the four major sports as part of the House of Collectible series: *The Official Price Guide to Baseball Cards, The Official Price Guide to Football Cards, The Official Price Guide to Basketball Cards,* and *The Official Price Guide to Hockey Cards.* Published in a convenient mass-market paperback format, these price guides provide information and accurate pricing on all the main issues by the major card manufacturers.

Advertising

Within this Price Guide you will find advertisements for sports memorabilia material, mail order, and retail sports collectibles establishments. All advertisements were accepted in good faith based on the reputation of the advertiser; however, neither the author, the publisher, the distributors, nor the other advertisers in this Price Guide accept any responsibility for any particular advertiser not complying with the terms of his or her ad.

Readers also should be aware that prices in advertisements are subject to change over the annual period before a new edition of this volume is issued each spring. When replying to an advertisement late in the basketball year, the reader should take this into account, and contact the dealer by phone or in writing for up-to-date price information. Should you come into contact with any of the advertisers in this guide as a result of their advertisement herein, please mention this source as your contact.

Prices in This Guide

Prices found in this guide reflect current retail rates just prior to the printing of this book. They do not reflect the FOR SALE prices of the author, the publisher, the distributors, the advertisers, or any card dealers associated with this guide. No one is obligated in any way to buy, sell or trade his or her cards based on these prices. The price listings were compiled by the author from actual buy/sell transactions at sports conventions, sports card shops, buy/sell advertisements in the hobby papers, for sale prices from dealer catalogs and price lists, and discussions with leading hobbyists in the U.S. and Canada. All prices are in U.S. dollars.

Acknowledgments

A great deal of diligence, hard work, and dedicated effort went into this year's volume. The high standards to which we hold ourselves, however, could not have been met without the expert input and generous amount of time contributed by many people. Our sincere thanks are extended to each and every one of you.

A complete list of these invaluable contributors appears after the price guide.

1948 Bowman

The 1948 Bowman set of 72 cards was the company's only basketball issue. Five cards were issued in each pack. It was also the only major basketball issue until 1957-58 when Topps released a set. Cards in the set measure 2 1/16" by 2 1/2". The set is in color and features both player cards and diagram cards. The player cards in the second series are sometimes found without the red or blue printing on the card front, leaving only a gray background. These gray versions are more difficult to find, as they are printing errors where the printer apparently ran out of red or blue ink that was supposed to print on the player's uniform. The key Rookie Card in this is George Mikan. Other Rookie Cards include Carl Braun, Joe Fulks, William "Red" Holzman, Jim Pollard, and Max Zaslofsky.

	EX-MT	VG-E	GOOD
COMPLETE SET (72)	8000.00	4000.00	800.00
COMMON CARD (1-36)	60.00	30.00	6.00
COMMON CARD (37-72)	100.00	50.00	4.50
COMMON PLAY CARD (1-36)	45.00	23.00	10.00
COMMON PLAY CARD (37-72)	80.00	40.00	8.00

		EX-MT	VG-E	GOOD
☐ 1	Ernie Calverley Providence Steamrollers	200.00	100.00	20.00
☐ 2	Ralph Hamilton Ft. Wayne Pistons	60.00	30.00	6.00
☐ 3	Gale Bishop Philadelphia Warriors	60.00	30.00	6.00
☐ 4	Fred Lewis CO Indianapolis Jets	70.00	35.00	7.00
☐ 5	Basketball Play Single cut off post	45.00	23.00	4.50
☐ 6	Bob Ferrick Washington Capitols	70.00	35.00	7.00
☐ 7	John Logan St. Louis Bombers	60.00	30.00	6.00
☐ 8	Mel Riebe Boston Celtics	60.00	30.00	6.00
☐ 9	Andy Phillip Chicago Stags	150.00	75.00	15.00
☐ 10	Bob Davies Rochester Royals	150.00	75.00	15.00
☐ 11	Basketball Play Single cut with return pass to post	45.00	23.00	4.50
☐ 12	Kenny Sailors Providence Steamrollers	70.00	35.00	7.00
☐ 13	Paul Armstrong	60.00	30.00	6.00

		EX-MT	VG-E	GOOD
	Ft. Wayne Pistons			
☐ 14	Howard Dallmar Philadelphia Warriors	70.00	35.00	7.00
☐ 15	Bruce Hale Indianapolis Jets	70.00	35.00	7.00
☐ 16	Sid Hertzberg Washington Capitols	60.00	30.00	6.00
☐ 17	Basketball Play Single cut	45.00	23.00	4.50
☐ 18	Red Rocha St. Louis Bombers	60.00	30.00	6.00
☐ 19	Eddie Ehlers Boston Celtics	60.00	30.00	6.00
☐ 20	Ellis(Gene) Vance Chicago Stags	60.00	30.00	6.00
☐ 21	Andrew(Fuzzy) Levane Rochester Royals	70.00	35.00	7.00
☐ 22	Earl Shannon Providence Steamrollers	60.00	30.00	6.00
☐ 23	Basketball Play Double cut off post	45.00	23.00	4.50
☐ 24	Leo(Crystal) Klier Ft. Wayne Pistons	60.00	30.00	6.00
☐ 25	George Senesky Philadelphia Warriors	60.00	30.00	6.00
☐ 26	Price Brookfield Indianapolis Jets	60.00	30.00	6.00
☐ 27	John Norlander Washington Capitols	60.00	30.00	6.00
☐ 28	Don Putman St. Louis Bombers	60.00	30.00	6.00
☐ 29	Basketball Play Double post	45.00	23.00	4.50
☐ 30	Jack Garfinkel Boston Celtics	60.00	30.00	6.00
☐ 31	Chuck Gilmur Chicago Stags	60.00	30.00	6.00
☐ 32	William Holzman Rochester Royals	425.00	210.00	42.50
☐ 33	Jack Smiley Ft. Wayne Pistons	60.00	30.00	6.00
☐ 34	Joe Fulks Philadelphia Warriors	425.00	210.00	42.50
☐ 35	Basketball Play Screen play	45.00	23.00	4.50
☐ 36	Hal Tidrick Indianapolis Jets	60.00	30.00	6.00
☐ 37	Don(Swede) Carlson Minneapolis Lakers	100.00	50.00	10.00
☐ 38	Buddy Jeanette CO Baltimore Bullets	150.00	75.00	15.00
☐ 39	Ray Kuka New York Knicks	100.00	50.00	10.00
☐ 40	Stan Miasek Chicago Stags	100.00	50.00	10.00
☐ 41	Basketball Play Double screen	80.00	40.00	8.00
☐ 42	George Nostrand Providence Steamrollers	100.00	50.00	10.00
☐ 43	Chuck Halbert Boston Celtics	130.00	65.00	13.00
☐ 44	Arnie Johnson Rochester Royals	100.00	50.00	10.00
☐ 45	Bob Doll St. Louis Bombers	100.00	50.00	10.00
☐ 46	Horace McKinney Washington Capitols	150.00	75.00	15.00
☐ 47	Basketball Play Out of bounds	80.00	40.00	8.00
☐ 48	Ed Sadowski Philadelphia Warriors	100.00	50.00	10.00

☐ 49	Bob Kinney Ft. Wayne Pistons	100.00	50.00	10.00
☐ 50	Charles(Hawk) Black Indianapolis Jets	100.00	50.00	10.00
☐ 51	Jack Dwan Minneapolis Lakers	100.00	50.00	10.00
☐ 52	Cornelius Simmons Baltimore Bullets	130.00	65.00	13.00
☐ 53	Basketball Play Out of bounds	80.00	40.00	8.00
☐ 54	Bud Palmer New York Knicks	150.00	75.00	15.00
☐ 55	Max Zaslofsky Chicago Stags	300.00	150.00	30.00
☐ 56	Lee Roy Robbins Providence Steamrollers	100.00	50.00	10.00
☐ 57	Arthur Spector Boston Celtics	100.00	50.00	10.00
☐ 58	Arnie Risen Rochester Royals	150.00	75.00	15.00
☐ 59	Basketball Play Out of bounds play	80.00	40.00	8.00
☐ 60	Ariel Maughan St. Louis Bombers	100.00	50.00	10.00
☐ 61	Dick O'Keefe Washington Capitols	100.00	50.00	10.00
☐ 62	Herman Schaefer Minneapolis Lakers	100.00	50.00	10.00
☐ 63	John Mahnken Baltimore Bullets	100.00	50.00	10.00
☐ 64	Tommy Byrnes New York Knicks	100.00	50.00	10.00
☐ 65	Basketball Play Held ball	80.00	40.00	8.00
☐ 66	Jim Pollard Minneapolis Lakers	400.00	200.00	40.00
☐ 67	Lee Mogus Baltimore Bullets	100.00	50.00	10.00
☐ 68	Lee Knorek New York Knicks	100.00	50.00	10.00
☐ 69	George Mikan Minneapolis Lakers	4500.00	1900.00	700.00
☐ 70	Walter Budko Baltimore Bullets	100.00	50.00	10.00
☐ 71	Basketball Play Guards Play	80.00	40.00	8.00
☐ 72	Carl Braun New York Knicks	350.00	112.00	28.00

1994-95 Collector's Choice

These 420 standard-size (2 1/2" by 3 1/2") cards, issued in two separate series of 210-cards each, comprise Upper Deck's '94-95 Collector's Choice set. Cards were issued in 12-card hobby packs (suggested retail of ninety-nine cents), 13-card retail packs (suggested retail of $1.18), and 20-card retail jumbo packs. White bordered fronts feature color player action shots. The player's name, team, and position appear in a lower corner. The back carries another color player action shot at the top, with statistics and career highlights displayed below. The cards are numbered on the

back. The following subsets are included in this set: Tip-Off (166-192), All-Star Advice (193-198), NBA Profiles (199-206), Blueprints (372-398), Trivia (399-406), and Draft Class (407-416).

	MINT	NRMT	EXC
COMPLETE SET (420)	30.00	13.50	3.80
COMPLETE SERIES 1 (210)	15.00	6.75	1.90
COMPLETE SERIES 2 (210)	15.00	6.75	1.90
COMMON CARD (1-420)	.05	.02	.01

☐ 1	Anfernee Hardaway Orlando Magic	1.00	.45	.13
☐ 2	Moses Malone Philadelphia 76ers	.15	.07	.02
☐ 3	Steve Smith Miami Heat	.08	.04	.01
☐ 4	Chris Webber Golden State Warriors	.40	.18	.05
☐ 5	Donald Royal Orlando Magic	.05	.02	.01
☐ 6	Avery Johnson Golden State Warriors	.05	.02	.01
☐ 7	Kevin Johnson Phoenix Suns	.15	.07	.02
☐ 8	Doug Christie Los Angeles Lakers	.05	.02	.01
☐ 9	Derrick McKey Indiana Pacers	.08	.04	.01
☐ 10	Dennis Rodman San Antonio Spurs	.15	.07	.02
☐ 11	Scott Skiles UER Orlando Magic (Listed as playing with Cavaliers instead of Pacers in '87-'88, '88-'89)	.05	.02	.01
☐ 12	Johnny Dawkins Philadelphia 76ers	.05	.02	.01
☐ 13	Kendall Gill Seattle Supersonics	.05	.02	.01
☐ 14	Jeff Hornacek Utah Jazz	.08	.04	.01
☐ 15	Latrell Sprewell Golden State Warriors	.30	.14	.04
☐ 16	Lucious Harris Dallas Mavericks	.05	.02	.01
☐ 17	Chris Mullin Golden State Warriors	.10	.04	.01
☐ 18	John Williams Cleveland Cavaliers	.08	.04	.01
☐ 19	Tony Campbell Dallas Mavericks	.05	.02	.01
☐ 20	LaPhonso Ellis Denver Nuggets	.05	.02	.01
☐ 21	Gerald Wilkins Cleveland Cavaliers	.05	.02	.01
☐ 22	Clyde Drexler	.25	.11	.03

	Portland Trail Blazers			
☐ 23	Michael Jordan	3.00	1.35	.40
	Chicago Bulls			
☐ 24	George Lynch	.05	.02	.01
	Los Angeles Lakers			
☐ 25	Mark Price	.10	.05	.01
	Cleveland Cavaliers			
☐ 26	James Robinson	.05	.02	.01
	Portland Trail Blazers			
☐ 27	Elmore Spencer	.05	.02	.01
	Los Angeles Clippers			
☐ 28	Stacey King	.05	.02	.01
	Minnesota Timberwolves			
☐ 29	Corie Blount	.05	.02	.01
	Chicago Bulls			
☐ 30	Dell Curry	.05	.02	.01
	Charlotte Hornets			
☐ 31	Reggie Miller	.25	.11	.03
	Indiana Pacers			
☐ 32	Karl Malone	.25	.11	.03
	Utah Jazz			
☐ 33	Scottie Pippen	.25	.11	.03
	Chicago Bulls			
☐ 34	Hakeem Olajuwon	.60	.25	.08
	Houston Rockets			
☐ 35	Clarence Weatherspoon	.08	.04	.01
	Philadelphia 76ers			
☐ 36	Kevin Edwards	.05	.02	.01
	New Jersey Nets			
☐ 37	Pete Myers	.05	.02	.01
	Chicago Bulls			
☐ 38	Jeff Turner	.05	.02	.01
	Orlando Magic			
☐ 39	Ennis Whatley	.05	.02	.01
	Atlanta Hawks			
☐ 40	Calbert Cheaney	.10	.05	.01
	Washington Bullets			
☐ 41	Glen Rice	.10	.05	.01
	Miami Heat			
☐ 42	Vin Baker	.25	.11	.03
	Milwaukee Bucks			
☐ 43	Grant Long	.05	.02	.01
	Miami Heat			
☐ 44	Derrick Coleman	.10	.05	.01
	New Jersey Nets			
☐ 45	Rik Smits	.10	.05	.01
	Indiana Pacers			
☐ 46	Chris Smith	.05	.02	.01
	Minnesota Timberwolves			
☐ 47	Carl Herrera	.05	.02	.01
	Houston Rockets			
☐ 48	Bob Martin	.05	.02	.01
	Los Angeles Clippers			
☐ 49	Terrell Brandon	.05	.02	.01
	Cleveland Cavaliers			
☐ 50	David Robinson	.50	.23	.06
	San Antonio Spurs			
☐ 51	Danny Ferry	.05	.02	.01
	Cleveland Cavaliers			
☐ 52	Buck Williams	.08	.04	.01
	Portland Trail Blazers			
☐ 53	Josh Grant	.05	.02	.01
	Golden State Warriors			
☐ 54	Ed Pinckney	.05	.02	.01
	Boston Celtics			
☐ 55	Dikembe Mutombo	.15	.07	.02
	Denver Nuggets			
☐ 56	Clifford Robinson	.08	.04	.01
	Portland Trail Blazers			
☐ 57	Luther Wright	.05	.02	.01
	Utah Jazz			
☐ 58	Scott Burrell	.05	.02	.01
	Charlotte Hornets			
☐ 59	Stacey Augmon	.08	.04	.01
	Atlanta Hawks			
☐ 60	Jeff Malone	.08	.04	.01
	Philadelphia 76ers			
☐ 61	Byron Houston	.05	.02	.01
	Golden State Warriors			
☐ 62	Anthony Peeler	.05	.02	.01
	Los Angeles Lakers			
☐ 63	Michael Adams	.05	.02	.01
	Washington Bullets			
☐ 64	Negele Knight	.05	.02	.01
	San Antonio Spurs			
☐ 65	Terry Cummings	.08	.04	.01
	San Antonio Spurs			
☐ 66	Christian Laettner	.08	.04	.01
	Minnesota Timberwolves			
☐ 67	Tracy Murray	.05	.02	.01
	Portland Trail Blazers			
☐ 68	Sedale Threatt	.05	.02	.01
	Los Angeles Lakers			
☐ 69	Dan Majerle	.08	.04	.01
	Phoenix Suns			
☐ 70	Frank Brickowski	.05	.02	.01
	Charlotte Hornets			
☐ 71	Ken Norman	.05	.02	.01
	Milwaukee Bucks			
☐ 72	Charles Smith	.05	.02	.01
	New York Knicks			
☐ 73	Adam Keefe	.05	.02	.01
	Atlanta Hawks			
☐ 74	P.J. Brown	.05	.02	.01
	New Jersey Nets			
☐ 75	Kevin Duckworth	.05	.02	.01
	Washington Bullets			
☐ 76	Shawn Bradley	.10	.05	.01
	Philadelphia 76ers			
☐ 77	Darnell Mee	.05	.02	.01
	Denver Nuggets			
☐ 78	Nick Anderson	.08	.04	.01
	Orlando Magic			
☐ 79	Mark West	.05	.02	.01
	Phoenix Suns			
☐ 80	B.J. Armstrong	.05	.02	.01
	Chicago Bulls			
☐ 81	Dennis Scott	.05	.02	.01
	Orlando Magic			
☐ 82	Lindsey Hunter	.05	.02	.01
	Detroit Pistons			
☐ 83	Derek Strong	.05	.02	.01
	Milwaukee Bucks			
☐ 84	Mike Brown	.05	.02	.01
	Minnesota Timberwolves			
☐ 85	Antonio Harvey	.05	.02	.01
	Los Angeles Lakers			
☐ 86	Anthony Bonner	.05	.02	.01
	New York Knicks			
☐ 87	Sam Cassell	.10	.05	.01
	Houston Rockets			
☐ 88	Harold Miner	.05	.02	.01
	Miami Heat			
☐ 89	Spud Webb	.08	.04	.01
	Sacramento Kings			
☐ 90	Mookie Blaylock	.08	.04	.01
	Atlanta Hawks			
☐ 91	Greg Anthony	.05	.02	.01
	New York Knicks			
☐ 92	Richard Petruska	.05	.02	.01
	Houston Rockets			
☐ 93	Sean Rooks	.05	.02	.01

Dallas Mavericks
☐ 94 Ervin Johnson .05 .02 .01
Seattle Supersonics
☐ 95 Randy Brown .05 .02 .01
Sacramento Kings
☐ 96 Orlando Woolridge .05 .02 .01
Philadelphia 76ers
☐ 97 Charles Oakley .08 .04 .01
New York Knicks
☐ 98 Craig Ehlo .05 .02 .01
Atlanta Hawks
☐ 99 Derek Harper .08 .04 .01
New York Knicks
☐ 100 Doug Edwards .05 .02 .01
Atlanta Hawks
☐ 101 Muggsy Bogues .10 .05 .01
Charlotte Hornets
☐ 102 Mitch Richmond .15 .07 .02
Sacramento Kings
☐ 103 Mahmoud Abdul-Rauf .08 .04 .01
Denver Nuggets
☐ 104 Joe Dumars .15 .07 .02
Detroit Pistons
☐ 105 Eric Riley .05 .02 .01
Houston Rockets
☐ 106 Terry Mills .05 .02 .01
Detroit Pistons
☐ 107 Toni Kukoc .10 .05 .01
Chicago Bulls
☐ 108 Jon Koncak .05 .02 .01
Atlanta Hawks
☐ 109 Haywoode Workman .05 .02 .01
Indiana Pacers
☐ 110 Todd Day .05 .02 .01
Milwaukee Bucks
☐ 111 Detlef Schrempf .10 .05 .01
Seattle Supersonics
☐ 112 David Wesley .05 .02 .01
New Jersey Nets
☐ 113 Mark Jackson .05 .02 .01
Los Angeles Clippers
☐ 114 Doug Overton .05 .02 .01
Washington Bullets
☐ 115 Vinny Del Negro .05 .02 .01
San Antonio Spurs
☐ 116 Loy Vaught .08 .04 .01
Los Angeles Clippers
☐ 117 Mike Peplowski .05 .02 .01
Sacramento Kings
☐ 118 Bimbo Coles .05 .02 .01
Miami Heat
☐ 119 Rex Walters .05 .02 .01
New Jersey Nets
☐ 120 Sherman Douglas .05 .02 .01
Boston Celtics
☐ 121 David Benoit .05 .02 .01
Utah Jazz
☐ 122 John Salley .05 .02 .01
Miami Heat
☐ 123 Cedric Ceballos .10 .05 .01
Phoenix Suns
☐ 124 Chris Mills .10 .05 .01
Cleveland Cavaliers
☐ 125 Robert Horry .10 .05 .01
Houston Rockets
☐ 126 Johnny Newman .05 .02 .01
New Jersey Nets
☐ 127 Malcolm Mackey .05 .02 .01
Phoenix Suns
☐ 128 Terry Dehere .05 .02 .01
Los Angeles Clippers

☐ 129 Dino Radja .10 .05 .01
Boston Celtics
☐ 130 Tree Rollins .05 .02 .01
Charlotte Hornets
☐ 131 Xavier McDaniel .08 .04 .01
Boston Celtics
☐ 132 Bobby Hurley .08 .04 .01
Sacramento Kings
☐ 133 Alonzo Mourning .30 .14 .04
Charlotte Hornets
☐ 134 Isaiah Rider .15 .07 .02
Minnesota Timberwolves
☐ 135 Antoine Carr .05 .02 .01
San Antonio Spurs
☐ 136 Robert Pack .05 .02 .01
Denver Nuggets
☐ 137 Walt Williams .08 .04 .01
Sacramento Kings
☐ 138 Tyrone Corbin .05 .02 .01
Utah Jazz
☐ 139 Popeye Jones .05 .02 .01
Dallas Mavericks
☐ 140 Shawn Kemp .50 .23 .06
Seattle Supersonics
☐ 141 Thurl Bailey .05 .02 .01
Minnesota Timberwolves
☐ 142 James Worthy .10 .05 .01
Los Angeles Lakers
☐ 143 Scott Haskin .05 .02 .01
Indiana Pacers
☐ 144 Hubert Davis .05 .02 .01
New York Knicks
☐ 145 A.C. Green .10 .05 .01
Phoenix Suns
☐ 146 Dale Davis .08 .04 .01
Indiana Pacers
☐ 147 Nate McMillan .05 .02 .01
Seattle Supersonics
☐ 148 Chris Morris .05 .02 .01
New Jersey Nets
☐ 149 Will Perdue .05 .02 .01
Chicago Bulls
☐ 150 Felton Spencer .05 .02 .01
Utah Jazz
☐ 151 Rod Strickland .08 .04 .01
Portland Trail Blazers
☐ 152 Blue Edwards .05 .02 .01
Milwaukee Bucks
☐ 153 John Williams .05 .02 .01
Los Angeles Clippers
☐ 154 Rodney Rogers .08 .04 .01
Denver Nuggets
☐ 155 Acie Earl .05 .02 .01
Boston Celtics
☐ 156 Hersey Hawkins .08 .04 .01
Charlotte Hornets
☐ 157 Jamal Mashburn .50 .23 .06
Dallas Mavericks
☐ 158 Don MacLean .05 .02 .01
Washington Bullets
☐ 159 Micheal Williams .05 .02 .01
Minnesota Timberwolves
☐ 160 Kenny Gattison .05 .02 .01
Charlotte Hornets
☐ 161 Rich King .05 .02 .01
Seattle Supersonics
☐ 162 Allan Houston .10 .05 .01
Detroit Pistons
☐ 163 Hoop-it up .05 .02 .01
Men's Champions
☐ 164 Hoop-it up .05 .02 .01

Women's Champions
☐ 165	Hoop-it up	.05	.02	.01

Slam-Dunk Champions
☐ 166	Danny Manning TO	.05	.02	.01
	Atlanta Hawks			
☐ 167	Robert Parish TO	.05	.02	.01
	Boston Celtics			
☐ 168	Alonzo Mourning TO	.10	.05	.01
	Charlotte Hornets			
☐ 169	Scottie Pippen TO	.10	.05	.01
	Chicago Bulls			
☐ 170	Mark Price TO	.05	.02	.01
	Cleveland Cavaliers			
☐ 171	Jamal Mashburn TO	.25	.11	.03
	Dallas Mavericks			
☐ 172	Dikembe Mutombo TO	.08	.04	.01
	Denver Nuggets			
☐ 173	Joe Dumars TO	.08	.04	.01
	Detroit Pistons			
☐ 174	Chris Webber TO	.20	.09	.03
	Golden State Warriors			
☐ 175	Hakeem Olajuwon TO	.30	.14	.04
	Houston Rockets			
☐ 176	Reggie Miller TO	.10	.05	.01
	Indiana Pacers			
☐ 177	Ron Harper TO	.05	.02	.01
	Los Angeles Clippers			
☐ 178	Nick Van Exel TO	.25	.11	.03
	Los Angeles Lakers			
☐ 179	Steve Smith TO	.05	.02	.01
	Miami Heat			
☐ 180	Vin Baker TO	.10	.05	.01
	Milwaukee Bucks			
☐ 181	Isaiah Rider TO	.08	.04	.01
	Minnesota Timberwolves			
☐ 182	Derrick Coleman TO	.05	.02	.01
	New Jersey Nets			
☐ 183	Patrick Ewing TO	.10	.05	.01
	New York Knicks			
☐ 184	Shaquille O'Neal TO	.60	.25	.08
	Orlando Magic			
☐ 185	Clarence Weatherspoon TO	.05	.02	.01
	Philadelphia 76ers			
☐ 186	Charles Barkley TO	.25	.11	.03
	Phoenix Suns			
☐ 187	Clyde Drexler TO	.10	.05	.01
	Portland Trail Blazers			
☐ 188	Mitch Richmond TO	.08	.04	.01
	Sacramento Kings			
☐ 189	David Robinson TO	.25	.11	.03
	San Antonio Spurs			
☐ 190	Shawn Kemp TO	.25	.11	.03
	Seattle Supersonics			
☐ 191	Karl Malone TO	.10	.05	.01
	Utah Jazz			
☐ 192	Tom Gugliotta TO	.05	.02	.01
	Washington Bullets			
☐ 193	Kenny Anderson ASA	.05	.02	.01
	New Jersey Nets			
☐ 194	Alonzo Mourning ASA	.10	.05	.01
	Charlotte Hornets			
☐ 195	Mark Price ASA	.05	.02	.01
	Cleveland Cavaliers			
☐ 196	John Stockton ASA	.10	.05	.01
	Utah Jazz			
☐ 197	Shaquille O'Neal ASA	.60	.25	.08
	Orlando Magic			
☐ 198	Latrell Sprewell ASA	.10	.05	.01
	Golden State Warriors			
☐ 199	Charles Barkley PRO	.25	.11	.03
	Phoenix Suns			
☐ 200	Chris Webber PRO	.20	.09	.03
	Golden State Warriors			
☐ 201	Patrick Ewing PRO	.10	.05	.01
	New York Knicks			
☐ 202	Dennis Rodman PRO	.08	.04	.01
	San Antonio Spurs			
☐ 203	Shawn Kemp PRO	.25	.11	.03
	Seattle Supersoncis			
☐ 204	Michael Jordan PRO	1.50	.65	.19
	Chicago Bulls			
☐ 205	Shaquille O'Neal PRO	.60	.25	.08
	Orlando Magic			
☐ 206	Larry Johnson PRO	.10	.05	.01
	Charlotte Hornets			
☐ 207	Tim Hardaway CL	.05	.02	.01
	Golden State Warriors			
☐ 208	John Stockton CL	.10	.05	.01
	Utah Jazz			
☐ 209	Harold Miner CL	.05	.02	.01
	Miami Heat			
☐ 210	B.J. Armstrong CL	.05	.02	.01
	Chicago Bulls			
☐ 211	Vernon Maxwell	.05	.02	.01
	Houston Rockets			
☐ 212	John Stockton	.25	.11	.03
	Utah Jazz			
☐ 213	Luc Longley	.05	.02	.01
	Chicago Bulls			
☐ 214	Sam Perkins	.08	.04	.01
	Seattle Supersonics			
☐ 215	Pooh Richardson	.05	.02	.01
	Los Angeles Clippers			
☐ 216	Tyrone Corbin	.05	.02	.01
	Atlanta Hawks			
☐ 217	Mario Elie	.05	.02	.01
	Houston Rockets			
☐ 218	Bobby Phills	.05	.02	.01
	Cleveland Cavaliers			
☐ 219	Grant Hill	4.00	1.80	.50
	Detroit Pistons			
☐ 220	Gary Payton	.10	.05	.01
	Seattle Supersonics			
☐ 221	Tom Hammonds	.05	.02	.01
	Denver Nuggets			
☐ 222	Danny Ainge	.08	.04	.01
	Phoenix Suns			
☐ 223	Gary Grant	.05	.02	.01
	Los Angeles Clippers			
☐ 224	Jimmy Jackson	.30	.14	.04
	Dallas Mavericks			
☐ 225	Chris Gatling	.05	.02	.01
	Golden State Warriors			
☐ 226	Sergei Bazarevich	.05	.02	.01
	Atlanta Hawks			
☐ 227	Tony Dumas	.08	.04	.01
	Dallas Mavericks			
☐ 228	Andrew Lang	.05	.02	.01
	Atlanta Hawks			
☐ 229	Wesley Person	.50	.23	.06
	Phoenix Suns			
☐ 230	Terry Porter	.08	.04	.01
	Phoenix Suns			
☐ 231	Duane Causwell	.05	.02	.01
	Sacramento Kings			
☐ 232	Shaquille O'Neal	1.25	.55	.16
	Orlando Magic			
☐ 233	Antonio Davis	.05	.02	.01
	Indiana Pacers			
☐ 234	Charles Barkley	.50	.23	.06
	Phoenix Suns			

☐ 235	Tony Massenberg .... .05	.02	.01
	Los Angeles Clippers		
☐ 236	Ricky Pierce .... .08	.04	.01
	Golden State Warriors		
☐ 237	Scott Skiles .... .05	.02	.01
	Washington Bullets		
☐ 238	Jalen Rose .... .50	.23	.06
	Denver Nuggets		
☐ 239	Charlie Ward .... .20	.09	.03
	New York Knicks		
☐ 240	Michael Jordan 1.50	.65	.19
	Chicago Bulls		
☐ 241	Elden Campbell .... .05	.02	.01
	Los Angeles Lakers		
☐ 242	Bill Cartwright .... .05	.02	.01
	Seattle Supersonics		
☐ 243	Armon Gilliam .... .05	.02	.01
	New Jersey Nets		
☐ 244	Rick Fox .... .05	.02	.01
	Boston Celtics		
☐ 245	Tim Breaux .... .05	.02	.01
	Houston Rockets		
☐ 246	Monty Williams .... .15	.07	.02
	New York Knicks		
☐ 247	Dominique Wilkins .... .15	.07	.02
	Boston Celtics		
☐ 248	Robert Parish............... .10	.05	.01
	Charlotte Hornets		
☐ 249	Mark Jackson .... .05	.02	.01
	Indiana Pacers		
☐ 250	Jason Kidd 2.50	1.15	.30
	Dallas Mavericks		
☐ 251	Andres Guibert............. .05	.02	.01
	Minnesota Timberwolves		
☐ 252	Matt Geiger.................. .05	.02	.01
	Miami Heat		
☐ 253	Stanley Roberts .... .05	.02	.01
	Los Angeles Clippers		
☐ 254	Jack Haley .... .05	.02	.01
	San Antonio Spurs		
☐ 255	David Wingate.............. .05	.02	.01
	Charlotte Hornets		
☐ 256	John Crotty .... .05	.02	.01
	Utah Jazz		
☐ 257	Brian Grant .... .75	.35	.09
	Sacramento Kings		
☐ 258	Otis Thorpe.................. .08	.04	.01
	Houston Rockets		
☐ 259	Clifford Rozier.............. .20	.09	.03
	Golden State Warriors		
☐ 260	Grant Long .... .05	.02	.01
	Atlanta Hawks		
☐ 261	Eric Mobley................. .15	.07	.02
	Milwaukee Bucks		
☐ 262	Dickey Simpkins .... .15	.07	.02
	Chicago Bulls		
☐ 263	J.R. Reid..................... .05	.02	.01
	San Antonio Spurs		
☐ 264	Kevin Willis................. .08	.04	.01
	Miami Heat		
☐ 265	Scott Brooks................ .05	.02	.01
	Houston Rockets		
☐ 266	Glenn Robinson 2.50	1.15	.30
	Milwaukee Bucks		
☐ 267	Dana Barros................. .10	.05	.01
	Philadelphia 76ers		
☐ 268	Kenny Norman.............. .05	.02	.01
	Atlanta Hawks		
☐ 269	Herb Williams .... .05	.02	.01
	New York Knicks		
☐ 270	Dee Brown................... .08	.04	.01
	Boston Celtics		
☐ 271	Steve Kerr.................... .05	.02	.01
	Chicago Bulls		
☐ 272	Jon Barry..................... .05	.02	.01
	Milwaukee Bucks		
☐ 273	Sean Elliott.................. .08	.04	.01
	San Antonio Spurs		
☐ 274	Elliot Perry .... .05	.02	.01
	Phoenix Suns		
☐ 275	Kenny Smith................. .05	.02	.01
	Houston Rockets		
☐ 276	Sean Rooks.................. .05	.02	.01
	Minnesota Timberwolves		
☐ 277	Gheorghe Muresan .... .08	.04	.01
	Washington Bullets		
☐ 278	Juwan Howard............. 1.00	.45	.13
	Washington Bullets		
☐ 279	Steve Smith.................. .08	.04	.01
	Atlanta Hawks		
☐ 280	Anthony Bowie.............. .05	.02	.01
	Orlando Magic		
☐ 281	Moses Malone .... .15	.07	.02
	San Antonio Spurs		
☐ 282	Olden Polynice............. .05	.02	.01
	Sacramento Kings		
☐ 283	Jo Jo English .... .05	.02	.01
	Chicago Bulls		
☐ 284	Marty Conlon .... .05	.02	.01
	Milwaukee Bucks		
☐ 285	Sam Mitchell................ .05	.02	.01
	Indiana Pacers		
☐ 286	Doug West................... .05	.02	.01
	Minnesota Timberwolves		
☐ 287	Cedric Ceballos............ .10	.05	.01
	Los Angeles Lakers		
☐ 288	Lorenzo Williams .... .05	.02	.01
	Dallas Mavericks		
☐ 289	Harold Ellis .... .05	.02	.01
	Los Angeles Clippers		
☐ 290	Doc Rivers .... .05	.02	.01
	New York Knicks		
☐ 291	Keith Tower.................. .05	.02	.01
	Orlando Magic		
☐ 292	Mark Bryant................. .05	.02	.01
	Portland Trail Blazers		
☐ 293	Oliver Miller .... .05	.02	.01
	Detroit Pistons		
☐ 294	Michael Adams............. .05	.02	.01
	Charlotte Hornets		
☐ 295	Tree Rollins.................. .05	.02	.01
	Orlando Magic		
☐ 296	Eddie Jones 1.50	.65	.19
	Los Angeles Lakers		
☐ 297	Malik Sealy.................. .05	.02	.01
	Los Angeles Clippers		
☐ 298	Blue Edwards............... .05	.02	.01
	Boston Celtics		
☐ 299	Brooks Thompson .... .08	.04	.01
	Orlando Magic		
☐ 300	Benoit Benjamin............ .05	.02	.01
	New Jersey Nets		
☐ 301	Avery Johnson.............. .05	.02	.01
	San Antonio Spurs		
☐ 302	Larry Johnson.............. .20	.09	.03
	Charlotte Hornets		
☐ 303	John Starks.................. .08	.04	.01
	New York Knicks		
☐ 304	Byron Scott.................. .08	.04	.01
	Indiana Pacers		
☐ 305	Eric Murdock................ .05	.02	.01
	Milwaukee Bucks		

☐ 306	Jay Humphries	.05	.02	.01
	Utah Jazz			
☐ 307	Kenny Anderson	.10	.05	.01
	New Jersey Nets			
☐ 308	Brian Williams	.05	.02	.01
	Denver Nuggets			
☐ 309	Nick Van Exel	.50	.23	.06
	Los Angeles Lakers			
☐ 310	Tim Hardaway	.10	.05	.01
	Golden State Warriors			
☐ 311	Lee Mayberry	.05	.02	.01
	Milwaukee Bucks			
☐ 312	Vlade Divac	.10	.05	.01
	Los Angeles Lakers			
☐ 313	Donyell Marshall	.50	.23	.06
	Minnesota Timberwolves			
☐ 314	Anthony Mason	.05	.02	.01
	New York Knicks			
☐ 315	Danny Manning	.10	.05	.01
	Phoenix Suns			
☐ 316	Tyrone Hill	.08	.04	.01
	Cleveland Cavaliers			
☐ 317	Vincent Askew	.05	.02	.01
	Seattle Supersonics			
☐ 318	Khalid Reeves	.40	.18	.05
	Miami Heat			
☐ 319	Ron Harper	.08	.04	.01
	Washington Bulls			
☐ 320	Brent Price	.05	.02	.01
	Washington Bullets			
☐ 321	Byron Houston	.05	.02	.01
	Seattle Supersonics			
☐ 322	Lamond Murray	.40	.18	.05
	Los Angeles Clippers			
☐ 323	Bryant Stith	.05	.02	.01
	Denver Nuggets			
☐ 324	Tom Gugliotta	.08	.04	.01
	Washington Bullets			
☐ 325	Jerome Kersey	.05	.02	.01
	Portland Trail Blazers			
☐ 326	B.J. Tyler	.08	.04	.01
	Philadelphia 76ers			
☐ 327	Antonio Lang	.08	.04	.01
	Phoenix Suns			
☐ 328	Carlos Rogers	.20	.09	.03
	Golden State Warriors			
☐ 329	Waymon Tisdale	.08	.04	.01
	Phoenix Suns			
☐ 330	Kevin Gamble	.05	.02	.01
	Miami Heat			
☐ 331	Eric Piatkowski	.15	.07	.02
	Los Angeles Clippers			
☐ 332	Mitchell Butler	.05	.02	.01
	Washington Bullets			
☐ 333	Patrick Ewing	.20	.09	.03
	New York Knicks			
☐ 334	Doug Smith	.05	.02	.01
	Dallas Mavericks			
☐ 335	Joe Kleine	.05	.02	.01
	Phoenix Suns			
☐ 336	Keith Jennings	.05	.02	.01
	Golden State Warriors			
☐ 337	Bill Curley	.15	.07	.02
	Detroit Pistons			
☐ 338	Johnny Newman	.05	.02	.01
	Milwaukee Bucks			
☐ 339	Howard Eisley	.05	.02	.01
	Minnesota Timberwolves			
☐ 340	Willie Anderson	.05	.02	.01
	San Antonio Spurs			
☐ 341	Aaron McKie	.20	.09	.03
	Portland Trail Blazers			
☐ 342	Tom Chambers	.08	.04	.01
	Utah Jazz			
☐ 343	Scott Williams	.05	.02	.01
	Philadelphia 76ers			
☐ 344	Harvey Grant	.05	.02	.01
	Portland Trail Blazers			
☐ 345	Billy Owens	.08	.04	.01
	Miami Heat			
☐ 346	Sharone Wright	.30	.14	.04
	Philadelphia 76ers			
☐ 347	Michael Cage	.05	.02	.01
	Cleveland Cavaliers			
☐ 348	Vern Fleming	.05	.02	.01
	Indiana Pacers			
☐ 349	Darrin Hancock	.05	.02	.01
	Charlotte Hornets			
☐ 350	Matt Fish	.05	.02	.01
	Los Angeles Clippers			
☐ 351	Rony Seikaly	.05	.02	.01
	Golden State Warriors			
☐ 352	Victor Alexander	.05	.02	.01
	Golden State Warriors			
☐ 353	Anthony Miller	.05	.02	.01
	Los Angeles Lakers			
☐ 354	Horace Grant	.15	.07	.02
	Orlando Magic			
☐ 355	Jayson Williams	.05	.02	.01
	New Jersey Nets			
☐ 356	Dale Ellis	.08	.04	.01
	Denver Nuggets			
☐ 357	Sarunas Marciulionis	.05	.02	.01
	Seattle Supersonics			
☐ 358	Anthony Avent	.05	.02	.01
	Orlando Magic			
☐ 359	Rex Chapman	.05	.02	.01
	Washington Bullets			
☐ 360	Askia Jones	.05	.02	.01
	Minnesota Timberwolves			
☐ 361	Charles Outlaw	.05	.02	.01
	Los Angeles Clippers			
☐ 362	Chuck Person	.08	.04	.01
	San Antonio Spurs			
☐ 363	Dan Schayes	.05	.02	.01
	Phoenix Suns			
☐ 364	Morlon Wiley	.05	.02	.01
	Dallas Mavericks			
☐ 365	Dontonio Wingfield	.10	.05	.01
	Seattle Supersonics			
☐ 366	Tony Smith	.05	.02	.01
	Los Angeles Lakers			
☐ 367	Bill Wennington	.05	.02	.01
	Chicago Bulls			
☐ 368	Bryon Russell	.05	.02	.01
	Utah Jazz			
☐ 369	Geert Hammink	.05	.02	.01
	Orlando Magic			
☐ 370	Eric Montross	.40	.18	.05
	Boston Celtics			
☐ 371	Cliff Levingston	.05	.02	.01
	Denver Nuggets			
☐ 372	Stacey Augmon BP	.05	.02	.01
	Atlanta Hawks			
☐ 373	Eric Montross BP	.15	.07	.02
	Boston Celtics			
☐ 374	Alonzo Mourning BP	.10	.05	.01
	Charlotte Hornets			
☐ 375	Scottie Pippen BP	.10	.05	.01
	Chicago Bulls			
☐ 376	Mark Price BP	.05	.02	.01
	Cleveland Cavaliers			

☐ 377	Jason Kidd BP 1.00	.45	.13	
	Dallas Mavericks			
☐ 378	Jalen Rose BP .... .20	.09	.03	
	Denver Nuggets			
☐ 379	Grant Hill BP 1.50	.65	.19	
	Detroit Pistons			
☐ 380	Latrell Sprewell BP .... .10	.05	.01	
	Golden State Warriors			
☐ 381	Hakeem Olajuwon BP... .30	.14	.04	
	Houston Rockets			
☐ 382	Reggie Miller BP .... .10	.05	.01	
	Indiana Pacers			
☐ 383	Lamond Murray BP...... .15	.07	.02	
	Los Angeles Clippers			
☐ 384	Eddie Jones BP .... .60	.25	.08	
	Los Angeles Lakers			
☐ 385	Khalid Reeves BP .... .10	.05	.01	
	Miami Heat			
☐ 386	Glenn Robinson BP... 1.00	.45	.13	
	Milwaukee Bucks			
☐ 387	Donyell Marshall BP .... .20	.09	.03	
	Minnesota Timberwolves			
☐ 388	Derrick Coleman BP ..... .05	.02	.01	
	New Jersey Nets			
☐ 389	Patrick Ewing BP .... .10	.05	.01	
	New York Knicks			
☐ 390	Shaquille O'Neal BP ..... .60	.25	.08	
	Orlando Magic			
☐ 391	Sharone Wright BP .... .10	.05	.01	
	Philadelphia 76ers			
☐ 392	Charles Barkley BP....... .25	.11	.03	
	Phoenix Suns			
☐ 393	Aaron McKie BP .... .10	.05	.01	
	Portland Trail Blazers			
☐ 394	Brian Grant BP .... .30	.14	.04	
	Sacramento Kings			
☐ 395	David Robinson BP .... .25	.11	.03	
	San Antonio Spurs			
☐ 396	Shawn Kemp BP .... .25	.11	.03	
	Seattle Supersonics			
☐ 397	Karl Malone BP .... .10	.05	.01	
	Utah Jazz			
☐ 398	Tom Gugliotta BP.......... .05	.02	.01	
	Washington Bullets			
☐ 399	Hakeem Olajuwon TRIV .30	.14	.04	
	Houston Rockets			
☐ 400	Shaquille O'Neal TRIV... .60	.25	.08	
	Orlando Magic			
☐ 401	Chris Webber TRIV ...... .20	.09	.03	
	Golden State Warriors			
☐ 402	Michael Jordan TRIV . 1.50	.65	.19	
	Chicago Bulls			
☐ 403	David Robinson TRIV... .25	.11	.03	
	San Antonio Spurs			
☐ 404	Shawn Kemp TRIV....... .25	.11	.03	
	Seattle Supersonics			
☐ 405	Patrick Ewing TRIV ...... .10	.05	.01	
	New York Knicks			
☐ 406	Charles Barkley TRIV ... .25	.11	.03	
	Phoenix Suns			
☐ 407	Glenn Robinson DC ... 1.00	.45	.13	
	Milwaukee Bucks			
☐ 408	Jason Kidd DC 1.00	.45	.13	
	Dallas Mavericks			
☐ 409	Grant Hill DC................ 1.50	.65	.19	
	Detroit Pistons			
☐ 410	Donyell Marshall DC .... .20	.09	.03	
	Minnesota Timberwolves			
☐ 411	Sharone Wright DC....... .10	.05	.01	
	Philadelphia 76ers			
☐ 412	Lamond Murray DC ...... .15	.07	.02	

	Los Angeles Clippers			
☐ 413	Brian Grant DC............. .30	.14	.04	
	Sacramento Kings			
☐ 414	Eric Montross DC.......... .15	.07	.02	
	Boston Celtics			
☐ 415	Eddie Jones DC............. .60	.25	.08	
	Los Angeles Lakers			
☐ 416	Carlos Rogers DC .... .10	.05	.01	
	Golden State Warriors			
☐ 417	Shawn Kemp CL .... .10	.05	.01	
	Seattle Supersonics			
☐ 418	Bobby Hurley CL........... .05	.02	.01	
	Sacramento Kings			
☐ 419	Shawn Bradley CL......... .05	.02	.01	
	Philadelphia 76ers			
☐ 420	Michael Jordan CL......... .75	.35	.09	

1994-95 Collector's Choice Gold Signature

Issued one in every thirty-six first series Collector's Choice 12-card hobby packs and 13-card retail packs, and one in every twenty 20-card retail jumbo packs, these 210 standard-size (2 1/2" by 3 1/2") cards parallel the basic 1994-95 Collector's Choice set. The difference is the player's facsimile autograph appears in gold-foil near the bottom and the front borders are colored in gold. Only the key cards within the set are listed below. Please refer to the multiplier provided (and the values listed for the regular-issue 1994-95 Collector's Choice cards) to ascertain the value of the other Gold cards within the set.

	MINT	NRMT	EXC
COMPLETE GOLD SET (420)	1500.00	700.00	190.00
COMPLETE SERIES 1 (210)	600.00	275.00	75.00
COMPLETE SERIES 2 (210)	900.00	400.00	115.00
COMMON GOLD CARD (1-420)	2.00	.90	.25
*STARS: 30X to 60X BASIC CARDS			
*ROOKIES: 12.5X to 25X BASIC CARDS			

☐ 1	Anfernee Hardaway...... 60.00	27.00	7.50	
	Orlando Magic			
☐ 23	Michael Jordan 150.00	70.00	19.00	
	Chicago Bulls			

		MINT	NRMT	EXC
☐ 34	Hakeem Olajuwon...... Houston Rockets	40.00	18.00	5.00
☐ 50	David Robinson .... San Antonio Spurs	30.00	13.50	3.80
☐ 140	Shawn Kemp............. Seattle Supersonics	30.00	13.50	3.80
☐ 157	Jamal Mashburn...... Dallas Mavericks	30.00	13.50	3.80
☐ 184	Shaquille O'Neal TO. Orlando Magic	40.00	18.00	5.00
☐ 197	Shaquille O'Neal ASA Orlando Magic	40.00	18.00	5.00
☐ 204	Michael Jordan PRO Chicago Bulls	80.00	36.00	10.00
☐ 205	Saquille O'Neal PRO Orlando Magic	40.00	18.00	5.00
☐ 219	Grant Hill................. Detroit Pistons	100.00	45.00	12.50
☐ 232	Shaquille O'Neal....... Orlando Magic	80.00	36.00	10.00
☐ 234	Charles Barkley........ Phoenix Suns	30.00	13.50	3.80
☐ 240	Michael Jordan .... Chicago Bulls	80.00	36.00	10.00
☐ 250	Jason Kidd............... Dallas Mavericks	60.00	27.00	7.50
☐ 266	Glenn Robinson .... Milwaukee Bucks	60.00	27.00	7.50
☐ 296	Eddie Jones .... Los Angeles Lakers	40.00	18.00	5.00
☐ 309	Nick Van Exel........... Los Angeles Lakers	30.00	13.50	3.80
☐ 379	Grant Hill BP .... Detroit Pistons	40.00	18.00	5.00
☐ 390	Shaquille O'Neal BP. Orlando Magic	40.00	18.00	5.00
☐ 400	Shaquille O'Neal TRIV Orlando Magic	40.00	18.00	5.00
☐ 402	Michael Jordan TRIV Chicago Bulls	80.00	36.00	10.00
☐ 409	Grant Hill DC............ Detroit Pistons	40.00	18.00	5.00
☐ 420	Michael Jordan CL ...	40.00	18.00	5.00

1994-95 Collector's Choice Silver Signature

Issued one per Collector's Choice 12-card hobby pack, two per 13-card retail pack, and three per 20-card retail jumbo pack, these 420 standard-size (2 1/2" by 3 1/2") cards parallel that of the basic 1994-95 Collector's Choice set. The difference is the player's facsimile autograph appears in silver-foil near the bottom and the front borders are colored in silver. A handful of first year players were not available for facsimile autographs and have team names scripted in silver foil instead. Please refer to the multiplier provided (and the values listed for the regular-issue 1994-95 Collector's Choice cards) to ascertain the value of the silver cards.

	MINT	NRMT	EXC
COMPLETE SET (420)	100.00	45.00	12.50
COMPLETE SERIES 1 (210)...	40.00	18.00	5.00
COMPLETE SERIES 2 (210)...	60.00	27.00	7.50
COMMON SILVER (1-420)......	.10	.05	.01
*STARS: 2X to 4X BASIC CARDS			
*ROOKIES: 1.5X to 3X BASIC CARDS			

1994-95 Collector's Choice Blow-Ups

One of these oversized (5" by 7") cards was inserted exclusively into each series 2 hobby box. Each Blow-Up is identical in design and numbering to their corresponding basic issue card. According to information provided by Upper Deck at least 3,000 of these cards were autographed and randomly seeded into boxes. There are far fewer autographed Michael Jordan Blow-Ups than the other four players featured.

		MINT	NRMT	EXC
COMPLETE SET (5)		10.00	4.50	1.25
COMMON CARD (40/76/132)		.50	.23	.06
☐ 23	Michael Jordan Baseball	8.00	3.60	1.00
☐ 140	Shawn Kemp...............	1.00	.45	.13
☐ A23	Michael Jordan AU	1500.00	700.00	190.00
☐ A40	Calbert Cheaney AU...	20.00	9.00	2.50
☐ A76	Shawn Bradley AU......	20.00	9.00	2.50
☐ A132	Bobby Hurley AU	20.00	9.00	2.50
☐ A140	Shawn Kemp AU..	100.00	45.00	12.50

1994-95 Collector's Choice Crash the Game Assists

These fifteen standard size Crash the Game Assists cards were randomly inserted exclusively into first series retail packs at a rate of one in 20. Cards that featured players who tallied 750 or more assists during the 1994-95 campaign were redeemable for a 15-card parallel Crash the Game Assists Redemption set. Only John Stockton eclipsed the mark. The fronts feature a color-action photo with the background of the game in black and white. The top has the player's name in a box the color of his team and the bottom has the words "You Crash The Game" in foil with the player's position behind it in his team's color. The back says 750 assists at the top below his name surrounded by the player's team color. Their are instructions on how to redeem your cards if you win. The exchange deadline was June 16th, 1995. The redemption cards were delayed in shipping until late October, 1995. The cards are numbered with an "A" prefix.

	MINT	NRMT	EXC
COMPLETE SET (15)	15.00	6.75	1.90
COMMON CARD (A1-A15)	.50	.23	.06
☐ A1 Michael Adams	.50	.23	.06
Washington Bullets			
☐ A2 Kenny Anderson	.50	.23	.06
New Jersey Nets			
☐ A3 Mookie Blaylock	.50	.23	.06
Atlanta Hawks			
☐ A4 Muggsy Bogues	.50	.23	.06
Charlotte Hornets			
☐ A5 Sherman Douglas	.50	.23	.06
Boston Celtics			
☐ A6 Anfernee Hardaway	8.00	3.60	1.00
Orlando Magic			
☐ A7 Tim Hardaway	.50	.23	.06
Golden State Warriors			
☐ A8 Lindsey Hunter	.50	.23	.06
Detroit Pistons			
☐ A9 Mark Jackson	.50	.23	.06
Los Angeles Clippers			
☐ A10 Kevin Johnson	.75	.35	.09
Phoenix Suns			
☐ A11 Eric Murdock	.50	.23	.06
Milwaukee Bucks			
☐ A12 Mark Price	.50	.23	.06
Cleveland Cavaliers			
☐ A13 John Stockton WIN	5.00	2.30	.60
Utah Jazz			
☐ A14 Rod Strickland	.50	.23	.06
Portland Trail Blazers			
☐ A15 Micheal Williams	.50	.23	.06
Minnesota Timberwolves			

1994-95 Collector's Choice Crash the Game Rebounds

These fifteen standard size Crash the Game Rebounds cards were randomly inserted exclusively into second series retail packs at a rate of one in 20. Cards that featured players who grabbed 1,000 or more rebounds during the 1994-95 campaign were redeemable for a 15-card parallel Crash the Game Rebounds Redemption set. The card design is the same as the Assists set except that it says 1,000 Rebounds. Only Dikembe Mutombo eclipsed the mark. The exchange deadline was June 30th, 1995. The redemption cards were delayed in shipping until late October, 1995. The cards are numbered with a "R" prefix.

	MINT	NRMT	EXC
COMPLETE SET (15)	20.00	9.00	2.50
COMMON CARD (R1-R15)	.50	.23	.06
☐ R1 Derrick Coleman	.75	.35	.09
New Jersey Nets			
☐ R2 Patrick Ewing	1.50	.65	.19
New York Knicks			
☐ R3 Horace Grant	.75	.35	.09
Orlando Magic			
☐ R4 Shawn Kemp	3.00	1.35	.40
Seattle Supersonics			
☐ R5 Karl Malone	1.50	.65	.19
Utah Jazz			
☐ R6 Alonzo Mourning	2.00	.90	.25
Charlotte Hornets			
☐ R7 Dikembe Mutombo WIN	3.00	1.35	.40

		MINT	NRMT	EXC
	Denver Nuggets			
☐ R8	Charles Oakley	.50	.23	.06
	New York Knicks			
☐ R9	Hakeem Olajuwon	4.00	1.80	.50
	Houston Rockets			
☐ R10	Shaquille O'Neal	8.00	3.60	1.00
	Orlando Magic			
☐ R11	Olden Polynice	.50	.23	.06
	Sacramento Kings			
☐ R12	David Robinson	3.00	1.35	.40
	San Antonio Spurs			
☐ R13	Dennis Rodman	1.00	.45	.13
	San Antonio Spurs			
☐ R14	Otis Thorpe	.75	.35	.09
	Houston Rockets			
☐ R15	Kevin Willis	.50	.23	.06
	Atlanta Hawks			

1994-95 Collector's Choice Crash the Game Rookie Scoring

These fifteen standard size Crash the Game Rookie Scoring cards were randomly inserted exclusively into second series hobby packs at a rate of one in 20. Cards that featured rookies who scored more than 1,250 points during the 1994-95 campaign were redeemable for a 15-card parallel Crash the Game Rookie Scoring Redemption set. The card design is the same as the Assists set except on the back it says 1,250 Points. Only Grant Hill and Glenn Robinson eclipsed the mark. The exchange deadline was June 30th, 1995. The redemption cards were delayed in shipping until late October, 1995. The cards are numbered with a "S" prefix.

		MINT	NRMT	EXC
COMPLETE SET (15)		30.00	13.50	3.80
COMMON CARD (S1-S15)		.50	.23	.06
☐ S1	Tony Dumas	.50	.23	.06
	Dallas Mavericks			
☐ S2	Brian Grant	1.50	.65	.19
	Sacramento Kings			
☐ S3	Grant Hill WIN	12.00	5.50	1.50

		MINT	NRMT	EXC
	Detroit Pistons			
☐ S4	Juwan Howard	2.00	.90	.25
	Washington Bullets			
☐ S5	Eddie Jones	3.00	1.35	.40
	Los Angeles Lakers			
☐ S6	Jason Kidd	5.00	2.30	.60
	Dallas Mavericks			
☐ S7	Donyell Marshall	1.00	.45	.13
	Minnesota Timberwolves			
☐ S8	Eric Montross	.75	.35	.09
	Boston Celtics			
☐ S9	Lamond Murray	.75	.35	.09
	Los Angeles Clippers			
☐ S10	Khalid Reeves	.75	.35	.09
	Miami Heat			
☐ S11	Glenn Robinson WIN	8.00	3.60	1.00
	Milwaukee Bucks			
☐ S12	Jalen Rose	1.00	.45	.13
	Denver Nuggets			
☐ S13	Dickey Simpkins	.50	.23	.06
	Chicago Bulls			
☐ S14	Charlie Ward	.50	.23	.06
	New York Knicks			
☐ S15	Sharone Wright	.75	.35	.09
	Philadelphia 76ers			

1994-95 Collector's Choice Crash the Game Scoring

These fifteen standard size Crash the Game Scoring cards were randomly inserted exclusively into first series hobby packs at a rate of one in 20. Cards that featured players who posted 2,000 or more points during the 1994-95 campaign were redeemable for a 15-card parallel Crash the Game Scoring Redemption set. The card design is the same as the Assists set except on the back it says 2,000 Points. Karl Malone, Shaquille O'Neal, Hakeem Olajuwon and David Robinson all eclipsed the mark. The exchange deadline was June 30th, 1995. The redemption cards were delayed in shipping until late October, 1995. The cards are numbered with a "S" prefix.

	MINT	NRMT	EXC
COMPLETE SET (15)	30.00	13.50	3.80
COMMON CARD (S1-S15)	.50	.23	.06

		MINT	NRMT	EXC
☐ S1	Charles Barkley Phoenix Suns	3.00	1.35	.40
☐ S2	Derrick Coleman New Jersey Nets	.50	.23	.06
☐ S3	Joe Dumars Detroit Pistons	.75	.35	.09
☐ S4	Patrick Ewing New York Knicks	1.50	.65	.19
☐ S5	Karl Malone WIN Utah Jazz	2.50	1.15	.30
☐ S6	Reggie Miller Indiana Pacers	1.50	.65	.19
☐ S7	Shaquille O'Neal WIN Orlando Magic	12.00	5.50	1.50
☐ S8	Hakeem Olajuwon WIN Houston Rockets	6.00	2.70	.75
☐ S9	Scottie Pippen Chicago Bulls	1.50	.65	.19
☐ S10	Glen Rice Miami Heat	.50	.23	.06
☐ S11	Mitch Richmond Sacramento Kings	.75	.35	.09
☐ S12	David Robinson WIN San Antonio Spurs	5.00	2.30	.60
☐ S13	Latrell Sprewell Golden State Warriors	2.00	.90	.25
☐ S14	Chris Webber Golden State Warriors	2.50	1.15	.30
☐ S15	Dominique Wilkins Los Angeles Clippers	.75	.35	.09

		MINT	NRMT	EXC
☐ 1	Glenn Robinson Milwaukee Bucks	2.50	1.15	.30
☐ 2	Jason Kidd Dallas Mavericks	2.50	1.15	.30
☐ 3	Grant Hill Detroit Pistons	4.00	1.80	.50
☐ 4	Donyell Marshall Minnesota Timberwolves	.50	.23	.06
☐ 5	Juwan Howard Washington Bullets	1.00	.45	.13
☐ 6	Sharone Wright Philadelphia 76ers	.30	.14	.04
☐ 7	Lamond Murray Los Angeles Clippers	.40	.18	.05
☐ 8	Brian Grant Sacramento Kings	.75	.35	.09
☐ 9	Eric Montross Boston Celtics	.40	.18	.05
☐ 10	Eddie Jones Los Angeles Lakers	1.50	.65	.19
☐ NNO	Draft Trade Card	.25	.11	.03

1995-96 Collector's Choice

These 210-standard size cards comprise Upper Deck's 1995-96 Collector's Choice first series. Cards were issued in 12-card hobby and retail packs (suggested retail price of ninety-nine cents) and five-card retail mini-packs. White-bordered fronts feature color player action shots. The backs have a color photo and statistics. The following subsets are included: Fun Facts (166-194) and Professor Dunk (195-208). Special Crash Packs containing only inserts (an assortion of Player's Club, Player's Club Platinum and Crash the Game cards) were randomly inserted into one in every 175 first series 12-card packs. A Draft Trade card, exchangeable for a set featuring the top 10 players selected in the 1995 NBA draft, was randomly inserted into one in every 144 first series 12-card packs.

1994-95 Collector's Choice Draft Trade

This 10-card set was available only by redeeming a Draft Trade card that was randomly seeded into one in every 36 first series Collector's Choice hobby or retail packs. The fronts have a color-action photo with the top-half having the background of the game in black and white. The bottom of the card has a white background. On the left side of the card are the words "NBA Draft Lottery Picks" with the player's name above it. The backs have the player's name and information set against the colors of his team. The expiration date on the redemption was June 16th, 1995.

	MINT	NRMT	EXC
COMPLETE SET (10)	8.00	3.60	1.00
COMMON CARD (1-10)	.30	.14	.04

	MINT	NRMT	EXC
COMPLETE SERIES 1 (210)	15.00	6.75	1.90
COMMON CARD (1-210)	.05	.02	.01
☐ 1 Rod Strickland Portland Trailblazers	.08	.04	.01

☐ 2	Larry Johnson	.20	.09	.03
	Charlotte Hornets			
☐ 3	Mahmoud Abdul-Rauf	.08	.04	.01
	Denver Nuggets			
☐ 4	Joe Dumars	.15	.07	.02
	Detroit Pistons			
☐ 5	Jason Kidd	.75	.35	.09
	Dallas Mavericks			
☐ 6	Avery Johnson	.05	.02	.01
	San Antonio Spurs			
☐ 7	Dee Brown	.05	.02	.01
	Boston Celtics			
☐ 8	Brian Williams	.05	.02	.01
	Denver Nuggets			
☐ 9	Nick Van Exel	.30	.14	.04
	Los Angeles Lakers			
☐ 10	Dennis Rodman	.15	.07	.02
	San Antonio Spurs			
☐ 11	Rony Seikaly	.05	.02	.01
	Golden State Warriors			
☐ 12	Harvey Grant	.05	.02	.01
	Portland Trailblazers			
☐ 13	Craig Ehlo	.05	.02	.01
	Atlanta Hawks			
☐ 14	Derek Harper	.08	.04	.01
	New York Knicks			
☐ 15	Oliver Miller	.05	.02	.01
	Detroit Pistons			
	Drafted by the Raptors			
☐ 16	Dennis Scott	.05	.02	.01
	Orlando Magic			
☐ 17	Ed Pinckney	.05	.02	.01
	Milwaukee Bucks			
	Drafted by the Raptors			
☐ 18	Eric Piatkowski	.05	.02	.01
	Los Angeles Clippers			
☐ 19	B.J. Armstrong	.05	.02	.01
	Chicago Bulls			
☐ 20	Tyrone Hill	.08	.04	.01
	Cleveland Cavaliers			
☐ 21	Malik Sealy	.05	.02	.01
	Los Angeles Clippers			
☐ 22	Clyde Drexler	.25	.11	.03
	Houston Rockets			
☐ 23	Aaron McKie	.08	.04	.01
	Portland Trailblazers			
☐ 24	Harold Miner	.05	.02	.01
	Miami Heat			
☐ 25	Bobby Hurley	.08	.04	.01
	Sacramento Kings			
☐ 26	Dell Curry	.05	.02	.01
	Sacramento Kings			
☐ 27	Micheal Williams	.05	.02	.01
	Minnesota Timberwolves			
☐ 28	Adam Keefe	.05	.02	.01
	Utah Jazz			
☐ 29	Antonio Harvey	.05	.02	.01
	Los Angeles Lakers			
	Drafted by the Grizzlies			
☐ 30	Billy Owens	.08	.04	.01
	Miami Heat			
☐ 31	Nate McMillan	.05	.02	.01
	Seattle Supersonics			
☐ 32	J.R. Reid	.05	.02	.01
	San Antonio Spurs			
☐ 33	Grant Hill	1.25	.55	.16
	Detroit Pistons			
☐ 34	Charles Barkley	.50	.23	.06
	Phoenix Suns			
☐ 35	Tyrone Corbin	.05	.02	.01
	Atlanta Hawks			

	Traded to the Kings			
☐ 36	Don MacLean	.05	.02	.01
	Washington Bullets			
☐ 37	Kenny Smith	.05	.02	.01
	Houston Rockets			
☐ 38	Juwan Howard	.30	.14	.04
	Washington Bullets			
☐ 39	Charles Smith	.05	.02	.01
	New York Knicks			
☐ 40	Shawn Kemp	.50	.23	.06
	Seattle Supersonics			
☐ 41	Dana Barros	.10	.05	.01
	Philadelphia 76ers			
☐ 42	Vin Baker	.15	.07	.02
	Milwaukee Bucks			
☐ 43	Armon Gilliam	.05	.02	.01
	New Jersey Nets			
☐ 44	Spud Webb	.08	.04	.01
	Sacramento Kings			
	Traded to the Hawks			
☐ 45	Michael Jordan	3.00	1.35	.40
	Chicago Bulls			
☐ 46	Scott Williams	.05	.02	.01
	Philadelphia 76ers			
☐ 47	Vlade Divac	.10	.05	.01
	Los Angeles Lakers			
☐ 48	Roy Tarpley	.05	.02	.01
	Dallas Mavericks			
☐ 49	Bimbo Coles	.05	.02	.01
	Miami Heat			
☐ 50	David Robinson	.50	.23	.06
	San Antonio Spurs			
☐ 51	Terry Dehere	.05	.02	.01
	Los Angeles Clippers			
☐ 52	Bobby Phills	.05	.02	.01
	Cleveland Cavaliers			
☐ 53	Sherman Douglas	.05	.02	.01
	Boston Celtics			
☐ 54	Rodney Rogers	.08	.04	.01
	Denver Nuggets			
	Traded to the Clippers			
☐ 55	Detlef Schrempf	.10	.05	.01
	Seattle Supersonics			
☐ 56	Calbert Cheaney	.08	.04	.01
	Washington Bullets			
☐ 57	Tom Gugliotta	.08	.04	.01
	Minnesota Timberwolves			
☐ 58	Jeff Turner	.05	.02	.01
	Orlando Magic			
☐ 59	Mookie Blaylock	.08	.04	.01
	Atlanta Hawks			
☐ 60	Bill Curley	.05	.02	.01
	Detroit Pistons			
☐ 61	Chris Dudley	.05	.02	.01
	Portland Trail Blazers			
☐ 62	Popeye Jones	.05	.02	.01
	Dallas Mavericks			
☐ 63	Scott Burrell	.05	.02	.01
	Charlotte Hornets			
☐ 64	Dale Davis	.08	.04	.01
	Indiana Pacers			
☐ 65	Mitchell Butler	.05	.02	.01
	Washington Bullets			
☐ 66	Pervis Ellison	.05	.02	.01
	Boston Celtics			
☐ 67	Todd Day	.05	.02	.01
	Milwaukee Bucks			
☐ 68	Carl Herrera	.05	.02	.01
	Houston Rockets			
☐ 69	Jeff Hornacek	.05	.02	.01
	Utah Jazz			

☐ 70	Vincent Askew	.05	.02	.01
	Seattle Supersonics			
☐ 71	A.C. Green	.10	.05	.01
	Phoenix Suns			
☐ 72	Kevin Gamble	.05	.02	.01
	Miami Heat			
☐ 73	Chris Gatling	.05	.02	.01
	Golden State Warriors			
☐ 74	Otis Thorpe	.08	.04	.01
	Portland Trail Blazers			
☐ 75	Michael Cage	.05	.02	.01
	Cleveland Cavaliers			
☐ 76	Carlos Rogers	.08	.04	.01
	Golden State Warriors			
☐ 77	Gheorghe Muresan	.05	.02	.01
	Washington Bullets			
☐ 78	Olden Polynice	.05	.02	.01
	Sacramento Kings			
☐ 79	Grant Long	.05	.02	.01
	Atlanta Hawks			
☐ 80	Allan Houston	.05	.02	.01
	Detroit Pistons			
☐ 81	Charles Outlaw	.05	.02	.01
	Los Angeles Clippers			
☐ 82	Clarence Weatherspoon	.08	.04	.01
	Philadelphia 76ers			
☐ 83	Tony Dumas	.05	.02	.01
	Dallas Mavericks			
☐ 84	Herb Williams	.05	.02	.01
	New York Knicks			
☐ 85	P.J. Brown	.05	.02	.01
	New Jersey Nets			
☐ 86	Robert Horry	.10	.05	.01
	Houston Rockets			
☐ 87	Byron Scott	.08	.04	.01
	Indiana Pacers			
	Drafted by the Grizzlies			
☐ 88	Horace Grant	.15	.07	.02
	Orlando Magic			
☐ 89	Dominique Wilkins	.15	.07	.02
	Boston Celtics			
☐ 90	Doug West	.05	.02	.01
	Minnesota Timberwolves			
☐ 91	Antoine Carr	.05	.02	.01
	Utah Jazz			
☐ 92	Dickey Simpkins	.05	.02	.01
	Washington Bullets			
☐ 93	Elden Campbell	.05	.02	.01
	Los Angeles Lakers			
☐ 94	Kevin Johnson	.15	.07	.02
	Phoenix Suns			
☐ 95	Rex Chapman	.05	.02	.01
	Washington Bullets			
	Traded to the Heat			
☐ 96	John Williams	.08	.04	.01
	Cleveland Cavaliers			
☐ 97	Tim Hardaway	.10	.05	.01
	Golden State Warriors			
☐ 98	Rik Smits	.10	.05	.01
	Indiana Pacers			
☐ 99	Rex Walters	.05	.02	.01
	New Jersey Nets			
☐ 100	Robert Parish	.10	.05	.01
	Charlotte Hornets			
☐ 101	Isaiah Rider	.10	.05	.01
	Minnesota Timberwolves			
☐ 102	Sarunas Marciulionis	.05	.02	.01
	Seattle Supersonics			
☐ 103	Andrew Lang	.05	.02	.01
	Atlanta Hawks			
☐ 104	Eric Mobley	.05	.02	.01
	Milwaukee Bucks			
☐ 105	Randy Brown	.05	.02	.01
	Sacramento Kings			
☐ 106	John Stockton	.25	.11	.03
	Utah Jazz			
☐ 107	Lamond Murray	.10	.05	.01
	Los Angeles Clippers			
☐ 108	Will Perdue	.05	.02	.01
	Washington Bulls			
☐ 109	Wayman Tisdale	.08	.04	.01
	Phoenix Suns			
☐ 110	John Starks	.05	.02	.01
	New York Knicks			
☐ 111	John Salley	.05	.02	.01
	Miami Heat			
☐ 112	Lucious Harris	.05	.02	.01
	Dallas Mavericks			
☐ 113	Jeff Malone	.08	.04	.01
	Philadelphia 76ers			
☐ 114	Anthony Bowie	.05	.02	.01
	Orlando Magic			
☐ 115	Vinny Del Negro	.05	.02	.01
	San Antonio Spurs			
☐ 116	Michael Adams	.05	.02	.01
	Charlotte Hornets			
☐ 117	Chris Mullin	.10	.05	.01
	Golden State Warriors			
☐ 118	Benoit Benjamin	.05	.02	.01
	New Jersey Nets			
	Drafted by the Grizzlies			
☐ 119	Byron Houston	.05	.02	.01
	Seattle Supersonics			
☐ 120	LaPhonso Ellis	.05	.02	.01
	Denver Nuggets			
☐ 121	Doug Overton	.05	.02	.01
	Washington Bullets			
☐ 122	Jerome Kersey	.05	.02	.01
	Portland Trail Blazers			
	Drafted by the Grizzlies			
☐ 123	Greg Minor	.05	.02	.01
	Boston Celtics			
☐ 124	Christian Laettner	.08	.04	.01
	Minnesota Timberwolves			
☐ 125	Mark Price	.10	.05	.01
	Cleveland Cavaliers			
☐ 126	Kevin Willis	.08	.04	.01
	Miami Heat			
☐ 127	Kenny Anderson	.10	.05	.01
	New Jersey Nets			
☐ 128	Marty Conlon	.05	.02	.01
	Milwaukee Bucks			
☐ 129	Blue Edwards	.05	.02	.01
	Utah Jazz			
	Drafted by the Grizzlies			
☐ 130	Dan Schayes	.05	.02	.01
	Phoenix Suns			
☐ 131	Duane Ferrell	.05	.02	.01
	Indiana Pacers			
☐ 132	Charles Oakley	.08	.04	.01
	New York Knicks			
☐ 133	Brian Grant	.25	.11	.03
	Sacramento Kings			
☐ 134	Reggie Williams	.05	.02	.01
	Denver Nuggets			
☐ 135	Steve Kerr	.05	.02	.01
	Chicago Bulls			
☐ 136	Khalid Reeves	.10	.05	.01
	Miami Heat			
☐ 137	David Benoit	.05	.02	.01
	Utah Jazz			
☐ 138	Derrick Coleman	.10	.05	.01

☐ 139	Anthony Peeler .... New Jersey Nets	.05	.02	.01
☐ 140	Jim Jackson.................. Los Angeles Lakers	.25	.11	.03
☐ 141	Stacey Augmon............. Dallas Mavericks	.08	.04	.01
☐ 142	Sam Cassell.................. Atlanta Hawks	.05	.02	.01
☐ 143	Derrick McKey............... Houston Rockets	.08	.04	.01
☐ 144	Danny Ferry .... Indiana Pacers	.05	.02	.01
☐ 145	Anfernee Hardaway...... Cleveland Cavaliers	.75	.35	.09
☐ 146	Clifford Robinson.......... Orlando Magic	.08	.04	.01
☐ 147	B.J. Tyler..................... Portland Trail Blazers	.05	.02	.01
☐ 148	Mark West .... Philadelphia 76ers Drafted by the Raptors	.05	.02	.01
☐ 149	David Wingate............... Detroit Pistons	.05	.02	.01
☐ 150	Willie Anderson............. Charlotte Hornets Traded to the Sonics	.05	.02	.01
☐ 151	Hersey Hawkins .... San Antonio Spurs Drafted by the Raptors	.08	.04	.01
☐ 152	Bryant Stith................. Charlotte Hornets Traded to the Sonics	.05	.02	.01
☐ 153	Dan Majerle................. Denver Nuggets	.08	.04	.01
☐ 154	Chris Smith.................. Phoenix Suns	.05	.02	.01
☐ 155	Donyell Marshall........... Minnesota Timberwolves	.15	.07	.02
☐ 156	Loy Vaught .... Golden State Warriors	.08	.04	.01
☐ 157	Reggie Miller................ Los Angeles Clippers	.25	.11	.03
☐ 158	Hubert Davis .... Indiana Pacers	.05	.02	.01
☐ 159	Ron Harper................... New York Knicks	.08	.04	.01
☐ 160	Lee Mayberry................ Chicago Bulls	.05	.02	.01
☐ 161	Eddie Jones .... Milwaukee Bucks	.50	.23	.06
☐ 162	Shawn Bradley .... Los Angeles Lakers	.08	.04	.01
☐ 163	Nick Anderson .... Philadelphia 76ers	.08	.04	.01
☐ 164	Ervin Johnson............... Orlando Magic	.05	.02	.01
☐ 165	Walt Williams................ Seattle Supersonics	.08	.04	.01
☐ 166	Steve Smith FF.............. Sacramento Kings	.05	.02	.01
☐ 167	Dino Radja FF............... Atlanta Hawks	.05	.02	.01
☐ 168	Alonzo Mourning FF....... Boston Celtics	.10	.05	.01
☐ 169	Michael Jordan FF...... Charlotte Hornets	1.50	.65	.19
☐ 170	Tyrone Hill FF............... Chicago Bulls	.05	.02	.01
☐ 171	Jamal Mashburn FF....... Cleveland Cavaliers	.15	.07	.02
	Dallas Mavericks			
☐ 172	Dikembe Mutombo FF.. Denver Nuggets	.08	.04	.01
☐ 173	Grant Hill FF................. Detroit Pistons with Jordan	.75	.35	.09
☐ 174	Latrell Sprewell FF........ Golden State Warriors	.10	.05	.01
☐ 175	Hakeem Olajuwon FF ... Houston Rockets	.30	.14	.04
☐ 176	Reggie Miller FF............ Indiana Pacers	.10	.05	.01
☐ 177	Pooh Richardson FF...... Los Angeles Clippers	.05	.02	.01
☐ 178	Cedric Ceballos FF........ Los Angeles Lakers	.05	.02	.01
☐ 179	Glen Rice FF................. Miami Heat	.05	.02	.01
☐ 180	Glenn Robinson FF........ Milwaukee Bucks	.40	.18	.05
☐ 181	Isaiah Rider FF.............. Minnesota Timberwolves	.05	.02	.01
☐ 182	Derrick Coleman FF....... New Jersey Nets	.05	.02	.01
☐ 183	Patrick Ewing FF........... New York Knicks	.10	.05	.01
☐ 184	Shaquille O'Neal FF....... Orlando Magic	.60	.25	.08
☐ 185	Dana Barros FF............. Philadelphia 76ers	.05	.02	.01
☐ 186	Dan Majerle FF............. Phoenix Suns	.05	.02	.01
☐ 187	Clifford Robinson FF .... Portland Trail Blazers	.05	.02	.01
☐ 188	Mitch Richmond FF....... Sacramento Kings	.08	.04	.01
☐ 189	David Robinson FF........ San Antonio Spurs	.25	.11	.03
☐ 190	Gary Payton FF............. Seattle Supersonics	.05	.02	.01
☐ 191	Oliver Miller FF............. Toronto Raptors	.05	.02	.01
☐ 192	Karl Malone FF.............. Utah Jazz	.10	.05	.01
☐ 193	Kevin Pritchard FF........ Vancouver Grizzlies	.05	.02	.01
☐ 194	Chris Webber FF .... Washington Bullets	.05	.02	.01
☐ 195	Michael Jordan PD.... Chicago Bulls	1.50	.65	.19
☐ 196	Hakeem Olajuwon PD .. Houston Rockets	.30	.14	.04
☐ 197	Vin Baker PD................ Milwaukee Bucks	.08	.04	.01
☐ 198	Grant Hill PD................ Detroit Pistons	.60	.25	.08
☐ 199	Clyde Drexler PD.......... Houston Rockets	.10	.05	.01
☐ 200	Chris Webber PD .... Washington Bullets	.10	.05	.01
☐ 201	Shawn Kemp PD............ Seattle Supersonics	.25	.11	.03
☐ 202	Shaquille O'Neal PD...... Orlando Magic	.60	.25	.08
☐ 203	Stacey Augmon PD........ Atlanta Hawks	.05	.02	.01
☐ 204	David Benoit PD............ Utah Jazz	.05	.02	.01
☐ 205	Rodney Rogers PD......... Denver Nuggets	.05	.02	.01
☐ 206	Latrell Sprewell PD .... Golden State Warriors	.10	.05	.01

☐ 207	Brian Grant PD .... .10	.05	.01
	Sacramento Kings		
☐ 208	Lamond Murray PD ...... .08	.04	.01
	Los Angeles Clippers		
☐ 209	Shawn Kemp CL .... .10	.05	.01
	Seattle Supersonics		
☐ 210	Michael Jordan CL .... .50	.23	.06
	Chicago Bulls		
☐ NNO	Draft Trade Card 20.00	9.00	2.50

1995-96 Collector's Choice Player's Club

Issued one per first series Collector's Choice 12-card pack, these 210 standard-size cards parallel the basic 1995-96 Collector's Choice series. Unlike the basic issue cards, Player's Club card fronts feature silver borders (except on the border-less subset cards) and a silver foil facsimile autograph and Player's Club logo. Please refer to the multiplier provided below (and the values listed for the regular issue 1995-96 Collector's Choice cards) to ascertain the value of individual Player's Club cards.

	MINT	NRMT	EXC
COMPLETE SERIES 1 (210)...	40.00	18.00	5.00
COMMON CARD (1-210)	.15	.07	.02
* STARS: 2X to 4X BASIC CARDS			

1995-96 Collector's Choice Player's Club Platinum

Issued randomly one in every thirty-five first series 12-card packs, these 210 standard-size cards parallel the basic 1995-96 Collector's Choice series. Unlike the basic issue cards, Player's Club Platinum card

fronts feature a special silver-foil paper stock and a silver foil facsimile autograph and Player's Club Platinum logo. Please refer to the multiplier provided below (and the values listed for the regular-issue 1995-96 Collector's Choice cards) to ascertain the value of individual Player's Club Platinum cards.

	MINT	NRMT	EXC
COMPLETE SET (210)	750.00	350.00	95.00
COMMON CARD (1-210)	2.00	.90	.25
*STARS: 25X to 50X BASIC CARDS .			

		MINT	NRMT	EXC
☐ 5	Jason Kidd....................	40.00	18.00	5.00
☐ 33	Grant Hill....................	60.00	27.00	7.50
☐ 34	Charles Barkley	25.00	11.50	3.10
☐ 40	Shawn Kemp............	25.00	11.50	3.10
☐ 45	Michael Jordan	125.00	57.50	15.50
☐ 50	David Robinson	25.00	11.50	3.10
☐ 145	Anfernee Hardaway..	40.00	18.00	5.00
☐ 161	Eddie Jones	25.00	11.50	3.10
☐ 169	Michael Jordan FF....	60.00	27.00	7.50
☐ 173	Grant Hill FF..............	40.00	18.00	5.00
	Michael Jordan			
☐ 184	Shaquille O'Neal FF....	30.00	13.50	3.80
☐ 195	Michael Jordan PD....	60.00	27.00	7.50
☐ 198	Grant Hill PD	30.00	13.50	3.80
☐ 202	Shaquille O'Neal PD.	30.00	13.50	3.80
☐ 210	Michael Jordan CL....	25.00	11.50	3.10

1995-96 Collector's Choice Crash The Game

Issued randomly one in every five first series 12-card packs, this 81-card set features three separate versions of twenty-seven different player cards. Each player is matched up against three different teams (two within their conference and one outside of their conference). If the player depicted on the card scored 30 or more points versus the team depicted on the card, the card was redeemable for a special 27-card Crash the Game Trade Silver set. Scarcer parallel gold versions of each card were also seeded one in every fifty first series packs. Winning gold cards were redeemable for a special 27-card Crash the Game Trade Gold set. Please refer to the multiplier provided within the header below for gold card values. Both regular and gold Crash the Game cards have an expiration date of May 8th, 1996.

	MINT	NRMT	EXC
COMPLETE SILVER SET (81)	150.00	70.00	19.00
COMMON SILVER (C1-C27)	1.00	.45	.13
COMPLETE GOLD SET (81)	500.00	230.00	65.00
COMMON GOLD (C1-C27)	3.00	1.35	.40
* GOLD: 1.5X to 3X BASIC CARDS...			

☐ C1A Michael Jordan HOU	15.00	6.75	1.90
Chicago Bulls			
☐ C1B Michael Jordan NY	15.00	6.75	1.90
Chicago Bulls			
☐ C1C Michael Jordan ORL	15.00	6.75	1.90
Chicago Bulls			
☐ C2A Kenny Anderson CLE.	1.00	.45	.13
New Jersey Nets			
☐ C2B Kenny Anderson LAC.	1.00	.45	.13
New Jersey Nets			
☐ C2C Kenny Anderson MIA.	1.00	.45	.13
New Jersey Nets			
☐ C3A Charles Barkley CLE	3.00	1.35	.40
Phoenix Suns			
☐ C3B Charles Barkley GS	3.00	1.35	.40
Phoenix Suns			
☐ C3C Charles Barkley SA	3.00	1.35	.40
Phoenix Suns			
☐ C4A Dana Barros ATL	1.00	.45	.13
Philadelphia 76ers			
☐ C4B Dana Barros BOS	1.00	.45	.13
Philadelphia 76ers			
☐ C4C Dana Barros LAL	1.00	.45	.13
Philadelphia 76ers			
☐ C5A Anfernee Hardaway CHI	5.00	2.30	.60
Orlando Magic			
☐ C5B Anfernee Hardaway SA	5.00	2.30	.60
Orlando Magic			
☐ C5C Anfernee Hardaway MIL	5.00	2.30	.60
Orlando Magic			
☐ C6A Mookie Blaylock DAL.	1.00	.45	.13
Atlanta Hawks			
☐ C6B Mookie Blaylock DET.	1.00	.45	.13
Atlanta Hawks			
☐ C6C Mookie Blaylock TOR	1.00	.45	.13
Atlanta Hawks			
☐ C7A Lamond Murray ATL.	1.00	.45	.13
Los Angeles Clippers			
☐ C7B Lamond Murray MIN.	1.00	.45	.13
Los Angeles Clippers			
☐ C7C Lamond Murray VAN.	1.00	.45	.13
Los Angeles Clippers			
☐ C8A Karl Malone HOU	1.50	.65	.19
Utah Jazz			
☐ C8B Karl Malone NY	1.50	.65	.19

Utah Jazz			
☐ C8C Karl Malone POR	1.50	.65	.19
Utah Jazz			
☐ C9A Alonzo Mourning CHI	1.50	.65	.19
Charlotte Hornets			
☐ C9B Alonzo Mourning IND	1.50	.65	.19
Charlotte Hornets			
☐ C9C Alonzo Mourning WASH	1.50	.65	.19
Charlotte Hornets			
☐ C10A Hakeem Olajuwon LAL	4.00	1.80	.50
Houston Rockets			
☐ C10B Hakeem Olajuwon ORL	4.00	1.80	.50
Houston Rockets			
☐ C10C Hakeem Olajuwon POR	4.00	1.80	.50
Houston Rockets			
☐ C11A Mark Price CHI	1.00	.45	.13
Cleveland Cavaliers			
☐ C11B Mark Price	1.00	.45	.13
Cleveland Cavaliers			
☐ C11C Mark Price SEA	1.00	.45	.13
Cleveland Cavaliers			
☐ C12A Isaiah Rider BOS	1.00	.45	.13
Minnesota Timberwolves			
☐ C12B Isaiah Rider PHO	1.00	.45	.13
Minnesota Timberwolves			
☐ C12C Isaiah Rider SAC	1.00	.45	.13
Minnesota Timberwolves			
☐ C13A Glen Rice NJ	1.00	.45	.13
Miami Heat			
☐ C13B Glen Rice SAC	1.00	.45	.13
Miami Heat			
☐ C13C Glen Rice WASH	1.00	.45	.13
Miami Heat			
☐ C14A Mitch Richmond LAL	1.00	.45	.13
Sacramento Kings			
☐ C14B Mitch Richmond MIN	1.00	.45	.13
Sacramento Kings			
☐ C14C Mitch Richmond NJ.	1.00	.45	.13
Sacramento Kings			
☐ C15A Chris Webber GS	1.50	.65	.19
Washington Bullets			
☐ C15B Chris Webber IND	1.50	.65	.19
Washington Bullets			
☐ C15C Chris Webber PHI	1.50	.65	.19
Washington Bullets			
☐ C16A Nick Van Exel DAL	2.00	.90	.25
Los Angeles Lakers			
☐ C16B Nick Van Exel MIL	2.00	.90	.25
Los Angeles Lakers			
☐ C16C Nick Van Exel SAC	2.00	.90	.25
Los Angeles Lakers			
☐ C17A Mah. Abdul-Rauf CHA	1.00	.45	.13
Denver Nuggets			
☐ C17B Mah. Abdul-Rauf PHO	1.00	.45	.13
Denver Nuggets			
☐ C17C Mah. Abdul-Rauf SEA	1.00	.45	.13
Denver Nuggets			
☐ C18A Dominique Wilkins PHI	1.00	.45	.13
Boston Celtics			
☐ C18B Dominique Wilkins POR	1.00	.45	.13
Boston Celtics			
☐ C18C Dominique Wilkins TOR	1.00	.45	.13
Boston Celtics			
☐ C19A Patrick Ewing BOS	1.50	.65	.19
New York Knicks			
☐ C19B Patrick Ewing CHA	1.50	.65	.19
New York Knicks			
☐ C19C Patrick Ewing PHO	1.50	.65	.19
New York Knicks			
☐ C20A David Robinson DEN	3.00	1.35	.40
San Antonio Spurs			

☐ C20B David Robinson SEA 3.00 1.35 .40
   San Antonio Spurs
☐ C20C David Robinson WASH 3.00 1.35 .40
   San Antonio Spurs
☐ C21A Shawn Kemp DEN ... 3.00 1.35 .40
   Seattle Supersonics
☐ C21B Shawn Kemp DET.... 3.00 1.35 .40
   Seattle Supersonics
☐ C21C Shawn Kemp UTAH. 3.00 1.35 .40
   Seattle Supersonics
☐ C22A Jason Kidd IND .... 5.00 2.30 .60
   Dallas Mavericks
☐ C22B Jason Kidd LAC....... 5.00 2.30 .60
   Dallas Mavericks
☐ C22C Jason Kidd SA......... 5.00 2.30 .60
   Dallas Mavericks
☐ C23A Glenn Robinson ATL 5.00 2.30 .60
   Milwaukee Bucks
☐ C23B Glenn Robinson CHA 5.00 2.30 .60
   Milwaukee Bucks
☐ C23C Glenn Robinson VAN 5.00 2.30 .60
   Milwaukee Bucks
☐ C24A Reggie Miller MIN ... 1.50 .65 .19
   Indiana Pacers
☐ C24B Reggie Miller NY ..... 1.50 .65 .19
   Indiana Pacers
☐ C24C Reggie Miller ORL .... 1.50 .65 .19
   Indiana Pacers
☐ C25A Joe Dumars CLE...... 1.00 .45 .13
   Detroit Pistons
☐ C25B Joe Dumars MIL....... 1.00 .45 .13
   Detroit Pistons
☐ C25C Joe Dumars UTAH... 1.00 .45 .13
   Detroit Pistons
☐ C26A Latrell Sprewell DAL 1.50 .65 .19
   Golden State Warriors
☐ C26B Latrell Sprewell HOU 1.50 .65 .19
   Golden State Warriors
☐ C26C Latrell Sprewell MIA 1.50 .65 .19
   Golden State Warriors
☐ C27A Clifford Robinson LAC 1.00 .45 .13
   Portland Trail Blazers
☐ C27B Clifford Robinson PHI 1.00 .45 .13
   Portland Trail Blazers
☐ C27C Clifford Robinson UTAH 1.00 .45 .13
   Portland Trail Blazers

1995-96 Collector's Choice Jordan Collection

Randomly inserted into one in every 11 first series 12-card packs, these four cards comprise the first part of a card-by-card chronology, spanning across all of Upper Deck's 1995-96 basketball products, highlighting the career of Michael Jordan. The fronts have a full-color photo with a gold-foil picture of Jordan in the lower left hand corner wearing number 45. The backs have a color photo at the top with information about the highlight and statistics from that year at the bottom. There is a silver hologram in the lower left hand corner.

	MINT	NRMT	EXC
COMPLETE SET (4)	20.00	9.00	2.50
COMMON CARD (JC1-JC4)	5.00	2.30	.60

☐ JC1 Michael Jordan .... 5.00 2.30 .60
   1985 NBA ROY
☐ JC2 Michael Jordan .... 5.00 2.30 .60
   1986-87 3
☐ JC3 Michael Jordan .... 5.00 2.30 .60
   '88 NBA Defensive POY
☐ JC4 Michael Jordan .... 5.00 2.30 .60
   Beginnings of a Superstar

1994-95 Embossed

Featuring 121 double-sided, standard size embossed cards, the 1994-95 Embossed set marks the premier of a new product for Topps. Each 6-card pack contained five cards and one Golden Idols parallel gold foil card, with a suggested retail of 3.00 per pack. The fronts display a color embossed player photo framed by a textured border. The backs carry a second embossed player photo, biography, statistics, and a special "Did You Know" section containing unique information not found on other Topps cards. The cards are grouped alphabetically within teams and checklisted below alphabetically according to teams as follows: Atlanta Hawks (1-4), Boston Celtics (5-8), Charlotte Hornets (9-12), Chicago Bulls (13-16), Cleveland Cavaliers (17-19), Dallas Mavericks (20-22), Denver Nuggets (23-26), Detroit Pistons (27-30), Golden State Warriors (31-34), Houston Rockets (35-39), Indiana Pacers (40-42), Los Angeles Clippers (43-45), Los Angeles Lakers (46-48), Miami Heat (49-51), Milwaukee Bucks (52-54), Minnesota Timberwolves (55-57),

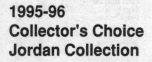

New Jersey Nets (58-61), New York Knicks (62-66), Orlando Magic (67-70), Philadelphia 76ers (71-73), Phoenix Suns (74-78), Portland Trail Blazers (79-81), Sacramento Kings (82-85), San Antonio Spurs (86-89), Seattle Supersonics (90-94), Utah Jazz (95-97), and Washington Bullets (98-100). The set closes with a silver foil Draft Picks (101-120) subset followed by a Michael Jordan card that was added at the last minute.

		MINT	NRMT	EXC
	COMPLETE SET (121)	30.00	13.50	3.80
	COMMON CARD (1-121)	.15	.07	.02
☐ 1	Stacey Augmon	.20	.09	.03
☐ 2	Mookie Blaylock	.20	.09	.03
☐ 3	Ken Norman	.15	.07	.02
☐ 4	Steve Smith	.20	.09	.03
☐ 5	Dee Brown	.20	.09	.03
☐ 6	Blue Edwards	.15	.07	.02
☐ 7	Dino Radja	.30	.14	.04
☐ 8	Dominique Wilkins	.40	.18	.05
☐ 9	Muggsy Bogues	.30	.14	.04
☐ 10	Dell Curry	.15	.07	.02
☐ 11	Larry Johnson	.60	.25	.08
☐ 12	Alonzo Mourning	1.00	.45	.13
☐ 13	B.J. Armstrong	.15	.07	.02
☐ 14	Ron Harper	.20	.09	.03
☐ 15	Toni Kukoc	.30	.14	.04
☐ 16	Scottie Pippen	.75	.35	.09
☐ 17	Tyrone Hill	.20	.09	.03
☐ 18	Mark Price	.30	.14	.04
☐ 19	John Williams	.20	.09	.03
☐ 20	Jim Jackson	1.00	.45	.13
☐ 21	Popeye Jones	.15	.07	.02
☐ 22	Jamal Mashburn	1.50	.65	.19
☐ 23	Mahmoud Abdul-Rauf	.20	.09	.03
☐ 24	LaPhonso Ellis	.15	.07	.02
☐ 25	Dikembe Mutombo	.50	.23	.06
☐ 26	Rodney Rogers	.30	.14	.04
☐ 27	Joe Dumars	.40	.18	.05
☐ 28	Lindsey Hunter	.15	.07	.02
☐ 29	Oliver Miller	.15	.07	.02
☐ 30	Terry Mills	.15	.07	.02
☐ 31	Tom Gugliotta	.20	.09	.03
☐ 32	Tim Hardaway	.30	.14	.04
☐ 33	Chris Mullin	.30	.14	.04
☐ 34	Latrell Sprewell	1.00	.45	.13
☐ 35	Sam Cassell	.30	.14	.04
☐ 36	Robert Horry	.30	.14	.04
☐ 37	Vernon Maxwell	.15	.07	.02
☐ 38	Hakeem Olajuwon	2.00	.90	.25
☐ 39	Otis Thorpe	.20	.09	.03
☐ 40	Mark Jackson	.15	.07	.02
☐ 41	Reggie Miller	.75	.35	.09
☐ 42	Rik Smits	.30	.14	.04
☐ 43	Terry Dehere	.15	.07	.02
☐ 44	Stanley Roberts	.15	.07	.02
☐ 45	Loy Vaught	.20	.09	.03
☐ 46	Vlade Divac	.30	.14	.04
☐ 47	George Lynch	.15	.07	.02
☐ 48	Nick Van Exel	1.50	.65	.19
☐ 49	Billy Owens	.20	.09	.03
☐ 50	Glen Rice	.30	.14	.04
☐ 51	Kevin Willis	.20	.09	.03
☐ 52	Vin Baker	.75	.35	.09
☐ 53	Todd Day	.15	.07	.02
☐ 54	Eric Murdock	.15	.07	.02
☐ 55	Christian Laettner	.20	.09	.03
☐ 56	Isaiah Rider	.50	.23	.06
☐ 57	Micheal Williams	.15	.07	.02
☐ 58	Kenny Anderson	.30	.14	.04
☐ 59	P.J. Brown	.15	.07	.02
☐ 60	Derrick Coleman	.30	.14	.04
☐ 61	Chris Morris	.15	.07	.02
☐ 62	Patrick Ewing	.75	.35	.09
☐ 63	Derek Harper	.20	.09	.03
☐ 64	Anthony Mason	.20	.09	.03
☐ 65	Charles Oakley	.20	.09	.03
☐ 66	John Starks	.20	.09	.03
☐ 67	Horace Grant	.40	.18	.05
☐ 68	Anfernee Hardaway	3.00	1.35	.40
☐ 69	Shaquille O'Neal	4.00	1.80	.50
☐ 70	Dennis Scott	.15	.07	.02
☐ 71	Shawn Bradley	.30	.14	.04
☐ 72	Jeff Malone	.20	.09	.03
☐ 73	Clarence Weatherspoon	.20	.09	.03
☐ 74	Charles Barkley	1.50	.65	.19
☐ 75	Kevin Johnson	.40	.18	.05
☐ 76	Dan Majerle	.20	.09	.03
☐ 77	Danny Manning	.30	.14	.04
☐ 78	Wayman Tisdale	.20	.09	.03
☐ 79	Clyde Drexler	.75	.35	.09
☐ 80	Clifford Robinson	.20	.09	.03
☐ 81	Rod Strickland	.20	.09	.03
☐ 82	Bobby Hurley	.20	.09	.03
☐ 83	Olden Polynice	.15	.07	.02
☐ 84	Mitch Richmond	.40	.18	.05
☐ 85	Spud Webb	.20	.09	.03
☐ 86	Sean Elliott	.20	.09	.03
☐ 87	Chuck Person	.20	.09	.03
☐ 88	David Robinson	1.50	.65	.19
☐ 89	Dennis Rodman	.50	.23	.06
☐ 90	Kendall Gill	.15	.07	.02
☐ 91	Shawn Kemp	1.50	.65	.19
☐ 92	Sarunas Marciulionis	.15	.07	.02
☐ 93	Gary Payton	.30	.14	.04
☐ 94	Detlef Schrempf	.30	.14	.04
☐ 95	Jeff Hornacek	.20	.09	.03
☐ 96	Karl Malone	.75	.35	.09
☐ 97	John Stockton	.75	.35	.09
☐ 98	Don MacLean	.15	.07	.02
☐ 99	Scott Skiles	.15	.07	.02
☐ 100	Chris Webber	1.25	.55	.16
☐ 101	Glenn Robinson FOIL.	6.00	2.70	.75
	Milwaukee Bucks			
☐ 102	Jason Kidd FOIL	6.00	2.70	.75
	Dallas Mavericks			
☐ 103	Grant Hill FOIL	10.00	4.50	1.25
	Detroit Pistons			
☐ 104	Donyell Marshall FOIL	1.25	.55	.16
	Minnesota Timberwolves			
☐ 105	Juwan Howard FOIL.	2.50	1.15	.30
	Washington Bullets			
☐ 106	Sharone Wright FOIL .75		.35	.09
	Philadelphia 76ers			
☐ 107	Lamond Murray FOIL.	1.00	.45	.13
	Los Angeles Clippers			
☐ 108	Brian Grant FOIL	2.00	.90	.25
	Sacramento Kings			
☐ 109	Eric Montross FOIL.	1.00	.45	.13
	Boston Celtics			
☐ 110	Eddie Jones FOIL	4.00	1.80	.50
	Los Angeles Lakers			
☐ 111	Carlos Rogers FOIL.	.50	.23	.06
	Golden State Warriors			
☐ 112	Khalid Reeves FOIL.	1.00	.45	.13
	Miami Heat			
☐ 113	Jalen Rose FOIL	1.25	.55	.16
	Denver Nuggets			

			MINT	NRMT	EXC
☐	114	Yinka Dare FOIL New Jersey Nets	.20	.09	.03
☐	115	Eric Piatkowski FOIL Los Angeles Clippers	.30	.14	.04
☐	116	Clifford Rozier FOIL Golden State Warriors	.50	.23	.06
☐	117	Aaron McKie FOIL Portland Trail Blazers	.50	.23	.06
☐	118	Eric Mobley FOIL Milwaukee Bucks	.30	.14	.04
☐	119	Tony Dumas FOIL Dallas Mavericks	.20	.09	.03
☐	120	B.J. Tyler FOIL Philadelphia 76ers	.20	.09	.03
☐	121	Michael Jordan Chicago Bulls	12.00	5.50	1.50

1994-95 Embossed Golden Idols

Inserted one per pack, this 121-card set parallels the regular 1994-95 Embossed issue. The only difference is the full gold foil treatment on each card front. Please refer to the multipliers provided below for individual card values.

	MINT	NRMT	EXC
COMPLETE SET (121)	90.00	40.00	11.50
COMMON CARD (1-121)	.40	.18	.05

*GOLD STARS: 1.25X TO 2.5X BASIC CARDS
*GOLD ROOKIES: 1X TO 2X BASIC CARDS

1994-95 Emotion

The complete 1994-95 Emotion set (produced by SkyBox) consists of 121 standard size cards. The cards were issued in eight-card packs with 36 packs per box. Suggested retail price was $4.99 per pack. The fronts have full-bleed color photos. Predominantly placed in the middle is a one word description of the player. The E in Emotion is a hologram at the bottom of the card. The player's name is printed in gold foil. The backs have career statistics and player information against a two photo background. There are two subsets,

Rookies (101-110) and Masters (111-120). The cards are grouped alphabetically within teams and checklisted below according to teams as follows: Atlanta Hawks (1-3), Boston Celtics (4-7), Charlotte Hornets (8-10), Chicago Bulls (11-14), Cleveland Cavaliers (15-17), Dallas Mavericks (18-21), Denver Nuggets (22-25), Detroit Pistons (26-28), Golden State Warriors (29-34), Houston Rockets (35-38), Indiana Pacers (39-41), Los Angeles Clippers (42-44), Los Angeles Lakers (45-48), Miami Heat (49-52), Milwaukee Bucks (53-56), Minnesota Timberwolves (57-59), New Jersey Nets (60-62), New York Knicks (63-66), Orlando Magic (67-71), Philadelphia 76ers (72-76), Phoenix Suns (77-81), Portland Trail Blazers (82-84), Sacramento Kings (85-87), San Antonio Spurs (88-90), Seattle Supersonics (91-93), Utah Jazz (94-96), and Washington Bullets (97-99). The set closes with two topical subsets: Rookies (101-110) and Masters (111-120). A Grant Hill SkyMotion card was offered to those who sent in two wrappers and a check or money order for 24.99 before December 31st, 1995. The card shows three seconds of a Hill dunk.

			MINT	NRMT	EXC
	COMPLETE SET (121)		50.00	23.00	6.25
	COMMON CARD (1-121)		.20	.09	.03
☐	1	Stacey Augmon	.30	.14	.04
☐	2	Mookie Blaylock	.30	.14	.04
☐	3	Steve Smith	.30	.14	.04
☐	4	Greg Minor	.30	.14	.04
☐	5	Eric Montross	1.25	.55	.16
☐	6	Dino Radja	.40	.18	.05
☐	7	Dominique Wilkins	.50	.23	.06
☐	8	Muggsy Bogues	.40	.18	.05
☐	9	Larry Johnson	.75	.35	.09
☐	10	Alonzo Mourning	1.25	.55	.16
☐	11	B.J. Armstrong	.20	.09	.03
☐	12	Toni Kukoc	.40	.18	.05
☐	13	Scottie Pippen	1.00	.45	.13
☐	14	Dickey Simpkins	.40	.18	.05
☐	15	Tyrone Hill	.30	.14	.04
☐	16	Chris Mills	.40	.18	.05
☐	17	Mark Price	.40	.18	.05
☐	18	Tony Dumas	.30	.14	.04
☐	19	Jim Jackson	1.25	.55	.16
☐	20	Jason Kidd	8.00	3.60	1.00
☐	21	Jamal Mashburn	2.00	.90	.25
☐	22	LaPhonso Ellis	.20	.09	.03
☐	23	Dikembe Mutombo	.60	.25	.08
☐	24	Rodney Rogers	.40	.18	.05

☐ 25	Jalen Rose	1.50	.65	.19
☐ 26	Bill Curley	.40	.18	.05
☐ 27	Joe Dumars	.50	.23	.06
☐ 28	Grant Hill	12.00	5.50	1.50
☐ 29	Tim Hardaway	.40	.18	.05
☐ 30	Donyell Marshall	1.50	.65	.19
☐ 31	Chris Mullin	.40	.18	.05
☐ 32	Carlos Rogers	.60	.25	.08
☐ 33	Clifford Rozier	.60	.25	.08
☐ 34	Latrell Sprewell	1.25	.55	.16
☐ 35	Sam Cassell	.40	.18	.05
☐ 36	Clyde Drexler	2.50	1.15	.30
☐ 37	Robert Horry	.40	.18	.05
☐ 38	Hakeem Olajuwon	2.50	1.15	.30
☐ 39	Mark Jackson	.20	.09	.03
☐ 40	Reggie Miller	1.00	.45	.13
☐ 41	Rik Smits	.40	.18	.05
☐ 42	Lamond Murray	1.25	.55	.16
☐ 43	Eric Piatkowski	.40	.18	.05
☐ 44	Loy Vaught	.30	.14	.04
☐ 45	Cedric Ceballos	.40	.18	.05
☐ 46	Eddie Jones	5.00	2.30	.60
☐ 47	George Lynch	.20	.09	.03
☐ 48	Nick Van Exel	2.00	.90	.25
☐ 49	Harold Miner	.20	.09	.03
☐ 50	Khalid Reeves	1.25	.55	.16
☐ 51	Glen Rice	.40	.18	.05
☐ 52	Kevin Willis	.30	.14	.04
☐ 53	Vin Baker	1.00	.45	.13
☐ 54	Eric Mobley	.40	.18	.05
☐ 55	Eric Murdock	.20	.09	.03
☐ 56	Glenn Robinson	8.00	3.60	1.00
☐ 57	Tom Gugliotta	.30	.14	.04
☐ 58	Christian Laettner	.30	.14	.04
☐ 59	Isaiah Rider	.60	.25	.08
☐ 60	Kenny Anderson	.40	.18	.05
☐ 61	Derrick Coleman	.40	.18	.05
☐ 62	Yinka Dare	.30	.14	.04
☐ 63	Patrick Ewing	1.00	.45	.13
☐ 64	John Starks	.30	.14	.04
☐ 65	Charlie Ward	.60	.25	.08
☐ 66	Monty Williams	.40	.18	.05
☐ 67	Nick Anderson	.30	.14	.04
☐ 68	Horace Grant	.50	.23	.06
☐ 69	Anfernee Hardaway	4.00	1.80	.50
☐ 70	Shaquille O'Neal	5.00	2.30	.60
☐ 71	Brooks Thompson	.30	.14	.04
☐ 72	Dana Barros	.40	.18	.05
☐ 73	Shawn Bradley	.40	.18	.05
☐ 74	B.J. Tyler	.30	.14	.04
☐ 75	Clarence Weatherspoon	.30	.14	.04
☐ 76	Sharone Wright	1.00	.45	.13
☐ 77	Charles Barkley	2.00	.90	.25
☐ 78	Kevin Johnson	.50	.23	.06
☐ 79	Dan Majerle	.30	.14	.04
☐ 80	Danny Manning	.40	.18	.05
☐ 81	Wesley Person	1.50	.65	.19
☐ 82	Aaron McKie	.60	.25	.08
☐ 83	Clifford Robinson	.30	.14	.04
☐ 84	Rod Strickland	.30	.14	.04
☐ 85	Brian Grant	2.50	1.15	.30
☐ 86	Bobby Hurley	.30	.14	.04
☐ 87	Mitch Richmond	.50	.23	.06
☐ 88	Sean Elliott	.30	.14	.04
☐ 89	David Robinson	2.00	.90	.25
☐ 90	Dennis Rodman	.60	.25	.08
☐ 91	Shawn Kemp	2.00	.90	.25
☐ 92	Gary Payton	.40	.18	.05
☐ 93	Dontonio Wingfield	.40	.18	.05
☐ 94	Jeff Hornacek	.30	.14	.04
☐ 95	Karl Malone	1.00	.45	.13

☐ 96	John Stockton	1.00	.45	.13
☐ 97	Calbert Cheaney	.40	.18	.05
☐ 98	Juwan Howard	3.00	1.35	.40
☐ 99	Chris Webber	1.50	.65	.19
☐ 100	Michael Jordan	15.00	6.75	1.90
☐ 101	Brian Grant ROO	1.00	.45	.13
	Sacramento Kings			
☐ 102	Grant Hill ROO	5.00	2.30	.60
	Detroit Pistons			
☐ 103	Juwan Howard ROO	1.25	.55	.16
	Washington Bullets			
☐ 104	Eddie Jones ROO	2.00	.90	.25
	Los Angeles Lakers			
☐ 105	Jason Kidd ROO	3.00	1.35	.40
	Dallas Mavericks			
☐ 106	Eric Montross ROO	.50	.23	.06
	Boston Celtics			
☐ 107	Lamond Murray ROO	.50	.23	.06
	Los Angeles Clippers			
☐ 108	Wesley Person ROO	.60	.25	.08
	Phoenix Suns			
☐ 109	Glenn Robinson ROO	3.00	1.35	.40
	Milwaukee Bucks			
☐ 110	Sharone Wright ROO	.40	.18	.05
	Philadelphia 76ers			
☐ 111	Anfernee Hardaway MAS	2.00	.90	.25
	Orlando Magic			
☐ 112	Shawn Kemp MAS	1.00	.45	.13
	Seattle Supersonics			
☐ 113	Karl Malone MAS	.50	.23	.06
	Utah Jazz			
☐ 114	Alonzo Mourning MAS	.60	.25	.08
	Charlotte Hornets			
☐ 115	Shaquille O'Neal MAS	2.50	1.15	.30
	Orlando Magic			
☐ 116	Hakeem Olajuwon MAS	1.25	.55	.16
	Houston Rockets			
☐ 117	Scottie Pippen MAS	.40	.18	.05
	Chicago Bulls			
☐ 118	David Robinson MAS	1.00	.45	.13
	San Antonio Spurs			
☐ 119	Latrell Sprewell MAS	.60	.25	.08
	Golden State Warriors			
☐ 120	Chris Webber MAS	.75	.35	.09
	Washington Bullets			
☐ 121	Checklist	.20	.09	.03
☐ NNO	Grant Hill SkyMotion	35.00	16.00	4.40
	Exchange			

1994-95 Emotion N-Tense

Cards from this 10-card standard-size set were randomly inserted in Emotion packs at a rate of one in 18. The set contains a selection of some of the top players in the NBA. The fronts have full-bleed color photos and the player's name down the left in a hologram set against a sparkling gold background. The N in Ntense is in a hologram at the bottom of the card. The backs have two color action photos with the players name across the middle against a black background.

	MINT	NRMT	EXC
COMPLETE SET (10)	175.00	80.00	22.00
COMMON CARD (N1-N10)	6.00	2.70	.75

		MINT	NRMT	EXC
☐ N1	Charles Barkley Phoenix Suns	12.00	5.50	1.50
☐ N2	Patrick Ewing New York Knicks	6.00	2.70	.75
☐ N3	Michael Jordan Chicago Bulls	90.00	40.00	11.50
☐ N4	Shawn Kemp Seattle Supersonics	12.00	5.50	1.50
☐ N5	Karl Malone Utah Jazz	6.00	2.70	.75
☐ N6	Alonzo Mourning Charlotte Hornets	8.00	3.60	1.00
☐ N7	Shaquille O'Neal Orlando Magic	35.00	16.00	4.40
☐ N8	Hakeem Olajuwon Houston Rockets	15.00	6.75	1.90
☐ N9	David Robinson San Antonio Spurs	12.00	5.50	1.50
☐ N10	Glenn Robinson Milwaukee Bucks	20.00	9.00	2.50

1994-95 Emotion X-Cited

Cards from this 20-card standard-size set were randomly inserted in Emotion packs at a rate of one in four. The set features a selection of the top guards and small forwards in the NBA. The fronts have full-bleed color photos and the player's last name across the top set against a sparkling background. The X in X-Cited is in a hologram at the bottom of the card. The backs have two color action photos set against a black background.

	MINT	NRMT	EXC
COMPLETE SET (20)	90.00	40.00	11.50
COMMON CARD (X1-X20)	1.00	.45	.13

		MINT	NRMT	EXC
☐ X1	Kenny Anderson New Jersey Nets	2.00	.90	.25
☐ X2	Anfernee Hardaway Orlando Magic	20.00	9.00	2.50
☐ X3	Tim Hardaway Golden State Warriors	2.00	.90	.25
☐ X4	Grant Hill Detroit Pistons	25.00	11.50	3.10
☐ X5	Jimmy Jackson Dallas Mavericks	6.00	2.70	.75
☐ X6	Eddie Jones Los Angeles Lakers	10.00	4.50	1.25
☐ X7	Jason Kidd Dallas Mavericks	15.00	6.75	1.90
☐ X8	Dan Majerle Phoenix Suns	1.00	.45	.13
☐ X9	Jamal Mashburn Dallas Mavericks	10.00	4.50	1.25
☐ X10	Lamond Murray Los Angeles Clippers	2.50	1.15	.30
☐ X11	Gary Payton Seattle Supersonics	2.00	.90	.25
☐ X12	Wesley Person Phoenix Suns	3.00	1.35	.40
☐ X13	Scottie Pippen Chicago Bulls	5.00	2.30	.60
☐ X14	Mark Price Cleveland Cavaliers	2.00	.90	.25
☐ X15	Mitch Richmond Sacramento Kings	2.50	1.15	.30
☐ X16	Isaiah Rider Minnesota Timberwolves	3.00	1.35	.40
☐ X17	Latrell Sprewell Golden State Warriors	6.00	2.70	.75
☐ X18	John Stockton Utah Jazz	5.00	2.30	.60
☐ X19	Rod Strickland Portland Trail Blazers	1.00	.45	.13
☐ X20	Nick Van Exel Los Angeles Lakers	10.00	4.50	1.25

1993-94 Finest

The premier edition of the 1993-94 Finest basketball set (produced by Topps) contains 220 cards. The set is comprised of 180 player cards and a 40-card subset of ten of the best players in each of the four divisions as follows: Atlantic (90-99), Central (100-109), Midwest (110-119), and

Pacific (120-129). The seven-card packs (24 per box) included six player cards plus one subset card and had a suggested retail price of 3.99. Topps also issued a 14-card jumbo pack for 7.99, which included 11 regulars, two subsets, and a jumbo-only Main Attraction chase card. Packs hit the market upon release well above the aforementioned prices. The rainbow colored metallic front features a color action cutout on a metallic marble background. The player's name appears in the blue horizontal bar in the upper left. The white bordered back features a color player cutout on the left inset in a marble textured background. The player's name and position appears in the gold bar in the upper right with the player's biography, statistics and profile below. The cards are numbered on the back.

	MINT	NRMT	EXC
COMPLETE SET (220)	100.00	45.00	12.50
COMMON CARD (1-220)	.25	.11	.03

		MINT	NRMT	EXC
☐ 1	Michael Jordan	25.00	11.50	3.10
☐ 2	Larry Bird	6.00	2.70	.75
☐ 3	Shaquille O'Neal	15.00	6.75	1.90
	Orlando Magic			
☐ 4	Benoit Benjamin	.25	.11	.03
	New Jersey Nets			
☐ 5	Ricky Pierce	.35	.16	.04
	Seattle Supersonics			
☐ 6	Ken Norman	.25	.11	.03
	Milwaukee Bucks			
☐ 7	Victor Alexander	.25	.11	.03
	Golden State Warriors			
☐ 8	Mark Jackson	.25	.11	.03
	Los Angeles Clippers			
☐ 9	Mark West	.25	.11	.03
	Phoenix Suns			
☐ 10	Don MacLean	.25	.11	.03
	Washington Bullets			
☐ 11	Reggie Miller	2.00	.90	.25
	Indiana Pacers			
☐ 12	Sarunas Marciulionis	.25	.11	.03
	Golden State Warriors			
☐ 13	Craig Ehlo	.25	.11	.03
	Atlanta Hawks			
☐ 14	Toni Kukoc	2.00	.90	.25
	Chicago Bulls			
☐ 15	Glen Rice	.50	.23	.06
	Miami Heat			
☐ 16	Otis Thorpe	.35	.16	.04
	Houston Rockets			
☐ 17	Reggie Williams	.25	.11	.03
	Denver Nuggets			
☐ 18	Charles Smith	.25	.11	.03
	New York Knicks			
☐ 19	Micheal Williams	.25	.11	.03
	Minnesota Timberwolves			
☐ 20	Tom Chambers	.35	.16	.04
	Utah Jazz			
☐ 21	David Robinson	4.00	1.80	.50
	San Antonio Spurs			
☐ 22	Jamal Mashburn	8.00	3.60	1.00
	Dallas Mavericks			
☐ 23	Clifford Robinson	.35	.16	.04
	Portland Trail Blazers			
☐ 24	Acie Earl	.25	.11	.03
	Boston Celtics			
☐ 25	Danny Ferry	.25	.11	.03
	Cleveland Cavaliers			
☐ 26	Bobby Hurley	.75	.35	.09
	Sacramento Kings			
☐ 27	Eddie Johnson	.35	.16	.04
	Charlotte Hornets			
☐ 28	Detlef Schrempf	.50	.23	.06
	Seattle Supersonics			
☐ 29	Mike Brown	.25	.11	.03
	Minnesota Timberwolves			
☐ 30	Latrell Sprewell	4.00	1.80	.50
	Golden State Warriors			
☐ 31	Derek Harper	.35	.16	.04
	New York Knicks			
☐ 32	Stacey Augmon	.35	.16	.04
	Atlanta Hawks			
☐ 33	Pooh Richardson	.25	.11	.03
	Indiana Pacers			
☐ 34	Larry Krystkowiak	.25	.11	.03
	Orlando Magic			
☐ 35	Pervis Ellison	.25	.11	.03
	Washington Bullets			
☐ 36	Jeff Malone	.35	.16	.04
	Philadelphia 76ers			
☐ 37	Sean Elliott	.35	.16	.04
	Detroit Pistons			
☐ 38	John Paxson	.25	.11	.03
	Chicago Bulls			
☐ 39	Robert Parish	.50	.23	.06
	Boston Celtics			
☐ 40	Mark Aguirre	.35	.16	.04
	Los Angeles Clippers			
☐ 41	Danny Ainge	.35	.16	.04
	Phoenix Suns			
☐ 42	Brian Shaw	.25	.11	.03
	Miami Heat			
☐ 43	LaPhonso Ellis	.35	.16	.04
	Denver Nuggets			
☐ 44	Carl Herrera	.25	.11	.03
	Houston Rockets			
☐ 45	Terry Cummings	.35	.16	.04
	San Antonio Spurs			
☐ 46	Chris Dudley	.25	.11	.03
	Portland Trail Blazers			
☐ 47	Anthony Mason	.35	.16	.04
	New York Knicks			
☐ 48	Chris Morris	.25	.11	.03
	New Jersey Nets			
☐ 49	Todd Day	.35	.16	.04
	Milwaukee Bucks			
☐ 50	Nick Van Exel	8.00	3.60	1.00
	Los Angeles Lakers			
☐ 51	Larry Nance	.35	.16	.04
	Cleveland Cavaliers			
☐ 52	Derrick McKey	.35	.16	.04
	Indiana Pacers			
☐ 53	Muggsy Bogues	.50	.23	.06
	Charlotte Hornets			
☐ 54	Andrew Lang	.25	.11	.03
	Atlanta Hawks			
☐ 55	Chuck Person	.35	.16	.04
	Minnesota Timberwolves			
☐ 56	Michael Adams	.25	.11	.03
	Washington Bullets			
☐ 57	Spud Webb	.35	.16	.04
	Sacramento Kings			
☐ 58	Scott Skiles	.25	.11	.03
	Orlando Magic			
☐ 59	A.C. Green	.50	.23	.06
	Phoenix Suns			
☐ 60	Terry Mills	.25	.11	.03
	Detroit Pistons			

☐ 61	Xavier McDaniel .35 .16 .04 Boston Celtics		
☐ 62	B.J. Armstrong .25 .11 .03 Chicago Bulls		
☐ 63	Donald Hodge .25 .11 .03 Dallas Mavericks		
☐ 64	Gary Grant .25 .11 .03 Los Angeles Clippers		
☐ 65	Billy Owens .35 .16 .04 Golden State Warriors		
☐ 66	Greg Anthony .25 .11 .03 New York Knicks		
☐ 67	Jay Humphries .25 .11 .03 Utah Jazz		
☐ 68	Lionel Simmons .25 .11 .03 Sacramento Kings		
☐ 69	Dana Barros .50 .23 .06 Philadelphia 76ers		
☐ 70	Steve Smith .35 .16 .04 Miami Heat		
☐ 71	Ervin Johnson .50 .23 .06 Seattle Supersonics		
☐ 72	Sleepy Floyd .25 .11 .03 San Antonio Spurs		
☐ 73	Blue Edwards .25 .11 .03 Milwaukee Bucks		
☐ 74	Clyde Drexler 2.00 .90 .25 Portland Trail Blazers		
☐ 75	Elden Campbell .25 .11 .03 Los Angeles Lakers		
☐ 76	Hakeem Olajuwon 5.00 2.30 .60 Houston Rockets		
☐ 77	Clarence Weatherspoon .50 .23 .06 Philadelphia 76ers		
☐ 78	Kevin Willis .35 .16 .04 Atlanta Hawks		
☐ 79	Isaiah Rider 2.50 1.15 .30 Minnesota Timberwolves		
☐ 80	Derrick Coleman .50 .23 .06 New Jersey Nets		
☐ 81	Nick Anderson .35 .16 .04 Orlando Magic		
☐ 82	Bryant Stith .25 .11 .03 Denver Nuggets		
☐ 83	Johnny Newman .25 .11 .03 New Jersey Nets		
☐ 84	Calbert Cheaney 2.00 .90 .25 Washington Bullets		
☐ 85	Oliver Miller .25 .11 .03 Phoenix Suns		
☐ 86	Loy Vaught .35 .16 .04 Los Angeles Clippers		
☐ 87	Isiah Thomas 1.00 .45 .13 Detroit Pistons		
☐ 88	Dee Brown .35 .16 .04 Boston Celtics		
☐ 89	Horace Grant 1.00 .45 .13 Chicago Bulls		
☐ 90	Patrick Ewing AF 1.25 .55 .16 New York Knicks		
☐ 91	Clarence Weatherspoon .50 .23 .06 AF Philadelphia 76ers		
☐ 92	Rony Seikaly AF .25 .11 .03 Miami Heat		
☐ 93	Dino Radja AF .50 .23 .06 Boston Celtics		
☐ 94	Kenny Anderson AF .25 .11 .03 New Jersey Nets		
☐ 95	John Starks AF .25 .11 .03 New York Knicks		
☐ 96	Tom Gugliotta AF .25 .11 .03 Washington Bullets		
☐ 97	Steve Smith AF .25 .11 .03 Miami Heat		
☐ 98	Derrick Coleman AF .25 .11 .03 New Jersey Nets		
☐ 99	Shaquille O'Neal AF 9.00 4.00 1.15 Orlando Magic		
☐ 100	Brad Daugherty CF .25 .11 .03 Cleveland Cavaliers		
☐ 101	Horace Grant CF .35 .16 .04 Chicago Bulls		
☐ 102	Dominique Wilkins CF .35 .16 .04 Atlanta Hawks		
☐ 103	Joe Dumars CF .35 .16 .04 Detroit Pistons		
☐ 104	Alonzo Mourning CF 2.50 1.15 .30 Charlotte Hornets		
☐ 105	Scottie Pippen CF 1.25 .55 .16 Chicago Bulls		
☐ 106	Reggie Miller CF .50 .23 .06 Indiana Pacers		
☐ 107	Mark Price CF .25 .11 .03 Cleveland Cavaliers		
☐ 108	Ken Norman CF .25 .11 .03 Milwaukee Bucks		
☐ 109	Larry Johnson CF 1.25 .55 .16 Charlotte Hornets		
☐ 110	Jamal Mashburn MF 3.00 1.35 .40 Dallas Mavericks		
☐ 111	Christian Laettner MF .25 .11 .03 Minnesota Timberwolves		
☐ 112	Karl Malone MF 1.25 .55 .16 Utah Jazz		
☐ 113	Dennis Rodman MF .35 .16 .04 San Antonio Spurs		
☐ 114	Mahmoud Abdul-Rauf MF .25 .11 .03 Denver Nuggets		
☐ 115	Hakeem Olajuwon MF 3.00 1.35 .40 Houston Rockets		
☐ 116	Jim Jackson MF 2.50 1.15 .30 Dallas Mavericks		
☐ 117	John Stockton MF 1.25 .55 .16 Utah Jazz		
☐ 118	David Robinson MF 2.50 1.15 .30 San Antonio Spurs		
☐ 119	Dikembe Mutombo MF 1.00 .45 .13 Denver Nuggets		
☐ 120	Vlade Divac PF .25 .11 .03 Los Angeles Lakers		
☐ 121	Dan Majerle PF .25 .11 .03 Phoenix Suns		
☐ 122	Chris Mullin PF .25 .11 .03 Golden State Warriors		
☐ 123	Shawn Kemp PF 2.50 1.15 .30 Seattle Supersonics		
☐ 124	Danny Manning PF .25 .11 .03 Los Angeles Clippers		
☐ 125	Charles Barkley PF 2.50 1.15 .30 Phoenix Suns		
☐ 126	Mitch Richmond PF .35 .16 .04 Sacramento Kings		
☐ 127	Tim Hardaway PF .25 .11 .03 Golden State Warriors		
☐ 128	Detlef Schrempf PF .25 .11 .03 Seattle Supersonics		
☐ 129	Clyde Drexler PF 1.25 .55 .16 Portland Trail Blazers		
☐ 130	Christian Laettner .50 .23 .06 Minnesota Timberwolves		
☐ 131	Rodney Rogers 1.50 .65 .19		

□ 132	Rik Smits	.50	.23	.06
	Denver Nuggets			
	Indiana Pacers			
□ 133	Chris Mills	1.50	.65	.19
	Cleveland Cavaliers			
□ 134	Corie Blount	.25	.11	.03
	Chicago Bulls			
□ 135	Mookie Blaylock	.35	.16	.04
	Atlanta Hawks			
□ 136	Jim Jackson	4.00	1.80	.50
	Dallas Mavericks			
□ 137	Tom Gugliotta	.50	.23	.06
	Washington Bullets			
□ 138	Dennis Scott	.25	.11	.03
	Orlando Magic			
□ 139	Vin Baker	4.00	1.80	.50
	Milwaukee Bucks			
□ 140	Gary Payton	.50	.23	.06
	Seattle Supersonics			
□ 141	Sedale Threatt	.25	.11	.03
	Los Angeles Lakers			
□ 142	Orlando Woolridge	.25	.11	.03
	Philadelphia 76ers			
□ 143	Avery Johnson	.25	.11	.03
	Golden State Warriors			
□ 144	Charles Oakley	.35	.16	.04
	New York Knicks			
□ 145	Harvey Grant	.25	.11	.03
	Portland Trail Blazers			
□ 146	Bimbo Coles	.25	.11	.03
	Miami Heat			
□ 147	Vernon Maxwell	.25	.11	.03
	Houston Rockets			
□ 148	Danny Manning	.50	.23	.06
	Los Angeles Clippers			
□ 149	Hersey Hawkins	.35	.16	.04
	Charlotte Hornets			
□ 150	Kevin Gamble	.25	.11	.03
	Boston Celtics			
□ 151	Johnny Dawkins	.25	.11	.03
	Philadelphia 76ers			
□ 152	Olden Polynice	.25	.11	.03
	Sacramento Kings			
□ 153	Kevin Edwards	.25	.11	.03
	New Jersey Nets			
□ 154	Willie Anderson	.25	.11	.03
	San Antonio Spurs			
□ 155	Wayman Tisdale	.35	.16	.04
	Sacramento Kings			
□ 156	Popeye Jones	1.25	.55	.16
	Dallas Mavericks			
□ 157	Dan Majerle	.35	.16	.04
	Phoenix Suns			
□ 158	Rex Chapman	.25	.11	.03
	Washington Bullets			
□ 159	Shawn Kemp	4.00	1.80	.50
	Seattle Supersonics			
□ 160	Eric Murdock	.25	.11	.03
	Milwaukee Bucks			
□ 161	Randy White	.25	.11	.03
	Dallas Mavericks			
□ 162	Larry Johnson	2.00	.90	.25
	Charlotte Hornets			
□ 163	Dominique Wilkins	1.00	.45	.13
	Atlanta Hawks			
□ 164	Dikembe Mutombo	1.50	.65	.19
	Denver Nuggets			
□ 165	Patrick Ewing	2.00	.90	.25
	New York Knicks			
□ 166	Jerome Kersey	.25	.11	.03
	Portland Trail Blazers			
□ 167	Dale Davis	.35	.16	.04
	Indiana Pacers			
□ 168	Ron Harper	.35	.16	.04
	Los Angeles Clippers			
□ 169	Sam Cassell	2.00	.90	.25
	Houston Rockets			
□ 170	Bill Cartwright	.25	.11	.03
	Chicago Bulls			
□ 171	John Williams	.35	.16	.04
	Cleveland Cavaliers			
□ 172	Dino Radja	1.50	.65	.19
	Boston Celtics			
□ 173	Dennis Rodman	1.25	.55	.16
	San Antonio Spurs			
□ 174	Kenny Anderson	.50	.23	.06
	New Jersey Nets			
□ 175	Robert Horry	.50	.23	.06
	Houston Rockets			
□ 176	Chris Mullin	.50	.23	.06
	Golden State Warriors			
□ 177	John Salley	.25	.11	.03
	Miami Heat			
□ 178	Scott Burrell	1.00	.45	.13
	Charlotte Hornets			
□ 179	Mitch Richmond	1.00	.45	.13
	Sacramento Kings			
□ 180	Lee Mayberry	.25	.11	.03
	Milwaukee Bucks			
□ 181	James Worthy	.50	.23	.06
	Los Angeles Lakers			
□ 182	Rick Fox	.25	.11	.03
	Boston Celtics			
□ 183	Kevin Johnson	1.00	.45	.13
	Phoenix Suns			
□ 184	Lindsey Hunter	.75	.35	.09
	Detroit Pistons			
□ 185	Marlon Maxey	.25	.11	.03
	Phoenix Suns			
□ 186	Sam Perkins	.35	.16	.04
	Seattle Supersonics			
□ 187	Kevin Duckworth	.25	.11	.03
	Washington Bullets			
□ 188	Jeff Hornacek	.35	.16	.04
	Utah Jazz			
□ 189	Anfernee Hardaway	15.00	6.75	1.90
	Orlando Magic			
□ 190	Rex Walters	.35	.16	.04
	New Jersey Nets			
□ 191	Mahmoud Abdul-Rauf..	.35	.16	.04
	Denver Nuggets			
□ 192	Terry Dehere	.35	.16	.04
	Los Angeles Clippers			
□ 193	Brad Daugherty	.35	.16	.04
	Cleveland Cavaliers			
□ 194	John Starks	.35	.16	.04
	New York Knicks			
□ 195	Rod Strickland	.35	.16	.04
	Portland Trail Blazers			
□ 196	Luther Wright	.25	.11	.03
	Utah Jazz			
□ 197	Vlade Divac	.50	.23	.06
	Los Angeles Lakers			
□ 198	Tim Hardaway	.50	.23	.06
	Golden State Warriors			
□ 199	Joe Dumars	1.00	.45	.13
	Detroit Pistons			
□ 200	Charles Barkley	4.00	1.80	.50
	Phoenix Suns			
□ 201	Alonzo Mourning	4.00	1.80	.50
	Orlando Magic			
□ 202	Doug West	.25	.11	.03

	Minnesota Timberwolves			
☐ 203	Anthony Avent	.25	.11	.03
	Orlando Magic			
☐ 204	Lloyd Daniels	.25	.11	.03
	San Antonio Spurs			
☐ 205	Mark Price	.50	.23	.06
	Cleveland Cavaliers			
☐ 206	Rumeal Robinson	.25	.11	.03
	Charlotte Hornets			
☐ 207	Kendall Gill	.25	.11	.03
	Seattle Supersonics			
☐ 208	Scottie Pippen	2.00	.90	.25
	Chicago Bulls			
☐ 209	Kenny Smith	.25	.11	.03
	Houston Rockets			
☐ 210	Walt Williams	.50	.23	.06
	Sacramento Kings			
☐ 211	Hubert Davis	.25	.11	.03
	New York Knicks			
☐ 212	Chris Webber	6.00	2.70	.75
	Golden State Warriors			
☐ 213	Rony Seikaly	.25	.11	.03
	Miami Heat			
☐ 214	Sam Bowie	.25	.11	.03
	Los Angeles Lakers			
☐ 215	Karl Malone	2.00	.90	.25
	Utah Jazz			
☐ 216	Malik Sealy	.25	.11	.03
	Indiana Pacers			
☐ 217	Dale Ellis	.35	.16	.04
	Indiana Pacers			
☐ 218	Harold Miner	.25	.11	.03
	Miami Heat			
☐ 219	John Stockton	2.00	.90	.25
	Utah Jazz			
☐ 220	Shawn Bradley	1.50	.65	.19
	Philadelphia 76ers			

1993-94 Finest Refractors

This set of Refractor cards parallels that of the 220-card Finest set. Information provided by Topps indicated the cards were randomly inserted in Finest packs at a rate of one in every nine seven-card Finest packs and one in approximately four 14-card jumbo packs. However, widespread evidence indicates the cards are easier to obtain. In addition, a good amount of the cards were included in retail "re-packs" at chains like Wal-Mart and Sams. The only

difference in design is refracting foil that creates a glossy shine to the card fronts when held under light. The rainbow-colored front features a color action cutout on a metallic background. The player's name appears in the blue horizontal bar at the upper left. The white-bordered back features a color player cutout on the left. The player's name and position appear in the gold bar at the upper right with the player's biography, statistics and profile below. The cards are numbered on the back. Only the top few cards within the set are listed below. Please refer to the multipliers provided below (coupled with the corresponding regular issue cards) to ascertain values on unlisted cards.

		MINT	NRMT	EXC
	COMPLETE SET (220)	2500.00	1150.00	325.00
	COMMON CARD (1-220)	4.00	1.80	.50
	*STARS: 6X to 12X BASIC CARDS ...			
	*ROOKIES: 5X to 10X BASIC CARDS			
☐ 1	Michael Jordan TRIB	275.00	125.00	34.00
☐ 2	Larry Bird TRIB	75.00	34.00	9.50
☐ 3	Shaquille O'Neal	175.00	80.00	22.00
	Orlando Magic			
☐ 11	Reggie Miller	50.00	23.00	6.25
☐ 21	David Robinson	50.00	23.00	6.25
	San Antonio Spurs			
☐ 22	Jamal Mashburn	75.00	34.00	9.50
	Dallas Mavericks			
☐ 30	Latrell Sprewell	50.00	23.00	6.25
	Golden State Warriors			
☐ 50	Nick Van Exel	90.00	40.00	11.50
	Los Angeles Lakers			
☐ 76	Hakeem Olajuwon	60.00	27.00	7.50
	Houston Rockets			
☐ 99	Shaquille O'Neal AF	90.00	40.00	11.50
	Orlando Magic			
☐ 136	Jim Jackson	50.00	23.00	6.25
	Dallas Mavericks			
☐ 159	Shawn Kemp UER	50.00	23.00	6.25
	Seattle Supersonics			
	(Misnumbered 136)			
☐ 189	Anfernee Hardaway	160.00	70.00	20.00
	Orlando Magic			
☐ 200	Charles Barkley	50.00	23.00	6.25
	Phoenix Suns			
☐ 201	Alonzo Mourning	50.00	23.00	6.25
	Orlando Magic			
☐ 212	Chris Webber	60.00	27.00	7.50
	Golden State Warriors			

1993-94 Finest Main Attraction

Distributed one per 14-card jumbo pack, a player from each of the 27 NBA teams is represented in this standard size (2 1/2" by 3 1/2") set. The rainbow colored metallic front features a semi-embossed color action cutout on textured metallic background. The players name appears in metallic gold on the orange colored hori-

		MINT	NRMT	EXC
☐ 24	David Robinson	10.00	4.50	1.25
	Sacramento Kings			
	San Antonio Spurs			
☐ 25	Shawn Kemp...............	10.00	4.50	1.25
	Seattle Supersonics			
☐ 26	Karl Malone.................	5.00	2.30	.60
	Utah Jazz			
☐ 27	Tom Gugliotta...............	2.00	.90	.25
	Washington Bullets			

1994-95 Finest

zontal bar in the lower left. The brick tex-
tured bordered back features a color action
shot with a gold border. The player's name
and position appear vertically in black on
the left side of the photo. Player's statistics
and profile appear below the photo. The
cards are numbered on the back "X of 27."

		MINT	NRMT	EXC
COMPLETE SET (27)		100.00	45.00	12.50
COMMON CARD (1-27)		1.00	.45	.13
☐ 1	Dominique Wilkins..........	2.50	1.15	.30
	Atlanta Hawks			
☐ 2	Dino Radja	3.00	1.35	.40
	Boston Celtics			
☐ 3	Larry Johnson..............	5.00	2.30	.60
	Charlotte Hornets			
☐ 4	Scottie Pippen..............	5.00	2.30	.60
	Chicago Bulls			
☐ 5	Mark Price	2.00	.90	.25
	Cleveland Cavaliers			
☐ 6	Jamal Mashburn	15.00	6.75	1.90
	Dallas Mavericks			
☐ 7	Mahmoud Abdul-Rauf....	1.00	.45	.13
	Denver Nuggets			
☐ 8	Joe Dumars	2.50	1.15	.30
	Detroit Pistons			
☐ 9	Chris Webber	12.00	5.50	1.50
	Golden State Warriors			
☐ 10	Hakeem Olajuwon	12.00	5.50	1.50
	Houston Rockets			
☐ 11	Reggie Miller................	5.00	2.30	.60
	Indiana Pacers			
☐ 12	Danny Manning............	2.00	.90	.25
	Los Angeles Clippers			
☐ 13	Doug Christie...............	1.00	.45	.13
	Los Angeles Lakers			
☐ 14	Steve Smith	1.50	.65	.19
	Miami Heat			
☐ 15	Eric Murdock	1.00	.45	.13
	Milwaukee Bucks			
☐ 16	Isaiah Rider..................	5.00	2.30	.60
	Minnesota Timberwolves			
☐ 17	Derrick Coleman	2.00	.90	.25
	New Jersey Nets			
☐ 18	Patrick Ewing...............	5.00	2.30	.60
	New York Knicks			
☐ 19	Shaquille O'Neal...........	40.00	18.00	5.00
	Orlando Magic			
☐ 20	Shawn Bradley.............	3.00	1.35	.40
	Philadelphia 76ers			
☐ 21	Charles Barkley	10.00	4.50	1.25
	Phoenix Suns			
☐ 22	Clyde Drexler	5.00	2.30	.60
	Portland Trail Blazers			
☐ 23	Mitch Richmond	2.50	1.15	.30

This 331-card standard size set was issued
in two series of 165 and 166 cards each.
Cards were distributed in 7-card packs.
Packs carried a suggested retail price of
$5.00 each. Metallic fronts feature a color
player photo against a prismatic back-
ground. The players name is at the bottom.
The backs have a small photo, stats, bio
and a "Finest Moment `93-94". The backs
have blue borders with the player's name
and position at the top. Topical subsets fea-
tured are City Legend-NYC (1-10), City
Legend-Balt/DC (51-55), City Legend-
Detroit (101-105), City Legend-Chicago
(106-110), City Legend-LA (151-155),
Finest's ACC's Best (201-209), Finest's Big
East's Best (226-234), Finest's Big Ten's
Best (250-259), and Finest's SEC's Best
(275-284). Each card features a protective
coating on front that was designed to pro-
tect the card from problems that may arise
from handling. The coating can be removed
by carefully peeling it from the card. Values
provided below are for unpeeled cards.
Peeled cards generally trade for about ten
to twenty-five percent less.

		MINT	NRMT	EXC
COMPLETE SET (1-331)		180.00	80.00	23.00
COMPLETE SERIES 1 (165)...		80.00	36.00	10.00
COMPLETE SERIES 2 (166).		100.00	45.00	12.50
COMMON CARD (1-165)		.50	.23	.06
COMMON CARD (166-331) ...		.30	.14	.04
☐ 1	Chris Mullin CY	.50	.23	.06
	Golden State Warriors			
☐ 2	Anthony Mason CY	.50	.23	.06
	New York Knicks			
☐ 3	John Salley CY..............	.50	.23	.06
	Miami Heat			

☐ 4 Jamal Mashburn CY	2.50	1.15	.30
Dallas Mavericks			
☐ 5 Mark Jackson CY	.50	.23	.06
Indiana Pacers			
☐ 6 Mario Elie CY	.50	.23	.06
Houston Rockets			
☐ 7 Kenny Anderson CY	.75	.35	.09
New Jersey Nets			
☐ 8 Rod Strickland CY	.50	.23	.06
Portland Trail Blazers			
☐ 9 Kenny Smith CY	.50	.23	.06
Houston Rockets			
☐ 10 Olden Polynice CY	.50	.23	.06
Sacramento Kings			
☐ 11 Derek Harper	.75	.35	.09
New York Knicks			
☐ 12 Danny Ainge	.75	.35	.09
Phoenix Suns			
☐ 13 Dino Radja	1.00	.45	.13
Boston Celtics			
☐ 14 Eric Murdock	.50	.23	.06
Milwaukee Bucks			
☐ 15 Sean Rooks	.50	.23	.06
Minnesota Timberwolves			
☐ 16 Dell Curry	.50	.23	.06
Charlotte Hornets			
☐ 17 Victor Alexander	.50	.23	.06
Golden State Warriors			
☐ 18 Rodney Rogers	1.00	.45	.13
Denver Nuggets			
☐ 19 John Salley	.50	.23	.06
Miami Heat			
☐ 20 Brad Daugherty	.75	.35	.09
Cleveland Cavaliers			
☐ 21 Elmore Spencer	.50	.23	.06
Los Angeles Clippers			
☐ 22 Mitch Richmond	1.25	.55	.16
Sacramento Kings			
☐ 23 Rex Walters	.50	.23	.06
New Jersey Nets			
☐ 24 Antonio Davis	.50	.23	.06
Indiana Pacers			
☐ 25 B.J. Armstrong	.50	.23	.06
Chicago Bulls			
☐ 26 Andrew Lang	.50	.23	.06
Atlanta Hawks			
☐ 27 Carl Herrera	.50	.23	.06
Houston Rockets			
☐ 28 Kevin Edwards	.50	.23	.06
New Jersey Nets			
☐ 29 Micheal Williams	.50	.23	.06
Minnesota Timberwolves			
☐ 30 Clyde Drexler	2.50	1.15	.30
Portland Trail Blazers			
☐ 31 Dana Barros	1.00	.45	.13
Philadelphia 76ers			
☐ 32 Shaquille O'Neal	12.00	5.50	1.50
Orlando Magic			
☐ 33 Patrick Ewing	2.50	1.15	.30
New York Knicks			
☐ 34 Charles Barkley	5.00	2.30	.60
Phoenix Suns			
☐ 35 J.R. Reid	.50	.23	.06
San Antonio Spurs			
☐ 36 Lindsey Hunter	.50	.23	.06
Detroit Pistons			
☐ 37 Jeff Malone	.75	.35	.09
Philadelphia 76ers			
☐ 38 Rik Smits	1.00	.45	.13
Indiana Pacers			
☐ 39 Brian Williams	.50	.23	.06
Denver Nuggets			
☐ 40 Shawn Kemp	5.00	2.30	.60
Seattle Supersonics			
☐ 41 Terry Porter	.75	.35	.09
Portland Trail Blazers			
☐ 42 James Worthy	1.00	.45	.13
Los Angeles Lakers			
☐ 43 Rex Chapman	.50	.23	.06
Washington Bullets			
☐ 44 Stanley Roberts	.50	.23	.06
Los Angeles Clippers			
☐ 45 Chris Smith	.50	.23	.06
Minnesota Timberwolves			
☐ 46 Dee Brown	.75	.35	.09
Boston Celtics			
☐ 47 Chris Gatling	.50	.23	.06
Golden State Warriors			
☐ 48 Donald Hodge	.50	.23	.06
Dallas Mavericks			
☐ 49 Bimbo Coles	.50	.23	.06
Miami Heat			
☐ 50 Derrick Coleman	1.00	.45	.13
New Jersey Nets			
☐ 51 Muggsy Bogues CY	.50	.23	.06
Charlotte Hornets			
☐ 52 Reggie Williams CY	.50	.23	.06
Denver Nuggets			
☐ 53 David Wingate CY	.50	.23	.06
Charlotte Hornets			
☐ 54 Sam Cassell CY	.75	.35	.09
Houston Rockets			
☐ 55 Sherman Douglas CY	.50	.23	.06
Boston Celtics			
☐ 56 Keith Jennings	.50	.23	.06
Golden State Warriors			
☐ 57 Kenny Gattison	.50	.23	.06
Charlotte Hornets			
☐ 58 Brent Price	.50	.23	.06
Washington Bullets			
☐ 59 Luc Longley	.50	.23	.06
Chicago Bulls			
☐ 60 Jamal Mashburn	5.00	2.30	.60
Dallas Mavericks			
☐ 61 Doug West	.50	.23	.06
Minnesota Timberwolves			
☐ 62 Walt Williams	.75	.35	.09
Sacramento Kings			
☐ 63 Tracy Murray	.50	.23	.06
Portland Trail Blazers			
☐ 64 Robert Pack	.50	.23	.06
Denver Nuggets			
☐ 65 Johnny Dawkins	.50	.23	.06
Detroit Pistons			
☐ 66 Vin Baker	2.50	1.15	.30
Milwaukee Bucks			
☐ 67 Sam Cassell	1.00	.45	.13
Houston Rockets			
☐ 68 Dale Davis	.75	.35	.09
Indiana Pacers			
☐ 69 Terrell Brandon	.50	.23	.06
Cleveland Cavaliers			
☐ 70 Billy Owens	.75	.35	.09
Golden State Warriors			
☐ 71 Ervin Johnson	.50	.23	.06
Seattle Supersonics			
☐ 72 Allan Houston	1.00	.45	.13
Detroit Pistons			
☐ 73 Craig Ehlo	.50	.23	.06
Atlanta Hawks			
☐ 74 Loy Vaught	.50	.23	.06
Los Angeles Clippers			

☐ 75 Scottie Pippen	2.50	1.15	.30
Chicago Bulls			
☐ 76 Sam Bowie	.50	.23	.06
Los Angeles Lakers			
☐ 77 Anthony Mason	.75	.35	.09
New York Knicks			
☐ 78 Felton Spencer	.50	.23	.06
Utah Jazz			
☐ 79 P.J. Brown	.50	.23	.06
New Jersey Nets			
☐ 80 Christian Laettner	.75	.35	.09
Minnesota Timberwolves			
☐ 81 Todd Day	.50	.23	.06
Milwaukee Bucks			
☐ 82 Sean Elliott	.75	.35	.09
San Antonio Spurs			
☐ 83 Grant Long	.50	.23	.06
Miami Heat			
☐ 84 Xavier McDaniel	.75	.35	.09
Boston Celtics			
☐ 85 David Benoit	.50	.23	.06
Utah Jazz			
☐ 86 Larry Stewart	.50	.23	.06
Washington Bullets			
☐ 87 Donald Royal	.50	.23	.06
Orlando Magic			
☐ 88 Duane Causwell	.50	.23	.06
Sacramento Kings			
☐ 89 Vlade Divac	1.00	.45	.13
Los Angeles Lakers			
☐ 90 Derrick McKey	.75	.35	.09
Indiana Pacers			
☐ 91 Kevin Johnson	1.25	.55	.16
Phoenix Suns			
☐ 92 LaPhonso Ellis	.50	.23	.06
Denver Nuggets			
☐ 93 Jerome Kersey	.50	.23	.06
Portland Trail Blazers			
☐ 94 Muggsy Bogues	1.00	.45	.13
Charlotte Hornets			
☐ 95 Tom Gugliotta	.75	.35	.09
Washington Bullets			
☐ 96 Jeff Hornacek	.75	.35	.09
Utah Jazz			
☐ 97 Kevin Willis	.75	.35	.09
Atlanta Hawks			
☐ 98 Chris Mills	1.00	.45	.13
Cleveland Cavaliers			
☐ 99 Sam Perkins	.75	.35	.09
Seattle Supersonics			
☐ 100 Alonzo Mourning	3.00	1.35	.40
Charlotte Hornets			
☐ 101 Derrick Coleman CY	.50	.23	.06
New Jersey Nets			
☐ 102 Glen Rice CY	.50	.23	.06
Miami Heat			
☐ 103 Kevin Willis CY	.50	.23	.06
Miami Heat			
☐ 104 Chris Webber CY	2.00	.90	.25
Golden State Warriors			
☐ 105 Terry Mills CY	.50	.23	.06
Detroit Pistons			
☐ 106 Tim Hardaway CY	.50	.23	.06
Golden State Warriors			
☐ 107 Nick Anderson CY	.50	.23	.06
Orlando Magic			
☐ 108 Terry Cummings CY	.50	.23	.06
San Antonio Spurs			
☐ 109 Hersey Hawkins CY	.50	.23	.06
Charlotte Hornets			
☐ 110 Ken Norman CY	.50	.23	.06

Atlanta Hawks			
☐ 111 Nick Anderson	.75	.35	.09
Orlando Magic			
☐ 112 Tim Perry	.50	.23	.06
Philadelphia 76ers			
☐ 113 Terry Dehere	.50	.23	.06
Los Angeles Clippers			
☐ 114 Chris Morris	.50	.23	.06
New Jersey Nets			
☐ 115 John Williams	.75	.35	.09
Cleveland Cavaliers			
☐ 116 Jon Barry	.50	.23	.06
Milwaukee Bucks			
☐ 117 Rony Seikaly	.50	.23	.06
Miami Heat			
☐ 118 Detlef Schrempf	1.00	.45	.13
Seattle Supersonics			
☐ 119 Terry Cummings	.75	.35	.09
San Antonio Spurs			
☐ 120 Chris Webber	4.00	1.80	.50
Washington Bullets			
☐ 121 David Wingate	.50	.23	.06
Charlotte Hornets			
☐ 122 Popeye Jones	.50	.23	.06
Dallas Mavericks			
☐ 123 Sherman Douglas	.50	.23	.06
Boston Celtics			
☐ 124 Greg Anthony	.50	.23	.06
New York Knicks			
☐ 125 Mookie Blaylock	.75	.35	.09
Atlanta Hawks			
☐ 126 Don MacLean	.50	.23	.06
Washington Bullets			
☐ 127 Lionel Simmons	.50	.23	.06
Sacramento Kings			
☐ 128 Scott Brooks	.50	.23	.06
Houston Rockets			
☐ 129 Jeff Turner	.50	.23	.06
Orlando Magic			
☐ 130 Bryant Stith	.50	.23	.06
Denver Nuggets			
☐ 131 Shawn Bradley	1.00	.45	.13
Philadelphia 76ers			
☐ 132 Byron Scott	.75	.35	.09
Indiana Pacers			
☐ 133 Doug Christie	.50	.23	.06
New York Knicks			
☐ 134 Dennis Rodman	.50	.23	.06
San Antonio Spurs			
☐ 135 Dan Majerle	.75	.35	.09
Phoenix Suns			
☐ 136 Gary Grant	.50	.23	.06
Los Angeles Clippers			
☐ 137 Bryon Russell	.50	.23	.06
Utah Jazz			
☐ 138 Will Perdue	.50	.23	.06
Chicago Bulls			
☐ 139 Gheorghe Muresan	.75	.35	.09
Washington Bullets			
☐ 140 Kendall Gill	.75	.35	.09
Seattle Supersonics			
☐ 141 Isaiah Rider	1.50	.65	.19
Minnesota Timberwolves			
☐ 142 Terry Mills	.50	.23	.06
Detroit Pistons			
☐ 143 Willie Anderson	.50	.23	.06
San Antonio Spurs			
☐ 144 Hubert Davis	.50	.23	.06
New York Knicks			
☐ 145 Lucious Harris	.50	.23	.06
Dallas Mavericks			

☐ 146	Spud Webb	.75	.35	.09
	Sacramento Kings			
☐ 147	Glen Rice	1.00	.45	.13
	Miami Heat			
☐ 148	Dennis Scott	.50	.23	.06
	Orlando Magic			
☐ 149	Robert Horry	1.00	.45	.13
	Houston Rockets			
☐ 150	John Stockton	2.50	1.15	.30
	Utah Jazz			
☐ 151	Stacey Augmon CY	.50	.23	.06
	Atlanta Hawks			
☐ 152	Chris Mills CY	.50	.23	.06
	Cleveland Cavaliers			
☐ 153	Elden Campbell CY	.50	.23	.06
	Los Angeles Lakers			
☐ 154	Jay Humphries CY	.50	.23	.06
	Utah Jazz			
☐ 155	Reggie Miller CY	1.00	.45	.13
	Indiana Pacers			
☐ 156	George Lynch	.50	.23	.06
	Los Angeles Lakers			
☐ 157	Tyrone Hill	.75	.35	.09
	Cleveland Cavaliers			
☐ 158	Lee Mayberry	.50	.23	.06
	Milwaukee Bucks			
☐ 159	Jon Koncak	.50	.23	.06
	Atlanta Hawks			
☐ 160	Joe Dumars	1.25	.55	.16
	Detroit Pistons			
☐ 161	Vernon Maxwell	.50	.23	.06
	Houston Rockets			
☐ 162	Joe Kleine	.50	.23	.06
	Phoenix Suns			
☐ 163	Acie Earl	.50	.23	.06
	Boston Celtics			
☐ 164	Steve Kerr	.50	.23	.06
	Chicago Bulls			
☐ 165	Rod Strickland	.75	.35	.09
	Portland Trail Blazers			
☐ 166	Glenn Robinson	12.00	5.50	1.50
	Milwaukee Bucks			
☐ 167	Anfernee Hardaway	6.00	2.70	.75
	Orlando Magic			
☐ 168	Latrell Sprewell	2.00	.90	.25
	Golden State Warriors			
☐ 169	Sergei Bazarevich	.30	.14	.04
	Atlanta Hawks			
☐ 170	Hakeem Olajuwon	4.00	1.80	.50
	Houston Rockets			
☐ 171	Nick Van Exel	3.00	1.35	.40
	Los Angeles Lakers			
☐ 172	Buck Williams	.45	.20	.06
	Portland Trail Blazers			
☐ 173	Antoine Carr	.30	.14	.04
	Utah Jazz			
☐ 174	Corie Blount	.30	.14	.04
	Chicago Bulls			
☐ 175	Dominique Wilkins	.75	.35	.09
	Boston Celtics			
☐ 176	Yinka Dare	.55	.25	.07
	New Jersey Nets			
☐ 177	Byron Houston	.30	.14	.04
	Seattle Supersonics			
☐ 178	LaSalle Thompson	.30	.14	.04
	Indiana Pacers			
☐ 179	Doug Smith	.30	.14	.04
	Dallas Mavericks			
☐ 180	David Robinson	3.00	1.35	.40
	San Antonio Spurs			
☐ 181	Eric Piatkowski	.75	.35	.09
	Sacramento Kings			
☐ 182	Scott Skiles	.30	.14	.04
	Washington Bullets			
☐ 183	Scott Burrell	.30	.14	.04
	Charlotte Hornets			
☐ 184	Mark West	.30	.14	.04
	Detroit Pistons			
☐ 185	Billy Owens	.45	.20	.06
	Miami Heat			
☐ 186	Brian Grant	4.00	1.80	.50
	Sacramento Kings			
☐ 187	Scott Williams	.30	.14	.04
	Philadelphia 76ers			
☐ 188	Gerald Madkins	.30	.14	.04
	Cleveland Cavaliers			
☐ 189	Reggie Williams	.30	.14	.04
	Denver Nuggets			
☐ 190	Danny Manning	.60	.25	.08
	Phoenix Suns			
☐ 191	Mike Brown	.30	.14	.04
	Minnesota Timberwolves			
☐ 192	Charles Smith	.30	.14	.04
	New York Knicks			
☐ 193	Elden Campbell	.30	.14	.04
	Los Angeles Lakers			
☐ 194	Ricky Pierce	.55	.25	.07
	Golden State Warriors			
☐ 195	Karl Malone	1.50	.65	.19
	Utah Jazz			
☐ 196	Brooks Thompson	.55	.25	.07
	Orlando Magic			
☐ 197	Alaa Abdelnaby	.30	.14	.04
	Sacramento Kings			
☐ 198	Tyrone Corbin	.30	.14	.04
	Utah Jazz			
☐ 199	Johnny Newman	.30	.14	.04
	New Jersey Nets			
☐ 200	Grant Hill FB	8.00	3.60	1.00
	Detroit Pistons			
☐ 201	Kenny Anderson FB	.30	.14	.04
	New Jersey Nets			
☐ 202	Olden Polynice FB	.30	.14	.04
	Sacramento Kings			
☐ 203	Horace Grant FB	.30	.14	.04
	Orlando Magic			
☐ 204	Muggsy Bogues FB	.30	.14	.04
	Charlotte Hornets			
☐ 205	Mark Price FB	.30	.14	.04
	Cleveland Cavaliers			
☐ 206	Tom Gugliotta FB	.30	.14	.04
	Golden State Warriors			
☐ 207	Christian Laettner FB	.30	.14	.04
	Minnesota Timberwolves			
☐ 208	Eric Montross FB	.60	.25	.08
	Boston Celtics			
☐ 209	Sam Cassell FB	.30	.14	.04
	Houston Rockets			
☐ 210	Charles Oakley	.45	.20	.06
	New York Knicks			
☐ 211	Harold Ellis	.30	.14	.04
	Los Angeles Clippers			
☐ 212	Nate McMillan	.30	.14	.04
	Seattle Supersonics			
☐ 213	Chuck Person	.45	.20	.06
	San Antonio Spurs			
☐ 214	Harold Miner	.30	.14	.04
	Miami Heat			
☐ 215	Clarence Weatherspoon	.45	.20	.06
	Philadelphia 76ers			
☐ 216	Robert Parish	.60	.25	.08
	Charlotte Hornets			

☐ 217	Michael Cage	.30	.14	.04
	Cleveland Cavaliers			
☐ 218	Kenny Smith	.30	.14	.04
	Houston Rockets			
☐ 219	Larry Krystkowiak	.30	.14	.04
	Orlando Magic			
☐ 220	Dikembe Mutombo	1.00	.45	.13
	Denver Nuggets			
☐ 221	Wayman Tisdale	.55	.25	.07
	Phoenix Suns			
☐ 222	Kevin Duckworth	.30	.14	.04
	Washington Bullets			
☐ 223	Vern Fleming	.30	.14	.04
	Indiana Pacers			
☐ 224	Eric Mobley	.75	.35	.09
	Milwaukee Bucks			
☐ 225	Patrick Ewing FB	.75	.35	.09
	New York Knicks			
☐ 226	Clifford Robinson FB	.30	.14	.04
	Portland Trail Blazers			
☐ 227	Eric Murdock FB	.30	.14	.04
	Milwaukee Bucks			
☐ 228	Derrick Coleman FB	.30	.14	.04
	New Jersey Nets			
☐ 229	Otis Thorpe FB	.30	.14	.04
	Houston Rockets			
☐ 230	Alonzo Mourning FB	1.00	.45	.13
	Charlotte Hornets			
☐ 231	Donyell Marshall FB	1.00	.45	.13
	Minnesota Timberwolves			
☐ 232	Dikembe Mutombo FB	.45	.20	.06
	Denver Nuggets			
☐ 233	Rony Seikaly FB	.30	.14	.04
	Miami Heat			
☐ 234	Chris Mullin FB	.30	.14	.04
	Golden State Warriors			
☐ 235	Reggie Miller	1.50	.65	.19
	Indiana Pacers			
☐ 236	Benoit Benjamin	.30	.14	.04
	New Jersey Nets			
☐ 237	Sean Rooks	.30	.14	.04
	Minnesota Timberwolves			
☐ 238	Terry Davis	.30	.14	.04
	Dallas Mavericks			
☐ 239	Anthony Avent	.30	.14	.04
	Orlando Magic			
☐ 240	Grant Hill	20.00	9.00	2.50
	Detroit Pistons			
☐ 241	Randy Woods	.30	.14	.04
	Los Angeles Clippers			
☐ 242	Tom Chambers	.45	.20	.06
	Utah Jazz			
☐ 243	Michael Adams	.30	.14	.04
	Charlotte Hornets			
☐ 244	Monty Williams	.75	.35	.09
	New York Knicks			
☐ 245	Chris Mullin	.60	.25	.08
	Golden State Warriors			
☐ 246	Bill Wennington	.30	.14	.04
	Chicago Bulls			
☐ 247	Mark Jackson	.30	.14	.04
	Indiana Pacers			
☐ 248	Blue Edwards	.30	.14	.04
	Boston Celtics			
☐ 249	Jalen Rose	2.50	1.15	.30
	Denver Nuggets			
☐ 250	Glenn Robinson FB	5.00	2.30	.60
	Milwaukee Bucks			
☐ 251	Kevin Willis FB	.30	.14	.04
	Miami Heat			
☐ 252	B.J. Armstrong FB	.30	.14	.04

	Chicago Bulls			
☐ 253	Jim Jackson FB	1.00	.45	.13
	Dallas Mavericks			
☐ 254	Steve Smith FB	.30	.14	.04
	Atlanta Hawks			
☐ 255	Chris Webber FB	1.25	.55	.16
	Washington Bullets			
☐ 256	Glen Rice FB	.30	.14	.04
	Miami Heat			
☐ 257	Derek Harper FB	.30	.14	.04
	New York Knicks			
☐ 258	Jalen Rose FB	.30	.14	.04
	Denver Nuggets			
☐ 259	Juwan Howard FB	2.00	.90	.25
	Washington Bullets			
☐ 260	Kenny Anderson	.60	.25	.08
	New Jersey Nets			
☐ 261	Calbert Cheaney	.60	.25	.08
	Washington Bullets			
☐ 262	Bill Cartwright	.30	.14	.04
	Seattle Supersonics			
☐ 263	Mario Elie	.30	.14	.04
	Houston Rockets			
☐ 264	Chris Dudley	.30	.14	.04
	Portland Trail Blazers			
☐ 265	Jim Jackson	2.00	.90	.25
	Dallas Mavericks			
☐ 266	Antonio Harvey	.30	.14	.04
	Los Angeles Lakers			
☐ 267	Bill Curley	.75	.35	.09
	Detroit Pistons			
☐ 268	Moses Malone	.75	.35	.09
	San Antonio Spurs			
☐ 269	A.C. Green	.60	.25	.08
	Phoenix Suns			
☐ 270	Larry Johnson	1.25	.55	.16
	Charlotte Hornets			
☐ 271	Marty Conlon	.30	.14	.04
	Milwaukee Bucks			
☐ 272	Greg Graham	.30	.14	.04
	Philadelphia 76ers			
☐ 273	Eric Montross	2.00	.90	.25
	Boston Celtics			
☐ 274	Stacey King	.30	.14	.04
	Minnesota Timberwolves			
☐ 275	Charles Barkley FB	1.50	.65	.19
	Phoenix Suns			
☐ 276	Chris Morris FB	.30	.14	.04
	New Jersey Nets			
☐ 277	Robert Horry FB	.45	.20	.06
	Houston Rockets			
☐ 278	Dominique Wilkins FB	.45	.20	.06
	Boston Celtics			
☐ 279	Latrell Sprewell FB	1.00	.45	.13
	Golden State Warriors			
☐ 280	Shaquille O'Neal FB	4.00	1.80	.50
	Orlando Magic			
☐ 281	Wesley Person FB	1.00	.45	.13
	Phoenix Suns			
☐ 282	Mahmoud Abdul-Rauf FB	.30	.14	.04
	Denver Nuggets			
☐ 283	Jamal Mashburn FB	1.50	.65	.19
	Dallas Mavericks			
☐ 284	Dale Ellis FB	.30	.14	.04
	San Antonio Spurs			
☐ 285	Gary Payton	.60	.25	.08
	Seattle Supersonics			
☐ 286	Jason Kidd	12.00	5.50	1.50
	Dallas Mavericks			
☐ 287	Ken Norman	.30	.14	.04
	Atlanta Hawks			

☐ 288	Juwan Howard 5.00	2.30	.60
	Washington Bullets		
☐ 289	Lamond Murray 2.00	.90	.25
	Los Angeles Clippers		
☐ 290	Clifford Robinson .... .45	.20	.06
	Portland Trail Blazers		
☐ 291	Frank Brickowski .... .30	.14	.04
	Sacramento Kings		
☐ 292	Adam Keefe .... .30	.14	.04
	Utah Jazz		
☐ 293	Ron Harper .... .45	.20	.06
	Chicago Bulls		
☐ 294	Tom Hammonds .... .30	.14	.04
	Denver Nuggets		
☐ 295	Otis Thorpe .... .45	.20	.06
	Houston Rockets		
☐ 296	Rick Mahorn .... .30	.14	.04
	New Jersey Nets		
☐ 297	Alton Lister .... .30	.14	.04
	Milwaukee Bucks		
☐ 298	Vinny Del Negro .... .30	.14	.04
	San Antonio Spurs		
☐ 299	Danny Ferry .... .30	.14	.04
	Cleveland Cavaliers		
☐ 300	John Starks .... .45	.20	.06
	New York Knicks		
☐ 301	Duane Ferrell .... .30	.14	.04
	Indiana Pacers		
☐ 302	Hersey Hawkins .... .55	.25	.07
	Charlotte Hornets		
☐ 303	Khalid Reeves 2.00	.90	.25
	Miami Heat		
☐ 304	Anthony Peeler .... .30	.14	.04
	Los Angeles Lakers		
☐ 305	Tim Hardaway .... .60	.25	.08
	Golden State Warriors		
☐ 306	Rick Fox .... .30	.14	.04
	Boston Celtics		
☐ 307	Jay Humphries .... .30	.14	.04
	Utah Jazz		
☐ 308	Brian Shaw .... .30	.14	.04
	Miami Heat		
☐ 309	Dan Schayes .... .30	.14	.04
	Phoenix Suns		
☐ 310	Stacey Augmon .... .45	.20	.06
	Atlanta Hawks		
☐ 311	Oliver Miller .... .30	.14	.04
	Detroit Pistons		
☐ 312	Pooh Richardson .... .30	.14	.04
	Los Angeles Clippers		
☐ 313	Donyell Marshall 2.50	1.15	.30
	Minnesota Timberwolves		
☐ 314	Aaron McKie 1.00	.45	.13
	Portland Trail Blazers		
☐ 315	Mark Price .... .60	.25	.08
	Cleveland Cavaliers		
☐ 316	B.J. Tyler .... .55	.25	.07
	Philadelphia 76ers		
☐ 317	Olden Polynice .... .30	.14	.04
	Sacramento Kings		
☐ 318	Avery Johnson .... .30	.14	.04
	San Antonio Spurs		
☐ 319	Derek Strong .... .30	.14	.04
	Boston Celtics		
☐ 320	Toni Kukoc .... .60	.25	.08
	Chicago Bulls		
☐ 321	Charlie Ward 1.00	.45	.13
	New York Knicks		
☐ 322	Wesley Person 2.50	1.15	.30
	Phoenix Suns		
☐ 323	Eddie Jones 8.00	3.60	1.00

	Los Angeles Lakers		
☐ 324	Horace Grant .... .75	.35	.09
	Orlando Magic		
☐ 325	Mahmoud Abdul-Rauf.. .45	.20	.06
	Denver Nuggets		
☐ 326	Sharone Wright 1.50	.65	.19
	Philadelphia 76ers		
☐ 327	Kevin Gamble .... .30	.14	.04
	Miami Heat		
☐ 328	Sarunas Marciulionis .. .30	.14	.04
	Seattle Supersonics		
☐ 329	Harvey Grant .... .30	.14	.04
	Portland Trail Blazers		
☐ 330	Bobby Hurley .... .45	.20	.06
	Sacramento Kings		
☐ 331	Michael Jordan 30.00	13.50	3.80
	Chicago Bulls		

1994-95 Finest Refractors

Parallel to the basic set, Refractors were randomly inserted in packs at a rate of one in 12. Refractors are distinguished from the basic cards by their rainbow-like appearance that refracts more light. Just like regular issue Finest cards, each Refractor comes with a protective coating designed to protect the card from wear and tear. Values provided below are for unpeeled cards. Peeled cards trade for about ten to twenty-five percent less. Only the top few cards are individually listed below. Please refer to the multipliers provided below (and the value of the corresponding regular issue card) for values on unlisted Refractors.

	MINT	NRMT	EXC
COMPLETE SET (331)	2700.00	1200.00	350.00
COMPLETE SERIES 1 (165)	1000.00	450.00	125.00
COMPLETE SERIES 2 (166)	1700.00	750.00	210.00
COMMON CARD (1-331)	3.00	1.35	.40
*SER.1 STARS: 4X to 8X BASIC CARDS			
*SER.2 STARS: 6X to 12X BASIC CARDS			
*ROOKIES: 3X to 6X BASIC CARDS			

☐ 32	Shaquille O'Neal....... 100.00	45.00	12.50
	Orlando Magic		
☐ 34	Charles Barkley......... 40.00	18.00	5.00
	Phoenix Suns		
☐ 40	Shawn Kemp............. 40.00	18.00	5.00

			MINT	NRMT	EXC
		Seattle Supersonics			
☐	60	Jamal Mashburn	40.00	18.00	5.00
		Dallas Mavericks			
☐	166	Glenn Robinson	80.00	36.00	10.00
		Milwaukee Bucks			
☐	167	Anfernee Hardaway	80.00	36.00	10.00
		Orlando Magic			
☐	170	Hakeem Olajuwon	50.00	23.00	6.25
		Houston Rockets			
☐	171	Nick Van Exel	40.00	18.00	5.00
		Los Angeles Lakers			
☐	180	David Robinson	40.00	18.00	5.00
		San Antonio Spurs			
☐	200	Grant Hill FB	50.00	23.00	6.25
		Detroit Pistons			
☐	240	Grant Hill	125.00	57.50	15.50
		Detroit Pistons			
☐	280	Shaquille O'Neal FB	50.00	23.00	6.25
		Orlando Magic			
☐	286	Jason Kidd	80.00	36.00	10.00
		Dallas Mavericks			
☐	323	Eddie Jones	50.00	23.00	6.25
		Los Angeles Lakers			
☐	331	Michael Jordan	350.00	160.00	45.00
		Chicago Bulls			

			MINT	NRMT	EXC
		New York Knicks			
☐	4	Karl Malone	10.00	4.50	1.25
		Utah Jazz			
☐	5	Kenny Anderson	3.00	1.35	.40
		New Jersey Nets			
☐	6	Latrell Sprewell	12.00	5.50	1.50
		Golden State Warriors			
☐	7	Dikembe Mutombo	6.00	2.70	.75
		Denver Nuggets			
☐	8	Charles Barkley	20.00	9.00	2.50
		Phoenix Suns			
☐	9	John Stockton	10.00	4.50	1.25
		Utah Jazz			
☐	10	Reggie Miller	10.00	4.50	1.25
		Indiana Pacers			
☐	11	Jamal Mashburn	20.00	9.00	2.50
		Dallas Mavericks			
☐	12	Anfernee Hardaway	40.00	18.00	5.00
		Orlando Magic			
☐	13	Jim Jackson	12.00	5.50	1.50
		Dallas Mavericks			
☐	14	David Robinson	20.00	9.00	2.50
		San Antonio Spurs			
☐	15	Hakeem Olajuwon	25.00	11.50	3.10
		Houston Rockets			

1994-95 Finest Cornerstone

1994-95 Finest Iron Men

Randomly inserted in second series packs at a rate of one in every 24, cards from this 15-card standard-size set highlight players who are foundations of their respective teams. The fronts have a color-action photo set against a multi-colored background. The word "Cornerstone" is at the bottom, jutting out from a wall. The backs have a color-photo and player information. Values provided below are for unpeeled cards. Peeled cards generally trade for ten to twenty-five percent less.

Randomly inserted in first series packs at a rate of one in 24, cards from this 10-card standard-size set spotlight players who played at least 3,000 minutes during the 1993-94 NBA season. These transparent cards have a front design much like the basic Finest cards with "Iron Man" at the top. The only design element on back is a small stat box at the bottom. Unlike most other 1994-95 Finest cards, Iron Men inserts have no protective coating.

	MINT	NRMT	EXC
COMPLETE SET (15)	200.00	90.00	25.00
COMMON CARD (1-15)	3.00	1.35	.40
☐ 1 Shaquille O'Neal	50.00	23.00	6.25
Orlando Magic			
☐ 2 Alonzo Mourning	12.00	5.50	1.50
Charlotte Hornets			
☐ 3 Patrick Ewing	10.00	4.50	1.25

	MINT	NRMT	EXC
COMPLETE SET (10)	75.00	34.00	9.50
COMMON CARD (1-10)	1.50	.65	.19
☐ 1 Shaquille O'Neal	30.00	13.50	3.80
Orlando Magic			
☐ 2 Kenny Anderson	1.50	.65	.19
New Jersey Nets			
☐ 3 Jim Jackson	8.00	3.60	1.00
Dallas Mavericks			

☐ 4	Clarence Weatherspoon. Philadelphia 76ers	1.50	.65	.19
☐ 5	Karl Malone. Utah Jazz	6.00	2.70	.75
☐ 6	Dan Majerle. Phoenix Suns	1.50	.65	.19
☐ 7	Anfernee Hardaway. Orlando Magic	25.00	11.50	3.10
☐ 8	David Robinson. San Antonio Spurs	12.00	5.50	1.50
☐ 9	Latrell Sprewell. Golden State Warriors	8.00	3.60	1.00
☐ 10	Hakeem Olajuwon. Houston Rockets	15.00	6.75	1.90

1994-95 Finest Lottery Prize

Randomly inserted in second series packs at a rate of one in six, cards from this 22-card standard-size set showcase lottery picks who went on to become impact players. The fronts have a color-action photo with background having a large basketball surrounded by a variety of colors and stars. At the top are the words "Lottery Prize." The backs have a color photo and player information with the words "Lottery Prize" set against a basketball. Values provided below are for unpeeled cards. Peeled cards generally trade for ten to twenty-five percent less.

	MINT	NRMT	EXC
COMPLETE SET (22)	75.00	34.00	9.50
COMMON CARD (1-22)	1.00	.45	.13
☐ 1 Patrick Ewing. New York Knicks	4.00	1.80	.50
☐ 2 Chris Mullin. Golden State Warriors	2.00	.90	.25
☐ 3 David Robinson. San Antonio Spurs	8.00	3.60	1.00
☐ 4 Scottie Pippen. Chicago Bulls	4.00	1.80	.50
☐ 5 Kevin Johnson. Phoenix Suns	2.00	.90	.25
☐ 6 Danny Manning. Phoenix Suns	2.00	.90	.25
☐ 7 Mitch Richmond. Sacramento Kings	1.00	.45	.13

☐ 8	Derrick Coleman. New Jersey Nets	2.00	.90	.25
☐ 9	Gary Payton. Seattle Supersonics	2.00	.90	.25
☐ 10	Mahmoud Abdul-Rauf.. Denver Nuggets	1.00	.45	.13
☐ 11	Larry Johnson. Charlotte Hornets	3.00	1.35	.40
☐ 12	Kenny Anderson. New Jersey Nets	2.00	.90	.25
☐ 13	Dikembe Mutombo. Denver Nuggets	2.00	.90	.25
☐ 14	Stacey Augmon. Atlanta Hawks	1.00	.45	.13
☐ 15	Shaquille O'Neal. Orlando Magic	20.00	9.00	2.50
☐ 16	Alonzo Mourning. Charlotte Hornets	5.00	2.30	.60
☐ 17	Clarence Weatherspoon Philadelphia 76ers	1.00	.45	.13
☐ 18	Robert Horry. Houston Rockets	2.00	.90	.25
☐ 19	Chris Webber. Washington Bullets	6.00	2.70	.75
☐ 20	Anfernee Hardaway. Orlando Magic	15.00	6.75	1.90
☐ 21	Jamal Mashburn. Dallas Mavericks	8.00	3.60	1.00
☐ 22	Vin Baker. Milwaukee Bucks	4.00	1.80	.50

1994-95 Finest Marathon Men

Randomly inserted into first series packs at a rate of one in 12, cards from this 12-card standard-size set highlight players who played in all 82 games during the 1993-94 NBA season. These transparent cards have a design on front that is similar to the basic issue with the words "Marathon Man" at the top. The back contains a small stat box at the bottom. Unlike most other 1994-95 Finest cards, Marathon Men inserts have no protective coatings.

	MINT	NRMT	EXC
COMPLETE SET (20)	75.00	34.00	9.50
COMMON CARD (1-20)	2.00	.90	.25
☐ 1 Latrell Sprewell. Golden State Warriors	12.00	5.50	1.50

☐ 2 Gary Payton	4.00	1.80	.50
Seattle Supersonics			
☐ 3 Kenny Anderson	4.00	1.80	.50
New Jersey Nets			
☐ 4 Jim Jackson	12.00	5.50	1.50
Dallas Mavericks			
☐ 5 Lindsey Hunter	2.00	.90	.25
Detroit Lions			
☐ 6 Rod Strickland	3.00	1.35	.40
Portland Trail Blazers			
☐ 7 Hersey Hawkins	2.00	.90	.25
Charlotte Hornets			
☐ 8 Gerald Wilkins	2.00	.90	.25
Cleveland Cavaliers			
☐ 9 B.J. Armstrong	2.00	.90	.25
Chicago Bulls			
☐ 10 Anfernee Hardaway	40.00	18.00	5.00
Orlando Magic			
☐ 11 Stacey Augmon	3.00	1.35	.40
Atlanta Hawks			
☐ 12 Eric Murdock	2.00	.90	.25
Milwaukee Bucks			
☐ 13 Clarence Weatherspoon	3.00	1.35	.40
Philadelphia 76ers			
☐ 14 Karl Malone	10.00	4.50	1.25
Utah Jazz			
☐ 15 Charles Oakley	3.00	1.35	.40
New York Knicks			
☐ 16 Rick Fox	2.00	.90	.25
Boston Celtics			
☐ 17 Otis Thorpe	3.00	1.35	.40
Houston Rockets			
☐ 18 Dikembe Mutombo	4.00	1.80	.50
Denver Nuggets			
☐ 19 Mike Brown	2.00	.90	.25
Minnesota Timberwolves			
☐ 20 A.C. Green	3.00	1.35	.40
Phoenix Suns			

1994-95 Finest Rack Pack

Randomly inserted in second series packs at a rate of one in every 72, cards from this seven-card standard-size set spotlight a selection of top performers from the 1994 NBA draft class. The fronts have a color-action photo with a basketball hoop and lights in the background. The words "Rack Pack" appear at the top in a red-foil. The backs have player information inside of a computer monitor.

	MINT	NRMT	EXC
COMPLETE SET (7)	250.00	115.00	31.00
COMMON CARD (1-7)	12.00	5.50	1.50
☐ RP1 Grant Hill	110.00	50.00	14.00
Detroit Pistons			
☐ RP2 Wesley Person	15.00	6.75	1.90
Phoenix Suns			
☐ RP3 Juwan Howard	30.00	13.50	3.80
Washington Bullets			
☐ RP4 Lamond Murray	12.00	5.50	1.50
Los Angeles Clippers			
☐ RP5 Glenn Robinson	70.00	32.00	8.75
Milwaukee Bucks			
☐ RP6 Donyell Marshall	15.00	6.75	1.90
Minnesota Timberwolves			
☐ RP7 Jason Kidd	70.00	32.00	8.75
Dallas Mavericks			

1994 Flair USA

The 120 standard-size (2 1/2" by 3 1/2") cards comprising this set pay tribute to the players of 1994 Team USA. Cards were distributed in 10-card packs (24 per box) with a suggested retail of $3.99. Each player has several cards highlighting various stages in his career. The cards are thicker than traditional basketball cards. The borderless fronts feature two blended color player photos. The player's name appears in gold-foil lettering near the bottom. The borderless backs carry a posed color photo with player information appearing in silver-foil lettering toward the bottom. The cards are numbered on the back. The set concludes with a USA Basketball Women's Team Legends (113-118) subset and checklists (119-120). A wrapper offer gave collectors the chance to receive an additional 10 Flair USA cards (eight of Kevin Johnson and two team cards) by sending in $4 to Fleer by October 31, 1994.

	MINT	NRMT	EXC
COMPLETE SET (120)	25.00	11.50	3.10
COMMON CARD (1-120)	.10	.05	.01
☐ 1 Don Chaney CO	.10	.05	.01
Career Highlights			
☐ 2 Don Chaney CO	.10	.05	.01
Personal Note			
☐ 3 Pete Gillen CO	.10	.05	.01
Career Highlights			

☐ 4	Pete Gillen CO Personal Note	.10	.05	.01
☐ 5	Rick Majerus CO Career Highlights	.10	.05	.01
☐ 6	Rick Majerus CO Personal Note	.10	.05	.01
☐ 7	Don Nelson CO Career Highlights	.10	.05	.01
☐ 8	Don Nelson CO Personal Note	.10	.05	.01
☐ 9	Derrick Coleman Strong Suit	.20	.09	.03
☐ 10	Derrick Coleman Career Highlights	.20	.09	.03
☐ 11	Derrick Coleman Golden Moment	.20	.09	.03
☐ 12	Derrick Coleman Biography	.20	.09	.03
☐ 13	Derrick Coleman Rookie Year	.20	.09	.03
☐ 14	Derrick Coleman Weights and Measures	.20	.09	.03
☐ 15	Derrick Coleman Personal Note	.20	.09	.03
☐ 16	Joe Dumars Dreamscapes	.25	.11	.03
☐ 17	Joe Dumars Strong Suit	.25	.11	.03
☐ 18	Joe Dumars Career Highlights	.25	.11	.03
☐ 19	Joe Dumars Golden Moment	.25	.11	.03
☐ 20	Joe Dumars Biography	.25	.11	.03
☐ 21	Joe Dumars Rookie Year	.25	.11	.03
☐ 22	Joe Dumars Weights and Measures	.25	.11	.03
☐ 23	Joe Dumars Personal Note	.25	.11	.03
☐ 24	Joe Dumars Dreamscapes	.25	.11	.03
☐ 25	Tim Hardaway Strong Suit	.20	.09	.03
☐ 26	Tim Hardaway Career Highlights	.20	.09	.03
☐ 27	Tim Hardaway Golden Moment	.20	.09	.03
☐ 28	Tim Hardaway Biography	.20	.09	.03
☐ 29	Tim Hardaway Rookie Year	.20	.09	.03
☐ 30	Tim Hardaway Weights and Measures	.20	.09	.03
☐ 31	Tim Hardaway Personal Note	.20	.09	.03
☐ 32	Tim Hardaway Dreamscapes	.20	.09	.03
☐ 33	Larry Johnson Strong Suit	.40	.18	.05
☐ 34	Larry Johnson Career Highlights	.40	.18	.05
☐ 35	Larry Johnson Golden Moments	.40	.18	.05
☐ 36	Larry Johnson Biography	.40	.18	.05
☐ 37	Larry Johnson Rookie Year	.40	.18	.05
☐ 38	Larry Johnson Weights and Measures	.40	.18	.05
☐ 39	Larry Johnson	.40	.18	.05
	Personal Note			
☐ 40	Larry Johnson Dreamscapes	.40	.18	.05
☐ 41	Shawn Kemp Strong Suit	1.00	.45	.13
☐ 42	Shawn Kemp Career Highlights	1.00	.45	.13
☐ 43	Shawn Kemp Golden Moment	1.00	.45	.13
☐ 44	Shawn Kemp Biography	1.00	.45	.13
☐ 45	Shawn Kemp Rookie Year	1.00	.45	.13
☐ 46	Shawn Kemp Weights and Measures	1.00	.45	.13
☐ 47	Shawn Kemp Personal Note	1.00	.45	.13
☐ 48	Shawn Kemp Dreamscapes	1.00	.45	.13
☐ 49	Dan Majerle Strong Suit	.10	.05	.01
☐ 50	Dan Majerle Career Highlights	.10	.05	.01
☐ 51	Dan Majerle Golden Moment	.10	.05	.01
☐ 52	Dan Majerle Biography	.10	.05	.01
☐ 53	Dan Majerle Rookie Year	.10	.05	.01
☐ 54	Dan Majerle Weights and Measures	.10	.05	.01
☐ 55	Dan Majerle Personal Note	.10	.05	.01
☐ 56	Dan Majerle Dreamscapes	.10	.05	.01
☐ 57	Reggie Miller Strong Suit	.50	.23	.06
☐ 58	Reggie Miller Career Highlights	.50	.23	.06
☐ 59	Reggie Miller Golden Moments	.50	.23	.06
☐ 60	Reggie Miller Biography	.50	.23	.06
☐ 61	Reggie Miller Rookie Year	.50	.23	.06
☐ 62	Reggie Miller Weights and Measures	.50	.23	.06
☐ 63	Reggie Miller Personal Note	.50	.23	.06
☐ 64	Reggie Miller Dreamscapes	.50	.23	.06
☐ 65	Alonzo Mourning Strong Suit	.60	.25	.08
☐ 66	Alonzo Mourning Career Highlights	.60	.25	.08
☐ 67	Alonzo Mourning Golden Moment	.60	.25	.08
☐ 68	Alonzo Mourning Biography	.60	.25	.08
☐ 69	Alonzo Mourning Rookie Year	.60	.25	.08
☐ 70	Alonzo Mourning Weights and Measures	.60	.25	.08
☐ 71	Alonzo Mourning Personal Note	.60	.25	.08
☐ 72	Alonzo Mourning Dreamscapes	.60	.25	.08
☐ 73	Shaquille O'Neal Strong Suit	2.50	1.15	.30
☐ 74	Shaquille O'Neal Career Highlights	2.50	1.15	.30

☐ 75	Shaquille O'Neal	2.50	1.15	.30
	Golden Moment			
☐ 76	Shaquille O'Neal	2.50	1.15	.30
	Biography			
☐ 77	Shaquille O'Neal	2.50	1.15	.30
	Rookie Year			
☐ 78	Shaquille O'Neal	2.50	1.15	.30
	Weights and Measures			
☐ 79	Shaquille O'Neal	2.50	1.15	.30
	Personal Note			
☐ 80	Shaquille O'Neal	2.50	1.15	.30
	Dreamscapes			
☐ 81	Mark Price	.20	.09	.03
	Strong Suit			
☐ 82	Mark Price	.20	.09	.03
	Career Highlights			
☐ 83	Mark Price	.20	.09	.03
	Golden Moment			
☐ 84	Mark Price	.20	.09	.03
	Biography			
☐ 85	Mark Price	.20	.09	.03
	Rookie Year			
☐ 86	Mark Price	.20	.09	.03
	Weights and Measures			
☐ 87	Mark Price	.20	.09	.03
	Personal Note			
☐ 88	Mark Price	.20	.09	.03
	Dreamscapes			
☐ 89	Steve Smith	.10	.05	.01
	Strong Suit			
☐ 90	Steve Smith	.10	.05	.01
	Career Highlights			
☐ 91	Steve Smith	.10	.05	.01
	Golden Moment			
☐ 92	Steve Smith	.10	.05	.01
	Biography			
☐ 93	Steve Smith	.10	.05	.01
	Rookie Year			
☐ 94	Steve Smith	.10	.05	.01
	Weights and Measures			
☐ 95	Steve Smith	.10	.05	.01
	Personal Note			
☐ 96	Steve Smith	.10	.05	.01
	Dreamscapes			
☐ 97	Isiah Thomas	.25	.11	.03
	Strong Suit			
☐ 98	Isiah Thomas	.25	.11	.03
	Career Highlights			
☐ 99	Isiah Thomas	.25	.11	.03
	Golden Moment			
☐ 100	Isiah Thomas	.25	.11	.03
	Biography			
☐ 101	Isiah Thomas	.25	.11	.03
	Rookie Year			
☐ 102	Isiah Thomas	.25	.11	.03
	Weights and Measures			
☐ 103	Isiah Thomas	.25	.11	.03
	Personal Note			
☐ 104	Isiah Thomas	.25	.11	.03
	Dreamscapes			
☐ 105	Dominique Wilkins	.25	.11	.03
	Strong Suit			
☐ 106	Dominique Wilkins	.25	.11	.03
	Career Highlights			
☐ 107	Dominique Wilkins	.25	.11	.03
	Golden Moment			
☐ 108	Dominique Wilkins	.25	.11	.03
	Biography			
☐ 109	Dominique Wilkins	.25	.11	.03
	Rookie Year			
☐ 110	Dominique Wilkins	.25	.11	.03

	Weights and Measures			
☐ 111	Dominique Wilkins	.25	.11	.03
	Personal Note			
☐ 112	Dominique Wilkins	.25	.11	.03
	Dreamscapes			
☐ 113	Carol Blazejowski	.20	.09	.03
☐ 114	Teresa Edwards	.10	.05	.01
☐ 115	Nancy Lieberman-Cline	.20	.09	.03
☐ 116	Ann Meyers	.10	.05	.01
☐ 117	Pat Summitt CO	.10	.05	.01
☐ 118	Lynette Woodard	.10	.05	.01
☐ 119	Checklist	.50	.23	.06
☐ 120	Checklist	.50	.23	.06

1994 Flair USA Kevin Johnson

This 10-card set was issued as a wrapper redemption offer. The collector sent in $4.00 to Fleer; the offer expired October 31, 1994. The final two cards are team checklist cards that picture on their fronts all the members of the U.S. Olympic basketball team. These reissued checklist cards include Johnson, who was added to the team later, in the team photo.

	MINT	NRMT	EXC
COMPLETE SET (10)	12.00	5.50	1.50
COMMON CARD (M1-M8)	1.25	.55	.16
☐ M1 Strong Suit	1.25	.55	.16
☐ M2 Career Highlights	1.25	.55	.16
☐ M3 Golden Moment	1.25	.55	.16
☐ M4 Biography	1.25	.55	.16
☐ M5 Rookie Year	1.25	.55	.16
☐ M6 Weights and Measures	1.25	.55	.16
☐ M7 Personal Note	1.25	.55	.16
☐ M8 Dreamscapes	1.25	.55	.16
☐ 119 Team Checklist	2.50	1.15	.30
☐ 120 Team Checklist	2.50	1.15	.30

1994-95 Flair

This 326-card super-premium standard size set (made by Fleer) was issued in two

series. The first series contains 175 cards while the second has 151 cards (including the late addition of Michael Jordan as card 326). Cards were distributed in 10-card "hardpacks" (featuring a two-piece protective design wrapper), each with a suggested retail price of $4.00. The cards have a polyester laminate protective coating on both sides and are made with 30 point stock. This stock gives the cards double thickness. The front has two color action photos blended. The back has one full color action photo with the player's statistics laid on top. Both sides have the player's name stamped in gold foil along with his team. The first series includes a "Dream Team II" subset commemorating the USA's team victory at the 1994 World Championships in Toronto. Key Rookie Cards in this set include Grant Hill, Jason Kidd, Glenn Robinson and Eddie Jones.

	MINT	NRMT	EXC
COMPLETE SET (326)	90.00	40.00	11.50
COMPLETE SERIES 1 (175)	40.00	18.00	5.00
COMPLETE SERIES 2 (151)	50.00	23.00	6.25
COMMON CARD (1-175)	.25	.11	.03
COMMON CARD (176-325)	.20	.09	.03

☐ 1 Stacey Augmon	.35	.16	.04
☐ 2 Mookie Blaylock	.35	.16	.04
☐ 3 Craig Ehlo	.25	.11	.03
☐ 4 Jon Koncak	.25	.11	.03
☐ 5 Andrew Lang	.25	.11	.03
☐ 6 Dee Brown	.35	.16	.04
☐ 7 Sherman Douglas	.25	.11	.03
☐ 8 Acie Earl	.25	.11	.03
☐ 9 Rick Fox	.25	.11	.03
☐ 10 Kevin Gamble	.25	.11	.03
☐ 11 Xavier McDaniel	.35	.16	.04
☐ 12 Dino Radja	.50	.23	.06
☐ 13 Tony Bennett	.25	.11	.03
☐ 14 Dell Curry	.25	.11	.03
☐ 15 Kenny Gattison	.25	.11	.03
☐ 16 Hersey Hawkins	.35	.16	.04
☐ 17 Larry Johnson	1.00	.45	.13
☐ 18 Alonzo Mourning	1.50	.65	.19
☐ 19 David Wingate	.25	.11	.03
☐ 20 B.J. Armstrong	.25	.11	.03
☐ 21 Steve Kerr	.25	.11	.03
☐ 22 Toni Kukoc	.50	.23	.06
☐ 23 Pete Myers	.25	.11	.03
☐ 24 Scottie Pippen	1.25	.55	.16
☐ 25 Bill Wennington	.25	.11	.03
☐ 26 Terrell Brandon	.25	.11	.03
☐ 27 Brad Daugherty	.35	.16	.04
☐ 28 Tyrone Hill	.35	.16	.04
☐ 29 Bobby Phills	.25	.11	.03
☐ 30 Mark Price	.50	.23	.06
☐ 31 Gerald Wilkins	.25	.11	.03
☐ 32 John Williams	.35	.16	.04
☐ 33 Lucious Harris	.25	.11	.03
☐ 34 Jim Jackson	1.50	.65	.19
☐ 35 Jamal Mashburn	2.50	1.15	.30
☐ 36 Sean Rooks	.25	.11	.03
☐ 37 Doug Smith	.25	.11	.03
☐ 38 Mahmoud Abdul-Rauf	.25	.11	.03
☐ 39 LaPhonso Ellis	.25	.11	.03
☐ 40 Dikembe Mutombo	.75	.35	.09
☐ 41 Robert Pack	.25	.11	.03
☐ 42 Rodney Rogers	.50	.23	.06
☐ 43 Brian Williams	.25	.11	.03
☐ 44 Reggie Williams	.25	.11	.03
☐ 45 Joe Dumars	.60	.25	.08
☐ 46 Allan Houston	.50	.23	.06
☐ 47 Lindsey Hunter	.25	.11	.03
☐ 48 Terry Mills	.25	.11	.03
☐ 49 Victor Alexander	.25	.11	.03
☐ 50 Chris Gatling	.25	.11	.03
☐ 51 Billy Owens	.35	.16	.04
☐ 52 Latrell Sprewell	1.50	.65	.19
☐ 53 Chris Webber	2.00	.90	.25
☐ 54 Sam Cassell	.50	.23	.06
☐ 55 Carl Herrera	.25	.11	.03
☐ 56 Robert Horry	.50	.23	.06
☐ 57 Hakeem Olajuwon	3.00	1.35	.40
☐ 58 Kenny Smith	.25	.11	.03
☐ 59 Otis Thorpe	.35	.16	.04
☐ 60 Antonio Davis	.25	.11	.03
☐ 61 Dale Davis	.35	.16	.04
☐ 62 Reggie Miller	1.25	.55	.16
☐ 63 Byron Scott	.35	.16	.04
☐ 64 Rik Smits	.50	.23	.06
☐ 65 Haywoode Workman	.25	.11	.03
☐ 66 Terry Dehere	.25	.11	.03
☐ 67 Harold Ellis	.25	.11	.03
☐ 68 Gary Grant	.25	.11	.03
☐ 69 Elmore Spencer	.25	.11	.03
☐ 70 Loy Vaught	.35	.16	.04
☐ 71 Elden Campbell	.25	.11	.03
☐ 72 Doug Christie	.25	.11	.03
☐ 73 Vlade Divac	.50	.23	.06
☐ 74 George Lynch	.25	.11	.03
☐ 75 Anthony Peeler	.25	.11	.03
☐ 76 Nick Van Exel	2.50	1.15	.30
☐ 77 James Worthy	.50	.23	.06
☐ 78 Bimbo Coles	.25	.11	.03
☐ 79 Harold Miner	.25	.11	.03
☐ 80 John Salley	.25	.11	.03
☐ 81 Rony Seikaly	.25	.11	.03
☐ 82 Steve Smith	.35	.16	.04
☐ 83 Vin Baker	1.25	.55	.16
☐ 84 Jon Barry	.25	.11	.03
☐ 85 Todd Day	.25	.11	.03
☐ 86 Lee Mayberry	.25	.11	.03
☐ 87 Eric Murdock	.25	.11	.03
☐ 88 Mike Brown	.25	.11	.03
☐ 89 Christian Laettner	.35	.16	.04
☐ 90 Isaiah Rider	.75	.35	.09
☐ 91 Doug West	.25	.11	.03
☐ 92 Micheal Williams	.25	.11	.03
☐ 93 Kenny Anderson	.50	.23	.06
☐ 94 Benoit Benjamin	.25	.11	.03
☐ 95 P.J. Brown	.25	.11	.03
☐ 96 Derrick Coleman	.50	.23	.06
☐ 97 Kevin Edwards	.25	.11	.03
☐ 98 Hubert Davis	.25	.11	.03
☐ 99 Patrick Ewing	1.25	.55	.16

☐	100	Derek Harper	.35	.16	.04	☐	171	Isiah Thomas USA	.35	.16	.04
☐	101	Anthony Mason	.25	.11	.03	☐	172	Dominique Wilkins USA	.35	.16	.04
☐	102	Charles Oakley	.35	.16	.04	☐	173	Checklist	.25	.11	.03
☐	103	Charles Smith	.25	.11	.03	☐	174	Checklist	.25	.11	.03
☐	104	John Starks	.35	.16	.04	☐	175	Checklist	.25	.11	.03
☐	105	Nick Anderson	.35	.16	.04	☐	176	Tyrone Corbin	.20	.09	.03
☐	106	Anfernee Hardaway	5.00	2.30	.60	☐	177	Grant Long	.20	.09	.03
☐	107	Shaquille O'Neal	6.00	2.70	.75	☐	178	Ken Norman	.20	.09	.03
☐	108	Dennis Scott	.25	.11	.03	☐	179	Steve Smith	.30	.14	.04
☐	109	Jeff Turner	.25	.11	.03	☐	180	Blue Edwards	.20	.09	.03
☐	110	Dana Barros	.50	.23	.06	☐	181	Pervis Ellison	.20	.09	.03
☐	111	Shawn Bradley	.50	.23	.06	☐	182	Greg Minor	.30	.14	.04
☐	112	Jeff Malone	.35	.16	.04	☐	183	Eric Montross	1.25	.55	.16
☐	113	Tim Perry	.25	.11	.03	☐	184	Derek Strong	.20	.09	.03
☐	114	Clarence Weatherspoon	.35	.16	.04	☐	185	David Wesley	.20	.09	.03
☐	115	Danny Ainge	.25	.11	.03	☐	186	Dominique Wilkins	.50	.23	.06
☐	116	Charles Barkley	2.50	1.15	.30	☐	187	Michael Adams	.20	.09	.03
☐	117	A.C. Green	.50	.23	.06	☐	188	Muggsy Bogues	.40	.18	.05
☐	118	Kevin Johnson	.60	.25	.08	☐	189	Scott Burrell	.20	.09	.03
☐	119	Dan Majerle	.35	.16	.04	☐	190	Darrin Hancock	.20	.09	.03
☐	120	Clyde Drexler	1.25	.55	.16	☐	191	Robert Parish	.40	.18	.05
☐	121	Harvey Grant	.25	.11	.03	☐	192	Jud Buechler	.20	.09	.03
☐	122	Jerome Kersey	.25	.11	.03	☐	193	Ron Harper	.30	.14	.04
☐	123	Clifford Robinson	.35	.16	.04	☐	194	Larry Krystkowiak	.20	.09	.03
☐	124	Rod Strickland	.35	.16	.04	☐	195	Will Perdue	.20	.09	.03
☐	125	Buck Williams	.35	.16	.04	☐	196	Dickey Simpkins	.40	.18	.05
☐	126	Randy Brown	.25	.11	.03	☐	197	Michael Cage	.20	.09	.03
☐	127	Olden Polynice	.25	.11	.03	☐	198	Tony Campbell	.20	.09	.03
☐	128	Mitch Richmond	.60	.25	.08	☐	199	Danny Ferry	.20	.09	.03
☐	129	Lionel Simmons	.25	.11	.03	☐	200	Chris Mills	.40	.18	.05
☐	130	Spud Webb	.35	.16	.04	☐	201	Popeye Jones	.20	.09	.03
☐	131	Walt Williams	.35	.16	.04	☐	202	Jason Kidd	8.00	3.60	1.00
☐	132	Willie Anderson	.25	.11	.03	☐	203	Roy Tarpley	.20	.09	.03
☐	133	Vinny Del Negro	.25	.11	.03	☐	204	Lorenzo Williams	.20	.09	.03
☐	134	Sean Elliott	.35	.16	.04	☐	205	Dale Ellis	.30	.14	.04
☐	135	Avery Johnson	.25	.11	.03	☐	206	Tom Hammonds	.20	.09	.03
☐	136	J.R. Reid	.25	.11	.03	☐	207	Jalen Rose	1.50	.65	.19
☐	137	David Robinson	2.50	1.15	.30	☐	208	Reggie Slater	.20	.09	.03
☐	138	Dennis Rodman	.75	.35	.09	☐	209	Bryant Stith	.20	.09	.03
☐	139	Kendall Gill	.25	.11	.03	☐	210	Rafael Addison	.20	.09	.03
☐	140	Ervin Johnson	.25	.11	.03	☐	211	Bill Curley	.40	.18	.05
☐	141	Shawn Kemp	2.50	1.15	.30	☐	212	Johnny Dawkins	.20	.09	.03
☐	142	Nate McMillan	.25	.11	.03	☐	213	Grant Hill	12.00	5.50	1.50
☐	143	Gary Payton	.50	.23	.06	☐	214	Mark Macon	.20	.09	.03
☐	144	Sam Perkins	.35	.16	.04	☐	215	Oliver Miller	.20	.09	.03
☐	145	David Benoit	.25	.11	.03	☐	216	Ivano Newbill	.20	.09	.03
☐	146	Jeff Hornacek	.35	.16	.04	☐	217	Mark West	.20	.09	.03
☐	147	Jay Humphries	.25	.11	.03	☐	218	Tom Gugliotta	.30	.14	.04
☐	148	Karl Malone	1.25	.55	.16	☐	219	Tim Hardaway	.40	.18	.05
☐	149	Bryon Russell	.25	.11	.03	☐	220	Keith Jennings	.20	.09	.03
☐	150	Felton Spencer	.25	.11	.03	☐	221	Dwayne Morton	.20	.09	.03
☐	151	John Stockton	1.25	.55	.16	☐	222	Chris Mullin	.40	.18	.05
☐	152	Rex Chapman	.25	.11	.03	☐	223	Ricky Pierce	.30	.14	.04
☐	153	Calbert Cheaney	.50	.23	.06	☐	224	Carlos Rogers	.60	.25	.08
☐	154	Tom Gugliotta	.35	.16	.04	☐	225	Clifford Rozier	.60	.25	.08
☐	155	Don MacLean	.25	.11	.03	☐	226	Rony Seikaly	.20	.09	.03
☐	156	Gheorghe Muresan	.35	.16	.04	☐	227	Tim Breaux	.20	.09	.03
☐	157	Doug Overton	.25	.11	.03	☐	228	Scott Brooks	.20	.09	.03
☐	158	Brent Price	.25	.11	.03	☐	229	Mario Elie	.20	.09	.03
☐	159	Derrick Coleman USA	.25	.11	.03	☐	230	Vernon Maxwell	.20	.09	.03
☐	160	Joe Dumars USA	.35	.16	.04	☐	231	Zan Tabak	.20	.09	.03
☐	161	Tim Hardaway USA	.25	.11	.03	☐	232	Mark Jackson	.20	.09	.03
☐	162	Kevin Johnson USA	.35	.16	.04	☐	233	Derrick McKey	.30	.14	.04
☐	163	Larry Johnson USA	.50	.23	.06	☐	234	Tony Massenburg	.20	.09	.03
☐	164	Shawn Kemp USA	.50	.55	.16	☐	235	Lamond Murray	1.25	.55	.16
☐	165	Dan Majerle USA	.25	.11	.03	☐	236	Charles Outlaw	.20	.09	.03
☐	166	Reggie Miller USA	.35	.16	.04	☐	237	Eric Piatkowski	.40	.18	.05
☐	167	Alonzo Mourning USA	.75	.35	.09	☐	238	Pooh Richardson	.20	.09	.03
☐	168	Shaquille O'Neal USA	3.00	1.35	.40	☐	239	Malik Sealy	.20	.09	.03
☐	169	Mark Price USA	.25	.11	.03	☐	240	Cedric Ceballos	.40	.18	.05
☐	170	Steve Smith USA	.25	.11	.03	☐	241	Eddie Jones	5.00	2.30	.60

☐ 242 Anthony Miller	.20	.09	.03
☐ 243 Tony Smith	.20	.09	.03
☐ 244 Sedale Threatt	.20	.09	.03
☐ 245 Ledell Eackles	.20	.09	.03
☐ 246 Kevin Gamble	.20	.09	.03
☐ 247 Matt Geiger	.20	.09	.03
☐ 248 Brad Lohaus	.20	.09	.03
☐ 249 Billy Owens	.30	.14	.04
☐ 250 Khalid Reeves	1.25	.55	.16
☐ 251 Glen Rice	.40	.18	.05
☐ 252 Kevin Willis	.30	.14	.04
☐ 253 Marty Conlon	.20	.09	.03
☐ 254 Eric Mobley	.40	.18	.05
☐ 255 Johnny Newman	.20	.09	.03
☐ 256 Ed Pinckney	.20	.09	.03
☐ 257 Glenn Robinson	8.00	3.60	1.00
☐ 258 Pat Durham	.20	.09	.03
☐ 259 Howard Eisley	.20	.09	.03
☐ 260 Winston Garland	.20	.09	.03
☐ 261 Stacey King	.20	.09	.03
☐ 262 Donyell Marshall	1.50	.65	.19
☐ 263 Sean Rooks	.20	.09	.03
☐ 264 Chris Smith	.20	.09	.03
☐ 265 Chris Childs	.20	.09	.03
☐ 266 Sleepy Floyd	.20	.09	.03
☐ 267 Armon Gilliam	.20	.09	.03
☐ 268 Sean Higgins	.20	.09	.03
☐ 269 Rex Walters	.20	.09	.03
☐ 270 Greg Anthony	.20	.09	.03
☐ 271 Charlie Ward	.60	.25	.08
☐ 272 Herb Williams	.20	.09	.03
☐ 273 Monty Williams	.40	.18	.05
☐ 274 Anthony Avent	.20	.09	.03
☐ 275 Anthony Bowie	.20	.09	.03
☐ 276 Horace Grant	.50	.23	.06
☐ 277 Donald Royal	.20	.09	.03
☐ 278 Brian Shaw	.20	.09	.03
☐ 279 Brooks Thompson	.30	.14	.04
☐ 280 Derrick Alston	.30	.14	.04
☐ 281 Willie Burton	.20	.09	.03
☐ 282 Greg Graham	.20	.09	.03
☐ 283 B.J. Tyler	.30	.14	.04
☐ 284 Scott Williams	.20	.09	.03
☐ 285 Sharone Wright	1.00	.45	.13
☐ 286 Joe Kleine	.20	.09	.03
☐ 287 Danny Manning	.40	.18	.05
☐ 288 Elliot Perry	.20	.09	.03
☐ 289 Wesley Person	1.50	.65	.19
☐ 290 Trevor Ruffin	.30	.14	.04
☐ 291 Wayman Tisdale	.30	.14	.04
☐ 292 Mark Bryant	.20	.09	.03
☐ 293 Chris Dudley	.20	.09	.03
☐ 294 Aaron McKie	.60	.25	.08
☐ 295 Tracy Murray	.20	.09	.03
☐ 296 Terry Porter	.30	.14	.04
☐ 297 James Robinson	.20	.09	.03
☐ 298 Alaa Abdelnaby	.20	.09	.03
☐ 299 Duane Causwell	.20	.09	.03
☐ 300 Brian Grant	2.50	1.15	.30
☐ 301 Bobby Hurley	.30	.14	.04
☐ 302 Michael Smith	.60	.25	.08
☐ 303 Terry Cummings	.30	.14	.04
☐ 304 Moses Malone	.50	.23	.06
☐ 305 Julius Nwosu	.20	.09	.03
☐ 306 Chuck Person	.30	.14	.04
☐ 307 Doc Rivers	.20	.09	.03
☐ 308 Vincent Askew	.20	.09	.03
☐ 309 Sarunas Marciulionis	.20	.09	.03
☐ 310 Detlef Schrempf	.40	.18	.05
☐ 311 Dontonio Wingfield	.45	.20	.06
☐ 312 Antoine Carr	.20	.09	.03

☐ 313 Tom Chambers	.30	.14	.04
☐ 314 John Crotty	.20	.09	.03
☐ 315 Adam Keefe	.20	.09	.03
☐ 316 Jamie Watson	.40	.18	.05
☐ 317 Mitchell Butler	.20	.09	.03
☐ 318 Kevin Duckworth	.20	.09	.03
☐ 319 Juwan Howard	3.00	1.35	.40
☐ 320 Jim McIlvaine	.20	.09	.03
☐ 321 Scott Skiles	.20	.09	.03
☐ 322 Anthony Tucker	.20	.09	.03
☐ 323 Chris Webber	1.50	.65	.19
☐ 324 Checklist	.20	.09	.03
☐ 325 Checklist	.20	.09	.03
☐ 326 Michael Jordan	15.00	6.75	1.90

1994-95 Flair
Center Spotlight

Randomly inserted at a rate of one in every 25 first series packs, cards from this 6-card set feature a selection of the game's dominant centers. The fronts have a 100% etched-foil design with a full color action photo with three shadows of him in red, green and blue. The bottom of the card has the player's name and the words "Center Spotlight" in gold-foil. The back also has a color photo with the red, green and blue shadowing on a white background along with player information. The cards are numbered on the back as "X of 6."

	MINT	NRMT	EXC
COMPLETE SET (6)	80.00	36.00	10.00
COMMON CARD (1-6)	6.00	2.70	.75
☐ 1 Patrick Ewing	6.00	2.70	.75
New York Knicks			
☐ 2 Alonzo Mourning	8.00	3.60	1.00
Charlotte Hornets			
☐ 3 Hakeem Olajuwon	15.00	6.75	1.90
Houston Rockets			
☐ 4 Shaquille O'Neal	35.00	16.00	4.40
Orlando Magic			
☐ 5 David Robinson	12.00	5.50	1.50
San Antonio Spurs			
☐ 6 Chris Webber	10.00	4.50	1.25
Golden State Warriors			

1994-95 Flair Hot Numbers

Randomly inserted into first series packs at a rate of one in six, cards from this 20-card set feature a selection of players who consistently produce big statistics. The player's top statistical numbers are shown on the front of the card without identifying which category. While some numbers are obvious, like the player's points per game, other statistics are not, like steals and blocks, particularly for multi-talented players. The fronts also have full-color action photos with the team's colors used as the background along with the words "Hot Numbers". Also in one of the bottom corners the words hot numbers are etched in gold-foil boxing in the player's number and his name is also in gold-foil. The backs also have a color picture with information on what type of player he is. The cards are numbered on the back as "X of 20."

	MINT	NRMT	EXC
COMPLETE SET (20)	75.00	34.00	9.50
COMMON CARD (1-20)	1.00	.45	.13
☐ 1 Vin Baker Milwaukee Bucks	3.00	1.35	.40
☐ 2 Sam Cassell Houston Rockets	1.50	.65	.19
☐ 3 Patrick Ewing New York Knicks	3.00	1.35	.40
☐ 4 Anfernee Hardaway Orlando Magic	12.00	5.50	1.50
☐ 5 Robert Horry Houston Rockets	1.50	.65	.19
☐ 6 Shawn Kemp Seattle Supersonics	6.00	2.70	.75
☐ 7 Toni Kukoc Chicago Bulls	1.50	.65	.19
☐ 8 Jamal Mashburn Dallas Mavericks	6.00	2.70	.75
☐ 9 Reggie Miller Indiana Pacers	3.00	1.35	.40
☐ 10 Dikembe Mutombo Denver Nuggets	2.00	.90	.25
☐ 11 Hakeem Olajuwon Houston Rockets	8.00	3.60	1.00
☐ 12 Shaquille O'Neal Orlando Magic	15.00	6.75	1.90
☐ 13 Scottie Pippen	3.00	1.35	.40
Chicago Bulls			
☐ 14 Isaiah Rider Minnesota Timberwolves	2.00	.90	.25
☐ 15 David Robinson San Antonio Spurs	6.00	2.70	.75
☐ 16 Latrell Sprewell Golden State Warriors	4.00	1.80	.50
☐ 17 John Starks New York Knicks	1.00	.45	.13
☐ 18 John Stockton Utah Jazz	3.00	1.35	.40
☐ 19 Nick Van Exel Los Angeles Lakers	6.00	2.70	.75
☐ 20 Chris Webber Golden State Warriors	5.00	2.30	.60

1994-95 Flair Playmakers

Randomly inserted into second series packs at a rate of one in four, cards from this 10-card set feature a selection of the best assist men in the NBA. The fronts have a full color action photo with a hardwood floor in the background. The word "Playmaker" with a ball going through a hoop is in gold-foil in one of the bottom corners. The back also has a color photo with player information set against a hardwood floor. The cards are numbered on the back as "X of 10."

	MINT	NRMT	EXC
COMPLETE SET (10)	15.00	6.75	1.90
COMMON CARD (1-10)	1.00	.45	.13
☐ 1 Kenny Anderson New Jersey Nets	1.00	.45	.13
☐ 2 Mookie Blaylock Atlanta Hawks	1.00	.45	.13
☐ 3 Sam Cassell Houston Rockets	1.00	.45	.13
☐ 4 Anfernee Hardaway Orlando Magic	8.00	3.60	1.00
☐ 5 Robert Pack Denver Nuggets	1.00	.45	.13
☐ 6 Scottie Pippen Chicago Bulls	2.00	.90	.25
☐ 7 Mark Price Cleveland Cavaliers	1.00	.45	.13
☐ 8 Mitch Richmond Sacramento Kings	1.00	.45	.13

☐ 9 John Stockton.............. 2.00 .90 .25
    Utah Jazz
☐ 10 Nick Van Exel............. 4.00 1.80 .50
    Los Angeles Lakers

1994-95 Flair Rejectors

Randomly inserted into second series packs at a rate of one in 25, cards from this six-card set feature a selection of top shot blockers in basketball. The fronts are 100% etched foil that have a full color action photo of the player. The background is three hands in red, green and blue seemingly up to reject a shot. One of the bottom corners has the word "Rejector" vertically with a hand blocking a shot. These along with the player's name at the bottom of card are in gold foil. The back also has a player photo along with information on him, such as his blocks per game. The background is nearly identical to the background on the front. The cards are numbered on the back as "X of 6."

	MINT	NRMT	EXC
COMPLETE SET (6)	75.00	34.00	9.50
COMMON CARD (1-6)	4.00	1.80	.50
☐ 1 Patrick Ewing......... New York Knicks	6.00	2.70	.75
☐ 2 Alonzo Mourning ..... Charlotte Hornets	8.00	3.60	1.00
☐ 3 Dikembe Mutombo ..... Denver Nuggets	4.00	1.80	.50
☐ 4 Hakeem Olajuwon ..... Houston Rockets	15.00	6.75	1.90
☐ 5 Shaquille O'Neal..... Orlando Magic	35.00	16.00	4.40
☐ 6 David Robinson....... San Antonio Spurs	12.00	5.50	1.50

1994-95 Flair Scoring Power

Randomly inserted into first series packs at a rate of one in eight, cards from this 20-

card set feature a selection of perennial NBA scoring leaders. The fronts emphasize the words scoring power as they are the size of the card laid out horizontally against a black background. There is a player photo in front of the words and another inside. The back also says "Scoring Power" across the entire card horizontally. There is also a player photo with information on him, namely about his scoring. The cards are numbered on the back as "X of 10."

	MINT	NRMT	EXC
COMPLETE SET (10)	40.00	18.00	5.00
COMMON CARD (1-10)	1.50	.65	.19
☐ 1 Charles Barkley............. Phoenix Suns	6.00	2.70	.75
☐ 2 Patrick Ewing................. New York Knicks	3.00	1.35	.40
☐ 3 Karl Malone.................... Utah Jazz	3.00	1.35	.40
☐ 4 Hakeem Olajuwon.......... Houston Rockets	8.00	3.60	1.00
☐ 5 Shaquille O'Neal........... Orlando Magic	15.00	6.75	1.90
☐ 6 Scottie Pippen................ Chicago Bulls	3.00	1.35	.40
☐ 7 Mitch Richmond............ Sacramento Kings	1.50	.65	.19
☐ 8 David Robinson .... San Antonio Spurs	6.00	2.70	.75
☐ 9 Latrell Sprewell............ Golden State Warriors	4.00	1.80	.50
☐ 10 Dominique Wilkins....... Boston Celtics	1.50	.65	.19

1994-95 Flair Wave of the Future

Randmly inserted into second series packs at a rate of one in seven, cards from this 10-card set feature a selection of top rookies from the 1994-95 season. Card fronts are laid out horizontally with three color photos of the player. The one in the middle has yellow glow surrounding it and the picture on the left is the same as the middle. The one on the left is a head shot of the color photo used on the back of the card. The words "Wave of the Future" are in the bottom left corner around a wave with a

basketball. These along with the player's name at the bottom are in gold-foil. The back has player information including some college statistics. Both sides of the card have a wave in the background in the team's colors. The cards are numbered on the back as "X of 10."

	MINT	NRMT	EXC
COMPLETE SET (10)	65.00	29.00	8.25
COMMON CARD (1-10)	2.00	.90	.25
□ 1 Brian Grant	4.00	1.80	.50
Sacramento Kings			
□ 2 Grant Hill	20.00	9.00	2.50
Detroit Pistons			
□ 3 Juwan Howard	5.00	2.30	.60
Washington Bullets			
□ 4 Eddie Jones	8.00	3.60	1.00
Los Angeles Lakers			
□ 5 Jason Kidd	12.00	5.50	1.50
Dallas Mavericks			
□ 6 Donyell Marshall	2.50	1.15	.30
Minnesota Timberwolves			
□ 7 Eric Montross	2.00	.90	.25
Boston Celtics			
□ 8 Lamond Murray	2.00	.90	.25
Los Angeles Clippers			
□ 9 Wesley Person	2.50	1.15	.30
Phoenix Suns			
□ 10 Glenn Robinson	12.00	5.50	1.50
Milwaukee Bucks			

1961-62 Fleer

The 1961-62 Fleer set was the company's only major basketball issue until the 1986-87 season. The cards were issued in five-cent wax packs. The cards in the set measure the standard 2 1/2" by 3 1/2". Cards numbered 45 to 66 are action shots (designated IA) of players elsewhere in the set. Both the regular cards and the IA cards are numbered alphabetically within that particular subset. No known scarcities exist, although the set is quite popular since it contains the first mainstream basketball cards of many of the game's all-time greats including Elgin Baylor, Wilt Chamberlain, Oscar Robertson and Jerry West. Most cards are frequently found with centering problems.

	NRMT	VG-E	GOOD
COMPLETE SET (66)	4000.00	1800.00	500.00
COMMON CARD (1-44)	15.00	6.75	1.90
COMMON CARD (45-66)	12.50	5.75	1.55
□ 1 Al Attles	100.00	22.00	5.00
Philadelphia Warriors			
□ 2 Paul Arizin	40.00	18.00	5.00
Philadelphia Warriors			
□ 3 Elgin Baylor	350.00	160.00	45.00
Los Angeles Lakers			
□ 4 Walt Bellamy	60.00	27.00	7.50
Chicago Packers			
□ 5 Arlen Bockhorn	15.00	6.75	1.90
Cincinnati Royals			
□ 6 Bob Boozer	20.00	9.00	2.50
Cincinnati Royals			
□ 7 Carl Braun	20.00	9.00	2.50
Boston Celtics			
□ 8 Wilt Chamberlain	1200.00	550.00	150.00
Philadelphia Warriors			
□ 9 Larry Costello	20.00	9.00	2.50
Syracuse Nationals			
□ 10 Bob Cousy	250.00	115.00	31.00
Boston Celtics			
□ 11 Walter Dukes	15.00	6.75	1.90
Detroit Pistons			
□ 12 Wayne Embry	30.00	13.50	3.80
Cincinnati Royals			
□ 13 Dave Gambee	15.00	6.75	1.90
Syracuse Nationals			
□ 14 Tom Gola	40.00	18.00	5.00
Philadelphia Warriors			
□ 15 Sihugo Green	15.00	6.75	1.90
St. Louis Hawks			
□ 16 Hal Greer	80.00	36.00	10.00
Syracuse Nationals			
□ 17 Richie Guerin	40.00	18.00	5.00
New York Knicks			
□ 18 Cliff Hagan	40.00	18.00	5.00
St. Louis Hawks			
□ 19 Tom Heinsohn	80.00	36.00	10.00
Boston Celtics			
□ 20 Bailey Howell	40.00	18.00	5.00
Detroit Pistons			
□ 21 Rod Hundley	40.00	18.00	5.00
Los Angeles Lakers			
□ 22 K.C. Jones	100.00	45.00	12.50
Boston Celtics			
□ 23 Sam Jones	100.00	45.00	12.50
Boston Celtics			
□ 24 Phil Jordan	15.00	6.75	1.90
New York Knicks			
□ 25 John Kerr	40.00	18.00	5.00
Syracuse Nationals			
□ 26 Rudy LaRusso	35.00	16.00	4.40
Los Angeles Lakers			
□ 27 George Lee	15.00	6.75	1.90

Detroit Pistons
☐ 28	Bob Leonard	20.00	9.00	2.50
	Chicago Packers			
☐ 29	Clyde Lovellette	50.00	23.00	6.25
	St. Louis Hawks			
☐ 30	John McCarthy	15.00	6.75	1.90
	St. Louis Hawks			
☐ 31	Tom Meschery	20.00	9.00	2.50
	Philadelphia Warriors			
☐ 32	Willie Naulls	25.00	11.50	3.10
	New York Knicks			
☐ 33	Don Ohl	20.00	9.00	2.50
	Detroit Pistons			
☐ 34	Bob Pettit	80.00	36.00	10.00
	St. Louis Hawks			
☐ 35	Frank Ramsey	40.00	18.00	5.00
	Boston Celtics			
☐ 36	Oscar Robertson	500.00	230.00	65.00
	Cincinnati Royals			
☐ 37	Guy Rodgers	25.00	11.50	3.10
	Philadelphia Warriors			
☐ 38	Bill Russell	500.00	230.00	65.00
	Boston Celtics			
☐ 39	Dolph Schayes	50.00	23.00	6.25
	Syracuse Nationals			
☐ 40	Frank Selvy	20.00	9.00	2.50
	Los Angeles Lakers			
☐ 41	Gene Shue	25.00	11.50	3.10
	Detroit Pistons			
☐ 42	Jack Twyman	40.00	18.00	5.00
	Cincinnati Royals			
☐ 43	Jerry West	650.00	300.00	80.00
	Los Angeles Lakers			
☐ 44	Len Wilkens UER	150.00	70.00	19.00
	St. Louis Hawks			
	(Misspelled Wilkins			
	on card front)			
☐ 45	Paul Arizin IA	25.00	11.50	3.10
	Philadelphia Warriors			
☐ 46	Elgin Baylor IA	100.00	45.00	12.50
	Los Angeles Lakers			
☐ 47	Wilt Chamberlain IA	400.00	180.00	50.00
	Philadelphia Warriors			
☐ 48	Larry Costello IA	12.50	5.75	1.55
	Syracuse Nationals			
☐ 49	Bob Cousy IA	110.00	50.00	14.00
	Boston Celtics			
☐ 50	Walter Dukes IA	12.50	5.75	1.55
	Detroit Pistons			
☐ 51	Tom Gola IA	25.00	11.50	3.10
	Philadelphia Warriors			
☐ 52	Richie Guerin IA	20.00	9.00	2.50
	New York Knicks			
☐ 53	Cliff Hagan IA	25.00	11.50	3.10
	St. Louis Hawks			
☐ 54	Tom Heinsohn IA	40.00	18.00	5.00
	Boston Celtics			
☐ 55	Bailey Howell IA	20.00	9.00	2.50
	Detroit Pistons			
☐ 56	John Kerr IA	25.00	11.50	3.10
	Syracuse Nationals			
☐ 57	Rudy LaRusso IA	17.50	8.00	2.20
	Los Angeles Lakers			
☐ 58	Clyde Lovellette IA	30.00	13.50	3.80
	St. Louis Hawks			
☐ 59	Bob Pettit IA	40.00	18.00	5.00
	St. Louis Hawks			
☐ 60	Frank Ramsey IA	25.00	11.50	3.10
	Boston Celtics			
☐ 61	Oscar Robertson IA	175.00	80.00	22.00
	Cincinnati Royals			

☐ 62	Bill Russell IA	250.00	115.00	31.00
	Boston Celtics			
☐ 63	Dolph Schayes IA	30.00	13.50	3.80
	Syracuse Nationals			
☐ 64	Gene Shue IA	17.50	8.00	2.20
	Detroit Pistons			
☐ 65	Jack Twyman IA	25.00	11.50	3.10
	Cincinnati Royals			
☐ 66	Jerry West IA	275.00	95.00	22.00
	Los Angeles Lakers			

1986-87 Fleer

This 132-card set marks Fleer's return to the basketball card industry after a 25-year hiatus. It also marks what is considered to be the beginning of the modern era of basketball cards. The cards were issued in 12-card wax packs (11 cards plus a sticker) that retailed for 50 cents. Wax boxes consisted of 36 packs. A stick of gum was also included in each pack. The set is checklisted alphabetically by the player's last name. Since only the Star Company had been issuing basketball cards nationally since 1983, most of the players in this Fleer set already had cards which are considered Extended Rookie Cards. However, since this Fleer set was the first nationally distributed through wax packs since the 1981-82 Topps issue, most of the players in the set are considered Rookie Cards including Michael Jordan. Other Rookie Cards, of those that had Star Company cards include Charles Barkley, Clyde Drexler, Patrick Ewing, Hakeem Olajuwon, Isiah Thomas and Dominique Wilkins. Rookie Cards of those that did not previously appear in a set include Joe Dumars, Karl Malone, Chris Mullin and Charles Oakley. Cards measure the standard 2 1/2" by 3 1/2". Red, white and blue borders surround a color photo that contains a Fleer "Premier" logo in an upper corner. The card backs are printed in red and blue on white card stock. Several cards have "Traded" notations on them if the player was traded subsequent to the photo selection process. It's important to note that some of the more expensive cards in this set (especially Michael Jordan) have been counterfeited in the past few years. Checking key detailed printing areas such

as the "Fleer Premier" logo on the front and the players' association logo on the back under eight or ten power magnification usually detects the legitimate from the counterfeits. The cards are condition sensitive due to dark borders and centering problems.

	NRMT-MT	EXC	VG
COMPLETE w/Stickers(143)	1200.00	550.00	150.00
COMPLETE SET (132)	1100.00	500.00	140.00
COMMON CARD (1-132)	2.00	.90	.25

☐ 1 Kareem Abdul-Jabbar ..	12.00	5.50	1.50
Los Angeles Lakers			
☐ 2 Alvan Adams	2.50	1.15	.30
Phoenix Suns			
☐ 3 Mark Aguirre	3.00	1.35	.40
Dallas Mavericks			
☐ 4 Danny Ainge	6.00	2.70	.75
Boston Celtics			
☐ 5 John Bagley	2.00	.90	.25
Cleveland Cavaliers			
☐ 6 Thurl Bailey	2.50	1.15	.30
Utah Jazz			
☐ 7 Charles Barkley	120.00	55.00	15.00
Philadelphia 76ers			
☐ 8 Benoit Benjamin	2.50	1.15	.30
Los Angeles Clippers			
☐ 9 Larry Bird	50.00	23.00	6.25
Boston Celtics			
☐ 10 Otis Birdsong	2.50	1.15	.30
New Jersey Nets			
☐ 11 Rolando Blackman	3.00	1.35	.40
Dallas Mavericks			
☐ 12 Manute Bol	2.50	1.15	.30
Washington Bullets			
☐ 13 Sam Bowie	2.50	1.15	.30
Portland Trail Blazers			
☐ 14 Joe Barry Carroll	2.50	1.15	.30
Golden State Warriors			
☐ 15 Tom Chambers	5.00	2.30	.60
Seattle Supersonics			
☐ 16 Maurice Cheeks	3.00	1.35	.40
Philadelphia 76ers			
☐ 17 Michael Cooper	3.00	1.35	.40
Los Angeles Lakers			
☐ 18 Wayne Cooper	2.00	.90	.25
Denver Nuggets			
☐ 19 Pat Cummings	2.00	.90	.25
New York Knicks			
☐ 20 Terry Cummings	3.00	1.35	.40
Milwaukee Bucks			
☐ 21 Adrian Dantley	3.00	1.35	.40
Utah Jazz			
☐ 22 Brad Davis	2.50	1.15	.30
Dallas Mavericks			
☐ 23 Walter Davis	3.00	1.35	.40
Phoenix Suns			
☐ 24 Darryl Dawkins	2.50	1.15	.30
New Jersey Nets			
☐ 25 Larry Drew	2.00	.90	.25
Sacramento Kings			
☐ 26 Clyde Drexler	60.00	27.00	7.50
Portland Trail Blazers			
☐ 27 Joe Dumars	30.00	13.50	3.80
Detroit Pistons			
☐ 28 Mark Eaton	2.50	1.15	.30
Utah Jazz			
☐ 29 James Edwards	2.50	1.15	.30
Phoenix Suns			
☐ 30 Alex English	3.00	1.35	.40

	Denver Nuggets			
☐ 31 Julius Erving	15.00	6.75	1.90
Philadelphia 76ers			
☐ 32 Patrick Ewing	60.00	27.00	7.50
New York Knicks			
☐ 33 Vern Fleming	2.50	1.15	.30
Indiana Pacers			
☐ 34 Sleepy Floyd	2.00	.90	.25
Golden State Warriors			
☐ 35 World B. Free	3.00	1.35	.40
Cleveland Cavaliers			
☐ 36 George Gervin	5.00	2.30	.60
Chicago Bulls			
☐ 37 Artis Gilmore	3.00	1.35	.40
San Antonio Spurs			
☐ 38 Mike Gminski	2.50	1.15	.30
New Jersey Nets			
☐ 39 Rickey Green	2.50	1.15	.30
Utah Jazz			
☐ 40 Sidney Green	2.00	.90	.25
Chicago Bulls			
☐ 41 David Greenwood	2.00	.90	.25
San Antonio Spurs			
☐ 42 Darrell Griffith	2.50	1.15	.30
Utah Jazz			
☐ 43 Bill Hanzlik	2.00	.90	.25
Denver Nuggets			
☐ 44 Derek Harper	5.00	2.30	.60
Dallas Mavericks			
☐ 45 Gerald Henderson	2.00	.90	.25
Seattle Supersonics			
☐ 46 Roy Hinson	2.00	.90	.25
Philadelphia 76ers			
☐ 47 Craig Hodges	2.50	1.15	.30
Milwaukee Bucks			
☐ 48 Phil Hubbard	2.00	.90	.25
Cleveland Cavaliers			
☐ 49 Jay Humphries	2.50	1.15	.30
Phoenix Suns			
☐ 50 Dennis Johnson	3.00	1.35	.40
Boston Celtics			
☐ 51 Eddie Johnson	2.50	1.15	.30
Sacramento Kings			
☐ 52 Frank Johnson	2.00	.90	.25
Washington Bullets			
☐ 53 Magic Johnson	30.00	13.50	3.80
Los Angeles Lakers			
☐ 54 Marques Johnson	3.00	1.35	.40
Los Angeles Clippers			
(Decimal point missing,			
rookie year scoring avg.)			
☐ 55 Steve Johnson UER	2.00	.90	.25
San Antonio Spurs			
(photo actually			
David Greenwood)			
☐ 56 Vinnie Johnson	2.50	1.15	.30
Detroit Pistons			
☐ 57 Michael Jordan	800.00	350.00	100.00
Chicago Bulls			
☐ 58 Clark Kellogg	2.50	1.15	.30
Indiana Pacers			
☐ 59 Albert King	2.00	.90	.25
New Jersey Nets			
☐ 60 Bernard King	3.00	1.35	.40
New York Knicks			
☐ 61 Bill Laimbeer	3.00	1.35	.40
Detroit Pistons			
☐ 62 Allen Leavell	2.00	.90	.25
Houston Rockets			
☐ 63 Lafayette Lever	2.50	1.15	.30
Denver Nuggets			

☐ 64	Alton Lister .... Seattle Supersonics	2.50	1.15	.30
☐ 65	Lewis Lloyd .... Houston Rockets	2.00	.90	.25
☐ 66	Maurice Lucas .... Los Angeles Lakers	3.00	1.35	.40
☐ 67	Jeff Malone .... Washington Bullets	3.00	1.35	.40
☐ 68	Karl Malone .... Utah Jazz	60.00	27.00	7.50
☐ 69	Moses Malone .... Washington Bullets	6.00	2.70	.75
☐ 70	Cedric Maxwell .... Los Angeles Clippers	2.00	.90	.25
☐ 71	Rodney McCray .... Houston Rockets	2.50	1.15	.30
☐ 72	Xavier McDaniel .... Seattle Supersonics	4.00	1.80	.50
☐ 73	Kevin McHale .... Boston Celtics	5.00	2.30	.60
☐ 74	Mike Mitchell .... San Antonio Spurs	2.00	.90	.25
☐ 75	Sidney Moncrief .... Milwaukee Bucks	3.00	1.35	.40
☐ 76	Johnny Moore .... San Antonio Spurs	2.00	.90	.25
☐ 77	Chris Mullin .... Golden State Warriors	15.00	6.75	1.90
☐ 78	Larry Nance .... Phoenix Suns	5.00	2.30	.60
☐ 79	Calvin Natt .... Denver Nuggets	2.00	.90	.25
☐ 80	Norm Nixon .... Los Angeles Clippers	2.50	1.15	.30
☐ 81	Charles Oakley .... Chicago Bulls	8.00	3.60	1.00
☐ 82	Hakeem Olajuwon .... Houston Rockets	150.00	70.00	19.00
☐ 83	Louis Orr .... New York Knicks	2.00	.90	.25
☐ 84	Robert Parish UER ...... Boston Celtics (Misspelled Parrish on both sides)	4.00	1.80	.50
☐ 85	Jim Paxson .... Portland Trail Blazers	2.00	.90	.25
☐ 86	Sam Perkins .... Dallas Mavericks	5.00	2.30	.60
☐ 87	Ricky Pierce .... Milwaukee Bucks	3.00	1.35	.40
☐ 88	Paul Pressey .... Milwaukee Bucks	2.00	.90	.25
☐ 89	Kurt Rambis .... Los Angeles Lakers	3.00	1.35	.40
☐ 90	Robert Reid .... Houston Rockets	2.00	.90	.25
☐ 91	Doc Rivers .... Atlanta Hawks	3.00	1.35	.40
☐ 92	Alvin Robertson .... San Antonio Spurs	2.50	1.15	.30
☐ 93	Cliff Robinson .... Philadelphia 76ers	2.00	.90	.25
☐ 94	Tree Rollins .... Atlanta Hawks	2.50	1.15	.30
☐ 95	Dan Roundfield .... Washington Bullets	3.00	1.35	.40
☐ 96	Jeff Ruland .... Philadelphia 76ers	2.50	1.15	.30
☐ 97	Ralph Sampson .... Houston Rockets	3.00	1.35	.40
☐ 98	Danny Schayes	2.50	1.15	.30
	Denver Nuggets			
☐ 99	Byron Scott .... Los Angeles Lakers	5.00	2.30	.60
☐ 100	Purvis Short .... Golden State Warriors	2.00	.90	.25
☐ 101	Jerry Sichting .... Boston Celtics	2.00	.90	.25
☐ 102	Jack Sikma .... Milwaukee Bucks	2.50	1.15	.30
☐ 103	Derek Smith .... Los Angeles Clippers	2.00	.90	.25
☐ 104	Larry Smith .... Golden State Warriors	2.00	.90	.25
☐ 105	Rory Sparrow .... New York Knicks	2.00	.90	.25
☐ 106	Steve Stipanovich .... Indiana Pacers	2.00	.90	.25
☐ 107	Terry Teagle .... Golden State Warriors	2.00	.90	.25
☐ 108	Reggie Theus .... Sacramento Kings	2.50	1.15	.30
☐ 109	Isiah Thomas .... Detroit Pistons	30.00	13.50	3.80
☐ 110	LaSalle Thompson ...... Sacramento Kings	2.00	.90	.25
☐ 111	Mychal Thompson .... Portland Trail Blazers	2.50	1.15	.30
☐ 112	Sedale Threatt .... Philadelphia 76ers	2.00	.90	.25
☐ 113	Wayman Tisdale .... Indiana Pacers	4.00	1.80	.50
☐ 114	Andrew Toney .... Philadelphia 76ers	2.00	.90	.25
☐ 115	Kelly Tripucka .... Detroit Pistons	2.00	.90	.25
☐ 116	Mel Turpin .... Cleveland Cavaliers	2.50	1.15	.30
☐ 117	Kiki Vandeweghe .... Portland Trail Blazers	3.00	1.35	.40
☐ 118	Jay Vincent .... Dallas Mavericks	2.00	.90	.25
☐ 119	Bill Walton .... Boston Celtics (Missing decimal points on four lines of FG Percentage)	6.00	2.70	.75
☐ 120	Spud Webb .... Atlanta Hawks	5.00	2.30	.60
☐ 121	Dominique Wilkins ... Atlanta Hawks	40.00	18.00	5.00
☐ 122	Gerald Wilkins .... New York Knicks	3.00	1.35	.40
☐ 123	Buck Williams .... New Jersey Nets	6.00	2.70	.75
☐ 124	Gus Williams .... Washington Bullets	2.50	1.15	.30
☐ 125	Herb Williams .... Indiana Pacers	2.50	1.15	.30
☐ 126	Kevin Willis .... Atlanta Hawks	6.00	2.70	.75
☐ 127	Randy Wittman .... Atlanta Hawks	2.00	.90	.25
☐ 128	Al Wood .... Seattle Supersonics	2.00	.90	.25
☐ 129	Mike Woodson .... Sacramento Kings	2.00	.90	.25
☐ 130	Orlando Woolridge ..... Chicago Bulls	2.50	1.15	.30
☐ 131	James Worthy .... Los Angeles Lakers	15.00	6.75	1.90
☐ 132	Checklist 1-132	10.00	1.15	.30

1986-87 Fleer Stickers

One of these eleven different stickers was inserted into each 1986-87 Fleer wax pack. The stickers are 2 1/2" by 3 1/2". The backs of the sticker cards are printed in blue and red on white card stock. The set numbering of the stickers is alphabetical by player's name. Based on the one-to-twelve proportion of stickers to regular cards in the wax packs, there are theoretically an equal number of sticker sets and regular sets. The cards are frequently found off-centered and most card backs are found with wax stains due to packaging.

	NRMT-MT	EXC	VG
COMPLETE SET (11)	150.00	70.00	19.00
COMMON STICKER (1-11)	2.00	.90	.25
☐ 1 Kareem Abdul-Jabbar	4.00	1.80	.50
Los Angeles Lakers			
☐ 2 Larry Bird	15.00	6.75	1.90
Boston Celtics			
☐ 3 Adrian Dantley	2.00	.90	.25
Utah Jazz			
☐ 4 Alex English	2.00	.90	.25
Denver Nuggets			
☐ 5 Julius Erving	5.00	2.30	.60
Philadelphia 76ers			
☐ 6 Patrick Ewing	12.00	5.50	1.50
New York Knicks			
☐ 7 Magic Johnson	10.00	4.50	1.25
Los Angeles Lakers			
☐ 8 Michael Jordan	100.00	45.00	12.50
Chicago Bulls			
☐ 9 Hakeem Olajuwon	25.00	11.50	3.10
Houston Rockets			
☐ 10 Isiah Thomas	5.00	2.30	.60
Detroit Pistons			
☐ 11 Dominique Wilkins	5.00	2.30	.60
Atlanta Hawks			

1987-88 Fleer

The 1987-88 Fleer basketball set contains 132 standard size (2 1/2" by 3 1/2") cards. The cards were issued in 12-card wax packs that retailed for 50 cents. A wax box consisted of 36 packs. A sticker card and stick of gum were included. The fronts are white, with gray horizontal stripes. The backs are red, white and blue and show each player's complete NBA statistics. The cards are numbered in alphabetical order by last name. Rookie Cards include Brad Daugherty, A.C. Green, Chuck Person, Terry Porter, Detlef Schrempf and Hot Rod Williams. Other key Rookie Cards in this set, who had already had cards in previous Star sets, are Dale Ellis, John Paxson, and Otis Thorpe. The cards are frequently found off-centered.

	MINT	NRMT	EXC
COMPLETE w/Stickers (143)	300.00	135.00	38.00
COMPLETE SET (132)	250.00	115.00	31.00
COMMON CARD (1-132)	1.00	.45	.13
☐ 1 Kareem Abdul-Jabbar	8.00	2.00	.50
Los Angeles Lakers			
☐ 2 Alvan Adams	1.25	.55	.16
Phoenix Suns			
☐ 3 Mark Aguirre	1.25	.55	.16
Dallas Mavericks			
☐ 4 Danny Ainge	1.00	.45	.13
Boston Celtics			
☐ 5 John Bagley	1.00	.45	.13
Cleveland Cavaliers			
☐ 6 Thurl Bailey UER	1.00	.45	.13
Utah Jazz			
(reverse negative)			
☐ 7 Greg Ballard	1.00	.45	.13
Golden State Warriors			
☐ 8 Gene Banks	1.00	.45	.13
Chicago Bulls			
☐ 9 Charles Barkley	30.00	13.50	3.80
Philadelphia 76ers			
☐ 10 Benoit Benjamin	1.00	.45	.13
Los Angeles Clippers			
☐ 11 Larry Bird	30.00	13.50	3.80
Boston Celtics			
☐ 12 Rolando Blackman	1.25	.55	.16
Dallas Mavericks			
☐ 13 Manute Bol	1.00	.45	.13
Washington Bullets			
☐ 14 Tony Brown	1.00	.45	.13
New Jersey Nets			
☐ 15 Michael Cage	1.00	.45	.13
Los Angeles Clippers			
☐ 16 Joe Barry Carroll	1.00	.45	.13
Golden State Warriors			
☐ 17 Bill Cartwright	1.00	.45	.13
New York Knicks			
☐ 18 Terry Catledge	1.00	.45	.13

☐ 19	Tom Chambers 1.50	.65	.19
	Seattle Supersonics
☐ 20	Maurice Cheeks 1.50	.65	.19
	Philadelphia 76ers
☐ 21	Michael Cooper 1.50	.65	.19
	Los Angeles Lakers
☐ 22	Dave Corzine 1.00	.45	.13
	Chicago Bulls
☐ 23	Terry Cummings 1.25	.55	.16
	Milwaukee Bucks
☐ 24	Adrian Dantley 1.50	.65	.19
	Detroit Pistons
☐ 25	Brad Daugherty 3.00	1.35	.40
	Cleveland Cavaliers
☐ 26	Walter Davis 1.50	.65	.19
	Phoenix Suns
☐ 27	Johnny Dawkins 1.00	.45	.13
	San Antonio Spurs
☐ 28	James Donaldson 1.00	.45	.13
	Dallas Mavericks
☐ 29	Larry Drew 1.00	.45	.13
	Los Angeles Clippers
☐ 30	Clyde Drexler 15.00	6.75	1.90
	Portland Trail Blazers
☐ 31	Joe Dumars 8.00	3.60	1.00
	Detroit Pistons
☐ 32	Mark Eaton 1.00	.45	.13
	Utah Jazz
☐ 33	Dale Ellis 3.00	1.35	.40
	Seattle Supersonics
☐ 34	Alex English 1.50	.65	.19
	Denver Nuggets
☐ 35	Julius Erving 12.00	5.50	1.50
	Philadelphia 76ers
☐ 36	Mike Evans 1.00	.45	.13
	Denver Nuggets
☐ 37	Patrick Ewing............... 15.00	6.75	1.90
	New York Knicks
☐ 38	Vern Fleming............... 1.00	.45	.13
	Indiana Pacers
☐ 39	Sleepy Floyd 1.00	.45	.13
	Golden State Warriors
☐ 40	Artis Gilmore 1.50	.65	.19
	San Antonio Spurs
☐ 41	Mike Gminski UER 1.00	.45	.13
	New Jersey Nets
	(reversed negative)
☐ 42	A.C. Green 10.00	4.50	1.25
	Los Angeles Lakers
☐ 43	Rickey Green 1.00	.45	.13
	Utah Jazz
☐ 44	Sidney Green 1.00	.45	.13
	Detroit Pistons
☐ 45	David Greenwood 1.00	.45	.13
	San Antonio Spurs
☐ 46	Darrell Griffith 1.25	.55	.16
	Utah Jazz
☐ 47	Bill Hanzlik 1.00	.45	.13
	Denver Nuggets
☐ 48	Derek Harper............... 1.50	.65	.19
	Dallas Mavericks
☐ 49	Ron Harper 3.00	1.35	.40
	Cleveland Cavaliers
☐ 50	Gerald Henderson 1.00	.45	.13
	New York Knicks
☐ 51	Roy Hinson 1.00	.45	.13
	Philadelphia 76ers
☐ 52	Craig Hodges 1.00	.45	.13
	Milwaukee Bucks
☐ 53	Phil Hubbard............... 1.00	.45	.13

☐ 54	Dennis Johnson 1.50	.65	.19
	Boston Celtics
☐ 55	Eddie Johnson 1.25	.55	.16
	Sacramento Kings
☐ 56	Magic Johnson 20.00	9.00	2.50
	Los Angeles Lakers
☐ 57	Steve Johnson 1.00	.45	.13
	Portland Trail Blazers
☐ 58	Vinnie Johnson 1.25	.55	.16
	Detroit Pistons
☐ 59	Michael Jordan 175.00	80.00	22.00
	Chicago Bulls
☐ 60	Jerome Kersey 1.00	.45	.13
	Portland Trail Blazers
☐ 61	Bill Laimbeer............... 1.25	.55	.16
	Detroit Pistons
☐ 62	Lafayette Lever UER..... 1.25	.55	.16
	Denver Nuggets
	(Photo actually
	Otis Smith)
☐ 63	Cliff Levingston 1.00	.45	.13
	Atlanta Hawks
☐ 64	Alton Lister 1.00	.45	.13
	Seattle Supersonics
☐ 65	John Long................... 1.00	.45	.13
	Indiana Pacers
☐ 66	John Lucas 1.25	.55	.16
	Milwaukee Bucks
☐ 67	Jeff Malone 1.25	.55	.16
	Washington Bullets
☐ 68	Karl Malone................ 15.00	6.75	1.90
	Utah Jazz
☐ 69	Moses Malone 4.00	1.80	.50
	Washington Bullets
☐ 70	Cedric Maxwell 1.00	.45	.13
	Houston Rockets
☐ 71	Tim McCormick 1.00	.45	.13
	Philadelphia 76ers
☐ 72	Rodney McCray 1.00	.45	.13
	Houston Rockets
☐ 73	Xavier McDaniel........... 1.25	.55	.16
	Seattle Supersonics
☐ 74	Kevin McHale 3.00	1.35	.40
	Boston Celtics
☐ 75	Nate McMillan.............. 3.00	1.35	.40
	Seattle Supersonics
☐ 76	Sidney Moncrief........... 1.50	.65	.19
	Milwaukee Bucks
☐ 77	Chris Mullin 4.00	1.80	.50
	Golden State Warriors
☐ 78	Larry Nance 1.50	.65	.19
	Phoenix Suns
☐ 79	Charles Oakley 2.50	1.15	.30
	Chicago Bulls
☐ 80	Hakeem Olajuwon 40.00	18.00	5.00
	Houston Rockets
☐ 81	Robert Parish UER....... 2.50	1.15	.30
	Boston Celtics
	(Misspelled Parrish
	on both sides)
☐ 82	Jim Paxson 1.00	.45	.13
	Portland Trail Blazers
☐ 83	John Paxson 3.00	1.35	.40
	Chicago Bulls
☐ 84	Sam Perkins 1.50	.65	.19
	Dallas Mavericks
☐ 85	Chuck Person 4.00	1.80	.50
	Indiana Pacers
☐ 86	Jim Peterson 1.00	.45	.13
	Houston Rockets

☐ 87	Ricky Pierce Milwaukee Bucks	1.25	.55	.16
☐ 88	Ed Pinckney Phoenix Suns	1.25	.55	.16
☐ 89	Terry Porter Portland Trail Blazers (College Wisconsin, should be Wisconsin - Stevens Point)	3.00	1.35	.40
☐ 90	Paul Pressey Milwaukee Bucks	1.00	.45	.13
☐ 91	Robert Reid Houston Rockets	1.00	.45	.13
☐ 92	Doc Rivers Atlanta Hawks	1.00	.45	.13
☐ 93	Alvin Robertson San Antonio Spurs	1.00	.45	.13
☐ 94	Tree Rollins Atlanta Hawks	1.00	.45	.13
☐ 95	Ralph Sampson Houston Rockets	1.25	.55	.16
☐ 96	Mike Sanders Phoenix Suns	1.00	.45	.13
☐ 97	Detlef Schrempf Dallas Mavericks	12.00	5.50	1.50
☐ 98	Byron Scott Los Angeles Lakers	1.50	.65	.19
☐ 99	Jerry Sichting Boston Celtics	1.00	.45	.13
☐ 100	Jack Sikma Milwaukee Bucks	1.25	.55	.16
☐ 101	Larry Smith Golden State Warriors	1.00	.45	.13
☐ 102	Rory Sparrow New York Knicks	1.00	.45	.13
☐ 103	Steve Stipanovich Indiana Pacers	1.00	.45	.13
☐ 104	Jon Sundvold San Antonio Spurs	1.00	.45	.13
☐ 105	Reggie Theus Sacramento Kings	1.25	.55	.16
☐ 106	Isiah Thomas Detroit Pistons	8.00	3.60	1.00
☐ 107	LaSalle Thompson Sacramento Kings	1.00	.45	.13
☐ 108	Mychal Thompson Los Angeles Lakers	1.00	.45	.13
☐ 109	Otis Thorpe Sacramento Kings	5.00	2.30	.60
☐ 110	Sedale Threatt Chicago Bulls	1.00	.45	.13
☐ 111	Waymon Tisdale Indiana Pacers	1.25	.55	.16
☐ 112	Kelly Tripucka Utah Jazz	1.00	.45	.13
☐ 113	Trent Tucker New York Knicks	1.00	.45	.13
☐ 114	Terry Tyler Sacramento Kings	1.00	.45	.13
☐ 115	Darnell Valentine Los Angeles Clippers	1.00	.45	.13
☐ 116	Kiki Vandeweghe Portland Trail Blazers	1.25	.55	.16
☐ 117	Darrell Walker Denver Nuggets	1.00	.45	.13
☐ 118	Dominique Wilkins Atlanta Hawks	8.00	3.60	1.00
☐ 119	Gerald Wilkins New York Knicks	1.25	.55	.16
☐ 120	Buck Williams New Jersey Nets	1.50	.65	.19
☐ 121	Herb Williams Indiana Pacers	1.00	.45	.13
☐ 122	John Williams Washington Bullets	1.00	.45	.13
☐ 123	John Williams Cleveland Cavaliers	3.00	1.35	.40
☐ 124	Kevin Willis Atlanta Hawks	1.00	.45	.13
☐ 125	David Wingate Philadelphia 76ers	1.25	.55	.16
☐ 126	Randy Wittman Atlanta Hawks	1.00	.45	.13
☐ 127	Leon Wood New Jersey Nets	1.00	.45	.13
☐ 128	Mike Woodson Los Angeles Clippers	1.00	.45	.13
☐ 129	Orlando Woolridge New Jersey Nets	1.00	.45	.13
☐ 130	James Worthy Los Angeles Lakers	4.00	1.80	.50
☐ 131	Danny Young Seattle Supersonics	1.00	.45	.13
☐ 132	Checklist 1-132	3.00	.45	.13

1987-88 Fleer Stickers

The 1987-88 Fleer Stickers is an 11-card standard size (2 1/2" by 3 1/2") set issued as an insert in wax packs with the regular 132-card set. The fronts are red, white, blue and yellow. The backs are white and blue and contain career highlights. One sticker was included in each wax pack. Based on the one-to-twelve proportion of stickers to regular cards in the wax packs, there are theoretically an equal number of sticker sets and regular sets. Virtually all cards from this set have wax-stained backs as a result of the packaging.

	MINT	NRMT	EXC
COMPLETE SET (11)	60.00	27.00	7.50
COMMON STICKER (1-11)	1.00	.45	.13
☐ 1 Magic Johnson Los Angeles Lakers	7.00	3.10	.85
☐ 2 Michael Jordan Chicago Bulls	50.00	23.00	6.25

(In text, votes mis-
spelled as voites)

		MINT	NRMT	EXC
☐ 3	Hakeem Olajuwon UER (Misspelled Olajuwan on card back) Houston Rockets	12.00	5.50	1.50
☐ 4	Larry Bird Boston Celtics	10.00	4.50	1.25
☐ 5	Kevin McHale Boston Celtics	1.50	.65	.19
☐ 6	Charles Barkley Philadelphia 76ers	10.00	4.50	1.25
☐ 7	Dominique Wilkins Atlanta Hawks	2.50	1.15	.30
☐ 8	Kareem Abdul-Jabbar Los Angeles Lakers	2.50	1.15	.30
☐ 9	Mark Aguirre Dallas Mavericks	1.25	.55	.16
☐ 10	Chuck Person Indiana Pacers	1.00	.45	.13
☐ 11	Alex English Denver Nuggets	1.25	.55	.16

1988-89 Fleer

The 1988-89 Fleer basketball set contains 132 standard size (2 1/2" by 3 1/2") cards. There are 119 regular cards, plus 12 All-Star cards and a checklist. This set was issued in wax packs of 12 cards, gum and a sticker. Wax boxes contained 36 wax packs. The outer borders are white and gray, while the inner borders correspond to the team colors. The backs are greenish and show full NBA statistics with limited biographical information. The set is ordered alphabetically by team with a few exceptions due to late trades. The numbering is: Atlanta Hawks (1-6, 98, 118), Boston Celtics (8-12), Charlotte Hornets (13-14), Chicago Bulls (15-17 and 19-21), Cleveland Cavaliers (22-26), Dallas Mavericks (27-32), Denver Nuggets (33-38), Detroit Pistons (39-45), Golden State Warriors (46-49), Houston Rockets (50-54, 63), Indiana Pacers (55-60), Los Angeles Clippers (61), Los Angeles Lakers (64-70), Miami Heat (71-72), Milwaukee Bucks (73-76), New Jersey Nets (77-79, 102), New York Knicks (18, 80-84), Philadelphia 76ers (85-88), Phoenix Suns (89-91, 106), Portland Trail Blazers (92-96), Sacramento Kings (7, 97, 99-100), San Antonio Spurs

(101, 103-105), Seattle Supersonics (62, 107-110), Utah Jazz (111-115), Washington Bullets (116-117, 119) and All-Stars (120-131). Rookie Cards include Michael Adams, Muggsy Bogues, Dell Curry, Horace Grant, Mark Jackson, Reggie Miller, Derrick McKey, Scottie Pippen, Mark Price, Dennis Rodman and Kenny Smith. There is also a Rookie Card of John Stockton who had previously only appeared in Star Company sets.

		MINT	NRMT	EXC
	COMPLETE w/Stickers (143)	175.00	80.00	22.00
	COMPLETE SET (132)	150.00	70.00	19.00
	COMMON CARD (1-132)	.25	.11	.03
☐ 1	Antoine Carr	1.00	.45	.13
☐ 2	Cliff Levingston	.25	.11	.03
☐ 3	Doc Rivers	.25	.11	.03
☐ 4	Spud Webb	.35	.16	.04
☐ 5	Dominique Wilkins	2.00	.90	.25
☐ 6	Kevin Willis	.35	.16	.04
☐ 7	Randy Wittman	.25	.11	.03
☐ 8	Danny Ainge	.25	.11	.03
☐ 9	Larry Bird	12.00	5.50	1.50
☐ 10	Dennis Johnson	.35	.16	.04
☐ 11	Kevin McHale	1.25	.55	.16
☐ 12	Robert Parish	1.00	.45	.13
☐ 13	Tyrone Bogues	4.00	1.80	.50
☐ 14	Dell Curry	2.00	.90	.25
☐ 15	Dave Corzine	.25	.11	.03
☐ 16	Horace Grant	15.00	6.75	1.90
☐ 17	Michael Jordan	50.00	23.00	6.25
☐ 18	Charles Oakley	.30	.14	.04
☐ 19	John Paxson	.35	.16	.04
☐ 20	Scottie Pippen UER (Misspelled Pippin on card back)	30.00	13.50	3.80
☐ 21	Brad Sellers	.25	.11	.03
☐ 22	Brad Daugherty	.35	.16	.04
☐ 23	Ron Harper	.35	.16	.04
☐ 24	Larry Nance	.35	.16	.04
☐ 25	Mark Price	8.00	3.60	1.00
☐ 26	Hot Rod Williams	.25	.11	.03
☐ 27	Mark Aguirre	.30	.14	.04
☐ 28	Rolando Blackman	.30	.14	.04
☐ 29	James Donaldson	.25	.11	.03
☐ 30	Derek Harper	.35	.16	.04
☐ 31	Sam Perkins	.35	.16	.04
☐ 32	Roy Tarpley	1.00	.45	.13
☐ 33	Michael Adams	1.00	.45	.13
☐ 34	Alex English	.35	.16	.04
☐ 35	Lafayette Lever	.25	.11	.03
☐ 36	Blair Rasmussen	.25	.11	.03
☐ 37	Danny Schayes	.25	.11	.03
☐ 38	Jay Vincent	.25	.11	.03
☐ 39	Adrian Dantley	.35	.16	.04
☐ 40	Joe Dumars	2.00	.90	.25
☐ 41	Vinnie Johnson	.30	.14	.04
☐ 42	Bill Laimbeer	.30	.14	.04
☐ 43	Dennis Rodman	18.00	8.00	2.30
☐ 44	John Salley	.25	.11	.03
☐ 45	Isiah Thomas	2.00	.90	.25
☐ 46	Winston Garland	.25	.11	.03
☐ 47	Rod Higgins	.25	.11	.03
☐ 48	Chris Mullin	1.00	.45	.13
☐ 49	Ralph Sampson	.25	.11	.03
☐ 50	Joe Barry Carroll	.25	.11	.03
☐ 51	Sleepy Floyd	.25	.11	.03
☐ 52	Rodney McCray	.25	.11	.03

☐ 53	Hakeem Olajuwon	10.00	4.50	1.25
☐ 54	Purvis Short	.25	.11	.03
☐ 55	Vern Fleming	.25	.11	.03
☐ 56	John Long	.25	.11	.03
☐ 57	Reggie Miller	30.00	13.50	3.80
☐ 58	Chuck Person	.35	.16	.04
☐ 59	Steve Stipanovich	.25	.11	.03
☐ 60	Waymon Tisdale	.30	.14	.04
☐ 61	Benoit Benjamin	.25	.11	.03
☐ 62	Michael Cage	.25	.11	.03
☐ 63	Mike Woodson	.25	.11	.03
☐ 64	Kareem Abdul-Jabbar	4.00	1.80	.50
☐ 65	Michael Cooper	.35	.16	.04
☐ 66	A.C. Green	1.00	.45	.13
☐ 67	Magic Johnson	8.00	3.60	1.00
☐ 68	Byron Scott	.30	.14	.04
☐ 69	Mychal Thompson	.30	.14	.04
☐ 70	James Worthy	1.00	.45	.13
☐ 71	Duane Washington	.25	.11	.03
☐ 72	Kevin Williams	.25	.11	.03
☐ 73	Randy Breuer	.25	.11	.03
☐ 74	Terry Cummings	.30	.14	.04
☐ 75	Paul Pressey	.25	.11	.04
☐ 76	Jack Sikma	.30	.14	.04
☐ 77	John Bagley	.25	.11	.03
☐ 78	Roy Hinson	.25	.11	.03
☐ 79	Buck Williams	.35	.16	.04
☐ 80	Patrick Ewing	4.00	1.80	.50
☐ 81	Sidney Green	.25	.11	.03
☐ 82	Mark Jackson	2.50	1.15	.30
☐ 83	Kenny Walker	.25	.11	.03
☐ 84	Gerald Wilkins	.25	.11	.03
☐ 85	Charles Barkley	8.00	3.60	1.00
☐ 86	Maurice Cheeks	.35	.16	.04
☐ 87	Mike Gminski	.30	.14	.04
☐ 88	Cliff Robinson	.25	.11	.03
☐ 89	Armon Gilliam	1.00	.45	.13
☐ 90	Eddie Johnson	.30	.14	.04
☐ 91	Mark West	.30	.14	.04
☐ 92	Clyde Drexler	4.00	1.80	.50
☐ 93	Kevin Duckworth	.25	.11	.03
☐ 94	Steve Johnson	.25	.11	.03
☐ 95	Jerome Kersey	.25	.11	.03
☐ 96	Terry Porter	.35	.16	.04
	(College Wisconsin, should be Wisconsin Stevens Point)			
☐ 97	Joe Kleine	1.00	.45	.13
☐ 98	Reggie Theus	.30	.14	.04
☐ 99	Otis Thorpe	.35	.16	.04
☐ 100	Kenny Smith	2.00	.90	.25
	(College NC State, should be North Carolina)			
☐ 101	Greg Anderson	.30	.14	.04
☐ 102	Walter Berry	.25	.11	.03
☐ 103	Frank Brickowski	.25	.11	.03
☐ 104	Johnny Dawkins	.30	.14	.04
☐ 105	Alvin Robertson	.25	.11	.03
☐ 106	Tom Chambers	.35	.16	.04
	(Born 6/2/59, should be 6/21/59)			
☐ 107	Dale Ellis	.35	.16	.04
☐ 108	Xavier McDaniel	.30	.14	.04
☐ 109	Derrick McKey	2.50	1.15	.30
☐ 110	Nate McMillan UER	.30	.14	.04
	(Photo actually Kevin Williams)			
☐ 111	Thurl Bailey	.25	.11	.03
☐ 112	Mark Eaton	.25	.11	.03
☐ 113	Bobby Hansen	.25	.11	.03

☐ 114	Karl Malone	4.00	1.80	.50
☐ 115	John Stockton	25.00	11.50	3.10
☐ 116	Bernard King	.35	.16	.04
☐ 117	Jeff Malone	.30	.14	.04
☐ 118	Moses Malone	1.50	.65	.19
☐ 119	John Williams	.25	.11	.03
☐ 120	Michael Jordan AS	20.00	9.00	2.50
	Chicago Bulls			
☐ 121	Mark Jackson AS	.25	.11	.03
	New York Knicks			
☐ 122	Byron Scott AS	.25	.11	.03
	Los Angeles Lakers			
☐ 123	Magic Johnson AS	3.00	1.35	.40
	Los Angeles Lakers			
☐ 124	Larry Bird AS	5.00	2.30	.60
	Boston Celtics			
☐ 125	Dominique Wilkins AS	.75	.35	.09
	Atlanta Hawks			
☐ 126	Hakeem Olajuwon AS	4.00	1.80	.50
	Houston Rockets			
☐ 127	John Stockton AS	5.00	2.30	.60
	Utah Jazz			
☐ 128	Alvin Robertson AS	.25	.11	.03
	San Antonio Spurs			
☐ 129	Charles Barkley AS	3.00	1.35	.40
	Philadelphia 76ers (Back says Buck Williams is member of Jets, should be Nets)			
☐ 130	Patrick Ewing AS	1.50	.65	.19
	New York Knicks			
☐ 131	Mark Eaton AS	.25	.11	.03
	Utah Jazz			
☐ 132	Checklist 1-132	.40	.11	.03

1988-89 Fleer Stickers

The 1988-89 Fleer Stickers is an 11-card standard size (2 1/2" by 3 1/2") set issued as a one per pack insert along with 12 cards from the regular 132-card set. The fronts are baby blue, red, and white. The backs are blue and pink and contain career highlights. The set is ordered alphabetically. Based on the one-to-twelve proportion of stickers to regular cards in the wax packs, there are theoretically an equal number of sticker sets and regular sets. Virtually all cards from this set have wax-stained backs as a result of the packaging.

	MINT	NRMT	EXC
COMPLETE SET (11)	25.00	11.50	3.10
COMMON STICKER (1-11)	.25	.11	.03
☐ 1 Mark Aguirre Dallas Mavericks	.25	.11	.03
☐ 2 Larry Bird Boston Celtics	5.00	2.30	.60
☐ 3 Clyde Drexler Portland Trail Blazers	1.50	.65	.19
☐ 4 Alex English Denver Nuggets	.25	.11	.03
☐ 5 Patrick Ewing New York Knicks	1.50	.65	.19
☐ 6 Magic Johnson Los Angeles Lakers	3.00	1.35	.40
☐ 7 Michael Jordan Chicago Bulls	20.00	9.00	2.50
☐ 8 Karl Malone Utah Jazz	1.50	.65	.19
☐ 9 Kevin McHale Boston Celtics	.50	.23	.06
☐ 10 Isiah Thomas Detroit Pistons	.75	.35	.09
☐ 11 Dominique Wilkins Atlanta Hawks	.75	.35	.09

1989-90 Fleer

The 1989-90 Fleer basketball set consists of 168 cards measuring the standard size (2 1/2" by 3 1/2"). The cards were distributed in 15-card wax packs (and one sticker) and in 36-card rack packs. Wax boxes contained 36 packs. The fronts feature color action player photos, with various color borders between white inner and outer borders. The player's name and position appear in the upper left corner, with the team logo superimposed over the upper right corner of the picture. The horizontally oriented backs have black lettering on red, pink, and white background and present career statistics, biographical information, and a performance index. The set is ordered alphabetically in team subsets (with a few exceptions due to late trades). The teams themselves are also presented in alphabetical order, Atlanta Hawks (1-7), Boston Celtics (8-14), Charlotte Hornets (15-18), Chicago Bulls (19-23), Cleveland Cavaliers (25-31), Dallas Mavericks (32-37), Denver Nuggets (38-43), Detroit Pistons (44-51), Golden State Warriors (52-57), Houston Rockets (58-63), Indiana

Pacers (64-68), Los Angeles Clippers (69-74), Los Angeles Lakers (75-80), Miami Heat (81-84), Milwaukee Bucks (85-91), Minnesota Timberwolves (92-94), New Jersey Nets (95-99), New York Knicks (100-107), Orlando Magic (108-111), Philadelphia 76ers (112-118), Phoenix Suns (119-125), Portland Trail Blazers (126-132), Sacramento Kings (133-139), San Antonio Spurs (140-144), Seattle Supersonics (24 and 145-150), Utah Jazz (151-156), Washington Bullets (157-162), and All-Star Game Combos (163-167). Rookie Cards included in this set are Willie Anderson, Rex Chapman, Kevin Edwards, Hersey Hawkins, Jeff Hornacek, Kevin Johnson, Reggie Lewis, Grant Long, Dan Majerle, Danny Manning, Vernon Maxwell, Chris Morris, Johnny Newman, Ken Norman, Mitch Richmond, Rony Seikaly, Brian Shaw, Scott Skiles, Charles Smith, Rik Smits, Rod Strickland, and Reggie Williams. Cards from this set are frequently found off-center.

	MINT	NRMT	EXC
COMPLETE w/Stickers (179)	35.00	16.00	4.40
COMPLETE SET (168)	30.00	13.50	3.80
COMMON CARD (1-168)	.10	.05	.01
☐ 1 John Battle	.10	.05	.01
☐ 2 Jon Koncak	.15	.07	.02
☐ 3 Cliff Levingston	.10	.05	.01
☐ 4 Moses Malone	.50	.23	.06
☐ 5 Doc Rivers	.15	.07	.02
☐ 6 Spud Webb UER (Points per 48 minutes incorrect at 2.6)	.15	.07	.02
☐ 7 Dominique Wilkins	.50	.23	.06
☐ 8 Larry Bird	3.00	1.35	.40
☐ 9 Dennis Johnson	.20	.09	.03
☐ 10 Reggie Lewis	1.00	.45	.13
☐ 11 Kevin McHale	.20	.09	.03
☐ 12 Robert Parish	.20	.09	.03
☐ 13 Ed Pinckney	.10	.05	.01
☐ 14 Brian Shaw	.75	.35	.09
☐ 15 Rex Chapman	.50	.23	.06
☐ 16 Kurt Rambis	.10	.05	.01
☐ 17 Robert Reid	.10	.05	.01
☐ 18 Kelly Tripucka	.10	.05	.01
☐ 19 Bill Cartwright UER (First season 1978-80, should be 1979-80)	.10	.05	.01
☐ 20 Horace Grant	1.25	.55	.16
☐ 21 Michael Jordan	12.00	5.50	1.50
☐ 22 John Paxson	.15	.07	.02
☐ 23 Scottie Pippen	2.50	1.15	.30
☐ 24 Brad Sellers	.10	.05	.01
☐ 25 Brad Daugherty	.15	.07	.02
☐ 26 Craig Ehlo	.15	.07	.02
☐ 27 Ron Harper	.15	.07	.02
☐ 28 Larry Nance	.15	.07	.02
☐ 29 Mark Price	.60	.25	.08
☐ 30 Mike Sanders	.10	.05	.01
☐ 31A John Williams ERR Washington Bullets	.50	.23	.06
☐ 31B John Williams COR Cleveland Cavaliers	.15	.07	.02
☐ 32 Rolando Blackman UER (Career blocks and points listed as 1961 and 2127,	.15	.07	.02

should be 196 and 12,127)

☐ 33	Adrian Dantley	.20	.09	.03
☐ 34	James Donaldson	.10	.05	.01
☐ 35	Derek Harper	.15	.07	.02
☐ 36	Sam Perkins	.15	.07	.02
☐ 37	Herb Williams	.10	.05	.01
☐ 38	Michael Adams	.10	.05	.01
☐ 39	Walter Davis	.20	.09	.03
☐ 40	Alex English	.20	.09	.03
☐ 41	Lafayette Lever	.10	.05	.01
☐ 42	Blair Rasmussen	.10	.05	.01
☐ 43	Dan Schayes	.10	.05	.01
☐ 44	Mark Aguirre	.15	.07	.02
☐ 45	Joe Dumars	.50	.23	.06
☐ 46	James Edwards	.10	.05	.01
☐ 47	Vinnie Johnson	.15	.07	.02
☐ 48	Bill Laimbeer	.15	.07	.02
☐ 49	Dennis Rodman	1.50	.65	.19
☐ 50	Isiah Thomas	.50	.23	.06
☐ 51	John Salley	.10	.05	.01
☐ 52	Manute Bol	.10	.05	.01
☐ 53	Winston Garland	.10	.05	.01
☐ 54	Rod Higgins	.10	.05	.01
☐ 55	Chris Mullin	.10	.05	.01
☐ 56	Mitch Richmond	3.00	1.35	.40
☐ 57	Terry Teagle	.10	.05	.01
☐ 58	Derrick Chievous UER	.10	.05	.01

(Stats correctly say
81 games in '88-89,
text says 82)

☐ 59	Sleepy Floyd	.10	.05	.01
☐ 60	Tim McCormick	.10	.05	.01
☐ 61	Hakeem Olajuwon	2.50	1.15	.30
☐ 62	Otis Thorpe	.15	.07	.02
☐ 63	Mike Woodson	.10	.05	.01
☐ 64	Vern Fleming	.10	.05	.01
☐ 65	Reggie Miller	2.50	1.15	.30
☐ 66	Chuck Person	.15	.07	.02
☐ 67	Detlef Schrempf	.60	.25	.08
☐ 68	Rik Smits	2.50	1.15	.30
☐ 69	Benoit Benjamin	.10	.05	.01
☐ 70	Gary Grant	.10	.05	.01
☐ 71	Danny Manning	2.50	1.15	.30
☐ 72	Ken Norman	.50	.23	.06
☐ 73	Charles Smith	.50	.23	.06
☐ 74	Reggie Williams	.50	.23	.06
☐ 75	Michael Cooper	.20	.09	.03
☐ 76	A.C. Green	.20	.09	.03
☐ 77	Magic Johnson	2.00	.90	.25
☐ 78	Byron Scott	.15	.07	.02
☐ 79	Mychal Thompson	.10	.05	.01
☐ 80	James Worthy	.20	.09	.03
☐ 81	Kevin Edwards	.10	.05	.01
☐ 82	Grant Long	.50	.23	.06
☐ 83	Rony Seikaly	.50	.23	.06
☐ 84	Rory Sparrow	.10	.05	.01
☐ 85	Greg Anderson UER	.10	.05	.01

(Stats show 1988-89
as 19888-89)

☐ 86	Jay Humphries	.10	.05	.01
☐ 87	Larry Krystkowiak	.10	.05	.01
☐ 88	Ricky Pierce	.15	.07	.02
☐ 89	Paul Pressey	.10	.05	.01
☐ 90	Alvin Robertson	.10	.05	.01
☐ 91	Jack Sikma	.15	.07	.02
☐ 92	Steve Johnson	.10	.05	.01
☐ 93	Rick Mahorn	.10	.05	.01
☐ 94	David Rivers	.10	.05	.01
☐ 95	Joe Barry Carroll	.10	.05	.01
☐ 96	Lester Conner UER	.10	.05	.01

(Garden State in stats,
should be Golden State)

☐ 97	Roy Hinson	.10	.05	.01
☐ 98	Mike McGee	.10	.05	.01
☐ 99	Chris Morris	.50	.23	.06
☐ 100	Patrick Ewing	1.00	.45	.13
☐ 101	Mark Jackson	.10	.05	.01
☐ 102	Johnny Newman	.10	.05	.01
☐ 103	Charles Oakley	.15	.07	.02
☐ 104	Rod Strickland	1.50	.65	.19
☐ 105	Trent Tucker	.10	.05	.01
☐ 106	Kiki Vandeweghe	.10	.05	.01
☐ 107A	Gerald Wilkins	.15	.07	.02

(U. of Tennesee)

☐ 107B	Gerald Wilkins	.15	.07	.02

(U. of Tenn.)

☐ 108	Terry Catledge	.10	.05	.01
☐ 109	Dave Corzine	.10	.05	.01
☐ 110	Scott Skiles	.15	.07	.02
☐ 111	Reggie Theus	.15	.07	.02
☐ 112	Ron Anderson	.10	.05	.01
☐ 113	Charles Barkley	2.00	.90	.25
☐ 114	Scott Brooks	.10	.05	.01
☐ 115	Maurice Cheeks	.20	.09	.03
☐ 116	Mike Gminski	.10	.05	.01
☐ 117	Hersey Hawkins UER	.75	.35	.09

(Born 9/29/65,
should be 9/9/65)

☐ 118	Christian Welp	.10	.05	.01
☐ 119	Tom Chambers	.15	.07	.02
☐ 120	Armon Gilliam	.10	.05	.01
☐ 121	Jeff Hornacek	1.00	.45	.13
☐ 122	Eddie Johnson	.15	.07	.02
☐ 123	Kevin Johnson	3.00	1.35	.40
☐ 124	Dan Majerle	2.00	.90	.25
☐ 125	Mark West	.10	.05	.01
☐ 126	Richard Anderson	.10	.05	.01
☐ 127	Mark Bryant	.10	.05	.01
☐ 128	Clyde Drexler	1.00	.45	.13
☐ 129	Kevin Duckworth	.10	.05	.01
☐ 130	Jerome Kersey	.10	.05	.01
☐ 131	Terry Porter	.15	.07	.02
☐ 132	Buck Williams	.15	.07	.02
☐ 133	Danny Ainge	.15	.07	.02
☐ 134	Ricky Berry	.10	.05	.01
☐ 135	Rodney McCray	.10	.05	.01
☐ 136	Jim Petersen	.10	.05	.01
☐ 137	Harold Pressley	.10	.05	.01
☐ 138	Kenny Smith	.10	.05	.01
☐ 139	Wayman Tisdale	.15	.07	.02
☐ 140	Willie Anderson	.10	.05	.01
☐ 141	Frank Brickowski	.10	.05	.01
☐ 142	Terry Cummings	.15	.07	.02
☐ 143	Johnny Dawkins	.15	.07	.02
☐ 144	Vern Maxwell	.50	.23	.06
☐ 145	Michael Cage	.10	.05	.01
☐ 146	Dale Ellis	.15	.07	.02
☐ 147	Alton Lister	.10	.05	.01
☐ 148	Xavier McDaniel UER	.15	.07	.02

(All-Rookie team in
1985, not 1988)

☐ 149	Derrick McKey	.20	.09	.03
☐ 150	Nate McMillan	.10	.05	.01
☐ 151	Thurl Bailey	.10	.05	.01
☐ 152	Mark Eaton	.10	.05	.01
☐ 153	Darrell Griffith	.15	.07	.02
☐ 154	Eric Leckner	.10	.05	.01
☐ 155	Karl Malone	1.00	.45	.13
☐ 156	John Stockton	2.50	1.15	.30
☐ 157	Mark Alarie	.10	.05	.01
☐ 158	Ledell Eackles	.10	.05	.01
☐ 159	Bernard King	.20	.09	.03

☐ 160	Jeff Malone	.15	.07	.02
☐ 161	Darrell Walker	.10	.05	.01
☐ 162A	John Williams ERR	.50	.23	.06
	Cleveland Cavaliers			
☐ 162B	John Williams COR	.10	.05	.01
	Washington Bullets			
☐ 163	All Star Game	.50	.23	.06
	Karl Malone			
	John Stockton			
☐ 164	All Star Game	1.00	.45	.13
	Hakeem Olajuwon			
	Clyde Drexler			
☐ 165	All Star Game	.10	.05	.01
	Dominique Wilkins			
	Moses Malone			
☐ 166	All Star Game UER	.10	.05	.01
	Brad Daugherty			
	Mark Price			
	(Bio says Nance had 204			
	blocks, should be 206)			
☐ 167	All Star Game	.25	.11	.03
	Patrick Ewing			
	Mark Jackson			
☐ 168	Checklist 1-168	.10	.05	.01

1989-90 Fleer Stickers

This set of 11 insert stickers features NBA All-Stars and measures the standard size (2 1/2" by 3 1/2"). One All-Star sticker was inserted in each 12-card wax pack. The front has a color action player photo. An aqua stripe with dark blue stars traverses the card top, and the same pattern reappears about halfway down the card face. The words "Fleer '89 All-Stars" appear at the top of the picture, with the player's name and position immediately below the picture. The back has a star pattern similar to the front. A career summary is printed in blue on a white background. The stickers are numbered on the back and checklisted below accordingly. Most card backs have problems with wax stains as a result of packaging.

	MINT	NRMT	EXC
COMPLETE SET (11)	6.00	2.70	.75
COMMON STICKER (1-11)	.10	.05	.01
☐ 1 Karl Malone	.40	.18	.05
Utah Jazz			

☐ 2	Hakeem Olajuwon	1.00	.45	.13
	Houston Rockets			
☐ 3	Michael Jordan	5.00	2.30	.60
	Chicago Bulls			
☐ 4	Charles Barkley	.75	.35	.09
	Philadelphia 76ers			
☐ 5	Magic Johnson	.75	.35	.09
	Los Angeles Lakers			
☐ 6	Isiah Thomas	.20	.09	.03
	Detroit Pistons			
☐ 7	Patrick Ewing	.40	.18	.05
	New York Knicks			
☐ 8	Dale Ellis	.15	.07	.02
	Seattle Supersonics			
☐ 9	Chris Mullin	.15	.07	.02
	Golden State Warriors			
☐ 10	Larry Bird	1.25	.55	.16
	Boston Celtics			
☐ 11	Tom Chambers	.10	.05	.01
	Phoenix Suns			

1990-91 Fleer

The 1990-91 Fleer set contains 198 cards measuring the standard size (2 1/2" by 3 1/2"). The cards were available in 15-card wax packs, 23-card cello packs and 36-card rack packs. Wax boxes contained 36 wax packs. There were also 43 card pre-priced packs ($1.49) which contained Rookie Sensation inserts. The fronts fea ture a color action player photo, with a white inner border and a two-color (red on top and bottom, blue on sides) outer border on a white card face. The team logo is superimposed at the upper left corner of the picture, with the player's name and position appearing below the picture. The backs are printed in black, gray, and yellow, and present biographical and statistical information. The cards are numbered on the back. The set is ordered alphabetically in team subsets (with a few exceptions due to late trades). The teams themselves are also presented in alphabetical order, Atlanta Hawks (1-7), Boston Celtics (8-15), Charlotte Hornets (16-21), Chicago Bulls (22-30 and 120), Cleveland Cavaliers (31-37), Dallas Mavericks (38-45 and 50), Denver Nuggets (46-53), Detroit Pistons (54-61), Golden State Warriors (62-68), Houston Rockets (69-75), Indiana Pacers (76-83), Los Angeles Clippers (84-89), Los Angeles Lakers (90-97), Miami Heat (98-103), Milwaukee Bucks (104-110),

Minnesota Timberwolves (111-116 and 140), New Jersey Nets (117-123 and 136), New York Knicks (124-131), Orlando Magic (132-135 and 137), Philadelphia 76ers (138-139 and 141-145), Phoenix Suns (146-153), Portland Trail Blazers (154-161), Sacramento Kings (162-167 and 186-187), San Antonio Spurs (168-174), Seattle Supersonics (175-181), Utah Jazz (182-189 and 195), and Washington Bullets (164, 190-194, and 196). The description, All-American, is properly capitalized on the back of cards 134 and 144, but is not capitalized on cards 20, 29, 51, 53, 59, 70, 119, 130, 178, and 192. Notable Rookie Cards in the set are Nick Anderson, B.J. Armstrong, Mookie Blaylock, Sherman Douglas, Sean Elliott, Tim Hardaway, Shawn Kemp, Glen Rice, and Cliff Robinson.

	MINT	NRMT	EXC
COMPLETE SET (198)	6.00	2.70	.75
COMMON CARD (1-198)	.05	.02	.01
☐ 1 John Battle UER	.05	.02	.01
(Drafted in '84, should be '85)			
☐ 2 Cliff Levingston	.05	.02	.01
☐ 3 Moses Malone	.15	.07	.02
☐ 4 Kenny Smith	.05	.02	.01
☐ 5 Spud Webb	.08	.04	.01
☐ 6 Dominique Wilkins	.15	.07	.02
☐ 7 Kevin Willis	.08	.04	.01
☐ 8 Larry Bird	.75	.35	.09
☐ 9 Dennis Johnson	.10	.05	.01
☐ 10 Joe Kleine	.05	.02	.01
☐ 11 Reggie Lewis	.10	.05	.01
☐ 12 Kevin McHale	.10	.05	.01
☐ 13 Robert Parish	.10	.05	.01
☐ 14 Jim Paxson	.05	.02	.01
☐ 15 Ed Pinckney	.05	.02	.01
☐ 16 Tyrone Bogues	.10	.05	.01
☐ 17 Rex Chapman	.05	.02	.01
☐ 18 Dell Curry	.05	.02	.01
☐ 19 Armon Gilliam	.05	.02	.01
☐ 20 J.R. Reid	.10	.05	.01
☐ 21 Kelly Tripucka	.05	.02	.01
☐ 22 B.J. Armstrong	.15	.07	.02
☐ 23A Bill Cartwright ERR	.50	.23	.06
(No decimal points in FGP and FTP)			
☐ 23B Bill Cartwright COR	.05	.02	.01
☐ 24 Horace Grant	.15	.07	.02
☐ 25 Craig Hodges	.05	.02	.01
☐ 26 Michael Jordan UER	3.00	1.35	.40
(Led NBA in scoring 4 years, not 3)			
☐ 27 Stacey King UER	.08	.04	.01
(Comma missing between progressed and Stacy)			
☐ 28 John Paxson	.05	.02	.01
☐ 29 Will Perdue	.05	.02	.01
☐ 30 Scottie Pippen UER	.30	.14	.04
(Born AR, not AK)			
☐ 31 Brad Daugherty	.08	.04	.01
☐ 32 Craig Ehlo	.05	.02	.01
☐ 33 Danny Ferry	.15	.07	.02
☐ 34 Steve Kerr	.05	.02	.01
☐ 35 Larry Nance	.08	.04	.01
☐ 36 Mark Price UER	.10	.05	.01
(Drafted by Cleveland, should be Dallas)			
☐ 37 Hot Rod Williams	.08	.04	.01
☐ 38 Rolando Blackman	.08	.04	.01
☐ 39A Adrian Dantley ERR	.50	.23	.06
(No decimal points in FGP and FTP)			
☐ 39B Adrian Dantley COR	.10	.05	.01
☐ 40 Brad Davis	.05	.02	.01
☐ 41 James Donaldson UER	.05	.02	.01
(Text says in committed, should be is committed)			
☐ 42 Derek Harper	.08	.04	.01
☐ 43 Sam Perkins UER	.08	.04	.01
(First line of text should be intact)			
☐ 44 Bill Wennington	.05	.02	.01
☐ 45 Herb Williams	.05	.02	.01
☐ 46 Michael Adams	.05	.02	.01
☐ 47 Walter Davis	.10	.05	.01
☐ 48 Alex English UER	.10	.05	.01
(Stats missing from '76-77 through '79-80)			
☐ 49 Bill Hanzlik	.05	.02	.01
☐ 50 Lafayette Lever UER	.05	.02	.01
(Born AR, not AK)			
☐ 51 Todd Lichti	.05	.02	.01
☐ 52 Blair Rasmussen	.05	.02	.01
☐ 53 Dan Schayes	.05	.02	.01
☐ 54 Mark Aguirre	.08	.04	.01
☐ 55 Joe Dumars	.15	.07	.02
☐ 56 James Edwards	.05	.02	.01
☐ 57 Vinnie Johnson	.05	.02	.01
☐ 58 Bill Laimbeer	.08	.04	.01
☐ 59 Dennis Rodman UER	.20	.09	.03
(College misspelled as coilege on back)			
☐ 60 John Salley	.05	.02	.01
☐ 61 Isiah Thomas	.15	.07	.02
☐ 62 Manute Bol	.05	.02	.01
☐ 63 Tim Hardaway	.60	.25	.08
☐ 64 Rod Higgins	.05	.02	.01
☐ 65 Sarunas Marciulionis	.10	.05	.01
☐ 66 Chris Mullin	.10	.05	.01
☐ 67 Mitch Richmond	.25	.11	.03
☐ 68 Terry Teagle	.05	.02	.01
☐ 69 Anthony Bowie UER	.08	.04	.01
(Seasons, not seeasons)			
☐ 70 Sleepy Floyd	.05	.02	.01
☐ 71 Buck Johnson	.05	.02	.01
☐ 72 Vernon Maxwell	.05	.02	.01
☐ 73 Hakeem Olajuwon	.60	.25	.08
☐ 74 Otis Thorpe	.08	.04	.01
☐ 75 Mitchell Wiggins	.05	.02	.01
☐ 76 Vern Fleming	.05	.02	.01
☐ 77 George McCloud	.05	.02	.01
☐ 78 Reggie Miller	.30	.14	.04
☐ 79 Chuck Person	.08	.04	.01
☐ 80 Mike Sanders	.05	.02	.01
☐ 81 Detlef Schrempf	.10	.05	.01
☐ 82 Rik Smits	.05	.02	.01
☐ 83 LaSalle Thompson	.05	.02	.01
☐ 84 Benoit Benjamin	.05	.02	.01
☐ 85 Winston Garland	.05	.02	.01
☐ 86 Ron Harper	.08	.04	.01
☐ 87 Danny Manning	.15	.07	.02
☐ 88 Ken Norman	.05	.02	.01
☐ 89 Charles Smith	.05	.02	.01
☐ 90 Michael Cooper	.08	.04	.01
☐ 91 Vlade Divac	.50	.23	.06
☐ 92 A.C. Green	.10	.05	.01

□ 93 Magic Johnson	.50	.23	.06
□ 94 Byron Scott	.08	.04	.01
□ 95 Mychal Thompson UER	.05	.02	.01
(Missing '78-79 stats from Portland)			
□ 96 Orlando Woolridge	.05	.02	.01
□ 97 James Worthy	.10	.05	.01
□ 98 Sherman Douglas	.15	.07	.02
□ 99 Kevin Edwards	.05	.02	.01
□ 100 Grant Long	.05	.02	.01
□ 101 Glen Rice	.50	.23	.06
□ 102 Rony Seikaly UER	.05	.02	.01
(Ron on front)			
□ 103 Billy Thompson	.05	.02	.01
□ 104 Jeff Grayer	.05	.02	.01
□ 105 Jay Humphries	.05	.02	.01
□ 106 Ricky Pierce	.08	.04	.01
□ 107 Paul Pressey	.05	.02	.01
□ 108 Fred Roberts	.05	.02	.01
□ 109 Alvin Robertson	.05	.02	.01
□ 110 Jack Sikma	.08	.04	.01
□ 111 Randy Breuer	.05	.02	.01
□ 112 Tony Campbell	.05	.02	.01
□ 113 Tyrone Corbin	.05	.02	.01
□ 114 Sam Mitchell UER	.05	.02	.01
(Mercer University, not Mercer College)			
□ 115 Tod Murphy UER	.05	.02	.01
(Born Long Beach, not Lakewood)			
□ 116 Pooh Richardson	.15	.07	.02
□ 117 Mookie Blaylock	.40	.18	.05
□ 118 Sam Bowie	.05	.02	.01
□ 119 Lester Conner	.05	.02	.01
□ 120 Dennis Hopson	.05	.02	.01
□ 121 Chris Morris	.05	.02	.01
□ 122 Charles Shackleford	.05	.02	.01
□ 123 Purvis Short	.05	.02	.01
□ 124 Maurice Cheeks	.10	.05	.01
□ 125 Patrick Ewing	.25	.11	.03
□ 126 Mark Jackson	.05	.02	.01
□ 127A Johnny Newman ERR	.50	.23	.06
(Jr. misprinted as J. on card back)			
□ 127B Johnny Newman COR	.05	.02	.01
□ 128 Charles Oakley	.08	.04	.01
□ 129 Trent Tucker	.05	.02	.01
□ 130 Kenny Walker	.05	.02	.01
□ 131 Gerald Wilkins	.05	.02	.01
□ 132 Nick Anderson	.40	.18	.05
□ 133 Terry Catledge	.05	.02	.01
□ 134 Sidney Green	.05	.02	.01
□ 135 Otis Smith	.05	.02	.01
□ 136 Reggie Theus	.08	.04	.01
□ 137 Sam Vincent	.05	.02	.01
□ 138 Ron Anderson	.05	.02	.01
□ 139 Charles Barkley UER	.50	.23	.06
(FG Percentage .545.)			
□ 140 Scott Brooks UER	.05	.02	.01
('89-89 Philadelphia in wrong typeface)			
□ 141 Johnny Dawkins	.05	.02	.01
□ 142 Mike Gminski	.05	.02	.01
□ 143 Hersey Hawkins	.08	.04	.01
□ 144 Rick Mahorn	.05	.02	.01
□ 145 Derek Smith	.05	.02	.01
□ 146 Tom Chambers	.08	.04	.01
□ 147 Jeff Hornacek	.10	.05	.01
□ 148 Eddie Johnson	.08	.04	.01
□ 149 Kevin Johnson	.25	.11	.03
□ 150A Dan Majerle ERR	1.00	.45	.13

(Award in 1988; three-time selection)			
□ 150B Dan Majerle COR	.15	.07	.02
(Award in 1989; three-time selection)			
□ 151 Tim Perry	.05	.02	.01
□ 152 Kurt Rambis	.05	.02	.01
□ 153 Mark West	.05	.02	.01
□ 154 Clyde Drexler	.25	.11	.03
□ 155 Kevin Duckworth	.05	.02	.01
□ 156 Byron Irvin	.05	.02	.01
□ 157 Jerome Kersey	.05	.02	.01
□ 158 Terry Porter	.08	.04	.01
□ 159 Cliff Robinson	.40	.18	.05
□ 160 Buck Williams	.08	.04	.01
□ 161 Danny Young	.05	.02	.01
□ 162 Danny Ainge	.08	.04	.01
□ 163 Antoine Carr	.05	.02	.01
□ 164 Pervis Ellison	.15	.07	.02
□ 165 Rodney McCray	.05	.02	.01
□ 166 Harold Pressley	.05	.02	.01
□ 167 Wayman Tisdale	.08	.04	.01
□ 168 Willie Anderson	.05	.02	.01
□ 169 Frank Brickowski	.05	.02	.01
□ 170 Terry Cummings	.08	.04	.01
□ 171 Sean Elliott	.40	.18	.05
□ 172 David Robinson	1.00	.45	.13
□ 173 Rod Strickland	.10	.05	.01
□ 174 David Wingate	.05	.02	.01
□ 175 Dana Barros	.50	.23	.06
□ 176 Michael Cage UER	.05	.02	.01
(Born AR, not AK)			
□ 177 Dale Ellis	.08	.04	.01
□ 178 Shawn Kemp	3.00	1.35	.40
□ 179 Xavier McDaniel	.08	.04	.01
□ 180 Derrick McKey	.05	.02	.01
□ 181 Nate McMillan	.05	.02	.01
□ 182 Thurl Bailey	.05	.02	.01
□ 183 Mike Brown	.05	.02	.01
□ 184 Mark Eaton	.05	.02	.01
□ 185 Blue Edwards	.08	.04	.01
□ 186 Bob Hansen	.05	.02	.01
□ 187 Eric Leckner	.05	.02	.01
□ 188 Karl Malone	.25	.11	.03
□ 189 John Stockton	.30	.14	.04
□ 190 Mark Alarie	.05	.02	.01
□ 191 Ledell Eackles	.05	.02	.01
□ 192A Harvey Grant	1.00	.45	.13
(First name on card front in black)			
□ 192B Harvey Grant	.05	.02	.01
(First name on card front in white)			
□ 193 Tom Hammonds	.05	.02	.01
□ 194 Bernard King	.10	.05	.01
□ 195 Jeff Malone	.08	.04	.01
□ 196 Darrell Walker	.05	.02	.01
□ 197 Checklist 1-99	.05	.02	.01
□ 198 Checklist 100-198	.05	.02	.01

1990-91 Fleer All-Stars

The 12-card All-Star insert set was randomly inserted in 1990-91 Fleer 12-card packs at a rate of one in five. They were more dif-

ficult to pull from packs than previous years. However, cards from previous years were printed in much smaller quantities. The cards measure the standard size (2 1/2" by 3 1/2"). The fronts feature a color action photo, framed by a basketball hoop and net on an aqua background. An orange stripe at the top represents the bottom of the backboard and has the words "Fleer '90 All-Stars." The player's name and position are given at the bottom between stars. The backs are printed in blue and pink with white borders and have career summaries. The cards are numbered on the back.

	MINT	NRMT	EXC
COMPLETE SET (12)	8.00	3.60	1.00
COMMON CARD (1-12)	.15	.07	.02
☐ 1 Charles Barkley .... Philadelphia 76ers	1.00	.45	.13
☐ 2 Larry Bird .... Boston Celtics	1.50	.65	.19
☐ 3 Hakeem Olajuwon .... Houston Rockets	1.25	.55	.16
☐ 4 Magic Johnson .... Los Angeles Lakers	1.00	.45	.13
☐ 5 Michael Jordan .... Chicago Bulls	6.00	2.70	.75
☐ 6 Isiah Thomas .... Detroit Pistons	.25	.11	.03
☐ 7 Karl Malone .... Utah Jazz	.50	.23	.06
☐ 8 Tom Chambers .... Phoenix Suns	.15	.07	.02
☐ 9 John Stockton .... Utah Jazz	.60	.25	.08
☐ 10 David Robinson .... San Antonio Spurs	2.00	.90	.25
☐ 11 Clyde Drexler .... Portland Trail Blazers	.50	.23	.06
☐ 12 Patrick Ewing .... New York Knicks	.50	.23	.06

1990-91 Fleer Rookie Sensations

Randomly inserted in 23-card cello packs, the 1990-91 Fleer Rookie Sensations set consists of 10 cards. Cards were inserted at a rate of approximately one in five packs.

The cards measure the standard size (2 1/2" by 3 1/2"). The fronts feature color action player photos, with white and red borders on an aqua background. A basketball overlays the lower left corner of the picture, with the words "Rookie Sensation" in yellow lettering, and the player's name appearing in white lettering in the bottom red border. The backs are printed in black and red on gray background (with white borders) and present summaries of their college careers and rookie seasons. The cards are numbered on the back. The key card is David Robinson's first insert.

	MINT	NRMT	EXC
COMPLETE SET (10)	40.00	18.00	5.00
COMMON CARD (1-10)	1.00	.45	.13
☐ 1 David Robinson UER ... San Antonio Spurs (Text has 1988-90 season, should be 1989-90)	30.00	13.50	3.80
☐ 2 Sean Elliott UER .... San Antonio Spurs (Misspelled Elliot on card front)	5.00	2.30	.60
☐ 3 Glen Rice .... Miami Heat	6.00	2.70	.75
☐ 4 J.R.Reid .... Charlotte Hornets	1.00	.45	.13
☐ 5 Stacey King .... Chicago Bulls	1.00	.45	.13
☐ 6 Pooh Richardson .... Minnesota Timberwolves	2.00	.90	.25
☐ 7 Nick Anderson .... Orlando Magic	5.00	2.30	.60
☐ 8 Tim Hardaway .... Golden State Warriors	8.00	3.60	1.00
☐ 9 Vlade Divac .... Los Angeles Lakers	6.00	2.70	.75
☐ 10 Sherman Douglas .... Miami Heat	2.00	.90	.25

1990-91 Fleer Update

These cards are the same size (2 1/2" by 3 1/2") and design as the regular issue. Factory sets were distributed exclusively through hobby dealers. The set numbering is arranged alphabetically by team as fol-

lows: Atlanta Hawks (1-5), Boston Celtics (6-10), Charlotte Hornets (11-13), Chicago Bulls (14-15), Cleveland Cavaliers (16-18), Dallas Mavericks (19-23), Cleveland Cavaliers (24-27), Detroit Pistons (28-30), Golden State Warriors (31-34), Houston Rockets (35-36), Indiana Pacers (37-39), Los Angeles Clippers (40-42), Los Angeles Lakers (43-46), Miami Heat (47-50), Milwaukee Bucks (51-55), Minnesota Timberwolves (56-58), New Jersey Nets (59-62), New York Knicks (63-66), Orlando Magic (67), Philadelphia 76ers (68-73), Phoenix Suns (74-77), Portland Trail Blazers (78-81), Sacramento Kings (82-87), San Antonio Spurs (88-91), Seattle Supersonics (92-93), Utah Jazz (94-96), and Washington Bullets (97-99). The card numbers have a "U" prefix. Rookie Cards include Dee Brown, Elden Campbell, Cedric Ceballos, Derrick Coleman, Kendall Gill, Tyrone Hill, Chris Jackson, Gary Payton, Drazen Petrovic, Dennis Scott, Lionel Simmons, Loy Vaught and Doug West.

	MINT	NRMT	EXC
COMPLETE SET (100)	5.00	2.30	.60
COMMON CARD (U1-U100)	.05	.02	.01

☐ U1	Jon Koncak	.05	.02	.01
☐ U2	Tim McCormick	.05	.02	.01
☐ U3	Doc Rivers	.08	.04	.01
☐ U4	Rumeal Robinson	.05	.02	.01
☐ U5	Trevor Wilson	.05	.02	.01
☐ U6	Dee Brown	.75	.35	.09
☐ U7	Dave Popson	.05	.02	.01
☐ U8	Kevin Gamble	.05	.02	.01
☐ U9	Brian Shaw	.05	.02	.01
☐ U10	Michael Smith	.05	.02	.01
☐ U11	Kendall Gill	.60	.25	.08
☐ U12	Johnny Newman	.05	.02	.01
☐ U13	Steve Scheffler	.05	.02	.01
☐ U14	Dennis Hopson	.05	.02	.01
☐ U15	Cliff Levingston	.05	.02	.01
☐ U16	Chucky Brown	.05	.02	.01
☐ U17	John Morton	.05	.02	.01
☐ U18	Gerald Paddio	.05	.02	.01
☐ U19	Alex English	.10	.05	.01
☐ U20	Fat Lever	.05	.02	.01
☐ U21	Rodney McCray	.05	.02	.01
☐ U22	Roy Tarpley	.05	.02	.01
☐ U23	Randy White	.05	.02	.01
☐ U24	Anthony Cook	.05	.02	.01
☐ U25	Chris Jackson	.60	.25	.08
☐ U26	Marcus Liberty	.05	.02	.01
☐ U27	Orlando Woolridge	.05	.02	.01
☐ U28	William Bedford	.05	.02	.01
☐ U29	Lance Blanks	.05	.02	.01
☐ U30	Scott Hastings	.05	.02	.01
☐ U31	Tyrone Hill	1.00	.45	.13
☐ U32	Les Jepsen	.05	.02	.01
☐ U33	Steve Johnson	.05	.02	.01
☐ U34	Kevin Pritchard	.05	.02	.01
☐ U35	Dave Jamerson	.05	.02	.01
☐ U36	Kenny Smith	.05	.02	.01
☐ U37	Greg Dreiling	.05	.02	.01
☐ U38	Kenny Williams	.05	.02	.01
☐ U39	Micheal Williams UER	.05	.02	.01
☐ U40	Gary Grant	.05	.02	.01
☐ U41	Bo Kimble	.05	.02	.01
☐ U42	Loy Vaught	.75	.35	.09
☐ U43	Elden Campbell	.75	.35	.09
☐ U44	Sam Perkins	.08	.04	.01
☐ U45	Tony Smith	.05	.02	.01
☐ U46	Terry Teagle	.05	.02	.01
☐ U47	Willie Burton	.40	.18	.05
☐ U48	Bimbo Coles	.08	.04	.01
☐ U49	Terry Davis	.08	.04	.01
☐ U50	Alec Kessler	.05	.02	.01
☐ U51	Greg Anderson	.05	.02	.01
☐ U52	Frank Brickowski	.05	.02	.01
☐ U53	Steve Henson	.05	.02	.01
☐ U54	Brad Lohaus	.05	.02	.01
☐ U55	Dan Schayes	.05	.02	.01
☐ U56	Gerald Glass	.05	.02	.01
☐ U57	Felton Spencer	.05	.02	.01
☐ U58	Doug West	.40	.18	.05
☐ U59	Jud Buechler	.05	.02	.01
☐ U60	Derrick Coleman	1.50	.65	.19
☐ U61	Tate George	.05	.02	.01
☐ U62	Reggie Theus	.08	.04	.01
☐ U63	Greg Grant	.05	.02	.01
☐ U64	Jerrod Mustaf	.05	.02	.01
☐ U65	Eddie Lee Wilkins	.05	.02	.01
☐ U66	Michael Ansley	.05	.02	.01
☐ U67	Jerry Reynolds	.05	.02	.01
☐ U68	Dennis Scott	.75	.35	.09
☐ U69	Manute Bol	.05	.02	.01
☐ U70	Armon Gilliam	.05	.02	.01
☐ U71	Brian Oliver	.05	.02	.01
☐ U72	Kenny Payne	.05	.02	.01
☐ U73	Jayson Williams	.10	.05	.01
☐ U74	Kenny Battle	.05	.02	.01
☐ U75	Cedric Ceballos	1.50	.65	.19
☐ U76	Negele Knight	.05	.02	.01
☐ U77	Xavier McDaniel	.08	.04	.01
☐ U78	Alaa Abdelnaby	.05	.02	.01
☐ U79	Danny Ainge	.08	.04	.01
☐ U80	Mark Bryant	.05	.02	.01
☐ U81	Drazen Petrovic	.40	.18	.05
☐ U82	Anthony Bonner	.05	.02	.01
☐ U83	Duane Causwell	.05	.02	.01
☐ U84	Bobby Hansen	.05	.02	.01
☐ U85	Eric Leckner	.05	.02	.01
☐ U86	Travis Mays	.05	.02	.01
☐ U87	Lionel Simmons	.10	.05	.01
☐ U88	Sidney Green	.05	.02	.01
☐ U89	Tony Massenburg	.05	.02	.01
☐ U90	Paul Pressey	.05	.02	.01
☐ U91	Dwayne Schintzius	.05	.02	.01
☐ U92	Gary Payton	1.50	.65	.19
☐ U93	Olden Polynice	.05	.02	.01
☐ U94	Jeff Malone	.08	.04	.01
☐ U95	Walter Palmer	.05	.02	.01
☐ U96	Delaney Rudd	.05	.02	.01
☐ U97	Pervis Ellison	.05	.02	.01

		MINT	NRMT	EXC
☐ U98 A.J. English		.05	.02	.01
☐ U99 Greg Foster		.05	.02	.01
☐ U100 Checklist 1-100		.05	.02	.01

1991-92 Fleer

The complete 1991-92 Fleer basketball card set contains 400 cards measuring the standard size (2 1/2" by 3 1/2"). The set was distributed in two series of 240 and 160 cards, respectively. The cards were distributed in 12-card wax packs, 23-card cello packs and 36-card rack packs. Wax boxes contained 36 packs. The fronts feature color action player photos, bordered by a red stripe on the bottom, and gray and red stripes on the top. A 3/4" blue stripe checkered with black NBA logos runs the length of the card and serves as the left border of the picture. The team logo, player's name, and position are printed in white lettering in this stripe. The picture is bordered on the right side by a thin gray stripe and a thicker blue one. The backs present career summaries and are printed with black lettering on various pastel colors, superimposed over a wooden basketball floor background. The cards are numbered and checklisted below alphabetically according to teams within each series as follows: Atlanta Hawks (1-7/241-246), Boston Celtics (8-16/247-251), Charlotte Hornets (17-24/252-255), Chicago Bulls (25-33/256-259), Cleveland Cavaliers (34-41/260-265), Dallas Mavericks (42-48/266-271), Denver Nuggets (49-56/272-277), Detroit Pistons (57-64/278-283), Golden State Warriors (65-72/284-288), Houston Rockets (73-80/289-292), Indiana Pacers (81-88/293-295), L.A. Clippers (86-96/296-299), L.A. Lakers (97-104/300-304), Miami Heat (105-112/305-309), Milwaukee Bucks (113-120/310-315), Minnesota Timberwolves (121-127/316-321), New Jersey Nets (128-134/322-325), New York Knicks (135-142/326-330), Orlando Magic (143-149/331-334), Philadelphia 76ers (150-157/335-338), Phoenix Suns (158-165/339-343), Portland Trail Blazers (166-173/344-346), Sacramento Kings (174-181/347-352), San Antonio Spurs (182-188/353-356), Seattle Supersonics (189-196/357-361), Utah Jazz (197-203/362-366) and Washington Bullets (204-209/367-371). Other subsets within the set are All-Stars (210-219), League Leaders (220-226), Slam Dunk (227-232), All Star Game Highlights (233-238) and Team Leaders (372-398). Rookie Cards include Kenny Anderson, Stacey Augmon, Larry Johnson, Dikembe Mutombo, Billy Owens, Steve Smith, and John Starks.

	MINT	NRMT	EXC
COMPLETE SET (400)	10.00	4.50	1.25
COMPLETE SERIES 1 (240)	5.00	2.30	.60
COMPLETE SERIES 2 (160)	5.00	2.30	.60
COMMON CARD (1-400)	.05	.02	.01

		MINT	NRMT	EXC
☐ 1	John Battle	.05	.02	.01
☐ 2	Jon Koncak	.05	.02	.01
☐ 3	Rumeal Robinson	.05	.02	.01
☐ 4	Spud Webb	.08	.04	.01
☐ 5	Bob Weiss CO	.05	.02	.01
☐ 6	Dominique Wilkins	.15	.07	.02
☐ 7	Kevin Willis	.08	.04	.01
☐ 8	Larry Bird	.75	.35	.09
☐ 9	Dee Brown	.10	.05	.01
☐ 10	Chris Ford CO	.05	.02	.01
☐ 11	Kevin Gamble	.05	.02	.01
☐ 12	Reggie Lewis	.10	.05	.01
☐ 13	Kevin McHale	.10	.05	.01
☐ 14	Robert Parish	.10	.05	.01
☐ 15	Ed Pinckney	.05	.02	.01
☐ 16	Brian Shaw	.05	.02	.01
☐ 17	Tyrone Bogues	.10	.05	.01
☐ 18	Rex Chapman	.05	.02	.01
☐ 19	Dell Curry	.05	.02	.01
☐ 20	Kendall Gill	.08	.04	.01
☐ 21	Eric Leckner	.05	.02	.01
☐ 22	Gene Littles CO	.05	.02	.01
☐ 23	Johnny Newman	.05	.02	.01
☐ 24	J.R. Reid	.05	.02	.01
☐ 25	B.J. Armstrong	.08	.04	.01
☐ 26	Bill Cartwright	.05	.02	.01
☐ 27	Horace Grant	.15	.07	.02
☐ 28	Phil Jackson CO	.08	.04	.01
☐ 29	Michael Jordan	3.00	1.35	.40
☐ 30	Cliff Levingston	.05	.02	.01
☐ 31	John Paxson	.05	.02	.01
☐ 32	Will Perdue	.05	.02	.01
☐ 33	Scottie Pippen	.25	.11	.03
☐ 34	Brad Daugherty	.08	.04	.01
☐ 35	Craig Ehlo	.05	.02	.01
☐ 36	Danny Ferry	.05	.02	.01
☐ 37	Larry Nance	.08	.04	.01
☐ 38	Mark Price	.10	.05	.01
☐ 39	Darnell Valentine	.05	.02	.01
☐ 40	Hot Rod Williams	.08	.04	.01
☐ 41	Lenny Wilkens CO	.08	.04	.01
☐ 42	Richie Adubato CO	.05	.02	.01
☐ 43	Rolando Blackman	.08	.04	.01
☐ 44	James Donaldson	.05	.02	.01
☐ 45	Derek Harper	.08	.04	.01
☐ 46	Rodney McCray	.05	.02	.01
☐ 47	Randy White	.05	.02	.01
☐ 48	Herb Williams	.05	.02	.01
☐ 49	Chris Jackson	.08	.04	.01
☐ 50	Marcus Liberty	.05	.02	.01
☐ 51	Todd Lichti	.05	.02	.01
☐ 52	Blair Rasmussen	.05	.02	.01
☐ 53	Paul Westhead CO	.05	.02	.01
☐ 54	Reggie Williams	.05	.02	.01

☐ 55	Joe Wolf	.05	.02	.01	☐ 126	Jim Rodgers CO	.05	.02	.01
☐ 56	Orlando Woolridge	.05	.02	.01	☐ 127	Felton Spencer	.05	.02	.01
☐ 57	Mark Aguirre	.08	.04	.01	☐ 128	Mookie Blaylock	.08	.04	.01
☐ 58	Chuck Daly CO	.08	.04	.01	☐ 129	Sam Bowie	.05	.02	.01
☐ 59	Joe Dumars	.15	.07	.02	☐ 130	Derrick Coleman	.10	.05	.01
☐ 60	James Edwards	.05	.02	.01	☐ 131	Chris Dudley	.05	.02	.01
☐ 61	Vinnie Johnson	.08	.04	.01	☐ 132	Bill Fitch CO	.05	.02	.01
☐ 62	Bill Laimbeer	.08	.04	.01	☐ 133	Chris Morris	.05	.02	.01
☐ 63	Dennis Rodman	.15	.07	.02	☐ 134	Drazen Petrovic	.08	.04	.01
☐ 64	Isiah Thomas	.15	.07	.02	☐ 135	Maurice Cheeks	.10	.05	.01
☐ 65	Tim Hardaway	.05	.02	.01	☐ 136	Patrick Ewing	.25	.11	.03
☐ 66	Rod Higgins	.05	.02	.01	☐ 137	Mark Jackson	.05	.02	.01
☐ 67	Tyrone Hill	.10	.05	.01	☐ 138	Charles Oakley	.08	.04	.01
☐ 68	Sarunas Marciulionis	.05	.02	.01	☐ 139	Pat Riley CO	.08	.04	.01
☐ 69	Chris Mullin	.10	.05	.01	☐ 140	Trent Tucker	.05	.02	.01
☐ 70	Don Nelson CO	.08	.04	.01	☐ 141	Kiki Vandeweghe	.05	.02	.01
☐ 71	Mitch Richmond	.15	.07	.02	☐ 142	Gerald Wilkins	.05	.02	.01
☐ 72	Tom Tolbert	.05	.02	.01	☐ 143	Nick Anderson	.10	.05	.01
☐ 73	Don Chaney CO	.05	.02	.01	☐ 144	Terry Catledge	.05	.02	.01
☐ 74	Eric(Sleepy) Floyd	.05	.02	.01	☐ 145	Matt Guokas CO	.05	.02	.01
☐ 75	Buck Johnson	.05	.02	.01	☐ 146	Jerry Reynolds	.05	.02	.01
☐ 76	Vernon Maxwell	.05	.02	.01	☐ 147	Dennis Scott	.08	.04	.01
☐ 77	Hakeem Olajuwon	.60	.25	.08	☐ 148	Scott Skiles	.05	.02	.01
☐ 78	Kenny Smith	.05	.02	.01	☐ 149	Otis Smith	.05	.02	.01
☐ 79	Larry Smith	.05	.02	.01	☐ 150	Ron Anderson	.05	.02	.01
☐ 80	Otis Thorpe	.08	.04	.01	☐ 151	Charles Barkley	.50	.23	.06
☐ 81	Vern Fleming	.05	.02	.01	☐ 152	Johnny Dawkins	.05	.02	.01
☐ 82	Bob Hill CO	.05	.02	.01	☐ 153	Armon Gilliam	.05	.02	.01
☐ 83	Reggie Miller	.25	.11	.03	☐ 154	Hersey Hawkins	.08	.04	.01
☐ 84	Chuck Person	.08	.04	.01	☐ 155	Jim Lynam CO	.05	.02	.01
☐ 85	Detlef Schrempf	.10	.05	.01	☐ 156	Rick Mahorn	.05	.02	.01
☐ 86	Rik Smits	.10	.05	.01	☐ 157	Brian Oliver	.05	.02	.01
☐ 87	LaSalle Thompson	.05	.02	.01	☐ 158	Tom Chambers	.08	.04	.01
☐ 88	Micheal Williams	.05	.02	.01	☐ 159	Cotton Fitzsimmons CO	.05	.02	.01
☐ 89	Gary Grant	.05	.02	.01	☐ 160	Jeff Hornacek	.08	.04	.01
☐ 90	Ron Harper	.08	.04	.01	☐ 161	Kevin Johnson	.15	.07	.02
☐ 91	Bo Kimble	.05	.02	.01	☐ 162	Negele Knight	.05	.02	.01
☐ 92	Danny Manning	.10	.05	.01	☐ 163	Dan Majerle	.10	.05	.01
☐ 93	Ken Norman	.05	.02	.01	☐ 164	Xavier McDaniel	.08	.04	.01
☐ 94	Olden Polynice	.05	.02	.01	☐ 165	Mark West	.05	.02	.01
☐ 95	Mike Schuler CO	.05	.02	.01	☐ 166	Rick Adelman CO	.05	.02	.01
☐ 96	Charles Smith	.05	.02	.01	☐ 167	Danny Ainge	.08	.04	.01
☐ 97	Vlade Divac	.10	.05	.01	☐ 168	Clyde Drexler	.25	.11	.03
☐ 98	Mike Dunleavy CO	.05	.02	.01	☐ 169	Kevin Duckworth	.05	.02	.01
☐ 99	A.C. Green	.08	.04	.01	☐ 170	Jerome Kersey	.05	.02	.01
☐ 100	Magic Johnson	.50	.23	.06	☐ 171	Terry Porter	.08	.04	.01
☐ 101	Sam Perkins	.08	.04	.01	☐ 172	Clifford Robinson	.05	.02	.01
☐ 102	Byron Scott	.08	.04	.01	☐ 173	Buck Williams	.08	.04	.01
☐ 103	Terry Teagle	.05	.02	.01	☐ 174	Antoine Carr	.05	.02	.01
☐ 104	James Worthy	.10	.05	.01	☐ 175	Duane Causwell	.05	.02	.01
☐ 105	Willie Burton	.05	.02	.01	☐ 176	Jim Les	.05	.02	.01
☐ 106	Bimbo Coles	.05	.02	.01	☐ 177	Travis Mays	.05	.02	.01
☐ 107	Sherman Douglas	.05	.02	.01	☐ 178	Dick Motta CO	.05	.02	.01
☐ 108	Kevin Edwards	.05	.02	.01	☐ 179	Lionel Simmons	.05	.02	.01
☐ 109	Grant Long	.05	.02	.01	☐ 180	Rory Sparrow	.05	.02	.01
☐ 110	Kevin Loughery CO	.05	.02	.01	☐ 181	Wayman Tisdale	.08	.04	.01
☐ 111	Glen Rice	.10	.05	.01	☐ 182	Willie Anderson	.05	.02	.01
☐ 112	Rony Seikaly	.05	.02	.01	☐ 183	Larry Brown CO	.08	.04	.01
☐ 113	Frank Brickowski	.05	.02	.01	☐ 184	Terry Cummings	.08	.04	.01
☐ 114	Dale Ellis	.08	.04	.01	☐ 185	Sean Elliott	.10	.05	.01
☐ 115	Del Harris CO	.05	.02	.01	☐ 186	Paul Pressey	.05	.02	.01
☐ 116	Jay Humphries	.05	.02	.01	☐ 187	David Robinson	.60	.25	.08
☐ 117	Fred Roberts	.05	.02	.01	☐ 188	Rod Strickland	.08	.04	.01
☐ 118	Alvin Robertson	.05	.02	.01	☐ 189	Benoit Benjamin	.05	.02	.01
☐ 119	Dan Schayes	.05	.02	.01	☐ 190	Eddie Johnson	.08	.04	.01
☐ 120	Jack Sikma	.08	.04	.01	☐ 191	K.C. Jones CO	.05	.02	.01
☐ 121	Tony Campbell	.05	.02	.01	☐ 192	Shawn Kemp	1.00	.45	.13
☐ 122	Tyrone Corbin	.05	.02	.01	☐ 193	Derrick McKey	.08	.04	.01
☐ 123	Sam Mitchell	.05	.02	.01	☐ 194	Gary Payton	.10	.05	.01
☐ 124	Tod Murphy	.05	.02	.01	☐ 195	Ricky Pierce	.08	.04	.01
☐ 125	Pooh Richardson	.05	.02	.01	☐ 196	Sedale Threatt	.05	.02	.01

☐ 197	Thurl Bailey	.05	.02	.01
☐ 198	Mark Eaton	.05	.02	.01
☐ 199	Blue Edwards	.05	.02	.01
☐ 200	Jeff Malone	.08	.04	.01
☐ 201	Karl Malone	.25	.11	.03
☐ 202	Jerry Sloan CO	.05	.02	.01
☐ 203	John Stockton	.25	.11	.03
☐ 204	Ledell Eackles	.05	.02	.01
☐ 205	Pervis Ellison	.05	.02	.01
☐ 206	A.J. English	.05	.02	.01
☐ 207	Harvey Grant	.05	.02	.01
☐ 208	Bernard King	.10	.05	.01
☐ 209	Wes Unseld CO	.08	.04	.01
☐ 210	Kevin Johnson AS	.08	.04	.01
☐ 211	Michael Jordan AS	1.50	.65	.19
☐ 212	Dominique Wilkins AS	.08	.04	.01
☐ 213	Charles Barkley AS	.25	.11	.03
☐ 214	Hakeem Olajuwon AS	.30	.14	.04
☐ 215	Patrick Ewing AS	.05	.02	.01
☐ 216	Tim Hardaway AS	.05	.02	.01
☐ 217	John Stockton AS	.10	.05	.01
☐ 218	Chris Mullin AS	.05	.02	.01
☐ 219	Karl Malone AS	.10	.05	.01
☐ 220	Michael Jordan LL	1.50	.65	.19
☐ 221	John Stockton LL	.10	.05	.01
☐ 222	Alvin Robertson LL	.05	.02	.01
☐ 223	Hakeem Olajuwon LL	.30	.14	.04
☐ 224	Buck Williams LL	.05	.02	.01
☐ 225	David Robinson LL	.30	.14	.04
☐ 226	Reggie Miller LL	.10	.05	.01
☐ 227	Blue Edwards SD	.05	.02	.01
☐ 228	Dee Brown SD	.05	.02	.01
☐ 229	Rex Chapman SD	.05	.02	.01
☐ 230	Kenny Smith SD	.05	.02	.01
☐ 231	Shawn Kemp SD	.50	.23	.06
☐ 232	Kendall Gill SD	.05	.02	.01
☐ 233	'91 All Star Game	.05	.02	.01
	Enemies - A Love Story			
	(East Bench Scene)			
☐ 234	'91 All Star Game	.08	.04	.01
	A Game of Contrasts			
	(Drexler over McHale)			
☐ 235	'91 All Star Game	.05	.02	.01
	Showtime			
	(Alvin Robertson)			
☐ 236	'91 All Star Game	.10	.05	.01
	Unstoppable Force			
	vs. Unbeatable Man			
	(Ewing rejects K.Malone)			
☐ 237	'91 All Star Game	.05	.02	.01
	Just Me and the Boys			
	(Rebounding Scene)			
☐ 238	'91 All Star Game	.10	.05	.01
	Unforgettable			
	(Jordan reverse lay-in)			
☐ 239	Checklist 1-120	.05	.02	.01
☐ 240	Checklist 121-240	.05	.02	.01
☐ 241	Stacey Augmon	.40	.18	.05
☐ 242	Maurice Cheeks	.10	.05	.01
☐ 243	Paul Graham	.05	.02	.01
☐ 244	Rodney Monroe	.05	.02	.01
☐ 245	Blair Rasmussen	.05	.02	.01
☐ 246	Alexander Volkov	.05	.02	.01
☐ 247	John Bagley	.05	.02	.01
☐ 248	Rick Fox	.08	.04	.01
☐ 249	Rickey Green	.05	.02	.01
☐ 250	Joe Kleine	.05	.02	.01
☐ 251	Stojko Vrankovic	.05	.02	.01
☐ 252	Allan Bristow CO	.05	.02	.01
☐ 253	Kenny Gattison	.05	.02	.01
☐ 254	Mike Gminski	.05	.02	.01

☐ 255	Larry Johnson	1.25	.55	.16
☐ 256	Bobby Hansen	.05	.02	.01
☐ 257	Craig Hodges	.05	.02	.01
☐ 258	Stacey King	.05	.02	.01
☐ 259	Scott Williams	.05	.02	.01
☐ 260	John Battle	.05	.02	.01
☐ 261	Winston Bennett	.05	.02	.01
☐ 262	Terrell Brandon	.25	.11	.03
☐ 263	Henry James	.05	.02	.01
☐ 264	Steve Kerr	.05	.02	.01
☐ 265	Jimmy Oliver	.05	.02	.01
☐ 266	Brad Davis	.05	.02	.01
☐ 267	Terry Davis	.05	.02	.01
☐ 268	Donald Hodge	.05	.02	.01
☐ 269	Mike Iuzzolino	.05	.02	.01
☐ 270	Fat Lever	.05	.02	.01
☐ 271	Doug Smith	.05	.02	.01
☐ 272	Greg Anderson	.05	.02	.01
☐ 273	Kevin Brooks	.05	.02	.01
☐ 274	Walter Davis	.10	.05	.01
☐ 275	Winston Garland	.05	.02	.01
☐ 276	Mark Macon	.05	.02	.01
☐ 277A	Dikembe Mutombo	1.00	.45	.13
	(Fleer '91 on front)			
☐ 277B	Dikembe Mutombo	1.00	.45	.13
	(Fleer '91-92 on front)			
☐ 278	William Bedford	.05	.02	.01
☐ 279	Lance Blanks	.05	.02	.01
☐ 280	John Salley	.05	.02	.01
☐ 281	Charles Thomas	.05	.02	.01
☐ 282	Darrell Walker	.05	.02	.01
☐ 283	Orlando Woolridge	.05	.02	.01
☐ 284	Victor Alexander	.08	.04	.01
☐ 285	Vincent Askew	.05	.02	.01
☐ 286	Mario Elie	.20	.09	.03
☐ 287	Alton Lister	.05	.02	.01
☐ 288	Billy Owens	.40	.18	.05
☐ 289	Matt Bullard	.05	.02	.01
☐ 290	Carl Herrera	.15	.07	.02
☐ 291	Tree Rollins	.05	.02	.01
☐ 292	John Turner	.05	.02	.01
☐ 293	Dale Davis UER	.40	.18	.05
	(Photo on back act-			
	ually Sean Green)			
☐ 294	Sean Green	.05	.02	.01
☐ 295	Kenny Williams	.05	.02	.01
☐ 296	James Edwards	.05	.02	.01
☐ 297	LeRon Ellis	.05	.02	.01
☐ 298	Doc Rivers	.05	.02	.01
☐ 299	Loy Vaught	.10	.05	.01
☐ 300	Elden Campbell	.08	.04	.01
☐ 301	Jack Haley	.05	.02	.01
☐ 302	Keith Owens	.05	.02	.01
☐ 303	Tony Smith	.05	.02	.01
☐ 304	Sedale Threatt	.05	.02	.01
☐ 305	Keith Askins	.05	.02	.01
☐ 306	Alec Kessler	.05	.02	.01
☐ 307	John Morton	.05	.02	.01
☐ 308	Alan Ogg	.05	.02	.01
☐ 309	Steve Smith	.40	.18	.05
☐ 310	Lester Conner	.05	.02	.01
☐ 311	Jeff Grayer	.05	.02	.01
☐ 312	Frank Hamblen CO	.05	.02	.01
☐ 313	Steve Henson	.05	.02	.01
☐ 314	Larry Krystkowiak	.05	.02	.01
☐ 315	Moses Malone	.15	.07	.02
☐ 316	Thurl Bailey	.05	.02	.01
☐ 317	Randy Breuer	.05	.02	.01
☐ 318	Scott Brooks	.05	.02	.01
☐ 319	Gerald Glass	.05	.02	.01
☐ 320	Luc Longley	.10	.05	.01

☐ 321	Doug West	.05	.02	.01
☐ 322	Kenny Anderson	.60	.25	.08
☐ 323	Tate George	.05	.02	.01
☐ 324	Terry Mills	.30	.14	.04
☐ 325	Greg Anthony	.10	.05	.01
☐ 326	Anthony Mason	.40	.18	.05
☐ 327	Tim McCormick	.05	.02	.01
☐ 328	Xavier McDaniel	.08	.04	.01
☐ 329	Brian Quinnett	.05	.02	.01
☐ 330	John Starks	.30	.14	.04
☐ 331	Stanley Roberts	.08	.04	.01
☐ 332	Jeff Turner	.05	.02	.01
☐ 333	Sam Vincent	.05	.02	.01
☐ 334	Brian Williams	.05	.02	.01
☐ 335	Manute Bol	.05	.02	.01
☐ 336	Kenny Payne	.05	.02	.01
☐ 337	Charles Shackleford	.05	.02	.01
☐ 338	Jayson Williams	.05	.02	.01
☐ 339	Cedric Ceballos	.10	.05	.01
☐ 340	Andrew Lang	.05	.02	.01
☐ 341	Jerrod Mustaf	.05	.02	.01
☐ 342	Tim Perry	.05	.02	.01
☐ 343	Kurt Rambis	.05	.02	.01
☐ 344	Alaa Abdelnaby	.05	.02	.01
☐ 345	Robert Pack	.05	.02	.01
☐ 346	Danny Young	.05	.02	.01
☐ 347	Anthony Bonner	.05	.02	.01
☐ 348	Pete Chilcutt	.05	.02	.01
☐ 349	Rex Hughes CO	.05	.02	.01
☐ 350	Mitch Richmond	.15	.07	.02
☐ 351	Dwayne Schintzius	.05	.02	.01
☐ 352	Spud Webb	.08	.04	.01
☐ 353	Antoine Carr	.05	.02	.01
☐ 354	Sidney Green	.05	.02	.01
☐ 355	Vinnie Johnson	.08	.04	.01
☐ 356	Greg Sutton	.05	.02	.01
☐ 357	Dana Barros	.10	.05	.01
☐ 358	Michael Cage	.05	.02	.01
☐ 359	Marty Conlon	.05	.02	.01
☐ 360	Rich King	.05	.02	.01
☐ 361	Nate McMillan	.05	.02	.01
☐ 362	David Benoit	.20	.09	.03
☐ 363	Mike Brown	.05	.02	.01
☐ 364	Tyrone Corbin	.05	.02	.01
☐ 365	Eric Murdock	.25	.11	.03
☐ 366	Delaney Rudd	.05	.02	.01
☐ 367	Michael Adams	.05	.02	.01
☐ 368	Tom Hammonds	.05	.02	.01
☐ 369	Larry Stewart	.05	.02	.01
☐ 370	Andre Turner	.05	.02	.01
☐ 371	David Wingate	.05	.02	.01
☐ 372	Dominique Wilkins TL	.08	.04	.01
	Atlanta Hawks			
☐ 373	Larry Bird TL	.40	.18	.05
	Boston Celtics			
☐ 374	Rex Chapman TL	.05	.02	.01
	Charlotte Hornets			
☐ 375	Michael Jordan TL	1.50	.65	.19
	Chicago Bulls			
☐ 376	Brad Daugherty TL	.05	.02	.01
	Cleveland Cavaliers			
☐ 377	Derek Harper TL	.05	.02	.01
	Dallas Mavericks			
☐ 378	Dikembe Mutombo TL	.20	.09	.03
	Denver Nuggets			
☐ 379	Joe Dumars TL	.08	.04	.01
	Detroit Pistons			
☐ 380	Chris Mullin TL	.05	.02	.01
	Golden State Warriors			
☐ 381	Hakeem Olajuwon TL	.30	.14	.04
	Houston Rockets			
☐ 382	Chuck Person TL	.05	.02	.01
	Indiana Pacers			
☐ 383	Charles Smith TL	.05	.02	.01
	Los Angeles Clippers			
☐ 384	James Worthy TL	.05	.02	.01
	Los Angeles Lakers			
☐ 385	Glen Rice TL	.05	.02	.01
	Miami Heat			
☐ 386	Alvin Robertson TL	.05	.02	.01
	Milwaukee Bucks			
☐ 387	Tony Campbell TL	.05	.02	.01
	Minnesota Timberwolves			
☐ 388	Derrick Coleman TL	.05	.02	.01
	New Jersey Nets			
☐ 389	Patrick Ewing TL	.10	.05	.01
	New York Knicks			
☐ 390	Scott Skiles TL	.05	.02	.01
	Orlando Magic			
☐ 391	Charles Barkley TL	.25	.11	.03
	Philadelphia 76ers			
☐ 392	Kevin Johnson TL	.08	.04	.01
	Phoenix Suns			
☐ 393	Clyde Drexler TL	.10	.05	.01
	Portland Trail Blazers			
☐ 394	Lionel Simmons TL	.05	.02	.01
	Sacramento Kings			
☐ 395	David Robinson TL	.30	.14	.04
	San Antonio Spurs			
☐ 396	Ricky Pierce TL	.05	.02	.01
	Seattle Supersonics			
☐ 397	John Stockton TL	.10	.05	.01
	Utah Jazz			
☐ 398	Michael Adams TL	.05	.02	.01
	Washington Bullets			
☐ 399	Checklist	.05	.02	.01
☐ 400	Checklist	.05	.02	.01

1991-92 Fleer Dikembe Mutombo

This 12-card set was randomly inserted in 1991-92 Fleer second series 12-card wax packs at a rate of approximately one in six. The set highlights the accomplishments of the Denver Nuggets' Dikembe Mutombo. The cards measure the standard size (2 1/2" by 3 1/2"). The front borders are dark red and checkered with miniature black NBA logos. The background of the color action photo is ghosted so that the featured player stands out, and the color of the lettering on the front is mustard. On a pink background, the back has a color close-up photo and a summary of the player's performance. The cards are numbered on the back. Mutombo autographed over 2,000 of these cards which were also randomly inserted into packs. Those cards inserted in packs feature embossed Fleer logos for authenticity.

	MINT	NRMT	EXC
COMPLETE SET (12)	5.00	2.30	.60
COMMON MUTOMBO (1-12)	.50	.23	.06
☐ 1 Dikembe Mutombo Childhood in Zaire	.50	.23	.06
☐ 2 Dikembe Mutombo Georgetown Start	.50	.23	.06
☐ 3 Dikembe Mutombo Arrival on college scene	.50	.23	.06
☐ 4 Dikembe Mutombo Capping college career	.50	.23	.06
☐ 5 Dikembe Mutombo NBA Draft	.50	.23	.06
☐ 6 Dikembe Mutombo First NBA games	.50	.23	.06
☐ 7 Dikembe Mutombo Offensive skills	.50	.23	.06
☐ 8 Dikembe Mutombo What he has meant to the Nuggets	.50	.23	.06
☐ 9 Dikembe Mutombo Work Habits	.50	.23	.06
☐ 10 Dikembe Mutombo Charmed Denver	.50	.23	.06
☐ 11 Dikembe Mutombo The Future	.50	.23	.06
☐ 12 Dikembe Mutombo The Mutombo Legend	.50	.23	.06
☐ AU Dikembe Mutombo (Certified autograph)	90.00	40.00	11.50

1991-92 Fleer Pro-Visions

This six-card set measures the standard size (2 1/2" by 3 1/2") and showcases outstanding NBA players. The set was distributed as a random insert in 1991-92 Fleer first series 12-card plastic-wrap packs at a rate of approximately one per six packs. The fronts feature a color player portrait by sports artist Terry Smith. The portrait is bordered on all sides by white, with the play-

er's name in red lettering below the picture. The backs present biographical information and career summary in black lettering on a color background (with white borders). The cards are numbered on the back.

	MINT	NRMT	EXC
COMPLETE SET (6)	5.00	2.30	.60
COMMON CARD (1-6)	.30	.14	.04
☐ 1 David Robinson San Antonio Spurs	.75	.35	.09
☐ 2 Michael Jordan Chicago Bulls	4.00	1.80	.50
☐ 3 Charles Barkley Philadelphia 76ers	.60	.25	.08
☐ 4 Patrick Ewing New York Knicks	.30	.14	.04
☐ 5 Karl Malone Utah Jazz	.30	.14	.04
☐ 6 Magic Johnson Los Angeles Lakers	.60	.25	.08

1991-92 Fleer Rookie Sensations

This 10-card set showcases outstanding rookies from the 1990-91 season and measures the standard size (2 1/2" by 3 1/2"). The set was distributed as a random insert in 1991-92 Fleer 23-card cello packs at a rate of approximately two in every three packs. The card fronts feature a color player photo inside a basketball rim and net. The picture is bordered in magenta on all sides. The words "Rookie Sensations" appear above the picture, and player information is given below the picture. An orange basketball with the words "Fleer '91" appears in the upper left corner on both sides of the card. The back has a magenta border and includes highlights of the player's rookie season. The cards are numbered on the back.

	MINT	NRMT	EXC
COMPLETE SET (10)	12.00	5.50	1.50
COMMON CARD (1-10)	.50	.23	.06
☐ 1 Lionel Simmons	.50	.23	.06
☐ 2 Dennis Scott	2.00	.90	.25
☐ 3 Derrick Coleman	4.00	1.80	.50

		MINT	NRMT	EXC
☐ 4	Kendall Gill	2.00	.90	.25
☐ 5	Travis Mays	.50	.23	.06
☐ 6	Felton Spencer	1.00	.45	.13
☐ 7	Willie Burton	.50	.23	.06
☐ 8	Chris Jackson	1.50	.65	.19
☐ 9	Gary Payton	4.00	1.80	.50
☐ 10	Dee Brown	2.50	1.15	.30

1991-92 Fleer Schoolyard

This six-card set of "Schoolyard Stars" measures the standard size (2 1/2" by 3 1/2"). The set was distributed only in 1991-92 Fleer 36-card rack packs at a rate of one per pack. The card front features color action player photos. The photos are bordered on the left and bottom by a black stripe and a broken pink stripe. Yellow stripes traverse the card top and bottom, and the background is a gray cement-colored design. The back has a similar layout and presents a basketball tip in black lettering on white. The cards are numbered on the back.

	MINT	NRMT	EXC
COMPLETE SET (6)	12.00	5.50	1.50
COMMON CARD (1-6)	.75	.35	.09

		MINT	NRMT	EXC
☐ 1	Chris Mullin Golden State Warriors	1.50	.65	.19
☐ 2	Isiah Thomas Detroit Pistons	3.00	1.35	.40
☐ 3	Kevin McHale Boston Celtics	1.50	.65	.19
☐ 4	Kevin Johnson Phoenix Suns	4.00	1.80	.50
☐ 5	Karl Malone Utah Jazz	6.00	2.70	.75
☐ 6	Alvin Robertson Milwaukee Bucks	.75	.35	.09

1991-92 Fleer Dominique Wilkins

Cards from this 12-card insert set were randomly inserted in 1991-92 Fleer second series 12-card wax packs at a rate of

approximately one per six. The set highlights the career of superstar Dominique Wilkins. The cards measure the standard size (2 1/2" by 3 1/2"). The front borders are dark red and checkered with miniature black NBA logos. The background of the color action photo is ghosted so that the featured player stands out, and the color of the lettering on the front is mustard. On a pink background, the back has a color close-up photo and a summary of the player's performance. The cards are numbered on the back. Wilkins personally autographed over 2,000 of these cards which were also randomly inserted in packs. Those cards inserted in packs feature embossed Fleer logos for authenticity.

	MINT	NRMT	EXC
COMPLETE SET (12)	4.00	1.80	.50
COMMON D.WILKINS (1-12)	.40	.18	.05

		MINT	NRMT	EXC
☐ 1	Dominique Wilkins Overview	.40	.18	.05
☐ 2	Dominique Wilkins College	.40	.18	.05
☐ 3	Dominique Wilkins Early years	.40	.18	.05
☐ 4	Dominique Wilkins Early Career	.40	.18	.05
☐ 5	Dominique Wilkins Dominique Emerges	.40	.18	.05
☐ 6	Dominique Wilkins Another milestone	.40	.18	.05
☐ 7	Dominique Wilkins Wilkins continues to shine	.40	.18	.05
☐ 8	Dominique Wilkins Best all-round season	.40	.18	.05
☐ 9	Dominique Wilkins Charitable Causes	.40	.18	.05
☐ 10	Dominique Wilkins Durability	.40	.18	.05
☐ 11	Dominique Wilkins Career Numbers	.40	.18	.05
☐ 12	Dominique Wilkins Future	.40	.18	.05
☐ AU	Dominique Wilkins (Certified autograph)	90.00	40.00	11.50

1992-93 Fleer

The complete 1992-93 Fleer basketball set contains 444 standard-size (2 1/2" by 3

1/2"). cards. The set was distributed in two series of 264 and 180 cards, respectively. First series cards were distributed in 17-card plastic-wrap packs, 32-card cello packs, and 42-card rack packs. Second series cards were distributed in 15-card plastic-wrap packs and 32-card cello packs. The fronts display color action player photos, enclosed by metallic bronze borders and accented on the right by two pebble-grain colored stripes. On a tan pebble-grain background, the horizontally oriented backs have a color close-up photo in the shape of the lane under the basket. Biography, career statistics, and player profile are included on the backs. The cards are numbered on the back and checklisted below alphabetically according to teams as follows: Atlanta Hawks (1-9/301-304), Boston Celtics (10-19/305-307), Charlotte Hornets (20-27/308-312), Chicago Bulls (28-37/313-316), Cleveland Cavaliers (38-46/317-320), Dallas Mavericks (47-53/321-326), Denver Nuggets (54-61/327-332), Detroit Pistons (62-71/333-337), Golden State Warriors (72-79/338-343), Houston Rockets (80-87/344-348), Indiana Pacers (88-96/349-354), Los Angeles Clippers (97-105/355-361), Los Angeles Lakers (106-114/362-365), Miami Heat (115-123/366-370), Milwaukee Bucks (124-130/371-377), Minnesota Timberwolves (131-139/378-384), New Jersey Nets (140-147/385-391), New York Knicks (148-157/392-398), Orlando Magic (158-165/399-403), Philadelphia 76ers (166-176/404-409), Phoenix Suns (177-184/410-414), Portland Trail Blazers (185-193/415-420), Sacramento Kings (194-200/421-424), San Antonio Spurs (201-208/425-429), Seattle Supersonics (209-217/430/431), Utah Jazz (218-227/432-436) and Washington Bullets (228-237/4367-442). Subsets include League Leaders (238-245), Award Winners (246-249), Pro-Visions (250-255), Schoolyard Stars (256-264) and Slam Dunk (265-300). The Slam Dunk subset is divided into five categories: Power, Grace, Champions, Little Big Men, and Great Defenders. Randomly inserted throughout the packs were more than 3,000 (Slam Dunk subset) cards signed by former NBA players Darryl Dawkins and Kenny Walker as well as by current NBA star Shawn Kemp. According to Fleer's advertising material, odds of finding a signed Slam Dunk card are one in 5,000 packs. Rookie

Cards include LaPhonso Ellis, Tom Gugliotta, Robert Horry, Christian Laettner, Don McLean, Harold Miner, Alonzo Mourning, Shaquille O'Neal, Latrell Sprewell, Clarence Weatherspoon and Walt Williams. A second series mail-in offer featuring an "All-Star Slam Dunk Team" card and an issue of Inside Stuff was available (expiring 6/30/93) in return for ten second series wrappers plus a dollar.

		MINT	NRMT	EXC
	COMPLETE SET (444)	30.00	13.50	3.80
	COMPLETE SERIES 1 (264)	10.00	4.50	1.25
	COMPLETE SERIES 2 (180)	20.00	9.00	2.50
	COMMON CARD (1-444)	.05	.02	.01
☐ 1	Stacey Augmon	.10	.05	.01
☐ 2	Duane Ferrell	.05	.02	.01
☐ 3	Paul Graham	.05	.02	.01
☐ 4A	Jon Koncak	.08	.04	.01
	(Shooting pose on back)			
☐ 4B	Jon Koncak	.08	.04	.01
	(No ball visible			
	in photo on back)			
☐ 5	Blair Rasmussen	.05	.02	.01
☐ 6	Rumeal Robinson	.05	.02	.01
☐ 7	Bob Weiss CO	.05	.02	.01
☐ 8	Dominique Wilkins	.15	.07	.02
☐ 9	Kevin Willis	.08	.04	.01
☐ 10	John Bagley	.05	.02	.01
☐ 11	Larry Bird	1.00	.45	.13
☐ 12	Dee Brown	.08	.04	.01
☐ 13	Chris Ford CO	.05	.02	.01
☐ 14	Rick Fox	.05	.02	.01
☐ 15	Kevin Gamble	.05	.02	.01
☐ 16	Reggie Lewis	.10	.05	.01
☐ 17	Kevin McHale	.10	.05	.01
☐ 18	Robert Parish	.10	.05	.01
☐ 19	Ed Pinckney	.05	.02	.01
☐ 20	Muggsy Bogues	.10	.05	.01
☐ 21	Allan Bristow CO	.05	.02	.01
☐ 22	Dell Curry	.05	.02	.01
☐ 23	Kenny Gattison	.05	.02	.01
☐ 24	Kendall Gill	.05	.02	.01
☐ 25	Larry Johnson	.50	.23	.06
☐ 26	Johnny Newman	.05	.02	.01
☐ 27	J.R. Reid	.05	.02	.01
☐ 28	B.J. Armstrong	.05	.02	.01
☐ 29	Bill Cartwright	.05	.02	.01
☐ 30	Horace Grant	.15	.07	.02
☐ 31	Phil Jackson CO	.08	.04	.01
☐ 32	Michael Jordan	4.00	1.80	.50
☐ 33	Stacey King	.05	.02	.01
☐ 34	Cliff Levingston	.05	.02	.01
☐ 35	John Paxson	.05	.02	.01
☐ 36	Scottie Pippen	.30	.14	.04
☐ 37	Scott Williams	.05	.02	.01
☐ 38	John Battle	.05	.02	.01
☐ 39	Terrell Brandon	.08	.04	.01
☐ 40	Brad Daugherty	.08	.04	.01
☐ 41	Craig Ehlo	.05	.02	.01
☐ 42	Larry Nance	.08	.04	.01
☐ 43	Mark Price	.10	.05	.01
☐ 44	Mike Sanders	.05	.02	.01
☐ 45	Lenny Wilkens CO	.08	.04	.01
☐ 46	John Hot Rod Williams	.08	.04	.01
☐ 47	Richie Adubato CO	.05	.02	.01
☐ 48	Terry Davis	.05	.02	.01
☐ 49	Derek Harper	.08	.04	.01
☐ 50	Donald Hodge	.05	.02	.01

☐ 51	Mike Iuzzolino	.05	.02	.01
☐ 52	Rodney McCray	.05	.02	.01
☐ 53	Doug Smith	.05	.02	.01
☐ 54	Greg Anderson	.05	.02	.01
☐ 55	Winston Garland	.05	.02	.01
☐ 56	Dan Issel CO	.08	.04	.01
☐ 57	Chris Jackson	.08	.04	.01
☐ 58	Marcus Liberty	.05	.02	.01
☐ 59	Mark Macon	.05	.02	.01
☐ 60	Dikembe Mutombo	.40	.18	.05
☐ 61	Reggie Williams	.05	.02	.01
☐ 62	Mark Aguirre	.08	.04	.01
☐ 63	Joe Dumars	.15	.07	.02
☐ 64	Bill Laimbeer	.08	.04	.01
☐ 65	Olden Polynice	.05	.02	.01
☐ 66	Dennis Rodman	.20	.09	.03
☐ 67	Ron Rothstein CO	.05	.02	.01
☐ 68	John Salley	.05	.02	.01
☐ 69	Isiah Thomas	.15	.07	.02
☐ 70	Darrell Walker	.05	.02	.01
☐ 71	Orlando Woolridge	.05	.02	.01
☐ 72	Victor Alexander	.05	.02	.01
☐ 73	Mario Elie	.05	.02	.01
☐ 74	Tim Hardaway	.10	.05	.01
☐ 75	Tyrone Hill	.08	.04	.01
☐ 76	Sarunas Marciulionis	.05	.02	.01
☐ 77	Chris Mullin	.10	.05	.01
☐ 78	Don Nelson CO	.08	.04	.01
☐ 79	Billy Owens	.10	.05	.01
☐ 80	Sleepy Floyd UER	.05	.02	.01
	(Went past 4000 assist mark, not 2000)			
☐ 81	Avery Johnson	.05	.02	.01
☐ 82	Buck Johnson	.05	.02	.01
☐ 83	Vernon Maxwell	.05	.02	.01
☐ 84	Hakeem Olajuwon	.75	.35	.09
☐ 85	Kenny Smith	.05	.02	.01
☐ 86	Otis Thorpe	.08	.04	.01
☐ 87	Rudy Tomjanovich CO	.10	.05	.01
☐ 88	Dale Davis	.10	.05	.01
☐ 89	Vern Fleming	.05	.02	.01
☐ 90	Bob Hill CO	.05	.02	.01
☐ 91	Reggie Miller	.30	.14	.04
☐ 92	Chuck Person	.08	.04	.01
☐ 93	Detlef Schrempf	.10	.05	.01
☐ 94	Rik Smits	.10	.05	.01
☐ 95	LaSalle Thompson	.05	.02	.01
☐ 96	Micheal Williams	.05	.02	.01
☐ 97	Larry Brown CO	.08	.04	.01
☐ 98	James Edwards	.05	.02	.01
☐ 99	Gary Grant	.05	.02	.01
☐ 100	Ron Harper	.08	.04	.01
☐ 101	Danny Manning	.10	.05	.01
☐ 102	Ken Norman	.05	.02	.01
☐ 103	Doc Rivers	.05	.02	.01
☐ 104	Charles Smith	.05	.02	.01
☐ 105	Loy Vaught	.08	.04	.01
☐ 106	Elden Campbell	.05	.02	.01
☐ 107	Vlade Divac	.10	.05	.01
☐ 108	A.C. Green	.05	.02	.01
☐ 109	Sam Perkins	.08	.04	.01
☐ 110	Randy Pfund CO	.05	.02	.01
☐ 111	Byron Scott	.08	.04	.01
☐ 112	Terry Teagle	.05	.02	.01
☐ 113	Sedale Threatt	.05	.02	.01
☐ 114	James Worthy	.10	.05	.01
☐ 115	Willie Burton	.05	.02	.01
☐ 116	Bimbo Coles	.05	.02	.01
☐ 117	Kevin Edwards	.05	.02	.01
☐ 118	Grant Long	.05	.02	.01
☐ 119	Kevin Loughery CO	.05	.02	.01
☐ 120	Glen Rice	.10	.05	.01
☐ 121	Rony Seikaly	.05	.02	.01
☐ 122	Brian Shaw	.05	.02	.01
☐ 123	Steve Smith	.10	.05	.01
☐ 124	Frank Brickowski	.05	.02	.01
☐ 125	Mike Dunleavy CO	.05	.02	.01
☐ 126	Blue Edwards	.05	.02	.01
☐ 127	Moses Malone	.15	.07	.02
☐ 128	Eric Murdock	.05	.02	.01
☐ 129	Fred Roberts	.05	.02	.01
☐ 130	Alvin Robertson	.05	.02	.01
☐ 131	Thurl Bailey	.05	.02	.01
☐ 132	Tony Campbell	.05	.02	.01
☐ 133	Gerald Glass	.05	.02	.01
☐ 134	Luc Longley	.05	.02	.01
☐ 135	Sam Mitchell	.05	.02	.01
☐ 136	Pooh Richardson	.05	.02	.01
☐ 137	Jimmy Rodgers CO	.05	.02	.01
☐ 138	Felton Spencer	.05	.02	.01
☐ 139	Doug West	.05	.02	.01
☐ 140	Kenny Anderson	.25	.11	.03
☐ 141	Mookie Blaylock	.08	.04	.01
☐ 142	Sam Bowie	.05	.02	.01
☐ 143	Derrick Coleman	.10	.05	.01
☐ 144	Chuck Daly CO	.08	.04	.01
☐ 145	Terry Mills	.08	.04	.01
☐ 146	Chris Morris	.05	.02	.01
☐ 147	Drazen Petrovic	.08	.04	.01
☐ 148	Greg Anthony	.05	.02	.01
☐ 149	Rolando Blackman	.08	.04	.01
☐ 150	Patrick Ewing	.30	.14	.04
☐ 151	Mark Jackson	.05	.02	.01
☐ 152	Anthony Mason	.10	.05	.01
☐ 153	Xavier McDaniel	.08	.04	.01
☐ 154	Charles Oakley	.08	.04	.01
☐ 155	Pat Riley CO	.08	.04	.01
☐ 156	John Starks	.10	.05	.01
☐ 157	Gerald Wilkins	.05	.02	.01
☐ 158	Nick Anderson	.08	.04	.01
☐ 159	Anthony Bowie	.05	.02	.01
☐ 160	Terry Catledge	.05	.02	.01
☐ 161	Matt Guokas CO	.05	.02	.01
☐ 162	Stanley Roberts	.05	.02	.01
☐ 163	Dennis Scott	.05	.02	.01
☐ 164	Scott Skiles	.05	.02	.01
☐ 165	Brian Williams	.05	.02	.01
☐ 166	Ron Anderson	.05	.02	.01
☐ 167	Manute Bol	.05	.02	.01
☐ 168	Johnny Dawkins	.05	.02	.01
☐ 169	Armon Gilliam	.05	.02	.01
☐ 170	Hersey Hawkins	.08	.04	.01
☐ 171	Jeff Hornacek	.08	.04	.01
☐ 172	Andrew Lang	.05	.02	.01
☐ 173	Doug Moe CO	.05	.02	.01
☐ 174	Tim Perry	.05	.02	.01
☐ 175	Jeff Ruland	.05	.02	.01
☐ 176	Charles Shackleford	.05	.02	.01
☐ 177	Danny Ainge	.08	.04	.01
☐ 178	Charles Barkley	.60	.25	.08
☐ 179	Cedric Ceballos	.10	.05	.01
☐ 180	Tom Chambers	.08	.04	.01
☐ 181	Kevin Johnson	.15	.07	.02
☐ 182	Dan Majerle	.08	.04	.01
☐ 183	Mark West UER	.05	.02	.01
	(Needs 33 blocks to reach 1000, not 31)			
☐ 184	Paul Westphal CO	.05	.02	.01
☐ 185	Rick Adelman CO	.05	.02	.01
☐ 186	Clyde Drexler	.30	.14	.04
☐ 187	Kevin Duckworth	.05	.02	.01
☐ 188	Jerome Kersey	.05	.02	.01

☐ 189	Robert Pack	.05	.02	.01
☐ 190	Terry Porter	.08	.04	.01
☐ 191	Clifford Robinson	.10	.05	.01
☐ 192	Rod Strickland	.08	.04	.01
☐ 193	Buck Williams	.08	.04	.01
☐ 194	Anthony Bonner	.05	.02	.01
☐ 195	Duane Causwell	.05	.02	.01
☐ 196	Mitch Richmond	.15	.07	.02
☐ 197	Garry St. Jean CO	.05	.02	.01
☐ 198	Lionel Simmons	.05	.02	.01
☐ 199	Wayman Tisdale	.08	.04	.01
☐ 200	Spud Webb	.08	.04	.01
☐ 201	Willie Anderson	.05	.02	.01
☐ 202	Antoine Carr	.05	.02	.01
☐ 203	Terry Cummings	.08	.04	.01
☐ 204	Sean Elliott	.08	.04	.01
☐ 205	Dale Ellis	.08	.04	.01
☐ 206	Vinnie Johnson	.08	.04	.01
☐ 207	David Robinson	.60	.25	.08
☐ 208	Jerry Tarkanian CO	.15	.07	.02
☐ 209	Benoit Benjamin	.05	.02	.01
☐ 210	Michael Cage	.05	.02	.01
☐ 211	Eddie Johnson	.08	.04	.01
☐ 212	George Karl CO	.05	.02	.01
☐ 213	Shawn Kemp	.75	.35	.09
☐ 214	Derrick McKey	.08	.04	.01
☐ 215	Nate McMillan	.05	.02	.01
☐ 216	Gary Payton	.10	.05	.01
☐ 217	Ricky Pierce	.08	.04	.01
☐ 218	David Benoit	.05	.02	.01
☐ 219	Mike Brown	.05	.02	.01
☐ 220	Tyrone Corbin	.05	.02	.01
☐ 221	Mark Eaton	.05	.02	.01
☐ 222	Jay Humphries	.05	.02	.01
☐ 223	Larry Krystkowiak	.05	.02	.01
☐ 224	Jeff Malone	.08	.04	.01
☐ 225	Karl Malone	.30	.14	.04
☐ 226	Jerry Sloan CO	.05	.02	.01
☐ 227	John Stockton	.30	.14	.04
☐ 228	Michael Adams	.05	.02	.01
☐ 229	Rex Chapman	.05	.02	.01
☐ 230	Ledell Eackles	.05	.02	.01
☐ 231	Pervis Ellison	.05	.02	.01
☐ 232	A.J. English	.05	.02	.01
☐ 233	Harvey Grant	.05	.02	.01
☐ 234	LaBradford Smith	.05	.02	.01
☐ 235	Larry Stewart	.05	.02	.01
☐ 236	Wes Unseld CO	.08	.04	.01
☐ 237	David Wingate	.05	.02	.01
☐ 238	Michael Jordan LL	2.00	.90	.25
	Scoring			
☐ 239	Dennis Rodman LL	.08	.04	.01
	Rebounding			
☐ 240	John Stockton LL	.10	.05	.01
	Assists/Steals			
☐ 241	Buck Williams LL	.05	.02	.01
	Field Goal Percentage			
☐ 242	Mark Price LL	.05	.02	.01
	Free Throw Percentage			
☐ 243	Dana Barros LL	.05	.02	.01
	Three Point Percentage			
☐ 244	David Robinson LL	.30	.14	.04
	Shots Blocked			
☐ 245	Chris Mullin LL	.05	.02	.01
	Minutes Played			
☐ 246	Michael Jordan MVP	2.00	.90	.25
☐ 247	Larry Johnson ROY UER	.25	.11	.03
	(Scoring average was 19.2, not 19.7)			
☐ 248	David Robinson	.30	.14	.04
	Defensive Player			

	of the Year			
☐ 249	Detlef Schrempf	.05	.02	.01
	Sixth Man of the Year			
☐ 250	Clyde Drexler PV	.10	.05	.01
☐ 251	Tim Hardaway PV	.05	.02	.01
☐ 252	Kevin Johnson PV	.08	.04	.01
☐ 253	Larry Johnson PV UER	.25	.11	.03
	(Scoring average was 19.2, not 19.7)			
☐ 254	Scottie Pippen PV	.10	.05	.01
☐ 255	Isiah Thomas PV	.08	.04	.01
☐ 256	Larry Bird SY	.50	.23	.06
☐ 257	Brad Daugherty SY	.05	.02	.01
☐ 258	Kevin Johnson SY	.08	.04	.01
☐ 259	Larry Johnson SY	.25	.11	.03
☐ 260	Scottie Pippen SY	.10	.05	.01
☐ 261	Dennis Rodman SY	.08	.04	.01
☐ 262	Checklist 1	.05	.02	.01
☐ 263	Checklist 2	.05	.02	.01
☐ 264	Checklist 3	.05	.02	.01
☐ 265	Charles Barkley SD	.30	.14	.04
☐ 266	Shawn Kemp SD	.40	.18	.05
	Seattle Supersonics			
☐ 267	Dan Majerle SD	.05	.02	.01
	Phoenix Suns			
☐ 268	Karl Malone SD	.10	.05	.01
	Utah Jazz			
☐ 269	Buck Williams SD	.05	.02	.01
	Portland Trail Blazers			
☐ 270	Clyde Drexler SD	.10	.05	.01
	Portland Trail Blazers			
☐ 271	Sean Elliott SD	.05	.02	.01
	San Antonio Spurs			
☐ 272	Ron Harper SD	.05	.02	.01
	Los Angeles Clippers			
☐ 273	Michael Jordan SD	2.00	.90	.25
	Chicago Bulls			
☐ 274	James Worthy SD	.05	.02	.01
	Los Angeles Lakers			
☐ 275	Cedric Ceballos SD	.05	.02	.01
	Phoenix Suns			
☐ 276	Larry Nance SD	.05	.02	.01
☐ 277	Kenny Walker SD	.05	.02	.01
	New York Knicks			
☐ 278	Spud Webb SD	.05	.02	.01
☐ 279	Dominique Wilkins SD	.08	.04	.01
	Atlanta Hawks			
☐ 280	Terrell Brandon SD	.05	.02	.01
	Cleveland Cavaliers			
☐ 281	Dee Brown SD	.05	.02	.01
	Boston Celtics			
☐ 282	Kevin Johnson SD	.08	.04	.01
	Phoenix Suns			
☐ 283	Doc Rivers SD	.05	.02	.01
☐ 284	Byron Scott SD	.05	.02	.01
	Los Angeles Lakers			
☐ 285	Manute Bol SD	.05	.02	.01
	Philadelphia 76ers			
☐ 286	Dikembe Mutombo SD	.20	.09	.03
	Denver Nuggets			
☐ 287	Robert Parish SD	.05	.02	.01
	Boston Celtics			
☐ 288	David Robinson SD	.30	.14	.04
	San Antonio Spurs			
☐ 289	Dennis Rodman SD	.08	.04	.01
	Detroit Pistons			
☐ 290	Blue Edwards SD	.05	.02	.01
☐ 291	Patrick Ewing SD	.10	.05	.01
	New York Knicks			
☐ 292	Larry Johnson SD	.25	.11	.03
	Charlotte Hornets			

☐ 293	Jerome Kersey SD .... Portland Trail Blazers	.05	.02	.01
☐ 294	Hakeem Olajuwon SD .. Houston Rockets	.40	.18	.05
☐ 295	Stacey Augmon SD .... Atlanta Hawks	.05	.02	.01
☐ 296	Derrick Coleman SD ..... New Jersey Nets	.05	.02	.01
☐ 297	Kendall Gill SD .... Charlotte Hornets	.05	.02	.01
☐ 298	Shaquille O'Neal SD ... Orlando Magic	2.50	1.15	.30
☐ 299	Scottie Pippen SD .... Chicago Bulls	.10	.05	.01
☐ 300	Darryl Dawkins SD........ Philadelphia 76ers	.05	.02	.01
☐ 301	Mookie Blaylock	.08	.04	.01
☐ 302	Adam Keefe	.15	.07	.02
☐ 303	Travis Mays	.05	.02	.01
☐ 304	Morlon Wiley	.05	.02	.01
☐ 305	Sherman Douglas	.05	.02	.01
☐ 306	Joe Kleine	.05	.02	.01
☐ 307	Xavier McDaniel	.08	.04	.01
☐ 308	Tony Bennett	.05	.02	.01
☐ 309	Tom Hammonds	.05	.02	.01
☐ 310	Kevin Lynch	.05	.02	.01
☐ 311	Alonzo Mourning	2.00	.90	.25
☐ 312	David Wingate	.05	.02	.01
☐ 313	Rodney McCray	.05	.02	.01
☐ 314	Will Perdue	.05	.02	.01
☐ 315	Trent Tucker	.05	.02	.01
☐ 316	Corey Williams	.05	.02	.01
☐ 317	Danny Ferry	.05	.02	.01
☐ 318	Jay Guidinger	.05	.02	.01
☐ 319	Jerome Lane	.05	.02	.01
☐ 320	Gerald Wilkins	.05	.02	.01
☐ 321	Stephen Bardo	.05	.02	.01
☐ 322	Walter Bond	.05	.02	.01
☐ 323	Brian Howard	.05	.02	.01
☐ 324	Tracy Moore	.05	.02	.01
☐ 325	Sean Rooks	.08	.04	.01
☐ 326	Randy White	.05	.02	.01
☐ 327	Kevin Brooks	.05	.02	.01
☐ 328	LaPhonso Ellis	.30	.14	.04
☐ 329	Scott Hastings	.05	.02	.01
☐ 330	Todd Lichti	.05	.02	.01
☐ 331	Robert Pack	.05	.02	.01
☐ 332	Bryant Stith	.25	.11	.03
☐ 333	Gerald Glass	.05	.02	.01
☐ 334	Terry Mills	.08	.04	.01
☐ 335	Isaiah Morris	.05	.02	.01
☐ 336	Mark Randall	.05	.02	.01
☐ 337	Danny Young	.05	.02	.01
☐ 338	Chris Gatling	.05	.02	.01
☐ 339	Jeff Grayer	.05	.02	.01
☐ 340	Byron Houston	.05	.02	.01
☐ 341	Keith Jennings	.05	.02	.01
☐ 342	Alton Lister	.05	.02	.01
☐ 343	Latrell Sprewell	2.00	.90	.25
☐ 344	Scott Brooks	.05	.02	.01
☐ 345	Matt Bullard	.05	.02	.01
☐ 346	Carl Herrera	.05	.02	.01
☐ 347	Robert Horry	.75	.35	.09
☐ 348	Tree Rollins	.05	.02	.01
☐ 349	Greg Dreiling	.05	.02	.01
☐ 350	George McCloud	.05	.02	.01
☐ 351	Sam Mitchell	.05	.02	.01
☐ 352	Pooh Richardson	.05	.02	.01
☐ 353	Malik Sealy	.20	.09	.03
☐ 354	Kenny Williams	.05	.02	.01
☐ 355	Jaren Jackson	.05	.02	.01
☐ 356	Mark Jackson	.05	.02	.01
☐ 357	Stanley Roberts	.05	.02	.01
☐ 358	Elmore Spencer	.05	.02	.01
☐ 359	Kiki Vandeweghe	.05	.02	.01
☐ 360	John S. Williams	.05	.02	.01
☐ 361	Randy Woods	.05	.02	.01
☐ 362	Duane Cooper	.05	.02	.01
☐ 363	James Edwards	.05	.02	.01
☐ 364	Anthony Peeler	.15	.07	.02
☐ 365	Tony Smith	.05	.02	.01
☐ 366	Keith Askins	.05	.02	.01
☐ 367	Matt Geiger	.05	.02	.01
☐ 368	Alec Kessler	.05	.02	.01
☐ 369	Harold Miner	.20	.09	.03
☐ 370	John Salley	.05	.02	.01
☐ 371	Anthony Avent	.05	.02	.01
☐ 372	Todd Day	.40	.18	.05
☐ 373	Blue Edwards	.05	.02	.01
☐ 374	Brad Lohaus	.05	.02	.01
☐ 375	Lee Mayberry	.08	.04	.01
☐ 376	Eric Murdock	.05	.02	.01
☐ 377	Dan Schayes	.05	.02	.01
☐ 378	Lance Blanks	.05	.02	.01
☐ 379	Christian Laettner	.60	.25	.08
☐ 380	Bob McCann	.05	.02	.01
☐ 381	Chuck Person	.08	.04	.01
☐ 382	Brad Sellers	.05	.02	.01
☐ 383	Chris Smith	.05	.02	.01
☐ 384	Micheal Williams	.05	.02	.01
☐ 385	Rafael Addison	.05	.02	.01
☐ 386	Chucky Brown	.05	.02	.01
☐ 387	Chris Dudley	.05	.02	.01
☐ 388	Tate George	.05	.02	.01
☐ 389	Rick Mahorn	.05	.02	.01
☐ 390	Rumeal Robinson	.05	.02	.01
☐ 391	Jayson Williams	.05	.02	.01
☐ 392	Eric Anderson	.05	.02	.01
☐ 393	Rolando Blackman	.08	.04	.01
☐ 394	Tony Campbell	.05	.02	.01
☐ 395	Hubert Davis	.15	.07	.02
☐ 396	Doc Rivers	.05	.02	.01
☐ 397	Charles Smith	.05	.02	.01
☐ 398	Herb Williams	.05	.02	.01
☐ 399	Litterial Green	.05	.02	.01
☐ 400	Greg Kite	.05	.02	.01
☐ 401	Shaquille O'Neal	8.00	3.60	1.00
☐ 402	Jerry Reynolds	.05	.02	.01
☐ 403	Jeff Turner	.05	.02	.01
☐ 404	Greg Grant	.05	.02	.01
☐ 405	Jeff Hornacek	.08	.04	.01
☐ 406	Andrew Lang	.05	.02	.01
☐ 407	Kenny Payne	.05	.02	.01
☐ 408	Tim Perry	.05	.02	.01
☐ 409	Clarence Weatherspoon	.60	.25	.08
☐ 410	Danny Ainge	.08	.04	.01
☐ 411	Charles Barkley	.60	.25	.08
☐ 412	Negele Knight	.05	.02	.01
☐ 413	Oliver Miller	.25	.11	.03
☐ 414	Jerrod Mustaf	.05	.02	.01
☐ 415	Mark Bryant	.05	.02	.01
☐ 416	Mario Elie	.05	.02	.01
☐ 417	Dave Johnson	.05	.02	.01
☐ 418	Tracy Murray	.08	.04	.01
☐ 419	Reggie Smith	.05	.02	.01
☐ 420	Rod Strickland	.08	.04	.01
☐ 421	Randy Brown	.05	.02	.01
☐ 422	Pete Chilcutt	.05	.02	.01
☐ 423	Jim Les	.05	.02	.01
☐ 424	Walt Williams	.60	.25	.08
☐ 425	Lloyd Daniels	.05	.02	.01
☐ 426	Vinny Del Negro	.05	.02	.01

☐ 427	Dale Ellis	.08	.04	.01
☐ 428	Sidney Green	.05	.02	.01
☐ 429	Avery Johnson	.05	.02	.01
☐ 430	Dana Barros	.10	.05	.01
☐ 431	Rich King	.05	.02	.01
☐ 432	Isaac Austin	.05	.02	.01
☐ 433	John Crotty	.05	.02	.01
☐ 434	Stephen Howard	.05	.02	.01
☐ 435	Jay Humphries	.05	.02	.01
☐ 436	Larry Krystkowiak	.05	.02	.01
☐ 437	Tom Gugliotta	.50	.23	.06
☐ 438	Buck Johnson	.05	.02	.01
☐ 439	Charles Jones	.05	.02	.01
☐ 440	Don MacLean	.15	.07	.02
☐ 441	Doug Overton	.05	.02	.01
☐ 442	Brent Price	.05	.02	.01
☐ 443	Checklist 1	.05	.02	.01
☐ 444	Checklist 2	.05	.02	.01
☐ NNO	Slam Dunk Wrapper	2.50	1.15	.30
	Exchange			
☐ SD266	Shawn Kemp AU	200.00	90.00	25.00
	(Certified Autograph)			
☐ SD277	Darrell Walker AU	20.00	9.00	2.50
	(Certified Autograph)			
☐ SD300	Darryl Dawkins AU	40.00	18.00	5.00
	(Certified Autograph)			

1992-93 Fleer All-Stars

This 24-card set was randomly inserted in first series 17-card packs and features outstanding players from the Eastern (1-12) and Western (13-24) Conference. According to Fleer's advertising materials, the odds of pulling an All-Star insert are approximately one per nine packs. The cards measure the standard size (2 1/2" by 3 1/2"). The horizontal fronts display two color images of the featured player against a gradated silver-blue background. The cards are bordered by a darker silver-blue, and the player's name is gold-foil stamped at the lower right corner. The Orlando All-Star Weekend logo is in the upper right and the team logo in the lower left corner. The backs are white with silver-blue borders and present career highlights, the player's name, and the Orlando All-Star Weekend

logo. The cards are numbered on the back in alphabetical order.

	MINT	NRMT	EXC
COMPLETE SET (24)	130.00	57.50	16.50
COMMON CARD (1-24)	2.00	.90	.25
☐ 1 Michael Adams	2.00	.90	.25
Washington Bullets			
☐ 2 Charles Barkley	15.00	6.75	1.90
Phoenix Suns			
☐ 3 Brad Daugherty	2.00	.90	.25
Cleveland Cavaliers			
☐ 4 Joe Dumars	4.00	1.80	.50
Detroit Pistons			
☐ 5 Patrick Ewing	8.00	3.60	1.00
New York Knicks			
☐ 6 Michael Jordan	100.00	45.00	12.50
Chicago Bulls			
☐ 7 Reggie Lewis	3.00	1.35	.40
Boston Celtics			
☐ 8 Scottie Pippen	8.00	3.60	1.00
Chicago Bulls			
☐ 9 Mark Price	3.00	1.35	.40
Cleveland Cavaliers			
☐ 10 Dennis Rodman	5.00	2.30	.60
Detroit Pistons			
☐ 11 Isiah Thomas	4.00	1.80	.50
Detroit Pistons			
☐ 12 Kevin Willis	2.00	.90	.25
Atlanta Hawks			
☐ 13 Clyde Drexler	8.00	3.60	1.00
Portland Trail Blazers			
☐ 14 Tim Hardaway	3.00	1.35	.40
Golden State Warriors			
☐ 15 Jeff Hornacek	2.00	.90	.25
Philadelphia 76ers			
☐ 16 Dan Majerle	2.00	.90	.25
Phoenix Suns			
☐ 17 Karl Malone	8.00	3.60	1.00
Utah Jazz			
☐ 18 Chris Mullin	3.00	1.35	.40
Golden State Warriors			
☐ 19 Dikembe Mutombo	6.00	2.70	.75
Denver Nuggets			
☐ 20 Hakeem Olajuwon	20.00	9.00	2.50
Houston Rockets			
☐ 21 David Robinson	15.00	6.75	1.90
San Antonio Spurs			
☐ 22 John Stockton	8.00	3.60	1.00
Utah Jazz			
☐ 23 Otis Thorpe	2.00	.90	.25
Houston Rockets			
☐ 24 James Worthy	3.00	1.35	.40
Los Angeles Lakers			

1992-93 Fleer Larry Johnson

Larry Johnson, the 1991-92 NBA Rookie of the Year, is featured in this 15-card signature series. The first 12 cards were available as random inserts in all forms of Fleer's first series packaging. The odds of

pulling a Larry Johnson insert from a 17-card pack were one in 18, from a 32-card cello pack were one in 13 and from a 42-card rack pack were one in six. In addition, Larry personally autographed more than 2,000 of these cards, which were randomly inserted in the wax packs. These cards feature embossed Fleer logos on front for authenticity. According to Fleer's advertising materials, the odds of finding a signed Larry Johnson were approximately one in 15,000 packs. Collectors were also able to receive three additional Johnson cards and the premiere edition of NBA Inside Stuff magazine by sending in ten wrappers and 1.00 in a mail-in offer expiring 6/30/93. These standard-size (2 1/2" by 3 1/2") cards feature color player photos framed by thin orange and blue borders on a silver-blue card face. The player's name and the words "NBA Rookie of the Year" are gold foil-stamped at the top. The backs feature an orange panel that summarizes Johnson's game and demeanor. His name and "NBA Rookie of the Year" appear at the top in a lighter orange. The cards are numbered on the back.

	MINT	NRMT	EXC
COMPLETE SET (12)	10.00	4.50	1.25
COMMON L.JOHNSON (1-12)	1.00	.45	.13
COMMON SEND-OFF (13-15)	4.00	1.80	.50
☐ 1 Larry Johnson (Holding up Hornets' home jersey)	1.00	.45	.13
☐ 2 Larry Johnson (Driving through traffic against Knicks)	1.00	.45	.13
☐ 3 Larry Johnson (Turned to the side, holding ball over head)	1.00	.45	.13
☐ 4 Larry Johnson (Shooting jumpshot)	1.00	.45	.13
☐ 5 Larry Johnson (Smiling, holding ball at chest level)	1.00	.45	.13
☐ 6 Larry Johnson (Dribbling into a no-look pass)	1.00	.45	.13
☐ 7 Larry Johnson (Posting up down low)	1.00	.45	.13
☐ 8 Larry Johnson (Shooting ball in lane)	1.00	.45	.13
☐ 9 Larry Johnson (Going for tip-in	1.00	.45	.13

in home jersey)			
☐ 10 Larry Johnson (In warm-up suit)	1.00	.45	.13
☐ 11 Larry Johnson (High-fiving during pre-game introductions)	1.00	.45	.13
☐ 12 Larry Johnson (Dribbling with his left hand)	1.00	.45	.13
☐ 13 Larry Johnson (Going up for a rebound)	4.00	1.80	.50
☐ 14 Larry Johnson (Away from ball photo)	4.00	1.80	.50
☐ 15 Larry Johnson (Charlotte skyline in background)	4.00	1.80	.50
☐ AU Larry Johnson AU (Certified autograph)	125.00	57.50	15.50

1992-93 Fleer Rookie Sensations

Randomly inserted in first series 32-card cello packs, this set features 12 of the top rookies from the 1991-92 season. According to information released by Fleer, the odds of pulling a Rookie Sensation is approximately one per five packs. Measuring the standard size (2 1/2" by 3 1/2"), the cards feature the player in action against a computer generated team emblem on a gradated purple background. The words "Rookie Sensations" and the player's name are gold foil-stamped at the bottom. The backs display career highlights on a mint-green face with a purple border. The cards are numbered on the back in alphabetical order.

	MINT	NRMT	EXC
COMPLETE SET (12)	40.00	18.00	5.00
COMMON CARD (1-12)	1.00	.45	.13
☐ 1 Greg Anthony New York Knicks	1.00	.45	.13
☐ 2 Stacey Augmon Atlanta Hawks	5.00	2.30	.60
☐ 3 Terrell Brandon Cleveland Cavaliers	2.00	.90	.25
☐ 4 Rick Fox Boston Celtics	1.00	.45	.13
☐ 5 Larry Johnson Charlotte Hornets	15.00	6.75	1.90

		MINT	NRMT	EXC
☐ 6	Mark Macon Denver Nuggets	1.00	.45	.13
☐ 7	Dikembe Mutombo Denver Nuggets	12.00	5.50	1.50
☐ 8	Billy Owens Golden State Warriors	5.00	2.30	.60
☐ 9	Stanley Roberts Orlando Magic	1.00	.45	.13
☐ 10	Doug Smith Dallas Mavericks	1.00	.45	.13
☐ 11	Steve Smith Miami Heat	5.00	2.30	.60
☐ 12	Larry Stewart Washington Bullets	1.00	.45	.13

1992-93 Fleer Sharpshooters

Randomly inserted in second series 15-card plastic-wrap packs, these 18 standard-size (2 1/2" by 3 1/2") cards feature some of the NBA's best shooters. According to Fleer's advertising materials, the odds of finding a Sharpshooter card are approximately one in three packs. The color action photos on the fronts are odd-shaped, overlaying a purple geometric shape and resting on a silver card face. The "Sharp Shooter" logo is gold-foil stamped at the upper left corner, while the player's name is gold-foil stamped below the picture. On a wheat-colored panel inside blue borders, the backs present a player profile. The cards are numbered on the back.

		MINT	NRMT	EXC
COMPLETE SET (18)		20.00	9.00	2.50
COMMON CARD (1-18)		.50	.23	.06
☐ 1	Reggie Miller Indiana Pacers	4.00	1.80	.50
☐ 2	Dana Barros Seattle Supersonics	1.50	.65	.19
☐ 3	Jeff Hornacek Philadelphia 76ers	.50	.23	.06
☐ 4	Drazen Petrovic New Jersey Nets	.50	.23	.06
☐ 5	Glen Rice Miami Heat	1.50	.65	.19
☐ 6	Terry Porter Portland Trail Blazers	.50	.23	.06

		MINT	NRMT	EXC
☐ 7	Mark Price Cleveland Cavaliers	1.00	.45	.13
☐ 8	Michael Adams Washington Bullets	.50	.23	.06
☐ 9	Hersey Hawkins Philadelphia 76ers	.50	.23	.06
☐ 10	Chuck Person Minnesota Timberwolves	.50	.23	.06
☐ 11	John Stockton Utah Jazz	4.00	1.80	.50
☐ 12	Dale Ellis San Antonio Spurs	.50	.23	.06
☐ 13	Clyde Drexler Portland Trail Blazers	4.00	1.80	.50
☐ 14	Mitch Richmond Golden State Warriors	2.00	.90	.25
☐ 15	Craig Ehlo Cleveland Cavaliers	.50	.23	.06
☐ 16	Dell Curry Charlotte Hornets	.50	.23	.06
☐ 17	Chris Mullin Golden State Warriors	1.00	.45	.13
☐ 18	Rolando Blackman New York Knicks	.50	.23	.06

1992-93 Fleer Team Leaders

The 1992-93 Fleer Team Leaders were inserted into five of every six first series 42-card rack packs. A Larry Johnson Signature Series insert card replaced a Team Leader in every sixth rack pack. These 27 standard size (2 1/2" by 3 1/2") cards feature a key member of each NBA team. The color action photos on the front are surrounded by thick dark blue borders, covered by a slick UV coating and stamped with gold foil printing. Because of the dark borders, these cards are condition sensitive. The full-color card backs include a player head shot accompanied by written text summarizing the player's career. The cards are numbered on the back in alphabetical order by team. A low production run of rack packs has contributed largely to the popularity of this set.

	MINT	NRMT	EXC
COMPLETE SET (27)	350.00	160.00	45.00
COMMON CARD (1-27)	3.00	1.35	.40

☐ 1	Dominique Wilkins........	10.00	4.50	1.25
	Atlanta Hawks			
☐ 2	Reggie Lewis	6.00	2.70	.75
	Boston Celtics			
☐ 3	Larry Johnson..............	20.00	9.00	2.50
	Charlotte Hornets			
☐ 4	Michael Jordan	225.00	100.00	28.00
	Chicago Bulls			
☐ 5	Mark Price	6.00	2.70	.75
	Cleveland Cavaliers			
☐ 6	Terry Davis	3.00	1.35	.40
	Dallas Mavericks			
☐ 7	Dikembe Mutombo	15.00	6.75	1.90
	Denver Nuggets			
☐ 8	Isiah Thomas	10.00	4.50	1.25
	Detroit Pistons			
☐ 9	Chris Mullin	6.00	2.70	.75
	Golden State Warriors			
☐ 10	Hakeem Olajuwon	50.00	23.00	6.25
	Houston Rockets			
☐ 11	Reggie Miller	20.00	9.00	2.50
	Indiana Pacers			
☐ 12	Danny Manning	8.00	3.60	1.00
	Los Angeles Clippers			
☐ 13	James Worthy	6.00	2.70	.75
	Los Angeles Lakers			
☐ 14	Glen Rice	8.00	3.60	1.00
	Miami Heat			
☐ 15	Alvin Robertson...........	3.00	1.35	.40
	Milwaukee Bucks			
☐ 16	Tony Campbell..............	3.00	1.35	.40
	Minnesota Timberwolves			
☐ 17	Derrick Coleman	8.00	3.60	1.00
	New Jersey Nets			
☐ 18	Patrick Ewing	20.00	9.00	2.50
	New York Knicks			
☐ 19	Scott Skiles	3.00	1.35	.40
	Orlando Magic			
☐ 20	Hersey Hawkins	3.00	1.35	.40
	Philadelphia 76ers			
☐ 21	Kevin Johnson	10.00	4.50	1.25
	Phoenix Suns			
☐ 22	Clyde Drexler	20.00	9.00	2.50
	Portland Trail Blazers			
☐ 23	Mitch Richmond	10.00	4.50	1.25
	Sacramento Kings			
☐ 24	David Robinson	40.00	18.00	5.00
	San Antonio Spurs			
☐ 25	Ricky Pierce.................	3.00	1.35	.40
	Seattle Supersonics			
☐ 26	Karl Malone.................	20.00	9.00	2.50
	Utah Jazz			
☐ 27	Pervis Ellison	3.00	1.35	.40
	Washington Bullets			

1992-93 Fleer Total D

The 1992-93 Fleer Total D cards were randomly inserted into second series 32-card cello packs. According to Fleer's advertising materials, the odds of pulling a Total D card were approximately one per five packs. These 15 standard size (2 1/2" by 3 1/2") cards feature some of the NBA's top

defensive players. Card fronts feature colorized players against a black border, covered with a slick UV coating and gold stamped lettering. Because of these black borders, the cards are condition sensitive. The full-color card backs feature small player head shots accompanied by text describing the player's defensive abilities. The cards are numbered on the back.

	MINT	NRMT	EXC
COMPLETE SET (15)	175.00	80.00	22.00
COMMON CARD (1-15)	1.50	.65	.19

☐ 1	David Robinson	20.00	9.00	2.50
	San Antonio Spurs			
☐ 2	Dennis Rodman............	6.00	2.70	.75
	Detroit Pistons			
☐ 3	Scottie Pippen.............	10.00	4.50	1.25
	Chicago Bulls			
☐ 4	Joe Dumars	5.00	2.30	.60
	Detroit Pistons			
☐ 5	Michael Jordan	125.00	57.50	15.50
	Chicago Bulls			
☐ 6	John Stockton..............	10.00	4.50	1.25
	Utah Jazz			
☐ 7	Patrick Ewing	10.00	4.50	1.25
	New York Knicks			
☐ 8	Micheal Williams.........	1.50	.65	.19
	Minnesota Timberwolves			
☐ 9	Larry Nance	3.00	1.35	.40
	Cleveland Cavaliers			
☐ 10	Buck Williams	3.00	1.35	.40
	Portland Trail Blazers			
☐ 11	Alvin Robertson...........	1.50	.65	.19
	Milwaukee Bucks			
☐ 12	Dikembe Mutombo	8.00	3.60	1.00
	Denver Nuggets			
☐ 13	Mookie Blaylock...........	3.00	1.35	.40
	Atlanta Hawks			
☐ 14	Hakeem Olajuwon......	25.00	11.50	3.10
	Houston Rockets			
☐ 15	Rony Seikaly	1.50	.65	.19
	Miami Heat			

1993-94 Fleer

The 1993-94 Fleer basketball card set contains 400 cards measuring the standard size (2 1/2" by 3 1/2"). The set was issued in two series consisting of 240 and 160 cards. Cards were primarily distributed in 15-card wax packs (1.29 suggested retail) and 21-card cello packs (1.99). Unlike the

first series packs, all second series packs
contained an insert card. There are 36
packs per wax box. The fronts are UV-coated and feature color action player photos
and are enclosed by white borders. The
player's name appears in the lower left and
is superimposed over a colorful florescent
background. The backs feature full-color
printing and bold graphics combining the
player's picture, name, and complete statistics. With the exception of card numbers
131, 174, and 216, the cards are numbered
and checklisted below alphabetically within
and according to teams as follows: Atlanta
Hawks (1-8), Boston Celtics (9-16),
Charlotte Hornets (17-24), Chicago Bulls
(25-33), Cleveland Cavaliers (34-42),
Dallas Mavericks (43-49), Denver Nuggets
(50-57), Detroit Pistons (58-65), Golden
State Warriors (66-73), Houston Rockets
(74-81), Indiana Pacers (82-89), Los
Angeles Clippers (90-97), Los Angeles
Lakers (98-105), Miami Heat (106-113),
Milwaukee Bucks (114-121), Minnesota
Timberwolves (122-128), New Jersey Nets
(129-136), New York Knicks (137-146),
Orlando Magic (147-154), Philadelphia
76ers (155-161), Phoenix Suns (162-171),
Portland Trail Blazers (172-180),
Sacramento Kings (181-187), San Antonio
Spurs (188-196), Seattle Supersonics (197-
204), Utah Jazz (205-212), Washington
Bullets (213-220), NBA League Leaders
(221-228), NBA Award Winners (229-232),
Pro-Visions (223-237), and checklists (238-
240). Players traded since the first series
are pictured with their new team in a 160-
card second series (241-400) offering.
Rookie Cards include Vin Baker, Shawn
Bradley, Sam Cassell, Calbert Cheaney,
Anfernee Hardaway, Bobby Hurley, Toni
Kukoc, Jamal Mashburn, Dino Radja,
Isaiah Rider, Nick Van Exel and Chris
Webber.

	MINT	NRMT	EXC
COMPLETE SET (400)	20.00	9.00	2.50
COMPLETE SERIES 1 (240)	10.00	4.50	1.25
COMPLETE SERIES 2 (160)	10.00	4.50	1.25
COMMON CARD (1-400)	.05	.02	.01

☐ 1	Stacey Augmon	.08	.04	.01
☐ 2	Mookie Blaylock	.08	.04	.01
☐ 3	Duane Ferrell	.05	.02	.01
☐ 4	Paul Graham	.05	.02	.01
☐ 5	Adam Keefe	.05	.02	.01
☐ 6	Jon Koncak	.05	.02	.01
☐ 7	Dominique Wilkins	.15	.07	.02
☐ 8	Kevin Willis	.08	.04	.01
☐ 9	Alaa Abdelnaby	.05	.02	.01
☐ 10	Dee Brown	.08	.04	.01
☐ 11	Sherman Douglas	.05	.02	.01
☐ 12	Rick Fox	.05	.02	.01
☐ 13	Kevin Gamble	.05	.02	.01
☐ 14	Reggie Lewis	.10	.05	.01
☐ 15	Xavier McDaniel	.08	.04	.01
☐ 16	Robert Parish	.10	.05	.01
☐ 17	Muggsy Bogues	.10	.05	.01
☐ 18	Dell Curry	.05	.02	.01
☐ 19	Kenny Gattison	.05	.02	.01
☐ 20	Kendall Gill	.05	.02	.01
☐ 21	Larry Johnson	.25	.11	.03
☐ 22	Alonzo Mourning	.50	.23	.06
☐ 23	Johnny Newman	.05	.02	.01
☐ 24	David Wingate	.05	.02	.01
☐ 25	B.J. Armstrong	.05	.02	.01
☐ 26	Bill Cartwright	.05	.02	.01
☐ 27	Horace Grant	.15	.07	.02
☐ 28	Michael Jordan	3.00	1.35	.40
☐ 29	Stacey King	.05	.02	.01
☐ 30	John Paxson	.05	.02	.01
☐ 31	Will Perdue	.05	.02	.01
☐ 32	Scottie Pippen	.25	.11	.03
☐ 33	Scott Williams	.05	.02	.01
☐ 34	Terrell Brandon	.05	.02	.01
☐ 35	Brad Daugherty	.08	.04	.01
☐ 36	Craig Ehlo	.05	.02	.01
☐ 37	Danny Ferry	.05	.02	.01
☐ 38	Larry Nance	.08	.04	.01
☐ 39	Mark Price	.10	.05	.01
☐ 40	Mike Sanders	.05	.02	.01
☐ 41	Gerald Wilkins	.05	.02	.01
☐ 42	John(Hot Rod) Williams	.08	.04	.01
☐ 43	Terry Davis	.05	.02	.01
☐ 44	Derek Harper	.08	.04	.01
☐ 45	Mike Iuzzolino	.05	.02	.01
☐ 46	Jim Jackson	.50	.23	.06
☐ 47	Sean Rooks	.05	.02	.01
☐ 48	Doug Smith	.05	.02	.01
☐ 49	Randy White	.05	.02	.01
☐ 50	Mahmoud Abdul-Rauf	.08	.04	.01
☐ 51	LaPhonso Ellis	.08	.04	.01
☐ 52	Marcus Liberty	.05	.02	.01
☐ 53	Mark Macon	.05	.02	.01
☐ 54	Dikembe Mutombo	.20	.09	.03
☐ 55	Robert Pack	.05	.02	.01
☐ 56	Bryant Stith	.05	.02	.01
☐ 57	Reggie Williams	.05	.02	.01
☐ 58	Mark Aguirre	.08	.04	.01
☐ 59	Joe Dumars	.15	.07	.02
☐ 60	Bill Laimbeer	.08	.04	.01
☐ 61	Terry Mills	.05	.02	.01
☐ 62	Olden Polynice	.05	.02	.01
☐ 63	Alvin Robertson	.05	.02	.01
☐ 64	Dennis Rodman	.15	.07	.02
☐ 65	Isiah Thomas	.15	.07	.02
☐ 66	Victor Alexander	.05	.02	.01
☐ 67	Tim Hardaway	.10	.05	.01
☐ 68	Tyrone Hill	.08	.04	.01
☐ 69	Byron Houston	.05	.02	.01
☐ 70	Sarunas Marciulionis	.05	.02	.01
☐ 71	Chris Mullin	.10	.05	.01
☐ 72	Billy Owens	.08	.04	.01
☐ 73	Latrell Sprewell	.50	.23	.06
☐ 74	Scott Brooks	.05	.02	.01
☐ 75	Matt Bullard	.05	.02	.01
☐ 76	Carl Herrera	.05	.02	.01
☐ 77	Robert Horry	.10	.05	.01

□	#	Player			
□	78	Vernon Maxwell	.05	.02	.01
□	79	Hakeem Olajuwon	.60	.25	.08
□	80	Kenny Smith	.05	.02	.01
□	81	Otis Thorpe	.08	.04	.01
□	82	Dale Davis	.08	.04	.01
□	83	Vern Fleming	.05	.02	.01
□	84	George McCloud	.05	.02	.01
□	85	Reggie Miller	.25	.11	.03
□	86	Sam Mitchell	.05	.02	.01
□	87	Pooh Richardson	.05	.02	.01
□	88	Detlef Schrempf	.10	.05	.01
□	89	Rik Smits	.10	.05	.01
□	90	Gary Grant	.05	.02	.01
□	91	Ron Harper	.08	.04	.01
□	92	Mark Jackson	.05	.02	.01
□	93	Danny Manning	.10	.05	.01
□	94	Ken Norman	.05	.02	.01
□	95	Stanley Roberts	.05	.02	.01
□	96	Loy Vaught	.08	.04	.01
□	97	John Williams	.05	.02	.01
□	98	Elden Campbell	.05	.02	.01
□	99	Doug Christie	.05	.02	.01
□	100	Duane Cooper	.05	.02	.01
□	101	Vlade Divac	.10	.05	.01
□	102	A.C. Green	.10	.05	.01
□	103	Anthony Peeler	.05	.02	.01
□	104	Sedale Threatt	.05	.02	.01
□	105	James Worthy	.10	.05	.01
□	106	Bimbo Coles	.05	.02	.01
□	107	Grant Long	.05	.02	.01
□	108	Harold Miner	.05	.02	.01
□	109	Glen Rice	.10	.05	.01
□	110	John Salley	.05	.02	.01
□	111	Rony Seikaly	.05	.02	.01
□	112	Brian Shaw	.05	.02	.01
□	113	Steve Smith	.08	.04	.01
□	114	Anthony Avent	.05	.02	.01
□	115	Jon Barry	.05	.02	.01
□	116	Frank Brickowski	.05	.02	.01
□	117	Todd Day	.08	.04	.01
□	118	Blue Edwards	.05	.02	.01
□	119	Brad Lohaus	.05	.02	.01
□	120	Lee Mayberry	.05	.02	.01
□	121	Eric Murdock	.05	.02	.01
□	122	Thurl Bailey	.05	.02	.01
□	123	Christian Laettner	.10	.05	.01
□	124	Luc Longley	.05	.02	.01
□	125	Chuck Person	.08	.04	.01
□	126	Felton Spencer	.05	.02	.01
□	127	Doug West	.05	.02	.01
□	128	Micheal Williams	.05	.02	.01
□	129	Rafael Addison	.05	.02	.01
□	130	Kenny Anderson	.10	.05	.01
□	131	Sam Bowie	.05	.02	.01
□	132	Chucky Brown	.05	.02	.01
□	133	Derrick Coleman	.10	.05	.01
□	134	Chris Dudley	.05	.02	.01
□	135	Chris Morris	.05	.02	.01
□	136	Rumeal Robinson	.05	.02	.01
□	137	Greg Anthony	.05	.02	.01
□	138	Rolando Blackman	.08	.04	.01
□	139	Tony Campbell	.05	.02	.01
□	140	Hubert Davis	.05	.02	.01
□	141	Patrick Ewing	.25	.11	.03
□	142	Anthony Mason	.08	.04	.01
□	143	Charles Oakley	.08	.04	.01
□	144	Doc Rivers	.05	.02	.01
□	145	Charles Smith	.05	.02	.01
□	146	John Starks	.08	.04	.01
□	147	Nick Anderson	.08	.04	.01
□	148	Anthony Bowie	.05	.02	.01
□	149	Shaquille O'Neal	2.00	.90	.25
□	150	Donald Royal	.05	.02	.01
□	151	Dennis Scott	.05	.02	.01
□	152	Scott Skiles	.05	.02	.01
□	153	Tom Tolbert	.05	.02	.01
□	154	Jeff Turner	.05	.02	.01
□	155	Ron Anderson	.05	.02	.01
□	156	Johnny Dawkins	.05	.02	.01
□	157	Hersey Hawkins	.08	.04	.01
□	158	Jeff Hornacek	.08	.04	.01
□	159	Andrew Lang	.05	.02	.01
□	160	Tim Perry	.05	.02	.01
□	161	Clarence Weatherspoon	.10	.05	.01
□	162	Danny Ainge	.08	.04	.01
□	163	Charles Barkley	.50	.23	.06
□	164	Cedric Ceballos	.10	.05	.01
□	165	Tom Chambers	.08	.04	.01
□	166	Richard Dumas	.05	.02	.01
□	167	Kevin Johnson	.15	.07	.02
□	168	Negele Knight	.05	.02	.01
□	169	Dan Majerle	.08	.04	.01
□	170	Oliver Miller	.05	.02	.01
□	171	Mark West	.05	.02	.01
□	172	Mark Bryant	.05	.02	.01
□	173	Clyde Drexler	.25	.11	.03
□	174	Kevin Duckworth	.05	.02	.01
□	175	Mario Elie	.05	.02	.01
□	176	Jerome Kersey	.05	.02	.01
□	177	Terry Porter	.08	.04	.01
□	178	Clifford Robinson	.08	.04	.01
□	179	Rod Strickland	.08	.04	.01
□	180	Buck Williams	.08	.04	.01
□	181	Anthony Bonner	.05	.02	.01
□	182	Duane Causwell	.05	.02	.01
□	183	Mitch Richmond	.15	.07	.02
□	184	Lionel Simmons	.05	.02	.01
□	185	Wayman Tisdale	.08	.04	.01
□	186	Spud Webb	.08	.04	.01
□	187	Walt Williams	.10	.05	.01
□	188	Antoine Carr	.05	.02	.01
□	189	Terry Cummings	.08	.04	.01
□	190	Lloyd Daniels	.05	.02	.01
□	191	Vinny Del Negro	.05	.02	.01
□	192	Sean Elliott	.08	.04	.01
□	193	Dale Ellis	.08	.04	.01
□	194	Avery Johnson	.05	.02	.01
□	195	J.R. Reid	.05	.02	.01
□	196	David Robinson	.50	.23	.06
□	197	Michael Cage	.05	.02	.01
□	198	Eddie Johnson	.08	.04	.01
□	199	Shawn Kemp	.50	.23	.06
□	200	Derrick McKey	.08	.04	.01
□	201	Nate McMillan	.05	.02	.01
□	202	Gary Payton	.10	.05	.01
□	203	Sam Perkins	.08	.04	.01
□	204	Ricky Pierce	.08	.04	.01
□	205	David Benoit	.05	.02	.01
□	206	Tyrone Corbin	.05	.02	.01
□	207	Mark Eaton	.05	.02	.01
□	208	Jay Humphries	.05	.02	.01
□	209	Larry Krystkowiak	.05	.02	.01
□	210	Jeff Malone	.08	.04	.01
□	211	Karl Malone	.25	.11	.03
□	212	John Stockton	.25	.11	.03
□	213	Michael Adams	.05	.02	.01
□	214	Rex Chapman	.05	.02	.01
□	215	Pervis Ellison	.05	.02	.01
□	216	Harvey Grant	.05	.02	.01
□	217	Tom Gugliotta	.10	.05	.01
□	218	Buck Johnson	.05	.02	.01
□	219	LaBradford Smith	.05	.02	.01

#	Player			
☐ 220	Larry Stewart	.05	.02	.01
☐ 221	B.J. Armstrong LL	.05	.02	.01
	Chicago Bulls			
	3-Pt Field Goal			
	Percentage Leader			
☐ 222	Cedric Ceballos LL	.05	.02	.01
	Phoenix Suns			
	FG Percentage Leader			
☐ 223	Larry Johnson LL	.10	.05	.01
	Charlotte Hornets			
	Minutes Played Leader			
☐ 224	Michael Jordan LL	1.50	.65	.19
	Chicago Bulls			
	Scoring/Steals Leader			
☐ 225	Hakeem Olajuwon LL	.30	.14	.04
	Houston Rockets			
	Shot Block Leader			
☐ 226	Mark Price LL	.05	.02	.01
	Cleveland Cavaliers			
	FT Percentage Leader			
☐ 227	Dennis Rodman LL	.08	.04	.01
	Detroit Pistons			
	Rebounding Leader			
☐ 228	John Stockton LL	.10	.05	.01
	Utah Jazz			
	Assists Leader			
☐ 229	Charles Barkley AW	.25	.11	.03
	Phoenix Suns			
	Most Valuable Player			
☐ 230	Hakeem Olajuwon AW	.30	.14	.04
	Houston Rockets			
	Defensive POY			
☐ 231	Shaquille O'Neal AW	1.00	.45	.13
	Orlando Magic			
	Rookie of the Year			
☐ 232	Clifford Robinson AW	.05	.02	.01
	Portland Trail Blazers			
	Sixth Man Award			
☐ 233	Shawn Kemp PV	.25	.11	.03
	Seattle Supersonics			
☐ 234	Alonzo Mourning PV	.25	.11	.03
	Charlotte Hornets			
☐ 235	Hakeem Olajuwon PV	.30	.14	.04
	Houston Rockets			
☐ 236	John Stockton PV	.10	.05	.01
	Utah Jazz			
☐ 237	Dominique Wilkins PV	.08	.04	.01
	Atlanta Hawks			
☐ 238	Checklist 1-85	.05	.02	.01
☐ 239	Checklist 86-165	.05	.02	.01
☐ 240	Checklist 166-240 UER	.05	.02	.01
	(237 listed as Cliff Robinson;			
	should be Dominique Wilkins)			
☐ 241	Doug Edwards	.08	.04	.01
☐ 242	Craig Ehlo	.05	.02	.01
☐ 243	Andrew Lang	.05	.02	.01
☐ 244	Ennis Whatley	.05	.02	.01
☐ 245	Chris Corchiani	.05	.02	.01
☐ 246	Acie Earl	.05	.02	.01
☐ 247	Jimmy Oliver	.05	.02	.01
☐ 248	Ed Pinckney	.05	.02	.01
☐ 249	Dino Radja	.30	.14	.04
☐ 250	Matt Wenstrom	.05	.02	.01
☐ 251	Tony Bennett	.05	.02	.01
☐ 252	Scott Burrell	.20	.09	.03
☐ 253	LeRon Ellis	.05	.02	.01
☐ 254	Hersey Hawkins	.08	.04	.01
☐ 255	Eddie Johnson	.08	.04	.01
☐ 256	Corie Blount	.05	.02	.01
☐ 257	Jo Jo English	.05	.02	.01
☐ 258	Dave Johnson	.05	.02	.01
☐ 259	Steve Kerr	.05	.02	.01
☐ 260	Toni Kukoc	.40	.18	.05
☐ 261	Pete Myers	.05	.02	.01
☐ 262	Bill Wennington	.05	.02	.01
☐ 263	John Battle	.05	.02	.01
☐ 264	Tyrone Hill	.08	.04	.01
☐ 265	Gerald Madkins	.05	.02	.01
☐ 266	Chris Mills	.30	.14	.04
☐ 267	Bobby Phills	.05	.02	.01
☐ 268	Greg Dreiling	.05	.02	.01
☐ 269	Lucious Harris	.10	.05	.01
☐ 270	Donald Hodge	.05	.02	.01
☐ 271	Popeye Jones	.25	.11	.03
☐ 272	Tim Legler	.05	.02	.01
☐ 273	Fat Lever	.05	.02	.01
☐ 274	Jamal Mashburn	1.50	.65	.19
☐ 275	Darren Morningstar	.05	.02	.01
☐ 276	Tom Hammonds	.05	.02	.01
☐ 277	Darnell Mee	.05	.02	.01
☐ 278	Rodney Rogers	.30	.14	.04
☐ 279	Brian Williams	.05	.02	.01
☐ 280	Greg Anderson	.05	.02	.01
☐ 281	Sean Elliott	.08	.04	.01
☐ 282	Allan Houston	.30	.14	.04
☐ 283	Lindsey Hunter	.15	.07	.02
☐ 284	Marcus Liberty	.05	.02	.01
☐ 285	Mark Macon	.05	.02	.01
☐ 286	David Wood	.05	.02	.01
☐ 287	Jud Buechler	.05	.02	.01
☐ 288	Chris Gatling	.05	.02	.01
☐ 289	Josh Grant	.05	.02	.01
☐ 290	Jeff Grayer	.05	.02	.01
☐ 291	Avery Johnson	.05	.02	.01
☐ 292	Chris Webber	1.25	.55	.16
☐ 293	Sam Cassell	.40	.18	.05
☐ 294	Mario Elie	.05	.02	.01
☐ 295	Richard Petruska	.05	.02	.01
☐ 296	Eric Riley	.05	.02	.01
☐ 297	Antonio Davis	.10	.05	.01
☐ 298	Scott Haskin	.05	.02	.01
☐ 299	Derrick McKey	.08	.04	.01
☐ 300	Byron Scott	.08	.04	.01
☐ 301	Malik Sealy	.05	.02	.01
☐ 302	LaSalle Thompson	.05	.02	.01
☐ 303	Kenny Williams	.05	.02	.01
☐ 304	Haywoode Workman	.05	.02	.01
☐ 305	Mark Aguirre	.08	.04	.01
☐ 306	Terry Dehere	.08	.04	.01
☐ 307	Bob Martin	.05	.02	.01
☐ 308	Elmore Spencer	.05	.02	.01
☐ 309	Tom Tolbert	.05	.02	.01
☐ 310	Randy Woods	.05	.02	.01
☐ 311	Sam Bowie	.05	.02	.01
☐ 312	James Edwards	.05	.02	.01
☐ 313	Antonio Harvey	.08	.04	.01
☐ 314	George Lynch	.08	.04	.01
☐ 315	Tony Smith	.05	.02	.01
☐ 316	Nick Van Exel	1.50	.65	.19
☐ 317	Manute Bol	.05	.02	.01
☐ 318	Willie Burton	.05	.02	.01
☐ 319	Matt Geiger	.05	.02	.01
☐ 320	Alec Kessler	.05	.02	.01
☐ 321	Vin Baker	.75	.35	.09
☐ 322	Ken Norman	.05	.02	.01
☐ 323	Dan Schayes	.05	.02	.01
☐ 324	Derek Strong	.05	.02	.01
☐ 325	Mike Brown	.05	.02	.01
☐ 326	Brian Davis	.05	.02	.01
☐ 327	Tellis Frank	.05	.02	.01
☐ 328	Marlon Maxey	.05	.02	.01
☐ 329	Isaiah Rider	.50	.23	.06

☐ 330	Chris Smith	.05	.02	.01
☐ 331	Benoit Benjamin	.05	.02	.01
☐ 332	P.J. Brown	.10	.05	.01
☐ 333	Kevin Edwards	.05	.02	.01
☐ 334	Armon Gilliam	.05	.02	.01
☐ 335	Rick Mahorn	.05	.02	.01
☐ 336	Dwayne Schintzius	.05	.02	.01
☐ 337	Rex Walters	.08	.04	.01
☐ 338	David Wesley	.08	.04	.01
☐ 339	Jayson Williams	.05	.02	.01
☐ 340	Anthony Bonner	.05	.02	.01
☐ 341	Herb Williams	.05	.02	.01
☐ 342	Litterial Green	.05	.02	.01
☐ 343	Anfernee Hardaway	3.00	1.35	.40
☐ 344	Greg Kite	.05	.02	.01
☐ 345	Larry Krystkowiak	.05	.02	.01
☐ 346	Todd Lichti	.05	.02	.01
☐ 347	Keith Tower	.05	.02	.01
☐ 348	Dana Barros	.10	.05	.01
☐ 349	Shawn Bradley	.30	.14	.04
☐ 350	Michael Curry	.05	.02	.01
☐ 351	Greg Graham	.05	.02	.01
☐ 352	Warren Kidd	.05	.02	.01
☐ 353	Moses Malone	.15	.07	.02
☐ 354	Orlando Woolridge	.05	.02	.01
☐ 355	Duane Cooper	.05	.02	.01
☐ 356	Joe Courtney	.05	.02	.01
☐ 357	A.C. Green	.10	.05	.01
☐ 358	Frank Johnson	.05	.02	.01
☐ 359	Joe Kleine	.05	.02	.01
☐ 360	Malcolm Mackey	.05	.02	.01
☐ 361	Jerrod Mustaf	.05	.02	.01
☐ 362	Chris Dudley	.05	.02	.01
☐ 363	Harvey Grant	.05	.02	.01
☐ 364	Tracy Murray	.05	.02	.01
☐ 365	James Robinson	.15	.07	.02
☐ 366	Reggie Smith	.05	.02	.01
☐ 367	Kevin Thompson	.05	.02	.01
☐ 368	Randy Breuer	.05	.02	.01
☐ 369	Randy Brown	.05	.02	.01
☐ 370	Evers Burns	.05	.02	.01
☐ 371	Pete Chilcutt	.05	.02	.01
☐ 372	Bobby Hurley	.15	.07	.02
☐ 373	Jim Les	.05	.02	.01
☐ 374	Mike Peplowski	.05	.02	.01
☐ 375	Willie Anderson	.05	.02	.01
☐ 376	Sleepy Floyd	.05	.02	.01
☐ 377	Negele Knight	.05	.02	.01
☐ 378	Dennis Rodman	.15	.07	.02
☐ 379	Chris Whitney	.05	.02	.01
☐ 380	Vincent Askew	.05	.02	.01
☐ 381	Kendall Gill	.05	.02	.01
☐ 382	Ervin Johnson	.10	.05	.01
☐ 383	Chris King	.05	.02	.01
☐ 384	Rich King	.05	.02	.01
☐ 385	Steve Scheffler	.05	.02	.01
☐ 386	Detlef Schrempf	.10	.05	.01
☐ 387	Tom Chambers	.08	.04	.01
☐ 388	John Crotty	.05	.02	.01
☐ 389	Bryon Russell	.05	.02	.01
☐ 390	Felton Spencer	.05	.02	.01
☐ 391	Luther Wright	.05	.02	.01
☐ 392	Mitchell Butler	.05	.02	.01
☐ 393	Calbert Cheaney	.40	.18	.05
☐ 394	Kevin Duckworth	.05	.02	.01
☐ 395	Don MacLean	.05	.02	.01
☐ 396	Gheorghe Muresan	.25	.11	.03
☐ 397	Doug Overton	.05	.02	.01
☐ 398	Brent Price	.05	.02	.01
☐ 399	Checklist	.05	.02	.01
☐ 400	Checklist	.05	.02	.01

1993-94 Fleer All-Stars

Randomly inserted in 1993-94 Fleer first series 15-card packs, this 24-card set feat ures 12 players from the Eastern Conference (1-12) and the Western Conference (13-24) that participated in the 1992-93 All-Star Game in Salt Lake City. According to information on the wrappers, All-Stars are randomly inserted into one of every 10 packs. The inserts measure the standard size (2 1/2" by 3 1/2"). The fronts are UV-coated and feature color action player photos enclosed by purple borders. The NBA All-Star logo appears in the lower left or right corner. The player's name is stamped in gold foil and appears at the bottom. The backs are also UV-coated and feature a full-color shot of the player along with a statistical performance sketch from the previous year.

	MINT	NRMT	EXC
COMPLETE SET (24)	100.00	45.00	12.50
COMMON CARD (1-24)	1.00	.45	.13
☐ 1 Brad Daugherty	1.00	.45	.13
Cleveland Cavaliers			
☐ 2 Joe Dumars	1.50	.65	.19
Detroit Pistons			
☐ 3 Patrick Ewing	3.00	1.35	.40
New York Knicks			
☐ 4 Larry Johnson	3.00	1.35	.40
Charlotte Hornets			
☐ 5 Michael Jordan	40.00	18.00	5.00
Chicago Bulls			
☐ 6 Larry Nance	1.00	.45	.13
Cleveland Cavaliers			
☐ 7 Shaquille O'Neal	25.00	11.50	3.10
Orlando Magic			
☐ 8 Scottie Pippen UER	3.00	1.35	.40
Chicago Bulls			
(Name spelled Pipen on front)			
☐ 9 Mark Price	1.00	.45	.13
Cleveland Cavaliers			
☐ 10 Detlef Schrempf	1.00	.45	.13
Indiana Pacers			
☐ 11 Isiah Thomas	1.50	.65	.19
Detroit Pistons			
☐ 12 Dominique Wilkins	1.50	.65	.19

Atlanta Hawks

		MINT	NRMT	EXC
☐ 13	Charles Barkley	6.00	2.70	.75
	Phoenix Suns			
☐ 14	Clyde Drexler	3.00	1.35	.40
	Portland Trail Blazers			
☐ 15	Sean Elliott.................	1.00	.45	.13
	San Antonio Spurs			
☐ 16	Tim Hardaway.............	1.00	.45	.13
	Golden State Warriors			
☐ 17	Shawn Kemp................	6.00	2.70	.75
	Seattle Supersonics			
☐ 18	Dan Majerle................	1.00	.45	.13
	Phoenix Suns			
☐ 19	Karl Malone.................	3.00	1.35	.40
	Utah Jazz			
☐ 20	Danny Manning...........	1.00	.45	.13
	Los Angeles Clippers			
☐ 21	Hakeem Olajuwon	8.00	3.60	1.00
	Houston Rockets			
☐ 22	Terry Porter................	1.00	.45	.13
	Portland Trail Blazers			
☐ 23	David Robinson............	6.00	2.70	.75
	San Antonio Spurs			
☐ 24	John Stockton..............	3.00	1.35	.40
	Utah Jazz			

1993-94 Fleer Clyde Drexler

Randomly inserted in all 1993-94 Fleer first series packs at an approximate rate of 1 in six, this 12-card standard-size (2 1/2" by 3 1/2") set captures the greatest moments in Drexler's career. Drexler autographed more than 2,000 of his cards. These cards are embossed with Fleer logos for authenticity. Odds of getting a signed card were approximately 1 in 7,000 packs. The collector could acquire three additional cards and an issue of NBA Inside Stuff magazine through a mail-in for ten wrappers plus 1.50. The offer expired June 10, 1994. An additional card (No. 16) was offered free to collectors who subscribed to NBA Inside Stuff magazine. Since 12 cards were issued through packs, a 12-card set is considered complete. All 16 cards have the same basic design with the front featuring a unique two photo design, one color, and the other red-

screened, serving as the background. The player's name as well as the Fleer logo appear at the top of the card in gold foil. The bottom of the card carries the words "Career Highlights," also stamped in gold foil. The back of the cards carry information about Drexler, with another red-screened photo again as the background. The cards are numbered on the back. The first twelve cards are numbered "X of 12" and the last four cards are simply numbered 13, 14, 15 and 16.

		MINT	NRMT	EXC
COMPLETE SET (12)		4.00	1.80	.50
COMMON DREXLER (1-12)........		.50	.23	.06
COMMON SEND-OFF (13-15) ..		1.50	.65	.19
☐ 1	Clyde Drexler	.50	.23	.06
	(Ball in right hand, pointing with left)			
☐ 2	Clyde Drexler	.50	.23	.06
	(Holding ball aloft with right hand)			
☐ 3	Clyde Drexler	.50	.23	.06
	(Wearing red shoes, left-hand dribble)			
☐ 4	Clyde Drexler	.50	.23	.06
	(Wearing red shoes, right-hand dribble)			
☐ 5	Clyde Drexler	.50	.23	.06
	(Making ready to slam dunk with both hands)			
☐ 6	Clyde Drexler	.50	.23	.06
	(Wearing white shoes, right-hand dribble)			
☐ 7	Clyde Drexler	.50	.23	.06
	(Right-hand dribble; half of ball visible)			
☐ 8	Clyde Drexler	.50	.23	.06
	(Right hand under ball, left hand alongside)			
☐ 9	Clyde Drexler	.50	.23	.06
	(Receiving or passing ball)			
☐ 10	Clyde Drexler	.50	.23	.06
	(Both hands above head; right hand near ball)			
☐ 11	Clyde Drexler	.50	.23	.06
	(Left foot off floor; right-hand dribble)			
☐ 12	Clyde Drexler	.50	.23	.06
	(In NBA All-Star uniform)			
☐ 13	Clyde Drexler	1.50	.65	.19
	(Right-hand dribble, looking over defense)			
☐ 14	Clyde Drexler	1.50	.65	.19
	(Dribbling down court with right hand)			
☐ 15	Clyde Drexler	1.50	.65	.19
	(Shooting, with Pippen defending)			
☐ 16	Clyde Drexler	5.00	2.30	.60
	(Bringing ball upcourt, black uniform)			
☐ AU	Clyde Drexler AU	90.00	40.00	11.50
	(Certified autograph)			

1993-94 Fleer First Year Phenoms

1993-94 Fleer Internationals

These 10 standard-size (2 1/2" by 3 1/2") cards feature top rookies from the 1993-94 season. Cards were randomly inserted in 1993-94 Fleer second-series 15-card wax and 21-card jumbo packs. The insertion rate was approximately one in four wax packs and one in three cello packs. The yellow-bordered fronts feature color player action cutouts superposed upon purple, yellow, and black florescent basketball court designs. The player's name appears vertically in gold foil near one corner, and the gold-foil set logo appears at the bottom left. The horizontal back sports a similar florescent design. A color player close-up cutout appears on one side; his name, team, and career highlights appear on the other. The cards are numbered on the back as "X of 10."

	MINT	NRMT	EXC
COMPLETE SET (10)	8.00	3.60	1.00
COMMON CARD (1-10)	.25	.11	.03
☐ 1 Shawn Bradley Philadelphia 76ers	.40	.18	.05
☐ 2 Anfernee Hardaway Orlando Magic	4.00	1.80	.50
☐ 3 Lindsey Hunter Detroit Pistons	.25	.11	.03
☐ 4 Bobby Hurley Sacramento Kings	.25	.11	.03
☐ 5 Toni Kukoc Chicago Bulls	.50	.23	.06
☐ 6 Jamal Mashburn Dallas Mavericks	2.00	.90	.25
☐ 7 Dino Radja Boston Celtics	.40	.18	.05
☐ 8 Isaiah Rider Minnesota Timberwolves	.60	.25	.08
☐ 9 Nick Van Exel Los Angeles Lakers	2.00	.90	.25
☐ 10 Chris Webber Golden State Warriors	1.50	.65	.19

This 12-card insert set features NBA players born outside the United States and measures the standard size (2 1/2" by 3 1/2"). The cards were randomly inserted in first series 15-card packs at a rate of one in 10. The fronts are UV-coated and feature a color player photo superimposed over a map of his country of origin. The player's name appears at the top of the card and is gold foil stamped. The backs are also UV-coated and feature a color shot of the player along with a brief biographical sketch. The cards are numbered on the back.

	MINT	NRMT	EXC
COMPLETE SET (12)	4.00	1.80	.50
COMMON CARD (1-12)	.25	.11	.03
☐ 1 Alaa Abdelnaby Boston Celtics	.25	.11	.03
☐ 2 Vlade Divac Los Angeles Lakers	.50	.23	.06
☐ 3 Patrick Ewing New York Knicks	1.25	.55	.16
☐ 4 Carl Herrera Houston Rockets	.25	.11	.03
☐ 5 Luc Longley Minnesota Timberwolves	.25	.11	.03
☐ 6 Sarunas Marciulionis Golden State Warriors	.25	.11	.03
☐ 7 Dikembe Mutombo Denver Nuggets	1.00	.45	.13
☐ 8 Rumeal Robinson New Jersey Nets	.25	.11	.03
☐ 9 Detlef Schrempf Indiana Pacers	.50	.23	.06
☐ 10 Rony Seikaly Miami Heat	.25	.11	.03
☐ 11 Rik Smits Indiana Pacers	.50	.23	.06
☐ 12 Dominique Wilkins Atlanta Hawks	.60	.25	.08

1993-94 Fleer
Living Legends

These six standard-size (2 1/2" by 3 1/2") cards honoring veteran superstars were randomly inserted in 1993-94 Fleer second series 15-card (ratio of one in 37) and 21-card (one in 24) packs. The horizontal fronts feature color player action cutouts superimposed upon a borderless metallic motion-streaked background. The player's name and the set's logo appear at the bottom in gold foil. The horizontal back carries a color player close-up cutout on one side; his name, team, and career highlights appear on the other. The cards are numbered on the back as "X of 6."

	MINT	NRMT	EXC
COMPLETE SET (6)	40.00	18.00	5.00
COMMON CARD (1-6)	1.25	.55	.16
☐ 1 Charles Barkley Phoenix Suns	5.00	2.30	.60
☐ 2 Larry Bird Boston Celtics	8.00	3.60	1.00
☐ 3 Patrick Ewing New York Knicks	2.50	1.15	.30
☐ 4 Michael Jordan Chicago Bulls	30.00	13.50	3.80
☐ 5 Hakeem Olajuwon Houston Rockets	6.00	2.70	.75
☐ 6 Dominique Wilkins Atlanta Hawks	1.25	.55	.16

1993-94 Fleer
Lottery Exchange

This 11-card standard-size (2 1/2" by 3 1/2") set features the top players from the 1993 NBA Draft. Card fronts resemble that of the basic Fleer issue with the exception of a notation of what number pick the player was. Backs have a photo and statistics. The set could be obtained in exchange for the Draft Exchange card that was randomly

inserted (one in .180) in first series packs. The expiration date was April 1, 1994. The cards are numbered on the back in the order the player was selected.

	MINT	NRMT	EXC
COMPLETE SET (11)	20.00	9.00	2.50
COMMON CARD (1-11)	.50	.23	.06
☐ 1 Chris Webber Golden State Warriors	4.00	1.80	.50
☐ 2 Shawn Bradley Philadelphia 76ers	1.00	.45	.13
☐ 3 Anfernee Hardaway Orlando Magic	10.00	4.50	1.25
☐ 4 Jamal Mashburn Dallas Mavericks	5.00	2.30	.60
☐ 5 Isaiah Rider Minnesota Timberwolves	1.50	.65	.19
☐ 6 Calbert Cheaney Washington Bullets	1.25	.55	.16
☐ 7 Bobby Hurley Sacramento Kings	.50	.23	.06
☐ 8 Vin Baker Milwaukee Bucks	2.50	1.15	.30
☐ 9 Rodney Rogers Denver Nuggets	1.00	.45	.13
☐ 10 Lindsey Hunter Detroit Pistons	.50	.23	.06
☐ 11 Allan Houston Detroit Pistons	1.00	.45	.13
☐ NNO Expired Exchange Card	1.50	.65	.19

1993-94 Fleer
NBA Superstars

These 20 standard-size (2 1/2" by 3 1/2") cards featuring stars of the NBA were ran-

domly inserted in 1993-94 Fleer second-series 15-card packs. The fronts feature color player action cutouts superimposed upon multiple color action shots on the right side and the player's name in team color-coded vertical block lettering on the left. The set's title appears vertically along the left edge in gold foil. The horizontal back carries a color player close-up cutout on one side; his name, team, and career highlights appear on the other. The cards are numbered on the back as "X of 20."

	MINT	NRMT	EXC
COMPLETE SET (20)	20.00	9.00	2.50
COMMON CARD (1-20)	.25	.11	.03
☐ 1 Mahmoud Abdul-Rauf Denver Nuggets	.25	.11	.03
☐ 2 Charles Barkley Phoenix Suns	1.50	.65	.19
☐ 3 Derrick Coleman New Jersey Nets	.25	.11	.03
☐ 4 Clyde Drexler Portland Trail Blazers	.75	.35	.09
☐ 5 Joe Dumars Detroit Pistons	.40	.18	.05
☐ 6 Patrick Ewing New York Knicks	.75	.35	.09
☐ 7 Michael Jordan Chicago Bulls	10.00	4.50	1.25
☐ 8 Shawn Kemp Seattle Supersonics	1.50	.65	.19
☐ 9 Christian Laettner Minnesota Timberwolves	.25	.11	.03
☐ 10 Karl Malone Utah Jazz	.75	.35	.09
☐ 11 Danny Manning Los Angeles Clippers	.25	.11	.03
☐ 12 Reggie Miller Indiana Pacers	.75	.35	.09
☐ 13 Alonzo Mourning Charlotte Hornets	1.50	.65	.19
☐ 14 Chris Mullin Golden State Warriors	.25	.11	.03
☐ 15 Hakeem Olajuwon Houston Rockets	2.00	.90	.25
☐ 16 Shaquille O'Neal Orlando Magic	6.00	2.70	.75
☐ 17 Mark Price Cleveland Cavaliers	.25	.11	.03
☐ 18 Mitch Richmond Sacramento Kings	.40	.18	.05
☐ 19 David Robinson San Antonio Spurs	1.50	.65	.19
☐ 20 Dominique Wilkins Atlanta Hawks	.40	.18	.05

1993-94 Fleer Rookie Sensations

Randomly inserted in 29-card series one jumbo packs, these 24 standard-size (2 1/2" by 3 1/2") UV-coated cards feature top rookies from the 1992-93 season. Odds of finding a Rookie Sensations card are approximately one in every five packs. The cards feature color player action photos on the fronts within silver-colored borders. Each player photo is superimposed upon a card design that has a basketball "earth" at the card bottom radiating "spotlight" beams that shade from yellow to magenta on a sky blue background. The player's name and the Rookie Sensations logo, both stamped in gold foil, appear in the lower left. Bordered in silver, the backs feature color close-ups of the players in the lower right or left. Blue "sky" and two intersecting yellow-to-magenta "spotlight" beams form the background. The player's name appears in silver-colored lettering at the top of the card above the player's NBA rookie-year highlights. The cards are numbered on the back.

	MINT	NRMT	EXC
COMPLETE SET (24)	70.00	32.00	8.75
COMMON CARD (1-24)	1.00	.45	.13
☐ 1 Anthony Avent Milwaukee Bucks	1.00	.45	.13
☐ 2 Doug Christie Los Angeles Lakers	1.00	.45	.13
☐ 3 Lloyd Daniels San Antonio Spurs	1.00	.45	.13
☐ 4 Hubert Davis New York Knicks	1.00	.45	.13
☐ 5 Todd Day Milwaukee Bucks	1.50	.65	.19
☐ 6 Richard Dumas Phoenix Suns	1.00	.45	.13
☐ 7 LaPhonso Ellis Denver Nuggets	1.50	.65	.19
☐ 8 Tom Gugliotta Washington Bullets	2.00	.90	.25
☐ 9 Robert Horry Houston Rockets	3.00	1.35	.40
☐ 10 Byron Houston Golden State Warriors	1.00	.45	.13
☐ 11 Jim Jackson UER Dallas Mavericks (Text on back states he played in Big East; he played in Big Ten)	8.00	3.60	1.00
☐ 12 Adam Keefe Atlanta Hawks	1.00	.45	.13
☐ 13 Christian Laettner Minnesota Timberwolves	2.50	1.15	.30
☐ 14 Lee Mayberry Milwaukee Bucks	1.00	.45	.13
☐ 15 Oliver Miller Phoenix Suns	1.00	.45	.13

		MINT	NRMT	EXC
☐ 16	Harold Miner Miami Heat	1.00	.45	.13
☐ 17	Alonzo Mourning Charlotte Hornets	8.00	3.60	1.00
☐ 18	Shaquille O'Neal Orlando Magic	30.00	13.50	3.80
☐ 19	Anthony Peeler Los Angeles Lakers	1.00	.45	.13
☐ 20	Sean Rooks Dallas Mavericks	1.00	.45	.13
☐ 21	Latrell Sprewell Golden State Warriors	8.00	3.60	1.00
☐ 22	Bryant Stith Denver Nuggets	1.00	.45	.13
☐ 23	Clarence Weatherspoon Philadelphia 76ers	2.50	1.15	.30
☐ 24	Walt Williams Sacramento Kings	2.50	1.15	.30

1993-94 Fleer Sharpshooters

These 10 standard-size (2 1/2" by 3 1/2") cards were randomly inserted in 1993-94 Fleer second-series 15-card packs. The fronts feature color player action cutouts superposed upon color-screened action shots. The player's name appears at the upper right in gold foil. The set's logo appears at the bottom left. The black horizontal back carries a color player close-up cutout on one side; his name, card title, and career highlights appear on the other. The cards are numbered on the back as "X of 10."

		MINT	NRMT	EXC
COMPLETE SET (10)		50.00	23.00	6.25
COMMON CARD (1-10)		1.00	.45	.13
☐ 1	Tom Gugliotta Washington Bullets	1.00	.45	.13
☐ 2	Jim Jackson Dallas Mavericks	6.00	2.70	.75
☐ 3	Michael Jordan Chicago Bulls	40.00	18.00	5.00
☐ 4	Dan Majerle Phoenix Suns	1.00	.45	.13
☐ 5	Mark Price Cleveland Cavaliers	1.00	.45	.13

		MINT	NRMT	EXC
☐ 6	Glen Rice Miami Heat	1.00	.45	.13
☐ 7	Mitch Richmond Sacramento Kings	1.50	.65	.19
☐ 8	Latrell Sprewell Golden State Warriors	6.00	2.70	.75
☐ 9	John Starks New York Knicks	1.00	.45	.13
☐ 10	Dominique Wilkins Atlanta Hawks	1.50	.65	.19

1993-94 Fleer Towers Of Power

These 30 standard-size (2 1/2" by 3 1/2") cards were randomly inserted in 1993-94 Fleer second series 21-card jumbo packs at an approximate rate of two in every three packs. The fronts feature color player action cutouts superposed upon borderless backgrounds of city skylines. The player's name appears in gold foil in a lower corner. The gold-foil set logo appears in an upper corner. The back has the same borderless skyline background photo as the front and carries a color player cutout on one side, and his career highlights on the other. The cards are numbered on the back as "X of 30.

		MINT	NRMT	EXC
COMPLETE SET (30)		75.00	34.00	9.50
COMMON CARD (1-30)		1.00	.45	.13
☐ 1	Charles Barkley Phoenix Suns	6.00	2.70	.75
☐ 2	Shawn Bradley Philadelphia 76ers	2.00	.90	.25
☐ 3	Derrick Coleman New Jersey Nets	1.50	.65	.19
☐ 4	Brad Daugherty Cleveland Cavaliers	1.00	.45	.13
☐ 5	Dale Davis Indiana Pacers	1.00	.45	.13
☐ 6	Vlade Divac Los Angeles Lakers	1.00	.45	.13
☐ 7	Patrick Ewing New York Knicks	3.00	1.35	.40
☐ 8	Horace Grant Chicago Bulls	1.50	.65	.19

		MINT	NRMT	EXC
☐ 9	Tom Gugliotta	1.00	.45	.13
	Washington Bullets			
☐ 10	Larry Johnson	3.00	1.35	.40
	Charlotte Hornets			
☐ 11	Shawn Kemp	6.00	2.70	.75
	Seattle Supersonics			
☐ 12	Christian Laettner	1.00	.45	.13
	Minnesota Timberwolves			
☐ 13	Karl Malone	3.00	1.35	.40
	Utah Jazz			
☐ 14	Danny Manning	1.00	.45	.13
	Los Angeles Clippers			
☐ 15	Jamal Mashburn	12.00	5.50	1.50
	Dallas Mavericks			
☐ 16	Oliver Miller	1.00	.45	.13
	Phoenix Suns			
☐ 17	Alonzo Mourning	6.00	2.70	.75
	Charlotte Hornets			
☐ 18	Dikembe Mutombo	2.50	1.15	.30
	Denver Nuggets			
☐ 19	Ken Norman	1.00	.45	.13
	Milwaukee Bucks			
☐ 20	Hakeem Olajuwon	8.00	3.60	1.00
	Houston Rockets			
☐ 21	Shaquille O'Neal	25.00	11.50	3.10
	Orlando Magic			
☐ 22	Robert Parish	1.00	.45	.13
	Boston Celtics			
☐ 23	Olden Polynice	1.00	.45	.13
	Detroit Pistons			
☐ 24	Clifford Robinson	1.00	.45	.13
	Portland Trail Blazers			
☐ 25	David Robinson	6.00	2.70	.75
	San Antonio Spurs			
☐ 26	Dennis Rodman	2.00	.90	.25
	San Antonio Spurs			
☐ 27	Rony Seikaly	1.00	.45	.13
	Miami Heat			
☐ 28	Wayman Tisdale	1.00	.45	.13
	Sacramento Kings			
☐ 29	Chris Webber	10.00	4.50	1.25
	Golden State Warriors			
☐ 30	Dominique Wilkins	1.50	.65	.19
	Atlanta Hawks			

1994-95 Fleer

The 390 cards comprising Fleer's '94-95 base-brand set were distributed in two separate series of 240 and 150 cards each. Cards were distributed in 15-card packs (SRP $1.29), 21-card magazine cello packs (SRP $1.99) and 23-card retail jumbo packs (SRP $2.27). Cards measure the standard size (2 1/2" by 3 1/2") and feature color player action shots on their white-bordered fronts. The player's name, team, and position appear in team-colored lettering set on an irregular team-colored foil patch at the lower left. The black-bordered back carries a color player action shot on the left side, with the player's name, biography, team logo, and statistics displayed on a team-colored background on the right. The cards are numbered on the back, grouped alphabetically within teams, and checklisted below alphabetically according to teams as follows: Atlanta Hawks (1-9/241-246), Boston Celtics (10-18/247-252), Charlotte Hornets (19-28/253-256), Chicago Bulls (29-37/257-263), Cleveland Cavaliers (38-46/264-265), Dallas Mavericks (47-55/266-271), Denver Nuggets (56-63/272-277), Detroit Pistons (64-69/278-284), Golden State Warriors (70-78/285-290), Houston Rockets (79-87/291-294), Indiana Pacers (88-96/295-297), Los Angeles Clippers (97-105/298-304), Los Angeles Lakers (106-114/305-309), Miami Heat (115-122/310-315), Milwaukee Bucks (123-130/316-320), Minnesota Timberwolves (131-138/321-326), New Jersey Nets (139-146/327-332), New York Knicks (147-156/333-335), Orlando Magic (157-164/336-341), Philadelphia 76ers (165-173/342-347), Phoenix Suns (174-182/348-355), Portland Trail Blazers (183-191/356-359), Sacramento Kings (192-200/360-365), San Antonio Spurs (201-209/366-371), Seattle Supersonics (210-218/372-375), Utah Jazz (219-227/376-379), and Washington Bullets (228-236/380-387). Each pack contained at least one insert card. One in every 72 packs (Hot Packs) contained only inserts.

		MINT	NRMT	EXC
	COMPLETE SET (390)	25.00	11.50	3.10
	COMPLETE SERIES 1 (240)	10.00	4.50	1.25
	COMPLETE SERIES 2 (150)	15.00	6.75	1.90
	COMMON CARD (1-390)	.05	.02	.01
☐ 1	Stacey Augmon	.08	.04	.01
☐ 2	Mookie Blaylock	.08	.04	.01
☐ 3	Craig Ehlo	.05	.02	.01
☐ 4	Duane Ferrell	.05	.02	.01
☐ 5	Adam Keefe	.05	.02	.01
☐ 6	Jon Koncak	.05	.02	.01
☐ 7	Andrew Lang	.05	.02	.01
☐ 8	Danny Manning	.10	.05	.01
☐ 9	Kevin Willis	.08	.04	.01
☐ 10	Dee Brown	.08	.04	.01
☐ 11	Sherman Douglas	.05	.02	.01
☐ 12	Acie Earl	.05	.02	.01
☐ 13	Rick Fox	.05	.02	.01
☐ 14	Kevin Gamble	.05	.02	.01
☐ 15	Xavier McDaniel	.08	.04	.01
☐ 16	Robert Parish	.10	.05	.01
☐ 17	Ed Pinckney	.05	.02	.01
☐ 18	Dino Radja	.10	.05	.01
☐ 19	Muggsy Bogues	.10	.05	.01
☐ 20	Frank Brickowski	.05	.02	.01
☐ 21	Scott Burrell	.05	.02	.01
☐ 22	Dell Curry	.05	.02	.01
☐ 23	Kenny Gattison	.05	.02	.01
☐ 24	Hersey Hawkins	.08	.04	.01
☐ 25	Eddie Johnson	.08	.04	.01

☐ 26	Larry Johnson	.20	.09	.03
☐ 27	Alonzo Mourning	.30	.14	.04
☐ 28	David Wingate	.05	.02	.01
☐ 29	B.J. Armstrong	.05	.02	.01
☐ 30	Horace Grant	.15	.07	.02
☐ 31	Steve Kerr	.05	.02	.01
☐ 32	Toni Kukoc	.10	.05	.01
☐ 33	Luc Longley	.05	.02	.01
☐ 34	Pete Myers	.05	.02	.01
☐ 35	Scottie Pippen	.25	.11	.03
☐ 36	Bill Wennington	.05	.02	.01
☐ 37	Scott Williams	.05	.02	.01
☐ 38	Terrell Brandon	.05	.02	.01
☐ 39	Brad Daugherty	.08	.04	.01
☐ 40	Tyrone Hill	.08	.04	.01
☐ 41	Chris Mills	.10	.05	.01
☐ 42	Larry Nance	.08	.04	.01
☐ 43	Bobby Phills	.05	.02	.01
☐ 44	Mark Price	.10	.05	.01
☐ 45	Gerald Wilkins	.05	.02	.01
☐ 46	John Williams	.08	.04	.01
☐ 47	Lucious Harris	.05	.02	.01
☐ 48	Donald Hodge	.05	.02	.01
☐ 49	Jim Jackson	.30	.14	.04
☐ 50	Popeye Jones	.05	.02	.01
☐ 51	Tim Legler	.05	.02	.01
☐ 52	Fat Lever	.05	.02	.01
☐ 53	Jamal Mashburn	.50	.23	.06
☐ 54	Sean Rooks	.05	.02	.01
☐ 55	Doug Smith	.05	.02	.01
☐ 56	Mahmoud Abdul-Rauf	.05	.02	.01
☐ 57	LaPhonso Ellis	.05	.02	.01
☐ 58	Dikembe Mutombo	.15	.07	.02
☐ 59	Robert Pack	.05	.02	.01
☐ 60	Rodney Rogers	.10	.05	.01
☐ 61	Bryant Stith	.05	.02	.01
☐ 62	Brian Williams	.05	.02	.01
☐ 63	Reggie Williams	.05	.02	.01
☐ 64	Greg Anderson	.05	.02	.01
☐ 65	Joe Dumars	.15	.07	.02
☐ 66	Sean Elliott	.08	.04	.01
☐ 67	Allan Houston	.10	.05	.01
☐ 68	Lindsey Hunter	.05	.02	.01
☐ 69	Terry Mills	.05	.02	.01
☐ 70	Victor Alexander	.05	.02	.01
☐ 71	Chris Gatling	.05	.02	.01
☐ 72	Tim Hardaway	.10	.05	.01
☐ 73	Keith Jennings	.05	.02	.01
☐ 74	Avery Johnson	.05	.02	.01
☐ 75	Chris Mullin	.10	.05	.01
☐ 76	Billy Owens	.08	.04	.01
☐ 77	Latrell Sprewell	.30	.14	.04
☐ 78	Chris Webber	.40	.18	.05
☐ 79	Scott Brooks	.05	.02	.01
☐ 80	Sam Cassell	.10	.05	.01
☐ 81	Mario Elie	.05	.02	.01
☐ 82	Carl Herrera	.05	.02	.01
☐ 83	Robert Horry	.10	.05	.01
☐ 84	Vernon Maxwell	.05	.02	.01
☐ 85	Hakeem Olajuwon	.60	.25	.08
☐ 86	Kenny Smith	.05	.02	.01
☐ 87	Otis Thorpe	.08	.04	.01
☐ 88	Antonio Davis	.05	.02	.01
☐ 89	Dale Davis	.08	.04	.01
☐ 90	Vern Fleming	.05	.02	.01
☐ 91	Derrick McKey	.08	.04	.01
☐ 92	Reggie Miller	.25	.11	.03
☐ 93	Pooh Richardson	.05	.02	.01
☐ 94	Byron Scott	.08	.04	.01
☐ 95	Rik Smits	.10	.05	.01
☐ 96	Haywoode Workman	.05	.02	.01
☐ 97	Terry Dehere	.05	.02	.01
☐ 98	Harold Ellis	.05	.02	.01
☐ 99	Gary Grant	.05	.02	.01
☐ 100	Ron Harper	.08	.04	.01
☐ 101	Mark Jackson	.05	.02	.01
☐ 102	Stanley Roberts	.05	.02	.01
☐ 103	Elmore Spencer	.05	.02	.01
☐ 104	Loy Vaught	.08	.04	.01
☐ 105	Dominique Wilkins	.15	.07	.02
☐ 106	Elden Campbell	.05	.02	.01
☐ 107	Doug Christie	.05	.02	.01
☐ 108	Vlade Divac	.10	.05	.01
☐ 109	George Lynch	.05	.02	.01
☐ 110	Anthony Peeler	.05	.02	.01
☐ 111	Tony Smith	.05	.02	.01
☐ 112	Sedale Threatt	.05	.02	.01
☐ 113	Nick Van Exel	.50	.23	.06
☐ 114	James Worthy	.10	.05	.01
☐ 115	Bimbo Coles	.05	.02	.01
☐ 116	Grant Long	.05	.02	.01
☐ 117	Harold Miner	.05	.02	.01
☐ 118	Glen Rice	.10	.05	.01
☐ 119	John Salley	.05	.02	.01
☐ 120	Rony Seikaly	.05	.02	.01
☐ 121	Brian Shaw	.05	.02	.01
☐ 122	Steve Smith	.08	.04	.01
☐ 123	Vin Baker	.25	.11	.03
☐ 124	Jon Barry	.05	.02	.01
☐ 125	Todd Day	.08	.04	.01
☐ 126	Blue Edwards	.05	.02	.01
☐ 127	Lee Mayberry	.05	.02	.01
☐ 128	Eric Murdock	.05	.02	.01
☐ 129	Ken Norman	.05	.02	.01
☐ 130	Derek Strong	.05	.02	.01
☐ 131	Thurl Bailey	.05	.02	.01
☐ 132	Stacey King	.05	.02	.01
☐ 133	Christian Laettner	.08	.04	.01
☐ 134	Chuck Person	.08	.04	.01
☐ 135	Isaiah Rider	.15	.07	.02
☐ 136	Chris Smith	.05	.02	.01
☐ 137	Doug West	.05	.02	.01
☐ 138	Micheal Williams	.05	.02	.01
☐ 139	Kenny Anderson	.10	.05	.01
☐ 140	Benoit Benjamin	.05	.02	.01
☐ 141	P.J. Brown	.05	.02	.01
☐ 142	Derrick Coleman	.10	.05	.01
☐ 143	Kevin Edwards	.05	.02	.01
☐ 144	Armon Gilliam	.05	.02	.01
☐ 145	Chris Morris	.05	.02	.01
☐ 146	Johnny Newman	.05	.02	.01
☐ 147	Greg Anthony	.05	.02	.01
☐ 148	Anthony Bonner	.05	.02	.01
☐ 149	Hubert Davis	.05	.02	.01
☐ 150	Patrick Ewing	.25	.11	.03
☐ 151	Derek Harper	.08	.04	.01
☐ 152	Anthony Mason	.08	.04	.01
☐ 153	Charles Oakley	.08	.04	.01
☐ 154	Doc Rivers	.05	.02	.01
☐ 155	Charles Smith	.05	.02	.01
☐ 156	John Starks	.08	.04	.01
☐ 157	Nick Anderson	.08	.04	.01
☐ 158	Anthony Avent	.05	.02	.01
☐ 159	Anfernee Hardaway	1.00	.45	.13
☐ 160	Shaquille O'Neal	1.25	.55	.16
☐ 161	Donald Royal	.05	.02	.01
☐ 162	Dennis Scott	.05	.02	.01
☐ 163	Scott Skiles	.05	.02	.01
☐ 164	Jeff Turner	.05	.02	.01
☐ 165	Dana Barros	.10	.05	.01
☐ 166	Shawn Bradley	.10	.05	.01
☐ 167	Greg Graham	.05	.02	.01

168 Eric Leckner	.05	.02	.01
169 Jeff Malone	.08	.04	.01
170 Moses Malone	.15	.07	.02
171 Tim Perry	.05	.02	.01
172 Clarence Weatherspoon	.10	.05	.01
173 Orlando Woolridge	.05	.02	.01
174 Danny Ainge	.08	.04	.01
175 Charles Barkley	.50	.23	.06
176 Cedric Ceballos	.10	.05	.01
177 A.C. Green	.10	.05	.01
178 Kevin Johnson	.15	.07	.02
179 Joe Kleine	.05	.02	.01
180 Dan Majerle	.08	.04	.01
181 Oliver Miller	.05	.02	.01
182 Mark West	.05	.02	.01
183 Clyde Drexler	.25	.11	.03
184 Harvey Grant	.05	.02	.01
185 Jerome Kersey	.05	.02	.01
186 Tracy Murray	.05	.02	.01
187 Terry Porter	.08	.04	.01
188 Clifford Robinson	.08	.04	.01
189 James Robinson	.05	.02	.01
190 Rod Strickland	.08	.04	.01
191 Buck Williams	.08	.04	.01
192 Duane Causwell	.05	.02	.01
193 Bobby Hurley	.08	.04	.01
194 Olden Polynice	.05	.02	.01
195 Mitch Richmond	.15	.07	.02
196 Lionel Simmons	.05	.02	.01
197 Wayman Tisdale	.08	.04	.01
198 Spud Webb	.08	.04	.01
199 Walt Williams	.08	.04	.01
200 Trevor Wilson	.05	.02	.01
201 Willie Anderson	.05	.02	.01
202 Antoine Carr	.05	.02	.01
203 Terry Cummings	.08	.04	.01
204 Vinny Del Negro	.05	.02	.01
205 Dale Ellis	.08	.04	.01
206 Negele Knight	.05	.02	.01
207 J.R. Reid	.05	.02	.01
208 David Robinson	.50	.23	.06
209 Dennis Rodman	.15	.07	.02
210 Vincent Askew	.05	.02	.01
211 Michael Cage	.05	.02	.01
212 Kendall Gill	.05	.02	.01
213 Shawn Kemp	.50	.23	.06
214 Nate McMillan	.05	.02	.01
215 Gary Payton	.10	.05	.01
216 Sam Perkins	.08	.04	.01
217 Ricky Pierce	.08	.04	.01
218 Detlef Schrempf	.10	.05	.01
219 David Benoit	.05	.02	.01
220 Tom Chambers	.08	.04	.01
221 Tyrone Corbin	.05	.02	.01
222 Jeff Hornacek	.08	.04	.01
223 Jay Humphries	.05	.02	.01
224 Karl Malone	.25	.11	.03
225 Bryon Russell	.05	.02	.01
226 Felton Spencer	.05	.02	.01
227 John Stockton	.25	.11	.03
228 Michael Adams	.05	.02	.01
229 Rex Chapman	.05	.02	.01
230 Calbert Cheaney	.10	.05	.01
231 Kevin Duckworth	.05	.02	.01
232 Pervis Ellison	.05	.02	.01
233 Tom Gugliotta	.08	.04	.01
234 Don MacLean	.05	.02	.01
235 Gheorghe Muresan	.05	.02	.01
236 Brent Price	.05	.02	.01
237 Toronto Raptors Logo Card	.10	.05	.01
238 Checklist	.05	.02	.01
239 Checklist	.05	.02	.01
240 Checklist	.05	.02	.01
241 Sergei Bazarevich	.05	.02	.01
242 Tyrone Corbin	.05	.02	.01
243 Grant Long	.05	.02	.01
244 Ken Norman	.05	.02	.01
245 Steve Smith	.08	.04	.01
246 Fred Vinson	.05	.02	.01
247 Blue Edwards	.05	.02	.01
248 Greg Minor	.08	.04	.01
249 Eric Montross	.40	.18	.05
250 Derek Strong	.05	.02	.01
251 David Wesley	.05	.02	.01
252 Dominique Wilkins	.15	.07	.02
253 Michael Adams	.05	.02	.01
254 Tony Bennett	.05	.02	.01
255 Darrin Hancock	.05	.02	.01
256 Robert Parish	.10	.05	.01
257 Corie Blount	.05	.02	.01
258 Jud Buechler	.05	.02	.01
259 Greg Foster	.05	.02	.01
260 Ron Harper	.08	.04	.01
261 Larry Krystkowiak	.05	.02	.01
262 Will Perdue	.05	.02	.01
263 Dickey Simpkins	.15	.07	.02
264 Michael Cage	.05	.02	.01
265 Tony Campbell	.05	.02	.01
266 Terry Davis	.05	.02	.01
267 Tony Dumas	.08	.04	.01
268 Jason Kidd	2.50	1.15	.30
269 Roy Tarpley	.05	.02	.01
270 Morlon Wiley	.05	.02	.01
271 Lorenzo Williams	.05	.02	.01
272 Dale Ellis	.08	.04	.01
273 Tom Hammonds	.05	.02	.01
274 Cliff Levingston	.05	.02	.01
275 Darnell Mee	.05	.02	.01
276 Jalen Rose	.50	.23	.06
277 Reggie Slater	.05	.02	.01
278 Bill Curley	.15	.07	.02
279 Johnny Dawkins	.05	.02	.01
280 Grant Hill	4.00	1.80	.50
281 Eric Leckner	.05	.02	.01
282 Mark Macon	.05	.02	.01
283 Oliver Miller	.05	.02	.01
284 Mark West	.05	.02	.01
285 Manute Bol	.05	.02	.01
286 Tom Gugliotta	.08	.04	.01
287 Ricky Pierce	.08	.04	.01
288 Carlos Rogers	.20	.09	.03
289 Clifford Rozier	.20	.09	.03
290 Rony Seikaly	.05	.02	.01
291 Tim Breaux	.05	.02	.01
292 Chris Jent	.05	.02	.01
293 Eric Riley	.05	.02	.01
294 Zan Tabak	.05	.02	.01
295 Duane Ferrell	.05	.02	.01
296 Mark Jackson	.05	.02	.01
297 John Williams	.05	.02	.01
298 Matt Fish	.05	.02	.01
299 Tony Massenburg	.05	.02	.01
300 Lamond Murray	.40	.18	.05
301 Charles Outlaw	.05	.02	.01
302 Eric Piatkowski	.15	.07	.02
303 Pooh Richardson	.05	.02	.01
304 Randy Woods	.05	.02	.01
305 Sam Bowie	.05	.02	.01
306 Cedric Ceballos	.10	.05	.01
307 Antonio Harvey	.05	.02	.01
308 Eddie Jones	1.50	.65	.19
309 Anthony Miller	.05	.02	.01

			MINT	NRMT	EXC
☐ 310	Ledell Eackles	.05	.02	.01
☐ 311	Kevin Gamble	.05	.02	.01
☐ 312	Brad Lohaus	.05	.02	.01
☐ 313	Billy Owens	.08	.04	.01
☐ 314	Khalid Reeves	.40	.18	.05
☐ 315	Kevin Willis	.08	.04	.01
☐ 316	Marty Conlon	.05	.02	.01
☐ 317	Eric Mobley	.15	.07	.02
☐ 318	Johnny Newman	.05	.02	.01
☐ 319	Ed Pinckney	.05	.02	.01
☐ 320	Glenn Robinson	2.50	1.15	.30
☐ 321	Mike Brown	.05	.02	.01
☐ 322	Pat Durham	.05	.02	.01
☐ 323	Howard Eisley	.05	.02	.01
☐ 324	Andres Guibert	.05	.02	.01
☐ 325	Donyell Marshall	.50	.23	.06
☐ 326	Sean Rooks	.05	.02	.01
☐ 327	Yinka Dare	.08	.04	.01
☐ 328	Sleepy Floyd	.05	.02	.01
☐ 329	Sean Higgins	.05	.02	.01
☐ 330	Rick Mahorn	.05	.02	.01
☐ 331	Rex Walters	.05	.02	.01
☐ 332	Jayson Williams	.05	.02	.01
☐ 333	Charlie Ward	.20	.09	.03
☐ 334	Herb Williams	.05	.02	.01
☐ 335	Monty Williams	.15	.07	.02
☐ 336	Anthony Bowie	.05	.02	.01
☐ 337	Horace Grant	.15	.07	.02
☐ 338	Geert Hammink	.05	.02	.01
☐ 339	Tree Rollins	.05	.02	.01
☐ 340	Brian Shaw	.05	.02	.01
☐ 341	Brooks Thompson	.08	.04	.01
☐ 342	Derrick Alston	.08	.04	.01
☐ 343	Willie Burton	.05	.02	.01
☐ 344	Jaren Jackson	.05	.02	.01
☐ 345	B.J. Tyler	.08	.04	.01
☐ 346	Scott Williams	.05	.02	.01
☐ 347	Sharone Wright	.30	.14	.04
☐ 348	Antonio Lang	.08	.04	.01
☐ 349	Danny Manning	.10	.05	.01
☐ 350	Elliot Perry	.08	.04	.01
☐ 351	Wesley Person	.50	.23	.06
☐ 352	Trevor Ruffin	.08	.04	.01
☐ 353	Dan Schayes	.05	.02	.01
☐ 354	Aaron Swinson	.05	.02	.01
☐ 355	Wayman Tisdale	.08	.04	.01
☐ 356	Mark Bryant	.05	.02	.01
☐ 357	Chris Dudley	.05	.02	.01
☐ 358	James Edwards	.05	.02	.01
☐ 359	Aaron McKie	.20	.09	.03
☐ 360	Alaa Abdelnaby	.05	.02	.01
☐ 361	Frank Brickowski	.05	.02	.01
☐ 362	Randy Brown	.05	.02	.01
☐ 363	Brian Grant	.75	.35	.09
☐ 364	Michael Smith	.20	.09	.03
☐ 365	Henry Turner	.05	.02	.01
☐ 366	Sean Elliott	.08	.04	.01
☐ 367	Avery Johnson	.05	.02	.01
☐ 368	Moses Malone	.15	.07	.02
☐ 369	Julius Nwosu	.05	.02	.01
☐ 370	Chuck Person	.08	.04	.01
☐ 371	Chris Whitney	.05	.02	.01
☐ 372	Bill Cartwright	.05	.02	.01
☐ 373	Byron Houston	.05	.02	.01
☐ 374	Ervin Johnson	.05	.02	.01
☐ 375	Sarunas Marciulionis	.05	.02	.01
☐ 376	Antoine Carr	.05	.02	.01
☐ 377	John Crotty	.05	.02	.01
☐ 378	Adam Keefe	.05	.02	.01
☐ 379	Jamie Watson	.15	.07	.02
☐ 380	Mitchell Butler	.05	.02	.01

			MINT	NRMT	EXC
☐ 381	Juwan Howard	1.00	.45	.13
☐ 382	Jim McIlvaine	.05	.02	.01
☐ 383	Doug Overton	.05	.02	.01
☐ 384	Scott Skiles	.05	.02	.01
☐ 385	Larry Stewart	.05	.02	.01
☐ 386	Kenny Walker	.05	.02	.01
☐ 387	Chris Webber	.40	.18	.05
☐ 388	Vancouver Grizzlies Logo Card	.10	.05	.01
☐ 389	Checklist	.05	.02	.01
☐ 390	Checklist	.05	.02	.01

1994-95 Fleer All-Defensive

Randomly inserted in all first-series packs at a rate of one in nine, these 10 standard-size (2 1/2" by 3 1/2") cards feature first and second All-NBA Defensive teams. Card fronts are borderless with color player action shots that have been faded to black-and-white. The player's name and first or second team designation appear in silver-foil lettering near the bottom. On a color-screened background, the back carries a color player cutout on one side and career highlights on the other. The cards are numbered on the back as "X of 10."

		MINT	NRMT	EXC
COMPLETE SET (10)		6.00	2.70	.75
COMMON CARD (1-10)		.25	.11	.03
☐ 1	Mookie Blaylock Atlanta Hawks	.25	.11	.03
☐ 2	Charles Oakley New York Knicks	.25	.11	.03
☐ 3	Hakeem Olajuwon Orlando Magic	2.50	1.15	.30
☐ 4	Gary Payton Seattle Seahawks	.25	.11	.03
☐ 5	Scottie Pippen Chicago Bulls	1.00	.45	.13
☐ 6	Horace Grant Chicago Bulls	.40	.18	.05
☐ 7	Nate McMillan Seattle Seahawks	.25	.11	.03
☐ 8	David Robinson San Antonio Spurs	2.00	.90	.25
☐ 9	Dennis Rodman San Antonio Spurs	.40	.18	.05
☐ 10	Latrell Sprewell Golden State Warriors	1.25	.55	.16

1994-95 Fleer All-Stars

Randomly inserted in 15-card first-series packs at a rate of one in two, these 10 standard-size (2 1/2" by 3 1/2") cards feature borderless fronts with color player action shots and backgrounds that fade to black-and-white. The player's name and first or second team designation appear in silver-foil lettering near the bottom. On a color-screened background, the back carries a color player cutout on one side and career highlights on the other. The cards are numbered on the back as "X of 10."

	MINT	NRMT	EXC
COMPLETE SET (26)	35.00	16.00	4.40
COMMON CARD (1-26)	.50	.23	.06
☐ 1 Kenny Anderson New Jersey Nets	.50	.23	.06
☐ 2 B.J. Armstrong Chicago Bulls	.50	.23	.06
☐ 3 Mookie Blaylock Atlanta Hawks	.50	.23	.06
☐ 4 Derrick Coleman New Jersey Nets	.50	.23	.06
☐ 5 Patrick Ewing New York Knicks	1.50	.65	.19
☐ 6 Horace Grant Chicago Bulls	.75	.35	.09
☐ 7 Alonzo Mourning Charlotte Hornets	2.00	.90	.25
☐ 8 Charles Oakley New York Knicks	.50	.23	.06
☐ 9 Shaquille O'Neal Orlando Magic	8.00	3.60	1.00
☐ 10 Scottie Pippen Chicago Bulls	1.50	.65	.19
☐ 11 Mark Price Cleveland Cavaliers	.50	.23	.06
☐ 12 John Starks New York Knicks	.50	.23	.06
☐ 13 Dominique Wilkins Atlanta Hawks	.75	.35	.09
☐ 14 Charles Barkley Phoenix Suns	3.00	1.35	.40
☐ 15 Clyde Drexler Portland Trail Blazers	1.50	.65	.19
☐ 16 Kevin Johnson Phoenix Suns	.75	.35	.09
☐ 17 Shawn Kemp Seattle Supersonics	3.00	1.35	.40
☐ 18 Karl Malone Utah Jazz	1.50	.65	.19
☐ 19 Danny Manning Los Angeles Clippers	.50	.23	.06
☐ 20 Hakeem Olajuwon Houston Rockets	4.00	1.80	.50
☐ 21 Gary Payton Seattle Supersonics	.50	.23	.06
☐ 22 Mitch Richmond Sacramento Kings	.75	.35	.09
☐ 23 Clifford Robinson Portland Trail Blazers	.50	.23	.06
☐ 24 David Robinson San Antonio Spurs	3.00	1.35	.40
☐ 25 Latrell Sprewell Golden State Warriors	2.00	.90	.25
☐ 26 John Stockton Utah Jazz	1.50	.65	.19

1994-95 Fleer Award Winners

These four standard size (2 1/2" by 3 1/2") cards were random inserts in all first series packs at an approximate rate of one in 22. The set highlights four NBA award winners from the 1993-94 season. The horizontal fronts feature multiple player images. The player's name and his award appear at the bottom in gold-foil lettering. The horizontal back carries a color player close-up on one side and career highlights on the other. The cards are numbered "X of 4".

	MINT	NRMT	EXC
COMPLETE SET (4)	4.00	1.80	.50
COMMON CARD (1-4)	.25	.11	.03
☐ 1 Dell Curry Charlotte Hornets	.25	.11	.03
☐ 2 Don MacLean Washington Bullets	.25	.11	.03
☐ 3 Hakeem Olajuwon Houston Rockets	2.50	1.15	.30
☐ 4 Chris Webber Golden State Warriors	1.50	.65	.19

1994-95 Fleer Career Achievement

Randomly inserted in all first series packs at rate of one in 37, these six standard-size (2 1/2" by 3 1/2") cards feature veteran NBA superstars. The fronts feature color player cutouts on their borderless metallic fronts. The player's name appears in gold-foil lettering in a lower corner. The back carries a color player close-up in a lower corner, with career highlights appearing above and alongside. The cards are numbered on the back as "X of 6".

	MINT	NRMT	EXC
COMPLETE SET (6)	20.00	9.00	2.50
COMMON CARD (1-6)	1.00	.45	.13
☐ 1 Patrick Ewing New York Knicks	4.00	1.80	.50
☐ 2 Karl Malone Utah Jazz	4.00	1.80	.50
☐ 3 Hakeem Olajuwon Houston Rockets	10.00	4.50	1.25
☐ 4 Robert Parish Boston Celtics	1.00	.45	.13
☐ 5 Scottie Pippen Chicago Bulls	4.00	1.80	.50
☐ 6 Dominique Wilkins Los Angeles Clippers	2.00	.90	.25

1994-95 Fleer First Year Phenoms

Randomly inserted into all second series packs at a rate of one in five, cards from

this 10-card set feature a selection of the top rookies from 1994. These borderless cards feature a full color, cut-out player photo bursting forth from the center of the card, against a multi-imaged, shaded photo background. Card backs feature brief text on each player.

	MINT	NRMT	EXC
COMPLETE SET (10)	20.00	9.00	2.50
COMMON CARD (1-10)	.60	.25	.08
☐ 1 Grant Hill Detroit Pistons	8.00	3.60	1.00
☐ 2 Jason Kidd Dallas Mavericks	5.00	2.30	.60
☐ 3 Donyell Marshall Minnesota Timberwolves	1.00	.45	.13
☐ 4 Eric Montross Boston Celtics	.75	.35	.09
☐ 5 Lamond Murray Los Angeles Clippers	.75	.35	.09
☐ 6 Wesley Person Phoenix Suns	1.00	.45	.13
☐ 7 Khalid Reeves Miami Heat	.75	.35	.09
☐ 8 Glenn Robinson Milwaukee Bucks	5.00	2.30	.60
☐ 9 Jalen Rose Denver Nuggets	1.00	.45	.13
☐ 10 Sharone Wright Philadelphia 76ers	.60	.25	.08

1994-95 Fleer League Leaders

Randomly inserted in all first series Fleer packs at an approximate rate of one in 11, these eight standard-size (2 1/2" by 3 1/2") cards showcase league statistical leaders from the 1993-94 season. Card fronts feature a horizontal design with color player cutouts set on hardwood backgrounds. The player's name and the category in which he led the NBA appear in gold-foil lettering at the bottom. On a hardwood background, the horizontal back carries a color player close-up on one side and career highlights on the other. The cards are numbered on the back as "X of 8."

	MINT	NRMT	EXC
COMPLETE SET (8)	8.00	3.60	1.00
COMMON CARD (1-8)	.25	.11	.03
☐ 1 Mahmoud Abdul-Rauf. Denver Nuggets	.25	.11	.03
☐ 2 Nate McMillan Seattle Seahawks	.25	.11	.03
☐ 3 Tracy Murray Portland Trail Blazers	.25	.11	.03
☐ 4 Dikembe Mutombo Denver Nuggets	.50	.23	.06
☐ 5 Shaquille O'Neal Orlando Magic	5.00	2.30	.60
☐ 6 David Robinson San Antonio Spurs	2.00	.90	.25
☐ 7 Dennis Rodman San Antonio Spurs	.50	.23	.06
☐ 8 John Stockton Utah Jazz	1.00	.45	.13

1994-95 Fleer Lottery Exchange

This 11-card set was available exclusively by redeeming the Fleer Lottery Exchange card, which was randomly inserted into all first series packs at a rate of one in 175. The expiration date for the redemption was April 1st, 1995. Card design is very similar to the basic issue Fleer cards except for the Lottery Pick logo on front.

	MINT	NRMT	EXC
COMPLETE SET (11)	25.00	11.50	3.10
COMMON CARD (1-11)	.50	.23	.06
☐ 1 Glenn Robinson Milwaukee Bucks	6.00	2.70	.75
☐ 2 Jason Kidd Dallas Mavericks	6.00	2.70	.75
☐ 3 Grant Hill Detroit Pistons	10.00	4.50	1.25
☐ 4 Donyell Marshall Minnesota Timberwolves	1.25	.55	.16
☐ 5 Juwan Howard Washington Bullets	2.50	1.15	.30
☐ 6 Sharone Wright Philadelphia 76ers	.75	.35	.09
☐ 7 Lamond Murray Los Angeles Clippers	1.00	.45	.13
☐ 8 Brian Grant Sacramento Kings	2.00	.90	.25

☐ 9 Eric Montross Boston Celtics	1.00	.45	.13
☐ 10 Eddie Jones Los Angeles Lakers	4.00	1.80	.50
☐ 11 Carlos Rogers Golden State Warriors	.50	.23	.06
☐ NNO Lottery Exchange Card	1.50	.65	.19

1994-95 Fleer Pro-Visions

Randomly inserted in all first-series packs at a rate of one in five, these nine standard-size (2 1/2" by 3 1/2") cards highlight some top NBA stars. Borderless fronts feature color paintings of the players on fanciful backgrounds. The player's name appears in gold-foil lettering in a lower corner. The back carries career highlights on a colorful ghosted abstract background. The cards are numbered on the back as "X of 10."

	MINT	NRMT	EXC
COMPLETE SET (9)	4.00	1.80	.50
COMMON CARD (1-9)	.20	.09	.03
☐ 1 Jamal Mashburn Dallas Mavericks	1.00	.45	.13
☐ 2 John Starks New York Knicks	.20	.09	.03
☐ 3 Toni Kukoc Chicago Bulls	.30	.14	.04
☐ 4 Derrick Coleman New Jersey Nets	.30	.14	.04
☐ 5 Chris Webber Golden State Warriors	.75	.35	.09
☐ 6 Dennis Rodman San Antonio Spurs	.40	.18	.05
☐ 7 Gary Payton Seattle Supersonics	.30	.14	.04
☐ 8 Anfernee Hardaway Orlando Magic	2.00	.90	.25
☐ 9 Dan Majerle Phoenix Suns	.20	.09	.03

1994-95 Fleer Rookie Sensations

Randomly inserted at a rate of one in three first-series 21-card cello packs, these 25

standard-size (2 1/2" by 3 1/2") cards feature a selection of the top rookies from the 1993-94 season. Card fronts feature color player action cutouts "breaking out" of borderless multicolored backgrounds. The player's name appears in gold-foil lettering in a lower corner. The back carries another color player action cutout on one side, and career highlights within a colored panel on the other. The cards are numbered on the back as "X"of 25.

	MINT	NRMT	EXC
COMPLETE SET (25)	40.00	18.00	5.00
COMMON CARD (1-25)	.75	.35	.09
☐ 1 Vin Baker	3.00	1.35	.40
Milwaukee Bucks			
☐ 2 Shawn Bradley	1.00	.45	.13
Philadelphia 76ers			
☐ 3 P.J. Brown	.75	.35	.09
New Jersey Nets			
☐ 4 Sam Cassell	1.00	.45	.13
Houston Rockets			
☐ 5 Calbert Cheaney	1.00	.45	.13
Washington Bullets			
☐ 6 Antonio Davis	.75	.35	.09
Indiana Pacers			
☐ 7 Acie Earl	.75	.35	.09
Boston Celtics			
☐ 8 Harold Ellis	.75	.35	.09
Los Angeles Clippers			
☐ 9 Anfernee Hardaway	12.00	5.50	1.50
Orlando Magic			
☐ 10 Allan Houston	1.00	.45	.13
Detroit Pistons			
☐ 11 Lindsey Hunter	.75	.35	.09
Detroit Pistons			
☐ 12 Bobby Hurley	.75	.35	.09
Sacramento Kings			
☐ 13 Popeye Jones	.75	.35	.09
Dallas Mavericks			
☐ 14 Toni Kukoc	1.00	.45	.13
Chicago Bulls			
☐ 15 George Lynch	.75	.35	.09
Los Angeles Lakers			
☐ 16 Jamal Mashburn	6.00	2.70	.75
Dallas Mavericks			
☐ 17 Chris Mills	1.00	.45	.13
Cleveland Cavaliers			
☐ 18 Gheorghe Muresan	.75	.35	.09
Washington Bullets			
☐ 19 Dino Radja	1.00	.45	.13
Boston Celtics			
☐ 20 Isaiah Rider	2.00	.90	.25
Minnesota Timberwolves			
☐ 21 James Robinson	.75	.35	.09
Portland Trail Blazers			
☐ 22 Rodney Rogers	1.00	.45	.13
Denver Nuggets			
☐ 23 Bryon Russell	.75	.35	.09
Utah Jazz			
☐ 24 Nick Van Exel	6.00	2.70	.75
Los Angeles Lakers			
☐ 25 Chris Webber	5.00	2.30	.60
Golden State Warriors			

1994-95 Fleer Sharpshooters

Randomly inserted exclusively into second series retail packs at a rate of one in seven, cards from this 10-card set feature a selection of the NBA's best long-distance shooters. Card fronts feature color player photos cut out against a neon basketball background overlapped by a basketball net.

	MINT	NRMT	EXC
COMPLETE SET (10)	12.00	5.50	1.50
COMMON CARD (1-10)	1.00	.45	.13
☐ 1 Dell Curry	1.00	.45	.13
Charlotte Hornets			
☐ 2 Joe Dumars	2.00	.90	.25
Detroit Pistons			
☐ 3 Dale Ellis	1.00	.45	.13
Denver Nuggets			
☐ 4 Dan Majerle	1.00	.45	.13
Phoenix Suns			
☐ 5 Reggie Miller	4.00	1.80	.50
Indiana Pacers			
☐ 6 Mark Price	1.50	.65	.19
Cleveland Cavaliers			
☐ 7 Glen Rice	1.50	.65	.19
Miami Heat			
☐ 8 Mitch Richmond	2.00	.90	.25
Sacramento Kings			
☐ 9 Dennis Scott	1.00	.45	.13
Orlando Magic			
☐ 10 Latrell Sprewell	5.00	2.30	.60
Golden State Warriors			

1994-95 Fleer Superstars

Randomly inserted into all second series packs at a rate of one in 37, cards from this

six-card set feature a selection of veteran NBA stars with true Hall of Fame potential. Card fronts feature psychedelic, etched-foil backgrounds against a full color, cut out player photo.

	MINT	NRMT	EXC
COMPLETE SET (6)	25.00	11.50	3.10
COMMON CARD (1-6)	1.00	.45	.13
☐ 1 Charles Barkley Phoenix Suns	8.00	3.60	1.00
☐ 2 Patrick Ewing New York Knicks	4.00	1.80	.50
☐ 3 Hakeem Olajuwon Houston Rockets	10.00	4.50	1.25
☐ 4 Robert Parish Charlotte Hornets	1.00	.45	.13
☐ 5 Scottie Pippen Chicago Bulls	4.00	1.80	.50
☐ 6 Dominique Wilkins Boston Celtics	2.00	.90	.25

1994-95 Fleer Team Leaders

Randomly inserted into all second series packs at a rate of one in three, cards from this nine-card set each feature three key players from an NBA team. Horizontal card fronts feature three full color, cut out player photos against a computer-enhanced graphic background. The backs have a head shot of all three players and information on them. The cards are numbered "X of 9."

	MINT	NRMT	EXC
COMPLETE SET (9)	4.00	1.80	.50
COMMON CARD (1-9)	.25	.11	.03
☐ 1 Mookie Blaylock Atlanta Hawks Dominique Wilkins Boston Celtics Alonzo Mourning Charlotte Hornets	.25	.11	.03
☐ 2 Scottie Pippen Chicago Bulls Mark Price Cleveland Cavaliers Jamal Mashburn Dallas Mavericks	1.00	.45	.13
☐ 3A Dikembe Mutombo Denver Nuggets Joe Dumars Detroit Pistons Latrell Sprewell Golden State Warriors (Card has Dumars with Rockets)	.50	.23	.06
☐ 3B Dikembe Mutombo COR Joe Dumars Latrell Sprewell	.50	.23	.06
☐ 4 Hakeem Olajuwon Houston Rockets Reggie Miller Indiana Pacers Loy Vaught Los Angeles Clippers	.50	.23	.06
☐ 5 Vlade Divac Los Angeles Lakers Glen Rice Miami Heat Vin Baker Milwaukee Bucks	.25	.11	.03
☐ 6 Isaiah Rider Minnesota Timberwolves Kenny Anderson New Jersey Nets Patrick Ewing New York Knicks	.25	.11	.03
☐ 7 Shaquille O'Neal Orlando Magic Clarence Weatherspoon Philadelphia 76ers Charles Barkley Phoenix Suns	2.00	.90	.25
☐ 8 Rod Strickland Portland Trail Blazers Mitch Richmond Sacramento Kings Rex Chapman Washington Bullets	.25	.11	.03
☐ 9 Shawn Kemp Seattle Supersonics John Stockton Utah Jazz Rex Chapman Washington Bullets	.50	.23	.06

1994-95 Fleer Total D

Randomly inserted exclusively into second series hobby packs at a rate of one in

seven, cards from this 10-card set feature a selection of the NBA's top defensive players. The fronts are laid out horizontally with a color photo and the player's name and team is in gold-foil at the bottom. "Total D" is in the background many times with a variety of colors set behind that. The backs have a head shot and information and why the player is so good defensively with a similar background to the front. The cards are numbered "X of 10."

	MINT	NRMT	EXC
COMPLETE SET (10)	10.00	4.50	1.25
COMMON CARD (1-10)	.50	.23	.06
☐ 1 Mookie Blaylock Atlanta Hawks	.50	.23	.06
☐ 2 Nate McMillan Seattle Supersonics	.50	.23	.06
☐ 3 Dikembe Mutombo Denver Nuggets	.75	.35	.09
☐ 4 Charles Oakley New York Knicks	.50	.23	.06
☐ 5 Hakeem Olajuwon Houston Rockets	3.00	1.35	.40
☐ 6 Gary Payton Seattle Supersonics	.60	.25	.08
☐ 7 Scottie Pippen Chicago Bulls	1.25	.55	.16
☐ 8 David Robinson San Antonio Spurs	2.50	1.15	.30
☐ 9 Latrell Sprewell Golden State Warriors	1.50	.65	.19
☐ 10 John Stockton Utah Jazz	1.25	.55	.16

1994-95 Fleer Towers of Power

Randomly inserted exclusively into second series 21-card retail packs at a rate of one

in five, cards from this 10-card set feature a selection of the top centers and power forwards in the NBA. The fronts have a color-action photo surrounded by a yellow glow with a tower in the background. The words "Tower of Power" are at the bottom in gold-foil. The backs are the same except for a different photo and player information at the bottom. The cards are numbered "X of 10."

	MINT	NRMT	EXC
COMPLETE SET (10)	40.00	18.00	5.00
COMMON CARD (1-10)	1.50	.65	.19
☐ 1 Charles Barkley Phoenix Suns	5.00	2.30	.60
☐ 2 Patrick Ewing New York Knicks	2.50	1.15	.30
☐ 3 Shawn Kemp Seattle Supersonics	5.00	2.30	.60
☐ 4 Karl Malone Utah Jazz	2.50	1.15	.30
☐ 5 Alonzo Mourning Charlotte Hornets	3.00	1.35	.40
☐ 6 Dikembe Mutombo Denver Nuggets	1.50	.65	.19
☐ 7 Hakeem Olajuwon Houston Rockets	6.00	2.70	.75
☐ 8 Shaquille O'Neal Orlando Magic	12.00	5.50	1.50
☐ 9 David Robinson San Antonio Spurs	5.00	2.30	.60
☐ 10 Chris Webber Washington Bullets	4.00	1.80	.50

1994-95 Fleer Triple Threats

Randomly inserted in all first-series packs at an approximate rate of one in nine, these 10 standard-size (2 1/2" by 3 1/2") cards spotlight some top NBA stars. Card fronts feature borderless fronts with multiple color player action cutouts on black backgrounds highlighted by colorful basketball court designs. The player's name appears in gold-foil lettering in a lower corner. This background design continues on the back, which carries a color player cutout on one side and career highlights in a ghosted strip on the other. The cards are numbered on the back as "X of 10."

	MINT	NRMT	EXC
COMPLETE SET (10)	6.00	2.70	.75
COMMON CARD (1-10)	.25	.11	.03
☐ 1 Mookie Blaylock	.25	.11	.03
Atlanta Hawks			
☐ 2 Patrick Ewing	.50	.23	.06
New York Knicks			
☐ 3 Shawn Kemp	1.00	.45	.13
Seattle Supersonics			
☐ 4 Karl Malone	.50	.23	.06
Utah Jazz			
☐ 5 Reggie Miller	.50	.23	.06
Indiana Pacers			
☐ 6 Hakeem Olajuwon	1.25	.55	.16
Houston Rockets			
☐ 7 Shaquille O'Neal	2.50	1.15	.30
Orlando Magic			
☐ 8 Scottie Pippen	.50	.23	.06
Chicago Bulls			
☐ 9 David Robinson	1.00	.45	.13
San Antonio Spurs			
☐ 10 Latrell Sprewell	.60	.25	.08
Golden State Warriors			

1994-95 Fleer Young Lions

Randomly inserted into all second series packs at a rate of one in five, cards from this 6-card set feature a selection of popular players with three years or less of NBA experience.

	MINT	NRMT	EXC
COMPLETE SET (6)	10.00	4.50	1.25
COMMON CARD (1-6)	1.00	.45	.13
☐ 1 Vin Baker	1.00	.45	.13
Milwaukee Bucks			
☐ 2 Anfernee Hardaway	4.00	1.80	.50
Orlando Magic			
☐ 3 Larry Johnson	1.00	.45	.13
Charlotte Hornets			
☐ 4 Alonzo Mourning	1.25	.55	.16
Charlotte Hornets			
☐ 5 Shaquille O'Neal	5.00	2.30	.60
Orlando Magic			
☐ 6 Chris Webber	1.50	.65	.19
Washington Bullets			

1995-96 Fleer

The 200 standard-size cards comprising Fleer's 1995-96 first series set were distributed in 11-card hobby and retail packs (SRP $1.49) and 17-card retail pre-priced packs (SRP $2.29). Each pack contains at least two insert cards. Special Hot Packs, containing a selection of only insert cards, were randomly seeded into one in every 72 packs. The borderless fronts feature four different background designs (one for each division) against a cut-out color player action shot. The backs have a color-action photo and the same picture set against a pixeled background, along with statistics. The cards are grouped alphabetically within teams and checklisted below alphabetically according to teams as follows: Atlanta Hawks (1-7), Boston Celtics (8-13), Charlotte Hornets (14-20), Chicago Bulls (21-26), Cleveland Cavaliers (27-32), Dallas Mavericks (33-40), Denver Nuggets (41-49), Detroit Pistons (50-56), Golden State Warriors (57-64), Houston Rockets (65-72), Indiana Pacers (73-79), Los Angeles Clippers (80-85), Los Angeles Lakers (86-92), Miami Heat (93-99), Milwaukee Bucks (100-105), Minnesota Timberwolves (106-111), New Jersey Nets (112-118), New York Knicks (119-125), Orlando Magic (126-133), Philadelphia 76ers (134-140), Phoenix Suns (141-149), Portland Trail Blazers (150-158), Sacramento Kings (159-165), San Antonio Spurs (166-174), Seattle Supersonics (175-182), Utah Jazz (183-190), and Washington Bullets (191-197). The set closes with checklists (198-200).

	MINT	NRMT	EXC
COMPLETE SERIES 1 (200)	15.00	6.75	1.90
COMMON CARD (1-200)	.05	.02	.01
☐ 1 Stacey Augmon	.05	.02	.01
☐ 2 Mookie Blaylock	.08	.04	.01
☐ 3 Craig Ehlo	.05	.02	.01
☐ 4 Andrew Lang	.05	.02	.01
☐ 5 Grant Long	.05	.02	.01
☐ 6 Ken Norman	.05	.02	.01
☐ 7 Steve Smith	.08	.04	.01
☐ 8 Dee Brown	.08	.04	.01
☐ 9 Sherman Douglas	.05	.02	.01

☐ 10 Eric Montross	.10	.05	.01
☐ 11 Dino Radja	.08	.04	.01
☐ 12 David Wesley	.05	.02	.01
☐ 13 Dominique Wilkins	.15	.07	.02
☐ 14 Muggsy Bogues	.10	.05	.01
☐ 15 Scott Burrell	.05	.02	.01
☐ 16 Dell Curry	.05	.02	.01
☐ 17 Hersey Hawkins	.08	.04	.01
☐ 18 Larry Johnson	.20	.09	.03
☐ 19 Alonzo Mourning	.25	.11	.03
☐ 20 Robert Parish	.10	.05	.01
☐ 21 B.J. Armstrong	.05	.02	.01
☐ 22 Michael Jordan	3.00	1.35	.40
☐ 23 Steve Kerr	.05	.02	.01
☐ 24 Toni Kukoc	.08	.04	.01
☐ 25 Will Perdue	.05	.02	.01
☐ 26 Scottie Pippen	.25	.11	.03
☐ 27 Terrell Brandon	.05	.02	.01
☐ 28 Tyrone Hill	.08	.04	.01
☐ 29 Chris Mills	.08	.04	.01
☐ 30 Bobby Phills	.05	.02	.01
☐ 31 Mark Price	.10	.05	.01
☐ 32 John Williams	.08	.04	.01
☐ 33 Lucious Harris	.05	.02	.01
☐ 34 Jim Jackson	.25	.11	.03
☐ 35 Popeye Jones	.05	.02	.01
☐ 36 Jason Kidd	.75	.35	.09
☐ 37 Jamal Mashburn	.30	.14	.04
☐ 38 George McCloud	.05	.02	.01
☐ 39 Roy Tarpley	.05	.02	.01
☐ 40 Lorenzo Williams	.05	.02	.01
☐ 41 Mahmoud Abdul-Rauf	.08	.04	.01
☐ 42 Dale Ellis	.05	.02	.01
☐ 43 LaPhonso Ellis	.05	.02	.01
☐ 44 Dikembe Mutombo	.15	.07	.02
☐ 45 Robert Pack	.05	.02	.01
☐ 46 Rodney Rogers	.08	.04	.01
☐ 47 Jalen Rose	.15	.07	.02
☐ 48 Bryant Stith	.05	.02	.01
☐ 49 Reggie Williams	.05	.02	.01
☐ 50 Joe Dumars	.15	.07	.02
☐ 51 Grant Hill	1.25	.55	.16
☐ 52 Allan Houston	.08	.04	.01
☐ 53 Lindsey Hunter	.05	.02	.01
☐ 54 Oliver Miller	.05	.02	.01
☐ 55 Terry Mills	.05	.02	.01
☐ 56 Mark West	.05	.02	.01
☐ 57 Chris Gatling	.05	.02	.01
☐ 58 Tim Hardaway	.10	.05	.01
☐ 59 Donyell Marshall	.15	.07	.02
☐ 60 Chris Mullin	.10	.05	.01
☐ 61 Carlos Rogers	.08	.04	.01
☐ 62 Clifford Rozier	.08	.04	.01
☐ 63 Rony Seikaly	.05	.02	.01
☐ 64 Latrell Sprewell	.25	.11	.03
☐ 65 Sam Cassell	.05	.02	.01
☐ 66 Clyde Drexler	.25	.11	.03
☐ 67 Mario Elie	.05	.02	.01
☐ 68 Carl Herrera	.05	.02	.01
☐ 69 Robert Horry	.10	.05	.01
☐ 70 Vernon Maxwell	.05	.02	.01
☐ 71 Hakeem Olajuwon	.60	.25	.08
☐ 72 Kenny Smith	.05	.02	.01
☐ 73 Dale Davis	.08	.04	.01
☐ 74 Mark Jackson	.05	.02	.01
☐ 75 Derrick McKey	.08	.04	.01
☐ 76 Reggie Miller	.25	.11	.03
☐ 77 Sam Mitchell	.05	.02	.01
☐ 78 Byron Scott	.05	.02	.01
☐ 79 Rik Smits	.10	.05	.01
☐ 80 Terry Dehere	.05	.02	.01
☐ 81 Tony Massenburg	.05	.02	.01
☐ 82 Lamond Murray	.08	.04	.01
☐ 83 Pooh Richardson	.05	.02	.01
☐ 84 Malik Sealy	.05	.02	.01
☐ 85 Loy Vaught	.08	.04	.01
☐ 86 Elden Campbell	.05	.02	.01
☐ 87 Cedric Ceballos	.10	.05	.01
☐ 88 Vlade Divac	.10	.05	.01
☐ 89 Eddie Jones	.50	.23	.06
☐ 90 Anthony Peeler	.05	.02	.01
☐ 91 Sedale Threatt	.05	.02	.01
☐ 92 Nick Van Exel	.30	.14	.04
☐ 93 Bimbo Coles	.05	.02	.01
☐ 94 Matt Geiger	.05	.02	.01
☐ 95 Billy Owens	.08	.04	.01
☐ 96 Khalid Reeves	.10	.05	.01
☐ 97 Glen Rice	.10	.05	.01
☐ 98 John Salley	.05	.02	.01
☐ 99 Kevin Willis	.08	.04	.01
☐ 100 Vin Baker	.15	.07	.02
☐ 101 Marty Conlon	.05	.02	.01
☐ 102 Todd Day	.05	.02	.01
☐ 103 Lee Mayberry	.05	.02	.01
☐ 104 Eric Murdock	.05	.02	.01
☐ 105 Glenn Robinson	.75	.35	.09
☐ 106 Winston Garland	.05	.02	.01
☐ 107 Tom Gugliotta	.08	.04	.01
☐ 108 Christian Laettner	.08	.04	.01
☐ 109 Isaiah Rider	.10	.05	.01
☐ 110 Sean Rooks	.05	.02	.01
☐ 111 Doug West	.05	.02	.01
☐ 112 Kenny Anderson	.10	.05	.01
☐ 113 Benoit Benjamin	.05	.02	.01
☐ 114 P.J. Brown	.05	.02	.01
☐ 115 Derrick Coleman	.10	.05	.01
☐ 116 Armon Gilliam	.05	.02	.01
☐ 117 Chris Morris	.05	.02	.01
☐ 118 Rex Walters	.05	.02	.01
☐ 119 Hubert Davis	.05	.02	.01
☐ 120 Patrick Ewing	.25	.11	.03
☐ 121 Derek Harper	.08	.04	.01
☐ 122 Anthony Mason	.08	.04	.01
☐ 123 Charles Oakley	.08	.04	.01
☐ 124 Charles Smith	.05	.02	.01
☐ 125 John Starks	.08	.04	.01
☐ 126 Nick Anderson	.08	.04	.01
☐ 127 Anthony Bowie	.05	.02	.01
☐ 128 Horace Grant	.15	.07	.02
☐ 129 Anfernee Hardaway	.75	.35	.09
☐ 130 Shaquille O'Neal	1.25	.55	.16
☐ 131 Donald Royal	.05	.02	.01
☐ 132 Dennis Scott	.05	.02	.01
☐ 133 Brian Shaw	.05	.02	.01
☐ 134 Derrick Alston	.05	.02	.01
☐ 135 Dana Barros	.10	.05	.01
☐ 136 Shawn Bradley	.08	.04	.01
☐ 137 Willie Burton	.05	.02	.01
☐ 138 Clarence Weatherspoon	.08	.04	.01
☐ 139 Scott Williams	.05	.02	.01
☐ 140 Sharone Wright	.08	.04	.01
☐ 141 Danny Ainge	.08	.04	.01
☐ 142 Charles Barkley	.50	.23	.06
☐ 143 A.C. Green	.10	.05	.01
☐ 144 Kevin Johnson	.15	.07	.02
☐ 145 Dan Majerle	.08	.04	.01
☐ 146 Danny Manning	.10	.05	.01
☐ 147 Elliot Perry	.05	.02	.01
☐ 148 Wesley Person	.15	.07	.02
☐ 149 Wayman Tisdale	.08	.04	.01
☐ 150 Chris Dudley	.05	.02	.01
☐ 151 Jerome Kersey	.05	.02	.01

		MINT	NRMT	EXC
☐ 152	Aaron McKie	.08	.04	.01
☐ 153	Terry Porter	.08	.04	.01
☐ 154	Clifford Robinson	.08	.04	.01
☐ 155	James Robinson	.05	.02	.01
☐ 156	Rod Strickland	.08	.04	.01
☐ 157	Otis Thorpe	.08	.04	.01
☐ 158	Buck Williams	.08	.04	.01
☐ 159	Brian Grant	.25	.11	.03
☐ 160	Bobby Hurley	.08	.04	.01
☐ 161	Olden Polynice	.05	.02	.01
☐ 162	Mitch Richmond	.15	.07	.02
☐ 163	Michael Smith	.08	.04	.01
☐ 164	Spud Webb	.05	.02	.01
☐ 165	Walt Williams	.08	.04	.01
☐ 166	Terry Cummings	.08	.04	.01
☐ 167	Vinny Del Negro	.05	.02	.01
☐ 168	Sean Elliott	.08	.04	.01
☐ 169	Avery Johnson	.05	.02	.01
☐ 170	Chuck Person	.08	.04	.01
☐ 171	J.R. Reid	.05	.02	.01
☐ 172	Doc Rivers	.05	.02	.01
☐ 173	David Robinson	.50	.23	.06
☐ 174	Dennis Rodman	.15	.07	.02
☐ 175	Vincent Askew	.05	.02	.01
☐ 176	Kendall Gill	.05	.02	.01
☐ 177	Shawn Kemp	.50	.23	.06
☐ 178	Sarunas Marciulionis	.05	.02	.01
☐ 179	Nate McMillan	.05	.02	.01
☐ 180	Gary Payton	.10	.05	.01
☐ 181	Sam Perkins	.08	.04	.01
☐ 182	Detlef Schrempf	.10	.05	.01
☐ 183	David Benoit	.05	.02	.01
☐ 184	Antoine Carr	.05	.02	.01
☐ 185	Blue Edwards	.05	.02	.01
☐ 186	Jeff Hornacek	.08	.04	.01
☐ 187	Adam Keefe	.05	.02	.01
☐ 188	Karl Malone	.25	.11	.03
☐ 189	Felton Spencer	.05	.02	.01
☐ 190	John Stockton	.25	.11	.03
☐ 191	Rex Chapman	.05	.02	.01
☐ 192	Calbert Cheaney	.08	.04	.01
☐ 193	Juwan Howard	.30	.14	.04
☐ 194	Don MacLean	.05	.02	.01
☐ 195	Gheorge Muresan	.05	.02	.01
☐ 196	Scott Skiles	.05	.02	.01
☐ 197	Chris Webber	.25	.11	.03
☐ 198	Checklist	.05	.02	.01
☐ 199	Checklist	.05	.02	.01
☐ 200	Checklist	.05	.02	.01

1995-96 Fleer All-Stars

the player's name and conference in gold-foil. The cards are numbered "X of 13."

	MINT	NRMT	EXC
COMPLETE SET (13)	8.00	3.60	1.00
COMMON CARD (1-13)	.25	.11	.03
☐ 1 Grant Hill	2.50	1.15	.30
Detroit Pistons			
Charles Barkley			
Phoenix Suns			
☐ 2 Scottie Pippen	1.00	.45	.13
Chicago Bulls			
Shawn Kemp			
Seattle Supersonics			
☐ 3 Shaquille O'Neal	2.50	1.15	.30
Orlando Magic			
Hakeem Olajuwon			
Houston Rockets			
☐ 4 Anfernee Hardaway	1.00	.45	.13
Orlando Magic			
Dan Majerle			
Phoenix Suns			
☐ 5 Reggie Miller	.60	.25	.08
Indiana Pacers			
Latrell Sprewell			
Golden State Warriors			
☐ 6 Vin Baker	.50	.23	.06
Milwaukee Bucks			
Cedric Ceballos			
Los Angeles Lakers			
☐ 7 Tyrone Hill	.25	.11	.03
Cleveland Cavaliers			
Karl Malone			
Utah Jazz			
☐ 8 Larry Johnson	.50	.23	.06
Charlotte Hornets			
Detlef Schrempf			
Seattle Supersonics			
☐ 9 Patrick Ewing	1.00	.45	.13
New York Knicks			
David Robinson			
San Antonio Spurs			
☐ 10 Alonzo Mourning	.50	.23	.06
Charlotte Hornets			
Dikembe Mutombo			
Denver Nuggets			
☐ 11 Dana Barros	.25	.11	.03
Philadelphia 76ers			
Gary Payton			
Seattle Supersonics			
☐ 12 Joe Dumars	.50	.23	.06
Detroit Pistons			
John Stockton			
Utah Jazz			
☐ 13 Mitch Richmond	.50	.23	.06
Sacramento Kings			
Most Valuable Player			

Randomly inserted in all first series packs at an approximate rate of one in three, these thirteen dual-player, double-sided cards feature members of the 1994-95 Eastern and Western Conference All-Star squads. Only All-Star MVP Mitch Richmond is given his own card. Both sides have a full-color action photo with the west havng a purple background of the actually photo and the east in green. The bottoms have the Phoenix All-Star Weekend insignia with

1995-96 Fleer Double Doubles

Randomly inserted in all first series packs at an approximate rate of one in three, these 12 cards feature players who averaged double figures per game in two statistical categories during the 1994-95 season. The fronts have to color-action photos of the player doing what he got double figures in, so for everybody but John Stockton it is scoring and rebounding. In the middle are the words "Double Double" while the player's name is in gold-foil. The backs have a full-color action photo with player-information, which is in a hazy, white background. The cards are numbered "X of 12."

	MINT	NRMT	EXC
COMPLETE SET (12)	8.00	3.60	1.00
COMMON CARD (1-12)	.25	.11	.03
☐ 1 Vin Baker Milwaukee Bucks	.40	.18	.05
☐ 2 Vlade Divac Los Angeles Lakers	.25	.11	.03
☐ 3 Patrick Ewing New York Knicks	.60	.25	.08
☐ 4 Tyrone Hill Cleveland Cavaliers	.25	.11	.03
☐ 5 Popeye Jones Dallas Mavericks	.25	.11	.03
☐ 6 Shawn Kemp Seattle Supersonics	1.25	.55	.16
☐ 7 Karl Malone Utah Jazz	.60	.25	.08
☐ 8 Dikembe Mutombo Denver Nuggets	.40	.18	.05
☐ 9 Hakeem Olajuwon Houston Rockets	1.50	.65	.19
☐ 10 Shaquille O'Neal Orlando Magic	3.00	1.35	.40
☐ 11 David Robinson San Antonio Spurs	1.25	.55	.16
☐ 12 John Stockton Utah Jazz	.60	.25	.08

1995-96 Fleer Flair Hardwood Leaders

Issued one per pack in all first series packs, these 27 super-premium, double-thick Flair

style cards feature each team's statistical leader or award winner from the 1994-95 season. The fronts have a color-action photo with the key the background. The words "Hardwood Leader" are on the sides of the card. The backs have a color-photo with a hardwood background and player information. The cards are numbered "X of 27."

	MINT	NRMT	EXC
COMPLETE SET (27)	20.00	9.00	2.50
COMMON CARD (1-27)	.25	.11	.03
☐ 1 Mookie Blaylock Atlanta Hawks	.25	.11	.03
☐ 2 Dominique Wilkins Boston Celtics	.50	.23	.06
☐ 3 Alonzo Mourning Charlotte Hornets	.75	.35	.09
☐ 4 Michael Jordan Chicago Bulls	10.00	4.50	1.25
☐ 5 Mark Price Cleveland Cavaliers	.25	.11	.03
☐ 6 Jim Jackson Dallas Mavericks	.75	.35	.09
☐ 7 Dikembe Mutombo Denver Nuggets	.50	.23	.06
☐ 8 Grant Hill Detroit Pistons	4.00	1.80	.50
☐ 9 Tim Hardaway Golden State Warriors	.25	.11	.03
☐ 10 Hakeem Olajuwon Houston Rockets	2.00	.90	.25
☐ 11 Reggie Miller Indiana Pacers	.75	.35	.09
☐ 12 Loy Vaught Los Angeles Clippers	.25	.11	.03
☐ 13 Cedric Ceballos Los Angeles Lakers	.25	.11	.03
☐ 14 Glen Rice Miami Heat	.25	.11	.03
☐ 15 Glenn Robinson Milwaukee Bucks	2.50	1.15	.30
☐ 16 Christian Laettner Minnesota Timberwolves	.25	.11	.03
☐ 17 Derrick Coleman New Jersey Nets	.25	.11	.03
☐ 18 Patrick Ewing New York Knicks	.75	.35	.09
☐ 19 Shaquille O'Neal Orlando Magic	4.00	1.80	.50
☐ 20 Dana Barros Philadelphia 76ers	.25	.11	.03
☐ 21 Charles Barkley	1.50	.65	.19

			MINT	NRMT	EXC
		Phoenix Suns			
☐	22	Clifford Robinson	.25	.11	.03
		Portland Trail Blazers			
☐	23	Mitch Richmond	.50	.23	.06
		Sacramento Kings			
☐	24	David Robinson	1.50	.65	.19
		San Antonio Spurs			
☐	25	Gary Payton	.25	.11	.03
		Seattle Supersonics			
☐	26	Karl Malone	.75	.35	.09
		Utah Jazz			
☐	27	Chris Webber	.75	.35	.09
		Washington Bullets			

1995-96 Fleer Franchise Futures

Randomly inserted into all first series packs at an approximate rate of one in 37, these nine etched-foil cards feature a selection of the games hottest young stars. The fronts have a full-color action photo with a huge basketball and fire underneath it in the background. The words "Franchise Futures" and the player's name are on the side in foil. The backs have a color photo with a similar yet less snazzy version of the fronts background. Their is also player information on the side and the card is numbered "X of 9."

			MINT	NRMT	EXC
		COMPLETE SET (9)	100.00	45.00	12.50
		COMMON CARD (1-9)	6.00	2.70	.75
☐	1	Vin Baker	6.00	2.70	.75
		Milwaukee Bucks			
☐	2	Anfernee Hardaway	25.00	11.50	3.10
		Orlando Magic			
☐	3	Jim Jackson	10.00	4.50	1.25
		Dallas Mavericks			
☐	4	Jamal Mashburn	12.00	5.50	1.50
		Dallas Mavericks			
☐	5	Alonzo Mourning	10.00	4.50	1.25
		Charlotte Hornets			
☐	6	Dikembe Mutombo	6.00	2.70	.75
		Denver Nuggets			
☐	7	Shaquille O'Neal	40.00	18.00	5.00
		Orlando Magic			
☐	8	Nick Van Exel	12.00	5.50	1.50
		Los Angeles Lakers			

			MINT	NRMT	EXC
☐	9	Chris Webber	10.00	4.50	1.25
		Washington Bullets			

1995-96 Fleer Rookie Sensations

Randomly inserted exclusively into first series 17-card retail pre-priced packs at an approximate rate of one in five, these 15 cards spotlight the top rookies from the 1994-95 season. The fronts have a full-color action photo with the words "Rookie Sensation" in gold-foil around a basketball. The backs have a full-color photo with player information at the bottom in a yellow haze. The cards are numbered "X of 15."

			MINT	NRMT	EXC
		COMPLETE SET (15)	40.00	18.00	5.00
		COMMON CARD (1-15)	1.00	.45	.13
☐	1	Brian Grant	3.00	1.35	.40
		Sacramento Kings			
☐	2	Grant Hill	15.00	6.75	1.90
		Detroit Pistons			
☐	3	Juwan Howard	4.00	1.80	.50
		Washington Bullets			
☐	4	Eddie Jones	6.00	2.70	.75
		Los Angeles Lakers			
☐	5	Jason Kidd	10.00	4.50	1.25
		Dallas Mavericks			
☐	6	Donyell Marshall	2.00	.90	.25
		Golden State Warriors			
☐	7	Eric Montross	1.50	.65	.19
		Boston Celtics			
☐	8	Lamond Murray	1.50	.65	.19
		Los Angeles Clippers			
☐	9	Wesley Person	2.00	.90	.25
		Phoenix Suns			
☐	10	Khalid Reeves	1.50	.65	.19
		Miami Heat			
☐	11	Glenn Robinson	10.00	4.50	1.25
		Milwaukee Bucks			
☐	12	Jalen Rose	2.00	.90	.25
		Denver Nuggets			
☐	13	Clifford Rozier	1.00	.45	.13
		Golden State Warriors			
☐	14	Michael Smith	1.00	.45	.13
		Sacramento Kings			
☐	15	Sharone Wright	1.50	.65	.19
		Philadelphia 76ers			

1995-96 Fleer Total D

Randomly inserted exclusively into first series 11-card hobby and retail packs at an approximate rate of one in five, these 12-cards feature a selection of the NBA's top defenders. The fronts have a color-action photo with the player's name and "Total D" on the side in gold-foil. The backs a color-photo with player information set against the player's team's colors. The cards are numbered "X of 12."

	MINT	NRMT	EXC
COMPLETE SET (12)	15.00	6.75	1.90
COMMON CARD (1-12)	.25	.11	.03
☐ 1 Mookie Blaylock	.25	.11	.03
Atlanta Hawks			
☐ 2 Patrick Ewing	.75	.35	.09
New York Knicks			
☐ 3 Michael Jordan	10.00	4.50	1.25
Chicago Bulls			
☐ 4 Alonzo Mourning	.75	.35	.09
Charlotte Hornets			
☐ 5 Dikembe Mutombo	.50	.23	.06
Denver Nuggets			
☐ 6 Hakeem Olajuwon	2.00	.90	.25
Houston Rockets			
☐ 7 Shaquille O'Neal	4.00	1.80	.50
Orlando Magic			
☐ 8 Gary Payton	.25	.11	.03
Seattle Supersonics			
☐ 9 Scottie Pippen	.75	.35	.09
Chicago Bulls			
☐ 10 David Robinson	1.50	.65	.19
San Antonio Spurs			
☐ 11 Dennis Rodman	.50	.23	.06
San Antonio Spurs			
☐ 12 John Stockton	.75	.35	.09
Utah Jazz			

1989-90 Hoops

The 1989-90 Hoops set contains 352 cards measuring the standard size (2 1/2" by 3 1/2"). The cards were issued in two series of 300 and 52 cards. Hoops' initial venture in the basketball market helped spark the basketball card boom of 1989-90. The cards were issued in 15-card packs. The fronts feature color action player photos, bordered by a basketball lane in one of the team's colors. On a white card face the player's name appears in black lettering above the picture. The backs have head shots of the players, biographical information and statistics printed on a pale yellow background with white borders. The cards are numbered on the back. The key Rookie Card in this set is David Robinson (138). This is his lone Rookie Card. Beware of Robinson counterfeits which are distinguishable primarily by comparison to a real card or under magnification. Other Rookie Cards include Hersey Hawkins, Jeff Hornacek, Kevin Johnson, Reggie Lewis, Dan Majerle, Danny Manning, Vernon Maxwell, Mitch Richmond, Rony Seikaly, Brian Shaw and Rod Strickland. The second series features the expansion teams (Minnesota and Orlando), traded players, a special NBA Championship card of the Detroit Pistons and a Robinson In Action (310) card. Since the original Detroit Pistons World Champs card (No. 353A) was so difficult for collectors to find in packs, Hoops produced another edition (353B) of the card that was available direct from the company free of charge. If a collector wished to acquire two or more from the company, additional copies were available for 35 cents per card. The set is considered complete with the less difficult version. The short prints (SP below) in the first series are those cards which were dropped to make room for the new second series cards on the printing sheet.

	MINT	NRMT	EXC
COMPLETE SET (352)	35.00	16.00	4.40
COMPLETE SERIES 1 (300)	30.00	13.50	3.80
COMPLETE SERIES 2 (52)	5.00	2.30	.60
COMMON CARD (1-352)	.05	.02	.01
☐ 1 Joe Dumars	.15	.07	.02
Detroit Pistons			
☐ 2 Tree Rollins	.05	.02	.01
Cleveland Cavaliers			
☐ 3 Kenny Walker	.05	.02	.01
New York Knicks			

☐ 4 Mychal Thompson	.05	.02	.01
Los Angeles Lakers			
☐ 5 Alvin Robertson SP	.15	.07	.02
San Antonio Spurs			
☐ 6 Vinny Del Negro	.15	.07	.02
Sacramento Kings			
☐ 7 Greg Anderson SP	.15	.07	.02
San Antonio Spurs			
☐ 8 Rod Strickland	.50	.23	.06
New York Knicks			
☐ 9 Ed Pinckney	.05	.02	.01
Boston Celtics			
☐ 10 Dale Ellis	.08	.04	.01
Seattle Supersonics			
☐ 11 Chuck Daly CO	.25	.11	.03
Detroit Pistons			
☐ 12 Eric Leckner	.05	.02	.01
Utah Jazz			
☐ 13 Charles Davis	.05	.02	.01
Chicago Bulls			
☐ 14 Cotton Fitzsimmons CO	.05	.02	.01
Phoenix Suns			
(No NBA logo on back			
in bottom right)			
☐ 15 Byron Scott	.08	.04	.01
Los Angeles Lakers			
☐ 16 Derrick Chievous	.05	.02	.01
Houston Rockets			
☐ 17 Reggie Lewis	.30	.14	.04
Boston Celtics			
☐ 18 Jim Paxson	.05	.02	.01
Boston Celtics			
☐ 19 Tony Campbell	.08	.04	.01
Los Angeles Lakers			
☐ 20 Rolando Blackman	.08	.04	.01
Dallas Mavericks			
☐ 21 Michael Jordan AS	2.00	.90	.25
Chicago Bulls			
☐ 22 Cliff Levingston	.05	.02	.01
Atlanta Hawks			
☐ 23 Roy Tarpley	.05	.02	.01
Dallas Mavericks			
☐ 24 Harold Pressley UER	.05	.02	.01
Sacramento Kings			
(Cinderella misspelled			
as cindarella)			
☐ 25 Larry Nance	.08	.04	.01
Cleveland Cavaliers			
☐ 26 Chris Morris	.15	.07	.02
New Jersey Nets			
☐ 27 Bob Hansen UER	.05	.02	.01
Utah Jazz			
(Drafted in '84,			
should say '83)			
☐ 28 Mark Price AS	.05	.02	.01
Cleveland Cavaliers			
☐ 29 Reggie Miller	.75	.35	.09
Indiana Pacers			
☐ 30 Karl Malone	.30	.14	.04
Utah Jazz			
☐ 31 Sidney Lowe SP	.15	.07	.02
Charlotte Hornets			
☐ 32 Ron Anderson	.05	.02	.01
Philadelphia 76ers			
☐ 33 Mike Gminski	.05	.02	.01
Philadelphia 76ers			
☐ 34 Scott Brooks	.08	.04	.01
Philadelphia 76ers			
☐ 35 Kevin Johnson	1.00	.45	.13
Phoenix Suns			
☐ 36 Mark Bryant	.05	.02	.01
Portland Trail Blazers			
☐ 37 Rik Smits	.75	.35	.09
Indiana Pacers			
☐ 38 Tim Perry	.08	.04	.01
Phoenix Suns			
☐ 39 Ralph Sampson	.05	.02	.01
Golden State Warriors			
☐ 40 Danny Manning UER	.75	.35	.09
Los Angeles Clippers			
(Missing 1988			
in draft info)			
☐ 41 Kevin Edwards	.05	.02	.01
Miami Heat			
☐ 42 Paul Mokeski	.05	.02	.01
Milwaukee Bucks			
☐ 43 Dale Ellis AS	.05	.02	.01
Seattle Supersonics			
☐ 44 Walter Berry	.05	.02	.01
Houston Rockets			
☐ 45 Chuck Person	.08	.04	.01
Indiana Pacers			
☐ 46 Rick Mahorn SP	.15	.07	.02
Detroit Pistons			
☐ 47 Joe Kleine	.05	.02	.01
Boston Celtics			
☐ 48 Brad Daugherty AS	.05	.02	.01
Cleveland Cavaliers			
☐ 49 Mike Woodson	.05	.02	.01
Houston Rockets			
☐ 50 Brad Daugherty	.08	.04	.01
Cleveland Cavaliers			
☐ 51 Shelton Jones SP	.15	.07	.02
Philadelphia 76ers			
☐ 52 Michael Adams	.05	.02	.01
Denver Nuggets			
☐ 53 Wes Unseld CO	.08	.04	.01
Washington Bullets			
☐ 54 Rex Chapman	.15	.07	.02
Charlotte Hornets			
☐ 55 Kelly Tripucka	.05	.02	.01
Charlotte Hornets			
☐ 56 Rickey Green	.05	.02	.01
Milwaukee Bucks			
☐ 57 Frank Johnson SP	.15	.07	.02
Houston Rockets			
☐ 58 Johnny Newman	.05	.02	.01
New York Knicks			
☐ 59 Billy Thompson	.05	.02	.01
Miami Heat			
☐ 60 Stu Jackson CO	.05	.02	.01
New York Knicks			
☐ 61 Walter Davis	.10	.05	.01
Denver Nuggets			
☐ 62 Brian Shaw SP UER	.75	.35	.09
Boston Celtics			
(Gary Grant led rookies			
in assists, not Shaw)			
☐ 63 Gerald Wilkins	.05	.02	.01
New York Knicks			
☐ 64 Armon Gilliam	.05	.02	.01
Phoenix Suns			
☐ 65 Maurice Cheeks SP	.25	.11	.03
Philadelphia 76ers			
☐ 66 Jack Sikma	.08	.04	.01
Milwaukee Bucks			
☐ 67 Harvey Grant	.15	.07	.02
Washington Bullets			
☐ 68 Jim Lynam CO	.05	.02	.01
Philadelphia 76ers			
☐ 69 Clyde Drexler AS	.15	.07	.02
Portland Trail Blazers			

☐ 70 Xavier McDaniel	.08	.04	.01
Seattle Supersonics			
☐ 71 Danny Young	.05	.02	.01
Portland Trail Blazers			
☐ 72 Fennis Dembo	.05	.02	.01
Detroit Pistons			
☐ 73 Mark Acres SP	.15	.07	.02
Boston Celtics			
☐ 74 Brad Lohaus SP	.15	.07	.02
Sacramento Kings			
☐ 75 Manute Bol	.05	.02	.01
Golden State Warriors			
☐ 76 Purvis Short	.05	.02	.01
Houston Rockets			
☐ 77 Allen Leavell	.05	.02	.01
Houston Rockets			
☐ 78 Johnny Dawkins SP	.25	.11	.03
San Antonio Spurs			
☐ 79 Paul Pressey	.05	.02	.01
Milwaukee Bucks			
☐ 80 Patrick Ewing	.30	.14	.04
New York Knicks			
☐ 81 Bill Wennington	.08	.04	.01
Dallas Mavericks			
☐ 82 Danny Schayes	.05	.02	.01
Denver Nuggets			
☐ 83 Derek Smith	.05	.02	.01
Philadelphia 76ers			
☐ 84 Moses Malone AS	.08	.04	.01
Atlanta Hawks			
☐ 85 Jeff Malone	.08	.04	.01
Washington Bullets			
☐ 86 Otis Smith SP	.15	.07	.02
Golden State Warriors			
☐ 87 Trent Tucker	.05	.02	.01
New York Knicks			
☐ 88 Robert Reid	.05	.02	.01
Charlotte Hornets			
☐ 89 John Paxson	.08	.04	.01
Chicago Bulls			
☐ 90 Chris Mullin	.10	.05	.01
Golden State Warriors			
☐ 91 Tom Garrick	.05	.02	.01
Los Angeles Clippers			
☐ 92 Willis Reed CO SP UER..	.15	.07	.02
New Jersey Nets			
(Gambling, should			
be Grambling)			
☐ 93 Dave Corzine SP	.15	.07	.02
Chicago Bulls			
☐ 94 Mark Alarie	.05	.02	.01
Washington Bullets			
☐ 95 Mark Aguirre	.08	.04	.01
Detroit Pistons			
☐ 96 Charles Barkley AS	.30	.14	.04
Philadelphia 76ers			
☐ 97 Sidney Green SP	.15	.07	.02
New York Knicks			
☐ 98 Kevin Willis	.08	.04	.01
Atlanta Hawks			
☐ 99 Dave Hoppen	.05	.02	.01
Charlotte Hornets			
☐ 100 Terry Cummings SP	.25	.11	.03
Milwaukee Bucks			
☐ 101 Dwayne Washington SP	.15	.07	.02
Miami Heat			
☐ 102 Larry Brown CO	.08	.04	.01
San Antonio Spurs			
☐ 103 Kevin Duckworth	.05	.02	.01
Portland Trail Blazers			
☐ 104 Uwe Blab SP	.15	.07	.02

Dallas Mavericks			
☐ 105 Terry Porter	.08	.04	.01
Portland Trail Blazers			
☐ 106 Craig Ehlo	.05	.02	.01
Cleveland Cavaliers			
☐ 107 Don Casey CO	.05	.02	.01
Los Angeles Clippers			
☐ 108 Pat Riley CO	.08	.04	.01
Los Angeles Lakers			
☐ 109 John Salley	.05	.02	.01
Detroit Pistons			
☐ 110 Charles Barkley	.60	.25	.08
Philadelphia 76ers			
☐ 111 Sam Bowie SP	.15	.07	.02
Portland Trail Blazers			
☐ 112 Earl Cureton	.05	.02	.01
Charlotte Hornets			
☐ 113 Craig Hodges UER	.05	.02	.01
Chicago Bulls			
(3-pointing shooting)			
☐ 114 Benoit Benjamin	.05	.02	.01
Los Angeles Clippers			
☐ 115A Spud Webb ERR SP ..	.30	.14	.04
Atlanta Hawks			
(Signed 9/27/89)			
☐ 115B Spud Webb COR	.05	.02	.01
Atlanta Hawks			
(Second series;			
signed 9/26/85)			
☐ 116 Karl Malone AS	.15	.07	.02
Utah Jazz			
☐ 117 Sleepy Floyd	.05	.02	.01
Houston Rockets			
☐ 118 John Williams	.08	.04	.01
Cleveland Cavaliers			
☐ 119 Michael Holton	.05	.02	.01
Charlotte Hornets			
☐ 120 Alex English	.10	.05	.01
Denver Nuggets			
☐ 121 Dennis Johnson	.10	.05	.01
Boston Celtics			
☐ 122 Wayne Cooper SP	.15	.07	.02
Denver Nuggets			
☐ 123A Don Chaney CO	.05	.02	.01
Houston Rockets			
(Line next to NBA			
coaching record)			
☐ 123B Don Chaney CO	.05	.02	.01
Houston Rockets			
(No line)			
☐ 124 A.C. Green	.10	.05	.01
Los Angeles Lakers			
☐ 125 Adrian Dantley	.10	.05	.01
Dallas Mavericks			
☐ 126 Del Harris CO	.05	.02	.01
Milwaukee Bucks			
☐ 127 Dick Harter CO	.05	.02	.01
Charlotte Hornets			
☐ 128 Reggie Williams	.15	.07	.02
Los Angeles Clippers			
☐ 129 Bill Hanzlik	.05	.02	.01
Denver Nuggets			
☐ 130 Dominique Wilkins	.15	.07	.02
Atlanta Hawks			
☐ 131 Herb Williams	.05	.02	.01
Dallas Mavericks			
☐ 132 Steve Johnson SP	.15	.07	.02
Portland Trail Blazers			
☐ 133 Alex English AS	.05	.02	.01
Denver Nuggets			
☐ 134 Darrell Walker	.05	.02	.01

	Washington Bullets			
☐ 135	Bill Laimbeer	.08	.04	.01
	Detroit Pistons			
☐ 136	Fred Roberts	.05	.02	.01
	Milwaukee Bucks			
☐ 137	Hersey Hawkins	.25	.11	.03
	Philadelphia 76ers			
☐ 138	David Robinson SP	18.00	8.00	2.30
	San Antonio Spurs			
☐ 139	Brad Sellers SP	.15	.07	.02
	Chicago Bulls			
☐ 140	John Stockton	.75	.35	.09
	Utah Jazz			
☐ 141	Grant Long	.15	.07	.02
	Miami Heat			
☐ 142	Marc Iavaroni SP	.15	.07	.02
	Utah Jazz			
☐ 143	Steve Alford SP	.50	.23	.06
	Golden State Warriors			
☐ 144	Jeff Lamp SP	.15	.07	.02
	Los Angeles Lakers			
☐ 145	Buck Williams SP UER	.25	.11	.03
	New Jersey Nets			
	(Won ROY in '81,			
	should say '82)			
☐ 146	Mark Jackson AS	.05	.02	.01
	New York Knicks			
☐ 147	Jim Petersen	.05	.02	.01
	Sacramento Kings			
☐ 148	Steve Stipanovich SP	.15	.07	.02
	Indiana Pacers			
☐ 149	Sam Vincent SP	.05	.02	.01
	Chicago Bulls			
☐ 150	Larry Bird	1.00	.45	.13
	Boston Celtics			
☐ 151	Jon Koncak	.08	.04	.01
	Atlanta Hawks			
☐ 152	Olden Polynice	.15	.07	.02
	Seattle Supersonics			
☐ 153	Randy Breuer	.05	.02	.01
	Milwaukee Bucks			
☐ 154	John Battle	.05	.02	.01
	Atlanta Hawks			
☐ 155	Mark Eaton	.05	.02	.01
	Utah Jazz			
☐ 156	Kevin McHale AS UER	.05	.02	.01
	Boston Celtics			
	(No TM on Celtics			
	logo on back)			
☐ 157	Jerry Sichting SP	.15	.07	.02
	Portland Trail Blazers			
☐ 158	Pat Cummings SP	.15	.07	.02
	Miami Heat			
☐ 159	Patrick Ewing AS	.15	.07	.02
	New York Knicks			
☐ 160	Mark Price	.20	.09	.03
	Cleveland Cavaliers			
☐ 161	Jerry Reynolds CO	.05	.02	.01
	Sacramento Kings			
☐ 162	Ken Norman	.15	.07	.02
	Los Angeles Clippers			
☐ 163	John Bagley SP UER	.15	.07	.02
	New Jersey Nets			
	(Picked in '83,			
	should say '82)			
☐ 164	Christian Welp SP	.15	.07	.02
	Philadelphia 76ers			
☐ 165	Reggie Theus SP	.25	.11	.03
	Atlanta Hawks			
☐ 166	Magic Johnson AS	.30	.14	.04
	Los Angeles Lakers			
☐ 167	John Long UER	.05	.02	.01
	Detroit Pistons			
	(Picked in '79,			
	should say '78)			
☐ 168	Larry Smith SP	.15	.07	.02
	Golden State Warriors			
☐ 169	Charles Shackleford	.05	.02	.01
	New Jersey Nets			
☐ 170	Tom Chambers	.08	.04	.01
	Phoenix Suns			
☐ 171A	John MacLeod CO SP	.15	.07	.02
	Dallas Mavericks			
	ERR (NBA logo in			
	wrong place)			
☐ 171B	John MacLeod CO	.15	.07	.02
	Dallas Mavericks			
	COR (Second series)			
☐ 172	Ron Rothstein CO	.05	.02	.01
	Miami Heat			
☐ 173	Joe Wolf	.05	.02	.01
	Los Angeles Clippers			
☐ 174	Mark Eaton AS	.05	.02	.01
	Utah Jazz			
☐ 175	Jon Sundvold	.05	.02	.01
	Miami Heat			
☐ 176	Scott Hastings SP	.15	.07	.02
	Miami Heat			
☐ 177	Isiah Thomas AS	.10	.05	.01
	Detroit Pistons			
☐ 178	Hakeem Olajuwon AS	.40	.18	.05
	Houston Rockets			
☐ 179	Mike Fratello CO	.05	.02	.01
	Atlanta Hawks			
☐ 180	Hakeem Olajuwon	.75	.35	.09
	Houston Rockets			
☐ 181	Randolph Keys	.05	.02	.01
	Cleveland Cavaliers			
☐ 182	Richard Anderson UER	.05	.02	.01
	Portland Trail Blazers			
	(Trail Blazers on front			
	should be all caps)			
☐ 183	Dan Majerle	.60	.25	.08
	Phoenix Suns			
☐ 184	Derek Harper	.08	.04	.01
	Dallas Mavericks			
☐ 185	Robert Parish	.10	.05	.01
	Boston Celtics			
☐ 186	Ricky Berry SP	.15	.07	.02
	Sacramento Kings			
☐ 187	Michael Cooper	.10	.05	.01
	Los Angeles Lakers			
☐ 188	Vinnie Johnson	.08	.04	.01
	Detroit Pistons			
☐ 189	James Donaldson	.05	.02	.01
	Dallas Mavericks			
☐ 190	Clyde Drexler UER	.30	.14	.04
	Portland Trail Blazers			
	(4th pick, should			
	be 14th)			
☐ 191	Jay Vincent SP	.15	.07	.02
	San Antonio Spurs			
☐ 192	Nate McMillan	.05	.02	.01
	Seattle Supersonics			
☐ 193	Kevin Duckworth AS	.05	.02	.01
	Portland Trail Blazers			
☐ 194	Ledell Eackles	.05	.02	.01
	Washington Bullets			
☐ 195	Eddie Johnson	.08	.04	.01
	Phoenix Suns			
☐ 196	Terry Teagle	.05	.02	.01
	Golden State Warriors			

☐ 197	Tom Chambers AS........ Phoenix Suns	.05	.02	.01
☐ 198	Joe Barry Carroll.......... New Jersey Nets	.05	.02	.01
☐ 199	Dennis Hopson .... New Jersey Nets	.05	.02	.01
☐ 200	Michael Jordan .... Chicago Bulls	4.00	1.80	.50
☐ 201	Jerome Lane .... Denver Nuggets	.05	.02	.01
☐ 202	Greg Kite .... Charlotte Hornets	.05	.02	.01
☐ 203	David Rivers SP............ Los Angeles Lakers	.15	.07	.02
☐ 204	Sylvester Gray.............. Miami Heat	.05	.02	.01
☐ 205	Ron Harper .... Cleveland Cavaliers	.08	.04	.01
☐ 206	Frank Brickowski........... San Antonio Spurs	.05	.02	.01
☐ 207	Rory Sparrow .... Miami Heat	.05	.02	.01
☐ 208	Gerald Henderson .... Philadelphia 76ers	.05	.02	.01
☐ 209	Rod Higgins UER .... Golden State Warriors ('85-86 stats should also include San Antonio and Seattle)	.05	.02	.01
☐ 210	James Worthy .... Los Angeles Lakers	.10	.05	.01
☐ 211	Dennis Rodman .... Detroit Pistons	.50	.23	.06
☐ 212	Ricky Pierce................. Milwaukee Bucks	.08	.04	.01
☐ 213	Charles Oakley .... New York Knicks	.08	.04	.01
☐ 214	Steve Colter .... Washington Bullets	.05	.02	.01
☐ 215	Danny Ainge .... Sacramento Kings	.08	.04	.01
☐ 216	Lenny Wilkens CO UER Cleveland Cavaliers (No NBA logo on back in bottom right)	.08	.04	.01
☐ 217	Larry Nance AS............. Cleveland Cavaliers	.05	.02	.01
☐ 218	Muggsy Bogues............ Charlotte Hornets	.10	.05	.01
☐ 219	James Worthy AS.......... Los Angeles Lakers	.05	.02	.01
☐ 220	Lafayette Lever .... Denver Nuggets	.05	.02	.01
☐ 221	Quintin Dailey SP .... Los Angeles Clippers	.15	.07	.02
☐ 222	Lester Conner .... New Jersey Nets	.05	.02	.01
☐ 223	Jose Ortiz.................... Utah Jazz	.05	.02	.01
☐ 224	Micheal Williams SP ..... Detroit Pistons UER (Misspelled Michael on card)	.15	.07	.02
☐ 225	Wayman Tisdale .... Sacramento Kings	.08	.04	.01
☐ 226	Mike Sanders SP .... Cleveland Cavaliers	.15	.07	.02
☐ 227	Jim Farmer SP .... Utah Jazz	.15	.07	.02
☐ 228	Mark West .... Phoenix Suns	.05	.02	.01
☐ 229	Jeff Hornacek............... Phoenix Suns	.30	.14	.04
☐ 230	Chris Mullin AS............. Golden State Warriors	.05	.02	.01
☐ 231	Vern Fleming .... Indiana Pacers	.05	.02	.01
☐ 232	Kenny Smith .... Sacramento Kings	.05	.02	.01
☐ 233	Derrick McKey .... Seattle Supersonics	.10	.05	.01
☐ 234	Dominique Wilkins AS . Atlanta Hawks	.08	.04	.01
☐ 235	Willie Anderson............. San Antonio Spurs	.05	.02	.01
☐ 236	Keith Lee SP .... New Jersey Nets	.15	.07	.02
☐ 237	Buck Johnson............... Houston Rockets	.05	.02	.01
☐ 238	Randy Wittman .... Indiana Pacers	.05	.02	.01
☐ 239	Terry Catledge SP .... Washington Bullets	.15	.07	.02
☐ 240	Bernard King .... Washington Bullets	.10	.05	.01
☐ 241	Darrell Griffith .... Utah Jazz	.08	.04	.01
☐ 242	Horace Grant................ Chicago Bulls	.40	.18	.05
☐ 243	Rony Seikaly .... Miami Heat	.15	.07	.02
☐ 244	Scottie Pippen .... Chicago Bulls	.75	.35	.09
☐ 245	Michael Cage UER .... Seattle Supersonics (Picked in '85, should say '84)	.05	.02	.01
☐ 246	Kurt Rambis .... Charlotte Hornets	.05	.02	.01
☐ 247	Morlon Wiley SP............ Dallas Mavericks	.15	.07	.02
☐ 248	Ronnie Grandison .... Boston Celtics	.05	.02	.01
☐ 249	Scott Skiles SP .... Indiana Pacers	.25	.11	.03
☐ 250	Isiah Thomas .... Detroit Pistons	.15	.07	.02
☐ 251	Thurl Bailey.................. Utah Jazz	.05	.02	.01
☐ 252	Doc Rivers .... Atlanta Hawks	.05	.02	.01
☐ 253	Stuart Gray SP .... Indiana Pacers	.15	.07	.02
☐ 254	John Williams............... Washington Bullets	.05	.02	.01
☐ 255	Bill Cartwright............... Chicago Bulls	.05	.02	.01
☐ 256	Terry Cummings AS..... Milwaukee Bucks	.05	.02	.01
☐ 257	Rodney McCray .... Sacramento Kings	.05	.02	.01
☐ 258	Larry Krystkowiak .... Milwaukee Bucks	.08	.04	.01
☐ 259	Will Perdue .... Chicago Bulls	.15	.07	.02
☐ 260	Mitch Richmond .... Golden State Warriors	1.00	.45	.13
☐ 261	Blair Rasmussen .... Denver Nuggets	.05	.02	.01
☐ 262	Charles Smith .... Los Angeles Clippers	.15	.07	.02
☐ 263	Tyrone Corbin SP..........	.15	.07	.02

	Phoenix Suns			
☐ 264	Kelvin Upshaw	.05	.02	.01
	Boston Celtics			
☐ 265	Otis Thorpe	.08	.04	.01
	Houston Rockets			
☐ 266	Phil Jackson CO	.08	.04	.01
	Chicago Bulls			
☐ 267	Jerry Sloan CO	.05	.02	.01
	Utah Jazz			
☐ 268	John Shasky	.05	.02	.01
	Miami Heat			
☐ 269A	B. Bickerstaff CO SP	.30	.14	.04
	Seattle Supersonics			
	ERR (Born 2/11/44)			
☐ 269B	B. Bickerstaff CO	.05	.02	.01
	Seattle Supersonics			
	COR (Second series;			
	Born 11/2/43)			
☐ 270	Magic Johnson	.60	.25	.08
	Los Angeles Lakers			
☐ 271	Vernon Maxwell	.15	.07	.02
	San Antonio Spurs			
☐ 272	Tim McCormick	.05	.02	.01
	Houston Rockets			
☐ 273	Don Nelson CO	.08	.04	.01
	Golden State Warriors			
☐ 274	Gary Grant	.08	.04	.01
	Los Angeles Clippers			
☐ 275	Sidney Moncrief SP	.25	.11	.03
	Milwaukee Bucks			
☐ 276	Roy Hinson	.05	.02	.01
	New Jersey Nets			
☐ 277	Jimmy Rodgers CO	.05	.02	.01
	Boston Celtics			
☐ 278	Antoine Carr	.05	.02	.01
	Atlanta Hawks			
☐ 279A	Orlando Woolridge SP	.15	.07	.02
	Los Angeles Lakers			
	ERR (No Trademark)			
☐ 279B	Orlando Woolridge	.05	.02	.01
	Los Angeles Lakers			
	COR (Second series)			
☐ 280	Kevin McHale	.10	.05	.01
	Boston Celtics			
☐ 281	LaSalle Thompson	.05	.02	.01
	Indiana Pacers			
☐ 282	Detlef Schrempf	.20	.09	.03
	Indiana Pacers			
☐ 283	Doug Moe CO	.05	.02	.01
	Denver Nuggets			
☐ 284A	James Edwards	.30	.14	.04
	Detroit Pistons			
	(Small black line			
	next to card number)			
☐ 284B	James Edwards	.05	.02	.01
	Detroit Pistons			
	(No small black line)			
☐ 285	Jerome Kersey	.05	.02	.01
	Portland Trail Blazers			
☐ 286	Sam Perkins	.08	.04	.01
	Dallas Mavericks			
☐ 287	Sedale Threatt	.05	.02	.01
	Seattle Supersonics			
☐ 288	Tim Kempton SP	.15	.07	.02
	Charlotte Hornets			
☐ 289	Mark McNamara	.05	.02	.01
	Los Angeles Lakers			
☐ 290	Moses Malone	.15	.07	.02
	Atlanta Hawks			
☐ 291	Rick Adelman CO UER	.05	.02	.01
	Portland Trail Blazers			

	(Chemekata misspelled			
	as Chemketa)			
☐ 292	Dick Versace CO	.05	.02	.01
	Indiana Pacers			
☐ 293	Alton Lister SP	.15	.07	.02
	Seattle Supersonics			
☐ 294	Winston Garland	.05	.02	.01
	Golden State Warriors			
☐ 295	Kiki Vandeweghe	.05	.02	.01
	New York Knicks			
☐ 296	Brad Davis	.05	.02	.01
	Dallas Mavericks			
☐ 297	John Stockton AS	.40	.18	.05
	Utah Jazz			
☐ 298	Jay Humphries	.05	.02	.01
	Milwaukee Bucks			
☐ 299	Dell Curry	.10	.05	.01
	Charlotte Hornets			
☐ 300	Mark Jackson	.05	.02	.01
	New York Knicks			
☐ 301	Morlon Wiley	.05	.02	.01
	Orlando Magic			
☐ 302	Reggie Theus	.08	.04	.01
	Orlando Magic			
☐ 303	Otis Smith	.05	.02	.01
	Orlando Magic			
☐ 304	Tod Murphy	.05	.02	.01
	Minnesota Timberwolves			
☐ 305	Sidney Green	.05	.02	.01
	Orlando Magic			
☐ 306	Shelton Jones	.05	.02	.01
	Milwaukee Bucks			
☐ 307	Mark Acres	.05	.02	.01
	Orlando Magic			
☐ 308	Terry Catledge	.05	.02	.01
	Orlando Magic			
☐ 309	Larry Smith	.05	.02	.01
	Houston Rockets			
☐ 310	David Robinson IA	3.00	1.35	.40
	San Antonio Spurs			
☐ 311	Johnny Dawkins	.08	.04	.01
	Philadelphia 76ers			
☐ 312	Terry Cummings	.08	.04	.01
	San Antonio Spurs			
☐ 313	Sidney Lowe	.05	.02	.01
	Minnesota Timberwolves			
☐ 314	Bill Musselman CO	.05	.02	.01
	Minnesota Timberwolves			
☐ 315	Buck Williams UER	.08	.04	.01
	Portland Trail Blazers			
	(Won ROY in '81,			
	should say '82)			
☐ 316	Mel Turpin	.05	.02	.01
	Washington Bullets			
☐ 317	Scott Hastings	.05	.02	.01
	Detroit Pistons			
☐ 318	Scott Skiles	.05	.02	.01
	Orlando Magic			
☐ 319	Tyrone Corbin	.08	.04	.01
	Minnesota Timberwolves			
☐ 320	Maurice Cheeks	.10	.05	.01
	San Antonio Spurs			
☐ 321	Matt Goukas CO	.05	.02	.01
	Orlando Magic			
☐ 322	Jeff Turner	.05	.02	.01
	Orlando Magic			
☐ 323	David Wingate	.05	.02	.01
	San Antonio Spurs			
☐ 324	Steve Johnson	.05	.02	.01
	Minnesota Timberwolves			
☐ 325	Alton Lister	.05	.02	.01

Golden State Warriors			
☐ 326 Ken Bannister	.05	.02	.01
Los Angeles Clippers			
☐ 327 Bill Fitch CO UER	.05	.02	.01
New Jersey Nets (Copyright missing on bottom of back)			
☐ 328 Sam Vincent	.05	.02	.01
Orlando Magic			
☐ 329 Larry Drew	.05	.02	.01
Los Angeles Lakers			
☐ 330 Rick Mahorn	.05	.02	.01
Minnesota Timberwolves			
☐ 331 Christian Welp	.05	.02	.01
San Antonio Spurs			
☐ 332 Brad Lohaus	.05	.02	.01
Minnesota Timberwolves			
☐ 333 Frank Johnson	.05	.02	.01
Orlando Magic			
☐ 334 Jim Farmer	.05	.02	.01
Minnesota Timberwolves			
☐ 335 Wayne Cooper	.05	.02	.01
Portland Trail Blazers			
☐ 336 Mike Brown	.05	.02	.01
Utah Jazz			
☐ 337 Sam Bowie	.05	.02	.01
New Jersey Nets			
☐ 338 Kevin Gamble	.08	.04	.01
Boston Celtics			
☐ 339 Jerry Ice Reynolds	.05	.02	.01
Orlando Magic			
☐ 340 Mike Sanders	.05	.02	.01
Indiana Pacers			
☐ 341 Bill Jones UER	.05	.02	.01
New Jersey Nets (Center on front, should be F)			
☐ 342 Greg Anderson	.05	.02	.01
Milwaukee Bucks			
☐ 343 Dave Corzine	.05	.02	.01
Orlando Magic			
☐ 344 Micheal Williams UER	.05	.02	.01
Phoenix Suns (Misspelled Michael on card)			
☐ 345 Jay Vincent	.05	.02	.01
Philadelphia 76ers			
☐ 346 David Rivers	.05	.02	.01
Minnesota Timberwolves			
☐ 347 Caldwell Jones UER	.05	.02	.01
San Antonio Spurs (He was not starting center on '83 Sixers)			
☐ 348 Brad Sellers	.05	.02	.01
Seattle Supersonics			
☐ 349 Scott Roth	.05	.02	.01
Minnesota Timberwolves			
☐ 350 Alvin Robertson	.05	.02	.01
Milwaukee Bucks			
☐ 351 Steve Kerr	.15	.07	.02
Cleveland Cavaliers			
☐ 352 Stuart Gray	.05	.02	.01
Charlotte Hornets			
☐ 353A World Champions SP	5.00	2.30	.60
Detroit Pistons			
☐ 353B World Champions UER	.50	.23	.06
Detroit Pistons (George Blaha misspelled Blanha)			

1990-91 Hoops

The complete 1990-91 Hoops basketball set contains 440 cards measuring the standard size (2 1/2" by 3 1/2"). The set was distributed in two series of 336 and 104 cards, respectively. The cards were issued in 15-card plastic-wrap packs which came 36 to a box. On the front the color action player photo appears in the shape of a basketball lane, bordered by gold on the All-Star cards (1-26) and by silver on the regular issues (27-331, 336). The player's name and the stripe below the picture are printed in one of the team's colors. The team logo at the lower right corner rounds out the card face. The back of the regular issue has a color head shot and biographical information as well as college and pro statistics, framed by a basketball lane. The cards are numbered on the back and arranged alphabetically according to teams as follows: Atlanta Hawks (27-37), Boston Celtics (38-48), Charlotte Hornets (49-59), Chicago Bulls (60-69), Cleveland Cavaliers (70-80), Dallas Mavericks (81-90), Denver Nuggets (91-100), Detroit Pistons (101-111), Golden State Warriors (112-122), Houston Rockets (123-131), Indiana Pacers (132-141), Los Angeles Clippers (142-152), Los Angeles Lakers (153-163), Miami Heat (164-172), Milwaukee Bucks (173-183), Minnesota Timberwolves (184-192), New Jersey Nets (193-201), New York Knicks (202-212), Orlando Magic (213-223), Philadelphia 76ers (224-232), Phoenix Suns (233-242), Portland Trail Blazers (243-252), Sacramento Kings (253-262), San Antonio Spurs (263-273), Seattle Supersonics (274-284), Utah Jazz (285-294), Washington Bullets (295-331), Coaches (305-331), NBA Finals (337-342), Coaches (343-354), Team checklists (355-381), Inside Stuff (382-385), Stay in School (386-387), Don't Foul Out (388-389), Lottery Selections (390-400), and Updates (401-438). Some of the All-Star cards (card numbers 2, 6, and 8) can be found with or without a printing mistake, i.e., no T in the trademark logo on the card back. A few of the cards (card numbers 14, 66, 144, and 279) refer to the player as "all America" rather than "All America". The following cards can be found with or without a black line under the card number, height, and birthplace: 20, 23, 24,

29, and 87. Rookie Cards included in the set are Nick Anderson, B.J. Armstrong, Mookie Blaylock, Derrick Coleman, Vlade Divac, Sherman Douglas, Sean Elliott, Kendall Gill, Tim Hardaway, Chris Jackson, Shawn Kemp, Gary Payton, Drazen Petrovic, Glen Rice, Cliff Robinson, Dennis Scott, and Lionel Simmons. The short prints (SP below) in the first series are those cards which were dropped to make room for the new second series cards on the printing sheet.

	MINT	NRMT	EXC
COMPLETE SET (440)	15.00	6.75	1.90
COMPLETE SERIES 1 (336)	10.00	4.50	1.25
COMPLETE SERIES 2 (104)	5.00	2.30	.60
COMMON CARD (1-440)	.05	.02	.01

☐ 1	Charles Barkley AS SP	.50	.23	.06
	Philadelphia 76ers			
☐ 2	Larry Bird AS SP	.75	.35	.09
	Boston Celtics			
☐ 3	Joe Dumars AS SP	.15	.07	.02
	Detroit Pistons			
☐ 4	Patrick Ewing AS SP	.25	.11	.03
	New York Knicks			
	(A-S blocks listed as			
	1, should be 5) UER			
☐ 5	Michael Jordan AS SP	3.00	1.35	.40
	Chicago Bulls			
	(Won Slam Dunk in			
	'87 and '88,			
	not '86 and '88) UER			
☐ 6	Kevin McHale AS SP	.10	.05	.01
	Boston Celtics			
☐ 7	Reggie Miller AS SP	.30	.14	.04
	Indiana Pacers			
☐ 8	Robert Parish AS SP	.10	.05	.01
	Boston Celtics			
☐ 9	Scottie Pippen AS SP	.30	.14	.04
	Chicago Bulls			
☐ 10	Dennis Rodman AS SP	.20	.09	.03
	Detroit Pistons			
☐ 11	Isiah Thomas AS SP	.15	.07	.02
	Detroit Pistons			
☐ 12	Dominique Wilkins	.15	.07	.02
	AS SP			
	Atlanta Hawks			
☐ 13A	All-Star Checklist P	.50	.23	.06
	ERR (No card number)			
☐ 13B	All-Star Checklist P	.10	.05	.01
	COR (Card number on back)			
☐ 14	Rolando Blackman AS SP	.10	.05	.01
	Dallas Mavericks			
☐ 15	Tom Chambers AS SP	.10	.05	.01
	Phoenix Suns			
☐ 16	Clyde Drexler AS SP	.25	.11	.03
	Portland Trail Blazers			
☐ 17	A.C. Green AS SP	.15	.07	.02
	Los Angeles Lakers			
☐ 18	Magic Johnson AS SP	.50	.23	.06
	Los Angeles Lakers			
☐ 19	Kevin Johnson AS SP	.25	.11	.03
	Phoenix Suns			
☐ 20	Lafayette Lever AS SP	.10	.05	.01
	Denver Nuggets			
☐ 21	Karl Malone AS SP	.25	.11	.03
	Utah Jazz			
☐ 22	Chris Mullin AS SP	.10	.05	.01
	Golden State Warriors			

☐ 23	Hakeem Olajuwon AS SP	.60	.25	.08
	Houston Rockets			
☐ 24	David Robinson AS SP	1.00	.45	.13
	San Antonio Spurs			
☐ 25	John Stockton AS SP	.30	.14	.04
	Utah Jazz			
☐ 26	James Worthy AS SP	.15	.07	.02
	Los Angeles Lakers			
☐ 27	John Battle	.05	.02	.01
☐ 28	Jon Koncak	.05	.02	.01
☐ 29	Cliff Levingston SP	.10	.05	.01
☐ 30	John Long SP	.10	.05	.01
☐ 31	Moses Malone	.15	.07	.02
☐ 32	Doc Rivers	.05	.02	.01
☐ 33	Kenny Smith SP	.10	.05	.01
☐ 34	Alexander Volkov	.05	.02	.01
☐ 35	Spud Webb	.08	.04	.01
☐ 36	Dominique Wilkins	.15	.07	.02
☐ 37	Kevin Willis	.08	.04	.01
☐ 38	John Bagley	.05	.02	.01
☐ 39	Larry Bird	.75	.35	.09
☐ 40	Kevin Gamble	.05	.02	.01
☐ 41	Dennis Johnson SP	.15	.07	.02
☐ 42	Joe Kleine	.05	.02	.01
☐ 43	Reggie Lewis	.10	.05	.01
☐ 44	Kevin McHale	.10	.05	.01
☐ 45	Robert Parish	.10	.05	.01
☐ 46	Jim Paxson SP	.10	.05	.01
☐ 47	Ed Pinckney	.05	.02	.01
☐ 48	Brian Shaw	.05	.02	.01
☐ 49	Richard Anderson SP	.10	.05	.01
☐ 50	Muggsy Bogues	.10	.05	.01
☐ 51	Rex Chapman	.05	.02	.01
☐ 52	Dell Curry	.05	.02	.01
☐ 53	Kenny Gattison	.05	.02	.01
☐ 54	Armon Gilliam	.05	.02	.01
☐ 55	Dave Hoppen	.05	.02	.01
☐ 56	Randolph Keys	.05	.02	.01
☐ 57	J.R. Reid	.10	.05	.01
☐ 58	Robert Reid SP	.10	.05	.01
☐ 59	Kelly Tripucka	.05	.02	.01
☐ 60	B.J. Armstrong	.15	.07	.02
☐ 61	Bill Cartwright	.05	.02	.01
☐ 62	Charles Davis SP	.10	.05	.01
☐ 63	Horace Grant	.15	.07	.02
☐ 64	Craig Hodges	.05	.02	.01
☐ 65	Michael Jordan	3.00	1.35	.40
☐ 66	Stacey King	.08	.04	.01
☐ 67	John Paxson	.05	.02	.01
☐ 68	Will Perdue	.05	.02	.01
☐ 69	Scottie Pippen	.30	.14	.04
☐ 70	Winston Bennett	.05	.02	.01
☐ 71	Chucky Brown	.05	.02	.01
☐ 72	Derrick Chievous	.05	.02	.01
☐ 73	Brad Daugherty	.08	.04	.01
☐ 74	Craig Ehlo	.08	.04	.01
☐ 75	Steve Kerr	.05	.02	.01
☐ 76	Paul Mokeski SP	.10	.05	.01
☐ 77	John Morton	.05	.02	.01
☐ 78	Larry Nance	.08	.04	.01
☐ 79	Mark Price	.10	.05	.01
☐ 80	Hot Rod Williams	.05	.02	.01
☐ 81	Steve Alford	.08	.04	.01
☐ 82	Rolando Blackman	.08	.04	.01
☐ 83	Adrian Dantley SP	.15	.07	.02
☐ 84	Brad Davis	.05	.02	.01
☐ 85	James Donaldson	.05	.02	.01
☐ 86	Derek Harper	.08	.04	.01
☐ 87	Sam Perkins SP	.15	.07	.02
☐ 88	Roy Tarpley	.05	.02	.01
☐ 89	Bill Wennington SP	.10	.05	.01

☐ 90	Herb Williams	.05	.02	.01
☐ 91	Michael Adams	.05	.02	.01
☐ 92	Joe Barry Carroll SP	.10	.05	.01
☐ 93	Walter Davis UER	.10	.05	.01
	(Born NC, not PA)			
☐ 94	Alex English SP	.15	.07	.02
☐ 95	Bill Hanzlik	.05	.02	.01
☐ 96	Jerome Lane	.05	.02	.01
☐ 97	Lafayette Lever SP	.10	.05	.01
☐ 98	Todd Lichti	.05	.02	.01
☐ 99	Blair Rasmussen	.05	.02	.01
☐ 100	Danny Schayes SP	.10	.05	.01
☐ 101	Mark Aguirre	.08	.04	.01
☐ 102	William Bedford	.05	.02	.01
☐ 103	Joe Dumars	.15	.07	.02
☐ 104	James Edwards	.05	.02	.01
☐ 105	Scott Hastings	.05	.02	.01
☐ 106	Gerald Henderson SP	.10	.05	.01
☐ 107	Vinnie Johnson	.08	.04	.01
☐ 108	Bill Laimbeer	.08	.04	.01
☐ 109	Dennis Rodman	.20	.09	.03
☐ 110	John Salley	.05	.02	.01
☐ 111	Isiah Thomas UER	.15	.07	.02
	(No position listed			
	on the card)			
☐ 112	Manute Bol SP	.10	.05	.01
☐ 113	Tim Hardaway	.60	.25	.08
☐ 114	Rod Higgins	.05	.02	.01
☐ 115	Sarunas Marciulionis	.10	.05	.01
☐ 116	Chris Mullin UER	.10	.05	.01
	(Born Brooklyn, NY,			
	not New York, NY)			
☐ 117	Jim Petersen	.05	.02	.01
☐ 118	Mitch Richmond	.25	.11	.03
☐ 119	Mike Smrek	.05	.02	.01
☐ 120	Terry Teagle SP	.10	.05	.01
☐ 121	Tom Tolbert	.05	.02	.01
☐ 122	Christian Welp SP	.10	.05	.01
☐ 123	Byron Dinkins SP	.10	.05	.01
☐ 124	Eric(Sleepy) Floyd	.08	.04	.01
☐ 125	Buck Johnson	.05	.02	.01
☐ 126	Vernon Maxwell	.05	.02	.01
☐ 127	Hakeem Olajuwon	.60	.25	.08
☐ 128	Larry Smith	.05	.02	.01
☐ 129	Otis Thorpe	.08	.04	.01
☐ 130	Mitchell Wiggins SP	.10	.05	.01
☐ 131	Mike Woodson	.05	.02	.01
☐ 132	Greg Dreiling	.05	.02	.01
☐ 133	Vern Fleming	.05	.02	.01
☐ 134	Rickey Green SP	.10	.05	.01
☐ 135	Reggie Miller	.30	.14	.04
☐ 136	Chuck Person	.08	.04	.01
☐ 137	Mike Sanders	.05	.02	.01
☐ 138	Detlef Schrempf	.10	.05	.01
☐ 139	Rik Smits	.10	.05	.01
☐ 140	LaSalle Thompson	.05	.02	.01
☐ 141	Randy Wittman	.05	.02	.01
☐ 142	Benoit Benjamin	.05	.02	.01
☐ 143	Winston Garland	.05	.02	.01
☐ 144	Tom Garrick	.05	.02	.01
☐ 145	Gary Grant	.05	.02	.01
☐ 146	Ron Harper	.08	.04	.01
☐ 147	Danny Manning	.15	.07	.02
☐ 148	Jeff Martin	.05	.02	.01
☐ 149	Ken Norman	.05	.02	.01
☐ 150	David Rivers SP	.10	.05	.01
☐ 151	Charles Smith	.05	.02	.01
☐ 152	Joe Wolf SP	.10	.05	.01
☐ 153	Michael Cooper SP	.15	.07	.02
☐ 154	Vlade Divac UER	.50	.23	.06
	(Height 6'11",			

	should be 7'1")			
☐ 155	Larry Drew	.05	.02	.01
☐ 156	A.C. Green	.10	.05	.01
☐ 157	Magic Johnson	.50	.23	.06
☐ 158	Mark McNamara SP	.10	.05	.01
☐ 159	Byron Scott	.08	.04	.01
☐ 160	Mychal Thompson	.08	.04	.01
☐ 161	Jay Vincent SP	.10	.05	.01
☐ 162	Orlando Woolridge SP	.10	.05	.01
☐ 163	James Worthy	.10	.05	.01
☐ 164	Sherman Douglas	.15	.07	.02
☐ 165	Kevin Edwards	.05	.02	.01
☐ 166	Tellis Frank SP	.10	.05	.01
☐ 167	Grant Long	.05	.02	.01
☐ 168	Glen Rice	.50	.23	.06
☐ 169A	Rony Seikaly	.05	.02	.01
	(Athens)			
☐ 169B	Rony Seikaly	.05	.02	.01
	(Beirut)			
☐ 170	Rory Sparrow SP	.10	.05	.01
☐ 171A	Jon Sundvold	.05	.02	.01
	(First series)			
☐ 171B	Billy Thompson	.05	.02	.01
	(Second series)			
☐ 172A	Billy Thompson	.05	.02	.01
	(First series)			
☐ 172B	Jon Sundvold	.05	.02	.01
	(Second series)			
☐ 173	Greg Anderson	.05	.02	.01
☐ 174	Jeff Grayer	.05	.02	.01
☐ 175	Jay Humphries	.05	.02	.01
☐ 176	Frank Kornet	.05	.02	.01
☐ 177	Larry Krystkowiak	.05	.02	.01
☐ 178	Brad Lohaus	.05	.02	.01
☐ 179	Ricky Pierce	.08	.04	.01
☐ 180	Paul Pressey SP	.10	.05	.01
☐ 181	Fred Roberts	.05	.02	.01
☐ 182	Alvin Robertson	.05	.02	.01
☐ 183	Jack Sikma	.08	.04	.01
☐ 184	Randy Breuer	.05	.02	.01
☐ 185	Tony Campbell	.05	.02	.01
☐ 186	Tyrone Corbin	.08	.04	.01
☐ 187	Sidney Lowe SP	.10	.05	.01
☐ 188	Sam Mitchell	.05	.02	.01
☐ 189	Tod Murphy	.05	.02	.01
☐ 190	Pooh Richardson	.15	.07	.02
☐ 191	Scott Roth SP	.10	.05	.01
☐ 192	Brad Sellers SP	.10	.05	.01
☐ 193	Mookie Blaylock	.40	.18	.05
☐ 194	Sam Bowie	.05	.02	.01
☐ 195	Lester Conner	.05	.02	.01
☐ 196	Derrick Gervin	.05	.02	.01
☐ 197	Jack Haley	.05	.02	.01
☐ 198	Roy Hinson	.05	.02	.01
☐ 199	Dennis Hopson SP	.10	.05	.01
☐ 200	Chris Morris	.05	.02	.01
☐ 201	Purvis Short SP	.10	.05	.01
☐ 202	Maurice Cheeks	.10	.05	.01
☐ 203	Patrick Ewing	.25	.11	.03
☐ 204	Stuart Gray	.05	.02	.01
☐ 205	Mark Jackson	.05	.02	.01
☐ 206	Johnny Newman SP	.10	.05	.01
☐ 207	Charles Oakley	.08	.04	.01
☐ 208	Trent Tucker	.05	.02	.01
☐ 209	Kiki Vandeweghe	.05	.02	.01
☐ 210	Kenny Walker	.05	.02	.01
☐ 211	Eddie Lee Wilkins	.05	.02	.01
☐ 212	Gerald Wilkins	.05	.02	.01
☐ 213	Mark Acres	.05	.02	.01
☐ 214	Nick Anderson	.40	.18	.05
☐ 215	Michael Ansley UER	.05	.02	.01

(Ranked first, not third)
☐ 216	Terry Catledge	.05	.02	.01
☐ 217	Dave Corzine SP	.10	.05	.01
☐ 218	Sidney Green SP	.10	.05	.01
☐ 219	Jerry Reynolds	.05	.02	.01
☐ 220	Scott Skiles	.05	.02	.01
☐ 221	Otis Smith	.05	.02	.01
☐ 222	Reggie Theus SP	.15	.07	.02
☐ 223A	Sam Vincent	1.50	.65	.19

(First series, shows
12 Michael Jordan)

☐ 223B	Sam Vincent	.05	.02	.01

(Second series, shows
Sam dribbling)

☐ 224	Ron Anderson	.05	.02	.01
☐ 225	Charles Barkley	.50	.23	.06
☐ 226	Scott Brooks SP UER	.10	.05	.01

(Born French Camp,
not Lathron, Cal.)

☐ 227	Johnny Dawkins	.05	.02	.01
☐ 228	Mike Gminski	.05	.02	.01
☐ 229	Hersey Hawkins	.08	.04	.01
☐ 230	Rick Mahorn	.05	.02	.01
☐ 231	Derek Smith SP	.10	.05	.01
☐ 232	Bob Thornton	.05	.02	.01
☐ 233	Kenny Battle	.05	.02	.01
☐ 234A	Tom Chambers	.08	.04	.01

(First series;
Forward on front)

☐ 234B	Tom Chambers	.08	.04	.01

(Second series;
Guard on front)

☐ 235	Greg Grant SP	.10	.05	.01
☐ 236	Jeff Hornacek	.10	.05	.01
☐ 237	Eddie Johnson	.08	.04	.01
☐ 238A	Kevin Johnson	.25	.11	.03

(First series;
Guard on front)

☐ 238B	Kevin Johnson	.25	.11	.03

(Second series;
Forward on front)

☐ 239	Dan Majerle	.10	.05	.01
☐ 240	Tim Perry	.05	.02	.01
☐ 241	Kurt Rambis	.05	.02	.01
☐ 242	Mark West	.05	.02	.01
☐ 243	Mark Bryant	.05	.02	.01
☐ 244	Wayne Cooper	.05	.02	.01
☐ 245	Clyde Drexler	.25	.11	.03
☐ 246	Kevin Duckworth	.05	.02	.01
☐ 247	Jerome Kersey	.05	.02	.01
☐ 248	Drazen Petrovic	.15	.07	.02
☐ 249A	Terry Porter ERR	1.00	.45	.13

(No NBA symbol on back)

☐ 249B	Terry Porter COR	.08	.04	.01
☐ 250	Cliff Robinson	.40	.18	.05
☐ 251	Buck Williams	.08	.04	.01
☐ 252	Danny Young	.05	.02	.01
☐ 253	Danny Ainge SP UER	.15	.07	.02

(Middle name Ray mis-
spelled as Rae on back)

☐ 254	Randy Allen SP	.10	.05	.01
☐ 255	Antoine Carr	.05	.02	.01
☐ 256	Vinny Del Negro SP	.10	.05	.01
☐ 257	Pervis Ellison SP	.20	.09	.03
☐ 258	Greg Kite SP	.10	.05	.01
☐ 259	Rodney McCray SP	.10	.05	.01
☐ 260	Harold Pressley SP	.10	.05	.01
☐ 261	Ralph Sampson	.05	.02	.01
☐ 262	Wayman Tisdale	.08	.04	.01
☐ 263	Willie Anderson	.05	.02	.01
☐ 264	Uwe Blab SP	.05	.02	.01

☐ 265	Frank Brickowski SP	.10	.05	.01
☐ 266	Terry Cummings	.08	.04	.01
☐ 267	Sean Elliott	.40	.18	.05
☐ 268	Caldwell Jones SP	.10	.05	.01
☐ 269	Johnny Moore SP	.10	.05	.01
☐ 270	David Robinson	1.00	.45	.13
☐ 271	Rod Strickland	.10	.05	.01
☐ 272	Reggie Williams	.05	.02	.01
☐ 273	David Wingate SP	.10	.05	.01
☐ 274	Dana Barros UER	.50	.23	.06

(Born April, not March)

☐ 275	Michael Cage UER	.05	.02	.01

(Drafted '84, not '85)

☐ 276	Quintin Dailey	.05	.02	.01
☐ 277	Dale Ellis	.08	.04	.01
☐ 278	Steve Johnson SP	.10	.05	.01
☐ 279	Shawn Kemp	3.00	1.35	.40
☐ 280	Xavier McDaniel	.08	.04	.01
☐ 281	Derrick McKey	.08	.04	.01
☐ 282	Nate McMillan	.05	.02	.01
☐ 283	Olden Polynice	.05	.02	.01
☐ 284	Sedale Threatt	.05	.02	.01
☐ 285	Thurl Bailey	.05	.02	.01
☐ 286	Mike Brown	.05	.02	.01
☐ 287	Mark Eaton UER	.05	.02	.01

(72nd pick, not 82nd)

☐ 288	Blue Edwards	.08	.04	.01
☐ 289	Darrell Griffith	.08	.04	.01
☐ 290	Robert Hansen SP	.10	.05	.01
☐ 291	Eric Leckner SP	.10	.05	.01
☐ 292	Karl Malone	.25	.11	.03
☐ 293	Delaney Rudd	.05	.02	.01
☐ 294	John Stockton	.30	.14	.04
☐ 295	Mark Alarie	.05	.02	.01
☐ 296	Ledell Eackles SP	.10	.05	.01
☐ 297	Harvey Grant	.05	.02	.01
☐ 298A	Tom Hammonds	.05	.02	.01

(No rookie logo on front)

☐ 298B	Tom Hammonds	.05	.02	.01

(Rookie logo on front)

☐ 299	Charles Jones	.05	.02	.01
☐ 300	Bernard King	.10	.05	.01
☐ 301	Jeff Malone SP	.15	.07	.02
☐ 302	Mel Turpin SP	.10	.05	.01
☐ 303	Darrell Walker	.05	.02	.01
☐ 304	John Williams	.05	.02	.01
☐ 305	Bob Weiss CO	.05	.02	.01
	Atlanta Hawks			
☐ 306	Chris Ford CO	.05	.02	.01
	Boston Celtics			
☐ 307	Gene Littles CO	.05	.02	.01
	Charlotte Hornets			
☐ 308	Phil Jackson CO	.08	.04	.01
	Chicago Bulls			
☐ 309	Lenny Wilkens CO	.08	.04	.01
	Cleveland Cavaliers			
☐ 310	Richie Adubato CO	.05	.02	.01
	Dallas Mavericks			
☐ 311	Doug Moe CO SP	.10	.05	.01
	Denver Nuggets			
☐ 312	Chuck Daly CO	.08	.04	.01
	Detroit Pistons			
☐ 313	Don Nelson CO	.08	.04	.01
	Golden State Warriors			
☐ 314	Don Chaney CO	.05	.02	.01
	Houston Rockets			
☐ 315	Dick Versace CO	.05	.02	.01
	Indiana Pacers			
☐ 316	Mike Schuler CO	.05	.02	.01
	Los Angeles Clippers			
☐ 317	Pat Riley CO SP	.15	.07	.02

	Los Angeles Lakers			
☐ 318	Ron Rothstein CO	.05	.02	.01
	Miami Heat			
☐ 319	Del Harris CO	.05	.02	.01
	Milwaukee Bucks			
☐ 320	Bill Musselman CO	.05	.02	.01
	Minnesota Timberwolves			
☐ 321	Bill Fitch CO	.05	.02	.01
	New Jersey Nets			
☐ 322	Stu Jackson CO	.05	.02	.01
	New York Knicks			
☐ 323	Matt Guokas CO	.05	.02	.01
	Orlando Magic			
☐ 324	Jim Lynam CO	.05	.02	.01
	Philadelphia 76ers			
☐ 325	Cotton Fitzsimmons CO	.05	.02	.01
	Phoenix Suns			
☐ 326	Rick Adelman CO	.05	.02	.01
	Portland Trail Blazers			
☐ 327	Dick Motta CO	.05	.02	.01
	Sacramento Kings			
☐ 328	Larry Brown CO	.08	.04	.01
	San Antonio Spurs			
☐ 329	K.C. Jones CO	.08	.04	.01
	Seattle Supersonics			
☐ 330	Jerry Sloan CO	.05	.02	.01
	Utah Jazz			
☐ 331	Wes Unseld CO	.08	.04	.01
	Washington Bullets			
☐ 332	Checklist 1 SP	.10	.05	.01
☐ 333	Checklist 2 SP	.10	.05	.01
☐ 334	Checklist 3 SP	.10	.05	.01
☐ 335	Checklist 4 SP	.10	.05	.01
☐ 336	Danny Ferry SP	.15	.07	.02
	Cleveland Cavaliers			
☐ 337	NBA Final Game 1	.05	.02	.01
☐ 338	NBA Final Game 2	.05	.02	.01
☐ 339	NBA Final Game 3	.05	.02	.01
☐ 340	NBA Final Game 4	.05	.02	.01
☐ 341A	NBA Final Game 5 ERR	.05	.02	.01
	(No headline on back)			
☐ 341B	NBA Final Game 5 COR	.05	.02	.01
☐ 342	Championship Card UER	.05	.02	.01
	(Player named as Sidney Green is really David Greenwood)			
☐ 343	K.C. Jones CO	.08	.04	.01
	Seattle Supersonics			
☐ 344	Wes Unseld CO	.08	.04	.01
	Washington Bullets			
☐ 345	Don Nelson CO	.08	.04	.01
	Golden State Warriors			
☐ 346	Bob Weiss CO	.05	.02	.01
	Atlanta Hawks			
☐ 347	Chris Ford CO	.05	.02	.01
	Boston Celtics			
☐ 348	Phil Jackson CO	.08	.04	.01
	Chicago Bulls			
☐ 349	Lenny Wilkens CO	.08	.04	.01
	Cleveland Cavaliers			
☐ 350	Don Chaney CO	.05	.02	.01
	Houston Rockets			
☐ 351	Mike Dunleavy CO	.05	.02	.01
	Los Angeles Lakers			
☐ 352	Matt Guokas CO	.05	.02	.01
	Orlando Magic			
☐ 353	Rick Adelman CO	.05	.02	.01
	Portland Trail Blazers			
☐ 354	Jerry Sloan CO	.05	.02	.01
	Utah Jazz			
☐ 355	Dominique Wilkins TC	.05	.02	.01
	Atlanta Hawks			
☐ 356	Larry Bird TC	.40	.18	.05
	Boston Celtics			
☐ 357	Rex Chapman TC	.05	.02	.01
	Charlotte Hornets			
☐ 358	Michael Jordan TC	1.50	.65	.19
	Chicago Bulls			
☐ 359	Mark Price TC	.05	.02	.01
	Cleveland Cavaliers			
☐ 360	Rolando Blackman TC	.05	.02	.01
	Dallas Mavericks			
☐ 361	Michael Adams TC UER	.05	.02	.01
	Denver Nuggets (Westhead should be card 422, not 440)			
☐ 362	Joe Dumars TC UER	.08	.04	.01
	Detroit Pistons (Gerald Henderson's name and number not listed)			
☐ 363	Chris Mullin TC	.05	.02	.01
	Golden State Warriors			
☐ 364	Hakeem Olajuwon TC	.30	.14	.04
	Houston Rockets			
☐ 365	Reggie Miller TC	.10	.05	.01
	Indiana Pacers			
☐ 366	Danny Manning TC	.05	.02	.01
	Los Angeles Clippers			
☐ 367	Magic Johnson TC UER	.25	.11	.03
	Los Angeles Lakers (Dunleavy listed as 439, should be 351)			
☐ 368	Rony Seikaly TC	.05	.02	.01
	Miami Heat			
☐ 369	Alvin Robertson TC	.05	.02	.01
	Milwaukee Bucks			
☐ 370	Pooh Richardson TC	.05	.02	.01
	Minnesota Timberwolves			
☐ 371	Chris Morris TC	.05	.02	.01
	New Jersey Nets			
☐ 372	Patrick Ewing TC	.10	.05	.01
	New York Knicks			
☐ 373	Nick Anderson TC	.15	.07	.02
	Orlando Magic			
☐ 374	Charles Barkley TC	.25	.11	.03
	Philadelphia 76ers			
☐ 375	Kevin Johnson TC	.08	.04	.01
	Phoenix Suns			
☐ 376	Clyde Drexler TC	.10	.05	.01
	Portland Trail Blazers			
☐ 377	Wayman Tisdale TC	.05	.02	.01
	Sacramento Kings			
☐ 378A	David Robinson TC	.50	.23	.06
	San Antonio Spurs (Basketball fully visible)			
☐ 378B	David Robinson TC	.50	.23	.06
	San Antonio Spurs (Basketball partially visible)			
☐ 379	Xavier McDaniel TC	.05	.02	.01
	Seattle Supersonics			
☐ 380	Karl Malone TC	.10	.05	.01
	Utah Jazz			
☐ 381	Bernard King TC	.05	.02	.01
	Washington Bullets			
☐ 382	Michael Jordan	1.50	.65	.19
	Playground			
☐ 383	Lights, Camera,	.10	.05	.01
	NBA Action (Karl Malone on horseback)			

☐ 384	European Imports (Vlade Divac and Sarunas Marciulionis)	.05	.02	.01
☐ 385	Super Streaks Stay In School (Magic Johnson and Michael Jordan)	1.00	.45	.13
☐ 386	Johnny Newman Charlotte Hornets (Stay in School)	.05	.02	.01
☐ 387	Dell Curry Charlotte Hornets (Stay in School)	.05	.02	.01
☐ 388	Patrick Ewing New York Knicks (Don't Foul Out)	.05	.02	.01
☐ 389	Isiah Thomas Detroit Pistons (Don't Foul Out)	.05	.02	.01
☐ 390	Derrick Coleman LS New Jersey Nets	.60	.25	.08
☐ 391	Gary Payton LS Seattle Supersonics	.60	.25	.08
☐ 392	Chris Jackson LS Denver Nuggets	.25	.11	.03
☐ 393	Dennis Scott LS Orlando Magic	.30	.14	.04
☐ 394	Kendall Gill LS Charlotte Hornets	.25	.11	.03
☐ 395	Felton Spencer LS Minnesota Timberwolves	.10	.05	.01
☐ 396	Lionel Simmons LS Sacramento Kings	.08	.04	.01
☐ 397	Bo Kimble LS Los Angeles Clippers	.05	.02	.01
☐ 398	Willie Burton LS Miami Heat	.15	.07	.02
☐ 399	Rumeal Robinson LS Atlanta Hawks	.08	.04	.01
☐ 400	Tyrone Hill LS Golden State Warriors	.40	.18	.05
☐ 401	Tim McCormick Atlanta Hawks	.05	.02	.01
☐ 402	Sidney Moncrief Atlanta Hawks	.10	.05	.01
☐ 403	Johnny Newman Charlotte Hornets	.05	.02	.01
☐ 404	Dennis Hopson Chicago Bulls	.05	.02	.01
☐ 405	Cliff Levingston Chicago Bulls	.05	.02	.01
☐ 406A	Danny Ferry ERR Cleveland Cavaliers (No position on front of card)	.50	.23	.06
☐ 406B	Danny Ferry COR Cleveland Cavaliers	.05	.02	.01
☐ 407	Alex English Dallas Mavericks	.10	.05	.01
☐ 408	Lafayette Lever Dallas Mavericks	.05	.02	.01
☐ 409	Rodney McCray Dallas Mavericks	.05	.02	.01
☐ 410	Mike Dunleavy CO Los Angeles Lakers	.05	.02	.01
☐ 411	Orlando Woolridge Denver Nuggets	.05	.02	.01
☐ 412	Joe Wolf Denver Nuggets	.05	.02	.01
☐ 413	Tree Rollins Detroit Pistons	.05	.02	.01

☐ 414	Kenny Smith Houston Rockets	.05	.02	.01
☐ 415	Sam Perkins Los Angeles Lakers	.08	.04	.01
☐ 416	Terry Teagle Los Angeles Lakers	.05	.02	.01
☐ 417	Frank Brickowski Milwaukee Bucks	.05	.02	.01
☐ 418	Danny Schayes Milwaukee Bucks	.05	.02	.01
☐ 419	Scott Brooks Minnesota Timberwolves	.05	.02	.01
☐ 420	Reggie Theus New Jersey Nets	.08	.04	.01
☐ 421	Greg Grant New York Knicks	.05	.02	.01
☐ 422	Paul Westhead CO Denver Nuggets	.08	.04	.01
☐ 423	Greg Kite Orlando Magic	.05	.02	.01
☐ 424	Manute Bol Philadelphia 76ers	.05	.02	.01
☐ 425	Rickey Green Philadelphia 76ers	.05	.02	.01
☐ 426	Ed Nealy Phoenix Suns	.05	.02	.01
☐ 427	Danny Ainge Portland Trail Blazers	.08	.04	.01
☐ 428	Bobby Hansen Sacramento Kings	.05	.02	.01
☐ 429	Eric Leckner Charlotte Hornets	.05	.02	.01
☐ 430	Rory Sparrow Sacramento Kings	.05	.02	.01
☐ 431	Bill Wennington Sacramento Kings	.05	.02	.01
☐ 432	Paul Pressey San Antonio Spurs	.05	.02	.01
☐ 433	David Greenwood San Antonio Spurs	.05	.02	.01
☐ 434	Mark McNamara Orlando Magic	.05	.02	.01
☐ 435	Sidney Green Orlando Magic	.05	.02	.01
☐ 436	Dave Corzine Orlando Magic	.05	.02	.01
☐ 437	Jeff Malone Utah Jazz	.08	.04	.01
☐ 438	Pervis Ellison Washington Bullets	.05	.02	.01
☐ 439	Checklist 5	.05	.02	.01
☐ 440	Checklist 6	.05	.02	.01
☐ NNO	David Robinson and All-Rookie Team (No stats on back)	1.50	.65	.19
☐ NNO	David Robinson and All-Rookie Team (Stats on back)	8.00	3.60	1.00

1991-92 Hoops

The complete 1991-92 Hoops basketball set contains 590 cards measuring the standard size (2 1/2" by 3 1/2"). The set was released in two series of 330 and 260 cards, respectively. For the first time, second series packs contained only second

series cards. The fronts feature color action player photos, with different color borders on a white card face. The player's name is printed in black lettering in the upper left corner, and the team logo is superimposed over the lower left corner of the picture. In a horizontal format the backs have color head shots and biographical information on the left side, while the right side presents college and pro statistics. The cards are numbered on the back and checklisted below alphabetically within and according to teams as follows: Atlanta Hawks (1-8/331-337), Boston Celtics (9-17/338-341), Charlotte Hornets (18-25/342-344), Chicago Bulls (26-34/345/346), Cleveland Cavaliers (35-42/347-351), Dallas Mavericks (43-50/352/353), Denver Nuggets (51-58/354-359), Detroit Pistons (59-66/360-367), Golden State Warriors (67-74), Houston Rockets (75-82/368-371), Indiana Pacers (83-90/372-375), Los Angeles Clippers (91-98/376-381), Los Angeles Lakers (99-106/382-385), Miami Heat (107-114/386-389), Milwaukee Bucks (115-122/390-394), Minnesota Timberwolves (123-130/395-397), New Jersey Nets (131-138/398-401), New York Knicks (139-146/402-406), Orlando Magic (147-154/407-410), Philadelphia 76ers (155-162/411-416), Phoenix Suns (163-170/417-422), Portland Trail Blazers (171-179/423-425), Sacramento Kings (180-187/426-431), San Antonio Spurs (188-196/432-437), Seattle Supersonics (197-204/438-441), Utah Jazz (205-212/442-448), Washington Bullets (213-220), Coaches (221-247), All-Stars East (248-260), All-Stars West (261-273), Teams (274-300), Centennial Card honoring James Naismith (301), Inside Stuff (302-305), League Leaders (306-313), Milestones (314-318), NBA yearbook (319-324), Public Service messages (325-327/544/545), Supreme Court (449-502), Art Cards (503-529), Active Leaders (530-537), NBA Hoops Tribune (538-543), Draft Picks (546-556), USA Basketball 1976 (557), USA Basketball 1984 (558-564), USA Basketball 1988 (565-574) and USA Basketball 1992 (575-588). Rookie Cards include Kenny Anderson, Stacey Augmon, Larry Johnson, Dikembe Mutombo, Billy Owens, Steve Smith, and John Starks. A short-printed Naismith card, numbered CC1, was inserted into wax packs. It features a colorized photo of Dr. Naismith standing between two peach baskets like those used in the first basketball game. The back narrates the invention of the game of basketball. An unnumbered Centennial card featuring the Centennial logo was also available via a mail-in offer. Second series packs featured a randomly inserted Gold Foil USA Basketball logo card. A special individually numbered (out of 10,000) "Head of the Class" (showing the top six draft picks from 1991) card was made available to the first 10,000 fans requesting one along with three wrappers from each series of 1991-92 Hoops cards.

		MINT	NRMT	EXC
	COMPLETE SET (590)	20.00	9.00	2.50
	COMPLETE SERIES 1 (330)	8.00	3.60	1.00
	COMPLETE SERIES 2 (260)	12.00	5.50	1.50
	COMMON CARD (1-590)	.05	.02	.01
☐ 1	John Battle	.05	.02	.01
☐ 2	Moses Malone UER (119 rebounds 1982-83, should be 1194)	.15	.07	.01
☐ 3	Sidney Moncrief	.10	.05	.01
☐ 4	Doc Rivers	.05	.02	.01
☐ 5	Rumeal Robinson UER (Back says 11th pick in 1990, should be 10th)	.05	.02	.01
☐ 6	Spud Webb	.08	.04	.01
☐ 7	Dominique Wilkins	.15	.07	.01
☐ 8	Kevin Willis	.08	.04	.01
☐ 9	Larry Bird	.75	.35	.09
☐ 10	Dee Brown	.10	.05	.01
☐ 11	Kevin Gamble	.05	.02	.01
☐ 12	Joe Kleine	.05	.02	.01
☐ 13	Reggie Lewis	.10	.05	.01
☐ 14	Kevin McHale	.10	.05	.01
☐ 15	Robert Parish	.10	.05	.01
☐ 16	Ed Pinckney	.05	.02	.01
☐ 17	Brian Shaw	.05	.02	.01
☐ 18	Muggsy Bogues	.10	.05	.01
☐ 19	Rex Chapman	.05	.02	.01
☐ 20	Dell Curry	.05	.02	.01
☐ 21	Kendall Gill	.08	.04	.01
☐ 22	Mike Gminski	.05	.02	.01
☐ 23	Johnny Newman	.05	.02	.01
☐ 24	J.R. Reid	.05	.02	.01
☐ 25	Kelly Tripucka	.05	.02	.01
☐ 26	B.J. Armstrong (B.J. on front, Benjamin Roy on back)	.08	.04	.01
☐ 27	Bill Cartwright	.05	.02	.01
☐ 28	Horace Grant	.15	.07	.02
☐ 29	Craig Hodges	.05	.02	.01
☐ 30	Michael Jordan	3.00	1.35	.40
☐ 31	Stacey King	.05	.02	.01
☐ 32	Cliff Levingston	.05	.02	.01
☐ 33	John Paxson	.05	.02	.01
☐ 34	Scottie Pippen	.25	.11	.03
☐ 35	Chucky Brown	.05	.02	.01
☐ 36	Brad Daugherty	.08	.04	.01
☐ 37	Craig Ehlo	.05	.02	.01
☐ 38	Danny Ferry	.05	.02	.01
☐ 39	Larry Nance	.08	.04	.01
☐ 40	Mark Price	.10	.05	.01
☐ 41	Darnell Valentine	.05	.02	.01
☐ 42	Hot Rod Williams	.05	.02	.01
☐ 43	Rolando Blackman	.08	.04	.01
☐ 44	Brad Davis	.05	.02	.01

□	No.	Name			
□	45	James Donaldson	.05	.02	.01
□	46	Derek Harper	.08	.04	.01
□	47	Fat Lever	.05	.02	.01
□	48	Rodney McCray	.05	.02	.01
□	49	Roy Tarpley	.05	.02	.01
□	50	Herb Williams	.05	.02	.01
□	51	Michael Adams	.05	.02	.01
□	52	Chris Jackson UER	.05	.02	.01
		(Born in Mississippi, not Michigan)			
□	53	Jerome Lane	.05	.02	.01
□	54	Todd Lichti	.05	.02	.01
□	55	Blair Rasmussen	.05	.02	.01
□	56	Reggie Williams	.05	.02	.01
□	57	Joe Wolf	.05	.02	.01
□	58	Orlando Woolridge	.05	.02	.01
□	59	Mark Aguirre	.08	.04	.01
□	60	Joe Dumars	.15	.07	.02
□	61	James Edwards	.05	.02	.01
□	62	Vinnie Johnson	.08	.04	.01
□	63	Bill Laimbeer	.08	.04	.01
□	64	Dennis Rodman	.15	.07	.02
□	65	John Salley	.05	.02	.01
□	66	Isiah Thomas	.15	.07	.02
□	67	Tim Hardaway	.15	.07	.02
□	68	Rod Higgins	.05	.02	.01
□	69	Tyrone Hill	.10	.05	.01
□	70	Alton Lister	.05	.02	.01
□	71	Sarunas Marciulionis	.05	.02	.01
□	72	Chris Mullin	.10	.05	.01
□	73	Mitch Richmond	.15	.07	.02
□	74	Tom Tolbert	.05	.02	.01
□	75	Eric(Sleepy) Floyd	.05	.02	.01
□	76	Buck Johnson	.05	.02	.01
□	77	Vernon Maxwell	.05	.02	.01
□	78	Hakeem Olajuwon	.60	.25	.08
□	79	Kenny Smith	.05	.02	.01
□	80	Larry Smith	.05	.02	.01
□	81	Otis Thorpe	.08	.04	.01
□	82	David Wood	.05	.02	.01
□	83	Vern Fleming	.05	.02	.01
□	84	Reggie Miller	.25	.11	.03
□	85	Chuck Person	.08	.04	.01
□	86	Mike Sanders	.05	.02	.01
□	87	Detlef Schrempf	.10	.05	.01
□	88	Rik Smits	.10	.05	.01
□	89	LaSalle Thompson	.05	.02	.01
□	90	Micheal Williams	.05	.02	.01
□	91	Winston Garland	.05	.02	.01
□	92	Gary Grant	.05	.02	.01
□	93	Ron Harper	.08	.04	.01
□	94	Danny Manning	.10	.05	.01
□	95	Jeff Martin	.05	.02	.01
□	96	Ken Norman	.05	.02	.01
□	97	Olden Polynice	.05	.02	.01
□	98	Charles Smith	.05	.02	.01
□	99	Vlade Divac	.10	.05	.01
□	100	A.C. Green	.10	.05	.01
□	101	Magic Johnson	.50	.23	.06
□	102	Sam Perkins	.08	.04	.01
□	103	Byron Scott	.08	.04	.01
□	104	Terry Teagle	.05	.02	.01
□	105	Mychal Thompson	.05	.02	.01
□	106	James Worthy	.10	.05	.01
□	107	Willie Burton	.05	.02	.01
□	108	Bimbo Coles	.05	.02	.01
□	109	Terry Davis	.05	.02	.01
□	110	Sherman Douglas	.05	.02	.01
□	111	Kevin Edwards	.05	.02	.01
□	112	Alec Kessler	.05	.02	.01
□	113	Glen Rice	.10	.05	.01
□	114	Rony Seikaly	.05	.02	.01
□	115	Frank Brickowski	.05	.02	.01
□	116	Dale Ellis	.08	.04	.01
□	117	Jay Humphries	.05	.02	.01
□	118	Brad Lohaus	.05	.02	.01
□	119	Fred Roberts	.05	.02	.01
□	120	Alvin Robertson	.05	.02	.01
□	121	Danny Schayes	.05	.02	.01
□	122	Jack Sikma	.08	.04	.01
□	123	Randy Breuer	.05	.02	.01
□	124	Tony Campbell	.05	.02	.01
□	125	Tyrone Corbin	.05	.02	.01
□	126	Gerald Glass	.05	.02	.01
□	127	Sam Mitchell	.05	.02	.01
□	128	Tod Murphy	.05	.02	.01
□	129	Pooh Richardson	.05	.02	.01
□	130	Felton Spencer	.05	.02	.01
□	131	Mookie Blaylock	.08	.04	.01
□	132	Sam Bowie	.05	.02	.01
□	133	Jud Buechler	.05	.02	.01
□	134	Derrick Coleman	.10	.05	.01
□	135	Chris Dudley	.05	.02	.01
□	136	Chris Morris	.05	.02	.01
□	137	Drazen Petrovic	.08	.04	.01
□	138	Reggie Theus	.08	.04	.01
□	139	Maurice Cheeks	.10	.05	.01
□	140	Patrick Ewing	.25	.11	.03
□	141	Mark Jackson	.05	.02	.01
□	142	Charles Oakley	.08	.04	.01
□	143	Trent Tucker	.05	.02	.01
□	144	Kiki Vandeweghe	.05	.02	.01
□	145	Kenny Walker	.05	.02	.01
□	146	Gerald Wilkins	.05	.02	.01
□	147	Nick Anderson	.10	.05	.01
□	148	Michael Ansley	.05	.02	.01
□	149	Terry Catledge	.05	.02	.01
□	150	Jerry Reynolds	.05	.02	.01
□	151	Dennis Scott	.08	.04	.01
□	152	Scott Skiles	.05	.02	.01
□	153	Otis Smith	.05	.02	.01
□	154	Sam Vincent	.05	.02	.01
□	155	Ron Anderson	.05	.02	.01
□	156	Charles Barkley	.50	.23	.06
□	157	Manute Bol	.05	.02	.01
□	158	Johnny Dawkins	.05	.02	.01
□	159	Armon Gilliam	.05	.02	.01
□	160	Rickey Green	.05	.02	.01
□	161	Hersey Hawkins	.08	.04	.01
□	162	Rick Mahorn	.05	.02	.01
□	163	Tom Chambers	.08	.04	.01
□	164	Jeff Hornacek	.08	.04	.01
□	165	Kevin Johnson	.15	.07	.02
□	166	Andrew Lang	.05	.02	.01
□	167	Dan Majerle	.08	.04	.01
□	168	Xavier McDaniel	.08	.04	.01
□	169	Kurt Rambis	.05	.02	.01
□	170	Mark West	.05	.02	.01
□	171	Danny Ainge	.08	.04	.01
□	172	Mark Bryant	.05	.02	.01
□	173	Walter Davis	.10	.05	.01
□	174	Clyde Drexler	.25	.11	.03
□	175	Kevin Duckworth	.05	.02	.01
□	176	Jerome Kersey	.05	.02	.01
□	177	Terry Porter	.08	.04	.01
□	178	Cliff Robinson	.05	.02	.01
□	179	Buck Williams	.08	.04	.01
□	180	Anthony Bonner	.05	.02	.01
□	181	Antoine Carr	.05	.02	.01
□	182	Duane Causwell	.05	.02	.01
□	183	Bobby Hansen	.05	.02	.01
□	184	Travis Mays	.05	.02	.01

☐ 185	Lionel Simmons	.05	.02	.01
☐ 186	Rory Sparrow	.05	.02	.01
☐ 187	Wayman Tisdale	.08	.04	.01
☐ 188	Willie Anderson	.05	.02	.01
☐ 189	Terry Cummings	.08	.04	.01
☐ 190	Sean Elliott	.10	.05	.01
☐ 191	Sidney Green	.05	.02	.01
☐ 192	David Greenwood	.05	.02	.01
☐ 193	Paul Pressey	.05	.02	.01
☐ 194	David Robinson	.60	.25	.08
☐ 195	Dwayne Schintzius	.05	.02	.01
☐ 196	Rod Strickland	.08	.04	.01
☐ 197	Benoit Benjamin	.05	.02	.01
☐ 198	Michael Cage	.05	.02	.01
☐ 199	Eddie Johnson	.08	.04	.01
☐ 200	Shawn Kemp	1.00	.45	.13
☐ 201	Derrick McKey	.08	.04	.01
☐ 202	Gary Payton	.10	.05	.01
☐ 203	Ricky Pierce	.08	.04	.01
☐ 204	Sedale Threatt	.05	.02	.01
☐ 205	Thurl Bailey	.05	.02	.01
☐ 206	Mike Brown	.05	.02	.01
☐ 207	Mark Eaton	.05	.02	.01
☐ 208	Blue Edwards UER	.05	.02	.01
	(Forward/guard on front, guard on back)			
☐ 209	Darrell Griffith	.08	.04	.01
☐ 210	Jeff Malone	.08	.04	.01
☐ 211	Karl Malone	.25	.11	.03
☐ 212	John Stockton	.25	.11	.03
☐ 213	Ledell Eackles	.05	.02	.01
☐ 214	Pervis Ellison	.05	.02	.01
☐ 215	A.J. English	.05	.02	.01
☐ 216	Harvey Grant	.05	.02	.01
	(Shown boxing out twin brother Horace)			
☐ 217	Charles Jones	.05	.02	.01
☐ 218	Bernard King	.10	.05	.01
☐ 219	Darrell Walker	.05	.02	.01
☐ 220	John Williams	.05	.02	.01
☐ 221	Bob Weiss CO	.05	.02	.01
☐ 222	Chris Ford CO	.05	.02	.01
☐ 223	Gene Littles CO	.05	.02	.01
☐ 224	Phil Jackson CO	.08	.04	.01
☐ 225	Lenny Wilkens CO	.08	.04	.01
☐ 226	Richie Adubato CO	.05	.02	.01
☐ 227	Paul Westhead CO	.08	.04	.01
☐ 228	Chuck Daly CO	.08	.04	.01
☐ 229	Don Nelson CO	.08	.04	.01
☐ 230	Don Chaney CO	.05	.02	.01
☐ 231	Bob Hill CO UER	.05	.02	.01
	(Coached under Ted Owens, not Ted Owen)			
☐ 232	Mike Schuler CO	.05	.02	.01
☐ 233	Mike Dunleavy CO	.05	.02	.01
☐ 234	Kevin Loughery CO	.05	.02	.01
☐ 235	Del Harris CO	.05	.02	.01
☐ 236	Jimmy Rodgers CO	.05	.02	.01
☐ 237	Bill Fitch CO	.05	.02	.01
☐ 238	Pat Riley CO	.08	.04	.01
☐ 239	Matt Guokas CO	.05	.02	.01
☐ 240	Jim Lynam CO	.05	.02	.01
☐ 241	Cotton Fitzsimmons CO	.05	.02	.01
☐ 242	Rick Adelman CO	.05	.02	.01
☐ 243	Dick Motta CO	.05	.02	.01
☐ 244	Larry Brown CO	.08	.04	.01
☐ 245	K.C. Jones CO	.08	.04	.01
☐ 246	Jerry Sloan CO	.05	.02	.01
☐ 247	Wes Unseld CO	.08	.04	.01
☐ 248	Charles Barkley AS	.25	.11	.03
☐ 249	Brad Daugherty AS	.05	.02	.01

☐ 250	Joe Dumars AS	.08	.04	.01
☐ 251	Patrick Ewing AS	.10	.05	.01
☐ 252	Hersey Hawkins AS	.05	.02	.01
☐ 253	Michael Jordan AS	1.50	.65	.19
☐ 254	Bernard King AS	.05	.02	.01
☐ 255	Kevin McHale AS	.05	.02	.01
☐ 256	Robert Parish AS	.05	.02	.01
☐ 257	Ricky Pierce AS	.05	.02	.01
☐ 258	Alvin Robertson AS	.05	.02	.01
☐ 259	Dominique Wilkins AS	.08	.04	.01
☐ 260	Chris Ford CO AS	.05	.02	.01
☐ 261	Tom Chambers AS	.05	.02	.01
☐ 262	Clyde Drexler AS	.10	.05	.01
☐ 263	Kevin Duckworth AS	.05	.02	.01
☐ 264	Tim Hardaway AS	.05	.02	.01
☐ 265	Kevin Johnson AS	.08	.04	.01
☐ 266	Magic Johnson AS	.25	.11	.03
☐ 267	Karl Malone AS	.10	.05	.01
☐ 268	Chris Mullin AS	.05	.02	.01
☐ 269	Terry Porter AS	.05	.02	.01
☐ 270	David Robinson AS	.30	.14	.04
☐ 271	John Stockton AS	.10	.05	.01
☐ 272	James Worthy AS	.05	.02	.01
☐ 273	Rick Adelman CO AS	.05	.02	.01
☐ 274	Atlanta Hawks	.05	.02	.01
	Team Card UER (Actually began as Tri-Cities Blackhawks)			
☐ 275	Boston Celtics	.05	.02	.01
	Team Card UER (No NBA Hoops logo on card front)			
☐ 276	Charlotte Hornets	.05	.02	.01
	Team Card			
☐ 277	Chicago Bulls	.05	.02	.01
	Team Card			
☐ 278	Cleveland Cavaliers	.05	.02	.01
	Team Card			
☐ 279	Dallas Mavericks	.05	.02	.01
	Team Card			
☐ 280	Denver Nuggets	.05	.02	.01
	Team Card			
☐ 281	Detroit Pistons	.05	.02	.01
	Team Card UER (Pistons not NBA Finalists until 1988; Ft. Ft. Wayne Pistons in Finals in 1955 and 1956)			
☐ 282	Golden State Warriors	.05	.02	.01
	Team Card			
☐ 283	Houston Rockets	.05	.02	.01
	Team Card			
☐ 284	Indiana Pacers	.05	.02	.01
	Team Card			
☐ 285	Los Angeles Clippers	.05	.02	.01
	Team Card			
☐ 286	Los Angeles Lakers	.05	.02	.01
	Team Card			
☐ 287	Miami Heat	.05	.02	.01
	Team Card			
☐ 288	Milwaukee Bucks	.05	.02	.01
	Team Card			
☐ 289	Minnesota Timberwolves	.05	.02	.01
	Team Card			
☐ 290	New Jersey Nets	.05	.02	.01
	Team Card			
☐ 291	New York Knicks	.05	.02	.01
	Team Card UER (Golden State not mentioned as an active charter member of NBA)			

☐ 292	Orlando Magic Team Card	.05	.02	.01
☐ 293	Philadelphia 76ers Team Card	.05	.02	.01
☐ 294	Phoenix Suns Team Card	.05	.02	.01
☐ 295	Portland Trail Blazers Team Card	.05	.02	.01
☐ 296	Sacramento Kings Team Card	.05	.02	.01
☐ 297	San Antonio Spurs Team Card	.05	.02	.01
☐ 298	Seattle Supersonics Team Card	.05	.02	.01
☐ 299	Utah Jazz Team Card	.05	.02	.01
☐ 300	Washington Bullets Team Card	.05	.02	.01
☐ 301	Centennial Card James Naismith	.05	.02	.01
☐ 302	Kevin Johnson IS	.08	.04	.01
☐ 303	Reggie Miller IS	.10	.05	.01
☐ 304	Hakeem Olajuwon IS	.30	.14	.04
☐ 305	Robert Parish IS	.05	.02	.01
☐ 306	Scoring Leaders Michael Jordan Karl Malone	1.00	.45	.13
☐ 307	3-Point FG Percent League Leaders Jim Les Trent Tucker	.05	.02	.01
☐ 308	Free Throw Percent League Leaders Reggie Miller Jeff Malone	.08	.04	.01
☐ 309	Blocks League Leaders Hakeem Olajuwon David Robinson	.50	.23	.06
☐ 310	Steals League Leaders Alvin Robertson John Stockton	.08	.04	.01
☐ 311	Rebounds LL UER David Robinson Dennis Rodman (Robinson credited as playing for Houston)	.25	.11	.03
☐ 312	Assists League Leaders John Stockton Magic Johnson	.25	.11	.03
☐ 313	Field Goal Percent League Leaders Buck Williams Robert Parish	.08	.04	.01
☐ 314	Larry Bird UER Milestone (Should be card 315 to fit Milestone sequence)	.40	.18	.05
☐ 315	A.English/M.Malone Milestone UER (Should be card 314 and be a League Leader card)	.05	.02	.01
☐ 316	Magic Johnson Milestone	.25	.11	.03
☐ 317	Michael Jordan Milestone	1.50	.65	.19
☐ 318	Moses Malone Milestone	.10	.05	.01
☐ 319	Larry Bird NBA Yearbook Look Back	.40	.18	.05
☐ 320	Maurice Cheeks NBA Yearbook Look Back	.05	.02	.01
☐ 321	Magic Johnson NBA Yearbook Look Back	.25	.11	.03
☐ 322	Bernard King NBA Yearbook Look Back	.05	.02	.01
☐ 323	Moses Malone NBA Yearbook Look Back	.08	.04	.01
☐ 324	Robert Parish NBA Yearbook Look Back	.05	.02	.01
☐ 325	All-Star Jam Jammin' With Will Smith (Stay in School)	.05	.02	.01
☐ 326	All-Star Jam Jammin' With The Boys and Will Smith (Stay in School)	.05	.02	.01
☐ 327	David Robinson Leave Alcohol Out	.30	.14	.04
☐ 328	Checklist 1	.05	.02	.01
☐ 329	Checklist 2 UER (Card front is from 330)	.05	.02	.01
☐ 330	Checklist 3 UER (Card front is from 329; card 327 listed operation, should be celebration)	.05	.02	.01
☐ 331	Maurice Cheeks	.10	.05	.01
☐ 332	Duane Ferrell	.05	.02	.01
☐ 333	Jon Koncak	.05	.02	.01
☐ 334	Gary Leonard	.05	.02	.01
☐ 335	Travis Mays	.05	.02	.01
☐ 336	Blair Rasmussen	.05	.02	.01
☐ 337	Alexander Volkov	.05	.02	.01
☐ 338	John Bagley	.05	.02	.01
☐ 339	Rickey Green UER (Ricky on front)	.05	.02	.01
☐ 340	Derek Smith	.05	.02	.01
☐ 341	Stojko Vrankovic	.05	.02	.01
☐ 342	Anthony Frederick	.05	.02	.01
☐ 343	Kenny Gattison	.05	.02	.01
☐ 344	Eric Leckner	.05	.02	.01
☐ 345	Will Perdue	.05	.02	.01
☐ 346	Scott Williams	.05	.02	.01
☐ 347	John Battle	.05	.02	.01
☐ 348	Winston Bennett	.05	.02	.01
☐ 349	Henry James	.05	.02	.01
☐ 350	Steve Kerr	.05	.02	.01
☐ 351	John Morton	.05	.02	.01
☐ 352	Terry Davis	.05	.02	.01
☐ 353	Randy White	.05	.02	.01
☐ 354	Greg Anderson	.05	.02	.01
☐ 355	Anthony Cook	.05	.02	.01
☐ 356	Walter Davis	.10	.05	.01
☐ 357	Winston Garland	.05	.02	.01
☐ 358	Scott Hastings	.05	.02	.01
☐ 359	Marcus Liberty	.05	.02	.01
☐ 360	William Bedford	.05	.02	.01
☐ 361	Lance Blanks	.05	.02	.01
☐ 362	Brad Sellers	.05	.02	.01
☐ 363	Darrell Walker	.05	.02	.01
☐ 364	Orlando Woolridge	.05	.02	.01
☐ 365	Vincent Askew	.10	.05	.01
☐ 366	Mario Elie	.20	.09	.03
☐ 367	Jim Petersen	.05	.02	.01
☐ 368	Matt Bullard	.05	.02	.01
☐ 369	Gerald Henderson	.05	.02	.01

☐	370 Dave Jamerson	.05	.02	.01	☐ 441 Nate McMillan	.05	.02	.01
☐	371 Tree Rollins	.05	.02	.01	☐ 442 Delaney Rudd	.05	.02	.01
☐	372 Greg Dreiling	.05	.02	.01	☐ 443 Michael Adams	.05	.02	.01
☐	373 George McCloud	.05	.02	.01	☐ 444 Mark Alarie	.05	.02	.01
☐	374 Kenny Williams	.05	.02	.01	☐ 445 Greg Foster	.05	.02	.01
☐	375 Randy Wittman	.05	.02	.01	☐ 446 Tom Hammonds	.05	.02	.01
☐	376 Tony Brown	.05	.02	.01	☐ 447 Andre Turner	.05	.02	.01
☐	377 Lanard Copeland	.10	.05	.01	☐ 448 David Wingate	.05	.02	.01
☐	378 James Edwards	.05	.02	.01	☐ 449 Dominique Wilkins SC	.08	.04	.01
☐	379 Bo Kimble	.05	.02	.01	☐ 450 Kevin Willis SC	.05	.02	.01
☐	380 Doc Rivers	.05	.02	.01	☐ 451 Larry Bird SC	.40	.18	.05
☐	381 Loy Vaught	.10	.05	.01	☐ 452 Robert Parish SC	.05	.02	.01
☐	382 Elden Campbell	.08	.04	.01	☐ 453 Rex Chapman SC	.05	.02	.01
☐	383 Jack Haley	.05	.02	.01	☐ 454 Kendall Gill SC	.05	.02	.01
☐	384 Tony Smith	.05	.02	.01	☐ 455 Michael Jordan SC	1.50	.65	.19
☐	385 Sedale Threatt	.05	.02	.01	☐ 456 Scottie Pippen SC	.10	.05	.01
☐	386 Keith Askins	.05	.02	.01	☐ 457 Brad Daugherty SC	.05	.02	.01
☐	387 Grant Long	.05	.02	.01	☐ 458 Larry Nance SC	.05	.02	.01
☐	388 Alan Ogg	.05	.02	.01	☐ 459 Rolando Blackman SC	.05	.02	.01
☐	389 Jon Sundvold	.05	.02	.01	☐ 460 Derek Harper SC	.05	.02	.01
☐	390 Lester Conner	.05	.02	.01	☐ 461 Chris Jackson SC	.05	.02	.01
☐	391 Jeff Grayer	.05	.02	.01	☐ 462 Todd Lichti SC	.05	.02	.01
☐	392 Steve Henson	.05	.02	.01	☐ 463 Joe Dumars SC	.08	.04	.01
☐	393 Larry Krystkowiak	.05	.02	.01	☐ 464 Isiah Thomas SC	.08	.04	.01
☐	394 Moses Malone	.15	.07	.02	☐ 465 Tim Hardaway SC	.05	.02	.01
☐	395 Scott Brooks	.05	.02	.01	☐ 466 Chris Mullin SC	.05	.02	.01
☐	396 Tellis Frank	.05	.02	.01	☐ 467 Hakeem Olajuwon SC	.30	.14	.04
☐	397 Doug West	.05	.02	.01	☐ 468 Otis Thorpe SC	.05	.02	.01
☐	398 Rafael Addison	.05	.02	.01	☐ 469 Reggie Miller SC	.10	.05	.01
☐	399 Dave Feitl	.05	.02	.01	☐ 470 Detlef Schrempf SC	.05	.02	.01
☐	400 Tate George	.05	.02	.01	☐ 471 Ron Harper SC	.05	.02	.01
☐	401 Terry Mills	.30	.14	.04	☐ 472 Charles Smith SC	.05	.02	.01
☐	402 Tim McCormick	.05	.02	.01	☐ 473 Magic Johnson SC	.25	.11	.03
☐	403 Xavier McDaniel	.08	.04	.01	☐ 474 James Worthy SC	.05	.02	.01
☐	404 Anthony Mason	.40	.18	.05	☐ 475 Sherman Douglas SC	.05	.02	.01
☐	405 Brian Quinnett	.05	.02	.01	☐ 476 Rony Seikaly SC	.05	.02	.01
☐	406 John Starks	.30	.14	.04	☐ 477 Jay Humphries SC	.05	.02	.01
☐	407 Mark Acres	.05	.02	.01	☐ 478 Alvin Robertson SC	.05	.02	.01
☐	408 Greg Kite	.05	.02	.01	☐ 479 Tyrone Corbin SC	.05	.02	.01
☐	409 Jeff Turner	.05	.02	.01	☐ 480 Pooh Richardson SC	.05	.02	.01
☐	410 Morlon Wiley	.05	.02	.01	☐ 481 Sam Bowie SC	.05	.02	.01
☐	411 Dave Hoppen	.05	.02	.01	☐ 482 Derrick Coleman SC	.08	.04	.01
☐	412 Brian Oliver	.05	.02	.01	☐ 483 Patrick Ewing SC	.10	.05	.01
☐	413 Kenny Payne	.05	.02	.01	☐ 484 Charles Oakley SC	.05	.02	.01
☐	414 Charles Shackleford	.05	.02	.01	☐ 485 Dennis Scott SC	.05	.02	.01
☐	415 Mitchell Wiggins	.05	.02	.01	☐ 486 Scott Skiles SC	.05	.02	.01
☐	416 Jayson Williams	.05	.02	.01	☐ 487 Charles Barkley SC	.25	.11	.03
☐	417 Cedric Ceballos	.10	.05	.01	☐ 488 Hersey Hawkins SC	.05	.02	.01
☐	418 Negele Knight	.05	.02	.01	☐ 489 Tom Chambers SC	.05	.02	.01
☐	419 Andrew Lang	.05	.02	.01	☐ 490 Kevin Johnson SC	.08	.04	.01
☐	420 Jerrod Mustaf	.05	.02	.01	☐ 491 Clyde Drexler SC	.05	.02	.01
☐	421 Ed Nealy	.05	.02	.01	☐ 492 Terry Porter SC	.05	.02	.01
☐	422 Tim Perry	.05	.02	.01	☐ 493 Lionel Simmons SC	.05	.02	.01
☐	423 Alaa Abdelnaby	.05	.02	.01	☐ 494 Wayman Tisdale SC	.05	.02	.01
☐	424 Wayne Cooper	.05	.02	.01	☐ 495 Terry Cummings SC	.05	.02	.01
☐	425 Danny Young	.05	.02	.01	☐ 496 David Robinson SC	.30	.14	.04
☐	426 Dennis Hopson	.05	.02	.01	☐ 497 Shawn Kemp SC	.50	.23	.06
☐	427 Les Jepsen	.05	.02	.01	☐ 498 Ricky Pierce SC	.05	.02	.01
☐	428 Jim Les	.05	.02	.01	☐ 499 Karl Malone SC	.10	.05	.01
☐	429 Mitch Richmond	.15	.07	.02	☐ 500 John Stockton SC	.10	.05	.01
☐	430 Dwayne Schintzius	.05	.02	.01	☐ 501 Harvey Grant SC	.05	.02	.01
☐	431 Spud Webb	.08	.04	.01	☐ 502 Bernard King SC	.05	.02	.01
☐	432 Jud Buechler	.05	.02	.01	☐ 503 Travis Mays Art	.05	.02	.01
☐	433 Antoine Carr	.05	.02	.01	☐ 504 Kevin McHale Art	.05	.02	.01
☐	434 Tom Garrick	.05	.02	.01	☐ 505 Muggsy Bogues Art	.05	.02	.01
☐	435 Sean Higgins	.05	.02	.01	☐ 506 Scottie Pippen Art	.10	.05	.01
☐	436 Avery Johnson	.05	.02	.01	☐ 507 Brad Daugherty Art	.05	.02	.01
☐	437 Tony Massenburg	.05	.02	.01	☐ 508 Derek Harper Art	.05	.02	.01
☐	438 Dana Barros	.10	.05	.01	☐ 509 Chris Jackson Art	.05	.02	.01
☐	439 Quintin Dailey	.05	.02	.01	☐ 510 Isiah Thomas Art	.08	.04	.01
☐	440 Bart Kofoed	.05	.02	.01	☐ 511 Tim Hardaway Art	.05	.02	.01

☐ 512 Otis Thorpe Art	.05	.02	.01	
☐ 513 Chuck Person Art	.05	.02	.01	
☐ 514 Ron Harper Art	.05	.02	.01	
☐ 515 James Worthy Art	.05	.02	.01	
☐ 516 Sherman Douglas Art	.05	.02	.01	
☐ 517 Dale Ellis Art	.05	.02	.01	
☐ 518 Tony Campbell Art	.05	.02	.01	
☐ 519 Derrick Coleman Art	.08	.04	.01	
☐ 520 Gerald Wilkins Art	.05	.02	.01	
☐ 521 Scott Skiles Art	.05	.02	.01	
☐ 522 Manute Bol Art	.05	.02	.01	
☐ 523 Tom Chambers Art	.05	.02	.01	
☐ 524 Terry Porter Art	.05	.02	.01	
☐ 525 Lionel Simmons Art	.05	.02	.01	
☐ 526 Sean Elliott Art	.05	.02	.01	
☐ 527 Shawn Kemp Art	.50	.23	.06	
☐ 528 John Stockton Art	.10	.05	.01	
☐ 529 Harvey Grant Art	.05	.02	.01	
☐ 530 Michael Adams Art All-Time Active Leader Three-Point Field Goals	.05	.02	.01	
☐ 531 Charles Barkley All-Time Active Leader Field Goal Percentage	.25	.11	.03	
☐ 532 Larry Bird All-Time Active Leader Free Throw Percentage	.40	.18	.05	
☐ 533 Maurice Cheeks All-Time Active Leader Steals	.05	.02	.01	
☐ 534 Mark Eaton All-Time Active Leader Blocks	.05	.02	.01	
☐ 535 Magic Johnson All-Time Active Leader Assists	.25	.11	.03	
☐ 536 Michael Jordan All-Time Active Leader Scoring Average	1.50	.65	.19	
☐ 537 Moses Malone All-Time Active Leader Rebounds	.08	.04	.01	
☐ 538 NBA Finals Game 1 Perkins' Three Pointer (Sam Perkins)	.05	.02	.01	
☐ 539 NBA Finals Game 2 Bulls Rout Lakers (Pippen against Worthy)	.05	.02	.01	
☐ 540 NBA Finals Game 3 Bulls Win OT Thriller (Vlade Divac lay-in)	.05	.02	.01	
☐ 541 NBA Finals Game 4 Bulls One Game Away (John Paxson jumper)	.05	.02	.01	
☐ 542 NBA Finals Game 5 Jordan, Bulls Win First Title (Jordan reverses over Vlade Divac)	1.50	.65	.19	
☐ 543 Championship Card Chicago Bulls Champs (Michael Jordan kissing trophy)	1.50	.65	.19	
☐ 544 Otis Smith Stay in School	.05	.02	.01	
☐ 545 Jeff Turner Stay in School	.05	.02	.01	
☐ 546 Larry Johnson	1.25	.55	.16	
☐ 547 Kenny Anderson	.60	.25	.08	
☐ 548 Billy Owens	.40	.18	.05	
☐ 549 Dikembe Mutombo	1.00	.45	.13	
☐ 550 Steve Smith	.40	.18	.05	
☐ 551 Doug Smith	.05	.02	.01	
☐ 552 Luc Longley	.10	.05	.01	
☐ 553 Mark Macon	.05	.02	.01	
☐ 554 Stacey Augmon	.40	.18	.05	
☐ 555 Brian Williams	.05	.02	.01	
☐ 556 Terrell Brandon	.25	.11	.03	
☐ 557 Walter Davis Team USA 1976	.05	.02	.01	
☐ 558 Vern Fleming Team USA 1984	.05	.02	.01	
☐ 559 Joe Kleine Team USA 1984	.05	.02	.01	
☐ 560 Jon Koncak Team USA 1984	.05	.02	.01	
☐ 561 Sam Perkins Team USA 1984	.05	.02	.01	
☐ 562 Alvin Robertson Team USA 1984	.05	.02	.01	
☐ 563 Wayman Tisdale Team USA 1984	.05	.02	.01	
☐ 564 Jeff Turner Team USA 1984	.05	.02	.01	
☐ 565 Willie Anderson Team USA 1988	.05	.02	.01	
☐ 566 Stacey Augmon Team USA 1988	.10	.05	.01	
☐ 567 Bimbo Coles Team USA 1988	.05	.02	.01	
☐ 568 Jeff Grayer Team USA 1988	.05	.02	.01	
☐ 569 Hersey Hawkins Team USA 1988	.05	.02	.01	
☐ 570 Dan Majerle Team USA 1988	.05	.02	.01	
☐ 571 Danny Manning Team USA 1988	.05	.02	.01	
☐ 572 J.R. Reid Team USA 1988	.05	.02	.01	
☐ 573 Mitch Richmond Team USA 1988	.08	.04	.01	
☐ 574 Charles Smith Team USA 1988	.05	.02	.01	
☐ 575 Charles Barkley Team USA 1992	1.00	.45	.13	
☐ 576 Larry Bird Team USA 1992	1.50	.65	.19	
☐ 577 Patrick Ewing Team USA 1992	.50	.23	.06	
☐ 578 Magic Johnson Team USA 1992	1.00	.45	.13	
☐ 579 Michael Jordan Team USA 1992	6.00	2.70	.75	
☐ 580 Karl Malone Team USA 1992	.50	.23	.06	
☐ 581 Chris Mullin Team USA 1992	.20	.09	.03	
☐ 582 Scottie Pippen Team USA 1992	.50	.23	.06	
☐ 583 David Robinson Team USA 1992	1.25	.55	.16	
☐ 584 John Stockton Team USA 1992	.50	.23	.06	
☐ 585 Chuck Daly CO Team USA 1992	.20	.09	.03	
☐ 586 Lenny Wilkens CO Team USA 1992	.20	.09	.03	
☐ 587 P.J. Carlesimo CO Team USA 1992	.20	.09	.03	
☐ 588 Mike Krzyzewski CO Team USA 1992	.75	.35	.09	

		MINT	NRMT	EXC
☐ 589	Checklist Card 1	.05	.02	.01
☐ 590	Checklist Card 2	.05	.02	.01
☐ CC1	Dr.James Naismith	1.50	.65	.19
☐ NNO	Team USA SP	.50	.23	.06
	Title Card			
☐ NNO	Centennial Card	1.00	.45	.13
	(Sendaway)			
☐ XX	Head of the Class	20.00	9.00	2.50
	Kenny Anderson			
	Larry Johnson			
	Dikembe Mutombo			
	Billy Owens			
	Doug Smith			
	Steve Smith			

1991-92 Hoops
All-Star MVP's

This six-card standard-size (2 1/2" by 3 1/2") insert set commemorates the most valuable player of the NBA All-Star games from 1986 to 1991. Two cards were inserted in each second series rack pack. On a white card face, the front features non-action color photos framed by either a blue (7, 9, 12) or red (8, 10, 11) border. The top thicker border is jagged and displays the player's name, while the year the award was received appears in a colored box in the lower left corner. The backs have the same design and feature a color action photo from the All-Star game. The cards are numbered on the back by Roman numerals.

	MINT	NRMT	EXC
COMPLETE SET (6)	25.00	11.50	3.10
COMMON CARD (7-12)	.50	.23	.06
☐ 7 Isiah Thomas	.75	.35	.09
(Numbered VII)			
☐ 8 Tom Chambers	.50	.23	.06
(Numbered VIII)			
☐ 9 Michael Jordan	20.00	9.00	2.50
(Numbered IX)			
☐ 10 Karl Malone	1.50	.65	.19
(Numbered X)			
☐ 11 Magic Johnson	3.00	1.35	.40
(Numbered XI)			
☐ 12 Charles Barkley	3.00	1.35	.40
(Numbered XII)			

1991-92 Hoops
Slam Dunk

This six-card standard size (2 1/2" by 3 1/2") insert set of "Slam Dunk Champions" features the winners of the All-Star weekend slam dunk competition from 1984 to 1991. The cards were issued two per first series 47-card rack pack. The front has a color photo of the player dunking the ball, with royal blue borders on a white card face. The player's name appears in orange lettering in a purple stripe above the picture, and the year the player won is given in a "Slam Dunk Champion" emblem overlaying the lower left corner of the picture. The design of the back is similar to the front, only with an extended caption on a yellow-green background. A drawing of a basketball entering a rim appears at the upper left corner. The cards are numbered on the back by Roman numerals.

	MINT	NRMT	EXC
COMPLETE SET (6)	22.00	10.00	2.80
COMMON CARD (1-6)	.50	.23	.06
☐ 1 Larry Nance	.50	.23	.06
(Numbered I)			
☐ 2 Dominique Wilkins	.75	.35	.09
(Numbered II)			
☐ 3 Spud Webb	.50	.23	.06
(Numbered III)			
☐ 4 Michael Jordan	20.00	9.00	2.50
(Numbered IV)			
☐ 5 Kenny Walker	.50	.23	.06
(Numbered V)			
☐ 6 Dee Brown	.75	.35	.09
(Numbered VI)			

1992-93 Hoops

The complete 1992-93 Hoops basketball set contains 490 cards measuring the standard size (2 1/2" by 3 1/2"). The set was released in two series of 350 and 140 cards, respectively. Both series packs contained 12 cards each with a suggested retail price of 79 cents each. Reported pro-

duction quantities were 20,000 20-box wax cases of the first series and approximately 14,000 20-box wax cases of the second series. The basic card fronts display color action player photos surrounded by white borders. A color stripe reflecting one of the team's colors cuts across the picture and the player's name is printed vertically in a transparent stripe bordering the left side of the picture. The horizontally oriented backs carry a color head shot, biography, career highlights, and complete statistics (college and pro). The cards are checklisted below alphabetically according to teams as follows: Atlanta Hawks (1-9/351-354), Boston Celtics (10-18/355-357), Charlotte Hornets (19-26/358-361), Chicago Bulls (27-35/362-364), Cleveland Cavaliers (36-44/365-369), Dallas Mavericks (45-53/370-373), Denver Nuggets (54-61/374-379), Detroit Pistons (62-70/380-385), Golden State Warriors (71-79/386-389), Houston Rockets (80-88/390-394), Indiana Pacers (89-97/395-400), Los Angeles Clippers (98-106/401-407), Los Angeles Lakers (107-115/408-410), Miami Heat (116-124/411-414), Milwaukee Bucks (125-133/415-420), Minnesota Timberwolves (134-142/421-426), New Jersey Nets (143-151/427-432), New York Knicks (152-159/433-438), Orlando Magic (160-168/439-443), Philadelphia 76ers (169-177/444-449), Phoenix Suns (178-186/450-453), Portland Trail Blazers (187-195/454-458), Sacramento Kings (196-203/459-463), San Antonio Spurs (204-211/464-469), Seattle Supersonics (212-220/470), Utah Jazz (221-229/471-475), Washington Bullets (230-238/476-480). Sunsets include Coaches (239-265), Team cards (266-292), NBA All-Stars East (293-305), NBA All-Stars West (306-319), League Leaders (320-327), Magic Moments (328-331), NBA Inside Stuff (332-333), NBA Stay in School (334-335), Basketball Tournament of the Americas (336-347) and Trivia (481-485). Rookie cards, scattered throughout the set, have a gold rather than a ghosted white stripe. The team logo appears in the lower left corner and intersects a team color-coded stripe that contains the player's position. The horizontal backs show a white background and include statistics (collegiate and pro), biographies, and career summaries. A close-up photo is at the upper left. Rookie Cards include LaPhonso Ellis, Tom Gugliotta, Robert Horry,

Christian Laettner, Don McLean, Harold Miner, Alonzo Mourning, Shaquille O'Neal, Latrell Sprewell, Clarence Weatherspoon and Walt Williams. A Magic Johnson "Commemorative Card" and a Patrick Ewing "Ultimate Game" card were randomly inserted in first series foil packs. One-thousand of each were autographed. The odds of pulling an autographed card were one in 14,400 packs. Also randomly inserted into second series foil packs were a Ewing Art card (reported odds were one per 21 packs), a Chicago Bulls Championship card (reported odds were one per 32 packs) and a John Stockton "Ultimate Game" card (reported odds were one per 92 packs). Stockton autographed 1,633 of these cards (reported odds were one per 5,732 packs). Also randomly inserted into first series packs was a USA Basketball Team card. A Barcelona Plastic card was also randomly inserted in first series packs at a rate of approximately one per 720 packs.

	MINT	NRMT	EXC
COMPLETE SET (490)	40.00	18.00	5.00
COMPLETE SERIES 1 (350)	15.00	6.75	1.90
COMPLETE SERIES 2 (140)	25.00	11.50	3.10
COMMON CARD (1-350)	.05	.02	.01
COMMON CARD (351-490)	.10	.05	.01
☐ 1 Stacey Augmon	.10	.05	.01
☐ 2 Maurice Cheeks	.10	.05	.01
☐ 3 Duane Ferrell	.05	.02	.01
☐ 4 Paul Graham	.05	.02	.01
☐ 5 Jon Koncak	.05	.02	.01
☐ 6 Blair Rasmussen	.05	.02	.01
☐ 7 Rumeal Robinson	.05	.02	.01
☐ 8 Dominique Wilkins	.15	.07	.02
☐ 9 Kevin Willis	.08	.04	.01
☐ 10 Larry Bird	1.00	.45	.13
☐ 11 Dee Brown	.08	.04	.01
☐ 12 Sherman Douglas	.05	.02	.01
☐ 13 Rick Fox	.05	.02	.01
☐ 14 Kevin Gamble	.05	.02	.01
☐ 15 Reggie Lewis	.10	.05	.01
☐ 16 Kevin McHale	.10	.05	.01
☐ 17 Robert Parish	.10	.05	.01
☐ 18 Ed Pinckney UER	.05	.02	.01
(Wrong trade info, Kleine to Sacramento and Lohaus to Boston)			
☐ 19 Muggsy Bogues	.10	.05	.01
☐ 20 Dell Curry	.05	.02	.01
☐ 21 Kenny Gattison	.05	.02	.01
☐ 22 Kendall Gill	.05	.02	.01
☐ 23 Mike Gminski	.05	.02	.01
☐ 24 Larry Johnson	.50	.23	.06
☐ 25 Johnny Newman	.05	.02	.01
☐ 26 J.R. Reid	.05	.02	.01
☐ 27 B.J. Armstrong	.05	.02	.01
☐ 28 Bill Cartwright	.05	.02	.01
☐ 29 Horace Grant	.15	.07	.02
☐ 30 Michael Jordan	4.00	1.80	.50
☐ 31 Stacey King	.05	.02	.01
☐ 32 John Paxson	.05	.02	.01
☐ 33 Will Perdue	.05	.02	.01
☐ 34 Scottie Pippen	.30	.14	.04
☐ 35 Scott Williams	.05	.02	.01

☐ 36	John Battle	.05	.02	.01
☐ 37	Terrell Brandon	.08	.04	.01
☐ 38	Brad Daugherty	.08	.04	.01
☐ 39	Craig Ehlo	.05	.02	.01
☐ 40	Danny Ferry	.05	.02	.01
☐ 41	Henry James	.05	.02	.01
☐ 42	Larry Nance	.08	.04	.01
☐ 43	Mark Price	.10	.05	.01
☐ 44	Hot Rod Williams	.05	.02	.01
☐ 45	Rolando Blackman	.08	.04	.01
☐ 46	Terry Davis	.05	.02	.01
☐ 47	Derek Harper	.08	.04	.01
☐ 48	Mike Iuzzolino	.05	.02	.01
☐ 49	Fat Lever	.05	.02	.01
☐ 50	Rodney McCray	.05	.02	.01
☐ 51	Doug Smith	.05	.02	.01
☐ 52	Randy White	.05	.02	.01
☐ 53	Herb Williams	.05	.02	.01
☐ 54	Greg Anderson	.05	.02	.01
☐ 55	Winston Garland	.05	.02	.01
☐ 56	Chris Jackson	.08	.04	.01
☐ 57	Marcus Liberty	.05	.02	.01
☐ 58	Todd Lichti	.05	.02	.01
☐ 59	Mark Macon	.05	.02	.01
☐ 60	Dikembe Mutombo	.40	.18	.05
☐ 61	Reggie Williams	.05	.02	.01
☐ 62	Mark Aguirre	.08	.04	.01
☐ 63	William Bedford	.05	.02	.01
☐ 64	Joe Dumars	.15	.07	.02
☐ 65	Bill Laimbeer	.08	.04	.01
☐ 66	Dennis Rodman	.20	.09	.03
☐ 67	John Salley	.05	.02	.01
☐ 68	Isiah Thomas	.15	.07	.02
☐ 69	Darrell Walker	.05	.02	.01
☐ 70	Orlando Woolridge	.05	.02	.01
☐ 71	Victor Alexander	.05	.02	.01
☐ 72	Mario Elie	.05	.02	.01
☐ 73	Chris Gatling	.05	.02	.01
☐ 74	Tim Hardaway	.10	.05	.01
☐ 75	Tyrone Hill	.08	.04	.01
☐ 76	Alton Lister	.05	.02	.01
☐ 77	Sarunas Marciulionis	.05	.02	.01
☐ 78	Chris Mullin	.10	.05	.01
☐ 79	Billy Owens	.10	.05	.01
☐ 80	Matt Bullard	.05	.02	.01
☐ 81	Sleepy Floyd	.05	.02	.01
☐ 82	Avery Johnson	.05	.02	.01
☐ 83	Buck Johnson	.05	.02	.01
☐ 84	Vernon Maxwell	.05	.02	.01
☐ 85	Hakeem Olajuwon	.75	.35	.09
☐ 86	Kenny Smith	.05	.02	.01
☐ 87	Larry Smith	.05	.02	.01
☐ 88	Otis Thorpe	.08	.04	.01
☐ 89	Dale Davis	.10	.05	.01
☐ 90	Vern Fleming	.05	.02	.01
☐ 91	George McCloud	.05	.02	.01
☐ 92	Reggie Miller	.30	.14	.04
☐ 93	Chuck Person	.08	.04	.01
☐ 94	Detlef Schrempf	.10	.05	.01
☐ 95	Rik Smits	.10	.05	.01
☐ 96	LaSalle Thompson	.05	.02	.01
☐ 97	Micheal Williams	.05	.02	.01
☐ 98	James Edwards	.05	.02	.01
☐ 99	Gary Grant	.05	.02	.01
☐ 100	Ron Harper	.08	.04	.01
☐ 101	Danny Manning	.10	.05	.01
☐ 102	Ken Norman	.05	.02	.01
☐ 103	Olden Polynice	.05	.02	.01
☐ 104	Doc Rivers	.05	.02	.01
☐ 105	Charles Smith	.05	.02	.01
☐ 106	Loy Vaught	.08	.04	.01
☐ 107	Elden Campbell	.05	.02	.01
☐ 108	Vlade Divac	.10	.05	.01
☐ 109	A.C. Green	.10	.05	.01
☐ 110	Sam Perkins	.08	.04	.01
☐ 111	Byron Scott	.08	.04	.01
☐ 112	Tony Smith	.05	.02	.01
☐ 113	Terry Teagle	.05	.02	.01
☐ 114	Sedale Threatt	.05	.02	.01
☐ 115	James Worthy	.10	.05	.01
☐ 116	Willie Burton	.05	.02	.01
☐ 117	Bimbo Coles	.05	.02	.01
☐ 118	Kevin Edwards	.05	.02	.01
☐ 119	Alec Kessler	.05	.02	.01
☐ 120	Grant Long	.05	.02	.01
☐ 121	Glen Rice	.10	.05	.01
☐ 122	Rony Seikaly	.05	.02	.01
☐ 123	Brian Shaw	.05	.02	.01
☐ 124	Steve Smith	.10	.05	.01
☐ 125	Frank Brickowski	.05	.02	.01
☐ 126	Dale Ellis	.08	.04	.01
☐ 127	Jeff Grayer	.05	.02	.01
☐ 128	Jay Humphries	.05	.02	.01
☐ 129	Larry Krystkowiak	.05	.02	.01
☐ 130	Moses Malone	.15	.07	.02
☐ 131	Fred Roberts	.05	.02	.01
☐ 132	Alvin Robertson	.05	.02	.01
☐ 133	Dan Schayes	.05	.02	.01
☐ 134	Thurl Bailey	.05	.02	.01
☐ 135	Scott Brooks	.05	.02	.01
☐ 136	Tony Campbell	.05	.02	.01
☐ 137	Gerald Glass	.05	.02	.01
☐ 138	Luc Longley	.05	.02	.01
☐ 139	Sam Mitchell	.05	.02	.01
☐ 140	Pooh Richardson	.05	.02	.01
☐ 141	Felton Spencer	.05	.02	.01
☐ 142	Doug West	.05	.02	.01
☐ 143	Rafael Addison	.05	.02	.01
☐ 144	Kenny Anderson	.25	.11	.03
☐ 145	Mookie Blaylock	.08	.04	.01
☐ 146	Sam Bowie	.05	.02	.01
☐ 147	Derrick Coleman	.10	.05	.01
☐ 148	Chris Dudley	.05	.02	.01
☐ 149	Terry Mills	.08	.04	.01
☐ 150	Chris Morris	.05	.02	.01
☐ 151	Drazen Petrovic	.08	.04	.01
☐ 152	Greg Anthony	.05	.02	.01
☐ 153	Patrick Ewing	.30	.14	.04
☐ 154	Mark Jackson	.05	.02	.01
☐ 155	Anthony Mason	.10	.05	.01
☐ 156	Xavier McDaniel	.08	.04	.01
☐ 157	Charles Oakley	.08	.04	.01
☐ 158	John Starks	.10	.05	.01
☐ 159	Gerald Wilkins	.05	.02	.01
☐ 160	Nick Anderson	.08	.04	.01
☐ 161	Terry Catledge	.05	.02	.01
☐ 162	Jerry Reynolds	.05	.02	.01
☐ 163	Stanley Roberts	.05	.02	.01
☐ 164	Dennis Scott	.05	.02	.01
☐ 165	Scott Skiles	.05	.02	.01
☐ 166	Jeff Turner	.05	.02	.01
☐ 167	Sam Vincent	.05	.02	.01
☐ 168	Brian Williams	.05	.02	.01
☐ 169	Ron Anderson	.05	.02	.01
☐ 170	Charles Barkley	.60	.25	.08
☐ 171	Manute Bol	.05	.02	.01
☐ 172	Johnny Dawkins	.05	.02	.01
☐ 173	Armon Gilliam	.05	.02	.01
☐ 174	Hersey Hawkins	.08	.04	.01
☐ 175	Brian Oliver	.05	.02	.01
☐ 176	Charles Shackleford	.05	.02	.01
☐ 177	Jayson Williams	.05	.02	.01

☐ 178	Cedric Ceballos	.10	.05	.01
☐ 179	Tom Chambers	.08	.04	.01
☐ 180	Jeff Hornacek	.08	.04	.01
☐ 181	Kevin Johnson	.15	.07	.02
☐ 182	Negele Knight	.05	.02	.01
☐ 183	Andrew Lang	.05	.02	.01
☐ 184	Dan Majerle	.08	.04	.01
☐ 185	Tim Perry	.05	.02	.01
☐ 186	Mark West	.05	.02	.01
☐ 187	Alaa Abdelnaby	.05	.02	.01
☐ 188	Danny Ainge	.08	.04	.01
☐ 189	Clyde Drexler	.30	.14	.04
☐ 190	Kevin Duckworth	.05	.02	.01
☐ 191	Jerome Kersey	.05	.02	.01
☐ 192	Robert Pack	.05	.02	.01
☐ 193	Terry Porter	.08	.04	.01
☐ 194	Clifford Robinson	.10	.05	.01
☐ 195	Buck Williams	.08	.04	.01
☐ 196	Anthony Bonner	.05	.02	.01
☐ 197	Duane Causwell	.05	.02	.01
☐ 198	Pete Chilcutt	.05	.02	.01
☐ 199	Dennis Hopson	.05	.02	.01
☐ 200	Mitch Richmond	.15	.07	.02
☐ 201	Lionel Simmons	.05	.02	.01
☐ 202	Wayman Tisdale	.08	.04	.01
☐ 203	Spud Webb	.08	.04	.01
☐ 204	Willie Anderson	.05	.02	.01
☐ 205	Antoine Carr	.05	.02	.01
☐ 206	Terry Cummings	.08	.04	.01
☐ 207	Sean Elliott	.08	.04	.01
☐ 208	Sidney Green	.05	.02	.01
☐ 209	David Robinson	.60	.25	.08
☐ 210	Rod Strickland	.08	.04	.01
☐ 211	Greg Sutton	.05	.02	.01
☐ 212	Dana Barros	.10	.05	.01
☐ 213	Benoit Benjamin	.05	.02	.01
☐ 214	Michael Cage	.05	.02	.01
☐ 215	Eddie Johnson	.08	.04	.01
☐ 216	Shawn Kemp	.75	.35	.09
☐ 217	Derrick McKey	.08	.04	.01
☐ 218	Nate McMillan	.05	.02	.01
☐ 219	Gary Payton	.10	.05	.01
☐ 220	Ricky Pierce	.08	.04	.01
☐ 221	David Benoit	.05	.02	.01
☐ 222	Mike Brown	.05	.02	.01
☐ 223	Tyrone Corbin	.05	.02	.01
☐ 224	Mark Eaton	.05	.02	.01
☐ 225	Blue Edwards	.05	.02	.01
☐ 226	Jeff Malone	.08	.04	.01
☐ 227	Karl Malone	.30	.14	.04
☐ 228	Eric Murdock	.05	.02	.01
☐ 229	John Stockton	.30	.14	.04
☐ 230	Michael Adams	.05	.02	.01
☐ 231	Rex Chapman	.05	.02	.01
☐ 232	Ledell Eackles	.05	.02	.01
☐ 233	Pervis Ellison	.05	.02	.01
☐ 234	A.J. English	.05	.02	.01
☐ 235	Harvey Grant	.05	.02	.01
☐ 236	Charles Jones	.05	.02	.01
☐ 237	LaBradford Smith	.05	.02	.01
☐ 238	Larry Stewart	.05	.02	.01
☐ 239	Bob Weiss CO	.05	.02	.01
☐ 240	Chris Ford CO	.05	.02	.01
☐ 241	Allan Bristow CO	.05	.02	.01
☐ 242	Phil Jackson CO	.08	.04	.01
☐ 243	Lenny Wilkens CO	.08	.04	.01
☐ 244	Richie Adubato CO	.05	.02	.01
☐ 245	Dan Issel CO	.08	.04	.01
☐ 246	Ron Rothstein CO	.05	.02	.01
☐ 247	Don Nelson CO	.08	.04	.01
☐ 248	Rudy Tomjanovich CO	.08	.04	.01
☐ 249	Bob Hill CO	.05	.02	.01
☐ 250	Larry Brown CO	.08	.04	.01
☐ 251	Randy Pfund CO	.05	.02	.01
☐ 252	Kevin Loughery CO	.05	.02	.01
☐ 253	Mike Dunleavy CO	.05	.02	.01
☐ 254	Jimmy Rodgers CO	.05	.02	.01
☐ 255	Chuck Daly CO	.08	.04	.01
☐ 256	Pat Riley CO	.08	.04	.01
☐ 257	Matt Guokas CO	.05	.02	.01
☐ 258	Doug Moe CO	.05	.02	.01
☐ 259	Paul Westphal CO	.08	.04	.01
☐ 260	Rick Adelman CO	.05	.02	.01
☐ 261	Garry St. Jean CO	.05	.02	.01
☐ 262	Jerry Tarkanian CO	.15	.07	.02
☐ 263	George Karl CO	.05	.02	.01
☐ 264	Jerry Sloan CO	.05	.02	.01
☐ 265	Wes Unseld CO	.08	.04	.01
☐ 266	Atlanta Hawks Team Card	.05	.02	.01
☐ 267	Boston Celtics Team Card	.05	.02	.01
☐ 268	Charlotte Hornets Team Card	.05	.02	.01
☐ 269	Chicago Bulls Team Card	.05	.02	.01
☐ 270	Cleveland Cavaliers Team Card	.05	.02	.01
☐ 271	Dallas Mavericks Team Card	.05	.02	.01
☐ 272	Denver Nuggets Team Card	.05	.02	.01
☐ 273	Detroit Pistons Team Card	.05	.02	.01
☐ 274	Golden State Warriors Team Card	.05	.02	.01
☐ 275	Houston Rockets Team Card	.05	.02	.01
☐ 276	Indiana Pacers Team Card	.05	.02	.01
☐ 277	Los Angeles Clippers Team Card	.05	.02	.01
☐ 278	Los Angeles Lakers Team Card	.05	.02	.01
☐ 279	Miami Heat Team Card	.05	.02	.01
☐ 280	Milwaukee Bucks Team Card	.05	.02	.01
☐ 281	Minnesota Timberwolves Team Card	.05	.02	.01
☐ 282	New Jersey Nets Team Card	.05	.02	.01
☐ 283	New York Knicks Team Card	.05	.02	.01
☐ 284	Orlando Magic Team Card	.05	.02	.01
☐ 285	Philadelphia 76ers Team Card	.05	.02	.01
☐ 286	Phoenix Suns Team Card	.05	.02	.01
☐ 287	Portland Trail Blazers Team Card	.05	.02	.01
☐ 288	Sacramento Kings Team Card	.05	.02	.01
☐ 289	San Antonio Spurs Team Card	.05	.02	.01
☐ 290	Seattle Supersonics Team Card	.05	.02	.01
☐ 291	Utah Jazz Team Card	.05	.02	.01
☐ 292	Washington Bullets Team Card	.05	.02	.01

☐ 293 Michael Adams AS	.05	.02	.01
☐ 294 Charles Barkley AS	.30	.14	.04
☐ 295 Brad Daugherty AS	.05	.02	.01
☐ 296 Joe Dumars AS	.08	.04	.01
☐ 297 Patrick Ewing AS	.10	.05	.01
☐ 298 Michael Jordan AS	2.00	.90	.25
☐ 299 Reggie Lewis AS	.05	.02	.01
☐ 300 Scottie Pippen AS	.10	.05	.01
☐ 301 Mark Price AS	.05	.02	.01
☐ 302 Dennis Rodman AS	.08	.04	.01
☐ 303 Isiah Thomas AS	.08	.04	.01
☐ 304 Kevin Willis AS	.05	.02	.01
☐ 305 Phil Jackson CO AS	.05	.02	.01
☐ 306 Clyde Drexler AS	.10	.05	.01
☐ 307 Tim Hardaway AS	.05	.02	.01
☐ 308 Jeff Hornacek AS	.05	.02	.01
☐ 309 Magic Johnson AS	.30	.14	.04
☐ 310 Dan Majerle AS	.05	.02	.01
☐ 311 Karl Malone AS	.10	.05	.01
☐ 312 Chris Mullin AS	.05	.02	.01
☐ 313 Dikembe Mutombo AS	.20	.09	.03
☐ 314 Hakeem Olajuwon AS	.40	.18	.05
☐ 315 David Robinson AS	.30	.14	.04
☐ 316 John Stockton AS	.10	.05	.01
☐ 317 Otis Thorpe AS	.05	.02	.01
☐ 318 James Worthy AS	.05	.02	.01
☐ 319 Don Nelson CO AS	.05	.02	.01
☐ 320 Scoring League Leaders	1.00	.45	.13
Michael Jordan			
Karl Malone			
☐ 321 Three-Point Field	.05	.02	.01
Goal Percent			
League Leaders			
Dana Barros			
Drazen Petrovic			
☐ 322 Free Throw Percent	.25	.11	.03
League Leaders			
Mark Price			
Larry Bird			
☐ 323 Blocks League Leaders	.40	.18	.05
David Robinson			
Hakeem Olajuwon			
☐ 324 Steals League Leaders	.08	.04	.01
John Stockton			
Micheal Williams			
☐ 325 Rebounds League	.08	.04	.01
Leaders			
Dennis Rodman			
Kevin Willis			
☐ 326 Assists League Leaders	.10	.05	.01
John Stockton			
Kevin Johnson			
☐ 327 Field Goal Percent	.05	.02	.01
League Leaders			
Buck Williams			
Otis Thorpe			
☐ 328 Magic Moments 1980	.25	.11	.03
☐ 329 Magic Moments 1985	.25	.11	.03
☐ 330 Magic Moments 87,88	.25	.11	.03
☐ 331 Magic Numbers	.25	.11	.03
☐ 332 Drazen Petrovic	.05	.02	.01
Inside Stuff			
☐ 333 Patrick Ewing	.10	.05	.01
Inside Stuff			
☐ 334 David Robinson	.30	.14	.04
Stay in School			
☐ 335 Kevin Johnson	.08	.04	.01
Stay in School			
☐ 336 Charles Barkley	.30	.14	.04
Tournament of			
The Americas			
☐ 337 Larry Bird	.50	.23	.06
Tournament of			
The Americas			
☐ 338 Clyde Drexler	.10	.05	.01
Tournament of			
The Americas			
☐ 339 Patrick Ewing	.05	.02	.01
Tournament of			
The Americas			
☐ 340 Magic Johnson	.30	.14	.04
Tournament of			
The Americas			
☐ 341 Michael Jordan	2.00	.90	.25
Tournament of			
The Americas			
☐ 342 Christian Laettner	.60	.25	.08
Tournament of			
The Americas			
☐ 343 Karl Malone	.10	.05	.01
Tournament of			
The Americas			
☐ 344 Chris Mullin	.05	.02	.01
Tournament of			
The Americas			
☐ 345 Scottie Pippen	.10	.05	.01
Tournament of			
The Americas			
☐ 346 David Robinson	.30	.14	.04
Tournament of			
The Americas			
☐ 347 John Stockton	.10	.05	.01
Tournament of			
The Americas			
☐ 348 Checklist 1	.05	.02	.01
☐ 349 Checklist 2	.05	.02	.01
☐ 350 Checklist 3	.05	.02	.01
☐ 351 Mookie Blaylock	.12	.05	.02
☐ 352 Adam Keefe	.25	.11	.03
☐ 353 Travis Mays	.10	.05	.01
☐ 354 Morlon Wiley	.10	.05	.01
☐ 355 Joe Kleine	.10	.05	.01
☐ 356 Bart Kofoed	.10	.05	.01
☐ 357 Xavier McDaniel	.12	.05	.02
☐ 358 Tony Bennett	.10	.05	.01
☐ 359 Tom Hammonds	.10	.05	.01
☐ 360 Kevin Lynch	.10	.05	.01
☐ 361 Alonzo Mourning	3.00	1.35	.40
☐ 362 Rodney McCray	.10	.05	.01
☐ 363 Trent Tucker	.10	.05	.01
☐ 364 Corey Williams	.10	.05	.01
☐ 365 Steve Kerr	.10	.05	.01
Traded to Orlando			
☐ 366 Jerome Lane	.10	.05	.01
☐ 367 Bobby Phills	.25	.11	.03
☐ 368 Mike Sanders	.10	.05	.01
☐ 369 Gerald Wilkins	.10	.05	.01
☐ 370 Donald Hodge	.10	.05	.01
☐ 371 Brian Howard	.10	.05	.01
☐ 372 Tracy Moore	.10	.05	.01
☐ 373 Sean Rooks	.12	.05	.02
☐ 374 Kevin Brooks	.10	.05	.01
☐ 375 LaPhonso Ellis	.50	.23	.06
☐ 376 Scott Hastings	.10	.05	.01
☐ 377 Robert Pack	.10	.05	.01
☐ 378 Bryant Stith	.40	.18	.05
☐ 379 Robert Werdann	.10	.05	.01
☐ 380 Lance Blanks	.10	.05	.01
Traded to Minnesota			
☐ 381 Terry Mills	.12	.05	.02
☐ 382 Isaiah Morris	.10	.05	.01
☐ 383 Olden Polynice	.10	.05	.01

☐ 384 Brad Sellers	.10	.05	.01
Traded to Minnesota			
☐ 385 Jud Buechler	.10	.05	.01
☐ 386 Jeff Grayer	.10	.05	.01
☐ 387 Byron Houston	.10	.05	.01
☐ 388 Keith Jennings	.10	.05	.01
☐ 389 Latrell Sprewell	3.00	1.35	.40
☐ 390 Scott Brooks	.10	.05	.01
☐ 391 Carl Herrera	.10	.05	.01
☐ 392 Robert Horry	1.25	.55	.16
☐ 393 Tree Rollins	.10	.05	.01
☐ 394 Kennard Winchester	.10	.05	.01
☐ 395 Greg Dreiling	.10	.05	.01
☐ 396 Sean Green	.10	.05	.01
☐ 397 Sam Mitchell	.10	.05	.01
☐ 398 Pooh Richardson	.10	.05	.01
☐ 399 Malik Sealy	.25	.11	.03
☐ 400 Kenny Williams	.10	.05	.01
☐ 401 Jaren Jackson	.10	.05	.01
☐ 402 Mark Jackson	.10	.05	.01
☐ 403 Stanley Roberts	.10	.05	.01
☐ 404 Elmore Spencer	.10	.05	.01
☐ 405 Kiki Vandeweghe	.10	.05	.01
☐ 406 John Williams	.10	.05	.01
☐ 407 Randy Woods	.10	.05	.01
☐ 408 Alex Blackwell	.10	.05	.01
☐ 409 Duane Cooper	.10	.05	.01
☐ 410 Anthony Peeler	.25	.11	.03
☐ 411 Keith Askins	.10	.05	.01
☐ 412 Matt Geiger	.10	.05	.01
☐ 413 Harold Miner	.30	.14	.04
☐ 414 John Salley	.10	.05	.01
☐ 415 Alaa Abdelnaby	.10	.05	.01
Traded to Boston			
☐ 416 Todd Day	.60	.25	.08
☐ 417 Blue Edwards	.10	.05	.01
☐ 418 Brad Lohaus	.10	.05	.01
☐ 419 Lee Mayberry	.13	.06	.02
☐ 420 Eric Murdock	.10	.05	.01
☐ 421 Christian Laettner	1.00	.45	.13
☐ 422 Bob McCann	.10	.05	.01
☐ 423 Chuck Person	.12	.05	.02
☐ 424 Chris Smith	.10	.05	.01
☐ 425 Gundars Vetra	.10	.05	.01
☐ 426 Micheal Williams	.10	.05	.01
☐ 427 Chucky Brown	.10	.05	.01
☐ 428 Tate George	.10	.05	.01
☐ 429 Rick Mahorn	.10	.05	.01
☐ 430 Rumeal Robinson	.10	.05	.01
☐ 431 Jayson Williams	.10	.05	.01
☐ 432 Eric Anderson	.10	.05	.01
☐ 433 Rolando Blackman	.12	.05	.02
☐ 434 Tony Campbell	.10	.05	.01
☐ 435 Hubert Davis	.25	.11	.03
☐ 436 Bo Kimble	.10	.05	.01
☐ 437 Doc Rivers	.10	.05	.01
☐ 438 Charles Smith	.10	.05	.01
☐ 439 Anthony Bowie	.10	.05	.01
☐ 440 Litterial Green	.10	.05	.01
☐ 441 Greg Kite	.10	.05	.01
☐ 442 Shaquille O'Neal	12.00	5.50	1.50
☐ 443 Donald Royal	.10	.05	.01
☐ 444 Greg Grant	.10	.05	.01
☐ 445 Jeff Hornacek	.12	.05	.02
☐ 446 Andrew Lang	.10	.05	.01
☐ 447 Kenny Payne	.10	.05	.01
☐ 448 Tim Perry	.10	.05	.01
☐ 449 Clarence Weatherspoon	1.00	.45	.13
☐ 450 Danny Ainge	.12	.05	.02
☐ 451 Charles Barkley	1.00	.45	.13
☐ 452 Tim Kempton	.10	.05	.01

☐ 453 Oliver Miller	.40	.18	.05
☐ 454 Mark Bryant	.10	.05	.01
☐ 455 Mario Elie	.10	.05	.01
☐ 456 Dave Jamerson	.10	.05	.01
☐ 457 Tracy Murray	.12	.05	.02
☐ 458 Rod Strickland	.12	.05	.02
☐ 459 Vincent Askew	.10	.05	.01
Traded to Seattle			
☐ 460 Randy Brown	.10	.05	.01
☐ 461 Marty Conlon	.10	.05	.01
☐ 462 Jim Les	.10	.05	.01
☐ 463 Walt Williams	1.00	.45	.13
☐ 464 William Bedford	.10	.05	.01
☐ 465 Lloyd Daniels	.10	.05	.01
☐ 466 Vinny Del Negro	.10	.05	.01
☐ 467 Dale Ellis	.12	.05	.02
☐ 468 Larry Smith	.10	.05	.01
☐ 469 David Wood	.10	.05	.01
☐ 470 Rich King	.10	.05	.01
☐ 471 Isaac Austin	.10	.05	.01
☐ 472 John Crotty	.10	.05	.01
☐ 473 Stephen Howard	.10	.05	.01
☐ 474 Jay Humphries	.10	.05	.01
☐ 475 Larry Krystowiak	.10	.05	.01
☐ 476 Tom Gugliotta	.75	.35	.09
☐ 477 Buck Johnson	.10	.05	.01
☐ 478 Don MacLean	.25	.11	.03
☐ 479 Doug Overton	.10	.05	.01
☐ 480 Brent Price	.10	.05	.01
☐ 481 David Robinson TRIV	.50	.23	.06
San Antonio Spurs			
Blocks			
☐ 482 Magic Johnson TRIV	.50	.23	.06
Los Angeles Lakers			
Assists			
☐ 483 John Stockton TRIV	.25	.11	.03
Utah Jazz			
Steals			
☐ 484 Patrick Ewing TRIV	.25	.11	.03
New York Knicks			
Points			
☐ 485 Answer Card TRIV	.25	.11	.03
Magic Johnson			
David Robinson			
Patrick Ewing			
John Stockton			
☐ 486 John Stockton	.25	.11	.03
Utah Jazz			
Stay in School			
☐ 487 Ahmad Rashad	.15	.07	.02
Willow Bay			
Inside Stuff			
☐ 488 Rookie Checklist	.10	.05	.01
☐ 489 Checklist 1	.10	.05	.01
☐ 490 Checklist 2	.10	.05	.01
☐ AC1 Patrick Ewing Art	1.00	.45	.13
☐ NNO Barcelona Plastic	20.00	9.00	2.50
☐ NNO Magic Johnson Comm	1.00	.45	.13
☐ NNO Patrick Ewing Game	200.00	90.00	25.00
☐ NNO Patrick Ewing AU	.75	.35	.09
(Certified autograph)			
☐ NNO Team USA	100.00	45.00	12.50
☐ NNO M. Johnson AU	200.00	90.00	25.00
☐ SU1 John Stockton Game	2.00	.90	.25
Utah Jazz			
His Ultimate Game			
☐ SU1AU John Stockton AU	100.00	45.00	12.50
(Certified autograph)			
☐ TR1 NBA Championship	2.00	.90	.25
Michael Jordan			
Clyde Drexler			

1992-93 Hoops Draft Redemption

A "Lottery Exchange Card" randomly inserted (reportedly at a rate of one per 360 packs) in 1992-93 Hoops first series 12-card foil packs entitled the collector to receive this NBA Draft Redemption Lottery Exchange set. It consists of ten standard size (2 1/2" by 3 1/2") cards of the top 1992 NBA Draft Picks. The first eleven players drafted are represented, with the exception of Jim Jackson, the late-signing fourth pick. Insert sets began to be mailed out during the week of January 4, 1993, and the redemption period expired on March 31, 1993. According to SkyBox International media releases a total of 25,876 sets were released to the public; 24,461 Lottery Exchange cards were redeemed. An additional 415 sets were claimed through a second chance drawing (selected from 149,166 mail-in entries). Finally, 1,000 more sets were released for public relations and promotional use. A reserve of 1,000 sets were held for replacement of damaged sets and 500 sets were kept for SkyBox International archives. In the color photos on the fronts, the players appear in dress attire in front of a gray studio background, except for cards C and J. The player's name is printed in white in a hardwood floor border design at the bottom of the card. A NBA Draft icon overlaps the border and the photo. A one inch tall hardwood design number at the upper left corner indicates the order the players were drafted. The horizontal backs display white backgrounds with a similar hardwood stripe containing the player's name across the top. A shadowed close-up photo is displayed next to college statistics and a player profile. The cards are lettered on the back. Sets still in the factory-sealed bags are valued at a premium of up to 20 percent above the complete set price below.

	MINT	NRMT	EXC
COMPLETE SET (10)	140.00	65.00	17.50
COMMON CARD (A-J)	1.50	.65	.19
☐ A Shaquille O'Neal Orlando Magic	90.00	40.00	11.50
☐ B Alonzo Mourning Charlotte Hornets	20.00	9.00	2.50
☐ C Christian Laettner Minnesota Timberwolves	6.00	2.70	.75
☐ D LaPhonso Ellis Denver Nuggets	3.00	1.35	.40
☐ E Tom Gugliotta Washington Bullets	5.00	2.30	.60
☐ F Walt Williams Sacramento Kings	6.00	2.70	.75
☐ G Todd Day Milwaukee Bucks	4.00	1.80	.50
☐ H Clarence Weatherspoon Philadelphia 76ers	6.00	2.70	.75
☐ I Adam Keefe Atlanta Hawks	1.50	.65	.19
☐ J Robert Horry Houston Rockets	8.00	3.60	1.00
☐ NNO Draft Redemption Card (Stamped)	1.00	.45	.13
☐ NNO Draft Redemption Card (Unstamped)	4.00	1.80	.50

1992-93 Hoops Magic's All-Rookies

This 10-card standard size (2 1/2" by 3 1/2") set was randomly inserted into Hoops second series 12-card foil packs. They were inserted at a rate of one in 30 packs. The set features Magic Johnson's selections of the top rookies from the 1992-93 season. The cards show color action player photos and have a gold foil stripe containing the player's name down the left edge and a thinner stripe across the bottom printed with the city's name. The Magic's All-Rookie Team logo appears in the lower left corner. The backs display a small close-up picture of Magic Johnson in a yellow Los Angeles Lakers' warm-up jacket. A yellow stripe down the left edge contains the set name (Magic's All-Rookie Team) and the card number. The white background is printed in black with Magic's evaluation of the player.

	MINT	NRMT	EXC
COMPLETE SET (10)	250.00	115.00	31.00
COMMON CARD (1-10)	4.00	1.80	.50

		MINT	NRMT	EXC
☐ 1	Shaquille O'Neal	175.00	80.00	22.00
	Orlando Magic			
☐ 2	Alonzo Mourning	40.00	18.00	5.00
	Charlotte Hornets			
☐ 3	Christian Laettner	12.00	5.50	1.50
	Minnesota Timberwolves			
☐ 4	LaPhonso Ellis	6.00	2.70	.75
	Denver Nuggets			
☐ 5	Tom Gugliotta	10.00	4.50	1.25
	Washington Bullets			
☐ 6	Walt Williams	12.00	5.50	1.50
	Sacramento Kings			
☐ 7	Todd Day	8.00	3.60	1.00
	Milwaukee Bucks			
☐ 8	Clarence Weatherspoon	12.00	5.50	1.50
	Philadelphia 76ers			
☐ 9	Robert Horry	15.00	6.75	1.90
	Houston Rockets			
☐ 10	Harold Miner	4.00	1.80	.50
	Miami Heat			

		MINT	NRMT	EXC
☐ M2	L.A. Lakers vs.	25.00	11.50	3.10
	Philadelphia			
	October 20, 1992			
☐ M3	L.A. Lakers vs.	25.00	11.50	3.10
	Cleveland			
	October 30, 1992			

1992-93 Hoops Supreme Court

This 10-card, standard size (2 1/2" by 3 1/2"), set was randomly inserted (at a reported rate of one card per 11 packs) in Hoops second series 12-card foil packs and features color action player photos on the front. A gold foil stripe frames the pictures which are surrounded by a hardwood floor design. The player's name is printed in gold foil down the left side. A gray and burnt-orange logo printed with the words "Supreme Court 1992-93" appears in the lower left corner. A purple stripe containing the phrase "The Fan's Choice" runs across the bottom of the picture. Hoops promoted The Supreme Court Sweepstakes, which offered fans the opportunity to select the ten players who appeared in this subset. The backs are white with black print. A small color player photo with rounded corners is displayed next to a personal profile. The cards are numbered on the back with an "SC" prefix.

1992-93 Hoops More Magic Moments

Randomly inserted (at a reported rate of one card per 195 packs) into 1992-93 Hoops second series 12-card packs, this three-card standard-size (2 1/2" by 3 1/2") set commemorates Magic Johnson's return to training camp and pre-season game action. Each card features a color player photo bordered in white. Team color-coded bars and lettering accent the picture on the left edge and below, and a team color-coded star overwritten with the words "More Magic" appears at the lower left corner. Over ghosted photos similar or identical to the front photos, the backs summarize Magic's return, his performance in his first game, his performance in his last game, and his decision to retire again. The cards are numbered on the back with an "M" prefix.

	MINT	NRMT	EXC
COMPLETE SET (3)	70.00	32.00	8.75
COMMON CARD (M1-M3)	25.00	11.50	3.10

		MINT	NRMT	EXC
☐ M1	Magic in Training Camp	25.00	11.50	3.10
	Fall 1992			

	MINT	NRMT	EXC
COMPLETE SET (10)	40.00	18.00	5.00
COMMON CARD (SC1-SC10)	.75	.35	.09

		MINT	NRMT	EXC
☐ SC1	Michael Jordan	25.00	11.50	3.10
	Chicago Bulls			
☐ SC2	Scottie Pippen	2.00	.90	.25
	Chicago Bulls			
☐ SC3	David Robinson	4.00	1.80	.50
	San Antonio Spurs			
☐ SC4	Patrick Ewing	2.00	.90	.25
	New York Knicks			
☐ SC5	Clyde Drexler	2.00	.90	.25
	Portland Trail Blazers			
☐ SC6	Karl Malone	2.00	.90	.25
	Utah Jazz			
☐ SC7	Charles Barkley	4.00	1.80	.50
	Phoenix Suns			

		MINT	NRMT	EXC
☐	SC8 John Stockton 2.00	.90	.25
	Utah Jazz		
☐	SC9 Chris Mullin .... .75	.35	.09
	Golden State Warriors		
☐	SC10 Magic Johnson 4.00	1.80	.50
	Los Angeles Lakers		

1993-94 Hoops

This 421-card standard-size (2 1/2" by 3 1/2") set was issued in separate series of 300 and 121 cards. Cards were distributed in 13-card foil (12 basic cards plus one Fifth Anniversary Gold) and 26-card jumbo (24 basic, two Fifth Anniv.) packs. Cards feature full-bleed glossy color player photos on the fronts. Each player's name and team logo appear in team colors along a ghosted band at the bottom. The back presents a color head shot of the player in a small rectangle bordered with a team color in the top right corner. Alongside is his jersey number and position within a team-colored bar. The player's name and a short biography are printed on a hardwood floor design at the top. Below, the player's college and NBA stats, displayed in separate tables on a white background, round out the card. The cards are numbered on the back and listed alphabetically according to and within teams as follows: Atlanta Hawks (1-8), Boston Celtics (9-16), Charlotte Hornets (17-24), Chicago Bulls (25-34), Cleveland Cavaliers (35-43), Dallas Mavericks (44-51), Denver Nuggets (52-59), Detroit Pistons (60-67), Golden State Warriors (68-75), Houston Rockets (76-83), Indiana Pacers (84-92), Los Angeles Clippers (93-102), Los Angeles Lakers (103-110), Miami Heat (111-118), Milwaukee Bucks (119-127), Minnesota Timberwolves (128-135), New Jersey Nets (136-142), New York Knicks (143-151), Orlando Magic (152-160), Philadelphia 76ers (161-167), Phoenix Suns (168-175), Portland Trail Blazers (176-185), Sacramento Kings (186-194), San Antonio Spurs (195-203), Seattle Supersonics (204-212), Utah Jazz (213-219), and Washington Bullets (220-229), Coaches (230-256), All-Stars (257-282), League Leaders (283-290), Boys and Girls Club (291), Hoops Tribune (292-297), and Checklists (298-300). Second series cards

(301-421) include rookies and traded players with their new teams. Rookie Cards include Vin Baker, Shawn Bradley, Sam Cassell, Calbert Cheaney, Anfernee Hardaway, Bobby Hurley, Jamal Mashburn and Chris Webber.

		MINT	NRMT	EXC
COMPLETE SET (421)	20.00	9.00	2.50
COMPLETE SERIES 1 (300)..	12.00	5.50	1.50
COMPLETE SERIES 2 (121)..	8.00	3.60	1.00
COMMON CARD (1-421)	.05	.02	.01

		MINT	NRMT	EXC
☐ 1	Stacey Augmon..................	.08	.04	.01
☐ 2	Mookie Blaylock................	.08	.04	.01
☐ 3	Duane Ferrell....................	.05	.02	.01
☐ 4	Paul Graham	.05	.02	.01
☐ 5	Adam Keefe......................	.05	.02	.01
☐ 6	Blair Rasmussen................	.05	.02	.01
☐ 7	Dominique Wilkins............	.15	.07	.02
☐ 8	Kevin Willis	.08	.04	.01
☐ 9	Alaa Abdelnaby	.05	.02	.01
☐ 10	Dee Brown	.08	.04	.01
☐ 11	Sherman Douglas	.05	.02	.01
☐ 12	Rick Fox	.05	.02	.01
☐ 13	Kevin Gamble	.05	.02	.01
☐ 14	Joe Kleine	.05	.02	.01
☐ 15	Xavier McDaniel	.08	.04	.01
☐ 16	Robert Parish	.10	.05	.01
☐ 17	Tony Bennett	.05	.02	.01
☐ 18	Muggsy Bogues	.10	.05	.01
☐ 19	Dell Curry	.05	.02	.01
☐ 20	Kenny Gattison	.05	.02	.01
☐ 21	Kendall Gill	.05	.02	.01
☐ 22	Larry Johnson..................	.25	.11	.03
☐ 23	Alonzo Mourning..............	.50	.23	.06
☐ 24	Johnny Newman	.05	.02	.01
☐ 25	B.J. Armstrong	.05	.02	.01
☐ 26	Bill Cartwright	.05	.02	.01
☐ 27	Horace Grant...................	.15	.07	.02
☐ 28	Michael Jordan	3.00	1.35	.40
☐ 29	Stacey King	.05	.02	.01
☐ 30	John Paxson	.05	.02	.01
☐ 31	Will Perdue	.05	.02	.01
☐ 32	Scottie Pippen	.25	.11	.03
☐ 33	Scott Williams	.05	.02	.01
☐ 34	Moses Malone	.15	.07	.02
☐ 35	John Battle	.05	.02	.01
☐ 36	Terrell Brandon	.08	.04	.01
☐ 37	Brad Daugherty	.08	.04	.01
☐ 38	Craig Ehlo	.05	.02	.01
☐ 39	Danny Ferry	.05	.02	.01
☐ 40	Larry Nance	.08	.04	.01
☐ 41	Mark Price	.10	.05	.01
☐ 42	Gerald Wilkins	.05	.02	.01
☐ 43	John Williams	.08	.04	.01
☐ 44	Terry Davis	.05	.02	.01
☐ 45	Derek Harper	.08	.04	.01
☐ 46	Donald Hodge	.05	.02	.01
☐ 47	Mike Iuzzolino..................	.05	.02	.01
☐ 48	Jim Jackson....................	.50	.23	.06
☐ 49	Sean Rooks.....................	.05	.02	.01
☐ 50	Doug Smith	.05	.02	.01
☐ 51	Randy White....................	.05	.02	.01
☐ 52	Mahmoud Abdul-Rauf....	.08	.04	.01
☐ 53	LaPhonso Ellis	.08	.04	.01
☐ 54	Marcus Liberty	.05	.02	.01
☐ 55	Mark Macon.....................	.05	.02	.01
☐ 56	Dikembe Mutombo	.20	.09	.03
☐ 57	Robert Pack	.05	.02	.01
☐ 58	Bryant Stith.....................	.05	.02	.01

☐ 59	Reggie Williams	.05	.02	.01
☐ 60	Mark Aguirre	.08	.04	.01
☐ 61	Joe Dumars	.15	.07	.02
☐ 62	Bill Laimbeer	.08	.04	.01
☐ 63	Terry Mills	.05	.02	.01
☐ 64	Olden Polynice	.05	.02	.01
☐ 65	Alvin Robertson	.05	.02	.01
☐ 66	Dennis Rodman	.15	.07	.02
☐ 67	Isiah Thomas	.15	.07	.02
☐ 68	Victor Alexander	.05	.02	.01
☐ 69	Tim Hardaway	.10	.05	.01
☐ 70	Tyrone Hill	.08	.04	.01
☐ 71	Byron Houston	.05	.02	.01
☐ 72	Sarunas Marciulionis	.05	.02	.01
☐ 73	Chris Mullin	.10	.05	.01
☐ 74	Billy Owens	.08	.04	.01
☐ 75	Latrell Sprewell	.50	.23	.06
☐ 76	Scott Brooks	.05	.02	.01
☐ 77	Matt Bullard	.05	.02	.01
☐ 78	Carl Herrera	.05	.02	.01
☐ 79	Robert Horry	.10	.05	.01
☐ 80	Vernon Maxwell	.05	.02	.01
☐ 81	Hakeem Olajuwon	.60	.25	.08
☐ 82	Kenny Smith	.05	.02	.01
☐ 83	Otis Thorpe	.08	.04	.01
☐ 84	Dale Davis	.08	.04	.01
☐ 85	Vern Fleming	.05	.02	.01
☐ 86	George McCloud	.05	.02	.01
☐ 87	Reggie Miller	.25	.11	.03
☐ 88	Sam Mitchell	.05	.02	.01
☐ 89	Pooh Richardson	.05	.02	.01
☐ 90	Detlef Schrempf	.10	.05	.01
☐ 91	Malik Sealy	.05	.02	.01
☐ 92	Rik Smits	.10	.05	.01
☐ 93	Gary Grant	.05	.02	.01
☐ 94	Ron Harper	.08	.04	.01
☐ 95	Mark Jackson	.05	.02	.01
☐ 96	Danny Manning	.10	.05	.01
☐ 97	Ken Norman	.05	.02	.01
☐ 98	Stanley Roberts	.05	.02	.01
☐ 99	Elmore Spencer	.05	.02	.01
☐ 100	Loy Vaught	.08	.04	.01
☐ 101	John Williams	.05	.02	.01
☐ 102	Randy Woods	.05	.02	.01
☐ 103	Benoit Benjamin	.05	.02	.01
☐ 104	Elden Campbell	.05	.02	.01
☐ 105	Doug Christie UER	.05	.02	.01
	(Has uniform on front and 35 on back)			
☐ 106	Vlade Divac	.10	.05	.01
☐ 107	Anthony Peeler	.05	.02	.01
☐ 108	Tony Smith	.05	.02	.01
☐ 109	Sedale Threatt	.05	.02	.01
☐ 110	James Worthy	.10	.05	.01
☐ 111	Bimbo Coles	.05	.02	.01
☐ 112	Grant Long	.05	.02	.01
☐ 113	Harold Miner	.05	.02	.01
☐ 114	Glen Rice	.10	.05	.01
☐ 115	John Salley	.05	.02	.01
☐ 116	Rony Seikaly	.05	.02	.01
☐ 117	Brian Shaw	.05	.02	.01
☐ 118	Steve Smith	.08	.04	.01
☐ 119	Anthony Avent	.05	.02	.01
☐ 120	Jon Barry	.05	.02	.01
☐ 121	Frank Brickowski	.05	.02	.01
☐ 122	Todd Day	.08	.04	.01
☐ 123	Blue Edwards	.05	.02	.01
☐ 124	Brad Lohaus	.05	.02	.01
☐ 125	Lee Mayberry	.05	.02	.01
☐ 126	Eric Murdock	.05	.02	.01
☐ 127	Derek Strong	.05	.02	.01
☐ 128	Thurl Bailey	.05	.02	.01
☐ 129	Christian Laettner	.10	.05	.01
☐ 130	Luc Longley	.05	.02	.01
☐ 131	Marlon Maxey	.05	.02	.01
☐ 132	Chuck Person	.08	.04	.01
☐ 133	Chris Smith	.05	.02	.01
☐ 134	Doug West	.05	.02	.01
☐ 135	Micheal Williams	.05	.02	.01
☐ 136	Rafael Addison	.05	.02	.01
☐ 137	Kenny Anderson	.10	.05	.01
☐ 138	Sam Bowie	.05	.02	.01
☐ 139	Chucky Brown	.05	.02	.01
☐ 140	Derrick Coleman	.10	.05	.01
☐ 141	Chris Morris	.05	.02	.01
☐ 142	Rumeal Robinson	.05	.02	.01
☐ 143	Greg Anthony	.05	.02	.01
☐ 144	Rolando Blackman	.08	.04	.01
☐ 145	Hubert Davis	.05	.02	.01
☐ 146	Patrick Ewing	.25	.11	.03
☐ 147	Anthony Mason	.08	.04	.01
☐ 148	Charles Oakley	.08	.04	.01
☐ 149	Doc Rivers	.05	.02	.01
☐ 150	Charles Smith	.05	.02	.01
☐ 151	John Starks	.08	.04	.01
☐ 152	Nick Anderson	.08	.04	.01
☐ 153	Anthony Bowie	.05	.02	.01
☐ 154	Litterial Green	.05	.02	.01
☐ 155	Shaquille O'Neal	2.00	.90	.25
☐ 156	Donald Royal	.05	.02	.01
☐ 157	Dennis Scott	.05	.02	.01
☐ 158	Scott Skiles	.05	.02	.01
☐ 159	Tom Tolbert	.05	.02	.01
☐ 160	Jeff Turner	.05	.02	.01
☐ 161	Ron Anderson	.05	.02	.01
☐ 162	Johnny Dawkins	.05	.02	.01
☐ 163	Hersey Hawkins	.08	.04	.01
☐ 164	Jeff Hornacek	.08	.04	.01
☐ 165	Andrew Lang	.05	.02	.01
☐ 166	Tim Perry	.05	.02	.01
☐ 167	Clarence Weatherspoon	.10	.05	.01
☐ 168	Danny Ainge	.08	.04	.01
☐ 169	Charles Barkley	.50	.23	.06
☐ 170	Cedric Ceballos	.10	.05	.01
☐ 171	Richard Dumas	.05	.02	.01
☐ 172	Kevin Johnson	.15	.07	.02
☐ 173	Dan Majerle	.08	.04	.01
☐ 174	Oliver Miller	.05	.02	.01
☐ 175	Mark West	.05	.02	.01
☐ 176	Clyde Drexler	.25	.11	.03
☐ 177	Kevin Duckworth	.05	.02	.01
☐ 178	Mario Elie	.05	.02	.01
☐ 179	Dave Johnson	.05	.02	.01
☐ 180	Jerome Kersey	.05	.02	.01
☐ 181	Tracy Murray	.05	.02	.01
☐ 182	Terry Porter	.08	.04	.01
☐ 183	Cliff Robinson	.08	.04	.01
☐ 184	Rod Strickland	.08	.04	.01
☐ 185	Buck Williams	.08	.04	.01
☐ 186	Anthony Bonner	.05	.02	.01
☐ 187	Randy Brown	.05	.02	.01
☐ 188	Duane Causwell	.05	.02	.01
☐ 189	Pete Chilcutt	.05	.02	.01
☐ 190	Mitch Richmond	.15	.07	.02
☐ 191	Lionel Simmons	.05	.02	.01
☐ 192	Wayman Tisdale	.08	.04	.01
☐ 193	Spud Webb	.08	.04	.01
☐ 194	Walt Williams	.10	.05	.01
☐ 195	Willie Anderson	.05	.02	.01
☐ 196	Antoine Carr	.05	.02	.01
☐ 197	Terry Cummings	.08	.04	.01
☐ 198	Lloyd Daniels	.05	.02	.01

☐	199	Sean Elliott	.08	.04	.01
☐	200	Dale Ellis	.08	.04	.01
☐	201	Avery Johnson	.05	.02	.01
☐	202	J.R. Reid	.05	.02	.01
☐	203	David Robinson	.50	.23	.06
☐	204	Dana Barros	.10	.05	.01
☐	205	Michael Cage	.05	.02	.01
☐	206	Eddie Johnson	.08	.04	.01
☐	207	Shawn Kemp	.50	.23	.06
☐	208	Derrick McKey	.08	.04	.01
☐	209	Nate McMillan	.05	.02	.01
☐	210	Gary Payton	.10	.05	.01
☐	211	Sam Perkins	.08	.04	.01
☐	212	Ricky Pierce	.08	.04	.01
☐	213	David Benoit	.05	.02	.01
☐	214	Tyrone Corbin	.05	.02	.01
☐	215	Mark Eaton	.05	.02	.01
☐	216	Jay Humphries	.05	.02	.01
☐	217	Jeff Malone	.08	.04	.01
☐	218	Karl Malone	.25	.11	.03
☐	219	John Stockton	.25	.11	.03
☐	220	Michael Adams	.05	.02	.01
☐	221	Rex Chapman	.05	.02	.01
☐	222	Pervis Ellison	.05	.02	.01
☐	223	Harvey Grant	.05	.02	.01
☐	224	Tom Gugliotta	.10	.05	.01
☐	225	Don MacLean	.05	.02	.01
☐	226	Doug Overton	.05	.02	.01
☐	227	Brent Price	.05	.02	.01
☐	228	LaBradford Smith	.05	.02	.01
☐	229	Larry Stewart	.05	.02	.01
☐	230	Lenny Wilkens CO	.08	.04	.01
☐	231	Chris Ford CO	.05	.02	.01
☐	232	Allan Bristow CO	.05	.02	.01
☐	233	Phil Jackson CO	.08	.04	.01
☐	234	Mike Fratello CO	.05	.02	.01
☐	235	Quinn Buckner CO	.05	.02	.01
☐	236	Dan Issel CO	.08	.04	.01
☐	237	Don Chaney CO	.05	.02	.01
☐	238	Don Nelson CO	.08	.04	.01
☐	239	Rudy Tomjanovich CO	.08	.04	.01
☐	240	Larry Brown CO	.08	.04	.01
☐	241	Bob Weiss CO	.05	.02	.01
☐	242	Randy Pfund CO	.05	.02	.01
☐	243	Kevin Loughery CO	.05	.02	.01
☐	244	Mike Dunleavy CO	.05	.02	.01
☐	245	Sidney Lowe CO	.05	.02	.01
☐	246	Chuck Daly CO	.08	.04	.01
☐	247	Pat Riley CO	.08	.04	.01
☐	248	Brian Hill CO	.05	.02	.01
☐	249	Fred Carter CO	.05	.02	.01
☐	250	Paul Westphal CO	.08	.04	.01
☐	251	Rick Adelman CO	.05	.02	.01
☐	252	Garry St. Jean CO	.05	.02	.01
☐	253	John Lucas CO	.08	.04	.01
☐	254	George Karl CO	.05	.02	.01
☐	255	Jerry Sloan CO	.05	.02	.01
☐	256	Wes Unseld CO	.08	.04	.01
☐	257	Michael Jordan AS	1.50	.65	.19
☐	258	Isiah Thomas AS	.08	.04	.01
☐	259	Scottie Pippen AS	.10	.05	.01
☐	260	Larry Johnson AS	.10	.05	.01
☐	261	Dominique Wilkins AS	.08	.04	.01
☐	262	Joe Dumars AS	.08	.04	.01
☐	263	Mark Price AS	.05	.02	.01
☐	264	Shaquille O'Neal AS	1.00	.45	.13
☐	265	Patrick Ewing AS	.10	.05	.01
☐	266	Larry Nance AS	.05	.02	.01
☐	267	Detlef Schrempf AS	.05	.02	.01
☐	268	Brad Daugherty AS	.05	.02	.01
☐	269	Charles Barkley AS	.25	.11	.03
☐	270	Clyde Drexler AS	.10	.05	.01
☐	271	Sean Elliott AS	.05	.02	.01
☐	272	Tim Hardaway AS	.05	.02	.01
☐	273	Shawn Kemp AS	.25	.11	.03
☐	274	Dan Majerle AS	.05	.02	.01
☐	275	Karl Malone AS	.10	.05	.01
☐	276	Danny Manning AS	.05	.02	.01
☐	277	Hakeem Olajuwon AS	.30	.14	.04
☐	278	Terry Porter AS	.05	.02	.01
☐	279	David Robinson AS	.25	.11	.03
☐	280	John Stockton AS	.10	.05	.01
☐	281	East Team Photo	.08	.04	.01
☐	282	West Team Photo	.08	.04	.01
☐	283	Scoring	.75	.35	.09
		Michael Jordan			
		Dominique Wilkins			
		Karl Malone			
☐	284	Rebounding	.50	.23	.06
		Dennis Rodman			
		Shaquille O'Neal			
		Dikembe Mutombo			
☐	285	Field Goal Percentage	.05	.02	.01
		Cedric Ceballos			
		Brad Daugherty			
		Dale Davis			
☐	286	Assists	.08	.04	.01
		John Stockton			
		Tim Hardaway			
		Scott Skiles			
☐	287	Free Throw Percentage	.08	.04	.01
		Mark Price			
		Mahmoud Abdul-Rauf			
		Eddie Johnson			
☐	288	3-point FG Percentage	.08	.04	.01
		B.J. Armstrong			
		Chris Mullin			
		Kenny Smith			
☐	289	Steals	.75	.35	.09
		Michael Jordan			
		Mookie Blaylock			
		John Stockton			
☐	290	Blocks	.50	.23	.06
		Hakeem Olajuwon			
		Shaquille O'Neal			
		Dikembe Mutombo			
☐	291	Boys and Girls Club	.25	.11	.03
		David Robinson			
☐	292	Tribune 1	.05	.02	.01
		B.J. Armstrong			
☐	293	Tribune 2	.10	.05	.01
		Scottie Pippen			
☐	294	Tribune 3	.08	.04	.01
		Kevin Johnson			
☐	295	Tribune 4	.25	.11	.03
		Charles Barkley			
☐	296	Tribune 5	.05	.02	.01
		Richard Dumas			
☐	297	Tribune 6	.08	.04	.01
		Horace Grant			
☐	298	Checklist 1	.10	.05	.01
		David Robinson			
☐	299	Checklist 2	.10	.05	.01
		David Robinson			
☐	300	Checklist 3	.10	.05	.01
		David Robinson			
☐	301	Craig Ehlo	.05	.02	.01
☐	302	Jon Koncak	.05	.02	.01
☐	303	Andrew Lang	.05	.02	.01
☐	304	Chris Corchiani	.05	.02	.01
☐	305	Acie Earl	.05	.02	.01
☐	306	Dino Radja	.30	.14	.04

☐ 307 Scott Burrell	.20	.09	.03
☐ 308 Hersey Hawkins	.08	.04	.01
☐ 309 Eddie Johnson	.08	.04	.01
☐ 310 David Wingate	.05	.02	.01
☐ 311 Corie Blount	.05	.02	.01
☐ 312 Steve Kerr	.05	.02	.01
☐ 313 Toni Kukoc	.40	.18	.05
☐ 314 Pete Myers	.05	.02	.01
☐ 315 Jay Guidinger	.05	.02	.01
☐ 316 Tyrone Hill	.08	.04	.01
☐ 317 Gerald Madkins	.05	.02	.01
☐ 318 Chris Mills	.30	.14	.04
☐ 319 Bobby Phills	.05	.02	.01
☐ 320 Lucious Harris	.10	.05	.01
☐ 321 Popeye Jones	.25	.11	.03
☐ 322 Fat Lever	.05	.02	.01
☐ 323 Jamal Mashburn	1.50	.65	.19
☐ 324 Darren Morningstar	.05	.02	.01
(See also 334)			
☐ 325 Kevin Brooks	.05	.02	.01
☐ 326 Tom Hammonds	.05	.02	.01
☐ 327 Darnell Mee	.05	.02	.01
☐ 328 Rodney Rodgers	.30	.14	.04
☐ 329 Brian Williams	.05	.02	.01
☐ 330 Greg Anderson	.05	.02	.01
☐ 331 Sean Elliott	.08	.04	.01
☐ 332 Allan Houston	.30	.14	.04
☐ 333 Lindsey Hunter	.15	.07	.02
☐ 334 David Wood UER	.05	.02	.01
(Card misnumbered 324)			
☐ 335 Jud Buechler	.05	.02	.01
☐ 336 Chris Gatling	.05	.02	.01
☐ 337 Josh Grant	.05	.02	.01
☐ 338 Jeff Grayer	.05	.02	.01
☐ 339 Keith Jennings	.05	.02	.01
☐ 340 Avery Johnson	.05	.02	.01
☐ 341 Chris Webber	1.25	.55	.16
☐ 342 Sam Cassell	.40	.18	.05
☐ 343 Mario Elie	.05	.02	.01
☐ 344 Eric Riley	.05	.02	.01
☐ 345 Antonio Davis	.10	.05	.01
☐ 346 Scott Haskin	.05	.02	.01
☐ 347 Gerald Paddio	.05	.02	.01
☐ 348 LaSalle Thompson	.05	.02	.01
☐ 349 Ken Williams	.05	.02	.01
☐ 350 Mark Aguirre	.08	.04	.01
☐ 351 Terry Dehere	.08	.04	.01
☐ 352 Henry James	.05	.02	.01
☐ 353 Sam Bowie	.05	.02	.01
☐ 354 George Lynch	.08	.04	.01
☐ 355 Kurt Rambis	.05	.02	.01
☐ 356 Nick Van Exel	1.50	.65	.19
☐ 357 Trevor Wilson	.05	.02	.01
☐ 358 Keith Askins	.05	.02	.01
☐ 359 Manute Bol	.05	.02	.01
☐ 360 Willie Burton	.05	.02	.01
☐ 361 Matt Geiger	.05	.02	.01
☐ 362 Alec Kessler	.05	.02	.01
☐ 363 Vin Baker	.75	.35	.09
☐ 364 Ken Norman	.05	.02	.01
☐ 365 Dan Schayes	.05	.02	.01
☐ 366 Mike Brown	.05	.02	.01
☐ 367 Isaiah Rider	.50	.23	.06
☐ 368 Benoit Benjamin	.05	.02	.01
☐ 369 P.J. Brown	.10	.05	.01
☐ 370 Kevin Edwards	.05	.02	.01
☐ 371 Armon Gilliam	.05	.02	.01
☐ 372 Rick Mahorn	.05	.02	.01
☐ 373 Dwayne Schintzius	.05	.02	.01
☐ 374 Rex Walters	.08	.04	.01
☐ 375 Jayson Williams	.05	.02	.01
☐ 376 Eric Anderson	.05	.02	.01
☐ 377 Anthony Bonner	.05	.02	.01
☐ 378 Tony Campbell	.05	.02	.01
☐ 379 Herb Williams	.05	.02	.01
☐ 380 Anfernee Hardaway	3.00	1.35	.40
☐ 381 Greg Kite	.05	.02	.01
☐ 382 Larry Krystkowiak	.05	.02	.01
☐ 383 Todd Lichti	.05	.02	.01
☐ 384 Dana Barros	.10	.05	.01
☐ 385 Shawn Bradley	.30	.14	.04
☐ 386 Greg Graham	.05	.02	.01
☐ 387 Warren Kidd	.05	.02	.01
☐ 388 Eric Leckner	.05	.02	.01
☐ 389 Moses Malone	.15	.07	.02
☐ 390 A.C. Green	.10	.05	.01
☐ 391 Frank Johnson	.05	.02	.01
☐ 392 Joe Kleine	.05	.02	.01
☐ 393 Malcolm Mackey	.05	.02	.01
☐ 394 Jerrod Mustaf	.05	.02	.01
☐ 395 Mark Bryant	.05	.02	.01
☐ 396 Chris Dudley	.05	.02	.01
☐ 397 Harvey Grant	.05	.02	.01
☐ 398 James Robinson	.15	.07	.02
☐ 399 Reggie Smith	.05	.02	.01
☐ 400 Randy Brown	.05	.02	.01
☐ 401 Bobby Hurley	.15	.07	.02
☐ 402 Jim Les	.05	.02	.01
☐ 403 Vinny Del Negro	.05	.02	.01
☐ 404 Sleepy Floyd	.05	.02	.01
☐ 405 Dennis Rodman	.15	.07	.02
☐ 406 Chris Whitney	.05	.02	.01
☐ 407 Vincent Askew	.05	.02	.01
☐ 408 Kendall Gill	.05	.02	.01
☐ 409 Ervin Johnson	.10	.05	.01
☐ 410 Rich King	.05	.02	.01
☐ 411 Detlef Schrempf	.10	.05	.01
☐ 412 Tom Chambers	.08	.04	.01
☐ 413 John Crotty	.05	.02	.01
☐ 414 Felton Spencer	.05	.02	.01
☐ 415 Luther Wright	.05	.02	.01
☐ 416 Calbert Cheaney	.40	.18	.05
☐ 417 Kevin Duckworth	.05	.02	.01
☐ 418 Gheorghe Muresan	.25	.11	.03
☐ 419 Checklist 1	.05	.02	.01
☐ 420 Checklist 2	.05	.02	.01
☐ 421 Rookie Checklist	.05	.02	.01
☐ DR1 David Robinson	.50	.23	.06
Commemorative 1989 Rookie Card			
☐ MB1 Magic Johnson	.50	.23	.06
Larry Bird Commemorative			
☐ David Robinson AU	150.00	70.00	19.00
☐ NNO David Robinson	30.00	13.50	3.80
Voucher			
☐ NNO Magic Johnson	100.00	45.00	12.00
Larry Bird Expired Voucher			
☐ NNO Magic Johnson	400.00	180.00	50.00
Larry Bird Autograph Card			

1993-94 Hoops Fifth Anniversary Gold

Inserted one per 13-card pack and two per 26-card jumbo pack, this 421-card set par-

allels the regular 1993-94 Hoops issue. The only differences are the Fifth Anniversary embossed gold-foil seal, gold-foil stripes highlighting the player's name on the front and UV coating. The cards are numbered on the back. Please refer to the multipliers below (coupled with the prices of the corresponding regular issue cards) to ascertain value.

	MINT	NRMT	EXC
COMPLETE SET (421)	60.00	27.00	7.50
COMPLETE SERIES 1 (300)	35.00	16.00	4.40
COMPLETE SERIES 2 (121)	25.00	11.50	3.10
COMMON CARD (1-421)	.10	.05	.01

*STARS: 1.5X to 3X BASIC CARDS
*ROOKIES: 1X to 2X BASIC CARDS

1993-94 Hoops
Admiral's Choice

Randomly inserted in second series 13-card foil and 26-card jumbo packs at a rate of one in 12, this five-card standard-size (2 1/2" by 3 1/2") set features David Robinson's selection of the best starting five players in the game today. The cards have borderless fronts with color player photos. The player's name appears in gold-foil lettering at the top. The white back features a color player photo on the left with the player profile on the right. The cards are numbered on the back with an "AC" prefix.

	MINT	NRMT	EXC
COMPLETE SET (5)	4.00	1.80	.50
COMMON CARD (AC1-AC5)	.25	.11	.03

		MINT	NRMT	EXC
☐ AC1	Shawn Kemp	.60	.25	.08
	Seattle Supersonics			
☐ AC2	Derrick Coleman	.25	.11	.03
	New Jersey Nets			
☐ AC3	Kenny Anderson	.25	.11	.03
	New Jersey Nets			
☐ AC4	Shaquille O'Neal	2.50	1.15	.30
	Orlando Magic			
☐ AC5	Chris Webber	1.00	.45	.13
	Golden State Warriors			

1993-94 Hoops
David's Best

Inserted into one in every ten first series 1993-94 Hoops 13-card foil packs, these UV-coated cards feature color action photos of David Robinson against featured opponents. The "David's Best" logo runs across the bottom of the card in "golden crystal-foil" lettering. The back of the cards present Robinson's stat line from the selected game and a brief synopsis of the highlights. The cards are numbered on the back with a "DB" prefix.

		MINT	NRMT	EXC
COMPLETE SET (5)		3.00	1.35	.40
COMMON ROBINSON (DB1-DB5)		.75	.35	.09
☐ DB1	David Robinson	.75	.35	.09
	(Vs. Lakers)			
☐ DB2	David Robinson	.75	.35	.09
	(Vs. Magic)			
☐ DB3	David Robinson	.75	.35	.09
	(Vs. Trail Blazers)			
☐ DB4	David Robinson	.75	.35	.09
	(Vs. Warriors)			
☐ DB5	David Robinson	.75	.35	.09
	(Vs. Hornets)			

1993-94 Hoops
Draft Redemption

For the second consecutive year, a redemption card was randomly inserted into series one packs at a rate of one in 360. The card could be sent in for this 11-card

standard-size (2 1/2" by 3 1/2") set by March 31, 1994. The cards feature a full-color head photo on the front. The player's name appears centered at the top in gold foil. The player's draft number also appears in gold foil at the upper right. The horizontal back features a color player head shot on the left, with player statistics and biography alongside on the right. The cards are numbered on the back with an "LP" prefix.

On both sides, the Face to Face logo and the player's name appears at the bottom. The cards are numbered on the second side with an "FTF" prefix.

	MINT	NRMT	EXC
COMPLETE SET (11)	40.00	18.00	5.00
COMMON CARD (LP1-LP11)	1.00	.45	.13
☐ LP1 Chris Webber	8.00	3.60	1.00
Golden State Warriors			
☐ LP2 Shawn Bradley	2.00	.90	.25
Philadelphia 76ers			
☐ LP3 Anfernee Hardaway	20.00	9.00	2.50
Orlando Magic			
☐ LP4 Jamal Mashburn	10.00	4.50	1.25
Dallas Mavericks			
☐ LP5 Isaiah Rider	3.00	1.35	.40
Minnesota Timberwolves			
☐ LP6 Calbert Cheaney	2.50	1.15	.30
Washington Bullets			
☐ LP7 Bobby Hurley	1.00	.45	.13
Sacramento Kings			
☐ LP8 Vin Baker	5.00	2.30	.60
Milwaukee Bucks			
☐ LP9 Rodney Rogers	2.00	.90	.25
Denver Nuggets			
☐ LP10 Lindsey Hunter	1.00	.45	.13
Detroit Pistons			
☐ LP11 Allan Houston	2.00	.90	.25
Detroit Pistons			
☐ NNO Redeemed Lottery Card	.25	.11	.03
☐ NNO Unred. Lottery Card	1.50	.65	.19

	MINT	NRMT	EXC
COMPLETE SET (12)	40.00	18.00	5.00
COMMON CARD (1-12)	.75	.35	.09
☐ 1 Shaquille O'Neal	12.00	5.50	1.50
David Robinson			
☐ 2 Alonzo Mourning	4.00	1.80	.50
Patrick Ewing			
☐ 3 Christian Laettner	3.00	1.35	.40
Shawn Kemp			
☐ 4 Jim Jackson	4.00	1.80	.50
Clyde Drexler			
☐ 5 LaPhonso Ellis	1.50	.65	.19
Larry Johnson			
☐ 6 Clarence Weatherspoon	3.00	1.35	.40
Charles Barkley			
☐ 7 Tom Gugliotta	2.00	.90	.25
Karl Malone			
☐ 8 Walt Williams	3.00	1.35	.40
Magic Johnson			
☐ 9 Robert Horry	2.50	1.15	.30
Scottie Pippen			
☐ 10 Harold Miner	15.00	6.75	1.90
Michael Jordan			
☐ 11 Todd Day	.75	.35	.09
Chris Mullin			
☐ 12 Richard Dumas	.75	.35	.09
Dominique Wilkins			

1993-94 Hoops Face to Face

Randomly inserted in first series 13-card foil packs at a rate of one in 20, these 12 standard-size (2 1/2" by 3 1/2") cards feature a standout rookie from 1992-93 on one side and a veteran All-Star with similar skills on the other. The full-bleed glossy color player action photos on both sides are reproduced over metallic-type backgrounds.

1993-94 Hoops Magic's All-Rookies

Randomly inserted in second-series 13-card foil and 26-card jumbo packs at a rate of one in 30, this 10-card standard size (2

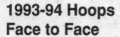

1/2" by 3 1/2") set features Magic
Johnson's projected All-Rookie team for
1993-94. The borderless front features a
full-color action shot with the player's name
in a gold-foil strip at the bottom. The borderless back features an italicized player
profile written by Magic Johnson set
against a ghosted background photo of
Magic. The cards are numbered on the
back.

	MINT	NRMT	EXC
COMPLETE SET (10)	60.00	27.00	7.50
COMMON CARD (1-10)	1.50	.65	.19
☐ 1 Chris Webber	12.00	5.50	1.50
Golden State Warriors			
☐ 2 Shawn Bradley	3.00	1.35	.40
Philadelphia 76ers			
☐ 3 Anfernee Hardaway	30.00	13.50	3.80
Orlando Magic			
☐ 4 Jamal Mashburn	15.00	6.75	1.90
Dallas Mavericks			
☐ 5 Isaiah Rider	5.00	2.30	.60
Minnesota Timberwolves			
☐ 6 Calbert Cheaney	4.00	1.80	.50
Washington Bullets			
☐ 7 Bobby Hurley	1.50	.65	.19
Sacramento Kings			
☐ 8 Vin Baker	8.00	3.60	1.00
Milwaukee Bucks			
☐ 9 Lindsey Hunter	1.50	.65	.19
Detroit Pistons			
☐ 10 Toni Kukoc	4.00	1.80	.50
Chicago Bulls			

1993-94 Hoops Scoops

*Randomly inserted in second series 13-
card foil packs, this 28-card set measures
the standard size (2 1/2" by 3 1/2").
Photos feature unique above the rim pho
tography of a star player from each of the
27 NBA teams. Cards are either horizontal
or vertical. The player's name, his team's
name, and logo appear in a black bar under
the photo, while the NBA Hoops Scoops
logo appears in the upper right or left corner. On a white background, the backs
carry trivia questions about the teams. The
cards are numbered on the back with an
"HS" prefix. These cards are as plentiful as
the regular issue cards.*

	MINT	NRMT	EXC
COMPLETE SET (28)	1.00	.45	.13
COMMON CARD (HS1-HS28)	.05	.02	.01
☐ HS1 Dominique Wilkins	.10	.05	.01
Atlanta Hawks			
☐ HS2 Robert Parish	.08	.04	.01
Boston Celtics			
☐ HS3 Alonzo Mourning	.25	.11	.03
Charlotte Hornets			
☐ HS4 Scottie Pippen	.15	.07	.02
Chicago Bulls			
☐ HS5 Larry Nance	.05	.02	.01
Cleveland Cavaliers			
☐ HS6 Derek Harper	.05	.02	.01
Dallas Mavericks			
☐ HS7 Reggie Williams	.05	.02	.01
Denver Nuggets			
☐ HS8 Bill Laimbeer	.05	.02	.01
Detroit Pistons			
☐ HS9 Tim Hardaway	.05	.02	.01
Golden State Warriors			
☐ HS10 Hakeem Olajuwon UER	.30	.14	.04
Houston Rockets			
(Robert Horry is featured player)			
☐ HS11 LaSalle Thompson	.05	.02	.01
Indiana Pacers			
☐ HS12 Danny Manning	.05	.02	.01
Los Angeles Clippers			
☐ HS13 James Worthy	.05	.02	.01
Los Angeles Lakers			
☐ HS14 Grant Long	.05	.02	.01
Miami Heat			
☐ HS15 Blue Edwards	.05	.02	.01
Milwaukee Bucks			
☐ HS16 Christian Laettner	.05	.02	.01
Minnesota Timberwolves			
☐ HS17 Derrick Coleman	.05	.02	.01
New Jersey Nets			
☐ HS18 Patrick Ewing	.15	.07	.02
New York Knicks			
☐ HS19 Nick Anderson	.05	.02	.01
Orlando Magic			
☐ HS20 Clarence Weatherspoon	.05	.02	.01
Philadelphia 76ers			
☐ HS21 Charles Barkley	.25	.11	.03
Phoenix Suns			
☐ HS22 Cliff Robinson	.05	.02	.01
Portland Trail Blazers			
☐ HS23 Lionel Simmons	.05	.02	.01
Sacramento Kings			
☐ HS24 David Robinson	.25	.11	.03
San Antonio Spurs			
☐ HS25 Shawn Kemp	.20	.09	.03
Seattle Supersonics			
☐ HS26 Karl Malone	.15	.07	.02
Utah Jazz			
☐ HS27 Rex Chapman	.05	.02	.01
Washington Bullets			
☐ HS28 Answer Card	.05	.02	.01

1993-94 Hoops Scoops Fifth Anniversary Gold

*Randomly inserted in second series 13-
card foil packs, this 28-card parallel set to*

the regular Hoops Scoops set measures the standard size (2 1/2" by 3 1/2"). Aside from the gold-foil logo and UV coating, the cards are identical to the regular issue Hoops Scoops cards. The cards are numbered on the back with an "HS" prefix. Please refer to the multiplier below (coupled with the price of the corresponding regular issue scoops card) to ascertain value.

	MINT	NRMT	EXC
COMPLETE SET (28)	4.00	1.80	.50
COMMON CARD (HS1-HS28)	.20	.05	.01
*STARS: 2X to 4X BASIC CARDS			

1993-94 Hoops Supreme Court

Randomly inserted into second series 13-card foil and 26-card jumbo packs, this 11-card standard size (2 1/2" by 3 1/2") set reflects the All-NBA team as chosen by media members that report on the hobby. Card fronts feature full-color action player photos set against a wood grain vertical bar with the player's name centered at the top in silver-foil lettering. The backs carry color player action shots along the left side and player statistics along the right side. The cards are numbered on the back with an "SC" prefix.

	MINT	NRMT	EXC
COMPLETE SET (11)	12.00	5.50	1.50
COMMON CARD (SC1-SC11)	.50	.23	.06
☐ SC1 Charles Barkley 1.00	.45	.13
Phoenix Suns			

☐ SC2 David Robinson 1.00	.45	.13
San Antonio Spurs			
☐ SC3 Patrick Ewing .... .50	.23	.06
New York Knicks			
☐ SC4 Shaquille O'Neal 4.00	1.80	.50
Orlando Magic			
☐ SC5 Larry Johnson .... .50	.23	.06
Charlotte Hornets			
☐ SC6 Karl Malone .... .50	.23	.06
Utah Jazz			
☐ SC7 Alonzo Mourning 1.00	.45	.13
Charlotte Hornets			
☐ SC8 John Stockton .... .50	.23	.06
Utah Jazz			
☐ SC9 Hakeem Olajuwon UER 1.25	.55	.16
Houston Rockets			
(Name spelled Olajwon on front)			
☐ SC10 Scottie Pippen .... .50	.23	.06
Chicago Bulls			
☐ SC11 Michael Jordan 6.00	2.70	.75
Chicago Bulls			

1994-95 Hoops

The 450 standard-size (2 1/2" by 3 1/2") cards comprising the '94-95 Hoops set were distributed in two separate series of 300 and 150 cards each. Cards were issued in 12-card hobby and retail packs (suggested retail price first series $0.99, second series $1.19) and 24-card retail jumbo packs. All second series packs contained at least one insert card (12-card packs had one insert and 24-card jumbo packs had two). Cards feature borderless color player action shots on the front. The player's name, position, and team name appear in white lettering within a team colored stripe near the bottom. The white back carries a color player head shot at the upper left, with the player's name and brief biography appearing alongside to the right. Statistics and career highlights follow below. The cards are numbered on the back, grouped alphabetically within teams, and checklisted below alphabetically according to teams as follows: Atlanta Hawks (1-7/301-305), Boston Celtics (8-14/306-309), Charlotte Hornets (15-22/310-312), Chicago Bulls (23-31/313-314), Cleveland Cavaliers (32-40/315), Dallas Mavericks (41-47/316-318), Denver Nuggets (48-55/319-320), Detroit Pistons (56-62/321-324), Golden State Warriors (63-71/325-329), Houston

Rockets (72-80/330), Indiana Pacers (81-89/331-332), Los Angeles Clippers (90-97/333-337), Los Angeles Lakers (98-106/338-340), Miami Heat (107-115/341-345), Milwaukee Bucks (116-121/346-349), Minnesota Timberwolves (122-129/350-351), New Jersey Nets (130-138/352), New York Knicks (139-147/353-354), Orlando Magic (148-156/355-357), Philadelphia 76ers (157-164/358-361), Phoenix Suns (165-173/362-366), Portland Trail Blazers (174-182/367), Sacramento Kings (183-190/368-369), San Antonio Spurs (191-197/370-372), Seattle Supersonics (198-206/373-375), Utah Jazz (207-215/376-377), and Washington Bullets (216-223/378-382). Subsets include All-Stars (224-251), League Leaders (252-258), Award Winners (259-265), Tribune (266-273), Coaches (274-295/383-388), Team Cards (391-420), Top This (421-430) and Gold Mine (431-450). A special Shaquille O'Neal Press Sheet (featuring 100 of his previously issued Hoops and SkyBox cards in an uncut poster-size format) was available by sending in thirty-two first series wrappers along with a check or money order for $1.50. As a special bonus 100 Press Sheets were autographed by O'Neal and randomly mailed out to collectors who responded to the promotion, which expired on March 1st, 1995. A special Grant Hill Commemorative card was available by sending in two second series wrappers along with a check or money order for $3.00 before the June 15th expiration date.

	MINT	NRMT	EXC
COMPLETE SET (450)	25.00	11.50	3.10
COMPLETE SERIES 1 (300)	10.00	4.50	1.25
COMPLETE SERIES 2 (150)	15.00	6.75	1.90
COMMON CARD (1-450)	.05	.02	.01

☐	1 Stacey Augmon	.08	.04	.01
☐	2 Mookie Blaylock	.08	.04	.01
☐	3 Doug Edwards	.05	.02	.01
☐	4 Craig Ehlo	.05	.02	.01
☐	5 Jon Koncak	.05	.02	.01
☐	6 Danny Manning	.10	.05	.01
☐	7 Kevin Willis	.08	.04	.01
☐	8 Dee Brown	.08	.04	.01
☐	9 Sherman Douglas	.05	.02	.01
☐	10 Acie Earl	.05	.02	.01
☐	11 Kevin Gamble	.05	.02	.01
☐	12 Xavier McDaniel	.08	.04	.01
☐	13 Robert Parish	.10	.05	.01
☐	14 Dino Radja	.10	.05	.01
☐	15 Tony Bennett	.05	.02	.01
☐	16 Muggsy Bogues	.10	.05	.01
☐	17 Scott Burrell	.05	.02	.01
☐	18 Dell Curry	.05	.02	.01
☐	19 Hersey Hawkins	.08	.04	.01
☐	20 Eddie Johnson	.08	.04	.01
☐	21 Larry Johnson	.20	.09	.03
☐	22 Alonzo Mourning	.30	.14	.04
☐	23 B.J. Armstrong	.05	.02	.01
☐	24 Corie Blount	.05	.02	.01
☐	25 Bill Cartwright	.05	.02	.01
☐	26 Horace Grant	.15	.07	.02
☐	27 Toni Kukoc	.10	.05	.01
☐	28 Luc Longley	.05	.02	.01
☐	29 Pete Myers	.05	.02	.01
☐	30 Scottie Pippen	.25	.11	.03
☐	31 Scott Williams	.05	.02	.01
☐	32 Terrell Brandon	.05	.02	.01
☐	33 Brad Daugherty	.08	.04	.01
☐	34 Tyrone Hill	.08	.04	.01
☐	35 Chris Mills	.08	.04	.01
☐	36 Larry Nance	.08	.04	.01
☐	37 Bobby Phills	.05	.02	.01
☐	38 Mark Price	.10	.05	.01
☐	39 Gerald Wilkins	.05	.02	.01
☐	40 John(Hot Rod) Williams	.08	.04	.01
☐	41 Terry Davis	.05	.02	.01
☐	42 Lucious Harris	.05	.02	.01
☐	43 Jim Jackson	.30	.14	.04
☐	44 Popeye Jones	.05	.02	.01
☐	45 Tim Legler	.05	.02	.01
☐	46 Jamal Mashburn	.50	.23	.06
☐	47 Sean Rooks	.05	.02	.01
☐	48 Mahmoud Abdul-Rauf	.08	.04	.01
☐	49 LaPhonso Ellis	.05	.02	.01
☐	50 Dikembe Mutombo	.15	.07	.02
☐	51 Robert Pack	.05	.02	.01
☐	52 Rodney Rogers	.10	.05	.01
☐	53 Bryant Stith	.05	.02	.01
☐	54 Brian Williams	.05	.02	.01
☐	55 Reggie Williams	.05	.02	.01
☐	56 Cadillac Anderson	.05	.02	.01
☐	57 Joe Dumars	.15	.07	.02
☐	58 Sean Elliott	.08	.04	.01
☐	59 Allan Houston	.10	.05	.01
☐	60 Lindsey Hunter	.05	.02	.01
☐	61 Mark Macon	.05	.02	.01
☐	62 Terry Mills	.05	.02	.01
☐	63 Victor Alexander	.05	.02	.01
☐	64 Chris Gatling	.05	.02	.01
☐	65 Tim Hardaway	.10	.05	.01
☐	66 Avery Johnson	.05	.02	.01
☐	67 Sarunas Marciulionis	.05	.02	.01
☐	68 Chris Mullin	.10	.05	.01
☐	69 Billy Owens	.08	.04	.01
☐	70 Latrell Sprewell	.30	.14	.04
☐	71 Chris Webber	.40	.18	.05
☐	72 Matt Bullard	.05	.02	.01
☐	73 Sam Cassell	.10	.05	.01
☐	74 Mario Elie	.05	.02	.01
☐	75 Carl Herrera	.05	.02	.01
☐	76 Robert Horry	.10	.05	.01
☐	77 Vernon Maxwell	.05	.02	.01
☐	78 Hakeem Olajuwon	.60	.25	.08
☐	79 Kenny Smith	.05	.02	.01
☐	80 Otis Thorpe	.08	.04	.01
☐	81 Antonio Davis	.05	.02	.01
☐	82 Dale Davis	.08	.04	.01
☐	83 Vern Fleming	.05	.02	.01
☐	84 Scott Haskin	.05	.02	.01
☐	85 Derrick McKey	.08	.04	.01
☐	86 Reggie Miller	.25	.11	.03
☐	87 Byron Scott	.08	.04	.01
☐	88 Rik Smits	.10	.05	.01
☐	89 Haywoode Workman	.05	.02	.01
☐	90 Terry Dehere	.05	.02	.01
☐	91 Harold Ellis	.05	.02	.01
☐	92 Gary Grant	.05	.02	.01
☐	93 Ron Harper	.08	.04	.01
☐	94 Mark Jackson	.05	.02	.01
☐	95 Stanley Roberts	.05	.02	.01
☐	96 Loy Vaught	.08	.04	.01
☐	97 Dominique Wilkins	.15	.07	.02
☐	98 Elden Campbell	.05	.02	.01
☐	99 Doug Christie	.05	.02	.01

☐ 100 Vlade Divac	.10	.05	.01
☐ 101 Reggie Jordan	.05	.02	.01
☐ 102 George Lynch	.05	.02	.01
☐ 103 Anthony Peeler	.05	.02	.01
☐ 104 Sedale Threatt	.05	.02	.01
☐ 105 Nick Van Exel	.50	.23	.06
☐ 106 James Worthy	.10	.05	.01
☐ 107 Bimbo Coles	.05	.02	.01
☐ 108 Matt Geiger	.05	.02	.01
☐ 109 Grant Long	.05	.02	.01
☐ 110 Harold Miner	.05	.02	.01
☐ 111 Glen Rice	.10	.05	.01
☐ 112 John Salley	.05	.02	.01
☐ 113 Rony Seikaly	.05	.02	.01
☐ 114 Brian Shaw	.05	.02	.01
☐ 115 Steve Smith	.08	.04	.01
☐ 116 Vin Baker	.25	.11	.03
☐ 117 Jon Barry	.05	.02	.01
☐ 118 Todd Day	.08	.04	.01
☐ 119 Lee Mayberry	.05	.02	.01
☐ 120 Eric Murdock	.05	.02	.01
☐ 121 Ken Norman	.05	.02	.01
☐ 122 Mike Brown	.05	.02	.01
☐ 123 Stacey King	.05	.02	.01
☐ 124 Christian Laettner	.08	.04	.01
☐ 125 Chuck Person	.08	.04	.01
☐ 126 Isaiah Rider	.15	.07	.02
☐ 127 Chris Smith	.05	.02	.01
☐ 128 Doug West	.05	.02	.01
☐ 129 Micheal Williams	.05	.02	.01
☐ 130 Kenny Anderson	.10	.05	.01
☐ 131 Benoit Benjamin	.05	.02	.01
☐ 132 P.J. Brown	.05	.02	.01
☐ 133 Derrick Coleman	.10	.05	.01
☐ 134 Kevin Edwards	.05	.02	.01
☐ 135 Armon Gilliam	.05	.02	.01
☐ 136 Chris Morris	.05	.02	.01
☐ 137 Rex Walters	.05	.02	.01
☐ 138 David Wesley	.05	.02	.01
☐ 139 Greg Anthony	.05	.02	.01
☐ 140 Anthony Bonner	.05	.02	.01
☐ 141 Hubert Davis	.05	.02	.01
☐ 142 Patrick Ewing	.25	.11	.03
☐ 143 Derek Harper	.08	.04	.01
☐ 144 Anthony Mason	.08	.04	.01
☐ 145 Charles Oakley	.08	.04	.01
☐ 146 Charles Smith	.05	.02	.01
☐ 147 John Starks	.08	.04	.01
☐ 148 Nick Anderson	.08	.04	.01
☐ 149 Anthony Avent	.05	.02	.01
☐ 150 Anthony Bowie	.05	.02	.01
☐ 151 Anfernee Hardaway	1.00	.45	.13
☐ 152 Shaquille O'Neal	1.25	.55	.16
☐ 153 Donald Royal	.05	.02	.01
☐ 154 Dennis Scott	.05	.02	.01
☐ 155 Scott Skiles	.05	.02	.01
☐ 156 Jeff Turner	.05	.02	.01
☐ 157 Dana Barros	.10	.05	.01
☐ 158 Shawn Bradley	.10	.05	.01
☐ 159 Greg Graham	.05	.02	.01
☐ 160 Warren Kidd	.05	.02	.01
☐ 161 Eric Leckner	.05	.02	.01
☐ 162 Jeff Malone	.08	.04	.01
☐ 163 Tim Perry	.05	.02	.01
☐ 164 Clarence Weatherspoon	.08	.04	.01
☐ 165 Danny Ainge	.08	.04	.01
☐ 166 Charles Barkley	.50	.23	.06
☐ 167 Cedric Ceballos	.10	.05	.01
☐ 168 A.C. Green	.10	.05	.01
☐ 169 Kevin Johnson	.15	.07	.02
☐ 170 Malcolm Mackey	.05	.02	.01
☐ 171 Dan Majerle	.08	.04	.01
☐ 172 Oliver Miller	.05	.02	.01
☐ 173 Mark West	.05	.02	.01
☐ 174 Clyde Drexler	.25	.11	.03
☐ 175 Chris Dudley	.05	.02	.01
☐ 176 Harvey Grant	.05	.02	.01
☐ 177 Tracy Murray	.05	.02	.01
☐ 178 Terry Porter	.08	.04	.01
☐ 179 Clifford Robinson	.08	.04	.01
☐ 180 James Robinson	.05	.02	.01
☐ 181 Rod Strickland	.08	.04	.01
☐ 182 Buck Williams	.08	.04	.01
☐ 183 Duane Causwell	.05	.02	.01
☐ 184 Bobby Hurley	.08	.04	.01
☐ 185 Olden Polynice	.05	.02	.01
☐ 186 Mitch Richmond	.15	.07	.02
☐ 187 Lionel Simmons	.05	.02	.01
☐ 188 Wayman Tisdale	.08	.04	.01
☐ 189 Spud Webb	.08	.04	.01
☐ 190 Walt Williams	.08	.04	.01
☐ 191 Willie Anderson	.05	.02	.01
☐ 192 Lloyd Daniels	.05	.02	.01
☐ 193 Vinny Del Negro	.05	.02	.01
☐ 194 Dale Ellis	.08	.04	.01
☐ 195 J.R. Reid	.05	.02	.01
☐ 196 David Robinson	.50	.23	.06
☐ 197 Dennis Rodman	.15	.07	.02
☐ 198 Kendall Gill	.05	.02	.01
☐ 199 Ervin Johnson	.05	.02	.01
☐ 200 Shawn Kemp	.50	.23	.06
☐ 201 Chris King	.05	.02	.01
☐ 202 Nate McMillan	.05	.02	.01
☐ 203 Gary Payton	.10	.05	.01
☐ 204 Sam Perkins	.08	.04	.01
☐ 205 Ricky Pierce	.08	.04	.01
☐ 206 Detlef Schrempf	.10	.05	.01
☐ 207 David Benoit	.05	.02	.01
☐ 208 Tom Chambers	.08	.04	.01
☐ 209 Tyrone Corbin	.05	.02	.01
☐ 210 Jeff Hornacek	.08	.04	.01
☐ 211 Karl Malone	.25	.11	.03
☐ 212 Bryon Russell	.05	.02	.01
☐ 213 Felton Spencer	.05	.02	.01
☐ 214 John Stockton	.25	.11	.03
☐ 215 Luther Wright	.05	.02	.01
☐ 216 Michael Adams	.05	.02	.01
☐ 217 Mitchell Butler	.05	.02	.01
☐ 218 Rex Chapman	.05	.02	.01
☐ 219 Calbert Cheaney	.10	.05	.01
☐ 220 Pervis Ellison	.05	.02	.01
☐ 221 Tom Gugliotta	.08	.04	.01
☐ 222 Don MacLean	.05	.02	.01
☐ 223 Gheorghe Muresan	.08	.04	.01
☐ 224 Kenny Anderson AS	.05	.02	.01
☐ 225 B.J. Armstrong AS	.05	.02	.01
☐ 226 Mookie Blaylock AS	.05	.02	.01
☐ 227 Derrick Coleman AS	.05	.02	.01
☐ 228 Patrick Ewing AS	.10	.05	.01
☐ 229 Horace Grant AS	.08	.04	.01
☐ 230 Alonzo Mourning AS	.15	.07	.02
☐ 231 Shaquille O'Neal AS	.60	.25	.08
☐ 232 Charles Oakley AS	.05	.02	.01
☐ 233 Scottie Pippen AS	.10	.05	.01
☐ 234 Mark Price AS	.05	.02	.01
☐ 235 John Starks AS	.05	.02	.01
☐ 236 Dominique Wilkins AS	.08	.04	.01
☐ 237 East Team	.05	.02	.01
☐ 238 Charles Barkley AS	.25	.11	.03
☐ 239 Clyde Drexler AS	.10	.05	.01
☐ 240 Kevin Johnson AS	.08	.04	.01
☐ 241 Shawn Kemp AS	.25	.11	.03

☐ 242	Karl Malone AS	.10	.05	.01
☐ 243	Danny Manning AS	.05	.02	.01
☐ 244	Hakeem Olajuwon AS	.30	.14	.04
☐ 245	Gary Payton AS	.05	.02	.01
☐ 246	Mitch Richmond AS	.08	.04	.01
☐ 247	Clifford Robinson AS	.05	.02	.01
☐ 248	David Robinson AS	.25	.11	.03
☐ 249	Latrell Sprewell AS	.15	.07	.01
☐ 250	John Stockton AS	.10	.05	.01
☐ 251	West Team	.05	.02	.01
☐ 252	Tracy Murray LL	.05	.02	.01

Portland Trail Blazers
B.J. Armstrong
Chicago Bulls
Reggie Miller
Indiana Pacers

☐ 253	John Stockton LL	.10	.05	.01

Utah Jazz
Muggsy Bogues
Charlotte Hornets
Mookie Blaylock
Atlanta Hawks

☐ 254	Dikembe Mutombo LL	.25	.11	.03

Denver Nuggets
Hakeem Olajuwon
Houston Rockets
David Robinson
San Antonio Spurs

☐ 255	Mahmoud Abdul-Rauf LL	.05	.02	.01

Denver Nuggets
Reggie Miller
Indiana Pacers
Ricky Pierce
Seattle SuperSonics

☐ 256	Dennis Rodman LL	.25	.11	.03

San Antonio Spurs
Shaquille O'Neal
Orlando Magic
Kevin Willis
Atlanta Hawks

☐ 257	David Robinson LL	.50	.23	.06

San Antonio Spurs
Shaquille O'Neal
Orlando Magic
Hakeem Olajuwon
Houston Rockets

☐ 258	Nate McMillan LL	.05	.02	.01

Seattle SuperSonics
Scottie Pippen
Chicago Bulls
Mookie Blaylock
Atlanta Hawks

☐ 259	Chris Webber AW	.20	.09	.03

Golden State Warriors

☐ 260	Hakeem Olajuwon AW	.30	.14	.04

Houston Rockets

☐ 261	Hakeem Olajuwon AW	.30	.14	.04

Houston Rockets

☐ 262	Dell Curry AW	.05	.02	.01

Charlotte Hornets

☐ 263	Scottie Pippen AW	.10	.05	.01

Chicago Bulls

☐ 264	Anfernee Hardaway AW	.50	.23	.06

Orlando Magic

☐ 265	Don MacLean AW	.05	.02	.01

Washington Bullets

☐ 266	Hakeem Olajuwon FINALS	.30	.14	.04

Houston Rockets

☐ 267	Derek Harper FINALS	.05	.02	.01

New York Knicks

☐ 268	Sam Cassell FINALS	.05	.02	.01

Houston Rockets

☐ 269	John Starks FINALS	.05	.02	.01

New York Knicks

☐ 270	Patrick Ewing FINALS	.10	.05	.01

New York Knicks
Hakeem Olajuwon
Houston Rockets

☐ 271	Carl Herrera FINALS	.05	.02	.01

Houston Rockets

☐ 272	Vernon Maxwell FINALS	.05	.02	.01

Houston Rockets

☐ 273	Hakeem Olajuwon FINALS	.30	.14	.04

Houston Rockets

☐ 274	Lenny Wilkens CO	.08	.04	.01

Atlanta Hawks

☐ 275	Chris Ford CO	.05	.02	.01

Boston Celtics

☐ 276	Allan Bristow CO	.05	.02	.01

Charlotte Hornets

☐ 277	Phil Jackson CO	.08	.04	.01

Chicago Bulls

☐ 278	Mike Fratello CO	.05	.02	.01

Cleveland Cavaliers

☐ 279	Dick Motta CO	.05	.02	.01

Dallas Mavericks

☐ 280	Dan Issel CO	.08	.04	.01

Denver Nuggets

☐ 281	Don Chaney CO	.05	.02	.01

Detroit Pistons

☐ 282	Don Nelson CO	.08	.04	.01

Golden State Warriors

☐ 283	Rudy Tomjanovich CO	.08	.04	.01

Houston Rockets

☐ 284	Larry Brown CO	.08	.04	.01

Indiana Pacers

☐ 285	Del Harris CO UER	.05	.02	.01

Los Angeles Lakers
(Back refers to Ralph Sampson and
Akeem Olajuwon as part of '80-'81 Rockets)

☐ 286	Kevin Loughery CO	.05	.02	.01

Miami Heat

☐ 287	Mike Dunleavy CO	.05	.02	.01

Milwaukee Bucks

☐ 288	Sidney Lowe CO	.05	.02	.01

Minnesota Timberwolves

☐ 289	Pat Riley CO	.08	.04	.01

New York Knicks

☐ 290	Brian Hill CO	.05	.02	.01

Orlando Magic

☐ 291	John Lucas CO	.08	.04	.01

Philadelphia 76ers

☐ 292	Paul Westphal CO	.08	.04	.01

Phoenix Suns

☐ 293	Garry St. Jean CO	.05	.02	.01

Sacramento Kings

☐ 294	George Karl CO	.05	.02	.01

Seattle SuperSonics

☐ 295	Jerry Sloan CO	.05	.02	.01

Utah Jazz

☐ 296	Magic Johnson	.50	.23	.06

Commemorative

☐ 297	Denzel Washington	.15	.07	.02
☐ 298	Checklist	.05	.02	.01
☐ 299	Checklist	.05	.02	.01
☐ 300	Checklist	.05	.02	.01
☐ 301	Sergei Bazarevich	.05	.02	.01
☐ 302	Tyrone Corbin	.05	.02	.01
☐ 303	Grant Long	.05	.02	.01
☐ 304	Ken Norman	.05	.02	.01
☐ 305	Steve Smith	.08	.04	.01
☐ 306	Blue Edwards	.05	.02	.01

☐ 307	Greg Minor	.08	.04	.01
☐ 308	Eric Montross	.40	.18	.05
☐ 309	Dominique Wilkins	.15	.07	.02
☐ 310	Michael Adams	.05	.02	.01
☐ 311	Darrin Hancock	.05	.02	.01
☐ 312	Robert Parish	.10	.05	.01
☐ 313	Ron Harper	.08	.04	.01
☐ 314	Dickey Simpkins	.15	.07	.02
☐ 315	Michael Cage	.05	.02	.01
☐ 316	Tony Dumas	.08	.04	.01
☐ 317	Jason Kidd	2.50	1.15	.30
☐ 318	Roy Tarpley	.05	.02	.01
☐ 319	Dale Ellis	.08	.04	.01
☐ 320	Jalen Rose	.50	.23	.06
☐ 321	Bill Curley	.15	.07	.02
☐ 322	Grant Hill	4.00	1.80	.50
☐ 323	Oliver Miller	.05	.02	.01
☐ 324	Mark West	.05	.02	.01
☐ 325	Tom Gugliotta	.08	.04	.01
☐ 326	Ricky Pierce	.08	.04	.01
☐ 327	Carlos Rogers	.20	.09	.03
☐ 328	Clifford Rozier	.20	.09	.03
☐ 329	Rony Seikaly	.05	.02	.01
☐ 330	Tim Breaux	.05	.02	.01
☐ 331	Duane Ferrell	.05	.02	.01
☐ 332	Mark Jackson	.05	.02	.01
☐ 333	Lamond Murray	.40	.18	.05
☐ 334	Charles Outlaw	.05	.02	.01
☐ 335	Eric Piatkowski	.15	.07	.02
☐ 336	Pooh Richardson	.05	.02	.01
☐ 337	Malik Sealy	.05	.02	.01
☐ 338	Cedric Ceballos	.10	.05	.01
☐ 339	Eddie Jones	1.50	.65	.19
☐ 340	Anthony Miller	.05	.02	.01
☐ 341	Kevin Gamble	.05	.02	.01
☐ 342	Brad Lohaus	.05	.02	.01
☐ 343	Billy Owens	.08	.04	.01
☐ 344	Khalid Reeves	.40	.18	.05
☐ 345	Kevin Willis	.08	.04	.01
☐ 346	Eric Mobley	.15	.07	.02
☐ 347	Johnny Newman	.05	.02	.01
☐ 348	Ed Pinckney	.05	.02	.01
☐ 349	Glenn Robinson	2.50	1.15	.30
☐ 350	Howard Eisley	.05	.02	.01
☐ 351	Donyell Marshall	.50	.23	.06
☐ 352	Yinka Dare	.08	.04	.01
☐ 353	Charlie Ward	.20	.09	.03
☐ 354	Monty Williams	.15	.07	.02
☐ 355	Horace Grant	.10	.05	.01
☐ 356	Brian Shaw	.05	.02	.01
☐ 357	Brooks Thompson	.08	.04	.01
☐ 358	Derrick Alston	.08	.04	.01
☐ 359	B.J. Tyler	.08	.04	.01
☐ 360	Scott Williams	.05	.02	.01
☐ 361	Sharone Wright	.30	.14	.04
☐ 362	Antonio Lang	.08	.04	.01
☐ 363	Danny Manning	.10	.05	.01
☐ 364	Wesley Person	.50	.23	.06
☐ 365	Wayman Tisdale	.08	.04	.01
☐ 366	Trevor Ruffin	.08	.04	.01
☐ 367	Aaron McKie	.20	.09	.03
☐ 368	Brian Grant	.75	.35	.09
☐ 369	Michael Smith	.20	.09	.03
☐ 370	Sean Elliott	.08	.04	.01
☐ 371	Avery Johnson	.05	.02	.01
☐ 372	Chuck Person	.08	.04	.01
☐ 373	Bill Cartwright	.05	.02	.01
☐ 374	Sarunas Marciulionis	.05	.02	.01
☐ 375	Dontonio Wingfield	.10	.05	.01
☐ 376	Antoine Carr	.05	.02	.01
☐ 377	Jamie Watson	.15	.07	.02

☐ 378	Juwan Howard	1.00	.45	.13
☐ 379	Jim McIlvaine	.05	.02	.01
☐ 380	Scott Skiles	.05	.02	.01
☐ 381	Anthony Tucker	.05	.02	.01
☐ 382	Chris Webber	.40	.18	.05
☐ 383	Bill Fitch CO	.05	.02	.01
☐ 384	Bill Blair CO	.05	.02	.01
☐ 385	Butch Beard CO	.05	.02	.01
☐ 386	P.J. Carlesimo CO	.05	.02	.01
☐ 387	Bob Hill CO	.05	.02	.01
☐ 388	Jim Lynam CO	.05	.02	.01
☐ 389	Checklist 4	.05	.02	.01
☐ 390	Checklist 5	.05	.02	.01
☐ 391	Atlanta Hawks TC	.05	.02	.01
☐ 392	Boston Celtics TC	.05	.02	.01
☐ 393	Charlotte Hornets TC	.05	.02	.01
☐ 394	Chicago Bulls TC	.05	.02	.01
☐ 395	Cleveland Cavaliers TC	.05	.02	.01
☐ 396	Dallas Mavericks TC	.05	.02	.01
☐ 397	Denver Nuggets TC	.05	.02	.01
☐ 398	Detroit Pistons TC	.05	.02	.01
☐ 399	Golden State Warriors TC	.05	.02	.01
☐ 400	Houston Rockets TC	.05	.02	.01
☐ 401	Indiana Pacers TC	.05	.02	.01
☐ 402	Los Angeles Clippers TC	.05	.02	.01
☐ 403	Los Angeles Lakers TC	.05	.02	.01
☐ 404	Miami Heat TC	.05	.02	.01
☐ 405	Milwaukee Bucks TC	.05	.02	.01
☐ 406	Minnesota Timberwolves TC	.05	.02	.01
☐ 407	New Jersey Nets TC	.05	.02	.01
☐ 408	New York Knicks TC	.05	.02	.01
☐ 409	Orlando Magic TC	.05	.02	.01
☐ 410	Philadelphia 76ers TC	.05	.02	.01
☐ 411	Phoenix Suns TC	.05	.02	.01
☐ 412	Portland Trail Blazers TC	.05	.02	.01
☐ 413	Sacramento Kings TC	.05	.02	.01
☐ 414	San Antonio Spurs TC	.05	.02	.01
☐ 415	Seattle Supersonics TC	.05	.02	.01
☐ 416	Utah Jazz TC	.05	.02	.01
☐ 417	Washington Bullets TC	.05	.02	.01
☐ 418	Toronto Raptors TC	.10	.05	.01
☐ 419	Vancouver Grizzlies TC	.10	.05	.01
☐ 420	NBA Logo Card	.05	.02	.01
☐ 421	Glenn Robinson	.50	.23	.06
	Milwaukee Bucks			
	Chris Webber			
	Washington Bullets			
☐ 422	Jason Kidd	.50	.23	.06
	Dallas Mavericks			
	Shawn Bradley			
	Philadelphia 76ers			
☐ 423	Grant Hill	1.00	.45	.13
	Detroit Pistons			
	Anfernee Hardaway			
	Orlando Magic			
☐ 424	Donyell Marshall	.20	.09	.03
	Minnesota Timberwolves			
	Jamal Mashburn			
	Dallas Mavericks			
☐ 425	Juwan Howard	.20	.09	.03
	Washington Bullets			
	Isaiah Rider			
	Minnesota Timberwolves			
☐ 426	Sharone Wright	.10	.05	.01
	Philadelphia 76ers			
	Calbert Cheaney			
	Washington Bullets			
☐ 427	Lamond Murray	.08	.04	.01

Los Angeles Clippers
Bobby Hurley
Sacramento Kings

		MINT	NRMT	EXC
☐ 428	Brian Grant	.20	.09	.03
	Sacramento Kings Vin Baker Milwaukee Bucks			
☐ 429	Eric Montross	.10	.05	.01
	Boston Celtics Rodney Rogers Denver Nuggets			
☐ 430	Eddie Jones	.25	.11	.03
	Los Angeles Lakers Lindsey Hunter Detroit Pistons			
☐ 431	Craig Ehlo GM	.05	.02	.01
	Atlanta Hawks			
☐ 432	Dino Radja GM	.05	.02	.01
	Boston Celtics			
☐ 433	Toni Kukoc GM	.05	.02	.01
	Chicago Bulls			
☐ 434	Mark Price GM	.05	.02	.01
	Cleveland Cavaliers			
☐ 435	Latrell Sprewell GM	.15	.07	.02
	Golden State Warriors			
☐ 436	Sam Cassell GM	.05	.02	.01
	Houston Rockets			
☐ 437	Vernon Maxwell GM	.05	.02	.01
	Houston Rockets			
☐ 438	Haywoode Workman GM	.05	.02	.01
	Indiana Pacers			
☐ 439	Harold Ellis GM	.05	.02	.01
	Los Angeles Clippers			
☐ 440	Cedric Ceballos GM	.05	.02	.01
	Los Angeles Lakers			
☐ 441	Vlade Divac GM	.05	.02	.01
	Los Angeles Lakers			
☐ 442	Nick Van Exel GM	.25	.11	.03
	Los Angeles Lakers			
☐ 443	John Starks GM	.05	.02	.01
	New York Knicks			
☐ 444	Scott Williams GM	.05	.02	.01
	Philadelphia 76ers			
☐ 445	Clifford Robinson GM	.05	.02	.01
	Portland Trail Blazers			
☐ 446	Spud Webb GM	.05	.02	.01
	Sacramento Kings			
☐ 447	Avery Johnson GM	.05	.02	.01
	San Antonio Spurs			
☐ 448	Dennis Rodman GM	.08	.04	.01
	San Antonio Spurs			
☐ 449	Sarunas Marciulionis GM	.05	.02	.01
	Seattle Supersonics			
☐ 450	Nate McMillan GM	.05	.02	.01
	Seattle Supersonics			
☐ NNO	G. Hill Wrapper Exch.	5.00	2.30	.60
☐ NNO	Shaq Sheet Wrapper	20.00	9.00	2.50
	Exchange			
☐ NNO	Shaq Sheet Wrapper Exchange Autograph	400.00	180.00	50.00

1994-95 Hoops Big Numbers

Randomly inserted in first series hobby and retail foil packs at a rate of one in 30, this

12 standard-size (2 1/2" by 3 1/2") set features color player action cutouts on their black horizontal and borderless fronts. The player's name and a number representing his Big Number accomplishment appear in silver-foil lettering offset to one side. The white horizontal back carries a color player head shot at the right, with a description of his Big Number accomplishment appearing alongside. The cards are numbered on the back with a "BN" prefix.

		MINT	NRMT	EXC
COMPLETE SET (12)		75.00	34.00	9.50
COMMON CARD (BN1-BN12)		2.50	1.15	.30
☐ BN1	David Robinson	8.00	3.60	1.00
	San Antonio Spurs			
☐ BN2	Jamal Mashburn	8.00	3.60	1.00
	Dallas Mavericks			
☐ BN3	Hakeem Olajuwon	10.00	4.50	1.25
	Houston Rockets			
☐ BN4	Patrick Ewing	4.00	1.80	.50
	New York Knicks			
☐ BN5	Shaquille O'Neal	20.00	9.00	2.50
	Orlando Magic			
☐ BN6	Latrell Sprewell	5.00	2.30	.60
	Golden State Warriors			
☐ BN7	Chris Webber	6.00	2.70	.75
	Golden State Warriors			
☐ BN8	Anfernee Hardaway	15.00	6.75	1.90
	Orlando Magic			
☐ BN9	Scottie Pippen	4.00	1.80	.50
	Chicago Bulls			
☐ BN10	Isaiah Rider	2.50	1.15	.30
	Minnesota Timberwolves			
☐ BN11	Alonzo Mourning	5.00	2.30	.60
	Charlotte Hornets			
☐ BN12	Charles Barkley	8.00	3.60	1.00
	Phoenix Suns			

1994-95 Hoops Big Numbers Rainbow

Inserted one per first series special retail pack, these 12 standard-size (2 1/2" by 3 1/2") cards are identical to their Big Numbers Silver counterparts, except for

	MINT	NRMT	EXC
☐ 8 Brian Grant	2.50	1.15	.30
☐ 9 Eric Montross	1.25	.55	.16
☐ 10 Eddie Jones	5.00	2.30	.60
☐ 11 Carlos Rogers	.60	.25	.08
☐ NNO Expired Exchange Card	1.50	.65	.19

their rainbow-colored foil numbers and highlights. The cards are numbered on the back with a "BN" prefix. Big Number Rainbow cards are valued equally to the regular issue silver-lettered "Big Numbers" inserts.

	MINT	NRMT	EXC
COMPLETE SET (12)	75.00	18.00	5.00
COMMON CARD (1-12)	2.50	1.15	.30
*RAINBOW CARDS: EQUAL VALUE TO SILVER			

1994-95 Hoops Draft Redemption

For the third straight year, a redemption card was randomly inserted into first series packs at a rate of one in 360. The card could be sent in for this 11-card standard size set on or before the June 15th, 1995 deadline. The cards feature a full-color player photo cut out against a computer-generated background with a big number (corresponding to the player's draft selection) zooming out of the side.

	MINT	NRMT	EXC
COMPLETE SET (11)	30.00	13.50	3.80
COMMON CARD (1-11)	.60	.25	.08
☐ 1 Glenn Robinson	8.00	3.60	1.00
☐ 2 Jason Kidd	8.00	3.60	1.00
☐ 3 Grant Hill	12.00	5.50	1.50
☐ 4 Donyell Marshall	1.50	.65	.19
☐ 5 Juwan Howard	3.00	1.35	.40
☐ 6 Sharone Wright	1.00	.45	.13
☐ 7 Lamond Murray	1.25	.55	.16

1994-95 Hoops Magic's All-Rookies

Randomly inserted into all second series packs (12-card hobby and retail packs at a rate of one in twelve, 24-card retail jumbo packs at an approximate rate of slightly greater than one per pack), cards from this 12-card set feature a selection of top rookies from the 1994-95 season. The fronts have a color action photo with different color backgrounds for each card with designs in them. The word "Magic's" is in the upper right corner and "All-Rookie" is three-dimensionally encompassing the player. The backs have a picture of Magic Johnson holding the card showing the front. On the left side it says "Magic's All-Rookie Team" and the their is player commentary at the bottom.

	MINT	NRMT	EXC
COMPLETE SET (10)	25.00	11.50	3.10
COMMON CARD (AR1-AR10)	.60	.25	.08
☐ AR1 Glenn Robinson	5.00	2.30	.60
Milwaukee Bucks			
☐ AR2 Jason Kidd	5.00	2.30	.60
Dallas Mavericks			
☐ AR3 Grant Hill	8.00	3.60	1.00
Detroit Pistons			
☐ AR4 Donyell Marshall	1.00	.45	.13
Minnesota Timberwolves			
☐ AR5 Juwan Howard	2.00	.90	.25
Washington Bullets			
☐ AR6 Sharone Wright	.60	.25	.08
Philadelphia 76ers			
☐ AR7 Brian Grant	1.50	.65	.19
Sacramento Kings			
☐ AR8 Eddie Jones	3.00	1.35	.40
Los Angeles Lakers			
☐ AR9 Jalen Rose	1.00	.45	.13
Dallas Mavericks			
☐ AR10 Wesley Person	1.00	.45	.13
San Antonio Spurs			

1994-95 Hoops Magic's All-Rookies Foil-Tech

	MINT	NRMT	EXC
COMPLETE SET (10)	50.00	23.00	6.25
COMMON CARD (AR1-AR10)	1.20	.55	.15

*JUMBO CARDS: 1X TO 2X BASIC CARDS

Randomly inserted into all series 2 packs at a rate of one in 36, these 10-cards parallel the basic Magic's All-Rookies insert cards. The difference is that each Foil-Tech card features a silver-foil background and has FAR numbering prefixes. Please refer to the multiplier provided below (coupled with the values of the basic Magic's All-Rookies inserts) to ascertain values.

	MINT	NRMT	EXC
COMPLETE SET (10)	100.00	45.00	12.50
COMMON CARD (1-10)	3.00	1.80	.50

*FOIL CARDS: 2.5X TO 5X BASIC CARDS

1994-95 Hoops Magic's All-Rookies Jumbos

One of these jumbo cards was inserted exclusively into second-series hobby boxes. The cards are an exact parallel of the corresponding Magic's All-Rookie inserts except that these measure 5" by 7". Please refer to the multiplier provided below (coupled with the values of the regular Magic's All-Rookie inserts) to ascertain value.

1994-95 Hoops Power Ratings

Inserted one per pack into all second series packs, cards from this 54-card set feature a selection of the top players in the NBA. Cards feature a photo of the player silhouetted over flame-thrower graphics. Backs present a second photo and colorful bar chart of the players stats in seven key categories.

	MINT	NRMT	EXC
COMPLETE SET (54)	10.00	4.50	1.25
COMMON CARD (PR1-PR54)	.10	.05	.01
☐ PR1 Mookie Blaylock	.15	.07	.02
Atlanta Hawks
☐ PR2 Stacey Augmon	.15	.07	.02
Atlanta Hawks
☐ PR3 Dino Radja	.15	.07	.02
Boston Celtics
☐ PR4 Dominique Wilkins	.25	.11	.03
Boston Celtics
☐ PR5 Larry Johnson	.40	.18	.05
Charlotte Hornets
☐ PR6 Alonzo Mourning	.60	.25	.08
Charlotte Hornets
☐ PR7 Toni Kukoc	.15	.07	.02
Chicago Bulls
☐ PR8 Scottie Pippen	.50	.23	.06
Chicago Bulls
☐ PR9 John Williams	.15	.07	.02
Cleveland Cavaliers
☐ PR10 Mark Price	.15	.07	.02
Cleveland Cavaliers
☐ PR11 Jim Jackson	.60	.25	.08
Dallas Mavericks
☐ PR12 Jamal Mashburn	1.00	.45	.13
Dallas Mavericks
☐ PR13 Dale Ellis	.15	.07	.02
Denver Nuggets
☐ PR14 LaPhonso Ellis	.15	.07	.02
Denver Nuggets
☐ PR15 Joe Dumars	.15	.07	.02
Detroit Pistons
☐ PR16 Lindsey Hunter	.10	.05	.01

Detroit Pistons			
☐ PR17 Latrell Sprewell	.60	.25	.08
Golden State Warriors			
☐ PR18 Chris Mullin...............	.15	.07	.02
Golden State Warriors			
☐ PR19 Vernon Maxwell	.10	.05	.01
Houston Rockets			
☐ PR20 Hakeem Olajuwon ...	1.25	.55	.16
Houston Rockets			
☐ PR21 Mark Jackson............	.10	.05	.01
Indiana Pacers			
☐ PR22 Reggie Miller..............	.50	.23	.06
Indiana Pacers			
☐ PR23 Pooh Richardson	.10	.05	.01
Los Angeles Clippers			
☐ PR24 Loy Vaught................	.15	.07	.02
Los Angeles Clippers			
☐ PR25 Vlade Divac................	.15	.07	.02
Los Angeles Lakers			
☐ PR26 Nick Van Exel	1.00	.45	.13
Los Angeles Lakers			
☐ PR27 Glen Rice....................	.15	.07	.02
Miami Heat			
☐ PR28 Billy Owens	.15	.07	.02
Miami Heat			
☐ PR29 Vin Baker....................	.50	.23	.06
Milwaukee Bucks			
☐ PR30 Eric Murdock.............	.10	.05	.01
Milwaukee Bucks			
☐ PR31 Christian Laettner.......	.15	.07	.02
Minnesota Timberwolves			
☐ PR32 Isaiah Rider...............	.15	.07	.02
Minnesota Timberwolves			
☐ PR33 Kenny Anderson........	.15	.07	.02
New Jersey Nets			
☐ PR34 Derrick Coleman.........	.15	.07	.02
New Jersey Nets			
☐ PR35 Patrick Ewing	.50	.23	.06
New York Knicks			
☐ PR36 John Starks................	.15	.07	.02
New York Knicks			
☐ PR37 Nick Anderson...........	.15	.07	.02
Orlando Magic			
☐ PR38 Anfernee Hardaway ..	2.00	.90	.25
Orlando Magic			
☐ PR39 Shawn Bradley	.15	.07	.02
Philadelphia 76ers			
☐ PR40 Clarence Weatherspoon	.15	.07	.02
Philadelphia 76ers			
☐ PR41 Charles Barkley	1.00	.45	.13
Phoenix Suns			
☐ PR42 Kevin Johnson	.25	.11	.03
Phoenix Suns			
☐ PR43 Clyde Drexler............	.50	.23	.06
Portland Trail Blazers			
☐ PR44 Clifford Robinson......	.15	.07	.02
Portland Trail Blazers			
☐ PR45 Mitch Richmond........	.25	.11	.03
Sacramento Kings			
☐ PR46 Olden Polynice...........	.10	.05	.01
Sacramento Kings			
☐ PR47 Sean Elliott...............	.15	.07	.02
San Antonio Spurs			
☐ PR48 Chuck Person............	.15	.07	.02
San Antonio Spurs			
☐ PR49 Shawn Kemp	1.00	.45	.13
Seattle Supersonics			
☐ PR50 Gary Payton..............	.15	.07	.02
Seattle Supersonics			
☐ PR51 Jeff Hornacek...........	.15	.07	.02
Utah Jazz			

☐ PR52 Karl Malone................	.50	.23	.06
Utah Jazz			
☐ PR53 Rex Chapman............	.10	.05	.01
Washington Bullets			
☐ PR54 Don MacLean............	.10	.05	.01
Washington Bullets			

1994-95 Hoops Predators

Randomly inserted into all second series packs (one in every twelve 12-card packs and two per 24-card jumbo pack), cards from this 8-card set feature eight league leaders from the 1993-94 season. Design is very similar to the Power Ratings inserts.

	MINT	NRMT	EXC
COMPLETE SET (8)	4.00	1.80	.50
COMMON CARD (P1-P8)........	.15	.07	.02
☐ P1 Mahmoud Abdul-Rauf ...	.15	.07	.02
Denver Nuggets			
☐ P2 Dikembe Mutombo........	.40	.18	.05
Denver Nuggets			
☐ P3 Shaquille O'Neal	3.00	1.35	.40
Orlando Magic			
☐ P4 Tracy Murray	.15	.07	.02
Portland Trail Blazers			
☐ P5 David Robinson	1.25	.55	.16
San Antonio Spurs			
☐ P6 Dennis Rodman............	.40	.18	.05
San Antonio Spurs			
☐ P7 Nate McMillan..............	.15	.07	.02
Seattle Supersonics			
☐ P8 John Stockton	.60	.25	.08
Utah Jazz			

1994-95 Hoops Supreme Court

Randomly inserted in first series hobby and retail packs at a rate of one in four, the 50 standard-size (2 1/2" by 3 1/2") parallel cards comprising the '94-95 Hoops Supreme Court set feature a selection of the top stars within the basic issue first

series Hoops set. Unlike the regular issue cards, each Supreme Court insert features a special embossed gold-foil logo on the card front. The cards are also numbered on the back with an "SC" prefix.

	MINT	NRMT	EXC
COMPLETE SERIES 1 (50)	20.00	9.00	2.50
COMMON CARD (SC1-SC50)	.25	.11	.03

☐ SC1	Mookie Blaylock	.35	.16	.04
	Atlanta Hawks			
☐ SC2	Danny Manning	.35	.16	.04
	Atlanta Hawks			
☐ SC3	Dino Radja	.35	.16	.04
	Boston Celtics			
☐ SC4	Larry Johnson	.60	.25	.08
	Charlotte Hornets			
☐ SC5	Alonzo Mourning	1.00	.45	.13
	Charlotte Hornets			
☐ SC6	B.J. Armstrong	.25	.11	.03
	Chicago Bulls			
☐ SC7	Horace Grant	.35	.16	.04
	Chicago Bulls			
☐ SC8	Toni Kukoc	.35	.16	.04
	Chicago Bulls			
☐ SC9	Brad Daugherty	.35	.16	.04
	Cleveland Cavaliers			
☐ SC10	Mark Price	.35	.16	.04
	Cleveland Cavaliers			
☐ SC11	Jim Jackson	1.00	.45	.13
	Dallas Mavericks			
☐ SC12	Jamal Mashburn	1.50	.65	.19
	Dallas Mavericks			
☐ SC13	Dikembe Mutombo	.50	.23	.06
	Denver Nuggets			
☐ SC14	Joe Dumars	.50	.23	.06
	Detroit Pistons			
☐ SC15	Lindsey Hunter	.25	.11	.03
	Detroit Pistons			
☐ SC16	Tim Hardaway	.35	.16	.04
	Golden State Warriors			
☐ SC17	Chris Mullin	.35	.16	.04
	Golden State Warriors			
☐ SC18	Sam Cassell	.35	.16	.04
	Houston Rockets			
☐ SC19	Hakeem Olajuwon	2.00	.90	.25
	Houston Rockets			
☐ SC20	Reggie Miller	.75	.35	.09
	Indiana Pacers			
☐ SC21	Dominique Wilkins	.50	.23	.06
	Los Angeles Clippers			
☐ SC22	Nick Van Exel	1.50	.65	.19
	Los Angeles Lakers			
☐ SC23	Harold Miner	.25	.11	.03
	Miami Heat			
☐ SC24	Steve Smith	.35	.16	.04
	Miami Heat			
☐ SC25	Vin Baker	.75	.35	.09
	Milwaukee Bucks			
☐ SC26	Christian Laettner	.35	.16	.04
	Minnesota Timberwolves			
☐ SC27	Isaiah Rider	.35	.16	.04
	Minnesota Timberwolves			
☐ SC28	Kenny Anderson	.35	.16	.04
	New Jersey Nets			
☐ SC29	Derrick Coleman	.35	.16	.04
	New Jersey Nets			
☐ SC30	Patrick Ewing	.75	.35	.09
	New York Knicks			
☐ SC31	John Starks	.35	.16	.04
	New York Knicks			
☐ SC32	Anfernee Hardaway	3.00	1.35	.40
	Orlando Magic			
☐ SC33	Shaquille O'Neal	4.00	1.80	.50
	Orlando Magic			
☐ SC34	Shawn Bradley	.35	.16	.04
	Philadelphia 76ers			
☐ SC35	Clarence Weatherspoon	.35	.16	.04
	Philadelphia 76ers			
☐ SC36	Charles Barkley	1.50	.65	.19
	Phoenix Suns			
☐ SC37	Kevin Johnson	.50	.23	.06
	Phoenix Suns			
☐ SC38	Oliver Miller	.25	.11	.03
	Phoenix Suns			
☐ SC39	Clyde Drexler	.75	.35	.09
	Portland Trail Blazers			
☐ SC40	Cliff Robinson	.35	.16	.04
	Portland Trail Blazers			
☐ SC41	Mitch Richmond	.50	.23	.06
	Sacramento Kings			
☐ SC42	Bobby Hurley	.35	.16	.04
	Sacramento Kings			
☐ SC43	David Robinson	1.50	.65	.19
	San Antonio Spurs			
☐ SC44	Dennis Rodman	.35	.16	.04
	San Antonio Spurs			
☐ SC45	Gary Payton	.35	.16	.04
	Seattle Supersonics			
☐ SC46	Shawn Kemp	1.50	.65	.19
	Seattle Supersonics			
☐ SC47	John Stockton	.75	.35	.09
	Utah Jazz			
☐ SC48	Karl Malone	.75	.35	.09
	Utah Jazz			
☐ SC49	Calbert Cheaney	.35	.16	.04
	Washington Bullets			
☐ SC50	Tom Gugliotta	.35	.16	.04
	Washington Bullets			

1995-96 Hoops

The 250 standard-size cards comprising the 1995-96 Hoops first series set were issued in 12-card hobby and retail packs (SRP $1.29) and 20-card retail jumbo packs (SRP $1.99). Series 1 packs (each of which contain an insert card) were released to the retail market in late August, 1995. The fronts have a full-color action photo with the player's name in gold-foil surrounded by his team's color. The backs have a color-photo with statistics from his pro and college car-

eer. The cards are grouped alphabetically within teams and checklisted below alphabetically according to teams as follows: Atlanta Hawks (1-7), Boston Celtics (8-13), Charlotte Hornets (14-19), Chicago Bulls (20-25), Cleveland Cavaliers (26-31), Dallas Mavericks (32-37), Denver Nuggets (38-44), Detroit Pistons (45-50), Golden State Warriors (51-58), Houston Rockets (59-64), Indiana Pacers (65-70), Los Angeles Clippers (71-76), Los Angeles Lakers (77-82), Miami Heat (83-88), Milwaukee Bucks (89-94), Minnesota Timberwolves (95-100), New Jersey Nets (101-106), New York Knicks (107-113), Orlando Magic (114-119), Philadelphia 76ers (120-125), Phoenix Suns (126-132), Portland Trail Blazers (133-138), Sacramento Kings (139-144), San Antonio Spurs (145-150), Seattle Supersonics (151-157), Utah Jazz (158-163), and Washington Bullets (164-197). Also includes subsets: Sizzlin' Sophs (198-207), Milestones (208-217), Buzzer Beaters (218-227), Pipeline (228-232), Class Acts (233-242) and Triple Threats (243-247). A special Grant Hill Tribute card, featuring a clear acetate center, was randomly inserted into one in every 360 first series packs. All series 1 insert cards feature 3-D technology. A pair of Grant Hill 3-D glasses was available by sending in two first series wrappers and a check or money order for $3.50. In addition, a limited edition Grant Hill Commemorative Co-Rookie of the Year card was available by sending in a check or money order for $9.95 plus two first series wrappers. Both promotions were detailed on first series wrappers and both expired December 31, 1995.

	MINT	NRMT	EXC
COMPLETE SERIES 1 (250)	15.00	6.75	1.90
COMMON CARD (1-250)	.05	.02	.01

☐ 1	Stacey Augmon	.08	.04	.01
☐ 2	Mookie Blaylock	.08	.04	.01
☐ 3	Craig Ehlo	.05	.02	.01
☐ 4	Andrew Lang	.05	.02	.01
☐ 5	Grant Long	.05	.02	.01
☐ 6	Ken Norman	.05	.02	.01
☐ 7	Steve Smith	.08	.04	.01
☐ 8	Dee Brown	.08	.04	.01
☐ 9	Sherman Douglas	.05	.02	.01
☐ 10	Pervis Ellison	.05	.02	.01
☐ 11	Eric Montross	.10	.05	.01
☐ 12	Dino Radja	.10	.05	.01
☐ 13	Dominique Wilkins	.15	.07	.02
☐ 14	Muggsy Bogues	.10	.05	.01
☐ 15	Scott Burrell	.05	.02	.01
☐ 16	Dell Curry	.05	.02	.01
☐ 17	Hersey Hawkins	.08	.04	.01
☐ 18	Larry Johnson	.20	.09	.03
☐ 19	Alonzo Mourning	.25	.11	.03
☐ 20	B.J. Armstrong	.05	.02	.01
☐ 21	Michael Jordan	3.00	1.35	.40
☐ 22	Toni Kukoc	.08	.04	.01
☐ 23	Will Perdue	.05	.02	.01
☐ 24	Scottie Pippen	.25	.11	.03
☐ 25	Dickey Simpkins	.05	.02	.01
☐ 26	Terrell Brandon	.05	.02	.01
☐ 27	Tyrone Hill	.08	.04	.01
☐ 28	Chris Mills	.08	.04	.01
☐ 29	Bobby Phills	.05	.02	.01
☐ 30	Mark Price	.10	.05	.01
☐ 31	John Williams	.08	.04	.01
☐ 32	Tony Dumas	.05	.02	.01
☐ 33	Jim Jackson	.25	.11	.03
☐ 34	Popeye Jones	.05	.02	.01
☐ 35	Jason Kidd	.75	.35	.09
☐ 36	Jamal Mashburn	.30	.14	.04
☐ 37	Roy Tarpley	.05	.02	.01
☐ 38	Mahmoud Abdul-Rauf	.08	.04	.01
☐ 39	LaPhonso Ellis	.05	.02	.01
☐ 40	Dikembe Mutombo	.15	.07	.02
☐ 41	Robert Pack	.05	.02	.01
☐ 42	Rodney Rogers	.08	.04	.01
☐ 43	Jalen Rose	.15	.07	.02
☐ 44	Bryant Stith	.05	.02	.01
☐ 45	Joe Dumars	.15	.07	.02
☐ 46	Grant Hill	1.25	.55	.16
☐ 47	Allan Houston	.08	.04	.01
☐ 48	Lindsey Hunter	.05	.02	.01
☐ 49	Oliver Miller	.05	.02	.01
☐ 50	Terry Mills	.05	.02	.01
☐ 51	Chris Gatling	.05	.02	.01
☐ 52	Tim Hardaway	.10	.05	.01
☐ 53	Donyell Marshall	.15	.07	.02
☐ 54	Chris Mullin	.10	.05	.01
☐ 55	Carlos Rogers	.10	.05	.01
☐ 56	Clifford Rozier	.08	.04	.01
☐ 57	Rony Seikaly	.05	.02	.01
☐ 58	Latrell Sprewell	.25	.11	.03
☐ 59	Sam Cassell	.05	.02	.01
☐ 60	Clyde Drexler	.25	.11	.03
☐ 61	Robert Horry	.10	.05	.01
☐ 62	Vernon Maxwell	.05	.02	.01
☐ 63	Hakeem Olajuwon	.60	.25	.08
☐ 64	Kenny Smith	.05	.02	.01
☐ 65	Dale Davis	.08	.04	.01
☐ 66	Mark Jackson	.05	.02	.01
☐ 67	Derrick McKey	.08	.04	.01
☐ 68	Reggie Miller	.25	.11	.03
☐ 69	Byron Scott	.08	.04	.01
☐ 70	Rik Smits	.05	.02	.01
☐ 71	Terry Dehere	.05	.02	.01
☐ 72	Lamond Murray	.05	.02	.01
☐ 73	Eric Piatkowski	.05	.02	.01
☐ 74	Pooh Richardson	.05	.02	.01
☐ 75	Malik Sealy	.05	.02	.01
☐ 76	Loy Vaught	.08	.04	.01
☐ 77	Elden Campbell	.05	.02	.01
☐ 78	Cedric Ceballos	.10	.05	.01
☐ 79	Vlade Divac	.10	.05	.01
☐ 80	Eddie Jones	.50	.23	.06
☐ 81	Sedale Threatt	.05	.02	.01
☐ 82	Nick Van Exel	.30	.14	.04
☐ 83	Bimbo Coles	.05	.02	.01

☐ 84	Harold Miner	.05	.02	.01
☐ 85	Billy Owens	.08	.04	.01
☐ 86	Khalid Reeves	.05	.02	.01
☐ 87	Glen Rice	.10	.05	.01
☐ 88	Kevin Willis	.10	.05	.01
☐ 89	Vin Baker	.15	.07	.02
☐ 90	Marty Conlon	.05	.02	.01
☐ 91	Todd Day	.05	.02	.01
☐ 92	Eric Mobley	.05	.02	.01
☐ 93	Eric Murdock	.05	.02	.01
☐ 94	Glenn Robinson	.75	.35	.09
☐ 95	Winston Garland	.05	.02	.01
☐ 96	Tom Gugliotta	.08	.04	.01
☐ 97	Christian Laettner	.08	.04	.01
☐ 98	Isaiah Rider	.10	.05	.01
☐ 99	Sean Rooks	.05	.02	.01
☐ 100	Doug West	.05	.02	.01
☐ 101	Kenny Anderson	.10	.05	.01
☐ 102	Benoit Benjamin	.05	.02	.01
☐ 103	Derrick Coleman	.10	.05	.01
☐ 104	Kevin Edwards	.05	.02	.01
☐ 105	Armon Gilliam	.05	.02	.01
☐ 106	Chris Morris	.05	.02	.01
☐ 107	Patrick Ewing	.25	.11	.03
☐ 108	Derek Harper	.08	.04	.01
☐ 109	Anthony Mason	.08	.04	.01
☐ 110	Charles Oakley	.08	.04	.01
☐ 111	Charles Smith	.05	.02	.01
☐ 112	John Starks	.08	.04	.01
☐ 113	Monty Williams	.05	.02	.01
☐ 114	Nick Anderson	.08	.04	.01
☐ 115	Horace Grant	.15	.07	.02
☐ 116	Anfernee Hardaway	.75	.35	.09
☐ 117	Shaquille O'Neal	1.25	.55	.16
☐ 118	Dennis Scott	.05	.02	.01
☐ 119	Brian Shaw	.05	.02	.01
☐ 120	Dana Barros	.10	.05	.01
☐ 121	Shawn Bradley	.05	.02	.01
☐ 122	Willie Burton	.05	.02	.01
☐ 123	Jeff Malone	.08	.04	.01
☐ 124	Clarence Weatherspoon	.08	.04	.01
☐ 125	Sharone Wright	.10	.05	.01
☐ 126	Charles Barkley	.50	.23	.06
☐ 127	A.C. Green	.10	.05	.01
☐ 128	Kevin Johnson	.15	.07	.02
☐ 129	Dan Majerle	.08	.04	.01
☐ 130	Danny Manning	.10	.05	.01
☐ 131	Elliot Perry	.05	.02	.01
☐ 132	Wesley Person	.15	.07	.02
☐ 133	Chris Dudley	.05	.02	.01
☐ 134	Clifford Robinson	.08	.04	.01
☐ 135	James Robinson	.05	.02	.01
☐ 136	Rod Strickland	.08	.04	.01
☐ 137	Otis Thorpe	.08	.04	.01
☐ 138	Buck Williams	.08	.04	.01
☐ 139	Brian Grant	.25	.11	.03
☐ 140	Olden Polynice	.05	.02	.01
☐ 141	Mitch Richmond	.15	.07	.02
☐ 142	Michael Smith	.08	.04	.01
☐ 143	Spud Webb	.05	.02	.01
☐ 144	Walt Williams	.08	.04	.01
☐ 145	Vinny Del Negro	.05	.02	.01
☐ 146	Sean Elliott	.05	.02	.01
☐ 147	Avery Johnson	.05	.02	.01
☐ 148	Chuck Person	.08	.04	.01
☐ 149	David Robinson	.50	.23	.06
☐ 150	Dennis Rodman	.15	.07	.02
☐ 151	Kendall Gill	.05	.02	.01
☐ 152	Ervin Johnson	.05	.02	.01
☐ 153	Shawn Kemp	.50	.23	.06
☐ 154	Nate McMillan	.05	.02	.01
☐ 155	Gary Payton	.10	.05	.01
☐ 156	Detlef Schrempf	.10	.05	.01
☐ 157	Dontonio Wingfield	.05	.02	.01
☐ 158	David Benoit	.05	.02	.01
☐ 159	Jeff Hornacek	.08	.04	.01
☐ 160	Karl Malone	.25	.11	.03
☐ 161	Felton Spencer	.05	.02	.01
☐ 162	John Stockton	.25	.11	.03
☐ 163	Jamie Watson	.05	.02	.01
☐ 164	Rex Chapman	.05	.02	.01
☐ 165	Calbert Cheaney	.08	.04	.01
☐ 166	Juwan Howard	.30	.14	.04
☐ 167	Don MacLean	.05	.02	.01
☐ 168	Gheorghe Muresan	.05	.02	.01
☐ 169	Scott Skiles	.05	.02	.01
☐ 170	Chris Webber	.25	.11	.03
☐ 171	Lenny Wilkens CO	.08	.04	.01
☐ 172	Allan Bristow CO	.05	.02	.01
☐ 173	Phil Jackson CO	.08	.04	.01
☐ 174	Mike Fratello CO	.05	.02	.01
☐ 175	Dick Motta CO	.05	.02	.01
☐ 176	Bernie Bickerstaff CO	.05	.02	.01
☐ 177	Doug Collins CO	.05	.02	.01
☐ 178	Rick Adelman CO	.05	.02	.01
☐ 179	Rudy Tomjanovich CO	.08	.04	.01
☐ 180	Larry Brown CO	.08	.04	.01
☐ 181	Bill Fitch CO	.05	.02	.01
☐ 182	Del Harris CO	.05	.02	.01
☐ 183	Mike Dunleavy CO	.05	.02	.01
☐ 184	Bill Blair CO	.05	.02	.01
☐ 185	Butch Beard CO	.05	.02	.01
☐ 186	Pat Riley CO	.08	.04	.01
☐ 187	Brian Hill CO	.05	.02	.01
☐ 188	John Lucas CO	.08	.04	.01
☐ 189	Paul Westphal CO	.08	.04	.01
☐ 190	P.J. Carlesimo CO	.05	.02	.01
☐ 191	Garry St. Jean CO	.05	.02	.01
☐ 192	Bob Hill CO	.05	.02	.01
☐ 193	George Karl CO	.05	.02	.01
☐ 194	Brendan Malone CO	.05	.02	.01
☐ 195	Jerry Sloan CO	.05	.02	.01
☐ 196	Brian Winters CO	.05	.02	.01
☐ 197	Jim Lynam CO	.05	.02	.01
☐ 198	Brian Grant SS	.10	.05	.01
☐ 199	Grant Hill SS	.60	.25	.08
☐ 200	Juwan Howard SS	.15	.07	.02
☐ 201	Eddie Jones SS	.25	.11	.03
☐ 202	Jason Kidd SS	.40	.18	.05
☐ 203	Donyell Marshall SS	.08	.04	.01
☐ 204	Eric Montross SS	.08	.04	.01
☐ 205	Glenn Robinson SS	.40	.18	.05
☐ 206	Jalen Rose SS	.08	.04	.01
☐ 207	Sharone Wright SS	.05	.02	.01
☐ 208	Dana Barros MS	.05	.02	.01
☐ 209	Joe Dumars MS	.08	.04	.01
☐ 210	A.C. Green MS	.05	.02	.01
☐ 211	Grant Hill MS	.60	.25	.08
☐ 212	Karl Malone MS	.05	.02	.01
☐ 213	Reggie Miller MS	.10	.05	.01
☐ 214	Glen Rice MS	.05	.02	.01
☐ 215	John Stockton MS	.10	.05	.01
☐ 216	Lenny Wilkens MS	.05	.02	.01
☐ 217	Dominique Wilkins MS	.08	.04	.01
☐ 218	Kenny Anderson MS	.05	.02	.01
☐ 219	Mookie Blaylock MS	.05	.02	.01
☐ 220	Larry Johnson BB	.10	.05	.01
☐ 221	Shawn Kemp BB	.25	.11	.03
☐ 222	Toni Kukoc BB	.05	.02	.01
☐ 223	Jamal Mashburn BB	.15	.07	.02
☐ 224	Glen Rice BB	.05	.02	.01
☐ 225	Mitch Richmond BB	.08	.04	.01

☐	226 Latrell Sprewell BB	.10	.05	.01
☐	227 Rod Strickland BB	.05	.02	.01
☐	228 Michael Adams PL	.05	.02	.01
	Darrick Martin			
☐	229 Craig Ehlo PL	.05	.02	.01
	Jerome Harmon			
☐	230 Mario Elie PL	.05	.02	.01
	George McCloud			
☐	231 Anthony Mason PL	.05	.02	.01
	Chucky Brown			
☐	232 John Starks PL	.05	.02	.01
	Tim Legler			
☐	233 Muggsy Bogues CA	.05	.02	.01
☐	234 Joe Dumars CA	.08	.04	.01
☐	235 LaPhonso Ellis CA	.05	.02	.01
☐	236 Patrick Ewing CA	.10	.05	.01
☐	237 Grant Hill CA	.60	.25	.08
☐	238 Kevin Johnson CA	.08	.04	.01
☐	239 Dan Majerle CA	.05	.02	.01
☐	240 Karl Malone CA	.10	.05	.01
☐	241 Hakeem Olajuwon CA	.30	.14	.04
☐	242 David Robinson CA	.25	.11	.03
☐	243 Dana Barros TT	.05	.02	.01
☐	244 Scott Burrell TT	.05	.02	.01
☐	245 Reggie Miller TT	.10	.05	.01
☐	246 Glen Rice TT	.05	.02	.01
☐	247 John Stockton TT	.10	.05	.01
☐	248 Checklist	.05	.02	.01
☐	249 Checklist	.05	.02	.01
☐	250 Checklist	.05	.02	.01
☐	NNO Grant Hill Tribute	50.00	23.00	6.25

1995-96 Hoops Block Party

Randomly inserted into all first series packs at an approximate rate of one in two packs, these 25 cards highlight the top shot-blockers in the NBA. The fronts have a full-color action photo with a multi-colored, 1970s looking background and the words "Block Party" at the top in gold-foil. The backs have a color photo on the left side with a similar background to the front with player information and statistics on the right. The cards are numbered "X of 25."

	MINT	NRMT	EXC
COMPLETE SET (25)	6.00	2.70	.75
COMMON CARD (1-25)	.15	.07	.02

☐	1 Oliver Miller	.15	.07	.02
	Detroit Pistons			
☐	2 Dennis Rodman	.30	.14	.04
	San Antonio Spurs			
☐	3 Scottie Pippen	.50	.23	.06
	Chicago Bulls			
☐	4 Dikembe Mutombo	.30	.14	.04
	Denver Nuggets			
☐	5 Vlade Divac	.20	.09	.03
	Los Angeles Lakers			
☐	6 Brian Grant	.50	.23	.06
	Sacramento Kings			
☐	7 Alonzo Mourning	.50	.23	.06
	Charlotte Hornets			
☐	8 Hakeem Olajuwon	1.25	.55	.16
	Houston Rockets			
☐	9 Patrick Ewing	.50	.23	.06
	New York Knicks			
☐	10 Shawn Kemp	1.00	.45	.13
	Seattle Supersonics			
☐	11 Vin Baker	.30	.14	.04
	Milwaukee Bucks			
☐	12 Horace Grant	.30	.14	.04
	Orlando Magic			
☐	13 Dale Davis	.15	.07	.02
	Indiana Pacers			
☐	14 Juwan Howard	.60	.25	.08
	Washington Bullets			
☐	15 Eddie Jones	1.00	.45	.13
	Los Angeles Lakers			
☐	16 Eric Montross	.20	.09	.03
	Boston Celtics			
☐	17 Tyrone Hill	.15	.07	.02
	Cleveland Cavaliers			
☐	18 Tom Gugliotta	.15	.07	.02
	Minnesota Timberwolves			
☐	19 Shawn Bradley	.15	.07	.02
	Philadelphia 76ers			
☐	20 Dan Majerle	.15	.07	.02
	Phoenix Suns			
☐	21 Loy Vaught	.15	.07	.02
	Los Angeles Clippers			
☐	22 Donyell Marshall	.20	.09	.03
	Golden State Warriors			
☐	23 Chris Webber	.50	.23	.06
	Washington Bullets			
☐	24 Derrick Coleman	.20	.09	.03
	New Jersey Nets			
☐	25 Walt Williams	.15	.07	.02
	Sacramento Kings			

1995-96 Hoops Grant Hill Dunks/Slams

Cards D1-D5 were randomly inserted exclusively in one in every thirty-six first series 12-card hobby packs, while cards S1-S5 were randomly inserted only in one in every thirty-six first series retail 12-card packs. All cards are foil-coated, featuring an assortion of Grant Hill dunking and slamming shots. The fronts each carry an oversized letter, so that cards D1-D5 spell

and statistics. The cards are numbered "X of 25."

out "DUNK!!!," and cards S1-S5 spell out "SLAM!".

	MINT	NRMT	EXC
COMPLETE DUNK SET (5)	40.00	18.00	5.00
COMPLETE SLAM SET (5)	40.00	18.00	5.00
COMMON CARD (D1-D5)	10.00	4.50	1.25
COMMON CARD (S1-S5)	10.00	4.50	1.25
☐ D1 D-Card	10.00	4.50	1.25
☐ D2 U-Card	10.00	4.50	1.25
☐ D3 N-Card	10.00	4.50	1.25
☐ D4 K-Card	10.00	4.50	1.25
☐ D5 !!!-Card	10.00	4.50	1.25
☐ S1 S-Card	10.00	4.50	1.25
☐ S2 L-Card	10.00	4.50	1.25
☐ S3 A-Card	10.00	4.50	1.25
☐ S4 M-Card	10.00	4.50	1.25
☐ S5 !-Card	10.00	4.50	1.25

1995-96 Hoops Number Crunchers

Randomly inserted into all first series packs at an approximate rate of one in two packs, these 25 cards highlight players that attained notable statistical achievements during the 1994-95 season. The fronts have a color-action photo with the player's number in a multi-color background and the word "Crunchers" spelled out in a tic-tac-toe board in the lower left hand corner in gold-foil. The backs have a color-action photo with a huge multi-colored ball in the background along with player information

		MINT	NRMT	EXC
COMPLETE SET (25)		15.00	6.75	1.90
COMMON CARD (1-25)		.15	.07	.02
☐ 1	Michael Jordan Chicago Bulls	6.00	2.70	.75
☐ 2	Shaquille O'Neal Orlando Magic	2.50	1.15	.30
☐ 3	Grant Hill Detroit Pistons	2.50	1.15	.30
☐ 4	Detlef Schrempf Seattle Supersonics	.20	.09	.03
☐ 5	Kenny Anderson New Jersey Nets	.20	.09	.03
☐ 6	Anfernee Hardaway Orlando Magic	1.50	.65	.19
☐ 7	Latrell Sprewell Golden State Warriors	.50	.23	.06
☐ 8	Jamal Mashburn Dallas Mavericks	.60	.25	.08
☐ 9	Nick Van Exel Los Angeles Lakers	.60	.25	.08
☐ 10	Charles Barkley Phoenix Suns	1.00	.45	.13
☐ 11	Mitch Richmond Sacramento Kings	.25	.11	.03
☐ 12	David Robinson San Antonio Spurs	1.00	.45	.13
☐ 13	Gary Payton Seattle Supersonics	.20	.09	.03
☐ 14	Rod Strickland Portland Trailblazers	.15	.07	.02
☐ 15	Glenn Robinson Milwaukee Bucks	1.50	.65	.19
☐ 16	Reggie Miller Indiana Pacers	.50	.23	.06
☐ 17	Karl Malone Utah Jazz	.50	.23	.06
☐ 18	Jim Jackson Dallas Mavericks	.50	.23	.06
☐ 19	Clyde Drexler Houston Rockets	.50	.23	.06
☐ 20	Glen Rice Miami Heat	.20	.09	.03
☐ 21	Isaiah Rider Minnesota Timberwolves	.20	.09	.03
☐ 22	Cedric Ceballos Los Angeles Lakers	.20	.09	.03
☐ 23	John Stockton Utah Jazz	.50	.23	.06
☐ 24	Jason Kidd Dallas Mavericks	1.50	.65	.19
☐ 25	Mookie Blaylock Atlanta Hawks	.15	.07	.02

1995-96 Hoops Top Ten

Randomly inserted into all first series packs at an approximate rate of one in 12 packs, these 10 cards feature a selection of former lottery picks that are on their way to or have already attained great success in the NBA.

The fronts are laid out horizontally with a color-action photo and a wide strip down the left side that reads "Top" with 10 in the middle of the O. The background on each card is different and has a multi-colored cloudy look. The backs have the same background as the front with a color-action photo and player information at the top.

	MINT	NRMT	EXC
COMPLETE SET (10)	50.00	23.00	6.25
COMMON CARD (AR1-AR10)	2.00	.90	.25
☐ AR1 Shaquille O'Neal	10.00	4.50	1.25
Orlando Magic			
☐ AR2 Grant Hill	10.00	4.50	1.25
Detroit Pistons			
☐ AR3 Chris Webber	2.00	.90	.25
Washington Bullets			
☐ AR4 Jamal Mashburn	2.50	1.15	.30
Dallas Mavericks			
☐ AR5 Anfernee Hardaway	6.00	2.70	.75
Orlando Magic			
☐ AR6 Alonzo Mourning	2.00	.90	.25
Charlotte Hornets			
☐ AR7 Michael Jordan	20.00	9.00	2.50
Chicago Bulls			
☐ AR8 Charles Barkley	4.00	1.80	.50
Phoenix Suns			
☐ AR9 Glenn Robinson	6.00	2.70	.75
Milwaukee Bucks			
☐ AR10 Jason Kidd	6.00	2.70	.75
Dallas Mavericks			

1993-94
Jam Session

This 240-card set was issued in 1993 by Fleer and features oversized cards measuring approximately 2 1/2" by 4 3/4". Cards were issued in 12-card packs (36 per box) with a suggested retail price of 1.59. The full-bleed fronts feature glossy color action player photos. Across the bottom edge of the picture appears a team color-coded bar with the player's name, position and team. The NBA Jam Session logo is superposed on the lower right corner. The backs are divided in half vertically with the

left side carrying a second action shot and on the right side a panel with a background that fades from green to white. On the panel appears biography, career highlights, statistics and team logo. The cards are numbered on the back and checklisted below alphabetically within and according to teams as follows: Atlanta Hawks (1-9), Boston Celtics (10-16), Charlotte Hornets (17-26), Chicago Bulls (27-35), Cleveland Cavaliers (36-44), Dallas Mavericks (45-51), Denver Nuggets (52-59), Detroit Pistons (60-66), Golden State Warriors (67-75), Houston Rockets (76-85), Indiana Pacers (86-94), Los Angeles Clippers (95-101), Los Angeles Lakers (102-110), Miami Heat (111-118), Milwaukee Bucks (119-128), Minnesota Timberwolves (129-136), New Jersey Nets (137-144), New York Knicks (145-155), Orlando Magic (156-164), Philadelphia 76ers (165-172), Phoenix Suns (173-183), Portland Trail Blazers (184-192), Sacramento Kings (193-200), San Antonio Spurs (201-210), Seattle Supersonics (211-219), Utah Jazz (220-229), and Washington Bullets (230-238).

	MINT	NRMT	EXC
COMPLETE SET (240)	30.00	13.50	3.80
COMMON CARD (1-240)	.10	.05	.01
☐ 1 Stacey Augmon	.15	.07	.02
☐ 2 Mookie Blaylock	.15	.07	.02
☐ 3 Doug Edwards	.15	.07	.02
☐ 4 Duane Ferrell	.10	.05	.01
☐ 5 Paul Graham	.10	.05	.01
☐ 6 Adam Keefe	.10	.05	.01
☐ 7 Jon Koncak	.10	.05	.01
☐ 8 Dominique Wilkins	.25	.11	.03
☐ 9 Kevin Willis	.15	.07	.02
☐ 10 Alaa Abdelnaby	.10	.05	.01
☐ 11 Dee Brown	.15	.07	.02
☐ 12 Sherman Douglas	.10	.05	.01
☐ 13 Rick Fox	.10	.05	.01
☐ 14 Kevin Gamble	.10	.05	.01
☐ 15 Xavier McDaniel	.10	.05	.01
☐ 16 Robert Parish	.20	.09	.03
☐ 17 Muggsy Bogues	.20	.09	.03
☐ 18 Scott Burrell	.40	.18	.05
☐ 19 Dell Curry	.10	.05	.01
☐ 20 Kenny Gattison	.10	.05	.01
☐ 21 Hersey Hawkins	.15	.07	.02

☐ 22	Eddie Johnson	.15	.07	.02
☐ 23	Larry Johnson	.50	.23	.06
☐ 24	Alonzo Mourning	1.00	.45	.13
☐ 25	Johnny Newman	.10	.05	.01
☐ 26	David Wingate	.10	.05	.01
☐ 27	B.J. Armstrong	.10	.05	.01
☐ 28	Corie Blount	.10	.05	.01
☐ 29	Bill Cartwright	.10	.05	.01
☐ 30	Horace Grant	.25	.11	.03
☐ 31	Stacey King	.10	.05	.01
☐ 32	John Paxson	.10	.05	.01
☐ 33	Michael Jordan	6.00	2.70	.75
☐ 34	Scottie Pippen	.50	.23	.06
☐ 35	Scott Williams	.10	.05	.01
☐ 36	Terrell Brandon	.10	.05	.01
☐ 37	Brad Daugherty	.15	.07	.02
☐ 38	Danny Ferry	.10	.05	.01
☐ 39	Tyrone Hill	.15	.07	.02
☐ 40	Chris Mills	.60	.25	.08
☐ 41	Larry Nance	.15	.07	.02
☐ 42	Mark Price	.20	.09	.03
☐ 43	Gerald Wilkins	.10	.05	.01
☐ 44	John Williams	.15	.07	.02
☐ 45	Terry Davis	.10	.05	.01
☐ 46	Derek Harper	.15	.07	.02
☐ 47	Donald Hodge	.10	.05	.01
☐ 48	Jim Jackson	1.00	.45	.13
☐ 49	Jamal Mashburn	3.00	1.35	.40
☐ 50	Sean Rooks	.10	.05	.01
☐ 51	Doug Smith	.10	.05	.01
☐ 52	Mahmoud Abdul-Rauf	.15	.07	.02
☐ 53	Kevin Brooks	.10	.05	.01
☐ 54	LaPhonso Ellis	.15	.07	.02
☐ 55	Mark Macon	.10	.05	.01
☐ 56	Dikembe Mutombo	.40	.18	.05
☐ 57	Rodney Rogers	.60	.25	.08
☐ 58	Bryant Stith	.10	.05	.01
☐ 59	Reggie Williams	.10	.05	.01
☐ 60	Joe Dumars	.25	.11	.03
☐ 61	Sean Elliott	.15	.07	.02
☐ 62	Bill Laimbeer	.15	.07	.02
☐ 63	Terry Mills	.10	.05	.01
☐ 64	Olden Polynice	.10	.05	.01
☐ 65	Alvin Robertson	.10	.05	.01
☐ 66	Isiah Thomas	.25	.11	.03
☐ 67	Victor Alexander	.10	.05	.01
☐ 68	Chris Gatling	.10	.05	.01
☐ 69	Tim Hardaway	.20	.09	.03
☐ 70	Byron Houston	.10	.05	.01
☐ 71	Sarunas Marciulionis	.10	.05	.01
☐ 72	Chris Mullin	.20	.09	.03
☐ 73	Billy Owens	.15	.07	.02
☐ 74	Latrell Sprewell	1.00	.45	.13
☐ 75	Chris Webber	2.50	1.15	.30
☐ 76	Scott Brooks	.10	.05	.01
☐ 77	Matt Bullard	.10	.05	.01
☐ 78	Sam Cassell	.75	.35	.09
☐ 79	Mario Elie	.10	.05	.01
☐ 80	Carl Herrera	.10	.05	.01
☐ 81	Robert Horry	.20	.09	.03
☐ 82	Vernon Maxwell	.10	.05	.01
☐ 83	Hakeem Olajuwon	1.25	.55	.16
☐ 84	Kenny Smith	.10	.05	.01
☐ 85	Otis Thorpe	.15	.07	.02
☐ 86	Dale Davis	.15	.07	.02
☐ 87	Vern Fleming	.10	.05	.01
☐ 88	Scott Haskin	.10	.05	.01
☐ 89	Reggie Miller	.50	.23	.06
☐ 90	Sam Mitchell	.10	.05	.01
☐ 91	Pooh Richardson	.10	.05	.01
☐ 92	Detlef Schrempf	.20	.09	.03
☐ 93	Malik Sealy	.10	.05	.01
☐ 94	Rik Smits	.20	.09	.03
☐ 95	Terry Dehere	.15	.07	.02
☐ 96	Ron Harper	.15	.07	.02
☐ 97	Mark Jackson	.10	.05	.01
☐ 98	Danny Manning	.20	.09	.03
☐ 99	Stanley Roberts	.10	.05	.01
☐ 100	Loy Vaught	.15	.07	.02
☐ 101	John Williams	.10	.05	.01
☐ 102	Sam Bowie	.10	.05	.01
☐ 103	Elden Campbell	.10	.05	.01
☐ 104	Doug Christie	.10	.05	.01
☐ 105	Vlade Divac	.20	.09	.03
☐ 106	James Edwards	.10	.05	.01
☐ 107	George Lynch	.15	.07	.02
☐ 108	Anthony Peeler	.10	.05	.01
☐ 109	Sedale Threatt	.10	.05	.01
☐ 110	James Worthy	.20	.09	.03
☐ 111	Bimbo Coles	.10	.05	.01
☐ 112	Grant Long	.10	.05	.01
☐ 113	Harold Miner	.10	.05	.01
☐ 114	Glen Rice	.20	.09	.03
☐ 115	John Salley	.10	.05	.01
☐ 116	Rony Seikaly	.10	.05	.01
☐ 117	Brian Shaw	.10	.05	.01
☐ 118	Steve Smith	.15	.07	.02
☐ 119	Anthony Avent	.10	.05	.01
☐ 120	Vin Baker	1.50	.65	.19
☐ 121	Jon Barry	.10	.05	.01
☐ 122	Frank Brickowski	.10	.05	.01
☐ 123	Todd Day	.15	.07	.02
☐ 124	Blue Edwards	.10	.05	.01
☐ 125	Brad Lohaus	.10	.05	.01
☐ 126	Lee Mayberry	.10	.05	.01
☐ 127	Eric Murdock	.10	.05	.01
☐ 128	Ken Norman	.10	.05	.01
☐ 129	Thurl Bailey	.10	.05	.01
☐ 130	Mike Brown	.10	.05	.01
☐ 131	Christian Laettner	.20	.09	.03
☐ 132	Luc Longley	.10	.05	.01
☐ 133	Chuck Person	.15	.07	.02
☐ 134	Chris Smith	.10	.05	.01
☐ 135	Doug West	.10	.05	.01
☐ 136	Micheal Williams	.10	.05	.01
☐ 137	Kenny Anderson	.20	.09	.03
☐ 138	Benoit Benjamin	.10	.05	.01
☐ 139	Derrick Coleman	.20	.09	.03
☐ 140	Armon Gilliam	.10	.05	.01
☐ 141	Rick Mahorn	.10	.05	.01
☐ 142	Chris Morris	.10	.05	.01
☐ 143	Rumeal Robinson	.10	.05	.01
☐ 144	Rex Walters	.15	.07	.02
☐ 145	Greg Anthony	.10	.05	.01
☐ 146	Rolando Blackman	.15	.07	.02
☐ 147	Tony Campbell	.10	.05	.01
☐ 148	Hubert Davis	.10	.05	.01
☐ 149	Patrick Ewing	.50	.23	.06
☐ 150	Anthony Mason	.15	.07	.02
☐ 151	Charles Oakley	.15	.07	.02
☐ 152	Doc Rivers	.10	.05	.01
☐ 153	Charles Smith	.10	.05	.01
☐ 154	John Starks	.15	.07	.02
☐ 155	Herb Williams	.10	.05	.01
☐ 156	Nick Anderson	.15	.07	.02
☐ 157	Anthony Bowie	.10	.05	.01
☐ 158	Litterial Green	.10	.05	.01
☐ 159	Anfernee Hardaway	6.00	2.70	.75
☐ 160	Shaquille O'Neal	4.00	1.80	.50
☐ 161	Donald Royal	.10	.05	.01
☐ 162	Dennis Scott	.10	.05	.01
☐ 163	Scott Skiles	.10	.05	.01

☐ 164	Jeff Turner	.10	.05	.01
☐ 165	Dana Barros	.20	.09	.03
☐ 166	Shawn Bradley	.60	.25	.08
☐ 167	Johnny Dawkins	.10	.05	.01
☐ 168	Greg Graham	.10	.05	.01
☐ 169	Jeff Hornacek	.15	.07	.02
☐ 170	Moses Malone	.25	.11	.03
☐ 171	Tim Perry	.10	.05	.01
☐ 172	Clarence Weatherspoon	.20	.09	.03
☐ 173	Danny Ainge	.15	.07	.02
☐ 174	Charles Barkley	1.00	.45	.13
☐ 175	Cedric Ceballos	.20	.09	.03
☐ 176	A.C. Green	.20	.09	.03
☐ 177	Frank Johnson	.10	.05	.01
☐ 178	Kevin Johnson	.25	.11	.03
☐ 179	Negele Knight	.10	.05	.01
☐ 180	Malcolm Mackey	.10	.05	.01
☐ 181	Dan Majerle	.15	.07	.02
☐ 182	Oliver Miller	.15	.07	.02
☐ 183	Mark West	.10	.05	.01
☐ 184	Clyde Drexler	.50	.23	.06
☐ 185	Chris Dudley	.10	.05	.01
☐ 186	Harvey Grant	.10	.05	.01
☐ 187	Jerome Kersey	.10	.05	.01
☐ 188	Terry Porter	.15	.07	.02
☐ 189	Clifford Robinson	.15	.07	.02
☐ 190	James Robinson	.25	.11	.03
☐ 191	Rod Strickland	.15	.07	.02
☐ 192	Buck Williams	.15	.07	.02
☐ 193	Randy Brown	.10	.05	.01
☐ 194	Duane Causwell	.10	.05	.01
☐ 195	Bobby Hurley	.30	.14	.04
☐ 196	Mitch Richmond	.25	.11	.03
☐ 197	Lionel Simmons	.10	.05	.01
☐ 198	Wayman Tisdale	.15	.07	.02
☐ 199	Spud Webb	.15	.07	.02
☐ 200	Walt Williams	.20	.09	.03
☐ 201	Willie Anderson	.10	.05	.01
☐ 202	Antoine Carr	.10	.05	.01
☐ 203	Terry Cummings	.15	.07	.02
☐ 204	Lloyd Daniels	.10	.05	.01
☐ 205	Vinny Del Negro	.10	.05	.01
☐ 206	Sleepy Floyd	.10	.05	.01
☐ 207	Avery Johnson	.10	.05	.01
☐ 208	J.R. Reid	.10	.05	.01
☐ 209	David Robinson	1.00	.45	.13
☐ 210	Dennis Rodman	.30	.14	.04
☐ 211	Michael Cage	.10	.05	.01
☐ 212	Kendall Gill	.10	.05	.01
☐ 213	Ervin Johnson	.20	.09	.03
☐ 214	Shawn Kemp	1.00	.45	.13
☐ 215	Derrick McKey	.15	.07	.02
☐ 216	Nate McMillan	.10	.05	.01
☐ 217	Gary Payton	.20	.09	.03
☐ 218	Sam Perkins	.15	.07	.02
☐ 219	Ricky Pierce	.15	.07	.02
☐ 220	Isaac Austin	.10	.05	.01
☐ 221	David Benoit	.10	.05	.01
☐ 222	Tom Chambers	.15	.07	.02
☐ 223	Tyrone Corbin	.10	.05	.01
☐ 224	Mark Eaton	.10	.05	.01
☐ 225	Jay Humphries	.10	.05	.01
☐ 226	Jeff Malone	.15	.07	.02
☐ 227	Karl Malone	.50	.23	.06
☐ 228	John Stockton	.50	.23	.06
☐ 229	Luther Wright	.10	.05	.01
☐ 230	Michael Adams	.10	.05	.01
☐ 231	Calbert Cheaney	.75	.35	.09
☐ 232	Kevin Duckworth	.10	.05	.01
☐ 233	Pervis Ellison	.10	.05	.01
☐ 234	Tom Gugliotta	.20	.09	.03

☐ 235	Buck Johnson	.10	.05	.01
☐ 236	Doug Overton	.10	.05	.01
☐ 237	LaBradford Smith	.10	.05	.01
☐ 238	Larry Stewart	.10	.05	.01
☐ 239	Checklist	.10	.05	.01
☐ 240	Checklist	.10	.05	.01

1993-94 Jam Session Gamebreakers

Randomly inserted into 12-card packs at a rate of one in four, this eight-card 2 1/2" by 4 3/4" set features some of the NBA's top players. The borderless fronts feature color action cutouts on multicolored backgrounds highlighted by grid lines. The player's name appears in gold foil at the lower left. The back features a color player head shot with a screened background similar to the front. The player's name appears above the photo, career highlights appear below. The cards are numbered on the back as "X of 8."

		MINT	NRMT	EXC
	COMPLETE SET (8)	4.00	1.80	.50
	COMMON CARD (1-8)	.25	.11	.03
☐ 1	Charles Barkley Phoenix Suns	1.50	.65	.19
☐ 2	Tim Hardaway Golden State Warriors	.25	.11	.03
☐ 3	Kevin Johnson Phoenix Suns	.40	.18	.05
☐ 4	Dan Majerle Phoenix Suns	.25	.11	.03
☐ 5	Scottie Pippen Chicago Bulls	.75	.35	.09
☐ 6	Mark Price Cleveland Cavaliers	.25	.11	.03
☐ 7	John Starks New York Knicks	.25	.11	.03
☐ 8	Dominique Wilkins Atlanta Hawks	.40	.18	.05

1993-94
Jam Session
Rookie Standouts

Randomly inserted in 12-card packs at a rate of one in four, this oversized (2 1/2" by 4 3/4") eight-card set features borderless fronts with full-color player action photos. The player's name appears in gold-foil lettering in the lower left corner. The back features a color player action head shot with the player's statistics below. The cards are numbered on the back as "X of 8."

	MINT	NRMT	EXC
COMPLETE SET (8)	20.00	9.00	2.50
COMMON CARD (1-8)	.50	.23	.06
☐ 1 Vin Baker	2.50	1.15	.30
Milwaukee Bucks			
☐ 2 Shawn Bradley	1.00	.45	.13
Philadelphia 76ers			
☐ 3 Calbert Cheaney	1.25	.55	.16
Washington Bullets			
☐ 4 Anfernee Hardaway UER	10.00	4.50	1.25
Orlando Magic			
(Text states he drafted after			
senior year instead of junior)			
☐ 5 Bobby Hurley	.50	.23	.06
Sacramento Kings			
☐ 6 Jamal Mashburn	5.00	2.30	.60
Dallas Mavericks			
☐ 7 Rodney Rogers	1.00	.45	.13
Denver Nuggets			
☐ 8 Chris Webber	4.00	1.80	.50
Golden State Warriors			

1993-94
Jam Session
Second Year Stars

Randomly inserted into Jam Session 12-card packs at a rate of one in four, this

eight-card 2 1/2" by 4 3/4" set features some of the NBA's top second-year players. The borderless fronts feature a color action cutout on a rainbow-colored background. The player's name appears in gold foil in the lower right. The back features a color player head shot with screened rainbow background. The players name appears above the photo with a player profile displayed below. The cards are numbered on the back as "X of 8."*

	MINT	NRMT	EXC
COMPLETE SET (8)	8.00	3.60	1.00
COMMON CARD (1-8)	.25	.11	.03
☐ 1 Tom Gugliotta	.50	.23	.06
Washington Bullets			
☐ 2 Jim Jackson	1.50	.65	.19
Dallas Mavericks			
☐ 3 Christian Laettner	.50	.23	.06
Minnesota Timberwolves			
☐ 4 Oliver Miller	.25	.11	.03
Phoenix Suns			
☐ 5 Harold Miner	.25	.11	.03
Miami Heat			
☐ 6 Alonzo Mourning	1.50	.65	.19
Charlotte Hornets			
☐ 7 Shaquille O'Neal	6.00	2.70	.75
Orlando Magic			
☐ 8 Walt Williams	.50	.23	.06
Sacramento Kings			

1993-94
Jam Session
Slam Dunk Heroes

Randomly inserted in 12-card Jam Session packs at a rate of one in four, this eight-card 2 1/2" by 4 3/4" set features some of the NBA's top slam dunkers. The borderless fronts feature color action cutouts on multicolored posterized background. The player's name appears vertically in gold foil near the bottom. The back features a color player head shot. The player's name

appears above the photo, a player profile is displayed below. The cards are numbered on the back as "X of 8."

cards. The cards were issued in 12-card packs with 36 packs per box. Each pack has one card from one of the four insert sets. Suggested retail price was $1.59 per pack. The fronts have full-bleed color action photos that are tightly cropped so the player takes up a larger percentage of the card than in most sets. The NBA Jam Session logo is superimposed on the lower right corner and the player's name and team is just above it in the teams color. The backs have color-action photos on the right side with statistics and information on the left that is set against the color of the player's team. The entire card is UV coated as are all the insert sets. The cards are numbered on the back, grouped alphabetically within teams, and checklisted below alphabetically according to teams as follows: Atlanta Hawks (1-6), Boston Celtics (7-16), Charlotte Hornets (17-24), Chicago Bulls (25-31), Cleveland Cavaliers (32-39), Dallas Mavericks (40-44), Denver Nuggets (45-52), Detroit Pistons (53-60), Golden State Warriors (61-67), Houston Rockets (68-75), Indiana Pacers (76-83), Los Angeles Clippers (84-88), Los Angeles Lakers (89-97), Miami Heat (98-103), Milwaukee Bucks (104-108), Minnesota Timberwolves (109-114), New Jersey Nets (115-121), New York Knicks (122-131), Orlando Magic (132-138), Philadelphia 76ers (139-145), Phoenix Suns (146-154), Portland Trail Blazers (155-161), Sacramento Kings (162-167), San Antonio Spurs (168-176), Seattle Supersonics (177-183), Utah Jazz (184-190), and Washington Bullets (191-197).

	MINT	NRMT	EXC
COMPLETE SET (8)	12.00	5.50	1.50
COMMON CARD (1-8)	.75	.35	.09
☐ 1 Patrick Ewing New York Knicks	.75	.35	.09
☐ 2 Larry Johnson Charlotte Hornets	.75	.35	.09
☐ 3 Shawn Kemp Seattle Supersonics	1.50	.65	.19
☐ 4 Karl Malone Utah Jazz	.75	.35	.09
☐ 5 Alonzo Mourning Charlotte Hornets	1.50	.65	.19
☐ 6 Hakeem Olajuwon Houston Rockets	2.00	.90	.25
☐ 7 Shaquille O'Neal Orlando Magic	6.00	2.70	.75
☐ 8 David Robinson San Antonio Spurs	1.50	.65	.19

1994-95 Jam Session

The complete 1994-95 Jam Session set consists of 200 oversized (2 1/2" by 4 3/4")

	MINT	NRMT	EXC
COMPLETE SET (200)	30.00	13.50	3.80
COMMON CARD (1-200)	.10	.05	.01
☐ 1 Stacey Augmon	.15	.07	.02
☐ 2 Mookie Blaylock	.15	.07	.02
☐ 3 Tyrone Corbin	.10	.05	.01
☐ 4 Craig Ehlo	.10	.05	.01
☐ 5 Ken Norman	.10	.05	.01
☐ 6 Kevin Willis	.15	.07	.02
☐ 7 Dee Brown	.15	.07	.02
☐ 8 Sherman Douglas	.10	.05	.01
☐ 9 Acie Earl	.10	.05	.01
☐ 10 Blue Edwards	.10	.05	.01
☐ 11 Pervis Ellison	.10	.05	.01
☐ 12 Rick Fox	.10	.05	.01
☐ 13 Xavier McDaniel	.15	.07	.02
☐ 14 Eric Montross	.75	.35	.09
☐ 15 Dino Radja	.20	.09	.03
☐ 16 Dominique Wilkins	.25	.11	.03
☐ 17 Michael Adams	.10	.05	.01
☐ 18 Muggsy Bogues	.20	.09	.03
☐ 19 Dell Curry	.10	.05	.01
☐ 20 Kenny Gattison	.10	.05	.01
☐ 21 Hersey Hawkins	.15	.07	.02
☐ 22 Larry Johnson	.40	.18	.05
☐ 23 Alonzo Mourning	.60	.25	.08
☐ 24 Robert Parish	.20	.09	.03
☐ 25 B.J. Armstrong	.10	.05	.01
☐ 26 Ron Harper	.15	.07	.02
☐ 27 Steve Kerr	.10	.05	.01
☐ 28 Toni Kukoc	.20	.09	.03

☐ 29	Pete Myers	.10	.05	.01
☐ 30	Will Perdue	.10	.05	.01
☐ 31	Scottie Pippen	.50	.23	.06
☐ 32	Terrell Brandon	.10	.05	.01
☐ 33	Michael Cage	.10	.05	.01
☐ 34	Brad Daugherty	.15	.07	.02
☐ 35	Chris Mills	.20	.09	.03
☐ 36	Bobby Phills	.10	.05	.01
☐ 37	Mark Price	.20	.09	.03
☐ 38	Gerald Wilkins	.10	.05	.01
☐ 39	John Williams	.15	.07	.02
☐ 40	Jim Jackson	.60	.25	.08
☐ 41	Jason Kidd	5.00	2.30	.60
☐ 42	Jamal Mashburn	1.00	.45	.13
☐ 43	Sean Rooks	.10	.05	.01
☐ 44	Doug Smith	.10	.05	.01
☐ 45	Mahmoud Abdul-Rauf	.10	.05	.01
☐ 46	LaPhonso Ellis	.10	.05	.01
☐ 47	Dikembe Mutombo	.30	.14	.04
☐ 48	Robert Pack	.10	.05	.01
☐ 49	Rodney Rogers	.20	.09	.03
☐ 50	Jalen Rose	1.00	.45	.13
☐ 51	Bryant Stith	.10	.05	.01
☐ 52	Reggie Williams	.10	.05	.01
☐ 53	Bill Curley	.25	.11	.03
☐ 54	Joe Dumars	.25	.11	.03
☐ 55	Grant Hill	8.00	3.60	1.00
☐ 56	Allan Houston	.20	.09	.03
☐ 57	Lindsey Hunter	.10	.05	.01
☐ 58	Oliver Miller	.10	.05	.01
☐ 59	Terry Mills	.10	.05	.01
☐ 60	Mark West	.10	.05	.01
☐ 61	Chris Gatling	.10	.05	.01
☐ 62	Tim Hardaway	.20	.09	.03
☐ 63	Chris Mullin	.20	.09	.03
☐ 64	Billy Owens	.15	.07	.02
☐ 65	Ricky Pierce	.15	.07	.02
☐ 66	Latrell Sprewell	.60	.25	.08
☐ 67	Chris Webber	.75	.35	.09
☐ 68	Sam Cassell	.20	.09	.03
☐ 69	Mario Elie	.10	.05	.01
☐ 70	Carl Herrera	.10	.05	.01
☐ 71	Robert Horry	.20	.09	.03
☐ 72	Vernon Maxwell	.10	.05	.01
☐ 73	Hakeem Olajuwon	1.25	.55	.16
☐ 74	Kenny Smith	.10	.05	.01
☐ 75	Otis Thorpe	.15	.07	.02
☐ 76	Antonio Davis	.10	.05	.01
☐ 77	Dale Davis	.15	.07	.02
☐ 78	Mark Jackson	.10	.05	.01
☐ 79	Derrick McKey	.15	.07	.02
☐ 80	Reggie Miller	.50	.23	.06
☐ 81	Byron Scott	.15	.07	.02
☐ 82	Rik Smits	.20	.09	.03
☐ 83	Haywoode Workman	.10	.05	.01
☐ 84	Gary Grant	.10	.05	.01
☐ 85	Pooh Richardson	.10	.05	.01
☐ 86	Stanley Roberts	.10	.05	.01
☐ 87	Elmore Spencer	.10	.05	.01
☐ 88	Loy Vaught	.10	.05	.01
☐ 89	Elden Campbell	.10	.05	.01
☐ 90	Cedric Ceballos	.20	.09	.03
☐ 91	Doug Christie	.10	.05	.01
☐ 92	Vlade Divac	.20	.09	.03
☐ 93	Eddie Jones	3.00	1.35	.40
☐ 94	George Lynch	.10	.05	.01
☐ 95	Anthony Peeler	.10	.05	.01
☐ 96	Nick Van Exel	1.00	.45	.13
☐ 97	James Worthy	.20	.09	.03
☐ 98	Grant Long	.10	.05	.01
☐ 99	Harold Miner	.10	.05	.01
☐ 100	Glen Rice	.20	.09	.03
☐ 101	John Salley	.10	.05	.01
☐ 102	Rony Seikaly	.10	.05	.01
☐ 103	Steve Smith	.15	.07	.02
☐ 104	Vin Baker	.50	.23	.06
☐ 105	Jon Barry	.10	.05	.01
☐ 106	Todd Day	.10	.05	.01
☐ 107	Lee Mayberry	.10	.05	.01
☐ 108	Eric Murdock	.10	.05	.01
☐ 109	Stacey King	.10	.05	.01
☐ 110	Christian Laettner	.15	.07	.02
☐ 111	Donyell Marshall	1.00	.45	.13
☐ 112	Isaiah Rider	.30	.14	.04
☐ 113	Doug West	.10	.05	.01
☐ 114	Micheal Williams	.10	.05	.01
☐ 115	Kenny Anderson	.20	.09	.03
☐ 116	P.J. Brown	.10	.05	.01
☐ 117	Derrick Coleman	.20	.09	.03
☐ 118	Yinka Dare	.15	.07	.02
☐ 119	Kevin Edwards	.10	.05	.01
☐ 120	Armon Gilliam	.10	.05	.01
☐ 121	Chris Morris	.10	.05	.01
☐ 122	Anthony Bonner	.10	.05	.01
☐ 123	Hubert Davis	.10	.05	.01
☐ 124	Patrick Ewing	.50	.23	.06
☐ 125	Derek Harper	.15	.07	.02
☐ 126	Anthony Mason	.10	.05	.01
☐ 127	Charles Oakley	.15	.07	.02
☐ 128	Doc Rivers	.10	.05	.01
☐ 129	Charles Smith	.10	.05	.01
☐ 130	John Starks	.15	.07	.02
☐ 131	Charlie Ward	.40	.18	.05
☐ 132	Nick Anderson	.15	.07	.02
☐ 133	Anthony Bowie	.10	.05	.01
☐ 134	Horace Grant	.25	.11	.03
☐ 135	Anfernee Hardaway	2.00	.90	.25
☐ 136	Shaquille O'Neal	2.50	1.15	.30
☐ 137	Dennis Scott	.10	.05	.01
☐ 138	Jeff Turner	.10	.05	.01
☐ 139	Dana Barros	.20	.09	.03
☐ 140	Shawn Bradley	.20	.09	.03
☐ 141	Johnny Dawkins	.10	.05	.01
☐ 142	Jeff Malone	.15	.07	.02
☐ 143	Tim Perry	.10	.05	.01
☐ 144	Clarence Weatherspoon	.15	.07	.02
☐ 145	Scott Williams	.10	.05	.01
☐ 146	Danny Ainge	.15	.07	.02
☐ 147	Charles Barkley	1.00	.45	.13
☐ 148	A.C. Green	.20	.09	.03
☐ 149	Kevin Johnson	.25	.11	.03
☐ 150	Joe Kleine	.10	.05	.01
☐ 151	Antonio Lang	.15	.07	.02
☐ 152	Dan Majerle	.15	.07	.02
☐ 153	Danny Manning	.20	.09	.03
☐ 154	Wayman Tisdale	.15	.07	.02
☐ 155	Clyde Drexler	.50	.23	.06
☐ 156	Harvey Grant	.10	.05	.01
☐ 157	Tracy Murray	.10	.05	.01
☐ 158	Terry Porter	.15	.07	.02
☐ 159	Clifford Robinson	.15	.07	.02
☐ 160	Rod Strickland	.15	.07	.02
☐ 161	Buck Williams	.15	.07	.02
☐ 162	Bobby Hurley	.15	.07	.02
☐ 163	Olden Polynice	.10	.05	.01
☐ 164	Mitch Richmond	.25	.11	.03
☐ 165	Lionel Simmons	.10	.05	.01
☐ 166	Spud Webb	.15	.07	.02
☐ 167	Walt Williams	.15	.07	.02
☐ 168	Willie Anderson	.10	.05	.01
☐ 169	Terry Cummings	.15	.07	.02
☐ 170	Vinny Del Negro	.10	.05	.01

☐ 171	Sean Elliott	.15	.07	.02
☐ 172	Avery Johnson	.10	.05	.01
☐ 173	Chuck Person	.15	.07	.02
☐ 174	J.R. Reid	.10	.05	.01
☐ 175	David Robinson	1.00	.45	.13
☐ 176	Dennis Rodman	.30	.14	.04
☐ 177	Bill Cartwright	.10	.05	.01
☐ 178	Kendall Gill	.10	.05	.01
☐ 179	Shawn Kemp	1.00	.45	.13
☐ 180	Nate McMillan	.10	.05	.01
☐ 181	Gary Payton	.20	.09	.03
☐ 182	Sam Perkins	.15	.07	.02
☐ 183	Detlef Schrempf	.20	.09	.03
☐ 184	David Benoit	.10	.05	.01
☐ 185	Jeff Hornacek	.15	.07	.02
☐ 186	Jay Humphries	.10	.05	.01
☐ 187	Karl Malone	.50	.23	.06
☐ 188	Bryon Russell	.10	.05	.01
☐ 189	Felton Spencer	.10	.05	.01
☐ 190	John Stockton	.50	.23	.06
☐ 191	Mitchell Butler	.10	.05	.01
☐ 192	Rex Chapman	.10	.05	.01
☐ 193	Calbert Cheaney	.20	.09	.03
☐ 194	Tom Gugliotta	.15	.07	.02
☐ 195	Don MacLean	.10	.05	.01
☐ 196	Gheorghe Muresan	.15	.07	.02
☐ 197	Scott Skiles	.10	.05	.01
☐ 198	Checklist	.10	.05	.01
☐ 199	Checklist	.10	.05	.01
☐ 200	Checklist	.10	.05	.01

right corner. The backs have color action photos and information explaining why he is a "Flashing star." The cards are numbered on the back as "X of 8."

	MINT	NRMT	EXC
COMPLETE SET (8)	6.00	2.70	.75
COMMON CARD (1-8)	.25	.11	.03

☐ 1	Anfernee Hardaway Orlando Magic	4.00	1.80	.50
☐ 2	Robert Horry Houston Rockets	.50	.23	.06
☐ 3	Dan Majerle Phoenix Suns	.25	.11	.03
☐ 4	Reggie Miller Indiana Pacers	1.00	.45	.13
☐ 5	Mitch Richmond Sacramento Kings	.50	.23	.06
☐ 6	Isaiah Rider Minnesota Timberwolves	.60	.25	.08
☐ 7	Latrell Sprewell Golden State Warriors	1.25	.55	.16
☐ 8	Dominique Wilkins Boston Celtics	.50	.23	.06

1994-95 Jam Session Gamebreakers

1994-95 Jam Session Flashing Stars

This eight card oversized (2 1/2" by 4 3/4") set was randomly inserted in 12-card packs at a rate of approximately one in two. The set is composed of the flashiest players in the game like Anfernee Hardaway and Reggie Miller. The fronts have full-bleed color action photos similar to the regular set but the background has swirling colors. The player's name and words "Flashing Star" are in gold foil at the bottom. The NBA Jam Session logo is superimposed on the upper

This eight card oversized (2 1/2" by 4 3/4") set was randomly inserted in 12-card packs at a rate of one in four. The set is composed of players who can take control of the game. The fronts have full-bleed color action photos similar to the regular set but the background is a basketball going through a net. The player image is also pushed out slightly which can also be seen from the back to give it a 3-D look. The NBA Jam Session logo is superimposed on the upper right corner. The backs have three layers to it. The background has two colors that are different on each card. A full-color action photo of the player is the middle layer. Up front is the player name in the middle and player information is a hazy white box underneath. The cards are numbered on the back as "X of 8."

color action photo also on a painted background and information on the rookie particularly about his college career. The cards are numbered on the back as "X of 20."

	MINT	NRMT	EXC
COMPLETE SET (8)	12.00	5.50	1.50
COMMON CARD (1-8)	1.00	.45	.13

		MINT	NRMT	EXC
☐ 1	Charles Barkley	2.00	.90	.25
	Phoenix Suns			
☐ 2	Patrick Ewing	1.00	.45	.13
	New York Knicks			
☐ 3	Karl Malone	1.00	.45	.13
	Utah Jazz			
☐ 4	Alonzo Mourning	1.25	.55	.16
	Charlotte Hornets			
☐ 5	Hakeem Olajuwon	2.50	1.15	.30
	Houston Rockets			
☐ 6	Shaquille O'Neal	5.00	2.30	.60
	Orlando Magic			
☐ 7	Scottie Pippen	1.00	.45	.13
	Chicago Bulls			
☐ 8	David Robinson	2.00	.90	.25
	San Antonio Spurs			

	MINT	NRMT	EXC
COMPLETE SET (20)	16.00	7.25	2.00
COMMON CARD (1-20)	.15	.07	.02

		MINT	NRMT	EXC
☐ 1	Brian Grant	1.00	.45	.13
☐ 2	Grant Hill	5.00	2.30	.60
☐ 3	Juwan Howard	1.25	.55	.16
☐ 4	Eddie Jones	2.00	.90	.25
☐ 5	Jason Kidd	3.00	1.35	.40
☐ 6	Donyell Marshall	.60	.25	.08
☐ 7	Eric Montross	.50	.23	.06
☐ 8	Lamond Murray	.50	.23	.06
☐ 9	Wesley Person	.60	.25	.08
☐ 10	Khalid Reeves	.50	.23	.06
☐ 11	Glenn Robinson	3.00	1.35	.40
☐ 12	Carlos Rogers	.25	.11	.03
☐ 13	Jalen Rose	.60	.25	.08
☐ 14	Clifford Rozier	.25	.11	.03
☐ 15	Dickey Simpkins	.15	.07	.02
☐ 16	Michael Smith	.25	.11	.03
☐ 17	Anthony Tucker	.15	.07	.02
☐ 18	Charlie Ward	.25	.11	.03
☐ 19	Monty Williams	.15	.07	.02
☐ 20	Sharone Wright	.40	.18	.05

1994-95 Jam Session Rookie Standouts

This 20-card oversized (2 1/2" by 4 3/4") set was available exclusively via mail. Information on obtaining the set was on the packs and you had to pay $3.95 to receive it. The wrapper offer expired on June 30th, 1995. The set contains a selection of the top rookies from the 1994-95 season. The fronts have full-bleed color action photos on a painted background with a black and white action photo in the looming behind. The NBA Jam Session logo is superimposed on the upper left corner. The player's name and the "Rookie Standout" with a basketball under it are in gold foil at the bottom of the card. The backs have a full

1994-95 Jam Session Second Year Stars

This eight card oversized (2 1/2" by 4 3/4") set was randomly inserted in 12-card packs at a rate of one in four. The set consists of the best rookies from the 93-94 crop. The fronts are laid out horizontally and have full-bleed color action photos. The player is surrounded by a glowing yellow. The background has a close-up of his face from the action shot and copies of the shot in television screens behind that. The bottom says the player's name and "Second Year Star"

in gold foil. The backs are laid out vertically with a full color action photo also surrounded by a glowing yellow on the left with player information on the right. The background is the same player photo set in numerous television screens similar to the front. The cards are numbered on the back as "X of 8."

	MINT	NRMT	EXC
COMPLETE SET (8)	8.00	3.60	1.00
COMMON CARD (1-8)	.50	.23	.06
☐ 1 Vin Baker	1.00	.45	.13
Milwaukee Bucks			
☐ 2 Anfernee Hardaway	4.00	1.80	.50
Orlando Magic			
☐ 3 Lindsey Hunter	.50	.23	.06
Detroit Pistons			
☐ 4 Toni Kukoc	.75	.35	.09
Chicago Bulls			
☐ 5 Jamal Mashburn	2.00	.90	.25
Dallas Mavericks			
☐ 6 Dino Radja	.75	.35	.09
Boston Celtics			
☐ 7 Isaiah Rider	.60	.25	.08
Minnesota Timberwolves			
☐ 8 Chris Webber	1.50	.65	.19
Golden State Warriors			

1994-95
Jam Session
Slam Dunk Heroes

Cards from this eight-card oversized (2 1/2" by 4 3/4") set were randomly inserted in packs at a rate of one in 36. The set is made up of players who jam with authority, namely centers and forwards. The cards have a 100% etched foil design. The fronts have a full color action photo with the player's name and the words "Slam Dunk Hero" boxing in a net are at the bottom in gold foil. The backs have a fuller color action photo on the left with player information on the right.

right. The background on both the fronts and backs have a psychedelic look to it with basketballs floating about. The cards are numbered on the back as "X of 8."

	MINT	NRMT	EXC
COMPLETE SET (8)	80.00	36.00	10.00
COMMON CARD (1-8)	4.00	1.80	.50
☐ 1 Charles Barkley	12.00	5.50	1.50
Phoenix Suns			
☐ 2 Larry Johnson	5.00	2.30	.60
Charlotte Hornets			
☐ 3 Shawn Kemp	12.00	5.50	1.50
Seattle Supersonics			
☐ 4 Jamal Mashburn	12.00	5.50	1.50
Dallas Mavericks			
☐ 5 Dikembe Mutombo	4.00	1.80	.50
Denver Nuggets			
☐ 6 Hakeem Olajuwon	15.00	6.75	1.90
Houston Rockets			
☐ 7 Shaquille O'Neal	30.00	13.50	3.80
Orlando Magic			
☐ 8 Chris Webber	10.00	4.50	1.25
Golden State Warriors			

1990-91 SkyBox

This 1990-91 set marks SkyBox's entry into the basketball card market. The complete set contains 423 cards featuring NBA players. The set was released in two series of 300 and 123 cards, respectively. Foil packs for each series contained 15 cards. However, the second series packs contained a mix of players from both series. The second series cards replaced 123 cards from the first series, which then became short-prints compared to other cards in the first series. The cards measure the standard size (2 1/2" by 3 1/2"). The front features an action shot of the player on a computer-generated background of various color schemes. The player's name appears in a black stripe at the bottom with the team logo superimposed at the left lower corner. The photo is bordered in gold. The back presents head shots of the player with gold borders on white background. Player statistics are given in a box below the photo. The cards are numbered on the back and checklisted below alphabetically *according to team names as follows: Atlanta Hawks (1-12), Boston Celtics (13-24), Charlotte Hornets (25-36), Chicago Bulls (37-47), Cleveland Cavaliers (48-58), Dallas Mavericks (59-70), Denver Nuggets (71-81), Detroit Pistons (82-93), Golden State Warriors (94-104), Houston Rockets (105-113), Indiana Pacers (114-123), Los Angeles Clippers (124-133), Los Angeles Lakers (134-143), Miami Heat (144-154), Milwaukee Bucks (155-166), Minnesota Timberwolves (167-175), New Jersey Nets (176-185), New York Knicks (186-197), Orlando Magic (198-209), Philadelphia 76ers (210-219), Phoenix Suns (220-230), Portland Trail Blazers (231-241), Sacramento Kings (242-251), San Antonio Spurs (252-262), Seattle Supersonics (263-273), Utah Jazz (274-284), Washington Bullets (285-294), Coaches (301-327), Team Checklists (328-354), Lottery Picks (355-365), Updates (366-420), and Checklists (421-423). Rookie Cards included in the set are Nick Anderson, B.J. Armstrong, Mookie Blaylock, Derrick Coleman, Vlade Divac, Sherman Douglas, Sean Elliott, Kendall Gill, Tim Hardaway, Chris Jackson, Shawn Kemp, Gary Payton, Drazen Petrovic, Glen Rice, Cliff Robinson, Dennis Scott, Lionel Simmons and Doug West. First series single prints (SP) are noted below.*

	MINT	NRMT	EXC
COMPLETE SET (423)	20.00	9.00	2.50
COMPLETE SERIES 1 (300)	12.00	5.50	1.50
COMPLETE SERIES 2 (123)	8.00	3.60	1.00
COMMON CARD (1-300)	.05	.02	.01
COMMON CARD (301-423)	.10	.05	.01

☐ 1	John Battle	.05	.02	.01
☐ 2	Duane Ferrell SP	.10	.05	.01
☐ 3	Jon Koncak	.05	.02	.01
☐ 4	Cliff Levingston SP	.10	.05	.01
☐ 5	John Long SP	.10	.05	.01
☐ 6	Moses Malone	.20	.09	.03
☐ 7	Doc Rivers	.08	.04	.01
☐ 8	Kenny Smith SP	.10	.05	.01
☐ 9	Alexander Volkov	.05	.02	.01
☐ 10	Spud Webb	.08	.04	.01
☐ 11	Dominique Wilkins	.20	.09	.03
☐ 12	Kevin Willis	.08	.04	.01
☐ 13	John Bagley	.05	.02	.01
☐ 14	Larry Bird	1.25	.55	.16
☐ 15	Kevin Gamble	.05	.02	.01
☐ 16	Dennis Johnson SP	.15	.07	.02
☐ 17	Joe Kleine	.05	.02	.01
☐ 18	Reggie Lewis	.10	.05	.01
☐ 19	Kevin McHale	.10	.05	.01
☐ 20	Robert Parish	.10	.05	.01
☐ 21	Jim Paxson SP	.10	.05	.01
☐ 22	Ed Pinckney	.05	.02	.01
☐ 23	Brian Shaw	.05	.02	.01
☐ 24	Michael Smith	.05	.02	.01
☐ 25	Richard Anderson SP	.10	.05	.01
☐ 26	Tyrone Bogues	.10	.05	.01
☐ 27	Rex Chapman	.05	.02	.01
☐ 28	Dell Curry	.05	.02	.01
☐ 29	Armon Gilliam	.05	.02	.01
☐ 30	Michael Holton SP	.10	.05	.01
☐ 31	Dave Hoppen	.05	.02	.01
☐ 32	J.R. Reid	.10	.05	.01
☐ 33	Robert Reid SP	.10	.05	.01
☐ 34	Brian Rowsom SP	.10	.05	.01
☐ 35	Kelly Tripucka	.05	.02	.01
☐ 36	Micheal Williams SP UER (Misspelled Michael on card)	.10	.05	.01
☐ 37	B.J. Armstrong	.25	.11	.03
☐ 38	Bill Cartwright	.05	.02	.01
☐ 39	Horace Grant	.25	.11	.03
☐ 40	Craig Hodges	.05	.02	.01
☐ 41	Michael Jordan	5.00	2.30	.60
☐ 42	Stacey King	.08	.04	.01
☐ 43	Ed Nealy SP	.10	.05	.01
☐ 44	John Paxson	.05	.02	.01
☐ 45	Will Perdue	.05	.02	.01
☐ 46	Scottie Pippen	.50	.23	.06
☐ 47	Jeff Sanders SP	.10	.05	.01
☐ 48	Winston Bennett	.05	.02	.01
☐ 49	Chucky Brown	.05	.02	.01
☐ 50	Brad Daugherty	.08	.04	.01
☐ 51	Craig Ehlo	.08	.04	.01
☐ 52	Steve Kerr	.05	.02	.01
☐ 53	Paul Mokeski SP	.10	.05	.01
☐ 54	John Morton	.08	.04	.01
☐ 55	Larry Nance	.08	.04	.01
☐ 56	Mark Price	.10	.05	.01
☐ 57	Tree Rollins SP	.10	.05	.01
☐ 58	Hot Rod Williams	.05	.02	.01
☐ 59	Steve Alford	.08	.04	.01
☐ 60	Rolando Blackman	.08	.04	.01
☐ 61	Adrian Dantley	.15	.07	.02
☐ 62	Brad Davis	.05	.02	.01
☐ 63	James Donaldson	.05	.02	.01
☐ 64	Derek Harper	.08	.04	.01
☐ 65	Anthony Jones SP	.10	.05	.01
☐ 66	Sam Perkins	.15	.07	.02
☐ 67	Roy Tarpley	.05	.02	.01
☐ 68	Bill Wennington SP	.10	.05	.01
☐ 69	Randy White	.05	.02	.01
☐ 70	Herb Williams	.05	.02	.01
☐ 71	Michael Adams	.05	.02	.01
☐ 72	Joe Barry Carroll SP	.10	.05	.01
☐ 73	Walter Davis	.10	.05	.01
☐ 74	Alex English SP	.10	.05	.01
☐ 75	Bill Hanzlik	.10	.05	.01
☐ 76	Tim Kempton SP	.10	.05	.01
☐ 77	Jerome Lane	.05	.02	.01
☐ 78	Lafayette Lever SP	.10	.05	.01
☐ 79	Todd Lichti	.05	.02	.01
☐ 80	Blair Rasmussen	.05	.02	.01
☐ 81	Dan Schayes SP	.10	.05	.01
☐ 82	Mark Aguirre	.08	.04	.01
☐ 83	William Bedford	.05	.02	.01
☐ 84	Joe Dumars	.20	.09	.03
☐ 85	James Edwards	.05	.02	.01
☐ 86	David Greenwood SP	.10	.05	.01
☐ 87	Scott Hastings	.05	.02	.01
☐ 88	Gerald Henderson SP	.10	.05	.01
☐ 89	Vinnie Johnson	.08	.04	.01
☐ 90	Bill Laimbeer	.08	.04	.01
☐ 91	Dennis Rodman (SkyBox logo in upper right or left)	.30	.14	.04
☐ 91B	Dennis Rodman (SkyBox logo in upper left corner)	.08	.04	.01
☐ 92	John Salley	.05	.02	.01
☐ 93	Isiah Thomas	.20	.09	.03
☐ 94	Manute Bol SP	.10	.05	.01
☐ 95	Tim Hardaway	1.00	.45	.13

☐ 96 Rod Higgins	.05	.02	.01
☐ 97 Sarunas Marciulionis	.10	.05	.01
☐ 98 Chris Mullin	.10	.05	.01
☐ 99 Jim Petersen	.05	.02	.01
☐ 100 Mitch Richmond	.40	.18	.05
☐ 101 Mike Smrek	.05	.02	.01
☐ 102 Terry Teagle SP	.10	.05	.01
☐ 103 Tom Tolbert	.05	.02	.01
☐ 104 Kelvin Upshaw SP	.10	.05	.01
☐ 105 Anthony Bowie SP	.10	.05	.01
☐ 106 Adrian Caldwell	.05	.02	.01
☐ 107 Eric(Sleepy) Floyd	.05	.02	.01
☐ 108 Buck Johnson	.05	.02	.01
☐ 109 Vernon Maxwell	.05	.02	.01
☐ 110 Hakeem Olajuwon	1.00	.45	.13
☐ 111 Larry Smith	.05	.02	.01
☐ 112A Otis Thorpe ERR	.50	.23	.06
(Front photo actually Mitchell Wiggins)			
☐ 112B Otis Thorpe COR	.08	.04	.01
☐ 113A M. Wiggins SP ERR	.50	.23	.06
(Front photo actually Otis Thorpe)			
☐ 113B M. Wiggins SP COR	.10	.05	.01
☐ 114 Vern Fleming	.05	.02	.01
☐ 115 Rickey Green SP	.10	.05	.01
☐ 116 George McCloud	.08	.04	.01
☐ 117 Reggie Miller	.50	.23	.06
☐ 118A Dyron Nix SP ERR	1.50	.65	.19
(Back photo actually Wayman Tisdale)			
☐ 118B Dyron Nix SP COR	.10	.05	.01
☐ 119 Chuck Person	.08	.04	.01
☐ 120 Mike Sanders	.05	.02	.01
☐ 121 Detlef Schrempf	.10	.05	.01
☐ 122 Rik Smits	.10	.05	.01
☐ 123 LaSalle Thompson	.05	.02	.01
☐ 124 Benoit Benjamin	.05	.02	.01
☐ 125 Winston Garland	.05	.02	.01
☐ 126 Tom Garrick	.05	.02	.01
☐ 127 Gary Grant	.05	.02	.01
☐ 128 Ron Harper	.08	.04	.01
☐ 129 Danny Manning	.20	.09	.03
☐ 130 Jeff Martin	.05	.02	.01
☐ 131 Ken Norman	.05	.02	.01
☐ 132 Charles Smith	.05	.02	.01
☐ 133 Joe Wolf SP	.10	.05	.01
☐ 134 Michael Cooper SP	.15	.07	.02
☐ 135 Vlade Divac	.75	.35	.09
☐ 136 Larry Drew	.08	.04	.01
☐ 137 A.C. Green	.10	.05	.01
☐ 138 Magic Johnson	.75	.35	.09
☐ 139 Mark McNamara SP	.10	.05	.01
☐ 140 Byron Scott	.08	.04	.01
☐ 141 Mychal Thompson	.08	.04	.01
☐ 142 Orlando Woolridge SP	.10	.05	.01
☐ 143 James Worthy	.10	.05	.01
☐ 144 Terry Davis	.08	.04	.01
☐ 145 Sherman Douglas	.25	.11	.03
☐ 146 Kevin Edwards	.05	.02	.01
☐ 147 Tellis Frank SP	.10	.05	.01
☐ 148 Scott Haffner SP	.10	.05	.01
☐ 149 Grant Long	.05	.02	.01
☐ 150 Glen Rice	.75	.35	.09
☐ 151 Rony Seikaly	.05	.02	.01
☐ 152 Rory Sparrow SP	.10	.05	.01
☐ 153 Jon Sundvold	.05	.02	.01
☐ 154 Billy Thompson	.05	.02	.01
☐ 155 Greg Anderson	.05	.02	.01
☐ 156 Ben Coleman	.10	.05	.01
☐ 157 Jeff Grayer	.05	.02	.01
☐ 158 Jay Humphries	.05	.02	.01
☐ 159 Frank Kornet	.05	.02	.01
☐ 160 Larry Krystkowiak	.05	.02	.01
☐ 161 Brad Lohaus	.05	.02	.01
☐ 162 Ricky Pierce	.08	.04	.01
☐ 163 Paul Pressey SP	.10	.05	.01
☐ 164 Fred Roberts	.05	.02	.01
☐ 165 Alvin Robertson	.08	.02	.01
☐ 166 Jack Sikma	.08	.04	.01
☐ 167 Randy Breuer	.05	.02	.01
☐ 168 Tony Campbell	.05	.02	.01
☐ 169 Tyrone Corbin	.08	.04	.01
☐ 170 Sidney Lowe SP	.10	.05	.01
☐ 171 Sam Mitchell	.05	.02	.01
☐ 172 Tod Murphy	.05	.02	.01
☐ 173 Pooh Richardson	.25	.11	.03
☐ 174 Donald Royal SP	.30	.14	.04
☐ 175 Brad Sellers SP	.10	.05	.01
☐ 176 Mookie Blaylock	.60	.25	.08
☐ 177 Sam Bowie	.05	.02	.01
☐ 178 Lester Conner	.05	.02	.01
☐ 179 Derrick Gervin	.05	.02	.01
☐ 180 Jack Haley	.05	.02	.01
☐ 181 Roy Hinson	.05	.02	.01
☐ 182 Dennis Hopson SP	.10	.05	.01
☐ 183 Chris Morris	.05	.02	.01
☐ 184 Pete Myers SP	.10	.05	.01
☐ 185 Purvis Short SP	.10	.05	.01
☐ 186 Maurice Cheeks	.10	.05	.01
☐ 187 Patrick Ewing	.40	.18	.05
☐ 188 Stuart Gray	.05	.02	.01
☐ 189 Mark Jackson	.05	.02	.01
☐ 190 Johnny Newman SP	.10	.05	.01
☐ 191 Charles Oakley	.08	.04	.01
☐ 192 Brian Quinnett	.05	.02	.01
☐ 193 Trent Tucker	.05	.02	.01
☐ 194 Kiki Vandeweghe	.05	.02	.01
☐ 195 Kenny Walker	.05	.02	.01
☐ 196 Eddie Lee Wilkins	.05	.02	.01
☐ 197 Gerald Wilkins	.05	.02	.01
☐ 198 Mark Acres	.05	.02	.01
☐ 199 Nick Anderson	.60	.25	.08
☐ 200 Michael Ansley	.05	.02	.01
☐ 201 Terry Catledge	.05	.02	.01
☐ 202 Dave Corzine SP	.10	.05	.01
☐ 203 Sidney Green SP	.10	.05	.01
☐ 204 Jerry Reynolds	.05	.02	.01
☐ 205 Scott Skiles	.05	.02	.01
☐ 206 Otis Smith	.05	.02	.01
☐ 207 Reggie Theus SP	.15	.07	.02
☐ 208 Jeff Turner	.05	.02	.01
☐ 209 Sam Vincent	.05	.02	.01
☐ 210 Ron Anderson	.05	.02	.01
☐ 211 Charles Barkley	.75	.35	.09
☐ 212 Scott Brooks SP	.10	.05	.01
☐ 213 Lanard Copeland SP	.20	.09	.03
☐ 214 Johnny Dawkins	.05	.02	.01
☐ 215 Mike Gminski	.05	.02	.01
☐ 216 Hersey Hawkins	.08	.04	.01
☐ 217 Rick Mahorn	.05	.02	.01
☐ 218 Derek Smith SP	.10	.05	.01
☐ 219 Bob Thornton	.05	.02	.01
☐ 220 Tom Chambers	.08	.04	.01
☐ 221 Greg Grant SP	.10	.05	.01
☐ 222 Jeff Hornacek	.10	.05	.01
☐ 223 Eddie Johnson	.08	.04	.01
☐ 224A Kevin Johnson	.40	.18	.05
(SkyBox logo in lower right corner)			
☐ 224B Kevin Johnson	.40	.18	.05
(SkyBox logo in upper			

☐ 225 Andrew Lang	.05	.02	.01
☐ 226 Dan Majerle	.10	.05	.01
☐ 227 Mike McGee SP	.10	.05	.01
☐ 228 Tim Perry	.05	.02	.01
☐ 229 Kurt Rambis	.05	.02	.01
☐ 230 Mark West	.05	.02	.01
☐ 231 Mark Bryant	.05	.02	.01
☐ 232 Wayne Cooper	.05	.02	.01
☐ 233 Clyde Drexler	.40	.18	.05
☐ 234 Kevin Duckworth	.05	.02	.01
☐ 235 Byron Irvin SP	.10	.05	.01
☐ 236 Jerome Kersey	.05	.02	.01
☐ 237 Drazen Petrovic	.25	.11	.03
☐ 238 Terry Porter	.08	.04	.01
☐ 239 Cliff Robinson	.75	.35	.09
☐ 240 Buck Williams	.08	.04	.01
☐ 241 Danny Young	.05	.02	.01
☐ 242 Danny Ainge SP	.15	.07	.02
☐ 243 Randy Allen SP	.10	.05	.01
☐ 244A Antoine Carr SP	.10	.05	.01
(Wearing Atlanta jersey on back)			
☐ 244B Antoine Carr	.05	.02	.01
(Wearing Sacramento jersey on back)			
☐ 245 Vinny Del Negro SP	.10	.05	.01
☐ 246 Pervis Ellison	.30	.14	.04
☐ 247 Greg Kite SP	.10	.05	.01
☐ 248 Rodney McCray SP	.10	.05	.01
☐ 249 Harold Pressley SP	.10	.05	.01
☐ 250 Ralph Sampson	.05	.02	.01
☐ 251 Wayman Tisdale	.08	.04	.01
☐ 252 Willie Anderson	.05	.02	.01
☐ 253 Uwe Blab SP	.10	.05	.01
☐ 254 Frank Brickowski SP	.10	.05	.01
☐ 255 Terry Cummings	.08	.04	.01
☐ 256 Sean Elliott	.60	.25	.08
☐ 257 Caldwell Jones SP	.15	.07	.02
☐ 258 Johnny Moore SP	.10	.05	.01
☐ 259 Zarko Paspalj SP	.10	.05	.01
☐ 260 David Robinson	1.50	.65	.19
☐ 261 Rod Strickland	.10	.05	.01
☐ 262 David Wingate SP	.10	.05	.01
☐ 263 Dana Barros	.75	.35	.09
☐ 264 Michael Cage	.05	.02	.01
☐ 265 Quintin Dailey	.05	.02	.01
☐ 266 Dale Ellis	.08	.04	.01
☐ 267 Steve Johnson SP	.10	.05	.01
☐ 268 Shawn Kemp	5.00	2.30	.60
☐ 269 Xavier McDaniel	.05	.02	.01
☐ 270 Derrick McKey	.08	.04	.01
☐ 271A Nate McMillan SP ERR	.10	.05	.01
(Back photo actually Olden Polynice; first series)			
☐ 271B Nate McMillan COR	.05	.02	.01
(second series)			
☐ 272 Olden Polynice	.05	.02	.01
☐ 273 Sedale Threatt	.05	.02	.01
☐ 274 Thurl Bailey	.05	.02	.01
☐ 275 Mike Brown	.05	.02	.01
☐ 276 Mark Eaton	.05	.02	.01
☐ 277 Blue Edwards	.08	.04	.01
☐ 278 Darrell Griffith	.08	.04	.01
☐ 279 Bobby Hansen SP	.10	.05	.01
☐ 280 Eric Johnson	.05	.02	.01
☐ 281 Eric Leckner SP	.10	.05	.01
☐ 282 Karl Malone	.40	.18	.05
☐ 283 Delaney Rudd	.05	.02	.01
☐ 284 John Stockton	.50	.23	.06
☐ 285 Mark Alarie	.05	.02	.01
☐ 286 Steve Colter SP	.10	.05	.01
☐ 287 Ledell Eackles SP	.10	.05	.01
☐ 288 Harvey Grant	.05	.02	.01
☐ 289 Tom Hammonds	.05	.02	.01
☐ 290 Charles Jones	.05	.02	.01
☐ 291 Bernard King	.10	.05	.01
☐ 292 Jeff Malone SP	.10	.05	.01
☐ 293 Darrell Walker	.05	.02	.01
☐ 294 John Williams	.05	.02	.01
☐ 295 Checklist 1 SP	.10	.05	.01
☐ 296 Checklist 2 SP	.10	.05	.01
☐ 297 Checklist 3 SP	.10	.05	.01
☐ 298 Checklist 4 SP	.10	.05	.01
☐ 299 Checklist 5 SP	.10	.05	.01
☐ 300 Danny Ferry SP	.30	.14	.04
Cleveland Cavaliers			
☐ 301 Bob Weiss CO	.10	.05	.01
Atlanta Hawks			
☐ 302 Chris Ford CO	.10	.05	.01
Boston Celtics			
☐ 303 Gene Littles CO	.10	.05	.01
Charlotte Hornets			
☐ 304 Phil Jackson CO	.15	.07	.02
Chicago Bulls			
☐ 305 Lenny Wilkens CO	.15	.07	.02
Cleveland Cavaliers			
☐ 306 Richie Adubato CO	.10	.05	.01
Dallas Mavericks			
☐ 307 Paul Westhead CO	.15	.07	.02
Denver Nuggets			
☐ 308 Chuck Daly CO	.15	.07	.02
Detroit Pistons			
☐ 309 Don Nelson CO	.15	.07	.02
Golden State Warriors			
☐ 310 Don Chaney CO	.10	.05	.01
Houston Rockets			
☐ 311 Dick Versace CO	.10	.05	.01
Indiana Pacers			
☐ 312 Mike Schuler CO	.10	.05	.01
Los Angeles Clippers			
☐ 313 Mike Dunleavy CO	.15	.07	.02
Los Angeles Lakers			
☐ 314 Ron Rothstein CO	.10	.05	.01
Miami Heat			
☐ 315 Del Harris CO	.10	.05	.01
Milwaukee Bucks			
☐ 316 Bill Musselman CO	.10	.05	.01
Minnesota Timberwolves			
☐ 317 Bill Fitch CO	.10	.05	.01
Houston Rockets			
☐ 318 Stu Jackson CO	.10	.05	.01
New York Knicks			
☐ 319 Matt Guokas CO	.10	.05	.01
Orlando Magic			
☐ 320 Jim Lynam CO	.10	.05	.01
Philadelphia 76ers			
☐ 321 Cotton Fitzsimmons CO	.10	.05	.01
Phoenix Suns			
☐ 322 Rick Adelman CO	.10	.05	.01
Portland Trail Blazers			
☐ 323 Dick Motta CO	.10	.05	.01
Sacramento Kings			
☐ 324 Larry Brown CO	.15	.07	.02
San Antonio Spurs			
☐ 325 K.C. Jones CO	.15	.07	.02
Seattle Supersonics			
☐ 326 Jerry Sloan CO	.10	.05	.01
Utah Jazz			
☐ 327 Wes Unseld CO	.15	.07	.02
Washington Bullets			

(right corner)

☐ 328 Atlanta Hawks TC	.10	.05	.01
☐ 329 Boston Celtics TC	.10	.05	.01
☐ 330 Charlotte Hornets TC	.10	.05	.01
☐ 331 Chicago Bulls TC	.10	.05	.01
☐ 332 Cleveland Cavaliers TC	.10	.05	.01
☐ 333 Dallas Mavericks TC	.10	.05	.01
☐ 334 Denver Nuggets TC	.10	.05	.01
☐ 335 Detroit Pistons TC	.10	.05	.01
☐ 336 Golden State Warriors TC	.10	.05	.01
☐ 337 Houston Rockets TC	.10	.05	.01
☐ 338 Indiana Pacers TC	.10	.05	.01
☐ 339 Los Angeles Clippers TC	.10	.05	.01
☐ 340 Los Angeles Lakers TC	.10	.05	.01
☐ 341 Miami Heat TC	.10	.05	.01
☐ 342 Milwaukee Bucks TC	.10	.05	.01
☐ 343 Minn. Timberwolves TC	.10	.05	.01
☐ 344 New Jersey Nets TC	.10	.05	.01
☐ 345 New York Knicks TC	.10	.05	.01
☐ 346 Orlando Magic TC	.10	.05	.01
☐ 347 Philadelphia 76ers TC	.10	.05	.01
☐ 348 Phoenix Suns TC	.10	.05	.01
☐ 349 Portland Trail Blazers TC	.10	.05	.01
☐ 350 Sacramento Kings TC	.10	.05	.01
☐ 351 San Antonio Spurs TC	.10	.05	.01
☐ 352 Seattle SuperSonics TC	.10	.05	.01
☐ 353 Utah Jazz TC	.10	.05	.01
☐ 354 Washington Bullets TC	.10	.05	.01
☐ 355 Rumeal Robinson LP	.10	.05	.01
Atlanta Hawks			
☐ 356 Kendall Gill LP	.75	.35	.09
Charlotte Hornets			
☐ 357 Chris Jackson LP	.75	.35	.09
Denver Nuggets			
☐ 358 Tyrone Hill LP	1.25	.55	.16
Golden State Warriors			
☐ 359 Bo Kimble LP	.10	.05	.01
Los Angeles Clippers			
☐ 360 Willie Burton LP	.50	.23	.06
Miami Heat			
☐ 361 Felton Spencer LP	.20	.09	.03
Minnesota Timberwolves			
☐ 362 Derrick Coleman LP	2.00	.90	.25
New Jersey Nets			
☐ 363 Dennis Scott LP	1.00	.45	.13
Orlando Magic			
☐ 364 Lionel Simmons LP	.20	.09	.03
Sacramento Kings			
☐ 365 Gary Payton LP	2.00	.90	.25
Seattle Supersonics			
☐ 366 Tim McCormick	.10	.05	.01
Atlanta Hawks			
☐ 367 Sidney Moncrief	.20	.09	.03
Atlanta Hawks			
☐ 368 Kenny Gattison	.10	.05	.01
Charlotte Hornets			
☐ 369 Randolph Keys	.10	.05	.01
Charlotte Hornets			
☐ 370 Johnny Newman	.10	.05	.01
Charlotte Hornets			
☐ 371 Dennis Hopson	.10	.05	.01
Chicago Bulls			
☐ 372 Cliff Levingston	.10	.05	.01
Chicago Bulls			
☐ 373 Derrick Chievous	.10	.05	.01
Cleveland Cavaliers			
☐ 374 Danny Ferry	.10	.05	.01
Cleveland Cavaliers			
☐ 375 Alex English	.20	.09	.03
Dallas Mavericks			
☐ 376 Lafayette Lever	.10	.05	.01
Dallas Mavericks			

☐ 377 Rodney McCray	.10	.05	.01
Dallas Mavericks			
☐ 378 T.R. Dunn	.10	.05	.01
Denver Nuggets			
☐ 379 Corey Gaines	.10	.05	.01
Denver Nuggets			
☐ 380 Avery Johnson	.75	.35	.09
San Antonio Spurs			
☐ 381 Joe Wolf	.10	.05	.01
Denver Nuggets			
☐ 382 Orlando Woolridge	.10	.05	.01
Denver Nuggets			
☐ 383 Tree Rollins	.10	.05	.01
Detroit Pistons			
☐ 384 Steve Johnson	.10	.05	.01
Seattle Supersonics			
☐ 385 Kenny Smith	.10	.05	.01
Houston Rockets			
☐ 386 Mike Woodson	.10	.05	.01
Cleveland Cavaliers			
☐ 387 Greg Dreiling	.10	.05	.01
Indiana Pacers			
☐ 388 Micheal Williams	.10	.05	.01
Indiana Pacers			
☐ 389 Randy Wittman	.10	.05	.01
Indiana Pacers			
☐ 390 Ken Bannister	.10	.05	.01
Los Angeles Clippers			
☐ 391 Sam Perkins	.15	.07	.02
Los Angeles Lakers			
☐ 392 Terry Teagle	.10	.05	.01
Los Angeles Lakers			
☐ 393 Milt Wagner	.10	.05	.01
Miami Heat			
☐ 394 Frank Brickowski	.10	.05	.01
Milwaukee Bucks			
☐ 395 Dan Schayes	.10	.05	.01
Milwaukee Bucks			
☐ 396 Scott Brooks	.10	.05	.01
Minnesota Timberwolves			
☐ 397 Doug West	.50	.23	.06
Minnesota Timberwolves			
☐ 398 Chris Dudley	.10	.05	.01
New Jersey Nets			
☐ 399 Reggie Theus	.15	.07	.02
New Jersey Nets			
☐ 400 Greg Grant	.10	.05	.01
New York Knicks			
☐ 401 Greg Kite	.10	.05	.01
Orlando Magic			
☐ 402 Mark McNamara	.10	.05	.01
Orlando Magic			
☐ 403 Manute Bol	.10	.05	.01
Philadelphia 76ers			
☐ 404 Rickey Green	.10	.05	.01
Philadelphia 76ers			
☐ 405 Kenny Battle	.10	.05	.01
Denver Nuggets			
☐ 406 Ed Nealy	.10	.05	.01
Phoenix Suns			
☐ 407 Danny Ainge	.15	.07	.02
Portland Trail Blazers			
☐ 408 Steve Colter	.10	.05	.01
Sacramento Kings			
☐ 409 Bobby Hansen	.10	.05	.01
Sacramento Kings			
☐ 410 Eric Leckner	.10	.05	.01
Charlotte Hornets			
☐ 411 Rory Sparrow	.10	.05	.01
Sacramento Kings			
☐ 412 Bill Wennington	.10	.05	.01

		MINT	NRMT	EXC
□ 413	Sidney Green San Antonio Spurs	.10	.05	.01
□ 414	David Greenwood San Antonio Spurs	.10	.05	.01
□ 415	Paul Pressey San Antonio Spurs	.10	.05	.01
□ 416	Reggie Williams San Antonio Spurs	.10	.05	.01
□ 417	Dave Corzine Orlando Magic	.10	.05	.01
□ 418	Jeff Malone Utah Jazz	.15	.07	.02
□ 419	Pervis Ellison Washington Bullets	.10	.05	.01
□ 420	Byron Irvin Washington Bullets	.10	.05	.01
□ 421	Checklist 1	.10	.05	.01
□ 422	Checklist 2	.10	.05	.01
□ 423	Checklist 3	.10	.05	.01
□ NNO	SkyBox Salutes the NBA	5.00	2.30	.60

1991-92 SkyBox

Earvin Johnson

The complete 1991-92 SkyBox basketball set contains 659 cards measuring the standard size (2 1/2" by 3 1/2"). The set was released in two series of 350 and 309 cards, respectively. This year SkyBox did not package both first and second series cards in second series packs. The cards were available in 15-card fin-sealed foil packs that feature four different mail-in offers on the back, or 62-card blister packs that contain two (of four) SkyBox logo cards not available in the 15-card foil packs. The fronts feature color action player photos overlaying multi-colored computer-generated geometric shapes and stripes. The pictures are borderless and the card face is white. The player's name appears in different color lettering at the bottom of each card, with the team logo in the lower right corner. In a trapezoid shape, the backs have non-action color player photos. At the bottom biographical and statistical information appear inside a color-striped diagonal. The cards are numbered and checklisted below alphabetically within and according to teams as follows: Atlanta Hawks (1-11), Boston Celtics (12-22), Charlotte Hornets (23-33), Chicago Bulls (34-44), Cleveland Cavaliers (45-55), Dallas Mavericks (56-66), Denver Nuggets (67-77), Detroit Pistons (78-88), Golden State Warriors (89-99), Houston Rockets (100-110), Indiana Pacers (111-121), Los Angeles Clippers (122-132), Los Angeles Lakers (133-143), Miami Heat (144-154), Milwaukee Bucks (155-165), Minnesota Timberwolves (166-176), New Jersey Nets (177-187), New York Knicks (188-198), Orlando Magic (199-209), Philadelphia 76ers (210-220), Phoenix Suns (221-231), Portland Trail Blazers (232-242), Sacramento Kings (243-253), San Antonio Spurs (254-264), Seattle Supersonics (265-275), Utah Jazz (276-286), Washington Bullets (287-297), Stats (298-307), Best Single Game Performance (308-312), NBA All-Star Weekend Highlights (313-317), NBA All-Rookie Team (318-322), GQ's "NBA All-Star Style Team" (323-327), Centennial Highlights (328-332), Great Moments from the NBA Finals (333-337), Stay in School (338-344), Checklists (345-350), Team Logos (351-377), Coaches (378-404), Game Frames (405-431), Sixth Man (432-458), Teamwork (459-485), Rising Stars (486-512), Lottery Picks (513-523), Centennial (524-529), 1992 USA Basketball Team (530-546), 1988 USA Basketball Team (547-556), 1984 USA Basketball Team (557-563), The Magic of SkyBox (564-571), SkyBox Salutes (572-576), Skymasters (577-588), Shooting Stars (589-602), Small School Sensations (603-609), NBA Stay in School (610-614), Player Updates (615-653), and Checklists (654-659). As part of a promotion with Cheerios, four SkyBox cards from the basic set were inserted into specially marked 10-ounce and 15-ounce cereal boxes. These cereal boxes appeared on store shelves in December 1991 and January 1992, and they depicted images of SkyBox cards on the front, back, and side panels. An unnumbered gold foil-stamped 1992 USA Basketball Team photo card was randomly inserted into second series foil packs, while the blister packs featured two-card sets of NBA MVPs from the same team for consecutive years. As a mail-in offer a limited Clyde Drexler Olympic card was sent to the first 10,000 respondents in return for ten SkyBox wrappers and 1.00 for postage and handling. Rookie Cards include Kenny Anderson, Stacey Augmon, Larry Johnson, Mike Krzyzewski (USA coach), Terry Mills, Dikembe Mutombo, Steve Smith and John Starks.

	MINT	NRMT	EXC
COMPLETE SET (659)	40.00	18.00	5.00
COMPLETE SERIES 1 (350)	12.00	5.50	1.50
COMPLETE SERIES 2 (309)	30.00	13.50	3.80
COMMON CARD (1-659)	.05	.02	.01
□ 1 John Battle	.05	.02	.01
□ 2 Duane Ferrell	.05	.02	.01
□ 3 Jon Koncak	.05	.02	.01
□ 4 Moses Malone	.20	.09	.03
□ 5 Tim McCormick	.05	.02	.01
□ 6 Sidney Moncrief	.15	.07	.02

☐ 7 Doc Rivers	.05	.02	.01
☐ 8 Rumeal Robinson UER	.05	.02	.01
(Drafted 11th,			
should say 10th)			
☐ 9 Spud Webb	.10	.05	.01
☐ 10 Dominique Wilkins	.20	.09	.03
☐ 11 Kevin Willis	.10	.05	.01
☐ 12 Larry Bird	1.25	.55	.16
☐ 13 Dee Brown	.15	.07	.02
☐ 14 Kevin Gamble	.05	.02	.01
☐ 15 Joe Kleine	.05	.02	.01
☐ 16 Reggie Lewis	.15	.07	.02
☐ 17 Kevin McHale	.15	.07	.02
☐ 18 Robert Parish	.15	.07	.02
☐ 19 Ed Pinckney	.05	.02	.01
☐ 20 Brian Shaw	.05	.02	.01
☐ 21 Michael Smith	.05	.02	.01
☐ 22 Stojko Vrankovic	.05	.02	.01
☐ 23 Muggsy Bogues	.15	.07	.02
☐ 24 Rex Chapman	.05	.02	.01
☐ 25 Dell Curry	.05	.02	.01
☐ 26 Kenny Gattison	.05	.02	.01
☐ 27 Kendall Gill	.10	.05	.01
☐ 28 Mike Gminski	.05	.02	.01
☐ 29 Randolph Keys	.05	.02	.01
☐ 30 Eric Leckner	.05	.02	.01
☐ 31 Johnny Newman	.05	.02	.01
☐ 32 J.R. Reid	.05	.02	.01
☐ 33 Kelly Tripucka	.05	.02	.01
☐ 34 B.J. Armstrong	.10	.05	.01
☐ 35 Bill Cartwright	.05	.02	.01
☐ 36 Horace Grant	.20	.09	.03
☐ 37 Craig Hodges	.05	.02	.01
☐ 38 Dennis Hopson	.05	.02	.01
☐ 39 Michael Jordan	5.00	2.30	.60
☐ 40 Stacey King	.05	.02	.01
☐ 41 Cliff Levingston	.05	.02	.01
☐ 42 John Paxson	.05	.02	.01
☐ 43 Will Perdue	.05	.02	.01
☐ 44 Scottie Pippen	.40	.18	.05
☐ 45 Winston Bennett	.05	.02	.01
☐ 46 Chucky Brown	.05	.02	.01
☐ 47 Brad Daugherty	.10	.05	.01
☐ 48 Craig Ehlo	.05	.02	.01
☐ 49 Danny Ferry	.05	.02	.01
☐ 50 Steve Kerr	.05	.02	.01
☐ 51 John Morton	.05	.02	.01
☐ 52 Larry Nance	.10	.05	.01
☐ 53 Mark Price	.15	.07	.02
☐ 54 Darnell Valentine	.05	.02	.01
☐ 55 John Williams	.10	.05	.01
☐ 56 Steve Alford	.05	.02	.01
☐ 57 Rolando Blackman	.05	.02	.01
☐ 58 Brad Davis	.05	.02	.01
☐ 59 James Donaldson	.05	.02	.01
☐ 60 Derek Harper	.10	.05	.01
☐ 61 Fat Lever	.05	.02	.01
☐ 62 Rodney McCray	.05	.02	.01
☐ 63 Roy Tarpley	.05	.02	.01
☐ 64 Kelvin Upshaw	.05	.02	.01
☐ 65 Randy White	.05	.02	.01
☐ 66 Herb Williams	.05	.02	.01
☐ 67 Michael Adams	.05	.02	.01
☐ 68 Greg Anderson	.05	.02	.01
☐ 69 Anthony Cook	.05	.02	.01
☐ 70 Chris Jackson	.15	.07	.02
☐ 71 Jerome Lane	.05	.02	.01
☐ 72 Marcus Liberty	.05	.02	.01
☐ 73 Todd Lichti	.05	.02	.01
☐ 74 Blair Rasmussen	.05	.02	.01
☐ 75 Reggie Williams	.05	.02	.01

☐ 76 Joe Wolf	.05	.02	.01
☐ 77 Orlando Woolridge	.05	.02	.01
☐ 78 Mark Aguirre	.10	.05	.01
☐ 79 William Bedford	.05	.02	.01
☐ 80 Lance Blanks	.05	.02	.01
☐ 81 Joe Dumars	.20	.09	.03
☐ 82 James Edwards	.05	.02	.01
☐ 83 Scott Hastings	.05	.02	.01
☐ 84 Vinnie Johnson	.10	.05	.01
☐ 85 Bill Laimbeer	.10	.05	.01
☐ 86 Dennis Rodman	.25	.11	.03
☐ 87 John Salley	.05	.02	.01
☐ 88 Isiah Thomas	.20	.09	.03
☐ 89 Mario Elie	.30	.14	.04
☐ 90 Tim Hardaway	.05	.02	.01
☐ 91 Rod Higgins	.05	.02	.01
☐ 92 Tyrone Hill	.15	.07	.02
☐ 93 Les Jepsen	.05	.02	.01
☐ 94 Alton Lister	.05	.02	.01
☐ 95 Sarunas Marciulionis	.05	.02	.01
☐ 96 Chris Mullin	.15	.07	.02
☐ 97 Jim Petersen	.05	.02	.01
☐ 98 Mitch Richmond	.25	.11	.03
☐ 99 Tom Tolbert	.05	.02	.01
☐ 100 Adrian Caldwell	.05	.02	.01
☐ 101 Eric(Sleepy) Floyd	.05	.02	.01
☐ 102 Dave Jamerson	.05	.02	.01
☐ 103 Buck Johnson	.05	.02	.01
☐ 104 Vernon Maxwell	.05	.02	.01
☐ 105 Hakeem Olajuwon	1.00	.45	.13
☐ 106 Kenny Smith	.05	.02	.01
☐ 107 Larry Smith	.05	.02	.01
☐ 108 Otis Thorpe	.10	.05	.01
☐ 109 Kennard Winchester	.05	.02	.01
☐ 110 David Wood	.05	.02	.01
☐ 111 Greg Dreiling	.05	.02	.01
☐ 112 Vern Fleming	.05	.02	.01
☐ 113 George McCloud	.05	.02	.01
☐ 114 Reggie Miller	.40	.18	.05
☐ 115 Chuck Person	.10	.05	.01
☐ 116 Mike Sanders	.05	.02	.01
☐ 117 Detlef Schrempf	.15	.07	.02
☐ 118 Rik Smits	.15	.07	.02
☐ 119 LaSalle Thompson	.05	.02	.01
☐ 120 Kenny Williams	.05	.02	.01
☐ 121 Micheal Williams	.05	.02	.01
☐ 122 Ken Bannister	.05	.02	.01
☐ 123 Winston Garland	.05	.02	.01
☐ 124 Gary Grant	.05	.02	.01
☐ 125 Ron Harper	.10	.05	.01
☐ 126 Bo Kimble	.05	.02	.01
☐ 127 Danny Manning	.15	.07	.02
☐ 128 Jeff Martin	.05	.02	.01
☐ 129 Ken Norman	.05	.02	.01
☐ 130 Olden Polynice	.05	.02	.01
☐ 131 Charles Smith	.05	.02	.01
☐ 132 Loy Vaught	.15	.07	.02
☐ 133 Elden Campbell	.10	.05	.01
☐ 134 Vlade Divac	.15	.07	.02
☐ 135 Larry Drew	.05	.02	.01
☐ 136 A.C. Green	.15	.07	.02
☐ 137 Magic Johnson	.75	.35	.09
☐ 138 Sam Perkins	.10	.05	.01
☐ 139 Byron Scott	.10	.05	.01
☐ 140 Tony Smith	.05	.02	.01
☐ 141 Terry Teagle	.05	.02	.01
☐ 142 Mychal Thompson	.05	.02	.01
☐ 143 James Worthy	.15	.07	.02
☐ 144 Willie Burton	.05	.02	.01
☐ 145 Bimbo Coles	.05	.02	.01
☐ 146 Terry Davis	.05	.02	.01

☐	147	Sherman Douglas	.05	.02	.01	☐	218	Brian Oliver	.05	.02	.01
☐	148	Kevin Edwards	.05	.02	.01	☐	219	Andre Turner	.05	.02	.01
☐	149	Alec Kessler	.05	.02	.01	☐	220	Jayson Williams	.05	.02	.01
☐	150	Grant Long	.05	.02	.01	☐	221	Joe Barry Carroll	.05	.02	.01
☐	151	Glen Rice	.15	.07	.02	☐	222	Cedric Ceballos	.15	.07	.02
☐	152	Rony Seikaly	.05	.02	.01	☐	223	Tom Chambers	.10	.05	.01
☐	153	Jon Sundvold	.05	.02	.01	☐	224	Jeff Hornacek	.10	.05	.01
☐	154	Billy Thompson	.05	.02	.01	☐	225	Kevin Johnson	.25	.11	.03
☐	155	Frank Brickowski	.05	.02	.01	☐	226	Negele Knight	.05	.02	.01
☐	156	Lester Conner	.05	.02	.01	☐	227	Andrew Lang	.05	.02	.01
☐	157	Jeff Grayer	.05	.02	.01	☐	228	Dan Majerle	.10	.05	.01
☐	158	Jay Humphries	.05	.02	.01	☐	229	Xavier McDaniel	.10	.05	.01
☐	159	Larry Krystkowiak	.05	.02	.01	☐	230	Kurt Rambis	.05	.02	.01
☐	160	Brad Lohaus	.05	.02	.01	☐	231	Mark West	.05	.02	.01
☐	161	Dale Ellis	.10	.05	.01	☐	232	Alaa Abdelnaby	.05	.02	.01
☐	162	Fred Roberts	.05	.02	.01	☐	233	Danny Ainge	.10	.05	.01
☐	163	Alvin Robertson	.05	.02	.01	☐	234	Mark Bryant	.05	.02	.01
☐	164	Danny Schayes	.05	.02	.01	☐	235	Wayne Cooper	.05	.02	.01
☐	165	Jack Sikma	.10	.05	.01	☐	236	Walter Davis	.15	.07	.02
☐	166	Randy Breuer	.05	.02	.01	☐	237	Clyde Drexler	.40	.18	.05
☐	167	Scott Brooks	.05	.02	.01	☐	238	Kevin Duckworth	.05	.02	.01
☐	168	Tony Campbell	.05	.02	.01	☐	239	Jerome Kersey	.05	.02	.01
☐	169	Tyrone Corbin	.05	.02	.01	☐	240	Terry Porter	.10	.05	.01
☐	170	Gerald Glass	.05	.02	.01	☐	241	Cliff Robinson	.05	.02	.01
☐	171	Sam Mitchell	.05	.02	.01	☐	242	Buck Williams	.10	.05	.01
☐	172	Tod Murphy	.05	.02	.01	☐	243	Anthony Bonner	.05	.02	.01
☐	173	Pooh Richardson	.05	.02	.01	☐	244	Antoine Carr	.05	.02	.01
☐	174	Felton Spencer	.05	.02	.01	☐	245	Duane Causwell	.05	.02	.01
☐	175	Bob Thornton	.05	.02	.01	☐	246	Bobby Hansen	.05	.02	.01
☐	176	Doug West	.05	.02	.01	☐	247	Jim Les	.05	.02	.01
☐	177	Mookie Blaylock	.15	.07	.02	☐	248	Travis Mays	.05	.02	.01
☐	178	Sam Bowie	.05	.02	.01	☐	249	Ralph Sampson	.05	.02	.01
☐	179	Jud Buechler	.05	.02	.01	☐	250	Lionel Simmons	.05	.02	.01
☐	180	Derrick Coleman	.15	.07	.02	☐	251	Rory Sparrow	.05	.02	.01
☐	181	Chris Dudley	.05	.02	.01	☐	252	Wayman Tisdale	.10	.05	.01
☐	182	Tate George	.05	.02	.01	☐	253	Bill Wennington	.05	.02	.01
☐	183	Jack Haley	.05	.02	.01	☐	254	Willie Anderson	.05	.02	.01
☐	184	Terry Mills	.50	.23	.06	☐	255	Terry Cummings	.10	.05	.01
☐	185	Chris Morris	.05	.02	.01	☐	256	Sean Elliott	.15	.07	.02
☐	186	Drazen Petrovic	.10	.05	.01	☐	257	Sidney Green	.05	.02	.01
☐	187	Reggie Theus	.10	.05	.01	☐	258	David Greenwood	.05	.02	.01
☐	188	Maurice Cheeks	.15	.07	.02	☐	259	Avery Johnson	.05	.02	.01
☐	189	Patrick Ewing	.40	.18	.05	☐	260	Paul Pressey	.05	.02	.01
☐	190	Mark Jackson	.05	.02	.01	☐	261	David Robinson	1.00	.45	.13
☐	191	Jerrod Mustaf	.05	.02	.01	☐	262	Dwayne Schintzius	.05	.02	.01
☐	192	Charles Oakley	.10	.05	.01	☐	263	Rod Strickland	.10	.05	.01
☐	193	Brian Quinnett	.05	.02	.01	☐	264	David Wingate	.05	.02	.01
☐	194	John Starks	.50	.23	.06	☐	265	Dana Barros	.15	.07	.02
☐	195	Trent Tucker	.05	.02	.01	☐	266	Benoit Benjamin	.05	.02	.01
☐	196	Kiki Vandeweghe	.05	.02	.01	☐	267	Michael Cage	.05	.02	.01
☐	197	Kenny Walker	.05	.02	.01	☐	268	Quintin Dailey	.05	.02	.01
☐	198	Gerald Wilkins	.05	.02	.01	☐	269	Ricky Pierce	.10	.05	.01
☐	199	Mark Acres	.05	.02	.01	☐	270	Eddie Johnson	.10	.05	.01
☐	200	Nick Anderson	.15	.07	.02	☐	271	Shawn Kemp	1.50	.65	.19
☐	201	Michael Ansley	.05	.02	.01	☐	272	Derrick McKey	.10	.05	.01
☐	202	Terry Catledge	.05	.02	.01	☐	273	Nate McMillan	.05	.02	.01
☐	203	Greg Kite	.05	.02	.01	☐	274	Gary Payton	.15	.07	.02
☐	204	Jerry Reynolds	.05	.02	.01	☐	275	Sedale Threatt	.05	.02	.01
☐	205	Dennis Scott	.10	.05	.01	☐	276	Thurl Bailey	.05	.02	.01
☐	206	Scott Skiles	.05	.02	.01	☐	277	Mike Brown	.05	.02	.01
☐	207	Otis Smith	.05	.02	.01	☐	278	Tony Brown	.05	.02	.01
☐	208	Jeff Turner	.05	.02	.01	☐	279	Mark Eaton	.05	.02	.01
☐	209	Sam Vincent	.05	.02	.01	☐	280	Blue Edwards	.05	.02	.01
☐	210	Ron Anderson	.05	.02	.01	☐	281	Darrell Griffith	.10	.05	.01
☐	211	Charles Barkley	.75	.35	.09	☐	282	Jeff Malone	.10	.05	.01
☐	212	Manute Bol	.05	.02	.01	☐	283	Karl Malone	.40	.18	.05
☐	213	Johnny Dawkins	.05	.02	.01	☐	284	Delaney Rudd	.05	.02	.01
☐	214	Armon Gilliam	.05	.02	.01	☐	285	John Stockton	.40	.18	.05
☐	215	Rickey Green	.05	.02	.01	☐	286	Andy Toolson	.05	.02	.01
☐	216	Hersey Hawkins	.10	.05	.01	☐	287	Mark Alarie	.05	.02	.01
☐	217	Rick Mahorn	.05	.02	.01	☐	288	Ledell Eackles	.05	.02	.01

☐	289	Pervis Ellison	.05	.02	.01
☐	290	A.J. English	.05	.02	.01
☐	291	Harvey Grant	.05	.02	.01
☐	292	Tom Hammonds	.05	.02	.01
☐	293	Charles Jones	.05	.02	.01
☐	294	Bernard King	.15	.07	.02
☐	295	Darrell Walker	.05	.02	.01
☐	296	John Williams	.05	.02	.01
☐	297	Haywoode Workman	.05	.02	.01
☐	298	Muggsy Bogues	.05	.02	.01
		Charlotte Hornets			
		Assist-to-Turnover			
		Ratio Leader			
☐	299	Lester Conner	.05	.02	.01
		Milwaukee Bucks			
		Steal-to Turnover			
		Ratio Leader			
☐	300	Michael Adams	.05	.02	.01
		Denver Nuggets			
		Largest One-Year			
		Scoring Improvement			
☐	301	Chris Mullin	.05	.02	.01
		Golden State Warriors			
		Most Minutes Per Game			
☐	302	Otis Thorpe	.05	.02	.01
		Houston Rockets			
		Most Consecutive			
		Games Played			
☐	303	Mitch Richmond	.05	.02	.01
		Chris Mullin			
		Tim Hardaway			
		Highest Scoring Trio			
☐	304	Darrell Walker	.05	.02	.01
		Washington Bullets			
		Top Rebounding Guard			
☐	305	Jerome Lane	.05	.02	.01
		Denver Nuggets			
		Rebounds Per 48 Minutes			
☐	306	John Stockton	.15	.07	.02
		Utah Jazz			
		Assists Per 48 Minutes			
☐	307	Michael Jordan	2.50	1.15	.30
		Chicago Bulls			
		Points Per 48 Minutes			
☐	308	Michael Adams	.05	.02	.01
		Denver Nuggets			
		Best Single Game			
		Performance: Points			
☐	309	Larry Smith	.05	.02	.01
		Houston Rockets			
		Jerome Lane			
		Denver Nuggets			
		Best Single Game			
		Performance: Rebounds			
☐	310	Scott Skiles	.05	.02	.01
		Orlando Magic			
		Best Single Game			
		Performance: Assists			
☐	311	Hakeem Olajuwon	.75	.35	.09
		David Robinson			
		Best Single Game			
		Performance: Blocks			
☐	312	Alvin Robertson	.05	.02	.01
		Milwaukee Bucks			
		Best Single Game			
		Performance: Steals			
☐	313	Stay In School Jam	.05	.02	.01
☐	314	Craig Hodges	.05	.02	.01
		Chicago Bulls			
		Three-Point Shootout			
☐	315	Dee Brown	.05	.02	.01

		Boston Celtics			
		Slam-Dunk Championship			
☐	316	Charles Barkley	.40	.18	.05
		Philadelphia 76ers			
		All-Star Game MVP			
☐	317	Behind the Scenes	.05	.02	.01
		Charles Barkley			
		Joe Dumars			
		Kevin McHale			
☐	318	Derrick Coleman ART	.05	.02	.01
		New Jersey Nets			
☐	319	Lionel Simmons ART	.05	.02	.01
		Sacramento Kings			
☐	320	Dennis Scott ART	.05	.02	.01
		Orlando Magic			
☐	321	Kendall Gill ART	.05	.02	.01
		Charlotte Hornets			
☐	322	Dee Brown ART	.05	.02	.01
		Boston Celtics			
☐	323	Magic Johnson	.40	.18	.05
		GQ All-Star Style Team			
☐	324	Hakeem Olajuwon	.50	.23	.06
		GQ All-Star Style Team			
☐	325	Kevin Willis	.05	.02	.01
		Dominique Wilkins			
		GQ All-Star Style Team			
☐	326	Kevin Willis	.05	.02	.01
		Dominique Wilkins			
		GQ All-Star Style Team			
☐	327	Gerald Wilkins	.05	.02	.01
		GQ All-Star Style Team			
☐	328	1891-1991 Basketball	.05	.02	.01
		Centennial Logo			
☐	329	Old-Fashioned Ball	.05	.02	.01
☐	330	Women Take the Court	.05	.02	.01
☐	331	The Peach Basket	.05	.02	.01
☐	332	James A. Naismith	.10	.05	.01
		Founder of Basketball			
☐	333	Magic Johnson	1.50	.65	.19
		and Michael Jordan			
		Great Moments from			
		the NBA Finals			
☐	334	Michael Jordan	2.50	1.15	.30
		Chicago Bulls			
		Great Moments from			
		the NBA Finals			
☐	335	Vlade Divac	.05	.02	.01
		Los Angeles Lakers			
		Great Moments from			
		the NBA Finals			
☐	336	John Paxson	.05	.02	.01
		Chicago Bulls			
		Great Moments from			
		the NBA Finals			
☐	337	Bulls Starting Five	1.00	.45	.13
		Great Moments from			
		the NBA Finals			
☐	338	Language Arts	.05	.02	.01
		Stay in School			
☐	339	Mathematics	.05	.02	.01
		Stay in School			
☐	340	Vocational Education	.05	.02	.01
		Stay in School			
☐	341	Social Studies	.05	.02	.01
		Stay in School			
☐	342	Physical Education	.05	.02	.01
		Stay in School			
☐	343	Art	.05	.02	.01
		Stay in School			
☐	344	Science	.05	.02	.01
		Stay in School			

☐ 345	Checklist 1 (1-60)	.05	.02	.01
☐ 346	Checklist 2 (61-120)	.05	.02	.01
☐ 347	Checklist 3 (121-180)	.05	.02	.01
☐ 348	Checklist 4 (181-244)	.05	.02	.01
☐ 349	Checklist 5 (245-305)	.05	.02	.01
☐ 350	Checklist 6 (306-350)	.05	.02	.01
☐ 351	Atlanta Hawks Team Logo	.05	.02	.01
☐ 352	Boston Celtics Team Logo	.05	.02	.01
☐ 353	Charlotte Hornets Team Logo	.05	.02	.01
☐ 354	Chicago Bulls Team Logo	.05	.02	.01
☐ 355	Cleveland Cavaliers Team Logo	.05	.02	.01
☐ 356	Dallas Mavericks Team Logo	.05	.02	.01
☐ 357	Denver Nuggets Team Logo	.05	.02	.01
☐ 358	Detroit Pistons Team Logo	.05	.02	.01
☐ 359	Golden State Warriors Team Logo	.05	.02	.01
☐ 360	Houston Rockets Team Logo	.05	.02	.01
☐ 361	Indiana Pacers Team Logo	.05	.02	.01
☐ 362	Los Angeles Clippers Team Logo	.05	.02	.01
☐ 363	Los Angeles Lakers Team Logo	.05	.02	.01
☐ 364	Miami Heat Team Logo	.05	.02	.01
☐ 365	Milwaukee Bucks Team Logo	.05	.02	.01
☐ 366	Minnesota Timberwolves Team Logo	.05	.02	.01
☐ 367	New Jersey Nets Team Logo	.05	.02	.01
☐ 368	New York Knicks Team Logo	.05	.02	.01
☐ 369	Orlando Magic Team Logo	.05	.02	.01
☐ 370	Philadelphia 76ers Team Logo	.05	.02	.01
☐ 371	Phoenix Suns Team Logo	.05	.02	.01
☐ 372	Portland Trail Blazers Team Logo	.05	.02	.01
☐ 373	Sacramento Kings Team Logo	.05	.02	.01
☐ 374	San Antonio Spurs Team Logo	.05	.02	.01
☐ 375	Seattle Supersonics Team Logo	.05	.02	.01
☐ 376	Utah Jazz Team Logo	.05	.02	.01
☐ 377	Washington Bullets Team Logo	.05	.02	.01
☐ 378	Bob Weiss CO Atlanta Hawks	.05	.02	.01
☐ 379	Chris Ford CO Boston Celtics	.05	.02	.01
☐ 380	Allan Bristow CO Charlotte Hornets	.05	.02	.01
☐ 381	Phil Jackson CO Chicago Bulls	.10	.05	.01
☐ 382	Lenny Wilkens CO Cleveland Cavaliers	.10	.05	.01
☐ 383	Richie Adubato CO Dallas Mavericks	.05	.02	.01
☐ 384	Paul Westhead CO Denver Nuggets	.05	.02	.01
☐ 385	Chuck Daly CO Detroit Pistons	.10	.05	.01
☐ 386	Don Nelson CO Golden State Warriors	.10	.05	.01
☐ 387	Don Chaney CO Houston Rockets	.05	.02	.01
☐ 388	Bob Hill CO Indiana Pacers	.05	.02	.01
☐ 389	Mike Schuler CO Los Angeles Clippers	.05	.02	.01
☐ 390	Mike Dunleavy CO Los Angeles Lakers	.05	.02	.01
☐ 391	Kevin Loughery CO Miami Heat	.05	.02	.01
☐ 392	Del Harris CO Milwaukee Bucks	.05	.02	.01
☐ 393	Jimmy Rodgers CO Minnesota Timberwolves	.05	.02	.01
☐ 394	Bill Fitch CO New Jersey Nets	.05	.02	.01
☐ 395	Pat Riley CO New York Knicks	.10	.05	.01
☐ 396	Matt Guokas CO Orlando Magic	.05	.02	.01
☐ 397	Jim Lynam CO Philadelphia 76ers	.05	.02	.01
☐ 398	Cotton Fitzsimmons CO Phoenix Suns	.05	.02	.01
☐ 399	Rick Adelman CO Portland Trail Blazers	.05	.02	.01
☐ 400	Dick Motta CO Sacramento Kings	.05	.02	.01
☐ 401	Larry Brown CO San Antonio Spurs	.10	.05	.01
☐ 402	K.C. Jones CO Seattle Supersonics	.10	.05	.01
☐ 403	Jerry Sloan CO Utah Jazz	.05	.02	.01
☐ 404	Wes Unseld CO Washington Bullets	.10	.05	.01
☐ 405	Mo Cheeks GF Atlanta Hawks	.05	.02	.01
☐ 406	Dee Brown GF Boston Celtics	.05	.02	.01
☐ 407	Rex Chapman GF Charlotte Hornets	.05	.02	.01
☐ 408	Michael Jordan GF Chicago Bulls	2.50	1.15	.30
☐ 409	John Williams GF Cleveland Cavaliers	.05	.02	.01
☐ 410	James Donaldson GF Dallas Mavericks	.05	.02	.01
☐ 411	Dikembe Mutombo GF Denver Nuggets	.50	.23	.06
☐ 412	Isiah Thomas GF Detroit Pistons	.10	.05	.01
☐ 413	Tim Hardaway GF Golden State Warriors	.05	.02	.01
☐ 414	Hakeem Olajuwon GF Houston Rockets	.50	.23	.06
☐ 415	Detlef Schrempf GF Indiana Pacers	.05	.02	.01
☐ 416	Danny Manning GF Los Angeles Clippers	.05	.02	.01
☐ 417	Magic Johnson GF Los Angeles Lakers	.40	.18	.05
☐ 418	Bimbo Coles GF Miami Heat	.05	.02	.01

☐ 419	Alvin Robertson GF ...... Milwaukee Bucks	.05	.02	.01
☐ 420	Sam Mitchell GF.......... Minnesota Timberwolves	.05	.02	.01
☐ 421	Sam Bowie GF .... New Jersey Nets	.05	.02	.01
☐ 422	Mark Jackson GF .... New York Knicks	.05	.02	.01
☐ 423	Orlando Magic .... Game Frame	.05	.02	.01
☐ 424	Charles Barkley GF....... Philadelphia 76ers	.40	.18	.05
☐ 425	Dan Majerle GF .... Phoenix Suns	.05	.02	.01
☐ 426	Robert Pack GF .... Portland Trail Blazers	.05	.02	.01
☐ 427	Wayman Tisdale GF...... Sacramento Kings	.05	.02	.01
☐ 428	David Robinson GF .... San Antonio Spurs	.50	.23	.06
☐ 429	Nate McMillan GF......... Seattle Supersonics)	.05	.02	.01
☐ 430	Karl Malone GF .... Utah Jazz	.15	.07	.02
☐ 431	Michael Adams GF........ Washington Bullets	.05	.02	.01
☐ 432	Duane Ferrell SM .... Atlanta Hawks	.05	.02	.01
☐ 433	Kevin McHale SM.......... Boston Celtics	.05	.02	.01
☐ 434	Dell Curry SM .... Charlotte Hornets	.05	.02	.01
☐ 435	B.J. Armstrong SM .... Chicago Bulls	.05	.02	.01
☐ 436	John Williams SM .... Cleveland Cavaliers	.05	.02	.01
☐ 437	Brad Davis SM .... Dallas Mavericks	.05	.02	.01
☐ 438	Marcus Liberty SM .... Denver Nuggets	.05	.02	.01
☐ 439	Mark Aguirre SM .... Detroit Pistons	.05	.02	.01
☐ 440	Rod Higgins SM............ Golden State Warriors	.05	.02	.01
☐ 441	Eric(Sleepy) Floyd SM .. Houston Rockets	.05	.02	.01
☐ 442	Detlef Schrempf SM...... Indiana Pacers	.05	.02	.01
☐ 443	Loy Vaught SM .... Los Angeles Clippers	.05	.02	.01
☐ 444	Terry Teagle SM........... Los Angeles Lakers	.05	.02	.01
☐ 445	Kevin Edwards SM........ Miami Heat	.05	.02	.01
☐ 446	Dale Ellis SM................ Milwaukee Bucks	.05	.02	.01
☐ 447	Tod Murphy SM............. Minnesota Timberwolves	.05	.02	.01
☐ 448	Chris Dudley SM........... New Jersey Nets	.05	.02	.01
☐ 449	Mark Jackson SM .... New York Knicks	.05	.02	.01
☐ 450	Jerry Reynolds SM .... Orlando Magic	.05	.02	.01
☐ 451	Ron Anderson SM .... Philadelphia 76ers	.05	.02	.01
☐ 452	Dan Majerle SM .... Phoenix Suns	.05	.02	.01
☐ 453	Danny Ainge SM .... Portland Trail Blazers	.05	.02	.01
☐ 454	Jim Les SM..................	.05	.02	.01

	Sacramento Kings			
☐ 455	Paul Pressey SM........... San Antonio Spurs	.05	.02	.01
☐ 456	Ricky Pierce SM............ Seattle Supersonics	.05	.02	.01
☐ 457	Mike Brown SM............. Utah Jazz	.05	.02	.01
☐ 458	Ledell Eackles SM......... Washington Bullets	.05	.02	.01
☐ 459	Atlanta Hawks.............. Teamwork (Dominique Wilkins and Kevin Willis)	.05	.02	.01
☐ 460	Boston Celtics.............. Teamwork (Larry Bird and Robert Parish)	.30	.14	.04
☐ 461	Charlotte Hornets.......... Teamwork (Rex Chapman and Kendall Gill)	.05	.02	.01
☐ 462	Chicago Bulls.............. Teamwork (Michael Jordan and Scottie Pippen)	1.25	.55	.16
☐ 463	Cleveland Cavaliers....... Teamwork (Craig Ehlo and Mark Price)	.05	.02	.01
☐ 464	Dallas Mavericks........... Teamwork (Derek Harper and Rolando Blackman)	.05	.02	.01
☐ 465	Denver Nuggets............ Teamwork (Reggie Williams and Chris Jackson)	.05	.02	.01
☐ 466	Detroit Pistons............. Teamwork (Isiah Thomas and Bill Laimbeer)	.05	.02	.01
☐ 467	Golden State Warriors . Teamwork (Tim Hardaway and Chris Mullin)	.05	.02	.01
☐ 468	Houston Rockets .... Teamwork (Vernon Maxwell and Kenny Smith)	.05	.02	.01
☐ 469	Indiana Pacers............. Teamwork (Detlef Schrempf and Reggie Miller)	.05	.02	.01
☐ 470	Los Angeles Clippers .... Teamwork (Charles Smith and Danny Manning)	.05	.02	.01
☐ 471	Los Angeles Lakers....... Teamwork (Magic Johnson and James Worthy)	.20	.09	.03
☐ 472	Miami Heat .... Teamwork (Glen Rice and Rony Seikaly)	.05	.02	.01
☐ 473	Milwaukee Bucks .... Teamwork (Jay Humphries and Alvin Robertson)	.05	.02	.01
☐ 474	Minnesota Timberwolves . Teamwork	.05	.02	.01

(Tony Campbell and
Pooh Richardson)

☐ 475 New Jersey Nets .... .05 .02 .01
Teamwork
(Derrick Coleman and
Sam Bowie)

☐ 476 New York Knicks .... .05 .02 .01
Teamwork
(Patrick Ewing and
Charles Oakley)

☐ 477 Orlando Magic .... .05 .02 .01
Teamwork
(Dennis Scott and
Scott Skiles)

☐ 478 Philadelphia 76ers .... .05 .02 .01
Teamwork
(Charles Barkley and
Hersey Hawkins)

☐ 479 Phoenix Suns .... .05 .02 .01
Teamwork
(Kevin Johnson and
Tom Chambers)

☐ 480 Portland Trail Blazers .... .05 .02 .01
Teamwork
(Clyde Drexler and
Terry Porter)

☐ 481 Sacramento Kings .... .05 .02 .01
Teamwork
(Lionel Simmons and
Wayman Tisdale)

☐ 482 San Antonio Spurs .... .05 .02 .01
Teamwork
(Terry Cummings and
Sean Elliott)

☐ 483 Seattle Supersonics ..... .05 .02 .01
Teamwork
(Eddie Johnson and
Ricky Pierce)

☐ 484 Utah Jazz .... .05 .02 .01
Teamwork
(Karl Malone and
John Stockton)

☐ 485 Washington Bullets .... .05 .02 .01
Teamwork
(Harvey Grant and
Bernard King)

☐ 486 Rumeal Robinson RS .... .05 .02 .01
Atlanta Hawks

☐ 487 Dee Brown RS .... .05 .02 .01
Boston Celtics

☐ 488 Kendall Gill RS .... .05 .02 .01
Charlotte Hornets

☐ 489 B.J. Armstrong RS .... .05 .02 .01
Chicago Bulls

☐ 490 Danny Ferry RS .... .05 .02 .01
Cleveland Cavaliers

☐ 491 Randy White RS .... .05 .02 .01
Dallas Mavericks

☐ 492 Chris Jackson RS .... .05 .02 .01
Denver Nuggets

☐ 493 Lance Blanks RS .... .05 .02 .01
Detroit Pistons

☐ 494 Tim Hardaway RS .... .05 .02 .01
Golden State Warriors

☐ 495 Vernon Maxwell RS .... .05 .02 .01
Houston Rockets

☐ 496 Micheal Williams RS ...... .05 .02 .01
Indiana Pacers

☐ 497 Charles Smith RS .... .05 .02 .01
Los Angeles Clippers

☐ 498 Vlade Divac RS .... .05 .02 .01
Los Angeles Lakers

☐ 499 Willie Burton RS .... .05 .02 .01
Miami Heat

☐ 500 Jeff Grayer RS .... .05 .02 .01
Milwaukee Bucks

☐ 501 Pooh Richardson RS .... .05 .02 .01
Minnesota Timberwolves

☐ 502 Derrick Coleman RS...... .10 .05 .01
New Jersey Nets

☐ 503 John Starks RS .... .05 .02 .01
New York Knicks

☐ 504 Dennis Scott RS............ .05 .02 .01
Orlando Magic

☐ 505 Hersey Hawkins RS ...... .05 .02 .01
Philadelphia 76ers

☐ 506 Negele Knight RS.......... .05 .02 .01
Phoenix Suns

☐ 507 Clifford Robinson RS .... .05 .02 .01
Portland Trail Blazers

☐ 508 Lionel Simmons RS....... .05 .02 .01
Sacramento Kings

☐ 509 David Robinson RS........ .50 .23 .06
San Antonio Spurs

☐ 510 Gary Payton RS .... .10 .05 .01
Seattle Supersonics

☐ 511 Blue Edwards RS .... .05 .02 .01
Utah Jazz

☐ 512 Harvey Grant RS .... .05 .02 .01
Washington Bullets

☐ 513 Larry Johnson.............. 2.00 .90 .25
Charlotte Hornets

☐ 514 Kenny Anderson .... 1.00 .45 .13
New Jersey Nets

☐ 515 Billy Owens................... .60 .25 .08
Golden State Warriors

☐ 516 Dikembe Mutombo .... 1.50 .65 .19
Denver Nuggets

☐ 517 Steve Smith .... .60 .25 .08
Miami Heat

☐ 518 Doug Smith.................. .05 .02 .01
Dallas Mavericks

☐ 519 Luc Longley .... .15 .07 .02
Minnesota Timberwolves

☐ 520 Mark Macon................. .05 .02 .01
Denver Nuggets

☐ 521 Stacey Augmon............. .60 .25 .08
Atlanta Hawks

☐ 522 Brian Williams............. .10 .05 .01
Orlando Magic

☐ 523 Terrell Brandon .... .40 .18 .05
Cleveland Cavaliers

☐ 524 The Ball....................... .05 .02 .01
☐ 525 The Basket................... .05 .02 .01
☐ 526 The 24-second Shot...... .05 .02 .01
Clock
☐ 527 The Game Program....... .05 .02 .01
☐ 528 The Championship Gift .05 .02 .01
☐ 529 Championship Trophy.. .05 .02 .01
☐ 530 Charles Barkley USA.. 1.50 .65 .19
☐ 531 Larry Bird USA.......... 2.50 1.15 .30
☐ 532 Patrick Ewing USA ...... .75 .35 .09
☐ 533 Magic Johnson USA .. 1.50 .65 .19
☐ 534 Michael Jordan USA 10.00 4.50 1.25
☐ 535 Karl Malone USA........... .75 .35 .09
☐ 536 Chris Mullin USA .... .25 .11 .03
☐ 537 Scottie Pippen USA ...... .75 .35 .09
☐ 538 David Robinson USA . 2.00 .90 .25
☐ 539 John Stockton USA .... .75 .35 .09
☐ 540 Chuck Daly CO USA ...... .25 .11 .03
☐ 541 P.J. Carlesimo CO USA .25 .11 .03
☐ 542 Mike Krzyzewski CO USA 1.00 .45 .13

☐ 543 Lenny Wilkens CO USA	.25	.11	.03
☐ 544 Team USA Card 1	2.50	1.15	.30
☐ 545 Team USA Card 2	2.50	1.15	.30
☐ 546 Team USA Card 3	2.50	1.15	.30
☐ 547 Willie Anderson USA	.05	.02	.01
☐ 548 Stacey Augmon USA	.10	.05	.01
☐ 549 Bimbo Coles USA	.05	.02	.01
☐ 550 Jeff Grayer USA	.05	.02	.01
☐ 551 Hersey Hawkins USA	.05	.02	.01
☐ 552 Dan Majerle USA	.05	.02	.01
☐ 553 Danny Manning USA	.05	.02	.01
☐ 554 J.R. Reid USA	.05	.02	.01
☐ 555 Mitch Richmond USA	.10	.05	.01
☐ 556 Charles Smith USA	.05	.02	.01
☐ 557 Vern Fleming USA	.05	.02	.01
☐ 558 Joe Kleine USA	.05	.02	.01
☐ 559 Jon Koncak USA	.05	.02	.01
☐ 560 Sam Perkins USA	.05	.02	.01
☐ 561 Alvin Robertson USA	.05	.02	.01
☐ 562 Wayman Tisdale USA	.05	.02	.01
☐ 563 Jeff Turner USA	.05	.02	.01
☐ 564 Tony Campbell	.05	.02	.01
Minnesota Timberwolves Magic of SkyBox			
☐ 565 Joe Dumars	.10	.05	.01
Detroit Pistons Magic of SkyBox			
☐ 566 Horace Grant	.15	.07	.02
Chicago Bulls Magic of SkyBox			
☐ 567 Reggie Lewis	.05	.02	.01
Boston Celtics Magic of SkyBox			
☐ 568 Hakeem Olajuwon	.50	.23	.06
Houston Rockets Magic of SkyBox			
☐ 569 Sam Perkins	.05	.02	.01
Los Angeles Lakers Magic of SkyBox			
☐ 570 Chuck Person	.05	.02	.01
Indiana Pacers Magic of SkyBox			
☐ 571 Buck Williams	.05	.02	.01
Portland Trail Blazers Magic of SkyBox			
☐ 572 Michael Jordan	2.50	1.15	.30
Chicago Bulls SkyBox Salutes			
☐ 573 Bernard King	.05	.02	.01
NBA All-Star SkyBox Salutes			
☐ 574 Moses Malone	.10	.05	.01
Milwaukee Bucks SkyBox Salutes			
☐ 575 Robert Parish	.05	.02	.01
Boston Celtics SkyBox Salutes			
☐ 576 Pat Riley CO	.05	.02	.01
Los Angeles Lakers SkyBox Salutes			
☐ 577 Dee Brown	.05	.02	.01
Boston Celtics SkyMaster			
☐ 578 Rex Chapman	.05	.02	.01
Charlotte Hornets SkyMaster			
☐ 579 Clyde Drexler	.15	.07	.02
Portland Trail Blazers SkyMaster			
☐ 580 Blue Edwards	.05	.02	.01
Utah Jazz			

SkyMaster			
☐ 581 Ron Harper	.05	.02	.01
Los Angeles Clippers SkyMaster			
☐ 582 Kevin Johnson	.10	.05	.01
Phoenix Suns SkyMaster			
☐ 583 Michael Jordan	2.50	1.15	.30
Chicago Bulls SkyMaster			
☐ 584 Shawn Kemp	.75	.35	.09
Seattle Supersonics SkyMaster			
☐ 585 Xavier McDaniel	.05	.02	.01
New York Knicks SkyMaster			
☐ 586 Scottie Pippen	.15	.07	.02
Chicago Bulls SkyMaster			
☐ 587 Kenny Smith	.05	.02	.01
Houston Rockets SkyMaster			
☐ 588 Dominique Wilkins	.10	.05	.01
Atlanta Hawks SkyMaster			
☐ 589 Michael Adams	.05	.02	.01
Denver Nuggets Shooting Star			
☐ 590 Danny Ainge	.05	.02	.01
Denver Nuggets Shooting Star			
☐ 591 Larry Bird	.60	.25	.08
Boston Celtics Shooting Star			
☐ 592 Dale Ellis	.05	.02	.01
Milwaukee Bucks Shooting Star			
☐ 593 Hersey Hawkins	.05	.02	.01
Philadelphia 76ers Shooting Star			
☐ 594 Jeff Hornacek	.05	.02	.01
Phoenix Suns Shooting Star			
☐ 595 Jeff Malone	.05	.02	.01
Utah Jazz Shooting Star			
☐ 596 Reggie Miller	.15	.07	.02
Indiana Pacers Shooting Star			
☐ 597 Chris Mullin	.05	.02	.01
Golden State Warriors Shooting Star			
☐ 598 John Paxson	.05	.02	.01
Chicago Bulls Shooting Star			
☐ 599 Drazen Petrovic	.05	.02	.01
New Jersey Nets Shooting Star			
☐ 600 Ricky Pierce	.05	.02	.01
Milwaukee Bucks Shooting Star			
☐ 601 Mark Price	.05	.02	.01
Cleveland Cavaliers Shooting Star			
☐ 602 Dennis Scott	.05	.02	.01
Orlando Magic Shooting Star			
☐ 603 Manute Bol	.05	.02	.01
Philadelphia 76ers Small School Sensation			
☐ 604 Jerome Kersey	.05	.02	.01

Portland Trail Blazers			
Small School Sensation			
☐ 605 Charles Oakley	.05	.02	.01
New York Knicks			
Small School Sensation			
☐ 606 Scottie Pippen	.15	.07	.02
Chicago Bulls			
Small School Sensation			
☐ 607 Terry Porter	.05	.02	.01
Portland Trail Blazers			
Small School Sensation			
☐ 608 Dennis Rodman	.10	.05	.01
Detroit Pistons			
Small School Sensation			
☐ 609 Sedale Threatt	.05	.02	.01
Los Angeles Lakers			
Small School Sensation			
☐ 610 Business	.05	.02	.01
Stay in School			
☐ 611 Engineering	.05	.02	.01
Stay in School			
☐ 612 Law	.05	.02	.01
Stay in School			
☐ 613 Liberal Arts	.05	.02	.01
Stay in School			
☐ 614 Medicine	.05	.02	.01
Stay in School			
☐ 615 Maurice Cheeks	.15	.07	.02
Atlanta Hawks			
☐ 616 Travis Mays	.05	.02	.01
Atlanta Hawks			
☐ 617 Blair Rasmussen	.05	.02	.01
Atlanta Hawks			
☐ 618 Alexander Volkov	.05	.02	.01
Atlanta Hawks			
☐ 619 Rickey Green	.05	.02	.01
Boston Celtics			
☐ 620 Bobby Hansen	.05	.02	.01
Chicago Bulls			
☐ 621 John Battle	.05	.02	.01
Cleveland Cavaliers			
☐ 622 Terry Davis	.05	.02	.01
Dallas Mavericks			
☐ 623 Walter Davis	.15	.07	.02
Denver Nuggets			
☐ 624 Winston Garland	.05	.02	.01
Denver Nuggets			
☐ 625 Scott Hastings	.05	.02	.01
Denver Nuggets			
☐ 626 Brad Sellers	.05	.02	.01
Denver Nuggets			
☐ 627 Darrell Walker	.05	.02	.01
Detroit Pistons			
☐ 628 Orlando Woolridge	.05	.02	.01
Detroit Pistons			
☐ 629 Tony Brown	.05	.02	.01
Los Angeles Clippers			
☐ 630 James Edwards	.05	.02	.01
Los Angeles Clippers			
☐ 631 Doc Rivers	.05	.02	.01
Los Angeles Clippers			
☐ 632 Jack Haley	.05	.02	.01
Los Angeles Lakers			
☐ 633 Sedale Threatt	.05	.02	.01
Los Angeles Lakers			
☐ 634 Moses Malone	.20	.09	.03
Milwaukee Bucks			
☐ 635 Thurl Bailey	.05	.02	.01
Minnesota Timberwolves			
☐ 636 Rafael Addison	.05	.02	.01
New Jersey Nets			

☐ 637 Tim McCormick	.05	.02	.01
New York Knicks			
☐ 638 Xavier McDaniel	.10	.05	.01
New York Knicks			
☐ 639 Charles Shackleford	.05	.02	.01
Philadelphia 76ers			
☐ 640 Mitchell Wiggins	.05	.02	.01
Philadelphia 76ers			
☐ 641 Jerrod Mustaf	.05	.02	.01
Phoenix Suns			
☐ 642 Dennis Hopson	.05	.02	.01
Sacramento Kings			
☐ 643 Les Jepsen	.05	.02	.01
Sacramento Kings			
☐ 644 Mitch Richmond	.25	.11	.03
Sacramento Kings			
☐ 645 Dwayne Schintzius	.05	.02	.01
Sacramento Kings			
☐ 646 Spud Webb	.10	.05	.01
Sacramento Kings			
☐ 647 Jud Buechler	.05	.02	.01
San Antonio Spurs			
☐ 648 Antoine Carr	.05	.02	.01
San Antonio Spurs			
☐ 649 Tyrone Corbin	.05	.02	.01
Utah Jazz			
☐ 650 Michael Adams	.05	.02	.01
Washington Bullets			
☐ 651 Ralph Sampson	.05	.02	.01
Washington Bullets			
☐ 652 Andre Turner	.05	.02	.01
Washington Bullets			
☐ 653 David Wingate	.05	.02	.01
Washington Bullets			
☐ 654 Checklist "S"	.05	.02	.01
(351-404)			
☐ 655 Checklist "K"	.05	.02	.01
(405-458)			
☐ 656 Checklist "Y"	.05	.02	.01
(459-512)			
☐ 657 Checklist "B"	.05	.02	.01
(513-563)			
☐ 658 Checklist "O"	.05	.02	.01
(564-614)			
☐ 659 Checklist "X"	.05	.02	.01
(615-659)			
☐ NNO Clyde Drexler USA	50.00	23.00	6.25
(Send-away)			
☐ NNO Team USA Card	12.00	5.50	1.50

1991-92 SkyBox Blister Inserts

The first four inserts were featured in series one blister packs, while the last two were inserted in series two blister packs. The cards measure the standard size (2 1/2" by 3 1/2"). The first four have logos on their front and comments on the back. The last two are double-sided cards and display most valuable players from the same team for two consecutive years. The cards are numbered on the back with Roman numerals.

Isiah Thomas
NBA Finals MVP 1989

Joe Dumars
NBA Finals MVP 1989

	MINT	NRMT	EXC
COMPLETE SET (6)	2.50	1.00	.25
COMMON CARD (1-4)	.25	.11	.03
COMMON CARD (5-6)	.50	.23	.06
☐ 1 USA Basketball (Numbered I)	.25	.11	.03
☐ 2 Stay in School It's Your Best Move (Numbered II)	.25	.11	.03
☐ 3 Orlando All-Star Weekend (Numbered III)	.25	.11	.03
☐ 4 Inside Stuff (Numbered IV)	.25	.11	.03
☐ 5 Magic Johnson and James Worthy Back to Back NBA Finals MVP 1987/1988 (Numbered V)	1.00	.40	.10
☐ 6 Joe Dumars and Isiah Thomas Back to Back NBA Finals MVP 1989/1990 (Numbered VI)	.50	.23	.06

1992 SkyBox USA

The 1992 SkyBox USA basketball set contains 110 cards which were distributed in foil-wrap packs. The set includes nine cards of each of the first ten NBA players named to the team, two cards of each coach, and two checklist cards. The set concludes with a "Magic On" subset, representing Johnson's thoughts on his teammates. The wax packs included randomly inserted cards autographed by Magic Johnson and David Robinson as well as a plastic trading card featuring a team photo. The standard-

size (2 1/2" by 3 1/2") cards feature on the fronts full-bleed glossy color action shots, with the player's name and the card's subtitle printed across the top of the picture. On the upper portion, the backs feature a color close-up photo, while the lower portion presents statistics or summarizes the player's professional career. The cards are numbered on the back.

	MINT	NRMT	EXC
COMPLETE SET (110)	20.00	9.00	2.50
COMMON CARD (1-110)	.05	.02	.01
☐ 1 Charles Barkley NBA Update	.25	.11	.03
☐ 2 Charles Barkley NBA Rookie	.25	.11	.03
☐ 3 Charles Barkley Game Strategy	.25	.11	.03
☐ 4 Charles Barkley NBA Best Game	.25	.11	.03
☐ 5 Charles Barkley Off the Court	.25	.11	.03
☐ 6 Charles Barkley NBA Playoffs	.25	.11	.03
☐ 7 Charles Barkley NBA All-Star Record	.25	.11	.03
☐ 8 Charles Barkley NBA Shooting	.25	.11	.03
☐ 9 Charles Barkley NBA Rebounds	.25	.11	.03
☐ 10 Larry Bird NBA Update	.40	.18	.05
☐ 11 Larry Bird NBA Rookie	.40	.18	.05
☐ 12 Larry Bird Game Strategy	.40	.18	.05
☐ 13 Larry Bird NBA Best Game	.40	.18	.05
☐ 14 Larry Bird Off the Court	.40	.18	.05
☐ 15 Larry Bird NBA Playoffs	.40	.18	.05
☐ 16 Larry Bird NBA All-Star Record	.40	.18	.05
☐ 17 Larry Bird NBA Shooting	.40	.18	.05
☐ 18 Larry Bird NBA Rebounds	.40	.18	.05
☐ 19 Patrick Ewing NBA Update	.15	.07	.02
☐ 20 Patrick Ewing NBA Rookie	.15	.07	.02
☐ 21 Patrick Ewing Game Strategy	.15	.07	.02
☐ 22 Patrick Ewing NBA Best Game	.15	.07	.02
☐ 23 Patrick Ewing Off the Court	.15	.07	.02
☐ 24 Patrick Ewing NBA Playoffs	.15	.07	.02
☐ 25 Patrick Ewing NBA All-Star Record	.15	.07	.02
☐ 26 Patrick Ewing NBA Shooting	.15	.07	.02
☐ 27 Patrick Ewing NBA Rebounds	.15	.07	.02
☐ 28 Magic Johnson NBA Update	.25	.11	.03
☐ 29 Magic Johnson	.25	.11	.03

☐ 30	Magic Johnson NBA Rookie	.25	.11		.03
☐ 31	Magic Johnson Game Strategy	.25	.11		.03
☐ 32	Magic Johnson NBA Best Game	.25	.11		.03
☐ 33	Magic Johnson Off the Court	.25	.11		.03
☐ 34	Magic Johnson NBA Playoffs	.25	.11		.03
☐ 35	Magic Johnson NBA All-Star Record	.25	.11		.03
☐ 36	Magic Johnson NBA Shooting	.25	.11		.03
☐ 37	Michael Jordan NBA Assists	1.50	.65		.19
☐ 38	Michael Jordan NBA Update	1.50	.65		.19
☐ 39	Michael Jordan NBA Rookie	1.50	.65		.19
☐ 40	Michael Jordan Game Strategy	1.50	.65		.19
☐ 41	Michael Jordan NBA Best Game	1.50	.65		.19
☐ 42	Michael Jordan Off the Court	1.50	.65		.19
☐ 43	Michael Jordan NBA Playoffs	1.50	.65		.19
☐ 44	Michael Jordan NBA All-Star Record	1.50	.65		.19
☐ 45	Michael Jordan NBA Shooting	1.50	.65		.19
☐ 46	Karl Malone NBA All-Time Records	.15	.07		.02
☐ 47	Karl Malone NBA Update	.15	.07		.02
☐ 48	Karl Malone NBA Rookie	.15	.07		.02
☐ 49	Karl Malone Game Strategy	.15	.07		.02
☐ 50	Karl Malone NBA Best Game	.15	.07		.02
☐ 51	Karl Malone Off the Court	.15	.07		.02
☐ 52	Karl Malone NBA Playoffs	.15	.07		.02
☐ 53	Karl Malone NBA All-Star Record	.15	.07		.02
☐ 54	Karl Malone NBA Shooting	.15	.07		.02
☐ 55	Chris Mullin NBA Rebounds	.05	.02		.01
☐ 56	Chris Mullin NBA Update	.05	.02		.01
☐ 57	Chris Mullin NBA Rookie	.05	.02		.01
☐ 58	Chris Mullin Game Strategy	.05	.02		.01
☐ 59	Chris Mullin NBA Best Game	.05	.02		.01
☐ 60	Chris Mullin Off the Court	.05	.02		.01
☐ 61	Chris Mullin NBA Playoffs	.05	.02		.01
☐ 62	Chris Mullin NBA All-Star Record	.05	.02		.01
☐ 63	Chris Mullin NBA Shooting	.05	.02		.01
☐ 64	Scottie Pippen NBA Minutes	.15	.07		.02
☐ 65	Scottie Pippen NBA Update	.15	.07		.02
☐ 66	Scottie Pippen NBA Rookie	.15	.07		.02
☐ 67	Scottie Pippen Game Strategy	.15	.07		.02
☐ 68	Scottie Pippen NBA Best Game	.15	.07		.02
☐ 69	Scottie Pippen Off the Court	.15	.07		.02
☐ 70	Scottie Pippen NBA Playoffs	.15	.07		.02
☐ 71	Scottie Pippen NBA All-Star Record	.15	.07		.02
☐ 72	Scottie Pippen NBA Shooting	.15	.07		.02
☐ 73	David Robinson NBA Steals and Blocks	.25	.11		.03
☐ 74	David Robinson NBA Update	.25	.11		.03
☐ 75	David Robinson NBA Rookie	.25	.11		.03
☐ 76	David Robinson Game Strategy	.25	.11		.03
☐ 77	David Robinson NBA Best Game	.25	.11		.03
☐ 78	David Robinson Off the Court	.25	.11		.03
☐ 79	David Robinson NBA Playoffs	.25	.11		.03
☐ 80	David Robinson NBA All-Star	.25	.11		.03
☐ 81	David Robinson NBA Shooting	.25	.11		.03
☐ 82	John Stockton NBA All-Around	.15	.07		.02
☐ 83	John Stockton NBA Update	.15	.07		.02
☐ 84	John Stockton NBA Rookie	.15	.07		.02
☐ 85	John Stockton Game Strategy	.15	.07		.02
☐ 86	John Stockton NBA Best Game	.15	.07		.02
☐ 87	John Stockton Off the Court	.15	.07		.02
☐ 88	John Stockton NBA Playoffs	.15	.07		.02
☐ 89	John Stockton NBA All-Star Record	.15	.07		.02
☐ 90	John Stockton NBA Shooting	.15	.07		.02
☐ 91	P.J. Carlesimo CO NBA Assists	.05	.02		.01
☐ 92	P.J. Carlesimo CO College Coaching	.05	.02		.01
☐ 93	Chuck Daly CO NCAA Coaching Record	.05	.02		.01
☐ 94	Chuck Daly CO NBA Coaching	.05	.02		.01
☐ 95	Mike Krzyzewski CO NCAA Coaching Record	.25	.11		.03
☐ 96	Mike Krzyzewski CO College Coaching	.25	.11		.03
☐ 97	Lenny Wilkens CO College Coaching Record	.05	.02		.01
☐ 98	Lenny Wilkens CO NBA Coaching	.05	.02		.01
☐ 99	Checklist 1-54 NBA Coaching Record	.05	.02		.01
☐ 100	Checklist 55-110	.05	.02		.01
☐ 101	Magic on Barkley	.25	.11		.03

☐	102	Magic on Bird	.40	.18	.05
☐	103	Magic on Ewing	.15	.07	.02
☐	104	Magic on Magic	.25	.11	.03
☐	105	Magic on Jordan	1.50	.65	.19
☐	106	Magic on Malone	.15	.07	.02
☐	107	Magic on Mullin	.05	.02	.01
☐	108	Magic on Pippen	.15	.07	.02
☐	109	Magic on Robinson	.25	.11	.03
☐	110	Magic on Stockton	.15	.07	.02
☐	NNO	Plastic Team Photo.	10.00	4.50	1.25

1992-93 SkyBox

The complete 1992-93 SkyBox basketball set contains 413 cards, measuring the standard size (2 1/2" by 3 1/2"). The set was released in two series of 327 and 86 cards, respectively. Both series foil packs contained 12 cards each with 36 packs to a box. Suggested retail price was 1.15 per pack. Reported production quantities were approximately 15,000 20-box cases for the first series and 15,000 20-box cases for the second series. The new front design features computer-generated screens of color blended with full-bleed color action photos. The backs carry full-bleed non-action close-up photos overlaid by a column displaying complete statistics and a color stripe with a personal "bio-bit." Cards of second series rookies have a gold seal in the other lower corner. In addition, the second series Draft Pick rookie cards were printed in shorter supply than the other cards in the second series set. First series cards are checklisted below alphabetically according to and within teams as follows: Atlanta Hawks (1-9), Boston Celtics (10-18), Charlotte Hornets (19-27), Chicago Bulls (28-36), Cleveland Cavaliers (37-46), Dallas Mavericks (47-56), Denver Nuggets (57-65), Detroit Pistons (66-75), Golden State Warriors (76-84), Houston Rockets (85-93), Indiana Pacers (94-102), Los Angeles Clippers (103-112), Los Angeles Lakers (113-121), Miami Heat (122-131), Milwaukee Bucks (132-140), Minnesota Timberwolves (141-149), New Jersey Nets (150-159), New York Knicks (160-168), Orlando Magic (169-177), Philadelphia 76ers (178-187), Phoenix Suns (188-197), Portland Trail Blazers (198-207),

Sacramento Kings (208-217), San Antonio Spurs (218-226), Seattle Supersonics (227-235), Utah Jazz (236-244), and Washington Bullets (245-254). Other cards featured include Coaches (255-281), Team Tix (282-308), 1992 NBA All-Star Weekend Highlights (309-313), 1992 NBA Finals (314-318), 1992 NBA All-Rookie Team (319), and Public Service (230-321). The set concludes with checklist cards (322-327). The cards are numbered on the back. Special gold-foil stamped cards of Magic Johnson and David Robinson, some personally autographed, were randomly inserted in first series foil packs. Versions of these Johnson and Robinson cards with sparkling silver foil were also produced and one of each accompanied the first 7,500 cases ordered exclusively by hobby accounts. According to SkyBox approximately one of every 36 packs contained either a Magic Johnson or David Robinson SP card. The "Head of the Class" mail-away card features the first six 1992 NBA draft picks. The card was made available to the first 20,000 fans through a mail-in offer for three wrappers from each series of 1992-93 SkyBox cards plus 3.25 for postage and handling. The horizontal front features three color, cut-out player photos against a black background. Three wide vertical stripes in shades of red and violet run behind the players. A gold bar near the bottom carries the phrase "Head of the Class 1992 Top NBA Draft Picks." The back features three player photos similar to the ones on the front. The background design is the same except the wide stripes are green, orange, and blue. A white bar at the lower right corner carries the serial number and production run (20,000). Rookie Cards include Tom Gugliotta, Robert Horry, Christian Laettner, Don McLean, Harold Miner, Alonzo Mourning, Shaquille O'Neal, Clarence Weatherspoon and Walt Williams.

	MINT	NRMT	EXC
COMPLETE SET (413)	50.00	23.00	6.25
COMPLETE SERIES 1 (327)	20.00	9.00	2.50
COMPLETE SERIES 2 (86)	30.00	13.50	3.80
COMMON CARD (1-413)	.10	.05	.01

☐	1	Stacey Augmon	.20	.09	.03
☐	2	Maurice Cheeks	.20	.09	.03
☐	3	Duane Ferrell	.10	.05	.01
☐	4	Paul Graham	.10	.05	.01
☐	5	Jon Koncak	.10	.05	.01
☐	6	Blair Rasmussen	.10	.05	.01
☐	7	Rumeal Robinson	.10	.05	.01
☐	8	Dominique Wilkins	.25	.11	.03
☐	9	Kevin Willis	.15	.07	.02
☐	10	Larry Bird	1.50	.65	.19
☐	11	Dee Brown	.15	.07	.02
☐	12	Sherman Douglas	.10	.05	.01
☐	13	Rick Fox	.10	.05	.01
☐	14	Kevin Gamble	.10	.05	.01
☐	15	Reggie Lewis	.20	.09	.03
☐	16	Kevin McHale	.20	.09	.03
☐	17	Robert Parish	.20	.09	.03
☐	18	Ed Pinckney	.10	.05	.01

☐ 19 Muggsy Bogues	.20	.09	.03
☐ 20 Dell Curry	.10	.05	.01
☐ 21 Kenny Gattison	.10	.05	.01
☐ 22 Kendall Gill	.10	.05	.01
☐ 23 Mike Gminski	.10	.05	.01
☐ 24 Tom Hammonds	.10	.05	.01
☐ 25 Larry Johnson	.75	.35	.09
☐ 26 Johnny Newman	.10	.05	.01
☐ 27 J.R. Reid	.10	.05	.01
☐ 28 B.J. Armstrong	.10	.05	.01
☐ 29 Bill Cartwright	.10	.05	.01
☐ 30 Horace Grant	.25	.11	.03
☐ 31 Michael Jordan	6.00	2.70	.75
☐ 32 Stacey King	.10	.05	.01
☐ 33 John Paxson	.10	.05	.01
☐ 34 Will Perdue	.10	.05	.01
☐ 35 Scottie Pippen	.50	.23	.06
☐ 36 Scott Williams	.10	.05	.01
☐ 37 John Battle	.10	.05	.01
☐ 38 Terrell Brandon	.15	.07	.02
☐ 39 Brad Daugherty	.15	.07	.02
☐ 40 Craig Ehlo	.10	.05	.01
☐ 41 Danny Ferry	.10	.05	.01
☐ 42 Henry James	.10	.05	.01
☐ 43 Larry Nance	.15	.07	.02
☐ 44 Mark Price	.20	.09	.03
☐ 45 Mike Sanders	.10	.05	.01
☐ 46 Hot Rod Williams	.15	.07	.02
☐ 47 Rolando Blackman	.15	.07	.02
☐ 48 Terry Davis	.10	.05	.01
☐ 49 Derek Harper	.15	.07	.02
☐ 50 Donald Hodge	.10	.05	.01
☐ 51 Mike Iuzzolino	.10	.05	.01
☐ 52 Fat Lever	.10	.05	.01
☐ 53 Rodney McCray	.10	.05	.01
☐ 54 Doug Smith	.10	.05	.01
☐ 55 Randy White	.10	.05	.01
☐ 56 Herb Williams	.10	.05	.01
☐ 57 Greg Anderson	.10	.05	.01
☐ 58 Walter Davis	.20	.09	.03
☐ 59 Winston Garland	.10	.05	.01
☐ 60 Chris Jackson	.15	.07	.02
☐ 61 Marcus Liberty	.10	.05	.01
☐ 62 Todd Lichti	.10	.05	.01
☐ 63 Mark Macon	.10	.05	.01
☐ 64 Dikembe Mutombo	.60	.25	.08
☐ 65 Reggie Williams	.10	.05	.01
☐ 66 Mark Aguirre	.15	.07	.02
☐ 67 William Bedford	.10	.05	.01
☐ 68 Lance Blanks	.10	.05	.01
☐ 69 Joe Dumars	.25	.11	.03
☐ 70 Bill Laimbeer	.15	.07	.02
☐ 71 Dennis Rodman	.30	.14	.04
☐ 72 John Salley	.10	.05	.01
☐ 73 Isiah Thomas	.25	.11	.03
☐ 74 Darrell Walker	.10	.05	.01
☐ 75 Orlando Woolridge	.10	.05	.01
☐ 76 Victor Alexander	.10	.05	.01
☐ 77 Mario Elie	.10	.05	.01
☐ 78 Chris Gatling	.10	.05	.01
☐ 79 Tim Hardaway	.20	.09	.03
☐ 80 Tyrone Hill	.15	.07	.02
☐ 81 Alton Lister	.10	.05	.01
☐ 82 Sarunas Marciulionis	.10	.05	.01
☐ 83 Chris Mullin	.20	.09	.03
☐ 84 Billy Owens	.15	.07	.02
☐ 85 Matt Bullard	.10	.05	.01
☐ 86 Sleepy Floyd	.10	.05	.01
☐ 87 Avery Johnson	.10	.05	.01
☐ 88 Buck Johnson	.10	.05	.01
☐ 89 Vernon Maxwell	.10	.05	.01
☐ 90 Hakeem Olajuwon	1.25	.55	.16
☐ 91 Kenny Smith	.10	.05	.01
☐ 92 Larry Smith	.10	.05	.01
☐ 93 Otis Thorpe	.15	.07	.02
☐ 94 Dale Davis	.20	.09	.03
☐ 95 Vern Fleming	.10	.05	.01
☐ 96 George McCloud	.10	.05	.01
☐ 97 Reggie Miller	.50	.23	.06
☐ 98 Chuck Person	.15	.07	.02
☐ 99 Detlef Schrempf	.20	.09	.03
☐ 100 Rik Smits	.20	.09	.03
☐ 101 LaSalle Thompson	.10	.05	.01
☐ 102 Micheal Williams	.10	.05	.01
☐ 103 James Edwards	.10	.05	.01
☐ 104 Gary Grant	.10	.05	.01
☐ 105 Ron Harper	.15	.07	.02
☐ 106 Bo Kimble	.10	.05	.01
☐ 107 Danny Manning	.20	.09	.03
☐ 108 Ken Norman	.10	.05	.01
☐ 109 Olden Polynice	.10	.05	.01
☐ 110 Doc Rivers	.10	.05	.01
☐ 111 Charles Smith	.10	.05	.01
☐ 112 Loy Vaught	.15	.07	.02
☐ 113 Elden Campbell	.10	.05	.01
☐ 114 Vlade Divac	.20	.09	.03
☐ 115 A.C. Green	.20	.09	.03
☐ 116 Jack Haley	.10	.05	.01
☐ 117 Sam Perkins	.15	.07	.02
☐ 118 Byron Scott	.15	.07	.02
☐ 119 Tony Smith	.10	.05	.01
☐ 120 Sedale Threatt	.10	.05	.01
☐ 121 James Worthy	.20	.09	.03
☐ 122 Keith Askins	.10	.05	.01
☐ 123 Willie Burton	.10	.05	.01
☐ 124 Bimbo Coles	.10	.05	.01
☐ 125 Kevin Edwards	.10	.05	.01
☐ 126 Alec Kessler	.10	.05	.01
☐ 127 Grant Long	.10	.05	.01
☐ 128 Glen Rice	.20	.09	.03
☐ 129 Rony Seikaly	.10	.05	.01
☐ 130 Brian Shaw	.10	.05	.01
☐ 131 Steve Smith	.20	.09	.03
☐ 132 Frank Brickowski	.10	.05	.01
☐ 133 Dale Ellis	.15	.07	.02
☐ 134 Jeff Grayer	.10	.05	.01
☐ 135 Jay Humphries	.10	.05	.01
☐ 136 Larry Krystkowiak	.10	.05	.01
☐ 137 Moses Malone	.25	.11	.03
☐ 138 Fred Roberts	.10	.05	.01
☐ 139 Alvin Robertson	.10	.05	.01
☐ 140 Dan Schayes	.10	.05	.01
☐ 141 Thurl Bailey	.10	.05	.01
☐ 142 Scott Brooks	.10	.05	.01
☐ 143 Tony Campbell	.10	.05	.01
☐ 144 Gerald Glass	.10	.05	.01
☐ 145 Luc Longley	.10	.05	.01
☐ 146 Sam Mitchell	.10	.05	.01
☐ 147 Pooh Richardson	.10	.05	.01
☐ 148 Felton Spencer	.10	.05	.01
☐ 149 Doug West	.10	.05	.01
☐ 150 Rafael Addison	.10	.05	.01
☐ 151 Kenny Anderson	.40	.18	.05
☐ 152 Mookie Blaylock	.20	.09	.03
☐ 153 Sam Bowie	.10	.05	.01
☐ 154 Derrick Coleman	.20	.09	.03
☐ 155 Chris Dudley	.10	.05	.01
☐ 156 Tate George	.10	.05	.01
☐ 157 Terry Mills	.15	.07	.02
☐ 158 Chris Morris	.10	.05	.01
☐ 159 Drazen Petrovic	.15	.07	.02
☐ 160 Greg Anthony	.10	.05	.01

□	#	Player			
□	161	Patrick Ewing	.50	.23	.06
□	162	Mark Jackson	.10	.05	.01
□	163	Anthony Mason	.20	.09	.03
□	164	Tim McCormick	.10	.05	.01
□	165	Xavier McDaniel	.15	.07	.02
□	166	Charles Oakley	.15	.07	.02
□	167	John Starks	.20	.09	.03
□	168	Gerald Wilkins	.10	.05	.01
□	169	Nick Anderson	.15	.07	.02
□	170	Terry Catledge	.10	.05	.01
□	171	Jerry Reynolds	.10	.05	.01
□	172	Stanley Roberts	.10	.05	.01
□	173	Dennis Scott	.10	.05	.01
□	174	Scott Skiles	.10	.05	.01
□	175	Jeff Turner	.10	.05	.01
□	176	Sam Vincent	.10	.05	.01
□	177	Brian Williams	.10	.05	.01
□	178	Ron Anderson	.10	.05	.01
□	179	Charles Barkley	1.00	.45	.13
□	180	Manute Bol	.10	.05	.01
□	181	Johnny Dawkins	.10	.05	.01
□	182	Armon Gilliam	.10	.05	.01
□	183	Greg Grant	.10	.05	.01
□	184	Hersey Hawkins	.15	.07	.02
□	185	Brian Oliver	.10	.05	.01
□	186	Charles Shackleford	.10	.05	.01
□	187	Jayson Williams	.10	.05	.01
□	188	Cedric Ceballos	.20	.09	.03
□	189	Tom Chambers	.15	.07	.02
□	190	Jeff Hornacek	.15	.07	.02
□	191	Kevin Johnson	.25	.11	.03
□	192	Negele Knight	.10	.05	.01
□	193	Andrew Lang	.10	.05	.01
□	194	Dan Majerle	.15	.07	.02
□	195	Jerrod Mustaf	.10	.05	.01
□	196	Tim Perry	.10	.05	.01
□	197	Mark West	.10	.05	.01
□	198	Alaa Abdelnaby	.10	.05	.01
□	199	Danny Ainge	.15	.07	.02
□	200	Mark Bryant	.10	.05	.01
□	201	Clyde Drexler	.50	.23	.06
□	202	Kevin Duckworth	.10	.05	.01
□	203	Jerome Kersey	.10	.05	.01
□	204	Robert Pack	.10	.05	.01
□	205	Terry Porter	.15	.07	.02
□	206	Cliff Robinson	.15	.07	.02
□	207	Buck Williams	.15	.07	.02
□	208	Anthony Bonner	.10	.05	.01
□	209	Randy Brown	.10	.05	.01
□	210	Duane Causwell	.10	.05	.01
□	211	Pete Chilcutt	.10	.05	.01
□	212	Dennis Hopson	.10	.05	.01
□	213	Jim Les	.10	.05	.01
□	214	Mitch Richmond	.25	.11	.03
□	215	Lionel Simmons	.10	.05	.01
□	216	Wayman Tisdale	.10	.05	.01
□	217	Spud Webb	.10	.05	.01
□	218	Willie Anderson	.10	.05	.01
□	219	Antoine Carr	.10	.05	.01
□	220	Terry Cummings	.15	.07	.02
□	221	Sean Elliott	.15	.07	.02
□	222	Sidney Green	.10	.05	.01
□	223	Vinnie Johnson	.15	.07	.02
□	224	David Robinson	1.00	.45	.13
□	225	Rod Strickland	.15	.07	.02
□	226	Greg Sutton	.10	.05	.01
□	227	Dana Barros	.20	.09	.03
□	228	Benoit Benjamin	.10	.05	.01
□	229	Michael Cage	.10	.05	.01
□	230	Eddie Johnson	.15	.07	.02
□	231	Shawn Kemp	1.25	.55	.16
□	232	Derrick McKey	.15	.07	.02
□	233	Nate McMillan	.10	.05	.01
□	234	Gary Payton	.20	.09	.03
□	235	Ricky Pierce	.15	.07	.02
□	236	David Benoit	.10	.05	.01
□	237	Mike Brown	.10	.05	.01
□	238	Tyrone Corbin	.10	.05	.01
□	239	Mark Eaton	.10	.05	.01
□	240	Blue Edwards	.10	.05	.01
□	241	Jeff Malone	.15	.07	.02
□	242	Karl Malone	.50	.23	.06
□	243	Eric Murdock	.10	.05	.01
□	244	John Stockton	.50	.23	.06
□	245	Michael Adams	.10	.05	.01
□	246	Rex Chapman	.10	.05	.01
□	247	Ledell Eackles	.10	.05	.01
□	248	Pervis Ellison	.10	.05	.01
□	249	A.J. English	.10	.05	.01
□	250	Harvey Grant	.10	.05	.01
□	251	Charles Jones	.10	.05	.01
□	252	Bernard King	.20	.09	.03
□	253	LaBradford Smith	.10	.05	.01
□	254	Larry Stewart	.10	.05	.01
□	255	Bob Weiss CO Atlanta Hawks	.10	.05	.01
□	256	Chris Ford CO Boston Celtics	.10	.05	.01
□	257	Allan Bristow CO Charlotte Hornets	.10	.05	.01
□	258	Phil Jackson CO Chicago Bulls	.15	.07	.02
□	259	Lenny Wilkens CO Cleveland Cavaliers	.15	.07	.02
□	260	Richie Adubato CO Dallas Mavericks	.10	.05	.01
□	261	Dan Issel CO Denver Nuggets	.15	.07	.02
□	262	Ron Rothstein CO Detroit Pistons	.10	.05	.01
□	263	Don Nelson CO Golden State Warriors	.15	.07	.02
□	264	Rudy Tomjanovich CO Houston Rockets	.15	.07	.02
□	265	Bob Hill CO Indiana Pacers	.10	.05	.01
□	266	Larry Brown CO Los Angeles Clippers	.15	.07	.02
□	267	Randy Pfund CO Los Angeles Lakers	.10	.05	.01
□	268	Kevin Loughery CO Miami Heat	.10	.05	.01
□	269	Mike Dunleavy CO Milwaukee Bucks	.10	.05	.01
□	270	Jimmy Rodgers CO Minnesota Timberwolves	.10	.05	.01
□	271	Chuck Daly CO New Jersey Nets	.15	.07	.02
□	272	Pat Riley CO New York Knicks	.15	.07	.02
□	273	Matt Guokas CO Orlando Magic	.10	.05	.01
□	274	Doug Moe CO Philadelphia 76ers	.10	.05	.01
□	275	Paul Westphal CO Phoenix Suns	.15	.07	.02
□	276	Rick Adelman CO Portland Trail Blazers	.10	.05	.01
□	277	Garry St. Jean CO Sacramento Kings	.10	.05	.01
□	278	Jerry Tarkanian CO San Antonio Spurs	.25	.11	.03

☐ 279	George Karl CO .10	.05	.01
	Seattle Supersonics		
☐ 280	Jerry Sloan CO .10	.05	.01
	Utah Jazz		
☐ 281	Wes Unseld CO .15	.07	.02
	Washington Bullets		
☐ 282	Dominique Wilkins TT .15	.07	.02
	Atlanta Hawks		
☐ 283	Reggie Lewis TT .10	.05	.01
	Boston Celtics		
☐ 284	Kendall Gill TT .10	.05	.01
	Charlotte Hornets		
☐ 285	Horace Grant TT .15	.07	.02
	Chicago Bulls		
☐ 286	Brad Daugherty TT .10	.05	.01
	Cleveland Cavaliers		
☐ 287	Derek Harper TT .10	.05	.01
	Dallas Mavericks		
☐ 288	Chris Jackson TT .10	.05	.01
	Denver Nuggets		
☐ 289	Isiah Thomas TT .15	.07	.02
	Detroit Pistons		
☐ 290	Chris Mullin TT .10	.05	.01
	Golden State Warriors		
☐ 291	Kenny Smith TT .10	.05	.01
	Houston Rockets		
☐ 292	Reggie Miller TT .20	.09	.03
	Indiana Pacers		
☐ 293	Ron Harper TT .10	.05	.01
	Los Angeles Clippers		
☐ 294	Vlade Divac TT .10	.05	.01
	Los Angeles Lakers		
☐ 295	Glen Rice TT .10	.05	.01
	Miami Heat		
☐ 296	Moses Malone TT .15	.07	.02
	Milwaukee Bucks		
☐ 297	Doug West TT .10	.05	.01
	Minnesota Timberwolves		
☐ 298	Derrick Coleman TT .10	.05	.01
	New Jersey Nets		
☐ 299	Patrick Ewing TT .25	.11	.03
	(See also card 305)		
	New York Knicks		
☐ 300	Scott Skiles TT .10	.05	.01
	Orlando Magic		
☐ 301	Hersey Hawkins TT .10	.05	.01
	Philadelphia 76ers		
☐ 302	Kevin Johnson TT .15	.07	.02
	Phoenix Suns		
☐ 303	Cliff Robinson TT .10	.05	.01
	Portland Trail Blazers		
☐ 304	Anthony Webb TT .10	.05	.01
	Sacramento Kings		
☐ 305A	David Robinson TT ERR .50	.23	.06
	(Card misnumbered as 299)		
	San Antonio Spurs		
☐ 305B	David Robinson TT COR .50	.23	.06
	San Antonio Spurs		
☐ 306	Shawn Kemp TT .60	.25	.08
	Seattle Supersonics		
☐ 307	John Stockton TT .20	.09	.03
	Utah Jazz		
☐ 308	Pervis Ellison TT .10	.05	.01
	Washington Bullets		
☐ 309	Craig Hodges .10	.05	.01
☐ 310	Magic Johnson A-S MVP .50	.23	.06
☐ 311	Cedric Ceballos .10	.05	.01
	Slam Dunk Champ		
☐ 312	West in Action .10	.05	.01
☐ 313	East in Action .10	.05	.01
☐ 314	Michael Jordan MVP.. 3.00	1.35	.40

☐ 315	Clyde Drexler .20	.09	.03
	NBA Finals		
☐ 316	Western Conference .10	.05	.01
	Danny Ainge		
☐ 317	Eastern Conference .25	.11	.03
	Scottie Pippen		
☐ 318	NBA Champs .20	.09	.03
	Chicago Bulls		
☐ 319	NBA Rookie of the Year .40	.18	.05
	All-Rookie Team		
	Larry Johnson		
	Dikembe Mutombo		
☐ 320	NBA Stay in School .10	.05	.01
☐ 321	Boys and Girls .10	.05	.01
	Clubs of America		
☐ 322	Checklist 1 .10	.05	.01
☐ 323	Checklist 2 .10	.05	.01
☐ 324	Checklist 3 .10	.05	.01
☐ 325	Checklist 4 .10	.05	.01
☐ 326	Checklist 5 .10	.05	.01
☐ 327	Checklist 6 .10	.05	.01
☐ 328	Adam Keefe .25	.11	.03
	Atlanta Hawks		
☐ 329	Sean Rooks .15	.07	.02
	Dallas Mavericks		
☐ 330	Xavier McDaniel .15	.07	.02
	Boston Celtics		
☐ 331	Kiki Vandeweghe .10	.05	.01
	Los Angeles Clippers		
☐ 332	Alonzo Mourning 3.00	1.35	.40
	Charlotte Hornets		
☐ 333	Rodney McCray .10	.05	.01
	Chicago Bulls		
☐ 334	Gerald Wilkins .10	.05	.01
	Cleveland Cavaliers		
☐ 335	Tony Bennett .10	.05	.01
	Charlotte Hornets		
☐ 336	LaPhonso Ellis .50	.23	.06
	Denver Nuggets		
☐ 337	Bryant Stith .40	.18	.05
	Denver Nuggets		
☐ 338	Isaiah Morris .10	.05	.01
	Detroit Pistons		
☐ 339	Olden Polynice .10	.05	.01
	Detroit Pistons		
☐ 340	Jeff Grayer .10	.05	.01
	Golden State Warriors		
☐ 341	Byron Houston .10	.05	.01
	Golden State Warriors		
☐ 342	Latrell Sprewell 3.00	1.35	.40
	Golden State Warriors		
☐ 343	Scott Brooks .10	.05	.01
	Houston Rockets		
☐ 344	Frank Johnson .15	.07	.02
	Phoenix Suns		
☐ 345	Robert Horry 1.25	.55	.16
	Houston Rockets		
☐ 346	David Wood .10	.05	.01
	San Antonio Spurs		
☐ 347	Sam Mitchell .10	.05	.01
	Indiana Pacers		
☐ 348	Pooh Richardson .10	.05	.01
	Indiana Pacers		
☐ 349	Malik Sealy .25	.11	.03
	Indiana Pacers		
☐ 350	Morlon Wiley .10	.05	.01
	Los Angeles Clippers		
☐ 351	Mark Jackson .10	.05	.01
	Los Angeles Clippers		
* ☐ 352	Stanley Roberts .10	.05	.01
	Los Angeles Clippers		

☐ 353	Elmore Spencer .10 Los Angeles Clippers	.05	.01
☐ 354	John Williams .10 Los Angeles Clippers	.05	.01
☐ 355	Randy Woods .10 Los Angeles Clippers	.05	.01
☐ 356	James Edwards .10 Los Angeles Lakers	.05	.01
☐ 357	Jeff Sanders .10 Atlanta Hawks	.05	.01
☐ 358	Magic Johnson .50 Los Angeles Lakers	.23	.06
☐ 359	Anthony Peeler .25 Los Angeles Lakers	.11	.03
☐ 360	Harold Miner .30 Miami Heat	.14	.04
☐ 361	John Salley .10 Miami Heat	.05	.01
☐ 362	Alaa Abdelnaby .10 Milwaukee Bucks	.05	.01
☐ 363	Todd Day .60 Milwaukee Bucks	.25	.08
☐ 364	Blue Edwards .10 Milwaukee Bucks	.05	.01
☐ 365	Lee Mayberry .15 Milwaukee Bucks	.07	.02
☐ 366	Eric Murdock .10 Milwaukee Bucks	.05	.01
☐ 367	Mookie Blaylock .15 Atlanta Hawks	.07	.02
☐ 368	Anthony Avent .10 Milwaukee Bucks	.05	.01
☐ 369	Christian Laettner .1.00 Minnesota Timberwolves	.45	.13
☐ 370	Chuck Person .15 Minnesota Timberwolves	.07	.02
☐ 371	Chris Smith .10 Minnesota Timberwolves	.05	.01
☐ 372	Micheal Williams .10 Minnesota Timberwolves	.05	.01
☐ 373	Rolando Blackman .15 New York Knicks	.07	.02
☐ 374	Tony Campbell UER .10 (Back photo actually Alvin Robertson) New York Knicks	.05	.01
☐ 375	Hubert Davis .25 New York Knicks	.11	.03
☐ 376	Travis Mays .10 Atlanta Hawks	.05	.01
☐ 377	Doc Rivers .10 New York Knicks	.05	.01
☐ 378	Charles Smith .10 New York Knicks	.05	.01
☐ 379	Rumeal Robinson .10 New Jersey Nets	.05	.01
☐ 380	Vinny Del Negro .10 San Antonio Spurs	.05	.01
☐ 381	Steve Kerr .10 Orlando Magic	.05	.01
☐ 382	Shaquille O'Neal .12.00 Orlando Magic	5.50	1.50
☐ 383	Donald Royal .10 Orlando Magic	.05	.01
☐ 384	Jeff Hornacek .15 Philadelphia 76ers	.07	.02
☐ 385	Andrew Lang .10 Philadelphia 76ers	.05	.01
☐ 386	Tim Perry UER .10 Philadelphia 76ers (Alvin Robertson pictured on back)	.05	.01

☐ 387	Clarence Weatherspoon 1.00 Philadelphia 76ers	.45	.13
☐ 388	Danny Ainge .15 Phoenix Suns	.07	.02
☐ 389	Charles Barkley .50 Phoenix Suns	.23	.06
☐ 390	Tim Kempton .10 Phoenix Suns	.05	.01
☐ 391	Oliver Miller .40 Phoenix Suns	.18	.05
☐ 392	Dave Johnson .10 Portland Trail Blazers	.05	.01
☐ 393	Tracy Murray .15 Portland Trail Blazers	.07	.02
☐ 394	Rod Strickland .15 Portland Trail Blazers	.07	.02
☐ 395	Marty Conlon .10 Sacramento Kings	.05	.01
☐ 396	Walt Williams .1.00 Sacramento Kings	.45	.13
☐ 397	Lloyd Daniels .10 San Antonio Spurs	.05	.01
☐ 398	Dale Ellis .15 San Antonio Spurs	.07	.02
☐ 399	Dave Hoppen .10 San Antonio Spurs	.05	.01
☐ 400	Larry Smith .10 San Antonio Spurs	.05	.01
☐ 401	Doug Overton .10 Washington Bullets	.05	.01
☐ 402	Isaac Austin .10 Utah Jazz	.05	.01
☐ 403	Jay Humphries .10 Utah Jazz	.05	.01
☐ 404	Larry Krystkowiak .10 Utah Jazz	.05	.01
☐ 405	Tom Gugliotta .75 Washington Bullets	.35	.09
☐ 406	Buck Johnson .10 Washington Bullets	.05	.01
☐ 407	Don MacLean .25 Washington Bullets	.11	.03
☐ 408	Marlon Maxey .10 Minnesota Timberwolves	.05	.01
☐ 409	Corey Williams .10 Chicago Bulls	.05	.01
☐ 410	Special Olympics .20 Dan Majerle Phoenix Suns	.09	.03
☐ 411	Checklist 1 .10	.05	.01
☐ 412	Checklist 2 .10	.05	.01
☐ 413	Checklist 3 .10	.05	.01
☐ NNO	David Robinson .10.00 The Admiral Comes Prepared	4.50	1.25
☐ NNO	Head of the Class .40.00 Alonzo Mourning Charlotte Hornets Shaquille O'Neal Orlando Magic Christian Laettner Minnesota Timberwolves LaPhonso Ellis Denver Nuggets Jim Jackson Dallas Mavericks Tom Gugliotta Washington Bullets	18.00	5.00
☐ NNO	Magic Johnson .10.00 The Magic Never Ends	4.50	1.25

1992-93 SkyBox Draft Picks

This 25-card insert set showcases the first round picks from the 1992 NBA Draft. The cards were randomly inserted into 12-card (both series) foil packs. According to SkyBox, approximately one out of every eight packs contained a Draft Pick card. The card numbering (1-27) reflects the actual order in which each player was selected. Six players (2, 10-11, 15-16, 18) available by the first series cut-off date were issued in first series foil packs, while the rest of the first round picks who signed NBA contracts were issued in second series packs. DP4 and DP17, intended for Jim Jackson and Doug Christie respectively, were not issued with this set because neither player signed a professional contract in time to be included in the second series. They were issued in 1993-94 first series packs. The fronts display an opaque metallic gold rectangle set off from the player. On a gradated gold background, the backs present player profiles. A white rectangle that runs vertically the length of the card contains statistics. The team logo is superimposed on this rectangle. The cards are numbered on the back with a "DP" prefix.

	MINT	NRMT	EXC
COMPLETE SET (25)	75.00	34.00	9.50
COMPLETE SERIES 1 (6)	15.00	6.75	1.90
COMPLETE SERIES 2 (19)	60.00	27.00	7.50
COMMON CARD	.50	.23	.06
☐ 1 Shaquille O'Neal	40.00	18.00	5.00
Orlando Magic			
☐ 2 Alonzo Mourning	10.00	4.50	1.25
Charlotte Hornets			
☐ 3 Christian Laettner	3.00	1.35	.40
Minnesota Timberwolves			
☐ 4 Not issued			
(Player unsigned)			
☐ 5 LaPhonso Ellis	1.50	.65	.19
Denver Nuggets			
☐ 6 Tom Gugliotta	2.50	1.15	.30
Washington Bullets			
☐ 7 Walt Williams	3.00	1.35	.40
Sacramento Kings			
☐ 8 Todd Day	2.00	.90	.25
Milwaukee Bucks			
☐ 9 Clarence Weatherspoon	3.00	1.35	.40
Philadelphia 76ers			
☐ 10 Adam Keefe	.50	.23	.06
Atlanta Hawks			
☐ 11 Robert Horry	4.00	1.80	.50
Houston Rockets			
☐ 12 Harold Miner	1.00	.45	.13
Miami Heat			
☐ 13 Bryant Stith	1.25	.55	.16
Denver Nuggets			
☐ 14 Malik Sealy	1.00	.45	.13
Indiana Pacers			
☐ 15 Anthony Peeler	1.00	.45	.13
Los Angeles Lakers			
☐ 16 Randy Woods	.50	.23	.06
San Diego Clippers			
☐ 17 Not issued			
(Player unsigned)			
☐ 18 Tracy Murray	.50	.23	.06
San Antonio Spurs			
☐ 19 Don MacLean	.50	.23	.06
Washington Bullets			
☐ 20 Hubert Davis	.50	.23	.06
New York Knicks			
☐ 21 Jon Barry	.50	.23	.06
Milwaukee Bucks			
☐ 22 Oliver Miller	1.25	.55	.16
Phoenix Suns			
☐ 23 Lee Mayberry	.50	.23	.06
Milwaukee Bucks			
☐ 24 Latrell Sprewell	10.00	4.50	1.25
Golden State Warriors			
☐ 25 Elmore Spencer	.50	.23	.06
Los Angeles Clippers			
☐ 26 Dave Johnson	.50	.23	.06
Portland Trail Blazers			
☐ 27 Byron Houston	.50	.23	.06
Golden State Warriors			

1992-93 SkyBox Olympic Team

Each card in this 12-card set features an action photo of a team member and his complete statistics from the Olympic Games. According to SkyBox, the cards were randomly inserted into 12-card first series foil packs at a rate of approximately one per six. The backs tell the story of U.S. Men's Olympic Team, from scrimmage in Monte Carlo to the medal ceremony in

Barcelona. These standard size (2 1/2" by 3 1/2") cards are numbered on the back with a "USA" prefix.

	MINT	NRMT	EXC
COMPLETE SET (12)	50.00	23.00	6.25
COMMON CARD (1-12)	1.00	.45	.13
☐ 1 Clyde Drexler	2.50	1.15	.30
☐ 2 Chris Mullin	1.00	.45	.13
☐ 3 John Stockton	2.50	1.15	.30
☐ 4 Karl Malone	2.50	1.15	.30
☐ 5 Scottie Pippen	2.50	1.15	.30
☐ 6 Larry Bird	8.00	3.60	1.00
☐ 7 Charles Barkley	5.00	2.30	.60
☐ 8 Patrick Ewing	2.50	1.15	.30
☐ 9 Christian Laettner	3.00	1.35	.40
☐ 10 David Robinson	5.00	2.30	.60
☐ 11 Michael Jordan	30.00	13.50	3.80
☐ 12 Magic Johnson	5.00	2.30	.60

1992-93 SkyBox David Robinson

This ten-card insert provides a look at Robinson at various stages of his life. Included are photos from his childhood, indulging in hobbies, with his family at the Naval Academy and his present day super stardom. The first five cards were randomly inserted in first series 12-card foil packs, while the second five were found in second series packs. According to SkyBox, approximately one of every eight packs contains a David Robinson insert card. The standard-size (2 1/2" by 3 1/2") cards feature a different design than the regular issue cards. The fronts display color photos tilted slightly to the left with a special seal overlaying the upper left corner. The surrounding card face shows two colors.

	MINT	NRMT	EXC
COMPLETE SET (10)	4.00	1.80	.50
COMPLETE SERIES 1 (5)	2.00	.90	.25
COMPLETE SERIES 2 (5)	2.00	.90	.25
COMMON D.ROBINSON (R1-R10)	.50	.23	.06
☐ R1 David Robinson Childhood	.50	.23	.06
☐ R2 David Robinson	.50	.23	.06
☐ R3 David Robinson College	.50	.23	.06
☐ R4 David Robinson College	.50	.23	.06
☐ R5 David Robinson At Ease	.50	.23	.06
☐ R6 David Robinson College	.50	.23	.06
☐ R7 David Robinson College	.50	.23	.06
☐ R8 David Robinson Awards	.50	.23	.06
☐ R9 David Robinson Awards	.50	.23	.06
☐ R10 David Robinson At Ease	.50	.23	.06

1992-93 SkyBox School Ties

Randomly inserted in 1992-93 SkyBox second series 12-card foil packs at a reported rate of one per four, this 18-card set consists of six different three-card "School Ties" interlocking cards. When the three cards in each puzzle are placed together, they create a montage of active NBA players from one particular college. The cards measure the standard size (2 1/2" by 3 1/2"). The fronts feature several color player photos that have team color-coded picture frames. The team logo appears in a team color-coded banner that is superimposed across the bottom of the picture. The backs have brightly colored backgrounds and display information about the college, the players, and a checklist of the players on the three-card puzzle. The cards are numbered on the back with an "ST" prefix.

	MINT	NRMT	EXC
COMPLETE SET (18)	15.00	6.75	1.90
COMMON CARD (ST1-ST18)	.25	.11	.03
☐ ST1 Patrick Ewing Alonzo Mourning Georgetown	3.00	1.35	.40
☐ ST2 Dikembe Mutombo Eric Floyd Georgetown	.50	.23	.06

☐ ST3 Reggie Williams	.25	.11	.03
David Wingate			
Georgetown			
☐ ST4 Kenny Anderson	.35	.16	.04
Duane Ferrell			
Georgia Tech			
☐ ST5 Tom Hammonds	.35	.16	.04
Jon Barry			
Mark Price			
Georgia Tech			
☐ ST6 John Salley	.25	.11	.03
Dennis Scott			
Georgia Tech			
☐ ST7 Rafael Addison	.25	.11	.03
Dave Johnson			
Syracuse			
☐ ST8 Billy Owens	.35	.10	.04
Derrick Coleman			
Rony Seikaly			
Syracuse			
☐ ST9 Sherman Douglas	.25	.11	.03
Danny Schayes			
Syracuse			
☐ ST10 Nick Anderson	.35	.16	.04
Kendall Gill			
Illinois			
☐ ST11 Derek Harper	.35	.16	.04
Eddie Johnson			
Illinois			
☐ ST12 Marcus Liberty	.25	.11	.03
Ken Norman			
Illinois			
☐ ST13 Greg Anthony	.35	.16	.04
Stacey Augmon			
Nevada-Las Vegas			
☐ ST14 Armon Gilliam	.75	.35	.09
Larry Johnson			
Sidney Green			
Nevada-Las Vegas			
☐ ST15 Elmore Spencer	.25	.11	.03
Gerald Paddio			
Nevada-Las Vegas			
☐ ST16 James Worthy	10.00	4.50	1.25
Michael Jordan			
Sam Perkins			
North Carolina			
☐ ST17 J.R. Reid	.25	.11	.03
Pete Chilcutt			
Brad Daugherty			
Rick Fox			
North Carolina			
☐ ST18 Hubert Davis	.25	.11	.03
Kenny Smith			
Scott Williams			
North Carolina			

1992-93 SkyBox Thunder and Lightning

Randomly inserted into second series 12-card foil packs at a reported rate of one per 40 packs, each card in this nine-card set features a pair of teammates. There is a photo on each side. The catchword on the front is "Thunder", referring to a dominant power player, while "Lightning" on the back captures the speed of a guard. The cards are highlighted by a litho-foil printing which gives a foil-look to the graphics around the basketball. The cards measure the standard size (2 1/2" by 3 1/2") and have color action player photos against a dark background, with computer enhancement around the ball and player. On the front, the power player's name appears at the bottom and is underlined by a thin yellow stripe. The word "Thunder" appears below the stripe. On the horizontal backs, the speed player's name is displayed in the upper right with the same yellow underline, but the word "Lightning" appears below it. The cards are numbered on the back with a "TL" prefix.

	MINT	NRMT	EXC
COMPLETE SET (9)	50.00	23.00	6.25
COMMON PAIR (TL1-TL9)	2.00	.90	.25
☐ TL1 Dikembe Mutombo	5.00	2.30	.60
Mark Macon			
Denver Nuggets			
☐ TL2 Buck Williams	6.00	2.70	.75
Clyde Drexler			
Portland Trail Blazers			
☐ TL3 Charles Barkley	15.00	6.75	1.90
Kevin Johnson			
Phoenix Suns			
☐ TL4 Pervis Ellison	2.00	.90	.25
Michael Adams			
Washington Bullets			
☐ TL5 Larry Johnson	6.00	2.70	.75
Tyrone Bogues			
Charlotte Hornets			
☐ TL6 Brad Daugherty	2.00	.90	.25
Mark Price			
Cleveland Cavaliers			
☐ TL7 Shawn Kemp	15.00	6.75	1.90
Gary Payton			
Seattle Supersonics			
☐ TL8 Karl Malone	12.00	5.50	1.50
John Stockton			
Utah Jazz			
☐ TL9 Billy Owens	2.00	.90	.25
Tim Hardaway			
Golden State Warriors			

1993-94 SkyBox

The 1993-94 SkyBox basketball set contains 341 cards that were issued in series

of 191 and 150 respectively. Cards were issued in 12-card packs with 36 packs per box. The cards measure standard size (2 1/2" by 3 1/2") and feature full-bleed color action photos with a wide white stripe down one side of the front containing the player's name, position, and team. The SkyBox Premium foil stamp logo appears superimposed on the front. The backs display a second player close-up shot on the top half, and the player's statistics and scouting report on the bottom half. The cards are numbered on the back, grouped alphabetically within teams, and checklisted below alphabetically according to teams as follows: Atlanta Hawks (24-29; 192-195), Boston Celtics (30-35; 196-199), Charlotte Hornets (36-41; 200-204), Chicago Bulls (42-48; 205-208), Cleveland Cavaliers (49-54; 209-212), Dallas Mavericks (55-59; 213-215), Denver Nuggets (60-65; 216-218), Detroit Pistons (66-71; 219-222), Golden State Warriors (72-78; 223-227), Houston Rockets (79-83; 228-231), Indiana Pacers (84-89; 232-234), Los Angeles Clippers (92-95; 235-238), Los Angeles Lakers (96-101; 239-241), Miami Heat (102-107; 242-243), Milwaukee Bucks (108-114; 244-248), Minnesota Timberwolves (115-119; 249-251), New Jersey Nets (120-124; 252-253), New York Knicks (125-131; 254-257), Orlando Magic (132-137; 258-261), Philadelphia 76ers (138-143; 262-265), Phoenix Suns (144-149; 266-268), Portland Trail Blazers (150-156; 269-272), Sacramento Kings (157-161; 273-275), San Antonio Spurs (162-168; 276-280), Seattle Supersonics (169-174; 281-284), Utah Jazz (175-179; 285-287), and Washington Bullets (180-185; 288-291). The following subsets are also included in this set: 1993 Playoff Performances (4-21), Changing Faces (292-318), and Costacos Brothers Poster Cards (319-338). The odds of finding a Head of the Class Exchange card are one in 360 first series packs. It was redeemable for a Head of the Class card featuring the top six 1993 draft picks. The redemption date was April 15, 1994.

	MINT	NRMT	EXC
COMPLETE SET (341)	30.00	13.50	3.80
COMPLETE SERIES 1 (191)	15.00	6.75	1.90
COMPLETE SERIES 2 (150)	15.00	6.75	1.90
COMMON CARD (1-341)	.05	.02	.01

☐	1 Checklist	.05	.02	.01
☐	2 Checklist	.05	.02	.01
☐	3 Checklist	.05	.02	.01
☐	4 Larry Johnson PO	.10	.05	.01
	Charlotte Hornets			
☐	5 Alonzo Mourning PO	.30	.14	.04
	Charlotte Hornets			
☐	6 Hakeem Olajuwon PO	.40	.18	.05
	Houston Rockets			
☐	7 Brad Daugherty PO	.05	.02	.01
	Cleveland Cavaliers			
☐	8 Oliver Miller PO	.05	.02	.01
	Phoenix Suns			
☐	9 David Robinson PO	.30	.14	.04
	San Antonio Spurs			
☐	10 Patrick Ewing PO	.10	.05	.01
	New York Knicks			
☐	11 Ricky Pierce PO	.05	.02	.01
	Seattle Supersonics			
☐	12 Sam Perkins PO	.05	.02	.01
	Seattle Supersonics			
☐	13 John Starks PO	.05	.02	.01
	New York Knicks			
☐	14 Michael Jordan PO	2.00	.90	.25
	Chicago Bulls			
☐	15 Dan Majerle PO	.05	.02	.01
	Phoenix Suns			
☐	16 Scottie Pippen PO	.10	.05	.01
	Chicago Bulls			
☐	17 Shawn Kemp PO	.30	.14	.04
	Seattle Supersonics			
☐	18 Charles Barkley PO	.30	.14	.04
	Phoenix Suns			
☐	19 Horace Grant PO	.08	.04	.01
	Chicago Bulls			
☐	20 Kevin Johnson PO	.08	.04	.01
	Phoenix Suns			
☐	21 John Paxson PO	.05	.02	.01
	Chicago Bulls			
☐	22 Inside Stuff	.05	.02	.01
☐	23 NBA On NBC	.05	.02	.01
☐	24 Stacey Augmon	.08	.04	.01
☐	25 Mookie Blaylock	.08	.04	.01
☐	26 Craig Ehlo	.05	.02	.01
☐	27 Adam Keefe	.05	.02	.01
☐	28 Dominique Wilkins	.15	.07	.02
☐	29 Kevin Willis	.08	.04	.01
☐	30 Dee Brown	.08	.04	.01
☐	31 Sherman Douglas	.05	.02	.01
☐	32 Rick Fox	.05	.02	.01
☐	33 Kevin Gamble	.05	.02	.01
☐	34 Xavier McDaniel	.08	.04	.01
☐	35 Robert Parish	.10	.05	.01
☐	36 Muggsy Bogues	.10	.05	.01
☐	37 Dell Curry	.05	.02	.01
☐	38 Kendall Gill	.05	.02	.01
☐	39 Larry Johnson	.30	.14	.04
☐	40 Alonzo Mourning	.60	.25	.08
☐	41 Johnny Newman	.05	.02	.01
☐	42 B.J. Armstrong	.05	.02	.01
☐	43 Bill Cartwright	.05	.02	.01
☐	44 Horace Grant	.15	.07	.02
☐	45 Michael Jordan	4.00	1.80	.50
☐	46 John Paxson	.05	.02	.01
☐	47 Scottie Pippen	.30	.14	.04
☐	48 Scott Williams	.05	.02	.01
☐	49 Terrell Brandon	.05	.02	.01
☐	50 Brad Daugherty	.08	.04	.01
☐	51 Larry Nance	.08	.04	.01
☐	52 Mark Price	.10	.05	.01
☐	53 Gerald Wilkins	.05	.02	.01

☐ 54	John Williams	.08	.04	.01	☐ 125	Rolando Blackman	.08	.04	.01
☐ 55	Terry Davis	.05	.02	.01	☐ 126	Patrick Ewing	.30	.14	.04
☐ 56	Derek Harper	.08	.04	.01	☐ 127	Anthony Mason	.08	.04	.01
☐ 57	Jim Jackson	.60	.25	.08	☐ 128	Charles Oakley	.08	.04	.01
☐ 58	Sean Rooks	.05	.02	.01	☐ 129	Doc Rivers	.05	.02	.01
☐ 59	Doug Smith	.05	.02	.01	☐ 130	Charles Smith	.05	.02	.01
☐ 60	Mahmoud Abdul-Rauf	.08	.04	.01	☐ 131	John Starks	.08	.04	.01
☐ 61	LaPhonso Ellis	.08	.04	.01	☐ 132	Nick Anderson	.08	.04	.01
☐ 62	Mark Macon	.05	.02	.01	☐ 133	Shaquille O'Neal	2.50	1.15	.30
☐ 63	Dikembe Mutombo	.25	.11	.03	☐ 134	Donald Royal	.05	.02	.01
☐ 64	Bryant Stith	.05	.02	.01	☐ 135	Dennis Scott	.05	.02	.01
☐ 65	Reggie Williams	.05	.02	.01	☐ 136	Scott Skiles	.05	.02	.01
☐ 66	Joe Dumars	.15	.07	.02	☐ 137	Brian Williams	.05	.02	.01
☐ 67	Bill Laimbeer	.08	.04	.01	☐ 138	Johnny Dawkins	.05	.02	.01
☐ 68	Terry Mills	.05	.02	.01	☐ 139	Hersey Hawkins	.08	.04	.01
☐ 69	Alvin Robertson	.05	.02	.01	☐ 140	Jeff Hornacek	.08	.04	.01
☐ 70	Dennis Rodman	.20	.09	.03	☐ 141	Andrew Lang	.05	.02	.01
☐ 71	Isiah Thomas	.15	.07	.02	☐ 142	Tim Perry	.05	.02	.01
☐ 72	Victor Alexander	.05	.02	.01	☐ 143	Clarence Weatherspoon	.10	.05	.01
☐ 73	Tim Hardaway	.10	.05	.01	☐ 144	Danny Ainge	.08	.04	.01
☐ 74	Tyrone Hill	.08	.04	.01	☐ 145	Charles Barkley	.60	.25	.08
☐ 75	Sarunas Marciulionis	.05	.02	.01	☐ 146	Cedric Ceballos	.10	.05	.01
☐ 76	Chris Mullin	.10	.05	.01	☐ 147	Kevin Johnson	.15	.07	.02
☐ 77	Billy Owens	.08	.04	.01	☐ 148	Oliver Miller	.05	.02	.01
☐ 78	Latrell Sprewell	.60	.25	.08	☐ 149	Dan Majerle	.08	.04	.01
☐ 79	Robert Horry	.10	.05	.01	☐ 150	Clyde Drexler	.30	.14	.04
☐ 80	Vernon Maxwell	.05	.02	.01	☐ 151	Harvey Grant	.05	.02	.01
☐ 81	Hakeem Olajuwon	.75	.35	.09	☐ 152	Jerome Kersey	.05	.02	.01
☐ 82	Kenny Smith	.05	.02	.01	☐ 153	Terry Porter	.08	.04	.01
☐ 83	Otis Thorpe	.08	.04	.01	☐ 154	Clifford Robinson	.08	.04	.01
☐ 84	Dale Davis	.08	.04	.01	☐ 155	Rod Strickland	.08	.04	.01
☐ 85	Reggie Miller	.30	.14	.04	☐ 156	Buck Williams	.08	.04	.01
☐ 86	Pooh Richardson	.05	.02	.01	☐ 157	Mitch Richmond	.15	.07	.02
☐ 87	Detlef Schrempf	.10	.05	.01	☐ 158	Lionel Simmons	.05	.02	.01
☐ 88	Malik Sealy	.05	.02	.01	☐ 159	Wayman Tisdale	.08	.04	.01
☐ 89	Rik Smits	.10	.05	.01	☐ 160	Spud Webb	.08	.04	.01
☐ 90	Ron Harper	.08	.04	.01	☐ 161	Walt Williams	.10	.05	.01
☐ 91	Mark Jackson	.05	.02	.01	☐ 162	Antoine Carr	.05	.02	.01
☐ 92	Danny Manning	.10	.05	.01	☐ 163	Lloyd Daniels	.05	.02	.01
☐ 93	Stanley Roberts	.05	.02	.01	☐ 164	Sean Elliott	.08	.04	.01
☐ 94	Loy Vaught	.08	.04	.01	☐ 165	Dale Ellis	.08	.04	.01
☐ 95	Randy Woods	.05	.02	.01	☐ 166	Avery Johnson	.05	.02	.01
☐ 96	Sam Bowie	.05	.02	.01	☐ 167	J.R. Reid	.05	.02	.01
☐ 97	Doug Christie	.05	.02	.01	☐ 168	David Robinson	.60	.25	.08
☐ 98	Vlade Divac	.10	.05	.01	☐ 169	Shawn Kemp	.60	.25	.08
☐ 99	Anthony Peeler	.05	.02	.01	☐ 170	Derrick McKey	.08	.04	.01
☐ 100	Sedale Threatt	.05	.02	.01	☐ 171	Nate McMillan	.05	.02	.01
☐ 101	James Worthy	.10	.05	.01	☐ 172	Gary Payton	.10	.05	.01
☐ 102	Grant Long	.05	.02	.01	☐ 173	Sam Perkins	.08	.04	.01
☐ 103	Harold Miner	.05	.02	.01	☐ 174	Ricky Pierce	.08	.04	.01
☐ 104	Glen Rice	.10	.05	.01	☐ 175	Tyrone Corbin	.05	.02	.01
☐ 105	John Salley	.05	.02	.01	☐ 176	Jay Humphries	.05	.02	.01
☐ 106	Rony Seikaly	.05	.02	.01	☐ 177	Jeff Malone	.08	.04	.01
☐ 107	Steve Smith	.08	.04	.01	☐ 178	Karl Malone	.30	.14	.04
☐ 108	Anthony Avent	.05	.02	.01	☐ 179	John Stockton	.30	.14	.04
☐ 109	Jon Barry	.05	.02	.01	☐ 180	Michael Adams	.05	.02	.01
☐ 110	Frank Brickowski	.05	.02	.01	☐ 181	Kevin Duckworth	.05	.02	.01
☐ 111	Blue Edwards	.05	.02	.01	☐ 182	Pervis Ellison	.05	.02	.01
☐ 112	Todd Day	.08	.04	.01	☐ 183	Tom Gugliotta	.10	.05	.01
☐ 113	Lee Mayberry	.05	.02	.01	☐ 184	Don MacLean	.05	.02	.01
☐ 114	Eric Murdock	.05	.02	.01	☐ 185	Brent Price	.05	.02	.01
☐ 115	Thurl Bailey	.05	.02	.01	☐ 186	George Lynch	.08	.04	.01
☐ 116	Christian Laettner	.10	.05	.01		Los Angeles Lakers			
☐ 117	Chuck Person	.08	.04	.01	☐ 187	Rex Walters	.08	.04	.01
☐ 118	Doug West	.05	.02	.01		New Jersey Nets			
☐ 119	Micheal Williams	.05	.02	.01	☐ 188	Shawn Bradley	.40	.18	.05
☐ 120	Kenny Anderson	.10	.05	.01		Philadelphia 76ers			
☐ 121	Benoit Benjamin	.05	.02	.01	☐ 189	Ervin Johnson	.10	.05	.01
☐ 122	Derrick Coleman	.10	.05	.01		Seattle Supersonics			
☐ 123	Chris Morris	.05	.02	.01	☐ 190	Luther Wright	.05	.02	.01
☐ 124	Rumeal Robinson	.05	.02	.01		Utah Jazz			

☐ 191	Calbert Cheaney	.50	.23	.06
	Washington Bullets			
☐ 192	Craig Ehlo	.05	.02	.01
☐ 193	Duane Ferrell	.05	.02	.01
☐ 194	Paul Graham	.05	.02	.01
☐ 195	Andrew Lang	.05	.02	.01
☐ 196	Chris Corchiani	.05	.02	.01
☐ 197	Acie Earl	.05	.02	.01
☐ 198	Dino Radja	.40	.18	.05
☐ 199	Ed Pinckney	.05	.02	.01
☐ 200	Tony Bennett	.05	.02	.01
☐ 201	Scott Burrell	.25	.11	.03
☐ 202	Kenny Gattison	.05	.02	.01
☐ 203	Hersey Hawkins	.08	.04	.01
☐ 204	Eddie Johnson	.08	.04	.01
☐ 205	Corie Blount	.05	.02	.01
☐ 206	Steve Kerr	.05	.02	.01
☐ 207	Toni Kukoc	.50	.23	.06
☐ 208	Pete Myers	.05	.02	.01
☐ 209	Danny Ferry	.05	.02	.01
☐ 210	Tyrone Hill	.08	.04	.01
☐ 211	Gerald Madkins	.05	.02	.01
☐ 212	Chris Mills	.40	.18	.05
☐ 213	Lucious Harris	.10	.05	.01
☐ 214	Ron Jones	.30	.14	.04
☐ 215	Jamal Mashburn	2.00	.90	.25
☐ 216	Darnell Mee	.05	.02	.01
☐ 217	Rodney Rodgers	.40	.18	.05
☐ 218	Brian Williams	.05	.02	.01
☐ 219	Greg Anderson	.05	.02	.01
☐ 220	Sean Elliott	.08	.04	.01
☐ 221	Allan Houston	.40	.18	.05
☐ 222	Lindsey Hunter	.15	.07	.02
☐ 223	Chris Gatling	.05	.02	.01
☐ 224	Josh Grant	.05	.02	.01
☐ 225	Keith Jennings	.05	.02	.01
☐ 226	Avery Johnson	.05	.02	.01
☐ 227	Chris Webber	1.50	.65	.19
☐ 228	Sam Cassell	.50	.23	.06
☐ 229	Mario Elie	.05	.02	.01
☐ 230	Richard Petruska	.05	.02	.01
☐ 231	Eric Riley	.05	.02	.01
☐ 232	Antonio Davis	.10	.05	.01
☐ 233	Scott Haskin	.05	.02	.01
☐ 234	Derrick McKey	.08	.04	.01
☐ 235	Mark Aguirre	.08	.04	.01
☐ 236	Terry Dehere	.08	.04	.01
☐ 237	Gary Grant	.05	.02	.01
☐ 238	Randy Woods	.05	.02	.01
☐ 239	Sam Bowie	.05	.02	.01
☐ 240	Elden Campbell	.05	.02	.01
☐ 241	Nick Van Exel	2.00	.90	.25
☐ 242	Manute Bol	.05	.02	.01
☐ 243	Brian Shaw	.05	.02	.01
☐ 244	Vin Baker	1.00	.45	.13
☐ 245	Brad Lohaus	.05	.02	.01
☐ 246	Ken Norman	.05	.02	.01
☐ 247	Derek Strong	.05	.02	.01
☐ 248	Dan Schayes	.05	.02	.01
☐ 249	Mike Brown	.05	.02	.01
☐ 250	Luc Longley	.05	.02	.01
☐ 251	Isaiah Rider	.60	.25	.08
☐ 252	Kevin Edwards	.05	.02	.01
☐ 253	Armon Gilliam	.05	.02	.01
☐ 254	Greg Anthony	.05	.02	.01
☐ 255	Anthony Bonner	.05	.02	.01
☐ 256	Tony Campbell	.05	.02	.01
☐ 257	Hubert Davis	.05	.02	.01
☐ 258	Litterial Green	.05	.02	.01
☐ 259	Anfernee Hardaway	4.00	1.80	.50
☐ 260	Larry Krystkowiak	.05	.02	.01
☐ 261	Todd Lichti	.05	.02	.01
☐ 262	Dana Barros	.10	.05	.01
☐ 263	Greg Graham	.05	.02	.01
☐ 264	Warren Kidd	.05	.02	.01
☐ 265	Moses Malone	.15	.07	.02
☐ 266	A.C. Green	.10	.05	.01
☐ 267	Joe Kleine	.05	.02	.01
☐ 268	Malcolm Mackey	.05	.02	.01
☐ 269	Mark Bryant	.05	.02	.01
☐ 270	Chris Dudley	.05	.02	.01
☐ 271	Harvey Grant	.05	.02	.01
☐ 272	James Robinson	.15	.07	.02
☐ 273	Duane Causwell	.05	.02	.01
☐ 274	Bobby Hurley	.20	.09	.03
☐ 275	Jim Les	.05	.02	.01
☐ 276	Willie Anderson	.05	.02	.01
☐ 277	Terry Cummings	.08	.04	.01
☐ 278	Vinny Del Negro	.05	.02	.01
☐ 279	Sleepy Floyd	.05	.02	.01
☐ 280	Dennis Rodman	.20	.09	.03
☐ 281	Vincent Askew	.05	.02	.01
☐ 282	Kendall Gill	.05	.02	.01
☐ 283	Steve Scheffler	.05	.02	.01
☐ 284	Detlef Schrempf	.10	.05	.01
☐ 285	David Benoit	.05	.02	.01
☐ 286	Tom Chambers	.08	.04	.01
☐ 287	Felton Spencer	.05	.02	.01
☐ 288	Rex Chapman	.05	.02	.01
☐ 289	Kevin Duckworth	.05	.02	.01
☐ 290	Gheorghe Muresan	.30	.14	.04
☐ 291	Kenny Walker	.05	.02	.01
☐ 292	Andrew Lang CF	.05	.02	.01
	Craig Ehlo			
	Atlanta Hawks			
☐ 293	Dino Radja CF	.08	.04	.01
	Acie Earl			
	Boston Celtics			
☐ 294	Eddie Johnson CF	.05	.02	.01
	Hersey Hawkins			
	Charlotte Hornets			
☐ 295	Toni Kukoc CF	.08	.04	.01
	Corie Blount			
	Chicago Bulls			
☐ 296	Tyrone Hill CF	.05	.02	.01
	Chris Mills			
	Cleveland Cavaliers			
☐ 297	Jamal Mashburn CF	.50	.23	.06
	Popeye Jones			
	Dallas Mavericks			
☐ 298	Darnell Mee CF	.08	.04	.01
	Rodney Rodgers			
	Denver Nuggets			
☐ 299	Lindsey Hunter CF	.08	.04	.01
	Allan Houston			
	Detroit Pistons			
☐ 300	Chris Webber CF	.40	.18	.05
	Avery Johnson			
	Golden State Warriors			
☐ 301	Sam Cassell CF	.08	.04	.01
	Mario Elie			
	Houston Rockets			
☐ 302	Derrick McKey CF	.05	.02	.01
	Antonio Davis			
	Indiana Pacers			
☐ 303	Terry Dehere CF	.05	.02	.01
	Mark Aguirre			
	Los Angeles Clippers			
☐ 304	Nick Van Exel CF	.50	.23	.06
	George Lynch			
	Los Angeles Lakers			
☐ 305	Harold Miner CF	.05	.02	.01

Steve Smith Miami Heat			
☐ 306 Ken Norman CF	.10	.05	.01
Vin Baker Milwaukee Bucks			
☐ 307 Mike Brown CF	.10	.05	.01
Isaiah Rider Minnesota Timberwolves			
☐ 308 Kevin Edwards CF	.05	.02	.01
Rex Walters New Jersey Nets			
☐ 309 Hubert Davis CF	.05	.02	.01
Anthony Bonner New York Knicks			
☐ 310 Anfernee Hardaway CF	1.00	.45	.13
Larry Krystkowiak Orlando Magic			
☐ 311 Moses Malone CF	.08	.04	.01
Shawn Bradley Philadelphia 76ers			
☐ 312 Joe Kleine CF	.05	.02	.01
A.C. Green Phoenix Suns			
☐ 313 Harvey Grant CF	.05	.02	.01
Chris Dudley Portland Trail Blazers			
☐ 314 Bobby Hurley CF	.08	.04	.01
Mitch Richmond Sacramento Kings			
☐ 315 Sleepy Floyd CF	.05	.02	.01
Dennis Rodman San Antonio Spurs			
☐ 316 Kendall Gill CF	.05	.02	.01
Detlef Schrempf Seattle Supersonics			
☐ 317 Felton Spencer CF	.05	.02	.01
Luther Wright Utah Jazz			
☐ 318 Calbert Cheaney CF	.05	.02	.01
Kevin Duckworth Washington Bullets			
☐ 319 Karl Malone PC	.10	.05	.01
Utah Jazz			
☐ 320 Alonzo Mourning PC	.30	.14	.04
Charlotte Hornets			
☐ 321 Scottie Pippen PC	.10	.05	.01
Chicago Bulls			
☐ 322 Mark Price PC	.05	.02	.01
Cleveland Cavaliers			
☐ 323 LaPhonso Ellis PC	.05	.02	.01
Denver Nuggets			
☐ 324 Joe Dumars PC	.08	.04	.01
Detroit Pistons			
☐ 325 Chris Mullin PC	.05	.02	.01
Golden State Warriors			
☐ 326 Ron Harper PC	.05	.02	.01
Los Angeles Clippers			
☐ 327 Glen Rice PC	.05	.02	.01
Miami Heat			
☐ 328 Christian Laettner PC	.05	.02	.01
Minnesota Timberwolves			
☐ 329 Kenny Anderson PC	.05	.02	.01
New Jersey Nets			
☐ 330 John Starks PC	.05	.02	.01
New York Knicks			
☐ 331 Shaquille O'Neal PC	1.25	.55	.16
Orlando Magic			
☐ 332 Charles Barkley PC	.30	.14	.04
Phoenix Suns			
☐ 333 Clifford Robinson PC	.05	.02	.01
Portland Trail Blazers			

☐ 334 Clyde Drexler PC	.05	.02	.01
Portland Trail Blazers			
☐ 335 Mitch Richmond PC	.08	.04	.01
Sacramento Kings			
☐ 336 David Robinson PC	.30	.14	.04
San Antonio Spurs			
☐ 337 Shawn Kemp PC	.30	.14	.04
Seattle Supersonics			
☐ 338 John Stockton PC	.10	.05	.01
Utah Jazz			
☐ 339 Checklist 4	.05	.02	.01
☐ 340 Checklist 5	.05	.02	.01
☐ 341 Checklist 6	.05	.02	.01
☐ DP4 Jim Jackson	5.00	2.30	.60
Dallas Mavericks			
☐ DP17 Doug Christie	.50	.23	.06
Los Angeles Lakers			
☐ NNO Expired Head of the Class Exchange Card	2.00	.90	.25
☐ NNO HOC Card	40.00	18.00	5.00

1993-94 SkyBox All-Rookies

Randomly inserted in first series 12-card packs at a rate of one in 36, this standard-size (2 1/2" by 3 1/2") 5-card set features five of the top rookies from the 1992-93 season. The design features borderless fronts with color action player cutouts set against metallic game-crowd backgrounds. The player's name appears in gold-foil lettering at the upper left. The white back carries a color player head shot along with career highlights.

	MINT	NRMT	EXC
COMPLETE SET (5)	25.00	11.50	3.10
COMMON CARD (AR1-AR5)	1.00	.45	.13
☐ AR1 Shaquille O'Neal	20.00	9.00	2.50
Orlando Magic			
☐ AR2 Alonzo Mourning	5.00	2.30	.60
Charlotte Hornets			
☐ AR3 Christian Laettner	1.50	.65	.19
Minnesota Timberwolves			
☐ AR4 Tom Gugliotta	1.50	.65	.19
Washington Bullets			
☐ AR5 LaPhonso Ellis	1.00	.45	.13
Denver Nuggets			

1993-94 SkyBox Center Stage

Randomly inserted in first series packs at a rate of one in 12, this 9-card standard-size (2 1/2" by 3 1/2") set showcases some of the best players in the NBA. Card fronts feature borderless fronts with color action player cutouts placed against black backgrounds. The player's name is centered at the top in prismatic silver-foil lettering. The white back features a color action player cutout and player biography.

	MINT	NRMT	EXC
COMPLETE SET (9)	55.00	25.00	7.00
COMMON CARD (CS1-CS9)	1.00	.45	.13
☐ CS1 Michael Jordan Chicago Bulls	30.00	13.50	3.80
☐ CS2 Shaquille O'Neal Orlando Magic	20.00	9.00	2.50
☐ CS3 Charles Barkley Phoenix Suns	5.00	2.30	.60
☐ CS4 John Starks New York Knicks	1.00	.45	.13
☐ CS5 Larry Johnson Charlotte Hornets	2.50	1.15	.30
☐ CS6 Hakeem Olajuwon Houston Rockets	6.00	2.70	.75
☐ CS7 Kenny Anderson New Jersey Nets	1.00	.45	.13
☐ CS8 Mahmoud Abdul-Rauf Denver Nuggets	1.00	.45	.13
☐ CS9 Cliff Robinson Portland Trail Blazers	1.00	.45	.13

1993-94 SkyBox Draft Picks

These 26 standard-size (2 1/2" by 3 1/2") cards were random inserts in both first series (Nos. 2, 6-8, 12, 15) and second series (the other 20) 12-card packs. The odds of finding one of these cards are one in every 12 packs. Card No. 26 was scheduled to be LSU center Geert Hammink. Hammink decided to play in Europe and his card was pulled. The fronts feature a color player action cutout set off to one side and superposed upon a ghosted posed color player photo. The player's name, the team that drafted him, and his draft pick number appear at the top. The white back carries the player's name, career highlights, and pre-NBA statistics. The cards are numbered on the back with a "DP" prefix.

	MINT	NRMT	EXC
COMPLETE SET (26)	60.00	27.00	7.50
COMPLETE SERIES 1 (6)	10.00	4.50	1.25
COMPLETE SERIES 2 (20)	50.00	23.00	6.25
COMMON CARD	.50	.23	.06
☐ 1 Chris Webber Golden State Warriors	8.00	3.60	1.00
☐ 2 Shawn Bradley Philadelphia 76ers	2.00	.90	.25
☐ 3 Anfernee Hardaway Orlando Magic	20.00	9.00	2.50
☐ 4 Jamal Mashburn Dallas Mavericks	10.00	4.50	1.25
☐ 5 Isaiah Rider Minnesota Timberwolves	3.00	1.35	.40
☐ 6 Calbert Cheaney Washington Bullets	2.50	1.15	.30
☐ 7 Bobby Hurley Seattle Supersonics	1.00	.45	.13
☐ 8 Vin Baker Minnesota Timberwolves	5.00	2.30	.60
☐ 9 Rodney Rodgers Denver Nuggets	2.00	.90	.25
☐ 10 Lindsey Hunter Detroit Pistons	.75	.35	.09
☐ 11 Allan Houston Detroit Pistons	2.00	.90	.25
☐ 12 George Lynch Los Angeles Lakers	.50	.23	.06
☐ 13 Terry Dehere Los Angeles Clippers	.50	.23	.06
☐ 14 Scott Haskin Indiana Pacers	.50	.23	.06
☐ 15 Doug Edwards Atlanta Hawks	.50	.23	.06
☐ 16 Rex Walters New Jersey Nets	.75	.35	.09
☐ 17 Greg Graham Philadelphia 76ers	.50	.23	.06
☐ 18 Luther Wright Utah Jazz	.50	.23	.06
☐ 19 Acie Earl Boston Celtics	.50	.23	.06
☐ 20 Scott Burrell Charlotte Hornets	1.25	.55	.16
☐ 21 James Robinson Portland Trail Blazers	.75	.35	.09

		MINT	NRMT	EXC
☐ 22	Chris Mills.................... Cleveland Cavaliers	2.00	.90	.25
☐ 23	Ervin Johnson............... Seattle Supersonics	.75	.35	.09
☐ 24	Sam Cassell.................. Houston Rockets	2.50	1.15	.30
☐ 25	Corie Blount.................. Chicago Bulls	.50	.23	.06
☐ 26	Not Issued			
☐ 27	Malcolm Mackey........... Phoenix Suns	.50	.23	.06

1993-94 SkyBox Dynamic Dunks

These nine standard-size (2 1/2" by 3 1/2") cards were random inserts in second series 12-card packs. The odds of finding one of these cards are one in every 36 packs. The horizontal fronts feature color dunking-action player cutouts superposed upon borderless black and gold metallic backgrounds. The player's name appears in gold lettering at the bottom right. The horizontal black back carries another color dunking-action player photo. The player's name and a comment on his dunking style appear in white lettering beneath the photo.

		MINT	NRMT	EXC
COMPLETE SET (9)		30.00	13.50	3.80
COMMON CARD (D1-D9)		.50	.23	.06
☐ D1	Nick Anderson............... Orlando Magic	.50	.23	.06
☐ D2	Charles Barkley............. Phoenix Suns	3.00	1.35	.40
☐ D3	Robert Horry .... Houston Rockets	1.25	.55	.16
☐ D4	Michael Jordan .... Chicago Bulls	20.00	9.00	2.50
☐ D5	Shawn Kemp .... Seattle Supersonics	3.00	1.35	.40
☐ D6	Anthony Mason .... New York Knicks	.50	.23	.06
☐ D7	Alonzo Mourning .... Charlotte Hornets	3.00	1.35	.40
☐ D8	Hakeem Olajuwon .... Houston Rockets	4.00	1.80	.50
☐ D9	Dominique Wilkins .... Atlanta Hawks	.75	.35	.09

1993-94 SkyBox Shaq Talk

The 1993-94 SkyBox Shaq Talk set consists of 10 cards that were randomly inserted in first (cards 1-5) and second series (6-10) 12-card packs. The odds of finding one of these cards are reportedly one in every 36 packs. The standard size (2 1/2" by 3 1/2") cards spotlight Shaquille O'Neal. The fronts feature cut-out action shots of Shaq over a ghosted background. The set title is superimposed across the top of the card in red lettering. The white backs have a ghosted SkyBox Premium logo. At the top is a quote from Shaquille regarding game strategy and below is player critique by a basketball analyst. The cards are numbered on the back with a "Shaq Talk" prefix.

		MINT	NRMT	EXC
COMPLETE SET (10)		40.00	18.00	5.00
COMPLETE SERIES 1 (5).......		20.00	9.00	2.50
COMPLETE SERIES 2 (5).......		20.00	9.00	2.50
COMMON O'NEAL (1-10)		5.00	2.30	.60
☐ 1	Shaq Talk 1..................... The Rebound	5.00	2.30	.60
☐ 2	Shaq Talk 2..................... The Block (Blocking David Robinson's shot)	5.00	2.30	.60
☐ 3	Shaq Talk 3..................... The Postup	5.00	2.30	.60
☐ 4	Shaq Talk 4..................... The Bunk	5.00	2.30	.60
☐ 5	Shaq Talk 5..................... Defense	5.00	2.30	.60
☐ 6	Shaq Talk 6..................... Scoring	5.00	2.30	.60
☐ 7	Shaq Talk 7..................... Passing	5.00	2.30	.60
☐ 8	Shaq Talk....................... Rejections	5.00	2.30	.60
☐ 9	Shaq Talk....................... Confidence	5.00	2.30	.60
☐ 10	Shaq Talk....................... Legends\	5.00	2.30	.60

1993-94 SkyBox Showdown Series

These 12 standard-size (2 1/2" by 3 1/2") cards were random inserts in first (cards 1-6) and second series (7-12) 12-card packs. The odds of finding one of these cards are one in every six packs. Each front features a borderless color action photo of the two players involved in the "Showdown." Both players' names appear, one vs. the other, in gold lettering within a metallic black stripe near the bottom. The horizontal white back carries a color player close-up for each player on each side. The players' names appear beneath each photo. Comparative statistics fill in the area between the two player photos.

	MINT	NRMT	EXC
COMPLETE SET (12)	6.00	2.70	.75
COMPLETE SERIES 1 (6)	3.00	1.35	.40
COMPLETE SERIES 2 (6)	3.00	1.35	.40
COMMON PAIR (SS1-SS6)	.40	.18	.05
COMMON PAIR (SS7-SS12)	.25	.11	.03
☐ SS1 Alonzo Mourning Patrick Ewing	.50	.23	.06
☐ SS2 Shaquille O'Neal Patrick Ewing	1.50	.65	.19
☐ SS3 Alonzo Mourning Shaquille O'Neal	1.50	.65	.19
☐ SS4 Hakeem Olajuwon Dikembe Mutombo	.50	.23	.06
☐ SS5 David Robinson Hakeem Olajuwon	.75	.35	.09
☐ SS6 David Robinson Dikembe Mutombo	.40	.18	.05
☐ SS7 Shawn Kemp Karl Malone	.50	.23	.06
☐ SS8 Larry Johnson Charles Barkley	.50	.23	.06
☐ SS9 Dominique Wilkins Scottie Pippen	.25	.11	.03
☐ SS10 Joe Dumars Reggie Miller	.25	.11	.03
☐ SS11 Clyde Drexler Michael Jordan	2.00	.90	.25
☐ SS12 Magic Johnson Larry Bird	.75	.35	.09

1993-94 SkyBox Thunder and Lightning

Randomly inserted in second series packs at a rate of one in 12 packs, this standard-size (2 1/2" by 3 1/2") nine-card set features players pictured on both sides. On one side a guard would be featured and a forward or center on the other side. Borderless on either side, the color action player cutouts set against metallic backgrounds.

	MINT	NRMT	EXC
COMPLETE SET (9)	30.00	13.50	3.80
COMMON PAIR (1-9)	1.00	.45	.13
☐ TL1 Jamal Mashburn Jim Jackson Dallas Mavericks	8.00	3.60	1.00
☐ TL2 Harold Miner Steve Smith Miami Heat	1.00	.45	.13
☐ TL3 Isaiah Rider Micheal Williams Minnesota Timberwolves	1.50	.65	.19
☐ TL4 Derrick Coleman Kenny Anderson New Jersey Nets	1.00	.45	.13
☐ TL5 Patrick Ewing John Starks New York Knicks	1.25	.55	.16
☐ TL6 Shaquille O'Neal Anfernee Hardaway Orlando Magic	20.00	9.00	2.50
☐ TL7 Shawn Bradley Jeff Hornacek Philadelphia 76ers	1.00	.45	.13
☐ TL8 Walt Williams Bobby Hurley Sacramento Kings	1.00	.45	.13
☐ TL9 Dennis Rodman David Robinson San Antonio Spurs	3.00	1.35	.40

1993-94 SkyBox USA Tip-Off

The 13-card 1993-94 SkyBox USA Tip-Off set could be only acquired by sending in

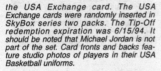

the USA Exchange card. The USA Exchange cards were randomly inserted in SkyBox series two packs. The Tip-Off redemption expiration was 6/15/94. It should be noted that Michael Jordan is not part of the set. Card fronts and backs feature studio photos of players in their USA Basketball uniforms.

rookie year, best game, NBA update, trademark move, and comments on the player by Magic Johnson. The cards are numbered on the back. In addition, a T-shirt exchange card (one in 300 packs) was available with this product. The offer was valid through October 31, 1994.

	MINT	NRMT	EXC
COMPLETE SET (14)	25.00	11.50	3.10
COMMON CARD (1-13)	.75	.35	.09
☐ 1 Steve Smith Magic Johnson	2.00	.90	.25
☐ 2 Larry Johnson Charles Barkley	3.00	1.35	.40
☐ 3 Patrick Ewing Alonzo Mourning	3.00	1.35	.40
☐ 4 Shawn Kemp Karl Malone	3.00	1.35	.40
☐ 5 Chris Mullin Dan Majerle	1.00	.45	.13
☐ 6 John Stockton Mark Price	1.25	.55	.16
☐ 7 Christian Laettner Derrick Coleman	.75	.35	.09
☐ 8 Dominique Wilkins Clyde Drexler	1.50	.65	.19
☐ 9 Joe Dumars Scottie Pippen	1.50	.65	.19
☐ 10 David Robinson Shaquille O'Neal	10.00	4.50	1.25
☐ 11 Reggie Miller Larry Bird	4.00	1.80	.50
☐ 12 Tim Hardaway	.75	.35	.09
☐ 13 Isiah Thomas	1.00	.45	.13
☐ NNO Checklist	1.50	.65	.19
☐ NNO Expired USA Exchange	1.50	.65	.19

1994 SkyBox USA

These 89 standard-size (2 1/2" by 3 1/2") cards honor the '94 Team USA players. Cards were issued in 10-card packs with 24 packs per box. The borderless fronts feature color posed and action player shots. The player's name appears in silver-foil lettering within a red stripe near the bottom. Each player has a subset of six cards, the backs of which carry information about each player's international experience, NBA

	MINT	NRMT	EXC
COMPLETE SET (89)	10.00	4.50	1.25
COMMON CARD (1-89)	.05	.02	.01
☐ 1 Alonzo Mourning International	.25	.11	.03
☐ 2 Alonzo Mourning NBA Rookie	.25	.11	.03
☐ 3 Alonzo Mourning Best Game	.25	.11	.03
☐ 4 Alonzo Mourning NBA Update	.25	.11	.03
☐ 5 Alonzo Mourning Trademark Move	.25	.11	.03
☐ 6 Alonzo Mourning Magic On	.15	.07	.02
☐ 7 Larry Johnson International	.15	.07	.02
☐ 8 Larry Johnson NBA Rookie	.15	.07	.02
☐ 9 Larry Johnson Best Game	.15	.07	.02
☐ 10 Larry Johnson NBA Update	.15	.07	.02
☐ 11 Larry Johnson Trademark Move	.15	.07	.02
☐ 12 Larry Johnson Magic On	.15	.07	.02
☐ 13 Shawn Kemp International	.40	.18	.05
☐ 14 Shawn Kemp NBA Rookie	.40	.18	.05
☐ 15 Shawn Kemp Best Game	.40	.18	.05
☐ 16 Shawn Kemp NBA Update	.40	.18	.05
☐ 17 Shawn Kemp Trademark Move	.40	.18	.05
☐ 18 Shawn Kemp Magic On	.40	.18	.05
☐ 19 Mark Price International	.05	.02	.01
☐ 20 Mark Price NBA Rookie	.05	.02	.01
☐ 21 Mark Price Best Game	.05	.02	.01
☐ 22 Mark Price NBA Update	.05	.02	.01

☐ 23	Mark Price	.05	.02	.01	
	Trademark Move				
☐ 24	Mark Price	.05	.02	.01	
	Magic On				
☐ 25	Steve Smith	.05	.02	.01	
	International				
☐ 26	Steve Smith	.05	.02	.01	
	NBA Rookie				
☐ 27	Steve Smith	.05	.02	.01	
	Best Game				
☐ 28	Steve Smith	.05	.02	.01	
	NBA Update				
☐ 29	Steve Smith	.05	.02	.01	
	Trademark Move				
☐ 30	Steve Smith	.05	.11	.03	
	Magic On				
☐ 31	Dominique Wilkins	.10	.05	.01	
	International				
☐ 32	Dominique Wilkins	.10	.05	.01	
	NBA Rookie				
☐ 33	Dominique Wilkins	.10	.05	.01	
	Best Game				
☐ 34	Dominique Wilkins	.10	.05	.01	
	NBA Update				
☐ 35	Dominique Wilkins	.10	.05	.01	
	Trademark Move				
☐ 36	Dominique Wilkins	.10	.05	.01	
	Magic On				
☐ 37	Derrick Coleman	.05	.02	.01	
	International				
☐ 38	Derrick Coleman	.05	.02	.01	
	NBA Rookie				
☐ 39	Derrick Coleman	.05	.02	.01	
	Best Game				
☐ 40	Derrick Coleman	.05	.02	.01	
	NBA Update				
☐ 41	Derrick Coleman	.05	.02	.01	
	Trademark Move				
☐ 42	Derrick Coleman	.05	.02	.01	
	Magic On				
☐ 43	Isiah Thomas	.10	.05	.01	
	International				
☐ 44	Isiah Thomas	.10	.05	.01	
	NBA Rookie				
☐ 45	Isiah Thomas	.10	.05	.01	
	Best Game				
☐ 46	Isiah Thomas	.10	.05	.01	
	NBA Update				
☐ 47	Isiah Thomas	.10	.05	.01	
	Trademark Move				
☐ 48	Isiah Thomas	.10	.05	.01	
	Magic On				
☐ 49	Joe Dumars	.10	.05	.01	
	International				
☐ 50	Joe Dumars	.10	.05	.01	
	NBA Rookie				
☐ 51	Joe Dumars	.10	.05	.01	
	Best Game				
☐ 52	Joe Dumars	.10	.05	.01	
	NBA Update				
☐ 53	Joe Dumars	.10	.05	.01	
	Trademark Move				
☐ 54	Joe Dumars	.10	.05	.01	
	Magic On				
☐ 55	Dan Majerle	.05	.02	.01	
	International				
☐ 56	Dan Majerle	.05	.02	.01	
	NBA Rookie				
☐ 57	Dan Majerle	.05	.02	.01	
	Best Game				
☐ 58	Dan Majerle	.05	.02	.01	

	NBA Update			
☐ 59	Dan Majerle	.05	.02	.01
	Trademark Move			
☐ 60	Dan Majerle	.05	.02	.01
	Magic On			
☐ 61	Tim Hardaway	.05	.02	.01
	International			
☐ 62	Tim Hardaway	.05	.02	.01
	NBA Rookie			
☐ 63	Tim Hardaway	.05	.02	.01
	Best Game			
☐ 64	Tim Hardaway	.05	.02	.01
	NBA Update			
☐ 65	Tim Hardaway	.05	.02	.01
	Trademark Move			
☐ 66	Tim Hardaway	.05	.02	.01
	Magic On			
☐ 67	Shaquille O'Neal	1.00	.45	.13
	International			
☐ 68	Shaquille O'Neal	1.00	.45	.13
	NBA Rookie			
☐ 69	Shaquille O'Neal	1.00	.45	.13
	Best Game			
☐ 70	Shaquille O'Neal	1.00	.45	.13
	NBA Update			
☐ 71	Shaquille O'Neal	1.00	.45	.13
	Trademark Move			
☐ 72	Shaquille O'Neal	1.00	.45	.13
	Magic On			
☐ 73	Reggie Miller	.20	.09	.03
	International			
☐ 74	Reggie Miller	.20	.09	.03
	NBA Rookie			
☐ 75	Reggie Miller	.20	.09	.03
	Best Game			
☐ 76	Reggie Miller	.20	.09	.03
	NBA Update			
☐ 77	Reggie Miller	.20	.09	.03
	Trademark Move			
☐ 78	Reggie Miller	.20	.09	.03
	Magic On			
☐ 79	Don Chaney CO	.05	.02	.01
☐ 80	Pete Gillen CO	.05	.02	.01
☐ 81	Rick Majerus CO	.05	.02	.01
☐ 82	Don Nelson CO	.05	.02	.01
☐ 83	'94 USA Team	.05	.02	.01
☐ 84	International Rules	.05	.02	.01
	Time			
☐ 85	International Rules	.05	.02	.01
	Court Dimensions			
☐ 86	International Rules	.05	.02	.01
	Rules			
☐ 87	Earvin(Magic) Johnson	.40	.18	.05
	Passing the Torch			
☐ 88	David Robinson	.40	.18	.05
	Passing the Torch			
☐ 89	Checklist	.05	.11	.03
☐ NNO	T-shirt Exchange Card	1.00	.45	.13

1994 SkyBox USA Champion Gold

Randomly inserted at a rate of 1 in 4 packs, this parallel set features standard-size (2 1/2" by 3 1/2") cards that differ from their '94 SkyBox USA counterparts only by the

	MINT	NRMT	EXC
☐ DP10 Dan Majerle	.75	.35	.09
☐ DP11 Tim Hardaway	1.25	.55	.16
☐ DP12 Shaquille O'Neal	15.00	6.75	1.90
☐ DP13 Reggie Miller	3.00	1.35	.40

embossed gold-foil highlights. The cards are numbered on the back. Please refer to the multiplier provided below (coupled with the prices of the corresponding regular issue cards) to ascertain value.

	MINT	NRMT	EXC
COMPLETE SET (89)	60.00	27.00	7.50
COMMON CARD (1-89)	.25	.11	.03
*STARS: 2.5X to 5X BASIC CARDS..			

1994 SkyBox USA
Kevin Johnson

1994 SkyBox USA
Dream Play

This 14-card set was issued through a wrapper redemption program. The collector received a complete set in exchange for nine wrappers. The offer expired October 31, 1994. The first six cards have the player's name in silver foil lettering, while the next six have the player's name and SkyBox logo in gold foil. The final two cards represent the Dream Play and Portrait insert sets. The silver and gold cards are distinguished in the listing below by "S" and "G" prefixes respectively.

	MINT	NRMT	EXC
COMPLETE SET (14)	25.00	11.50	3.10
COMMON CARD	.50	.23	.06
☐ 90G International	2.00	.90	.25
☐ 90S International	.50	.23	.06
☐ 91G NBA Rookie	2.00	.90	.25
☐ 91S NBA Rookie	.50	.23	.06
☐ 92G Best Game	2.00	.90	.25
☐ 92S Best Game	.50	.23	.06
☐ 93G NBA Update	2.00	.90	.25
☐ 93S NBA Update	.50	.23	.06
☐ 94G Trademark Move	2.00	.90	.25
☐ 94S Trademark Move	.50	.23	.06
☐ 95G Magic on Johnson	2.00	.90	.25
☐ 95S Magic on Johnson	.50	.23	.06
☐ DP14 Dream Play	3.00	1.35	.40
☐ PT14 Portrait	12.00	5.50	1.40

Randomly inserted in packs at a rate of one in 35, these 13 standard-size (2 1/2" by 3 1/2") cards feature on their borderless fronts posed action color cutouts of the players in their Team USA uniforms set on a dark play diagram background. The player's name appears in prismatic silver-foil lettering at the top. The white back carries play diagrams and descriptions.

	MINT	NRMT	EXC
COMPLETE SET (13)	25.00	11.50	3.10
COMMON CARD (DP1-DP13)	.75	.35	.09
☐ DP1 Alonzo Mourning	4.00	1.80	.50
☐ DP2 Larry Johnson	2.50	1.15	.30
☐ DP3 Shawn Kemp	6.00	2.70	.75
☐ DP4 Mark Price	1.25	.55	.16
☐ DP5 Steve Smith	.75	.35	.09
☐ DP6 Dominique Wilkins	1.50	.65	.19
☐ DP7 Derrick Coleman	1.25	.55	.16
☐ DP8 Isiah Thomas	1.50	.65	.19
☐ DP9 Joe Dumars	1.50	.65	.19

1994 SkyBox USA
On The Court

This 14 card standard-size set was available exclusively by exchanging the SkyBox

USA On the Court trade card before the November 15th, 1994 deadline. The trade card was randomly inserted into one in every 300 SkyBox USA packs. Each member of Dream Team II is represented in this set. The set is called as "On the Court" as all photos were all taken in Toronto during the World Championships in 1994.

	MINT	NRMT	EXC
COMPLETE SET (14)	30.00	13.50	3.80
COMMON CARD (1-14)	.60	.25	.08
☐ 1 Isiah Thomas	1.50	.65	.19
☐ 2 Tim Hardaway	1.25	.55	.16
☐ 3 Reggie Miller	3.00	1.35	.40
☐ 4 Steve Smith	.60	.25	.08
☐ 5 Joe Dumars	1.50	.65	.19
☐ 6 Shawn Kemp	6.00	2.70	.75
☐ 7 Mark Price	1.25	.55	.16
☐ 8 Dan Majerle	.60	.25	.08
☐ 9 Kevin Johnson	1.50	.65	.19
☐ 10 Derrick Coleman	1.25	.55	.16
☐ 11 Alonzo Mourning	4.00	1.80	.50
☐ 12 Dominique Wilkins	1.50	.65	.19
☐ 13 Larry Johnson	2.50	1.15	.30
☐ 14 Shaquille O'Neal	15.00	6.75	1.90
☐ NNO Expired--On The Court Exchange	1.00	.45	.13

1994 SkyBox USA Portraits

Randomly inserted at a rate of one in 100 packs, these 13 standard-size (2 1/2" by 3 1/2") cards feature embossed gold foil-bordered fronts with posed color portraits of the players in their Team USA uniforms. The player's name appears in embossed lettering within the gold-foil lower margin. The red, white, and blue back carries a quote from the player.

	MINT	NRMT	EXC
COMPLETE SET (13)	150.00	70.00	19.00
COMMON CARD (PT1-PT13)	4.00	1.80	.50
☐ PT1 Alonzo Mourning	20.00	9.00	2.50
☐ PT2 Larry Johnson	12.00	5.50	1.50
☐ PT3 Shawn Kemp	30.00	13.50	3.80
☐ PT4 Mark Price	6.00	2.70	.75
☐ PT5 Steve Smith	4.00	1.80	.50
☐ PT6 Dominique Wilkins	8.00	3.60	1.00
☐ PT7 Derrick Coleman	6.00	2.70	.75
☐ PT8 Isiah Thomas	8.00	3.60	1.00
☐ PT9 Joe Dumars	8.00	3.60	1.00
☐ PT10 Dan Majerle	4.00	1.80	.50
☐ PT11 Tim Hardaway	6.00	2.70	.75
☐ PT12 Shaquille O'Neal	75.00	34.00	9.50
☐ PT13 Reggie Miller	15.00	6.75	1.90

1994-95 SkyBox

The 350-cards that comprise the 1994-95 SkyBox set were issued in two separate series of 200 and 150 cards respectively. Cards were distributed in 12-card hobby and retail packs with a suggested retail price of $1.99 each. Unlike first series packs, each second series pack contained an insert card. Card fronts feature full-bleed action photos with the player's name running down the upper-left corner. The cards are grouped alphabetically within teams and checklisted below alphabetically according to teams as follows: Atlanta Hawks (1-7, 201-205), Boston Celtics (8-13, 206-209), Charlotte Hornets (14-20, 210-213), Chicago Bulls (21-27, 214-217), Cleveland Cavaliers (28-34, 218-219), Dallas Mavericks (35-39, 220-222), Denver Nuggets (40-46, 223-224), Detroit Pistons (47-51, 225-228), Golden State Warriors (52-57, 229-233), Houston Rockets (58-64, 234), Indiana Pacers (65-71, 235-238), Los Angeles Clippers (72-77, 239-242), Los Angeles Lakers (78-84, 243-246), Miami Heat (85-90, 247-251), Milwaukee Bucks (91-96, 252-255), Minnesota Timberwolves (97-102, 256-257), New Jersey Nets (103-

108, 258-260), New York Knicks (109-115, 261-262), Orlando Magic (116-121, 263-265), Philadelphia 76ers (122-126, 266-269), Phoenix Suns (127-133, 270-274), Portland Trail Blazers (134-140, 275-276), Sacramento Kings (141-147, 277-279), San Antonio Spurs (148-153, 280-284), Seattle Supersonics (154-160, 285-288), Utah Jazz (161-168, 289-291), and Washington Bullets (169-175, 292-297). Topical subsets featured are NBA on NBC (176-185), Dynamic Duals (186-197), USA Basketball (198), Checklists (298-300), SkySlams (301-313), SkyShots (314-325), SkySwats (326-338), and SkyPilots (339-350). Every first series pack contained an Action and Drama Instant Win game card, offering the chance to play one-on-one with Magic Johnson, or receive a number of other prizes including autographed Hakeem Olajuwon or David Robinson jerseys, a dual autographed Olajuwon/Robinson card or an exclusive Magic Johnson exchange card available only through this promotion. A special three-card panel featuring Johnson, Olajuwon and Robinson was available by mailing in forty first series wrappers before the June 30th, 1995 deadline. Also, three Master Series Preview Press Sheet Exchange cards were randomly seeded into one in every 360 first series packs. The cards were redeemable for 50-card uncut press sheets of SkyBox's new super-premium Emotion cards. The expiration date for the Emotion Press Sheets was March 1, 1995. As a final note, approximately one in every 360 first series retail packs contained an unannounced Hakeem Olajuwon Gold "stealth" card. Approximately one in every 360 second series retail packs contained an unannounced Grant Hill Gold "stealth" card.

	MINT	NRMT	EXC
COMPLETE SET (350)	30.00	13.50	3.80
COMPLETE SERIES 1 (200)	15.00	6.75	1.90
COMPLETE SERIES 2 (150)	15.00	6.75	1.90
COMMON CARD (1-200)	.10	.05	.01
COMMON CARD (201-350)	.05	.02	.01

☐	1 Stacey Augmon	.12	.05	.02
☐	2 Mookie Blaylock	.12	.05	.02
☐	3 Doug Edwards	.10	.05	.01
☐	4 Craig Ehlo	.10	.05	.01
☐	5 Adam Keefe	.10	.05	.01
☐	6 Danny Manning	.15	.07	.02
☐	7 Kevin Willis	.12	.05	.02
☐	8 Dee Brown	.12	.05	.02
☐	9 Sherman Douglas	.10	.05	.01
☐	10 Acie Earl	.10	.05	.01
☐	11 Kevin Gamble	.10	.05	.01
☐	12 Xavier McDaniel	.12	.05	.02
☐	13 Dino Radja	.15	.07	.02
☐	14 Muggsy Bogues	.15	.07	.02
☐	15 Scott Burrell	.10	.05	.01
☐	16 Dell Curry	.10	.05	.01
☐	17 LeRon Ellis	.10	.05	.01
☐	18 Hersey Hawkins	.12	.05	.02
☐	19 Larry Johnson	.30	.14	.04
☐	20 Alonzo Mourning	.50	.23	.06
☐	21 B.J. Armstrong	.10	.05	.01
☐	22 Corie Blount	.10	.05	.01
☐	23 Horace Grant	.20	.09	.03
☐	24 Toni Kukoc	.15	.07	.02
☐	25 Luc Longley	.10	.05	.01
☐	26 Scottie Pippen	.40	.18	.05
☐	27 Scott Williams	.10	.05	.01
☐	28 Terrell Brandon	.10	.05	.01
☐	29 Brad Daugherty	.12	.05	.02
☐	30 Tyrone Hill	.12	.05	.02
☐	31 Chris Mills	.15	.07	.02
☐	32 Bobby Phills	.10	.05	.01
☐	33 Mark Price	.15	.07	.02
☐	34 Gerald Wilkins	.10	.05	.01
☐	35 Lucious Harris	.10	.05	.01
☐	36 Jim Jackson	.50	.23	.06
☐	37 Popeye Jones	.10	.05	.01
☐	38 Jamal Mashburn	.75	.35	.09
☐	39 Sean Rooks	.10	.05	.01
☐	40 Mahmoud Abdul-Rauf	.12	.05	.02
☐	41 LaPhonso Ellis	.10	.05	.01
☐	42 Dikembe Mutombo	.25	.11	.03
☐	43 Robert Pack	.10	.05	.01
☐	44 Rodney Rogers	.15	.07	.02
☐	45 Bryant Stith	.10	.05	.01
☐	46 Reggie Williams	.10	.05	.01
☐	47 Joe Dumars	.20	.09	.03
☐	48 Sean Elliott	.12	.05	.02
☐	49 Allan Houston	.15	.07	.02
☐	50 Lindsey Hunter	.10	.05	.01
☐	51 Terry Mills	.10	.05	.01
☐	52 Victor Alexander	.10	.05	.01
☐	53 Tim Hardaway	.15	.07	.02
☐	54 Chris Mullin	.15	.07	.02
☐	55 Billy Owens	.12	.05	.02
☐	56 Latrell Sprewell	.50	.23	.06
☐	57 Chris Webber	.60	.25	.08
☐	58 Sam Cassell	.15	.07	.02
☐	59 Carl Herrera	.10	.05	.01
☐	60 Robert Horry	.15	.07	.02
☐	61 Vernon Maxwell	.10	.05	.01
☐	62 Hakeem Olajuwon	1.00	.45	.13
☐	63 Kenny Smith	.10	.05	.01
☐	64 Otis Thorpe	.12	.05	.02
☐	65 Antonio Davis	.10	.05	.01
☐	66 Dale Davis	.12	.05	.02
☐	67 Derrick McKey	.12	.05	.02
☐	68 Reggie Miller	.40	.18	.05
☐	69 Pooh Richardson	.10	.05	.01
☐	70 Rik Smits	.15	.07	.02
☐	71 Haywoode Workman	.10	.05	.01
☐	72 Terry Dehere	.10	.05	.01
☐	73 Harold Ellis	.10	.05	.01
☐	74 Ron Harper	.12	.05	.02
☐	75 Mark Jackson	.10	.05	.01
☐	76 Loy Vaught	.12	.05	.02
☐	77 Dominique Wilkins	.20	.09	.03
☐	78 Elden Campbell	.10	.05	.01
☐	79 Doug Christie	.10	.05	.01
☐	80 Vlade Divac	.15	.07	.02
☐	81 George Lynch	.10	.05	.01
☐	82 Anthony Peeler	.10	.05	.01
☐	83 Sedale Threatt	.10	.05	.01
☐	84 Nick Van Exel	.75	.35	.09
☐	85 Harold Miner	.10	.05	.01
☐	86 Glen Rice	.15	.07	.02
☐	87 John Salley	.10	.05	.01
☐	88 Rony Seikaly	.10	.05	.01
☐	89 Brian Shaw	.10	.05	.01
☐	90 Steve Smith	.12	.05	.02
☐	91 Vin Baker	.40	.18	.05
☐	92 Jon Barry	.10	.05	.01

☐ 93	Todd Day	.12	.05	.02
☐ 94	Blue Edwards	.10	.05	.01
☐ 95	Lee Mayberry	.10	.05	.01
☐ 96	Eric Murdock	.10	.05	.01
☐ 97	Mike Brown	.10	.05	.01
☐ 98	Stacey King	.10	.05	.01
☐ 99	Christian Laettner	.12	.05	.02
☐ 100	Isaiah Rider	.25	.11	.03
☐ 101	Doug West	.10	.05	.01
☐ 102	Micheal Williams	.10	.05	.01
☐ 103	Kenny Anderson	.15	.07	.02
☐ 104	P.J. Brown	.10	.05	.01
☐ 105	Derrick Coleman	.15	.07	.02
☐ 106	Kevin Edwards	.10	.05	.01
☐ 107	Chris Morris	.10	.05	.01
☐ 108	Rex Walters	.10	.05	.01
☐ 109	Hubert Davis	.10	.05	.01
☐ 110	Patrick Ewing	.40	.18	.05
☐ 111	Derek Harper	.12	.05	.02
☐ 112	Anthony Mason	.10	.05	.01
☐ 113	Charles Oakley	.12	.05	.02
☐ 114	Charles Smith	.10	.05	.01
☐ 115	John Starks	.12	.05	.02
☐ 116	Nick Anderson	.12	.05	.02
☐ 117	Anfernee Hardaway	1.50	.65	.19
☐ 118	Shaquille O'Neal	2.00	.90	.25
☐ 119	Donald Royal	.10	.05	.01
☐ 120	Dennis Scott	.10	.05	.01
☐ 121	Scott Skiles	.10	.05	.01
☐ 122	Dana Barros	.15	.07	.02
☐ 123	Shawn Bradley	.15	.07	.02
☐ 124	Johnny Dawkins	.10	.05	.01
☐ 125	Greg Graham	.10	.05	.01
☐ 126	Clarence Weatherspoon	.12	.05	.02
☐ 127	Danny Ainge	.12	.05	.02
☐ 128	Charles Barkley	.75	.35	.09
☐ 129	Cedric Ceballos	.15	.07	.02
☐ 130	A.C. Green	.15	.07	.02
☐ 131	Kevin Johnson	.20	.09	.03
☐ 132	Dan Majerle	.12	.05	.02
☐ 133	Oliver Miller	.10	.05	.01
☐ 134	Clyde Drexler	.40	.18	.05
☐ 135	Harvey Grant	.10	.05	.01
☐ 136	Tracy Murray	.10	.05	.01
☐ 137	Terry Porter	.12	.05	.02
☐ 138	Clifford Robinson	.12	.05	.02
☐ 139	James Robinson	.10	.05	.01
☐ 140	Rod Strickland	.12	.05	.02
☐ 141	Bobby Hurley	.12	.05	.02
☐ 142	Olden Polynice	.10	.05	.01
☐ 143	Mitch Richmond	.20	.09	.03
☐ 144	Lionel Simmons	.10	.05	.01
☐ 145	Wayman Tisdale	.12	.05	.02
☐ 146	Spud Webb	.12	.05	.02
☐ 147	Walt Williams	.12	.05	.02
☐ 148	Willie Anderson	.10	.05	.01
☐ 149	Vinny Del Negro	.10	.05	.01
☐ 150	Dale Ellis	.12	.05	.02
☐ 151	J.R. Reid	.10	.05	.01
☐ 152	David Robinson	.75	.35	.09
☐ 153	Dennis Rodman	.25	.11	.03
☐ 154	Kendall Gill	.10	.05	.01
☐ 155	Shawn Kemp	.75	.35	.09
☐ 156	Nate McMillan	.10	.05	.01
☐ 157	Gary Payton	.15	.07	.02
☐ 158	Sam Perkins	.12	.05	.02
☐ 159	Ricky Pierce	.12	.05	.02
☐ 160	Detlef Schrempf	.15	.07	.02
☐ 161	David Benoit	.10	.05	.01
☐ 162	Tyrone Corbin	.10	.05	.01
☐ 163	Jeff Hornacek	.12	.05	.02

☐ 164	Jay Humphries	.10	.05	.01
☐ 165	Karl Malone	.40	.18	.05
☐ 166	Bryon Russell	.10	.05	.01
☐ 167	Felton Spencer	.10	.05	.01
☐ 168	John Stockton	.40	.18	.05
☐ 169	Michael Adams	.10	.05	.01
☐ 170	Rex Chapman	.10	.05	.01
☐ 171	Calbert Cheaney	.15	.07	.02
☐ 172	Pervis Ellison	.10	.05	.01
☐ 173	Tom Gugliotta	.12	.05	.02
☐ 174	Don MacLean	.10	.05	.01
☐ 175	Gheorghe Muresan	.12	.05	.02
☐ 176	Charles Barkley NBC	.40	.18	.05
☐ 177	Charles Oakley NBC	.10	.05	.01
☐ 178	Hakeem Olajuwon NBC	.50	.23	.06
☐ 179	Dikembe Mutombo NBC	.12	.05	.02
☐ 180	Scottie Pippen NBC	.15	.07	.02
☐ 181	Sam Cassell NBC	.10	.05	.01
☐ 182	Karl Malone NBC	.15	.07	.02
☐ 183	Reggie Miller NBC	.15	.07	.02
☐ 184	Patrick Ewing NBC	.15	.07	.02
☐ 185	Vernon Maxwell NBC	.10	.05	.01
☐ 186	Anfernee Hardaway DD Steve Smith	.30	.14	.04
☐ 187	Chris Webber DD Shaquille O'Neal	.50	.23	.06
☐ 188	Jamal Mashburn DD Rodney Rogers	.15	.07	.02
☐ 189	Toni Kukoc DD Dino Radja	.12	.05	.02
☐ 190	Lindsey Hunter DD Kenny Anderson	.10	.05	.01
☐ 191	Latrell Sprewell DD Jimmy Jackson	.20	.09	.03
☐ 192	Clarence Weatherspoon Vin Baker DD	.12	.05	.02
☐ 193	Calbert Cheaney DD Chris Mills	.10	.05	.01
☐ 194	Isaiah Rider DD Robert Horry	.12	.05	.02
☐ 195	Sam Cassell DD Nick Van Exel	.15	.07	.02
☐ 196	Gheorghe Muresan DD Shawn Bradley	.10	.05	.01
☐ 197	LaPhonso Ellis DD Tony Gugliotta	.10	.05	.01
☐ 198	USA Basketball Card	.12	.05	.02
☐ 199	Checklist	.10	.05	.01
☐ 200	Checklist	.10	.05	.01
☐ 201	Sergei Bazarevich	.05	.02	.01
☐ 202	Tyrone Corbin	.05	.02	.01
☐ 203	Grant Long	.05	.02	.01
☐ 204	Ken Norman	.05	.02	.01
☐ 205	Steve Smith	.08	.04	.01
☐ 206	Blue Edwards	.05	.02	.01
☐ 207	Greg Minor	.08	.04	.01
☐ 208	Eric Montross	.40	.18	.05
☐ 209	Dominique Wilkins	.15	.07	.02
☐ 210	Michael Adams	.05	.02	.01
☐ 211	Kenny Gattison	.05	.02	.01
☐ 212	Darrin Hancock	.05	.02	.01
☐ 213	Robert Parish	.10	.05	.01
☐ 214	Ron Harper	.08	.04	.01
☐ 215	Steve Kerr	.05	.02	.01
☐ 216	Will Perdue	.05	.02	.01
☐ 217	Dickey Simpkins	.15	.07	.02
☐ 218	John Battle	.05	.02	.01
☐ 219	Michael Cage	.05	.02	.01
☐ 220	Tony Dumas	.08	.04	.01
☐ 221	Jason Kidd	2.50	1.15	.30
☐ 222	Roy Tarpley	.05	.02	.01

☐ 223	Dale Ellis	.08	.04	.01
☐ 224	Jalen Rose	.50	.23	.06
☐ 225	Bill Curley	.15	.07	.02
☐ 226	Grant Hill	4.00	1.80	.50
☐ 227	Oliver Miller	.05	.02	.01
☐ 228	Mark West	.05	.02	.01
☐ 229	Tom Gugliotta	.08	.04	.01
☐ 230	Ricky Pierce	.08	.04	.01
☐ 231	Carlos Rogers	.20	.09	.03
☐ 232	Clifford Rozier	.20	.09	.03
☐ 233	Rony Seikaly	.05	.02	.01
☐ 234	Tim Breaux	.05	.02	.01
☐ 235	Duane Ferrell	.05	.02	.01
☐ 236	Mark Jackson	.05	.02	.01
☐ 237	Byron Scott	.08	.04	.01
☐ 238	John Williams	.05	.02	.01
☐ 239	Lamond Murray	.40	.18	.05
☐ 240	Eric Piatkowski	.15	.07	.02
☐ 241	Pooh Richardson	.05	.02	.01
☐ 242	Malik Sealy	.05	.02	.01
☐ 243	Cedric Ceballos	.10	.05	.01
☐ 244	Eddie Jones	1.50	.65	.19
☐ 245	Anthony Miller	.05	.02	.01
☐ 246	Tony Smith	.05	.02	.01
☐ 247	Kevin Gamble	.05	.02	.01
☐ 248	Brad Lohaus	.05	.02	.01
☐ 249	Billy Owens	.08	.04	.01
☐ 250	Khalid Reeves	.40	.18	.05
☐ 251	Kevin Willis	.08	.04	.01
☐ 252	Eric Mobley	.15	.07	.02
☐ 253	Johnny Newman	.05	.02	.01
☐ 254	Ed Pinckney	.05	.02	.01
☐ 255	Glenn Robinson	2.50	1.15	.30
☐ 256	Howard Eisley	.05	.02	.01
☐ 257	Donyell Marshall	.50	.23	.06
☐ 258	Yinka Dare	.07	.03	.01
☐ 259	Sean Higgins	.05	.02	.01
☐ 260	Jayson Williams	.05	.02	.01
☐ 261	Charlie Ward	.20	.09	.03
☐ 262	Monty Williams	.15	.07	.02
☐ 263	Horace Grant	.15	.07	.02
☐ 264	Brian Shaw	.05	.02	.01
☐ 265	Brooks Thompson	.08	.04	.01
☐ 266	Derrick Alston	.08	.04	.01
☐ 267	B.J. Tyler	.08	.04	.01
☐ 268	Scott Williams	.05	.02	.01
☐ 269	Sharone Wright	.30	.14	.04
☐ 270	Antonio Lang	.07	.03	.01
☐ 271	Danny Manning	.10	.05	.01
☐ 272	Wesley Person	.50	.23	.06
☐ 273	Trevor Ruffin	.08	.04	.01
☐ 274	Wayman Tisdale	.08	.04	.01
☐ 275	Jerome Kersey	.05	.02	.01
☐ 276	Aaron McKie	.20	.09	.03
☐ 277	Frank Brickowski	.05	.02	.01
☐ 278	Brian Grant	.75	.35	.09
☐ 279	Michael Smith	.20	.09	.03
☐ 280	Terry Cummings	.07	.03	.01
☐ 281	Sean Elliott	.08	.04	.01
☐ 282	Avery Johnson	.05	.02	.01
☐ 283	Moses Malone	.15	.07	.02
☐ 284	Chuck Person	.08	.04	.01
☐ 285	Vincent Askew	.05	.02	.01
☐ 286	Bill Cartwright	.05	.02	.01
☐ 287	Sarunas Marciulionis	.05	.02	.01
☐ 288	Dontonio Wingfield	.10	.05	.01
☐ 289	Jay Humphries	.05	.02	.01
☐ 290	Adam Keefe	.05	.02	.01
☐ 291	Jamie Watson	.15	.07	.02
☐ 292	Kevin Duckworth	.05	.02	.01
☐ 293	Juwan Howard	1.00	.45	.13

☐ 294	Jim McIlvaine	.05	.02	.01
☐ 295	Scott Skiles	.05	.02	.01
☐ 296	Anthony Tucker	.05	.02	.01
☐ 297	Chris Webber	.40	.18	.05
☐ 298	Checklist 201-265	.05	.02	.01
☐ 299	Checklist 266-345	.05	.02	.01
☐ 300	Checklist 346-350/Inserts	.05	.02	.01
☐ 301	Vin Baker SSL	.10	.05	.01
	Milwaukee Bucks			
☐ 302	Charles Barkley SSL	.25	.11	.03
	Phoenix Suns			
☐ 303	Derrick Coleman SSL	.05	.02	.01
	New Jersey Nets			
☐ 304	Clyde Drexler SSL	.10	.05	.01
	Portland Trail Blazers			
☐ 305	LaPhonso Ellis SSL	.05	.02	.01
	Denver Nuggets			
☐ 306	Larry Johnson SSL	.08	.04	.01
	Charlotte Hornets			
☐ 307	Shawn Kemp SSL	.25	.11	.03
	Seattle Supersonics			
☐ 308	Karl Malone SSL	.10	.05	.01
	Utah Jazz			
☐ 309	Jamal Mashburn SSL	.25	.11	.03
	Dallas Mavericks			
☐ 310	Scottie Pippen SSL	.10	.05	.01
	Chicago Bulls			
☐ 311	Dominique Wilkins SSL	.08	.04	.01
	Boston Celtics			
☐ 312	Walt Williams SSL	.05	.02	.01
	Sacramento Kings			
☐ 313	Sharone Wright SSL	.10	.05	.01
	Philadelphia 76ers			
☐ 314	B.J. Armstrong SSH	.05	.02	.01
	Chicago Bulls			
☐ 315	Joe Dumars SSH	.08	.04	.01
	Detroit Pistons			
☐ 316	Tony Dumas SSH	.05	.02	.01
	Dallas Mavericks			
☐ 317	Tim Hardaway SSH	.05	.02	.01
	Golden State Warriors			
☐ 318	Toni Kukoc SSH	.05	.02	.01
	Chicago Bulls			
☐ 319	Danny Manning SSH	.05	.02	.01
	Phoenix Suns			
☐ 320	Reggie Miller SSH	.10	.05	.01
	Indiana Pacers			
☐ 321	Chris Mullin SSH	.05	.02	.01
	Golden State Warriors			
☐ 322	Wesley Person SSH	.20	.09	.03
	Phoenix Suns			
☐ 323	John Starks SSH	.05	.02	.01
	New York Knicks			
☐ 324	John Stockton SSH	.10	.05	.01
	Utah Jazz			
☐ 325	C. Weatherspoon SSH	.05	.02	.01
	Philadelphia 76ers			
☐ 326	Shawn Bradley SSW	.05	.02	.01
	Philadelphia 76ers			
☐ 327	Vlade Divac SSW	.05	.02	.01
	Los Angeles Lakers			
☐ 328	Patrick Ewing SSW	.10	.05	.01
	New York Knicks			
☐ 329	Christian Laettner SSW	.05	.02	.01
	Minnesota Timberwolves			
☐ 330	Eric Montross SSW	.15	.07	.02
	Boston Celtics			
☐ 331	Gheorghe Muresan SSW	.05	.02	.01
	Washington Bullets			
☐ 332	Dikembe Mutombo SSW	.08	.04	.01
	Denver Nuggets			

			MINT	NRMT	EXC
☐	333	Hakeem Olajuwon SSW	.30	.14	.04
		Houston Rockets			
☐	334	Robert Parish SSW	.05	.02	.01
		Charlotte Hornets			
☐	335	David Robinson SSW	.25	.11	.03
		San Antonio Spurs			
☐	336	Dennis Rodman SSW	.08	.04	.01
		San Antonio Spurs			
☐	337	Rony Seikaly SSW	.05	.02	.01
		Golden State Warriors			
☐	338	Rik Smits SSW	.05	.02	.01
		Indiana Pacers			
☐	339	Kenny Anderson SPI	.05	.02	.01
		New Jersey Nets			
☐	340	Dee Brown SPI	.05	.02	.01
		Boston Celtics			
☐	341	Bobby Hurley SPI	.05	.02	.01
		Sacramento Kings			
☐	342	Kevin Johnson SPI	.08	.04	.01
		Phoenix Suns			
☐	343	Jason Kidd SPI	1.00	.45	.13
		Dallas Mavericks			
☐	344	Gary Payton SPI	.05	.02	.01
		Seattle Supersonics			
☐	345	Mark Price SPI	.05	.02	.01
		Cleveland Cavaliers			
☐	346	Khalid Reeves SPI	.15	.07	.02
		Miami Heat			
☐	347	Jalen Rose SPI	.20	.09	.03
		Denver Nuggets			
☐	348	Latrell Sprewell SPI	.15	.07	.02
		Golden State Warriors			
☐	349	B.J. Tyler SPI	.05	.02	.01
		Philadelphia 76ers			
☐	350	Charlie Ward SPI	.05	.02	.01
		New York Knicks			
☐	GHO	Grant Hill Gold	50.00	23.00	6.25
☐	NNO	Hakeem Olajuwon Gold	25.00	11.50	3.10
☐	NNO	Emotion Sheet A	30.00	13.50	3.80
☐	NNO	Emotion Sheet B	30.00	13.50	3.80
☐	NNO	Exp. Emotion Exch. A	1.50	.65	.19
☐	NNO	Exp. Emotion Exch. B	1.50	.65	.19
☐	NNO	Exp. Emotion Exch. C	1.50	.65	.19
☐	NNO	Exp. 3rd Prize Game Card	.25	.11	.03
☐	NNO	H. Olajuwon/			
		D. Robinson AU	250.00	115.00	31.00
☐	NNO	M.Johnson Exch. Card	3.00	1.35	.40
☐	NNO	Three-Card Panel Exch.	3.00	1.35	.40

1994-95 SkyBox Center Stage

Randomly inserted in all first series packs at a rate of one in 72, cards from this 9-card set feature a selection of the game's top stars. Card fronts feature full-color player photos over etched-foil backgrounds.

	MINT	NRMT	EXC
COMPLETE SET (9)	175.00	80.00	22.00
COMMON CARD (CS1-CS9)	10.00	4.50	1.25
☐ CS1 Hakeem Olajuwon	25.00	11.50	3.10
Houston Rockets			
☐ CS2 Shaquille O'Neal	50.00	23.00	6.25

		MINT	NRMT	EXC
	Orlando Magic			
☐	CS3 Anfernee Hardaway	40.00	18.00	5.00
	Orlando Magic			
☐	CS4 Chris Webber	15.00	6.75	1.90
	Golden State Warriors			
☐	CS5 Scottie Pippen	10.00	4.50	1.25
	Chicago Bulls			
☐	CS6 David Robinson	20.00	9.00	2.50
	San Antonio Spurs			
☐	CS7 Latrell Sprewell	12.00	5.50	1.50
	Golden State Warriors			
☐	CS8 Charles Barkley	20.00	9.00	2.50
	Phoenix Suns			
☐	CS9 Alonzo Mourning	12.00	5.50	1.50
	Charlotte Hornets			

1994-95 SkyBox Draft Picks

These 27 standard size cards were random inserts in both first series (Nos. 2, 9, 10, 14 and 23) and second series (the other 22) packs. The first series cards were randomly seeded into one in every 45 packs. The second series cards were randomly seeded into one in every 18 packs. The set features all twenty-seven first round draft selections from the 1994 NBA draft. The foil card fronts feature a head shot of each player.

	MINT	NRMT	EXC
COMPLETE SET (27)	175.00	80.00	22.00
COMPLETE SERIES 1 (5)	50.00	23.00	6.25
COMPLETE SERIES 2 (22)	125.00	57.50	15.50
COMMON CARD	1.50	.65	.19

		MINT	NRMT	EXC
☐ 1	Glenn Robinson	30.00	13.50	3.80
	Milwaukee Bucks			
☐ 2	Jason Kidd	30.00	13.50	3.80
	Dallas Mavericks			
☐ 3	Grant Hill	50.00	23.00	6.25
	Detroit Pistons			
☐ 4	Donyell Marshall	6.00	2.70	.75
	Minnesota Timberwolves			
☐ 5	Juwan Howard	12.00	5.50	1.50
	Washington Bullets			
☐ 6	Sharone Wright	4.00	1.80	.50
	Philadelphia 76ers			
☐ 7	Lamond Murray	5.00	2.30	.60
	Los Angeles Clippers			
☐ 8	Brian Grant	10.00	4.50	1.25
	Sacramento Kings			
☐ 9	Eric Montross	5.00	2.30	.60
	Boston Celtics			
☐ 10	Eddie Jones	20.00	9.00	2.50
	Los Angeles Lakers			
☐ 11	Carlos Rogers	2.50	1.15	.30
	Golden State Warriors			
☐ 12	Kahlid Reeves	5.00	2.30	.60
	Miami Heat			
☐ 13	Jalen Rose	6.00	2.70	.75
	Denver Nuggets			
☐ 14	Yinka Dare	1.50	.65	.19
	New Jersey Nets			
☐ 15	Eric Piatkowski	1.50	.65	.19
	Los Angeles Clippers			
☐ 16	Clifford Rozier	2.50	1.15	.30
	Golden State Warriors			
☐ 17	Aaron McKie	2.50	1.15	.30
	Portland Trail Blazers			
☐ 18	Eric Mobley	1.50	.65	.19
	Milwaukee Bucks			
☐ 19	Tony Dumas	1.50	.65	.19
	Dallas Mavericks			
☐ 20	B.J. Tyler	1.50	.65	.19
	Philadelphia 76ers			
☐ 21	Dickey Simpkins	1.50	.65	.19
	Chicago Bulls			
☐ 22	Bill Curley	1.50	.65	.19
	Detroit Pistons			
☐ 23	Wesley Person	6.00	2.70	.75
	Phoenix Suns			
☐ 24	Monty Williams	1.50	.65	.19
	New York Knicks			
☐ 25	Greg Minor	1.50	.65	.19
	Indiana Pacers			
☐ 26	Charlie Ward	2.50	1.15	.30
	New York Knicks			
☐ 27	Brooks Thompson	1.50	.65	.19
	Orlando Magic			

1994-95 SkyBox Head of the Class

This 6-card set was available exclusively by mailing in the SkyBox Head of the Class exchange card before the June 15th, 1995 deadline. The Head of the Class exchange card was randomly inserted into one in every 480 first series packs. SkyBox selected six top rookies from the 1994-95 NBA season to be featured in the set. Card

fronts feature a full-color player photo against a computer generated textured background.

	MINT	NRMT	EXC
COMPLETE SET (7)	50.00	23.00	6.25
COMMON CARD (1-6)	2.00	.90	.25
☐ 1 Grant Hill	25.00	11.50	3.10
☐ 2 Juwan Howard	6.00	2.70	.75
☐ 3 Jason Kidd	15.00	6.75	1.90
☐ 4 Donyell Marshall	3.00	1.35	.40
☐ 5 Glenn Robinson	15.00	6.75	1.90
☐ 6 Sharone Wright	2.00	.90	.25
☐ NNO Checklist Card	.25	.11	.03
☐ NNO Exp. HOC Exch. Card	3.00	1.35	.40

1994-95 SkyBox Grant Hill

Randomly inserted exclusively into one in every 36 second series hobby packs, cards from this 5-card set highlight the Detroit rookie in various action shots. Full-color photos are set against a psychedelic background.

	MINT	NRMT	EXC
COMPLETE SET (5)	60.00	27.00	7.50
COMMON HILL (GH1-GH5)	15.00	6.75	1.90
☐ GH1 Grant Hill	15.00	6.75	1.90
(Two-handed jam; back turned)			
☐ GH2 Grant Hill	15.00	6.75	1.90
(One arm jam)			
☐ GH3 Grant Hill	15.00	6.75	1.90
(Dribbling)			

	MINT	NRMT	EXC
☐ GH4 Grant Hill..............	15.00	6.75	1.90
(Driving to hoop at left)			
☐ GH5 Grant Hill..............	15.00	6.75	1.90
(Two-handed jam)			

1994-95 SkyBox Ragin' Rookies

Randomly inserted into all first series packs at a rate of one in five, cards from this 24-card set feature a selection of the top rookies from the 1993 NBA draft. Full-color action photos feature a scratched border design.

	MINT	NRMT	EXC
COMPLETE SET (24)	40.00	18.00	5.00
COMMON CARD (RR1-RR24)	.75	.35	.09
☐ RR1 Dino Radja	1.50	.65	.19
Boston Celtics			
☐ RR2 Corie Blount..............	.75	.35	.09
Chicago Bulls			
☐ RR3 Toni Kukoc................	1.50	.65	.19
Chicago Bulls			
☐ RR4 Chris Mills................	1.50	.65	.19
Cleveland Cavaliers			
☐ RR5 Jamal Mashburn........	6.00	2.70	.75
Dallas Mavericks			
☐ RR6 Rodney Rogers..........	1.50	.65	.19
Denver Nuggets			
☐ RR7 Allan Houston	1.50	.65	.19
Detroit Pistons			
☐ RR8 Lindsey Hunter..........	.75	.35	.09
Detroit Pistons			
☐ RR9 Chris Webber............	5.00	2.30	.60
Golden State Warriors			
☐ RR10 Sam Cassell	1.50	.65	.19
Houston Rockets			
☐ RR11 Antonio Davis............	.75	.35	.09
Indiana Pacers			
☐ RR12 Terry Dehere	.75	.35	.09
Los Angeles Clippers			
☐ RR13 Nick Van Exel...........	6.00	2.70	.75
Los Angeles Lakers			
☐ RR14 George Lynch.............	.75	.35	.09
Los Angeles Lakers			
☐ RR15 Vin Baker	3.00	1.35	.40
Milwaukee Bucks			
☐ RR16 Isaiah Rider..............	2.00	.90	.25
Minnesota Timberwolves			
☐ RR17 P.J. Brown	.75	.35	.09
New Jersey Nets			
☐ RR18 Anfernee Hardaway	12.00	5.50	1.50
Orlando Magic			
☐ RR19 Shawn Bradley........	1.50	.65	.19
Philadelphia 76ers			
☐ RR20 James Robinson.......	.75	.35	.09
Portland Trailblazers			
☐ RR21 Bobby Hurley............	1.00	.45	.13
Sacramento Kings			
☐ RR22 Ervin Johnson............	.75	.35	.09
Seattle Supersonics			
☐ RR23 Bryon Russell.............	.75	.35	.09
Utah Jazz			
☐ RR24 Calbert Cheaney	1.50	.65	.19
Washington Bullets			

1994-95 SkyBox Revolution

Randomly inserted into second series packs at a rate of one in 72, cards from this 10-card set feature a selection of NBA stars. The horizontal fronts feature full-color player photos against etched-foil backgrounds featuring team colors.

	MINT	NRMT	EXC
COMPLETE SET (10)	175.00	80.00	22.00
COMMON CARD (R1-R10) ...	6.00	2.70	.75
☐ R1 Patrick Ewing	10.00	4.50	1.25
New York Knicks			
☐ R2 Grant Hill	50.00	23.00	6.25
Detroit Pistons			
☐ R3 Jamal Mashburn........	20.00	9.00	2.50
Dallas Mavericks			
☐ R4 Alonzo Mourning.......	12.00	5.50	1.50
Charlotte Hornets			
☐ R5 Dikembe Mutombo......	6.00	2.70	.75
Denver Nuggets			
☐ R6 Shaquille O'Neal.......	50.00	23.00	6.25
Orlando Magic			
☐ R7 Scottie Pippen...........	10.00	4.50	1.25
Chicago Bulls			
☐ R8 Glenn Robinson.......	30.00	13.50	3.80
Milwaukee Bucks			
☐ R9 Latrell Sprewell........	12.00	5.50	1.50
Golden State Warriors			
☐ R10 Chris Webber	15.00	6.75	1.90
Washington Bullets			

1994-95 SkyBox SkyTech Force

Randomly inserted into second series packs at a rate of one in two, cards from this 30-card set feature a selection of the NBA's top stars. Card fronts feature foil backgrounds. The player's name is in gold foil on the bottom while the words "SkyTech Force" is printed vertically on the right. The backs contain some career information as well as a color action photo. The cards are numbered in the upper right with an "SF" prefix.

	MINT	NRMT	EXC
COMPLETE SET (30)	10.00	4.50	1.25
COMMON CARD (SF1-SF30)	.20	.09	.03
☐ SF1 Kenny Anderson New Jersey Nets	.30	.14	.04
☐ SF2 B.J. Armstrong Chicago Bulls	.20	.09	.03
☐ SF3 Charles Barkley Phoenix Suns	1.25	.55	.16
☐ SF4 Shawn Bradley Philadelphia 76ers	.30	.14	.04
☐ SF5 LaPhonso Ellis Denver Nuggets	.20	.09	.03
☐ SF6 Anfernee Hardaway Orlando Magic	2.50	1.15	.30
☐ SF7 Bobby Hurley Sacramento Kings	.20	.09	.03
☐ SF8 Kevin Johnson Phoenix Suns	.40	.18	.05
☐ SF9 Larry Johnson Charlotte Hornets	.50	.23	.06
☐ SF10 Shawn Kemp Seattle Supersonics	1.25	.55	.16
☐ SF11 Jason Kidd Dallas Mavericks	5.00	2.30	.60
☐ SF12 Christian Laettner Minnesota Timberwolves	.30	.14	.04
☐ SF13 Karl Malone Utah Jazz	.60	.25	.08
☐ SF14 Danny Manning Phoenix Suns	.30	.14	.04
☐ SF15 Chris Mills Cleveland Cavaliers	.30	.14	.04
☐ SF16 Chris Mullin Golden State Warriors	.30	.14	.04
☐ SF17 Lamond Murray Los Angeles Clippers	.75	.35	.09
☐ SF18 Charles Oakley New York Knicks	.20	.09	.03
☐ SF19 Hakeem Olajuwon Houston Rockets	1.50	.65	.19
☐ SF20 Gary Payton Seattle Supersonics	.30	.14	.04
☐ SF21 Mark Price Cleveland Cavaliers	.30	.14	.04
☐ SF22 Dino Radja Boston Celtics	.30	.14	.04
☐ SF23 Mitch Richmond Sacramento Kings	.30	.14	.04
☐ SF24 Clifford Robinson Portland Trail Blazers	.20	.09	.03
☐ SF25 David Robinson San Antonio Spurs	1.25	.55	.16
☐ SF26 Dennis Rodman San Antonio Spurs	.40	.18	.05
☐ SF27 Dickey Simpkins Chicago Bulls	.20	.09	.03
☐ SF28 John Starks New York Knicks	.20	.09	.03
☐ SF29 John Stockton Utah Jazz	.60	.25	.08
☐ SF30 Charlie Ward New York Knicks	.30	.14	.04

1994-95 SkyBox Slammin' Universe

Randomly inserted into second series packs at a rate of one in two, cards from this 30-card set feature a selection of the NBA's top dunkers. The horizontal card fronts feature full-color player action shots against a foil "galaxy" background.

	MINT	NRMT	EXC
COMPLETE SET (30)	20.00	9.00	2.50
COMMON CARD (SU1-SU30)	.20	.09	.03
☐ SU1 Vin Baker Milwaukee Bucks	.60	.25	.08
☐ SU2 Dee Brown Boston Celtics	.20	.09	.03
☐ SU3 Derrick Coleman New Jersey Nets	.30	.14	.04
☐ SU4 Clyde Drexler Portland Trail Blazers	.60	.25	.08
☐ SU5 Joe Dumars Detroit Pistons	.40	.18	.05

☐ SU6	Tony Dumas	.20	.09	.03
	Dallas Mavericks			
☐ SU7	Patrick Ewing	.60	.25	.08
	New York Knicks			
☐ SU8	Horace Grant	.40	.18	.05
	Orlando Magic			
☐ SU9	Tom Gugliotta	.20	.09	.03
	Golden State Warriors			
☐ SU10	Grant Hill	8.00	3.60	1.00
	Detroit Pistons			
☐ SU11	Jim Jackson	.75	.35	.09
	Dallas Mavericks			
☐ SU12	Toni Kukoc	.30	.14	.04
	Chicago Bulls			
☐ SU13	Donyell Marshall	1.00	.45	.13
	Minnesota Timberwolves			
☐ SU14	Jamal Mashburn	1.25	.55	.16
	Dallas Mavericks			
☐ SU15	Reggie Miller	.60	.25	.08
	Indiana Pacers			
☐ SU16	Eric Montross	.75	.35	.09
	Boston Celtics			
☐ SU17	Alonzo Mourning	.75	.35	.09
	Charlotte Hornets			
☐ SU18	Dikembe Mutombo	.40	.18	.05
	Denver Nuggets			
☐ SU19	Shaquille O'Neal	3.00	1.35	.40
	Orlando Magic			
☐ SU20	Glen Rice	.30	.14	.04
	Miami Heat			
☐ SU21	Isaiah Rider	.40	.18	.05
	Minnesota Timberwolves			
☐ SU22	Glenn Robinson	5.00	2.30	.60
	Milwaukee Bucks			
☐ SU23	Jalen Rose	1.00	.45	.13
	Denver Nuggets			
☐ SU24	Detlef Schrempf	.30	.14	.04
	Seattle Supersonics			
☐ SU25	Steve Smith	.20	.09	.03
	Atlanta Hawks			
☐ SU26	Latrell Sprewell	.75	.35	.09
	Golden State Warriors			
☐ SU27	Rod Strickland	.20	.09	.03
	Portland Trail Blazers			
☐ SU28	B.J. Tyler	.20	.09	.03
	Philadelphia 76ers			
☐ SU29	Nick Van Exel	1.25	.55	.16
	Los Angeles Lakers			
☐ SU30	Dominique Wilkins	.40	.18	.05
	Boston Celtics			

1994-95 SP

The complete 1994-95 SP set (by Upper Deck) consists of 165-card standard size

cards issued in eight-card packs (suggested retail price $3.99). Boxes were distributed from Upper Deck exclusively to hobby dealers. The set features full-bleed fronts with color action photos. There is a gold strip down the left side with the player name while the team name is at the bottom. . The backs feature another color action photo with the statistics at the bottom and a gold hologram at the bottom left. The only subset is Premier Prospects (1-30) which highlights rookies. These cards are designed differently. They have a full-bleed gold foil background with a silver foil pyramid at the bottom with the player's name in it. The backs have a vertical color player photo on the right and statistics on the left. After the Premier Prospects subset, the cards are grouped alphabetically within teams and checklisted below alphabetically according to teams as follows: Atlanta Hawks (31-35), Boston Celtics (36-40), Charlotte Hornets (41-45), Chicago Bulls (46-50), Cleveland Cavaliers (51-55), Dallas Mavericks (56-60), Detroit Pistons (66-70), Golden State Warriors (71-74), Houston Rockets (76-80), Indiana Pacers (81-85), Los Angeles Clippers (86-90), Los Angeles Lakers (91-95), Miami Heat (96-100), Milwaukee Bucks (101-105), Minnesota Timberwolves (75,106-110), New Jersey Nets (111-115), New York Knicks (116-120), Orlando Magic (121-125), Philadelphia 76ers (126-130), Phoenix Suns (131-135), Portland Trail Blazers (136-140), Sacramento Kings (141-145), San Antonio Spurs (146-150), Seattle Supersonics (151-155), Utah Jazz (156-160), and Washington Bullets (161-165). Two parallel Michael Jordan cards (red and silver), both numbered MJ1, were randomly inserted into packs. The cards feature feature photos from Jordan's return with the words "He's Back March 19, 1995" in red foil. The red version was inserted at a ratio of one in every 30 packs. The silver version was inserted at a ratio of one in every 192 packs.

	MINT	NRMT	EXC
COMPLETE SET (165)	50.00	23.00	6.25
COMMON CARD (1-165)	.20	.09	.03

☐ 1	Glenn Robinson FOIL	10.00	4.50	1.25
	Milwaukee Bucks			
☐ 2	Jason Kidd FOIL	10.00	4.50	1.25
	Dallas Mavericks			
☐ 3	Grant Hill FOIL	15.00	6.75	1.90
	Detroit Pistons			
☐ 4	Donyell Marshall FOIL	2.00	.90	.25
	Minnesota Timberwolves			
☐ 5	Juwan Howard FOIL	4.00	1.80	.50
	Washington Bullets			
☐ 6	Sharone Wright FOIL	1.25	.55	.16
	Philadelphia 76ers			
☐ 7	Lamond Murray FOIL	1.50	.65	.19
	Los Angeles Clippers			
☐ 8	Brian Grant FOIL	3.00	1.35	.40
	Sacramento Kings			
☐ 9	Eric Montross FOIL	1.50	.65	.19

Boston Celtics

☐ 10	Eddie Jones FOIL	6.00	2.70	.75
	Los Angeles Lakers			
☐ 11	Carlos Rogers FOIL	.75	.35	.09
	Golden State Warriors			
☐ 12	Khalid Reeves FOIL	1.50	.65	.19
	Miami Heat			
☐ 13	Jalen Rose FOIL	2.00	.90	.25
	Denver Nuggets			
☐ 14	Eric Piatkowski FOIL	.50	.23	.06
	Los Angeles Clippers			
☐ 15	Clifford Rozier FOIL	.75	.35	.09
	Golden State Warriors			
☐ 16	Aaron McKie FOIL	.75	.35	.09
	Portland Trail Blazers			
☐ 17	Eric Mobley FOIL	.50	.23	.06
	Milwaukee Bucks			
☐ 18	Tony Dumas FOIL	.40	.18	.05
	Dallas Mavericks			
☐ 19	B.J. Tyler FOIL	.50	.23	.06
	Philadelphia 76ers			
☐ 20	Dickey Simpkins FOIL	.50	.23	.06
	Chicago Bulls			
☐ 21	Bill Curley FOIL	.50	.23	.06
	Detroit Pistons			
☐ 22	Wesley Person FOIL	2.00	.90	.25
	Phoenix Suns			
☐ 23	Monty Williams FOIL	.50	.23	.06
	New York Knicks			
☐ 24	Greg Minor FOIL	.50	.23	.06
	Boston Celtics			
☐ 25	Charlie Ward FOIL	.75	.35	.09
	New York Knicks			
☐ 26	Brooks Thompson FOIL	.50	.23	.06
	Orlando Magic			
☐ 27	Trevor Ruffin FOIL	.50	.23	.06
	Phoenix Suns			
☐ 28	Derrick Alston FOIL	.50	.23	.06
	Philadelphia 76ers			
☐ 29	Michael Smith FOIL	.75	.35	.09
	Sacramento Kings			
☐ 30	Dontonio Wingfield FOIL	.60	.25	.08
	Seattle Supersonics			
☐ 31	Stacey Augmon	.30	.14	.04
☐ 32	Steve Smith	.30	.14	.04
☐ 33	Mookie Blaylock	.30	.14	.04
☐ 34	Grant Long	.20	.09	.03
☐ 35	Ken Norman	.20	.09	.03
☐ 36	Dominique Wilkins	.50	.23	.06
☐ 37	Dino Radja	.40	.18	.05
☐ 38	Dee Brown	.30	.14	.04
☐ 39	David Wesley	.20	.09	.03
☐ 40	Rick Fox	.20	.09	.03
☐ 41	Alonzo Mourning	1.25	.55	.16
☐ 42	Larry Johnson	.75	.35	.09
☐ 43	Hersey Hawkins	.30	.14	.04
☐ 44	Scott Burrell	.20	.09	.03
☐ 45	Muggsy Bogues	.40	.18	.05
☐ 46	Scottie Pippen	1.00	.45	.13
☐ 47	Toni Kukoc	.40	.18	.05
☐ 48	B.J. Armstrong	.20	.09	.03
☐ 49	Will Perdue	.20	.09	.03
☐ 50	Ron Harper	.30	.14	.04
☐ 51	Mark Price	.40	.18	.05
☐ 52	Tyrone Hill	.30	.14	.04
☐ 53	Chris Mills	.40	.18	.05
☐ 54	John Williams	.30	.14	.04
☐ 55	Bobby Phills	.20	.09	.03
☐ 56	Jim Jackson	1.25	.55	.16
☐ 57	Jamal Mashburn	2.00	.90	.25
☐ 58	Popeye Jones	.20	.09	.03

☐ 59	Roy Tarpley	.20	.09	.03
☐ 60	Lorenzo Williams	.20	.09	.03
☐ 61	Mahmoud Abdul-Rauf	.30	.14	.04
☐ 62	Rodney Rogers	.40	.18	.05
☐ 63	Bryant Stith	.20	.09	.03
☐ 64	Dikembe Mutombo	.60	.25	.08
☐ 65	Robert Pack	.20	.09	.03
☐ 66	Joe Dumars	.50	.23	.06
☐ 67	Terry Mills	.20	.09	.03
☐ 68	Oliver Miller	.20	.09	.03
☐ 69	Lindsey Hunter	.20	.09	.03
☐ 70	Mark West	.20	.09	.03
☐ 71	Latrell Sprewell	1.25	.55	.16
☐ 72	Tim Hardaway	.40	.18	.05
☐ 73	Ricky Pierce	.30	.14	.04
☐ 74	Rony Seikaly	.20	.09	.03
☐ 75	Tom Gugliotta	.30	.14	.04
☐ 76	Hakeem Olajuwon	2.50	1.15	.30
☐ 77	Clyde Drexler	1.00	.45	.13
☐ 78	Vernon Maxwell	.20	.09	.03
☐ 79	Robert Horry	.40	.18	.05
☐ 80	Sam Cassell	.40	.18	.05
☐ 81	Reggie Miller	1.00	.45	.13
☐ 82	Rik Smits	.40	.18	.05
☐ 83	Derrick McKey	.30	.14	.04
☐ 84	Mark Jackson	.20	.09	.03
☐ 85	Dale Davis	.30	.14	.04
☐ 86	Loy Vaught	.30	.14	.04
☐ 87	Terry Dehere	.20	.09	.03
☐ 88	Malik Sealy	.20	.09	.03
☐ 89	Pooh Richardson	.20	.09	.03
☐ 90	Tony Massenburg	.20	.09	.03
☐ 91	Cedric Ceballos	.40	.18	.05
☐ 92	Nick Van Exel	2.00	.90	.25
☐ 93	George Lynch	.20	.09	.03
☐ 94	Vlade Divac	.40	.18	.05
☐ 95	Elden Campbell	.20	.09	.03
☐ 96	Glen Rice	.40	.18	.05
☐ 97	Kevin Willis	.30	.14	.04
☐ 98	Billy Owens	.30	.14	.04
☐ 99	Bimbo Coles	.20	.09	.03
☐ 100	Harold Miner	.20	.09	.03
☐ 101	Vin Baker	1.00	.45	.13
☐ 102	Todd Day	.30	.14	.04
☐ 103	Marty Conlon	.20	.09	.03
☐ 104	Lee Mayberry	.20	.09	.03
☐ 105	Eric Murdock	.20	.09	.03
☐ 106	Isaiah Rider	.60	.25	.08
☐ 107	Doug West	.20	.09	.03
☐ 108	Christian Laettner	.30	.14	.04
☐ 109	Sean Rooks	.20	.09	.03
☐ 110	Stacey King	.20	.09	.03
☐ 111	Derrick Coleman	.40	.18	.05
☐ 112	Kenny Anderson	.40	.18	.05
☐ 113	Chris Morris	.20	.09	.03
☐ 114	Armon Gilliam	.20	.09	.03
☐ 115	Benoit Benjamin	.20	.09	.03
☐ 116	Patrick Ewing	1.00	.45	.13
☐ 117	Charles Oakley	.30	.14	.04
☐ 118	John Starks	.30	.14	.04
☐ 119	Derek Harper	.30	.14	.04
☐ 120	Charles Smith	.20	.09	.03
☐ 121	Shaquille O'Neal	5.00	2.30	.60
☐ 122	Anfernee Hardaway	4.00	1.80	.50
☐ 123	Nick Anderson	.30	.14	.04
☐ 124	Horace Grant	.50	.23	.06
☐ 125	Donald Royal	.20	.09	.03
☐ 126	Clarence Weatherspoon	.40	.18	.05
☐ 127	Dana Barros	.40	.18	.05
☐ 128	Jeff Malone	.30	.14	.04
☐ 129	Willie Burton	.20	.09	.03

		MINT	NRMT	EXC
COMPLETE SET (165)	140.00	64.00	16.00
COMMON CARD (1-165)	.50	.23	.06

*DIE CUT STARS: 1.25X to 2.5X BASIC CARDS
*DIE CUT ROOKIES: 1X to 2X BASIC CARDS

☐ 130	Shawn Bradley	.40	.18	.05
☐ 131	Charles Barkley	2.00	.90	.25
☐ 132	Kevin Johnson	.50	.23	.06
☐ 133	Danny Manning	.40	.18	.05
☐ 134	Dan Majerle	.30	.14	.04
☐ 135	A.C. Green	.40	.18	.05
☐ 136	Otis Thorpe	.30	.14	.04
☐ 137	Clifford Robinson	.30	.14	.04
☐ 138	Rod Strickland	.30	.14	.04
☐ 139	Buck Williams	.30	.14	.04
☐ 140	James Robinson	.20	.09	.03
☐ 141	Mitch Richmond	.50	.23	.06
☐ 142	Walt Williams	.30	.14	.04
☐ 143	Olden Polynice	.20	.09	.03
☐ 144	Spud Webb	.30	.14	.04
☐ 145	Duane Causwell	.20	.09	.03
☐ 146	David Robinson	2.00	.90	.25
☐ 147	Dennis Rodman	.60	.25	.08
☐ 148	Sean Elliott	.30	.14	.04
☐ 149	Avery Johnson	.20	.09	.03
☐ 150	J.R. Reid	.20	.09	.03
☐ 151	Shawn Kemp	2.00	.90	.25
☐ 152	Gary Payton	.40	.18	.05
☐ 153	Detlef Schrempf	.40	.18	.05
☐ 154	Nate McMillan	.20	.09	.03
☐ 155	Kendall Gill	.20	.09	.03
☐ 156	Karl Malone	1.00	.45	.13
☐ 157	John Stockton	1.00	.45	.13
☐ 158	Jeff Hornacek	.30	.14	.04
☐ 159	Felton Spencer	.20	.09	.03
☐ 160	David Benoit	.20	.09	.03
☐ 161	Chris Webber	1.50	.65	.19
☐ 162	Rex Chapman	.20	.09	.03
☐ 163	Don MacLean	.20	.09	.03
☐ 164	Calbert Cheaney	.40	.18	.05
☐ 165	Scott Skiles	.20	.09	.03
☐ MJ1R	Michael Jordan Red	15.00	6.75	1.90
☐ MJ1S	Michael Jordan Silver	80.00	36.00	10.00

1994-95 SP Premium Collection Holoviews

Cards from this 36-card standard size set were randomly inserted in packs at a rate of one in five. The set features a mixture of NBA stars coupled with a wide selection of 1994-95 rookies. The fronts feature color action photos with a hologram of company spokesperson Shawn Kemp on the left with the player's name in silver just to the right. In addition, a holographic head shot of each player is placed in the lower left corner. The backs have a black and white photo on the right and player information on the left.

		MINT	NRMT	EXC
COMPLETE SET (36)	150.00	70.00	19.00
COMMON CARD (PC1-PC36)	1.50	.65	.19

☐ PC1	Eric Montross Boston Celtics	3.00	1.35	.40
☐ PC2	Dominique Wilkins Boston Celtics	3.00	1.35	.40
☐ PC3	Larry Johnson Charlotte Hornets	5.00	2.30	.60
☐ PC4	Dickey Simpkins Chicago Bulls	1.50	.65	.19
☐ PC5	Jalen Rose Denver Nuggets	4.00	1.80	.50
☐ PC6	Latrell Sprewell Golden State Warriors	8.00	3.60	1.00
☐ PC7	Carlos Rogers Golden State Warriors	2.00	.90	.25
☐ PC8	Lamond Murray Los Angeles Clippers	3.00	1.35	.40
☐ PC9	Eddie Jones Los Angeles Lakers	12.00	5.50	1.50
☐ PC10	Cedric Ceballos Los Angeles Lakers	2.50	1.15	.30

1994-95 SP Die-Cut

This is a parallel set to the regular SP issue. These die cuts appear one per pack. The only difference other than the die cut is there is a silver hologram in the bottom left of the back instead of the gold hologram in the regular set. Please refer to the multipliers provided below (coupled with prices of the regular issue SP cards) to ascertain value.

☐ PC11 Khalid Reeves........... 3.00		1.35	.40
Miami Heat			
☐ PC12 Glenn Robinson...... 20.00		9.00	2.50
Milwaukee Bucks			
☐ PC13 Christian Laettner.... 2.00		.90	.25
Minnesota Timberwolves			
☐ PC14 Derrick Coleman..... 2.50		1.15	.30
New Jersey Nets			
☐ PC15 Vin Baker................ 6.00		2.70	.75
Milwaukee Bucks			
☐ PC16 Donyell Marshall...... 4.00		1.80	.50
Minnesota Timberwolves			
☐ PC17 Kenny Anderson...... 2.50		1.15	.30
New Jersey Nets			
☐ PC18 Sharone Wright....... 2.50		1.15	.30
Philadelphia 76ers			
☐ PC19 Wesley Person........ 4.00		1.80	.50
Phoenix Suns			
☐ PC20 Brian Grant............. 6.00		2.70	.75
Sacramento Kings			
☐ PC21 Mitch Richmond....... 3.00		1.35	.40
Sacramento Kings			
☐ PC22 Shawn Kemp.......... 12.00		5.50	1.50
Seattle Supersonics			
☐ PC23 Gary Payton........... 2.50		1.15	.30
Seattle Supersonics			
☐ PC24 Juwan Howard......... 8.00		3.60	1.00
Washington Bullets			
☐ PC25 Stacey Augmon....... 2.00		.90	.25
Atlanta Hawks			
☐ PC26 Aaron McKie........... 2.00		.90	.25
Portland Trail Blazers			
☐ PC27 Clifford Rozier........ 2.00		.90	.25
Golden State Warriors			
☐ PC28 Eric Piatkowski....... 1.50		.65	.19
Los Angeles Clippers			
☐ PC29 Shaquille O'Neal..... 35.00		16.00	4.40
Orlando Magic			
☐ PC30 Charlie Ward.......... 2.00		.90	.25
New York Knicks			
☐ PC31 Monty Williams....... 1.50		.65	.19
New York Knicks			
☐ PC32 Jason Kidd............. 20.00		9.00	2.50
Dallas Mavericks			
☐ PC33 Bill Curley............... 1.50		.65	.19
Detroit Pistons			
☐ PC34 Grant Hill............... 35.00		16.00	4.40
Detroit Pistons			
☐ PC35 Jamal Mashburn...... 12.00		5.50	1.50
Dallas Mavericks			
☐ PC36 Nick Van Exel......... 12.00		5.50	1.50
Los Angeles Lakers			

1994-95 SP Premium Collection Holoview Die Cuts

This is a parallel set to the SP Premium Collection Holoviews. These die cuts appear one per 75 packs. The cards are similar to the regular Premium Collection Holoviews except for their die cut design and DPC prefixed numbering.

	MINT	NRMT	EXC
COMPLETE SET (36) 2000.00		900.00	250.00
COMMON CARD (1-36) 15.00		6.75	1.90
☐ 1 Eric Montross............ 25.00		11.50	3.10
Boston Celtics			
☐ 2 Dominique Wilkins....... 25.00		11.50	3.10
Boston Celtics			
☐ 3 Larry Johnson............ 40.00		18.00	5.00
Charlotte Hornets			
☐ 5 Jalen Rose................ 30.00		13.50	3.80
Denver Nuggets			
☐ 6 Latrell Sprewell.......... 60.00		27.00	7.50
Golden State Warriors			
☐ 8 Lamond Murray........... 25.00		11.50	3.10
Los Angeles Clippers			
☐ 9 Eddie Jones.............. 100.00		45.00	12.50
Los Angeles Lakers			
☐ 11 Khalid Reeves.......... 25.00		11.50	3.10
Miami Heat			
☐ 12 Glenn Robinson....... 175.00		80.00	22.00
Milwaukee Bucks			
☐ 15 Vin Baker................ 50.00		23.00	6.25
Milwaukee Bucks			
☐ 16 Donyell Marshall....... 40.00		18.00	5.00
Minnesota Timberwolves			
☐ 19 Wesley Person......... 30.00		13.50	3.80
Phoenix Suns			
☐ 20 Brian Grant.............. 50.00		23.00	6.25
Sacramento Kings			
☐ 21 Mitch Richmond....... 25.00		11.50	3.10
Sacramento Kings			
☐ 22 Shawn Kemp........... 100.00		45.00	12.50
Seattle Supersonics			
☐ 24 Juwan Howard........... 60.00		27.00	7.50
Washington Bullets			
☐ 29 Shaquille O'Neal...... 350.00		160.00	45.00
Orlando Magic			
☐ 32 Jason Kidd............. 175.00		80.00	22.00
Dallas Mavericks			
☐ 34 Grant Hill............... 250.00		115.00	31.00
Detroit Pistons			
☐ 35 Jamal Mashburn...... 100.00		45.00	12.50
Dallas Mavericks			
☐ 36 Nick Van Exel.......... 100.00		45.00	12.50
Los Angeles Lakers			

1994-95 SP Championship

The premier edition of the 1994-95 SP Championship series (made by Upper

Deck) consists of 135 standard size cards issued in six-card foil packs, each with a suggested retail price of $2.99. SP Championship cards were shipped by Upper Deck exclusively to retail outlets. Card fronts feature full-bleed, color action photos with a foil SP Championship logo. The player's name runs up the side of the card in small gold foil print. Team name is contained in a foil oval. After a Road to the Finals (1-27) subset, the cards are grouped alphabetically within teams and checklisted below alphabetically according to teams as follows: Atlanta Hawks (28-31), Boston Celtics (32-35), Charlotte Hornets (36-39), Chicago Bulls (40-43), Cleveland Cavaliers (44-47), Dallas Mavericks (48-51), Denver Nuggets (52-55), Detroit Pistons (56-59), Golden State Warriors (60-63), Houston Rockets (64-67), Indiana Pacers (68-71), Los Angeles Clippers (72-75), Los Angeles Lakers (76-79), Miami Heat (80-83), Milwaukee Bucks (84-87), Minnesota Timberwolves (88-91), New Jersey Nets (92-95), New York Knicks (96-99), Orlando Magic (100-103), Philadelphia 76ers (104-107), Phoenix Suns (108-111), Portland Trail Blazers (112-115), Sacramento Kings (116-119), San Antonio Spurs (120-123), Seattle Supersonics (124-127), Utah Jazz (128-131), and Washington Bullets (132-135).

	MINT	NRMT	EXC
COMPLETE SET (135)	40.00	18.00	5.00
COMMON CARD (1-135)	.10	.05	.01
☐ 1 Mookie Blaylock RF Atlanta Hawks	.10	.05	.01
☐ 2 Dominique Wilkins RF Boston Celtics	.15	.07	.02
☐ 3 Alonzo Mourning RF Charlotte Hornets	.40	.18	.05
☐ 4 Michael Jordan RF Chicago Bulls	10.00	4.50	1.25
☐ 5 Mark Price RF Cleveland Cavaliers	.10	.05	.01
☐ 6 Jamal Mashburn RF Dallas Mavericks	.60	.25	.08
☐ 7 Dikembe Mutombo RF Denver Nuggets	.15	.07	.02
☐ 8 Grant Hill RF Detroit Pistons	3.00	1.35	.40
☐ 9 Latrell Sprewell RF Golden State Warriors	.40	.18	.05
☐ 10 Hakeem Olajuwon RF Houston Rockets	.75	.35	.09
☐ 11 Reggie Miller RF Indiana Pacers	.25	.11	.03
☐ 12 Loy Vaught RF Los Angeles Clippers	.10	.05	.01
☐ 13 Nick Van Exel RF Los Angeles Lakers	.60	.25	.08
☐ 14 Glen Rice RF Miami Heat	.10	.05	.01
☐ 15 Glenn Robinson RF Milwaukee Bucks	2.00	.90	.25
☐ 16 Isaiah Rider RF Minnesota Timberwolves	.25	.11	.03
☐ 17 Kenny Anderson RF New Jersey Nets	.10	.05	.01
☐ 18 Patrick Ewing RF New York Knicks	.30	.14	.04
☐ 19 Shaquille O'Neal RF Orlando Magic	1.50	.65	.19
☐ 20 Dana Barros RF Philadelphia 76ers	.10	.05	.01
☐ 21 Charles Barkley RF Phoenix Suns	.60	.25	.08
☐ 22 Clifford Robinson RF Portland Trail Blazers	.10	.05	.01
☐ 23 Mitch Richmond RF Sacramento Kings	.15	.07	.02
☐ 24 David Robinson RF San Antonio Spurs	.60	.25	.08
☐ 25 Shawn Kemp RF Seattle SuperSonics	.60	.25	.08
☐ 26 Karl Malone RF Utah Jazz	.25	.11	.03
☐ 27 Chris Webber RF Washington Bullets	.50	.23	.06
☐ 28 Stacey Augmon	.15	.07	.02
☐ 29 Mookie Blaylock	.15	.07	.02
☐ 30 Grant Long	.10	.05	.01
☐ 31 Steve Smith	.15	.07	.02
☐ 32 Dee Brown	.15	.07	.02
☐ 33 Eric Montross	.75	.35	.09
☐ 34 Dino Radja	.25	.11	.03
☐ 35 Dominique Wilkins	.30	.14	.04
☐ 36 Muggsy Bogues	.25	.11	.03
☐ 37 Scott Burrell	.10	.05	.01
☐ 38 Larry Johnson	.50	.23	.06
☐ 39 Alonzo Mourning	.75	.35	.09
☐ 40 B.J. Armstrong	.10	.05	.01
☐ 41 Michael Jordan	10.00	4.50	1.25
☐ 42 Toni Kukoc	.25	.11	.03
☐ 43 Scottie Pippen	.60	.25	.08
☐ 44 Tyrone Hill	.15	.07	.02
☐ 45 Chris Mills	.25	.11	.03
☐ 46 Mark Price	.25	.11	.03
☐ 47 John Williams	.15	.07	.02
☐ 48 Jim Jackson	.75	.35	.09
☐ 49 Jason Kidd	5.00	2.30	.60
☐ 50 Jamal Mashburn	1.25	.55	.16
☐ 51 Roy Tarpley	.10	.05	.01
☐ 52 Mahmoud Abdul-Rauf	.15	.07	.02
☐ 53 Dikembe Mutombo	.40	.18	.05
☐ 54 Rodney Rogers	.25	.11	.03
☐ 55 Bryant Stith	.10	.05	.01
☐ 56 Joe Dumars	.30	.14	.04
☐ 57 Grant Hill	8.00	3.60	1.00
☐ 58 Lindsey Hunter	.10	.05	.01
☐ 59 Terry Mills	.10	.05	.01
☐ 60 Tim Hardaway	.25	.11	.03
☐ 61 Donyell Marshall	1.00	.45	.13
☐ 62 Chris Mullin	.25	.11	.03
☐ 63 Latrell Sprewell	.75	.35	.09
☐ 64 Sam Cassell	.25	.11	.03

☐ 65 Clyde Drexler	.60	.25	.08
☐ 66 Vernon Maxwell	.10	.05	.01
☐ 67 Hakeem Olajuwon	1.50	.65	.19
☐ 68 Dale Davis	.15	.07	.02
☐ 69 Mark Jackson	.10	.05	.01
☐ 70 Reggie Miller	.60	.25	.08
☐ 71 Rik Smits	.25	.11	.03
☐ 72 Terry Dehere	.10	.05	.01
☐ 73 Lamond Murray	.75	.35	.09
☐ 74 Pooh Richardson	.10	.05	.01
☐ 75 Loy Vaught	.10	.05	.01
☐ 76 Cedric Ceballos	.25	.11	.03
☐ 77 Vlade Divac	.25	.11	.03
☐ 78 Eddie Jones	3.00	1.35	.40
☐ 79 Nick Van Exel	1.25	.55	.16
☐ 80 Bimbo Coles	.10	.05	.01
☐ 81 Billy Owens	.15	.07	.02
☐ 82 Glen Rice	.25	.11	.03
☐ 83 Kevin Willis	.15	.07	.02
☐ 84 Vin Baker	.60	.25	.08
☐ 85 Marty Conlon	.10	.05	.01
☐ 86 Eric Murdock	.10	.05	.01
☐ 87 Glenn Robinson	5.00	2.30	.60
☐ 88 Tom Gugliotta	.15	.07	.02
☐ 89 Christian Laettner	.15	.07	.02
☐ 90 Isaiah Rider	.40	.18	.05
☐ 91 Doug West	.10	.05	.01
☐ 92 Kenny Anderson	.25	.11	.03
☐ 93 Benoit Benjamin	.10	.05	.01
☐ 94 Derrick Coleman	.25	.11	.03
☐ 95 Armon Gilliam	.10	.05	.01
☐ 96 Patrick Ewing	.60	.25	.08
☐ 97 Derek Harper	.15	.07	.02
☐ 98 Charles Oakley	.15	.07	.02
☐ 99 John Starks	.15	.07	.02
☐ 100 Nick Anderson	.15	.07	.02
☐ 101 Horace Grant	.30	.14	.04
☐ 102 Anfernee Hardaway	2.50	1.15	.30
☐ 103 Shaquille O'Neal	3.00	1.35	.40
☐ 104 Dana Barros	.25	.11	.03
☐ 105 Shawn Bradley	.25	.11	.03
☐ 106 Clarence Weatherspoon	.25	.11	.03
☐ 107 Sharone Wright	.60	.25	.08
☐ 108 Charles Barkley	1.25	.55	.16
☐ 109 Kevin Johnson	.30	.14	.04
☐ 110 Dan Majerle	.15	.07	.02
☐ 111 Wesley Person	1.00	.45	.13
☐ 112 Terry Porter	.15	.07	.02
☐ 113 Clifford Robinson	.15	.07	.02
☐ 114 Rod Strickland	.15	.07	.02
☐ 115 Buck Williams	.15	.07	.02
☐ 116 Brian Grant	1.50	.65	.19
☐ 117 Mitch Richmond	.30	.14	.04
☐ 118 Spud Webb	.15	.07	.02
☐ 119 Walt Williams	.15	.07	.02
☐ 120 Vinny Del Negro	.10	.05	.01
☐ 121 Sean Elliott	.15	.07	.02
☐ 122 David Robinson	1.25	.55	.16
☐ 123 Dennis Rodman	.40	.18	.05
☐ 124 Kendall Gill	.10	.05	.01
☐ 125 Shawn Kemp	1.25	.55	.16
☐ 126 Gary Payton	.25	.11	.03
☐ 127 Detlef Schrempf	.25	.11	.03
☐ 128 David Benoit	.10	.05	.01
☐ 129 Jeff Hornacek	.15	.07	.02
☐ 130 Karl Malone	.60	.25	.08
☐ 131 John Stockton	.60	.25	.08
☐ 132 Rex Chapman	.10	.05	.01
☐ 133 Calbert Cheaney	.25	.11	.03
☐ 134 Juwan Howard	2.00	.90	.25
☐ 135 Chris Webber	1.00	.45	.13

1994-95
SP Championship
Die Cuts

This 135-card parallel set is identical to the regular SP Championship series except for the die cut design on the cards as well as the silver hologram on their backs. One die cut card was inserted in each pack.

	MINT	NRMT	EXC
COMPLETE SET (135)	120.00	54.00	15.00
COMMON CARD (1-135)	.40	.18	.05

*DIE CUT STARS: 1.25X to 2.5X BASIC CARDS
*DIE CUT ROOKIES: 1X to 2X BASIC CARDS

1994-95
SP Championship
Future Playoff
Heroes

Randomly inserted at a rate of 1 in every 40 foil packs, this 10-card standard-size set spotlights up-and-coming NBA stars who figure to be Playoff Heroes in the coming years. Unlike the glossy regular issue cards, these inserts feature a throwback design element incorporating basic card-board-style backgrounds against glossy color player action photos.

	MINT	NRMT	EXC
COMPLETE SET (10)	100.00	45.00	12.50
COMMON CARD (F1-F10)	3.00	1.35	.40
☐ F1 Brian Grant Sacramento Kings	5.00	2.30	.60
☐ F2 Anfernee Hardaway Orlando Magic	20.00	9.00	2.50
☐ F3 Grant Hill Detroit Pistons	25.00	11.50	3.10
☐ F4 Eddie Jones Los Angeles Lakers	10.00	4.50	1.25
☐ F5 Jamal Mashburn Dallas Mavericks	10.00	4.50	1.25
☐ F6 Shaquille O'Neal Orlando Magic	25.00	11.50	3.10
☐ F7 Isaiah Rider Minnesota Timberwolves	3.00	1.35	.40
☐ F8 Glenn Robinson Milwaukee Bucks	15.00	6.75	1.90
☐ F9 Latrell Sprewell Golden State Warriors	6.00	2.70	.75
☐ F10 Chris Webber Washington Bullets	8.00	3.60	1.00

1994-95
SP Championship
Future Playoff
Heroes Die Cuts

Randomly inserted at a rate of 1 in every 300 foil packs, this 10 card standard-size set spotlights up-and-coming NBA stars who figure to be Playoff Heroes in the coming years. They differ from the basic inserts in their die cut design and the presence of silver (rather than gold) holograms on their backs.

	MINT	NRMT	EXC
COMPLETE SET (10)	700.00	325.00	90.00
COMMON CARD (F1-F10)	20.00	9.00	2.50
☐ F1 Brian Grant Sacramento Kings	30.00	13.50	3.80
☐ F2 Anfernee Hardaway Orlando Magic	125.00	57.50	15.50
☐ F3 Grant Hill Detroit Pistons	150.00	70.00	19.00
☐ F4 Eddie Jones Los Angeles Lakers	60.00	27.00	7.50
☐ F5 Jamal Mashburn Dallas Mavericks	60.00	27.00	7.50
☐ F6 Shaquille O'Neal Orlando Magic	150.00	70.00	19.00
☐ F7 Isaiah Rider Minnesota Timberwolves	20.00	9.00	2.50
☐ F8 Glenn Robinson Milwaukee Bucks	100.00	45.00	12.50

	MINT	NRMT	EXC
☐ F9 Latrell Sprewell Golden State Warriors	40.00	18.00	5.00
☐ F10 Chris Webber Washington Bullets	50.00	23.00	6.25

1994-95
SP Championship
Playoff Heroes

Randomly inserted at a rate of one in every 15 packs, this 10-card standard size set features some of the greatest active NBA Playoff performers. Unlike, the glossy regular issue cards, these inserts feature a throwback design element incorporating basic cardboard-style backgrounds against glossy color player action photos. A number of cards slipped through production with scuffed logos on front. In addition, some others also had "Future Playoff Heroes" logos rather than the regular "Playoff Heroes" logos. None of these variations trade for a premium.

	MINT	NRMT	EXC
COMPLETE SET (10)	75.00	34.00	9.50
COMMON CARD (P1-P10)	2.00	.90	.25
☐ P1 Charles Barkley Phoenix Suns	10.00	4.50	1.25
☐ P2 Michael Jordan Chicago Bulls	60.00	27.00	7.50
☐ P3 Shawn Kemp Seattle Supersonics	10.00	4.50	1.25
☐ P4 Moses Malone San Antonio Spurs	2.50	1.15	.30
☐ P5 Reggie Miller Indiana Pacers	5.00	2.30	.60
☐ P6 Alonzo Mourning Charlotte Hornets	6.00	2.70	.75
☐ P7 Dikembe Mutombo Denver Nuggets	3.00	1.35	.40
☐ P8 Hakeem Olajuwon Houston Rockets	12.00	5.50	1.50
☐ P9 Robert Parish Charlotte Hornets	2.00	.90	.25
☐ P10 John Stockton Utah Jazz	5.00	2.30	.60

1994-95
SP Championship
Playoff Heroes
Die Cuts

Randomly inserted at a rate of 1 in every 225 foil packs, this 10 card set features some of the greatest active NBA Playoff performers. They differ from the basic inserts in their die cut design and the presence of silver (rather than gold) holograms on their backs.

	MINT	NRMT	EXC
COMPLETE SET (10)	500.00	230.00	65.00
COMMON CARD (P1-P10)	10.00	4.50	1.25
☐ P1 Charles Barkley Phoenix Suns	50.00	23.00	6.25
☐ P2 Michael Jordan Chicago Bulls	300.00	135.00	38.00
☐ P3 Shawn Kemp Seattle Supersonics	50.00	23.00	6.25
☐ P4 Moses Malone San Antonio Spurs	12.00	5.50	1.50
☐ P5 Reggie Miller Indiana Pacers	25.00	11.50	3.10
☐ P6 Alonzo Mourning Charlotte Hornets	30.00	13.50	3.80
☐ P7 Dikembe Mutombo Denver Nuggets	15.00	6.75	1.90
☐ P8 Hakeem Olajuwon Houston Rockets	60.00	27.00	7.50
☐ P9 Robert Parish Charlotte Hornets	10.00	4.50	1.25
☐ P10 John Stockton Utah Jazz	25.00	11.50	3.10

1992-93
Stadium Club

The complete 1992-93 Stadium Club basketball set (created by Topps) consists of 400 cards, having been issued in two 200-card series. Both first and second series packs contained 15 cards with a suggested retail price of 1.79 per pack. Topps also issued, late in the season, second series 23-card jumbo packs. The cards measure the standard size (2 1/2" by 3 1/2" inches). A Stadium Club membership form (also standard size) was inserted in every 15-card pack. The basic card fronts feature full-bleed color action player photos. The team name and player's name appear in gold foil stripes that cut across the bottom of the card and intersect the Stadium Club logo. On a colorful background of a basketball in a net, the horizontal backs present biography, The Sporting News Skills Rating System, player evaluation, 1991-92 season and career statistics, and a miniature representation of the player's first Topps card, which is confusingly referenced as "Topps Rookie Card" by Topps. The first series closes and the second series begins with a Members Choice (191-211) subset. The cards are numbered on the back. Rookie Cards include LaPhonso Ellis, Tom Gugliotta, Robert Horry, Christian Laettner, Alonzo Mourning, Shaquille O'Neal, Latrell Sprewell, Clarence Weatherspoon, and Walt Williams.

	MINT	NRMT	EXC
COMPLETE SET (400)	60.00	27.00	7.50
COMPLETE SERIES 1 (200)	20.00	9.00	2.50
COMPLETE SERIES 2 (200)	40.00	18.00	5.00
COMMON CARD (1-400)	.10	.05	.01
☐ 1 Michael Jordan Chicago Bulls	8.00	3.60	1.00
☐ 2 Greg Anthony New York Knicks	.10	.05	.01
☐ 3 Otis Thorpe Houston Rockets	.15	.07	.02
☐ 4 Jim Les Sacramento Kings	.10	.05	.01
☐ 5 Kevin Willis Atlanta Hawks	.15	.07	.02
☐ 6 Derek Harper Dallas Mavericks	.15	.07	.02
☐ 7 Elden Campbell Los Angeles Lakers	.10	.05	.01
☐ 8 A.J. English Washington Bullets	.10	.05	.01
☐ 9 Kenny Gattison Charlotte Hornets	.10	.05	.01
☐ 10 Drazen Petrovic New Jersey Nets	.15	.07	.02
☐ 11 Chris Mullin Golden State Warriors	.25	.11	.03

☐ 12 Mark Price	.25	.11	.03
Cleveland Cavaliers			
☐ 13 Karl Malone	.60	.25	.08
Utah Jazz			
☐ 14 Gerald Glass	.10	.05	.01
Minnesota Timberwolves			
☐ 15 Negele Knight	.10	.05	.01
Phoenix Suns			
☐ 16 Mark Macon	.10	.05	.01
Denver Nuggets			
☐ 17 Michael Cage	.10	.05	.01
Seattle Supersonics			
☐ 18 Kevin Edwards	.10	.05	.01
Miami Heat			
☐ 19 Sherman Douglas	.10	.05	.01
Boston Celtics			
☐ 20 Ron Harper	.15	.07	.02
Los Angeles Clippers			
☐ 21 Clifford Robinson	.25	.11	.03
Portland Trail Blazers			
☐ 22 Byron Scott	.15	.07	.02
Los Angeles Lakers			
☐ 23 Antoine Carr	.10	.05	.01
San Antonio Spurs			
☐ 24 Greg Dreiling	.10	.05	.01
Indiana Pacers			
☐ 25 Bill Laimbeer	.15	.07	.02
Detroit Pistons			
☐ 26 Hersey Hawkins	.15	.07	.02
Philadelphia 76ers			
☐ 27 Will Perdue	.10	.05	.01
Chicago Bulls			
☐ 28 Todd Lichti	.10	.05	.01
Denver Nuggets			
☐ 29 Gary Grant	.10	.05	.01
Los Angeles Clippers			
☐ 30 Sam Perkins	.15	.07	.02
Los Angeles Lakers			
☐ 31 Jayson Williams	.10	.05	.01
Philadelphia 76ers			
☐ 32 Magic Johnson	1.25	.55	.16
Los Angeles Lakers			
☐ 33 Larry Bird	2.00	.90	.25
Boston Celtics			
☐ 34 Chris Morris	.10	.05	.01
New Jersey Nets			
☐ 35 Nick Anderson	.15	.07	.02
Orlando Magic			
☐ 36 Scott Hastings	.10	.05	.01
Denver Nuggets			
☐ 37 Ledell Eackles	.10	.05	.01
Washington Bullets			
☐ 38 Robert Pack	.10	.05	.01
Portland Trail Blazers			
☐ 39 Dana Barros	.25	.11	.03
Seattle Supersonics			
☐ 40 Anthony Bonner	.10	.05	.01
Sacramento Kings			
☐ 41 J.R. Reid	.10	.05	.01
Charlotte Hornets			
☐ 42 Tyrone Hill	.15	.07	.02
Golden State Warriors			
☐ 43 Rik Smits	.25	.11	.03
Indiana Pacers			
☐ 44 Kevin Duckworth	.10	.05	.01
Portland Trail Blazers			
☐ 45 LaSalle Thompson	.10	.05	.01
Indiana Pacers			
☐ 46 Brian Williams	.10	.05	.01
Orlando Magic			
☐ 47 Willie Anderson	.10	.05	.01
San Antonio Spurs			
☐ 48 Ken Norman	.10	.05	.01
Los Angeles Clippers			
☐ 49 Mike Iuzzolino	.10	.05	.01
Dallas Mavericks			
☐ 50 Isiah Thomas	.30	.14	.04
Detroit Pistons			
☐ 51 Alec Kessler	.10	.05	.01
Miami Heat			
☐ 52 Johnny Dawkins	.10	.05	.01
Philadelphia 76ers			
☐ 53 Avery Johnson	.10	.05	.01
Houston Rockets			
☐ 54 Stacey Augmon	.25	.11	.03
Atlanta Hawks			
☐ 55 Charles Oakley	.15	.07	.02
New York Knicks			
☐ 56 Rex Chapman	.10	.05	.01
Washington Bullets			
☐ 57 Charles Shackleford	.10	.05	.01
Philadelphia 76ers			
☐ 58 Jeff Ruland	.10	.05	.01
Philadelphia 76ers			
☐ 59 Craig Ehlo	.10	.05	.01
Cleveland Cavaliers			
☐ 60 Jon Koncak	.10	.05	.01
Atlanta Hawks			
☐ 61 Danny Schayes	.10	.05	.01
Milwaukee Bucks			
☐ 62 David Benoit	.10	.05	.01
Utah Jazz			
☐ 63 Robert Parish	.25	.11	.03
Boston Celtics			
☐ 64 Mookie Blaylock	.15	.07	.02
New Jersey Nets			
☐ 65 Sean Elliott	.15	.07	.02
San Antonio Spurs			
☐ 66 Mark Aguirre	.15	.07	.02
Detroit Pistons			
☐ 67 Scott Williams	.10	.05	.01
Chicago Bulls			
☐ 68 Doug West	.10	.05	.01
Minnesota Timberwolves			
☐ 69 Kenny Anderson	.50	.23	.06
New Jersey Nets			
☐ 70 Randy Brown	.10	.05	.01
Sacramento Kings			
☐ 71 Muggsy Bogues	.25	.11	.03
Charlotte Hornets			
☐ 72 Spud Webb	.15	.07	.02
Sacramento Kings			
☐ 73 Sedale Threatt	.10	.05	.01
Los Angeles Lakers			
☐ 74 Chris Gatling	.10	.05	.01
Golden State Warriors			
☐ 75 Derrick McKey	.15	.07	.02
Seattle Supersonics			
☐ 76 Sleepy Floyd	.10	.05	.01
Houston Rockets			
☐ 77 Chris Jackson	.15	.07	.02
Denver Nuggets			
☐ 78 Thurl Bailey	.10	.05	.01
Minnesota Timberwolves			
☐ 79 Steve Smith	.25	.11	.03
Miami Heat			
☐ 80 Jerrod Mustaf	.10	.05	.01
Phoenix Suns			
☐ 81 Anthony Bowie	.10	.05	.01
Orlando Magic			
☐ 82 John Williams	.10	.05	.01
Washington Bullets			

☐ 83 Paul Graham .... .10	.05	.01
Atlanta Hawks		
☐ 84 Willie Burton .... .10	.05	.01
Miami Heat		
☐ 85 Vernon Maxwell .... .10	.05	.01
Houston Rockets		
☐ 86 Stacey King .... .10	.05	.01
Chicago Bulls		
☐ 87 B.J. Armstrong .... .10	.05	.01
Chicago Bulls		
☐ 88 Kevin Gamble................. .10	.05	.01
Boston Celtics		
☐ 89 Terry Catledge................ .10	.05	.01
Orlando Magic		
☐ 90 Jeff Malone..................... .15	.07	.02
Utah Jazz		
☐ 91 Sam Bowie .... .10	.05	.01
New Jersey Nets		
☐ 92 Orlando Woolridge.......... .10	.05	.01
Detroit Pistons		
☐ 93 Steve Kerr .... .10	.05	.01
Cleveland Cavaliers		
☐ 94 Eric Leckner .... .10	.05	.01
Charlotte Hornets		
☐ 95 Loy Vaught .... .15	.07	.02
Los Angeles Clippers		
☐ 96 Jud Buechler.................. .10	.05	.01
Golden State Warriors		
☐ 97 Doug Smith..................... .10	.05	.01
Dallas Mavericks		
☐ 98 Sidney Green .... .10	.05	.01
San Antonio Spurs		
☐ 99 Jerome Kersey................ .10	.05	.01
Portland Trail Blazers		
☐ 100 Patrick Ewing................ .60	.25	.08
New York Knicks		
☐ 101 Ed Nealy....................... .10	.05	.01
Phoenix Suns		
☐ 102 Shawn Kemp 1.50	.65	.19
Seattle Supersonics		
☐ 103 Luc Longley .... .10	.05	.01
Minnesota Timberwolves		
☐ 104 George McCloud .... .10	.05	.01
Indiana Pacers		
☐ 105 Ron Anderson................ .10	.05	.01
Philadelphia 76ers		
☐ 106 Moses Malone UER ...... .30	.14	.04
(Rookie Card is 1975-76,		
not 1976-77)		
Milwaukee Bucks		
☐ 107 Tony Smith .... .10	.05	.01
Los Angeles Lakers		
☐ 108 Terry Porter................... .15	.07	.02
Portland Trail Blazers		
☐ 109 Blair Rasmussen............ .10	.05	.01
Atlanta Hawks		
☐ 110 Bimbo Coles .... .10	.05	.01
Miami Heat		
☐ 111 Grant Long.................... .10	.05	.01
Miami Heat		
☐ 112 John Battle.................... .10	.05	.01
Cleveland Cavaliers		
☐ 113 Brian Oliver .... .10	.05	.01
Philadelphia 76ers		
☐ 114 Tyrone Corbin .... .10	.05	.01
Utah Jazz		
☐ 115 Benoit Benjamin............. .10	.05	.01
Seattle Supersonics		
☐ 116 Rick Fox .... .10	.05	.01
Boston Celtics		
☐ 117 Rafael Addison.............. .10	.05	.01

New Jersey Nets		
☐ 118 Danny Young............... .10	.05	.01
Los Angeles Clippers		
☐ 119 Fat Lever .... .10	.05	.01
Dallas Mavericks		
☐ 120 Terry Cummings .... .15	.07	.02
San Antonio Spurs		
☐ 121 Felton Spencer.............. .10	.05	.01
Minnesota Timberwolves		
☐ 122 Joe Kleine .... .10	.05	.01
Boston Celtics		
☐ 123 Johnny Newman............. .10	.05	.01
Charlotte Hornets		
☐ 124 Gary Payton................. .25	.11	.03
Seattle Supersonics		
☐ 125 Kurt Rambis................. .10	.05	.01
Phoenix Suns		
☐ 126 Vlade Divac................. .25	.11	.03
Los Angeles Lakers		
☐ 127 John Paxson................ .10	.05	.01
Chicago Bulls		
☐ 128 Lionel Simmons............ .10	.05	.01
Sacramento Kings		
☐ 129 Randy Wittman............. .10	.05	.01
Indiana Pacers		
☐ 130 Winston Garland .... .10	.05	.01
Denver Nuggets		
☐ 131 Jerry Reynolds.............. .10	.05	.01
Orlando Magic		
☐ 132 Dell Curry .... .10	.05	.01
Charlotte Hornets		
☐ 133 Fred Roberts .... .10	.05	.01
Milwaukee Bucks		
☐ 134 Michael Adams .... .10	.05	.01
Washington Bullets		
☐ 135 Charles Jones .... .10	.05	.01
Washington Bullets		
☐ 136 Frank Brickowski.......... .10	.05	.01
Milwaukee Bucks		
☐ 137 Alton Lister .... .10	.05	.01
Golden State Warriors		
☐ 138 Horace Grant................ .30	.14	.04
Chicago Bulls		
☐ 139 Greg Sutton .... .10	.05	.01
San Antonio Spurs		
☐ 140 John Starks................... .25	.11	.03
New York Knicks		
☐ 141 Detlef Schrempf............ .25	.11	.03
Indiana Pacers		
☐ 142 Rodney Monroe .... .10	.05	.01
Atlanta Hawks		
☐ 143 Pete Chilcutt .... .10	.05	.01
Sacramento Kings		
☐ 144 Mike Brown.................. .10	.05	.01
Utah Jazz		
☐ 145 Rony Seikaly................. .10	.05	.01
Miami Heat		
☐ 146 Donald Hodge............... .10	.05	.01
Dallas Mavericks		
☐ 147 Kevin McHale .... .25	.11	.03
Boston Celtics		
☐ 148 Ricky Pierce.................. .15	.07	.02
Seattle Supersonics		
☐ 149 Brian Shaw .... .10	.05	.01
Miami Heat		
☐ 150 Reggie Williams .... .10	.05	.01
Denver Nuggets		
☐ 151 Kendall Gill .... .10	.05	.01
Charlotte Hornets		
☐ 152 Tom Chambers .... .15	.07	.02
Phoenix Suns		

☐ 153	Jack Haley	.10	.05	.01
	Los Angeles Lakers			
☐ 154	Terrell Brandon	.10	.05	.01
	Cleveland Cavaliers			
☐ 155	Dennis Scott	.10	.05	.01
	Orlando Magic			
☐ 156	Mark Randall	.10	.05	.01
	Minnesota Timberwolves			
☐ 157	Kenny Payne	.10	.05	.01
	Philadelphia 76ers			
☐ 158	Bernard King	.25	.11	.03
	Washington Bullets			
☐ 159	Tate George	.10	.05	.01
	New Jersey Nets			
☐ 160	Scott Skiles	.10	.05	.01
	Orlando Magic			
☐ 161	Pervis Ellison	.10	.05	.01
	Washington Bullets			
☐ 162	Marcus Liberty	.10	.05	.01
	Denver Nuggets			
☐ 163	Rumeal Robinson	.10	.05	.01
	Atlanta Hawks			
☐ 164	Anthony Mason	.25	.11	.03
	New York Knicks			
☐ 165	Les Jepsen	.10	.05	.01
	Sacramento Kings			
☐ 166	Kenny Smith	.10	.05	.01
	Houston Rockets			
☐ 167	Randy White	.10	.05	.01
	Dallas Mavericks			
☐ 168	Dee Brown	.15	.07	.02
	Boston Celtics			
☐ 169	Chris Dudley	.10	.05	.01
	New Jersey Nets			
☐ 170	Armon Gilliam	.10	.05	.01
	Philadelphia 76ers			
☐ 171	Eddie Johnson	.15	.07	.02
	Seattle Supersonics			
☐ 172	A.C. Green	.25	.11	.03
	Los Angeles Lakers			
☐ 173	Darrell Walker	.10	.05	.01
	Detroit Pistons			
☐ 174	Bill Cartwright	.10	.05	.01
	Chicago Bulls			
☐ 175	Mike Gminski	.10	.05	.01
	Charlotte Hornets			
☐ 176	Tom Tolbert	.10	.05	.01
	Golden State Warriors			
☐ 177	Buck Williams	.15	.07	.02
	Portland Trail Blazers			
☐ 178	Mark Eaton	.10	.05	.01
	Utah Jazz			
☐ 179	Danny Manning	.25	.11	.03
	Los Angeles Clippers			
☐ 180	Glen Rice	.25	.11	.03
	Miami Heat			
☐ 181	Sarunas Marciulionis	.10	.05	.01
	Golden State Warriors			
☐ 182	Danny Ferry	.10	.05	.01
	Cleveland Cavaliers			
☐ 183	Chris Corchiani	.10	.05	.01
	Orlando Magic			
☐ 184	Dan Majerle	.15	.07	.02
	Phoenix Suns			
☐ 185	Alvin Robertson	.10	.05	.01
	Milwaukee Bucks			
☐ 186	Vern Fleming	.10	.05	.01
	Indiana Pacers			
☐ 187	Kevin Lynch	.10	.05	.01
	Charlotte Hornets			
☐ 188	John Williams	.15	.07	.02
	Cleveland Cavaliers			
☐ 189	Checklist 1-100	.10	.05	.01
☐ 190	Checklist 101-200	.10	.05	.01
☐ 191	David Robinson MC	.60	.25	.08
	San Antonio Spurs			
☐ 192	Larry Johnson MC	.50	.23	.06
	Charlotte Hornets			
☐ 193	Derrick Coleman MC	.10	.05	.01
	New Jersey Nets			
☐ 194	Larry Bird MC	1.00	.45	.13
	Boston Celtics			
☐ 195	Billy Owens MC	.10	.05	.01
	Golden State Warriors			
☐ 196	Dikembe Mutombo MC	.40	.18	.05
	Denver Nuggets			
☐ 197	Charles Barkley MC	.60	.25	.08
	Philadelphia 76ers			
☐ 198	Scottie Pippen MC	.30	.14	.04
	Chicago Bulls			
☐ 199	Clyde Drexler MC	.30	.14	.04
	Portland Trail Blazers			
☐ 200	John Stockton MC	.30	.14	.04
	Utah Jazz			
☐ 201	Shaquille O'Neal MC	5.00	2.30	.60
	Orlando Magic			
☐ 202	Chris Mullin MC	.10	.05	.01
	Golden State Warriors			
☐ 203	Glen Rice MC	.10	.05	.01
	Miami Heat			
☐ 204	Isiah Thomas MC	.15	.07	.02
	Detroit Pistons			
☐ 205	Karl Malone MC	.30	.14	.04
	Utah Jazz			
☐ 206	Christian Laettner MC	.40	.18	.05
	Minnesota Timberwolves			
☐ 207	Patrick Ewing MC	.30	.14	.04
	New York Knicks			
☐ 208	Dominique Wilkins MC	.25	.11	.03
	Atlanta Hawks			
☐ 209	Alonzo Mourning MC	1.25	.55	.16
	Charlotte Hornets			
☐ 210	Michael Jordan MC	4.00	1.80	.50
	Chicago Bulls			
☐ 211	Tim Hardaway MC	.10	.05	.01
	Golden State Warriors			
☐ 212	Rodney McCray	.10	.05	.01
	Chicago Bulls			
☐ 213	Larry Johnson	1.00	.45	.13
	Charlotte Hornets			
☐ 214	Charles Smith	.10	.05	.01
	New York Knicks			
☐ 215	Kevin Brooks	.10	.05	.01
	Indiana Pacers			
☐ 216	Kevin Johnson	.30	.14	.04
	Phoenix Suns			
☐ 217	Duane Cooper	.10	.05	.01
	Los Angeles Lakers			
☐ 218	Christian Laettner UER	1.25	.55	.16
	(Missing '92 Draft			
	Pick logo)			
	Minnesota Timberwolves			
☐ 219	Tim Perry	.10	.05	.01
	Philadelphia 76ers			
☐ 220	Hakeem Olajuwon	1.50	.65	.19
	Houston Rockets			
☐ 221	Lee Mayberry	.15	.07	.02
	Milwaukee Bucks			
☐ 222	Mark Bryant	.10	.05	.01
	Portland Trail Blazers			
☐ 223	Robert Horry	1.50	.65	.19
	Houston Rockets			

☐ 224	Tracy Murray UER .... (Missing '92 Draft Pick logo) Portland Trail Blazers	.15	.07	.02
☐ 225	Greg Grant .... Philadelphia 76ers	.10	.05	.01
☐ 226	Rolando Blackman .... New York Knicks	.15	.07	.02
☐ 227	James Edwards UER.... (Rookie Card is 1978-79, not 1980-81) Los Angeles Lakers	.10	.05	.01
☐ 228	Sean Green .... Indiana Pacers	.10	.05	.01
☐ 229	Buck Johnson .... Washington Bullets	.10	.05	.01
☐ 230	Andrew Lang .... Philadelphia 76ers	.10	.05	.01
☐ 231	Tracy Moore .... Dallas Mavericks	.10	.05	.01
☐ 232	Adam Keefe UER .... (Missing '92 Draft Pick logo) Atlanta Hawks	.30	.14	.04
☐ 233	Tony Campbell .... New York Knicks	.10	.05	.01
☐ 234	Rod Strickland .... Portland Trail Blazers	.15	.07	.02
☐ 235	Terry Mills .... Detroit Pistons	.15	.07	.02
☐ 236	Billy Owens .... Golden State Warriors	.25	.11	.03
☐ 237	Bryant Stith UER .... (Missing '92 Draft Pick logo) Denver Nuggets	.50	.23	.06
☐ 238	Tony Bennett UER......... (Missing '92 Draft Pick logo) Charlotte Hornets	.10	.05	.01
☐ 239	David Wood .... San Antonio Spurs	.10	.05	.01
☐ 240	Jay Humphries............. Utah Jazz	.10	.05	.01
☐ 241	Doc Rivers .... New York Knicks	.10	.05	.01
☐ 242	Wayman Tisdale .... Sacramento Kings	.15	.07	.02
☐ 243	Litterial Green .... Orlando Magic	.10	.05	.01
☐ 244	Jon Barry .... Milwaukee Bucks	.15	.07	.02
☐ 245	Brad Daugherty............ Cleveland Cavaliers	.15	.07	.02
☐ 246	Nate McMillan.............. Seattle Supersonics	.10	.05	.01
☐ 247	Shaquille O'Neal........... Orlando Magic	15.00	6.75	1.90
☐ 248	Chris Smith .... Minnesota Timberwolves	.10	.05	.01
☐ 249	Duane Ferrell............... Atlanta Hawks	.10	.05	.01
☐ 250	Anthony Peeler .... Los Angeles Lakers	.30	.14	.04
☐ 251	Gundars Vetra............. Minnesota Timberwolves	.10	.05	.01
☐ 252	Danny Ainge .... Phoenix Suns	.15	.07	.02
☐ 253	Mitch Richmond .... Sacramento Kings	.30	.14	.04
☐ 254	Malik Sealy .... Indiana Pacers	.30	.14	.04
☐ 255	Brent Price.................. Washington Bullets	.10	.05	.01
☐ 256	Xavier McDaniel .... Boston Celtics	.15	.07	.02
☐ 257	Bobby Phills................ Cleveland Cavaliers	.30	.14	.04
☐ 258	Donald Royal .... Orlando Magic	.10	.05	.01
☐ 259	Olden Polynice............. Detroit Pistons	.10	.05	.01
☐ 260	Dominique Wilkins UER (Scoring 10,000th point, should be 20,000th) Atlanta Hawks	.30	.14	.04
☐ 261	Larry Krystkowiak......... Utah Jazz	.10	.05	.01
☐ 262	Duane Causwell .... Sacramento Kings	.10	.05	.01
☐ 263	Todd Day .... Milwaukee Bucks	.75	.35	.09
☐ 264	Sam Mack.................... San Antonio Spurs	.10	.05	.01
☐ 265	John Stockton.............. Utah Jazz	.60	.25	.08
☐ 266	Eddie Lee Wilkins......... Philadelphia 76ers	.10	.05	.01
☐ 267	Gerald Glass .... Detroit Pistons	.10	.05	.01
☐ 268	Robert Pack .... Denver Nuggets	.10	.05	.01
☐ 269	Gerald Wilkins............. Cleveland Cavaliers	.10	.05	.01
☐ 270	Reggie Lewis .... Boston Celtics	.25	.11	.03
☐ 271	Scott Brooks .... Houston Rockets	.10	.05	.01
☐ 272	Randy Woods UER .... (Missing '92 Draft Pick logo) Los Angeles Clippers	.10	.05	.01
☐ 273	Dikembe Mutombo .... Denver Nuggets	.75	.35	.09
☐ 274	Kiki Vandeweghe........... Los Angeles Clippers	.10	.05	.01
☐ 275	Rich King .... Seattle Supersonics	.10	.05	.01
☐ 276	Jeff Turner.................. Orlando Magic	.10	.05	.01
☐ 277	Vinny Del Negro .... San Antonio Spurs	.10	.05	.01
☐ 278	Marlon Maxey............... Minnesota Timberwolves	.10	.05	.01
☐ 279	Elmore Spencer UER .... (Missing '92 Draft Pick logo) Los Angeles Clippers	.10	.05	.01
☐ 280	Cedric Ceballos............ Phoenix Suns	.25	.11	.03
☐ 281	Alex Blackwell.............. Los Angeles Lakers	.10	.05	.01
☐ 282	Terry Davis .... Dallas Mavericks	.10	.05	.01
☐ 283	Morlon Wiley .... Atlanta Hawks	.10	.05	.01
☐ 284	Trent Tucker .... Washington Bullets	.10	.05	.01
☐ 285	Carl Herrera .... Houston Rockets	.10	.05	.01
☐ 286	Eric Anderson .... New York Knicks	.10	.05	.01

☐ 287	Clyde Drexler	.60	.25	.08
	Portland Trail Blazers			
☐ 288	Tom Gugliotta	1.00	.45	.13
	Washington Bullets			
☐ 289	Dale Ellis	.15	.07	.02
	San Antonio Spurs			
☐ 290	Lance Blanks	.10	.05	.01
	Minnesota Timberwolves			
☐ 291	Tom Hammonds	.10	.05	.01
	Charlotte Hornets			
☐ 292	Eric Murdock	.10	.05	.01
	Milwaukee Bucks			
☐ 293	Walt Williams	1.25	.55	.16
	Sacramento Kings			
☐ 294	Gerald Paddio	.10	.05	.01
	Seattle Supersonics			
☐ 295	Brian Howard	.10	.05	.01
	Dallas Mavericks			
☐ 296	Ken Williams	.10	.05	.01
	Indiana Pacers			
☐ 297	Alonzo Mourning	4.00	1.80	.50
	Charlotte Hornets			
☐ 298	Larry Nance	.15	.07	.02
	Cleveland Cavaliers			
☐ 299	Jeff Grayer	.10	.05	.01
	Golden State Warriors			
☐ 300	Dave Johnson	.10	.05	.01
	Portland Trail Blazers			
☐ 301	Bob McCann	.10	.05	.01
	Minnesota Timberwolves			
☐ 302	Bart Kofoed	.10	.05	.01
	Boston Celtics			
☐ 303	Anthony Cook	.10	.05	.01
	Denver Nuggets			
☐ 304	Radisav Curcic	.10	.05	.01
	Dallas Mavericks			
☐ 305	John Crotty	.10	.05	.01
	Utah Jazz			
☐ 306	Brad Sellers	.10	.05	.01
	Detroit Pistons			
☐ 307	Marcus Webb	.10	.05	.01
	Boston Celtics			
☐ 308	Winston Garland	.10	.05	.01
	Houston Rockets			
☐ 309	Walter Palmer	.10	.05	.01
	Dallas Mavericks			
☐ 310	Rod Higgins	.10	.05	.01
	Sacramento Kings			
☐ 311	Travis Mays	.10	.05	.01
	Atlanta Hawks			
☐ 312	Alex Stivrins	.10	.05	.01
	Atlanta Hawks			
☐ 313	Greg Kite	.10	.05	.01
	Orlando Magic			
☐ 314	Dennis Rodman	.40	.18	.05
	Detroit Pistons			
☐ 315	Mike Sanders	.10	.05	.01
	Cleveland Cavaliers			
☐ 316	Ed Pinckney	.10	.05	.01
	Boston Celtics			
☐ 317	Harold Miner	.40	.18	.05
	Miami Heat			
☐ 318	Pooh Richardson	.10	.05	.01
	Indiana Pacers			
☐ 319	Oliver Miller	.50	.23	.06
	Phoenix Suns			
☐ 320	Latrell Sprewell	4.00	1.80	.50
	Golden State Warriors			
☐ 321	Anthony Pullard	.10	.05	.01
	Milwaukee Bucks			
☐ 322	Mark Randall	.10	.05	.01

	Detroit Pistons			
☐ 323	Jeff Hornacek	.15	.07	.02
	Philadelphia 76ers			
☐ 324	Rick Mahorn UER	.10	.05	.01
	(Rookie Card is 1981-82,			
	not 1992-93)			
	New Jersey Nets			
☐ 325	Sean Rooks	.15	.07	.02
	Dallas Mavericks			
☐ 326	Paul Pressey	.10	.05	.01
	Golden State Warriors			
☐ 327	James Worthy	.25	.11	.03
	Los Angeles Lakers			
☐ 328	Matt Bullard	.10	.05	.01
	Houston Rockets			
☐ 329	Reggie Smith	.10	.05	.01
	Portland Trail Blazers			
☐ 330	Don MacLean UER	.30	.14	.04
	(Missing '92 Draft			
	Pick logo)			
	Washington Bullets			
☐ 331	John Williams UER	.10	.05	.01
	(Rookie Card erroneously			
	shows Hot Rod)			
	Los Angeles Clippers			
☐ 332	Frank Johnson	.15	.07	.02
	Phoenix Suns			
☐ 333	Hubert Davis UER	.30	.14	.04
	(Missing '92 Draft			
	Pick logo)			
	New York Knicks			
☐ 334	Lloyd Daniels	.10	.05	.01
	San Antonio Spurs			
☐ 335	Steve Bardo	.10	.05	.01
	Dallas Mavericks			
☐ 336	Jeff Sanders	.10	.05	.01
	Atlanta Hawks			
☐ 337	Tree Rollins	.10	.05	.01
	Houston Rockets			
☐ 338	Micheal Williams	.10	.05	.01
	Minnesota Timberwolves			
☐ 339	Lorenzo Williams	.10	.05	.01
	Boston Celtics			
☐ 340	Harvey Grant	.10	.05	.01
	Washington Bullets			
☐ 341	Avery Johnson	.10	.05	.01
	San Antonio Spurs			
☐ 342	Bo Kimble	.10	.05	.01
	New York Knicks			
☐ 343	LaPhonso Ellis UER	.60	.25	.08
	(Missing '92 Draft			
	Pick logo)			
	Denver Nuggets			
☐ 344	Mookie Blaylock	.15	.07	.02
	Atlanta Hawks			
☐ 345	Isaiah Morris UER	.10	.05	.01
	(Missing '92 Draft			
	Pick logo)			
	Detroit Pistons			
☐ 346	Clarence Weatherspoon	1.25	.55	.16
	Philadelphia 76ers			
☐ 347	Manute Bol	.10	.05	.01
	Philadelphia 76ers			
☐ 348	Victor Alexander	.10	.05	.01
	Golden State Warriors			
☐ 349	Corey Williams	.10	.05	.01
	Washington Bullets			
☐ 350	Byron Houston	.10	.05	.01
	Golden State Warriors			
☐ 351	Stanley Roberts	.10	.05	.01
	Los Angeles Clippers			

☐ 352	Anthony Avent	.10	.05	.01
	Milwaukee Bucks			
☐ 353	Vincent Askew	.10	.05	.01
	Golden State Warriors			
☐ 354	Herb Williams	.10	.05	.01
	New York Knicks			
☐ 355	J.R. Reid	.10	.05	.01
	San Antonio Spurs			
☐ 356	Brad Lohaus	.10	.05	.01
	Milwaukee Bucks			
☐ 357	Reggie Miller	.60	.25	.08
	Indiana Pacers			
☐ 358	Blue Edwards	.10	.05	.01
	Milwaukee Bucks			
☐ 359	Tom Tolbert	.10	.05	.01
	Orlando Magic			
☐ 360	Charles Barkley	1.25	.55	.16
	Phoenix Suns			
☐ 361	David Robinson	1.25	.55	.16
	San Antonio Spurs			
☐ 362	Dale Davis	.25	.11	.03
	Indiana Pacers			
☐ 363	Robert Werdann UER	.10	.05	.01
	(Missing '92 Draft			
	Pick logo)			
	Denver Nuggets			
☐ 364	Chuck Person	.15	.07	.02
	Minnesota Timberwolves			
☐ 365	Alaa Abdelnaby	.10	.05	.01
	Boston Celtics			
☐ 366	Dave Jamerson	.10	.05	.01
	Houston Rockets			
☐ 367	Scottie Pippen	.60	.25	.08
	Washington Bullets			
☐ 368	Mark Jackson	.10	.05	.01
	Los Angeles Clippers			
☐ 369	Keith Askins	.10	.05	.01
	Miami Heat			
☐ 370	Marty Conlon	.10	.05	.01
	Sacramento Kings			
☐ 371	Chucky Brown	.10	.05	.01
	New Jersey Nets			
☐ 372	LaBradford Smith	.10	.05	.01
	Washington Bullets			
☐ 373	Tim Kempton	.10	.05	.01
	Phoenix Suns			
☐ 374	Sam Mitchell	.10	.05	.01
	Indiana Pacers			
☐ 375	John Salley	.10	.05	.01
	Miami Heat			
☐ 376	Mario Elie	.10	.05	.01
	Portland Trail Blazers			
☐ 377	Mark West	.10	.05	.01
	Phoenix Suns			
☐ 378	David Wingate	.10	.05	.01
	Charlotte Hornets			
☐ 379	Jaren Jackson	.10	.05	.01
	Los Angeles Clippers			
☐ 380	Rumeal Robinson	.10	.05	.01
	New Jersey Nets			
☐ 381	Kennard Winchester	.10	.05	.01
	Houston Rockets			
☐ 382	Walter Bond	.10	.05	.01
	Dallas Mavericks			
☐ 383	Isaac Austin	.10	.05	.01
	Utah Jazz			
☐ 384	Derrick Coleman	.25	.11	.03
	New Jersey Nets			
☐ 385	Larry Smith	.10	.05	.01
	San Antonio Spurs			
☐ 386	Joe Dumars	.30	.14	.04
	Detroit Pistons			
☐ 387	Matt Geiger UER	.10	.05	.01
	(Missing '92 Draft			
	Pick logo)			
	Miami Heat			
☐ 388	Stephen Howard	.10	.05	.01
	Utah Jazz			
☐ 389	William Bedford	.10	.05	.01
	Los Angeles Clippers			
☐ 390	Jayson Williams	.10	.05	.01
	New Jersey Nets			
☐ 391	Kurt Rambis	.10	.05	.01
	Sacramento Kings			
☐ 392	Keith Jennings	.10	.05	.01
	Golden State Warriors			
☐ 393	Steve Kerr UER	.10	.05	.01
	(The words key stat			
	are repeated on back)			
	Orlando Magic			
☐ 394	Larry Stewart	.10	.05	.01
	Washington Bullets			
☐ 395	Danny Young	.10	.05	.01
	Los Angeles Clippers			
☐ 396	Doug Overton	.10	.05	.01
	Washington Bullets			
☐ 397	Mark Acres	.10	.05	.01
	Orlando Magic			
☐ 398	John Bagley	.10	.05	.01
	Boston Celtics			
☐ 399	Checklist 201-300	.10	.05	.01
☐ 400	Checklist 301-400	.10	.05	.01

1992-93 Stadium Club Beam Team

Comprised of some of the NBA's biggest stars, "Beam Team" cards commemorate Topps' 1993 sponsorship of a six-minute NBA laser animation show called Beams Above the Rim. The show premiered at the 1993 NBA All-Star Game. Afterwards, the laser show embarked on a ten-city tour and was featured in either the pre-game or half-time events in ten NBA arenas. These cards were randomly inserted in second series 15-card packs at a rate of one in 36. The cards measure the standard size (2 1/2" by 3 1/2"). The color action player pho-

tos on the fronts are bordered on two sides by an angled silver light beam border design with a light refracting pattern. The player's name appears on a white-outlined burnt orange bar superimposed over a basketball icon at the bottom. The backs present a color head shot and, on a basketball icon, career highlights. The cards are numbered on the back.

	MINT	NRMT	EXC
COMPLETE SET (21)	250.00	115.00	31.00
COMMON CARD (1-21)	2.00	.90	.25
☐ 1 Michael Jordan	100.00	45.00	12.50
Chicago Bulls			
☐ 2 Dominique Wilkins	4.00	1.80	.50
Atlanta Hawks			
☐ 3 Shawn Kemp	20.00	9.00	2.50
Seattle Supersonics			
☐ 4 Clyde Drexler	8.00	3.60	1.00
Portland Trail Blazers			
☐ 5 Scottie Pippen	8.00	3.60	1.00
Chicago Bulls			
☐ 6 Chris Mullin	3.00	1.35	.40
Golden State Warriors			
☐ 7 Reggie Miller	8.00	3.60	1.00
Indiana Pacers			
☐ 8 Glen Rice	3.00	1.35	.40
Miami Heat			
☐ 9 Jeff Hornacek	2.00	.90	.25
Philadelphia 76ers			
☐ 10 Jeff Malone	2.00	.90	.25
Utah Jazz			
☐ 11 John Stockton	8.00	3.60	1.00
Utah Jazz			
☐ 12 Kevin Johnson	4.00	1.80	.50
Phoenix Suns			
☐ 13 Mark Price	3.00	1.35	.40
Cleveland Cavaliers			
☐ 14 Tim Hardaway	3.00	1.35	.40
Golden State Warriors			
☐ 15 Charles Barkley	15.00	6.75	1.90
Phoenix Suns			
☐ 16 Hakeem Olajuwon	20.00	9.00	2.50
Houston Rockets			
☐ 17 Karl Malone	8.00	3.60	1.00
Utah Jazz			
☐ 18 Patrick Ewing	8.00	3.60	1.00
New York Knicks			
☐ 19 Dennis Rodman	5.00	2.30	.60
Detroit Pistons			
☐ 20 David Robinson	15.00	6.75	1.90
San Antonio Spurs			
☐ 21 Shaquille O'Neal	150.00	70.00	19.00
Orlando Magic			

1993-94
Stadium Club

The 1993-94 Stadium Club set consists of 360 standard-size (2 1/2" by 3 1/2") cards issued in two series of 180 cards. Cards

were issued in 12 and 20-card packs. There were 24 twelve-card packs per box. The full-bleed fronts feature glossy color action photos. The player's name is super imposed on the lower portion of the picture in white and gold foil lettering. The borderless backs are divided in half vertically with a torn effect. The left side sports a vertical player photo and on the right side, over a purple background, is biography and player's name and team. A brief section named "The Buzz" provides career highlights. A multi-colored box lists the 1992-93 statistics, career statistics and a Topps Skills Rating System that provides a score including player intimidation, mobility, shooting range and defense. Subsets featured are Triple Double (1-11, 101-111) and High Court (61-69, 170-178) and interspersed NBA Draft Picks. The cards are numbered on the back.

	MINT	NRMT	EXC
COMPLETE SET (360)	40.00	18.00	5.00
COMPLETE SERIES 1 (180)	25.00	11.50	3.10
COMPLETE SERIES 2 (180)	15.00	6.75	1.90
COMMON CARD (1-180)	.10	.05	.01
COMMON CARD (181-360)	.05	.02	.01
☐ 1 Michael Jordan TD	3.00	1.35	.40
Chicago Bulls			
☐ 2 Kenny Anderson	.10	.05	.01
New Jersey Nets			
☐ 3 Steve Smith TD	.10	.05	.01
Miami Heat			
☐ 4 Kevin Gamble TD	.10	.05	.01
Boston Celtics			
☐ 5 Detlef Schrempf TD	.10	.05	.01
Indiana Pacers			
☐ 6 Larry Johnson TD	.25	.11	.03
Charlotte Hornets			
☐ 7 Brad Daugherty TD	.10	.05	.01
Cleveland Cavaliers			
☐ 8 Rumeal Robinson TD	.10	.05	.01
Atlanta Hawks			
☐ 9 Micheal Williams TD	.10	.05	.01
Minnesota Timberwolves			
☐ 10 David Robinson TD	.50	.23	.06
San Antonio Spurs			
☐ 11 Sam Perkins TD	.10	.05	.01
San Antonio Spurs			
☐ 12 Thurl Bailey	.10	.05	.01
Minnesota Timberwolves			
☐ 13 Sherman Douglas	.10	.05	.01
Boston Celtics			
☐ 14 Larry Stewart	.10	.05	.01
Washington Bullets			

☐ 15 Kevin Johnson	.25	.11	.03
Phoenix Suns			
☐ 16 Bill Cartwright	.10	.05	.01
Chicago Bulls			
☐ 17 Larry Nance	.15	.07	.02
Cleveland Cavaliers			
☐ 18 P.J. Brown	.20	.09	.03
New Jersey Nets			
☐ 19 Tony Bennett	.10	.05	.01
Charlotte Hornets			
☐ 20 Robert Parish	.20	.09	.03
Boston Celtics			
☐ 21 David Benoit	.10	.05	.01
Utah Jazz			
☐ 22 Detlef Schrempf	.20	.09	.03
Indiana Pacers			
☐ 23 Hubert Davis	.10	.05	.01
New York Knicks			
☐ 24 Donald Hodge	.10	.05	.01
Dallas Mavericks			
☐ 25 Hersey Hawkins	.15	.07	.02
Philadelphia 76ers			
☐ 26 Mark Jackson	.10	.05	.01
Los Angeles Clippers			
☐ 27 Reggie Williams	.10	.05	.01
Denver Nuggets			
☐ 28 Lionel Simmons	.10	.05	.01
Sacramento Kings			
☐ 29 Ron Harper	.15	.07	.02
Los Angeles Clippers			
☐ 30 Chris Mills DP	.60	.25	.08
Cleveland Cavaliers			
☐ 31 Danny Schayes	.10	.05	.01
Milwaukee Bucks			
☐ 32 J.R. Reid	.10	.05	.01
San Antonio Spurs			
☐ 33 Willie Burton	.10	.05	.01
Miami Heat			
☐ 34 Greg Anthony	.10	.05	.01
New York Knicks			
☐ 35 Elden Campbell	.10	.05	.01
Los Angeles Lakers			
☐ 36 Ervin Johnson DP	.20	.09	.03
Seattle Supersonics			
☐ 37 Scott Brooks	.10	.05	.01
Houston Rockets			
☐ 38 Johnny Newman	.10	.05	.01
Charlotte Hornets			
☐ 39 Rex Chapman	.10	.05	.01
Washington Bullets			
☐ 40 Chuck Person	.15	.07	.02
Minnesota Timberwolves			
☐ 41 John Williams	.15	.07	.02
Cleveland Cavaliers			
☐ 42 Anthony Bowie	.10	.05	.01
Orlando Magic			
☐ 43 Negele Knight	.10	.05	.01
Phoenix Suns			
☐ 44 Tyrone Corbin	.10	.05	.01
Utah Jazz			
☐ 45 Jud Buechler	.10	.05	.01
Golden State Warriors			
☐ 46 Adam Keefe	.10	.05	.01
Atlanta Hawks			
☐ 47 Glen Rice	.20	.09	.03
Miami Heat			
☐ 48 Tracy Murray	.10	.05	.01
Portland Trail Blazers			
☐ 49 Rick Mahorn	.10	.05	.01
New Jersey Nets			
☐ 50 Vlade Divac	.20	.09	.03

Los Angeles Lakers			
☐ 51 Eric Murdock	.10	.05	.01
Milwaukee Bucks			
☐ 52 Isaiah Morris	.10	.05	.01
Detroit Pistons			
☐ 53 Bobby Hurley DP	.30	.14	.04
Sacramento Kings			
☐ 54 Mitch Richmond	.25	.11	.03
Golden State Warriors			
☐ 55 Danny Ainge	.15	.07	.02
Phoenix Suns			
☐ 56 Dikembe Mutombo	.40	.18	.05
Denver Nuggets			
☐ 57 Jeff Hornacek	.15	.07	.02
Philadelphia 76ers			
☐ 58 Tony Campbell	.10	.05	.01
New York Knicks			
☐ 59 Vinny Del Negro	.10	.05	.01
San Antonio Spurs			
☐ 60 Xavier McDaniel HC	.10	.05	.01
Boston Celtics			
☐ 61 Scottie Pippen HC	.25	.11	.03
Chicago Bulls			
☐ 62 Larry Nance HC	.10	.05	.01
Cleveland Cavaliers			
☐ 63 Dikembe Mutombo HC	.15	.07	.02
Denver Nuggets			
☐ 64 Hakeem Olajuwon HC	.60	.25	.08
Houston Rockets			
☐ 65 Dominique Wilkins HC	.15	.07	.02
Atlanta Hawks			
☐ 66 Clarence Weatherspoon HC	.10	.05	.01
Philadelphia 76ers			
☐ 67 Chris Morris HC	.10	.05	.01
New Jersey Nets			
☐ 68 Patrick Ewing HC	.25	.11	.03
New York Knicks			
☐ 69 Kevin Willis HC	.10	.05	.01
Atlanta Hawks			
☐ 70 Jon Barry	.10	.05	.01
Milwaukee Bucks			
☐ 71 Jerry Reynolds	.10	.05	.01
Orlando Magic			
☐ 72 Sarunas Marciulionis	.10	.05	.01
Golden State Warriors			
☐ 73 Mark West	.10	.05	.01
Phoenix Suns			
☐ 74 B.J. Armstrong	.10	.05	.01
Chicago Bulls			
☐ 75 Greg Kite	.10	.05	.01
Orlando Magic			
☐ 76 LaSalle Thompson	.10	.05	.01
Indiana Pacers			
☐ 77 Randy White	.10	.05	.01
Dallas Mavericks			
☐ 78 Alaa Abdelnaby	.10	.05	.01
Boston Celtics			
☐ 79 Kevin Brooks	.10	.05	.01
Denver Nuggets			
☐ 80 Vern Fleming	.10	.05	.01
Indiana Pacers			
☐ 81 Doc Rivers	.10	.05	.01
New York Knicks			
☐ 82 Shawn Bradley DP	.60	.25	.08
Philadelphia 76ers			
☐ 83 Wayman Tisdale	.15	.07	.02
Sacramento Kings			
☐ 84 Olden Polynice	.10	.05	.01
Detroit Pistons			
☐ 85 Michael Cage	.10	.05	.01
Seattle Supersonics			

☐ 86	Harold Miner	.10	.05	.01
	Orlando Magic			
☐ 87	Doug Smith	.10	.05	.01
	Dallas Mavericks			
☐ 88	Tom Gugliotta	.20	.09	.03
	Washington Bullets			
☐ 89	Hakeem Olajuwon	1.25	.55	.16
	Houston Rockets			
☐ 90	Loy Vaught	.15	.07	.02
	Los Angeles Clippers			
☐ 91	James Worthy	.20	.09	.03
	Los Angeles Lakers			
☐ 92	John Paxson	.10	.05	.01
	Chicago Bulls			
☐ 93	Jon Koncak	.10	.05	.01
	Atlanta Hawks			
☐ 94	Lee Mayberry	.10	.05	.01
	Milwaukee Bucks			
☐ 95	Clarence Weatherspoon	.20	.09	.03
	Philadelphia 76ers			
☐ 96	Mark Eaton	.10	.05	.01
	Utah Jazz			
☐ 97	Rex Walters DP	.15	.07	.02
	New Jersey Nets			
☐ 98	Alvin Robertson	.10	.05	.01
	Detroit Pistons			
☐ 99	Dan Majerle	.15	.07	.02
	Phoenix Suns			
☐ 100	Shaquille O'Neal	4.00	1.80	.50
	Orlando Magic			
☐ 101	Derrick Coleman TD	.10	.05	.01
	New Jersey Nets			
☐ 102	Hersey Hawkins TD	.10	.05	.01
	Philadelphia 76ers			
☐ 103	Scottie Pippen TD	.25	.11	.03
	Chicago Bulls			
☐ 104	Scott Skiles TD	.10	.05	.01
	Orlando Magic			
☐ 105	Rod Strickland TD	.10	.05	.01
	Portland Trail Blazers			
☐ 106	Pooh Richardson TD	.10	.05	.01
	Indiana Pacers			
☐ 107	Tom Gugliotta TD	.10	.05	.01
	Washington Bullets			
☐ 108	Mark Jackson TD	.10	.05	.01
	Los Angeles Clippers			
☐ 109	Dikembe Mutombo TD	.15	.07	.02
	Denver Nuggets			
☐ 110	Charles Barkley TD	.50	.23	.06
	Phoenix Suns			
☐ 111	Otis Thorpe TD	.10	.05	.01
	Houston Rockets			
☐ 112	Malik Sealy	.10	.05	.01
	Indiana Pacers			
☐ 113	Mark Macon	.10	.05	.01
	Denver Nuggets			
☐ 114	Dee Brown	.15	.07	.02
	Boston Celtics			
☐ 115	Nate McMillan	.10	.05	.01
	Seattle Supersonics			
☐ 116	John Starks	.15	.07	.02
	New York Knicks			
☐ 117	Clyde Drexler	.50	.23	.06
	Portland Trail Blazers			
☐ 118	Antoine Carr	.10	.05	.01
	San Antonio Spurs			
☐ 119	Doug West	.10	.05	.01
	Minnesota Timberwolves			
☐ 120	Victor Alexander	.10	.05	.01
	Golden State Warriors			
☐ 121	Kenny Gattison	.10	.05	.01
	Charlotte Hornets			
☐ 122	Spud Webb	.15	.07	.02
	Atlanta Hawks			
☐ 123	Rumeal Robinson	.10	.05	.01
	New Jersey Nets			
☐ 124	Tim Kempton	.10	.05	.01
	Phoenix Suns			
☐ 125	Karl Malone	.50	.23	.06
	Utah Jazz			
☐ 126	Randy Woods	.10	.05	.01
	Los Angeles Clippers			
☐ 127	Calbert Cheaney DP	.75	.35	.09
	Washington Bullets			
☐ 128	Johnny Dawkins	.10	.05	.01
	Philadelphia 76ers			
☐ 129	Dominique Wilkins	.25	.11	.03
	Atlanta Hawks			
☐ 130	Horace Grant	.25	.11	.03
	Chicago Bulls			
☐ 131	Bill Laimbeer	.15	.07	.02
	Detroit Pistons			
☐ 132	Kenny Smith	.10	.05	.01
	Houston Rockets			
☐ 133	Sedale Threatt	.10	.05	.01
	Los Angeles Lakers			
☐ 134	Brian Shaw	.10	.05	.01
	Miami Heat			
☐ 135	Dennis Scott	.10	.05	.01
	Orlando Magic			
☐ 136	Mark Bryant	.10	.05	.01
	Portland Trail Blazers			
☐ 137	Xavier McDaniel	.15	.07	.02
	Boston Celtics			
☐ 138	David Wood	.10	.05	.01
	Houston Rockets			
☐ 139	Luther Wright DP	.10	.05	.01
	Utah Jazz			
☐ 140	Lloyd Daniels	.10	.05	.01
	San Antonio Spurs			
☐ 141	Marlon Maxey UER	.10	.05	.01
	Minnesota Timberwolves			
	(Name spelled Maxley on the front)			
☐ 142	Pooh Richardson	.10	.05	.01
	Indiana Pacers			
☐ 143	Jeff Grayer	.10	.05	.01
	Golden State Warriors			
☐ 144	LaPhonso Ellis	.15	.07	.02
	Denver Nuggets			
☐ 145	Gerald Wilkins	.10	.05	.01
	Cleveland Cavaliers			
☐ 146	Dell Curry	.10	.05	.01
	Charlotte Hornets			
☐ 147	Duane Causwell	.10	.05	.01
	Sacramento Kings			
☐ 148	Tim Hardaway	.20	.09	.03
	Golden State Warriors			
☐ 149	Isiah Thomas	.25	.11	.03
	Detroit Pistons			
☐ 150	Doug Edwards DP	.15	.07	.02
	Atlanta Hawks			
☐ 151	Anthony Peeler	.10	.05	.01
	Los Angeles Lakers			
☐ 152	Tate George	.10	.05	.01
	New Jersey Nets			
☐ 153	Terry Davis	.10	.05	.01
	Dallas Mavericks			
☐ 154	Sam Perkins	.15	.07	.02
	Seattle Supersonics			
☐ 155	John Salley	.10	.05	.01
	Miami Heat			
☐ 156	Vernon Maxwell	.10	.05	.01

	Houston Rockets			
☐ 157	Anthony Avent	.10	.05	.01
	Milwaukee Bucks			
☐ 158	Clifford Robinson	.15	.07	.02
	Portland Trail Blazers			
☐ 159	Corie Blount DP	.10	.05	.01
	Chicago Bulls			
☐ 160	Gerald Paddio	.10	.05	.01
	Seattle Supersonics			
☐ 161	Blair Rasmussen	.10	.05	.01
	Atlanta Hawks			
☐ 162	Carl Herrera	.10	.05	.01
	Houston Rockets			
☐ 163	Chris Smith	.10	.05	.01
	Minnesota Timberwolves			
☐ 164	Pervis Ellison	.10	.05	.01
	Washington Bullets			
☐ 165	Rod Strickland	.15	.07	.02
	Portland Trail Blazers			
☐ 166	Jeff Malone	.15	.07	.02
	Utah Jazz			
☐ 167	Danny Ferry	.10	.05	.01
	Cleveland Cavaliers			
☐ 168	Kevin Lynch	.10	.05	.01
	Charlotte Hornets			
☐ 169	Michael Jordan	6.00	2.70	.75
	Chicago Bulls			
☐ 170	Derrick Coleman HC	.10	.05	.01
	New Jersey Nets			
☐ 171	Jerome Kersey HC	.10	.05	.01
	Portland Trail Blazers			
☐ 172	David Robinson HC	.50	.23	.06
	San Antonio Spurs			
☐ 173	Shawn Kemp HC	.50	.23	.06
	Seattle Supersonics			
☐ 174	Karl Malone HC	.25	.11	.03
	Utah Jazz			
☐ 175	Shaquille O'Neal HC	2.00	.90	.25
	Orlando Magic			
☐ 176	Alonzo Mourning HC	.50	.23	.06
	Charlotte Hornets			
☐ 177	Charles Barkley HC	.50	.23	.06
	Phoenix Suns			
☐ 178	Larry Johnson HC	.25	.11	.03
	Charlotte Hornets			
☐ 179	Checklist 1-90	.10	.05	.01
☐ 180	Checklist 91-180	.10	.05	.01
☐ 181	Michael Jordan FF	2.00	.90	.25
	Chicago Bulls			
☐ 182	Dominique Wilkins FF	.08	.04	.01
	Atlanta Hawks			
☐ 183	Dennis Rodman FF	.08	.04	.01
	San Antonio Spurs			
☐ 184	Scottie Pippen FF	.10	.05	.01
	Chicago Bulls			
☐ 185	Larry Johnson FF	.10	.05	.01
	Charlotte Hornets			
☐ 186	Karl Malone FF	.10	.05	.01
	Utah Jazz			
☐ 187	Clarence Weatherspoon FF	.05	.02	.01
	Philadelphia 76ers			
☐ 188	Charles Barkley FF	.30	.14	.04
	Phoenix Suns			
☐ 189	Patrick Ewing FF	.10	.05	.01
	New York Knicks			
☐ 190	Derrick Coleman FF	.05	.02	.01
	New Jersey Nets			
☐ 191	LaBradford Smith	.05	.02	.01
	San Antonio Spurs			
☐ 192	Derek Harper	.08	.04	.01
	New York Knicks			
☐ 193	Ken Norman	.05	.02	.01
	Milwaukee Bucks			
☐ 194	Rodney Rogers	.40	.18	.05
	Denver Nuggets			
☐ 195	Chris Dudley	.05	.02	.01
	Portland Trail Blazers			
☐ 196	Gary Payton	.10	.05	.01
	Seattle Supersonics			
☐ 197	Andrew Lang	.05	.02	.01
	Atlanta Hawks			
☐ 198	Billy Owens	.08	.04	.01
	Golden State Warriors			
☐ 199	Bryon Russell	.05	.02	.01
	Utah Jazz			
☐ 200	Patrick Ewing	.30	.14	.04
	New York Knicks			
☐ 201	Stacey King	.05	.02	.01
	Chicago Bulls			
☐ 202	Grant Long	.05	.02	.01
	Miami Heat			
☐ 203	Sean Elliott	.08	.04	.01
	Detroit Pistons			
☐ 204	Muggsy Bogues	.10	.05	.01
	Charlotte Hornets			
☐ 205	Kevin Edwards	.05	.02	.01
	New Jersey Nets			
☐ 206	Dale Davis	.08	.04	.01
	Indiana Pacers			
☐ 207	Dale Ellis	.08	.04	.01
	San Antonio Spurs			
☐ 208	Terrell Brandon	.05	.02	.01
	Cleveland Cavaliers			
☐ 209	Kevin Gamble	.05	.02	.01
	Boston Celtics			
☐ 210	Robert Horry	.10	.05	.01
	Houston Rockets			
☐ 211	Moses Malone UER	.15	.07	.02
	Philadelphia 76ers			
	(Birthdate on back is 1993)			
☐ 212	Gary Grant	.05	.02	.01
	Los Angeles Clippers			
☐ 213	Bobby Hurley	.08	.04	.01
	Sacramento Kings			
☐ 214	Larry Krystkowiak	.05	.02	.01
	Orlando Magic			
☐ 215	A.C. Green	.10	.05	.01
	Phoenix Suns			
☐ 216	Christian Laettner	.05	.02	.01
	Minnesota Timberwolves			
☐ 217	Orlando Woolridge	.05	.02	.01
	Philadelphia 76ers			
☐ 218	Craig Ehlo	.05	.02	.01
	Atlanta Hawks			
☐ 219	Terry Porter	.08	.04	.01
	Portland Trail Blazers			
☐ 220	Jamal Mashburn	2.00	.90	.25
	Dallas Mavericks			
☐ 221	Kevin Duckworth	.05	.02	.01
	Washington Bullets			
☐ 222	Shawn Kemp	.60	.25	.08
	Seattle Supersonics			
☐ 223	Frank Brickowski	.05	.02	.01
	Milwaukee Bucks			
☐ 224	Chris Webber	1.50	.65	.19
	Golden State Warriors			
☐ 225	Charles Oakley	.08	.04	.01
	New York Knicks			
☐ 226	Jay Humphries	.05	.02	.01
	Utah Jazz			
☐ 227	Steve Kerr	.05	.02	.01
	Chicago Bulls			

☐ 228 Tim Perry	.05	.02	.01
Philadelphia 76ers			
☐ 229 Sleepy Floyd	.05	.02	.01
San Antonio Spurs			
☐ 230 Bimbo Coles	.05	.02	.01
Miami Heat			
☐ 231 Eddie Johnson	.08	.04	.01
Charlotte Hornets			
☐ 232 Terry Mills	.05	.02	.01
Detroit Pistons			
☐ 233 Danny Manning	.10	.05	.01
Los Angeles Clippers			
☐ 234 Isaiah Rider	.60	.25	.08
Minnesota Timberwolves			
☐ 235 Darnell Mee	.05	.02	.01
Denver Nuggets			
☐ 236 Haywoode Workman	.05	.02	.01
Indiana Pacers			
☐ 237 Scott Skiles	.05	.02	.01
Orlando Magic			
☐ 238 Otis Thorpe	.08	.04	.01
Houston Rockets			
☐ 239 Mike Peplowski	.05	.02	.01
Sacramento Kings			
☐ 240 Eric Leckner	.05	.02	.01
Philadelphia 76ers			
☐ 241 Johnny Newman	.05	.02	.01
New Jersey Nets			
☐ 242 Benoit Benjamin	.05	.02	.01
New Jersey Nets			
☐ 243 Doug Christie	.05	.02	.01
Los Angeles Lakers			
☐ 244 Acie Earl	.05	.02	.01
Boston Celtics			
☐ 245 Luc Longley	.05	.02	.01
Minnesota Timberwolves			
☐ 246 Tyrone Hill	.08	.04	.01
Cleveland Cavaliers			
☐ 247 Allan Houston	.40	.18	.05
Detroit Pistons			
☐ 248 Joe Kleine	.05	.02	.01
Phoenix Suns			
☐ 249 Mookie Blaylock	.08	.04	.01
Atlanta Hawks			
☐ 250 Anthony Bonner	.05	.02	.01
New York Knicks			
☐ 251 Luther Wright	.05	.02	.01
Utah Jazz			
☐ 252 Todd Day	.08	.04	.01
Milwaukee Bucks			
☐ 253 Kendall Gill	.05	.02	.01
Seattle Supersonics			
☐ 254 Mario Elie	.05	.02	.01
Houston Rockets			
☐ 255 Pete Myers	.05	.02	.01
Chicago Bulls			
☐ 256 Jim Les	.05	.02	.01
Sacramento Kings			
☐ 257 Stanley Roberts	.05	.02	.01
Los Angeles Clippers			
☐ 258 Michael Adams	.05	.02	.01
Washington Bullets			
☐ 259 Hersey Hawkins	.10	.05	.01
Charlotte Hornets			
☐ 260 Shawn Bradley	.15	.07	.02
Philadelphia 76ers			
☐ 261 Scott Haskin	.05	.02	.01
Indiana Pacers			
☐ 262 Corie Blount	.05	.02	.01
Chicago Bulls			
☐ 263 Charles Smith	.05	.02	.01
New York Knicks			
☐ 264 Armon Gilliam	.05	.02	.01
New Jersey Nets			
☐ 265 Jamal Mashburn NW	.75	.35	.09
Dallas Mavericks			
☐ 266 Anfernee Hardaway NW	1.50	.65	.19
Orlando Magic			
☐ 267 Shawn Bradley NW	.10	.05	.01
Philadelphia 76ers			
☐ 268 Chris Webber NW	.60	.25	.08
Golden State Warriors			
☐ 269 Bobby Hurley NW	.08	.04	.01
Sacramento Kings			
☐ 270 Isaiah Rider NW	.25	.11	.03
Minnesota Timberwolves			
☐ 271 Dino Radja NW	.10	.05	.01
Boston Celtics			
☐ 272 Chris Mills NW	.10	.05	.01
Cleveland Cavaliers			
☐ 273 Nick Van Exel NW	.75	.35	.09
Los Angeles Lakers			
☐ 274 Lindsey Hunter NW	.05	.02	.01
Detroit Pistons			
☐ 275 Toni Kukoc NW	.10	.05	.01
Chicago Bulls			
☐ 276 Popeye Jones NW	.08	.04	.01
Dallas Mavericks			
☐ 277 Chris Mills	.15	.07	.02
Cleveland Cavaliers			
☐ 278 Ricky Pierce	.08	.04	.01
Seattle Supersonics			
☐ 279 Negele Knight	.05	.02	.01
San Antonio Spurs			
☐ 280 Kenny Walker	.05	.02	.01
New Jersey Nets			
☐ 281 Nick Van Exel	2.00	.90	.25
Los Angeles Lakers			
☐ 282 Derrick Coleman UER	.10	.05	.01
New Jersey Nets			
(Career stats listed under '92-93)			
☐ 283 Popeye Jones	.30	.14	.04
Dallas Mavericks			
☐ 284 Derrick McKey	.08	.04	.01
Indiana Pacers			
☐ 285 Rick Fox	.05	.02	.01
Boston Celtics			
☐ 286 Jerome Kersey	.05	.02	.01
Portland Trail Blazers			
☐ 287 Steve Smith	.08	.04	.01
Miami Heat			
☐ 288 Brian Williams	.05	.02	.01
Denver Nuggets			
☐ 289 Chris Mullin	.10	.05	.01
Golden State Warriors			
☐ 290 Terry Cummings	.08	.04	.01
San Antonio Spurs			
☐ 291 Donald Royal	.05	.02	.01
Orlando Magic			
☐ 292 Alonzo Mourning	.60	.25	.08
Charlotte Hornets			
☐ 293 Mike Brown	.05	.02	.01
Minnesota Timberwolves			
☐ 294 Latrell Sprewell	.60	.25	.08
Golden State Warriors			
☐ 295 Oliver Miller	.05	.02	.01
Phoenix Suns			
☐ 296 Terry Dehere	.08	.04	.01
Los Angeles Clippers			
☐ 297 Detlef Schrempf	.10	.05	.01
Seattle Supersonics			
☐ 298 Sam Bowie UER	.05	.02	.01

	Los Angeles Lakers (Last name Bowe on front)			
☐ 299	Chris Morris	.05	.02	.01
	New Jersey Nets			
☐ 300	Scottie Pippen	.30	.14	.04
	Chicago Bulls			
☐ 301	Warren Kidd	.05	.02	.01
	Philadelphia 76ers			
☐ 302	Don MacLean	.05	.02	.01
	Washington Bullets			
☐ 303	Sean Rooks	.05	.02	.01
	Dallas Mavericks			
☐ 304	Matt Geiger	.05	.02	.01
	Miami Heat			
☐ 305	Dennis Rodman	.20	.09	.03
	San Antonio Spurs			
☐ 306	Reggie Miller	.30	.14	.04
	Indiana Pacers			
☐ 307	Vin Baker	1.00	.45	.13
	Miami Heat			
☐ 308	Anfernee Hardaway	4.00	1.80	.50
	Orlando Magic			
☐ 309	Lindsey Hunter	.15	.07	.02
	Detroit Pistons			
☐ 310	Stacey Augmon	.08	.04	.01
	Atlanta Hawks			
☐ 311	Randy Brown	.05	.02	.01
	Sacramento Kings			
☐ 312	Anthony Mason	.08	.04	.01
	New York Knicks			
☐ 313	John Stockton	.30	.14	.04
	Utah Jazz			
☐ 314	Sam Cassell	.50	.23	.06
	Houston Rockets			
☐ 315	Buck Williams	.08	.04	.01
	Portland Trail Blazers			
☐ 316	Bryant Stith	.05	.02	.01
	Denver Nuggets			
☐ 317	Brad Daugherty	.08	.04	.01
	Cleveland Cavaliers			
☐ 318	Dino Radja	.40	.18	.05
	Boston Celtics			
☐ 319	Rony Seikaly	.05	.02	.01
	Miami Heat			
☐ 320	Charles Barkley	.60	.25	.08
	Phoenix Suns			
☐ 321	Avery Johnson	.05	.02	.01
	Golden State Warriors			
☐ 322	Mahmoud Abdul Rauf	.08	.04	.01
	Denver Nuggets			
☐ 323	Larry Johnson	.30	.14	.04
	Charlotte Hornets			
☐ 324	Micheal Williams	.05	.02	.01
	Minnesota Timberwolves			
☐ 325	Mark Aguirre	.08	.04	.01
	Los Angeles Clippers			
☐ 326	Jim Jackson	.60	.25	.08
	Dallas Mavericks			
☐ 327	Antonio Harvey	.08	.04	.01
	Los Angeles Lakers			
☐ 328	David Robinson	.60	.25	.08
	San Antonio Spurs			
☐ 329	Calbert Cheaney	.15	.07	.02
	Washington Bullets			
☐ 330	Kenny Anderson	.10	.05	.01
	New Jersey Nets			
☐ 331	Walt Williams	.10	.05	.01
	Sacramento Kings			
☐ 332	Kevin Willis	.08	.04	.01
	Atlanta Hawks			
☐ 333	Nick Anderson	.08	.04	.01

	Orlando Magic			
☐ 334	Rik Smits	.10	.05	.01
	Indiana Pacers			
☐ 335	Joe Dumars	.15	.07	.02
	Detroit Pistons			
☐ 336	Toni Kukoc	.50	.23	.06
	Chicago Bulls			
☐ 337	Harvey Grant	.05	.02	.01
	Portland Trail Blazers			
☐ 338	Tom Chambers	.08	.04	.01
	Utah Jazz			
☐ 339	Blue Edwards	.05	.02	.01
	Milwaukee Bucks			
☐ 340	Mark Price	.10	.05	.01
	Cleveland Cavaliers			
☐ 341	Ervin Johnson	.05	.02	.01
	Seattle Supersonics			
☐ 342	Rolando Blackman	.08	.04	.01
	New York Knicks			
☐ 343	Scott Burrell	.25	.11	.03
	Charlotte Hornets			
☐ 344	Gheorghe Muresan	.30	.14	.04
	Washington Bullets			
☐ 345	Chris Corchiani	.05	.02	.01
	Boston Celtics			
☐ 346	Richard Petruska	.05	.02	.01
	Houston Rockets			
☐ 347	Dana Barros	.10	.05	.01
	Philadelphia 76ers			
☐ 348	Hakeem Olajuwon FF	.40	.18	.05
	Houston Rockets			
☐ 349	Dee Brown FF	.05	.02	.01
	Boston Celtics			
☐ 350	John Starks FF	.05	.02	.01
	New York Knicks			
☐ 351	Ron Harper FF	.05	.02	.01
	Los Angeles Clippers			
☐ 352	Chris Webber FF	.60	.25	.08
	Golden State Warriors			
☐ 353	Dan Majerle FF	.05	.02	.01
	Phoenix Suns			
☐ 354	Clyde Drexler FF	.10	.05	.01
	Portland Trail Blazers			
☐ 355	Shawn Kemp FF	.30	.14	.04
	Seattle Supersonics			
☐ 356	David Robinson FF	.30	.14	.04
	San Antonio Spurs			
☐ 357	Chris Morris FF	.05	.02	.01
	New Jersey Nets			
☐ 358	Shaquille O'Neal FF	1.25	.55	.16
	Orlando Magic			
☐ 359	Checklist	.05	.02	.01
☐ 360	Checklist	.05	.02	.01

1993-94
Stadium Club
First Day Issue

Randomly inserted in first and second series foil packs at a rate of 1 in 24, the First Day Issue set parallels that of the basic Stadium Club set. Each of the 360 standard size (2 1/2" by 3 1/2") cards have a prismatic silver First Day logo in one

1993-94 Stadium Club Big Tips

upper corner. Topps announced that there were 1,000 of each card produced. Only the top few cards in the set are individually priced below. Please refer to the multipliers provided below (coupled with the price of the corresponding regular issue card) to ascertain value.

	MINT	NRMT	EXC
COMPLETE SET (360)	2000.00	900.00	250.00
COMPLETE SERIES 1 (180)	1000.00	450.00	125.00
COMPLETE SERIES 2 (180)	1000.00	450.00	125.00
COMMON CARD (1-360)	2.50	1.15	.30

*SER.1 STARS: 25X to 40X BASIC CARDS
*SER.2 STARS: 35X to 65X BASIC CARDS
*SER.1 ROOKIES: 12X to 20X BASIC CARDS
*SER.2 ROOKIES: 18X to 30X BASIC CARDS

		MINT	NRMT	EXC
☐ 1	Michael Jordan TD.... Chicago Bulls	100.00	45.00	12.50
☐ 89	Hakeem Olajuwon...... Houston Rockets	50.00	23.00	6.25
☐ 100	Shaquille O'Neal...... Orlando Magic	150.00	70.00	19.00
☐ 169	Michael Jordan ...... Chicago Bulls	200.00	90.00	25.00
☐ 175	Shaquille O'Neal HC.. Orlando Magic	75.00	34.00	9.50
☐ 181	Michael Jordan ...... Chicago Bulls	100.00	45.00	12.50
☐ 220	Jamal Mashburn...... Dallas Mavericks	60.00	27.00	7.50
☐ 222	Shawn Kemp........... Seattle Supersonics	40.00	18.00	5.00
☐ 224	Chris Webber......... Golden State Warriors	50.00	23.00	6.25
☐ 266	Anfernee Hardaway.. Orlando Magic	50.00	23.00	6.25
☐ 281	Nick Van Exel........ Los Angeles Lakers	60.00	27.00	7.50
☐ 292	Alonzo Mourning ..... Charlotte Hornets	40.00	18.00	5.00
☐ 294	Latrell Sprewell...... Golden State Warriors	40.00	18.00	5.00
☐ 308	Anfernee Hardaway Orlando Magic	125.00	57.50	15.50
☐ 320	Charles Barkley...... Phoenix Suns	40.00	18.00	5.00
☐ 326	Jim Jackson.......... Dallas Mavericks	40.00	18.00	5.00
☐ 328	David Robinson...... San Antonio Spurs	40.00	18.00	5.00
☐ 358	Shaquille O'Neal..... Orlando Magic	75.00	34.00	9.50

Randomly inserted about one in every four packs, these 27 team logo cards measure the standard size (2 1/2" by 3 1/2"). The horizontal black fronts are framed by a thin white line and carry the words "NBA Showdown '94," the NBA logo and the team name and logo within a team-colored stripe across the bottom. The back carries game hints for the Electronic Arts NBA Showdown '94 and a videogame offer. The logo cards are unnumbered and checklisted below in alphabetical team order.

		MINT	NRMT	EXC
COMPLETE SET (27)		5.00	2.30	.60
COMMON CARD (1-27)		.25	.11	.03

		MINT	NRMT	EXC
☐ 1	Atlanta Hawks..............	.25	.11	.03
☐ 2	Boston Celtics.............	.25	.11	.03
☐ 3	Charlotte Hornets..........	.25	.11	.03
☐ 4	Chicago Bulls.............	.25	.11	.03
☐ 5	Cleveland Cavaliers........	.25	.11	.03
☐ 6	Dallas Mavericks..........	.25	.11	.03
☐ 7	Denver Nuggets...........	.25	.11	.03
☐ 8	Detroit Pistons............	.25	.11	.03
☐ 9	Golden State Warriors......	.25	.11	.03
☐ 10	Houston Rockets..........	.25	.11	.03
☐ 11	Indiana Pacers............	.25	.11	.03
☐ 12	Los Angeles Clippers......	.25	.11	.03
☐ 13	Los Angeles Lakers.......	.25	.11	.03
☐ 14	Miami Heat...............	.25	.11	.03
☐ 15	Milwaukee Bucks..........	.25	.11	.03
☐ 16	Minnesota Timberwolves	.25	.11	.03
☐ 17	New Jersey Nets..........	.25	.11	.03
☐ 18	New York Knicks..........	.25	.11	.03
☐ 19	Orlando Magic............	.25	.11	.03
☐ 20	Philadelphia 76ers........	.25	.11	.03
☐ 21	Phoenix Suns.............	.25	.11	.03
☐ 22	Portland Trail Blazers......	.25	.11	.03
☐ 23	Sacramento Kings.........	.25	.11	.03
☐ 24	San Antonio Spurs........	.25	.11	.03
☐ 25	Seattle Supersonics.......	.25	.11	.03
☐ 26	Utah Jazz................	.25	.11	.03
☐ 27	Washington Bullets........	.25	.11	.03

1993-94 Stadium Club Beam Team

Randomly inserted in first and second series 12-card and 20-card foil packs at a rate of one in 24, cards from this standard-size (2 1/2" by 3 1/2") 27-card set features a selection of top NBA stars and rookies. Cards were issued in two series of 13 and 14, respectively. The design consists of borderless fronts with color player action photos set against game-crowd backgrounds. Silver metallic beams appear near the bottom above the player's name. The horizontal back carries a color action photo on one side, with player profile on the other. The cards are numbered on the back as "X of 27."

		MINT	NRMT	EXC
COMPLETE SET (27)		225.00	100.00	28.00
COMPLETE SERIES 1 (13)		135.00	60.00	17.00
COMPLETE SERIES 2 (14)		90.00	40.00	11.50
COMMON CARD (1-27)		1.00	.45	.13
☐ 1	Shaquille O'Neal	30.00	13.50	3.80
	Orlando Magic			
☐ 2	Mark Price	1.50	.65	.19
	Cleveland Cavaliers			
☐ 3	Patrick Ewing	4.00	1.80	.50
	New York Knicks			
☐ 4	Michael Jordan	55.00	25.00	7.00
	Chicago Bulls			
☐ 5	Charles Barkley	8.00	3.60	1.00
	Phoenix Suns			
☐ 6	Reggie Miller	4.00	1.80	.50
	Indiana Pacers			
☐ 7	Derrick Coleman	1.50	.65	.19
	New Jersey Nets			
☐ 8	Dominique Wilkins	2.00	.90	.25
	Atlanta Hawks			
☐ 9	Karl Malone	4.00	1.80	.50
	Utah Jazz			
☐ 10	Alonzo Mourning	8.00	3.60	1.00
	Charlotte Hornets			
☐ 11	Tim Hardaway	1.50	.65	.19
	Golden State Warriors			
☐ 12	Hakeem Olajuwon	10.00	4.50	1.25
	Houston Rockets			
☐ 13	David Robinson	8.00	3.60	1.00
	San Antonio Spurs			
☐ 14	Dan Majerle	1.00	.45	.13
	Phoenix Suns			
☐ 15	Larry Johnson	4.00	1.80	.50
	Charlotte Hornets			
☐ 16	LaPhonso Ellis	1.00	.45	.13
	Denver Nuggets			
☐ 17	Nick Van Exel	15.00	6.75	1.90
	Los Angeles Lakers			
☐ 18	Scottie Pippen	4.00	1.80	.50
	Chicago Bulls			
☐ 19	John Stockton	4.00	1.80	.50
	Utah Jazz			
☐ 20	Bobby Hurley	1.00	.45	.13
	Sacramento Kings			
☐ 21	Chris Webber	12.00	5.50	1.50
	Golden State Warriors			
☐ 22	Jamal Mashburn	15.00	6.75	1.90
	Dallas Mavericks			
☐ 23	Anfernee Hardaway	30.00	13.50	3.80
	Orlando Magic			
☐ 24	Isaiah Rider	5.00	2.30	.60
	Minnesota Timberwolves			
☐ 25	Ken Norman	1.00	.45	.13
	Milwaukee Bucks			
☐ 26	Danny Manning	1.50	.65	.19
	Los Angeles Clippers			
☐ 27	Calbert Cheaney	4.00	1.80	.50
	Washington Bullets			

1993-94 Stadium Club Frequent Flyer Upgrades

Cards from this 20-card standard size set are based upon the Frequent Flyer subsets in the basic 1993-94 Stadium Club issue. Upgrades are identical to the basic cards with the exception of a chromium like metallic gloss and Upgrade logo on front. Upgrades were available only through a mail offer based on Frequent Flyer Point cards which were randomly inserted at a rate of 1 in every 6 second series packs. Each of the 21 players featured in the Frequent Flyer subsets (except for Michael Jordan) had five different point cards

(based upon point totals derived from actual games during the season) making for a total of 100 different point cards. To obtain a Frequent Flyer Upgrade card, collectors had to accumulate 50 points or more of an individual player and redeem them by September 15, 1994.

	MINT	NRMT	EXC
COMPLETE SET (20)	75.00	34.00	9.50
COMMON (182-190/348-358)	1.00	.45	.13
☐ 182 Dominique Wilkins Atlanta Hawks	2.00	.90	.25
☐ 183 Dennis Rodman San Antonio Spurs	2.50	1.15	.30
☐ 184 Scottie Pippen Chicago Bulls	4.00	1.80	.50
☐ 185 Larry Johnson Charlotte Hornets	4.00	1.80	.50
☐ 186 Karl Malone Utah Jazz	4.00	1.80	.50
☐ 187 Clarence Weatherspoon Philadelphia 76ers	1.50	.65	.19
☐ 188 Charles Barkley Phoenix Suns	8.00	3.60	1.00
☐ 189 Patrick Ewing New York Knicks	4.00	1.80	.50
☐ 190 Derrick Coleman New Jersey Nets	1.50	.65	.19
☐ 348 Hakeem Olajuwon Houston Rockets	10.00	4.50	1.25
☐ 349 Dee Brown Boston Celtics	1.00	.45	.13
☐ 350 John Starks New York Knicks	1.00	.45	.13
☐ 351 Ron Harper Los Angeles Clippers	1.00	.45	.13
☐ 352 Chris Webber Golden State Warriors	12.00	5.50	1.50
☐ 353 Dan Majerle Phoenix Suns	1.00	.45	.13
☐ 354 Clyde Drexler Portland Trail Blazers	4.00	1.80	.50
☐ 355 Shawn Kemp Seattle Supersonics	8.00	3.60	1.00
☐ 356 David Robinson San Antonio Spurs	8.00	3.60	1.00
☐ 357 Chris Morris New Jersey Nets	1.00	.45	.13
☐ 358 Shaquille O'Neal Orlando Magic	30.00	13.50	3.80
☐ NNO Expired Point Cards	.25	.11	.03

1993-94 Stadium Club Rim Rockers

Randomly inserted in second series 12-card packs at a rate of one in 24, these six standard-size (2 1/2" by 3 1/2") cards feature some of the NBA's top dunkers. Fronts contain color player action shots. The player's name appears near the bottom. His

first name is printed in white lowercase lettering; his last is gold-foil stamped in uppercase lettering. The back carries another borderless color player action shot, but its right side is ghosted, blue-screened, and overprinted with career highlights in white lettering. The cards are numbered on the back as "X of 6."

	MINT	NRMT	EXC
COMPLETE SET (6)	12.00	5.50	1.50
COMMON CARD (1-6)	.25	.11	.03
☐ 1 Shaquille O'Neal Orlando Magic	8.00	3.60	1.00
☐ 2 Harold Miner Miami Heat	.25	.11	.03
☐ 3 Charles Barkley Phoenix Suns	2.00	.90	.25
☐ 4 Dominique Wilkins Atlanta Hawks	.50	.23	.06
☐ 5 Shawn Kemp Seattle Supersonics	2.00	.90	.25
☐ 6 Robert Horry Houston Rockets	.75	.35	.09

1993-94 Stadium Club Super Teams

Randomly inserted in first series 12 and 20-card foil packs at a rate of one in 24, cards from this standard-size (2 1/2" by 3 1/2") 27-card set feature borderless fronts with color team action photos. The team name appears in gold-foil lettering at the bottom. The back features the NBA Super Team

Card rules. If the team shown on the card won its division, conference or league championship, the collector could have redeemed it for special prizes until Nov. 1, 1994. Atlanta, Houston, New York and Seattle were all winners. Their cards are currently in shorter supply than non-winner Super Team cards. The four winning teams are designated below with a "W". In addition, Conference, Division and Finals winner cards have "C", "D" and "F" designations.

1993-94 Stadium Club Super Teams Division Winners

Super Team cards were randomly inserted into 1993-94 Stadium Club first series packs. Through a mail-in offer, collectors could exchange this card for an 11-card Division Winner set. The offer expired November 1, 1994. The cards are identical to their regular issue counterparts, except for the gold-foil Division Winner logo on their fronts. In the listing below, the suffixes H, K, R, and S have been added to denote Hawks, Knicks, Rockets and Supersonics.

	MINT	NRMT	EXC
COMPLETE SET (27)	75.00	34.00	9.50
COMMON CARD (1-27)	1.00	.45	.13
☐ 1 Atlanta Hawks WD	2.50	1.15	.30
(Kevin Willis/Dominique Wilkins)			
☐ 2 Boston Celtics	1.00	.45	.13
(Xavier McDaniel/Robert Parish)			
☐ 3 Charlotte Hornets	8.00	3.60	1.00
(Larry Johnson/Alonzo Mourning)			
☐ 4 Chicago Bulls	1.00	.45	.13
(Harvey Grant)			
☐ 5 Cleveland Cavaliers	1.00	.45	.13
(Brad Daugherty/John Williams)			
☐ 6 Dallas Mavericks	1.00	.45	.13
(Group photo)			
☐ 7 Denver Nuggets	2.00	.90	.25
(Dikembe Mutombo/Kevin Brooks)			
☐ 8 Detroit Pistons	1.00	.45	.13
(Group photo)			
☐ 9 Golden State Warriors	1.00	.45	.13
(Group photo)			
☐ 10 Houston Rockets WCDF	15.00	6.75	1.90
(Group photo)			
☐ 11 Indiana Pacers	1.00	.45	.13
(Group photo)			
☐ 12 Los Angeles Clippers	1.50	.65	.19
(Danny Manning/Ron Harper)			
☐ 13 Los Angeles Lakers	1.00	.45	.13
(Group photo)			
☐ 14 Miami Heat	1.00	.45	.13
(John Salley/Willie Burton)			
☐ 15 Milwaukee Bucks	1.00	.45	.13
(Group photo)			
☐ 16 Minnesota Timberwolves	2.00	.90	.25
(Christian Laettner/Felton Spencer)			
☐ 17 New Jersey Nets	2.00	.90	.25
(Derrick Coleman)			
☐ 18 New York Knicks WCD	5.00	2.30	.60
(Patrick Ewing)			
☐ 19 Orlando Magic	15.00	6.75	1.90
(Shaquille O'Neal)			
☐ 20 Philadelphia 76ers	1.50	.65	.19
(Clarence Weatherspoon/Jeff Hornacek)			
☐ 21 Phoenix Suns	5.00	2.30	.60
(Charles Barkley Dan Majerle)			
☐ 22 Portland Trail Blazers	1.00	.45	.13
(Buck Williams)			
☐ 23 Sacramento Kings	1.00	.45	.13
(Lionel Simmons)			
☐ 24 San Antonio Spurs	5.00	2.30	.60
☐ 25 Seattle Supersonics WD	10.00	4.50	1.25
(Shawn Kemp)			
☐ 26 Utah Jazz	1.00	.45	.13
(Group photo)			
☐ 27 Washington Bullets	1.00	.45	.13
(Group photo)			

	MINT	EXC	G-VG
COMP.BAG HAWKS (11)	6.00	2.70	.75
COMP.BAG KNICKS (11)	6.00	2.70	.75
COMP.BAG ROCKETS (11)	10.00	4.50	1.25
COMP.BAG SONICS (11)	10.00	4.50	1.25
COMMON CARD	.50	.23	.06
☐ H46 Adam Keefe	.50	.23	.06
☐ H93 Jon Koncak	.50	.23	.06
☐ H129 Dominique Wilkins	1.25	.55	.16
☐ H150 Doug Edwards DP	.75	.35	.09
☐ H197 Andrew Lang	.50	.23	.06
☐ H218 Craig Ehlo	.50	.23	.06
☐ H233 Danny Manning	1.00	.45	.13
☐ H249 Mookie Blaylock	.75	.35	.09
☐ H310 Stacey Augmon	.75	.35	.09
☐ H332 Kevin Willis	.75	.35	.09
☐ HD1 Hawks DW Super Team	1.00	.45	.13
☐ K23 Hubert Davis	.50	.23	.06
☐ K34 Greg Anthony	.50	.23	.06
☐ K81 Doc Rivers	.50	.23	.06
☐ K116 John Starks	.75	.35	.09
☐ K192 Derek Harper	.75	.35	.09
☐ K200 Patrick Ewing	2.50	1.15	.30
☐ K225 Charles Oakley	.75	.35	.09
☐ K250 Anthony Bonner	.50	.23	.06
☐ K263 Charles Smith	.50	.23	.06
☐ K312 Anthony Mason	.75	.35	.09
☐ KD18 Knicks DW Super Team	1.00	.45	.13
☐ R37 Scott Brooks	.50	.23	.06
☐ R89 Hakeem Olajuwon	6.00	2.70	.75
☐ R132 Kenny Smith	.50	.23	.06
☐ R156 Vernon Maxwell	.50	.23	.06
☐ R162 Carl Herrera	.50	.23	.06
☐ R210 Robert Horry	2.00	.90	.25

		MINT	EXC	G-VG
☐ R238	Otis Thorpe	.75	.35	.09
☐ R254	Mario Elie	.50	.23	.06
☐ R314	Sam Cassell	2.50	1.15	.30
☐ R346	Richard Petruska	.50	.23	.06
☐ RD10	Rocket DW Super Team	1.00	.45	.13
☐ S85	Michael Cage	.50	.23	.06
☐ S115	Nate McMillan	.50	.23	.06
☐ S154	Sam Perkins	.75	.35	.09
☐ S173	Shawn Kemp HC	2.50	1.15	.30
☐ S196	Gary Payton	1.00	.45	.13
☐ S222	Shawn Kemp	5.00	2.30	.60
☐ S253	Kendall Gill	.50	.23	.06
☐ S278	Ricky Pierce	.75	.35	.09
☐ S297	Detlef Schrempf	1.00	.45	.13
☐ S341	Ervin Johnson	.75	.35	.09
☐ SD25	Division Winner Card	1.00	.45	.13

1993-94 Stadium Club Super Teams Master Photos

Collectors who pulled either a Knicks or Rockets Super Team insert card (randomly inserted in 1993-94 Stadium Club series 1 packs) could exchange the card via mail for a 11-card Master Photo set. The expiration date for the offer was November 1, 1994. Measuring 5" by 7", the cards are numbered on the back "X of 10." In the listing below, the suffixes K and R have been added to denote Knicks and Rockets.

		MINT	EXC	G-VG
COMP.BAG KNICKS (11)		10.00	4.50	1.25
COMP.BAG ROCKETS (11)		15.00	6.75	1.90
COMMON CARD		.75	.35	.09

☐ K1	Greg Anthony	.75	.35	.09
☐ K2	Anthony Bonner	.75	.35	.09
☐ K3	Hubert Davis	.75	.35	.09
☐ K4	Patrick Ewing	4.00	1.80	.50
☐ K5	Derek Harper	.75	.35	.09
☐ K6	Anthony Mason	1.00	.45	.13
☐ K7	Charles Oakley	1.00	.45	.13
☐ K8	Doc Rivers	.75	.35	.09
☐ K9	Charles Smith	.75	.35	.09
☐ K10	John Starks	1.00	.45	.13
☐ KMP	Knicks MP Super Team	1.50	.65	.19
☐ R1	Scott Brooks	.75	.35	.09

☐ R2	Sam Cassell	4.00	1.80	.50
☐ R3	Mario Elie	.75	.35	.09
☐ R4	Carl Herrera	.75	.35	.09
☐ R5	Robert Horry	3.00	1.35	.40
☐ R6	Vernon Maxwell	.75	.35	.09
☐ R7	Hakeem Olajuwon	10.00	4.50	1.25
☐ R8	Richard Petruska	.75	.35	.09
☐ R9	Kenny Smith	.75	.35	.09
☐ R10	Otis Thorpe	1.00	.45	.13
☐ RMP	Rockets MP Super Team	1.50	.65	.19

1993-94 Stadium Club Super Teams NBA Finals

This parallel issue to the 1993-94 Stadium Club set was redeemable only by mail in exchange for the Houston Rockets Super Team card (randomly inserted into 1993-94 Stadium Club series 1 packs.) The card had to be mailed in before the Nov. 1st, 1994 deadline. A gold-foil NBA Finals logo on the front distinguishes these cards from their regular issue counterparts. Only the top few cards are individually priced below. Please refer to the multipliers provided below (coupled with the prices of the corresponding regular issue cards) to ascertain value.

	MINT	NRMT	EXC
COMPLETE SET (361)	80.00	36.00	10.00
COMMON CARD (1-360)	.15	.07	.02
*SER.1 STARS: 1X to 2X BASIC CARDS			
*SER.2 STARS: 1.5X to 3X BASIC CARDS			
*SER.1 ROOKIES: .75X to 1.5X BASIC CARDS			
*SER.2 ROOKIES: 1X to 2X BASIC CARDS			

		MINT	NRMT	EXC
☐ 1	Michael Jordan TD Chicago Bulls	6.00	2.70	.75
☐ 89	Hakeem Olajuwon Houston Rockets	2.50	1.15	.30
☐ 100	Shaquille O'Neal Orlando Magic	8.00	3.60	1.00
☐ 169	Michael Jordan Chicago Bulls	12.00	5.50	1.50
☐ 175	Shaquille O'Neal HC Orlando Magic	4.00	1.80	.50
☐ 181	Michael Jordan FF Chicago Bulls	6.00	2.70	.75

☐	220	Jamal Mashburn	4.00	1.80	.50
		Dallas Mavericks			
☐	222	Shawn Kemp	2.00	.90	.25
		Seattle Supersonics			
☐	224	Chris Webber	3.00	1.35	.40
		Golden State Warriors			
☐	266	Anfernee Hardaway NW	3.00	1.35	.40
		Orlando Magic			
☐	281	Nick Van Exel	4.00	1.80	.50
		Los Angeles Lakers			
☐	292	Alonzo Mourning	2.00	.90	.25
		Charlotte Hornets			
☐	294	Latrell Sprewell	2.00	.90	.25
		Golden State Warriors			
☐	308	Anfernee Hardaway	8.00	3.60	1.00
		Orlando Magic			
☐	320	Charles Barkley	2.00	.90	.25
		Phoenix Suns			
☐	326	Jim Jackson	2.00	.90	.25
		Dallas Mavericks			
☐	328	David Robinson	2.00	.90	.25
		San Antonio Spurs			
☐	358	Shaquille O'Neal FF	4.00	1.80	.50
		Orlando Magic			
☐	NF10	Rockets Super Team NF	1.00	.45	.13

1994-95 Stadium Club

The 362 standard size cards that comprise the 1994-95 Stadium Club set were issued in two separate series of 182 and 180 cards each. Cards were primarily distributed in 12-card packs, each with a suggested retail price of 2.00. Full-bleed fronts feature full-color action shots with player's name placed along the bottom in foil. Topical subsets featured are College Teammates (100-114), Draft Picks (172, 179-182), All-Import (201-205, 251-255), Back Court Tandem (226-230, 276-280, 326-330), and Faces of the Game (353-362). Other topical subsets, such as Thru the Glass as well as First and Second Round '94 Draft Picks, are scattered throughout the set.

	MINT	NRMT	EXC
COMPLETE SET (362)	40.00	18.00	5.00
COMPLETE SERIES 1 (182)	20.00	9.00	2.50
COMPLETE SERIES 2 (180)	20.00	9.00	2.50
COMMON CARD (1-362)	.10	.05	.01

☐	1	Patrick Ewing	.40	.18	.05
		New York Knicks			
☐	2	Patrick Ewing TTG	.15	.07	.02
		New York Knicks			
☐	3	Bimbo Coles	.10	.05	.01
		Miami Heat			
☐	4	Elden Campbell	.10	.05	.01
		Los Angeles Lakers			
☐	5	Brent Price	.10	.05	.01
		Washington Bullets			
☐	6	Hubert Davis	.10	.05	.01
		New York Knicks			
☐	7	Donald Royal	.10	.05	.01
		Orlando Magic			
☐	8	Tim Perry	.10	.05	.01
		Philadelphia 76ers			
☐	9	Chris Webber	.60	.25	.08
		Golden State Warriors			
☐	10	Chris Webber TTG	.30	.14	.04
		Golden State Warriors			
☐	11	Brad Daugherty	.12	.05	.02
		Cleveland Cavaliers			
☐	12	P.J. Brown	.10	.05	.01
		New Jersey Nets			
☐	13	Charles Barkley	.75	.35	.09
		Phoenix Suns			
☐	14	Mario Elie	.10	.05	.01
		Houston Rockets			
☐	15	Tyrone Hill	.12	.05	.02
		Cleveland Cavaliers			
☐	16	Anfernee Hardaway	1.50	.65	.19
		Orlando Magic			
☐	17	Anfernee Hardaway TTG	.75	.35	.09
		Orlando Magic			
☐	18	Toni Kukoc	.15	.07	.02
		Chicago Bulls			
☐	19	Chris Morris	.10	.05	.01
		New Jersey Nets			
☐	20	Gerald Wilkins	.10	.05	.01
		Cleveland Cavaliers			
☐	21	David Benoit	.10	.05	.01
		Utah Jazz			
☐	22	Kevin Duckworth	.10	.05	.01
		Washington Bullets			
☐	23	Derrick Coleman	.15	.07	.02
		New Jersey Nets			
☐	24	Adam Keefe	.10	.05	.01
		Atlanta Hawks			
☐	25	Marlon Maxey	.10	.05	.01
		Minnesota Timberwolves			
☐	26	Vern Fleming	.10	.05	.01
		Indiana Pacers			
☐	27	Jeff Malone	.12	.05	.02
		Philadelphia 76ers			
☐	28	Rodney Rogers	.15	.07	.02
		Denver Nuggets			
☐	29	Terry Mills	.10	.05	.01
		Detroit Pistons			
☐	30	Doug West	.10	.05	.01
		Minnesota Timberwolves			
☐	31	Doug West TTG	.10	.05	.01
		Minnesota Timberwolves			
☐	32	Shaquille O'Neal	2.00	.90	.25
		Orlando Magic			
☐	33	Scottie Pippen	.40	.18	.05
		Chicago Bulls			
☐	34	Lee Mayberry	.10	.05	.01
		Milwaukee Bucks			
☐	35	Dale Ellis	.12	.05	.02
		San Antonio Spurs			
☐	36	Cedric Ceballos	.15	.07	.02

☐ 37	Lionel Simmons	.10	.05	.01
	Sacramento Kings			
☐ 38	Kenny Gattison	.10	.05	.01
	Charlotte Hornets			
☐ 39	Popeye Jones	.10	.05	.01
	Dallas Mavericks			
☐ 40	Jerome Kersey	.10	.05	.01
	Portland Trail Blazers			
☐ 41	Jerome Kersey TTG	.10	.05	.01
	Portland Trail Blazers			
☐ 42	Larry Stewart	.10	.05	.01
	Washington Bullets			
☐ 43	Rod Strickland	.12	.05	.02
	Portland Trail Blazers			
☐ 44	Chris Mills	.15	.07	.02
	Cleveland Cavaliers			
☐ 45	Latrell Sprewell	.50	.23	.06
	Golden State Warriors			
☐ 46	Haywoode Workman	.10	.05	.01
	Indiana Pacers			
☐ 47	Charles Smith	.10	.05	.01
	New York Knicks			
☐ 48	Detlef Schrempf	.15	.07	.02
	Seattle Supersonics			
☐ 49	Gary Grant	.10	.05	.01
	Los Angeles Clippers			
☐ 50	Gary Grant TTG	.10	.05	.01
	Los Angeles Clippers			
☐ 51	Tom Chambers	.12	.05	.02
	Utah Jazz			
☐ 52	J.R. Reid	.10	.05	.01
	San Antonio Spurs			
☐ 53	Mookie Blaylock	.12	.05	.02
	Atlanta Hawks			
☐ 54	Mookie Blaylock TTG	.10	.05	.01
	Atlanta Hawks			
☐ 55	Rony Seikaly	.10	.05	.01
	Miami Heat			
☐ 56	Isaiah Rider	.25	.11	.03
	Minnesota Timberwolves			
☐ 57	Isaiah Rider TTG	.12	.05	.02
	Minnesota Timberwolves			
☐ 58	Nick Anderson	.12	.05	.02
	Orlando Magic			
☐ 59	Victor Alexander	.10	.05	.01
	Golden State Warriors			
☐ 60	Lucious Harris	.10	.05	.01
	Dallas Mavericks			
☐ 61	Mark Macon	.10	.05	.01
	Detroit Pistons			
☐ 62	Otis Thorpe	.12	.05	.02
	Houston Rockets			
☐ 63	Randy Woods	.10	.05	.01
	Los Angeles Clippers			
☐ 64	Clyde Drexler	.40	.18	.05
	Portland Trail Blazers			
☐ 65	Dikembe Mutombo	.25	.11	.03
	Denver Nuggets			
☐ 66	Todd Day	.12	.05	.02
	Milwaukee Bucks			
☐ 67	Greg Anthony	.10	.05	.01
	New York Knicks			
☐ 68	Sherman Douglas	.10	.05	.01
	Boston Celtics			
☐ 69	Chris Mullin	.15	.07	.02
	Golden State Warriors			
☐ 70	Kevin Johnson	.20	.09	.03
	Phoenix Suns			
☐ 71	Kendall Gill	.10	.05	.01
	Seattle Supersonics			
☐ 72	Dennis Rodman	.25	.11	.03
	San Antonio Spurs			
☐ 73	Dennis Rodman TTG	.12	.05	.02
	San Antonio Spurs			
☐ 74	Jeff Turner	.10	.05	.01
	Orlando Magic			
☐ 75	John Stockton	.40	.18	.05
	Utah Jazz			
☐ 76	John Stockton TTG	.15	.07	.02
	Utah Jazz			
☐ 77	Doug Edwards	.10	.05	.01
	Atlanta Hawks			
☐ 78	Jim Jackson	.50	.23	.06
	Dallas Mavericks			
☐ 79	Hakeem Olajuwon	1.00	.45	.13
	Houston Rockets			
☐ 80	Glen Rice	.15	.07	.02
	Miami Heat			
☐ 81	Christian Laettner	.12	.05	.02
	Minnesota Timberwolves			
☐ 82	Terry Porter	.12	.05	.02
	Portland Trail Blazers			
☐ 83	Joe Dumars	.20	.09	.03
	Detroit Pistons			
☐ 84	David Wingate	.10	.05	.01
	Charlotte Hornets			
☐ 85	B.J. Armstrong	.10	.05	.01
	Chicago Bulls			
☐ 86	Derrick McKey	.12	.05	.02
	Indiana Pacers			
☐ 87	Elmore Spencer	.10	.05	.01
	Los Angeles Clippers			
☐ 88	Walt Williams	.12	.05	.02
	Sacramento Kings			
☐ 89	Shawn Bradley	.15	.07	.02
	Philadelphia 76ers			
☐ 90	Acie Earl	.10	.05	.01
	Boston Celtics			
☐ 91	Acie Earl TTG	.10	.05	.01
	Boston Celtics			
☐ 92	Randy Brown	.10	.05	.01
	Sacramento Kings			
☐ 93	Grant Long	.10	.05	.01
	Miami Heat			
☐ 94	Terry Dehere	.10	.05	.01
	Los Angeles Clippers			
☐ 95	Spud Webb	.12	.05	.02
	Sacramento Kings			
☐ 96	Lindsey Hunter	.10	.05	.01
	Detroit Pistons			
☐ 97	Blair Rasmussen	.10	.05	.01
	Atlanta Hawks			
☐ 98	Tim Hardaway	.15	.07	.02
	Golden State Warriors			
☐ 99	Kevin Edwards	.10	.05	.01
	New Jersey Nets			
☐ 100	Patrick Ewing CT	.12	.05	.02
	Reggie Williams CT			
	Georgetown Hoyas			
☐ 101	Chuck Person CT	.15	.07	.02
	Charles Barkley CT			
	Auburn Tigers			
☐ 102	Mahmoud Abdul-Rauf CT	.50	.23	.06
	Shaquille O'Neal CT			
	LSU Tigers			
☐ 103	Rony Seikaly CT	.10	.05	.01
	Derrick Coleman CT			
	Syracuse Orangemen			
☐ 104	Hakeem Olajuwon CT	.40	.18	.05
	Clyde Drexler CT			
	Houston Cougars			

☐ 105	Chris Mullin CT	.10	.05	.01
	Mark Jackson CT			
	St. John Red Storm			
☐ 106	Robert Horry CT	.12	.05	.02
	Latrell Sprewell CT			
	Alabama Crimson Tide			
☐ 107	Pooh Richardson CT	.12	.05	.02
	Reggie Miller CT			
	UCLA Bruins			
☐ 108	Dennis Scott CT	.10	.05	.01
	Kenny Anderson CT			
	GA Tech Yellow Jackets			
☐ 109	Kendall Gill CT	.10	.05	.01
	Ken Norman CT			
	Illinois Fightin' Illini			
☐ 110	Scott Skiles CT	.10	.05	.01
	Kevin Willis CT			
	Michigan State Spartans			
☐ 111	Terry Mills CT	.12	.05	.02
	Glen Rice CT			
	Michigan Wolverines			
☐ 112	Christian Laettner CT	.12	.05	.02
	Bobby Hurley CT			
	Duke Blue Devils			
☐ 113	Stacey Augmon CT	.12	.05	.02
	Larry Johnson CT			
	UNLV Runnin' Rebels			
☐ 114	Sam Perkins CT	.12	.05	.02
	James Worthy CT			
	North Carolina Tar Heels			
☐ 115	Carl Herrera	.10	.05	.01
	Houston Rockets			
☐ 116	Sam Bowie	.10	.05	.01
	Los Angeles Lakers			
☐ 117	Gary Payton	.15	.07	.02
	Seattle Supersonics			
☐ 118	Danny Ainge	.12	.05	.02
	Phoenix Suns			
☐ 119	Danny Ainge TTG	.10	.05	.01
	Phoenix Suns			
☐ 120	Luc Longley	.10	.05	.01
	Chicago Bulls			
☐ 121	Antonio Davis	.10	.05	.01
	Indiana Pacers			
☐ 122	Terry Cummings	.12	.05	.02
	San Antonio Spurs			
☐ 123	Terry Cummings TTG	.10	.05	.01
	San Antonio Spurs			
☐ 124	Mark Price	.15	.07	.02
	Cleveland Cavaliers			
☐ 125	Jamal Mashburn	.75	.35	.09
	Dallas Mavericks			
☐ 126	Mahmoud Abdul-Rauf	.12	.05	.02
	Denver Nuggets			
☐ 127	Charles Oakley	.12	.05	.02
	New York Knicks			
☐ 128	Steve Smith	.12	.05	.02
	Miami Heat			
☐ 129	Vin Baker	.40	.18	.05
	Milwaukee Bucks			
☐ 130	Robert Horry	.15	.07	.02
	Houston Rockets			
☐ 131	Doug Christie	.10	.05	.01
	Los Angeles Lakers			
☐ 132	Wayman Tisdale	.12	.05	.02
	Sacramento Kings			
☐ 133	Wayman Tisdale TTG	.10	.05	.01
	Sacramento Kings			
☐ 134	Muggsy Bogues	.15	.07	.02
	Charlotte Hornets			
☐ 135	Dino Radja	.15	.07	.02
	Boston Celtics			
☐ 136	Jeff Hornacek	.12	.05	.02
	Utah Jazz			
☐ 137	Gheorghe Muresan	.12	.05	.02
	Washington Bullets			
☐ 138	Loy Vaught	.12	.05	.02
	Los Angeles Clippers			
☐ 139	Loy Vaught TTG	.10	.05	.01
	Los Angeles Clippers			
☐ 140	Benoit Benjamin	.10	.05	.01
	New Jersey Nets			
☐ 141	Johnny Dawkins	.10	.05	.01
	Philadelphia 76ers			
☐ 142	Allan Houston	.15	.07	.02
	Detroit Pistons			
☐ 143	Jon Barry	.10	.05	.01
	Milwaukee Bucks			
☐ 144	Reggie Miller	.40	.18	.05
	Indiana Pacers			
☐ 145	Kevin Willis	.12	.05	.02
	Atlanta Hawks			
☐ 146	James Worthy	.15	.07	.02
	Los Angeles Lakers			
☐ 147	James Worthy TTG	.10	.05	.01
	Los Angeles Lakers			
☐ 148	Scott Burrell	.10	.05	.01
	Charlotte Hornets			
☐ 149	Tom Gugliotta	.12	.05	.02
	Washington Bullets			
☐ 150	LaPhonso Ellis	.10	.05	.01
	Denver Nuggets			
☐ 151	Doug Smith	.10	.05	.01
	Dallas Mavericks			
☐ 152	A.C. Green	.15	.07	.02
	Phoenix Suns			
☐ 153	A.C. Green TTG	.10	.05	.01
	Phoenix Suns			
☐ 154	George Lynch	.10	.05	.01
	Los Angeles Lakers			
☐ 155	Sam Perkins	.12	.05	.02
	Seattle Supersonics			
☐ 156	Corie Blount	.10	.05	.01
	Chicago Bulls			
☐ 157	Xavier McDaniel	.12	.05	.02
	Boston Celtics			
☐ 158	Xavier McDaniel TTG	.10	.05	.01
	Boston Celtics			
☐ 159	Eric Murdock	.10	.05	.01
	Milwaukee Bucks			
☐ 160	David Robinson	.75	.35	.09
	San Antonio Spurs			
☐ 161	Karl Malone	.40	.18	.05
	Utah Jazz			
☐ 162	Karl Malone TTG	.15	.07	.02
	Utah Jazz			
☐ 163	Clarence Weatherspoon	.15	.07	.02
	Philadelphia 76ers			
☐ 164	Calbert Cheaney	.15	.07	.02
	Washington Bullets			
☐ 165	Tom Hammonds	.10	.05	.01
	Denver Nuggets			
☐ 166	Tom Hammonds TTG	.10	.05	.01
	Denver Nuggets			
☐ 167	Alonzo Mourning	.50	.23	.06
	Charlotte Hornets			
☐ 168	Clifford Robinson	.12	.05	.02
	Portland Trail Blazers			
☐ 169	Micheal Williams	.10	.05	.01
	Minnesota Timberwolves			
☐ 170	Ervin Johnson	.10	.05	.01
	Seattle Supersonics			

☐ 171	Mike Gminski — Milwaukee Bucks	.10	.05	.01
☐ 172	Jason Kidd DP — Dallas Mavericks	4.00	1.80	.50
☐ 173	Anthony Bonner — New York Knicks	.10	.05	.01
☐ 174	Stacey King — Minnesota Timberwolves	.10	.05	.01
☐ 175	Rex Chapman — Washington Bullets	.10	.05	.01
☐ 176	Greg Graham — Philadelphia 76ers	.10	.05	.01
☐ 177	Stanley Roberts — Los Angeles Clippers	.10	.05	.01
☐ 178	Mitch Richmond — Sacramento Kings	.20	.09	.03
☐ 179	Eric Montross DP — Boston Celtics	.60	.25	.08
☐ 180	Eddie Jones DP — Los Angeles Lakers	2.50	1.15	.30
☐ 181	Grant Hill — Detroit Pistons	6.00	2.70	.75
☐ 182	Donyell Marshall DP — Minnesota Timberwolves	.75	.35	.09
☐ 183	Glenn Robinson — Milwaukee Bucks	4.00	1.80	.50
☐ 184	Dominique Wilkins — Boston Celtics	.20	.09	.03
☐ 185	Mark Price — Cleveland Cavaliers	.15	.07	.02
☐ 186	Anthony Mason — New York Knicks	.12	.05	.02
☐ 187	Tyrone Corbin — Utah Jazz	.10	.05	.01
☐ 188	Dale Davis — Indiana Pacers	.12	.05	.02
☐ 189	Nate McMillan — Seattle Supersonics	.10	.05	.01
☐ 190	Jason Kidd — Dallas Mavericks	2.00	.90	.25
☐ 191	John Salley — Miami Heat	.10	.05	.01
☐ 192	Keith Jennings — Golden State Warriors	.10	.05	.01
☐ 193	Mark Bryant — Portland Trail Blazers	.10	.05	.01
☐ 194	Sleepy Floyd — New Jersey Nets	.10	.05	.01
☐ 195	Grant Hill — Detroit Pistons	3.00	1.35	.40
☐ 196	Joe Kleine — Phoenix Suns	.10	.05	.01
☐ 197	Anthony Peeler — Los Angeles Lakers	.10	.05	.01
☐ 198	Malik Sealy — Los Angeles Clippers	.10	.05	.01
☐ 199	Kenny Walker — Washington Bullets	.10	.05	.01
☐ 200	Donyell Marshall — Minnesota Timberwolves	.40	.18	.05
☐ 201	Vlade Divac AI — Los Angeles Lakers	.10	.05	.01
☐ 202	Dino Radja AI — Boston Celtics	.10	.05	.01
☐ 203	Carl Herrera AI — Houston Oilers	.10	.05	.01
☐ 204	Olden Polynice AI — Sacramento Kings	.10	.05	.01
☐ 205	Patrick Ewing AI — New York Knicks	.15	.07	.02
☐ 206	Willie Anderson — San Antonio Spurs	.10	.05	.01
☐ 207	Mitch Richmond — Sacramento Kings	.20	.09	.03
☐ 208	John Crotty — Utah Jazz	.10	.05	.01
☐ 209	Tracy Murray — Portland Trail Blazers	.10	.05	.01
☐ 210	Juwan Howard — Washington Bullets	1.50	.65	.19
☐ 211	Robert Parish — Charlotte Hornets	.15	.07	.02
☐ 212	Steve Kerr — Chicago Bulls	.10	.05	.01
☐ 213	Anthony Bowie — Orlando Magic	.10	.05	.01
☐ 214	Tim Breaux — Houston Rockets	.10	.05	.01
☐ 215	Sharone Wright — Philadelphia 76ers	.50	.23	.06
☐ 216	Brian Williams — Denver Nuggets	.10	.05	.01
☐ 217	Rick Fox — Boston Celtics	.10	.05	.01
☐ 218	Harold Miner — Miami Heat	.10	.05	.01
☐ 219	Duane Ferrell — Indiana Pacers	.10	.05	.01
☐ 220	Lamond Murray — Los Angeles Clippers	.60	.25	.08
☐ 221	Blue Edwards — Boston Celtics	.10	.05	.01
☐ 222	Bill Cartwright — Seattle Supersonics	.10	.05	.01
☐ 223	Sergei Bazarevich — Atlanta Hawks	.10	.05	.01
☐ 224	Herb Williams — New York Knicks	.10	.05	.01
☐ 225	Brian Grant — Sacramento Kings	1.25	.55	.16
☐ 226	Derek Harper BCT / John Starks — New York Knicks	.10	.05	.01
☐ 227	Rod Strickland BCT / Clyde Drexler — Portland Trail Blazers	.12	.05	.02
☐ 228	Kevin Johnson BCT / Dan Majerle — Phoenix Suns	.10	.05	.01
☐ 229	Lindsey Hunter BCT / Joe Dumars — Detroit Pistons	.10	.05	.01
☐ 230	Tim Hardaway BCT / Latrell Sprewell — Golden State Warriors	.15	.07	.02
☐ 231	Bill Wennington — Chicago Bulls	.10	.05	.01
☐ 232	Brian Shaw — Orlando Magic	.10	.05	.01
☐ 233	Jamie Watson — Utah Jazz	.20	.09	.03
☐ 234	Chris Whitney — San Antonio Spurs	.10	.05	.01
☐ 235	Eric Montross — Boston Celtics	.30	.14	.04
☐ 236	Kenny Smith — Houston Rockets	.10	.05	.01
☐ 237	Andrew Lang — Atlanta Hawks	.10	.05	.01
☐ 238	Lorenzo Williams — Dallas Mavericks	.10	.05	.01
☐ 239	Dana Barros	.15	.07	.02

☐ 240	Eddie Jones Philadelphia 76ers Los Angeles Lakers	1.25	.55	.16
☐ 241	Harold Ellis Los Angeles Clippers	.10	.05	.01
☐ 242	James Edwards Portland Trail Blazers	.10	.05	.01
☐ 243	Don MacLean Washington Bullets	.10	.05	.01
☐ 244	Ed Pinckney Milwaukee Bucks	.10	.05	.01
☐ 245	Carlos Rogers Golden State Warriors	.30	.14	.04
☐ 246	Michael Adams Charlotte Hornets	.10	.05	.01
☐ 247	Rex Walters New Jersey Nets	.10	.05	.01
☐ 248	John Starks New York Knicks	.12	.05	.02
☐ 249	Terrell Brandon Cleveland Cavaliers	.10	.05	.01
☐ 250	Khalid Reeves Miami Heat	.60	.25	.08
☐ 251	Dominique Wilkins AI Boston Celtics	.12	.05	.02
☐ 252	Toni Kukoc AI Chicago Bulls	.10	.05	.01
☐ 253	Rick Fox AI Boston Celtics	.10	.05	.01
☐ 254	Detlef Schrempf AI Seattle Supersonics	.10	.05	.01
☐ 255	Rik Smits AI Indiana Pacers	.10	.05	.01
☐ 256	Johnny Dawkins Detroit Pistons	.10	.05	.01
☐ 257	Dan Majerle Phoenix Suns	.12	.05	.02
☐ 258	Mike Brown Minnesota Timberwolves	.10	.05	.01
☐ 259	Byron Scott Indiana Pacers	.12	.05	.02
☐ 260	Jalen Rose Denver Nuggets	.75	.35	.09
☐ 261	Byron Houston Seattle Supersonics	.10	.05	.01
☐ 262	Frank Brickowski Sacramento Kings	.10	.05	.01
☐ 263	Vernon Maxwell Houston Rockets	.10	.05	.01
☐ 264	Craig Ehlo Atlanta Hawks	.10	.05	.01
☐ 265	Yinka Dare New Jersey Nets	.12	.05	.02
☐ 266	Dee Brown Boston Celtics	.12	.05	.02
☐ 267	Felton Spencer Utah Jazz	.10	.05	.01
☐ 268	Harvey Grant Portland Trail Blazers	.10	.05	.01
☐ 269	Nick Van Exel Los Angeles Lakers	.75	.35	.09
☐ 270	Bob Martin Los Angeles Clippers	.10	.05	.01
☐ 271	Hersey Hawkins Charlotte Hornets	.12	.05	.02
☐ 272	Scott Williams Philadelphia 76ers	.10	.05	.01
☐ 273	Sarunas Marciulionis Seattle Supersonics	.10	.05	.01
☐ 274	Kevin Gamble Miami Heat	.10	.05	.01
☐ 275	Clifford Rozier Golden State Warriors	.30	.14	.04
☐ 276	B.J. Armstrong BCT Ron Harper Chicago Bulls	.10	.05	.01
☐ 277	John Stockton BCT Jeff Hornacek Utah Jazz	.15	.07	.02
☐ 278	Bobby Hurley BCT Mitch Richmond Sacramento Kings	.12	.05	.02
☐ 279	Anfernee Hardaway BCT Dennis Scott Orlando Magic	.30	.14	.04
☐ 280	Jason Kidd BCT Jim Jackson Dallas Mavericks	.75	.35	.09
☐ 281	Ron Harper Chicago Bulls	.12	.05	.02
☐ 282	Chuck Person San Antonio Spurs	.12	.05	.02
☐ 283	John Williams Cleveland Cavaliers	.12	.05	.02
☐ 284	Robert Pack Denver Nuggets	.10	.05	.01
☐ 285	Aaron McKie Portland Trail Blazers	.30	.14	.04
☐ 286	Chris Smith Minnesota Timberwolves	.10	.05	.01
☐ 287	Horace Grant Orlando Magic	.20	.09	.03
☐ 288	Oliver Miller Detroit Pistons	.10	.05	.01
☐ 289	Derek Harper New York Knicks	.10	.05	.01
☐ 290	Eric Mobley Milwaukee Bucks	.20	.09	.03
☐ 291	Scott Skiles Washington Bullets	.10	.05	.01
☐ 292	Olden Polynice Sacramento Kings	.10	.05	.01
☐ 293	Mark Jackson Indiana Pacers	.10	.05	.01
☐ 294	Wayman Tisdale Phoenix Suns	.12	.05	.02
☐ 295	Tony Dumas Dallas Mavericks	.12	.05	.02
☐ 296	Bryon Russell Utah Jazz	.10	.05	.01
☐ 297	Vlade Divac Los Angeles Lakers	.15	.07	.02
☐ 298	David Wesley Boston Celtics	.10	.05	.01
☐ 299	Askia Jones Minnesota Timberwolves	.10	.05	.01
☐ 300	B.J. Tyler Philadelphia 76ers	.12	.05	.02
☐ 301	Hakeem Olajuwon AI Houston Rockets	.50	.23	.06
☐ 302	Luc Longley AI Chicago Bulls	.10	.05	.01
☐ 303	Rony Seikaly AI Golden State Warriors	.10	.05	.01
☐ 304	Sarunas Marciulionis AI Seattle Supersonics	.10	.05	.01
☐ 305	Dikembe Mutombo AI Denver Nuggets	.12	.05	.02
☐ 306	Ken Norman Atlanta Hawks	.10	.05	.01
☐ 307	Dell Curry Charlotte Hornets	.10	.05	.01

☐ 308 Danny Ferry .... .10	.05	.01
Cleveland Cavaliers		
☐ 309 Shawn Kemp .... .75	.35	.09
Seattle Supersonics		
☐ 310 Dickey Simpkins .... .20	.09	.03
Chicago Bulls		
☐ 311 Johnny Newman .... .10	.05	.01
Milwaukee Bucks		
☐ 312 Dwayne Schintzius ...... .10	.05	.01
New Jersey Nets		
☐ 313 Sean Elliott .... .12	.05	.02
San Antonio Spurs		
☐ 314 Sean Rooks .... .10	.05	.01
Minnesota Timberwolves		
☐ 315 Bill Curley .... .20	.09	.03
Detroit Pistons		
☐ 316 Bryant Stith .... .10	.05	.01
Denver Nuggets		
☐ 317 Pooh Richardson .... .10	.05	.01
Los Angeles Clippers		
☐ 318 Jim McIlvaine .... .10	.05	.01
Washington Bullets		
☐ 319 Dennis Scott .... .10	.05	.01
Orlando Magic		
☐ 320 Wesley Person .... .75	.35	.09
Phoenix Suns		
☐ 321 Bobby Hurley .... .12	.05	.02
Sacramento Kings		
☐ 322 Armon Gilliam .... .10	.05	.01
New Jersey Nets		
☐ 323 Rik Smits .... .15	.07	.02
Indiana Pacers		
☐ 324 Tony Smith .... .10	.05	.01
Los Angeles Lakers		
☐ 325 Monty Williams .... .20	.09	.03
New York Knicks		
☐ 326 Gary Payton BCT .... .10	.05	.01
Kendall Gill		
Seattle Supersonics		
☐ 327 Mookie Blaylock BCT ... .10	.05	.01
Stacey Augmon		
Atlanta Hawks		
☐ 328 Mark Jackson BCT .... .12	.05	.02
Reggie Miller		
Indiana Pacers		
☐ 329 Sam Cassell BCT......... .10	.05	.01
Vernon Maxwell		
Houston Rockets		
☐ 330 Harold Miner BCT .... .12	.05	.02
Khalid Reeves		
Miami Heat		
☐ 331 Vinny Del Negro .... .10	.05	.01
San Antonio Spurs		
☐ 332 Billy Owens .... .12	.05	.02
Miami Heat		
☐ 333 Mark West .... .10	.05	.01
Detroit Pistons		
☐ 334 Matt Geiger .... .10	.05	.01
Miami Heat		
☐ 335 Greg Minor .... .10	.05	.01
Boston Celtics		
☐ 336 Larry Johnson .... .30	.14	.04
Charlotte Hornets		
☐ 337 Donald Hodge .... .10	.05	.01
Dallas Mavericks		
☐ 338 Aaron Williams .... .10	.05	.01
Milwaukee Bucks		
☐ 339 Jay Humphries .... .10	.05	.01
Utah Jazz		
☐ 340 Charlie Ward .... .30	.14	.04
New York Knicks		

☐ 341 Scott Brooks .... .10	.05	.01
Houston Rockets		
☐ 342 Stacey Augmon .... .12	.05	.02
Atlanta Hawks		
☐ 343 Will Perdue .... .10	.05	.01
Chicago Bulls		
☐ 344 Dale Ellis .... .12	.05	.02
Denver Nuggets		
☐ 345 Brooks Thompson .... .12	.05	.02
Orlando Magic		
☐ 346 Manute Bol .... .10	.05	.01
Golden State Warriors		
☐ 347 Kenny Anderson .... .15	.07	.02
New Jersey Nets		
☐ 348 Willie Burton .... .10	.05	.01
Philadelphia 76ers		
☐ 349 Michael Cage .... .10	.05	.01
Cleveland Cavaliers		
☐ 350 Danny Manning .... .15	.07	.02
Phoenix Suns		
☐ 351 Ricky Pierce .... .12	.05	.02
Golden State Warriors		
☐ 352 Sam Cassell .... .15	.07	.02
Houston Rockets		
☐ 353 Reggie Miller FG .... .15	.07	.02
Indiana Pacers		
☐ 354 David Robinson FG ...... .40	.18	.05
San Antonio Spurs		
☐ 355 Shaquille O'Neal FG ... 1.00	.45	.13
Orlando Magic		
☐ 356 Scottie Pippen FG .... .15	.07	.02
Chicago Bulls		
☐ 357 Alonzo Mourning FG .... .25	.11	.03
Charlotte Hornets		
☐ 358 Clarence Weatherspoon FG .10	.05	.01
Philadelphia 76ers		
☐ 359 Derrick Coleman FG ..... .10	.05	.01
New Jersey Nets		
☐ 360 Charles Barkley FG ...... .40	.18	.05
Phoenix Suns		
☐ 361 Karl Malone FG .... .15	.07	.02
Utah Jazz		
☐ 362 Chris Webber FG .... .30	.14	.04
Washington Bullets		

1994-95
Stadium Club
First Day Issue

This set parallels the basic issue 1994-95 Stadium Club set. First Day cards were ran-

domly inserted into both series packs at a rate of one in 24. The cards differ from their regular issue counterparts in that each First Day card has a gold-foil "First Day Issue" logo on front. Only the top few cards are priced below individually. Please refer to the multipliers provided below (coupled with the values of the corresponding regular issue cards) to ascertain value of unlisted singles.

	MINT	NRMT	EXC
COMPLETE SET (362)	1250.00	575.00	160.00
COMPLETE SERIES 1 (182).	750.00	350.00	95.00
COMPLETE SERIES 2 (180).	500.00	230.00	65.00
COMMON CARD (1-362)	2.00	.90	.25

STARS: 20X to 40X BASIC CARDS
ROOKIES: 7.5X to 15X BASIC CARDS

		MINT	NRMT	EXC
☐ 13	Charles Barkley .... Phoenix Suns	30.00	13.50	3.80
☐ 16	Anfernee Hardaway .... Orlando Magic	60.00	27.00	7.50
☐ 32	Shaquille O'Neal .... Orlando Magic	80.00	36.00	10.00
☐ 79	Hakeem Olajuwon ...... Houston Rockets	40.00	18.00	5.00
☐ 125	Jamal Mashburn ...... Dallas Mavericks	30.00	13.50	3.80
☐ 160	David Robinson .... San Antonio Spurs	30.00	13.50	3.80
☐ 172	Jason Kidd .... Dallas Mavericks	60.00	27.00	7.50
☐ 180	Eddie Jones .... Los Angeles Lakers	40.00	18.00	5.00
☐ 181	Grant Hill .... Detroit Pistons	100.00	45.00	12.50
☐ 183	Glenn Robinson .... Milwaukee Bucks	60.00	27.00	7.50
☐ 190	Jason Kidd .... Dallas Mavericks	30.00	13.50	3.80
☐ 195	Grant Hill................. Detroit Pistons	50.00	23.00	6.25
☐ 269	Nick Van Exel .... Los Angeles Lakers	30.00	13.50	3.80
☐ 309	Shawn Kemp............ Seattle Supersonics	30.00	13.50	3.80
☐ 355	Shaquille O'Neal FG . Orlando Magic	40.00	18.00	5.00

1994-95 Stadium Club Beam Team

Randomly inserted at a rate of 1 in every 24 second series packs, this 27-card standard-size set features a star player from each NBA team showcased by lazer light foil. The borderless fronts feature a player photo with his name in the upper left corner and the words "Beam Team" in funky lettering on the bottom. The backs are split between a player photo and some notes. Vital statistics are in the lower left corner

and the cards are numbered in the lower corner as "X" of 27. The set is sequenced in alphabetical order by team.

		MINT	NRMT	EXC
COMPLETE SET (27)		120.00	55.00	15.00
COMMON CARD (1-27)		1.00	.45	.13
☐ 1	Mookie Blaylock .... Atlanta Hawks	1.50	.65	.19
☐ 2	Dominique Wilkins ...... Boston Celtics	2.50	1.15	.30
☐ 3	Alonzo Mourning .... Charlotte Hornets	6.00	2.70	.75
☐ 4	Toni Kukoc .... Chicago Bulls	2.00	.35	.25
☐ 5	Mark Price .... Cleveland Cavaliers	2.00	.35	.25
☐ 6	Jason Kidd .... Dallas Mavericks	15.00	6.75	1.90
☐ 7	Jalen Rose .... Denver Nuggets	3.00	1.35	.40
☐ 8	Grant Hill .... Detroit Pistons	25.00	11.50	3.10
☐ 9	Latrell Sprewell.......... Golden State Warriors	6.00	2.70	.75
☐ 10	Hakeem Olajuwon ...... Houston Rockets	12.00	5.50	1.50
☐ 11	Reggie Miller .... Indiana Pacers	5.00	2.30	.60
☐ 12	Lamond Murray .... Los Angeles Clippers	2.50	1.15	.30
☐ 13	George Lynch .... Los Angeles Lakers	1.00	.45	.13
☐ 14	Khalid Reeves .... Miami Heat	2.50	1.15	.30
☐ 15	Glenn Robinson .... Milwaukee Bucks	15.00	6.75	1.90
☐ 16	Donyell Marshall .... Minnesota Timberwolves	3.00	1.35	.40
☐ 17	Derrick Coleman .... New Jersey Nets	3.00	1.35	.40
☐ 18	Patrick Ewing .... New York Knicks	5.00	2.30	.60
☐ 19	Shaquille O'Neal .... Orlando Magic	25.00	11.50	3.10
☐ 20	Clarence Weatherspoon Philadelphia 76ers	1.50	.65	.19
☐ 21	Charles Barkley .... Phoenix Suns	10.00	4.50	1.25
☐ 22	Clifford Robinson .... Portland Trail Blazers	2.00	.90	.25
☐ 23	Bobby Hurley .... Sacramento Kings	1.50	.65	.19
☐ 24	David Robinson .... San Antonio Spurs	10.00	4.50	1.25
☐ 25	Shawn Kemp................	10.00	4.50	1.25

	Seattle Supersonics		
☐ 26	Karl Malone.................. 5.00	2.30	.60
	Utah Jazz		
☐ 27	Chris Webber............... 8.00	3.60	1.00
	Washington Bullets		

1994-95 Stadium Club Clear Cut

Randomly inserted in all first series packs at a rate of one in 12, cards from this 27-card acetate set spotlight one key player from each NBA team. The set has "see through" fronts with some statistical information on the back. The player is identified on the right side of the card and the words "Clear Cut" are located in the bottom right. The set is sequenced in alphabetical order by teams.

	MINT	NRMT	EXC
COMPLETE SET (27)	75.00	34.00	9.50
COMMON CARD (1-27)	1.00	.45	.13

☐ 1	Stacey Augmon.............. 1.50	.65	.19	
	Atlanta Hawks			
☐ 2	Dino Radja 2.00	.90	.25	
	Boston Celtics			
☐ 3	Alonzo Mourning 6.00	2.70	.75	
	Charlotte Hornets			
☐ 4	Scottie Pippen............... 5.00	2.30	.60	
	Chicago Bulls			
☐ 5	Gerald Wilkins................ 1.00	.45	.13	
	Cleveland Cavaliers			
☐ 6	Jamal Mashburn 10.00	4.50	1.25	
	Dallas Mavericks			
☐ 7	Dikembe Mutombo 3.00	1.35	.40	
	Denver Nuggets			
☐ 8	Lindsey Hunter 1.00	.45	.13	
	Detroit Pistons			
☐ 9	Chris Mullin 2.00	.90	.25	
	Golden State Warriors			
☐ 10	Hakeem Olajuwon 12.00	5.50	1.50	
	Houston Rockets			
☐ 11	Reggie Miller.................. 5.00	2.30	.60	
	Indiana Pacers			
☐ 12	Gary Grant 1.00	.45	.13	
	Los Angeles Clippers			

☐ 13	Doug Christie................. 1.00	.45	.13	
	Los Angeles Lakers			
☐ 14	Steve Smith 1.50	.65	.19	
	Miami Heat			
☐ 15	Vin Baker 5.00	2.30	.60	
	Milwaukee Bucks			
☐ 16	Christian Laettner 1.50	.65	.19	
	Minnesota Timberwolves			
☐ 17	Derrick Coleman 2.00	.90	.25	
	New Jersey Nets			
☐ 18	Charles Oakley............... 1.50	.65	.19	
	New York Knicks			
☐ 19	Dennis Scott 1.00	.45	.13	
	Orlando Magic			
☐ 20	Clarence Weatherspoon 1.50	.65	.19	
	Philadelphia 76ers			
☐ 21	Charles Barkley 10.00	4.50	1.25	
	Phoenix Suns			
☐ 22	Clifford Robinson 1.50	.65	.19	
	Portland Trail Blazers			
☐ 23	Mitch Richmond 2.50	1.15	.30	
	Sacramento Kings			
☐ 24	David Robinson 10.00	4.50	1.25	
	San Antonio Spurs			
☐ 25	Shawn Kemp.............. 10.00	4.50	1.25	
	Seattle Supersonics			
☐ 26	Karl Malone.................... 5.00	2.30	.60	
	Utah Jazz			
☐ 27	Don MacLean.................. 1.00	.45	.13	
	Washington Bullets			

1994-95 Stadium Club Dynasty and Destiny

This 20-card standard-size set was randomly inserted in first series foil packs at a rate of one in six and were also inserted one per first series rack pack. This set features a mixture of youthful phenoms paired up with a matching veteran star. The borderless fronts feature player photos, the player's name in the upper left corner and either the word "Destiny" or "Dynasty" in the lower right. The back has a player photo in a lower corner with a brief note and stats on the other side.

	MINT	NRMT	EXC
COMPLETE SET (20)	12.00	5.50	1.50
COMMON DYNASTY (1A-10A)	.25	.11	.03
COMMON DESTINY (1B-10B)	.25	.11	.03
☐ 1A Mark Price	.25	.11	.03
Cleveland Cavaliers			
☐ 1B Kenny Anderson	.25	.11	.03
New Jersey Nets			
☐ 2A Karl Malone	.60	.25	.08
Utah Jazz			
☐ 2B Derrick Coleman	.25	.11	.03
New Jersey Nets			
☐ 3A John Stockton	.60	.25	.08
Utah Jazz			
☐ 3B Anfernee Hardaway	2.50	1.15	.30
Orlando Magic			
☐ 4A Mitch Richmond	.25	.11	.03
Sacramento Kings			
☐ 4B Jim Jackson	.75	.35	.09
Dallas Mavericks			
☐ 5A James Worthy	.25	.11	.03
Los Angeles Lakers			
☐ 5B Jamal Mashburn	1.25	.55	.16
Dallas Mavericks			
☐ 6A Patrick Ewing	.60	.25	.08
New York Knicks			
☐ 6B Alonzo Mourning	.75	.35	.09
Charlotte Hornets			
☐ 7A Hakeem Olajuwon	1.50	.65	.19
Houston Rockets			
☐ 7B Shaquille O'Neal	3.00	1.35	.40
Orlando Magic			
☐ 8A Clyde Drexler	.60	.25	.08
Portland Trail Blazers			
☐ 8B Isaiah Rider	.40	.18	.05
Minnesota Timberwolves			
☐ 9A Scottie Pippen	.60	.25	.08
Chicago Bulls			
☐ 9B Latrell Sprewell	.75	.35	.09
Golden State Warriors			
☐ 10A Charles Barkley	1.25	.55	.16
Phoenix Suns			
☐ 10B Chris Webber	1.00	.45	.13
Golden State Warriors			

1994-95 Stadium Club Rising Stars

Randomly inserted in all first series packs at a rate of one in 24, cards from this 10-card set feature a selection of young NBA stars. Card fronts feature full-color player action shots cut out against etched-foil backgrounds, with a prismatic galaxy design.

	MINT	NRMT	EXC
COMPLETE SET (12)	80.00	36.00	10.00
COMMON CARD (1-12)	1.50	.65	.19
☐ 1 Kenny Anderson	2.50	1.15	.30
New Jersey Nets			
☐ 2 Latrell Sprewell	8.00	3.60	1.00
Golden State Warriors			
☐ 3 Jamal Mashburn	12.00	5.50	1.50
Dallas Mavericks			
☐ 4 Alonzo Mourning	8.00	3.60	1.00
Charlotte Hornets			
☐ 5 Shaquille O'Neal	30.00	13.50	3.80
Orlando Magic			
☐ 6 LaPhonso Ellis	1.50	.65	.19
Denver Nuggets			
☐ 7 Chris Webber	10.00	4.50	1.25
Golden State Warriors			
☐ 8 Isaiah Rider	4.00	1.80	.50
Minnesota Timberwolves			
☐ 9 Dikembe Mutombo	4.00	1.80	.50
Denver Nuggets			
☐ 10 Anfernee Hardaway	25.00	11.50	3.10
Orlando Magic			
☐ 11 Antonio Davis	1.50	.65	.19
Indiana Pacers			
☐ 12 Robert Horry	2.50	1.15	.30
Houston Rockets			

1994-95 Stadium Club Super Skills

Randomly inserted at a rate of 1 in every 24 second series 12-card packs and seeded one per second series retail rack pack, cards from this 25-card set feature Topps selection of the five top players at each position in the NBA. Card fronts feature a multi-hued rainbow foil background.

	MINT	NRMT	EXC
COMPLETE SET (25)	60.00	27.00	7.50
COMMON CARD (1-25)	1.00	.45	.13

		MINT	NRMT	EXC
☐ 1	Mark Price	1.50	.65	.19
	Cleveland Cavaliers			
☐ 2	Tim Hardaway	1.50	.65	.19
	Golden State Warriors			
☐ 3	Kevin Johnson	2.00	.90	.25
	Phoenix Suns			
☐ 4	John Stockton	4.00	1.80	.50
	Utah Jazz			
☐ 5	Mookie Blaylock	1.00	.45	.13
	New Jersey Nets			
☐ 6	Reggie Miller	4.00	1.80	.50
	Indiana Pacers			
☐ 7	Jeff Hornacek	1.00	.45	.13
	Utah Jazz			
☐ 8	Latrell Sprewell	5.00	2.30	.60
	Golden State Warriors			
☐ 9	John Starks	1.00	.45	.13
	New York Knicks			
☐ 10	Nate McMillan	1.00	.45	.13
	Seattle Supersonics			
☐ 11	Chris Mullin	1.50	.65	.19
	Golden State Warriors			
☐ 12	Toni Kukoc	1.50	.65	.19
	Chicago Bulls			
☐ 13	Anthony Mason	1.00	.45	.13
	New York Knicks			
☐ 14	Robert Horry	1.50	.65	.19
	Houston Rockets			
☐ 15	Scottie Pippen	4.00	1.80	.50
	Chicago Bulls			
☐ 16	Charles Barkley	8.00	3.60	1.00
	Phoenix Suns			
☐ 17	Dennis Rodman	2.50	1.15	.30
	San Antonio Spurs			
☐ 18	Karl Malone	4.00	1.80	.50
	Utah Jazz			
☐ 19	Chris Webber	6.00	2.70	.75
	Washington Bullets			
☐ 20	Charles Oakley	1.00	.45	.13
	New York Knicks			
☐ 21	Patrick Ewing	4.00	1.80	.50
	New York Knicks			
☐ 22	Shaquille O'Neal	20.00	9.00	2.50
	Orlando Magic			
☐ 23	Dikembe Mutombo	2.50	1.15	.30
	Denver Nuggets			
☐ 24	David Robinson	8.00	3.60	1.00
	San Antonio Spurs			
☐ 25	Hakeem Olajuwon	10.00	4.50	1.25
	Houston Rockets			

winning cards (Houston, Indiana, Orlando, Phoenix and San Antonio) carry "W" designations. In addition "C", "D" and "F" designations are used to denote conference, division and finals winners.

	MINT	NRMT	EXC
COMPLETE SET (27)	100.00	45.00	12.50
COMMON TEAM (1-27)	1.00	.45	.13

		MINT	NRMT	EXC
☐ 1	Atlanta/K.Willis	1.00	.45	.13
☐ 2	Boston/Group	1.00	.45	.13
☐ 3	Charlotte/M.Bogues	1.50	.65	.19
☐ 4	Chicago/Group	1.00	.45	.13
☐ 5	Cleveland/D.Ferry	1.00	.45	.13
☐ 6	Dallas/J.Jackson	3.00	1.35	.40
☐ 7	Denver/R.Rogers	1.50	.65	.19
☐ 8	Detroit/Dumars	1.50	.65	.19
☐ 9	Golden State/C.Webber..	4.00	1.80	.50
☐ 10	Houston/Olajuwon WCF	50.00	23.00	6.25
☐ 11	Indiana/R.Smits WD	3.00	1.35	.40
☐ 12	LA Clippers/Group	1.00	.45	.13
☐ 13	LA Lakers/N.Van Exel...	5.00	2.30	.60
☐ 14	Miami/G.Rice	1.50	.65	.19
☐ 15	Milwaukee/V.Baker	2.50	1.15	.30
☐ 16	Minnesota/Laettner	1.50	.65	.19
☐ 17	New Jersey/C.Morris	1.00	.45	.13
☐ 18	New York/Group	1.00	.45	.13
☐ 19	Orlando/O'Neal WCD..	20.00	9.00	2.50
☐ 20	Philadelphia/D.Barros..	1.50	.65	.19
☐ 21	Phoenix/C.Barkley WB .	6.00	2.70	.75
☐ 22	Portland/Group	1.00	.45	.13
☐ 23	Sacramento/O.Polynice	1.00	.45	.13
☐ 24	San Antonio/Group WD	5.00	2.30	.60
☐ 25	Seattle/Group	1.00	.45	.13
☐ 26	Utah/J.Stockton	2.50	1.15	.30
☐ 27	Washington/Group	1.00	.45	.13

1994-95 Stadium Club Super Teams

Randomly inserted in all first series packs at a rate of one in 24, cards from this 27-card set feature an action shot or group photo from each team in the league. Teams that won either their Division, their Conference or the NBA Finals were redeemable for special team sets or other prizes. The expiration date for Super Team cards was December 31st, 1995. The five

1994-95 Stadium Club Super Teams Division Winners

Each of these four team sets was available exclusively by mailing in the corresponding winning Super Team card before the December 31st, 1995 deadline. Super Team cards were randomly seeded in all first series Stadium Club packs at a rate of

The card design parallels the regular issue Stadium Club cards. In fact, the only way to tell these cards apart is by the gold foil "Division Winner" logo on each card front. The cards are listed below alphabetically according to teams; the prefixes M, P, SP, and SU have been added to denote Magic, Pacers, Spurs and Suns respectively.

	MINT	NRMT	EXC
COMP.BAG MAGIC (11)	10.00	4.50	1.25
COMP.BAG PACERS (11)	3.00	1.35	.40
COMP.BAG SPURS (11)	5.00	2.30	.60
COMP.BAG SUNS (11)	6.00	2.70	.75
COMMON CARD	.25	.11	.03

☐	M7 Donald Royal Orlando Magic	.25	.11	.03
☐	M16 Anfernee Hardaway Orlando Magic	4.00	1.80	.50
☐	M32 Shaquille O'Neal Orlando Magic	6.00	2.70	.75
☐	M58 Nick Anderson Orlando Magic	.35	.16	.04
☐	M74 Jeff Turner Orlando Magic	.25	.11	.03
☐	M213 Anthony Bowie Orlando Magic	.25	.11	.03
☐	M232 Brian Shaw Orlando Magic	.25	.11	.03
☐	M287 Horace Grant Orlando Magic	.60	.25	.08
☐	M319 Dennis Scott Orlando Magic	.25	.11	.03
☐	M345 Brooks Thompson Orlando Magic	.25	.11	.03
☐	MD19 Magic DW Super Team	1.00	.45	.13
☐	P26 Vern Fleming Indiana Pacers	.25	.11	.03
☐	P46 Haywoode Workman Indiana Pacers	.25	.11	.03
☐	P86 Derrick McKey Indiana Pacers	.35	.16	.04
☐	P121 Antonio Davis Indiana Pacers	.25	.11	.03
☐	P144 Reggie Miller Indiana Pacers	1.25	.55	.16
☐	P188 Dale Davis Indiana Pacers	.35	.16	.04
☐	P219 Duane Ferrell Indiana Pacers	.25	.11	.03
☐	P259 Byron Scott Indiana Pacers	.35	.16	.04
☐	P293 Mark Jackson Indiana Pacers	.25	.11	.03
☐	P323 Rik Smits Indiana Pacers	.50	.23	.06
☐	PD11 Pacers DW Super Team	1.00	.45	.13
☐	SP52 J.R. Reid San Antonio Spurs	.25	.11	.03
☐	SP72 Dennis Rodman San Antonio Spurs	.75	.35	.09
☐	SP73 Dennis Rodman San Antonio Spurs	.35	.16	.04
☐	SP122 Terry Cummings San Antonio Spurs	.35	.16	.04
☐	SP160 David Robinson San Antonio Spurs	2.50	1.15	.30
☐	SP206 Willie Anderson San Antonio Spurs	.25	.11	.03

one in 24. The card design parallels the

☐	SP282 Chuck Person San Antonio Spurs	.35	.16	.04
☐	SP313 Sean Elliott San Antonio Spurs	.35	.16	.04
☐	SP331 Vinny Del Negro San Antonio Spurs	.25	.11	.03
☐	SP354 David Robinson San Antonio Spurs	1.25	.55	.16
☐	SPD24 Spurs DW Super Team	1.00	.45	.13
☐	SU13 Charles Barkley Phoenix Suns	2.50	1.15	.30
☐	SU70 Kevin Johnson Phoenix Suns	.60	.25	.08
☐	SU118 Danny Ainge Orlando Magic	.35	.16	.04
☐	SU152 A.C. Green Phoenix Suns	.35	.16	.04
☐	SU196 Joe Kleine Phoenix Suns	.25	.11	.03
☐	SU257 Dan Majerle Phoenix Suns	.35	.16	.04
☐	SU294 Wayman Tisdale Phoenix Suns	.35	.16	.04
☐	SU320 Wesley Person Phoenix Suns	2.00	.90	.25
☐	SU350 Danny Manning Phoenix Suns	.50	.23	.06
☐	SU360 Charles Barkley Phoenix Suns	1.25	.55	.16
☐	SUD21 Suns DW Super Team	1.00	.45	.13

1994-95 Stadium Club Super Teams Master Photos

Each of these two over-sized (5" by 7") team sets were available exclusively by mailing in the corresponding winning Super Team card before the December 31st, 1995 deadline. Super Team cards were randomly seeded in all first series Stadium Club packs at a rate of one in 24. The card design loosely parallels the corresponding regular issue Stadium Club cards but the bold, wildly designed borders and separate numbering sequences create distinctive differences. The cards are listed below alpha-

betically according to teams; the prefixes M and R have been added to denote Magic and Rockets respectively.

	MINT	NRMT	EXC
COMP.BAG MAGIC (11)	15.00	6.75	1.90
COMP.BAG ROCKETS (11)	8.00	3.60	1.00
COMMON CARD	.40	.18	.05
☐ M1 Nick Anderson	.60	.25	.08
☐ M2 Anthony Bowie	.40	.18	.05
☐ M3 Jeff Turner	.40	.18	.05
☐ M4 Dennis Scott	.40	.18	.05
☐ M5 Horace Grant	1.00	.45	.13
☐ M6 Shaquille O'Neal	10.00	4.50	1.25
☐ M7 Brooks Thompson	.40	.18	.05
☐ M8 Anfernee Hardaway	6.00	2.70	.75
☐ M9 Donald Royal	.40	.18	.05
☐ M10 Brian Shaw	.40	.18	.05
☐ MM19 Magic MP Super Team	1.00	.45	.13
☐ R1 Tim Breaux	.40	.18	.05
☐ R2 Scott Brooks	.40	.18	.05
☐ R3 Clyde Drexler Hakeem Olajuwon	3.00	1.35	.40
☐ R4 Hakeem Olajuwon	5.00	2.30	.60
☐ R5 Sam Cassell	.60	.25	.08
☐ R6 Vernon Maxwell	.40	.18	.05
☐ R7 Mario Ellie	.40	.18	.05
☐ R8 Carl Herrera	.40	.18	.05
☐ R9 Kenny Smith	.40	.18	.05
☐ R10 Robert Horry	.75	.35	.09
☐ MR10 Rockets MP Super Team	1.00	.45	.13

1994-95 Stadium Club Super Teams NBA Finals

Available exclusively by redeeming the Stadium Club Super Teams Houston Rockets card before the December 31st, 1995 deadline, this 362-card set parallels the basic issue 1994-95 Stadium Club set. In fact, the only difference between Super Teams NBA Finals cards and basic issue Stadium Club cards is the gold foil NBA Finals logo placed on each card front. Only the top few cards are priced below individually. Please refer to the multipliers provided

below (coupled with the value of the corresponding regular issue card) to ascertain value.

	MINT	NRMT	EXC
COMPLETE SET (363)	50.00	23.00	6.25
COMMON CARD (1-362)	.15	.07	.02
*STARS: 1.25X to 2.5X BASIC CARDS			
*ROOKIES: 1X to 2X BASIC CARDS			
☐ 13 Charles Barkley Phoenix Suns	2.00	.90	.25
☐ 16 Anfernee Hardaway Orlando Magic	4.00	1.80	.50
☐ 32 Shaquille O'Neal Orlando Magic	5.00	2.30	.60
☐ 79 Hakeem Olajuwon Houston Rockets	2.50	1.15	.30
☐ 125 Jamal Mashburn Dallas Mavericks	2.00	.90	.25
☐ 160 David Robinson San Antonio Spurs	2.00	.90	.25
☐ 180 Eddie Jones Los Angeles Lakers	5.00	2.30	.60
☐ 181 Grant Hill Detroit Pistons	12.00	5.50	1.50
☐ 183 Glenn Robinson Milwaukee Bucks	8.00	3.60	1.00
☐ 190 Jason Kidd Dallas Mavericks	4.00	1.80	.50
☐ 195 Grant Hill Detroit Pistons	6.00	2.70	.75
☐ 269 Nick Van Exel Los Angeles Lakers	2.00	.90	.25
☐ 309 Shawn Kemp Seattle Supersonics	2.00	.90	.25
☐ 355 Shaquille O'Neal FG Orlando Magic	2.50	1.15	.30
☐ NF10 Rockets NF Super Team	1.00	.45	.13

1994-95 Stadium Club Team of the Future

Randomly inserted at a rate of 1 in every 24 second series packs, this 10-card standard-size set is comprised of tomorrow's superstars. Card fronts feature color player action shots against brilliant gold, etched-foil backgrounds.

	MINT	NRMT	EXC
COMPLETE SET (10)	75.00	34.00	9.50
COMMON CARD (1-10)	5.00	2.30	.60

☐ 1	Anfernee Hardaway Orlando Magic	15.00	6.75	1.90
☐ 2	Latrell Sprewell Golden State Warriors	5.00	2.30	.60
☐ 3	Grant Hill Detroit Pistons	20.00	9.00	2.50
☐ 4	Chris Webber Washington Bullets	6.00	2.70	.75
☐ 5	Shaquille O'Neal Orlando Magic	20.00	9.00	2.50
☐ 6	Jason Kidd Dallas Mavericks	12.00	5.50	1.50
☐ 7	Jim Jackson Dallas Mavericks	5.00	2.30	.60
☐ 8	Jamal Mashburn Dallas Mavericks	8.00	3.60	1.00
☐ 9	Glenn Robinson Milwaukee Bucks	12.00	5.50	1.50
☐ 10	Alonzo Mourning Charlotte Hornets	5.00	2.30	.60

1983 Star All-Star Game

This was the first NBA set issued by Star Company. The 30-card set was issued in a clear, sealed plastic bag and distributed through hobby dealers. According to information provided on the order forms, Star Company printed 15,000 sets. The sets originally retailed for $2.50 to $5.00 each. Each card measures 2 1/2" by 3 1/2". Each card has a blue border on the front and blue print on the back. The set commemorates the 1983 NBA All-Star Game held in Los Angeles. Many of the cards feature players in their All-Star uniforms. There are two unnumbered cards in the set listed at the end of the checklist below. The cards are numbered on the back with the order of the numbering essentially alphabetical according to the player's name. The set features the first professional card of Isiah Thomas.

	NRMT-MT	EXC	VG
COMPLETE BAG SET (32)	75.00	34.00	9.50
COMMON CARD (1-30)	2.00	.90	.25
*OPENED SET: .75X to 1.0X VALUE.			

☐ 1	Checklist (Julius Erving on front)	9.00	4.00	1.15
☐ 2	Larry Bird	30.00	13.50	3.80
☐ 3	Maurice Cheeks	2.50	1.15	.30
☐ 4	Julius Erving	14.00	6.25	1.75
☐ 5	Marques Johnson	2.50	1.15	.30
☐ 6	Bill Laimbeer	3.00	1.35	.40
☐ 7	Moses Malone	5.00	2.30	.60
☐ 8	Sidney Moncrief	2.50	1.15	.30
☐ 9	Robert Parish	5.00	2.30	.60
☐ 10	Reggie Theus	2.50	1.15	.30
☐ 11	Isiah Thomas	20.00	9.00	2.50
☐ 12	Andrew Toney	2.00	.90	.25
☐ 13	Buck Williams	4.00	1.80	.50
☐ 14	Kareem Abdul-Jabbar	12.00	5.50	1.50
☐ 15	Alex English	2.50	1.15	.30
☐ 16	George Gervin	6.00	2.70	.75
☐ 17	Artis Gilmore	3.00	1.35	.40
☐ 18	Magic Johnson	20.00	9.00	2.50
☐ 19	Maurice Lucas	2.50	1.15	.30
☐ 20	Jim Paxson	2.00	.90	.25
☐ 21	Jack Sikma	3.00	1.35	.40
☐ 22	David Thompson	5.00	2.30	.60
☐ 23	Kiki Vandeweghe	2.00	.90	.25
☐ 24	Jamaal Wilkes	2.50	1.15	.30
☐ 25	Gus Williams	2.00	.90	.25
☐ 26	All-Star MVPs (Dr. J, '77, '83)	9.00	4.00	1.15
☐ 27	One Player, Single-Game Records (Theus and Malone)	2.50	1.15	.30
☐ 28	All-Star All-Time Leaders (East Coast Line)	2.00	.90	.25
☐ 29	East Box Score (Boston Bombers: Bird and Parish)	18.00	8.00	2.30
☐ 30	West Box Score (Moncrief Soars)	2.00	.90	.25
☐ xx	Gilmore and English (Ad on back)	2.50	1.15	.30
☐ xx	Kareem Abdul-Jabbar (Uncut sheet offer on back)	12.00	5.50	1.50

1983-84 Star

This set of 276 cards was issued in four series during the first six months of 1984. Several teams in the first series (1-100) are difficult to obtain due to extensive miscuts (all of which, according to the company,

were destroyed) in the initial production process. The team sets were issued in clear sealed bags. Many of the team bags were distributed to hobby dealers through a small group of Star Co. master distributors. According to Star Company's original sales materials and order forms, reportedly 5,000 team bags were printed for each team although quality control problems with the early sets apparently reduced that number considerably. The retail price per bag was $2.50 to $5 for most of the teams. Cards measure 2 1/2" by 3 1/2". Color borders around the fronts and color printing on the backs correspond to team colors. Cards are numbered according to team order, e.g., Philadelphia 76ers (1-12), Los Angeles Lakers (13-25), Boston Celtics (26-37), Milwaukee Bucks (38-48), Dallas Mavericks (49-60), New York Knicks (61-72), Houston Rockets (73-84), Detroit Pistons (85-96), Portland Trail Blazers (97-108), Phoenix Suns (109-120), San Diego Clippers (121-132), Utah Jazz (133-144), New Jersey Nets (145-156), Indiana Pacers (157-168), Chicago Bulls (169-180), Denver Nuggets (181-192), Seattle Supersonics (193-203), Washington Bullets (204-215), Kansas City Kings (216-227), Cleveland Cavaliers (228-240), San Antonio Spurs (241-251), Golden State Warriors (252-263), and Atlanta Hawks (264-275). Extended Rookie Cards include Mark Aguirre, Danny Ainge, Rolando Blackman, Tom Chambers, Clyde Drexler, Dale Ellis, Derek Harper, Larry Nance, Rickey Pierce, Isiah Thomas, Dominique Wilkins, Buck Williams and James Worthy. A promotional card of Sidney Moncrief was produced in limited quantities, but it was numbered 39 rather than 38 as it was in the regular set. There is typically a slight discount on sales of opened team bags.

	NRMT-MT	EXC	VG
COMPLETE BAG SET (276)	2400.00	1100.00	300.00
COMP.BAG 76ERS (12)	120.00	55.00	15.00
COMP.BAG LAKERS (13)	200.00	90.00	25.00
COMP.BAG CELTICS (12)	600.00	275.00	75.00
COMP.BAG BUCKS (11)	60.00	27.00	7.50
COMP.BAG MAVS (12)	425.00	190.00	52.50
COMP.BAG KNICKS (12)	20.00	9.00	2.50
COMP.BAG ROCKETS (12)	15.00	6.75	1.90
COMP.BAG PISTONS (12)	160.00	70.00	20.00
COMP.BAG BLAZERS (12)	250.00	115.00	31.00
COMP.BAG SUNS (12)	60.00	27.00	7.50
COMP.BAG CLIPPERS (12)	60.00	27.00	7.50
COMP.BAG JAZZ (12)	20.00	9.00	2.50
COMP.BAG NETS (12)	20.00	9.00	2.50
COMP.BAG PACERS (12)	15.00	6.75	1.90
COMP.BAG BULLS (12)	25.00	11.50	3.10
COMP.BAG NUGGETS (12)	20.00	9.00	2.50
COMP.BAG SONICS (11)	50.00	23.00	6.25
COMP.BAG BULLETS (12)	25.00	11.50	3.10
COMP.BAG KINGS (12)	20.00	9.00	2.50
COMP.BAG CAVS (13)	20.00	9.00	2.50
COMP.BAG SPURS (11)	25.00	11.50	3.10
COMP.BAG WARRIORS (11)	15.00	6.75	1.90
COMP.BAG HAWKS (14)	200.00	90.00	25.00
COMMON 76ERS SP (1-12)	4.00	1.80	.50
COMMON LAKERS SP (13-25)	4.00	1.80	.50
COMMON CELTICS SP (26-37)	8.00	3.60	1.00
COMMON BUCKS SP (38-48)	4.00	1.80	.50
COMMON MAVS SP (49-60) !	20.00	9.00	2.50
COMMON KNICKS (61-72)	2.00	.90	.25
COMMON ROCKETS (73-84)	2.00	.90	.25
COMMON PISTONS (85-96)	2.00	.90	.25
COMMON BLAZERS (97-108)	2.00	.90	.25
COMMON SUNS (109-120)	2.00	.90	.25
COMMON CLIPPERS (121-132)	2.00	.90	.25
COMMON JAZZ (133-144)	2.00	.90	.25
COMMON NETS (145-156)	2.00	.90	.25
COMMON PACERS (157-168)	2.00	.90	.25
COMMON BULLS (169-180)	2.00	.90	.25
COMMON NUGGETS (181-192)	2.00	.90	.25
COMMON SONICS (193-203)	2.00	.90	.25
COMMON BULLETS (204-215)	2.00	.90	.25
COMMON KINGS (216-227)	2.00	.90	.25
COMMON CAVS (228-240)	2.00	.90	.25
COMMON SPURS (241-251)	2.00	.90	.25
COMMON WARRIORS (252-262)	2.00	.90	.25
COMMON HAWKS (263-276)	2.00	.90	.25
OPENED TEAM SETS: .75X to 1.0 VALUE			

		NRMT-MT	EXC	VG
☐	1 Julius Erving	75.00	34.00	9.50
☐	2 Maurice Cheeks	12.00	5.50	1.50
☐	3 Franklin Edwards	4.00	1.80	.50
☐	4 Marc Iavaroni	4.00	1.80	.50
☐	5 Clemon Johnson	4.00	1.80	.50
☐	6 Bobby Jones	10.00	4.50	1.25
☐	7 Moses Malone	25.00	11.50	3.10
☐	8 Leo Rautins	4.00	1.80	.50
☐	9 Clint Richardson	4.00	1.80	.50
☐	10 Sedale Threatt	15.00	6.75	1.90
☐	11 Andrew Toney	10.00	4.50	1.25
☐	12 Sam Williams	4.00	1.80	.50
☐	13 Magic Johnson	150.00	70.00	19.00
☐	14 Kareem Abdul-Jabbar	40.00	18.00	5.00
☐	15 Michael Cooper	10.00	4.50	1.25
☐	16 Calvin Garrett	4.00	1.80	.50
☐	17 Mitch Kupchak	4.00	1.80	.50
☐	18 Bob McAdoo	12.00	5.50	1.50
☐	19 Mike McGee	4.00	1.80	.50
☐	20 Swen Nater	4.00	1.80	.50
☐	21 Kurt Rambis	8.00	3.60	1.00
☐	22 Byron Scott	25.00	11.50	3.10
☐	23 Larry Spriggs	4.00	1.80	.50
☐	24 Jamaal Wilkes	8.00	3.60	1.00
☐	25 James Worthy	45.00	20.00	5.75
☐	26 Larry Bird	400.00	180.00	50.00
☐	27 Danny Ainge	50.00	23.00	6.25
☐	28 Quinn Buckner	9.00	4.00	1.15
☐	29 M.L. Carr	9.00	4.00	1.15
☐	30 Carlos Clark	8.00	3.60	1.00
☐	31 Gerald Henderson	8.00	3.60	1.00
☐	32 Dennis Johnson	15.00	6.75	1.90
☐	33 Cedric Maxwell	10.00	4.50	1.25
☐	34 Kevin McHale	55.00	25.00	7.00
☐	35 Robert Parish	45.00	20.00	5.75
☐	36 Scott Wedman	8.00	3.60	1.00
☐	37 Greg Kite	8.00	3.60	1.00
☐	38 Sidney Moncrief	15.00	6.75	1.90
☐	39A Sidney Moncrief (Promotional card)	30.00	13.50	3.80
☐	39B Nate Archibald	15.00	6.75	1.90
☐	40 Randy Breuer	4.00	1.80	.50
☐	41 Junior Bridgeman	5.00	2.30	.60
☐	42 Harvey Catchings	4.00	1.80	.50
☐	43 Kevin Grevey	4.00	1.80	.50
☐	44 Marques Johnson	10.00	4.50	1.25
☐	45 Bob Lanier	20.00	9.00	2.50
☐	46 Alton Lister	4.00	1.80	.50

☐ 47	Paul Mokeski	4.00	1.80	.50
☐ 48	Paul Pressey	5.00	2.30	.60
☐ 49	Mark Aguirre	40.00	18.00	5.00
☐ 50	Rolando Blackman	40.00	18.00	5.00
☐ 51	Pat Cummings	20.00	9.00	2.50
☐ 52	Brad Davis	25.00	11.50	3.10
☐ 53	Dale Ellis	40.00	18.00	5.00
☐ 54	Bill Garnett	20.00	9.00	2.50
☐ 55	Derek Harper	80.00	36.00	10.00
☐ 56	Kurt Nimphius	20.00	9.00	2.50
☐ 57	Jim Spanarkel	20.00	9.00	2.50
☐ 58	Elston Turner	20.00	9.00	2.50
☐ 59	Jay Vincent	20.00	9.00	2.50
☐ 60	Mark West	25.00	11.50	3.10
☐ 61	Bernard King	8.00	3.60	1.00
☐ 62	Bill Cartwright	5.00	2.30	.60
☐ 63	Len Elmore	2.00	.90	.25
☐ 64	Eric Fernsten	2.00	.90	.25
☐ 65	Ernie Grunfeld	2.00	.90	.25
☐ 66	Louis Orr	2.00	.90	.25
☐ 67	Leonard Robinson	3.00	1.35	.40
☐ 68	Rory Sparrow	2.00	.90	.25
☐ 69	Trent Tucker	2.00	.90	.25
☐ 70	Darrell Walker	3.00	1.35	.40
☐ 71	Marvin Webster	4.00	1.80	.50
☐ 72	Ray Williams	2.00	.90	.25
☐ 73	Ralph Sampson	6.00	2.70	.75
☐ 74	James Bailey	2.00	.90	.25
☐ 75	Phil Ford	3.00	1.35	.40
☐ 76	Elvin Hayes	10.00	4.50	1.25
☐ 77	Caldwell Jones	3.00	1.35	.40
☐ 78	Major Jones	2.00	.90	.25
☐ 79	Allen Leavell	2.00	.90	.25
☐ 80	Lewis Lloyd	2.00	.90	.25
☐ 81	Rodney McCray	2.00	.90	.25
☐ 82	Robert Reid	2.00	.90	.25
☐ 83	Terry Teagle	2.00	.90	.25
☐ 84	Wally Walker	2.00	.90	.25
☐ 85	Kelly Tripucka	2.00	.90	.25
☐ 86	Kent Benson	3.00	1.35	.40
☐ 87	Earl Cureton	2.00	.90	.25
☐ 88	Lionel Hollins	2.00	.90	.25
☐ 89	Vinnie Johnson	3.00	1.35	.40
☐ 90	Bill Laimbeer	5.00	2.30	.60
☐ 91	Cliff Levingston	2.00	.90	.25
☐ 92	John Long	2.00	.90	.25
☐ 93	David Thirdkill	2.00	.90	.25
☐ 94	Isiah Thomas	120.00	55.00	15.00
☐ 95	Ray Tolbert	2.00	.90	.25
☐ 96	Terry Tyler	2.00	.90	.25
☐ 97	Jim Paxson	2.00	.90	.25
☐ 98	Kenny Carr	2.00	.90	.25
☐ 99	Wayne Cooper	2.00	.90	.25
☐ 100	Clyde Drexler	225.00	100.00	28.00
☐ 101	Jeff Lamp	2.00	.90	.25
☐ 102	Lafayette Lever	4.00	1.80	.50
☐ 103	Calvin Natt	2.00	.90	.25
☐ 104	Audie Norris	2.00	.90	.25
☐ 105	Tom Piotrowski	2.00	.90	.25
☐ 106	Mychal Thompson	3.00	1.35	.40
☐ 107	Darnell Valentine	2.00	.90	.25
☐ 108	Pete Verhoeven	2.00	.90	.25
☐ 109	Walter Davis	6.00	2.70	.75
☐ 110	Alvan Adams	3.00	1.35	.40
☐ 111	James Edwards	3.00	1.35	.40
☐ 112	Rod Foster	2.00	.90	.25
☐ 113	Maurice Lucas	3.00	1.35	.40
☐ 114	Kyle Macy	3.00	1.35	.40
☐ 115	Larry Nance	30.00	13.50	3.80
☐ 116	Charles Pittman	2.00	.90	.25
☐ 117	Rick Robey	3.00	1.35	.40
☐ 118	Mike Sanders	2.00	.90	.25
☐ 119	Alvin Scott	2.00	.90	.25
☐ 120	Paul Westphal	10.00	4.50	1.25
☐ 121	Bill Walton	20.00	9.00	2.50
☐ 122	Michael Brooks	2.00	.90	.25
☐ 123	Terry Cummings	12.00	5.50	1.50
☐ 124	James Donaldson	3.00	1.35	.40
☐ 125	Craig Hodges	4.00	1.80	.50
☐ 126	Greg Kelser	2.00	.90	.25
☐ 127	Hank McDowell	2.00	.90	.25
☐ 128	Billy McKinney	2.00	.90	.25
☐ 129	Norm Nixon	3.00	1.35	.40
☐ 130	Ricky Pierce UER	15.00	6.75	1.90
	(Misspelled Rickey on both sides)			
☐ 131	Derek Smith	2.00	.90	.25
☐ 132	Jerome Whitehead	2.00	.90	.25
☐ 133	Adrian Dantley	8.00	3.60	1.00
☐ 134	Mitch Anderson	2.00	.90	.25
☐ 135	Thurl Bailey	4.00	1.80	.50
☐ 136	Tom Boswell	2.00	.90	.25
☐ 137	John Drew	2.00	.90	.25
☐ 138	Mark Eaton	5.00	2.30	.60
☐ 139	Jerry Eaves	2.00	.90	.25
☐ 140	Rickey Green	3.00	1.35	.40
☐ 141	Darrell Griffith	3.00	1.35	.40
☐ 142	Bobby Hansen	2.00	.90	.25
☐ 143	Rich Kelley	2.00	.90	.25
☐ 144	Jeff Wilkins	2.00	.90	.25
☐ 145	Buck Williams	20.00	9.00	2.50
☐ 146	Otis Birdsong	3.00	1.35	.40
☐ 147	Darwin Cook	2.00	.90	.25
☐ 148	Darryl Dawkins	5.00	2.30	.60
☐ 149	Mike Gminski	3.00	1.35	.40
☐ 150	Reggie Johnson	2.00	.90	.25
☐ 151	Albert King	2.00	.90	.25
☐ 152	Mike O'Koren	3.00	1.35	.40
☐ 153	Kelvin Ransey	2.00	.90	.25
☐ 154	Micheal Ray Richardson	2.00	.90	.25
☐ 155	Clarence Walker	2.00	.90	.25
☐ 156	Bill Willoughby	2.00	.90	.25
☐ 157	Steve Stipanovich	3.00	1.35	.40
☐ 158	Butch Carter	2.00	.90	.25
☐ 159	Edwin Leroy Combs	2.00	.90	.25
☐ 160	George L. Johnson	2.00	.90	.25
☐ 161	Clark Kellogg	3.00	1.35	.40
☐ 162	Sidney Lowe	2.00	.90	.25
☐ 163	Kevin McKenna	2.00	.90	.25
☐ 164	Jerry Sichting	2.00	.90	.25
☐ 165	Brook Steppe	2.00	.90	.25
☐ 166	Jimmy Thomas	2.00	.90	.25
☐ 167	Granville Waiters	2.00	.90	.25
☐ 168	Herb Williams	3.00	1.35	.40
☐ 169	Dave Corzine	3.00	1.35	.40
☐ 170	Wallace Bryant	2.00	.90	.25
☐ 171	Quintin Dailey	2.00	.90	.25
☐ 172	Sidney Green	3.00	1.35	.40
☐ 173	David Greenwood	3.00	1.35	.40
☐ 174	Rod Higgins	2.00	.90	.25
☐ 175	Clarence Johnson	2.00	.90	.25
☐ 176	Ronnie Lester	2.00	.90	.25
☐ 177	Jawann Oldham	2.00	.90	.25
☐ 178	Ennis Whatley	2.00	.90	.25
☐ 179	Mitchell Wiggins	2.00	.90	.25
☐ 180	Orlando Woolridge	8.00	3.60	1.00
☐ 181	Kiki Vandeweghe	6.00	2.70	.75
☐ 182	Richard Anderson	2.00	.90	.25
☐ 183	Howard Carter	2.00	.90	.25
☐ 184	T.R. Dunn	2.00	.90	.25
☐ 185	Keith Edmonson	2.00	.90	.25
☐ 186	Alex English	8.00	3.60	1.00

☐ 187	Mike Evans	2.00	.90	.25
☐ 188	Bill Hanzlik	2.00	.90	.25
☐ 189	Dan Issel	10.00	4.50	1.25
☐ 190	Anthony Roberts	2.00	.90	.25
☐ 191	Danny Schayes	4.00	1.80	.50
☐ 192	Rob Williams	2.00	.90	.25
☐ 193	Jack Sikma	3.00	1.35	.40
☐ 194	Fred Brown	3.00	1.35	.40
☐ 195	Tom Chambers	18.00	8.00	2.30
☐ 196	Steve Hawes	2.00	.90	.25
☐ 197	Steve Hayes	2.00	.90	.25
☐ 198	Reggie King	2.00	.90	.25
☐ 199	Scooter McCray	3.00	1.35	.40
☐ 200	Jon Sundvold	2.00	.90	.25
☐ 201	Danny Vranes	2.00	.90	.25
☐ 202	Gus Williams	3.00	1.35	.40
☐ 203	Al Wood	2.00	.90	.25
☐ 204	Jeff Ruland	3.00	1.35	.40
☐ 205	Greg Ballard	2.00	.90	.25
☐ 206	Darren Davis	2.00	.90	.25
☐ 207	Darren Daye	2.00	.90	.25
☐ 208	Michael Gibson	2.00	.90	.25
☐ 209	Frank Johnson	3.00	1.35	.40
☐ 210	Joe Kopicki	2.00	.90	.25
☐ 211	Rick Mahorn	2.00	.90	.25
☐ 212	Jeff Malone	14.00	6.25	1.75
☐ 213	Tom McMillen	3.00	1.35	.40
☐ 214	Ricky Sobers	2.00	.90	.25
☐ 215	Bryan Warrick	2.00	.90	.25
☐ 216	Billy Knight	3.00	1.35	.40
☐ 217	Don Buse	3.00	1.35	.40
☐ 218	Larry Drew	3.00	1.35	.40
☐ 219	Eddie Johnson	6.00	2.70	.75
☐ 220	Joe Meriweather	2.00	.90	.25
☐ 221	Larry Micheaux	2.00	.90	.25
☐ 222	Ed Nealy	2.00	.90	.25
☐ 223	Mark Olberding	2.00	.90	.25
☐ 224	Dave Robisch	3.00	1.35	.40
☐ 225	Reggie Theus	3.00	1.35	.40
☐ 226	LaSalle Thompson	2.00	.90	.25
☐ 227	Mike Woodson	2.00	.90	.25
☐ 228	World B. Free	3.00	1.35	.40
☐ 229	John Bagley	2.00	.90	.25
☐ 230	Jeff Cook	2.00	.90	.25
☐ 231	Geoff Crompton	2.00	.90	.25
☐ 232	John Garris	2.00	.90	.25
☐ 233	Stewart Granger	2.00	.90	.25
☐ 234	Roy Hinson	2.00	.90	.25
☐ 235	Phil Hubbard	2.00	.90	.25
☐ 236	Geoff Huston	2.00	.90	.25
☐ 237	Ben Poquette	2.00	.90	.25
☐ 238	Cliff Robinson	2.00	.90	.25
☐ 239	Lonnie Shelton	3.00	1.35	.40
☐ 240	Paul Thompson	2.00	.90	.25
☐ 241	George Gervin	15.00	6.75	1.90
☐ 242	Gene Banks	2.00	.90	.25
☐ 243	Ron Brewer	2.00	.90	.25
☐ 244	Artis Gilmore	6.00	2.70	.75
☐ 245	Edgar Jones	2.00	.90	.25
☐ 246	John Lucas	4.00	1.80	.50
☐ 247A	Mike Mitchell ERR	3.00	1.35	.40
	(Photo actually Mark McNamara)			
☐ 247B	Mike Mitchell COR	5.00	2.30	.60
☐ 248A	Mark McNamara ERR	3.00	1.35	.40
	(Photo actually Mike Mitchell)			
☐ 248B	Mark McNamara COR	5.00	2.30	.60
☐ 249	Johnny Moore	2.00	.90	.25
☐ 250	John Paxson	12.00	5.50	1.50
☐ 251	Fred Roberts	2.00	.90	.25

☐ 252	Joe Barry Carroll	3.00	1.35	.40
☐ 253	Mike Bratz	2.00	.90	.25
☐ 254	Don Collins	2.00	.90	.25
☐ 255	Lester Conner	2.00	.90	.25
☐ 256	Chris Engler	2.00	.90	.25
☐ 257	Sleepy Floyd	8.00	3.60	1.00
☐ 258	Wallace Johnson	2.00	.90	.25
☐ 259	Pace Mannion	2.00	.90	.25
☐ 260	Purvis Short	2.00	.90	.25
☐ 261	Larry Smith	2.00	.90	.25
☐ 262	Darren Tillis	2.00	.90	.25
☐ 263	Dominique Wilkins	180.00	80.00	23.00
☐ 264	Rickey Brown	2.00	.90	.25
☐ 265	Johnny Davis	2.00	.90	.25
☐ 266	Mike Glenn	3.00	1.35	.40
☐ 267	Scott Hastings	2.00	.90	.25
☐ 268	Eddie Johnson	2.00	.90	.25
☐ 269	Mark Landsberger	2.00	.90	.25
☐ 270	Billy Paultz	3.00	1.35	.40
☐ 271	Doc Rivers	12.00	5.50	1.50
☐ 272	Tree Rollins	3.00	1.35	.40
☐ 273	Dan Roundfield	3.00	1.35	.40
☐ 274	Sly Williams	2.00	.90	.25
☐ 275	Randy Wittman	2.00	.90	.25

1983-84 Star All-Rookies

This set features the ten members of the 1982-83 NBA All-Rookie Team. Cards measure 2 1/2" by 3 1/2" and have a yellow border around the fronts of the cards. The set was issued in a sealed plastic bag and distributed through hobby dealers. It originally retailed for about $2.50 to $5. The set was issued late summer of 1983 and features the Star '84 logo on the front of each card. The cards are numbered on the backs with the order of the numbering alphabetical according to the player's last name.

	NRMT-MT	EXC	VG
COMPLETE BAG SET (10)	50.00	23.00	6.25
COMMON CARD (1-10)	2.00	.90	.25
*OPENED SET: .75X to 1.0X VALUE			

☐ 1	Terry Cummings	5.00	2.30	.60
☐ 2	Quintin Dailey	2.00	.90	.25
☐ 3	Roderick Higgins	2.00	.90	.25
☐ 4	Clark Kellogg	2.00	.90	.25

		NRMT-MT	EXC	VG
☐ 5	Lafayette Lever	2.50	1.15	.30
☐ 6	Paul Pressey	2.00	.90	.25
☐ 7	Trent Tucker	2.00	.90	.25
☐ 8	Dominique Wilkins	25.00	11.50	3.10
☐ 9	Rob Williams	2.00	.90	.25
☐ 10	James Worthy	10.00	4.50	1.25

1983-84 Star
Sixers Champs

This set of 25 cards is devoted to Philadelphia's NBA Championship victory over the Los Angeles Lakers in 1983. Reportedly 10,000 sets were printed. Majority of the distribution was done at the Spectrum, the 76ers home arena. Cards measure 2 1/2" by 3 1/2" and have a red border around the fronts of the cards and red printing on the backs. The set was issued in late summer of 1983 and features the Star '84 logo on the front of each card.

	NRMT-MT	EXC	VG
COMPLETE BAG SET (25)	40.00	18.00	5.00
COMMON CARD (1-25)	2.00	.90	.25
*OPENED SET: .75X to 1.0X VALUE.			

		NRMT-MT	EXC	VG
☐ 1	Sixers 1982-83 NBA World Champs (Checklist back)	3.00	1.35	.40
☐ 2	Billy Cunningham Head Coach	2.50	1.15	.30
☐ 3	Clash of the Titans Malone vs. Abdul-Jabbar	5.00	2.30	.60
☐ 4	The Quest Begins Julius Erving	7.00	3.10	.85
☐ 5	Philly Super-Sub Clint Richardson	2.00	.90	.25
☐ 6	Laker Killer Andrew Toney	2.00	.90	.25
☐ 7	Phila. 113, LA 107 Game 1 Boxscore	2.00	.90	.25
☐ 8	Secretary of Defense Bobby Jones	2.50	1.15	.30
☐ 9	Mo Can Go Maurice Cheeks	2.50	1.15	.30
☐ 10	Doc for 2 Julius Erving	7.00	3.10	.85
☐ 11	Toney on the Drive Andrew Toney	2.00	.90	.25
☐ 12	Phila. 103, LA 93 Game 2 Boxscore	2.00	.90	.25
☐ 13	Serious Sixers (Pre-Game Lineup)	2.00	.90	.25
☐ 14	Moses Leads Sixers Moses Malone	3.00	1.35	.40
☐ 15	Bench Strength Clemon Johnson	2.00	.90	.25
☐ 16	One Mo Time Maurice Cheeks	2.50	1.15	.30
☐ 17	Phila. 111, LA 94 Game 3 Boxscore	2.00	.90	.25
☐ 18	Julius Scoops Julius Erving	7.00	3.10	.85
☐ 19	Sixth Man of Year Bobby Jones	2.50	1.15	.30
☐ 20	Coast to Coast Moses Malone	3.00	1.35	.40
☐ 21	World Champs Phila. 115, LA 108 Game 4 Boxscore	2.00	.90	.25
☐ 22	Doc Gets the Ring (Julius Erving) Series Stats	7.00	3.10	.85
☐ 23	Philly in a Sweep Prior World Champs	3.00	1.35	.40
☐ 24	Basking in Glory Profile: Dr.J	7.00	3.10	.85
☐ 25	The NBA's MVP Profile: Moses Malone	3.00	1.35	.40

1984 Star
All-Star Game

This set of 25 cards features participants in the 34th Annual NBA All-Star Game held in Denver. Cards measure 2 1/2" by 3 1/2" and have a white border around the fronts of the cards and blue printing on the backs. Cards feature the Star '84 logo on the front. The cards are ordered with the East All-Stars on cards 2-13 and the West All-Stars on cards 14-25. The cards are numbered on the backs and are in order by division. Within each division, the cards are alphabetical by player's last name.

	NRMT-MT	EXC	VG
COMPLETE BAG SET (1-25)	100.00	45.00	12.50
COMMON CARD (1-25)	2.00	.90	.25
*OPENED SET: .75X to 1.0X VALUE.			

		NRMT-MT	EXC	VG
☐	1 1984 NBA All-Star Game Checklist (Isiah Thomas)	5.00	2.30	.60
☐	2 Larry Bird	50.00	23.00	6.25
☐	3 Otis Birdsong	2.00	.90	.25
☐	4 Julius Erving	20.00	9.00	2.50
☐	5 Bernard King	3.00	1.35	.40
☐	6 Bill Laimbeer	3.00	1.35	.40
☐	7 Kevin McHale	10.00	4.50	1.25
☐	8 Sidney Moncrief	2.50	1.15	.30
☐	9 Robert Parish	7.00	3.10	.85
☐	10 Jeff Ruland	2.00	.90	.25
☐	11 Isiah Thomas (Magic Johnson also shown on card)	8.00	3.60	1.00
☐	12 Andrew Toney	2.00	.90	.25
☐	13 Kelly Tripucka	2.00	.90	.25
☐	14 Kareem Abdul-Jabbar	15.00	6.75	1.90
☐	15 Mark Aguirre	3.00	1.35	.40
☐	16 Adrian Dantley	3.00	1.35	.40
☐	17 Walter Davis	3.00	1.35	.40
☐	18 Alex English	3.00	1.35	.40
☐	19 George Gervin	5.00	2.30	.60
☐	20 Rickey Green	2.00	.90	.25
☐	21 Magic Johnson	30.00	13.50	3.80
☐	22 Jim Paxson	2.00	.90	.25
☐	23 Ralph Sampson	2.50	1.15	.30
☐	24 Jack Sikma	3.00	1.35	.40
☐	25 Kiki Vandeweghe	2.50	1.15	.30

		NRMT-MT	EXC	VG
☐	1 Checklist Card	5.00	2.30	.60
☐	2 Larry Bird	50.00	23.00	6.25
☐	3 Otis Birdsong	2.00	.90	.25
☐	4 Julius Erving	20.00	9.00	2.50
☐	5 Bernard King	3.00	1.35	.40
☐	6 Bill Laimbeer	3.00	1.35	.40
☐	7 Kevin McHale	12.00	5.50	1.50
☐	8 Sidney Moncrief	2.50	1.15	.30
☐	9 Robert Parish	8.00	3.60	1.00
☐	10 Jeff Ruland	2.00	.90	.25
☐	11 Isiah Thomas (Magic Johnson also shown on card)	14.00	6.25	1.75
☐	12 Andrew Toney	2.00	.90	.25
☐	13 Kelly Tripucka	2.00	.90	.25
☐	14 Kareem Abdul-Jabbar	15.00	6.75	1.90
☐	15 Mark Aguirre	3.00	1.35	.40
☐	16 Adrian Dantley	3.00	1.35	.40
☐	17 Walter Davis	3.00	1.35	.40
☐	18 Alex English	3.00	1.35	.40
☐	19 George Gervin	6.00	2.70	.75
☐	20 Rickey Green	2.00	.90	.25
☐	21 Magic Johnson	35.00	16.00	4.40
☐	22 Jim Paxson	2.00	.90	.25
☐	23 Ralph Sampson	2.50	1.15	.30
☐	24 Jack Sikma	3.00	1.35	.40
☐	25 Kiki Vandeweghe	2.00	.90	.25
☐	26 Michael Cooper	2.50	1.15	.30
☐	27 Clyde Drexler	30.00	13.50	3.80
☐	28 Julius Erving	20.00	9.00	2.50
☐	29 Darrell Griffith	2.50	1.15	.30
☐	30 Edgar Jones	2.00	.90	.25
☐	31 Larry Nance	6.00	2.70	.75
☐	32 Ralph Sampson	2.50	1.15	.30
☐	33 Dominique Wilkins	20.00	9.00	2.50
☐	34 Orlando Woolridge	2.00	.90	.25

1984 Star All-Star Game Denver Police

This 34-card set was distributed as individual cards by the Denver Police in the months following the NBA All-Star Game held in Denver. Reportedly 10,000 sets were produced. The set was composed of participants in the All-Star Game (1-25) and the Slam Dunk contest (26-34). Cards measure 2 1/2" by 3 1/2" and have a white border around the fronts and blue printing on the backs. Cards feature the Star '84 logo on the fronts and safety tips on the backs.

	NRMT-MT	EXC	VG
COMPLETE SET (34)	200.00	90.00	25.00
COMMON CARD (1-25)	2.00	.90	.25
COMMON CARD (26-34)	2.00	.90	.25

1984 Star Award Banquet

This 24-card set was produced for the NBA to be given away at the Awards Banquet which took place following the conclusion of the 1983-84 season. According to a 1984 Star Company press release, only 3,000 sets were produced. The cards highlighted award winners from the 1983-84 season. Cards measure 2 1/2" by 3 1/2" and have a blue border around the fronts of the cards and pink and blue printing on the backs. The set was issued in June of 1984 and features the Star '84 logo on the front of each card.

	NRMT-MT	EXC	VG
COMPLETE BAG SET (24)	75.00	34.00	9.50
COMMON CARD (1-24)	2.00	.90	.25
*OPENED SET: .75X to 1.0X VALUE.			

		NRMT-MT	EXC	VG
☐ 1	1984 Award Winners ..... Checklist	2.00	.90	.25
☐ 2	Frank Layden CO............	2.00	.90	.25
☐ 3	Ralph Sampson ROY	2.50	1.15	.30
☐ 4	Comeback Player .... of the Year; Adrian Dantley	2.50	1.15	.30
☐ 5	Sixth Man: .... Kevin McHale	6.00	2.70	.75
☐ 6	Pivotal Player .... of the Year; Magic Johnson	15.00	6.75	1.90
☐ 7	Defensive Player: .... Sidney Moncrief	2.50	1.15	.30
☐ 8	MVP: Larry Bird	25.00	11.50	3.10
☐ 9	Slam Dunk Champ; .... Larry Nance	4.00	1.80	.50
☐ 10	Statistical Leaders......	10.00	4.50	1.25
☐ 11	Statistical Leaders II	5.00	2.30	.60
☐ 12	All-Star Game MVP;..... Isiah Thomas	5.00	2.30	.60
☐ 13	Leading Scorer; .... Adrian Dantley	2.50	1.15	.30
☐ 14	Field Goal Percent...... Leader; Artis Gilmore	2.50	1.15	.30
☐ 15	Free Throw Percent... Leader; Larry Bird	25.00	11.50	3.10
☐ 16	Three Point Field Goal.. Percent Leader; Darrell Griffith	2.00	.90	.25
☐ 17	Assists Leader; .... Magic Johnson	15.00	6.75	1.90
☐ 18	Steals Leader; .... Rickey Green	2.00	.90	.25
☐ 19	Most Blocked Shots;.... Mark Eaton	2.00	.90	.25
☐ 20	Leading Rebounder;..... Moses Malone	4.00	1.80	.50
☐ 21	Most Career Points; ... Kareem Abdul-Jabbar	12.00	5.50	1.50
☐ 22	NBA All-Defensive Team	2.50	1.15	.30
☐ 23	NBA All-Rookie Team...	5.00	2.30	.60
☐ 24	NBA All-NBA Team.....	15.00	6.75	1.90

1984 Star Larry Bird

This set contains 18 cards highlighting the career of basketball great Larry Bird. Cards measure 2 1/2" by 3 1/2" and have a green border around the fronts of the cards and green printing on the backs. Cards feature Star '84 logo on the front as they were released in May of 1984.

	NRMT-MT	EXC	VG
COMPLETE BAG SET (18) ...	100.00	45.00	12.50
COMMON L.BIRD (1-18) -	7.00	3.10	.85
*OPENED SET: .75X to 1.0X VALUE.			

		NRMT-MT	EXC	VG
☐ 1	Checklist	7.00	3.10	.85
☐ 2	Collegiate Stats	7.00	3.10	.85
☐ 3	1980 Rookie .... of the Year	7.00	3.10	.85
☐ 4	Regular Season Stats.....	7.00	3.10	.85
☐ 5	Playoff Stats	7.00	3.10	.85
☐ 6	All-Star Stats.................	7.00	3.10	.85
☐ 7	The 1979-80 Season......	7.00	3.10	.85
☐ 8	The 1980-81 Season......	7.00	3.10	.85
☐ 9	The 1981-82 Season......	7.00	3.10	.85
☐ 10	The 1982-83 Season.....	7.00	3.10	.85
☐ 11	The 1983-84 Season.....	7.00	3.10	.85
☐ 12	The 1984 NBA MVP	7.00	3.10	.85
☐ 13	Member - 1984 .... All NBA Team	7.00	3.10	.85
☐ 14	World Champions 1981, 1984	7.00	3.10	.85
☐ 15	1984 Free Throw.......... Percentage Leader	7.00	3.10	.85
☐ 16	Career Data	7.00	3.10	.85
☐ 17	Personal Data	7.00	3.10	.85
☐ 18	The Future....................	7.00	3.10	.85

1984 Star Celtics Champs

This set of 25 cards is devoted to Boston's NBA Championship victory over the Los Angeles Lakers in 1984. Cards measure 2 1/2" by 3 1/2" and have a green border around the fronts of the cards and green printing on the backs. The set was issued in summer of 1984 and features the Star '84 logo on the front of each card. The set includes two of the three Red Auerbach cards ever printed.

	NRMT-MT	EXC	VG
COMPLETE BAG SET (25) ...	275.00	125.00	34.00
COMMON CARD (1-25)	3.00	1.35	.40
*OPENED SET: .75X to 1.0X VALUE.			

☐ 1	Celtics Champs .... (Red Auerbach/Maxwell) (Checklist back)	12.00	5.50	1.50
☐ 2	Game 1 (Abdul-Jabbar over Parish)	10.00	4.50	1.25
☐ 3	Game 1 (McHale drives)	8.00	3.60	1.00
☐ 4	LA 115, Boston 109 .... (Larry Bird)	40.00	18.00	5.00
☐ 5	Game 2 .... (Magic Johnson)	25.00	11.50	3.10
☐ 6	Game 2 (K.C. Jones and Danny Ainge)	7.00	3.10	.85
☐ 7	Boston 124, LA 121 (OT) (Larry Bird)	40.00	18.00	5.00
☐ 8	Game 3 (Abdul-Jabbar and McHale)	12.00	5.50	1.50
☐ 9	Game 3 (J.Worthy)	6.00	2.70	.75
☐ 10	LA 137, Boston 104 .... (Magic Johnson)	25.00	11.50	3.10
☐ 11	Game 4 (Magic blocks Bird)	60.00	27.00	7.50
☐ 12	Game 4 .... (Ainge scuffle)	6.00	2.70	.75
☐ 13	Boston 129, LA 125 .... Overtime (Carr and Maxwell)	3.00	1.35	.40
☐ 14	Game 5 (Larry Bird)	40.00	18.00	5.00
☐ 15	Game 5 (Pat Riley)	6.00	2.70	.75
☐ 16	Boston 121, LA 103 .... (Kareem Abdul-Jabbar)	14.00	6.25	1.75
☐ 17	Game 6 .... (Parish sandwich)	6.00	2.70	.75
☐ 18	Game 6 .... (Kareem Abdul-Jabbar)	10.00	4.50	1.25
☐ 19	LA 119, Boston 108 .... (Dennis Johnson)	4.00	1.80	.50
☐ 20	Game 7 .... (Kareem sky hook)	10.00	4.50	1.25
☐ 21	Game 7 (K.C. Jones)	4.00	1.80	.50
☐ 22	World Champs; Boston 111, LA 102 (M.L. Carr)	3.00	1.35	.40
☐ 23	Prior Celtic .... Championships (Red Auerbach)	10.00	4.50	1.25
☐ 24	Bird: Championship ... Series MVP	45.00	20.00	5.75
☐ 25	The Road to the Title... (Boston Garden)	12.00	5.50	1.50

1984 Star Slam Dunk

An 11-card set highlighting the revival of the Slam Dunk contest (during the 1984 All-Star Weekend in Denver) was produced by the Star Company in 1984. Cards measure 2 1/2" by 3 1/2" and have a white border around the fronts and blue printing on the backs. The Star '84 logo are featured on the front. The cards are numbered on the back.

	NRMT-MT	EXC	VG
COMPLETE BAG SET (11)	90.00	40.00	11.50
COMMON CARD (1-11)	2.00	.90	.25
*OPENED SET: .75X to 1.0X VALUE			

☐ 1	Group Photo .... (checklist back)	12.00	5.50	1.50
☐ 2	Michael Cooper	3.00	1.35	.40
☐ 3	Clyde Drexler	30.00	13.50	3.80
☐ 4	Julius Erving	25.00	11.50	3.10
☐ 5	Darrell Griffith	3.00	1.35	.40
☐ 6	Edgar Jones	2.00	.90	.25
☐ 7	Larry Nance	6.00	2.70	.75
☐ 8	Ralph Sampson	3.00	1.35	.40
☐ 9	Dominique Wilkins	20.00	9.00	2.50
☐ 10	Orlando Woolridge.......	3.00	1.35	.40
☐ 11	Larry Nance .... 1984 Slam Dunk Champ	6.00	2.70	.75

1984-85 Star

This set of 288 cards was issued in three series during the first five months of 1985 by Star Company. The set is comprised of team sets that were issued in clear sealed bags. Many of these team bags were distributed to hobby dealers through a small group of Star Company master distributors and retailed for $2.50-$5. According to Star Company's original sales materials and order forms, reportedly 3,000 team bags were printed for each team. Cards measure 2 1/2" by 3 1/2" and have a colored border around the fronts of the cards according to the team with corresponding color printing on the backs. Cards are organized numerically by team, i.e., Boston Celtics (1-12), Los Angeles Clippers (13-24), New York Knicks (25-37), Phoenix Suns (38-51), Indiana Pacers (52-63), San Antonio Spurs (64-75), Atlanta Hawks (76-87), New Jersey Nets (88-100), Chicago Bulls (101-112), Seattle Supersonics (113-124), Milwaukee Bucks (125-136), Denver

Nuggets (137-148), Golden State Warriors (149-160), Portland Trail Blazers (161-171), Los Angeles Lakers (172-184), Washington Bullets (185-194), Philadelphia 76ers (201-212), Cleveland Cavaliers (213-224), Utah Jazz (225-236), Houston Rockets (237-249), Dallas Mavericks (250-260), Detroit Pistons (261-269) and Sacramento Kings (270-280). The set also features a special subset (195-200) honoring Gold Medal-winning players from the 1984 Olympic basketball competition as well as a subset of NBA specials (281-288). Michael Jordan's Extended Rookie Card appears in this set. Other Extended Rookie's include Charles Barkley, Craig Ehlo, Hakeem Olajuwon, Alvin Robertson, Sam Perkins, John Stockton and Otis Thorpe. There is typically a slight discount on sales of opened team bags.

	NRMT-MT	EXC	VG
COMPLETE BAG SET (288)	5500.00	2500.00	700.00
COMP.BAG CELTICS (12)	275.00	125.00	34.00
COMP.BAG CLIPPERS (12)	15.00	6.75	1.90
COMP.BAG KNICKS (13)	20.00	9.00	2.50
COMP.BAG SUNS (14)	25.00	11.50	3.10
COMP.BAG PACERS SP (12)	60.00	27.00	7.50
COMP.BAG SPURS (12)	25.00	11.50	3.10
COMP.BAG HAWKS (12)	110.00	50.00	14.00
COMP.BAG NETS (13)	15.00	6.75	1.90
COMP.BAG BULLS (12)	3000.00	1350.00	375.00
COMP.BAG SONICS (12)	20.00	9.00	2.50
COMP.BAG BUCKS (12)	15.00	6.75	1.90
COMP.BAG NUGGETS (12)	15.00	6.75	1.90
COMP.BAG WARRIORS (12)	15.00	6.75	1.90
COMP.BAG BLAZERS (11)	125.00	57.50	15.50
COMP.BAG LAKERS (13)	150.00	70.00	19.00
COMP.BAG BULLETS (12)	15.00	6.75	1.90
COMP.BAG OLY/SPEC (14)	850.00	375.00	105.00
COMP.BAG 76ERS (12)	325.00	145.00	40.00
COMP.BAG CAVS (12)	15.00	6.75	1.90
COMP.BAG JAZZ (12)	250.00	115.00	31.00
COMP.BAG ROCKETS (13)	400.00	180.00	50.00
COMP.BAG MAVS (11)	50.00	23.00	6.25
COMP.BAG PISTONS (9)	50.00	23.00	6.25
COMP.BAG KINGS (11)	25.00	11.50	3.10
COMMON CELTICS (1-12)	2.00	.90	.25
COMMON CLIPPERS (13-24)	2.00	.90	.25
COMMON KNICKS (25-37)	2.00	.90	.25
COMMON SUNS (38-51)	2.00	.90	.25
COMMON PACERS SP (52-63)	5.00	2.30	.60
COMMON SPURS (64-75)	2.00	.90	.25
COMMON HAWKS (76-87)	2.00	.90	.25
COMMON NETS (88-100)	2.00	.90	.25
COMMON BULLS (101-112)	2.00	.90	.25
COMMON SONICS (113-124)	2.00	.90	.25
COMMON BUCKS (125-136)	2.00	.90	.25
COMMON NUGGETS (137-148)	2.00	.90	.25
COMMON WARRIORS (149-160)	2.00	.90	.25
COMMON BLAZERS (161-171)	2.00	.90	.25
COMMON LAKERS (172-184)	2.00	.90	.25
COMMON BULLETS (185-194)	2.00	.90	.25
COMMON OLYMPIANS (195-200)	2.00	.90	.25
COMMON 76ERS (201-212)	2.00	.90	.25
COMMON CAVS (213-224)	2.00	.90	.25
COMMON JAZZ (225-236)	2.00	.90	.25
COMMON ROCKETS (237-249)	2.00	.90	.25
COMMON MAVS (250-260)	2.00	.90	.25
COMMON PISTONS (261-269)	2.00	.90	.25
COMMON KINGS (270-280)	2.00	.90	.25

		NRMT-MT	EXC	VG
	COMMON SPECIALS (281-288)	2.00	.90	.25
	*OPENED TEAM SETS: .75X to 1.0X VALUE			
☐ 1	Larry Bird	175.00	80.00	22.00
☐ 2	Danny Ainge	14.00	6.25	1.75
☐ 3	Quinn Buckner	3.00	1.35	.40
☐ 4	Rick Carlisle	2.00	.90	.25
☐ 5	M.L. Carr	3.00	1.35	.40
☐ 6	Dennis Johnson	6.00	2.70	.75
☐ 7	Greg Kite	2.00	.90	.25
☐ 8	Cedric Maxwell	3.00	1.35	.40
☐ 9	Kevin McHale	16.00	7.25	2.00
☐ 10	Robert Parish	12.00	5.50	1.50
☐ 11	Scott Wedman	2.00	.90	.25
☐ 12	Larry Bird	90.00	40.00	11.50
	1983-84 NBA MVP			
☐ 13	Marques Johnson	3.00	1.35	.40
☐ 14	Junior Bridgeman	3.00	1.35	.40
☐ 15	Michael Cage	5.00	2.30	.60
☐ 16	Harvey Catchings	2.00	.90	.25
☐ 17	James Donaldson	2.00	.90	.25
☐ 18	Lancaster Gordon	2.00	.90	.25
☐ 19	Jay Murphy	2.00	.90	.25
☐ 20	Norm Nixon	3.00	1.35	.40
☐ 21	Derek Smith	2.00	.90	.25
☐ 22	Bill Walton	20.00	9.00	2.50
☐ 23	Bryan Warrick	2.00	.90	.25
☐ 24	Rory White	2.00	.90	.25
☐ 25	Bernard King	6.00	2.70	.75
☐ 26	James Bailey	2.00	.90	.25
☐ 27	Ken Bannister	2.00	.90	.25
☐ 28	Butch Carter	2.00	.90	.25
☐ 29	Bill Cartwright	4.00	1.80	.50
☐ 30	Pat Cummings	2.00	.90	.25
☐ 31	Ernie Grunfeld	2.00	.90	.25
☐ 32	Louis Orr	2.00	.90	.25
☐ 33	Leonard Robinson	3.00	1.35	.40
☐ 34	Rory Sparrow	2.00	.90	.25
☐ 35	Trent Tucker	2.00	.90	.25
☐ 36	Darrell Walker	2.00	.90	.25
☐ 37	Eddie Lee Wilkins	2.00	.90	.25
☐ 38	Alvan Adams	3.00	1.35	.40
☐ 39	Walter Davis	6.00	2.70	.75
☐ 40	James Edwards	3.00	1.35	.40
☐ 41	Rod Foster	2.00	.90	.25
☐ 42	Michael Holton	2.00	.90	.25
☐ 43	Jay Humphries	4.00	1.80	.50
☐ 44	Charles Jones	2.00	.90	.25
☐ 45	Maurice Lucas	3.00	1.35	.40
☐ 46	Kyle Macy	3.00	1.35	.40
☐ 47	Larry Nance	10.00	4.50	1.25
☐ 48	Charles Pittman	2.00	.90	.25
☐ 49	Rick Robey	2.00	.90	.25
☐ 50	Mike Sanders	2.00	.90	.25
☐ 51	Alvin Scott	2.00	.90	.25
☐ 52	Clark Kellogg	5.00	2.30	.60
☐ 53	Tony Brown	5.00	2.30	.60
☐ 54	Devin Durrant	5.00	2.30	.60
☐ 55	Vern Fleming	8.00	3.60	1.00
☐ 56	Bill Garnett	5.00	2.30	.60
☐ 57	Stuart Gray UER	5.00	2.30	.60
	(Photo actually Tony Brown)			
☐ 58	Jerry Sichting	6.00	2.70	.75
☐ 59	Terence Stansbury	5.00	2.30	.60
☐ 60	Steve Stipanovich	6.00	2.70	.75
☐ 61	Jimmy Thomas	5.00	2.30	.60
☐ 62	Granville Waiters	5.00	2.30	.60
☐ 63	Herb Williams	6.00	2.70	.75
☐ 64	Artis Gilmore	6.00	2.70	.75
☐ 65	Gene Banks	2.00	.90	.25

☐ 66 Ron Brewer	2.00	.90	.25
☐ 67 George Gervin	14.00	6.25	1.75
☐ 68 Edgar Jones	2.00	.90	.25
☐ 69 Ozell Jones	2.00	.90	.25
☐ 70 Mark McNamara	2.00	.90	.25
☐ 71 Mike Mitchell	2.00	.90	.25
☐ 72 Johnny Moore	2.00	.90	.25
☐ 73 John Paxson	4.00	1.80	.50
☐ 74 Fred Roberts	2.00	.90	.25
☐ 75 Alvin Robertson	5.00	2.30	.60
☐ 76 Dominique Wilkins	80.00	36.00	10.00
☐ 77 Rickey Brown	2.00	.90	.25
☐ 78 Antoine Carr	4.00	1.80	.50
☐ 79 Mike Glenn	2.00	.90	.25
☐ 80 Scott Hastings	2.00	.90	.25
☐ 81 Eddie Johnson	2.00	.90	.25
☐ 82 Cliff Levingston	2.00	.90	.25
☐ 83 Leo Rautins	2.00	.90	.25
☐ 84 Doc Rivers	5.00	2.30	.60
☐ 85 Tree Rollins	3.00	1.35	.40
☐ 86 Randy Wittman	2.00	.90	.25
☐ 87 Sly Williams	2.00	.90	.25
☐ 88 Darryl Dawkins	5.00	2.30	.60
☐ 89 Otis Birdsong	3.00	1.35	.40
☐ 90 Darwin Cook	2.00	.90	.25
☐ 91 Mike Gminski	3.00	1.35	.40
☐ 92 George L. Johnson	2.00	.90	.25
☐ 93 Albert King	2.00	.90	.25
☐ 94 Mike O'Koren	2.00	.90	.25
☐ 95 Kelvin Ransey	2.00	.90	.25
☐ 96 M.R. Richardson	2.00	.90	.25
☐ 97 Wayne Sappleton	2.00	.90	.25
☐ 98 Jeff Turner	2.00	.90	.25
☐ 99 Buck Williams	6.00	2.70	.75
☐ 100 Michael Wilson	2.00	.90	.25
☐ 101 Michael Jordan	2700.00	1200.00	350.00
☐ 102 Dave Corzine	2.00	.90	.25
☐ 103 Quintin Dailey	2.00	.90	.25
☐ 104 Sidney Green	2.00	.90	.25
☐ 105 David Greenwood	3.00	1.35	.40
☐ 106 Rod Higgins	2.00	.90	.25
☐ 107 Steve Johnson	2.00	.90	.25
☐ 108 Caldwell Jones	3.00	1.35	.40
☐ 109 Wes Matthews	2.00	.90	.25
☐ 110 Jawann Oldham	2.00	.90	.25
☐ 111 Ennis Whatley	2.00	.90	.25
☐ 112 Orlando Woolridge	3.00	1.35	.40
☐ 113 Tom Chambers	6.00	2.70	.75
☐ 114 Cory Blackwell	2.00	.90	.25
☐ 115 Frank Brickowski	5.00	2.30	.60
☐ 116 Gerald Henderson	2.00	.90	.25
☐ 117 Reggie King	2.00	.90	.25
☐ 118 Tim McCormick	2.00	.90	.25
☐ 119 John Schweitz	2.00	.90	.25
☐ 120 Jack Sikma	2.00	.90	.25
☐ 121 Ricky Sobers	2.00	.90	.25
☐ 122 Jon Sundvold	2.00	.90	.25
☐ 123 Danny Vranes	2.00	.90	.25
☐ 124 Al Wood	2.00	.90	.25
☐ 125 Terry Cummings UER (Robert Cummings on card back)	5.00	2.30	.60
☐ 126 Randy Breuer	2.00	.90	.25
☐ 127 Charles Davis	2.00	.90	.25
☐ 128 Mike Dunleavy	3.00	1.35	.40
☐ 129 Kenny Fields	2.00	.90	.25
☐ 130 Kevin Grevey	2.00	.90	.25
☐ 131 Craig Hodges	2.00	.90	.25
☐ 132 Alton Lister	2.00	.90	.25
☐ 133 Larry Micheaux	2.00	.90	.25
☐ 134 Paul Mokeski	2.00	.90	.25
☐ 135 Sidney Moncrief	5.00	2.30	.60
☐ 136 Paul Pressey	2.00	.90	.25
☐ 137 Alex English	6.00	2.70	.75
☐ 138 Wayne Cooper	2.00	.90	.25
☐ 139 T.R. Dunn	2.00	.90	.25
☐ 140 Mike Evans	2.00	.90	.25
☐ 141 Bill Hanzlik	2.00	.90	.25
☐ 142 Dan Issel	10.00	4.50	1.25
☐ 143 Joe Kopicki	2.00	.90	.25
☐ 144 Lafayette Lever	3.00	1.35	.40
☐ 145 Calvin Natt	2.00	.90	.25
☐ 146 Danny Schayes	3.00	1.35	.40
☐ 147 Elston Turner	2.00	.90	.25
☐ 148 Willie White	2.00	.90	.25
☐ 149 Purvis Short	2.00	.90	.25
☐ 150 Chuck Aleksinas	2.00	.90	.25
☐ 151 Mike Bratz	2.00	.90	.25
☐ 152 Steve Burtt	2.00	.90	.25
☐ 153 Lester Conner	2.00	.90	.25
☐ 154 Sleepy Floyd	2.00	.90	.25
☐ 155 Mickey Johnson	2.00	.90	.25
☐ 156 Gary Plummer	2.00	.90	.25
☐ 157 Larry Smith	2.00	.90	.25
☐ 158 Peter Thibeaux	2.00	.90	.25
☐ 159 Jerome Whitehead	2.00	.90	.25
☐ 160 Othell Wilson	2.00	.90	.25
☐ 161 Kiki Vandeweghe	2.00	.90	.25
☐ 162 Sam Bowie	5.00	2.30	.60
☐ 163 Kenny Carr	2.00	.90	.25
☐ 164 Steve Colter	2.00	.90	.25
☐ 165 Clyde Drexler	110.00	50.00	14.00
☐ 166 Audie Norris	2.00	.90	.25
☐ 167 Jim Paxson	2.00	.90	.25
☐ 168 Tom Scheffler	2.00	.90	.25
☐ 169 Bernard Thompson	2.00	.90	.25
☐ 170 Mychal Thompson	3.00	1.35	.40
☐ 171 Darnell Valentine	2.00	.90	.25
☐ 172 Magic Johnson	125.00	57.50	15.50
☐ 173 Kareem Abdul-Jabbar	35.00	16.00	4.40
☐ 174 Michael Cooper	3.00	1.35	.40
☐ 175 Earl Jones	2.00	.90	.25
☐ 176 Mitch Kupchak	2.00	.90	.25
☐ 177 Ronnie Lester	2.00	.90	.25
☐ 178 Bob McAdoo	6.00	2.70	.75
☐ 179 Mike McGee	2.00	.90	.25
☐ 180 Kurt Rambis	2.00	.90	.25
☐ 181 Byron Scott	7.00	3.10	.85
☐ 182 Larry Spriggs	2.00	.90	.25
☐ 183 Jamaal Wilkes	4.00	1.80	.50
☐ 184 James Worthy	12.00	5.50	1.50
☐ 185 Gus Williams	3.00	1.35	.40
☐ 186 Greg Ballard	2.00	.90	.25
☐ 187 Dudley Bradley	2.00	.90	.25
☐ 188 Darren Daye	2.00	.90	.25
☐ 189 Frank Johnson	2.00	.90	.25
☐ 190 Charles Jones	2.00	.90	.25
☐ 191 Rick Mahorn	2.00	.90	.25
☐ 192 Jeff Malone	5.00	2.30	.60
☐ 193 Tom McMillen	3.00	1.35	.40
☐ 194 Jeff Ruland	2.00	.90	.25
☐ 195 Michael Jordan	400.00	180.00	50.00
☐ 196 Vern Fleming	3.00	1.35	.40
☐ 197 Sam Perkins	7.00	3.10	.85
☐ 198 Alvin Robertson	2.00	.90	.25
☐ 199 Jeff Turner	2.00	.90	.25
☐ 200 Leon Wood	2.00	.90	.25
☐ 201 Moses Malone	15.00	6.75	1.90
☐ 202 Charles Barkley	275.00	125.00	34.00
☐ 203 Maurice Cheeks	5.00	2.30	.60
☐ 204 Julius Erving	35.00	16.00	4.40
☐ 205 Clemon Johnson	2.00	.90	.25

☐ 206	George Johnson	2.00	.90	.25
☐ 207	Bobby Jones	5.00	2.30	.60
☐ 208	Clint Richardson	2.00	.90	.25
☐ 209	Sedale Threatt	2.00	.90	.25
☐ 210	Andrew Toney	2.00	.90	.25
☐ 211	Sam Williams	2.00	.90	.25
☐ 212	Leon Wood	2.00	.90	.25
☐ 213	Mel Turpin	2.00	.90	.25
☐ 214	Ron Anderson	2.00	.90	.25
☐ 215	John Bagley	2.00	.90	.25
☐ 216	Johnny Davis	2.00	.90	.25
☐ 217	World B. Free	4.00	1.80	.50
☐ 218	Roy Hinson	2.00	.90	.25
☐ 219	Phil Hubbard	2.00	.90	.25
☐ 220	Edgar Jones	2.00	.90	.25
☐ 221	Ben Poquette	2.00	.90	.25
☐ 222	Lonnie Shelton	2.00	.90	.25
☐ 223	Mark West	2.00	.90	.25
☐ 224	Kevin Williams	2.00	.90	.25
☐ 225	Mark Eaton	3.00	1.35	.40
☐ 226	Mitchell Anderson	2.00	.90	.25
☐ 227	Thurl Bailey	2.00	.90	.25
☐ 228	Adrian Dantley	6.00	2.70	.75
☐ 229	Rickey Green	3.00	1.35	.40
☐ 230	Darrell Griffith	4.00	1.80	.50
☐ 231	Rich Kelley	2.00	.90	.25
☐ 232	Pace Mannion	2.00	.90	.25
☐ 233	Billy Paultz	3.00	1.35	.40
☐ 234	Fred Roberts	2.00	.90	.25
☐ 235	John Stockton	200.00	90.00	25.00
☐ 236	Jeff Wilkins	2.00	.90	.25
☐ 237	Hakeem Olajuwon	350.00	160.00	45.00
☐ 238	Craig Ehlo	16.00	7.25	2.00
☐ 239	Lionel Hollins	2.00	.90	.25
☐ 240	Allen Leavell	2.00	.90	.25
☐ 241	Lewis Lloyd	2.00	.90	.25
☐ 242	John Lucas	4.00	1.80	.50
☐ 243	Rodney McCray	3.00	1.35	.40
☐ 244	Hank McDowell	2.00	.90	.25
☐ 245	Larry Micheaux	2.00	.90	.25
☐ 246	Jim Peterson	2.00	.90	.25
☐ 247	Robert Reid	2.00	.90	.25
☐ 248	Ralph Sampson	4.00	1.80	.50
☐ 249	Mitchell Wiggins	2.00	.90	.25
☐ 250	Mark Aguirre	6.00	2.70	.75
☐ 251	Rolando Blackman	4.00	1.80	.50
☐ 252	Wallace Bryant	2.00	.90	.25
☐ 253	Brad Davis	2.00	.90	.25
☐ 254	Dale Ellis	4.00	1.80	.50
☐ 255	Derek Harper	10.00	4.50	1.25
☐ 256	Kurt Nimphius	2.00	.90	.25
☐ 257	Sam Perkins	20.00	9.00	2.50
☐ 258	Charlie Sitton	2.00	.90	.25
☐ 259	Tom Sluby	2.00	.90	.25
☐ 260	Jay Vincent	2.00	.90	.25
☐ 261	Isiah Thomas	40.00	18.00	5.00
☐ 262	Kent Benson	3.00	1.35	.40
☐ 263	Earl Cureton	2.00	.90	.25
☐ 264	Vinnie Johnson	3.00	1.35	.40
☐ 265	Bill Laimbeer	4.00	1.80	.50
☐ 266	John Long	2.00	.90	.25
☐ 267	Dan Roundfield	3.00	1.35	.40
☐ 268	Kelly Tripucka	2.00	.90	.25
☐ 269	Terry Tyler	2.00	.90	.25
☐ 270	Reggie Theus	3.00	1.35	.40
☐ 271	Don Buse	2.00	.90	.25
☐ 272	Larry Drew	3.00	1.35	.40
☐ 273	Eddie Johnson	2.00	.90	.25
☐ 274	Billy Knight	3.00	1.35	.40
☐ 275	Joe Meriweather	2.00	.90	.25
☐ 276	Mark Olberding	2.00	.90	.25

☐ 277	LaSalle Thompson	2.00	.90	.25
☐ 278	Otis Thorpe	20.00	9.00	2.50
☐ 279	Pete Verhoeven	2.00	.90	.25
☐ 280	Mike Woodson	2.00	.90	.25
☐ 281	Julius Erving	20.00	9.00	2.50
☐ 282	Kareem Abdul-Jabbar	18.00	8.00	2.30
☐ 283	Dan Issel	6.00	2.70	.75
☐ 284	Bernard King	4.00	1.80	.50
☐ 285	Moses Malone	8.00	3.60	1.00
☐ 286	Mark Eaton	3.00	1.35	.40
☐ 287	Isiah Thomas	18.00	8.00	2.30
☐ 288	Michael Jordan	400.00	180.00	50.00

1984-85 Star Arena

These sets were produced to be sold in the arena of each of the five teams featured in this set. The teams are Boston, Dallas, Milwaukee, Los Angeles Lakers and Philadelphia. Each set is different from the team's regular issue set in that the photography and card backs are different. Shortly after distribution began, Bob Lanier announced his retirement and his cards were withdrawn from the Milwaukee set. Cards measure 2 1/2" by 3 1/2" and have a colored border around the fronts according to team. Corresponding color printing is on the backs. Celtics feature Star '85 logo on the front while the other four teams feature the Star '84 logo on the front. The cards are ordered alphabetically by team using prefixes A-E.

	NRMT-MT	EXC	VG
COMPLETE BAG SET (48)	300.00	135.00	38.00
COMPLETE SET (49) w/Lanier	550.00	250.00	70.00
COMP.BAG CELTICS (9)	110.00	50.00	14.00
COMP.BAG MAVERICKS (11)	20.00	9.00	2.50
COMP.BAG BUCKS (8)	20.00	9.00	2.50
COMP.BAG LAKERS (10)	100.00	45.00	12.50
COMP.BAG 76ERS (10)	40.00	18.00	5.00
COMMON CELTICS (A1-A9)	2.00	.90	.25
COMMON MAVS (B1-B11)	2.00	.90	.25
COMMON BUCKS (C1-C9)	2.00	.90	.25
COMMON LAKERS (D1-D10)	2.00	.90	.25
COMMON 76ERS (E1-E10)	2.00	.90	.25
*OPENED TEAM SETS: .75X to 1.0X VALUE			

☐ A1	Larry Bird	60.00	27.00	7.50
☐ A2	Danny Ainge	7.00	3.10	.85
☐ A3	Rick Carlisle	2.00	.90	.25

			NRMT-MT	EXC	VG
☐ A4	Dennis Johnson	4.00	1.80	.50
☐ A5	Cedric Maxwell	2.00	.90	.25
☐ A6	Kevin McHale	8.00	3.60	1.00
☐ A7	Robert Parish	6.00	2.70	.75
☐ A8	Scott Wedman	2.00	.90	.25
☐ A9	World Champs	30.00	13.50	3.80

1981, 1984
Robert Parish
Larry Bird
Kevin McHale
Jimmy Rodgers CO
K.C. Jones CO
Chris Ford CO

☐ B1	Mark Aguirre	4.00	1.80	.50
☐ B2	Rolando Blackman	3.00	1.35	.40
☐ B3	Brad Davis	2.00	.90	.25
☐ B4	Dale Ellis	3.00	1.35	.40
☐ B5	Bill Garnett	2.00	.90	.25
☐ B6	Derek Harper UER	5.00	2.30	.60

(Mike Harper on both
sides with Mike's
birthdate, etc.)

☐ B7	Kurt Nimphius	2.00	.90	.25
☐ B8	Jim Spanarkel	2.00	.90	.25
☐ B9	Elston Turner	2.00	.90	.25
☐ B10	Jay Vincent	2.00	.90	.25
☐ B11	Mark West	3.00	1.35	.40
☐ C1	Nate Archibald	6.00	2.70	.75
☐ C2	Junior Bridgeman	2.00	.90	.25
☐ C3	Mike Dunleavy	2.00	.90	.25
☐ C4	Kevin Grevey	2.00	.90	.25
☐ C5	Marques Johnson	3.00	1.35	.40
☐ C6	Bob Lanier SP	300.00	135.00	38.00
☐ C7	Alton Lister	2.00	.90	.25
☐ C8	Sidney Moncrief	4.00	1.80	.50
☐ C9	Paul Pressey	2.00	.90	.25
☐ D1	Kareem Abdul-Jabbar	20.00	9.00	2.50
☐ D2	Michael Cooper	3.00	1.35	.40
☐ D3	Magic Johnson	45.00	20.00	5.75
☐ D4	Mike McGee	2.00	.90	.25
☐ D5	Swen Nater	2.00	.90	.25
☐ D6	Kurt Rambis	2.00	.90	.25
☐ D7	Byron Scott	3.00	1.35	.40
☐ D8	James Worthy	7.00	3.10	.85
☐ D9	Laker All-Stars	30.00	13.50	3.80

(Magic Johnson and
Kareem Abdul-Jabbar)

☐ D10	Kareem Abdul-Jabbar	15.00	6.75	1.90

NBA Scoring Leader

☐ E1	Julius Erving	25.00	11.50	3.10
☐ E2	Maurice Cheeks	3.00	1.35	.40
☐ E3	Franklin Edwards	2.00	.90	.25
☐ E4	Marc Iavaroni	2.00	.90	.25
☐ E5	Clemon Johnson	2.00	.90	.25
☐ E6	Bobby Jones	3.00	1.35	.40
☐ E7	Moses Malone	8.00	3.60	1.00
☐ E8	Clint Richardson	2.00	.90	.25
☐ E9	Andrew Toney	2.00	.90	.25
☐ E10	Sam Williams	2.00	.90	.25

1984-85 Star
Court Kings 5x7

*This over-sized 50-card set was issued as
two series of 25. Cards measure approximately 5" by 7" and have a yellow (first*

*series 1-25) or blue (second series 26-50)
colored border around the fronts of the
cards and blue and yellow printing on the
backs. These large cards feature the Star
'85 logo on the front. The set features early
professional cards of Charles Barkley,
Michael Jordan and Hakeem Olajuwon.*

	NRMT-MT	EXC	VG
COMPLETE BAG SET (50)	450.00	200.00	57.50
COMP.BAG SER.1 (25)	125.00	57.50	15.50
COMP.BAG SER.2 (25)	325.00	145.00	40.00
COMMON CARD (1-25)	2.00	.90	.25
COMMON CARD (26-50)	2.50	1.15	.30

*OPENED TEAM SETS: .75X TO 1.0X VALUE

☐ 1	Kareem Abdul-Jabbar	20.00	9.00	2.50
☐ 2	Jeff Ruland	2.00	.90	.25
☐ 3	Mark Aguirre	3.00	1.35	.40
☐ 4	Julius Erving	20.00	9.00	2.50
☐ 5	Kelly Tripucka	2.00	.90	.25
☐ 6	Buck Williams	2.00	.90	.25
☐ 7	Sidney Moncrief	3.00	1.35	.40
☐ 8	World B. Free	3.00	1.35	.40
☐ 9	Bill Walton	6.00	2.70	.75
☐ 10	Purvis Short	2.00	.90	.25
☐ 11	Rickey Green	2.00	.90	.25
☐ 12	Dominique Wilkins	20.00	9.00	2.50
☐ 13	Jim Paxson	2.00	.90	.25
☐ 14	Ralph Sampson	3.00	1.35	.40
☐ 15	Magic Johnson	40.00	18.00	5.00
☐ 16	Reggie Theus	3.00	1.35	.40
☐ 17	Moses Malone	6.00	2.70	.75
☐ 18	Larry Bird	50.00	23.00	6.25
☐ 19	Larry Nance	2.00	.90	.25
☐ 20	Clark Kellogg	2.00	.90	.25
☐ 21	Jack Sikma	3.00	1.35	.40
☐ 22	Alex English	4.00	1.80	.50
☐ 23	Bernard King	4.00	1.80	.50
☐ 24	Dave Corzine	2.00	.90	.25
☐ 25	George Gervin	6.00	2.70	.75
☐ 26	Michael Jordan	200.00	90.00	25.00
☐ 27	Rolando Blackman	3.50	1.55	.45
☐ 28	Dan Issel	2.50	1.15	.30
☐ 29	Maurice Cheeks	3.50	1.55	.45
☐ 30	Isiah Thomas	12.00	5.50	1.50
☐ 31	Robert Parish	6.00	2.70	.75
☐ 32	Mark Eaton	3.50	1.55	.45
☐ 33	Sam Perkins	2.50	1.15	.30
☐ 34	Artis Gilmore	4.00	1.80	.50
☐ 35	Andrew Toney	2.50	1.15	.30
☐ 36	Adrian Dantley	4.00	1.80	.50
☐ 37	Terry Cummings	3.50	1.55	.45
☐ 38	Orlando Woolridge	2.50	1.15	.30
☐ 39	Tom Chambers	2.50	1.15	.30

		NRMT-MT	EXC	VG
☐ 40	Gus Williams	3.50	1.55	.45
☐ 41	Charles Barkley	50.00	23.00	6.25
☐ 42	Kevin McHale	7.00	3.10	.85
☐ 43	Otis Birdsong	3.50	1.55	.45
☐ 44	Sam Bowie	3.50	1.55	.45
☐ 45	Darrell Griffith	3.50	1.55	.45
☐ 46	Kiki Vandeweghe	3.50	1.55	.45
☐ 47	Hakeem Olajuwon	60.00	27.00	7.50
☐ 48	Marques Johnson	3.50	1.55	.45
☐ 49	James Worthy	6.00	2.70	.75
☐ 50	Mel Turpin	2.50	1.15	.30

1984-85 Star Julius Erving

This set contains 18 cards highlighting the career of basketball great Julius Erving. Cards measure 2 1/2" by 3 1/2" and have a red border around the fronts of the cards and red printing on the backs. Cards feature Star '85 logo on the front although they were released in the summer of 1984.

		NRMT-MT	EXC	VG
COMPLETE BAG SET (18)		90.00	40.00	11.50
COMMON J.ERVING (1-18)		7.00	3.10	.85
*OPENED SET: .75X to 1.0X VALUE.				

		NRMT-MT	EXC	VG
☐ 1	Checklist	7.00	3.10	.85
☐ 2	NBA Regular Season Stats	7.00	3.10	.85
☐ 3	ABA Regular Season Stats	7.00	3.10	.85
☐ 4	NBA All-Star Eight Times	7.00	3.10	.85
☐ 5	ABA All-Star Five Times	7.00	3.10	.85
☐ 6	NBA Playoff Stats	7.00	3.10	.85
☐ 7	ABA Playoff Stats	7.00	3.10	.85
☐ 8	NBA MVP, 1981	7.00	3.10	.85
☐ 9	ABA MVP, 1974, 1975, and 1976	7.00	3.10	.85
☐ 10	Collegiate Stats	7.00	3.10	.85
☐ 11	NBA All-Star MVP, 1977 and 1983	7.00	3.10	.85
☐ 12	NBA Career Highlights	7.00	3.10	.85
☐ 13	ABA Career Highlights	7.00	3.10	.85
☐ 14	1983 World Champs	7.00	3.10	.85
☐ 15	ABA Champions 1974 and 1976	7.00	3.10	.85
☐ 16	All-Time Scoring	7.00	3.10	.85
☐ 17	Personal Data	7.00	3.10	.85
☐ 18	The Future	7.00	3.10	.85

1985 Star Kareem Abdul-Jabbar

The 1985 Star Kareem Abdul-Jabbar set is an 18-card tribute highlighting his career. Most of the photos on the fronts are from the early 1980s. Card backs provide various statistics and tidbits of information about Abdul-Jabbar. The set's basic design is identical to those of the Star Company's regular NBA sets. The cards show a Star '85 logo in the upper right corner. The cards measure approximately 2 1/2" by 3 1/2". The front borders are Lakers' purple.

		NRMT-MT	EXC	VG
COMPLETE BAG SET (18)		50.00	23.00	6.25
COMMON JABBAR (1-18)		3.50	1.55	.45
*OPENED SET: .75X to 1.0X VALUE.				

		NRMT-MT	EXC	VG
☐ 1	Checklist Card	3.50	1.55	.45
☐ 2	Collegiate Stats	3.50	1.55	.45
☐ 3	Regular Season Stats	3.50	1.55	.45
☐ 4	Playoff Stats	3.50	1.55	.45
☐ 5	All Star Stats	3.50	1.55	.45
☐ 6	All-Time Scoring King	3.50	1.55	.45
☐ 7	NBA MVP 71/72/74	3.50	1.55	.45
☐ 8	NBA MVP 76/77/80	3.50	1.55	.45
☐ 9	Defensive Star	3.50	1.55	.45
☐ 10	World Champs 71	3.50	1.55	.45
☐ 11	World Champs 80/82/85	3.50	1.55	.45
☐ 12	All-Time Records	3.50	1.55	.45
☐ 13	Rookie-of-the-Year 70	3.50	1.55	.45
☐ 14	Playoff MVP 71/85	3.50	1.55	.45
☐ 15	The League Leader	3.50	1.55	.45
☐ 16	Career Highlights	3.50	1.55	.45
☐ 17	Personal Data	3.50	1.55	.45
☐ 18	The Future	3.50	1.55	.45

1985 Star Crunch'n'Munch All-Stars

The 1985 Star Crunch'n'Munch NBA All-Stars set is an 11-card set featuring the ten starting players in the 1985 NBA All-Star Game plus a checklist card. The set was produced for the Crunch 'n' Munch Food Company and was originally available to

the hobby exclusively through Don Guilbert of Woonsocket, Rhode Island. The set's basic design is identical to those of the Star Company's regular NBA sets. The cards measure approximately 2 1/2" by 3 1/2". The cards show a Star '85 logo in the upper right corner. The front borders are yellowish orange and the backs show each player's All-Star Game record.

	NRMT-MT	EXC	VG
COMPLETE BAG SET (11) ...	525.00	240.00	65.00
COMMON CARD (1-11)	5.00	2.30	.60

*OPENED SET: .75X to 1.0X VALUE.

		NRMT-MT	EXC	VG
☐	1 Checklist Card...............	10.00	4.50	1.25
☐	2 Larry Bird.....................	100.00	45.00	12.50
☐	3 Julius Erving.................	30.00	13.50	3.80
☐	4 Michael Jordan	325.00	145.00	40.00
☐	5 Moses Malone	10.00	4.50	1.25
☐	6 Isiah Thomas	15.00	6.75	1.90
☐	7 Kareem Abdul-Jabbar ..	25.00	11.50	3.10
☐	8 Adrian Dantley	6.00	2.70	.75
☐	9 George Gervin	12.00	5.50	1.50
☐	10 Magic Johnson	70.00	32.00	8.75
☐	11 Ralph Sampson	5.00	2.30	.60

1985 Star Gatorade Slam Dunk

This nine-card set was given to the people who attended the 1985 All-Star Weekend Banquet at Indianapolis. Cards measure the standard size and have a green border around the fronts of the cards and green printing on the backs. Cards feature the Star '85 and Gatorade logos on the fronts. Since Terence Stansbury was a late substitute in the Slam Dunk contest for Charles Barkley. Both cards were produced, but the

Barkley card was never released. However, the card has since surfaced in the marketplace. The Barkley card is unnumbered and shows him dunking.

	NRMT-MT	EXC	VG
COMPLETE BAG SET (9)	300.00	135.00	38.00
COMMON CARD (1-9)	3.00	1.35	.40

*OPENED SET: .75X to 1.0X VALUE.

		NRMT-MT	EXC	VG
☐	1 Gatorade 2nd Annual ..... Slam Dunk Championship (Checklist back)	6.00	2.70	.75
☐	2 Larry Nance	6.00	2.70	.75
☐	3 Terence Stansbury.........	3.00	1.35	.40
☐	4 Clyde Drexler	35.00	16.00	4.40
☐	5 Julius Erving.................	25.00	11.50	3.10
☐	6 Darrell Griffith	3.50	1.55	.45
☐	7 Michael Jordan	225.00	100.00	28.00
☐	8 Dominique Wilkins.........	25.00	11.50	3.10
☐	9 Orlando Woolridge	3.50	1.55	.45
☐	NNO Charles Barkley SP (Withdrawn)	300.00	135.00	38.00

1985 Star Last 11 ROY's

The 1985 Star Rookies of the Year set is an 11-card set depicting each of the NBA's ROY award winners from the 1974-75 through 1984-85 seasons. Michael Jordan's card only shows his collegiate statistics while all others provide NBA statistics up through the 1983-84 season. Cards of Darrell Griffith and Jamaal Wilkes show the Star '86 logo in the upper right corner while all others in the set show Star '85. The set's basic design is identical to those of the Star Company's regular NBA sets and the front borders are off-white. The cards measure approximately 2 1/2" by 3 1/2". The cards are numbered on the back in reverse chronological order according to when each player won the ROY.

	NRMT-MT	EXC	VG
COMPLETE BAG SET (11) ...	300.00	135.00	38.00
COMMON CARD (1-11)	3.00	1.35	.40

*OPENED SET: .75X to 1.0X VALUE.

		NRMT-MT	EXC	VG
☐	1 Michael Jordan	225.00	100.00	28.00
☐	2 Ralph Sampson	3.00	1.35	.40

		NRMT-MT	EXC	VG
☐	3 Terry Cummings	3.00	1.35	.40
☐	4 Buck Williams	3.00	1.35	.40
☐	5 Darrell Griffith	3.00	1.35	.40
☐	6 Larry Bird	90.00	40.00	11.50
☐	7 Phil Ford	3.00	1.35	.40
☐	8 Walter Davis	3.00	1.35	.40
☐	9 Adrian Dantley	3.00	1.35	.40
☐	10 Alvan Adams	3.00	1.35	.40
☐	11 Keith/Jamaal Wilkes	3.00	1.35	.40

1985 Star
Lite All-Stars

This 13-card set was given to the people who attended the 1985 All-Star Weekend Banquet at Indianapolis. The set was issued in a clear, sealed plastic bag. Cards measure 2 1/2" by 3 1/2" and have a blue border around the fronts of the cards and blue printing on the backs. Cards feature the Star '85 and Lite Beer logos on the fronts. Players featured are the 1985 NBA All-Star starting line-ups and coaches.

		NRMT-MT	EXC	VG
	COMPLETE BAG SET (13)	350.00	160.00	45.00
	COMMON CARD (1-13)	4.00	1.80	.50
	*OPENED SET: .75X to 1.0X VALUE.			

		NRMT-MT	EXC	VG
☐	1 1985 NBA All-Stars Starting Line-Ups	4.00	1.80	.50
☐	2 Larry Bird	90.00	40.00	11.50
☐	3 Julius Erving	25.00	11.50	3.10
☐	4 Michael Jordan	225.00	100.00	28.00
☐	5 Moses Malone	8.00	3.60	1.00
☐	6 Isiah Thomas	12.00	5.50	1.50
☐	7 K.C. Jones CO	4.00	1.80	.50
☐	8 Kareem Abdul-Jabbar	20.00	9.00	2.50
☐	9 Adrian Dantley	5.00	2.30	.60
☐	10 George Gervin	10.00	4.50	1.25
☐	11 Magic Johnson	60.00	27.00	7.50
☐	12 Ralph Sampson	5.00	2.30	.60
☐	13 Pat Riley CO	8.00	3.60	1.00

1985 Star
Team Supers 5x7

This 40-card set is actually eight team sets of five each except for the Sixers having ten

players included. Cards measure approximately 5" by 7" and have a colored border around the fronts of the cards according to the team with corresponding color printing on the backs. Cards feature Star '85 logo on the front. Cards are numbered below by assigning a team prefix based on the initials of the team, for example, BC for Boston Celtics.

	NRMT-MT	EXC	VG
COMPLETE BAG SET (40)	525.00	240.00	65.00
COMP.BAG 76ERS (10)	80.00	36.00	10.00
COMP.BAG BULLS (5)	225.00	100.00	28.00
COMP.BAG PISTONS (5)	25.00	11.50	3.10
COMP.BAG ROCKETS (5)	70.00	32.00	8.75
COMP.BAG LAKERS (5)	75.00	34.00	9.50
COMP.BAG BUCKS (5)	10.00	4.50	1.25
COMP.BAG 76ERS (10)	80.00	36.00	10.00
COMMON CELTICS (BC1-BC5)	2.00	.90	.25
COMMON BULLS (CB1-CB5)	2.00	.90	.25
COMMON PISTONS (DP1-DP5)	2.00	.90	.25
COMMON ROCKETS (HR1-HR5)	2.00	.90	.25
COMMON LAKERS (LA1-LA5)	2.00	.90	.25
COMMON BUCKS (MB1-MB5)	2.00	.90	.25
COMMON 76ERS (PS1-PS10)	2.00	.90	.25
*OPENED TEAM SETS: .75X to 1.0X VALUE			

		NRMT-MT	EXC	VG
☐	BC1 Larry Bird	50.00	23.00	6.25
☐	BC2 Robert Parish	5.00	2.30	.60
☐	BC3 Kevin McHale	6.00	2.70	.75
☐	BC4 Dennis Johnson	3.00	1.35	.40
☐	BC5 Danny Ainge	5.00	2.30	.60
☐	CB1 Michael Jordan	200.00	90.00	25.00
☐	CB2 Orlando Woolridge	2.50	1.15	.30
☐	CB3 Quintin Dailey	2.00	.90	.25
☐	CB4 Dave Corzine	2.00	.90	.25
☐	CB5 Steve Johnson	2.00	.90	.25
☐	DP1 Isiah Thomas	12.00	5.50	1.50
☐	DP2 Kelly Tripucka	2.00	.90	.25
☐	DP3 Vinnie Johnson	2.50	1.15	.30
☐	DP4 Bill Laimbeer	2.50	1.15	.30
☐	DP5 John Long	2.00	.90	.25
☐	HR1 Ralph Sampson	2.50	1.15	.30
☐	HR2 Hakeem Olajuwon	60.00	27.00	7.50
☐	HR3 Lewis Lloyd	2.00	.90	.25
☐	HR4 Rodney McCray	2.50	1.15	.30
☐	HR5 Lionel Hollins	2.00	.90	.25
☐	LA1 Kareem Abdul-Jabbar	18.00	8.00	2.30
☐	LA2 Magic Johnson	40.00	18.00	5.00
☐	LA3 James Worthy	5.00	2.30	.60
☐	LA4 Byron Scott	2.50	1.15	.30
☐	LA5 Bob McAdoo	3.00	1.35	.40
☐	MB1 Terry Cummings	2.50	1.15	.30
☐	MB2 Sidney Moncrief	2.50	1.15	.30
☐	MB3 Paul Pressey	2.00	.90	.25
☐	MB4 Mike Dunleavy	2.00	.90	.25

		NRMT-MT	EXC	VG
☐	MB5 Alton Lister	2.00	.90	.25
☐	PS1 Julius Erving	20.00	9.00	2.50
☐	PS2 Maurice Cheeks	2.50	1.15	.30
☐	PS3 Bobby Jones	2.50	1.15	.30
☐	PS4 Clemon Johnson	2.00	.90	.25
☐	PS5 Leon Wood	2.00	.90	.25
☐	PS6 Moses Malone	5.00	2.30	.60
☐	PS7 Andrew Toney	2.00	.90	.25
☐	PS8 Charles Barkley	50.00	23.00	6.25
☐	PS9 Clint Richardson	2.00	.90	.25
☐	PS10 Sedale Threatt	2.00	.90	.25

1985 Star Slam Dunk Supers 5x7

This ten-card set uses actual photography from the 1985 Slam Dunk contest in Indianapolis held during the NBA All-Star Weekend. Cards measure approximately 5" by 7" and have a red border around the fronts of the cards and red printing on the backs. Cards feature Star '85 logo on the fronts. The set ordering for these numbered cards is alphabetical by subject's name.

		NRMT-MT	EXC	VG
	COMPLETE BAG SET (10)	250.00	115.00	31.00
	COMMON CARD (1-10)	2.00	.90	.25
	*OPENED SET: .75X to 1.0X VALUE.			
☐	1 Checklist Card (Group photo)	45.00	20.00	5.75
☐	2 Clyde Drexler	30.00	13.50	3.80
☐	3 Julius Erving	25.00	11.50	3.10
☐	4 Darrell Griffith	3.00	1.35	.40
☐	5 Michael Jordan	200.00	90.00	25.00
☐	6 Larry Nance	6.00	2.70	.75
☐	7 Terence Stansbury	2.00	.90	.25
☐	8 Dominique Wilkins	20.00	9.00	2.50
☐	9 Orlando Woolridge	3.00	1.35	.40
☐	10 Dominique Wilkins (1985 Slam Dunk Champ)	15.00	6.75	1.90

1985-86 Star

This 172-card set was produced by the Star Company and features players in the NBA. Cards were released in two groups, 1-94

and 95-172. The team sets were issued in clear sealed bags. Many of these team bags were distributed to hobby dealers through a small group of Star Company master distributors. The original wholesale price per bag was $2-$3 for most of the teams. According to Star Company's original sales materials and order forms, reportedly 2,000 team bags were printed for each team and an additional 2,200 team sets were printed for the more popular teams of that time. Cards are numbered in team order and measure the standard 2 1/2" by 3 1/2". The team ordering is as follows, Philadelphia 76ers (1-9), Detroit Pistons (10-17), Houston Rockets (18-25), Los Angeles Lakers (26-33), Phoenix Suns (34-41), Atlanta Hawks (42-49), Denver Nuggets (50-57), New Jersey Nets (58-65), Seattle Supersonics (66-73), Sacramento Kings (74-80), Indiana Pacers (81-87), Los Angeles Clippers (88-94), Boston Celtics (95-102), Portland Trail Blazers (103-109), Washington Bullets (110-116), Chicago Bulls (117-123), Milwaukee Bucks (124-130), Golden State Warriors (131-136), Utah Jazz (137-144), San Antonio Spurs (145-151), Cleveland Cavaliers (152-158), Dallas Mavericks (159-165) and New York Knicks (166-172). Borders are colored according to team. Card backs are very similar to the other Star basketball sets except that the player statistics go up through the 1984-85 season. Extended Rookie Cards in this set include Patrick Ewing and Kevin Willis. There is typically a slight discount on sales of opened team bags. Cards of Celtics players (95-102) have either green or white borders. Many cards in this set (particularly 95-176) have been counterfeited and are prevalent on the market. Among those affected are the Ewing Extended Rookie Card (166) and Jordan (117).

	NRMT-MT	EXC	VG
COMPLETE BAG SET (172)	1800.00	800.00	230.00
COMP.BAG 76ERS (9)	160.00	70.00	20.00
COMP.BAG PISTONS (8)	45.00	20.00	5.75
COMP.BAG ROCKETS (8)	175.00	80.00	22.00
COMP.BAG LAKERS SP (8)	275.00	125.00	34.00
COMP.BAG SUNS (8)	15.00	6.75	1.90
COMP.BAG HAWKS (8)	100.00	45.00	12.50
COMP.BAG NUGGETS (8)	15.00	6.75	1.90
COMP.BAG NETS (8)	15.00	6.75	1.90
COMP.BAG SONICS (8)	15.00	6.75	1.90
COMP.BAG KINGS (7)	15.00	6.75	1.90

COMP.BAG PACERS (7)	15.00	6.75	1.90
COMP.BAG CLIPPERS (7)	15.00	6.75	1.90
COMP.BAG CELTICS (8)	140.00	65.00	17.50
COMP.BAG BLAZERS (7)	120.00	55.00	15.00
COMP.BAG BULLETS (7)	15.00	6.75	1.90
COMP.BAG BULLS (7)	900.00	400.00	115.00
COMP.BAG BUCKS (7)	15.00	6.75	1.90
COMP.BAG WARRIORS (7)	15.00	6.75	1.90
COMP.BAG JAZZ (7)	90.00	40.00	11.50
COMP.BAG SPURS (7)	15.00	6.75	1.90
COMP.BAG CAVS (7)	15.00	6.75	1.90
COMP.BAG MAVS (7)	15.00	6.75	1.90
COMP.BAG KNICKS (7)	200.00	90.00	25.00
COMMON 76ERS (1-9)	2.00	.90	.25
COMMON PISTONS (10-17)	2.00	.90	.25
COMMON ROCKETS (18-25)	2.00	.90	.25
COMMON LAKERS SP (26-33)	5.00	2.30	.60
COMMON SUNS (34-41)	2.00	.90	.25
COMMON HAWKS (42-49)	2.00	.90	.25
COMMON NUGGETS (50-57)	2.00	.90	.25
COMMON NETS (58-65)	2.00	.90	.25
COMMON SONICS (66-73)	2.00	.90	.25
COMMON KINGS (74-80)	2.00	.90	.25
COMMON PACERS (81-87)	2.00	.90	.25
COMMON CLIPPERS (88-94)	2.00	.90	.25
COMMON CELTICS (95-102)	2.00	.90	.25
COMMON BLAZERS (103-109)	2.00	.90	.25
COMMON BULLETS (110-116)	2.00	.90	.25
COMMON BULLS (117-123)	2.00	.90	.25
COMMON BUCKS (124-130)	2.00	.90	.25
COMMON WARRIORS (131-137)	2.00	.90	.25
COMMON JAZZ (138-144)	2.00	.90	.25
COMMON SPURS (145-151)	2.00	.90	.25
COMMON CAVS (152-158)	2.00	.90	.25
COMMON MAVS (159-165)	2.00	.90	.25
COMMON KNICKS (166-172) !	2.00	.90	.25

*OPENED TEAM SETS: .75X to 1.0
*WHITE CELTICS LISTED BELOW
*GREEN CELTICS: 1.25X VALUE OF WHITE

☐ 1	Maurice Cheeks	5.00	2.30	.60
☐ 2	Charles Barkley	125.00	57.50	15.50
☐ 3	Julius Erving	30.00	13.50	3.80
☐ 4	Clemon Johnson	2.00	.90	.25
☐ 5	Bobby Jones	3.00	1.35	.40
☐ 6	Moses Malone	10.00	4.50	1.25
☐ 7	Sedale Threatt	2.00	.90	.25
☐ 8	Andrew Toney	2.00	.90	.25
☐ 9	Leon Wood	2.00	.90	.25
☐ 10	Isiah Thomas UER	25.00	11.50	3.10
	(No Pistons logo on card front)			
☐ 11	Kent Benson	2.00	.90	.25
☐ 12	Earl Cureton	2.00	.90	.25
☐ 13	Vinnie Johnson	3.00	1.35	.40
☐ 14	Bill Laimbeer	4.00	1.80	.50
☐ 15	John Long	2.00	.90	.25
☐ 16	Rick Mahorn	2.00	.90	.25
☐ 17	Kelly Tripucka	2.00	.90	.25
☐ 18	Hakeem Olajuwon	160.00	70.00	20.00
☐ 19	Allen Leavell	2.00	.90	.25
☐ 20	Lewis Lloyd	2.00	.90	.25
☐ 21	John Lucas	3.00	1.35	.40
☐ 22	Rodney McCray	2.00	.90	.25
☐ 23	Robert Reid	2.00	.90	.25
☐ 24	Ralph Sampson	4.00	1.80	.50
☐ 25	Mitchell Wiggins	2.00	.90	.25
☐ 26	Kareem Abdul-Jabbar	50.00	23.00	6.25
☐ 27	Michael Cooper	10.00	4.50	1.25
☐ 28	Magic Johnson	200.00	90.00	25.00
☐ 29	Mitch Kupchak	5.00	2.30	.60
☐ 30	Maurice Lucas	6.00	2.70	.75
☐ 31	Kurt Rambis	6.00	2.70	.75
☐ 32	Byron Scott	8.00	3.60	1.00
☐ 33	James Worthy	18.00	8.00	2.30
☐ 34	Larry Nance	9.00	4.00	1.15
☐ 35	Alvan Adams	3.00	1.35	.40
☐ 36	Walter Davis	4.00	1.80	.50
☐ 37	James Edwards	3.00	1.35	.40
☐ 38	Jay Humphries	2.00	.90	.25
☐ 39	Charles Pittman	2.00	.90	.25
☐ 40	Rick Robey	2.00	.90	.25
☐ 41	Mike Sanders	2.00	.90	.25
☐ 42	Dominique Wilkins	45.00	20.00	5.75
☐ 43	Scott Hastings	2.00	.90	.25
☐ 44	Eddie Johnson	2.00	.90	.25
☐ 45	Cliff Levingston	2.00	.90	.25
☐ 46	Tree Rollins	4.00	1.80	.50
☐ 47	Doc Rivers UER	4.00	1.80	.50
	(Ray Williams is pictured on the front)			
☐ 48	Kevin Willis	18.00	8.00	2.30
☐ 49	Randy Wittman	2.00	.90	.25
☐ 50	Alex English	5.00	2.30	.60
☐ 51	Wayne Cooper	2.00	.90	.25
☐ 52	T.R. Dunn	2.00	.90	.25
☐ 53	Mike Evans	2.00	.90	.25
☐ 54	Lafayette Lever	3.00	1.35	.40
☐ 55	Calvin Natt	2.00	.90	.25
☐ 56	Danny Schayes	3.00	1.35	.40
☐ 57	Elston Turner	2.00	.90	.25
☐ 58	Buck Williams	5.00	2.30	.60
☐ 59	Otis Birdsong	3.00	1.35	.40
☐ 60	Darwin Cook	2.00	.90	.25
☐ 61	Darryl Dawkins	4.00	1.80	.50
☐ 62	Mike Gminski	3.00	1.35	.40
☐ 63	Mickey Johnson	2.00	.90	.25
☐ 64	Mike O'Koren	3.00	1.35	.40
☐ 65	Micheal R. Richardson	2.00	.90	.25
☐ 66	Tom Chambers	5.00	2.30	.60
☐ 67	Gerald Henderson	2.00	.90	.25
☐ 68	Tim McCormick	2.00	.90	.25
☐ 69	Jack Sikma	3.00	1.35	.40
☐ 70	Ricky Sobers	2.00	.90	.25
☐ 71	Danny Vranes	2.00	.90	.25
☐ 72	Al Wood	2.00	.90	.25
☐ 73	Danny Young	2.00	.90	.25
☐ 74	Reggie Theus	3.00	1.35	.40
☐ 75	Larry Drew	2.00	.90	.25
☐ 76	Eddie Johnson	3.00	1.35	.40
☐ 77	Mark Olberding	2.00	.90	.25
☐ 78	LaSalle Thompson	2.00	.90	.25
☐ 79	Otis Thorpe	7.00	3.10	.85
☐ 80	Mike Woodson	2.00	.90	.25
☐ 81	Clark Kellogg	2.00	.90	.25
☐ 82	Quinn Buckner	3.00	1.35	.40
☐ 83	Vern Fleming	3.00	1.35	.40
☐ 84	Bill Garnett	2.00	.90	.25
☐ 85	Terence Stansbury	2.00	.90	.25
☐ 86	Steve Stipanovich	2.00	.90	.25
☐ 87	Herb Williams	3.00	1.35	.40
☐ 88	Marques Johnson	3.00	1.35	.40
☐ 89	Michael Cage	2.00	.90	.25
☐ 90	Franklin Edwards	2.00	.90	.25
☐ 91	Cedric Maxwell	3.00	1.35	.40
☐ 92	Derek Smith	2.00	.90	.25
☐ 93	Rory White	2.00	.90	.25
☐ 94	Jamaal Wilkes	4.00	1.80	.50
☐ 95	Larry Bird	125.00	57.50	15.50
☐ 96	Danny Ainge	10.00	4.50	1.25
☐ 97	Dennis Johnson	4.00	1.80	.50
☐ 98	Kevin McHale	14.00	6.25	1.75

			NRMT-MT	EXC	VG
☐	99	Robert Parish ERR	10.00	4.50	1.25
☐	100	Jerry Sichting	2.00	.90	.25
☐	101	Bill Walton	12.00	5.50	1.50
☐	102	Scott Wedman	2.00	.90	.25
☐	103	Kiki Vandeweghe	2.00	.90	.25
☐	104	Sam Bowie	3.00	1.35	.40
☐	105	Kenny Carr	2.00	.90	.25
☐	106	Clyde Drexler	75.00	34.00	9.50
☐	107	Jerome Kersey	4.00	1.80	.50
☐	108	Jim Paxson	2.00	.90	.25
☐	109	Mychal Thompson	3.00	1.35	.40
☐	110	Gus Williams	3.00	1.35	.40
☐	111	Darren Daye	2.00	.90	.25
☐	112	Jeff Malone	4.00	1.80	.50
☐	113	Tom McMillen	3.00	1.35	.40
☐	114	Cliff Robinson	2.00	.90	.25
☐	115	Dan Roundfield	3.00	1.35	.40
☐	116	Jeff Ruland	3.00	1.35	.40
☐	117	Michael Jordan	850.00	375.00	105.00
☐	118	Gene Banks	2.00	.90	.25
☐	119	Dave Corzine	2.00	.90	.25
☐	120	Quintin Dailey	2.00	.90	.25
☐	121	George Gervin	12.00	5.50	1.50
☐	122	Jawann Oldham	2.00	.90	.25
☐	123	Orlando Woolridge	4.00	1.80	.50
☐	124	Terry Cummings	4.00	1.80	.50
☐	125	Craig Hodges	2.00	.90	.25
☐	126	Alton Lister	2.00	.90	.25
☐	127	Paul Mokeski	2.00	.90	.25
☐	128	Sidney Moncrief	4.00	1.80	.50
☐	129	Ricky Pierce	5.00	2.30	.60
☐	130	Paul Pressey	2.00	.90	.25
☐	131	Purvis Short	2.00	.90	.25
☐	132	Joe Barry Carroll	3.00	1.35	.40
☐	133	Lester Conner	2.00	.90	.25
☐	134	Sleepy Floyd	2.00	.90	.25
☐	135	Geoff Huston	2.00	.90	.25
☐	136	Larry Smith	2.00	.90	.25
☐	137	Jerome Whitehead	2.00	.90	.25
☐	138	Adrian Dantley	4.00	1.80	.50
☐	139	Mitchell Anderson	2.00	.90	.25
☐	140	Thurl Bailey	2.00	.90	.25
☐	141	Mark Eaton	3.00	1.35	.40
☐	142	Rickey Green	3.00	1.35	.40
☐	143	Darrell Griffith	3.00	1.35	.40
☐	144	John Stockton	100.00	45.00	12.50
☐	145	Artis Gilmore	4.00	1.80	.50
☐	146	Marc Iavaroni	2.00	.90	.25
☐	147	Steve Johnson	2.00	.90	.25
☐	148	Mike Mitchell	2.00	.90	.25
☐	149	Johnny Moore	2.00	.90	.25
☐	150	Alvin Robertson	2.00	.90	.25
☐	151	Jon Sundvold	2.00	.90	.25
☐	152	World B. Free	4.00	1.80	.50
☐	153	John Bagley	2.00	.90	.25
☐	154	Johnny Davis	2.00	.90	.25
☐	155	Roy Hinson	2.00	.90	.25
☐	156	Phil Hubbard	2.00	.90	.25
☐	157	Ben Poquette	2.00	.90	.25
☐	158	Mel Turpin	2.00	.90	.25
☐	159	Rolando Blackman	3.00	1.35	.40
☐	160	Mark Aguirre	4.00	1.80	.50
☐	161	Brad Davis	2.00	.90	.25
☐	162	Dale Ellis	3.00	1.35	.40
☐	163	Derek Harper	7.00	3.10	.85
☐	164	Sam Perkins	7.00	3.10	.85
☐	165	Jay Vincent	2.00	.90	.25
☐	166	Patrick Ewing	175.00	80.00	22.00
☐	167	Bill Cartwright	3.00	1.35	.40
☐	168	Pat Cummings	2.00	.90	.25
☐	169	Ernie Grunfeld	2.00	.90	.25
☐	170	Rory Sparrow	2.00	.90	.25
☐	171	Trent Tucker	2.00	.90	.25
☐	172	Darrell Walker	2.00	.90	.25

1985-86 Star All-Rookie Team

The 1985-86 Star NBA All-Rookie Team is an 11-card set that features 11 top rookies from the previous (1984-85) season. The set's basic design is identical to those of the Star Company's regular NBA sets. The cards measure approximately 2 1/2" by 3 1/2". The front borders are red and the backs include each player's collegiate statistics. Alvin Robertson's card shows the Star '86 logo in the upper right corner. All others in the set show Star '85.

	NRMT-MT	EXC	VG
COMPLETE BAG SET (11)	500.00	230.00	65.00
COMMON CARD (1-11)	5.00	2.30	.60
*OPENED SET: .75X to 1.0X VALUE.			

			NRMT-MT	EXC	VG
☐	1	Hakeem Olajuwon	80.00	36.00	10.00
☐	2	Michael Jordan	325.00	145.00	40.00
☐	3	Charles Barkley	60.00	27.00	7.50
☐	4	Sam Bowie	5.00	2.30	.60
☐	5	Sam Perkins	6.00	2.70	.75
☐	6	Vern Fleming	5.00	2.30	.60
☐	7	Otis Thorpe	6.00	2.70	.75
☐	8	John Stockton	50.00	23.00	6.25
☐	9	Kevin Willis	6.00	2.70	.75
☐	10	Tim McCormick	5.00	2.30	.60
☐	11	Alvin Robertson	5.00	2.30	.60

1985-86 Star Lakers Champs

The 1985-86 Star Lakers NBA Champs set is an 18-card set commemorating the Los Angeles Lakers' 1985 NBA Championship. Each card depicts action from the Championship series. The front borders are off-white. The backs feature game and series summaries plus other related information. The set's basic design is identical to those of the Star Company's regular NBA sets. The cards show a Star '86 logo in the upper right corner. The cards measure approximately 2 1/2" by 3 1/2". The cards are numbered in the upper left corner of the reverse.

	NRMT-MT	EXC	VG
COMPLETE BAG SET (18) ...	100.00	45.00	12.50
COMMON CARD (1-18)	2.00	.90	.25

*OPENED SET: .75X to 1.0X VALUE.

		NRMT-MT	EXC	VG
☐ 1	Lakers 1985 NBA Champs (Kareem and Buss with trophy)	12.00	5.50	1.50
☐ 2	Boston 148, L.A. 114... (Bird under basket)	30.00	13.50	3.80
☐ 3	L.A. 109, Boston 102..... (Dennis Johnson)	2.00	.90	.25
☐ 4	L.A. 136, Boston 111..... (Danny Ainge)	5.00	2.30	.60
☐ 5	Boston 107, L.A. 105..... (Byron Scott driving)	3.00	1.35	.40
☐ 6	L.A. 120, Boston 111 .... (McHale under basket)	7.00	3.10	.85
☐ 7	L.A. 111, Boston 100 ... (Magic driving)	20.00	9.00	2.50
☐ 8	Kareem 1985 Series MVP	7.00	3.10	.85
☐ 9	Playoff Highs .... (Larry Bird)	30.00	13.50	3.80
☐ 10	Top Playoff Scorers ... (Kareem holding ball)	10.00	4.50	1.25
☐ 11	Title Fight .... (Ainge/Michael Cooper)	4.00	1.80	.50
☐ 12	Laker Series Stats........ (Riley in huddle)	6.00	2.70	.75
☐ 13	Boston Series Stats ..... (K.C. Jones in huddle)	2.00	.90	.25
☐ 14	L.A. Playoff Stats .... (Magic driving)	20.00	9.00	2.50
☐ 15	Boston Playoff Stats .... (action under basket)	3.00	1.35	.40
☐ 16	Road To The Title........	2.00	.90	.25
☐ 17	Prior World Champs I... (riding on float)	2.00	.90	.25
☐ 18	Prior World Champs II (with Ronald Reagan)	30.00	13.50	3.80

1986 Star
Best of the Best

The Star Company reportedly produced only 1,400 sets and planned to release them in 1986. However, they were not issued until as late as 1990. This set and the Magic Johnson set were printed on the same uncut sheet. No factory-sealed bags exist for this set due to the fact that the sets were cut from the sheets years after the original printing. It is understood that the uncut sheets were sold to hobbyists who cut the sheets and packaged sets to be sold into the hobby. The cards measure standard size (2 1/2" by 3 1/2"). The fronts feature color action photos with white inner borders and a blue card face. The player's name, position, and team name appear at the bottom. The set title "Best of the Best" appears in a white circle at the lower left corner. The backs are white with blue borders and contain biography and statistics. The cards are numbered and arranged in alphabetical order.

		NRMT-MT	EXC	VG
COMPLETE SET (15)		700.00	325.00	90.00
COMMON CARD (1-15)		7.00	3.10	.85
☐ 1	Kareem Abdul-Jabbar ..	30.00	13.50	3.80
☐ 2	Charles Barkley	60.00	27.00	7.50
☐ 3	Larry Bird	100.00	45.00	12.50
☐ 4	Tom Chambers	7.00	3.10	.85
☐ 5	Terry Cummings	7.00	3.10	.85
☐ 6	Julius Erving	35.00	16.00	4.40
☐ 7	Patrick Ewing	50.00	23.00	6.25
☐ 8	Magic Johnson	60.00	27.00	7.50
☐ 9	Michael Jordan	325.00	145.00	40.00
☐ 10	Moses Malone	10.00	4.50	1.25
☐ 11	Hakeem Olajuwon	80.00	36.00	10.00
☐ 12	John Stockton.............	50.00	23.00	6.25
☐ 13	Isiah Thomas	18.00	8.00	2.30
☐ 14	Dominique Wilkins.......	25.00	11.50	3.10
☐ 15	James Worthy.............	10.00	4.50	1.25

1986 Star
Court Kings

The 1986 Star Court Kings set contains 33 cards which feature many of the NBA's top players. The set's basic design is identical to those of the Star Company's regular NBA sets. The front borders are yellow, and the backs have career narrative summaries of each player but no statistics. The cards show a Star '86 logo in the upper right corner. The cards measure approximately 2

1/2" by 3 1/2". The cards are numbered in the upper left corner of the reverse. The numbering is alphabetical by last name.

	NRMT-MT	EXC	VG
COMPLETE BAG SET (33)	350.00	160.00	45.00
COMMON CARD (1-33)	2.00	.90	.25
*OPENED SET: .75X to 1.0X VALUE.			

		NRMT-MT	EXC	VG
☐	1 Mark Aguirre	2.50	1.15	.30
☐	2 Kareem Abdul-Jabbar	12.00	5.50	1.50
☐	3 Charles Barkley	40.00	18.00	5.00
☐	4 Larry Bird	60.00	27.00	7.50
☐	5 Rolando Blackman	2.50	1.15	.30
☐	6 Tom Chambers	2.50	1.15	.30
☐	7 Maurice Cheeks	2.50	1.15	.30
☐	8 Terry Cummings	2.50	1.15	.30
☐	9 Adrian Dantley	3.00	1.35	.40
☐	10 Darryl Dawkins	3.00	1.35	.40
☐	11 Mark Eaton	2.00	.90	.25
☐	12 Alex English	3.00	1.35	.40
☐	13 Julius Erving	15.00	6.75	1.90
☐	14 Patrick Ewing	20.00	9.00	2.50
☐	15 George Gervin	6.00	2.70	.75
☐	16 Darrell Griffith	2.00	.90	.25
☐	17 Magic Johnson	40.00	18.00	5.00
☐	18 Michael Jordan	200.00	90.00	25.00
☐	19 Clark Kellogg	2.00	.90	.25
☐	20 Bernard King	3.00	1.35	.40
☐	21 Moses Malone	6.00	2.70	.75
☐	22 Kevin McHale	7.00	3.10	.85
☐	23 Sidney Moncrief	2.50	1.15	.30
☐	24 Larry Nance	5.00	2.30	.60
☐	25 Hakeem Olajuwon	50.00	23.00	6.25
☐	26 Robert Parish	5.00	2.30	.60
☐	27 Ralph Sampson	2.50	1.15	.30
☐	28 Isiah Thomas	8.00	3.60	1.00
☐	29 Andrew Toney	2.00	.90	.25
☐	30 Kelly Tripucka	2.00	.90	.25
☐	31 Kiki Vandeweghe	2.00	.90	.25
☐	32 Dominique Wilkins	15.00	6.75	1.90
☐	33 James Worthy	5.00	2.30	.60

1986 Star Magic Johnson

This 10-card set highlights the career of Magic Johnson. The Star Company reportedly produced only 1,400 sets of these cards and planned to release them in 1986. However, they were not issued until perhaps as late as 1990. This set and the Best

of the Best set were printed on the same uncut sheet. Star directly sold sheets to hobbyists who cut them and sold sets to the hobby. The cards measure the standard size (2 1/2" by 3 1/2"). The cards are unnumbered and checklisted below in alphabetical order.

		NRMT-MT	EXC	VG
COMPLETE SET (10)		125.00	57.50	15.50
COMMON M.JOHNSON (1-10)		15.00	6.75	1.90

		NRMT-MT	EXC	VG
☐	1 Checklist	15.00	6.75	1.90
☐	2 Collegiate Stats	15.00	6.75	1.90
☐	3 Regular Season Stats	15.00	6.75	1.90
☐	4 Playoff Stats	15.00	6.75	1.90
☐	5 All-Star Stats	15.00	6.75	1.90
☐	6 Career Info 1	15.00	6.75	1.90
☐	7 Career Info 2	15.00	6.75	1.90
☐	8 Top Performance	15.00	6.75	1.90
☐	9 1980 Playoff MVP	15.00	6.75	1.90
☐	10 1982 Playoff MVP	15.00	6.75	1.90

1986 Star Michael Jordan

The 1986 Star Michael Jordan set contains ten cards highlighting his career. There were reportedly only 2,800 sets produced. They were originally available to the hobby exclusively through Dan Stickney of Michigan. Sets were originally issued in sealed plastic bags. The card backs contain various bits of information about Jordan. The set's basic design is identical to those of the Star Company's regular NBA sets. The front borders are red. The cards show a Star '86 logo in the upper right corner. The cards measure approximately 2 1/2" by 3 1/2". The cards are numbered in the upper left corner of the reverse. Collectors should beware of counterfeits.

	NRMT-MT	EXC	VG
COMPLETE BAG SET (10) ...	750.00	350.00	95.00
COMMON M.JORDAN (1-10).	90.00	40.00	11.50

*OPENED SET: .75X to 1.0X VALUE.

☐ 1 Michael Jordan	90.00	40.00	11.50
☐ 2 Collegiate Stats	90.00	40.00	11.50
☐ 3 1984 Olympian	90.00	40.00	11.50
☐ 4 Pro Stats	90.00	40.00	11.50
☐ 5 1985 All-Star..............	90.00	40.00	11.50
☐ 6 1985 Rookie of Year	90.00	40.00	11.50
☐ 7 Career Highlights.........	90.00	40.00	11.50
☐ 8 The 1986 Playoffs.........	90.00	40.00	11.50
☐ 9 Personal Data	90.00	40.00	11.50
☐ 10 The Future..................	90.00	40.00	11.50

1986 Star Best of the New/Old

It was reported that Star Company produced only 440 of these sets. They were distributed to dealers who purchased 1985-86 complete sets. Dealers received one set for every five regular sets purchased. The cards measure the standard size (2 1/2" by 3 1/2"). The cards are unnumbered and checklisted below in alphabetical order. The Best of the New are numbered 1-4 and the Best of the Old are numbered 5-8. The numbering is alphabetical within each group. Counterfeiting has been a problem with Best of the New.

	NRMT-MT	EXC	VG
COMPLETE SET (8)	1300.00	575.00	160.00
COMPLETE NEW SET (4).....	900.00	400.00	115.00
COMPLETE OLD SET (4).....	400.00	180.00	50.00
COMMON NEW CARD (1-4) ..	25.00	11.50	3.10
COMMON OLD CARD (5-8) ...	75.00	34.00	9.50

*BAGGED SETS: 1.0X to 1.5X VALUE

☐ 1 Patrick Ewing.............	110.00	50.00	14.00
☐ 2 Michael Jordan	600.00	275.00	75.00
☐ 3 Hakeem Olajuwon......	180.00	80.00	23.00

☐ 4 Ralph Sampson	25.00	11.50	3.10
☐ 5 Kareem Abdul-Jabbar	125.00	57.50	15.50
☐ 6 Julius Erving	150.00	70.00	19.00
☐ 7 George Gervin	75.00	34.00	9.50
☐ 8 Bill Walton..................	75.00	34.00	9.50

1957-58 Topps

The 1957-58 Topps basketball set of 80 cards was Topps' first basketball issue. Topps did not produce another basketball set until it released a test issue in 1968. A major set followed in 1969. Cards were issued in 5-cent packs (six cards per pack, 24 per box) and measure the standard 2 1/2" by 3 1/2". A number of cards in the set were double printed (indicated by DP in checklist below). The set contains 49 double prints, 30 single prints and one quadruple print (No. 24 Bob Pettit). Card backs give statistical information from the 1956-57 NBA season. Bill Russell's Rookie Card is part of the set. Other Rookie Cards include Paul Arizin, Nat Clifton, Bob Cousy, Cliff Hagan, Tom Heinsohn, Rod Hundley, Red Kerr, Clyde Lovellette, Pettit, Dolph Schayes, Bill Sharman and Jack Twyman. The set contains the only card of Maurice Stokes. Topps also produced a three-card advertising panel featuring the fronts of Walt Davis, Joe Graboski and Cousy with an advertisement for the upcoming Topps basketball set on the combined reverse.

	EX-MT	VG-E	GOOD
COMPLETE SET (80)	5500.00	2500.00	700.00
COMMON CARD (1-80)	35.00	16.00	4.40

☐ 1 Nat Clifton DP....... Detroit Pistons	250.00	115.00	31.00
☐ 2 George Yardley DP....... Detroit Pistons	50.00	23.00	6.25
☐ 3 Neil Johnston DP....... Philadelphia Warriors	55.00	25.00	7.00
☐ 4 Carl Braun DP....... New York Knicks	50.00	23.00	6.25
☐ 5 Bill Sharman DP......... Boston Celtics	175.00	80.00	22.00
☐ 6 George King DP .... Cincinnati Royals	35.00	16.00	4.40
☐ 7 Kenny Sears DP .... New York Knicks	35.00	16.00	4.40
☐ 8 Dick Ricketts DP	35.00	16.00	4.40

☐ 9	Jack Nichols DP .... Cincinnati Royals	25.00	11.50	3.10
☐ 10	Paul Arizin DP .... Boston Celtics	110.00	50.00	14.00
☐ 11	Chuck Noble DP .... Philadelphia Warriors	25.00	11.50	3.10
☐ 12	Slater Martin DP .... Detroit Pistons	55.00	25.00	7.00
☐ 13	Dolph Schayes DP ... St. Louis Hawks	125.00	57.50	15.50
☐ 14	Dick Atha DP .... Syracuse Nationals	25.00	11.50	3.10
☐ 15	Frank Ramsey DP ...... Detroit Pistons	75.00	34.00	9.50
☐ 16	Dick McGuire DP .... Boston Celtics	50.00	23.00	6.25
☐ 17	Bob Cousy DP .... Detroit Pistons	500.00	230.00	65.00
☐ 18	Larry Foust DP .... Boston Celtics	35.00	16.00	4.40
☐ 19	Tom Heinsohn .... Minneapolis Lakers	300.00	135.00	38.00
☐ 20	Bill Thieben DP .... Boston Celtics	25.00	11.50	3.10
☐ 21	Don Meineke DP .... Detroit Pistons	35.00	16.00	4.40
☐ 22	Tom Marshall .... Cincinnati Royals	35.00	16.00	4.40
☐ 23	Dick Garmaker .... Cincinnati Royals	35.00	16.00	4.40
☐ 24	Bob Pettit QP .... Minneapolis Lakers	175.00	80.00	22.00
☐ 25	Jim Krebs DP .... St. Louis Hawks	35.00	16.00	4.40
☐ 26	Gene Shue DP .... Minneapolis Lakers	55.00	25.00	7.00
☐ 27	Ed Macauley DP .... Detroit Pistons	55.00	25.00	7.00
☐ 28	Vern Mikkelsen .... St. Louis Hawks	75.00	34.00	9.50
☐ 29	Willie Nauls .... Minneapolis Lakers	55.00	25.00	7.00
☐ 30	Walter Dukes DP .... New York Knicks	35.00	16.00	4.40
☐ 31	Dave Piontek DP .... Detroit Pistons	25.00	11.50	3.10
☐ 32	John Kerr .... Cincinnati Royals	125.00	57.50	15.50
☐ 33	Larry Costello DP ...... Syracuse Nationals	50.00	23.00	6.25
☐ 34	Woody Sauldsberry DP	35.00	16.00	4.40
	Syracuse Nationals			
☐ 35	Ray Felix .... Philadelphia Warriors	40.00	18.00	5.00
☐ 36	Ernie Beck.............. New York Knicks	35.00	16.00	4.40
☐ 37	Cliff Hagan .... Philadelphia Warriors	125.00	57.50	15.50
☐ 38	Guy Sparrow DP .... St. Louis Hawks	25.00	11.50	3.10
☐ 39	Jim Loscutoff .... New York Knicks	45.00	20.00	5.75
☐ 40	Arnie Risen DP .... Boston Celtics	40.00	18.00	5.00
☐ 41	Joe Graboski .... Boston Celtics	35.00	16.00	4.40
☐ 42	Maurice Stokes DP UER Philadelphia Warriors	120.00	55.00	15.00
	Cincinnati Royals			
	(Text refers to			
	N.F.L. Record)			
☐ 43	Rod Hundley DP ...... Cincinnati Royals	120.00	55.00	15.00
☐ 44	Tom Gola DP .... Minneapolis Lakers	75.00	34.00	9.50
☐ 45	Med Park .... Philadelphia Warriors	40.00	18.00	5.00
☐ 46	Mel Hutchins DP .... St. Louis Hawks	25.00	11.50	3.10
☐ 47	Larry Friend DP .... New York Knicks	25.00	11.50	3.10
☐ 48	Lennie Rosenbluth DP	55.00	25.00	7.00
	New York Knicks			
☐ 49	Walt Davis .... Philadelphia Warriors	35.00	16.00	4.40
☐ 50	Richie Regan............ Philadelphia Warriors	40.00	18.00	5.00
☐ 51	Frank Selvy DP.......... Cincinnati Royals	50.00	23.00	6.25
☐ 52	Art Spoelstra DP .... St. Louis Hawks	25.00	11.50	3.10
☐ 53	Bob Hopkins .... Minneapolis Lakers	40.00	18.00	5.00
☐ 54	Earl Lloyd .... Syracuse Nationals	40.00	18.00	5.00
☐ 55	Phil Jordan DP .... Syracuse Nationals	25.00	11.50	3.10
☐ 56	Bob Houbregs DP .... New York Knicks	40.00	18.00	5.00
☐ 57	Lou Tsioupoulas DP . Detroit Pistons	25.00	11.50	3.10
☐ 58	Ed Conlin .... Boston Celtics	40.00	18.00	5.00
☐ 59	Al Bianchi............... Syracuse Nationals	75.00	34.00	9.50
☐ 60	George Dempsey .... Syracuse Nationals	40.00	18.00	5.00
☐ 61	Chuck Share .... Philadelphia Warriors	35.00	16.00	4.40
☐ 62	Harry Gallatin DP ...... St. Louis Hawks	45.00	20.00	5.75
☐ 63	Bob Harrison............ Detroit Pistons	35.00	16.00	4.40
☐ 64	Bob Burrow DP .... Syracuse Nationals	25.00	11.50	3.10
☐ 65	Win Wilfong DP .... Minneapolis Lakers	25.00	11.50	3.10
☐ 66	Jack McMahon DP ...... St. Louis Hawks	35.00	16.00	4.40
☐ 67	Jack George .... St. Louis Hawks	35.00	16.00	4.40
☐ 68	Charlie Tyra DP .... Philadelphia Warriors	25.00	11.50	3.10
☐ 69	Ron Sobie .... New York Knicks	35.00	16.00	4.40
☐ 70	Jack Coleman .... New York Knicks	35.00	16.00	4.40
☐ 71	Jack Twyman DP ...... St. Louis Hawks	110.00	50.00	14.00
☐ 72	Paul Seymour............ Cincinnati Royals	40.00	18.00	5.00
☐ 73	Jim Paxson DP .... Syracuse Nationals	50.00	23.00	6.25
☐ 74	Bob Leonard .... Cincinnati Royals	40.00	18.00	5.00
☐ 75	Andy Phillip............. Minneapolis Lakers	45.00	20.00	5.75
☐ 76	Joe Holup .... Boston Celtics	35.00	16.00	4.40
☐ 77	Bill Russell .... Syracuse Nationals	1800.00	800.00	230.00
☐ 78	Clyde Lovellette DP .. Boston Celtics	110.00	50.00	14.00

		NRMT-MT	EXC	VG
☐ 79	Ed Fleming DP	25.00	11.50	3.10
	Cincinnati Royals			
	Minneapolis Lakers			
☐ 80	Dick Schnittker	100.00	45.00	12.50
	Minneapolis Lakers			

1969-70 Topps

The 1969-70 Topps set of 99 cards was Topps' first major basketball issue since 1957. Cards were issued in 10-cent packs (10 cards per pack, 24 packs per box) and measure 2 1/2" by 4 11/16". The set features the first card of Lew Alcindor (later Kareem Abdul-Jabbar). Other notable Rookie Cards in the set are Dave Bing, Bill Bradley, Billy Cunningham, Dave DeBusschere, Walt Frazier, John Havlicek, Connie Hawkins, Elvin Hayes, Jerry Lucas, Earl Monroe, Don Nelson, Willis Reed, Nate Thurmond and Wes Unseld. The set was printed on a sheet of 99 cards (nine rows of eleven across) with the checklist card occupying the lower right corner of the sheet. As a result, the checklist is prone to wear and very difficult to obtain in Near Mint or better condition.

		NRMT-MT	EXC	VG
COMPLETE SET (99)		1600.00	700.00	200.00
COMMON CARD (1-99)		4.00	1.80	.50
☐ 1	Wilt Chamberlain	200.00	65.00	20.00
	Los Angeles Lakers			
☐ 2	Gail Goodrich	30.00	13.50	3.80
	Phoenix Suns			
☐ 3	Cazzie Russell	15.00	6.75	1.90
	New York Knicks			
☐ 4	Darrall Imhoff	5.00	2.30	.60
	Philadelphia 76ers			
☐ 5	Bailey Howell	5.00	2.30	.60
	Boston Celtics			
☐ 6	Lucius Allen	8.00	3.60	1.00
	Seattle Supersonics			
☐ 7	Tom Boerwinkle	6.00	2.70	.75
	Chicago Bulls			
☐ 8	Jimmy Walker	8.00	3.60	1.00
	Detroit Pistons			
☐ 9	John Block	5.00	2.30	.60
	San Diego Rockets			
☐ 10	Nate Thurmond	30.00	13.50	3.80
	San Francisco Warriors			
☐ 11	Gary Gregor	4.00	1.80	.50
	Atlanta Hawks			
☐ 12	Gus Johnson	15.00	6.75	1.90
	Baltimore Bullets			
☐ 13	Luther Rackley	4.00	1.80	.50
	Cincinnati Royals			
☐ 14	Jon McGlocklin	6.00	2.70	.75
	Milwaukee Bucks			
☐ 15	Connie Hawkins	40.00	18.00	5.00
	Phoenix Suns			
☐ 16	Johnny Egan	4.00	1.80	.50
	Los Angeles Lakers			
☐ 17	Jim Washington	4.00	1.80	.50
	Philadelphia 76ers			
☐ 18	Dick Barnett	8.00	3.60	1.00
	New York Knicks			
☐ 19	Tom Meschery	4.00	1.80	.50
	Seattle Supersonics			
☐ 20	John Havlicek	160.00	70.00	20.00
	Boston Celtics			
☐ 21	Eddie Miles	4.00	1.80	.50
	Detroit Pistons			
☐ 22	Walt Wesley	4.00	1.80	.50
	Chicago Bulls			
☐ 23	Rick Adelman	8.00	3.60	1.00
	San Diego Rockets			
☐ 24	Al Attles	5.00	2.30	.60
	San Francisco Warriors			
☐ 25	Lew Alcindor	600.00	275.00	75.00
	Milwaukee Bucks			
☐ 26	Jack Marin	10.00	4.50	1.25
	Baltimore Bullets			
☐ 27	Walt Hazzard	12.00	5.50	1.50
	Atlanta Hawks			
☐ 28	Connie Dierking	4.00	1.80	.50
	Cincinnati Royals			
☐ 29	Keith Erickson	10.00	4.50	1.25
	Los Angeles Lakers			
☐ 30	Bob Rule	8.00	3.60	1.00
	Seattle Supersonics			
☐ 31	Dick Van Arsdale	10.00	4.50	1.25
	Phoenix Suns			
☐ 32	Archie Clark	12.00	5.50	1.50
	Philadelphia 76ers			
☐ 33	Terry Dischinger	4.00	1.80	.50
	Detroit Pistons			
☐ 34	Henry Finkel	4.00	1.80	.50
	Boston Celtics			
☐ 35	Elgin Baylor	50.00	23.00	6.25
	Los Angeles Lakers			
☐ 36	Ron Williams	4.00	1.80	.50
	San Francisco Warriors			
☐ 37	Loy Petersen	4.00	1.80	.50
	Chicago Bulls			
☐ 38	Guy Rodgers	5.00	2.30	.60
	Milwaukee Bucks			
☐ 39	Toby Kimball	4.00	1.80	.50
	San Diego Rockets			
☐ 40	Billy Cunningham	50.00	23.00	6.25
	Philadelphia 76ers			
☐ 41	Joe Caldwell	6.00	2.70	.75
	Atlanta Hawks			
☐ 42	Leroy Ellis	6.00	2.70	.75
	Baltimore Bullets			
☐ 43	Bill Bradley	140.00	65.00	17.50
	New York Knicks			

☐ 44	Len Wilkens UER .... Seattle Supersonics (Misspelled Wilkins on card back)	40.00	18.00	5.00
☐ 45	Jerry Lucas .... San Francisco Warriors	30.00	13.50	3.80
☐ 46	Neal Walk .... Phoenix Suns	6.00	2.70	.75
☐ 47	Emmette Bryant .... Boston Celtics	5.00	2.30	.60
☐ 48	Bob Kauffman .... Chicago Bulls	4.00	1.80	.50
☐ 49	Mel Counts .... Los Angeles Lakers	5.00	2.30	.60
☐ 50	Oscar Robertson .... Cincinnati Royals	70.00	32.00	8.75
☐ 51	Jim Barnett .... San Diego Rockets	5.00	2.30	.60
☐ 52	Don Smith .... Milwaukee Bucks	4.00	1.80	.50
☐ 53	Jim Davis .... Atlanta Hawks	4.00	1.80	.50
☐ 54	Wally Jones .... Philadelphia 76ers	6.00	2.70	.75
☐ 55	Dave Bing .... Detroit Pistons	40.00	18.00	5.00
☐ 56	Wes Unseld .... Baltimore Bullets	40.00	18.00	5.00
☐ 57	Joe Ellis .... San Francisco Warriors	4.00	1.80	.50
☐ 58	John Tresvant .... Seattle Supersonics	4.00	1.80	.50
☐ 59	Larry Siegfried .... Boston Celtics	6.00	2.70	.75
☐ 60	Willis Reed .... New York Knicks	50.00	23.00	6.25
☐ 61	Paul Silas .... Phoenix Suns	15.00	6.75	1.90
☐ 62	Bob Weiss .... Chicago Bulls	8.00	3.60	1.00
☐ 63	Willie McCarter .... Los Angeles Lakers	4.00	1.80	.50
☐ 64	Don Kojis .... San Diego Rockets	4.00	1.80	.50
☐ 65	Lou Hudson .... Atlanta Hawks	18.00	8.00	2.30
☐ 66	Jim King .... Cincinnati Royals	4.00	1.80	.50
☐ 67	Luke Jackson .... Philadelphia 76ers	5.00	2.30	.60
☐ 68	Len Chappell .... Milwaukee Bucks	4.00	1.80	.50
☐ 69	Ray Scott .... Baltimore Bullets	4.00	1.80	.50
☐ 70	Jeff Mullins .... San Francisco Warriors	8.00	3.60	1.00
☐ 71	Howie Komives .... Detroit Pistons	4.00	1.80	.50
☐ 72	Tom Sanders .... Boston Celtics	8.00	3.60	1.00
☐ 73	Dick Snyder .... Seattle Supersonics	4.00	1.80	.50
☐ 74	Dave Stallworth .... New York Knicks	5.00	2.30	.60
☐ 75	Elvin Hayes .... San Diego Rockets	70.00	32.00	8.75
☐ 76	Art Harris .... Phoenix Suns	4.00	1.80	.50
☐ 77	Don Ohl .... Atlanta Hawks	4.00	1.80	.50
☐ 78	Bob Love......................	30.00	13.50	3.80

	Chicago Bulls			
☐ 79	Tom Van Arsdale .... Cincinnati Royals	10.00	4.50	1.25
☐ 80	Earl Monroe .... Baltimore Bullets	40.00	18.00	5.00
☐ 81	Greg Smith .... Milwaukee Bucks	4.00	1.80	.50
☐ 82	Don Nelson .... Boston Celtics	35.00	16.00	4.40
☐ 83	Happy Hairston .... Detroit Pistons	8.00	3.60	1.00
☐ 84	Hal Greer .... Philadelphia 76ers	10.00	4.50	1.25
☐ 85	Dave DeBusschere ...... New York Knicks	40.00	18.00	5.00
☐ 86	Bill Bridges .... Atlanta Hawks	8.00	3.60	1.00
☐ 87	Herm Gilliam................. Cincinnati Royals	5.00	2.30	.60
☐ 88	Jim Fox .... Phoenix Suns	4.00	1.80	.50
☐ 89	Bob Boozer .... Seattle Supersonics	5.00	2.30	.60
☐ 90	Jerry West .... Los Angeles Lakers	90.00	40.00	11.50
☐ 91	Chet Walker .... Chicago Bulls	15.00	6.75	1.90
☐ 92	Flynn Robinson .... Milwaukee Bucks	5.00	2.30	.60
☐ 93	Clyde Lee .... San Francisco Warriors	5.00	2.30	.60
☐ 94	Kevin Loughery .... Baltimore Bullets	12.00	5.50	1.50
☐ 95	Walt Bellamy............... Detroit Pistons	10.00	4.50	1.25
☐ 96	Art Williams .... San Diego Rockets	4.00	1.80	.50
☐ 97	Adrian Smith .... Cincinnati Royals	6.00	2.70	.75
☐ 98	Walt Frazier .... New York Knicks	70.00	32.00	8.75
☐ 99	Checklist 1-99..........	275.00	33.00	8.25

1970-71 Topps

The 1970-71 Topps basketball card set of 175 color cards continued the larger-size (2

1/2" by 4 11/16") format established the previous year. Cards were issued in 10-cent wax packs with 10 cards in a pack and 24 packs per box. Cards numbered 106 to 115 contain the previous season's NBA first and second team All-Star selections. The first six cards in the set (1-6) feature the statistical league leaders from the previous season. The last eight cards in the set (168-175) summarize the results of the previous season's NBA championship playoff series won by the Knicks over the Lakers. The key Rookie Cards in this set are Pete Maravich, Calvin Murphy and Pat Riley. There are 22 short-printed cards in the first series which are marked SP in the checklist below.

	MINT	NRMT	EXC
COMPLETE SET (175)	1000.00	450.00	125.00
COMMON CARD (1-110)	2.50	1.15	.30
COMMON CARD (111-175)	3.00	1.35	.40

		MINT	NRMT	EXC
☐ 1	NBA Scoring Leaders	35.00	8.75	1.75
	Lew Alcindor			
	Jerry West			
	Elvin Hayes			
☐ 2	NBA Scoring SP	30.00	13.50	3.80
	Average Leaders			
	Jerry West			
	Lew Alcindor			
	Elvin Hayes			
☐ 3	NBA FG Pct Leaders	5.00	2.30	.60
	Johnny Green			
	Darrall Imhoff			
	Lou Hudson			
☐ 4	NBA FT Pct Leaders SP	10.00	4.50	1.25
	Flynn Robinson			
	Chet Walker			
	Jeff Mullins			
☐ 5	NBA Rebound Leaders	20.00	9.00	2.50
	Elvin Hayes			
	Wes Unseld			
	Lew Alcindor			
☐ 6	NBA Assist Leaders SP	10.00	4.50	1.25
	Len Wilkens			
	Walt Frazier			
	Clem Haskins			
☐ 7	Bill Bradley	40.00	18.00	5.00
	New York Knicks			
☐ 8	Ron Williams	2.50	1.15	.30
	San Francisco Warriors			
☐ 9	Otto Moore	2.50	1.15	.30
	Detroit Pistons			
☐ 10	John Havlicek SP	70.00	32.00	8.75
	Boston Celtics			
☐ 11	George Wilson	2.50	1.15	.30
	Buffalo Braves			
☐ 12	John Trapp	2.50	1.15	.30
	San Diego Rockets			
☐ 13	Pat Riley	45.00	20.00	5.75
	Portland Trail Blazers			
☐ 14	Jim Washington	2.50	1.15	.30
	Philadelphia 76ers			
☐ 15	Bob Rule	4.00	1.80	.50
	Seattle Supersonics			
☐ 16	Bob Weiss	4.00	1.80	.50
	Chicago Bulls			
☐ 17	Neil Johnson	2.50	1.15	.30
	Phoenix Suns			
☐ 18	Walt Bellamy	7.00	3.10	.85
	Atlanta Hawks			
☐ 19	McCoy McLemore	2.50	1.15	.30
	Cleveland Cavaliers			
☐ 20	Earl Monroe	12.00	5.50	1.50
	Baltimore Bullets			
☐ 21	Wally Anderzunas	2.50	1.15	.30
	Cincinnati Royals			
☐ 22	Guy Rodgers	4.00	1.80	.50
	Milwaukee Bucks			
☐ 23	Rick Roberson	2.50	1.15	.30
	Los Angeles Lakers			
☐ 24	Checklist 1-110	50.00	7.50	2.50
☐ 25	Jimmy Walker	4.00	1.80	.50
	Detroit Pistons			
☐ 26	Mike Riordan	5.00	2.30	.60
	New York Knicks			
☐ 27	Henry Finkel	2.50	1.15	.30
	Boston Celtics			
☐ 28	Joe Ellis	2.50	1.15	.30
	San Francisco Warriors			
☐ 29	Mike Davis	2.50	1.15	.30
	Buffalo Braves			
☐ 30	Lou Hudson	5.00	2.30	.60
	Atlanta Hawks			
☐ 31	Lucius Allen SP	7.00	3.10	.85
	Seattle Supersonics			
☐ 32	Toby Kimball SP	5.00	2.30	.60
	San Diego Rockets			
☐ 33	Luke Jackson SP	5.00	2.30	.60
	Philadelphia 76ers			
☐ 34	Johnny Egan	2.50	1.15	.30
	Cleveland Cavaliers			
☐ 35	Leroy Ellis SP	5.00	2.30	.60
	Portland Trail Blazers			
☐ 36	Jack Marin SP	7.00	3.10	.85
	Baltimore Bullets			
☐ 37	Joe Caldwell SP	7.00	3.10	.85
	Atlanta Hawks			
☐ 38	Keith Erickson	4.00	1.80	.50
	Los Angeles Lakers			
☐ 39	Don Smith	2.50	1.15	.30
	Milwaukee Bucks			
☐ 40	Flynn Robinson	4.00	1.80	.50
	Cincinnati Royals			
☐ 41	Bob Boozer	2.50	1.15	.30
	Seattle Supersonics			
☐ 42	Howie Komives	2.50	1.15	.30
	Detroit Pistons			
☐ 43	Dick Barnett	3.50	1.55	.45
	New York Knicks			
☐ 44	Stu Lantz	2.50	1.15	.30
	San Diego Rockets			
☐ 45	Dick Van Arsdale	6.00	2.70	.75
	Phoenix Suns			
☐ 46	Jerry Lucas	8.00	3.60	1.00
	San Francisco Warriors			
☐ 47	Don Chaney	8.00	3.60	1.00
	Boston Celtics			
☐ 48	Ray Scott	2.50	1.15	.30
	Buffalo Bullets			
☐ 49	Dick Cunningham SP	5.00	2.30	.60
	Milwaukee Bucks			
☐ 50	Wilt Chamberlain	90.00	40.00	11.50
	Los Angeles Lakers			
☐ 51	Kevin Loughery	5.00	2.30	.60
	Baltimore Bullets			
☐ 52	Stan McKenzie	2.50	1.15	.30
	Portland Trail Blazers			
☐ 53	Fred Foster	2.50	1.15	.30
	Cincinnati Royals			
☐ 54	Jim Davis	2.50	1.15	.30

Atlanta Hawks
- ☐ 55 Walt Wesley .... 2.50   1.15   .30
  Cleveland Cavaliers
- ☐ 56 Bill Hewitt .... 2.50   1.15   .30
  Detroit Pistons
- ☐ 57 Darrall Imhoff .... 2.50   1.15   .30
  Philadelphia 76ers
- ☐ 58 John Block .... 2.50   1.15   .30
  San Diego Rockets
- ☐ 59 Al Attles SP .... 7.00   3.10   .85
  San Francisco Warriors
- ☐ 60 Chet Walker .... 6.00   2.70   .75
  Chicago Bulls
- ☐ 61 Luther Rackley .... 2.50   1.15   .30
  Cleveland Cavaliers
- ☐ 62 Jerry Chambers SP ... 6.00   2.70   .75
  Atlanta Hawks
- ☐ 63 Bob Dandridge 8.00   3.60   1.00
  Milwaukee Bucks
- ☐ 64 Dick Snyder .... 2.50   1.15   .30
  Seattle Supersonics
- ☐ 65 Elgin Baylor 30.00   13.50   3.80
  Los Angeles Lakers
- ☐ 66 Connie Dierking .... 2.50   1.15   .30
  Cincinnati Royals
- ☐ 67 Steve Kuberski .... 2.50   1.15   .30
  Boston Celtics
- ☐ 68 Tom Boerwinkle .... 2.50   1.15   .30
  Chicago Bulls
- ☐ 69 Paul Silas .... 6.00   2.70   .75
  Phoenix Suns
- ☐ 70 Elvin Hayes 25.00   11.50   3.10
  San Diego Rockets
- ☐ 71 Bill Bridges .... 4.00   1.80   .50
  Atlanta Hawks
- ☐ 72 Wes Unseld 12.00   5.50   1.50
  Baltimore Bullets
- ☐ 73 Herm Gilliam .... 2.50   1.15   .30
  Buffalo Braves
- ☐ 74 Bobby Smith SP 8.00   3.60   1.00
  Cleveland Cavaliers
- ☐ 75 Lew Alcindor 100.00 45.00   12.50
  Milwaukee Bucks
- ☐ 76 Jeff Mullins .... 4.00   1.80   .50
  San Francisco Warriors
- ☐ 77 Happy Hairston .... 4.00   1.80   .50
  Los Angeles Lakers
- ☐ 78 Dave Stallworth SP .... 5.00   2.30   .60
  New York Knicks
- ☐ 79 Fred Hetzel .... 2.50   1.15   .30
  Portland Trail Blazers
- ☐ 80 Len Wilkens SP 25.00   11.50   3.10
  Seattle Supersonics
- ☐ 81 Johnny Green .... 5.00   2.30   .60
  Cincinnati Royals
- ☐ 82 Erwin Mueller............ 2.50   1.15   .30
  Detroit Pistons
- ☐ 83 Wally Jones .... 4.00   1.80   .50
  Philadelphia 76ers
- ☐ 84 Bob Love 8.00   3.60   1.00
  Chicago Bulls
- ☐ 85 Dick Garrett .... 2.50   1.15   .30
  Buffalo Braves
- ☐ 86 Don Nelson SP 25.00   11.50   3.10
  Boston Celtics
- ☐ 87 Neal Walk SP .... 5.00   2.30   .60
  Phoenix Suns
- ☐ 88 Larry Siegfried .... 2.50   1.15   .30
  San Diego Rockets
- ☐ 89 Gary Gregor .... 2.50   1.15   .30
  Portland Trail Blazers

- ☐ 90 Nate Thurmond 8.00   3.60   1.00
  San Francisco Warriors
- ☐ 91 John Warren .... 2.50   1.15   .30
  Cleveland Cavaliers
- ☐ 92 Gus Johnson .... 6.00   2.70   .75
  Baltimore Bullets
- ☐ 93 Gail Goodrich 8.00   3.60   1.00
  Los Angeles Lakers
- ☐ 94 Dorrie Murrey .... 2.50   1.15   .30
  Portland Trail Blazers
- ☐ 95 Cazzie Russell SP 10.00   4.50   1.25
  New York Knicks
- ☐ 96 Terry Dischinger .... 2.50   1.15   .30
  Detroit Pistons
- ☐ 97 Norm Van Lier SP 15.00   6.75   1.90
  Cincinnati Royals
- ☐ 98 Jim Fox .... 2.50   1.15   .30
  Chicago Bulls
- ☐ 99 Tom Meschery .... 2.50   1.15   .30
  Seattle Supersonics
- ☐ 100 Oscar Robertson 40.00   18.00   5.00
  Milwaukee Bucks
- ☐ 101A Checklist 111-175.. 30.00   4.50   1.50
  (1970-71 in black)
- ☐ 101B Checklist 111-175.. 30.00   4.50   1.50
  (1970-71 in white)
- ☐ 102 Rich Johnson .... 2.50   1.15   .30
  Boston Celtics
- ☐ 103 Mel Counts .... 4.00   1.80   .50
  Phoenix Suns
- ☐ 104 Bill Hosket SP .... 6.00   2.70   .75
  Buffalo Braves
- ☐ 105 Archie Clark .... 4.00   1.80   .50
  Philadelphia 76ers
- ☐ 106 Walt Frazier AS 10.00   4.50   1.25
  New York Knicks
- ☐ 107 Jerry West AS 30.00   13.50   3.80
  Los Angeles Lakers
- ☐ 108 Bill Cunningham AS. 12.00   5.50   1.50
  Philadelphia 76ers
- ☐ 109 Connie Hawkins AS.... 6.00   2.70   .75
  Phoenix Suns
- ☐ 110 Willis Reed AS 9.00   4.00   1.15
  New York Knicks
- ☐ 111 Nate Thurmond AS .... 5.50   2.50   .70
  San Francisco Warriors
- ☐ 112 John Havlicek AS 25.00   11.50   3.10
  Boston Celtics
- ☐ 113 Elgin Baylor AS 18.00   8.00   2.30
  Los Angeles Lakers
- ☐ 114 Oscar Robertson AS 25.00   11.50   3.10
  Milwaukee Bucks
- ☐ 115 Lou Hudson AS.......... 4.00   1.80   .50
  Atlanta Hawks
- ☐ 116 Emmette Bryant .... 3.00   1.35   .40
  Buffalo Braves
- ☐ 117 Greg Howard............. 3.00   1.35   .40
  Phoenix Suns
- ☐ 118 Rick Adelman........... 4.50   2.00   .55
  Portland Trail Blazers
- ☐ 119 Barry Clemens .... 3.00   1.35   .40
  Seattle Supersonics
- ☐ 120 Walt Frazier.............. 25.00   11.50   3.10
  New York Knicks
- ☐ 121 Jim Barnes.............. 3.00   1.35   .40
  Boston Celtics
- ☐ 122 Bernie Williams......... 3.00   1.35   .40
  San Diego Rockets
- ☐ 123 Pete Maravich 200.00 90.00   25.00
  Atlanta Hawks
- ☐ 124 Matt Guokas 8.00   3.60   1.00

☐ 125	Dave Bing .... Detroit Pistons	12.00	5.50	1.50
☐ 126	John Tresvant .... Los Angeles Lakers	3.00	1.35	.40
☐ 127	Shaler Halimon .... Chicago Bulls	3.00	1.35	.40
☐ 128	Don Ohl .... Cleveland Cavaliers	3.00	1.35	.40
☐ 129	Fred Carter .... Baltimore Bullets	5.00	2.30	.60
☐ 130	Connie Hawkins .... Phoenix Suns	12.00	5.50	1.50
☐ 131	Jim King .... Cincinnati Royals	3.00	1.35	.40
☐ 132	Ed Manning .... Portland Trail Blazers	5.00	2.30	.60
☐ 133	Adrian Smith .... San Francisco Warriors	3.00	1.35	.40
☐ 134	Walt Hazzard .... Atlanta Hawks	5.00	2.30	.60
☐ 135	Dave DeBusschere... New York Knicks	12.00	5.50	1.50
☐ 136	Don Kojis .... Seattle Supersonics	3.00	1.35	.40
☐ 137	Calvin Murphy .... San Diego Rockets	25.00	11.50	3.10
☐ 138	Nate Bowman .... Buffalo Braves	3.00	1.35	.40
☐ 139	Jon McGlocklin .... Milwaukee Bucks	3.00	1.35	.40
☐ 140	Billy Cunningham ..... Philadelphia 76ers	15.00	6.75	1.90
☐ 141	Willie McCarter .... Los Angeles Lakers	3.00	1.35	.40
☐ 142	Jim Barnett .... Portland Trail Blazers	3.00	1.35	.40
☐ 143	JoJo White .... Boston Celtics	18.00	8.00	2.30
☐ 144	Clyde Lee .... San Francisco Warriors	3.00	1.35	.40
☐ 145	Tom Van Arsdale ...... Cincinnati Royals	6.00	2.70	.75
☐ 146	Len Chappell .... Cleveland Cavaliers	3.00	1.35	.40
☐ 147	Lee Winfield .... Seattle Supersonics	3.00	1.35	.40
☐ 148	Jerry Sloan .... Chicago Bulls	15.00	6.75	1.90
☐ 149	Art Harris .... Phoenix Suns	3.00	1.35	.40
☐ 150	Willis Reed .... New York Knicks	15.00	6.75	1.90
☐ 151	Art Williams .... San Diego Rockets	3.00	1.35	.40
☐ 152	Don May .... Buffalo Braves	3.00	1.35	.40
☐ 153	Loy Petersen .... Cleveland Cavaliers	3.00	1.35	.40
☐ 154	Dave Gambee .... San Francisco Warriors	3.00	1.35	.40
☐ 155	Hal Greer .... Philadelphia 76ers	6.00	2.70	.75
☐ 156	Dave Newmark .... Atlanta Hawks	3.00	1.35	.40
☐ 157	Jimmy Collins .... Chicago Bulls	3.00	1.35	.40
☐ 158	Bill Turner .... Cincinnati Royals	3.00	1.35	.40
☐ 159	Eddie Miles .... Baltimore Bullets	3.00	1.35	.40
☐ 160	Jerry West .... Los Angeles Lakers	50.00	23.00	6.25
☐ 161	Bob Quick .... Detroit Pistons	3.00	1.35	.40
☐ 162	Fred Crawford .... Buffalo Braves	3.00	1.35	.40
☐ 163	Tom Sanders .... Boston Celtics	5.00	2.30	.60
☐ 164	Dale Schlueter .... Portland Trail Blazers	3.00	1.35	.40
☐ 165	Clem Haskins .... Phoenix Suns	9.00	4.00	1.15
☐ 166	Greg Smith .... Milwaukee Bucks	3.00	1.35	.40
☐ 167	Rod Thorn .... Seattle Supersonics	8.00	3.60	1.00
☐ 168	Playoff Game 1 .... (Willis Reed)	8.00	3.60	1.00
☐ 169	Playoff Game 2 .... (Dick Garrett)	5.00	2.30	.60
☐ 170	Playoff Game 3 .... (Dave DeBusschere)	8.00	3.60	1.00
☐ 171	Playoff Game 4 .... (Jerry West)	15.00	6.75	1.90
☐ 172	Playoff Game 5 .... (Bill Bradley)	15.00	6.75	1.90
☐ 173	Playoff Game 6 .... (Wilt Chamberlain)	18.00	8.00	2.30
☐ 174	Playoff Game 7 .... (Walt Frazier)	10.00	4.50	1.25
☐ 175	Knicks Celebrate ...... (New York Knicks, World Champs)	20.00	5.00	1.00

1971-72 Topps

The 1971-72 Topps basketball set of 233 witnessed a return to the standard-sized card, i.e., 2 1/2" by 3 1/2". Cards were issued in 10-card, 10 cent packs with 24 packs per box. National Basketball Association players are depicted on cards 1 to 144 and American Basketball Association players are depicted on cards 145 to 233. The set was produced on two sheets. The second production sheet contained the ABA players (145-233) as well as 31 double-printed cards (NBA players) from the first sheet. These DP's are indicated in the checklist below. Subsets include NBA Playoffs (133-137), NBA Statistical Leaders (138-143) and ABA Statistical Leaders

(146-151). The key Rookie Cards in this set are Nate Archibald, Rick Barry, Larry Brown, Dave Cowens, Spencer Haywood, Dan Issel, Bob Lanier, Rudy Tomjanovich and Doug Moe.

	NRMT-MT	EXC	VG
COMPLETE SET (233)	750.00	350.00	95.00
COMMON NBA CARD (1-144)	1.50	.65	.19
COMMON ABA CARD (145-233)	2.00	.90	.25

☐ 1	Oscar Robertson	40.00	13.00	2.40
	Milwaukee Bucks			
☐ 2	Bill Bradley	25.00	11.50	3.10
	New York Knicks			
☐ 3	Jim Fox	1.50	.65	.19
	Chicago Bulls			
☐ 4	John Johnson	2.00	.90	.25
	Cleveland Cavaliers			
☐ 5	Luke Jackson	1.50	.65	.19
	Philadelphia 76ers			
☐ 6	Don May DP	1.50	.65	.19
	Atlanta Hawks			
☐ 7	Kevin Loughery	2.00	.90	.25
	Baltimore Bullets			
☐ 8	Terry Dischinger	2.00	.90	.25
	Detroit Pistons			
☐ 9	Neal Walk	2.00	.90	.25
	Phoenix Suns			
☐ 10	Elgin Baylor	25.00	11.50	3.10
	Los Angeles Lakers			
☐ 11	Rick Adelman	2.00	.90	.25
	Portland Trail Blazers			
☐ 12	Clyde Lee	1.50	.65	.19
	Golden State Warriors			
☐ 13	Jerry Chambers	1.50	.65	.19
	Buffalo Braves			
☐ 14	Fred Carter	1.50	.65	.19
	Baltimore Bullets			
☐ 15	Tom Boerwinkle DP	1.50	.65	.19
	Chicago Bulls			
☐ 16	John Block	1.50	.65	.19
	Houston Rockets			
☐ 17	Dick Barnett	2.00	.90	.25
	New York Knicks			
☐ 18	Henry Finkel	1.50	.65	.19
	Boston Celtics			
☐ 19	Norm Van Lier	4.00	1.80	.50
	Cincinnati Royals			
☐ 20	Spencer Haywood	12.00	5.50	1.50
	Seattle Supersonics			
☐ 21	George Johnson	1.50	.65	.19
	Baltimore Bullets			
☐ 22	Bobby Lewis	1.50	.65	.19
	Cleveland Cavaliers			
☐ 23	Bill Hewitt	1.50	.65	.19
	Detroit Pistons			
☐ 24	Walt Hazzard DP	3.00	1.35	.40
	Buffalo Braves			
☐ 25	Happy Hairston	2.00	.90	.25
	Los Angeles Lakers			
☐ 26	George Wilson	1.50	.65	.19
	Buffalo Braves			
☐ 27	Lucius Allen	2.00	.90	.25
	Milwaukee Bucks			
☐ 28	Jim Washington	1.50	.65	.19
	Philadelphia 76ers			
☐ 29	Nate Archibald	25.00	11.50	3.10
	Cincinnati Royals			
☐ 30	Willis Reed	10.00	4.50	1.25
	New York Knicks			
☐ 31	Erwin Mueller	1.50	.65	.19
	Detroit Pistons			
☐ 32	Art Harris	1.50	.65	.19
	Phoenix Suns			
☐ 33	Pete Cross	1.50	.65	.19
	Seattle Supersonics			
☐ 34	Geoff Petrie	6.00	2.70	.75
	Portland Trail Blazers			
☐ 35	John Havlicek	30.00	13.50	3.80
	Boston Celtics			
☐ 36	Larry Siegfried	1.50	.65	.19
	Houston Rockets			
☐ 37	John Tresvant DP	1.50	.65	.19
	Baltimore Bullets			
☐ 38	Ron Williams	1.50	.65	.19
	Golden State Warriors			
☐ 39	Lamar Green DP	1.50	.65	.19
	Phoenix Suns			
☐ 40	Bob Rule DP	1.50	.65	.19
	Seattle Supersonics			
☐ 41	Jim McMillian	1.50	.65	.19
	Los Angeles Lakers			
☐ 42	Wally Jones	2.00	.90	.25
	Philadelphia 76ers			
☐ 43	Bob Boozer	2.00	.90	.25
	Milwaukee Bucks			
☐ 44	Eddie Miles	1.50	.65	.19
	Baltimore Bullets			
☐ 45	Bob Love DP	4.00	1.80	.50
	Chicago Bulls			
☐ 46	Claude English	1.50	.65	.19
	Portland Trail Blazers			
☐ 47	Dave Cowens	50.00	23.00	6.25
	Boston Celtics			
☐ 48	Emmette Bryant	1.50	.65	.19
	Buffalo Braves			
☐ 49	Dave Stallworth	1.50	.65	.19
	New York Knicks			
☐ 50	Jerry West	40.00	18.00	5.00
	Los Angeles Lakers			
☐ 51	Joe Ellis	1.50	.65	.19
	Golden State Warriors			
☐ 52	Walt Wesley DP	1.50	.65	.19
	Cleveland Cavaliers			
☐ 53	Howie Komives	1.50	.65	.19
	Detroit Pistons			
☐ 54	Paul Silas	4.00	1.80	.50
	Phoenix Suns			
☐ 55	Pete Maravich DP	40.00	18.00	5.00
	Atlanta Hawks			
☐ 56	Gary Gregor	1.50	.65	.19
	Portland Trail Blazers			
☐ 57	Sam Lacey	3.00	1.35	.40
	Cincinnati Royals			
☐ 58	Calvin Murphy DP	6.00	2.70	.75
	Houston Rockets			
☐ 59	Bob Dandridge	2.00	.90	.25
	Milwaukee Bucks			
☐ 60	Hal Greer	4.00	1.80	.50
	Philadelphia 76ers			
☐ 61	Keith Erickson	2.00	.90	.25
	Los Angeles Lakers			
☐ 62	Joe Cooke	1.50	.65	.19
	Cleveland Cavaliers			
☐ 63	Bob Lanier	40.00	18.00	5.00
	Detroit Pistons			
☐ 64	Don Kojis	1.50	.65	.19
	Seattle Supersonics			
☐ 65	Walt Frazier	14.00	6.25	1.75
	New York Knicks			
☐ 66	Chet Walker DP	3.00	1.35	.40

	Chicago Bulls			
☐ 67	Dick Garrett	1.50	.65	.19
	Buffalo Braves			
☐ 68	John Trapp	2.00	.90	.25
	Houston Rockets			
☐ 69	JoJo White	6.00	2.70	.75
	Boston Celtics			
☐ 70	Wilt Chamberlain	50.00	23.00	6.25
	Los Angeles Lakers			
☐ 71	Dave Sorenson	1.50	.65	.19
	Cleveland Cavaliers			
☐ 72	Jim King	1.50	.65	.19
	Chicago Bulls			
☐ 73	Cazzie Russell	4.00	1.80	.50
	Golden State Warriors			
☐ 74	Jon McGlocklin	2.00	.90	.25
	Milwaukee Bucks			
☐ 75	Tom Van Arsdale	2.00	.90	.25
	Cincinnati Royals			
☐ 76	Dale Schlueter	1.50	.65	.19
	Portland Trail Blazers			
☐ 77	Gus Johnson DP	2.00	.90	.25
	Baltimore Bullets			
☐ 78	Dave Bing	8.00	3.60	1.00
	Detroit Pistons			
☐ 79	Billy Cunningham	10.00	4.50	1.25
	Philadelphia 76ers			
☐ 80	Len Wilkens	12.00	5.50	1.50
	Seattle Supersonics			
☐ 81	Jerry Lucas DP	4.00	1.80	.50
	New York Knicks			
☐ 82	Don Chaney	2.00	.90	.25
	Boston Celtics			
☐ 83	McCoy McLemore	1.50	.65	.19
	Milwaukee Bucks			
☐ 84	Bob Kauffman DP	1.50	.65	.19
	Buffalo Braves			
☐ 85	Dick Van Arsdale	2.00	.90	.25
	Phoenix Suns			
☐ 86	Johnny Green	1.50	.65	.19
	Cincinnati Royals			
☐ 87	Jerry Sloan	4.00	1.80	.50
	Chicago Bulls			
☐ 88	Luther Rackley DP	1.50	.65	.19
	Cleveland Cavaliers			
☐ 89	Shaler Halimon	1.50	.65	.19
	Portland Trail Blazers			
☐ 90	Jimmy Walker	1.50	.65	.19
	Detroit Pistons			
☐ 91	Rudy Tomjanovich	25.00	11.50	3.10
	Houston Rockets			
☐ 92	Levi Fontaine	1.50	.65	.19
	Golden State Warriors			
☐ 93	Bobby Smith	2.00	.90	.25
	Cleveland Cavaliers			
☐ 94	Bob Arnzen	1.50	.65	.19
	Cincinnati Royals			
☐ 95	Wes Unseld DP	6.00	2.70	.75
	Baltimore Bullets			
☐ 96	Clem Haskins DP	2.00	.90	.25
	Phoenix Suns			
☐ 97	Jim Davis	1.50	.65	.19
	Atlanta Hawks			
☐ 98	Steve Kuberski	1.50	.65	.19
	Boston Celtics			
☐ 99	Mike Davis DP	1.50	.65	.19
	Buffalo Braves			
☐ 100	Lew Alcindor	55.00	25.00	7.00
	Milwaukee Bucks			
☐ 101	Willie McCarter	1.50	.65	.19
	Los Angeles Lakers			
☐ 102	Charlie Paulk	1.50	.65	.19
	Chicago Bulls			
☐ 103	Lee Winfield	1.50	.65	.19
	Seattle Supersonics			
☐ 104	Jim Barnett	1.50	.65	.19
	Golden State Warriors			
☐ 105	Connie Hawkins DP	6.00	2.70	.75
	Phoenix Suns			
☐ 106	Archie Clark DP	2.00	.90	.25
	Philadelphia 76ers			
☐ 107	Dave DeBusschere	8.00	3.60	1.00
	New York Knicks			
☐ 108	Stu Lantz DP	2.00	.90	.25
	Houston Rockets			
☐ 109	Don Smith	1.50	.65	.19
	Seattle Supersonics			
☐ 110	Lou Hudson	3.00	1.35	.40
	Atlanta Hawks			
☐ 111	Leroy Ellis	2.00	.90	.25
	Portland Trail Blazers			
☐ 112	Jack Marin	2.00	.90	.25
	Baltimore Bullets			
☐ 113	Matt Guokas	3.00	1.35	.40
	Cincinnati Royals			
☐ 114	Don Nelson	6.00	2.70	.75
	Boston Celtics			
☐ 115	Jeff Mullins DP	1.50	.65	.19
	Golden State Warriors			
☐ 116	Walt Bellamy	4.00	1.80	.50
	Atlanta Hawks			
☐ 117	Bob Quick	1.50	.65	.19
	Detroit Pistons			
☐ 118	John Warren	1.50	.65	.19
	Cleveland Cavaliers			
☐ 119	Barry Clemens	1.50	.65	.19
	Seattle Supersonics			
☐ 120	Elvin Hayes DP	10.00	4.50	1.25
	Houston Rockets			
☐ 121	Gail Goodrich	6.00	2.70	.75
	Los Angeles Lakers			
☐ 122	Ed Manning	2.00	.90	.25
	Portland Trail Blazers			
☐ 123	Herm Gilliam DP	1.50	.65	.19
	Atlanta Hawks			
☐ 124	Dennis Awtrey	2.00	.90	.25
	Philadelphia 76ers			
☐ 125	John Hummer DP	1.50	.65	.19
	Buffalo Braves			
☐ 126	Mike Riordan	2.00	.90	.25
	New York Knicks			
☐ 127	Mel Counts	2.00	.90	.25
	Phoenix Suns			
☐ 128	Bob Weiss DP	2.00	.90	.25
	Chicago Bulls			
☐ 129	Greg Smith DP	1.50	.65	.19
	Milwaukee Bucks			
☐ 130	Earl Monroe	8.00	3.60	1.00
	Baltimore Bullets			
☐ 131	Nate Thurmond DP	4.00	1.80	.50
	Golden State Warriors			
☐ 132	Bill Bridges DP	2.00	.90	.25
	Atlanta Hawks			
☐ 133	NBA Playoffs G1	12.00	5.50	1.50
	Alcindor scores 31			
☐ 134	NBA Playoffs G2	3.00	1.35	.40
	Bucks make it Two Straight			
☐ 135	NBA Playoffs G3	3.00	1.35	.40
	Dandridge makes It Three in a Row			
☐ 136	NBA Playoffs G4	8.00	3.60	1.00

	A Clean Sweep (Oscar Robertson)			
☐ 137	NBA Champs Celebrate Bucks sweep Bullets	3.50	1.55	.45
☐ 138	NBA Scoring Leaders Lew Alcindor Elvin Hayes John Havlicek	18.00	8.00	2.30
☐ 139	NBA Scoring Average Leaders Lew Alcindor John Havlicek Elvin Hayes	18.00	8.00	2.30
☐ 140	NBA FG Pct Leaders. Johnny Green Lew Alcindor Wilt Chamberlain	14.00	6.25	1.75
☐ 141	NBA FT Pct Leaders .... Chet Walker Oscar Robertson Ron Williams	3.00	1.35	.40
☐ 142	NBA Rebound Leaders Wilt Chamberlain Elvin Hayes Lew Alcindor	25.00	11.50	3.10
☐ 143	NBA Assist Leaders . Norm Van Lier Oscar Robertson Jerry West	12.00	5.50	1.50
☐ 144A	NBA Checklist 1-144 (Copyright notation extends up to card 110)	18.00	2.30	.45
☐ 144B	NBA Checklist 1-144 (Copyright notation extends up to card 108)	18.00	2.30	.45
☐ 145	ABA Checklist 145-233	18.00	2.30	.45
☐ 146	ABA Scoring Leaders . Dan Issel John Brisker Charlie Scott	8.00	3.60	1.00
☐ 147	ABA Scoring Average Leaders Dan Issel Rick Barry John Brisker	12.00	5.50	1.50
☐ 148	ABA 2pt FG Pct Leaders Zelmo Beaty Bill Paultz Roger Brown	4.00	1.80	.50
☐ 149	ABA FT Pct Leaders . Rick Barry Darrell Carrier Billy Keller	10.00	4.50	1.25
☐ 150	ABA Rebound Leaders Mel Daniels Julius Keye Mike Lewis	4.00	1.80	.50
☐ 151	ABA Assist Leaders.... Bill Melchionni Mack Calvin Charlie Scott	4.00	1.80	.50
☐ 152	Larry Brown Denver Rockets	25.00	11.50	3.10
☐ 153	Bob Bedell Dallas Chaparrals	2.00	.90	.25
☐ 154	Merv Jackson Utah Stars	2.00	.90	.25
☐ 155	Joe Caldwell Carolina Cougars	2.50	1.15	.30
☐ 156	Billy Paultz New York Nets	4.00	1.80	.50
☐ 157	Les Hunter Kentucky Colonels	2.00	.90	.25
☐ 158	Charlie Williams Memphis Pros	2.00	.90	.25
☐ 159	Stew Johnson Pittsburgh Condors	2.00	.90	.25
☐ 160	Mack Calvin Florida Floridians	5.00	2.30	.60
☐ 161	Don Sidle Indiana Pacers	2.00	.90	.25
☐ 162	Mike Barrett Virginia Squires	2.00	.90	.25
☐ 163	Tom Workman Denver Rockets	2.00	.90	.25
☐ 164	Joe Hamilton Dallas Chaparrals	2.00	.90	.25
☐ 165	Zelmo Beaty Utah Stars	8.00	3.60	1.00
☐ 166	Dan Hester Kentucky Colonels	2.00	.90	.25
☐ 167	Bob Verga Carolina Cougars	2.00	.90	.25
☐ 168	Wilbert Jones Memphis Pros	2.00	.90	.25
☐ 169	Skeeter Swift Pittsburgh Condors	2.00	.90	.25
☐ 170	Rick Barry New York Nets	50.00	23.00	6.25
☐ 171	Billy Keller Indiana Pacers	4.00	1.80	.50
☐ 172	Ron Franz Florida Floridians	2.00	.90	.25
☐ 173	Roland Taylor Virginia Squires	2.00	.90	.25
☐ 174	Julian Hammond Denver Rockets	2.00	.90	.25
☐ 175	Steve Jones Dallas Chaparrals	5.00	2.30	.60
☐ 176	Gerald Govan Memphis Pros	2.00	.90	.25
☐ 177	Darrell Carrier Kentucky Colonels	2.00	.90	.25
☐ 178	Ron Boone Utah Stars	4.00	1.80	.50
☐ 179	George Peeples Carolina Cougars	2.00	.90	.25
☐ 180	John Brisker Pittsburgh Condors	2.50	1.15	.30
☐ 181	Doug Moe Virginia Squires	6.00	2.70	.75
☐ 182	Ollie Taylor New York Nets	2.00	.90	.25
☐ 183	Bob Netolicky Indiana Pacers	2.50	1.15	.30
☐ 184	Sam Robinson Florida Floridians	2.00	.90	.25
☐ 185	James Jones Memphis Pros	2.50	1.15	.30
☐ 186	Julius Keye Denver Rockets	2.00	.90	.25
☐ 187	Wayne Hightower Dallas Chaparrals	2.00	.90	.25
☐ 188	Warren Armstrong Indiana Pacers	2.50	1.15	.30
☐ 189	Mike Lewis Pittsburgh Condors	2.00	.90	.25
☐ 190	Charlie Scott Virginia Squires	8.00	3.60	1.00
☐ 191	Jim Ard	2.00	.90	.25

New York Nets
☐ 192	George Lehmann	2.00	.90	.25

Carolina Cougars
☐ 193	Ira Harge	2.00	.90	.25

Florida Floridians
☐ 194	Willie Wise	5.00	2.30	.60

Utah Stars
☐ 195	Mel Daniels	8.00	3.60	1.00

Indiana Pacers
☐ 196	Larry Cannon	2.00	.90	.25

Denver Rockets
☐ 197	Jim Eakins	2.00	.90	.25

Virginia Squires
☐ 198	Rich Jones	2.00	.90	.25

Dallas Chaparrals
☐ 199	Bill Melchionni	4.00	1.80	.50

New York Nets
☐ 200	Dan Issel	40.00	18.00	5.00

Kentucky Colonels
☐ 201	George Stone	2.00	.90	.25

Utah Stars
☐ 202	George Thompson	2.00	.90	.25

Pittsburgh Condors
☐ 203	Craig Raymond	2.00	.90	.25

Memphis Pros
☐ 204	Freddie Lewis	4.00	1.80	.50

Indiana Pacers
☐ 205	George Carter	2.00	.90	.25

Virginia Squires
☐ 206	Lonnie Wright	2.00	.90	.25

Florida Floridians
☐ 207	Cincy Powell	2.00	.90	.25

Kentucky Colonels
☐ 208	Larry Miller	2.00	.90	.25

Carolina Cougars
☐ 209	Sonny Dove	2.50	1.15	.30

New York Nets
☐ 210	Byron Beck	2.50	1.15	.30

Denver Rockets
☐ 211	John Beasley	2.00	.90	.25

Dallas Chaparrals
☐ 212	Lee Davis	2.00	.90	.25

Memphis Pros
☐ 213	Rick Mount	8.00	3.60	1.00

Indiana Pacers
☐ 214	Walt Simon	2.00	.90	.25

Kentucky Colonels
☐ 215	Glen Combs	2.00	.90	.25

Utah Stars
☐ 216	Neil Johnson	2.00	.90	.25

Virginia Squires
☐ 217	Manny Leaks	2.00	.90	.25

New York Nets
☐ 218	Chuck Williams	2.00	.90	.25

Pittsburgh Condors
☐ 219	Warren Davis	2.00	.90	.25

Florida Floridians
☐ 220	Donnie Freeman	4.00	1.80	.50

Dallas Chaparrals
☐ 221	Randy Mahaffey	2.00	.90	.25

Carolina Cougars
☐ 222	John Barnhill	2.00	.90	.25

Denver Rockets
☐ 223	Al Cueto	2.00	.90	.25

Memphis Pros
☐ 224	Louie Dampier	8.00	3.60	1.00

Kentucky Colonels
☐ 225	Roger Brown	4.00	1.80	.50

Indiana Pacers
☐ 226	Joe DePre	2.00	.90	.25

New York Nets
☐ 227	Ray Scott	2.00	.90	.25

Virginia Squires
☐ 228	Arvesta Kelly	2.00	.90	.25

Pittsburgh Condors
☐ 229	Vann Williford	2.00	.90	.25

Carolina Cougars
☐ 230	Larry Jones	2.50	1.15	.30

Florida Floridians
☐ 231	Gene Moore	2.00	.90	.25

Dallas Chaparrals
☐ 232	Ralph Simpson	4.00	1.80	.50

Denver Rockets
☐ 233	Red Robbins	4.00	1.20	.35

Utah Stars

1972-73 Topps

The 1972-73 Topps set of 264 cards contains NBA players (1-176) and ABA players (177-264). Cards were issued in 10-card packs with 24 packs per box. The cards in the set measure standard size, 2 1/2" by 3 1/2". All-Star selections are depicted for the NBA on cards 161-170 and for the ABA on cards 249-258. Subsets include NBA Playoffs (154-159), NBA Statistical Leaders (171-176), ABA Playoffs (241-247) and ABA Statistical Leaders (259-264). The key Rookie Card is Julius Erving. Other Rookie Cards include Artis Gilmore and Phil Jackson.

	NRMT-MT	EXC	VG
COMPLETE SET (264)	750.00	350.00	95.00
COMMON NBA CARD (1-176)	1.00	.45	.13
COMMON ABA CARD (177-264)	1.50	.65	.19

☐ 1	Wilt Chamberlain	40.00	12.50	2.50

Los Angeles Lakers
☐ 2	Stan Love	1.00	.45	.13

Baltimore Bullets
☐ 3	Geoff Petrie	1.50	.65	.19

Portland Trail Blazers
☐ 4	Curtis Perry	1.50	.65	.19

Milwaukee Bucks
☐ 5	Pete Maravich	35.00	16.00	4.40

Atlanta Hawks
☐ 6	Gus Johnson	1.50	.65	.19

Phoenix Suns
☐ 7	Dave Cowens	15.00	6.75	1.90

Boston Celtics
☐ 8	Randy Smith	4.00	1.80	.50

	Buffalo Braves			
☐ 9	Matt Guokas	1.50	.65	.19
	Kansas City-Omaha Kings			
☐ 10	Spencer Haywood	4.00	1.80	.50
	Seattle Supersonics			
☐ 11	Jerry Sloan	1.50	.65	.19
	Chicago Bulls			
☐ 12	Dave Sorenson	1.00	.45	.13
	Cleveland Cavaliers			
☐ 13	Howie Komives	1.00	.45	.13
	Detroit Pistons			
☐ 14	Joe Ellis	1.00	.45	.13
	Golden State Warriors			
☐ 15	Jerry Lucas	4.00	1.80	.50
	New York Knicks			
☐ 16	Stu Lantz	1.50	.65	.19
	Detroit Pistons			
☐ 17	Bill Bridges	1.50	.65	.19
	Philadelphia 76ers			
☐ 18	Leroy Ellis	1.50	.65	.19
	Los Angeles Lakers			
☐ 19	Art Williams	1.00	.45	.13
	Boston Celtics			
☐ 20	Sidney Wicks	8.00	3.60	1.00
	Portland Trail Blazers			
☐ 21	Wes Unseld	6.00	2.70	.75
	Baltimore Bullets			
☐ 22	Jim Washington	1.00	.45	.13
	Atlanta Hawks			
☐ 23	Fred Hilton	1.00	.45	.13
	Buffalo Braves			
☐ 24	Curtis Rowe	1.00	.45	.13
	Detroit Pistons			
☐ 25	Oscar Robertson	20.00	9.00	2.50
	Milwaukee Bucks			
☐ 26	Larry Steele	1.50	.65	.19
	Portland Trail Blazers			
☐ 27	Charlie Davis	1.00	.45	.13
	Cleveland Cavaliers			
☐ 28	Nate Thurmond	4.00	1.80	.50
	Golden State Warriors			
☐ 29	Fred Carter	1.50	.65	.19
	Philadelphia 76ers			
☐ 30	Connie Hawkins	6.00	2.70	.75
	Phoenix Suns			
☐ 31	Calvin Murphy	5.00	2.30	.60
	Houston Rockets			
☐ 32	Phil Jackson	20.00	9.00	2.50
	New York Knicks			
☐ 33	Lee Winfield	1.00	.45	.13
	Seattle Supersonics			
☐ 34	Jim Fox	1.00	.45	.13
	Seattle Supersonics			
☐ 35	Dave Bing	6.00	2.70	.75
	Detroit Pistons			
☐ 36	Gary Gregor	1.00	.45	.13
	Portland Trail Blazers			
☐ 37	Mike Riordan	1.50	.65	.19
	Baltimore Bullets			
☐ 38	George Trapp	1.00	.45	.13
	Atlanta Hawks			
☐ 39	Mike Davis	1.00	.45	.13
	Buffalo Braves			
☐ 40	Bob Rule	1.00	.45	.13
	Philadelphia 76ers			
☐ 41	John Block	1.00	.45	.13
	Philadelphia 76ers			
☐ 42	Bob Dandridge	1.50	.65	.19
	Milwaukee Bucks			
☐ 43	John Johnson	1.00	.45	.13
	Cleveland Cavaliers			
☐ 44	Rick Barry	15.00	6.75	1.90
	Golden State Warriors			
☐ 45	JoJo White	3.00	1.35	.40
	Boston Celtics			
☐ 46	Cliff Meely	1.00	.45	.13
	Houston Rockets			
☐ 47	Charlie Scott	2.50	1.15	.30
	Phoenix Suns			
☐ 48	Johnny Green	1.00	.45	.13
	Kansas City-Omaha Kings			
☐ 49	Pete Cross	1.00	.45	.13
	Kansas City-Omaha Kings			
☐ 50	Gail Goodrich	4.00	1.80	.50
	Los Angeles Lakers			
☐ 51	Jim Davis	1.00	.45	.13
	Detroit Pistons			
☐ 52	Dick Barnett	1.50	.65	.19
	New York Knicks			
☐ 53	Bob Christian	1.00	.45	.13
	Atlanta Hawks			
☐ 54	Jon McGlocklin	1.50	.65	.19
	Milwaukee Bucks			
☐ 55	Paul Silas	3.00	1.35	.40
	Boston Celtics			
☐ 56	Hal Greer	3.00	1.35	.40
	Philadelphia 76ers			
☐ 57	Barry Clemens	1.00	.45	.13
	Seattle Supersonics			
☐ 58	Nick Jones	1.00	.45	.13
	Golden State Warriors			
☐ 59	Cornell Warner	1.00	.45	.13
	Buffalo Braves			
☐ 60	Walt Frazier	10.00	4.50	1.25
	New York Knicks			
☐ 61	Dorie Murray	1.00	.45	.13
	Baltimore Bullets			
☐ 62	Dick Cunningham	1.00	.45	.13
	Houston Rockets			
☐ 63	Sam Lacey	1.50	.65	.19
	Kansas City-Omaha Kings			
☐ 64	John Warren	1.00	.45	.13
	Cleveland Cavaliers			
☐ 65	Tom Boerwinkle	1.50	.65	.19
	Chicago Bulls			
☐ 66	Fred Foster	1.00	.45	.13
	Detroit Pistons			
☐ 67	Mel Counts	1.50	.65	.19
	Phoenix Suns			
☐ 68	Toby Kimball	1.00	.45	.13
	Milwaukee Bucks			
☐ 69	Dale Schlueter	1.00	.45	.13
	Portland Trail Blazers			
☐ 70	Jack Marin	1.50	.65	.19
	Houston Rockets			
☐ 71	Jim Barnett	1.00	.45	.13
	Golden State Warriors			
☐ 72	Clem Haskins	1.50	.65	.19
	Phoenix Suns			
☐ 73	Earl Monroe	6.00	2.70	.75
	New York Knicks			
☐ 74	Tom Sanders	1.00	.45	.13
	Boston Celtics			
☐ 75	Jerry West	25.00	11.50	3.10
	Los Angeles Lakers			
☐ 76	Elmore Smith	1.50	.65	.19
	Buffalo Braves			
☐ 77	Don Adams	1.00	.45	.13
	Atlanta Hawks			
☐ 78	Wally Jones	1.00	.45	.13
	Milwaukee Bucks			
☐ 79	Tom Van Arsdale	1.50	.65	.19

	Kansas City-Omaha Kings			
☐ 80	Bob Lanier 12.00	5.50	1.50
	Detroit Pistons			
☐ 81	Len Wilkens 8.00	3.60	1.00
	Seattle Supersonics			
☐ 82	Neal Walk 1.50	.65	.19
	Phoenix Suns			
☐ 83	Kevin Loughery 1.50	.65	.19
	Philadelphia 76ers			
☐ 84	Stan McKenzie 1.00	.45	.13
	Portland Trail Blazers			
☐ 85	Jeff Mullins 1.50	.65	.19
	Golden State Warriors			
☐ 86	Otto Moore 1.00	.45	.13
	Houston Rockets			
☐ 87	John Tresvant 1.00	.45	.13
	Baltimore Bullets			
☐ 88	Dean Meminger 1.00	.45	.13
	New York Knicks			
☐ 89	Jim McMillian 1.00	.45	.13
	Los Angeles Lakers			
☐ 90	Austin Carr 6.00	2.70	.75
	Cleveland Cavaliers			
☐ 91	Clifford Ray 1.00	.45	.13
	Chicago Bulls			
☐ 92	Don Nelson 4.00	1.80	.50
	Boston Celtics			
☐ 93	Mahdi Abdul-Rahman .. 1.50	.65	.19
	Buffalo Braves			
	(formerly Walt Hazzard)			
☐ 94	Willie Norwood 1.00	.45	.13
	Detroit Pistons			
☐ 95	Dick Van Arsdale 1.50	.65	.19
	Phoenix Suns			
☐ 96	Don May 1.00	.45	.13
	Atlanta Hawks			
☐ 97	Walt Bellamy 2.50	1.15	.30
	Atlanta Hawks			
☐ 98	Garfield Heard 4.00	1.80	.50
	Seattle Supersonics			
☐ 99	Dave Wohl 1.00	.45	.13
	Philadelphia 76ers			
☐ 100	Kareem Abdul-Jabbar 40.00	18.00	5.00
	Milwaukee Bucks			
☐ 101	Ron Knight 1.00	.45	.13
	Portland Trail Blazers			
☐ 102	Phil Chenier 4.00	1.80	.50
	Baltimore Bullets			
☐ 103	Rudy Tomjanovich 8.00	3.60	1.00
	Houston Rockets			
☐ 104	Flynn Robinson 1.00	.45	.13
	Los Angeles Lakers			
☐ 105	Dave DeBusschere 6.00	2.70	.75
	New York Knicks			
☐ 106	Dennis Layton 1.00	.45	.13
	Phoenix Suns			
☐ 107	Bill Hewitt 1.00	.45	.13
	Detroit Pistons			
☐ 108	Dick Garrett 1.00	.45	.13
	Buffalo Braves			
☐ 109	Walt Wesley 1.00	.45	.13
	Cleveland Cavaliers			
☐ 110	John Havlicek 20.00	9.00	2.50
	Boston Celtics			
☐ 111	Norm Van Lier 1.50	.65	.19
	Chicago Bulls			
☐ 112	Cazzie Russell 2.50	1.15	.30
	Golden State Warriors			
☐ 113	Herm Gilliam 1.00	.45	.13
	Atlanta Hawks			
☐ 114	Greg Smith 1.00	.45	.13

	Houston Rockets			
☐ 115	Nate Archibald 7.00	3.10	.85
	Kansas City-Omaha Kings			
☐ 116	Don Kojis 1.00	.45	.13
	Kansas City-Omaha Kings			
☐ 117	Rick Adelman 1.50	.65	.19
	Portland Trail Blazers			
☐ 118	Luke Jackson 1.50	.65	.19
	Philadelphia 76ers			
☐ 119	Lamar Green 1.00	.45	.13
	Phoenix Suns			
☐ 120	Archie Clark 1.50	.65	.19
	Baltimore Bullets			
☐ 121	Happy Hairston 1.50	.65	.19
	Los Angeles Lakers			
☐ 122	Bill Bradley 20.00	9.00	2.50
	New York Knicks			
☐ 123	Ron Williams 1.00	.45	.13
	Golden State Warriors			
☐ 124	Jimmy Walker 1.50	.65	.19
	Houston Rockets			
☐ 125	Bob Kauffman 1.00	.45	.13
	Buffalo Braves			
☐ 126	Rick Roberson 1.00	.45	.13
	Cleveland Cavaliers			
☐ 127	Howard Porter 2.50	1.15	.30
	Chicago Bulls			
☐ 128	Mike Newlin 1.50	.65	.19
	Houston Rockets			
☐ 129	Willis Reed 7.00	3.10	.85
	New York Knicks			
☐ 130	Lou Hudson 2.50	1.15	.30
	Atlanta Hawks			
☐ 131	Don Chaney 1.50	.65	.19
	Boston Celtics			
☐ 132	Dave Stallworth 1.00	.45	.13
	Baltimore Bullets			
☐ 133	Charlie Yelverton 1.00	.45	.13
	Portland Trail Blazers			
☐ 134	Ken Durrett 1.00	.45	.13
	Kansas City-Omaha Kings			
☐ 135	John Brisker 1.00	.45	.13
	Seattle Supersonics			
☐ 136	Dick Snyder 1.00	.45	.13
	Seattle Supersonics			
☐ 137	Jim McDaniels 1.00	.45	.13
	Seattle Supersonics			
☐ 138	Clyde Lee 1.00	.45	.13
	Golden State Warriors			
☐ 139	Dennis Awtrey UER 1.50	.65	.19
	Philadelphia 76ers			
	(Misspelled Awtry			
	on card front)			
☐ 140	Keith Erickson 1.00	.45	.13
	Los Angeles Lakers			
☐ 141	Bob Weiss 1.00	.45	.13
	Chicago Bulls			
☐ 142	Butch Beard 3.00	1.35	.40
	Cleveland Cavaliers			
☐ 143	Terry Dischinger 1.50	.65	.19
	Portland Trail Blazers			
☐ 144	Pat Riley 12.00	5.50	1.50
	Los Angeles Lakers			
☐ 145	Lucius Allen 1.00	.45	.13
	Milwaukee Bucks			
☐ 146	John Mengelt 1.00	.45	.13
	Kansas City-Omaha Kings			
☐ 147	John Hummer 1.00	.45	.13
	Buffalo Braves			
☐ 148	Bob Love 4.00	1.80	.50
	Chicago Bulls			

☐ 149	Bobby Smith	1.50	.65	.19
	Cleveland Cavaliers			
☐ 150	Elvin Hayes	10.00	4.50	1.25
	Baltimore Bullets			
☐ 151	Nate Williams	1.00	.45	.13
	Kansas City-Omaha Kings			
☐ 152	Chet Walker	2.50	1.15	.30
	Chicago Bulls			
☐ 153	Steve Kuberski	1.50	.65	.19
	Boston Celtics			
☐ 154	NBA Playoffs G1	3.00	1.35	.40
	Knicks win Opener			
	(Earl Monroe)			
☐ 155	NBA Playoffs G2	2.50	1.15	.30
	Lakers Come Back			
	(under the basket)			
☐ 156	NBA Playoffs G3	2.50	1.15	.30
	Two in a Row			
	(under the basket)			
☐ 157	NBA Playoffs G4	2.50	1.15	.30
	Ellis provides			
	bench strength			
☐ 158	NBA Playoffs G5	8.00	3.60	1.00
	Jerry drives in			
	(Jerry West)			
☐ 159	NBA Champs-Lakers	10.00	4.50	1.25
	(Wilt rebounding)			
☐ 160	NBA Checklist 1-176	16.00	1.90	.50
	UER (135 Jim King)			
☐ 161	John Havlicek AS	10.00	4.50	1.25
	Boston Celtics			
☐ 162	Spencer Haywood AS	2.50	1.15	.30
	Seattle Supersonics			
☐ 163	Kareem Abdul-Jabbar AS	25.00	11.50	3.10
	Milwaukee Bucks			
☐ 164	Jerry West AS	15.00	6.75	1.90
	Los Angeles Lakers			
☐ 165	Walt Frazier AS	5.00	2.30	.60
	New York Knicks			
☐ 166	Bob Love AS	2.50	1.15	.30
	Chicago Bulls			
☐ 167	Billy Cunningham AS .	4.00	1.80	.50
	Philadelphia 76ers			
☐ 168	Wilt Chamberlain AS	20.00	9.00	2.50
	Los Angeles Lakers			
☐ 169	Nate Archibald AS	4.00	1.80	.50
	Kansas City-Omaha Kings			
☐ 170	Archie Clark AS	2.50	1.15	.30
	Baltimore Bullets			
☐ 171	NBA Scoring Leaders	12.00	5.50	1.50
	Kareem Abdul-Jabbar			
	John Havlicek			
	Nate Archibald			
☐ 172	NBA Scoring Average	12.00	5.50	1.50
	Leaders			
	Kareem Abdul-Jabbar			
	Nate Archibald			
	John Havlicek			
☐ 173	NBA FG Pct Leaders.	15.00	6.75	1.90
	Wilt Chamberlain			
	Kareem Abdul-Jabbar			
	Walt Bellamy			
☐ 174	NBA FT Pct Leaders ...	2.50	1.15	.30
	Jack Marin			
	Calvin Murphy			
	Gail Goodrich			
☐ 175	NBA Rebound Leaders	15.00	6.75	1.90
	Wilt Chamberlain			
	Kareem Abdul-Jabbar			
	Wes Unseld			
☐ 176	NBA Assist Leaders .	12.00	5.50	1.50
	Len Wilkens			
	Jerry West			
	Nate Archibald			
☐ 177	Roland Taylor	1.50	.65	.19
	Virginia Squires			
☐ 178	Art Becker	1.50	.65	.19
	San Diego Conquistadors			
☐ 179	Mack Calvin	2.00	.90	.25
	Carolina Cougars			
☐ 180	Artis Gilmore	20.00	9.00	2.50
	Kentucky Colonels			
☐ 181	Collis Jones	1.50	.65	.19
	Dallas Chaparrals			
☐ 182	John Roche	2.50	1.15	.30
	New York Nets			
☐ 183	George McGinnis	12.00	5.50	1.50
	Indiana Pacers			
☐ 184	Johnny Neumann	2.00	.90	.25
	Memphis Tams			
☐ 185	Willie Wise	2.00	.90	.25
	Utah Stars			
☐ 186	Bernie Williams	1.50	.65	.19
	Virginia Squires			
☐ 187	Byron Beck	2.00	.90	.25
	Denver Rockets			
☐ 188	Larry Miller	1.50	.65	.19
	San Diego Conquistadors			
☐ 189	Cincy Powell	1.50	.65	.19
	Kentucky Colonels			
☐ 190	Donnie Freeman	2.00	.90	.25
	Dallas Chaparrals			
☐ 191	John Baum	1.50	.65	.19
	New York Nets			
☐ 192	Billy Keller	2.00	.90	.25
	Indiana Pacers			
☐ 193	Wilbert Jones	1.50	.65	.19
	Memphis Tams			
☐ 194	Glen Combs	1.50	.65	.19
	Utah Stars			
☐ 195	Julius Erving	275.00	125.00	34.00
	Virginia Squires			
	(Forward on front,			
	but Center on back)			
☐ 196	Al Smith	1.50	.65	.19
	Denver Rockets			
☐ 197	George Carter	1.50	.65	.19
	New York Nets			
☐ 198	Louie Dampier	3.00	1.35	.40
	Kentucky Colonels			
☐ 199	Rich Jones	1.50	.65	.19
	Dallas Chaparrals			
☐ 200	Mel Daniels	3.00	1.35	.40
	Indiana Pacers			
☐ 201	Gene Moore	1.50	.65	.19
	San Diego Conquistadors			
☐ 202	Randy Denton	1.50	.65	.19
	Memphis Tams			
☐ 203	Larry Jones	2.00	.90	.25
	Utah Stars			
☐ 204	Jim Ligon	1.50	.65	.19
	Virginia Squires			
☐ 205	Warren Jabali	1.50	.65	.19
	Denver Rockets			
☐ 206	Joe Caldwell	2.00	.90	.25
	Carolina Cougars			
☐ 207	Darrell Carrier	2.00	.90	.25
	Kentucky Colonels			
☐ 208	Gene Kennedy	1.50	.65	.19
	Dallas Chaparrals			
☐ 209	Ollie Taylor	1.50	.65	.19
	San Diego Conquistadors			

☐ 210	Roger Brown	2.00	.90	.25
	Indiana Pacers			
☐ 211	George Lehmann	1.50	.65	.19
	Memphis Tams			
☐ 212	Red Robbins	1.50	.65	.19
	San Diego Conquistadors			
☐ 213	Jim Eakins	1.50	.65	.19
	Virginia Squires			
☐ 214	Willie Long	1.50	.65	.19
	Denver Rockets			
☐ 215	Billy Cunningham	8.00	3.60	1.00
	Carolina Cougars			
☐ 216	Steve Jones	2.00	.90	.25
	Dallas Chaparrals			
☐ 217	Les Hunter	1.50	.65	.19
	San Diego Conquistadors			
☐ 218	Billy Paultz	2.00	.90	.25
	New York Nets			
☐ 219	Freddie Lewis	2.00	.90	.25
	Indiana Pacers			
☐ 220	Zelmo Beaty	1.50	.65	.19
	Utah Stars			
☐ 221	George Thompson	1.50	.65	.19
	Memphis Tams			
☐ 222	Neil Johnson	1.50	.65	.19
	Virginia Squires			
☐ 223	Dave Robisch	2.50	1.15	.30
	Denver Rockets			
☐ 224	Walt Simon	1.50	.65	.19
	Kentucky Colonels			
☐ 225	Bill Melchionni	2.00	.90	.25
	New York Nets			
☐ 226	Wendell Ladner	2.50	1.15	.30
	Memphis Tams			
☐ 227	Joe Hamilton	1.50	.65	.19
	Dallas Chaparrals			
☐ 228	Bob Netolicky	2.00	.90	.25
	Dallas Chaparrals			
☐ 229	James Jones	2.00	.90	.25
	Utah Stars			
☐ 230	Dan Issel	12.00	5.50	1.50
	Kentucky Colonels			
☐ 231	Charlie Williams	1.50	.65	.19
	San Diego Conquistadors			
☐ 232	Willie Sojourner	1.50	.65	.19
	Virginia Squires			
☐ 233	Merv Jackson	1.50	.65	.19
	Utah Stars			
☐ 234	Mike Lewis	1.50	.65	.19
	Carolina Cougars			
☐ 235	Ralph Simpson	2.00	.90	.25
	Denver Rockets			
☐ 236	Darnell Hillman	2.00	.90	.25
	Indiana Pacers			
☐ 237	Rick Mount	3.00	1.35	.40
	Kentucky Colonels			
☐ 238	Gerald Govan	1.50	.65	.19
	Memphis Tams			
☐ 239	Ron Boone	2.00	.90	.25
	Utah Stars			
☐ 240	Tom Washington	1.50	.65	.19
	New York Nets			
☐ 241	ABA Playoffs G1	2.50	1.15	.30
	Pacers take lead (under the basket)			
☐ 242	ABA Playoffs G2	5.00	2.30	.60
	Barry evens things			
☐ 243	ABA Playoffs G3	4.00	1.80	.50
	McGinnis blocks a jumper			
☐ 244	ABA Playoffs G4	5.00	2.30	.60

	Rick (Barry) scores on fast break			
☐ 245	ABA Playoffs G5	2.50	1.15	.30
	Keller becomes Net killer			
☐ 246	ABA Playoffs G6	2.50	1.15	.30
	Tight Defense			
☐ 247	ABA Champs: Pacers	3.00	1.35	.40
☐ 248	ABA Checklist 177-264	16.00	1.90	.50
	UER (236 John Brisker)			
☐ 249	Dan Issel AS	6.00	2.70	.75
	Kentucky Colonels			
☐ 250	Rick Barry AS	8.00	3.60	1.00
	New York Nets			
☐ 251	Artis Gilmore AS	6.00	2.70	.75
	Kentucky Colonels			
☐ 252	Donnie Freeman AS	2.00	.90	.25
	Dallas Chaparrals			
☐ 253	Bill Melchionni AS	2.00	.90	.25
	New York Nets			
☐ 254	Willie Wise AS	2.50	1.15	.30
	Utah Stars			
☐ 255	Julius Erving AS	60.00	27.00	7.50
	Virginia Squires			
☐ 256	Zelmo Beaty AS	2.50	1.15	.30
	Utah Stars			
☐ 257	Ralph Simpson AS	2.50	1.15	.30
	Denver Rockets			
☐ 258	Charlie Scott AS	2.50	1.15	.30
	Virginia Squires			
☐ 259	ABA Scoring Average	6.00	2.70	.75
	Leaders			
	Charlie Scott			
	Rick Barry			
	Dan Issel			
☐ 260	ABA 2pt FG Pct.	4.00	1.80	.50
	Leaders			
	Artis Gilmore			
	Tom Washington			
	Larry Jones			
☐ 261	ABA 3pt FG Pct.	2.50	1.15	.30
	Leaders			
	Glen Combs			
	Louie Dampier			
	Warren Jabali			
☐ 262	ABA FT Pct Leaders	4.00	1.80	.50
	Rick Barry			
	Mack Calvin			
	Steve Jones			
☐ 263	ABA Rebound Leaders	20.00	9.00	2.50
	Artis Gilmore			
	Julius Erving			
	Mel Daniels			
☐ 264	ABA Assist Leaders	6.00	2.40	.50
	Bill Melchionni			
	Larry Brown			
	Louie Dampier			

1973-74 Topps

The 1973-74 Topps set of 264 contains NBA players on cards numbered 1 to 176 and ABA players on cards numbered 177 to 264. Cards were issued in 10-card packs with 24 packs per box. The cards in the set measure the standard 2 1/2" by 3 1/2". All-Star selections (first and second team) for

both leagues are noted on the respective player's regular cards. Card backs are printed in red and green on gray card stock. The backs feature year-by-year both ABA and NBA statistics. Subsets include NBA Playoffs (62-68), NBA League Leaders (153-158), ABA Playoffs (202-208) and ABA League Leaders (234-239). The only notable Rookie Cards in this set are Chris Ford, Bob McAdoo, and Paul Westphal.

		NRMT-MT	EXC	VG
COMPLETE SET (264)		350.00	160.00	45.00
COMMON NBA CARD (1-176)		.50	.23	.06
COMMON ABA CARD (177-264)		1.00	.45	.13

			NRMT-MT	EXC	VG
☐	1	Nate Archibald AS1 KC-Omaha Kings	8.00	2.20	.50
☐	2	Steve Kuberski Boston Celtics	1.00	.45	.13
☐	3	John Mengelt Detroit Pistons	.50	.23	.06
☐	4	Jim McMillian Los Angeles Lakers	1.00	.45	.13
☐	5	Nate Thurmond Golden State Warriors	3.00	1.35	.40
☐	6	Dave Wohl Buffalo Braves	.50	.23	.06
☐	7	John Brisker Seattle Supersonics	.50	.23	.06
☐	8	Charlie Davis Portland Trail Blazers	.50	.23	.06
☐	9	Lamar Green Phoenix Suns	.50	.23	.06
☐	10	Walt Frazier AS2 New York Knicks	7.00	3.10	.85
☐	11	Bob Christian Atlanta Hawks	.50	.23	.06
☐	12	Cornell Warner Cleveland Cavaliers	.50	.23	.06
☐	13	Calvin Murphy Houston Rockets	4.00	1.80	.50
☐	14	Dave Sorenson Philadelphia 76ers	.50	.23	.06
☐	15	Archie Clark Capital Bullets	1.00	.45	.13
☐	16	Clifford Ray Chicago Bulls	1.00	.45	.13
☐	17	Terry Driscoll Milwaukee Bucks	.50	.23	.06
☐	18	Matt Guokas Kansas City-Omaha Kings	1.00	.45	.13
☐	19	Elmore Smith Buffalo Braves	.50	.23	.06
☐	20	John Havlicek AS1 Boston Celtics	14.00	6.25	1.75
☐	21	Pat Riley	6.00	2.70	.75

			NRMT-MT	EXC	VG
		Los Angeles Lakers			
☐	22	George Trapp Detroit Pistons	.50	.23	.06
☐	23	Ron Williams Golden State Warriors	.50	.23	.06
☐	24	Jim Fox Seattle Supersonics	.50	.23	.06
☐	25	Dick Van Arsdale Phoenix Suns	1.00	.45	.13
☐	26	John Tresvant Capital Bullets	.50	.23	.06
☐	27	Rick Adelman Portland Trail Blazers	1.00	.45	.13
☐	28	Eddie Mast Atlanta Hawks	.50	.23	.06
☐	29	Jim Cleamons Cleveland Cavaliers	.50	.23	.06
☐	30	Dave DeBusschere AS2 New York Knicks	5.00	2.30	.60
☐	31	Norm Van Lier Chicago Bulls	.50	.23	.06
☐	32	Stan McKenzie Houston Rockets	.50	.23	.06
☐	33	Bob Dandridge Milwaukee Bucks	1.00	.45	.13
☐	34	Leroy Ellis Philadelphia 76ers	1.00	.45	.13
☐	35	Mike Riordan Capital Bullets	1.00	.45	.13
☐	36	Fred Hilton Buffalo Braves	.50	.23	.06
☐	37	Toby Kimball Kansas City-Omaha Kings	.50	.23	.06
☐	38	Jim Price Los Angeles Lakers	.50	.23	.06
☐	39	Willie Norwood Detroit Pistons	.50	.23	.06
☐	40	Dave Cowens AS2 Boston Celtics	8.00	3.60	1.00
☐	41	Cazzie Russell Golden State Warriors	.50	.23	.06
☐	42	Lee Winfield Seattle Supersonics	.50	.23	.06
☐	43	Connie Hawkins Phoenix Suns	4.00	1.80	.50
☐	44	Mike Newlin Houston Rockets	1.00	.45	.13
☐	45	Chet Walker Chicago Bulls	1.00	.45	.13
☐	46	Walt Bellamy Atlanta Hawks	2.50	1.15	.30
☐	47	John Johnson Portland Trail Blazers	1.00	.45	.13
☐	48	Henry Bibby New York Knicks	3.00	1.35	.40
☐	49	Bobby Smith Cleveland Cavaliers	.50	.23	.06
☐	50	Kareem Abdul-Jabbar AS1 Milwaukee Bucks	30.00	13.50	3.80
☐	51	Mike Price Philadelphia 76ers	.50	.23	.06
☐	52	John Hummer Buffalo Braves	.50	.23	.06
☐	53	Kevin Porter Capital Bullets	5.00	2.30	.60
☐	54	Nate Williams Kansas City-Omaha Kings	.50	.23	.06
☐	55	Gail Goodrich Los Angeles Lakers	3.00	1.35	.40
☐	56	Fred Foster Detroit Pistons	.50	.23	.06

☐ 57 Don Chaney	1.00	.45	.13
Boston Celtics			
☐ 58 Bud Stallworth	.50	.23	.06
Seattle Supersonics			
☐ 59 Clem Haskins	1.00	.45	.13
Phoenix Suns			
☐ 60 Bob Love AS2	3.00	1.35	.40
Chicago Bulls			
☐ 61 Jimmy Walker	1.00	.45	.13
Houston Rockets			
☐ 62 NBA Eastern Semis	1.00	.45	.13
Knicks shoot down			
Bullets in 5			
☐ 63 NBA Eastern Semis	1.00	.45	.13
Celts oust Hawks			
2nd Straight Year			
☐ 64 NBA Western Semis	8.00	3.60	1.00
Lakers outlast			
Bulls at Wire			
(W.Chamberlain)			
☐ 65 NBA Western Semis	1.00	.45	.13
Warriors over-			
whelm Milwaukee			
☐ 66 NBA Eastern Finals	3.00	1.35	.40
Knicks stun			
Celtics at Boston			
(W.Reed/Finkel)			
☐ 67 NBA Western Finals	1.00	.45	.13
Lakers Breeze Past			
Golden State			
☐ 68 NBA Championship	4.00	1.80	.50
Knicks Do It,			
Repeat '70 Miracle			
(W.Frazier/Erickson)			
☐ 69 Larry Steele	1.00	.45	.13
Portland Trail Blazers			
☐ 70 Oscar Robertson	14.00	6.25	1.75
Milwaukee Bucks			
☐ 71 Phil Jackson	5.00	2.30	.60
New York Knicks			
☐ 72 John Wetzel	.50	.23	.06
Atlanta Hawks			
☐ 73 Steve Patterson	2.50	1.15	.30
Cleveland Cavaliers			
☐ 74 Manny Leaks	.50	.23	.06
Philadelphia 76ers			
☐ 75 Jeff Mullins	1.00	.45	.13
Golden State Warriors			
☐ 76 Stan Love	.50	.23	.06
Capital Bullets			
☐ 77 Dick Garrett	.50	.23	.06
Buffalo Braves			
☐ 78 Don Nelson	3.00	1.35	.40
Boston Celtics			
☐ 79 Chris Ford	3.00	1.35	.40
Detroit Pistons			
☐ 80 Wilt Chamberlain	25.00	11.50	3.10
Los Angeles Lakers			
☐ 81 Dennis Layton	.50	.23	.06
Phoenix Suns			
☐ 82 Bill Bradley	12.00	5.50	1.50
New York Knicks			
☐ 83 Jerry Sloan	1.00	.45	.13
Chicago Bulls			
☐ 84 Cliff Meely	.50	.23	.06
Houston Rockets			
☐ 85 Sam Lacey	.50	.23	.06
Kansas City-Omaha Kings			
☐ 86 Dick Snyder	.50	.23	.06
Seattle Supersonics			
☐ 87 Jim Washington	.50	.23	.06
Atlanta Hawks			
☐ 88 Lucius Allen	.50	.23	.06
Milwaukee Bucks			
☐ 89 LaRue Martin	.50	.23	.06
Portland Trail Blazers			
☐ 90 Rick Barry	8.00	3.60	1.00
Golden State Warriors			
☐ 91 Fred Boyd	.50	.23	.06
Philadelphia 76ers			
☐ 92 Barry Clemens	.50	.23	.06
Cleveland Cavaliers			
☐ 93 Dean Meminger	.50	.23	.06
New York Knicks			
☐ 94 Henry Finkel	.50	.23	.06
Boston Celtics			
☐ 95 Elvin Hayes	7.00	3.10	.85
Capital Bullets			
☐ 96 Stu Lantz	1.00	.45	.13
Detroit Pistons			
☐ 97 Bill Hewitt	.50	.23	.06
Buffalo Braves			
☐ 98 Neal Walk	1.00	.45	.13
Phoenix Suns			
☐ 99 Garfield Heard	1.00	.45	.13
Chicago Bulls			
☐ 100 Jerry West AS1	20.00	9.00	2.50
Los Angeles Lakers			
☐ 101 Otto Moore	.50	.23	.06
Houston Rockets			
☐ 102 Don Kojis	.50	.23	.06
Kansas City-Omaha Kings			
☐ 103 Fred Brown	4.00	1.80	.50
Seattle Supersonics			
☐ 104 Dwight Davis	.50	.23	.06
Cleveland Cavaliers			
☐ 105 Willis Reed	5.00	2.30	.60
New York Knicks			
☐ 106 Herm Gilliam	.50	.23	.06
Atlanta Hawks			
☐ 107 Mickey Davis	.50	.23	.06
Milwaukee Bucks			
☐ 108 Jim Barnett	.50	.23	.06
Golden State Warriors			
☐ 109 Ollie Johnson	.50	.23	.06
Portland Trail Blazers			
☐ 110 Bob Lanier	6.00	2.70	.75
Detroit Pistons			
☐ 111 Fred Carter	1.00	.45	.13
Philadelphia 76ers			
☐ 112 Paul Silas	2.00	.90	.25
Boston Celtics			
☐ 113 Phil Chenier	1.00	.45	.13
Capital Bullets			
☐ 114 Dennis Awtrey	.50	.23	.06
Chicago Bulls			
☐ 115 Austin Carr	1.00	.45	.13
Cleveland Cavaliers			
☐ 116 Bob Kauffman	.50	.23	.06
Buffalo Braves			
☐ 117 Keith Erickson	1.00	.45	.13
Los Angeles Lakers			
☐ 118 Walt Wesley	.50	.23	.06
Phoenix Suns			
☐ 119 Steve Bracey	.50	.23	.06
Atlanta Hawks			
☐ 120 Spencer Haywood AS1	2.50	1.15	.30
Seattle Supersonics			
☐ 121 NBA Checklist 1-176	12.00	1.00	.20
☐ 122 Jack Marin	1.00	.45	.13
Houston Rockets			
☐ 123 Jon McGlocklin	.50	.23	.06

		Milwaukee Bucks		
☐	124	Johnny Green .50	.23	.06
		Kansas City-Omaha Kings		
☐	125	Jerry Lucas 3.00	1.35	.40
		New York Knicks		
☐	126	Paul Westphal 20.00	9.00	2.50
		Boston Celtics		
☐	127	Curtis Rowe 1.00	.45	.13
		Detroit Pistons		
☐	128	Mahdi Abdul-Rahman 1.00	.45	.13
		Seattle Supersonics		
		(formerly Walt Hazzard)		
☐	129	Lloyd Neal .50	.23	.06
		Portland Trail Blazers		
☐	130	Pete Maravich AS1 25.00	11.50	3.10
		Atlanta Hawks		
☐	131	Don May .50	.23	.06
		Philadelphia 76ers		
☐	132	Bob Weiss .50	.23	.06
		Chicago Bulls		
☐	133	Dave Stallworth .50	.23	.06
		Capital Bullets		
☐	134	Dick Cunningham .50	.23	.06
		Milwaukee Bucks		
☐	135	Bob McAdoo 20.00	9.00	2.50
		Buffalo Braves		
☐	136	Butch Beard 1.00	.45	.13
		Golden State Warriors		
☐	137	Happy Hairston 1.00	.45	.13
		Los Angeles Lakers		
☐	138	Bob Rule .50	.23	.06
		Cleveland Cavaliers		
☐	139	Don Adams .50	.23	.06
		Detroit Pistons		
☐	140	Charlie Scott 1.00	.45	.13
		Phoenix Suns		
☐	141	Ron Riley .50	.23	.06
		Kansas City-Omaha Kings		
☐	142	Earl Monroe 4.00	1.80	.50
		New York Knicks		
☐	143	Clyde Lee .50	.23	.06
		Golden State Warriors		
☐	144	Rick Roberson .50	.23	.06
		Portland Trail Blazers		
☐	145	Rudy Tomjanovich 6.00	2.70	.75
		Houston Rockets		
		(Printed without		
		Houston on basket)		
☐	146	Tom Van Arsdale 1.00	.45	.13
		Philadelphia 76ers		
☐	147	Art Williams .50	.23	.06
		Boston Celtics		
☐	148	Curtis Perry .50	.23	.06
		Milwaukee Bucks		
☐	149	Rich Rinaldi .50	.23	.06
		Capital Bullets		
☐	150	Lou Hudson 1.00	.45	.13
		Atlanta Hawks		
☐	151	Mel Counts 1.00	.45	.13
		Los Angeles Lakers		
☐	152	Jim McDaniels .50	.23	.06
		Seattle Supersonics		
☐	153	NBA Scoring Leaders. 8.00	3.60	1.00
		Nate Archibald		
		Kareem Abdul-Jabbar		
		Spencer Haywood		
☐	154	NBA Scoring Average. 8.00	3.60	1.00
		Leaders		
		Nate Archibald		
		Kareem Abdul-Jabbar		
		Spencer Haywood		
☐	155	NBA FG Pct Leaders. 12.00	5.50	1.50
		Wilt Chamberlain		
		Matt Guokas		
		Kareem Abdul-Jabbar		
☐	156	NBA FT Pct Leaders 3.00	1.35	.40
		Rick Barry		
		Calvin Murphy		
		Mike Newlin		
☐	157	NBA Rebound Leaders 7.00	3.10	.85
		Wilt Chamberlain		
		Nate Thurmond		
		Dave Cowens		
☐	158	NBA Assist Leaders 4.00	1.80	.50
		Nate Archibald		
		Len Wilkens		
		Dave Bing		
☐	159	Don Smith .50	.23	.06
		Houston Rockets		
☐	160	Sidney Wicks 2.50	1.15	.30
		Portland Trail Blazers		
☐	161	Howie Komives .50	.23	.06
		Buffalo Braves		
☐	162	John Gianelli .50	.23	.06
		New York Knicks		
☐	163	Jeff Halliburton .50	.23	.06
		Philadelphia 76ers		
☐	164	Kennedy McIntosh .50	.23	.06
		Seattle Supersonics		
☐	165	Len Wilkens 7.00	3.10	.85
		Cleveland Cavaliers		
☐	166	Corky Calhoun 1.00	.45	.13
		Phoenix Suns		
☐	167	Howard Porter .50	.23	.06
		Chicago Bulls		
☐	168	JoJo White 2.50	1.15	.30
		Boston Celtics		
☐	169	John Block .50	.23	.06
		Kansas City-Omaha Kings		
☐	170	Dave Bing 4.00	1.80	.50
		Detroit Pistons		
☐	171	Joe Ellis .50	.23	.06
		Golden State Warriors		
☐	172	Chuck Terry .50	.23	.06
		Milwaukee Bucks		
☐	173	Randy Smith 1.00	.45	.13
		Buffalo Braves		
☐	174	Bill Bridges 1.00	.45	.13
		Los Angeles Lakers		
☐	175	Geoff Petrie 1.00	.45	.13
		Portland Trail Blazers		
☐	176	Wes Unseld 4.00	1.80	.50
		Capital Bullets		
☐	177	Skeeter Swift 1.00	.45	.13
		San Antonio Spurs		
☐	178	Jim Eakins 1.00	.45	.13
		Virginia Squires		
☐	179	Steve Jones 1.50	.65	.19
		Carolina Cougars		
☐	180	George McGinnis AS1 3.00	1.35	.40
		Indiana Pacers		
☐	181	Al Smith 1.00	.45	.13
		Denver Rockets		
☐	182	Tom Washington 1.00	.45	.13
		New York Nets		
☐	183	Louie Dampier 1.50	.65	.19
		Kentucky Colonels		
☐	184	Simmie Hill 1.00	.45	.13
		San Diego Conquistadors		
☐	185	George Thompson 1.00	.45	.13
		Memphis Tams		
☐	186	Cincy Powell 1.00	.45	.13

☐ 187	Larry Jones.................. Utah Stars	1.50	.65	.19
☐ 188	Neil Johnson............... Virginia Squires	1.00	.45	.13
☐ 189	Tom Owens................. Carolina Cougars	1.00	.45	.13
☐ 190	Ralph Simpson AS2.... Denver Rockets	1.50	.65	.19
☐ 191	George Carter .... Virginia Squires	1.00	.45	.13
☐ 192	Rick Mount .... Kentucky Colonels	1.50	.65	.19
☐ 193	Red Robbins .... San Diego Conquistadors	1.00	.45	.13
☐ 194	George Lehmann .... Memphis Tams	1.00	.45	.13
☐ 195	Mel Daniels AS2......... Indiana Pacers	1.00	.45	.13
☐ 196	Bob Warren .... Utah Stars	1.00	.45	.13
☐ 197	Gene Kennedy............. San Antonio Spurs	1.00	.45	.13
☐ 198	Mike Barr .... Virginia Squires	1.00	.45	.13
☐ 199	Dave Robisch............... Denver Rockets	1.50	.65	.19
☐ 200	Billy Cunningham AS1 Carolina Cougars	5.00	2.30	.60
☐ 201	John Roche.................. New York Nets	1.50	.65	.19
☐ 202	ABA Western Semis... Pacers Oust Injured Rockets	2.00	.90	.25
☐ 203	ABA Western Semis... Stars sweep Q's in Four Straight	2.00	.90	.25
☐ 204	ABA Eastern Semis .... Kentucky overcomes Squires and Dr. J. (Issel jump shot)	2.00	.90	.25
☐ 205	ABA Eastern Semis .... Cougars in strong finish over Nets	2.00	.90	.25
☐ 206	ABA Western Finals ... Pacers nip bitter rival, Stars	2.00	.90	.25
☐ 207	ABA Eastern Finals..... Colonels prevail in grueling Series (Gilmore shooting)	3.00	1.35	.40
☐ 208	ABA Championship.... McGinnis leads Pacers to Title (center jump)	2.00	.90	.25
☐ 209	Glen Combs .... Utah Stars	1.00	.45	.13
☐ 210	Dan Issel AS2 .... Kentucky Colonels	6.00	2.70	.75
☐ 211	Randy Denton............. Memphis Tams	1.00	.45	.13
☐ 212	Freddie Lewis .... Indiana Pacers	1.50	.65	.19
☐ 213	Stew Johnson .... San Diego Conquistadors	1.00	.45	.13
☐ 214	Roland Taylor .... Virginia Squires	1.00	.45	.13
☐ 215	Rich Jones .... San Antonio Spurs	1.00	.45	.13
☐ 216	Billy Paultz.................. New York Nets	1.50	.65	.19
☐ 217	Ron Boone .... Utah Stars	1.50	.65	.19
☐ 218	Walt Simon .... Kentucky Colonels	1.00	.45	.13
☐ 219	Mike Lewis .... Carolina Cougars	1.00	.45	.13
☐ 220	Warren Jabali AS1 .... Denver Rockets	1.50	.65	.19
☐ 221	Wilbert Jones.............. Memphis Tams	1.00	.45	.13
☐ 222	Don Buse .... Indiana Pacers	2.00	.90	.25
☐ 223	Gene Moore .... San Diego Conquistadors	1.00	.45	.13
☐ 224	Joe Hamilton............... San Antonio Spurs	1.00	.45	.13
☐ 225	Zelmo Beaty .... Utah Stars	1.50	.65	.19
☐ 226	Brian Taylor .... New York Nets	2.00	.90	.25
☐ 227	Julius Keye .... Denver Rockets	1.00	.45	.13
☐ 228	Mike Gale..................... Kentucky Colonels	1.50	.65	.19
☐ 229	Warren Davis .... Memphis Tams	1.00	.45	.13
☐ 230	Mack Calvin AS2......... Carolina Cougars	1.50	.65	.19
☐ 231	Roger Brown................ Indiana Pacers	1.50	.65	.19
☐ 232	Chuck Williams .... San Diego Conquistadors	1.00	.45	.13
☐ 233	Gerald Govan .... Utah Stars	1.00	.45	.13
☐ 234	ABA Scoring Average Leaders Julius Erving George McGinnis Dan Issel	10.00	4.50	1.25
☐ 235	ABA 2 Pt. Pct. .... Leaders Artis Gilmore Gene Kennedy Tom Owens	2.50	1.15	.30
☐ 236	ABA 3 Pt. Pct. .... Leaders Glen Combs Roger Brown Louie Dampier	2.00	.90	.25
☐ 237	ABA F.T. Pct. Leaders Billy Keller Ron Boone Bob Warren	2.00	.90	.25
☐ 238	ABA Rebound Leaders Artis Gilmore Mel Daniels Bill Paultz	2.50	1.15	.30
☐ 239	ABA Assist Leaders.... Bill Melchionni Chuck Williams Warren Jabali		.90	.25
☐ 240	Julius Erving AS2........ Virginia Squires	60.00	27.00	7.50
☐ 241	Jimmy O'Brien .... Kentucky Colonels	1.00	.45	.13
☐ 242	ABA Checklist 177-264	12.00	1.20	.24
☐ 243	Johnny Neumann........ Memphis Tams	1.50	.65	.19
☐ 244	Darnell Hillman .... Indiana Pacers	1.50	.65	.19
☐ 245	Willie Wise..................	1.50	.65	.19

		NRMT-MT	EXC	VG
	Utah Stars			
☐ 246	Collis Jones	1.00	.45	.13
	San Antonio Spurs			
☐ 247	Ted McClain	1.00	.45	.13
	Carolina Cougars			
☐ 248	George Irvine	1.00	.45	.13
	Virginia Squires			
☐ 249	Bill Melchionni	1.50	.65	.19
	New York Nets			
☐ 250	Artis Gilmore AS1	5.00	2.30	.60
	Kentucky Colonels			
☐ 251	Willie Long	1.00	.45	.13
	Denver Rockets			
☐ 252	Larry Miller	1.00	.45	.13
	San Diego Conquistadors			
☐ 253	Lee Davis	1.00	.45	.13
	Memphis Tams			
☐ 254	Donnie Freeman	1.00	.45	.13
	Indiana Pacers			
☐ 255	Joe Caldwell	1.50	.65	.19
	Carolina Cougars			
☐ 256	Bob Netolicky	1.50	.65	.19
	San Antonio Spurs			
☐ 257	Bernie Williams	1.00	.45	.13
	Virginia Squires			
☐ 258	Byron Beck	1.50	.65	.19
	Denver Rockets			
☐ 259	Jim Chones	3.00	1.35	.40
	New York Nets			
☐ 260	James Jones AS1	1.50	.65	.19
	Utah Stars			
☐ 261	Wendell Ladner	1.50	.65	.19
	Kentucky Colonels			
☐ 262	Ollie Taylor	1.00	.45	.13
	San Diego Conquistadors			
☐ 263	Les Hunter	1.00	.45	.13
	Memphis Tams			
☐ 264	Billy Keller	2.50	1.15	.30
	Indiana Pacers			

1974-75 Topps

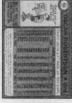

The 1974-75 Topps set of 264 cards contains NBA players on cards numbered 1 to 176 and ABA players on cards numbered 177 to 264. For the first time Team Leader (TL) cards are provided for each team. The cards in the set measure the standard 2 1/2" by 3 1/2" and were issued in 10-card packs with 24 packs per box. All-Star selections (first and second team) for both leagues are noted on the respective player's regular cards. The card backs are print-ed in blue and red on gray card stock. Subsets include NBA Team Leaders (81-98), NBA Statistical Leaders (144-149), NBA Playoffs (161-164), ABA Statistical Leaders (207-212), ABA Team Leaders (221-230) and ABA Playoffs (246-249). The key Rookie Cards in this set are Doug Collins, George Gervin and Bill Walton.

		NRMT-MT	EXC	VG
COMPLETE SET (264)		350.00	160.00	45.00
COMMON NBA CARD (1-176)		.50	.23	.06
COMMON ABA CARD (177-264)		1.00	.45	.13
☐ 1	Kareem Abdul-Jabbar AS1	35.00	10.50	2.10
	Milwaukee Bucks			
☐ 2	Don May	.50	.23	.06
	Philadelphia 76ers			
☐ 3	Bernie Fryer	1.00	.45	.13
	Portland Trail Blazers			
☐ 4	Don Adams	.50	.23	.06
	Detroit Pistons			
☐ 5	Herm Gilliam	.50	.23	.06
	Atlanta Hawks			
☐ 6	Jim Chones	1.00	.45	.13
	Cleveland Cavaliers			
☐ 7	Rick Adelman	.50	.23	.06
	Chicago Bulls			
☐ 8	Randy Smith	1.00	.45	.13
	Buffalo Braves			
☐ 9	Paul Silas	2.00	.90	.25
	Boston Celtics			
☐ 10	Pete Maravich	20.00	9.00	2.50
	New Orleans Jazz			
☐ 11	Ron Behagen	.50	.23	.06
	Kansas City-Omaha Kings			
☐ 12	Kevin Porter	1.00	.45	.13
	Washington Bullets			
☐ 13	Bill Bridges	1.00	.45	.13
	Los Angeles Lakers			
	(On back team shown as			
	Los And., should			
	be Los Ang.)			
☐ 14	Charles Johnson	1.00	.45	.13
	Golden State Warriors			
☐ 15	Bob Love	1.00	.45	.13
	Chicago Bulls			
☐ 16	Henry Bibby	.50	.23	.06
	New York Knicks			
☐ 17	Neal Walk	1.00	.45	.13
	Phoenix Suns			
☐ 18	John Brisker	.50	.23	.06
	Seattle Supersonics			
☐ 19	Lucius Allen	1.00	.45	.13
	Milwaukee Bucks			
☐ 20	Tom Van Arsdale	1.00	.45	.13
	Philadelphia 76ers			
☐ 21	Larry Steele	.50	.23	.06
	Portland Trail Blazers			
☐ 22	Curtis Rowe	1.00	.45	.13
	Detroit Pistons			
☐ 23	Dean Meminger	.50	.23	.06
	Atlanta Hawks			
☐ 24	Steve Patterson	.50	.23	.06
	Cleveland Cavaliers			
☐ 25	Earl Monroe	3.00	1.35	.40
	New York Knicks			
☐ 26	Jack Marin	1.00	.45	.13
	Buffalo Braves			
☐ 27	JoJo White	2.00	.90	.25
	Boston Celtics			

☐ 28	Rudy Tomjanovich	6.00	2.70	.75
	Houston Rockets			
☐ 29	Otto Moore	.50	.23	.06
	Kansas City-Omaha Kings			
☐ 30	Elvin Hayes AS2	6.00	2.70	.75
	Washington Bullets			
☐ 31	Pat Riley	6.00	2.70	.75
	Los Angeles Lakers			
☐ 32	Clyde Lee	.50	.23	.06
	Golden State Warriors			
☐ 33	Bob Weiss	1.00	.45	.13
	Chicago Bulls			
☐ 34	Jim Fox	.50	.23	.06
	Seattle Supersonics			
☐ 35	Charlie Scott	1.00	.45	.13
	Phoenix Suns			
☐ 36	Cliff Meely	.50	.23	.06
	Houston Rockets			
☐ 37	Jon McGlocklin	.50	.23	.06
	Milwaukee Bucks			
☐ 38	Jim McMillian	1.00	.45	.13
	Buffalo Braves			
☐ 39	Bill Walton	60.00	27.00	7.50
	Portland Trail Blazers			
☐ 40	Dave Bing AS2	3.00	1.35	.40
	Detroit Pistons			
☐ 41	Jim Washington	.50	.23	.06
	Atlanta Hawks			
☐ 42	Jim Cleamons	.50	.23	.06
	Cleveland Cavaliers			
☐ 43	Mel Davis	.50	.23	.06
	New York Knicks			
☐ 44	Garfield Heard	1.00	.45	.13
	Buffalo Braves			
☐ 45	Jimmy Walker	1.00	.45	.13
	Kansas City-Omaha Kings			
☐ 46	Don Nelson	.50	.23	.06
	Boston Celtics			
☐ 47	Jim Barnett	.50	.23	.06
	New Orleans Jazz			
☐ 48	Manny Leaks	.50	.23	.06
	Washington Bullets			
☐ 49	Elmore Smith	1.00	.45	.13
	Los Angeles Lakers			
☐ 50	Rick Barry AS1	6.00	2.70	.75
	Golden State Warriors			
☐ 51	Jerry Sloan	1.00	.45	.13
	Chicago Bulls			
☐ 52	John Hummer	.50	.23	.06
	Seattle Supersonics			
☐ 53	Keith Erickson	1.00	.45	.13
	Phoenix Suns			
☐ 54	George E. Johnson	.50	.23	.06
	Houston Rockets			
☐ 55	Oscar Robertson	12.00	5.50	1.50
	Milwaukee Bucks			
☐ 56	Steve Mix	1.00	.45	.13
	Philadelphia 76ers			
☐ 57	Rick Roberson	.50	.23	.06
	Portland Trail Blazers			
☐ 58	John Mengelt	.50	.23	.06
	Detroit Pistons			
☐ 59	Dwight Jones	1.00	.45	.13
	Atlanta Hawks			
☐ 60	Austin Carr	1.00	.45	.13
	Cleveland Cavaliers			
☐ 61	Nick Weatherspoon	1.00	.45	.13
	Washington Bullets			
☐ 62	Clem Haskins	1.00	.45	.13
	Phoenix Suns			
☐ 63	Don Kojis	.50	.23	.06
	Kansas City-Omaha Kings			
☐ 64	Paul Westphal	6.00	2.70	.75
	Boston Celtics			
☐ 65	Walt Bellamy	2.00	.90	.25
	New Orleans Jazz			
☐ 66	John Johnson	1.00	.45	.13
	Portland Trail Blazers			
☐ 67	Butch Beard	1.00	.45	.13
	Golden State Warriors			
☐ 68	Happy Hairston	1.00	.45	.13
	Los Angeles Lakers			
☐ 69	Tom Boerwinkle	.50	.23	.06
	Chicago Bulls			
☐ 70	Spencer Haywood AS2	2.00	.90	.25
	Seattle Supersonics			
☐ 71	Gary Melchionni	.50	.23	.06
	Phoenix Suns			
☐ 72	Ed Ratleff	1.00	.45	.13
	Houston Rockets			
☐ 73	Mickey Davis	.50	.23	.06
	Milwaukee Bucks			
☐ 74	Dennis Awtrey	.50	.23	.06
	New Orleans Jazz			
☐ 75	Fred Carter	1.00	.45	.13
	Philadelphia 76ers			
☐ 76	George Trapp	.50	.23	.06
	Detroit Pistons			
☐ 77	John Wetzel	.50	.23	.06
	Atlanta Hawks			
☐ 78	Bobby Smith	1.00	.45	.13
	Cleveland Cavaliers			
☐ 79	John Gianelli	.50	.23	.06
	New York Knicks			
☐ 80	Bob McAdoo AS2	7.00	3.10	.85
	Buffalo Braves			
☐ 81	Atlanta Hawks TL	5.00	2.30	.60
	Pete Maravich			
	Lou Hudson			
	Walt Bellamy			
	Pete Maravich			
☐ 82	Boston Celtics TL	5.00	2.30	.60
	John Havlicek			
	JoJo White			
	Dave Cowens			
	JoJo White			
☐ 83	Buffalo Braves TL	1.50	.65	.19
	Bob McAdoo			
	Ernie DiGregorio			
	Bob McAdoo			
	Ernie DiGregorio			
☐ 84	Chicago Bulls TL	2.50	1.15	.30
	Bob Love			
	Chet Walker			
	Clifford Ray			
	Norm Van Lier			
☐ 85	Cleveland Cavs TL	1.50	.65	.19
	Austin Carr			
	Austin Carr			
	Dwight Davis			
	Len Wilkens			
☐ 86	Detroit Pistons TL	1.50	.65	.19
	Bob Lanier			
	Stu Lantz			
	Bob Lanier			
	Dave Bing			
☐ 87	Golden State	2.50	1.15	.30
	Warriors TL			
	Rick Barry			
	Rick Barry			
	Nate Thurmond			
	Rick Barry			

□ 88	Houston Rockets TL	1.50	.65	.19
	Rudy Tomjanovich			
	Calvin Murphy			
	Don Smith			
	Calvin Murphy			
□ 89	Kansas City Omaha TL.	1.00	.45	.13
	Jimmy Walker			
	Jimmy Walker			
	Sam Lacey			
	Jimmy Walker			
□ 90	Los Angeles Lakers TL.	1.00	.45	.13
	Gail Goodrich			
	Gail Goodrich			
	Happy Hairston			
	Gail Goodrich			
□ 91	Milwaukee Bucks TL ..	12.00	5.50	1.50
	Kareem Abdul-Jabbar			
	Oscar Robertson			
	Kareem Abdul-Jabbar			
	Oscar Robertson			
□ 92	New Orleans Jazz	1.00	.45	.13
	Emblem; Expansion			
	Draft Picks on Back			
□ 93	New York Knicks TL	5.00	2.30	.60
	Walt Frazier			
	Bill Bradley			
	Dave DeBusschere			
	Walt Frazier			
□ 94	Philadelphia 76ers TL ..	1.50	.65	.19
	Fred Carter			
	Tom Van Arsdale			
	Leroy Ellis			
	Fred Carter			
□ 95	Phoenix Suns TL	1.50	.65	.19
	Charlie Scott			
	Dick Van Arsdale			
	Neal Walk			
	Neal Walk			
□ 96	Portland Trail	1.50	.65	.19
	Blazers TL			
	Geoff Petrie			
	Geoff Petrie			
	Rick Roberson			
	Sidney Wicks			
□ 97	Seattle Supersonics TL	1.50	.65	.19
	Spencer Haywood			
	Dick Snyder			
	Spencer Haywood			
	Fred Brown			
□ 98	Capitol Bullets TL	1.50	.65	.19
	Phil Chenier			
	Phil Chenier			
	Elvin Hayes			
	Kevin Porter			
□ 99	Sam Lacey	.50	.23	.06
	Kansas City-Omaha Kings			
□ 100	John Havlicek AS1 ..	10.00	4.50	1.25
	Boston Celtics			
□ 101	Stu Lantz	1.00	.45	.13
	New Orleans Jazz			
□ 102	Mike Riordan	1.00	.45	.13
	Washington Bullets			
□ 103	Larry Jones	1.00	.45	.13
	Philadelphia 76ers			
□ 104	Connie Hawkins	3.00	1.35	.40
	Los Angeles Lakers			
□ 105	Nate Thurmond	2.00	.90	.25
	Golden State Warriors			
□ 106	Dick Gibbs	.50	.23	.06
	Seattle Supersonics			
□ 107	Corky Calhoun	1.00	.45	.13

	Phoenix Suns			
□ 108	Dave Wohl	.50	.23	.06
	Houston Rockets			
□ 109	Cornell Warner	.50	.23	.06
	Milwaukee Bucks			
□ 110	Geoff Petrie UER	.50	.23	.06
	Portland Trail Blazers			
	(Misspelled Patrie			
	on card front)			
□ 111	Leroy Ellis	1.00	.45	.13
	Philadelphia 76ers			
□ 112	Chris Ford	2.00	.90	.25
	Detroit Pistons			
□ 113	Bill Bradley	10.00	4.50	1.25
	New York Knicks			
□ 114	Clifford Ray	1.00	.45	.13
	Chicago Bulls			
□ 115	Dick Snyder	.50	.23	.06
	Cleveland Cavaliers			
□ 116	Nate Williams	.50	.23	.06
	Kansas City-Omaha Kings			
□ 117	Matt Guokas	.50	.23	.06
	Buffalo Braves			
□ 118	Henry Finkel	.50	.23	.06
	Boston Celtics			
□ 119	Curtis Perry	.50	.23	.06
	New Orleans Jazz			
□ 120	Gail Goodrich AS1	2.50	1.15	.30
	Los Angeles Lakers			
□ 121	Wes Unseld	3.00	1.35	.40
	Washington Bullets			
□ 122	Howard Porter	1.00	.45	.13
	New York Knicks			
□ 123	Jeff Mullins	1.00	.45	.13
	Golden State Warriors			
□ 124	Mike Bantom	1.00	.45	.13
	Phoenix Suns			
□ 125	Fred Brown	.50	.23	.06
	Seattle Supersonics			
□ 126	Bob Dandridge	1.00	.45	.13
	Milwaukee Bucks			
□ 127	Mike Newlin	1.00	.45	.13
	Houston Rockets			
□ 128	Greg Smith	.50	.23	.06
	Portland Trail Blazers			
□ 129	Doug Collins	14.00	6.25	1.75
	Philadelphia 76ers			
□ 130	Lou Hudson	1.00	.45	.13
	Atlanta Hawks			
□ 131	Bob Lanier	5.00	2.30	.60
	Detroit Pistons			
□ 132	Phil Jackson	4.00	1.80	.50
	New York Knicks			
□ 133	Don Chaney	1.00	.45	.13
	Boston Celtics			
□ 134	Jim Brewer	1.00	.45	.13
	Cleveland Cavaliers			
□ 135	Ernie DiGregorio	4.00	1.80	.50
	Buffalo Braves			
□ 136	Steve Kuberski	.50	.23	.06
	New Orleans Jazz			
□ 137	Jim Price	.50	.23	.06
	Los Angeles Lakers			
□ 138	Mike D'Antoni	.50	.23	.06
	Kansas City-Omaha Kings			
□ 139	John Brown	.50	.23	.06
	Atlanta Hawks			
□ 140	Norm Van Lier AS2	.50	.23	.06
	Chicago Bulls			
□ 141	NBA Checklist 1-176	10.00	1.00	.20
□ 142	Don(Slick) Watts	2.00	.90	.25

	Seattle Supersonics			
☐ 143	Walt Wesley................. .50	.23	.06
	Washington Bullets			
☐ 144	NBA Scoring Leaders 12.00	5.50	1.50
	Bob McAdoo			
	Kareem Abdul-Jabbar			
	Pete Maravich			
☐ 145	NBA Scoring 12.00	5.50	1.50
	Average Leaders			
	Bob McAdoo			
	Pete Maravich			
	Kareem Abdul-Jabbar			
☐ 146	NBA F.G. Pct. Leaders 10.00	4.50	1.25
	Bob McAdoo			
	Kareem Abdul-Jabbar			
	Rudy Tomjanovich			
☐ 147	NBA F.T. Pct. Leaders 1.00	.45	.13
	Ernie DiGregorio			
	Rick Barry			
	Jeff Mullins			
☐ 148	NBA Rebound Leaders 4.00	1.80	.50
	Elvin Hayes			
	Dave Cowens			
	Bob McAdoo			
☐ 149	NBA Assist Leaders 1.00	.45	.13
	Ernie DiGregorio			
	Calvin Murphy			
	Len Wilkens			
☐ 150	Walt Frazier AS1 .... 6.00	2.70	.75
	New York Knicks			
☐ 151	Cazzie Russell .... .50	.23	.06
	Golden State Warriors			
☐ 152	Calvin Murphy............ 3.00	1.35	.40
	Houston Rockets			
☐ 153	Bob Kauffman .... .50	.23	.06
	Atlanta Hawks			
☐ 154	Fred Boyd .... .50	.23	.06
	Philadelphia 76ers			
☐ 155	Dave Cowens 6.00	2.70	.75
	Boston Celtics			
☐ 156	Willie Norwood .... .50	.23	.06
	Detroit Pistons			
☐ 157	Lee Winfield................. .50	.23	.06
	Buffalo Braves			
☐ 158	Dwight Davis................ .50	.23	.06
	Cleveland Cavaliers			
☐ 159	George T. Johnson .... .50	.23	.06
	Golden State Warriors			
☐ 160	Dick Van Arsdale........ 1.00	.45	.13
	Phoenix Suns			
☐ 161	NBA Eastern Semis.... 1.00	.45	.13
	Celts over Braves			
	Knicks edge Bullets			
☐ 162	NBA Western Semis.... 1.00	.45	.13
	Bucks over Lakers			
	Bulls edge Pistons			
☐ 163	NBA Div. Finals 1.00	.45	.13
	Celts over Knicks			
	Bucks sweep Bulls			
☐ 164	NBA Championship.... 1.50	.65	.19
	Celtics over Bucks			
☐ 165	Phil Chenier 1.00	.45	.13
	Washington Bullets			
☐ 166	Kermit Washington 2.00	.90	.25
	Los Angeles Lakers			
☐ 167	Dale Schlueter............. .50	.23	.06
	Atlanta Hawks			
☐ 168	John Block.................. .50	.23	.06
	New Orleans Jazz			
☐ 169	Don Smith..................... .50	.23	.06
	Houston Rockets			

☐ 170	Nate Archibald 4.00	1.80	.50
	Kansas City-Omaha Kings			
☐ 171	Chet Walker 1.00	.45	.13
	Chicago Bulls			
☐ 172	Archie Clark 1.00	.45	.13
	Washington Bullets			
☐ 173	Kennedy McIntosh....... .50	.23	.06
	Seattle Supersonics			
☐ 174	George Thompson .... .50	.23	.06
	Milwaukee Bucks			
☐ 175	Sidney Wicks 2.00	.90	.25
	Portland Trail Blazers			
☐ 176	Jerry West 20.00	9.00	2.50
	Los Angeles Lakers			
☐ 177	Dwight Lamar 1.50	.65	.19
	San Diego Conquistadors			
☐ 178	George Carter 1.00	.45	.13
	Virginia Squires			
☐ 179	Wil Robinson 1.00	.45	.13
	Memphis Sounds			
☐ 180	Artis Gilmore AS1 .... 4.00	1.80	.50
	Kentucky Colonels			
☐ 181	Brian Taylor 1.50	.65	.19
	New York Nets			
☐ 182	Darnell Hillman 1.50	.65	.19
	Indiana Pacers			
☐ 183	Dave Robisch.............. 1.50	.65	.19
	Denver Nuggets			
☐ 184	Gene Littles................. 2.00	.90	.25
	St. Louis Spirits			
☐ 185	Willie Wise AS2 .... 1.50	.65	.19
	Utah Stars			
☐ 186	James Silas................. 2.50	1.15	.30
	San Antonio Spurs			
☐ 187	Caldwell Jones 3.00	1.35	.40
	San Diego Conquistadors			
☐ 188	Roland Taylor 1.00	.45	.13
	Virginia Squires			
☐ 189	Randy Denton 1.00	.45	.13
	Memphis Sounds			
☐ 190	Dan Issel AS2 .... 5.00	2.30	.60
	Kentucky Colonels			
☐ 191	Mike Gale................... 1.00	.45	.13
	New York Nets			
☐ 192	Mel Daniels................. 1.00	.45	.13
	Memphis Sounds			
☐ 193	Steve Jones 1.50	.65	.19
	Denver Nuggets			
☐ 194	Marv Roberts............... 1.00	.45	.13
	St. Louis Spirits			
☐ 195	Ron Boone AS2 .... 1.50	.65	.19
	Utah Stars			
☐ 196	George Gervin........... 35.00	16.00	4.40
	San Antonio Spurs			
☐ 197	Flynn Robinson 1.00	.45	.13
	San Diego Conquistadors			
☐ 198	Cincy Powell 1.00	.45	.13
	Virginia Squires			
☐ 199	Glen Combs 1.00	.45	.13
	Memphis Sounds			
☐ 200	Julius Erving AS1 UER 50.00	23.00	6.25
	New York Nets			
	(Misspelled Irving			
	on card back)			
☐ 201	Billy Keller.................. 1.50	.65	.19
	Indiana Pacers			
☐ 202	Willie Long.................. 1.00	.45	.13
	Denver Nuggets			
☐ 203	ABA Checklist 177-264 10.00	1.00	.20
☐ 204	Joe Caldwell................ 1.50	.65	.19
	St. Louis Spirits			

☐ 205	Swen Nater AS2	2.50	1.15	.30
	San Antonio Spurs			
☐ 206	Rick Mount	1.00	.45	.13
	Utah Stars			
☐ 207	ABA Scoring	10.00	4.50	1.25
	Avg. Leaders			
	Julius Erving			
	George McGinnis			
	Dan Issel			
☐ 208	ABA Two-Point Field	2.00	.90	.25
	Goal Percent Leaders			
	Swen Nater			
	James Jones			
	Tom Owens			
☐ 209	ABA Three-Point Field	2.00	.90	.25
	Goal Percent Leaders			
	Louie Dampier			
	Billy Keller			
	Roger Brown			
☐ 210	ABA Free Throw	2.00	.90	.25
	Percent Leaders			
	James Jones			
	Mack Calvin			
	Ron Boone			
☐ 211	ABA Rebound Leaders	2.50	1.15	.30
	Artis Gilmore			
	George McGinnis			
	Caldwell Jones			
☐ 212	ABA Assist Leaders	2.00	.90	.25
	Al Smith			
	Chuck Williams			
	Louie Dampier			
☐ 213	Larry Miller	1.00	.45	.13
	Virginia Squires			
☐ 214	Stew Johnson	1.00	.45	.13
	San Diego Conquistadors			
☐ 215	Larry Finch	2.50	1.15	.30
	Memphis Sounds			
☐ 216	Larry Kenon	3.00	1.35	.40
	New York Nets			
☐ 217	Joe Hamilton	1.00	.45	.13
	Kentucky Colonels			
☐ 218	Gerald Govan	1.00	.45	.13
	Utah Stars			
☐ 219	Ralph Simpson	1.50	.65	.19
	Denver Nuggets			
☐ 220	George McGinnis AS1	2.50	1.15	.30
	Indiana Pacers			
☐ 221	Carolina Cougars TL	2.50	1.15	.30
	Billy Cunningham			
	Mack Calvin			
	Tom Owens			
	Joe Caldwell			
☐ 222	Denver Nuggets TL	2.50	1.15	.30
	Ralph Simpson			
	Byron Beck			
	Dave Robisch			
	Al Smith			
☐ 223	Indiana Pacers TL	2.50	1.15	.30
	George McGinnis			
	Billy Keller			
	George McGinnis			
	Freddie Lewis			
☐ 224	Kentucky Colonels TL	3.00	1.35	.40
	Dan Issel			
	Louie Dampier			
	Artis Gilmore			
	Louie Dampier			
☐ 225	Memphis Sounds TL	2.00	.90	.25
	George Thompson			
	Larry Finch			

	Randy Denton			
	George Thompson			
☐ 226	New York Nets TL	10.00	4.50	1.25
	Julius Erving			
	John Roche			
	Larry Kenon			
	Julius Erving			
☐ 227	San Antonio Spurs TL	5.00	2.30	.60
	George Gervin			
	George Gervin			
	Swen Nater			
	James Silas			
☐ 228	San Diego Conq. TL	2.00	.90	.25
	Dwight Lamar			
	Stew Johnson			
	Caldwell Jones			
	Chuck Williams			
☐ 229	Utah Stars TL	2.50	1.15	.30
	Willie Wise			
	James Jones			
	Gerald Govan			
	James Jones			
☐ 230	Virginia Squires TL	2.00	.90	.25
	George Carter			
	George Irvine			
	Jim Eakins			
	Roland Taylor			
☐ 231	Bird Averitt	1.00	.45	.13
	Kentucky Colonels			
☐ 232	John Roche	1.00	.45	.13
	Kentucky Colonels			
☐ 233	George Irvine	1.00	.45	.13
	Virginia Squires			
☐ 234	John Williamson	1.00	.45	.13
	New York Nets			
☐ 235	Billy Cunningham	4.00	1.80	.50
	St. Louis Spirits			
☐ 236	Jimmy O'Brien	1.00	.45	.13
	San Diego Conquistadors			
☐ 237	Wilbert Jones	1.00	.45	.13
	Kentucky Colonels			
☐ 238	Johnny Neumann	1.50	.65	.19
	Utah Stars			
☐ 239	Al Smith	1.00	.45	.13
	Denver Nuggets			
☐ 240	Roger Brown	1.50	.65	.19
	Memphis Sounds			
☐ 241	Chuck Williams	1.00	.45	.13
	Kentucky Colonels			
☐ 242	Rich Jones	1.00	.45	.13
	San Antonio Spurs			
☐ 243	Dave Twardzik	2.00	.90	.25
	Virginia Squires			
☐ 244	Wendell Ladner	1.50	.65	.19
	New York Nets			
☐ 245	Mack Calvin AS1	1.50	.65	.19
	St. Louis Spirits			
☐ 246	ABA Eastern Semis	2.00	.90	.25
	Nets over Squires			
	Colonels sweep Cougars			
☐ 247	ABA Western Semis	2.00	.90	.25
	Stars over Conquistadors			
	Pacers over Spurs			
☐ 248	ABA Div. Finals	2.00	.90	.25
	Nets sweep Colonels			
	Stars edge Pacers			
☐ 249	ABA Championship	10.00	4.50	1.25
	Nets over Stars			
	(Julius Erving)			
☐ 250	Wilt Chamberlain CO	25.00	11.50	3.10
	San Diego Conquistadors			

		NRMT-MT	EXC	VG
☐ 251	Ron Robinson............ Memphis Sounds	1.00	.45	.13
☐ 252	Zelmo Beaty............... Utah Stars	1.50	.65	.19
☐ 253	Donnie Freeman........ Indiana Pacers	1.50	.65	.19
☐ 254	Mike Green................ Denver Nuggets	1.00	.45	.13
☐ 255	Louie Dampier AS2..... Kentucky Colonels	1.50	.65	.19
☐ 256	Tom Owens................ St. Louis Spirits	1.00	.45	.13
☐ 257	George Karl............... San Antonio Spurs	5.00	2.30	.60
☐ 258	Jim Eakins................ Virginia Squires	1.00	.45	.13
☐ 259	Travis Grant.............. San Diego Conquistadors	1.50	.65	.19
☐ 260	James Jones AS1........ Utah Stars	1.50	.65	.19
☐ 261	Mike Jackson............ Memphis Sounds	1.00	.45	.13
☐ 262	Billy Paultz............... New York Nets	1.50	.65	.19
☐ 263	Freddie Lewis............ Memphis Sounds	1.50	.65	.19
☐ 264	Byron Beck .... Denver Nuggets (Back refers to ANA, should be ABA)	2.00	.90	.25

1975-76 Topps

The 1975-76 Topps basketball card set of 330 was the largest basketball set ever produced up to that time. Cards were issued in 10-card packs with 24 packs per box. NBA players are depicted on cards 1-220 and ABA players on cards 221-330. The cards in the set measure the standard 2 1/2" by 3 1/2". Team Leaders (TL) cards are 116-133 (NBA teams) and 278-287 (ABA). Other subsets include NBA Statistical Leaders (1-6), NBA Playoffs (188-189), NBA Team Checklists (203-220), ABA Statistical Leaders (221-226), ABA Playoffs (309-310) and ABA Team Checklists (321-330). All-Star selections (first and second team) for both leagues are noted on the respective player's regular cards. Card backs are printed in blue and green on gray card stock. The set is particularly hard to

sort numerically, as the small card number on the back is printed in blue on a dark green background. The set was printed on three large sheets each containing 110 different cards. Investigation of the second (series) sheet reveals that 22 of the cards were double printed; they are marked DP in the checklist below. Rookie Cards in this set include Bobby Jones, Maurice Lucas, Moses Malone and Keith (Jamaal) Wilkes.

		NRMT-MT	EXC	VG
	COMPLETE SET (330)	450.00	200.00	57.50
	COMMON NBA CARD (1-110) ...	.75	.35	.09
	COMMON NBA CARD (111-220)	.75	.35	.09
	COMMON ABA CARD (221-330)	1.50	.65	.19
☐ 1	NBA Scoring Average... Leaders Bob McAdoo Rick Barry Kareem Abdul-Jabbar	12.00	3.40	.70
☐ 2	NBA Field Goal .... Percentage Leaders Don Nelson Butch Beard Rudy Tomjanovich	4.00	1.80	.50
☐ 3	NBA Free Throw........... Percentage Leaders Rick Barry Calvin Murphy Bill Bradley	5.00	2.30	.60
☐ 4	NBA Rebounds Leaders . Wes Unseld Dave Cowens Sam Lacey	1.50	.65	.19
☐ 5	NBA Assists Leaders ...... Kevin Porter Dave Bing Nate Archibald	3.00	1.35	.40
☐ 6	NBA Steals Leaders .... Rick Barry Walt Frazier Larry Steele	4.00	1.80	.50
☐ 7	Tom Van Arsdale .... Atlanta Hawks	1.25	.55	.16
☐ 8	Paul Silas .... Boston Celtics	1.25	.55	.16
☐ 9	Jerry Sloan .... Chicago Bulls	1.25	.55	.16
☐ 10	Bob McAdoo AS1......... Buffalo Braves	6.00	2.70	.75
☐ 11	Dwight Davis................ Golden State Warriors	.75	.35	.09
☐ 12	John Mengelt............... Detroit Pistons	.75	.35	.09
☐ 13	George Johnson........... Golden State Warriors	.75	.35	.09
☐ 14	Ed Ratleff.................. Houston Rockets	.75	.35	.09
☐ 15	Nate Archibald AS1 .... Kansas City Kings	4.00	1.80	.50
☐ 16	Elmore Smith.............. Milwaukee Bucks	1.25	.55	.16
☐ 17	Bob Dandridge............ Milwaukee Bucks	1.25	.55	.16
☐ 18	Louie Nelson............... New Orleans Jazz	.75	.35	.09
☐ 19	Neal Walk .... New York Knicks	1.25	.55	.16
☐ 20	Billy Cunningham......... 	4.00	1.80	.50

	Philadelphia 76ers			
☐ 21	Gary Melchionni	.75	.35	.09
	Phoenix Suns			
☐ 22	Barry Clemens	.75	.35	.09
	Portland Trail Blazers			
☐ 23	Jimmy Jones	.75	.35	.09
	Washington Bullets			
☐ 24	Tom Burleson	2.50	1.15	.30
	Seattle Supersonics			
☐ 25	Lou Hudson	1.25	.55	.16
	Atlanta Hawks			
☐ 26	Henry Finkel	.75	.35	.09
	Boston Celtics			
☐ 27	Jim McMillian	1.25	.55	.16
	Buffalo Braves			
☐ 28	Matt Guokas	.75	.35	.09
	Chicago Bulls			
☐ 29	Fred Foster DP	.75	.35	.09
	Cleveland Cavaliers			
☐ 30	Bob Lanier	5.00	2.30	.60
	Detroit Pistons			
☐ 31	Jimmy Walker	1.25	.55	.16
	Kansas City Kings			
☐ 32	Cliff Meely	.75	.35	.09
	Houston Rockets			
☐ 33	Butch Beard	1.25	.55	.16
	Cleveland Cavaliers			
☐ 34	Cazzie Russell	1.25	.55	.16
	Los Angeles Lakers			
☐ 35	Jon McGlocklin	.75	.35	.09
	Milwaukee Bucks			
☐ 36	Bernie Fryer	1.25	.55	.16
	New Orleans Jazz			
☐ 37	Bill Bradley	10.00	4.50	1.25
	New York Knicks			
☐ 38	Fred Carter	1.25	.55	.16
	Philadelphia 76ers			
☐ 39	Dennis Awtrey DP	.75	.35	.09
	Phoenix Suns			
☐ 40	Sidney Wicks	1.25	.55	.16
	Portland Trail Blazers			
☐ 41	Fred Brown	.75	.35	.09
	Seattle Supersonics			
☐ 42	Rowland Garrett	.75	.35	.09
	Chicago Bulls			
☐ 43	Herm Gilliam	.75	.35	.09
	Atlanta Hawks			
☐ 44	Don Nelson	1.25	.55	.16
	Boston Celtics			
☐ 45	Ernie DiGregorio	1.25	.55	.16
	Buffalo Braves			
☐ 46	Jim Brewer	.75	.35	.09
	Cleveland Cavaliers			
☐ 47	Chris Ford	1.25	.55	.16
	Detroit Pistons			
☐ 48	Nick Weatherspoon	1.25	.55	.16
	Washington Bullets			
☐ 49	Zaid Abdul-Aziz	.75	.35	.09
	(formerly Don Smith)			
	Houston Rockets			
☐ 50	Keith Wilkes	8.00	3.60	1.00
	Golden State Warriors			
☐ 51	Ollie Johnson DP	.75	.35	.09
	Kansas City Kings			
☐ 52	Lucius Allen	.75	.35	.09
	Los Angeles Lakers			
☐ 53	Mickey Davis	.75	.35	.09
	Milwaukee Bucks			
☐ 54	Otto Moore	.75	.35	.09
	New Orleans Jazz			
☐ 55	Walt Frazier AS1	6.00	2.70	.75
	New York Knicks			
☐ 56	Steve Mix	1.25	.55	.16
	Philadelphia 76ers			
☐ 57	Nate Hawthorne	.75	.35	.09
	Phoenix Suns			
☐ 58	Lloyd Neal	1.25	.55	.16
	Portland Trail Blazers			
☐ 59	Don Watts	1.25	.55	.16
	Seattle Supersonics			
☐ 60	Elvin Hayes	6.00	2.70	.75
	Washington Bullets			
☐ 61	Checklist 1-110	8.00	.80	.15
☐ 62	Mike Sojourner	.75	.35	.09
	Atlanta Hawks			
☐ 63	Randy Smith	1.25	.55	.16
	Buffalo Braves			
☐ 64	John Block DP	.75	.35	.09
	Chicago Bulls			
☐ 65	Charlie Scott	1.25	.55	.16
	Boston Celtics			
☐ 66	Jim Chones	1.25	.55	.16
	Cleveland Cavaliers			
☐ 67	Rick Adelman	.75	.35	.09
	Kansas City Kings			
☐ 68	Curtis Rowe	1.25	.55	.16
	Detroit Pistons			
☐ 69	Derrek Dickey	1.25	.55	.16
	Golden State Warriors			
☐ 70	Rudy Tomjanovich	5.00	2.30	.60
	Houston Rockets			
☐ 71	Pat Riley	5.00	2.30	.60
	Los Angeles Lakers			
☐ 72	Cornell Warner	.75	.35	.09
	Milwaukee Bucks			
☐ 73	Earl Monroe	3.00	1.35	.40
	New York Knicks			
☐ 74	Allan Bristow	4.00	1.80	.50
	Philadelphia 76ers			
☐ 75	Pete Maravich DP	14.00	6.25	1.75
	New Orleans Jazz			
☐ 76	Curtis Perry	.75	.35	.09
	Phoenix Suns			
☐ 77	Bill Walton	25.00	11.50	3.10
	Portland Trail Blazers			
☐ 78	Leonard Gray	.75	.35	.09
	Seattle Supersonics			
☐ 79	Kevin Porter	1.25	.55	.16
	Washington Bullets			
☐ 80	John Havlicek AS2	10.00	4.50	1.25
	Boston Celtics			
☐ 81	Dwight Jones	.75	.35	.09
	Atlanta Hawks			
☐ 82	Jack Marin	1.25	.55	.16
	Buffalo Braves			
☐ 83	Dick Snyder	.75	.35	.09
	Cleveland Cavaliers			
☐ 84	George Trapp	.75	.35	.09
	Detroit Pistons			
☐ 85	Nate Thurmond	2.50	1.15	.30
	Chicago Bulls			
☐ 86	Charles Johnson	.75	.35	.09
	Golden State Warriors			
☐ 87	Ron Riley	.75	.35	.09
	Houston Rockets			
☐ 88	Stu Lantz	1.25	.55	.16
	Los Angeles Lakers			
☐ 89	Scott Wedman	2.50	1.15	.30
	Kansas City Kings			
☐ 90	Kareem Abdul-Jabbar	25.00	11.50	3.10
	Los Angeles Lakers			
☐ 91	Aaron James	.75	.35	.09

	New Orleans Jazz			
☐ 92	Jim Barnett	.75	.35	.09
	New York Knicks			
☐ 93	Clyde Lee	.75	.35	.09
	Philadelphia 76ers			
☐ 94	Larry Steele	.75	.35	.09
	Portland Trail Blazers			
☐ 95	Mike Riordan	1.25	.55	.16
	Washington Bullets			
☐ 96	Archie Clark	1.25	.55	.16
	Seattle Supersonics			
☐ 97	Mike Bantom	1.25	.55	.16
	Phoenix Suns			
☐ 98	Bob Kauffman	.75	.35	.09
	Atlanta Hawks			
☐ 99	Kevin Stacom	1.25	.55	.16
	Boston Celtics			
☐ 100	Rick Barry AS1	6.00	2.70	.75
	Golden State Warriors			
☐ 101	Ken Charles	.75	.35	.09
	Buffalo Braves			
☐ 102	Tom Boerwinkle	.75	.35	.09
	Chicago Bulls			
☐ 103	Mike Newlin	1.25	.55	.16
	Houston Rockets			
☐ 104	Leroy Ellis	1.25	.55	.16
	Philadelphia 76ers			
☐ 105	Austin Carr	1.25	.55	.16
	Cleveland Cavaliers			
☐ 106	Ron Behagen	.75	.35	.09
	New Orleans Jazz			
☐ 107	Jim Price	.75	.35	.09
	Milwaukee Bucks			
☐ 108	Bud Stallworth	.75	.35	.09
	New Orleans Jazz			
☐ 109	Earl Williams	.75	.35	.09
	Detroit Pistons			
☐ 110	Gail Goodrich	2.50	1.15	.30
	Los Angeles Lakers			
☐ 111	Phil Jackson	4.00	1.80	.50
	New York Knicks			
☐ 112	Rod Derline	.75	.35	.09
	Seattle Supersonics			
☐ 113	Keith Erickson	1.25	.55	.16
	Phoenix Suns			
☐ 114	Phil Lumpkin	.75	.35	.09
	Phoenix Suns			
☐ 115	Wes Unseld	3.00	1.35	.40
	Washington Bullets			
☐ 116	Atlanta Hawks TL	1.50	.65	.19
	Lou Hudson			
	Lou Hudson			
	John Drew			
	Dean Meminger			
☐ 117	Boston Celtics TL	2.50	1.15	.30
	Dave Cowens			
	Kevin Stacom			
	Paul Silas			
	JoJo White			
☐ 118	Buffalo Braves TL	2.00	.90	.25
	Bob McAdoo			
	Jack Marin			
	Bob McAdoo			
	Randy Smith			
☐ 119	Chicago Bulls TL	2.50	1.15	.30
	Bob Love			
	Chet Walker			
	Nate Thurmond			
	Norm Van Lier			
☐ 120	Cleveland Cavs TL	1.50	.65	.19
	Bobby Smith			
	Dick Snyder			
	Jim Chones			
	Jim Cleamons			
☐ 121	Detroit Pistons TL	3.00	1.35	.40
	Bob Lanier			
	John Mengelt			
	Bob Lanier			
	Dave Bing			
☐ 122	Golden State TL	2.50	1.15	.30
	Rick Barry			
	Rick Barry			
	Clifford Ray			
	Rick Barry			
☐ 123	Houston Rockets TL	2.00	.90	.25
	Rudy Tomjanovich			
	Calvin Murphy			
	Kevin Kunnert			
	Mike Newlin			
☐ 124	Kansas City Kings TL	2.00	.90	.25
	Nate Archibald			
	Ollie Johnson			
	Sam Lacey UER			
	(Lacy on front)			
	Nate Archibald			
☐ 125	Los Angeles Lakers TL	1.50	.65	.19
	Gail Goodrich			
	Cazzie Russell			
	Happy Hairston			
	Gail Goodrich			
☐ 126	Milwaukee Bucks TL	6.00	2.70	.75
	Kareem Abdul-Jabbar			
	Mickey Davis			
	Kareem Abdul-Jabbar			
	Kareem Abdul-Jabbar			
☐ 127	New Orleans Jazz TL	5.00	2.30	.60
	Pete Maravich			
	Stu Lantz			
	E.C. Coleman			
	Pete Maravich			
☐ 128	New York Knicks TL DP	3.00	1.35	.40
	Walt Frazier			
	Bill Bradley			
	John Gianelli			
	Walt Frazier			
☐ 129	Phila. 76ers TL DP	2.00	.90	.25
	Fred Carter			
	Doug Collins			
	Billy Cunningham			
	Billy Cunningham			
☐ 130	Phoenix Suns TL DP	1.50	.65	.19
	Charlie Scott			
	Keith Erickson			
	Curtis Perry			
	Dennis Awtrey			
☐ 131	Portland Blazers TL DP	1.50	.65	.19
	Sidney Wicks			
	Geoff Petrie			
	Sidney Wicks			
	Geoff Petrie			
☐ 132	Seattle Sonics TL	2.00	.90	.25
	Spencer Haywood			
	Archie Clark			
	Spencer Haywood			
	Don Watts			
☐ 133	Washington Bullets TL	3.00	1.35	.40
	Elvin Hayes			
	Clem Haskins			
	Wes Unseld			
	Kevin Porter			
☐ 134	John Drew	2.00	.90	.25
	Atlanta Hawks			

☐ 135	JoJo White AS2 Boston Celtics	2.00	.90	.25
☐ 136	Garfield Heard Buffalo Braves	1.25	.55	.16
☐ 137	Jim Cleamons Cleveland Cavaliers	.75	.35	.09
☐ 138	Howard Porter Detroit Pistons	1.25	.55	.16
☐ 139	Phil Smith Golden State Warriors	1.25	.55	.16
☐ 140	Bob Love Chicago Bulls	1.25	.55	.16
☐ 141	John Gianelli DP New York Knicks	.75	.35	.09
☐ 142	Larry McNeill Kansas City Kings	.75	.35	.09
☐ 143	Brian Winters Milwaukee Bucks	3.00	1.35	.40
☐ 144	George Thompson Milwaukee Bucks	.75	.35	.09
☐ 145	Kevin Kunnert Houston Rockets	.75	.35	.09
☐ 146	Henry Bibby New Orleans Jazz	1.25	.55	.16
☐ 147	John Johnson Portland Trail Blazers	.75	.35	.09
☐ 148	Doug Collins Philadelphia 76ers	5.00	2.30	.60
☐ 149	John Brisker Seattle Supersonics	.75	.35	.09
☐ 150	Dick Van Arsdale Phoenix Suns	1.25	.55	.16
☐ 151	Leonard Robinson Washington Bullets	2.50	1.15	.30
☐ 152	Dean Meminger Atlanta Hawks	.75	.35	.09
☐ 153	Phil Hankinson Boston Celtics	.75	.35	.09
☐ 154	Dale Schlueter Buffalo Braves	.75	.35	.09
☐ 155	Norm Van Lier Chicago Bulls	1.25	.55	.16
☐ 156	Campy Russell Cleveland Cavaliers	3.00	1.35	.40
☐ 157	Jeff Mullins Golden State Warriors	1.25	.55	.16
☐ 158	Sam Lacey Kansas City Kings	.75	.35	.09
☐ 159	Happy Hairston Los Angeles Lakers	1.25	.55	.16
☐ 160	Dave Bing DP Detroit Pistons	2.50	1.15	.30
☐ 161	Kevin Restani Milwaukee Bucks	.75	.35	.09
☐ 162	Dave Wohl Houston Rockets	.75	.35	.09
☐ 163	E.C. Coleman New Orleans Jazz	.75	.35	.09
☐ 164	Jim Fox Seattle Supersonics	.75	.35	.09
☐ 165	Geoff Petrie Portland Trail Blazers	1.25	.55	.16
☐ 166	Hawthorne Wingo DP UER New York Knicks (Misspelled Harthorne on card front)	.75	.35	.09
☐ 167	Fred Boyd Philadelphia 76ers	.75	.35	.09
☐ 168	Willie Norwood Phoenix Suns	.75	.35	.09
☐ 169	Bob Wilson	.75	.35	.09
	Chicago Bulls			
☐ 170	Dave Cowens Boston Celtics	6.00	2.70	.75
☐ 171	Tom Henderson Atlanta Hawks	.75	.35	.09
☐ 172	Jim Washington Buffalo Braves	.75	.35	.09
☐ 173	Clem Haskins Washington Bullets	1.25	.55	.16
☐ 174	Jim Davis Detroit Pistons	.75	.35	.09
☐ 175	Bobby Smith DP Cleveland Cavaliers	.75	.35	.09
☐ 176	Mike D'Antoni Kansas City Kings	.75	.35	.09
☐ 177	Zelmo Beaty Los Angeles Lakers	1.25	.55	.16
☐ 178	Gary Brokaw Milwaukee Bucks	.75	.35	.09
☐ 179	Mel Davis New York Knicks	.75	.35	.09
☐ 180	Calvin Murphy Houston Rockets	3.00	1.35	.40
☐ 181	Checklist 111-220 DP	8.00	.80	.15
☐ 182	Nate Williams New Orleans Jazz	.75	.35	.09
☐ 183	LaRue Martin Portland Trail Blazers	.75	.35	.09
☐ 184	George McGinnis Philadelphia 76ers	2.50	1.15	.30
☐ 185	Clifford Ray Golden State Warriors	1.25	.55	.16
☐ 186	Paul Westphal Phoenix Suns	5.00	2.30	.60
☐ 187	Talvin Skinner Seattle Supersonics	.75	.35	.09
☐ 188	NBA Playoff Semis DP Warriors edge Bulls Bullets over Celts	1.50	.65	.19
☐ 189	NBA Playoff Finals Warriors sweep Bullets (C.Ray blocks shot)	1.50	.65	.19
☐ 190	Phil Chenier AS2 DP Washington Bullets	1.25	.55	.16
☐ 191	John Brown Atlanta Hawks	.75	.35	.09
☐ 192	Lee Winfield Buffalo Braves	.75	.35	.09
☐ 193	Steve Patterson Cleveland Cavaliers	.75	.35	.09
☐ 194	Charles Dudley Golden State Warriors	.75	.35	.09
☐ 195	Connie Hawkins DP Los Angeles Lakers	2.50	1.15	.30
☐ 196	Leon Benbow Chicago Bulls	.75	.35	.09
☐ 197	Don Kojis Kansas City Kings	.75	.35	.09
☐ 198	Ron Williams Milwaukee Bucks	.75	.35	.09
☐ 199	Mel Counts New Orleans Jazz	1.25	.55	.16
☐ 200	Spencer Haywood AS2 Seattle Supersonics	2.00	.90	.25
☐ 201	Greg Jackson Phoenix Suns	.75	.35	.09
☐ 202	Tom Kozelko DP Washington Bullets	.75	.35	.09
☐ 203	Atlanta Hawks Checklist	1.50	.65	.19
☐ 204	Boston Celtics	3.00	1.35	.40

☐ 205	Buffalo Braves Checklist	1.50	.65	.19
☐ 206	Chicago Bulls Checklist	2.50	1.15	.30
☐ 207	Cleveland Cavs Checklist	1.50	.65	.19
☐ 208	Detroit Pistons Checklist	1.50	.65	.19
☐ 209	Golden State Checklist	1.50	.65	.19
☐ 210	Houston Rockets Checklist	1.50	.65	.19
☐ 211	Kansas City Kings DP Checklist	1.50	.65	.19
☐ 212	Los Angeles Lakers DP Checklist	1.50	.65	.19
☐ 213	Milwaukee Bucks Checklist	1.50	.65	.19
☐ 214	New Orleans Jazz Checklist	1.50	.65	.19
☐ 215	New York Knicks Checklist	1.50	.65	.19
☐ 216	Philadelphia 76ers Checklist	1.50	.65	.19
☐ 217	Phoenix Suns DP Checklist	1.50	.65	.19
☐ 218	Portland Blazers Checklist	1.50	.65	.19
☐ 219	Seattle Sonics DP Checklist	10.00	4.50	1.25
☐ 220	Washington Bullets Checklist	1.50	.65	.19
☐ 221	ABA Scoring Average Leaders George McGinnis Julius Erving Ron Boone	8.00	3.60	1.00
☐ 222	ABA 2 Pt. Field Goal Percentage Leaders Bobby Jones Artis Gilmore Moses Malone	8.00	3.60	1.00
☐ 223	ABA 3 Pt. Field Goal Percentage Leaders Billy Shepherd Louie Dampier Al Smith	2.00	.90	.25
☐ 224	ABA Free Throw Percentage Leaders Mack Calvin James Silas Dave Robisch	2.00	.90	.25
☐ 225	ABA Rebounds Leaders Swen Nater Artis Gilmore Marvin Barnes	2.00	.90	.25
☐ 226	ABA Assists Leaders Mack Calvin Chuck Williams George McGinnis	2.00	.90	.25
☐ 227	Mack Calvin AS1 Virginia Squires	2.00	.90	.25
☐ 228	Billy Knight AS1 Indiana Pacers	4.00	1.80	.50
☐ 229	Bird Averitt Kentucky Colonels	1.50	.65	.19
☐ 230	George Carter Memphis Sounds	1.50	.65	.19
☐ 231	Swen Nater AS2 New York Nets	2.00	.90	.25
☐ 232	Steve Jones St. Louis Spirits	2.00	.90	.25
☐ 233	George Gervin San Antonio Spurs	16.00	7.25	2.00
☐ 234	Lee Davis San Diego Sails	1.50	.65	.19
☐ 235	Ron Boone AS1 Utah Stars	2.00	.90	.25
☐ 236	Mike Jackson Virginia Squires	1.50	.65	.19
☐ 237	Kevin Joyce Indiana Pacers	2.00	.90	.25
☐ 238	Marv Roberts Kentucky Colonels	1.50	.65	.19
☐ 239	Tom Owens Memphis Sounds	1.50	.65	.19
☐ 240	Ralph Simpson Denver Nuggets	2.00	.90	.25
☐ 241	Gus Gerard St. Louis Spirits	2.00	.90	.25
☐ 242	Brian Taylor AS2 New York Nets	1.50	.65	.19
☐ 243	Rich Jones San Antonio Spurs	1.50	.65	.19
☐ 244	John Roche Utah Stars	2.00	.90	.25
☐ 245	Travis Grant San Diego Sails	2.00	.90	.25
☐ 246	Dave Twardzik Virginia Squires	2.00	.90	.25
☐ 247	Mike Green Virginia Squires	1.50	.65	.19
☐ 248	Billy Keller Indiana Pacers	2.00	.90	.25
☐ 249	Stew Johnson Memphis Sounds	1.50	.65	.19
☐ 250	Artis Gilmore AS1 Kentucky Colonels	4.00	1.80	.50
☐ 251	John Williamson New York Nets	2.00	.90	.25
☐ 252	Marvin Barnes AS2 St. Louis Spirits	5.00	2.30	.60
☐ 253	James Silas AS2 San Antonio Spurs	2.00	.90	.25
☐ 254	Moses Malone Utah Stars	50.00	23.00	6.25
☐ 255	Willie Wise Virginia Squires	2.00	.90	.25
☐ 256	Dwight Lamar San Diego Sails	1.50	.65	.19
☐ 257	Checklist 221-330	8.00	.80	.15
☐ 258	Byron Beck Denver Nuggets	2.00	.90	.25
☐ 259	Len Elmore Indiana Pacers	4.00	1.80	.50
☐ 260	Dan Issel Kentucky Colonels	5.00	2.30	.60
☐ 261	Rick Mount Memphis Sounds	2.00	.90	.25
☐ 262	Billy Paultz New York Nets	2.00	.90	.25
☐ 263	Donnie Freeman San Antonio Spurs	2.00	.90	.25
☐ 264	George Adams San Diego Sails	1.50	.65	.19
☐ 265	Don Chaney St. Louis Spirits	2.00	.90	.25
☐ 266	Randy Denton Utah Stars	1.50	.65	.19
☐ 267	Don Washington Denver Nuggets	1.50	.65	.19

☐ 268	Roland Taylor .... Denver Nuggets	1.50	.65	.19
☐ 269	Charlie Edge .... Indiana Pacers	1.50	.65	.19
☐ 270	Louie Dampier .... Kentucky Colonels	2.00	.90	.25
☐ 271	Collis Jones .... Memphis Sounds	1.50	.65	.19
☐ 272	Al Skinner .... New York Nets	1.50	.65	.19
☐ 273	Coby Dietrick .... San Antonio Spurs	1.50	.65	.19
☐ 274	Tim Bassett .... San Diego Sails	1.50	.65	.19
☐ 275	Freddie Lewis .... St. Louis Spirits	2.00	.90	.25
☐ 276	Gerald Govan .... Utah Stars	1.50	.65	.19
☐ 277	Ron Thomas .... Kentucky Colonels	1.50	.65	.19
☐ 278	Denver Nuggets TL .... Ralph Simpson Mack Calvin Mike Green Mack Calvin	2.00	.90	.25
☐ 279	Indiana Pacers TL ...... George McGinnis Billy Keller George McGinnis George McGinnis	2.50	1.15	.30
☐ 280	Kentucky Colonels TL	2.50	1.15	.30
	Artis Gilmore Louie Dampier Artis Gilmore Louie Dampier			
☐ 281	Memphis Sounds TL... George Carter Larry Finch Tom Owens Chuck Williams	2.00	.90	.25
☐ 282	New York Nets TL ...... Julius Erving John Williamson Julius Erving Julius Erving	10.00	4.50	1.25
☐ 283	St. Louis Spirits TL .... Marvin Barnes Freddie Lewis Marvin Barnes Freddie Lewis	2.50	1.15	.30
☐ 284	San Antonio Spurs TL	5.00	2.30	.60
	George Gervin James Silas Swen Nater James Silas			
☐ 285	San Diego Sails TL...... Travis Grant Jimmy O'Brien Caldwell Jones Jimmy O'Brien	2.00	.90	.25
☐ 286	Utah Stars TL .... Ron Boone Ron Boone Moses Malone Al Smith	8.00	3.60	1.00
☐ 287	Virginia Squires TL .... Willie Wise Red Robbins Dave Vaughn Dave Twardzik	2.00	.90	.25
☐ 288	Claude Terry	1.50	.65	.19
☐ 289	Denver Nuggets Wilbert Jones............. Kentucky Colonels	1.50	.65	.19
☐ 290	Darnell Hillman .... Indiana Pacers	2.00	.90	.25
☐ 291	Bill Melchionni .... New York Nets	2.00	.90	.25
☐ 292	Mel Daniels .... Memphis Sounds	2.00	.90	.25
☐ 293	Fly Williams .... St. Louis Spirits	2.00	.90	.25
☐ 294	Larry Kenon .... San Antonio Spurs	2.00	.90	.25
☐ 295	Red Robbins .... Virginia Squires	1.50	.65	.19
☐ 296	Warren Jabali............. San Diego Sails	1.50	.65	.19
☐ 297	Jim Eakins .... Utah Stars	1.50	.65	.19
☐ 298	Bobby Jones .... Denver Nuggets	10.00	4.50	1.25
☐ 299	Don Buse .... Indiana Pacers	2.00	.90	.25
☐ 300	Julius Erving AS1.... New York Nets	50.00	23.00	6.25
☐ 301	Billy Shepherd .... Memphis Sounds	1.50	.65	.19
☐ 302	Maurice Lucas .... St. Louis Spirits	8.00	3.60	1.00
☐ 303	George Karl .... San Antonio Spurs	2.50	1.15	.30
☐ 304	Jim Bradley .... Kentucky Colonels	1.50	.65	.19
☐ 305	Caldwell Jones .... San Diego Sails	2.00	.90	.25
☐ 306	Al Smith.................... Utah Stars	1.50	.65	.19
☐ 307	Jan Van Breda Kolff ... Virginia Squires	2.00	.90	.25
☐ 308	Darrell Elston .... Virginia Squires	1.50	.65	.19
☐ 309	ABA Playoff Semifinals Colonels over Spirits; Pacers edge Nuggets	2.00	.90	.25
☐ 310	ABA Playoff Finals...... Colonels over Pacers (Gilmore hooking)	2.00	.90	.25
☐ 311	Ted McClain .... Kentucky Colonels	1.50	.65	.19
☐ 312	Willie Sojourner .... New York Nets	1.50	.65	.19
☐ 313	Bob Warren .... San Antonio Spurs	1.50	.65	.19
☐ 314	Bob Netolicky............. Indiana Pacers	2.00	.90	.25
☐ 315	Chuck Williams .... Memphis Sounds	1.50	.65	.19
☐ 316	Gene Kennedy .... St. Louis Spirits	1.50	.65	.19
☐ 317	Jimmy O'Brien .... San Diego Sails	1.50	.65	.19
☐ 318	Dave Robisch .... Denver Nuggets	2.00	.90	.25
☐ 319	Wali Jones .... Utah Stars	1.50	.65	.19
☐ 320	George Irvine .... Denver Nuggets	1.50	.65	.19
☐ 321	Denver Nuggets .... Checklist	2.00	.90	.25
☐ 322	Indiana Pacers .... Checklist	2.00	.90	.25

			NRMT-MT	EXC	VG
☐ 323	Kentucky Colonels Checklist		2.00	.90	.25
☐ 324	Memphis Sounds Checklist		2.00	.90	.25
☐ 325	New York Nets Checklist		2.00	.90	.25
☐ 326	St. Louis Spirits Checklist (Spirits of St. Louis on card back)		2.00	.90	.25
☐ 327	San Antonio Spurs Checklist		2.00	.90	.25
☐ 328	San Diego Sails Checklist		2.00	.90	.25
☐ 329	Utah Stars Checklist		2.00	.90	.25
☐ 330	Virginia Squires Checklist		4.00	1.00	.22

1976-77 Topps

DAVID THOMPSON • FORWARD

Perhaps the most popular set of the seventies, the 144-card 1976-77 Topps set witnessed a return to the larger-size at 3 1/8" by 5 1/4". The larger size and excellent photo quality are appealing to collectors. Also, because of the size, they are attractive to autograph collectors. Cards were issued in 10-card packs with 24 packs per box. The fronts have a large color photo with the team name vertical on the left border. The player's name and position are at the bottom. Backs have statistical and biographical data. Cards numbered 126-135 are the previous season's NBA All-Star selections. The cards were printed on two large sheets, each with eight rows and nine columns. The checklist card was located in the lower right corner of the second sheet. Card No. 1, Julius Erving, is rarely found centered. Rookie Cards include Alvan Adams, Lloyd Free, Gus Johnson and David Thompson.

	NRMT-MT	EXC	VG
COMPLETE SET (144)	350.00	160.00	45.00
COMMON CARD (1-144)	1.75	.80	.22

		NRMT-MT	EXC	VG
☐ 1	Julius Erving New York Nets	65.00	24.00	5.25
☐ 2	Dick Snyder	1.75	.80	.22
☐ 3	Paul Silas Cleveland Cavaliers	2.50	1.15	.30
☐ 4	Keith Erickson Boston Celtics	2.00	.90	.25
☐ 5	Wes Unseld Phoenix Suns	4.00	1.80	.50
☐ 6	Butch Beard Washington Bullets	2.00	.90	.25
☐ 7	Lloyd Neal New York Knicks	2.00	.90	.25
☐ 8	Tom Henderson Portland Trail Blazers	1.75	.80	.22
☐ 9	Jim McMillian Atlanta Hawks	2.00	.90	.25
☐ 10	Bob Lanier Buffalo Braves	6.00	2.70	.75
☐ 11	Junior Bridgeman Detroit Pistons	3.00	1.35	.40
☐ 12	Corky Calhoun Milwaukee Bucks	1.75	.80	.22
☐ 13	Billy Keller Los Angeles Lakers	1.75	.80	.22
☐ 14	Mickey Johnson Indiana Pacers	2.00	.90	.25
☐ 15	Fred Brown Chicago Bulls	2.50	1.15	.30
☐ 16	Jamaal Wilkes Seattle Supersonics	4.00	1.80	.50
☐ 17	Louie Nelson Golden State Warriors	1.75	.80	.22
☐ 18	Ed Ratleff New Orleans Jazz	1.75	.80	.22
☐ 19	Billy Paultz Houston Rockets	2.50	1.15	.30
☐ 20	Nate Archibald San Antonio Spurs	5.00	2.30	.60
☐ 21	Steve Mix Kansas City Kings	2.00	.90	.25
☐ 22	Ralph Simpson Philadelphia 76ers	2.00	.90	.25
☐ 23	Campy Russell Denver Nuggets	2.00	.90	.25
☐ 24	Charlie Scott Cleveland Cavaliers	2.00	.90	.25
☐ 25	Artis Gilmore Boston Celtics	5.00	2.30	.60
☐ 26	Dick Van Arsdale Chicago Bulls	2.00	.90	.25
☐ 27	Phil Chenier Phoenix Suns	2.00	.90	.25
☐ 28	Spencer Haywood Washington Bullets	3.00	1.35	.40
☐ 29	Chris Ford New York Knicks	2.00	.90	.25
☐ 30	Dave Cowens Detroit Pistons	8.00	3.60	1.00
☐ 31	Sidney Wicks Boston Celtics	2.00	.90	.25
☐ 32	Jim Price Portland Trail Blazers	1.75	.80	.22
☐ 33	Dwight Jones Milwaukee Bucks	1.75	.80	.22
☐ 34	Lucius Allen Houston Rockets	2.00	.90	.25
☐ 35	Marvin Barnes Los Angeles Lakers	2.00	.90	.25
☐ 36	Henry Bibby Detroit Pistons	2.00	.90	.25
☐ 37	Joe Meriweather New Orleans Jazz	1.75	.80	.22

☐ 38	Doug Collins	6.00	2.70	.75
	Philadelphia 76ers			
☐ 39	Garfield Heard	2.00	.90	.25
	Phoenix Suns			
☐ 40	Randy Smith	2.00	.90	.25
	Buffalo Braves			
☐ 41	Tom Burleson	2.00	.90	.25
	Seattle Supersonics			
☐ 42	Dave Twardzik	2.00	.90	.25
	Portland Trail Blazers			
☐ 43	Bill Bradley	12.00	5.50	1.50
	New York Knicks			
☐ 44	Calvin Murphy	4.00	1.80	.50
	Houston Rockets			
☐ 45	Bob Love	2.00	.90	.25
	Chicago Bulls			
☐ 46	Brian Winters	3.00	1.35	.40
	Milwaukee Bucks			
☐ 47	Glenn McDonald	1.75	.80	.22
	Boston Celtics			
☐ 48	Checklist 1-144	20.00	2.20	.55
☐ 49	Bird Averitt	1.75	.80	.22
	Buffalo Braves			
☐ 50	Rick Barry	8.00	3.60	1.00
	Golden State Warriors			
☐ 51	Ticky Burden	1.75	.80	.22
	New York Knicks			
☐ 52	Rich Jones	1.75	.80	.22
	New York Nets			
☐ 53	Austin Carr	2.00	.90	.25
	Cleveland Cavaliers			
☐ 54	Steve Kuberski	1.75	.80	.22
	Boston Celtics			
☐ 55	Paul Westphal	6.00	2.70	.75
	Phoenix Suns			
☐ 56	Mike Riordan	2.00	.90	.25
	Washington Bullets			
☐ 57	Bill Walton	30.00	13.50	3.80
	Portland Trail Blazers			
☐ 58	Eric Money	1.75	.80	.22
	Detroit Pistons			
☐ 59	John Drew	2.00	.90	.25
	Atlanta Hawks			
☐ 60	Pete Maravich	35.00	16.00	4.40
	New Orleans Jazz			
☐ 61	John Shumate	3.00	1.35	.40
	Buffalo Braves			
☐ 62	Mack Calvin	2.00	.90	.25
	Los Angeles Lakers			
☐ 63	Bruce Seals	1.75	.80	.22
	Seattle Supersonics			
☐ 64	Walt Frazier	6.00	2.70	.75
	New York Knicks			
☐ 65	Elmore Smith	2.00	.90	.25
	Milwaukee Bucks			
☐ 66	Rudy Tomjanovich	6.00	2.70	.75
	Houston Rockets			
☐ 67	Sam Lacey	1.75	.80	.22
	Kansas City Kings			
☐ 68	George Gervin	20.00	9.00	2.50
	San Antonio Spurs			
☐ 69	Gus Williams	5.00	2.30	.60
	Golden State Warriors			
☐ 70	George McGinnis	2.50	1.15	.30
	Philadelphia 76ers			
☐ 71	Len Elmore	1.75	.80	.22
	Indiana Pacers			
☐ 72	Jack Marin	2.00	.90	.25
	Chicago Bulls			
☐ 73	Brian Taylor	1.75	.80	.22
	New York Nets			
☐ 74	Jim Brewer	1.75	.80	.22
	Cleveland Cavaliers			
☐ 75	Alvan Adams	6.00	2.70	.75
	Phoenix Suns			
☐ 76	Dave Bing	4.00	1.80	.50
	Washington Bullets			
☐ 77	Phil Jackson	5.00	2.30	.60
	New York Knicks			
☐ 78	Geoff Petrie	2.00	.90	.25
	Portland Trail Blazers			
☐ 79	Mike Sojourner	1.75	.80	.22
	Atlanta Hawks			
☐ 80	James Silas	2.00	.90	.25
	San Antonio Spurs			
☐ 81	Bob Dandridge	2.00	.90	.25
	Milwaukee Bucks			
☐ 82	Ernie DiGregorio	2.00	.90	.25
	Buffalo Braves			
☐ 83	Cazzie Russell	2.00	.90	.25
	Los Angeles Lakers			
☐ 84	Kevin Porter	2.00	.90	.25
	Detroit Pistons			
☐ 85	Tom Boerwinkle	1.75	.80	.22
	Chicago Bulls			
☐ 86	Darnell Hillman	2.00	.90	.25
	Indiana Pacers			
☐ 87	Herm Gilliam	1.75	.80	.22
	Seattle Supersonics			
☐ 88	Nate Williams	1.75	.80	.22
	New Orleans Jazz			
☐ 89	Phil Smith	1.75	.80	.22
	Golden State Warriors			
☐ 90	John Havlicek	18.00	8.00	2.30
	Boston Celtics			
☐ 91	Kevin Kunnert	1.75	.80	.22
	Houston Rockets			
☐ 92	Jimmy Walker	2.00	.90	.25
	Kansas City Kings			
☐ 93	Billy Cunningham	5.00	2.30	.60
	Philadelphia 76ers			
☐ 94	Dan Issel	6.00	2.70	.75
	Denver Nuggets			
☐ 95	Ron Boone	2.00	.90	.25
	Kansas City Kings			
☐ 96	Lou Hudson	2.00	.90	.25
	Atlanta Hawks			
☐ 97	Jim Chones	2.00	.90	.25
	Cleveland Cavaliers			
☐ 98	Earl Monroe	4.00	1.80	.50
	New York Knicks			
☐ 99	Tom Van Arsdale	2.00	.90	.25
	Buffalo Braves			
☐ 100	Kareem Abdul-Jabbar	35.00	16.00	4.40
	Los Angeles Lakers			
☐ 101	Moses Malone	25.00	11.50	3.10
	Portland Trail Blazers			
☐ 102	Ricky Sobers	1.75	.80	.22
	Phoenix Suns			
☐ 103	Swen Nater	2.00	.90	.25
	Milwaukee Bucks			
☐ 104	Leonard Robinson	2.50	1.15	.30
	Washington Bullets			
☐ 105	Don Watts	2.00	.90	.25
	Seattle Supersonics			
☐ 106	Otto Moore	1.75	.80	.22
	New Orleans Jazz			
☐ 107	Maurice Lucas	3.00	1.35	.40
	Portland Trail Blazers			
☐ 108	Norm Van Lier	2.00	.90	.25
	Chicago Bulls			
☐ 109	Clifford Ray	2.00	.90	.25

1977-78 Topps

		NRMT-MT	EXC	VG
	Golden State Warriors			
☐ 110	David Thompson...... 30.00	13.50	3.80
	Denver Nuggets			
☐ 111	Fred Carter.................. 2.00	.90	.25
	Philadelphia 76ers			
☐ 112	Caldwell Jones............ 2.00	.90	.25
	Philadelphia 76ers			
☐ 113	John Williamson........ 2.00	.90	.25
	New York Nets			
☐ 114	Bobby Smith................ 1.75	.80	.22
	Cleveland Cavaliers			
☐ 115	JoJo White.................. 2.50	1.15	.30
	Boston Celtics			
☐ 116	Curtis Perry................ 1.75	.80	.22
	Phoenix Suns			
☐ 117	John Gianelli................ 1.75	.80	.22
	New York Knicks			
☐ 118	Curtis Rowe................ 2.00	.90	.25
	Detroit Pistons			
☐ 119	Lionel Hollins.............. 3.00	1.35	.40
	Portland Trail Blazers			
☐ 120	Elvin Hayes................ 6.00	2.70	.75
	Washington Bullets			
☐ 121	Ken Charles................ 1.75	.80	.22
	Atlanta Hawks			
☐ 122	Dave Meyers................ 3.00	1.35	.40
	Milwaukee Bucks			
☐ 123	Jerry Sloan 2.00	.90	.25
	Chicago Bulls			
☐ 124	Billy Knight 2.00	.90	.25
	Indiana Pacers			
☐ 125	Gail Goodrich.............. 1.75	.80	.22
	Los Angeles Lakers			
☐ 126	Kareem Abdul-Jabbar AS 20.00	9.00	2.50
	Los Angeles Lakers			
☐ 127	Julius Erving AS....... 25.00	11.50	3.10
	New York Nets			
☐ 128	George McGinnis AS.. 2.75	1.25	.35
	Philadelphia 76ers			
☐ 129	Nate Archibald AS...... 3.00	1.35	.40
	Kansas City Kings			
☐ 130	Pete Maravich AS...... 20.00	9.00	2.50
	New Orleans Jazz			
☐ 131	Dave Cowens AS....... 5.00	2.30	.60
	Boston Celtics			
☐ 132	Rick Barry AS............ 5.00	2.30	.60
	Golden State Warriors			
☐ 133	Elvin Hayes AS............ 4.00	1.80	.50
	Washington Bullets			
☐ 134	James Silas AS............ 2.00	.90	.25
	San Antonio Spurs			
☐ 135	Randy Smith AS............ 2.00	.90	.25
	Buffalo Braves			
☐ 136	Leonard Gray.............. 1.75	.80	.22
	Seattle Supersonics			
☐ 137	Charles Johnson........ 1.75	.80	.22
	Golden State Warriors			
☐ 138	Ron Behagen................ 1.75	.80	.22
	New Orleans Jazz			
☐ 139	Mike Newlin................ 2.00	.90	.25
	Houston Rockets			
☐ 140	Bob McAdoo................ 6.00	2.70	.75
	Buffalo Braves			
☐ 141	Mike Gale.................. 1.75	.80	.22
	San Antonio Spurs			
☐ 142	Scott Wedman.............. 2.00	.90	.25
	Kansas City Kings			
☐ 143	Lloyd Free.................. 6.00	2.70	.75
	Philadelphia 76ers			
☐ 144	Bobby Jones.............. 6.00	2.10	.50
	Denver Nuggets			

The 1977-78 Topps basketball card set consists of 132 standard-size (2 1/2" by 3 1/2") cards. Cards were issued in 10-card packs with 24 packs per box. Fronts feature team and player name at the bottom with the player's position in a basketball at bottom left of the photo. Card backs are printed in green and black on either white or gray card stock. The white card stock is considered more desirable by most collectors and may even be a little tougher to find. Rookie Cards include Adrian Dantley, Darryl Dawkins, John Lucas, Tom McMillen and Robert Parish.

	NRMT-MT	EXC	VG
COMPLETE SET (132) 110.00	50.00	14.00
COMMON CARD (1-132) .... .30	.14	.04
*GRAY AND WHITE BACKS: EQUAL VALUE		

☐ 1	Kareem Abdul-Jabbar .. 15.00	5.50	1.45
	Los Angeles Lakers		
☐ 2	Henry Bibby .... .40	.18	.05
	Philadelphia 76ers		
☐ 3	Curtis Rowe .... .30	.14	.04
	Boston Celtics		
☐ 4	Norm Van Lier .... .40	.18	.05
	Chicago Bulls		
☐ 5	Darnell Hillman .... .40	.18	.05
	New Jersey Nets		
☐ 6	Earl Monroe 1.50	.65	.19
	New York Knicks		
☐ 7	Leonard Gray .... .30	.14	.04
	Washington Bullets		
☐ 8	Bird Averitt.................. .30	.14	.04
	Buffalo Braves		
☐ 9	Jim Brewer .... .30	.14	.04
	Cleveland Cavaliers		
☐ 10	Paul Westphal.............. 1.50	.65	.19
	Phoenix Suns		
☐ 11	Bob Gross.................... .40	.18	.05
	Portland Trail Blazers		
☐ 12	Phil Smith .... .30	.14	.04
	Golden State Warriors		
☐ 13	Dan Roundfield............ .75	.35	.09
	Indiana Pacers		
☐ 14	Brian Taylor .... .30	.14	.04
	Denver Nuggets		
☐ 15	Rudy Tomjanovich....... 2.00	.90	.25
	Houston Rockets		
☐ 16	Kevin Porter.................. .60	.25	.08
	Detroit Pistons		

☐ 17	Scott Wedman .... .40	.18	.05
	Kansas City Kings		
☐ 18	Lloyd Free .... .60	.25	.08
	Philadelphia 76ers		
☐ 19	Tom Boswell .... .30	.14	.04
	Boston Celtics		
☐ 20	Pete Maravich 10.00	4.50	1.25
	New Orleans Jazz		
☐ 21	Cliff Poindexter .... .30	.14	.04
	Chicago Bulls		
☐ 22	Bubbles Hawkins .... .40	.18	.05
	New Jersey Nets		
☐ 23	Kevin Grevey 1.50	.65	.19
	Washington Bullets		
☐ 24	Ken Charles .... .30	.14	.04
	Atlanta Hawks		
☐ 25	Bob Dandridge .... .40	.18	.05
	Washington Bullets		
☐ 26	Lonnie Shelton .... .30	.14	.04
	New York Knicks		
☐ 27	Don Chaney .... .30	.14	.04
	Los Angeles Lakers		
☐ 28	Larry Kenon .... .40	.18	.05
	San Antonio Spurs		
☐ 29	Checklist 1-132 .... 3.00	.30	.06
☐ 30	Fred Brown .... .40	.18	.05
	Seattle Supersonics		
☐ 31	John Gianelli UER .... .30	.14	.04
	Cleveland Cavaliers		
	(Listed as Cavaliers,		
	should be Buffalo Braves)		
☐ 32	Austin Carr .... .40	.18	.05
	Cleveland Cavaliers		
☐ 33	Jamaal Wilkes .... .60	.25	.08
	Los Angeles Lakers		
☐ 34	Caldwell Jones .... .40	.18	.05
	Philadelphia 76ers		
☐ 35	JoJo White .... .60	.25	.08
	Boston Celtics		
☐ 36	Scott May 1.50	.65	.19
	Chicago Bulls		
☐ 37	Mike Newlin .... .40	.18	.05
	Houston Rockets		
☐ 38	Mel Davis .... .30	.14	.04
	New Jersey Nets		
☐ 39	Lionel Hollins .... .60	.25	.08
	Portland Trail Blazers		
☐ 40	Elvin Hayes 3.00	1.35	.40
	Washington Bullets		
☐ 41	Dan Issel 2.00	.90	.25
	Denver Nuggets		
☐ 42	Ricky Sobers .... .30	.14	.04
	Phoenix Suns		
☐ 43	Don Ford .... .30	.14	.04
	Los Angeles Lakers		
☐ 44	John Williamson .... .40	.18	.05
	Indiana Pacers		
☐ 45	Bob McAdoo 2.00	.90	.25
	New York Knicks		
☐ 46	Geoff Petrie .... .40	.18	.05
	Atlanta Hawks		
☐ 47	M.L. Carr 3.00	1.35	.40
	Detroit Pistons		
☐ 48	Brian Winters .... .40	.18	.05
	Milwaukee Bucks		
☐ 49	Sam Lacey .... .30	.14	.04
	Kansas City Kings		
☐ 50	George McGinnis .... .60	.25	.08
	Philadelphia 76ers		
☐ 51	Don Watts .... .40	.18	.05
	Seattle Supersonics		
☐ 52	Sidney Wicks .... .60	.25	.08
	Boston Celtics		
☐ 53	Wilbur Holland .... .30	.14	.04
	Chicago Bulls		
☐ 54	Tim Bassett .... .30	.14	.04
	New Jersey Nets		
☐ 55	Phil Chenier .... .40	.18	.05
	Washington Bullets		
☐ 56	Adrian Dantley 8.00	3.60	1.00
	Buffalo Braves		
☐ 57	Jim Chones .... .40	.18	.05
	Cleveland Cavaliers		
☐ 58	John Lucas 6.00	2.70	.75
	Houston Rockets		
☐ 59	Cazzie Russell .... .60	.25	.08
	Los Angeles Lakers		
☐ 60	David Thompson 3.00	1.35	.40
	Denver Nuggets		
☐ 61	Bob Lanier 2.00	.90	.25
	Detroit Pistons		
☐ 62	Dave Twardzik .... .40	.18	.05
	Portland Trail Blazers		
☐ 63	Wilbert Jones .... .40	.18	.05
	Indiana Pacers		
☐ 64	Clifford Ray .... .40	.18	.05
	Golden State Warriors		
☐ 65	Doug Collins 1.50	.65	.19
	Philadelphia 76ers		
☐ 66	Tom McMillen 2.50	1.15	.30
	New York Knicks		
☐ 67	Rich Kelley .... .30	.14	.04
	New Orleans Jazz		
☐ 68	Mike Bantom .... .30	.14	.04
	New Jersey Nets		
☐ 69	Tom Boerwinkle .... .30	.14	.04
	Chicago Bulls		
☐ 70	John Havlicek 6.00	2.70	.75
	Boston Celtics		
☐ 71	Marvin Webster .... .40	.18	.05
	Seattle Supersonics		
☐ 72	Curtis Perry .... .30	.14	.04
	Phoenix Suns		
☐ 73	George Gervin 6.00	2.70	.75
	San Antonio Spurs		
☐ 74	Leonard Robinson .... .60	.25	.08
	New Orleans Jazz		
☐ 75	Wes Unseld 1.50	.65	.19
	Washington Bullets		
☐ 76	Dave Meyers .... .40	.18	.05
	Milwaukee Bucks		
☐ 77	Gail Goodrich .... .60	.25	.08
	New Orleans Jazz		
☐ 78	Richard Washington .... .75	.35	.09
	Kansas City Kings		
☐ 79	Mike Gale .... .30	.14	.04
	San Antonio Spurs		
☐ 80	Maurice Lucas .... .60	.25	.08
	Portland Trail Blazers		
☐ 81	Harvey Catchings .... .30	.14	.04
	Philadelphia 76ers		
☐ 82	Randy Smith .... .40	.18	.05
	Buffalo Braves		
☐ 83	Campy Russell .... .40	.18	.05
	Cleveland Cavaliers		
☐ 84	Kevin Kunnert .... .30	.14	.04
	Houston Rockets		
☐ 85	Lou Hudson .... .60	.25	.08
	Atlanta Hawks		
☐ 86	Mickey Johnson .... .40	.18	.05
	Chicago Bulls		
☐ 87	Lucius Allen .... .40	.18	.05

			NRMT-MT	EXC	VG
☐ 88	Spencer Haywood	Kansas City Kings	1.00	.45	.13
☐ 89	Gus Williams	New York Knicks	.60	.25	.08
☐ 90	Dave Cowens	Golden State Warriors	3.00	1.35	.40
☐ 91	Al Skinner	Boston Celtics	.30	.14	.04
☐ 92	Swen Nater	New Jersey Nets	.30	.14	.04
☐ 93	Tom Henderson	Buffalo Braves	.40	.18	.05
☐ 94	Don Buse	Washington Bullets	.40	.18	.05
☐ 95	Alvan Adams	Indiana Pacers	.30	.14	.04
☐ 96	Mack Calvin	Phoenix Suns	.60	.25	.08
☐ 97	Tom Burleson	Denver Nuggets	.40	.18	.05
☐ 98	John Drew	Kansas City Kings	.40	.18	.05
☐ 99	Mike Green	Atlanta Hawks	.30	.14	.04
☐ 100	Julius Erving	Seattle Supersonics	16.00	7.25	2.00
☐ 101	John Mengelt	Philadelphia 76ers	.30	.14	.04
☐ 102	Howard Porter	Chicago Bulls	.40	.18	.05
☐ 103	Billy Paultz	Detroit Pistons	.60	.25	.08
☐ 104	John Shumate	San Antonio Spurs	.60	.25	.08
☐ 105	Calvin Murphy	Buffalo Braves	1.50	.65	.19
☐ 106	Elmore Smith	Houston Rockets	.40	.18	.05
☐ 107	Jim McMillian	Cleveland Cavaliers	.40	.18	.05
☐ 108	Kevin Stacom	New York Knicks	.30	.14	.04
☐ 109	Jan Van Breda Kolff	Boston Celtics	.30	.14	.04
☐ 110	Billy Knight	New Jersey Nets	.40	.18	.05
☐ 111	Robert Parish	Indiana Pacers	35.00	16.00	4.40
☐ 112	Larry Wright	Golden State Warriors	.30	.14	.04
☐ 113	Bruce Seals	Washington Bullets	.30	.14	.04
☐ 114	Junior Bridgeman	Seattle Supersonics	.40	.18	.05
☐ 115	Artis Gilmore	Milwaukee Bucks	1.50	.65	.19
☐ 116	Steve Mix	Chicago Bulls	.40	.18	.05
☐ 117	Ron Lee	Philadelphia 76ers	.30	.14	.04
☐ 118	Bobby Jones	Phoenix Suns	.60	.25	.08
☐ 119	Ron Boone	Denver Nuggets	.40	.18	.05
☐ 120	Bill Walton	Kansas City Kings	10.00	4.50	1.25
☐ 121	Chris Ford	Portland Trail Blazers	.40	.18	.05
☐ 122	Earl Tatum	Detroit Pistons	.30	.14	.04
		Los Angeles Lakers			
☐ 123	E.C. Coleman	New Orleans Jazz	.30	.14	.04
☐ 124	Moses Malone	Houston Rockets	10.00	4.50	1.25
☐ 125	Charlie Scott	Boston Celtics	.40	.18	.05
☐ 126	Bobby Smith	Cleveland Cavaliers	.30	.14	.04
☐ 127	Nate Archibald	New Jersey Nets	1.50	.65	.19
☐ 128	Mitch Kupchak	Washington Bullets	1.50	.65	.19
☐ 129	Walt Frazier	New York Knicks	3.00	1.35	.40
☐ 130	Rick Barry	Golden State Warriors	3.00	1.35	.40
☐ 131	Ernie DiGregorio	Buffalo Braves	.40	.18	.05
☐ 132	Darryl Dawkins	Philadelphia 76ers	8.00	2.00	.40

1978-79 Topps

The 1978-79 Topps basketball card set contains 132 cards. Cards were issued in 10-card packs with 36 packs per box. The cards in the set measure the standard 2 1/2" by 3 1/2". Card fronts feature the player and team name down the left border and a small head shot inserted at bottom right. Card backs are printed in orange and brown on gray card stock. The key Rookie Cards in this set are Quinn Buckner, Walter Davis, Dennis Johnson, Marques Johnson, Bernard King, Norm Nixon and Jack Sikma.

			NRMT-MT	EXC	VG
COMPLETE SET (132)			75.00	34.00	9.50
COMMON CARD (1-132)			.30	.14	.04
☐ 1	Bill Walton	Portland Trail Blazers	12.00	3.60	.70
☐ 2	Doug Collins	Philadelphia 76ers	1.25	.55	.16
☐ 3	Jamaal Wilkes	Los Angeles Lakers	.60	.25	.08
☐ 4	Wilbur Holland	Chicago Bulls	.30	.14	.04
☐ 5	Bob McAdoo	New York Knicks	1.25	.55	.16
☐ 6	Lucius Allen	Kansas City Kings	.40	.18	.05

☐ 7	Wes Unseld	1.25	.55	.16
	Washington Bullets			
☐ 8	Dave Meyers	.40	.18	.05
	Milwaukee Bucks			
☐ 9	Austin Carr	.40	.18	.05
	Cleveland Cavaliers			
☐ 10	Walter Davis	6.00	2.70	.75
	Phoenix Suns			
☐ 11	John Williamson	.40	.18	.05
	New Jersey Nets			
☐ 12	E.C. Coleman	.30	.14	.04
	Golden State Warriors			
☐ 13	Calvin Murphy	1.00	.45	.13
	Houston Rockets			
☐ 14	Bobby Jones	.30	.14	.04
	Denver Nuggets			
☐ 15	Chris Ford	.40	.18	.05
	Detroit Pistons			
☐ 16	Kermit Washington	.40	.18	.05
	Boston Celtics			
☐ 17	Butch Beard	.40	.18	.05
	New York Knicks			
☐ 18	Steve Mix	.40	.18	.05
	Philadelphia 76ers			
☐ 19	Marvin Webster	.60	.25	.08
	Seattle Supersonics			
☐ 20	George Gervin	6.00	2.70	.75
	San Antonio Spurs			
☐ 21	Steve Hawes	.30	.14	.04
	Atlanta Hawks			
☐ 22	Johnny Davis	.30	.14	.04
	Portland Trail Blazers			
☐ 23	Swen Nater	.30	.14	.04
	San Diego Clippers			
☐ 24	Lou Hudson	.60	.25	.08
	Los Angeles Lakers			
☐ 25	Elvin Hayes	2.00	.90	.25
	Washington Bullets			
☐ 26	Nate Archibald	1.00	.45	.13
	San Diego Clippers			
☐ 27	James Edwards	2.00	.90	.25
	Indiana Pacers			
☐ 28	Howard Porter	.30	.14	.04
	New Jersey Nets			
☐ 29	Quinn Buckner	1.50	.65	.19
	Milwaukee Bucks			
☐ 30	Leonard Robinson	.60	.25	.08
	New Orleans Jazz			
☐ 31	Jim Cleamons	.30	.14	.04
	New York Knicks			
☐ 32	Campy Russell	.40	.18	.05
	Cleveland Cavaliers			
☐ 33	Phil Smith	.30	.14	.04
	Golden State Warriors			
☐ 34	Darryl Dawkins	1.50	.65	.19
	Philadelphia 76ers			
☐ 35	Don Buse	.40	.18	.05
	Phoenix Suns			
☐ 36	Mickey Johnson	.30	.14	.04
	Chicago Bulls			
☐ 37	Mike Gale	.30	.14	.04
	San Antonio Spurs			
☐ 38	Moses Malone	6.00	2.70	.75
	Houston Rockets			
☐ 39	Gus Williams	.30	.14	.04
	Seattle Supersonics			
☐ 40	Dave Cowens	2.00	.90	.25
	Boston Celtics			
☐ 41	Bobby Wilkerson	.40	.18	.05
	Denver Nuggets			
☐ 42	Wilbert Jones	.30	.14	.04
	San Diego Clippers			
☐ 43	Charlie Scott	.40	.18	.05
	Los Angeles Lakers			
☐ 44	John Drew	.40	.18	.05
	Atlanta Hawks			
☐ 45	Earl Monroe	1.25	.55	.16
	New York Knicks			
☐ 46	John Shumate	.40	.18	.05
	Detroit Pistons			
☐ 47	Earl Tatum	.30	.14	.04
	Indiana Pacers			
☐ 48	Mitch Kupchak	.40	.18	.05
	Washington Bullets			
☐ 49	Ron Boone	.40	.18	.05
	Kansas City Kings			
☐ 50	Maurice Lucas	.60	.25	.08
	Portland Trail Blazers			
☐ 51	Louie Dampier	.40	.18	.05
	San Antonio Spurs			
☐ 52	Aaron James	.30	.14	.04
	New Orleans Jazz			
☐ 53	John Mengelt	.30	.14	.04
	Chicago Bulls			
☐ 54	Garfield Heard	.40	.18	.05
	Phoenix Suns			
☐ 55	George Johnson	.30	.14	.04
	New Jersey Nets			
☐ 56	Junior Bridgeman	.40	.18	.05
	Milwaukee Bucks			
☐ 57	Elmore Smith	.40	.18	.05
	Cleveland Cavaliers			
☐ 58	Rudy Tomjanovich	1.50	.65	.19
	Houston Rockets			
☐ 59	Fred Brown	.40	.18	.05
	Seattle Supersonics			
☐ 60	Rick Barry UER	2.00	.90	.25
	Golden State Warriors			
	(reversed negative)			
☐ 61	Dave Bing	1.25	.55	.16
	Boston Celtics			
☐ 62	Anthony Roberts	.30	.14	.04
	Denver Nuggets			
☐ 63	Norm Nixon	2.50	1.15	.30
	Los Angeles Lakers			
☐ 64	Leon Douglas	.30	.14	.04
	Detroit Pistons			
☐ 65	Henry Bibby	.40	.18	.05
	Philadelphia 76ers			
☐ 66	Lonnie Shelton	.40	.18	.05
	New York Knicks			
☐ 67	Checklist 1-132	2.00	.25	.05
☐ 68	Tom Henderson	.30	.14	.04
	Washington Bullets			
☐ 69	Dan Roundfield	.40	.18	.05
	Indiana Pacers			
☐ 70	Armond Hill	.40	.18	.05
	Atlanta Hawks			
☐ 71	Larry Kenon	.40	.18	.05
	San Antonio Spurs			
☐ 72	Billy Knight	.40	.18	.05
	San Diego Clippers			
☐ 73	Artis Gilmore	1.00	.45	.13
	Chicago Bulls			
☐ 74	Lionel Hollins	.40	.18	.05
	Portland Trail Blazers			
☐ 75	Bernard King	8.00	3.60	1.00
	New Jersey Nets			
☐ 76	Brian Winters	.60	.25	.08
	Milwaukee Bucks			
☐ 77	Alvan Adams	.40	.18	.05
	Phoenix Suns			

☐ 78 Dennis Johnson 7.00	3.10	.85
Seattle Supersonics		
☐ 79 Scott Wedman .... .30	.14	.04
Kansas City Kings		
☐ 80 Pete Maravich 6.00	2.70	.75
New Orleans Jazz		
☐ 81 Dan Issel 1.50	.65	.19
Denver Nuggets		
☐ 82 M.L. Carr .... .60	.25	.08
Detroit Pistons		
☐ 83 Walt Frazier 2.00	.90	.25
Cleveland Cavaliers		
☐ 84 Dwight Jones .... .30	.14	.04
Houston Rockets		
☐ 85 JoJo White .... .60	.25	.08
Boston Celtics		
☐ 86 Robert Parish 5.00	2.30	.60
Golden State Warriors		
☐ 87 Charlie Criss .... .40	.18	.05
Atlanta Hawks		
☐ 88 Jim McMillian .... .40	.18	.05
New York Knicks		
☐ 89 Chuck Williams .... .30	.14	.04
San Diego Clippers		
☐ 90 George McGinnis .... .60	.25	.08
Philadelphia 76ers		
☐ 91 Billy Paultz .... .60	.25	.08
San Antonio Spurs		
☐ 92 Bob Dandridge .... .40	.18	.05
Washington Bullets		
☐ 93 Ricky Sobers .... .30	.14	.04
Indiana Pacers		
☐ 94 Paul Silas .... .40	.18	.05
Seattle Supersonics		
☐ 95 Gail Goodrich .... .60	.25	.08
New Orleans Jazz		
☐ 96 Tim Bassett .... .30	.14	.04
New Jersey Nets		
☐ 97 Ron Lee .... .30	.14	.04
Phoenix Suns		
☐ 98 Bob Gross .... .30	.14	.04
Portland Trail Blazers		
☐ 99 Sam Lacey .... .30	.14	.04
Kansas City Kings		
☐ 100 David Thompson 2.00	.90	.25
Denver Nuggets		
(College North Carolina,		
should be NC State)		
☐ 101 John Gianelli .... .30	.14	.04
Milwaukee Bucks		
☐ 102 Norm Van Lier .... .40	.18	.05
Chicago Bulls		
☐ 103 Caldwell Jones .... .40	.18	.05
Philadelphia 76ers		
☐ 104 Eric Money .... .30	.14	.04
Detroit Pistons		
☐ 105 Jim Chones .... .40	.18	.05
Cleveland Cavaliers		
☐ 106 John Lucas 1.50	.65	.19
Houston Rockets		
☐ 107 Spencer Haywood ...... .60	.25	.08
New York Knicks		
☐ 108 Eddie Johnson .... .30	.14	.04
Atlanta Hawks		
☐ 109 Sidney Wicks .... .60	.25	.08
Boston Celtics		
☐ 110 Kareem Abdul-Jabbar 10.00	4.50	1.25
Los Angeles Lakers		
☐ 111 Sonny Parker .... .30	.14	.04
Golden State Warriors		
☐ 112 Randy Smith .... .40	.18	.05

San Diego Clippers		
☐ 113 Kevin Grevey............. .40	.18	.05
Washington Bullets		
☐ 114 Rich Kelley .... .30	.14	.04
New Orleans Jazz		
☐ 115 Scott May .... .40	.18	.05
Chicago Bulls		
☐ 116 Lloyd Free .... .60	.25	.08
Philadelphia 76ers		
☐ 117 Jack Sikma 2.00	.90	.25
Seattle Supersonics		
☐ 118 Kevin Porter .... .60	.25	.08
New Jersey Nets		
☐ 119 Darnell Hillman .... .40	.18	.05
Denver Nuggets		
☐ 120 Paul Westphal............ 1.50	.65	.19
Phoenix Suns		
☐ 121 Richard Washington .... .30	.14	.04
Kansas City Kings		
☐ 122 Dave Twardzik........... .40	.18	.05
Portland Trail Blazers		
☐ 123 Mike Bantom............. .30	.14	.04
Indiana Pacers		
☐ 124 Mike Newlin .... .40	.18	.05
Houston Rockets		
☐ 125 Bob Lanier 1.50	.65	.19
Detroit Pistons		
☐ 126 Marques Johnson 3.00	1.35	.40
Milwaukee Bucks		
☐ 127 Foots Walker .... .40	.18	.05
Cleveland Cavaliers		
☐ 128 Cedric Maxwell 1.50	.65	.19
Boston Celtics		
☐ 129 Ray Williams .... .40	.18	.05
New York Knicks		
☐ 130 Julius Erving 12.00	5.50	1.50
Philadelphia 76ers		
☐ 131 Clifford Ray .... .40	.18	.05
Golden State Warriors		
☐ 132 Adrian Dantley 3.00	1.00	.25
Los Angeles Lakers		

1979-80 Topps

The 1979-80 Topps basketball set contains 132 cards. The cards in the set measure the standard size. Cards were issued in 12-card packs along with a stick of bubble gum. The player's name, team and position are at the bottom. The team name is wrapped around a basketball. Card backs are printed in red and black on gray card stock. All-Star selections are designated as

AS1 for first team selections and AS2 for second team selections and are denoted on the front of the player's regular card. Notable Rookie Cards in this set include Alex English, Reggie Theus, and Mychal Thompson.

	NRMT-MT	EXC	VG
COMPLETE SET (132)	75.00	34.00	9.50
COMMON CARD (1-132)	.30	.14	.04

☐ 1	George Gervin	5.00	1.65	.40
	San Antonio Spurs			
☐ 2	Mitch Kupchak	.40	.18	.05
	Washington Bullets			
☐ 3	Henry Bibby	.40	.18	.05
	Philadelphia 76ers			
☐ 4	Bob Gross	.40	.18	.05
	Portland Trail Blazers			
☐ 5	Dave Cowens	2.00	.90	.25
	Boston Celtics			
☐ 6	Dennis Johnson	1.50	.65	.19
	Seattle Supersonics			
☐ 7	Scott Wedman	.30	.14	.04
	Kansas City Kings			
☐ 8	Earl Monroe	1.25	.55	.16
	New York Knicks			
☐ 9	Mike Bantom	.30	.14	.04
	Indiana Pacers			
☐ 10	Kareem Abdul-Jabbar AS	10.00	4.50	1.25
	Los Angeles Lakers			
☐ 11	JoJo White	.60	.25	.08
	Golden State Warriors			
☐ 12	Spencer Haywood	.60	.25	.08
	Utah Jazz			
☐ 13	Kevin Porter	.40	.18	.05
	Detroit Pistons			
☐ 14	Bernard King	1.50	.65	.19
	New Jersey Nets			
☐ 15	Mike Newlin	.40	.18	.05
	Houston Rockets			
☐ 16	Sidney Wicks	.40	.18	.05
	San Diego Clippers			
☐ 17	Dan Issel	1.25	.55	.16
	Denver Nuggets			
☐ 18	Tom Henderson	.30	.14	.04
	Washington Bullets			
☐ 19	Jim Chones	.40	.18	.05
	Cleveland Cavaliers			
☐ 20	Julius Erving	12.00	5.50	1.50
	Philadelphia 76ers			
☐ 21	Brian Winters	.30	.14	.04
	Milwaukee Bucks			
☐ 22	Billy Paultz	.40	.18	.05
	San Antonio Spurs			
☐ 23	Cedric Maxwell	.40	.18	.05
	Boston Celtics			
☐ 24	Eddie Johnson	.30	.14	.04
	Atlanta Hawks			
☐ 25	Artis Gilmore	.75	.35	.09
	Chicago Bulls			
☐ 26	Maurice Lucas	.60	.25	.08
	Portland Trail Blazers			
☐ 27	Gus Williams	.60	.25	.08
	Seattle Supersonics			
☐ 28	Sam Lacey	.30	.14	.04
	Kansas City Kings			
☐ 29	Toby Knight	.30	.14	.04
	New York Knicks			
☐ 30	Paul Westphal AS1	1.00	.45	.13
	Phoenix Suns			
☐ 31	Alex English	8.00	3.60	1.00
	Indiana Pacers			
☐ 32	Gail Goodrich	.60	.25	.08
	Utah Jazz			
☐ 33	Caldwell Jones	.40	.18	.05
	Philadelphia 76ers			
☐ 34	Kevin Grevey	.30	.14	.04
	Washington Bullets			
☐ 35	Jamaal Wilkes	.60	.25	.08
	Los Angeles Lakers			
☐ 36	Sonny Parker	.30	.14	.04
	Golden State Warriors			
☐ 37	John Gianelli	.30	.14	.04
	New Jersey Nets			
☐ 38	John Long	.40	.18	.05
	Detroit Pistons			
☐ 39	George Johnson	.30	.14	.04
	New Jersey Nets			
☐ 40	Lloyd Free AS2	.60	.25	.08
	San Diego Clippers			
☐ 41	Rudy Tomjanovich	1.25	.55	.16
	Houston Rockets			
☐ 42	Foots Walker	.40	.18	.05
	Cleveland Cavaliers			
☐ 43	Dan Roundfield	.60	.25	.08
	Atlanta Hawks			
☐ 44	Reggie Theus	2.00	.90	.25
	Chicago Bulls			
☐ 45	Bill Walton	4.00	1.80	.50
	San Diego Clippers			
☐ 46	Fred Brown	.40	.18	.05
	Seattle Supersonics			
☐ 47	Darnell Hillman	.40	.18	.05
	Kansas City Kings			
☐ 48	Ray Williams	.40	.18	.05
	New York Knicks			
☐ 49	Larry Kenon	.40	.18	.05
	San Antonio Spurs			
☐ 50	David Thompson	2.00	.90	.25
	Denver Nuggets			
☐ 51	Billy Knight	.40	.18	.05
	Indiana Pacers			
☐ 52	Alvan Adams	.60	.25	.08
	Phoenix Suns			
☐ 53	Phil Smith	.30	.14	.04
	Golden State Warriors			
☐ 54	Adrian Dantley	1.25	.55	.16
	Los Angeles Lakers			
☐ 55	John Williamson	.40	.18	.05
	New Jersey Nets			
☐ 56	Campy Russell	.40	.18	.05
	Cleveland Cavaliers			
☐ 57	Armond Hill	.40	.18	.05
	Atlanta Hawks			
☐ 58	Bob Lanier	1.25	.55	.16
	Detroit Pistons			
☐ 59	Mickey Johnson	.30	.14	.04
	Chicago Bulls			
☐ 60	Pete Maravich	6.00	2.70	.75
	Utah Jazz			
☐ 61	Nick Weatherspoon	.30	.14	.04
	San Diego Clippers			
☐ 62	Robert Reid	.60	.25	.08
	Houston Rockets			
☐ 63	Mychal Thompson	2.00	.90	.25
	Portland Trail Blazers			
☐ 64	Doug Collins	1.00	.45	.13
	Philadelphia 76ers			
☐ 65	Wes Unseld	1.25	.55	.16
	Washington Bullets			
☐ 66	Jack Sikma	.60	.25	.08

	Seattle Supersonics			
☐ 67	Bobby Wilkerson	.30	.14	.04
	Denver Nuggets			
☐ 68	Bill Robinzine	.30	.14	.04
	Kansas City Kings			
☐ 69	Joe Meriweather	.30	.14	.04
	New York Knicks			
☐ 70	Marques Johnson AS1	.40	.18	.05
	Milwaukee Bucks			
☐ 71	Ricky Sobers	.30	.14	.04
	Indiana Pacers			
☐ 72	Clifford Ray	.40	.18	.05
	Golden State Warriors			
☐ 73	Tim Bassett	.30	.14	.04
	New Jersey Nets			
☐ 74	James Silas	.40	.18	.05
	San Antonio Spurs			
☐ 75	Bob McAdoo	.75	.35	.09
	Boston Celtics			
☐ 76	Austin Carr	.40	.18	.05
	Cleveland Cavaliers			
☐ 77	Don Ford	.30	.14	.04
	Los Angeles Lakers			
☐ 78	Steve Hawes	.30	.14	.04
	Atlanta Hawks			
☐ 79	Ron Brewer	.30	.14	.04
	Portland Trail Blazers			
☐ 80	Walter Davis	1.25	.55	.16
	Phoenix Suns			
☐ 81	Calvin Murphy	.75	.35	.09
	Houston Rockets			
☐ 82	Tom Boswell	.30	.14	.04
	Denver Nuggets			
☐ 83	Lonnie Shelton	.40	.18	.05
	Seattle Supersonics			
☐ 84	Terry Tyler	.30	.14	.04
	Detroit Pistons			
☐ 85	Randy Smith	.40	.18	.05
	San Diego Clippers			
☐ 86	Rich Kelley	.30	.14	.04
	Utah Jazz			
☐ 87	Otis Birdsong	.40	.18	.05
	Kansas City Kings			
☐ 88	Marvin Webster	.60	.25	.08
	New York Knicks			
☐ 89	Eric Money	.30	.14	.04
	Philadelphia 76ers			
☐ 90	Elvin Hayes AS1	2.00	.90	.25
	Washington Bullets			
☐ 91	Junior Bridgeman	.40	.18	.05
	Milwaukee Bucks			
☐ 92	Johnny Davis	.30	.14	.04
	Indiana Pacers			
☐ 93	Robert Parish	4.00	1.80	.50
	Golden State Warriors			
☐ 94	Eddie Jordan	.40	.18	.05
	New Jersey Nets			
☐ 95	Leonard Robinson	.40	.18	.05
	Phoenix Suns			
☐ 96	Rick Robey	.40	.18	.05
	Boston Celtics			
☐ 97	Norm Nixon	.60	.25	.08
	Los Angeles Lakers			
☐ 98	Mark Olberding	.30	.14	.04
	San Antonio Spurs			
☐ 99	Wilbur Holland	.30	.14	.04
	Utah Jazz			
☐ 100	Moses Malone AS1	4.00	1.80	.50
	Houston Rockets			
☐ 101	Checklist 1-132	2.00	.16	.04
☐ 102	Tom Owens	.30	.14	.04
	Portland Trail Blazers			
☐ 103	Phil Chenier	.40	.18	.05
	Washington Bullets			
☐ 104	John Johnson	.30	.14	.04
	Seattle Supersonics			
☐ 105	Darryl Dawkins	.75	.35	.09
	Philadelphia 76ers			
☐ 106	Charlie Scott	.40	.18	.05
	Denver Nuggets			
☐ 107	M.L. Carr	.40	.18	.05
	Detroit Pistons			
☐ 108	Phil Ford	2.00	.90	.25
	Kansas City Kings			
☐ 109	Swen Nater	.30	.14	.04
	San Diego Clippers			
☐ 110	Nate Archibald	1.25	.55	.16
	Boston Celtics			
☐ 111	Aaron James	.30	.14	.04
	Utah Jazz			
☐ 112	Jim Cleamons	.30	.14	.04
	New York Knicks			
☐ 113	James Edwards	.60	.25	.08
	Indiana Pacers			
☐ 114	Don Buse	.40	.18	.05
	Phoenix Suns			
☐ 115	Steve Mix	.40	.18	.05
	Philadelphia 76ers			
☐ 116	Charles Johnson	.30	.14	.04
	Washington Bullets			
☐ 117	Elmore Smith	.40	.18	.05
	Cleveland Cavaliers			
☐ 118	John Drew	.40	.18	.05
	Atlanta Hawks			
☐ 119	Lou Hudson	.40	.18	.05
	Los Angeles Lakers			
☐ 120	Rick Barry	2.00	.90	.25
	Houston Rockets			
☐ 121	Kent Benson	.30	.14	.04
	Milwaukee Bucks			
☐ 122	Mike Gale	.30	.14	.04
	San Antonio Spurs			
☐ 123	Jan Van Breda Kolff	.30	.14	.04
	New Jersey Nets			
☐ 124	Chris Ford	.40	.18	.05
	Boston Celtics			
☐ 125	George McGinnis	.60	.25	.08
	Denver Nuggets			
☐ 126	Leon Douglas	.30	.14	.04
	Detroit Pistons			
☐ 127	John Lucas	.40	.18	.05
	Golden State Warriors			
☐ 128	Kermit Washington	.40	.18	.05
	San Diego Clippers			
☐ 129	Lionel Hollins	.40	.18	.05
	Portland Trail Blazers			
☐ 130	Bob Dandridge AS2	.40	.18	.05
	Washington Bullets			
☐ 131	James McElroy	.30	.14	.04
	Utah Jazz			
☐ 132	Bobby Jones	1.50	.50	.12
	Philadelphia 76ers			

1980-81 Topps

The 1980-81 Topps basketball card set contains 264 different individual players (1 1/6" by 2 1/2") on 176 different panels of

three (2 1/2" by 3 1/2"). This set was issued in packs of eight cards with 36 packs per box. The cards come with three individual players per standard card. A perforation line segments each card into three players. In all, there are 176 different complete cards, however, the same player will be on more than one card. The variations stem from the fact that the cards in this set were printed on two separate sheets. In the checklist below, the first 88 cards comprise a complete set of all 264 players. The second 88 cards (89-176) provide a slight rearrangement of players within the card, but still contain the same 264 players. The cards are numbered within each series of 88 by any ordering of the left-hand player's number when the card is viewed from the back. In the checklist below, SD refers to a "Slam Dunk" star card. The letters AS in the checklist refer to an All-Star selection pictured on the front of the checklist card. There are a number of Team Leader (TL) cards which depict the team's leader in assists, scoring or rebounds. Prices given below are for complete panels, that is the typical way these cards are collected. Cards which have been separated into the three parts are relatively valueless. The key card in this set features Larry Bird, Julius Erving and Magic Johnson. It the Rookie Card for Bird and Magic. In addition to Bird and Magic, other noteworthy players making their first card appearance in this set include Bill Cartwright, Maurice Cheeks, Michael Cooper, Sidney Moncrief and Tree Rollins.

	NRMT-MT	EXC	VG
COMPLETE SET (176)	550.00	250.00	70.00
COMMON PANEL (1-176)	.30	.14	.04

☐ 1	3 Dan Roundfield AS 181 Julius Erving 258 Ron Brewer SD	5.00	2.30	.60
☐ 2	7 Moses Malone AS 185 Steve Mix 92 Robert Parish TL	1.50	.65	.19
☐ 3	12 Gus Williams AS 67 Geoff Huston 5 John Drew AS	.40	.18	.05
☐ 4	24 Steve Hawes 32 Nate Archibald TL 248 Elvin Hayes	1.00	.45	.13
☐ 5	29 Dan Roundfield 73 Dan Issel TL 152 Brian Winters	.60	.25	.08
☐ 6	34 Larry Bird 174 Julius Erving TL 139 Magic Johnson	400.00	180.00	50.00
☐ 7	36 Dave Cowens 186 Paul Westphal TL 142 Jamaal Wilkes	1.00	.45	.13
☐ 8	38 Pete Maravich 264 Lloyd Free SD 194 Dennis Johnson	3.00	1.35	.40
☐ 9	40 Rick Robey 234 Ad.Dantley TL 26 Eddie Johnson	.60	.25	.08
☐ 10	47 Scott May 196 K.Washington TL 177 Henry Bibby	.30	.14	.04
☐ 11	55 Don Ford 145 Quinn Buckner TL 138 Brad Holland	.30	.14	.04
☐ 12	58 Campy Russell 247 Kevin Grevey 52 Dave Robisch TL	.30	.14	.04
☐ 13	60 Foots Walker 113 Mick.Johnson TL 130 Bill Robinzine	.30	.14	.04
☐ 14	61 Austin Carr 8 Kareem Abdul-Jabbar AS 200 Calvin Natt	3.00	1.35	.40
☐ 15	63 Jim Cleamons 256 Robert Reid SD 22 Charlie Criss	.30	.14	.04
☐ 16	69 Tom LaGarde 215 Swen Nater TL 213 James Silas	.30	.14	.04
☐ 17	71 Jerome Whitehead 259 Artis Gilmore SD 184 Caldwell Jones	.60	.25	.08
☐ 18	74 John Roche TL 99 Clifford Ray 235 Ben Poquette TL	.30	.14	.04
☐ 19	75 Alex English 2 Marques Johnson AS 68 Jeff Judkins	2.00	.90	.25
☐ 20	82 Terry Tyler TL 21 Armond Hill TL 171 M.R. Richardson	.30	.14	.04
☐ 21	84 Kent Benson 212 John Shumate 229 Paul Westphal	.60	.25	.08
☐ 22	86 Phil Hubbard 93 Robert Parish TL 126 Tom Burleson	1.50	.65	.19
☐ 23	88 John Long 1 Julius Erving AS 49 Ricky Sobers	3.50	1.55	.45
☐ 24	90 Eric Money 57 Dave Robisch 254 Rick Robey SD	.30	.14	.04
☐ 25	95 Wayne Cooper 226 John Johnson TL 45 David Greenwood	.30	.14	.04
☐ 26	97 Robert Parish 187 Leon.Robinson TL 46 Dwight Jones	3.00	1.35	.40
☐ 27	98 Sonny Parker 197 Dave Twardzik TL 39 Cedric Maxwell	.30	.14	.04
☐ 28	105 Rick Barry 122 Otis Birdsong TL 48 John Mengelt	1.00	.45	.13
☐ 29	106 Allen Leavell 53 Foots Walker TL	.30	.14	.04

	223 Freeman Williams			
☐ 30	108 Calvin Murphy.........	.60	.25	.08
	176 Maur.Cheeks TL			
	87 Greg Kelser			
☐ 31	110 Robert Reid.............	.60	.25	.08
	243 Wes Unseld TL			
	50 Reggie Theus			
☐ 32	111 Rudy Tomjanovich..	.60	.25	.08
	13 Eddie Johnson AS			
	179 Doug Collins			
☐ 33	112 Mickey Johnson TL..	.30	.14	.04
	28 Wayne Rollins			
	15 M.R.Richardson AS			
☐ 34	115 Mike Bantom.............	.40	.18	.05
	6 Adrian Dantley AS			
	227 James Bailey			
☐ 35	116 Dudley Bradley.........	.30	.14	.04
	155 Eddie Jordan TL			
	239 Allan Bristow			
☐ 36	118 James Edwards.......	.30	.14	.04
	153 Mike Newlin TL			
	182 Lionel Hollins			
☐ 37	119 Mickey Johnson........	.30	.14	.04
	154 Geo.Johnson TL			
	193 Leonard Robinson			
☐ 38	120 Billy Knight	.60	.25	.08
	16 Paul Westphal AS			
	59 Randy Smith			
☐ 39	121 George McGinnis	.40	.18	.05
	83 Eric Money TL			
	65 Mike Bratz			
☐ 40	124 Phil Ford TL............	.30	.14	.04
	101 Phil Smith			
	224 Gus Williams TL			
☐ 41	127 Phil Ford	.30	.14	.04
	19 John Drew TL			
	209 Larry Kenon			
☐ 42	131 Scott Wedman.........	.40	.18	.05
	164 B.Cartwright TL			
	23 John Drew			
☐ 43	132 K.Abdul-Jabbar TL	3.00	1.35	.40
	56 Mike Mitchell			
	81 Terry Tyler TL			
☐ 44	135 K.Abdul-Jabbar......	5.00	2.30	.60
	79 David Thompson			
	216 Brian Taylor TL			
☐ 45	137 Michael Cooper.....	2.00	.90	.25
	103 Moses Malone TL			
	148 George Johnson			
☐ 46	140 Mark Landsberger.	1.50	.65	.19
	10 Bob Lanier AS			
	222 Bill Walton			
☐ 47	141 Norm Nixon	.30	.14	.04
	123 Sam Lacey TL			
	54 Kenny Carr			
☐ 48	143 Marq.Johnson TL	15.00	6.75	1.90
	30 Larry Bird TL			
	232 Jack Sikma			
☐ 49	146 Junior Bridgeman	15.00	6.75	1.90
	31 Larry Bird TL			
	198 Ron Brewer			
☐ 50	147 Quinn Buckner	3.00	1.35	.40
	133 K.Abdul-Jabbar TL			
	207 Mike Gale			
☐ 51	149 Marques Johnson.	3.50	1.55	.45
	262 Julius Erving SD			
	62 Abdul Jeelani			
☐ 52	151 Sidney Moncrief....	3.50	1.55	.45
	260 Lonnie Shelton SD			
	220 Paul Silas			
☐ 53	156 George Johnson	.40	.18	.05

	9 Bill Cartwright AS			
	199 Bob Gross			
☐ 54	158 Maurice Lucas	.40	.18	.05
	261 James Edwards SD			
	157 Eddie Jordan			
☐ 55	159 Mike Newlin	.30	.14	.04
	134 Norm Nixon TL			
	180 Darryl Dawkins			
☐ 56	160 Roger Phegley	.30	.14	.04
	206 James Silas TL			
	91 Terry Tyler UER			
	(First name spelled Jams)			
☐ 57	161 Cliff Robinson	.30	.14	.04
	51 Mike Mitchell TL			
	80 Bobby Wilkerson			
☐ 58	162 Jan V.Breda Kolff ...	.40	.18	.05
	204 George Gervin TL			
	117 Johnny Davis			
☐ 59	165 M.R.Richardson TL..	.30	.14	.04
	214 Lloyd Free TL			
	44 Artis Gilmore			
☐ 60	166 Bill Cartwright	1.50	.65	.19
	244 Kevin Porter TL			
	25 Armond Hill			
☐ 61	168 Toby Knight	.30	.14	.04
	14 Lloyd Free AS			
	240 Adrian Dantley			
☐ 62	169 Joe Meriweather	.40	.18	.05
	218 Lloyd Free			
	42 D.Greenwood TL			
☐ 63	170 Earl Monroe	.60	.25	.08
	27 James McElroy			
	85 Leon Douglas			
☐ 64	172 Marvin Webster	.40	.18	.05
	175 Caldwell Jones TL			
	129 Sam Lacey			
☐ 65	173 Ray Williams	.30	.14	.04
	94 John Lucas TL			
	202 Dave Twardzik			
☐ 66	178 Maurice Cheeks ..	15.00	6.75	1.90
	18 Magic Johnson AS			
	237 Ron Boone			
☐ 67	183 Bobby Jones............	.60	.25	.08
	37 Chris Ford			
	66 Joe Hassett			
☐ 68	189 Alvan Adams............	.60	.25	.08
	163 B.Cartwright TL			
	76 Dan Issel			
☐ 69	190 Don Buse.................	.40	.18	.05
	242 Elvin Hayes TL			
	35 M.L. Carr			
☐ 70	191 Walter Davis	.60	.25	.08
	11 George Gervin AS			
	136 Jim Chones			
☐ 71	192 Rich Kelley.............	1.00	.45	.13
	102 Moses Malone TL			
	64 Winford Boynes			
☐ 72	201 Tom Owens............	.30	.14	.04
	225 Jack Sikma TL			
	100 Purvis Short			
☐ 73	208 George Gervin	1.50	.65	.19
	72 Dan Issel TL			
	249 Mitch Kupchak			
☐ 74	217 Joe Bryant.............	1.50	.65	.19
	263 Bobby Jones SD			
	107 Moses Malone			
☐ 75	219 Swen Nater	.40	.18	.05
	17 Calvin Murphy AS			
	70 Rich.Washington			
☐ 76	221 Brian Taylor	.30	.14	.04
	253 John Shumate SD			

☐ 124	118 James Edwards... 32 Nate Archibald TL 248 Elvin Hayes	1.00	.45	.13
☐ 125	119 Mickey Johnson.... 72 Dan Issel TL 249 Mitch Kupchak	.60	.25	.08
☐ 126	120 Billy Knight ..... 104 Allen Leavell TL 96 John Lucas	.30	.14	.04
☐ 127	121 George McGinnis 10 Bob Lanier AS 222 Bill Walton	1.50	.65	.19
☐ 128	124 Phil Ford TL ...... 234 Adr.Dantley TL 26 Eddie Johnson	.40	.18	.05
☐ 129	127 Phil Ford .... 43 Reggie Theus TL 252 John Williamson	.40	.18	.05
☐ 130	131 Scott Wedman ... 244 Kevin Porter TL 25 Armond Hill	.30	.14	.04
☐ 131	132 K.Abdul-Jabbar TL 93 Robert Parish TL 126 Tom Burleson	4.00	1.80	.50
☐ 132	135 K.Abdul-Jabbar ... 253 John Shumate SD 167 Larry Demic	5.00	2.30	.60
☐ 133	137 Michael Cooper.... 212 John Shumate 229 Paul Westphal	1.00	.45	.13
☐ 134	140 Mark Landsberger. 214 Lloyd Free TL 44 Artis Gilmore	.40	.18	.05
☐ 135	141 Norm Nixon .... 242 Elvin Hayes TL 35 M.L. Carr	.40	.18	.05
☐ 136	143 Marq.Johnson TL.. 57 Dave Robisch 254 Rick Robey SD	.30	.14	.04
☐ 137	146 Junior Bridgeman 1 Julius Erving AS 49 Ricky Sobers	3.50	1.55	.45
☐ 138	147 Quinn Buckner ...... 2 Marques Johnson AS 68 Jeff Judkins	.40	.18	.05
☐ 139	149 Marques Johnson . 83 Eric Money TL 65 Mike Bratz	.30	.14	.04
☐ 140	151 Sidney Moncrief.. 133 K.Abdul-Jabbar TL 207 Mike Gale	5.00	2.30	.60
☐ 141	156 George Johnson ... 175 Caldw.Jones TL 129 Sam Lacey	.30	.14	.04
☐ 142	158 Maurice Lucas ... 262 Julius Erving SD 62 Abdul Jeelani	3.50	1.55	.45
☐ 143	159 Mike Newlin .... 243 Wes Unseld TL 50 Reggie Theus	.40	.18	.05
☐ 144	160 Roger Phegley ...... 145 Quinn Buckner TL 138 Brad Holland	.30	.14	.04
☐ 145	161 Cliff Robinson ...... 114 Johnny Davis TL 125 Otis Birdsong	.30	.14	.04
☐ 146	162 Jan V.Breda Kolff 174 Julius Erving TL 139 Magic Johnson	40.00	18.00	5.00
☐ 147	165 M.R.Richardson TL 185 Steve Mix	1.50	.65	.19
☐ 148	92 Robert Parish TL 166 Bill Cartwright..... 13 Eddie Johnson AS 179 Doug Collins	1.00	.45	.13
☐ 149	168 Toby Knight .... 188 Paul Westphal TL 77 Charlie Scott	.60	.25	.08
☐ 150	169 Joe Meriweather ... 196 K.Washington TL 177 Henry Bibby	.30	.14	.04
☐ 151	170 Earl Monroe .... 206 James Silas TL 91 Terry Tyler	.30	.14	.04
☐ 152	172 Marvin Webster .... 155 Eddie Jordan TL 239 Allan Bristow	.40	.18	.05
☐ 153	173 Ray Williams........ 225 Jack Sikma TL 100 Purvis Short	.30	.14	.04
☐ 154	178 Maurice Cheeks .. 11 George Gervin AS 136 Jim Chones	4.00	1.80	.50
☐ 155	183 Bobby Jones........ 99 Clifford Ray 235 Ben Poquette TL	.40	.18	.05
☐ 156	189 Alvan Adams........ 14 Lloyd Free AS 240 Adrian Dantley	.40	.18	.05
☐ 157	190 Don Buse .... 6 Adrian Dantley AS 227 James Bailey	.40	.18	.05
☐ 158	191 Walter Davis .... 9 Bill Cartwright AS 199 Bob Gross	.40	.18	.05
☐ 159	192 Rich Kelley .... 263 Bobby Jones SD 107 Moses Malone	1.50	.65	.19
☐ 160	201 Tom Owens.......... 134 Norm Nixon TL 180 Darryl Dawkins	.40	.18	.05
☐ 161	208 George Gervin..... 53 Foots Walker TL 223 Freeman Williams	1.50	.65	.19
☐ 162	217 Joe Bryant........... 8 K.Abdul-Jabbar AS 200 Calvin Natt	3.00	1.35	.40
☐ 163	219 Swen Nater .... 101 Phil Smith 224 Gus Williams TL	.30	.14	.04
☐ 164	221 Brian Taylor .... 256 Robert Reid SD 22 Charlie Criss	.30	.14	.04
☐ 165	228 Fred Brown .... 31 Larry Bird TL 198 Ron Brewer	15.00	6.75	1.90
☐ 166	230 John Johnson....... 163 B.Cartwright TL 76 Dan Issel	.60	.25	.08
☐ 167	231 Lonnie Shelton...... 205 Larry Kenon TL 203 Kermit Washington	.30	.14	.04
☐ 168	233 Gus Williams.......... 41 Reggie Theus TL 128 Reggie King	.40	.18	.05
☐ 169	236 Allan Bristow TL.... 260 Lonnie Shelton SD 220 Paul Silas	.30	.14	.04
☐ 170	238 Tom Boswell .... 27 James McElroy 85 Leon Douglas	.30	.14	.04
☐ 171	241 Ben Poquette	.60	.25	.08

		NRMT-MT	EXC	VG
	176 Maurice Cheeks TL			
	87 Greg Kelser			
☐ 172	245 Greg Ballard	.60	.25	.08
	4 Walter Davis AS			
	33 Nate Archibald			
☐ 173	246 Bob Dandridge	.30	.14	.04
	19 John Drew TL			
	209 Larry Kenon			
☐ 174	250 Kevin Porter	.30	.14	.04
	20 Dan Roundfield TL			
	211 Kevin Restani			
☐ 175	251 Wes Unseld	.60	.25	.08
	67 Geoff Huston			
	5 John Drew AS			
☐ 176	257 Elvin Hayes SD	5.00	2.30	.60
	181 Julius Erving			
	258 Ron Brewer SD			

1981-82 Topps

The 1981-82 Topps basketball card set contains a total of 198 cards that were issued in 10-card, 30-cent wax packs with 36 packs per box. The cards in the set measure the standard 2 1/2" by 3 1/2". These cards are numbered depending upon the regional distribution used in the issue. A 66-card national set was issued to all parts of the country, however, subsets of 44 cards each were issued in the East, Midwest and West. Card numbers over 66 are prefaced on the card by the region in which they were distributed, e.g., East 96. The cards feature the Topps logo in the frame line and a quarter-round sunburst in the lower left-hand corner which lists the name, position and team of the player depicted. Cards 44-66 are Team Leader (TL) cards picturing each team's statistical leaders. The back, printed in orange and brown on gray stock, features standard Topps biographical data and career statistics. There are a number of Super Action (SA) cards in the set. Rookie Cards include Joe Barry Carroll, Mike Dunleavy, Mike Gminski, Darrell Griffith, Ernie Grunfeld, Vinnie Johnson, Bill Laimbeer, Rick Mahorn, Kevin McHale, Jim Paxson and Larry Smith. The card numbering sequence is alphabetical within team within each series. This was Topps' last basketball card issue until 1992.

		NRMT-MT	EXC	VG
	COMPLETE SET (198)	80.00	36.00	10.00
	COMMON CARD (1-66)	.10	.05	.01
	COMMON CARD (E67-E110)	.15	.07	.02
	COMMON CARD (MW67-MW110)	.15	.07	.02
	COMMON CARD (W67-W110)	.15	.07	.02
☐ 1	John Drew	.15	.07	.02
	Atlanta Hawks			
☐ 2	Dan Roundfield	.15	.07	.02
	Atlanta Hawks			
☐ 3	Nate Archibald	.60	.25	.08
	Boston Celtics			
☐ 4	Larry Bird	25.00	11.50	3.10
	Boston Celtics			
☐ 5	Cedric Maxwell	.15	.07	.02
	Boston Celtics			
☐ 6	Robert Parish	2.00	.90	.25
	Boston Celtics			
☐ 7	Artis Gilmore	.60	.25	.08
	Chicago Bulls			
☐ 8	Ricky Sobers	.10	.05	.01
	Chicago Bulls			
☐ 9	Mike Mitchell	.15	.07	.02
	Cleveland Cavaliers			
☐ 10	Tom LaGarde	.10	.05	.01
	Dallas Mavericks			
☐ 11	Dan Issel	.75	.35	.09
	Denver Nuggets			
☐ 12	David Thompson	.50	.23	.06
	Denver Nuggets			
☐ 13	Lloyd Free	.20	.09	.03
	Golden State Warriors			
☐ 14	Moses Malone	2.00	.90	.25
	Houston Rockets			
☐ 15	Calvin Murphy	.20	.09	.03
	Houston Rockets			
☐ 16	Johnny Davis	.10	.05	.01
	Indiana Pacers			
☐ 17	Otis Birdsong	.20	.09	.03
	Milwaukee Bucks			
☐ 18	Phil Ford	.15	.07	.02
	Kansas City Kings			
☐ 19	Scott Wedman	.10	.05	.01
	Cleveland Cavaliers			
☐ 20	Kareem Abdul-Jabbar	4.00	1.80	.50
	Los Angeles Lakers			
☐ 21	Magic Johnson	20.00	9.00	2.50
	Los Angeles Lakers			
☐ 22	Norm Nixon	.20	.09	.03
	Los Angeles Lakers			
☐ 23	Jamaal Wilkes	.20	.09	.03
	Los Angeles Lakers			
☐ 24	Marques Johnson	.20	.09	.03
	Milwaukee Bucks			
☐ 25	Bob Lanier	.75	.35	.09
	Milwaukee Bucks			
☐ 26	Bill Cartwright	.50	.23	.06
	New York Knicks			
☐ 27	Michael Ray Richardson	.15	.07	.02
	New York Knicks			
☐ 28	Ray Williams	.15	.07	.02
	New York Knicks			
☐ 29	Darryl Dawkins	.20	.09	.03
	Philadelphia 76ers			
☐ 30	Julius Erving	4.00	1.80	.50
	Philadelphia 76ers			
☐ 31	Lionel Hollins	.10	.05	.01
	Philadelphia 76ers			
☐ 32	Bobby Jones	.25	.11	.03
	Philadelphia 76ers			

☐ 33 Walter Davis	.50	.23	.06
Phoenix Suns			
☐ 34 Dennis Johnson	.50	.23	.06
Phoenix Suns			
☐ 35 Leonard Robinson	.20	.09	.03
Phoenix Suns			
☐ 36 Mychal Thompson	.20	.09	.03
Portland Trail Blazers			
☐ 37 George Gervin	1.25	.55	.16
San Antonio Spurs			
☐ 38 Swen Nater	.10	.05	.01
San Diego Clippers			
☐ 39 Jack Sikma	.20	.09	.03
Seattle Supersonics			
☐ 40 Adrian Dantley	.60	.25	.08
Utah Jazz			
☐ 41 Darrell Griffith	1.00	.45	.13
Utah Jazz			
☐ 42 Elvin Hayes	1.00	.45	.13
Houston Rockets			
☐ 43 Fred Brown	.25	.11	.03
Seattle Supersonics			
☐ 44 Atlanta Hawks TL	.15	.07	.02
John Drew			
Dan Roundfield			
Eddie Johnson			
☐ 45 Boston Celtics TL	2.00	.90	.25
Larry Bird			
Larry Bird			
Nate Archibald			
☐ 46 Chicago Bulls TL	.25	.11	.03
Reggie Theus			
Artis Gilmore			
Reggie Theus			
☐ 47 Cleveland Cavs TL	.15	.07	.02
Mike Mitchell			
Kenny Carr			
Mike Bratz			
☐ 48 Dallas Mavericks TL	.15	.07	.02
Jim Spanarkel			
Tom LaGarde			
Brad Davis			
☐ 49 Denver Nuggets TL	.25	.11	.03
David Thompson			
Dan Issel			
Kenny Higgs			
☐ 50 Detroit Pistons TL	.15	.07	.02
John Long			
Phil Hubbard			
Ron Lee			
☐ 51 Golden State TL	.25	.11	.03
Lloyd Free			
Larry Smith			
John Lucas			
☐ 52 Houston Rockets TL	.40	.18	.05
Moses Malone			
Moses Malone			
Allen Leavell			
☐ 53 Indiana Pacers TL	.20	.09	.03
Billy Knight			
James Edwards			
Johnny Davis			
☐ 54 Kansas City Kings TL	.15	.07	.02
Otis Birdsong			
Reggie King			
Phil Ford			
☐ 55 Los Angeles Lakers TL.	1.00	.45	.13
Kareem Abdul-Jabbar			
Kareem Abdul-Jabbar			
Norm Nixon			
☐ 56 Milwaukee Bucks TL	.25	.11	.03
Marques Johnson			
Mickey Johnson			
Quinn Buckner			
☐ 57 New Jersey Nets TL	.15	.07	.02
Mike Newlin			
Maurice Lucas			
Mike Newlin			
☐ 58 New York Knicks TL	.20	.09	.03
Bill Cartwright			
Bill Cartwright			
M.R. Richardson			
☐ 59 Philadelphia 76ers TL	1.25	.55	.16
Julius Erving			
Caldwell Jones			
Maurice Cheeks			
☐ 60 Phoenix Suns TL	.20	.09	.03
Truck Robinson			
Truck Robinson			
Alvan Adams			
☐ 61 Portland Blazers TL	.15	.07	.02
Jim Paxson			
Mychal Thompson			
Kermit Washington			
Kelvin Ransey			
☐ 62 San Antonio Spurs TL	.20	.09	.03
George Gervin			
Dave Corzine			
Johnny Moore			
☐ 63 San Diego Clippers TL	.15	.07	.02
Freeman Williams			
Swen Nater			
Brian Taylor			
☐ 64 Seattle Sonics TL	.25	.11	.03
Jack Sikma			
Jack Sikma			
Vinnie Johnson			
☐ 65 Utah Jazz TL	.25	.11	.03
Adrian Dantley			
Ben Poquette			
Allan Bristow			
☐ 66 Washington Bullets TL	.25	.11	.03
Elvin Hayes			
Elvin Hayes			
Kevin Porter			
☐ E67 Charlie Criss	.20	.09	.03
Atlanta Hawks			
☐ E68 Eddie Johnson	.15	.07	.02
Atlanta Hawks			
☐ E69 Wes Matthews	.15	.07	.02
Atlanta Hawks			
☐ E70 Tom McMillen	.40	.18	.05
Atlanta Hawks			
☐ E71 Tree Rollins	.40	.18	.05
Atlanta Hawks			
☐ E72 M.L. Carr	.25	.11	.03
Boston Celtics			
☐ E73 Chris Ford	.15	.07	.02
Boston Celtics			
☐ E74 Gerald Henderson	.40	.18	.05
Boston Celtics			
☐ E75 Kevin McHale	20.00	9.00	2.50
Boston Celtics			
☐ E76 Rick Robey	.20	.09	.03
Boston Celtics			
☐ E77 Darwin Cook	.15	.07	.02
Milwaukee Bucks			
☐ E78 Mike Gminski	.75	.35	.09
Milwaukee Bucks			
☐ E79 Maurice Lucas	.25	.11	.03
Milwaukee Bucks			
☐ E80 Mike Newlin	.20	.09	.03

New York Knicks				
☐ E81 Mike O'Koren	.25	.11	.03	
Milwaukee Bucks				
☐ E82 Steve Hawes	.15	.07	.02	
Atlanta Hawks				
☐ E83 Foots Walker	.20	.09	.03	
Milwaukee Bucks				
☐ E84 Campy Russell	.20	.09	.03	
New York Knicks				
☐ E85 DeWayne Scales	.15	.07	.02	
New York Knicks				
☐ E86 Randy Smith	.20	.09	.03	
New York Knicks				
☐ E87 Marvin Webster	.25	.11	.03	
New York Knicks				
☐ E88 Sly Williams	.15	.07	.02	
New York Knicks				
☐ E89 Mike Woodson	.25	.11	.03	
Milwaukee Bucks				
☐ E90 Maurice Cheeks	1.50	.65	.19	
Philadelphia 76ers				
☐ E91 Caldwell Jones	.25	.11	.03	
Philadelphia 76ers				
☐ E92 Steve Mix	.20	.09	.03	
Philadelphia 76ers				
☐ E93A Checklist 1-110 ERR	2.00	.90	.25	
(WEST above card number)				
☐ E93B Checklist 1-110 COR	1.00	.45	.13	
Washington Bullets				
☐ E94 Greg Ballard	.15	.07	.02	
Washington Bullets				
☐ E95 Don Collins	.15	.07	.02	
Washington Bullets				
☐ E96 Kevin Grevey	.20	.09	.03	
Washington Bullets				
☐ E97 Mitch Kupchak	.20	.09	.03	
Washington Bullets				
☐ E98 Rick Mahorn	.75	.35	.09	
Washington Bullets				
☐ E99 Kevin Porter	.20	.09	.03	
Washington Bullets				
☐ E100 Nate Archibald SA	.20	.09	.03	
Boston Celtics				
☐ E101 Larry Bird SA	12.00	5.50	1.50	
Boston Celtics				
☐ E102 Bill Cartwright SA	.15	.07	.02	
New York Knicks				
☐ E103 Darryl Dawkins SA	.25	.11	.03	
Philadelphia 76ers				
☐ E104 Julius Erving SA	2.50	1.15	.30	
Philadelphia 76ers				
☐ E105 Kevin Porter SA	.20	.09	.03	
Washington Bullets				
☐ E106 Bobby Jones SA	.25	.11	.03	
Philadelphia 76ers				
☐ E107 Cedric Maxwell SA	.20	.09	.03	
Boston Celtics				
☐ E108 Robert Parish SA	1.00	.45	.13	
Boston Celtics				
☐ E109 M.R.Richardson SA	.20	.09	.03	
New York Knicks				
☐ E110 Dan Roundfield SA	.20	.09	.03	
Atlanta Hawks				
☐ MW67 David Greenwood	.20	.09	.03	
Chicago Bulls				
☐ MW68 Dwight Jones	.15	.07	.02	
Chicago Bulls				
☐ MW69 Reggie Theus	.25	.11	.03	
Chicago Bulls				
☐ MW70 Bobby Wilkerson	.15	.07	.02	
Cleveland Cavaliers				
☐ MW71 Mike Bratz	.15	.07	.02	

Cleveland Cavaliers			
☐ MW72 Kenny Carr	.15	.07	.02
Cleveland Cavaliers			
☐ MW73 Geoff Huston	.15	.07	.02
Cleveland Cavaliers			
☐ MW74 Bill Laimbeer	4.00	1.80	.50
Cleveland Cavaliers			
☐ MW75 Roger Phegley	.15	.07	.02
Cleveland Cavaliers			
☐ MW76 Checklist 1-110	1.00	.45	.13
☐ MW77 Abdul Jeelani	.15	.07	.02
Dallas Mavericks			
☐ MW78 Bill Robinzine	.15	.07	.02
Dallas Mavericks			
☐ MW79 Jim Spanarkel	.15	.07	.02
Dallas Mavericks			
☐ MW80 Kent Benson	.20	.09	.03
Detroit Pistons			
☐ MW81 Keith Herron	.15	.07	.02
Detroit Pistons			
☐ MW82 Phil Hubbard	.15	.07	.02
Detroit Pistons			
☐ MW83 John Long	.15	.07	.02
Detroit Pistons			
☐ MW84 Terry Tyler	.15	.07	.02
Detroit Pistons			
☐ MW85 Mike Dunleavy	1.50	.65	.19
Houston Rockets			
☐ MW86 Tom Henderson	.15	.07	.02
Houston Rockets			
☐ MW87 Billy Paultz	.20	.09	.03
Houston Rockets			
☐ MW88 Robert Reid	.15	.07	.02
Houston Rockets			
☐ MW89 Mike Bantom	.15	.07	.02
Indiana Pacers			
☐ MW90 James Edwards	.25	.11	.03
Cleveland Cavaliers			
☐ MW91 Billy Knight	.20	.09	.03
Indiana Pacers			
☐ MW92 George McGinnis	.25	.11	.03
Indiana Pacers			
☐ MW93 Louis Orr	.15	.07	.02
Indiana Pacers			
☐ MW94 Ernie Grunfeld	.40	.18	.05
Kansas City Kings			
☐ MW95 Reggie King	.15	.07	.02
Kansas City Kings			
☐ MW96 Sam Lacey	.15	.07	.02
Kansas City Kings			
☐ MW97 Junior Bridgeman	.20	.09	.03
Milwaukee Bucks			
☐ MW98 Mickey Johnson	.20	.09	.03
Milwaukee Bucks			
☐ MW99 Sidney Moncrief	1.25	.55	.16
Milwaukee Bucks			
☐ MW100 Brian Winters	.25	.11	.03
Milwaukee Bucks			
☐ MW101 Dave Corzine	.15	.07	.02
San Antonio Spurs			
☐ MW102 Paul Griffin	.15	.07	.02
San Antonio Spurs			
☐ MW103 Johnny Moore	.20	.09	.03
San Antonio Spurs			
☐ MW104 Mark Olberding	.15	.07	.02
San Antonio Spurs			
☐ MW105 James Silas	.20	.09	.03
Cleveland Cavaliers			
☐ MW106 George Gervin SA	.75	.35	.09
San Antonio Spurs			
☐ MW107 Artis Gilmore SA	.25	.11	.03

Chicago Bulls
- ☐ MW108 Marques Johnson SA .20 .09 .03
  Milwaukee Bucks
- ☐ MW109 Bob Lanier SA .... .50 .23 .06
  Milwaukee Bucks
- ☐ MW110 Moses Malone SA 1.00 .45 .13
  Houston Rockets
- ☐ W67 T.R. Dunn .... .15 .07 .02
  Denver Nuggets
- ☐ W68 Alex English .... 1.50 .65 .19
  Denver Nuggets
- ☐ W69 Billy McKinney .... .20 .09 .03
  Denver Nuggets
- ☐ W70 Dave Robisch .... .20 .09 .03
  Denver Nuggets
- ☐ W71 Joe Barry Carroll......... .50 .23 .06
  Golden State Warriors
- ☐ W72 Bernard King .... 1.00 .45 .13
  Golden State Warriors
- ☐ W73 Sonny Parker.............. .15 .07 .02
  Golden State Warriors
- ☐ W74 Purvis Short .... .20 .09 .03
  Golden State Warriors
- ☐ W75 Larry Smith .... .50 .23 .06
  Golden State Warriors
- ☐ W76 Jim Chones .... .20 .09 .03
  Los Angeles Lakers
- ☐ W77 Michael Cooper .... 1.00 .45 .13
  Los Angeles Lakers
- ☐ W78 Mark Landsberger ... .15 .07 .02
  Los Angeles Lakers
- ☐ W79 Alvan Adams .... .25 .11 .03
  Phoenix Suns
- ☐ W80 Jeff Cook .... .15 .07 .02
  Phoenix Suns
- ☐ W81 Rich Kelley .... .15 .07 .02
  Phoenix Suns
- ☐ W82 Kyle Macy .... .50 .23 .06
  Phoenix Suns
- ☐ W83 Billy Ray Bates.......... .15 .07 .02
  Portland Trail Blazers
- ☐ W84 Bob Gross .... .20 .09 .03
  Portland Trail Blazers
- ☐ W85 Calvin Natt............... .20 .09 .03
  Portland Trail Blazers
- ☐ W86 Lonnie Shelton .... .20 .09 .03
  Seattle Supersonics
- ☐ W87 Jim Paxson .... .75 .35 .09
  Portland Trail Blazers
- ☐ W88 Kelvin Ransey........... .15 .07 .02
  Portland Trail Blazers
- ☐ W89 Kermit Washington .... .20 .09 .03
  Portland Trail Blazers
- ☐ W90 Henry Bibby .... .20 .09 .03
  San Diego Clippers
- ☐ W91 Michael Brooks........... .15 .07 .02
  San Diego Clippers
- ☐ W92 Joe Bryant .... .15 .07 .02
  San Diego Clippers
- ☐ W93 Phil Smith.................. .15 .07 .02
  San Diego Clippers
- ☐ W94 Brian Taylor .... .15 .07 .02
  San Diego Clippers
- ☐ W95 Freeman Williams .... .20 .09 .03
  San Diego Clippers
- ☐ W96 James Bailey .... .15 .07 .02
  Seattle Supersonics
- ☐ W97 Checklist 1-110 ...... 1.00 .45 .13
- ☐ W98 John Johnson............. .15 .07 .02
  Seattle Supersonics
- ☐ W99 Vinnie Johnson......... 1.50 .65 .19

Seattle Supersonics
- ☐ W100 Wally Walker .... .25 .11 .03
  Seattle Supersonics
- ☐ W101 Paul Westphal .... .25 .11 .03
  Seattle Supersonics
- ☐ W102 Allan Bristow .... .25 .11 .03
  Utah Jazz
- ☐ W103 Wayne Cooper........... .15 .07 .02
  Utah Jazz
- ☐ W104 Carl Nicks................. .15 .07 .02
  Utah Jazz
- ☐ W105 Ben Poquette............. .15 .07 .02
  Utah Jazz
- ☐ W106 Kareem Abdul-Jabbar SA 2.50 1.15 .30
  Los Angeles Lakers
- ☐ W107 Dan Issel SA.............. .50 .23 .06
  Denver Nuggets
- ☐ W108 Dennis Johnson SA.. .20 .09 .03
  Phoenix Suns
- ☐ W109 Magic Johnson SA 10.00 4.50 1.25
  Los Angeles Lakers
- ☐ W110 Jack Sikma SA.......... .20 .09 .03
  Seattle Supersonics

1992-93 Topps

*The complete 1992-93 Topps basketball
set consists of 396 cards, issued in two
198-card series. Each card measures the
standard size (2 1/2" by 3 1/2"). Cards were
issued in 15-card plastic wrap packs (suggested retail 79 cents, 36 packs per box),
18-card mini-jumbo packs, 45-card retail
packs and 41-card magazine jumbo packs.
In addition, factory sets were also released.
On a white card face, the fronts display
color action player photos framed by two-
color border stripes. The player's name and
team name appear in two different colored
bars across the bottom of the picture. In
addition to a color close-up photo, the horizontal backs have biography on a light blue
panel as well as statistics and brief player
profile on a yellow panel. Most Rookie
Cards have the gold-foil "92 Draft Pix"
emblem on their card fronts. Topical subsets included are Highlight (2-4), All-Star
(100-126), 50 Point Club (199-215), and 20
Assist Club (216-224). The cards are numbered on the back in a basketball icon at
the upper left corner. Rookie Cards include
LaPhonso Ellis, Tom Gugliotta, Robert
Horry, Christian Laettner, Alonzo Mourning,
Shaquille O'Neal, Latrell Sprewell, Clarence
Weatherspoon and Walt Williams.*

	MINT	NRMT	EXC
COMPLETE SET (396)	12.00	5.50	1.50
COMPLETE FACT.SET (408)	15.00	6.75	1.90
COMPLETE SERIES 1 (198)	4.00	1.80	.50
COMPLETE SERIES 2 (198)	8.00	3.60	1.00
COMMON CARD (1-396)	.05	.02	.01

☐ 1	Larry Bird	.50	.23	.06
	Boston Celtics			
☐ 2	Magic Johnson HL	.15	.07	.02
	Earvin's Magical Moment 2/9/92 Los Angeles Lakers			
☐ 3	Michael Jordan HL	1.00	.45	.13
	Michael Lights It Up 6/3/92 Chicago Bulls			
☐ 4	David Robinson HL	.15	.07	.02
	Admiral Ranks High In Five 4/19/92 San Antonio Spurs			
☐ 5	Johnny Newman	.05	.02	.01
	Charlotte Hornets			
☐ 6	Mike Iuzzolino	.05	.02	.01
	Dallas Mavericks			
☐ 7	Ken Norman	.05	.02	.01
	Los Angeles Clippers			
☐ 8	Chris Jackson	.06	.03	.01
	Denver Nuggets			
☐ 9	Duane Ferrell	.05	.02	.01
	Atlanta Hawks			
☐ 10	Sean Elliott	.06	.03	.01
	San Antonio Spurs			
☐ 11	Bernard King	.08	.04	.01
	Washington Bullets			
☐ 12	Armon Gilliam	.05	.02	.01
	Philadelphia 76ers			
☐ 13	Reggie Williams	.05	.02	.01
	Denver Nuggets			
☐ 14	Steve Kerr	.05	.02	.01
	Cleveland Cavaliers			
☐ 15	Anthony Bowie	.05	.02	.01
	Orlando Magic			
☐ 16	Alton Lister	.05	.02	.01
	Golden State Warriors			
☐ 17	Dee Brown	.06	.03	.01
	Boston Celtics			
☐ 18	Tom Chambers	.06	.03	.01
	Phoenix Suns			
☐ 19	Otis Thorpe	.06	.03	.01
	Houston Rockets			
☐ 20	Karl Malone	.15	.07	.02
	Utah Jazz			
☐ 21	Kenny Gattison	.05	.02	.01
	Charlotte Hornets			
☐ 22	Lionel Simmons UER	.05	.02	.01
	(Misspelled Lionell on card front) Sacramento Kings			
☐ 23	Vern Fleming	.05	.02	.01
	Indiana Pacers			
☐ 24	John Paxson	.05	.02	.01
	Chicago Bulls			
☐ 25	Mitch Richmond	.10	.05	.01
	Sacramento Kings			
☐ 26	Danny Schayes	.05	.02	.01
	Milwaukee Bucks			
☐ 27	Derrick McKey	.06	.03	.01
	Seattle Supersonics			
☐ 28	Mark Randall	.05	.02	.01
	Minnesota Timberwolves			
☐ 29	Bill Laimbeer	.06	.03	.01
	Detroit Pistons			
☐ 30	Chris Morris	.05	.02	.01
	New Jersey Nets			
☐ 31	Alec Kessler	.05	.02	.01
	Miami Heat			
☐ 32	Vlade Divac	.08	.04	.01
	Los Angeles Lakers			
☐ 33	Rick Fox	.05	.02	.01
	Boston Celtics			
☐ 34	Charles Shackleford	.05	.02	.01
	Philadelphia 76ers			
☐ 35	Dominique Wilkins	.10	.05	.01
	Atlanta Hawks			
☐ 36	Sleepy Floyd	.05	.02	.01
	Houston Rockets			
☐ 37	Doug West	.05	.02	.01
	Minnesota Timberwolves			
☐ 38	Pete Chilcutt	.05	.02	.01
	Sacramento Kings			
☐ 39	Orlando Woolridge	.05	.02	.01
	Detroit Pistons			
☐ 40	Eric Leckner	.05	.02	.01
	Charlotte Hornets			
☐ 41	Joe Kleine	.05	.02	.01
	Boston Celtics			
☐ 42	Scott Skiles	.05	.02	.01
	Orlando Magic			
☐ 43	Jerrod Mustaf	.05	.02	.01
	Phoenix Suns			
☐ 44	John Starks	.08	.04	.01
	New York Knicks			
☐ 45	Sedale Threatt	.05	.02	.01
	Los Angeles Lakers			
☐ 46	Doug Smith	.05	.02	.01
	Dallas Mavericks			
☐ 47	Byron Scott	.06	.03	.01
	Los Angeles Lakers			
☐ 48	Willie Anderson	.05	.02	.01
	San Antonio Spurs			
☐ 49	David Benoit	.05	.02	.01
	Utah Jazz			
☐ 50	Scott Hastings	.05	.02	.01
	Denver Nuggets			
☐ 51	Terry Porter	.06	.03	.01
	Portland Trail Blazers			
☐ 52	Sidney Green	.05	.02	.01
	San Antonio Spurs			
☐ 53	Danny Young	.05	.02	.01
	Los Angeles Clippers			
☐ 54	Magic Johnson	.30	.14	.04
	Los Angeles Lakers			
☐ 55	Brian Williams	.05	.02	.01
	Orlando Magic			
☐ 56	Randy Wittman	.05	.02	.01
	Indiana Pacers			
☐ 57	Kevin McHale	.08	.04	.01
	Boston Celtics			
☐ 58	Dana Barros	.08	.04	.01
	Seattle Supersonics			
☐ 59	Thurl Bailey	.05	.02	.01
	Minnesota Timberwolves			
☐ 60	Kevin Duckworth	.05	.02	.01
	Portland Trail Blazers			
☐ 61	John Williams	.06	.03	.01
	Cleveland Cavaliers			
☐ 62	Willie Burton	.05	.02	.01
	Miami Heat			
☐ 63	Spud Webb	.06	.03	.01
	Sacramento Kings			
☐ 64	Detlef Schrempf	.08	.04	.01

	Indiana Pacers			
☐ 65	Sherman Douglas	.05	.02	.01
	Boston Celtics			
☐ 66	Patrick Ewing	.15	.07	.02
	New York Knicks			
☐ 67	Michael Adams	.05	.02	.01
	Washington Bullets			
☐ 68	Vernon Maxwell	.05	.02	.01
	Houston Rockets			
☐ 69	Terrell Brandon	.05	.02	.01
	Cleveland Cavaliers			
☐ 70	Terry Catledge	.05	.02	.01
	Orlando Magic			
☐ 71	Mark Eaton	.05	.02	.01
	Utah Jazz			
☐ 72	Tony Smith	.05	.02	.01
	Los Angeles Lakers			
☐ 73	B.J. Armstrong	.05	.02	.01
	Chicago Bulls			
☐ 74	Moses Malone	.10	.05	.01
	Milwaukee Bucks			
☐ 75	Anthony Bonner	.05	.02	.01
	Sacramento Kings			
☐ 76	George McCloud	.05	.02	.01
	Indiana Pacers			
☐ 77	Glen Rice	.08	.04	.01
	Miami Heat			
☐ 78	Jon Koncak	.05	.02	.01
	Atlanta Hawks			
☐ 79	Michael Cage	.05	.02	.01
	Seattle Supersonics			
☐ 80	Ron Harper	.06	.03	.01
	Los Angeles Clippers			
☐ 81	Tom Tolbert	.05	.02	.01
	Golden State Warriors			
☐ 82	Brad Sellers	.05	.02	.01
	Detroit Pistons			
☐ 83	Winston Garland	.05	.02	.01
	Denver Nuggets			
☐ 84	Negele Knight	.05	.02	.01
	Phoenix Suns			
☐ 85	Ricky Pierce	.06	.03	.01
	Seattle Supersonics			
☐ 86	Mark Aguirre	.06	.03	.01
	Detroit Pistons			
☐ 87	Ron Anderson	.05	.02	.01
	Philadelphia 76ers			
☐ 88	Loy Vaught	.06	.03	.01
	Los Angeles Clippers			
☐ 89	Luc Longley	.05	.02	.01
	Minnesota Timberwolves			
☐ 90	Jerry Reynolds	.05	.02	.01
	Orlando Magic			
☐ 91	Terry Cummings	.06	.03	.01
	San Antonio Spurs			
☐ 92	Rony Seikaly	.05	.02	.01
	Miami Heat			
☐ 93	Derek Harper	.06	.03	.01
	Dallas Mavericks			
☐ 94	Cliff Robinson	.08	.04	.01
	Portland Trail Blazers			
☐ 95	Kenny Anderson	.15	.07	.02
	New Jersey Nets			
☐ 96	Chris Gatling	.05	.02	.01
	Golden State Warriors			
☐ 97	Stacey Augmon	.08	.04	.01
	Atlanta Hawks			
☐ 98	Chris Corchiani	.05	.02	.01
	Orlando Magic			
☐ 99	Pervis Ellison	.05	.02	.01
	Washington Bullets			
☐ 100	Larry Bird AS	.25	.11	.03
	Boston Celtics			
☐ 101	John Stockton AS UER	.08	.04	.01
	(Listed as Center			
	on card back)			
	Phoenix Suns			
☐ 102	Clyde Drexler AS	.08	.04	.01
	Portland Trail Blazers			
☐ 103	Scottie Pippen AS	.08	.04	.01
	Chicago Bulls			
☐ 104	Reggie Lewis AS	.05	.02	.01
	Boston Celtics			
☐ 105	Hakeem Olajuwon AS	.20	.09	.03
	Houston Rockets			
☐ 106	David Robinson AS	.15	.07	.02
	San Antonio Spurs			
☐ 107	Charles Barkley AS	.15	.07	.02
	Philadelphia 76ers			
☐ 108	James Worthy AS	.05	.02	.01
	Los Angeles Lakers			
☐ 109	Kevin Willis AS	.05	.02	.01
	Atlanta Hawks			
☐ 110	Dikembe Mutombo AS	.08	.04	.01
	Denver Nuggets			
☐ 111	Joe Dumars AS	.06	.03	.01
	Detroit Pistons			
☐ 112	Jeff Hornacek AS UER	.05	.02	.01
	(5 or 7 shots should			
	be 5 of 7 shots)			
	Phoenix Suns			
☐ 113	Mark Price AS	.05	.02	.01
	Cleveland Cavaliers			
☐ 114	Michael Adams AS	.05	.02	.01
	Washington Bullets			
☐ 115	Michael Jordan AS	1.00	.45	.13
	Chicago Bulls			
☐ 116	Brad Daugherty AS	.05	.02	.01
	Cleveland Cavaliers			
☐ 117	Dennis Rodman AS	.06	.03	.01
	Detroit Pistons			
☐ 118	Isiah Thomas AS	.06	.03	.01
	Detroit Pistons			
☐ 119	Tim Hardaway AS	.05	.02	.01
	Golden State Warriors			
☐ 120	Chris Mullin AS	.05	.02	.01
	Golden State Warriors			
☐ 121	Patrick Ewing AS	.06	.03	.01
	New York Knicks			
☐ 122	Dan Majerle AS	.05	.02	.01
	Phoenix Suns			
☐ 123	Karl Malone AS	.08	.04	.01
	Utah Jazz			
☐ 124	Otis Thorpe AS	.05	.02	.01
	Houston Rockets			
☐ 125	Dominique Wilkins AS	.06	.03	.01
	Atlanta Hawks			
☐ 126	Magic Johnson AS	.15	.07	.02
	Los Angeles Lakers			
☐ 127	Charles Oakley AS	.06	.03	.01
	New York Knicks			
☐ 128	Robert Pack	.05	.02	.01
	Portland Trail Blazers			
☐ 129	Billy Owens	.08	.04	.01
	Golden State Warriors			
☐ 130	Jeff Malone	.06	.03	.01
	Utah Jazz			
☐ 131	Danny Ferry	.05	.02	.01
	Cleveland Cavaliers			
☐ 132	Sam Bowie	.05	.02	.01
	New Jersey Nets			
☐ 133	Avery Johnson	.05	.02	.01

☐ 134	Houston Rockets Jayson Williams	.05	.02	.01
☐ 135	Philadelphia 76ers Fred Roberts	.05	.02	.01
☐ 136	Milwaukee Bucks Greg Sutton	.05	.02	.01
☐ 137	San Antonio Spurs Dennis Rodman	.10	.05	.01
☐ 138	Detroit Pistons John Williams	.05	.02	.01
☐ 139	Washington Bullets Greg Dreiling	.05	.02	.01
☐ 140	Indiana Pacers Rik Smits	.08	.04	.01
☐ 141	Indiana Pacers Michael Jordan	2.00	.90	.25
☐ 142	Chicago Bulls Nick Anderson	.06	.03	.01
☐ 143	Orlando Magic Jerome Kersey	.05	.02	.01
☐ 144	Portland Trail Blazers Fat Lever	.05	.02	.01
☐ 145	Dallas Mavericks Tyrone Corbin	.05	.02	.01
☐ 146	Utah Jazz Robert Parish	.08	.04	.01
☐ 147	Boston Celtics Steve Smith	.08	.04	.01
☐ 148	Miami Heat Chris Dudley	.05	.02	.01
☐ 149	New Jersey Nets Antoine Carr	.05	.02	.01
☐ 150	San Antonio Spurs Elden Campbell	.05	.02	.01
☐ 151	Los Angeles Lakers Randy White	.05	.02	.01
☐ 152	Dallas Mavericks Felton Spencer	.05	.02	.01
☐ 153	Minnesota Timberwolves Cedric Ceballos	.08	.04	.01
☐ 154	Phoenix Suns Mark Macon	.05	.02	.01
☐ 155	Denver Nuggets Jack Haley	.05	.02	.01
☐ 156	Los Angeles Lakers Bimbo Coles	.05	.02	.01
☐ 157	Miami Heat A.J. English	.05	.02	.01
☐ 158	Washington Bullets Kendall Gill	.05	.02	.01
☐ 159	Charlotte Hornets A.C. Green	.08	.04	.01
☐ 160	Los Angeles Lakers Mark West	.05	.02	.01
☐ 161	Phoenix Suns Benoit Benjamin	.05	.02	.01
☐ 162	Seattle Supersonics Tyrone Hill	.06	.03	.01
☐ 163	Golden State Warriors Larry Nance	.06	.03	.01
☐ 164	Cleveland Cavaliers Gary Grant	.05	.02	.01
☐ 165	Los Angeles Clippers Bill Cartwright	.05	.02	.01
☐ 166	Chicago Bulls Greg Anthony	.05	.02	.01
☐ 167	New York Knicks Jim Les	.05	.02	.01
☐ 168	Sacramento Kings Johnny Dawkins	.05	.02	.01
	Philadelphia 76ers			

☐ 169	Alvin Robertson	.05	.02	.01
☐ 170	Milwaukee Bucks Kenny Smith	.05	.02	.01
☐ 171	Houston Rockets Gerald Glass	.05	.02	.01
☐ 172	Minnesota Timberwolves Harvey Grant	.05	.02	.01
☐ 173	Washington Bullets Paul Graham	.05	.02	.01
☐ 174	Atlanta Hawks Sam Perkins	.06	.03	.01
☐ 175	Los Angeles Lakers Manute Bol	.05	.02	.01
☐ 176	Philadelphia 76ers Muggsy Bogues	.08	.04	.01
☐ 177	Charlotte Hornets Mike Brown	.05	.02	.01
☐ 178	Utah Jazz Donald Hodge	.05	.02	.01
☐ 179	Dallas Mavericks Dave Jamerson	.05	.02	.01
☐ 180	Houston Rockets Mookie Blaylock	.06	.03	.01
☐ 181	New Jersey Nets Randy Brown	.05	.02	.01
☐ 182	Sacramento Kings Todd Lichti	.05	.02	.01
☐ 183	Denver Nuggets Kevin Gamble	.05	.02	.01
☐ 184	Boston Celtics Gary Payton	.08	.04	.01
☐ 185	Seattle Supersonics Brian Shaw	.05	.02	.01
☐ 186	Miami Heat Grant Long	.05	.02	.01
☐ 187	Miami Heat Frank Brickowski	.05	.02	.01
☐ 188	Milwaukee Bucks Tim Hardaway	.08	.04	.01
☐ 189	Golden State Warriors Danny Manning	.08	.04	.01
☐ 190	Los Angeles Clippers Kevin Johnson	.10	.05	.01
☐ 191	Phoenix Suns Craig Ehlo	.05	.02	.01
☐ 192	Cleveland Cavaliers Dennis Scott	.05	.02	.01
☐ 193	Orlando Magic Reggie Miller	.15	.07	.02
☐ 194	Indiana Pacers Darrell Walker	.05	.02	.01
☐ 195	Detroit Pistons Anthony Mason	.08	.04	.01
☐ 196	New York Knicks Buck Williams	.06	.03	.01
☐ 197	Portland Trail Blazers Checklist 1-99	.05	.02	.01
☐ 198	Checklist 100-198	.05	.02	.01
☐ 199	Karl Malone 50P	.08	.04	.01
☐ 200	Utah Jazz Dominique Wilkins 50P	.06	.03	.01
☐ 201	Atlanta Hawks Tom Chambers 50P	.05	.02	.01
☐ 202	Phoenix Suns Bernard King 50P	.05	.02	.01
☐ 203	Washington Bullets Kiki Vandeweghe 50P	.05	.02	.01
☐ 204	Los Angeles Clippers Dale Ellis 50P	.05	.02	.01
☐ 205	San Antonio Spurs Michael Jordan 50P	1.00	.45	.13

	Chicago Bulls			
☐ 206	Michael Adams 50P	.05	.02	.01
	Washington Bullets			
☐ 207	Charles Smith 50P	.05	.02	.01
	New York Knicks			
☐ 208	Moses Malone 50P	.06	.03	.01
	Milwaukee Bucks			
☐ 209	Terry Cummings 50P	.05	.02	.01
	San Antonio Spurs			
☐ 210	Vernon Maxwell 50P	.05	.02	.01
	Houston Rockets			
☐ 211	Patrick Ewing 50P	.08	.04	.01
	New York Knicks			
☐ 212	Clyde Drexler 50P	.08	.04	.01
	Portland Trail Blazers			
☐ 213	Kevin McHale 50P	.05	.02	.01
	Boston Celtics			
☐ 214	Hakeem Olajuwon 50P	.20	.09	.03
	Houston Rockets			
☐ 215	Reggie Miller 50P	.08	.04	.01
	Indiana Pacers			
☐ 216	Gary Grant 20A	.05	.02	.01
	Los Angeles Clippers			
☐ 217	Doc Rivers 20A	.05	.02	.01
	New York Knicks			
☐ 218	Mark Price 20A	.05	.02	.01
	Cleveland Cavaliers			
☐ 219	Isiah Thomas 20A	.06	.03	.01
	Detroit Pistons			
☐ 220	Nate McMillan 20A	.05	.02	.01
	Seattle Supersonics			
☐ 221	Fat Lever 20A	.05	.02	.01
	Dallas Mavericks			
☐ 222	Kevin Johnson 20A	.06	.03	.01
	Phoenix Suns			
☐ 223	John Stockton 20A	.08	.04	.01
	Utah Jazz			
☐ 224	Scott Skiles 20A	.05	.02	.01
	Orlando Magic			
☐ 225	Kevin Brooks	.05	.02	.01
	Indiana Pacers			
☐ 226	Bobby Phills	.10	.05	.01
	Cleveland Cavaliers			
☐ 227	Oliver Miller	.15	.07	.02
	Phoenix Suns			
☐ 228	John Williams	.05	.02	.01
	Los Angeles Clippers			
☐ 229	Brad Lohaus	.05	.02	.01
	Milwaukee Bucks			
☐ 230	Derrick Coleman	.08	.04	.01
	New Jersey Nets			
☐ 231	Ed Pinckney	.05	.02	.01
	Boston Celtics			
☐ 232	Trent Tucker	.05	.02	.01
	Chicago Bulls			
☐ 233	Lance Blanks	.05	.02	.01
	Minnesota Timberwolves			
☐ 234	Drazen Petrovic	.06	.03	.01
	New Jersey Nets			
☐ 235	Mark Bryant	.05	.02	.01
	Portland Trail Blazers			
☐ 236	Lloyd Daniels	.05	.02	.01
	San Antonio Spurs			
☐ 237	Dale Davis	.08	.04	.01
	Indiana Pacers			
☐ 238	Jayson Williams	.05	.02	.01
	New Jersey Nets			
☐ 239	Mike Sanders	.05	.02	.01
	Cleveland Cavaliers			
☐ 240	Mike Gminski	.05	.02	.01
	Charlotte Hornets			
☐ 241	William Bedford	.05	.02	.01
	Los Angeles Clippers			
☐ 242	Dell Curry	.05	.02	.01
	Charlotte Hornets			
☐ 243	Gerald Paddio	.05	.02	.01
	Seattle Supersonics			
☐ 244	Chris Smith	.05	.02	.01
	Minnesota Timberwolves			
☐ 245	Jud Buechler	.05	.02	.01
	Golden State Warriors			
☐ 246	Walter Palmer	.05	.02	.01
	Dallas Mavericks			
☐ 247	Larry Krystkowiak	.05	.02	.01
	Utah Jazz			
☐ 248	Marcus Liberty	.05	.02	.01
	Denver Nuggets			
☐ 249	Sam Mitchell	.05	.02	.01
	Indiana Pacers			
☐ 250	Kiki Vandeweghe	.05	.02	.01
	Los Angeles Clippers			
☐ 251	Vincent Askew	.05	.02	.01
	Seattle Supersonics			
☐ 252	Travis Mays	.05	.02	.01
	Atlanta Hawks			
☐ 253	Charles Smith	.05	.02	.01
	New York Knicks			
☐ 254	John Bagley	.05	.02	.01
	Boston Celtics			
☐ 255	James Worthy	.08	.04	.01
	Los Angeles Lakers			
☐ 256	Paul Pressey P/CO	.05	.02	.01
	Golden State Warriors			
☐ 257	Rumeal Robinson	.05	.02	.01
	New Jersey Nets			
☐ 258	Tom Gugliotta	.25	.11	.03
	Washington Bullets			
☐ 259	Eric Anderson	.05	.02	.01
	New York Knicks			
☐ 260	Hersey Hawkins	.06	.03	.01
	Philadelphia 76ers			
☐ 261	Terry Davis	.05	.02	.01
	Dallas Mavericks			
☐ 262	Rex Chapman	.05	.02	.01
	Washington Bullets			
☐ 263	Chucky Brown	.05	.02	.01
	New Jersey Nets			
☐ 264	Danny Young	.05	.02	.01
	Detroit Pistons			
☐ 265	Olden Polynice	.05	.02	.01
	Detroit Pistons			
☐ 266	Kevin Willis	.06	.03	.01
	Atlanta Hawks			
☐ 267	Shawn Kemp	.40	.18	.05
	Seattle Supersonics			
☐ 268	Mookie Blaylock	.06	.03	.01
	Atlanta Hawks			
☐ 269	Malik Sealy	.10	.05	.01
	Indiana Pacers			
☐ 270	Charles Barkley	.30	.14	.04
	Phoenix Suns			
☐ 271	Corey Williams	.05	.02	.01
	Chicago Bulls			
☐ 272	Stephen Howard	.05	.02	.01
	(See also card 286)			
	Utah Jazz			
☐ 273	Keith Askins	.05	.02	.01
	Miami Heat			
☐ 274	Matt Bullard	.05	.02	.01
	Houston Rockets			
☐ 275	John Battle	.05	.02	.01
	Cleveland Cavaliers			

☐ 276	Andrew Lang	.05	.02	.01
	Philadelphia 76ers			
☐ 277	David Robinson	.30	.14	.04
	San Antonio Spurs			
☐ 278	Harold Miner	.10	.05	.01
	Miami Heat			
☐ 279	Tracy Murray	.06	.03	.01
	Portland Trail Blazers			
☐ 280	Pooh Richardson	.05	.02	.01
	Indiana Pacers			
☐ 281	Dikembe Mutombo	.20	.09	.03
	Denver Nuggets			
☐ 282	Wayman Tisdale	.06	.03	.01
	Sacramento Kings			
☐ 283	Larry Johnson	.25	.11	.03
	Charlotte Hornets			
☐ 284	Todd Day	.20	.09	.03
	Milwaukee Bucks			
☐ 285	Stanley Roberts	.05	.02	.01
	Los Angeles Clippers			
☐ 286	Randy Woods UER	.05	.02	.01
	Los Angeles Clippers			
	(Card misnumbered 272;			
	run he show should			
	be run the show)			
☐ 287	Avery Johnson	.05	.02	.01
	San Antonio Spurs			
☐ 288	Anthony Peeler	.10	.05	.01
	Los Angeles Lakers			
☐ 289	Mario Elie	.05	.02	.01
	Portland Trail Blazers			
☐ 290	Doc Rivers	.05	.02	.01
	New York Knicks			
☐ 291	Blue Edwards	.05	.02	.01
	Milwaukee Bucks			
☐ 292	Sean Rooks	.06	.03	.01
	Dallas Mavericks			
☐ 293	Xavier McDaniel	.06	.03	.01
	Boston Celtics			
☐ 294	Clarence Weatherspoon	.30	.14	.04
	Philadelphia 76ers			
☐ 295	Morlon Wiley	.05	.02	.01
	Atlanta Hawks			
☐ 296	LaBradford Smith	.05	.02	.01
	Washington Bullets			
☐ 297	Reggie Lewis	.08	.04	.01
	Boston Celtics			
☐ 298	Chris Mullin	.08	.04	.01
	Golden State Warriors			
☐ 299	Litterial Green	.05	.02	.01
	Orlando Magic			
☐ 300	Elmore Spencer	.05	.02	.01
	Los Angeles Clippers			
☐ 301	John Stockton	.15	.07	.02
	Utah Jazz			
☐ 302	Walt Williams	.30	.14	.04
	Sacramento Kings			
☐ 303	Anthony Pullard	.05	.02	.01
	Milwaukee Bucks			
☐ 304	Gundars Vetra	.05	.02	.01
	Minnesota Timberwolves			
☐ 305	LaSalle Thompson	.05	.02	.01
	Indiana Pacers			
☐ 306	Nate McMillan	.05	.02	.01
	Seattle Supersonics			
☐ 307	Steve Bardo	.05	.02	.01
	Dallas Mavericks			
☐ 308	Robert Horry	.40	.18	.05
	Houston Rockets			
☐ 309	Scott Williams	.05	.02	.01
	Chicago Bulls			
☐ 310	Bo Kimble	.05	.02	.01
	New York Knicks			
☐ 311	Tree Rollins	.05	.02	.01
	Houston Rockets			
☐ 312	Tim Perry	.05	.02	.01
	Philadelphia 76ers			
☐ 313	Isaac Austin	.05	.02	.01
	Utah Jazz			
☐ 314	Tate George	.05	.02	.01
	New Jersey Nets			
☐ 315	Kevin Lynch	.05	.02	.01
	Charlotte Hornets			
☐ 316	Victor Alexander	.05	.02	.01
	Golden State Warriors			
☐ 317	Doug Overton	.05	.02	.01
	Washington Bullets			
☐ 318	Tom Hammonds	.05	.02	.01
	Charlotte Hornets			
☐ 319	LaPhonso Ellis	.15	.07	.02
	Denver Nuggets			
☐ 320	Scott Brooks	.05	.02	.01
	Houston Rockets			
☐ 321	Anthony Avent UER	.05	.02	.01
	(Front photo act-			
	ually Blue Edwards)			
	Milwaukee Bucks			
☐ 322	Matt Geiger	.05	.02	.01
	Miami Heat			
☐ 323	Duane Causwell	.05	.02	.01
	Sacramento Kings			
☐ 324	Horace Grant	.10	.05	.01
	Chicago Bulls			
☐ 325	Mark Jackson	.05	.02	.01
	Los Angeles Clippers			
☐ 326	Dan Majerle	.06	.03	.01
	Phoenix Suns			
☐ 327	Chuck Person	.06	.03	.01
	Minnesota Timberwolves			
☐ 328	Buck Johnson	.05	.02	.01
	Washington Bullets			
☐ 329	Duane Cooper	.05	.02	.01
	Los Angeles Lakers			
☐ 330	Rod Strickland	.06	.03	.01
	Portland Trail Blazers			
☐ 331	Isiah Thomas	.10	.05	.01
	Detroit Pistons			
☐ 332	Greg Kite	.05	.02	.01
	(See also card 387)			
	Orlando Magic			
☐ 333	Don MacLean	.10	.05	.01
	Washington Bullets			
☐ 334	Christian Laettner	.30	.14	.04
	Minnesota Timberwolves			
☐ 335	John Crotty	.05	.02	.01
	Utah Jazz			
☐ 336	Tracy Moore	.05	.02	.01
	Dallas Mavericks			
☐ 337	Hakeem Olajuwon	.40	.18	.05
	Houston Rockets			
☐ 338	Byron Houston	.05	.02	.01
	Golden State Warriors			
☐ 339	Walter Bond	.05	.02	.01
	Dallas Mavericks			
☐ 340	Brent Price	.05	.02	.01
	Washington Bullets			
☐ 341	Bryant Stith	.15	.07	.02
	Denver Nuggets			
☐ 342	Will Perdue	.05	.02	.01
	Chicago Bulls			
☐ 343	Jeff Hornacek	.06	.03	.01
	Philadelphia 76ers			

☐ 344	Adam Keefe	.10	.05	.01
	Atlanta Hawks			
☐ 345	Rafael Addison	.05	.02	.01
	New Jersey Nets			
☐ 346	Marlon Maxey	.05	.02	.01
	Minnesota Timberwolves			
☐ 347	Joe Dumars	.10	.05	.01
	Detroit Pistons			
☐ 348	Jon Barry	.06	.03	.01
	Milwaukee Bucks			
☐ 349	Marty Conlon	.05	.02	.01
	Sacramento Kings			
☐ 350	Alaa Abdelnaby	.05	.02	.01
	Boston Celtics			
☐ 351	Micheal Williams	.05	.02	.01
	Minnesota Timberwolves			
☐ 352	Brad Daugherty	.06	.03	.01
	Cleveland Cavaliers			
☐ 353	Tony Bennett	.05	.02	.01
	Charlotte Hornets			
☐ 354	Clyde Drexler	.15	.07	.02
	Portland Trail Blazers			
☐ 355	Rolando Blackman	.06	.03	.01
	New York Knicks			
☐ 356	Tom Tolbert	.05	.02	.01
	Orlando Magic			
☐ 357	Sarunas Marciulionis	.05	.02	.01
	Golden State Warriors			
☐ 358	Jaren Jackson	.05	.02	.01
	Los Angeles Clippers			
☐ 359	Stacey King	.05	.02	.01
	Chicago Bulls			
☐ 360	Danny Ainge	.06	.03	.01
	Phoenix Suns			
☐ 361	Dale Ellis	.06	.03	.01
	San Antonio Spurs			
☐ 362	Shaquille O'Neal	4.00	1.80	.50
	Orlando Magic			
☐ 363	Bob McCann	.05	.02	.01
	Minnesota Timberwolves			
☐ 364	Reggie Smith	.05	.02	.01
	Portland Trail Blazers			
☐ 365	Vinny Del Negro	.05	.02	.01
	San Antonio Spurs			
☐ 366	Robert Pack	.05	.02	.01
	Denver Nuggets			
☐ 367	David Wood	.05	.02	.01
	San Antonio Spurs			
☐ 368	Rodney McCray	.05	.02	.01
	Chicago Bulls			
☐ 369	Terry Mills	.06	.03	.01
	Detroit Pistons			
☐ 370	Eric Murdock UER	.05	.02	.01
	Milwaukee Bucks			
	(Jazz on back spelled Jass)			
☐ 371	Alex Blackwell	.05	.02	.01
	Los Angeles Lakers			
☐ 372	Jay Humphries	.05	.02	.01
	Utah Jazz			
☐ 373	Eddie Lee Wilkins	.05	.02	.01
	Philadelphia 76ers			
☐ 374	James Edwards	.05	.02	.01
	Los Angeles Lakers			
☐ 375	Tim Kempton	.05	.02	.01
	Phoenix Suns			
☐ 376	J.R. Reid	.05	.02	.01
	San Antonio Spurs			
☐ 377	Sam Mack	.05	.02	.01
	San Antonio Spurs			
☐ 378	Donald Royal	.05	.02	.01
	Orlando Magic			

☐ 379	Mark Price	.08	.04	.01
	Cleveland Cavaliers			
☐ 380	Mark Acres	.05	.02	.01
	Orlando Magic			
☐ 381	Hubert Davis	.10	.05	.01
	New York Knicks			
☐ 382	Dave Johnson	.05	.02	.01
	Portland Trail Blazers			
☐ 383	John Salley	.05	.02	.01
	Miami Heat			
☐ 384	Eddie Johnson	.06	.03	.01
	Seattle Supersonics			
☐ 385	Brian Howard	.05	.02	.01
	Dallas Mavericks			
☐ 386	Isaiah Morris	.05	.02	.01
	Detroit Pistons			
☐ 387	Frank Johnson	.05	.02	.01
	Phoenix Suns			
	(Card misnumbered 332)			
☐ 388	Rick Mahorn	.05	.02	.01
	New Jersey Nets			
☐ 389	Scottie Pippen	.15	.07	.02
	Chicago Bulls			
☐ 390	Lee Mayberry	.06	.03	.01
	Milwaukee Bucks			
☐ 391	Tony Campbell	.05	.02	.01
	New York Knicks			
☐ 392	Latrell Sprewell	1.00	.45	.13
	Golden State Warriors			
☐ 393	Alonzo Mourning	1.00	.45	.13
	Charlotte Hornets			
☐ 394	Robert Werdann	.05	.02	.01
	Denver Nuggets			
☐ 395	Checklist 199-297 UER	.05	.02	.01
	(286 Kennard Winchester; should be Randy Woods)			
☐ 396	Checklist 298-396	.05	.02	.01

1992-93 Topps Gold

Gold foil versions of the regular cards were inserted one per 15-card plastic-wrap pack, except if the pack contained a randomly inserted Topps Beam Team card. Gold foil cards were also inserted two per 18-card mini-jumbo pack, three per 45-card retail rack pack, five per 41-card magazine jumbo pack, and 12 per factory set. In addition, complete Gold factory sets were made at the end of the season. These sets include all 396 cards, plus a 7-card Gold Beam Team insert set. The cards are identical in

design to the regular issue, except that on the fronts the team color-coded stripes carrying player information are replaced by gold foil stripes. The cards are numbered on the back without a "G" suffix. The cards are standard size, 2 1/2" by 3 1/2". Reportedly only 10,000 factory sets were produced. Four different player cards replaced the checklist cards found in the regular 396-card set. Please refer to the multiplier provided below (coupled with the prices of the corresponding regular issue cards) to ascertain the value.

	MINT	NRMT	EXC
COMPLETE GOLD SET (396)	60.00	27.00	7.50
COMPLETE FACT.SET (403)	75.00	36.00	10.00
COMPLETE SERIES 1 (198)	20.00	9.00	2.50
COMPLETE SERIES 2 (198)	40.00	18.00	5.00
COMMON CARD (1-396)	.10	.05	.01
*STARS: 2.5X to 5X BASIC CARDS..			
*ROOKIES: 1.5X to 3X BASIC CARDS			

		MINT	NRMT	EXC
☐	197G Jeff Sanders	.50	.23	.06
	Atlanta Hawks			
☐	198G Elliott Perry UER	.50	.23	.06
	Charlotte Hornets			
	(Misspelled Elliot			
	on front)			
☐	395G David Wingate	.50	.23	.06
	Washington Bullets			
☐	396G Carl Herrera	.50	.23	.06
	Houston Rockets			

1992-93 Topps Beam Team

Comprised of some of the NBA's biggest stars, the Topps Beam Team set contains seven standard size (2 1/2" by 3 1/2") cards. Inserted in 15-card second series packs at a ratio of one in 18, these special "Topps Beam Team" bonus cards commemorate Topps' 1993 sponsorship of a six-minute NBA laser animation show. Called Beams Above the Rim, the show premiered at the NBA All-Star Game on Feb. 21. Afterwards, the laser show embarked on a ten-city tour and was featured in either the pre-game or half-time events in ten NBA arenas. Three players

are featured on each Topps Beam Team card. The horizontal fronts display three color action player photos on a dark blue background with a grid of brightly colored light beams. The set title "Beam Team" appears in pastel green block lettering across the top. The backs carry three light blue panels, with a close-up color photo, biography, and player profile on each panel. The cards are numbered on the back.

		MINT	NRMT	EXC
COMPLETE SET (7)		5.00	2.30	.60
COMMON TRIO (1-7)		.50	.23	.06
☐ 1	Reggie Miller	.75	.35	.09
	Indiana Pacers			
	Charles Barkley			
	Phoenix Suns			
	Clyde Drexler			
	Portland Trail Blazers			
☐ 2	Patrick Ewing	.50	.23	.06
	New York Knicks			
	Tim Hardaway			
	Golden State Warriors			
	Jeff Hornacek			
	Philadelphia 76ers			
☐ 3	Kevin Johnson	2.50	1.15	.30
	Phoenix Suns			
	Michael Jordan			
	Chicago Bulls			
	Dennis Rodman			
	Detroit Pistons			
☐ 4	Dominique Wilkins	.50	.23	.06
	Atlanta Hawks			
	John Stockton			
	Utah Jazz			
	Karl Malone			
	Utah Jazz			
☐ 5	Hakeem Olajuwon	1.00	.45	.13
	Houston Rockets			
	Mark Price			
	Cleveland Cavaliers			
	Shawn Kemp			
	Seattle Supersonics			
☐ 6	Scottie Pippen	.75	.35	.09
	Chicago Bulls			
	David Robinson			
	San Antonio Spurs			
	Jeff Malone			
	Utah Jazz			
☐ 7	Chris Mullin	4.00	1.80	.50
	Golden State Warriors			
	Shaquille O'Neal			
	Orlando Magic			
	Glen Rice			
	Miami Heat			

1992-93 Topps Beam Team Gold

Topps also produced a 7-card gold parallel version to the regular issue Beam Team series. These gold cards command 1.5 to 3 times the values of their nongold counterparts. One of these gold Beam Team sets

was included with the purchase of a 1992-93 Topps Gold factory set. Please refer to the multiplier provided below (coupled with the corresponding regular Beam Team inserts) to ascertain value.

	MINT	NRMT	EXC
COMPLETE SET (7)	20.00	9.00	2.50
COMMON CARD (1-7)	3.00		

*GOLD BT CARDS: 2X to 4X BASIC CARDS

1992-93 Topps Archives

Featuring the missing years of Topps basketball from 1981 through 1991, this 150-card set consists of 139 current NBA players and an 11-card subset of the Number One draft picks from 1981 to 1991. Production was limited to 10,000 24-box cases (24 packs per box). Each pack contained 14 cards and one Stadium Club membership card. The cards measure the standard size (2 1/2" by 3 1/2"). Since Topps did not produce basketball cards when the photos were taken, the front designs are patterned after the Topps baseball cards issued during the same year. The horizontal backs display a small, square, current action player photo that overlaps a red, yellow, and white box containing biographical information, and statistics from college and the NBA. The set name, player's name, and team are printed in the upper left portion. The background is in varying shades of blue with a light beam design. After opening with a No. 1 Draft

Pick (1-11) subset, the player cards are arranged by year in ascending chronological order and alphabetically within each season as follows: 1981-82 (12-22), 1982-83 (23-31), 1983-84 (32-42), 1984-85 (43-59), 1985-86 (60-76), 1986-87 (77-88), 1987-88 (89-100), 1988-89 (101-114), 1989-90 (115-130), 1990-91 (131-139), and 1991-92 (140-148). The set closes with checklist (149-150) cards.

	MINT	NRMT	EXC
COMPLETE SET (150)	8.00	3.60	1.00
COMMON CARD (1-150)	.05	.02	.01
☐ 1 Mark Aguirre FDP Dallas Mavericks	.05	.02	.01
☐ 2 James Worthy FDP Los Angeles Lakers	.10	.05	.01
☐ 3 Ralph Sampson FDP Houston Rockets	.05	.02	.01
☐ 4 Hakeem Olajuwon FDP Houston Rockets	.40	.18	.05
☐ 5 Patrick Ewing FDP New York Knicks	.10	.05	.01
☐ 6 Brad Daugherty FDP Cleveland Cavaliers	.05	.02	.01
☐ 7 David Robinson FDP San Antonio Spurs	.30	.14	.04
☐ 8 Danny Manning FDP Los Angeles Clippers	.05	.02	.01
☐ 9 Pervis Ellison FDP UER Sacramento Kings (Text on back: Clippers not Lakers had 2nd pick)	.05	.02	.01
☐ 10 Derrick Coleman FDP New Jersey Nets	.05	.02	.01
☐ 11 Larry Johnson FDP Charlotte Hornets	.25	.11	.03
☐ 12 Mark Aguirre Dallas Mavericks	.08	.04	.01
☐ 13 Danny Ainge Boston Celtics	.08	.04	.01
☐ 14 Rolando Blackman Dallas Mavericks	.05	.02	.01
☐ 15 Tom Chambers San Diego Clippers	.08	.04	.01
☐ 16 Eddie Johnson Kansas City Kings	.08	.04	.01
☐ 17 Alton Lister Milwaukee Bucks	.05	.02	.01
☐ 18 Larry Nance Phoenix Suns	.08	.04	.01
☐ 19 Kurt Rambis Los Angeles Lakers	.05	.02	.01
☐ 20 Isiah Thomas Detroit Pistons	.15	.07	.02
☐ 21 Buck Williams New Jersey Nets	.08	.04	.01
☐ 22 Orlando Woolridge Chicago Bulls	.05	.02	.01
☐ 23 John Bagley Cleveland Cavaliers	.05	.02	.01
☐ 24 Terry Cummings San Diego Clippers	.08	.04	.01
☐ 25 Mark Eaton Utah Jazz	.05	.02	.01
☐ 26 Sleepy Floyd New Jersey Nets	.05	.02	.01
☐ 27 Fat Lever Portland Trail Blazers	.05	.02	.01

☐ 28 Ricky Pierce	.08	.04	.01
Detroit Pistons			
☐ 29 Trent Tucker	.05	.02	.01
New York Knicks			
☐ 30 Dominique Wilkins	.15	.07	.02
Atlanta Hawks			
☐ 31 James Worthy	.10	.05	.01
Los Angeles Lakers			
☐ 32 Thurl Bailey	.05	.02	.01
Utah Jazz			
☐ 33 Clyde Drexler	.30	.14	.04
Portland Trail Blazers			
☐ 34 Dale Ellis	.08	.04	.01
Dallas Mavericks			
☐ 35 Sidney Green	.05	.02	.01
Chicago Bulls			
☐ 36 Derek Harper	.08	.04	.01
Dallas Mavericks			
☐ 37 Jeff Malone	.08	.04	.01
Washington Bullets			
☐ 38 Rodney McCray	.05	.02	.01
Houston Rockets			
☐ 39 John Paxson	.05	.02	.01
San Antonio Spurs			
☐ 40 Doc Rivers	.05	.02	.01
Atlanta Hawks			
☐ 41 Byron Scott	.08	.04	.01
Los Angeles Lakers			
☐ 42 Sedale Threatt	.05	.02	.01
Philadelphia 76ers			
☐ 43 Ron Anderson	.05	.02	.01
Cleveland Cavaliers			
☐ 44 Charles Barkley	.60	.25	.08
Philadelphia 76ers			
☐ 45 Sam Bowie	.05	.02	.01
Portland Trail Blazers			
☐ 46 Michael Cage	.05	.02	.01
Los Angeles Clippers			
☐ 47 Tony Campbell	.05	.02	.01
Detroit Pistons			
☐ 48 Antoine Carr	.05	.02	.01
Atlanta Hawks			
☐ 49 Craig Ehlo	.05	.02	.01
Houston Rockets			
☐ 50 Vern Fleming	.05	.02	.01
Indiana Pacers			
☐ 51 Jay Humphries	.05	.02	.01
Phoenix Suns			
☐ 52 Michael Jordan	4.00	1.80	.50
Chicago Bulls			
☐ 53 Jerome Kersey	.05	.02	.01
Portland Trail Blazers			
☐ 54 Hakeem Olajuwon	.75	.35	.09
Houston Rockets			
☐ 55 Sam Perkins	.08	.04	.01
Dallas Mavericks			
☐ 56 Alvin Robertson	.05	.02	.01
San Antonio Spurs			
☐ 57 John Stockton	.30	.14	.04
Utah Jazz			
☐ 58 Otis Thorpe	.08	.04	.01
Kansas City Kings			
☐ 59 Kevin Willis	.08	.04	.01
Atlanta Hawks			
☐ 60 Michael Adams	.05	.02	.01
Sacramento Kings			
☐ 61 Benoit Benjamin	.05	.02	.01
Los Angeles Clippers			
☐ 62 Terry Catledge	.05	.02	.01
Philadelphia 76ers			
☐ 63 Joe Dumars	.15	.07	.02

Detroit Pistons			
☐ 64 Patrick Ewing	.30	.14	.04
New York Knicks			
☐ 65 A.C. Green	.10	.05	.01
Los Angeles Lakers			
☐ 66 Karl Malone	.30	.14	.04
Utah Jazz			
☐ 67 Reggie Miller	.30	.14	.04
Indiana Pacers			
☐ 68 Chris Mullin	.10	.05	.01
Golden State Warriors			
☐ 69 Xavier McDaniel	.08	.04	.01
Seattle Supersonics			
☐ 70 Charles Oakley	.08	.04	.01
Chicago Bulls			
☐ 71 Terry Porter	.08	.04	.01
Portland Trail Blazers			
☐ 72 Jerry Reynolds	.05	.02	.01
Milwaukee Bucks			
☐ 73 Detlef Schrempf	.10	.05	.01
Dallas Mavericks			
☐ 74 Wayman Tisdale	.08	.04	.01
Indiana Pacers			
☐ 75 Spud Webb	.08	.04	.01
Atlanta Hawks			
☐ 76 Gerald Wilkins	.05	.02	.01
New York Knicks			
☐ 77 Dell Curry	.05	.02	.01
Utah Jazz			
☐ 78 Brad Daugherty	.08	.04	.01
Cleveland Cavaliers			
☐ 79 Johnny Dawkins	.05	.02	.01
San Antonio Spurs			
☐ 80 Kevin Duckworth	.05	.02	.01
Portland Trail Blazers			
☐ 81 Ron Harper	.08	.04	.01
Cleveland Cavaliers			
☐ 82 Jeff Hornacek	.08	.04	.01
Phoenix Suns			
☐ 83 Johnny Newman	.05	.02	.01
Cleveland Cavaliers			
☐ 84 Chuck Person	.08	.04	.01
Indiana Pacers			
☐ 85 Mark Price	.10	.05	.01
Cleveland Cavaliers			
☐ 86 Dennis Rodman	.20	.09	.03
Detroit Pistons			
☐ 87 John Salley	.05	.02	.01
Detroit Pistons			
☐ 88 Scott Skiles	.05	.02	.01
Milwaukee Bucks			
☐ 89 Muggsy Bogues	.10	.05	.01
Washington Bullets			
☐ 90 Armon Gilliam	.05	.02	.01
Phoenix Suns			
☐ 91 Horace Grant	.15	.07	.02
Chicago Bulls			
☐ 92 Mark Jackson	.05	.02	.01
New York Knicks			
☐ 93 Kevin Johnson	.15	.07	.02
Cleveland Cavaliers			
☐ 94 Reggie Lewis	.10	.05	.01
Boston Celtics			
☐ 95 Derrick McKey	.08	.04	.01
Seattle Supersonics			
☐ 96 Ken Norman	.05	.02	.01
Los Angeles Clippers			
☐ 97 Scottie Pippen	.30	.14	.04
Chicago Bulls			
☐ 98 Olden Polynice	.05	.02	.01
Seattle Supersonics			

☐ 99	Kenny Smith .... Sacramento Kings	.05	.02	.01
☐ 100	John Williams .... Cleveland Cavaliers	.08	.04	.01
☐ 101	Willie Anderson .... San Antonio Spurs	.05	.02	.01
☐ 102	Rex Chapman .... Charlotte Hornets	.05	.02	.01
☐ 103	Harvey Grant .... Washington Bullets	.05	.02	.01
☐ 104	Hersey Hawkins .... Philadelphia 76ers	.08	.04	.01
☐ 105	Dan Majerle .... Phoenix Suns	.08	.04	.01
☐ 106	Danny Manning .... Los Angeles Clippers	.10	.05	.01
☐ 107	Vernon Maxwell .... San Antonio Spurs	.05	.02	.01
☐ 108	Chris Morris .... New Jersey Nets	.05	.02	.01
☐ 109	Mitch Richmond UER .. Golden State Warriors (Tim Hardaway pictured on front)	.15	.07	.02
☐ 110	Rony Seikaly .... Miami Heat	.05	.02	.01
☐ 111	Brian Shaw .... Boston Celtics	.05	.02	.01
☐ 112	Charles Smith .... Los Angeles Clippers	.05	.02	.01
☐ 113	Rod Strickland .... New York Knicks	.08	.04	.01
☐ 114	Micheal Williams .... Detroit Pistons	.05	.02	.01
☐ 115	Nick Anderson .... Orlando Magic	.05	.02	.01
☐ 116	B.J. Armstrong .... Chicago Bulls	.05	.02	.01
☐ 117	Mookie Blaylock .... New Jersey Nets	.08	.04	.01
☐ 118	Vlade Divac .... Los Angeles Lakers	.10	.05	.01
☐ 119	Sherman Douglas .... Miami Heat	.05	.02	.01
☐ 120	Blue Edwards .... Utah Jazz	.05	.02	.01
☐ 121	Sean Elliott .... San Antonio Spurs	.08	.04	.01
☐ 122	Pervis Ellison .... Sacramento Kings	.05	.02	.01
☐ 123	Tim Hardaway .... Golden State Warriors	.10	.05	.01
☐ 124	Sarunas Marciulionis ... Golden State Warriors	.05	.02	.01
☐ 125	Drazen Petrovic .... Portland Trail Blazers	.08	.04	.01
☐ 126	J.R. Reid .... Charlotte Hornets	.05	.02	.01
☐ 127	Glen Rice .... Miami Heat	.10	.05	.01
☐ 128	Pooh Richardson .... Minnesota Timberwolves	.05	.02	.01
☐ 129	Clifford Robinson .... Portland Trail Blazers	.10	.05	.01
☐ 130	David Robinson .... San Antonio Spurs	.60	.25	.08
☐ 131	Dee Brown .... Boston Celtics	.08	.04	.01
☐ 132	Cedric Ceballos .... Phoenix Suns	.10	.05	.01
☐ 133	Derrick Coleman .... New Jersey Nets	.10	.05	.01
☐ 134	Kendall Gill .... Charlotte Hornets	.05	.02	.01
☐ 135	Chris Jackson .... Denver Nuggets	.08	.04	.01
☐ 136	Shawn Kemp .... Seattle Supersonics	.75	.35	.09
☐ 137	Gary Payton .... Seattle Supersonics	.10	.05	.01
☐ 138	Dennis Scott .... Orlando Magic	.05	.02	.01
☐ 139	Lionel Simmons .... Sacramento Kings	.05	.02	.01
☐ 140	Kenny Anderson .... New Jersey Nets	.25	.11	.03
☐ 141	Greg Anthony .... New York Knicks	.05	.02	.01
☐ 142	Stacey Augmon .... Atlanta Hawks	.10	.05	.01
☐ 143	Rick Fox .... Boston Celtics	.05	.02	.01
☐ 144	Larry Johnson .... Charlotte Hornets	.50	.23	.06
☐ 145	Luc Longley .... Minnesota Timberwolves	.05	.02	.01
☐ 146	Dikembe Mutombo .... Denver Nuggets	.40	.18	.05
☐ 147	Billy Owens .... Golden State Warriors	.10	.05	.01
☐ 148	Steve Smith .... Miami Heat	.10	.05	.01
☐ 149	Checklist 1-75	.05	.02	.01
☐ 150	Checklist 76-150	.05	.02	.01

1992-93 Topps Archives Gold

10,000 factory sets were made of the 1992-93 Topps Archives Gold. The factory sets were sold to dealers in eight-set cases. The 150 cards comprising this set have identical player selection and numbering as the regular-issue Topps Archives set, except that the checklist cards from the regular Archives set (149 and 150) have been replaced by cards of Rumeal Robinson and Shaquille O'Neal, respectively. Like the regular-issue Archive cards, the fronts are designed to mimic the layouts of several Topps' baseball issues of the 1980s; the only differences being that the Topps Archives logo, which doesn't appear on the regular-issue set, and the player's name are stamped in gold foil. The horizontal backs, however, all have the same design, with player action photos displayed in the upper right, the NBA and Topps Archives logos to the left of the picture, and the player's name and team beneath the logos. A brief biography is printed within a red rectangle, a complete college record appears beneath within a yellow rectangle, and the player's record of his NBA rookie year on the bottom rounds out the back. The cards are standard size, 2 1/2" by 3 1/2". Please refer to the multiplier provided below (coupled with the prices of the corresponding regular issue card) to ascertain value.

	MINT	NRMT	EXC
COMPLETE FACT.SET (150)	40.00	18.00	5.00
COMMON CARD (1-150)	.10	.05	.01
*STARS: 2X TO 4X BASIC CARDS			

		MINT	NRMT	EXC
☐	149G Rumeal Robinson	.50	.23	.06
☐	150G Shaquille O'Neal	15.00	6.75	1.90

1992-93 Topps Archives Master Photos

In one out of 24 '92-93 Archives packs, the Stadium Club membership card was replaced by a mini-Master Photo Trade card (2 1/2" by 3 1/2") good for three of these full-size (5" by 7") Master Photos. The expiration date was January 31, 1994. Showcasing the 11 No. 1 NBA draft picks from the missing years of Topps basketball from 1981 through 1991, these 12 over-sized cards feature white-bordered color player action shots framed by prismatic silver-foil lines. The player's name, team name and year of his being the No. 1 pick appear in diagonal red, yellow, and blue stripes near the bottom. The words "1 Draft Pick" followed by a curving comet like prismatic silver-foil tail appear in one of the

photo's upper corners. Aside from the Topps and NBA trademarks, the backs are blank. The cards are numbered on the front by year. The mini Master Photo cards are presently valued the same as the large.

	MINT	NRMT	EXC
COMPLETE SET (12)	10.00	4.50	1.25
COMMON CARD (1981-1991)	.25	.11	.03
COMPLETE MP TRADE SET (12)	10.00	4.50	1.25

			MINT	NRMT	EXC
☐	1981	Mark Aguirre Dallas Mavericks 1981 No. 1 Draft Pick	.35	.16	.04
☐	1982	James Worthy Los Angeles Lakers 1982 No. 1 Draft Pick	.50	.23	.06
☐	1983	Ralph Sampson Houston Rockets 1983 No. 1 Draft Pick	.25	.11	.03
☐	1984	Hakeem Olajuwon Houston Rockets 1984 No. 1 Draft Pick	3.00	1.35	.40
☐	1985	Patrick Ewing New York Knicks 1985 No. 1 Draft Pick	1.25	.55	.16
☐	1986	Brad Daugherty Cleveland Cavaliers 1986 No. 1 Draft Pick	.35	.16	.04
☐	1987	David Robinson San Antonio Spurs 1987 No. 1 Draft Pick	2.50	1.15	.30
☐	1988	Danny Manning Los Angeles Clippers 1988 No. 1 Draft Pick	.50	.23	.06
☐	1989	Pervis Ellison Sacramento Kings 1989 No. 1 Draft Pick	.25	.11	.03
☐	1990	Derrick Coleman New Jersey Nets 1990 No. 1 Draft Pick	.50	.23	.06
☐	1991	Larry Johnson Charlotte Hornets 1991 No. 1 Draft Pick	1.25	.55	.16
☐	NNO	First Picks 1981-91	.50	.23	.06

1993-94 Topps

The complete 1993-94 Topps basketball set consists of 396 cards issued in two 198-

card series. Cards were issued in 12, 15 and 29-card packs. Factory sets contain 410 cards including 10 Gold, three Black Gold and one Finest Redemption card. The cards are standard size (2 1/2" by 3 1/2"). The white bordered fronts display color action player photos with a team color coded inner border. The player's name is printed in white script at the lower left corner with the team name appearing on a team color coded bar at the very bottom. The horizontal backs carry a close-up player photo on the right with complete NBA statistics, biography, and career highlights on the left on a beige panel. Subsets featured are Highlights (1-5), 50 Point Club (50, 57, 64), Topps All-Star 1st Team (100-104), Topps All-Star 2nd Team (115-119), Topps All-Star 3rd Team (130-134), Topps All-Rookie 1st Team (150-154), and Topps All-Rookie 2nd Team (175-179). The cards are numbered on the back.

	MINT	NRMT	EXC
COMPLETE SET (396)	20.00	9.00	2.50
COMPLETE FACT.SET (410)	25.00	11.50	3.10
COMPLETE SERIES 1 (198)	10.00	4.50	1.25
COMPLETE SERIES 2 (198)	10.00	4.50	1.25
COMMON CARD (1-396)	.05	.02	.01
☐ 1 Charles Barkley HL	.25	.11	.03
Phoenix Suns			
☐ 2 Hakeem Olajuwon HL	.30	.14	.04
Houston Rockets			
☐ 3 Shaquille O'Neal HL	1.00	.45	.13
Orlando Magic			
☐ 4 Chris Jackson HL	.05	.02	.01
Denver Nuggets			
☐ 5 Cliff Robinson HL	.05	.02	.01
Portland Trail Blazers			
☐ 6 Donald Hodge	.05	.02	.01
Dallas Mavericks			
☐ 7 Victor Alexander	.05	.02	.01
Golden State Warriors			
☐ 8 Chris Morris	.05	.02	.01
New Jersey Nets			
☐ 9 Muggsy Bogues	.10	.05	.01
Charlotte Hornets			
☐ 10 Steve Smith UER	.08	.04	.01
Miami Heat			
(Listed with Kings in '90-91;			
was not in NBA that year)			
☐ 11 Dave Johnson	.05	.02	.01
Portland Trail Blazers			
☐ 12 Tom Gugliotta	.10	.05	.01
Washington Bullets			
☐ 13 Doug Edwards	.08	.04	.01
Atlanta Hawks			
☐ 14 Vlade Divac	.10	.05	.01
Los Angeles Lakers			
☐ 15 Corie Blount	.05	.02	.01
Chicago Bulls			
☐ 16 Derek Harper	.08	.04	.01
Dallas Mavericks			
☐ 17 Matt Bullard	.05	.02	.01
Houston Rockets			
☐ 18 Terry Catledge	.05	.02	.01
Orlando Magic			
☐ 19 Mark Eaton	.05	.02	.01
Utah Jazz			
☐ 20 Mark Jackson	.05	.02	.01
Los Angeles Clippers			
☐ 21 Terry Mills	.05	.02	.01
Detroit Pistons			
☐ 22 Johnny Dawkins	.05	.02	.01
Philadelphia 76ers			
☐ 23 Michael Jordan UER	3.00	1.35	.40
Chicago Bulls			
(Listed as a forward with birthdate			
of 1968; he is a guard with			
bithdate of 1963)			
☐ 24 Rick Fox UER	.05	.02	.01
Boston Celtics			
(Listed with Kings in '91-92)			
☐ 25 Charles Oakley	.08	.04	.01
New York Knicks			
☐ 26 Derrick McKey	.08	.04	.01
Seattle Supersonics			
☐ 27 Christian Laettner	.10	.05	.01
Minnesota Timberwolves			
☐ 28 Todd Day	.08	.04	.01
Milwaukee Bucks			
☐ 29 Danny Ferry	.05	.02	.01
Cleveland Cavaliers			
☐ 30 Kevin Johnson	.15	.07	.02
Phoenix Suns			
☐ 31 Vinny Del Negro	.05	.02	.01
San Antonio Spurs			
☐ 32 Kevin Brooks	.05	.02	.01
Denver Nuggets			
☐ 33 Pete Chilcutt	.05	.02	.01
Sacramento Kings			
☐ 34 Larry Stewart	.05	.02	.01
Washington Bullets			
☐ 35 Dave Jamerson	.05	.02	.01
Houston Rockets			
☐ 36 Sidney Green	.05	.02	.01
Philadelphia 76ers			
☐ 37 J.R. Reid	.05	.02	.01
San Antonio Spurs			
☐ 38 Jimmy Jackson	.50	.23	.06
Dallas Mavericks			
☐ 39 Micheal Williams UER	.05	.02	.01
Minnesota Timberwolves			
(350.2 minutes per game)			
☐ 40 Rex Walters	.08	.04	.01
New Jersey Nets			
☐ 41 Shawn Bradley	.30	.14	.04
Philadelphia 76ers			
☐ 42 Jon Koncak	.05	.02	.01
Atlanta Hawks			
☐ 43 Byron Houston	.05	.02	.01
Golden State Warriors			
☐ 44 Brian Shaw	.05	.02	.01
Miami Heat			
☐ 45 Bill Cartwright	.05	.02	.01
Chicago Bulls			
☐ 46 Jerome Kersey	.05	.02	.01
Portland Trail Blazers			
☐ 47 Danny Schayes	.05	.02	.01
Milwaukee Bucks			
☐ 48 Olden Polynice	.05	.02	.01
Detroit Pistons			
☐ 49 Anthony Peeler	.05	.02	.01
Los Angeles Lakers			
☐ 50 Nick Anderson 50	.10	.05	.01
Orlando Magic			
☐ 51 David Benoit	.05	.02	.01
Utah Jazz			
☐ 52 David Robinson	.25	.11	.03
San Antonio Spurs			

□ 53	Greg Kite	.05	.02	.01
	Orlando Magic			
□ 54	Gerald Paddio	.05	.02	.01
	Seattle Supersonics			
□ 55	Don MacLean	.05	.02	.01
	Washington Bullets			
□ 56	Randy Woods	.05	.02	.01
	Los Angeles Clippers			
□ 57	Reggie Miller 50	.10	.05	.01
	Indiana Pacers			
□ 58	Kevin Gamble	.05	.02	.01
	Boston Celtics			
□ 59	Sean Green	.05	.02	.01
	Indiana Pacers			
□ 60	Jeff Hornacek	.08	.04	.01
	Philadelphia 76ers			
□ 61	John Starks	.08	.04	.01
	New York Knicks			
□ 62	Gerald Wilkins	.05	.02	.01
	Cleveland Cavaliers			
□ 63	Jim Les	.05	.02	.01
	Sacramento Kings			
□ 64	Michael Jordan 50	1.50	.65	.19
	Chicago Bulls			
□ 65	Alvin Robertson	.05	.02	.01
	Detroit Pistons			
□ 66	Tim Kempton	.05	.02	.01
	Phoenix Suns			
□ 67	Bryant Stith	.05	.02	.01
	Denver Nuggets			
□ 68	Jeff Turner	.05	.02	.01
	Orlando Magic			
□ 69	Malik Sealy	.05	.02	.01
	Indiana Pacers			
□ 70	Dell Curry	.05	.02	.01
	Charlotte Hornets			
□ 71	Brent Price	.05	.02	.01
	Washington Bullets			
□ 72	Kevin Lynch	.05	.02	.01
	Charlotte Hornets			
□ 73	Bimbo Coles	.05	.02	.01
	Miami Heat			
□ 74	Larry Nance	.08	.04	.01
	Cleveland Cavaliers			
□ 75	Luther Wright	.05	.02	.01
	Utah Jazz			
□ 76	Willie Anderson	.05	.02	.01
	San Antonio Spurs			
□ 77	Dennis Rodman	.15	.07	.02
	Detroit Pistons			
□ 78	Anthony Mason	.08	.04	.01
	New York Knicks			
□ 79	Chris Gatling	.05	.02	.01
	Golden State Warriors			
□ 80	Antoine Carr	.05	.02	.01
	San Antonio Spurs			
□ 81	Kevin Willis	.08	.04	.01
	Atlanta Hawks			
□ 82	Thurl Bailey	.05	.02	.01
	Minnesota Timberwolves			
□ 83	Reggie Williams	.05	.02	.01
	Denver Nuggets			
□ 84	Rod Strickland	.08	.04	.01
	Portland Trail Blazers			
□ 85	Rolando Blackman	.08	.04	.01
	New York Knicks			
□ 86	Bobby Hurley	.15	.07	.02
	Sacramento Kings			
□ 87	Jeff Malone	.08	.04	.01
	Utah Jazz			
□ 88	James Worthy	.10	.05	.01
	Los Angeles Lakers			
□ 89	Alaa Abdelnaby	.05	.02	.01
	Boston Celtics			
□ 90	Duane Ferrell	.05	.02	.01
	Atlanta Hawks			
□ 91	Anthony Avent	.05	.02	.01
	Milwaukee Bucks			
□ 92	Scottie Pippen	.25	.11	.03
	Chicago Bulls			
□ 93	Ricky Pierce	.08	.04	.01
	Seattle Supersonics			
□ 94	P.J. Brown	.10	.05	.01
	New Jersey Nets			
□ 95	Jeff Grayer	.05	.02	.01
	Golden State Warriors			
□ 96	Jerrod Mustaf	.05	.02	.01
	Phoenix Suns			
□ 97	Elmore Spencer	.05	.02	.01
	Los Angeles Clippers			
□ 98	Walt Williams	.10	.05	.01
	Sacramento Kings			
□ 99	Otis Thorpe	.08	.04	.01
	Houston Rockets			
□ 100	Patrick Ewing AS	.10	.05	.01
	New York Knicks			
□ 101	Michael Jordan AS	1.50	.65	.19
	Chicago Bulls			
□ 102	John Stockton AS	.10	.05	.01
	Utah Jazz			
□ 103	Dominique Wilkins AS	.08	.04	.01
	Atlanta Hawks			
□ 104	Charles Barkley AS	.25	.11	.03
	Phoenix Suns			
□ 105	Lee Mayberry	.05	.02	.01
	Milwaukee Bucks			
□ 106	James Edwards	.05	.02	.01
	Los Angeles Lakers			
□ 107	Scott Brooks	.05	.02	.01
	Houston Rockets			
□ 108	John Battle	.05	.02	.01
	Cleveland Cavaliers			
□ 109	Kenny Gattison	.05	.02	.01
	Charlotte Hornets			
□ 110	Pooh Richardson	.05	.02	.01
	Indiana Pacers			
□ 111	Rony Seikaly	.05	.02	.01
	Miami Heat			
□ 112	Mahmoud Abdul-Rauf	.05	.02	.01
	Denver Nuggets			
□ 113	Nick Anderson	.08	.04	.01
	Orlando Magic			
□ 114	Gundars Vetra	.05	.02	.01
	Minnesota Timberwolves			
□ 115	Joe Dumars AS	.08	.04	.01
	Detroit Pistons			
□ 116	Hakeem Olajuwon AS	.30	.14	.04
	Houston Rockets			
□ 117	Scottie Pippen AS	.10	.05	.01
	Chicago Bulls			
□ 118	Mark Price AS	.05	.02	.01
	Cleveland Cavaliers			
□ 119	Karl Malone AS	.10	.05	.01
	Utah Jazz			
□ 120	Michael Cage	.05	.02	.01
	Seattle Supersonics			
□ 121	Ed Pinckney	.05	.02	.01
	Boston Celtics			
□ 122	Jay Humphries	.05	.02	.01
	Utah Jazz			
□ 123	Dale Davis	.08	.04	.01
	Indiana Pacers			

☐ 124	Sean Rooks	.05	.02	.01
	Dallas Mavericks			
☐ 125	Mookie Blaylock	.08	.04	.01
	Atlanta Hawks			
☐ 126	Buck Williams	.08	.04	.01
	Portland Trail Blazers			
☐ 127	John Williams	.05	.02	.01
	Los Angeles Clippers			
☐ 128	Stacey King	.05	.02	.01
	Chicago Bulls			
☐ 129	Tim Perry	.05	.02	.01
	Philadelphia 76ers			
☐ 130	Tim Hardaway AS	.05	.02	.01
	Golden State Warriors			
☐ 131	Larry Johnson AS	.10	.05	.01
	Charlotte Hornets			
☐ 132	Detlef Schrempf AS	.05	.02	.01
	Indiana Pacers			
☐ 133	Reggie Miller AS	.10	.05	.01
	Indiana Pacers			
☐ 134	Shaquille O'Neal	1.00	.45	.13
	Orlando Magic			
☐ 135	Dale Ellis	.08	.04	.01
	San Antonio Spurs			
☐ 136	Duane Causwell	.05	.02	.01
	Sacramento Kings			
☐ 137	Rumeal Robinson	.05	.02	.01
	New Jersey Nets			
☐ 138	Billy Owens	.08	.04	.01
	Golden State Warriors			
☐ 139	Malcolm Mackey	.05	.02	.01
	Phoenix Suns			
☐ 140	Vernon Maxwell	.05	.02	.01
	Houston Rockets			
☐ 141	LaPhonso Ellis	.08	.04	.01
	Denver Nuggets			
☐ 142	Robert Parish	.10	.05	.01
	Boston Celtics			
☐ 143	LaBradford Smith	.05	.02	.01
	Washington Bullets			
☐ 144	Charles Smith	.05	.02	.01
	New York Knicks			
☐ 145	Terry Porter	.08	.04	.01
	Portland Trail Blazers			
☐ 146	Elden Campbell	.05	.02	.01
	Los Angeles Lakers			
☐ 147	Bill Laimbeer	.08	.04	.01
	Detroit Pistons			
☐ 148	Chris Mills	.30	.14	.04
	Cleveland Cavaliers			
☐ 149	Brad Lohaus	.05	.02	.01
	Milwaukee Bucks			
☐ 150	Jimmy Jackson ART	.25	.11	.03
	Dallas Mavericks			
☐ 151	Tom Gugliotta ART	.05	.02	.01
	Washington Bullets			
☐ 152	Shaquille O'Neal ART.	1.00	.45	.13
	Orlando Magic			
☐ 153	Latrell Sprewell ART	.25	.11	.03
	Golden State Warriors			
☐ 154	Walt Williams ART	.05	.02	.01
	Sacramento Kings			
☐ 155	Gary Payton	.10	.05	.01
	Seattle Supersonics			
☐ 156	Orlando Woolridge	.05	.02	.01
	Milwaukee Bucks			
☐ 157	Adam Keefe	.05	.02	.01
	Atlanta Hawks			
☐ 158	Calbert Cheaney	.40	.18	.05
	Washington Bullets			
☐ 159	Rick Mahorn	.05	.02	.01
	New Jersey Nets			
☐ 160	Robert Horry	.10	.05	.01
	Houston Rockets			
☐ 161	John Salley	.05	.02	.01
	Miami Heat			
☐ 162	Sam Mitchell	.05	.02	.01
	Indiana Pacers			
☐ 163	Stanley Roberts	.05	.02	.01
	Los Angeles Clippers			
☐ 164	Clarence Weatherspoon	.10	.05	.01
	Philadelphia 76ers			
☐ 165	Anthony Bowie	.05	.02	.01
	Orlando Magic			
☐ 166	Derrick Coleman	.10	.05	.01
	New Jersey Nets			
☐ 167	Negele Knight	.05	.02	.01
	Phoenix Suns			
☐ 168	Marlon Maxey	.05	.02	.01
	Minnesota Timberwolves			
☐ 169	Spud Webb UER	.08	.04	.01
	Sacramento Kings			
	(Listed as center instead of guard)			
☐ 170	Alonzo Mourning	.50	.23	.06
	Charlotte Hornets			
☐ 171	Ervin Johnson	.10	.05	.01
	Seattle Supersonics			
☐ 172	Sedale Threatt	.05	.02	.01
	Los Angeles Lakers			
☐ 173	Mark Macon	.05	.02	.01
	Denver Nuggets			
☐ 174	B.J. Armstrong	.05	.02	.01
	Chicago Bulls			
☐ 175	Harold Miner ART	.05	.02	.01
	Miami Heat			
☐ 176	Anthony Peeler ART	.05	.02	.01
	Los Angeles Lakers			
☐ 177	Alonzo Mourning ART..	.25	.11	.03
	Charlotte Hornets			
☐ 178	Christian Laettner ART.	.05	.02	.01
	Minnesota Timberwolves			
☐ 179	C. Weatherspoon ART..	.05	.02	.01
	Philadelphia 76ers			
☐ 180	Dee Brown	.08	.04	.01
	Boston Celtics			
☐ 181	Shaquille O'Neal	2.00	.90	.25
	Orlando Magic			
☐ 182	Loy Vaught	.08	.04	.01
	Los Angeles Clippers			
☐ 183	Terrell Brandon	.05	.02	.01
	Cleveland Cavaliers			
☐ 184	Lionel Simmons	.05	.02	.01
	Sacramento Kings			
☐ 185	Mark Aguirre	.08	.04	.01
	Detroit Pistons			
☐ 186	Danny Ainge	.08	.04	.01
	Phoenix Suns			
☐ 187	Reggie Miller	.25	.11	.03
	Indiana Pacers			
☐ 188	Terry Davis	.05	.02	.01
	Dallas Mavericks			
☐ 189	Mark Bryant	.05	.02	.01
	Portland Trail Blazers			
☐ 190	Tyrone Corbin	.05	.02	.01
	Utah Jazz			
☐ 191	Chris Mullin	.10	.05	.01
	Golden State Warriors			
☐ 192	Johnny Newman	.05	.02	.01
	Charlotte Hornets			
☐ 193	Doug West	.05	.02	.01
	Minnesota Timberwolves			
☐ 194	Keith Askins	.05	.02	.01

Miami Heat
- [ ] 195 Bo Kimble .05 .02 .01
New York Knicks
- [ ] 196 Sean Elliott .08 .04 .01
San Antonio Spurs
- [ ] 197 Checklist 1-99 UER .05 .02 .01
(No. 18 listed as Terry Mills
instead of Terry Cummings and
No. 23 listed as Sam Mitchell
instead of Michael Jordan)
- [ ] 198 Checklist 100-198 .05 .02 .01
- [ ] 199 Michael Jordan FPM .. 1.50 .65 .19
Chicago Bulls
- [ ] 200 Patrick Ewing FPM .10 .05 .01
New York Knicks
- [ ] 201 John Stockton FPM .10 .05 .01
Utah Jazz
- [ ] 202 Shawn Kemp FPM .25 .11 .03
Seattle Supersonics
- [ ] 203 Mark Price FPM .05 .02 .01
Cleveland Cavaliers
- [ ] 204 Charles Barkley FPM .25 .11 .03
Phoenix Suns
- [ ] 205 Hakeem Olajuwon FPM .30 .14 .04
Houston Rockets
- [ ] 206 Clyde Drexler FPM .10 .05 .01
Portland Trail Blazers
- [ ] 207 Kevin Johnson FPM .08 .04 .01
Phoenix Suns
- [ ] 208 John Starks FPM .05 .02 .01
New York Knicks
- [ ] 209 Chris Mullin FPM .05 .02 .01
Golden State Warriors
- [ ] 210 Doc Rivers .05 .02 .01
New York Knicks
- [ ] 211 Kenny Walker .05 .02 .01
Washington Bullets
- [ ] 212 Doug Christie .05 .02 .01
Los Angeles Lakers
- [ ] 213 James Robinson .15 .07 .02
Portland Trail Blazers
- [ ] 214 Larry Krystkowiak .05 .02 .01
Orlando Magic
- [ ] 215 Manute Bol .05 .02 .01
Miami Heat
- [ ] 216 Carl Herrera .05 .02 .01
Houston Rockets
- [ ] 217 Paul Graham .05 .02 .01
Atlanta Hawks
- [ ] 218 Jud Buechler .05 .02 .01
Golden State Warriors
- [ ] 219 Mike Brown .05 .02 .01
Minnesota Timberwolves
- [ ] 220 Tom Chambers .08 .04 .01
Utah Jazz
- [ ] 221 Kendall Gill .05 .02 .01
Seattle Supersonics
- [ ] 222 Kenny Anderson .10 .05 .01
New Jersey Nets
- [ ] 223 Larry Johnson .25 .11 .03
Charlotte Hornets
- [ ] 224 Chris Webber 1.25 .55 .16
Golden State Warriors
- [ ] 225 Randy White .05 .02 .01
Dallas Mavericks
- [ ] 226 Rik Smits .10 .05 .01
Indiana Pacers
- [ ] 227 A.C. Green .10 .05 .01
Phoenix Suns
- [ ] 228 David Robinson .50 .23 .06
San Antonio Spurs

- [ ] 229 Sean Elliott .08 .04 .01
Detroit Pistons
- [ ] 230 Gary Grant .05 .02 .01
Los Angeles Clippers
- [ ] 231 Dana Barros .10 .05 .01
Philadelphia 76ers
- [ ] 232 Bobby Hurley .08 .04 .01
Sacramento Kings
- [ ] 233 Blue Edwards .05 .02 .01
Milwaukee Bucks
- [ ] 234 Tom Hammonds .05 .02 .01
Denver Nuggets
- [ ] 235 Pete Myers .05 .02 .01
Chicago Bulls
- [ ] 236 Acie Earl .05 .02 .01
Boston Celtics
- [ ] 237 Tony Smith .05 .02 .01
Los Angeles Lakers
- [ ] 238 Bill Wennington .05 .02 .01
Chicago Bulls
- [ ] 239 Andrew Lang .05 .02 .01
Atlanta Hawks
- [ ] 240 Ervin Johnson .05 .02 .01
Seattle Supersonics
- [ ] 241 Byron Scott .08 .04 .01
Indiana Pacers
- [ ] 242 Eddie Johnson .08 .04 .01
Charlotte Hornets
- [ ] 243 Anthony Bonner .05 .02 .01
New York Knicks
- [ ] 244 Luther Wright .05 .02 .01
Utah Jazz
- [ ] 245 LaSalle Thompson .05 .02 .01
Indiana Pacers
- [ ] 246 Harold Miner .05 .02 .01
Miami Heat
- [ ] 247 Chris Smith .05 .02 .01
Minnesota Timberwolves
- [ ] 248 John Williams .08 .04 .01
Cleveland Cavaliers
- [ ] 249 Clyde Drexler .25 .11 .03
Portland Trail Blazers
- [ ] 250 Calbert Cheaney .05 .02 .01
Washington Bullets
- [ ] 251 Avery Johnson .05 .02 .01
Golden State Warriors
- [ ] 252 Steve Kerr .05 .02 .01
Chicago Bulls
- [ ] 253 Warren Kidd .05 .02 .01
Philadelphia 76ers
- [ ] 254 Wayman Tisdale .08 .04 .01
Sacramento Kings
- [ ] 255 Bob Martin .05 .02 .01
Milwaukee Bucks
- [ ] 256 Popeye Jones .25 .11 .03
Dallas Mavericks
- [ ] 257 Jimmy Oliver .05 .02 .01
Boston Celtics
- [ ] 258 Kevin Edwards .05 .02 .01
New Jersey Nets
- [ ] 259 Dan Majerle .08 .04 .01
Phoenix Suns
- [ ] 260 Jon Barry .05 .02 .01
Milwaukee Bucks
- [ ] 261 Allan Houston .30 .14 .04
Detroit Pistons
- [ ] 262 Dikembe Mutombo .20 .09 .03
Denver Nuggets
- [ ] 263 Sleepy Floyd .05 .02 .01
San Antonio Spurs
- [ ] 264 George Lynch .08 .04 .01

☐ 265	Los Angeles Lakers Stacey Augmon UER....	.08	.04	.01
	Atlanta Hawks (Listed with Heat in stats)			
☐ 266	Hakeem Olajuwon	.60	.25	.08
	Houston Rockets			
☐ 267	Scott Skiles	.05	.02	.01
	Orlando Magic			
☐ 268	Detlef Schrempf	.10	.05	.01
	Seattle Supersonics			
☐ 269	Brian Davis	.05	.02	.01
	Minnesota Timberwolves			
☐ 270	Tracy Murray	.05	.02	.01
	Portland Trail Blazers			
☐ 271	Gheorghe Muresan	.25	.11	.03
	Washington Bullets			
☐ 272	Terry Dehere	.08	.04	.01
	Los Angeles Clippers			
☐ 273	Terry Cummings	.08	.04	.01
	San Antonio Spurs			
☐ 274	Keith Jennings	.05	.02	.01
	Golden State Warriors			
☐ 275	Tyrone Hill	.08	.04	.01
	Cleveland Cavaliers			
☐ 276	Hersey Hawkins	.08	.04	.01
	Charlotte Hornets			
☐ 277	Grant Long	.05	.02	.01
	Miami Heat			
☐ 278	Herb Williams	.05	.02	.01
	New York Knicks			
☐ 279	Karl Malone	.25	.11	.03
	Utah Jazz			
☐ 280	Mitch Richmond	.15	.07	.02
	Sacramento Kings			
☐ 281	Derek Strong	.05	.02	.01
	Milwaukee Bucks			
☐ 282	Dino Radja	.30	.14	.04
	Boston Celtics			
☐ 283	Jack Haley	.05	.02	.01
	San Antonio Spurs			
☐ 284	Derek Harper	.08	.04	.01
	New York Knicks			
☐ 285	Dwayne Schintzius	.05	.02	.01
	New Jersey Nets			
☐ 286	Michael Curry	.05	.02	.01
	Philadelphia 76ers			
☐ 287	Rodney Rogers	.30	.14	.04
	Denver Nuggets			
☐ 288	Horace Grant	.15	.07	.02
	Chicago Bulls			
☐ 289	Oliver Miller	.08	.04	.01
	Phoenix Suns			
☐ 290	Luc Longley	.05	.02	.01
	Minnesota Timberwolves			
☐ 291	Walter Bond	.05	.02	.01
	Utah Jazz			
☐ 292	Dominique Wilkins	.15	.07	.02
	Atlanta Hawks			
☐ 293	Vern Fleming	.05	.02	.01
	Indiana Pacers			
☐ 294	Mark Price	.10	.05	.01
	Cleveland Cavaliers			
☐ 295	Mark Aguirre	.08	.04	.01
	Los Angeles Clippers			
☐ 296	Shawn Kemp................	.50	.23	.06
	Seattle Supersonics			
☐ 297	Pervis Ellison	.05	.02	.01
	Washington Bullets			
☐ 298	Josh Grant	.05	.02	.01
	Golden State Warriors			
☐ 299	Scott Burrell	.20	.09	.03

☐ 300	Charlotte Hornets Patrick Ewing	.25	.11	.03
	New York Knicks			
☐ 301	Sam Cassell	.40	.18	.05
	Houston Rockets			
☐ 302	Nick Van Exel	1.50	.65	.19
	Los Angeles Lakers			
☐ 303	Clifford Robinson	.10	.05	.01
	Portland Trail Blazers			
☐ 304	Frank Johnson	.05	.02	.01
	Phoenix Suns			
☐ 305	Matt Geiger	.05	.02	.01
	Miami Heat			
☐ 306	Vin Baker	.75	.35	.09
	Milwaukee Bucks			
☐ 307	Benoit Benjamin............	.05	.02	.01
	New Jersey Nets			
☐ 308	Shawn Bradley	.05	.02	.01
	Philadelphia 76ers			
☐ 309	Chris Whitney	.05	.02	.01
	San Antonio Spurs			
☐ 310	Eric Riley	.05	.02	.01
	Houston Rockets			
☐ 311	Isiah Thomas	.15	.07	.02
	Detroit Pistons			
☐ 312	Jamal Mashburn	1.50	.65	.19
	Dallas Mavericks			
☐ 313	Xavier McDaniel	.05	.02	.01
	Boston Celtics			
☐ 314	Mike Peplowski............	.05	.02	.01
	Sacramento Kings			
☐ 315	Darnell Mee................	.05	.02	.01
	Denver Nuggets			
☐ 316	Toni Kukoc	.40	.18	.05
	Chicago Bulls			
☐ 317	Felton Spencer	.05	.02	.01
	Utah Jazz			
☐ 318	Sam Bowie	.05	.02	.01
	Los Angeles Lakers			
☐ 319	Mario Elie................	.05	.02	.01
	Houston Rockets			
☐ 320	Tim Hardaway	.10	.05	.01
	Golden State Warriors			
☐ 321	Ken Norman................	.05	.02	.01
	Milwaukee Bucks			
☐ 322	Isaiah Rider	.50	.23	.06
	Minnesota Timberwolves			
☐ 323	Rex Chapman	.05	.02	.01
	Washington Bullets			
☐ 324	Dennis Rodman	.15	.07	.02
	San Antonio Spurs			
☐ 325	Derrick McKey	.08	.04	.01
	Indiana Pacers			
☐ 326	Corie Blount	.05	.02	.01
	Chicago Bulls			
☐ 327	Fat Lever	.05	.02	.01
	Dallas Mavericks			
☐ 328	Ron Harper	.08	.04	.01
	Los Angeles Clippers			
☐ 329	Eric Anderson	.05	.02	.01
	New York Knicks			
☐ 330	Armon Gilliam	.05	.02	.01
	New Jersey Nets			
☐ 331	Lindsey Hunter	.15	.07	.02
	Detroit Pistons			
☐ 332	Eric Leckner................	.05	.02	.01
	Philadelphia 76ers			
☐ 333	Chris Corchiani	.05	.02	.01
	Boston Celtics			
☐ 334	Anfernee Hardaway....	3.00	1.35	.40
	Orlando Magic			

☐ 335	Randy Brown	.05	.02	.01
	Sacramento Kings			
☐ 336	Sam Perkins	.08	.04	.01
	Seattle Supersonics			
☐ 337	Glen Rice	.10	.05	.01
	Miami Heat			
☐ 338	Orlando Woolridge	.05	.02	.01
	Philadelphia 76ers			
☐ 339	Mike Gminski	.05	.02	.01
	Charlotte Hornets			
☐ 340	Latrell Sprewell	.50	.23	.06
	Golden State Warriors			
☐ 341	Harvey Grant	.05	.02	.01
	Portland Trail Blazers			
☐ 342	Doug Smith	.05	.02	.01
	Dallas Mavericks			
☐ 343	Kevin Duckworth	.05	.02	.01
	Washington Bullets			
☐ 344	Cedric Ceballos	.10	.05	.01
	Phoenix Suns			
☐ 345	Chuck Person	.08	.04	.01
	Minnesota Timberwolves			
☐ 346	Scott Haskin	.05	.02	.01
	Indiana Pacers			
☐ 347	Frank Brickowski	.05	.02	.01
	Milwaukee Bucks			
☐ 348	Scott Williams	.05	.02	.01
	Chicago Bulls			
☐ 349	Brad Daugherty	.08	.04	.01
	Cleveland Cavaliers			
☐ 350	Willie Burton	.05	.02	.01
	Miami Heat			
☐ 351	Joe Dumars	.15	.07	.02
	Detroit Pistons			
☐ 352	Craig Ehlo	.05	.02	.01
	Atlanta Hawks			
☐ 353	Lucious Harris	.10	.05	.01
	Dallas Mavericks			
☐ 354	Danny Manning	.10	.05	.01
	Los Angeles Clippers			
☐ 355	Litterial Green	.05	.02	.01
	Orlando Magic			
☐ 356	John Stockton	.25	.11	.03
	Utah Jazz			
☐ 357	Nate McMillan	.05	.02	.01
	Seattle Supersonics			
☐ 358	Greg Graham	.05	.02	.01
	Philadelphia 76ers			
☐ 359	Rex Walters	.05	.02	.01
	New Jersey Nets			
☐ 360	Lloyd Daniels	.05	.02	.01
	San Antonio Spurs			
☐ 361	Antonio Harvey	.08	.04	.01
	Los Angeles Lakers			
☐ 362	Brian Williams	.05	.02	.01
	Denver Nuggets			
☐ 363	LeRon Ellis	.05	.02	.01
	Charlotte Hornets			
☐ 364	Chris Dudley	.05	.02	.01
	Portland Trail Blazers			
☐ 365	Hubert Davis	.05	.02	.01
	New York Knicks			
☐ 366	Evers Burns	.05	.02	.01
	Sacramento Kings			
☐ 367	Sherman Douglas	.05	.02	.01
	Boston Celtics			
☐ 368	Sarunas Marciulionis	.05	.02	.01
	Golden State Warriors			
☐ 369	Tom Tolbert	.05	.02	.01
	Orlando Magic			
☐ 370	Robert Pack	.05	.02	.01
	Denver Nuggets			
☐ 371	Michael Adams	.05	.02	.01
	Washington Bullets			
☐ 372	Negele Knight	.05	.02	.01
	San Antonio Spurs			
☐ 373	Charles Barkley	.50	.23	.06
	Phoenix Suns			
☐ 374	Bryon Russell	.05	.02	.01
	Utah Jazz			
☐ 375	Greg Anthony	.05	.02	.01
	New York Knicks			
☐ 376	Ken Williams	.05	.02	.01
	Indiana Pacers			
☐ 377	John Paxson	.05	.02	.01
	Chicago Bulls			
☐ 378	Corey Gaines	.05	.02	.01
	New York Knicks			
☐ 379	Eric Murdock	.05	.02	.01
	Milwaukee Bucks			
☐ 380	Kevin Thompson	.05	.02	.01
	Portland Trail Blazers			
☐ 381	Moses Malone	.15	.07	.02
	Philadelphia 76ers			
☐ 382	Kenny Smith	.05	.02	.01
	Houston Rockets			
☐ 383	Dennis Scott	.05	.02	.01
	Orlando Magic			
☐ 384	Michael Jordan FSL	1.50	.65	.19
	Chicago Bulls			
☐ 385	Hakeem Olajuwon FSL	.30	.14	.04
	Houston Rockets			
☐ 386	Shaquille O'Neal FSL	1.00	.45	.13
	Orlando Magic			
☐ 387	David Robinson FSL	.25	.11	.03
	San Antonio Spurs			
☐ 388	Derrick Coleman FSL	.05	.02	.01
	New Jersey Nets			
☐ 389	Karl Malone FSL	.10	.05	.01
	Utah Jazz			
☐ 390	Patrick Ewing FSL	.10	.05	.01
	New York Knicks			
☐ 391	Scottie Pippen FSL	.10	.05	.01
	Chicago Bulls			
☐ 392	Dominique Wilkins FSL	.08	.04	.01
	Atlanta Hawks			
☐ 393	Charles Barkley FSL	.25	.11	.03
	Phoenix Suns			
☐ 394	Larry Johnson FSL	.10	.05	.01
	Charlotte Hornets			
☐ 395	Checklist	.05	.02	.01
☐ 396	Checklist	.05	.02	.01
☐ NNO	Expired Finest	1.00	.45	.13
	Redemption Card			

1993-94 Topps Gold

The cards of this parallel set were distributed through various means. Each pack of '93-94 Topps contained one Gold card with two Gold cards inserted in every fourth pack. Three Gold cards were inserted in every rack pack and 10 in every factory set. Aside from the gold-foil highlights, the 396 standard-size (2 1/2" by 3 1/2") Gold cards are identical to their regular issue counterparts, except the four regular issue check

list cards were replaced by Gold cards featuring the players listed below. The cards are numbered on the back. Please refer to the multipliers provided below (coupled with the prices of the corresponding regular issue card) to ascertain value.

	MINT	NRMT	EXC
COMPLETE SET (396)	75.00	34.00	9.50
COMPLETE SERIES 1 (198)	30.00	13.50	3.80
COMPLETE SERIES 2 (198)	45.00	20.00	5.75
COMMON CARD (1-396)	.10	.05	.01
*STARS: 2X to 4X BASIC CARDS			
*ROOKIES: 1.25X to 2.5X BASIC CARDS			

		MINT	NRMT	EXC
☐ 197G	Frank Johnson Phoenix Suns	.50	.23	.06
☐ 198G	David Wingate Charlotte Hornets	.50	.23	.06
☐ 395G	Will Perdue Chicago Bulls	.50	.23	.06
☐ 396G	Mark West Phoenix Suns	.50	.23	.06

1993-94 Topps Black Gold

Randomly inserted in first and second series packs and three per factory set, this 25-card standard size (2 1/2" by 3 1/2") set features the top five draft picks each year from 1989-1993. Thirteen cards were inserts in series one and 12 in series two. They were inserted at a rate of one in 72 for 12-card packs and one in 18 for 29-card packs. Winner A cards, redeemable for a series 1 set, were randomly inserted into 1 in every 144 series 1 packs. Winner B cards, redeemable for a series 2 set, were randomly inserted into 1 in every 144 series 2 packs. The A/B Winner card (randomly inserted into 1 in every 288 series 2 packs only) was redeemable for a complete set. Each white-bordered front displays a color action player shot with the background tinted in black. Gold prismatic wavy stripes appear above and below the photo with the player's name reversed out of the black bar near the bottom. The white-bordered horizontal backs carry a close-up color cutout on a black background with white concentric stripes. The player's name appears in gold-foil lettering on a wood textured bar with the team name directly to the right in black lettering. Player statistics appear below in an orange background. The cards are numbered on the back.

		MINT	NRMT	EXC
COMPLETE SET (25)		25.00	11.50	3.10
COMPLETE SERIES 1 (13)		5.00	2.30	.60
COMPLETE SERIES 2 (12)		20.00	9.00	2.50
COMMON CARD (1-25)		.25	.11	.03

		MINT	NRMT	EXC
☐ 1	Sean Elliott San Antonio Spurs	.35	.16	.04
☐ 2	Dennis Scott Orlando Magic	.25	.11	.03
☐ 3	Kenny Anderson New Jersey Nets	.50	.23	.06
☐ 4	Alonzo Mourning Charlotte Hornets	2.00	.90	.25
☐ 5	Glen Rice Miami Heat	.50	.23	.06
☐ 6	Billy Owens Golden State Warriors	.35	.16	.04
☐ 7	Jim Jackson Dallas Mavericks	2.00	.90	.25
☐ 8	Derrick Coleman New Jersey Nets	.25	.11	.03
☐ 9	Larry Johnson Charlotte Hornets	1.00	.45	.13
☐ 10	Gary Payton Seattle Supersonics	.50	.23	.06
☐ 11	Christian Laettner Minnesota Timberwolves	.50	.23	.06
☐ 12	Dikembe Mutombo Denver Nuggets	.75	.35	.09
☐ 13	Mahmoud Abdul-Rauf Denver Nuggets	.35	.16	.04
☐ 14	Isaiah Rider Minnesota Timberwolves	1.25	.55	.16
☐ 15	Steve Smith Miami Heat	.35	.16	.04
☐ 16	LaPhonso Ellis Denver Nuggets	.35	.16	.04
☐ 17	Danny Ferry Cleveland Cavaliers	.25	.11	.03
☐ 18	Shaquille O'Neal Orlando Magic	8.00	3.60	1.00
☐ 19	Anfernee Hardaway Orlando Magic	8.00	3.60	1.00
☐ 20	J.R. Reid San Antonio Spurs	.25	.11	.03
☐ 21	Shawn Bradley Philadelphia 76ers	.50	.23	.06
☐ 22	Pervis Ellison	.25	.11	.03

Washington Bullets
☐ 23	Chris Webber	3.00	1.35	.40
	Golden State Warriors			
☐ 24	Jamal Mashburn	4.00	1.80	.50
	Dallas Mavericks			
☐ 25	Kendall Gill	.25	.11	.03
	Seattle Supersonics			
☐ A	Expired Winner A	.75	.35	.09
☐ AX	Redeemed Winner A	.25	.11	.03
☐ B	Expired Winner B	.75	.35	.09
☐ BX	Redeemed Winner B	.25	.11	.03
☐ AB	Expired Winner A/B	1.50	.65	.19

1994-95 Topps

The 396 cards that comprise the 1994-95 Topps set were issued in two separate series of 198 cards each. Cards were dis tributed primarily in 12-card packs that car ried a suggested retail price of 1.00 each. Fronts feature full-color action photos framed by a jagged white border. Player's name and team are placed in gold foil along the bottom. The following subsets are included in this set: Eastern All-Star (1-13), Paint Patrol (100-109), and Western All-Star (183-195). In addition, various From the Roof subsets cards are intermingled within the set.

	MINT	NRMT	EXC
COMPLETE SET (396)	30.00	13.50	3.80
COMPLETE SERIES 1 (198)	12.00	5.50	1.50
COMPLETE SERIES 2 (198)	18.00	8.00	2.30
COMMON CARD (1-396)	.05	.02	.01

☐ 1	Patrick Ewing AS	.10	.05	.01
	New York Knicks			
☐ 2	Mookie Blaylock AS	.05	.02	.01
	Atlanta Hawks			
☐ 3	Charles Oakley AS	.05	.02	.01
	New York Knicks			
☐ 4	Mark Price AS	.05	.02	.01
	Cleveland Cavaliers			
☐ 5	John Starks AS	.05	.02	.01
	New York Knicks			
☐ 6	Dominique Wilkins AS	.08	.04	.01
	Atlanta Hawks			
☐ 7	Horace Grant AS	.08	.04	.01
	Chicago Bulls			
☐ 8	Alonzo Mourning AS	.15	.07	.02
	Charlotte Hornets			
☐ 9	B.J. Armstrong AS	.05	.02	.01
	Chicago Bulls			

☐ 10	Kenny Anderson AS	.05	.02	.01
	New Jersey Nets			
☐ 11	Scottie Pippen AS	.10	.05	.01
	Chicago Bulls			
☐ 12	Derrick Coleman AS	.05	.02	.01
	New Jersey Nets			
☐ 13	Shaquille O'Neal AS	.60	.25	.08
	Orlando Magic			
☐ 14	Anfernee Hardaway SPEC	.50	.23	.06
	Orlando Magic			
☐ 15	Isaiah Rider SPEC	.08	.04	.01
	Minnesota Timberwolves			
☐ 16	John Williams	.08	.04	.01
	Cleveland Cavaliers			
☐ 17	Todd Day	.08	.04	.01
	Milwaukee Bucks			
☐ 18	Dale Davis	.08	.04	.01
	Indiana Pacers			
☐ 19	Sean Rooks	.05	.02	.01
	Dallas Mavericks			
☐ 20	George Lynch	.05	.02	.01
	Los Angeles Lakers			
☐ 21	Mitchell Butler	.05	.02	.01
	Washington Bullets			
☐ 22	Stacey King	.05	.02	.01
	Minnesota Timberwolves			
☐ 23	Sherman Douglas	.05	.02	.01
	Boston Celtics			
☐ 24	Derrick McKey	.08	.04	.01
	Indiana Pacers			
☐ 25	Joe Dumars	.15	.07	.02
	Detroit Pistons			
☐ 26	Scott Brooks	.05	.02	.01
	Houston Rockets			
☐ 27	Clarence Weatherspoon	.10	.05	.01
	Philadelphia 76ers			
☐ 28	Jayson Williams	.05	.02	.01
	New Jersey Nets			
☐ 29	Scottie Pippen	.25	.11	.03
	Chicago Bulls			
☐ 30	John Starks	.08	.04	.01
	New York Knicks			
☐ 31	Robert Pack	.05	.02	.01
	Denver Nuggets			
☐ 32	Donald Royal	.05	.02	.01
	Orlando Magic			
☐ 33	Haywoode Workman	.05	.02	.01
	Indiana Pacers			
☐ 34	Greg Graham	.05	.02	.01
	Philadelphia 76ers			
☐ 35	Terry Cummings	.08	.04	.01
	San Antonio Spurs			
☐ 36	Andrew Lang	.05	.02	.01
	Atlanta Hawks			
☐ 37	Jason Kidd	2.50	1.15	.30
	Dallas Mavericks			
☐ 38	Terry Mills	.05	.02	.01
	Detroit Pistons			
☐ 39	Alonzo Mourning	.30	.14	.04
	Charlotte Hornets			
☐ 40	Shawn Kemp	.50	.23	.06
	Seattle Supersonics			
☐ 41	Kevin Willis FTR	.05	.02	.01
	Atlanta Hawks			
☐ 42	Kevin Willis	.08	.04	.01
	Atlanta Hawks			
☐ 43	Armon Gilliam	.05	.02	.01
	New Jersey Nets			
☐ 44	Bobby Hurley	.08	.04	.01
	Sacramento Kings			
☐ 45	Jerome Kersey	.05	.02	.01

	Portland Trail Blazers			
☐ 46	Xavier McDaniel	.08	.04	.01
	Boston Celtics			
☐ 47	Chris Webber	.40	.18	.05
	Golden State Warriors			
☐ 48	Chris Webber FTR	.20	.09	.03
	Golden State Warriors			
☐ 49	Jeff Malone	.08	.04	.01
	Philadelphia 76ers			
☐ 50	Dikembe Mutombo SPEC	.08	.04	.01
	Denver Nuggets			
☐ 51	Dan Majerle SPEC	.05	.02	.01
	Phoenix Suns			
☐ 52	Dee Brown SPEC	.05	.02	.01
	Boston Celtics			
☐ 53	John Stockton SPEC	.10	.05	.01
	Utah Jazz			
☐ 54	Dennis Rodman SPEC	.08	.04	.01
	San Antonio Spurs			
☐ 55	Eric Murdock SPEC	.05	.02	.01
	Milwaukee Bucks			
☐ 56	Glen Rice	.10	.05	.01
	Miami Heat			
☐ 57	Glen Rice FTR	.05	.02	.01
	Miami Heat			
☐ 58	Dino Radja	.10	.05	.01
	Boston Celtics			
☐ 59	Billy Owens	.08	.04	.01
	Golden State Warriors			
☐ 60	Doc Rivers	.05	.02	.01
	New York Knicks			
☐ 61	Don MacLean	.05	.02	.01
	Washington Bullets			
☐ 62	Lindsey Hunter	.05	.02	.01
	Detroit Pistons			
☐ 63	Sam Cassell	.10	.05	.01
	Houston Rockets			
☐ 64	James Worthy	.10	.05	.01
	Los Angeles Lakers			
☐ 65	Christian Laettner	.08	.04	.01
	Minnesota Timberwolves			
☐ 66	Wesley Person	.50	.23	.06
	Phoenix Suns			
☐ 67	Rich King	.05	.02	.01
	Seattle Supersonics			
☐ 68	Jon Koncak	.05	.02	.01
	Atlanta Hawks			
☐ 69	Muggsy Bogues	.10	.05	.01
	Charlotte Hornets			
☐ 70	Jamal Mashburn	.50	.23	.06
	Dallas Mavericks			
☐ 71	Gary Grant	.05	.02	.01
	Los Angeles Clippers			
☐ 72	Eric Murdock	.05	.02	.01
	Milwaukee Bucks			
☐ 73	Scott Burrell	.05	.02	.01
	Charlotte Hornets			
☐ 74	Scott Burrell FTR	.05	.02	.01
	Charlotte Hornets			
☐ 75	Anfernee Hardaway	1.00	.45	.13
	Orlando Magic			
☐ 76	Anfernee Hardaway FTR	.50	.23	.06
	Orlando Magic			
☐ 77	Yinka Dare	.08	.04	.01
	New Jersey Nets			
☐ 78	Anthony Avent	.05	.02	.01
	Orlando Magic			
☐ 79	Jon Barry	.05	.02	.01
	Milwaukee Bucks			
☐ 80	Rodney Rogers	.10	.05	.01
	Denver Nuggets			
☐ 81	Chris Mills	.10	.05	.01
	Cleveland Cavaliers			
☐ 82	Antonio Davis	.05	.02	.01
	Indiana Pacers			
☐ 83	Steve Smith	.08	.04	.01
	Miami Heat			
☐ 84	Buck Williams	.08	.04	.01
	Portland Trail Blazers			
☐ 85	Spud Webb	.08	.04	.01
	Sacramento Kings			
☐ 86	Stacey Augmon	.08	.04	.01
	Atlanta Hawks			
☐ 87	Allan Houston	.10	.05	.01
	Detroit Pistons			
☐ 88	Will Perdue	.05	.02	.01
	Chicago Bulls			
☐ 89	Chris Gatling	.05	.02	.01
	Golden State Warriors			
☐ 90	Danny Ainge	.08	.04	.01
	Phoenix Suns			
☐ 91	Rick Mahorn	.05	.02	.01
	New Jersey Nets			
☐ 92	Elmore Spencer	.05	.02	.01
	Los Angeles Clippers			
☐ 93	Vin Baker	.25	.11	.03
	Milwaukee Bucks			
☐ 94	Rex Chapman	.05	.02	.01
	Washington Bullets			
☐ 95	Dale Ellis	.08	.04	.01
	San Antonio Spurs			
☐ 96	Doug Smith	.05	.02	.01
	Dallas Mavericks			
☐ 97	Tim Perry	.05	.02	.01
	Philadelphia 76ers			
☐ 98	Toni Kukoc	.10	.05	.01
	Chicago Bulls			
☐ 99	Terry Dehere	.05	.02	.01
	Los Angeles Clippers			
☐ 100	Shaquille O'Neal PP	.60	.25	.08
	Orlando Magic			
☐ 101	Shawn Kemp PP	.25	.11	.03
	Seattle Supersonics			
☐ 102	Hakeem Olajuwon PP	.30	.14	.04
	Houston Rockets			
☐ 103	Derrick Coleman PP	.05	.02	.01
	New Jersey Nets			
☐ 104	Alonzo Mourning PP	.15	.07	.02
	Charlotte Hornets			
☐ 105	Dikembe Mutombo PP	.08	.04	.01
	Denver Nuggets			
☐ 106	Chris Webber PP	.20	.09	.03
	Golden State Warriors			
☐ 107	Dennis Rodman PP	.08	.04	.01
	San Antonio Spurs			
☐ 108	David Robinson PP	.25	.11	.03
	San Antonio Spurs			
☐ 109	Charles Barkley PP	.25	.11	.03
	Phoenix Suns			
☐ 110	Brad Daugherty	.08	.04	.01
	Cleveland Cavaliers			
☐ 111	Derek Harper	.08	.04	.01
	New York Knicks			
☐ 112	Detlef Schrempf	.10	.05	.01
	Seattle Supersonics			
☐ 113	Harvey Grant	.05	.02	.01
	Portland Trail Blazers			
☐ 114	Vlade Divac	.10	.05	.01
	Los Angeles Lakers			
☐ 115	Isaiah Rider	.15	.07	.02
	Minnesota Timberwolves			
☐ 116	Mitch Richmond	.15	.07	.02

	Sacramento Kings			
☐ 117	Tom Chambers	.08	.04	.01
	Utah Jazz			
☐ 118	Kenny Gattison	.05	.02	.01
	Charlotte Hornets			
☐ 119	Kenny Gattison FTR	.05	.02	.01
	Charlotte Hornets			
☐ 120	Vernon Maxwell	.05	.02	.01
	Houston Rockets			
☐ 121	Reggie Williams	.05	.02	.01
	Denver Nuggets			
☐ 122	Chris Mullin	.10	.05	.01
	Golden State Warriors			
☐ 123	Harold Miner	.05	.02	.01
	Miami Heat			
☐ 124	Harold Miner FTR	.05	.02	.01
	Miami Heat			
☐ 125	Calbert Cheaney	.10	.05	.01
	Washington Bullets			
☐ 126	Randy Woods	.05	.02	.01
	Los Angeles Clippers			
☐ 127	Mike Gminski	.05	.02	.01
	Milwaukee Bucks			
☐ 128	Willie Anderson	.05	.02	.01
	San Antonio Spurs			
☐ 129	Mark Macon	.05	.02	.01
	Detroit Pistons			
☐ 130	Avery Johnson	.05	.02	.01
	San Antonio Spurs			
☐ 131	Bimbo Coles	.05	.02	.01
	Miami Heat			
☐ 132	Kenny Smith	.05	.02	.01
	Houston Rockets			
☐ 133	Dennis Scott	.05	.02	.01
	Orlando Magic			
☐ 134	Lionel Simmons	.05	.02	.01
	Sacramento Kings			
☐ 135	Nate McMillan	.05	.02	.01
	Seattle Supersonics			
☐ 136	Eric Montross	.40	.18	.05
	Boston Celtics			
☐ 137	Sedale Threatt	.05	.02	.01
	Los Angeles Lakers			
☐ 138	Kenny Anderson	.10	.05	.01
	New Jersey Nets			
☐ 139	Micheal Williams	.05	.02	.01
	Minnesota Timberwolves			
☐ 140	Grant Long	.05	.02	.01
	Miami Heat			
☐ 141	Grant Long FTR	.05	.02	.01
	Miami Heat			
☐ 142	Tyrone Corbin	.05	.02	.01
	Utah Jazz			
☐ 143	Craig Ehlo	.05	.02	.01
	Atlanta Hawks			
☐ 144	Gerald Wilkins	.05	.02	.01
	Cleveland Cavaliers			
☐ 145	LaPhonso Ellis	.05	.02	.01
	Denver Nuggets			
☐ 146	Reggie Miller	.25	.11	.03
	Indiana Pacers			
☐ 147	Tracy Murray	.05	.02	.01
	Portland Trail Blazers			
☐ 148	Victor Alexander	.05	.02	.01
	Golden State Warriors			
☐ 149	Victor Alexander FTR	.05	.02	.01
	Golden State Warriors			
☐ 150	Clifford Robinson	.08	.04	.01
	Portland Trail Blazers			
☐ 151	Anthony Mason FTR	.05	.02	.01
	New York Knicks			
☐ 152	Anthony Mason	.08	.04	.01
	New York Knicks			
☐ 153	Jim Jackson	.30	.14	.04
	Dallas Mavericks			
☐ 154	Jeff Hornacek	.08	.04	.01
	Utah Jazz			
☐ 155	Nick Anderson	.08	.04	.01
	Orlando Magic			
☐ 156	Mike Brown	.05	.02	.01
	Minnesota Timberwolves			
☐ 157	Kevin Johnson	.15	.07	.02
	Phoenix Suns			
☐ 158	John Paxson	.05	.02	.01
	Chicago Bulls			
☐ 159	Loy Vaught	.08	.04	.01
	Los Angeles Clippers			
☐ 160	Carl Herrera	.05	.02	.01
	Houston Rockets			
☐ 161	Shawn Bradley	.10	.05	.01
	Philadelphia 76ers			
☐ 162	Hubert Davis	.05	.02	.01
	New York Knicks			
☐ 163	David Benoit	.05	.02	.01
	Utah Jazz			
☐ 164	Dell Curry	.05	.02	.01
	Charlotte Hornets			
☐ 165	Dee Brown	.08	.04	.01
	Boston Celtics			
☐ 166	LaSalle Thompson	.05	.02	.01
	Indiana Pacers			
☐ 167	Eddie Jones	1.50	.65	.19
	Los Angeles Lakers			
☐ 168	Walt Williams	.08	.04	.01
	Sacramento Kings			
☐ 169	A.C. Green	.10	.05	.01
	Phoenix Suns			
☐ 170	Kendall Gill	.05	.02	.01
	Seattle Supersonics			
☐ 171	Kendall Gill FTR	.05	.02	.01
	Seattle Supersonics			
☐ 172	Danny Ferry	.05	.02	.01
	Cleveland Cavaliers			
☐ 173	Bryant Stith	.05	.02	.01
	Denver Nuggets			
☐ 174	John Salley	.05	.02	.01
	Miami Heat			
☐ 175	Cedric Ceballos	.10	.05	.01
	Phoenix Suns			
☐ 176	Derrick Coleman	.10	.05	.01
	New Jersey Nets			
☐ 177	Tony Bennett	.05	.02	.01
	Charlotte Hornets			
☐ 178	Kevin Duckworth	.05	.02	.01
	Washington Bullets			
☐ 179	Jay Humphries	.05	.02	.01
	Utah Jazz			
☐ 180	Sean Elliott	.08	.04	.01
	San Antonio Spurs			
☐ 181	Sam Perkins	.08	.04	.01
	Seattle Supersonics			
☐ 182	Luc Longley	.05	.02	.01
	Chicago Bulls			
☐ 183	Mitch Richmond AS	.08	.04	.01
	Sacramento Kings			
☐ 184	Clyde Drexler AS	.10	.05	.01
	Portland Trail Blazers			
☐ 185	Karl Malone AS	.10	.05	.01
	Utah Jazz			
☐ 186	Shawn Kemp AS	.25	.11	.03
	Seattle Supersonics			
☐ 187	Hakeem Olajuwon AS	.30	.14	.04

	Houston Rockets			
☐ 188	Danny Manning AS	.05	.02	.01
	Los Angeles Clippers			
☐ 189	Kevin Johnson AS	.08	.04	.01
	Phoenix Suns			
☐ 190	John Stockton AS	.10	.05	.01
	Utah Jazz			
☐ 191	Latrell Sprewell AS	.15	.07	.02
	Golden State Warriors			
☐ 192	Gary Payton AS	.05	.02	.01
	Seattle Supersonics			
☐ 193	Clifford Robinson AS	.05	.02	.01
	Portland Trail Blazers			
☐ 194	David Robinson AS	.25	.11	.03
	San Antonio Spurs			
☐ 195	Charles Barkley AS	.25	.11	.03
	Phoenix Suns			
☐ 196	Mark Price SPEC	.05	.02	.01
	Cleveland Cavaliers			
☐ 197	Checklist 1-99	.05	.02	.01
☐ 198	Checklist 100-198	.05	.02	.01
☐ 199	Patrick Ewing	.25	.11	.03
	New York Knicks			
☐ 200	Patrick Ewing FR	.10	.05	.01
	New York Knicks			
☐ 201	Tracy Murray PP	.05	.02	.01
	Portland Trail Blazers			
☐ 202	Craig Ehlo PP	.05	.02	.01
	Atlanta Hawks			
☐ 203	Nick Anderson PP	.05	.02	.01
	Orlando Magic			
☐ 204	John Starks PP	.05	.02	.01
	New York Knicks			
☐ 205	Rex Chapman PP	.05	.02	.01
	Washington Bullets			
☐ 206	Hersey Hawkins PP	.05	.02	.01
	Charlotte Hornets			
☐ 207	Glen Rice PP	.05	.02	.01
	Miami Heat			
☐ 208	Jeff Malone PP	.05	.02	.01
	Philadelphia 76ers			
☐ 209	Dan Majerle PP	.05	.02	.01
	Phoenix Suns			
☐ 210	Chris Mullin PP	.05	.02	.01
	Golden State Warriors			
☐ 211	Grant Hill	4.00	1.80	.50
	Detroit Pistons			
☐ 212	Bobby Phills	.05	.02	.01
	Cleveland Cavaliers			
☐ 213	Dennis Rodman	.15	.07	.02
	San Antonio Spurs			
☐ 214	Doug West	.05	.02	.01
	Minnesota Timberwolves			
☐ 215	Harold Ellis	.05	.02	.01
	Los Angeles Clippers			
☐ 216	Kevin Edwards	.05	.02	.01
	New Jersey Nets			
☐ 217	Lorenzo Williams	.05	.02	.01
	Dallas Mavericks			
☐ 218	Rick Fox	.05	.02	.01
	Boston Celtics			
☐ 219	Mookie Blaylock	.08	.04	.01
	Atlanta Hawks			
☐ 220	Mookie Blaylock FR	.05	.02	.01
	Atlanta Hawks			
☐ 221	John Williams	.05	.02	.01
	Indiana Pacers			
☐ 222	Keith Jennings	.05	.02	.01
	Golden State Warriors			
☐ 223	Nick Van Exel	.50	.23	.06
	Los Angeles Lakers			
☐ 224	Gary Payton	.10	.05	.01
	Seattle Supersonics			
☐ 225	John Stockton	.25	.11	.03
	Utah Jazz			
☐ 226	Ron Harper	.08	.04	.01
	Chicago Bulls			
☐ 227	Monty Williams	.15	.07	.02
	New York Knicks			
☐ 228	Marty Conlon	.05	.02	.01
	Milwaukee Bucks			
☐ 229	Hersey Hawkins	.08	.04	.01
	Charlotte Hornets			
☐ 230	Rik Smits	.10	.05	.01
	Indiana Pacers			
☐ 231	James Robinson	.05	.02	.01
	Portland Trail Blazers			
☐ 232	Malik Sealy	.05	.02	.01
	Los Angeles Clippers			
☐ 233	Sergei Bazarevich	.05	.02	.01
	Atlanta Hawks			
☐ 234	Brad Lohaus	.05	.02	.01
	Miami Heat			
☐ 235	Olden Polynice	.05	.02	.01
	Sacramento Kings			
☐ 236	Brian Williams	.05	.02	.01
	Denver Nuggets			
☐ 237	Tyrone Hill	.08	.04	.01
	Cleveland Cavaliers			
☐ 238	Jim McIlvaine	.05	.02	.01
	Washington Bullets			
☐ 239	Latrell Sprewell	.30	.14	.04
	Golden State Warriors			
☐ 240	Latrell Sprewell FR	.15	.07	.02
	Golden State Warriors			
☐ 241	Popeye Jones	.05	.02	.01
	Dallas Mavericks			
☐ 242	Scott Williams	.05	.02	.01
	Philadelphia 76ers			
☐ 243	Eddie Jones	.75	.35	.09
	Los Angeles Lakers			
☐ 244	Moses Malone	.15	.07	.02
	San Antonio Spurs			
☐ 245	B.J. Armstrong	.05	.02	.01
	Chicago Bulls			
☐ 246	Jim Les	.05	.02	.01
	Atlanta Hawks			
☐ 247	Greg Grant	.05	.02	.01
	Orlando Magic			
☐ 248	Lee Mayberry	.05	.02	.01
	Milwaukee Bucks			
☐ 249	Mark Jackson	.05	.02	.01
	Indiana Pacers			
☐ 250	Larry Johnson	.20	.09	.03
	Charlotte Hornets			
☐ 251	Terrell Brandon	.05	.02	.01
	Cleveland Cavaliers			
☐ 252	Ledell Eackles	.05	.02	.01
	Miami Heat			
☐ 253	Yinka Dare	.05	.02	.01
	New Jersey Nets			
☐ 254	Dontonio Wingfield	.10	.05	.01
	Seattle Supersonics			
☐ 255	Clyde Drexler	.25	.11	.03
	Portland Trail Blazers			
☐ 256	Andres Guibert	.05	.02	.01
	Minnesota Timberwolves			
☐ 257	Gheorghe Muresan	.08	.04	.01
	Washington Bullets			
☐ 258	Tom Hammonds	.05	.02	.01
	Denver Nuggets			
☐ 259	Charles Barkley	.50	.23	.06

Phoenix Suns			
☐ 260 Charles Barkley FR	.25	.11	.03
Phoenix Suns			
☐ 261 Acie Earl	.05	.02	.01
Boston Celtics			
☐ 262 Lamond Murray	.40	.18	.05
Los Angeles Clippers			
☐ 263 Dana Barros	.10	.05	.01
Philadelphia 76ers			
☐ 264 Greg Anthony	.05	.02	.01
New York Knicks			
☐ 265 Dan Majerle	.08	.04	.01
Phoenix Suns			
☐ 266 Zan Tabak	.05	.02	.01
Houston Rockets			
☐ 267 Ricky Pierce	.08	.04	.01
Golden State Warriors			
☐ 268 Eric Leckner	.05	.02	.01
Detroit Pistons			
☐ 269 Duane Ferrell	.05	.02	.01
Indiana Pacers			
☐ 270 Mark Price	.05	.02	.01
Cleveland Cavaliers			
☐ 271 Anthony Peeler	.05	.02	.01
Los Angeles Lakers			
☐ 272 Adam Keefe	.05	.02	.01
Utah Jazz			
☐ 273 Rex Walters	.05	.02	.01
New Jersey Nets			
☐ 274 Scott Skiles	.05	.02	.01
Washington Bullets			
☐ 275 Glenn Robinson	2.50	1.15	.30
Milwaukee Bucks			
☐ 276 Tony Dumas	.08	.04	.01
Dallas Mavericks			
☐ 277 Elliot Perry	.05	.02	.01
Phoenix Suns			
☐ 278 Bo Outlaw	.05	.02	.01
Los Angeles Clippers			
☐ 279 Karl Malone	.25	.11	.03
Utah Jazz			
☐ 280 Karl Malone FR	.10	.05	.01
Utah Jazz			
☐ 281 Herb Williams	.05	.02	.01
New York Knicks			
☐ 282 Vincent Askew	.05	.02	.01
Seattle Supersonics			
☐ 283 Askia Jones	.05	.02	.01
Minnesota Timberwolves			
☐ 284 Shawn Bradley	.10	.05	.01
Philadelphia 76ers			
☐ 285 Tim Hardaway	.10	.05	.01
Golden State Warriors			
☐ 286 Mark West	.05	.02	.01
Detroit Pistons			
☐ 287 Chuck Person	.08	.04	.01
San Antonio Spurs			
☐ 288 James Edwards	.05	.02	.01
Portland Trail Blazers			
☐ 289 Antonio Lang	.08	.04	.01
Phoenix Suns			
☐ 290 Dominique Wilkins	.15	.07	.02
Boston Celtics			
☐ 291 Khalid Reeves	.40	.18	.05
Miami Heat			
☐ 292 Jamie Watson	.15	.07	.02
Utah Jazz			
☐ 293 Darnell Mee	.05	.02	.01
Denver Nuggets			
☐ 294 Brian Grant	.75	.35	.09
Sacramento Kings			
☐ 295 Hakeem Olajuwon	.60	.25	.08
Houston Rockets			
☐ 296 Dickey Simpkins	.15	.07	.02
Chicago Bulls			
☐ 297 Tyrone Corbin	.05	.02	.01
Atlanta Hawks			
☐ 298 David Wingate	.05	.02	.01
Charlotte Hornets			
☐ 299 Shaquille O'Neal	1.25	.55	.16
Orlando Magic			
☐ 300 Shaquille O'Neal FR	.60	.25	.08
Orlando Magic			
☐ 301 B.J. Armstrong PP	.05	.02	.01
Chicago Bulls			
☐ 302 Mitch Richmond PP	.08	.04	.01
Sacramento Kings			
☐ 303 Jim Jackson PP	.15	.07	.02
Dallas Mavericks			
☐ 304 Jeff Hornacek PP	.05	.02	.01
Utah Jazz			
☐ 305 Mark Price PP	.05	.02	.01
Cleveland Cavaliers			
☐ 306 Kendall Gill PP	.05	.02	.01
Seattle Supersonics			
☐ 307 Dale Ellis PP	.05	.02	.01
Denver Nuggets			
☐ 308 Vernon Maxwell PP	.05	.02	.01
Houston Rockets			
☐ 309 Joe Dumars PP	.08	.04	.01
Detroit Pistons			
☐ 310 Reggie Miller PP	.10	.05	.01
Indina Pacers			
☐ 311 Geert Hammink	.05	.02	.01
Orlando Magic			
☐ 312 Charles Smith	.05	.02	.01
New York Knicks			
☐ 313 Bill Cartwright	.05	.02	.01
Seattle Supersonics			
☐ 314 Aaron McKie	.20	.09	.03
Portland Trail Blazers			
☐ 315 Tom Gugliotta	.08	.04	.01
Golden State Warriors			
☐ 316 P.J. Brown	.05	.02	.01
New Jersey Nets			
☐ 317 David Wesley	.05	.02	.01
Boston Celtics			
☐ 318 Felton Spencer	.05	.02	.01
Utah Jazz			
☐ 319 Robert Horry	.10	.05	.01
Houston Rockets			
☐ 320 Robert Horry FR	.05	.02	.01
Houston Rockets			
☐ 321 Larry Krystkowiak	.05	.02	.01
Chicago Bulls			
☐ 322 Eric Piatkowski	.15	.07	.02
Los Angeles Clippers			
☐ 323 Anthony Bonner	.05	.02	.01
New York Knicks			
☐ 324 Keith Askins	.05	.02	.01
Miami Heat			
☐ 325 Mahmoud Abdul-Rauf..	.08	.04	.01
Denver Nuggets			
☐ 326 Darrin Hancock	.05	.02	.01
Charlotte Hornets			
☐ 327 Vern Fleming	.05	.02	.01
Indiana Pacers			
☐ 328 Wayman Tisdale	.08	.04	.01
Phoenix Suns			
☐ 329 Sam Bowie	.05	.02	.01
Los Angeles Lakers			
☐ 330 Billy Owens	.08	.04	.01

	Miami Heat			
☐ 331	Donald Hodge	.05	.02	.01
	Dallas Mavericks			
☐ 332	Derrick Alston	.08	.04	.01
	Philadelphia 76ers			
☐ 333	Doug Edwards	.05	.02	.01
	Atlanta Hawks			
☐ 334	Johnny Newman	.05	.02	.01
	Milwaukee Bucks			
☐ 335	Otis Thorpe	.08	.04	.01
	Houston Rockets			
☐ 336	Bill Curley	.15	.07	.02
	Detroit Pistons			
☐ 337	Michael Cage	.05	.02	.01
	Cleveland Cavaliers			
☐ 338	Chris Smith	.05	.02	.01
	Minnesota Timberwolves			
☐ 339	Dikembe Mutombo	.15	.07	.02
	Denver Nuggets			
☐ 340	Dikembe Mutombo FR.	.08	.04	.01
	Denver Nuggets			
☐ 341	Duane Causwell	.05	.02	.01
	Sacramento Kings			
☐ 342	Sean Higgins	.05	.02	.01
	New Jersey Nets			
☐ 343	Steve Kerr	.05	.02	.01
	Chicago Bulls			
☐ 344	Eric Montross	.20	.09	.03
	Boston Celtics			
☐ 345	Charles Oakley	.08	.04	.01
	New York Knicks			
☐ 346	Brooks Thompson	.08	.04	.01
	Orlando Magic			
☐ 347	Rony Seikaly	.05	.02	.01
	Golden State Warriors			
☐ 348	Chris Dudley	.05	.02	.01
	Portland Trail Blazers			
☐ 349	Sharone Wright	.30	.14	.04
	Philadelphia 76ers			
☐ 350	Sarunas Marciulionis	.05	.02	.01
	Seattle Supersonics			
☐ 351	Anthony Miller	.05	.02	.01
	Los Angeles Lakers			
☐ 352	Pooh Richardson	.05	.02	.01
	Los Angeles Clippers			
☐ 353	Byron Scott	.08	.04	.01
	Indiana Pacers			
☐ 354	Michael Adams	.05	.02	.01
	Charlotte Hornets			
☐ 355	Ken Norman	.05	.02	.01
	Atlanta Hawks			
☐ 356	Clifford Rozier	.20	.09	.03
	Golden State Warriors			
☐ 357	Tim Breaux	.05	.02	.01
	Houston Rockets			
☐ 358	Derek Strong	.05	.02	.01
	Boston Celtics			
☐ 359	David Robinson	.50	.23	.06
	San Antonio Spurs			
☐ 360	David Robinson FR	.25	.11	.03
	San Antonio Spurs			
☐ 361	Benoit Benjamin	.05	.02	.01
	New Jersey Nets			
☐ 362	Terry Porter	.08	.04	.01
	Portland Trail Blazers			
☐ 363	Ervin Johnson	.05	.02	.01
	Seattle Supersonics			
☐ 364	Alaa Abdelnaby	.05	.02	.01
	Sacramento Kings			
☐ 365	Robert Parish	.10	.05	.01
	Charlotte Hornets			

☐ 366	Mario Elie	.05	.02	.01
	Houston Rockets			
☐ 367	Antonio Harvey	.05	.02	.01
	Los Angeles Lakers			
☐ 368	Charlie Ward	.20	.09	.03
	New York Knicks			
☐ 369	Kevin Gamble	.05	.02	.01
	Miami Heat			
☐ 370	Rod Strickland	.08	.04	.01
	Portland Trail Blazers			
☐ 371	Jason Kidd	1.25	.55	.16
	Dallas Mavericks			
☐ 372	Oliver Miller	.05	.02	.01
	Detroit Pistons			
☐ 373	Eric Mobley	.15	.07	.02
	Milwaukee Bucks			
☐ 374	Brian Shaw	.05	.02	.01
	Orlando Magic			
☐ 375	Horace Grant	.15	.07	.02
	Orlando Magic			
☐ 376	Corie Blount	.05	.02	.01
	Chicago Bulls			
☐ 377	Sam Mitchell	.05	.02	.01
	Indiana Pacers			
☐ 378	Jalen Rose	.50	.23	.06
	Denver Nuggets			
☐ 379	Elden Campbell	.05	.02	.01
	Los Angeles Lakers			
☐ 380	Elden Campbell FR	.05	.02	.01
	Los Angeles Lakers			
☐ 381	Donyell Marshall	.50	.23	.06
	Minnesota Timberwolves			
☐ 382	Frank Brickowski	.05	.02	.01
	Sacramento Kings			
☐ 383	B.J. Tyler	.08	.04	.01
	Philadelphia 76ers			
☐ 384	Bryon Russell	.05	.02	.01
	Utah Jazz			
☐ 385	Danny Manning	.10	.05	.01
	Phoenix Suns			
☐ 386	Manute Bol	.05	.02	.01
	Golden State Warriors			
☐ 387	Brent Price	.05	.02	.01
	Washington Bullets			
☐ 388	J.R. Reid	.05	.02	.01
	San Antonio Spurs			
☐ 389	Byron Houston	.05	.02	.01
	Seattle Supersonics			
☐ 390	Blue Edwards	.05	.02	.01
	Boston Celtics			
☐ 391	Adrian Caldwell	.05	.02	.01
	Houston Rockets			
☐ 392	Wesley Person	.25	.11	.03
	Phoenix Suns			
☐ 393	Juwan Howard	1.00	.45	.13
	Washington Bullets			
☐ 394	Chris Morris	.05	.02	.01
	New Jersey Nets			
☐ 395	Checklist 199-296	.05	.02	.01
☐ 396	Checklist 297-396	.05	.02	.01

1994-95 Topps Spectralight

Randomly inserted into both first and second series packs at a rate of one in four, cards from this set parallel the basic issue

1994-95 Topps set. Unlike the basic issue cards, fronts feature a full foil-treatment on the pictures. Also, card numbers 197-198 and 395-396 feature players on them (in replacement of the checklist cards that are part of the regular issue set). Please refer to the multipliers provided below (coupled with the prices of the corresponding regular issue card) to ascertain value.

	MINT	NRMT	EXC
COMPLETE SET (396)	300.00	135.00	38.00
COMPLETE SERIES 1 (198)	125.00	57.50	15.50
COMPLETE SERIES 2 (198)	175.00	80.00	22.00
COMMON CARD (1-396)	.25	.11	.03
*STARS: 5X to 10X BASIC CARDS			
*ROOKIES: 3X to 6X BASIC CARDS			

		MINT	NRMT	EXC
☐ 197S	Keith Jennings	.50	.23	.06
☐ 198S	Mark Price	.50	.23	.06
☐ 395S	Chris Webber	4.00	1.80	.50
	Washington Bullets			
☐ 396S	Mitch Richmond	1.25	.55	.16
	Sacramento Kings			

		MINT	NRMT	EXC
☐ 1	Mookie Blaylock	1.50	.65	.19
	Atlanta Hawks			
☐ 2	Stacey Augmon	1.50	.65	.19
	Atlanta Hawks			
☐ 3	Dominique Wilkins	3.00	1.35	.40
	Boston Celtics			
☐ 4	Eric Montross	3.00	1.35	.40
	Boston Celtics			
☐ 5	Dikembe Mutombo	4.00	1.80	.50
	Denver Nuggets			
☐ 6	Jalen Rose	4.00	1.80	.50
	Denver Nuggets			
☐ 7	Joe Dumars	3.00	1.35	.40
	Detroit Pistons			
☐ 8	Grant Hill	30.00	13.50	3.80
	Detroit Pistons			
☐ 9	Chris Mullin	2.50	1.15	.30
	Golden State Warriors			
☐ 10	Latrell Sprewell	8.00	3.60	1.00
	Golden State Warriors			
☐ 11	Glen Rice	2.50	1.15	.30
	Miami Heat			
☐ 12	Khalid Reeves	3.00	1.35	.40
	Miami Heat			
☐ 13	Derrick Coleman	2.50	1.15	.30
	New Jersey Nets			
☐ 14	Yinka Dare	1.50	.65	.19
	New Jersey Nets			
☐ 15	Patrick Ewing	6.00	2.70	.75
	New York Knicks			
☐ 16	Monty Williams	1.50	.65	.19
	New York Knicks			
☐ 17	Shaquille O'Neal	30.00	13.50	3.80
	Orlando Magic			
☐ 18	Anfernee Hardaway	25.00	11.50	3.10
	Orlando Magic			
☐ 19	Charles Barkley	12.00	5.50	1.50
	Phoenix Suns			
☐ 20	Wesley Person	4.00	1.80	.50
	Phoenix Suns			

1994-95 Topps Franchise/Futures

Randomly inserted into all second series packs at a rate of one in 18, cards from this 20-card set feature a selection of promising youngsters coupled with established stars from the same team.

	MINT	NRMT	EXC
COMPLETE SET (20)	125.00	57.50	15.50
COMMON CARD (1-20)	1.50	.65	.19

1994-95 Topps Own the Game

Randomly inserted in all first series packs (12-card packs one in 18, jumbo packs one in 9), cards from this 50-card unnumbered set featured nine top players in five different statistical categories (Super Passers, Super Rebounders, Super Scorers, Super

Stealers and Super Swatters) in addition to five Field Cards. If the player pictured on the card (Field Card represented all other players in the league) led the league in that respective category, it became redeemable for a special 10-card Own the Game redemption set for that category. The Own the Game redemption expires on February 7th, 1996. Cards are listed below in alphabetical order with a number assigned to them for checklisting purposes.

	MINT	NRMT	EXC
COMPLETE SET (50)	30.00	13.50	3.80
COMMON CARD (1-50)	.25	.11	.03

		MINT	NRMT	EXC
☐ 1	Kenny Anderson PASS.... New Jersey Nets	.35	.16	.04
☐ 2	Charles Barkley SCORE.. Phoenix Suns	1.50	.65	.19
☐ 3	Mookie Blaylock PASS.... Atlanta Hawks	.25	.11	.03
☐ 4	Mookie Blaylock STEAL ... Atlanta Hawks	.25	.11	.03
☐ 5	Muggsy Bogues PASS .... Charlotte Hornets	.35	.16	.04
☐ 6	Shawn Bradley SWAT ...... Philadelphia 76ers	.35	.16	.04
☐ 7	Derrick Coleman REB....... New Jersey Nets	.35	.16	.04
☐ 8	Sherman Douglas PASS .. Boston Celtics	.25	.11	.03
☐ 9	Patrick Ewing REB .... New York Knicks	.75	.35	.09
☐ 10	Patrick Ewing SCORE..... New York Knicks	.75	.35	.09
☐ 11	Patrick Ewing SWAT ...... New York Knicks	.75	.35	.09
☐ 12	Tom Gugliotta STEAL..... Washington Bullets	.25	.11	.03
☐ 13	Anfernee Hardaway STEAL Charlotte Hornets	3.00	1.35	.40
☐ 14	Mark Jackson PASS........ Los Angeles Clippers	.25	.11	.03
☐ 15	Kevin Johnson PASS ...... Phoenix Suns	.50	.23	.06
☐ 16	Karl Malone REB.............. Utah Jazz	.75	.35	.09
☐ 17	Karl Malone SCORE .... Utah Jazz	.75	.35	.09
☐ 18	Nate McMillan STEAL .... Seattle Supersonics	.25	.11	.03
☐ 19	Oliver Miller SWAT........ Phoenix Suns	.25	.11	.03
☐ 20	Alonzo Mourning SWAT Charlotte Hornets	1.00	.45	.13
☐ 21	Eric Murdock STEAL....... Milwaukee Bucks	.25	.11	.03
☐ 22	Dikembe Mutombo REB.. Denver Nuggets	.50	.23	.06
☐ 23	D. Mutombo SWAT W .. Denver Nuggets	4.00	1.80	.50
☐ 24	Charles Oakley REB ...... New York Knicks	.25	.11	.03
☐ 25	Hakeem Olajuwon REB Houston Rockets	2.00	.90	.25
☐ 26	Hakeem Olajuwon SCORE Houston Rockets	2.00	.90	.25
☐ 27	Hakeem Olajuwon SWAT Houston Rockets	2.00	.90	.25
☐ 28	Shaquille O'Neal REB.... Charlotte Hornets	4.00	1.80	.50
☐ 29	S. O'Neal SCORE W ..... Charlotte Hornets	6.00	2.70	.75
☐ 30	Shaquille O'Neal SWAT Charlotte Hornets	4.00	1.80	.50
☐ 31	Gary Payton STEAL......... Seattle Supersonics	.35	.16	.04
☐ 32	Scottie Pippen SCORE .. Chicago Bulls	.75	.35	.09
☐ 33	Scottie Pippen STEAL W Chicago Bulls	4.00	1.80	.50
☐ 34	Mark Price PASS .... Cleveland Cavaliers	.35	.16	.04
☐ 35	Mitch Richmond SCORE Sacramento Kings	.50	.23	.06
☐ 36	David Robinson SCORE San Antonio Spurs	1.50	.65	.19
☐ 37	David Robinson SWAT. San Antonio Spurs	1.50	.65	.19
☐ 38	Dennis Rodman REB W San Antonio Spurs	4.00	1.80	.50
☐ 39	Latrell Sprewell STEAL.. Golden State Warriors	1.00	.45	.13
☐ 40	John Stockton PASS W Utah Jazz	4.00	1.80	.50
☐ 41	John Stockton STEAL.... Utah Jazz	.75	.35	.09
☐ 42	Rod Strickland PASS ..... Portland Trail Blazers	.25	.11	.03
☐ 43	Chris Webber SWAT .... Golden State Warriors	1.25	.55	.16
☐ 44	Kevin Willis REB .... Atlanta Hawks	.25	.11	.03
☐ 45	Dominique Wilkins SCORE Boston Celtics	.50	.23	.06
☐ 46	Passers Field Card	.25	.11	.03
☐ 47	Rebounders Field Card...	.25	.11	.03
☐ 48	Scorers Field Card	.25	.11	.03
☐ 49	Stealers Field Card	.25	.11	.03
☐ 50	Swatters Field Card........	.25	.11	.03

1994-95 Topps Super Sophomores

Randomly inserted into all second series packs at a rate of one in 36, cards from this 10-card set spotlight a selection of young phenoms in their second NBA season. Fronts feature full-color player action shots cut out against silver-foil backgrounds.

	MINT	NRMT	EXC
COMPLETE SET (10)	80.00	36.00	10.00
COMMON CARD (1-10)	2.50	1.15	.30
☐ 1 Chris Webber	12.00	5.50	1.50
Washington Bullets			
☐ 2 Anfernee Hardaway	30.00	13.50	3.80
Orlando Magic			
☐ 3 Vin Baker	8.00	3.60	1.00
Milwaukee Bucks			
☐ 4 Sam Cassell	3.50	1.55	.45
Houston Rockets			
☐ 5 Jamal Mashburn	15.00	6.75	1.90
Dallas Mavericks			
☐ 6 Isaiah Rider	5.00	2.30	.60
Minnesota Timberwolves			
☐ 7 Chris Mills	3.50	1.55	.45
Cleveland Cavaliers			
☐ 8 Antonio Davis	2.50	1.15	.30
Indiana Pacers			
☐ 9 Nick Van Exel	15.00	6.75	1.90
Los Angeles Lakers			
☐ 10 Lindsey Hunter	2.50	1.15	.30
Detroit Pistons			

1995-96 Topps

The 176 standard size cards comprising the 1995-96 Topps first series set were issued in 12-card hobby and retail packs (SRP $1.29). The white bordered fronts have a full-color action photo with the player's name in gold set against a black shadow. The backs are laid out horizontally and have a color head-shot with statistics and information. Subsets include Active Leaders (1-5), Scoring Leaders (6-10), Rebound Leaders (11-15), Assist Leaders (16-20), Steal Leaders (21-25) and Block Leaders (26-30).

	MINT	NRMT	EXC
COMPLETE SERIES 1 (181)	15.00	6.75	1.90
COMMON CARD (1-181)	.05	.02	.01
☐ 1 Michael Jordan AL	1.50	.65	.19
Chicago Bulls			
☐ 2 Dennis Rodman AL	.08	.04	.01
San Antonio Spurs			
☐ 3 John Stockton AL	.10	.05	.01
Utah Jazz			
☐ 4 Michael Jordan AL	1.50	.65	.19
Chicago Bulls			
☐ 5 David Robinson AL	.25	.11	.03

San Antonio Spurs			
☐ 6 Shaquille O'Neal LL	.60	.25	.08
Orlando Magic			
☐ 7 Hakeem Olajuwon LL	.30	.14	.04
Houston Rockets			
☐ 8 David Robinson LL	.25	.11	.03
San Antonio Spurs			
☐ 9 Karl Malone LL	.10	.05	.01
Utah Jazz			
☐ 10 Jamal Mashburn LL	.15	.07	.02
Dallas Mavericks			
☐ 11 Dennis Rodman LL	.08	.04	.01
San Antonio Spurs			
☐ 12 Dikembe Mutombo LL	.08	.04	.01
Denver Nuggets			
☐ 13 Shaquille O'Neal LL	.60	.25	.08
Orlando Magic			
☐ 14 Patrick Ewing LL	.10	.05	.01
New York Knicks			
☐ 15 Tyrone Hill LL	.05	.02	.01
Cleveland Cavaliers			
☐ 16 John Stockton LL	.10	.05	.01
Utah Jazz			
☐ 17 Kenny Anderson LL	.05	.02	.01
New Jersey Nets			
☐ 18 Tim Hardaway LL	.05	.02	.01
Golden State Warriors			
☐ 19 Rod Strickland LL	.05	.02	.01
Portland Trailblazers			
☐ 20 Muggsy Bogues LL	.05	.02	.01
Charlotte Hornets			
☐ 21 Scottie Pippen LL	.10	.05	.01
Chicago Bulls			
☐ 22 Mookie Blaylock LL	.05	.02	.01
Atlanta Hawks			
☐ 23 Gary Payton LL	.05	.02	.01
Seattle Supersonics			
☐ 24 John Stockton LL	.10	.05	.01
Utah Jazz			
☐ 25 Nate McMillan LL	.05	.02	.01
Seattle Supersonics			
☐ 26 Dikembe Mutombo LL	.08	.04	.01
Denver Nuggets			
☐ 27 Hakeem Olajuwon LL	.30	.14	.04
Houston Rockets			
☐ 28 Shawn Bradley LL	.05	.02	.01
Philadelphia 76ers			
☐ 29 David Robinson LL	.25	.11	.03
San Antonio Spurs			
☐ 30 Alonzo Mourning LL	.10	.05	.01
Charlotte Hornets			
☐ 31 Reggie Miller LL	.25	.11	.03
Indiana Pacers			
☐ 32 Karl Malone	.25	.11	.03
Utah Jazz			
☐ 33 Grant Hill	1.25	.55	.16
Detroit Pistons			
☐ 34 Charles Barkley	.50	.23	.06
Phoenix Suns			
☐ 35 Cedric Ceballos	.10	.05	.01
Los Angeles Lakers			
☐ 36 Gheorghe Muresan	.05	.02	.01
Washington Bullets			
☐ 37 Doug West	.05	.02	.01
Minnesota Timberwolves			
☐ 38 Tony Dumas	.05	.02	.01
Dallas Mavericks			
☐ 39 Kenny Gattison	.05	.02	.01
Charlotte Hornets			
☐ 40 Chris Mullin	.10	.05	.01
Golden State Warriors			

☐ 41	Pervis Ellison	.05	.02	.01
	Boston Celtics			
☐ 42	Vinny Del Negro	.05	.02	.01
	San Antonio Spurs			
☐ 43	Mario Elie	.05	.02	.01
	Houston Rockets			
☐ 44	Todd Day	.05	.02	.01
	Milwaukee Bucks			
☐ 45	Scottie Pippen	.25	.11	.03
	Chicago Bulls			
☐ 46	Buck Williams	.08	.04	.01
	Portland Trailblazers			
☐ 47	P.J. Brown	.05	.02	.01
	New Jersey Nets			
☐ 48	Bimbo Coles	.05	.02	.01
	Miami Heat			
☐ 49	Terrell Brandon	.05	.02	.01
	Cleveland Cavaliers			
☐ 50	Charles Oakley	.08	.04	.01
	New York Knicks			
☐ 51	Sam Perkins	.08	.04	.01
	Seattle Supersonics			
☐ 52	Dale Ellis	.08	.04	.01
	Denver Nuggets			
☐ 53	Andrew Lang	.05	.02	.01
	Atlanta Hawks			
☐ 54	Harold Ellis	.05	.02	.01
	Los Angeles Clippers			
☐ 55	Clarence Weatherspoon	.08	.04	.01
	Philadelphia 76ers			
☐ 56	Bill Curley	.05	.02	.01
	Detroit Pistons			
☐ 57	Robert Parish	.10	.05	.01
	Charlotte Hornets			
☐ 58	David Benoit	.05	.02	.01
	Utah Jazz			
☐ 59	Anthony Avent	.05	.02	.01
	Orlando Magic			
☐ 60	Jamal Mashburn	.30	.14	.04
	Dallas Mavericks			
☐ 61	Duane Ferrell	.05	.02	.01
	Indiana Pacers			
☐ 62	Elden Campbell	.05	.02	.01
	Los Angeles Lakers			
☐ 63	Rex Chapman	.05	.02	.01
	Washington Bullets			
☐ 64	Wesley Person	.15	.07	.02
	Phoenix Suns			
☐ 65	Mitch Richmond	.15	.07	.02
	Sacramento Kings			
☐ 66	Micheal Williams	.05	.02	.01
	Minnesota Timberwolves			
☐ 67	Clifford Rozier	.10	.05	.01
	Golden State Warriors			
☐ 68	Eric Montross	.10	.05	.01
	Boston Celtics			
☐ 69	Dennis Rodman	.15	.07	.02
	San Antonio Spurs			
☐ 70	Vin Baker	.15	.07	.02
	Milwaukee Bucks			
☐ 71	Tyrone Hill	.08	.04	.01
	Cleveland Cavaliers			
☐ 72	Tyrone Corbin	.05	.02	.01
	Atlanta Hawks			
☐ 73	Chris Dudley	.05	.02	.01
	Portland Trailblazers			
☐ 74	Nate McMillan	.05	.02	.01
	Seattle Supersonics			
☐ 75	Kenny Anderson	.10	.05	.01
	New Jersey Nets			
☐ 76	Monty Williams	.05	.02	.01
	New York Knicks			
☐ 77	Kenny Smith	.05	.02	.01
	Houston Rockets			
☐ 78	Rodney Rogers	.08	.04	.01
	Denver Nuggets			
☐ 79	Corie Blount	.05	.02	.01
	Chicago Bulls			
☐ 80	Glen Rice	.10	.05	.01
	Miami Heat			
☐ 81	Walt Williams	.08	.04	.01
	Sacramento Kings			
☐ 82	Scott Williams	.05	.02	.01
	Philadelphia 76ers			
☐ 83	Michael Adams	.05	.02	.01
	Charlotte Hornets			
☐ 84	Terry Mills	.05	.02	.01
	Detroit Pistons			
☐ 85	Horace Grant	.15	.07	.02
	Orlando Magic			
☐ 86	Chuck Person	.08	.04	.01
	San Antonio Spurs			
☐ 87	Adam Keefe	.05	.02	.01
	Utah Jazz			
☐ 88	Scott Brooks	.05	.02	.01
	Dallas Mavericks			
☐ 89	George Lynch	.05	.02	.01
	Los Angeles Lakers			
☐ 90	Kevin Johnson	.15	.07	.02
	Phoenix Suns			
☐ 91	Armon Gilliam	.05	.02	.01
	New Jersey Nets			
☐ 92	Greg Minor	.05	.02	.01
	Boston Celtics			
☐ 93	Derrick McKey	.08	.04	.01
	Indiana Pacers			
☐ 94	Victor Alexander	.05	.02	.01
	Golden State Warriors			
☐ 95	B.J. Armstrong	.05	.02	.01
	Chicago Bulls			
☐ 96	Terry Dehere	.05	.02	.01
	Los Angeles Clippers			
☐ 97	Christian Laettner	.08	.04	.01
	Minnesota Timberwolves			
☐ 98	Hubert Davis	.05	.02	.01
	New York Knicks			
☐ 99	Aaron McKie	.05	.02	.01
	Portland Trailblazers			
☐ 100	Hakeem Olajuwon	.60	.25	.08
	Houston Rockets			
☐ 101	Michael Cage	.05	.02	.01
	Cleveland Cavaliers			
☐ 102	Grant Long	.05	.02	.01
	Atlanta Hawks			
☐ 103	Calbert Cheaney	.08	.04	.01
	Washington Bullets			
☐ 104	Olden Polynice	.05	.02	.01
	Sacramento Kings			
☐ 105	Sharone Wright	.08	.04	.01
	Philadelphia 76ers			
☐ 106	Lee Mayberry	.05	.02	.01
	Milwaukee Bucks			
☐ 107	Robert Pack	.05	.02	.01
	Denver Nuggets			
☐ 108	Loy Vaught	.08	.04	.01
	Los Angeles Clippers			
☐ 109	Khalid Reeves	.10	.05	.01
	Miami Heat			
☐ 110	Shawn Kemp	.50	.23	.06
	Seattle Supersonics			
☐ 111	Lindsey Hunter	.05	.02	.01
	Detroit Pistons			

New York Knicks

☐ 112	Dell Curry Charlotte Hornets	.05	.02	.01
☐ 113	Dan Majerle Phoenix Suns	.08	.04	.01
☐ 114	Bryon Russell Utah Jazz	.05	.02	.01
☐ 115	John Starks New York Knicks	.08	.04	.01
☐ 116	Roy Tarpley Dallas Mavericks	.05	.02	.01
☐ 117	Dale Davis Indiana Pacers	.08	.04	.01
☐ 118	Nick Anderson Orlando Magic	.08	.04	.01
☐ 119	Rex Walters New Jersey Nets	.05	.02	.01
☐ 120	Dominique Wilkins Boston Celtics	.15	.07	.02
☐ 121	Sam Cassell Houston Rockets	.05	.02	.01
☐ 122	Sean Elliott San Antonio Spurs	.05	.02	.01
☐ 123	B.J. Tyler Philadelphia 76ers	.05	.02	.01
☐ 124	Eric Mobley Milwaukee Bucks	.05	.02	.01
☐ 125	Toni Kukoc Chicago Bulls	.08	.04	.01
☐ 126	Pooh Richardson Los Angeles Clippers	.05	.02	.01
☐ 127	Isaiah Rider Minnesota Timberwolves	.10	.05	.01
☐ 128	Steve Smith Atlanta Hawks	.08	.04	.01
☐ 129	Chris Mills Cleveland Cavaliers	.08	.04	.01
☐ 130	Detlef Schrempf Seattle Supersonics	.10	.05	.01
☐ 131	Donyell Marshall Golden State Warriors	.15	.07	.02
☐ 132	Eddie Jones Los Angeles Lakers	.50	.23	.06
☐ 133	Otis Thorpe Portland Trailblazers	.08	.04	.01
☐ 134	Lionel Simmons Sacramento Kings	.05	.02	.01
☐ 135	Jeff Hornacek Utah Jazz	.08	.04	.01
☐ 136	Jalen Rose Denver Nuggets	.15	.07	.02
☐ 137	Kevin Willis Miami Heat	.08	.04	.01
☐ 138	Don MacLean Washington Bullets	.05	.02	.01
☐ 139	Dee Brown Boston Celtics	.08	.04	.01
☐ 140	Glenn Robinson Milwaukee Bucks	.75	.35	.09
☐ 141	Joe Kleine Phoenix Suns	.05	.02	.01
☐ 142	Ron Harper Chicago Bulls	.08	.04	.01
☐ 143	Antonio Davis Indiana Pacers	.05	.02	.01
☐ 144	Jeff Malone Philadelphia 76ers	.08	.04	.01
☐ 145	Joe Dumars Detroit Pistons	.15	.07	.02
☐ 146	Jason Kidd Dallas Mavericks	.75	.35	.09
☐ 147	J.R. Reid San Antonio Spurs	.05	.02	.01
☐ 148	Lamond Murray Los Angeles Clippers	.10	.05	.01
☐ 149	Derrick Coleman New Jersey Nets	.10	.05	.01
☐ 150	Alonzo Mourning Charlotte Hornets	.25	.11	.03
☐ 151	Clifford Robinson Portland Trailblazers	.08	.04	.01
☐ 152	Kendall Gill Seattle Supersonics	.05	.02	.01
☐ 153	Doug Christie New York Knicks	.05	.02	.01
☐ 154	Stacey Augmon Atlanta Hawks	.08	.04	.01
☐ 155	Anfernee Hardaway Orlando Magic	.75	.35	.09
☐ 156	Mahmoud Abdul-Rauf.. Denver Nuggets	.08	.04	.01
☐ 157	Latrell Sprewell Golden State Warriors	.25	.11	.03
☐ 158	Mark Price Cleveland Cavaliers	.10	.05	.01
☐ 159	Brian Grant Sacramento Kings	.25	.11	.03
☐ 160	Clyde Drexler Houston Rockets	.25	.11	.03
☐ 161	Juwan Howard Washington Bullets	.30	.14	.04
☐ 162	Tom Gugliotta Minnesota Timberwolves	.08	.04	.01
☐ 163	Nick Van Exel Los Angeles Lakers	.30	.14	.04
☐ 164	Billy Owens Miami Heat	.08	.04	.01
☐ 165	Brooks Thompson Orlando Magic	.05	.02	.01
☐ 166	Acie Earl Toronto Raptors	.05	.02	.01
☐ 167	Ed Pinckney Toronto Raptors	.05	.02	.01
☐ 168	Oliver Miller Toronto Raptors	.05	.02	.01
☐ 169	John Salley Toronto Raptors	.05	.02	.01
☐ 170	Jerome Kersey Toronto Raptors	.05	.02	.01
☐ 171	Willie Anderson Toronto Raptors	.05	.02	.01
☐ 172	Keith Jennings Toronto Raptors	.05	.02	.01
☐ 173	Doug Smith Toronto Raptors	.05	.02	.01
☐ 174	Gerald Wilkins Vancouver Grizzlies	.05	.02	.01
☐ 175	Byron Scott Vancouver Grizzlies	.08	.04	.01
☐ 176	Benoit Benjamin Vancouver Grizzlies	.05	.02	.01
☐ 177	Blue Edwards Vancouver Grizzlies	.05	.02	.01
☐ 178	Greg Anthony Vancouver Grizzlies	.05	.02	.01
☐ 179	Trevor Ruffin Vancouver Grizzlies	.05	.02	.01
☐ 180	Kenny Gattison Vancouver Grizzlies	.05	.02	.01
☐ 181	Checklist 1-181	.05	.02	.01

1992-93 Ultra

The complete 1992-93 Ultra basketball set consists of 375 standard-size (2 1/2" by 3 1/2") cards. The set was released in two series of 200 and 175 cards, respectively. Both series packs contained 14 cards each with 36 packs to a box. Suggested retail pack price was 1.79. The glossy color action player photos on the fronts are full-bleed except at the bottom where a diagonal gold-foil stripe edges a pale green variegated border. The player's name and team appear on two team color-coded bars that overlay the bottom border. The horizontal backs display action and close-up cut-out player photos against a basketball court background. The team logo and biographical information appear in a pale green bar like that on the front that edges the right side, while the player's name and statistics are given in bars running across the card bottom. The cards are numbered on the back, grouped alphabetically within teams, and checklisted below alphabetically according to teams as follows: Atlanta Hawks (1-7), Boston Celtics (8-16), Charlotte Hornets (17-23), Chicago Bulls (24-32), Cleveland Cavaliers (33-40), Dallas Mavericks (41-47), Denver Nuggets (48-54), Detroit Pistons (55-61), Golden State Warriors (62-68), Houston Rockets (69-74), Indiana Pacers (75-81), Los Angeles Clippers (82-88), Los Angeles Lakers (89-96), Miami Heat (97-104), Milwaukee Bucks (105-108), Minnesota Timberwolves (109-113), New Jersey Nets (114-120), New York Knicks (121-127), Orlando Magic (128-134), Philadelphia 76ers (135-141), Phoenix Suns (142-147), Portland Trail Blazers (148-155), Sacramento Kings (156-161), San Antonio Spurs (162-167), Seattle Supersonics (168-176), Utah Jazz (177-183), and Washington Bullets (184-192). The first series closes with NBA Draft Picks (193-198) and checklists (199-200). The second series contains more than 40 rookies, 30 trades, free agent signings, and other veterans omitted from the first series. The second series opens with an NBA Jam Session (201-220) subset. Three players from this Jam Session subset, Duane Causwell, Pervis Ellison, and Stacey Augmon, autographed a total of more than 2,500 cards that were randomly inserted in second series foil packs. These cards were embossed with Fleer logos for

authenticity. On each series two pack, a mail-in offer provided the opportunity to acquire two more exclusive Jam Session cards, showing all 20 players in the set, for ten wrappers and 1.00 for postage and handling. According to Fleer, they anticipated about 100,000 requests. Key Rookie Cards include Tom Gugliotta, Robert Horry, Christian Laettner, Alonzo Mourning, Shaquille O'Neal, Latrell Sprewell and Clarence Weatherspoon.

		MINT	NRMT	EXC
	COMPLETE SET (375)	40.00	18.00	5.00
	COMPLETE SERIES 1 (200)	20.00	9.00	2.50
	COMPLETE SERIES 2 (175)	20.00	9.00	2.50
	COMMON CARD (1-200)	.10	.05	.01
	COMMON CARD (201-375)	.05	.02	.01
☐ 1	Stacey Augmon	.20	.09	.03
☐ 2	Duane Ferrell	.10	.05	.01
☐ 3	Paul Graham	.10	.05	.01
☐ 4	Blair Rasmussen	.10	.05	.01
☐ 5	Rumeal Robinson	.10	.05	.01
☐ 6	Dominique Wilkins	.25	.11	.03
☐ 7	Kevin Willis	.15	.07	.02
☐ 8	John Bagley	.10	.05	.01
☐ 9	Dee Brown	.15	.07	.02
☐ 10	Rick Fox	.10	.05	.01
☐ 11	Kevin Gamble	.10	.05	.01
☐ 12	Joe Kleine	.10	.05	.01
☐ 13	Reggie Lewis	.20	.09	.03
☐ 14	Kevin McHale	.20	.09	.03
☐ 15	Robert Parish	.20	.09	.03
☐ 16	Ed Pinckney	.10	.05	.01
☐ 17	Muggsy Bogues	.20	.09	.03
☐ 18	Dell Curry	.10	.05	.01
☐ 19	Kenny Gattison	.10	.05	.01
☐ 20	Kendall Gill	.10	.05	.01
☐ 21	Larry Johnson	.75	.35	.09
☐ 22	Johnny Newman	.10	.05	.01
☐ 23	J.R. Reid	.10	.05	.01
☐ 24	B.J. Armstrong	.10	.05	.01
☐ 25	Bill Cartwright	.10	.05	.01
☐ 26	Horace Grant	.25	.11	.03
☐ 27	Michael Jordan	6.00	2.70	.75
☐ 28	Stacey King	.10	.05	.01
☐ 29	John Paxson	.10	.05	.01
☐ 30	Will Perdue	.10	.05	.01
☐ 31	Scottie Pippen	.50	.23	.06
☐ 32	Scott Williams	.10	.05	.01
☐ 33	John Battle	.10	.05	.01
☐ 34	Terrell Brandon	.10	.05	.01
☐ 35	Brad Daugherty	.15	.07	.02
☐ 36	Craig Ehlo	.10	.05	.01
☐ 37	Larry Nance	.15	.07	.02
☐ 38	Mark Price	.20	.09	.03
☐ 39	Mike Sanders	.10	.05	.01
☐ 40	John Williams	.15	.07	.02
☐ 41	Terry Davis	.10	.05	.01
☐ 42	Derek Harper	.15	.07	.02
☐ 43	Donald Hodge	.10	.05	.01
☐ 44	Mike Iuzzolino	.10	.05	.01
☐ 45	Fat Lever	.10	.05	.01
☐ 46	Doug Smith	.10	.05	.01
☐ 47	Randy White	.10	.05	.01
☐ 48	Winston Garland	.10	.05	.01
☐ 49	Chris Jackson	.15	.07	.02
☐ 50	Marcus Liberty	.10	.05	.01
☐ 51	Todd Lichti	.10	.05	.01
☐ 52	Mark Macon	.10	.05	.01

☐	53	Dikembe Mutombo	.60	.25	.08			
☐	54	Reggie Williams	.10	.05	.01			
☐	55	Mark Aguirre	.15	.07	.02			
☐	56	Joe Dumars	.25	.11	.03			
☐	57	Bill Laimbeer	.15	.07	.02			
☐	58	Dennis Rodman	.30	.14	.04			
☐	59	Isiah Thomas	.25	.11	.03			
☐	60	Darrell Walker	.10	.05	.01			
☐	61	Orlando Woolridge	.10	.05	.01			
☐	62	Victor Alexander	.10	.05	.01			
☐	63	Chris Gatling	.10	.05	.01			
☐	64	Tim Hardaway	.20	.09	.03			
☐	65	Tyrone Hill	.15	.07	.02			
☐	66	Sarunas Marciulionis	.10	.05	.01			
☐	67	Chris Mullin	.20	.09	.03			
☐	68	Billy Owens	.20	.09	.03			
☐	69	Sleepy Floyd	.10	.05	.01			
☐	70	Avery Johnson	.10	.05	.01			
☐	71	Vernon Maxwell	.10	.05	.01			
☐	72	Hakeem Olajuwon	1.25	.55	.16			
☐	73	Kenny Smith	.10	.05	.01			
☐	74	Otis Thorpe	.15	.07	.02			
☐	75	Dale Davis	.20	.09	.03			
☐	76	Vern Fleming	.10	.05	.01			
☐	77	George McCloud	.10	.05	.01			
☐	78	Reggie Miller	.50	.23	.06			
☐	79	Detlef Schrempf	.20	.09	.03			
☐	80	Rik Smits	.20	.09	.03			
☐	81	LaSalle Thompson	.10	.05	.01			
☐	82	Gary Grant	.10	.05	.01			
☐	83	Ron Harper	.15	.07	.02			
☐	84	Mark Jackson	.10	.05	.01			
☐	85	Danny Manning	.20	.09	.03			
☐	86	Ken Norman	.10	.05	.01			
☐	87	Stanley Roberts	.10	.05	.01			
☐	88	Loy Vaught	.15	.07	.02			
☐	89	Elden Campbell	.10	.05	.01			
☐	90	Vlade Divac	.20	.09	.03			
☐	91	A.C. Green	.20	.09	.03			
☐	92	Sam Perkins	.15	.07	.02			
☐	93	Byron Scott	.15	.07	.02			
☐	94	Tony Smith	.10	.05	.01			
☐	95	Sedale Threatt	.10	.05	.01			
☐	96	James Worthy	.20	.09	.03			
☐	97	Willie Burton	.10	.05	.01			
☐	98	Bimbo Coles	.10	.05	.01			
☐	99	Kevin Edwards	.10	.05	.01			
☐	100	Grant Long	.10	.05	.01			
☐	101	Glen Rice	.20	.09	.03			
☐	102	Rony Seikaly	.10	.05	.01			
☐	103	Brian Shaw	.10	.05	.01			
☐	104	Steve Smith	.20	.09	.03			
☐	105	Frank Brickowski	.10	.05	.01			
☐	106	Moses Malone	.25	.11	.03			
☐	107	Fred Roberts	.10	.05	.01			
☐	108	Alvin Robertson	.10	.05	.01			
☐	109	Thurl Bailey	.10	.05	.01			
☐	110	Gerald Glass	.10	.05	.01			
☐	111	Luc Longley	.10	.05	.01			
☐	112	Felton Spencer	.10	.05	.01			
☐	113	Doug West	.10	.05	.01			
☐	114	Kenny Anderson	.40	.18	.05			
☐	115	Mookie Blaylock	.15	.07	.02			
☐	116	Sam Bowie	.10	.05	.01			
☐	117	Derrick Coleman	.20	.09	.03			
☐	118	Chris Dudley	.10	.05	.01			
☐	119	Chris Morris	.10	.05	.01			
☐	120	Drazen Petrovic	.15	.07	.02			
☐	121	Greg Anthony	.10	.05	.01			
☐	122	Patrick Ewing	.50	.23	.06			
☐	123	Anthony Mason	.20	.09	.03			
☐	124	Charles Oakley	.15	.07	.02
☐	125	Doc Rivers	.15	.07	.02
☐	126	Charles Smith	.10	.05	.01
☐	127	John Starks	.20	.09	.03
☐	128	Nick Anderson	.15	.07	.02
☐	129	Anthony Bowie	.10	.05	.01
☐	130	Terry Catledge	.10	.05	.01
☐	131	Jerry Reynolds	.10	.05	.01
☐	132	Dennis Scott	.10	.05	.01
☐	133	Scott Skiles	.10	.05	.01
☐	134	Brian Williams	.10	.05	.01
☐	135	Ron Anderson	.10	.05	.01
☐	136	Manute Bol	.10	.05	.01
☐	137	Johnny Dawkins	.10	.05	.01
☐	138	Armon Gilliam	.10	.05	.01
☐	139	Hersey Hawkins	.15	.07	.02
☐	140	Jeff Ruland	.10	.05	.01
☐	141	Charles Shackleford	.10	.05	.01
☐	142	Cedric Ceballos	.20	.09	.03
☐	143	Tom Chambers	.15	.07	.02
☐	144	Kevin Johnson	.25	.11	.03
☐	145	Negele Knight	.10	.05	.01
☐	146	Dan Majerle	.15	.07	.02
☐	147	Mark West	.10	.05	.01
☐	148	Mark Bryant	.10	.05	.01
☐	149	Clyde Drexler	.50	.23	.06
☐	150	Kevin Duckworth	.10	.05	.01
☐	151	Jerome Kersey	.10	.05	.01
☐	152	Robert Pack	.10	.05	.01
☐	153	Terry Porter	.15	.07	.02
☐	154	Cliff Robinson	.20	.09	.03
☐	155	Buck Williams	.15	.07	.02
☐	156	Anthony Bonner	.10	.05	.01
☐	157	Duane Causwell	.10	.05	.01
☐	158	Mitch Richmond	.25	.11	.03
☐	159	Lionel Simmons	.10	.05	.01
☐	160	Wayman Tisdale	.15	.07	.02
☐	161	Spud Webb	.15	.07	.02
☐	162	Willie Anderson	.10	.05	.01
☐	163	Antoine Carr	.10	.05	.01
☐	164	Terry Cummings	.15	.07	.02
☐	165	Sean Elliott	.15	.07	.02
☐	166	Sidney Green	.10	.05	.01
☐	167	David Robinson	1.00	.45	.13
☐	168	Dana Barros	.20	.09	.03
☐	169	Benoit Benjamin	.10	.05	.01
☐	170	Michael Cage	.10	.05	.01
☐	171	Eddie Johnson	.15	.07	.02
☐	172	Shawn Kemp	1.25	.55	.16
☐	173	Derrick McKey	.15	.07	.02
☐	174	Nate McMillan	.10	.05	.01
☐	175	Gary Payton	.20	.09	.03
☐	176	Ricky Pierce	.15	.07	.02
☐	177	David Benoit	.10	.05	.01
☐	178	Mike Brown	.10	.05	.01
☐	179	Tyrone Corbin	.10	.05	.01
☐	180	Mark Eaton	.10	.05	.01
☐	181	Jeff Malone	.15	.07	.02
☐	182	Karl Malone	.50	.23	.06
☐	183	John Stockton	.50	.23	.06
☐	184	Michael Adams	.10	.05	.01
☐	185	Ledell Eackles	.10	.05	.01
☐	186	Pervis Ellison	.10	.05	.01
☐	187	A.J. English	.10	.05	.01
☐	188	Harvey Grant	.10	.05	.01
☐	189	Buck Johnson	.10	.05	.01
☐	190	LaBradford Smith	.10	.05	.01
☐	191	Larry Stewart	.10	.05	.01
☐	192	David Wingate	.10	.05	.01
☐	193	Alonzo Mourning	3.00	1.35	.40
☐	194	Adam Keefe	.25	.11	.03

☐ 195	Robert Horry	1.25	.55	.16
☐ 196	Anthony Peeler	.25	.11	.03
☐ 197	Tracy Murray	.15	.07	.02
☐ 198	Dave Johnson	.10	.05	.01
☐ 199	Checklist 1-104	.10	.05	.01
☐ 200	Checklist 105-200	.10	.05	.01
☐ 201	David Robinson JS	.30	.14	.04
	San Antonio Spurs			
☐ 202	Dikembe Mutombo JS	.20	.09	.03
	Denver Nuggets			
☐ 203	Otis Thorpe JS	.05	.02	.01
	Houston Rockets			
☐ 204	Hakeem Olajuwon JS	.40	.18	.05
	Houston Rockets			
☐ 205	Shawn Kemp JS	.40	.18	.05
	Seattle Supersonics			
☐ 206	Charles Barkley JS	.30	.14	.04
	Phoenix Suns			
☐ 207	Pervis Ellison JS	.05	.02	.01
	Washington Bullets			
☐ 208	Chris Morris JS	.05	.02	.01
	New Jersey Nets			
☐ 209	Brad Daugherty JS	.05	.02	.01
	Cleveland Cavaliers			
☐ 210	Derrick Coleman JS	.05	.02	.01
	New Jersey Nets			
☐ 211	Tim Perry JS	.05	.02	.01
	Philadelphia 76ers			
☐ 212	Duane Causwell JS	.05	.02	.01
	Sacramento Kings			
☐ 213	Scottie Pippen JS	.10	.05	.01
	Chicago Bulls			
☐ 214	Robert Parish JS	.05	.02	.01
	Boston Celtics			
☐ 215	Stacey Augmon JS	.05	.02	.01
	Atlanta Hawks			
☐ 216	Michael Jordan JS	2.00	.90	.25
	Chicago Bulls			
☐ 217	Karl Malone JS	.10	.05	.01
	Utah Jazz			
☐ 218	John Williams JS	.05	.02	.01
	Cleveland Cavaliers			
☐ 219	Horace Grant JS	.05	.02	.01
	Chicago Bulls			
☐ 220	Orlando Woolridge JS	.05	.02	.01
	Detroit Pistons			
☐ 221	Mookie Blaylock	.08	.04	.01
☐ 222	Greg Foster	.05	.02	.01
☐ 223	Steve Henson	.05	.02	.01
☐ 224	Adam Keefe	.05	.02	.01
☐ 225	Jon Koncak	.05	.02	.01
☐ 226	Travis Mays	.05	.02	.01
☐ 227	Alaa Abdelnaby	.05	.02	.01
☐ 228	Sherman Douglas	.05	.02	.01
☐ 229	Xavier McDaniel	.10	.05	.01
☐ 230	Marcus Webb	.05	.02	.01
☐ 231	Tony Bennett	.05	.02	.01
☐ 232	Mike Gminski	.05	.02	.01
☐ 233	Kevin Lynch	.05	.02	.01
☐ 234	Alonzo Mourning	1.00	.45	.13
☐ 235	David Wingate	.05	.02	.01
☐ 236	Rodney McCray	.05	.02	.01
☐ 237	Trent Tucker	.05	.02	.01
☐ 238	Corey Williams	.05	.02	.01
☐ 239	Danny Ferry	.05	.02	.01
☐ 240	Jay Guidinger	.05	.02	.01
☐ 241	Jerome Lane	.05	.02	.01
☐ 242	Bobby Phills	.15	.07	.02
☐ 243	Gerald Wilkins	.05	.02	.01
☐ 244	Walter Bond	.05	.02	.01
☐ 245	Dexter Cambridge	.05	.02	.01

☐ 246	Radisav Curcic UER	.05	.02	.01
	(Misspelled Radislav			
	on card front)			
☐ 247	Brian Howard	.05	.02	.01
☐ 248	Tracy Moore	.05	.02	.01
☐ 249	Sean Rooks	.10	.05	.01
☐ 250	Kevin Brooks	.05	.02	.01
☐ 251	LaPhonso Ellis	.30	.14	.04
☐ 252	Scott Hastings	.05	.02	.01
☐ 253	Robert Pack	.05	.02	.01
☐ 254	Gary Plummer	.05	.02	.01
☐ 255	Bryant Stith	.25	.11	.03
☐ 256	Robert Werdann	.05	.02	.01
☐ 257	Gerald Glass	.05	.02	.01
☐ 258	Terry Mills	.10	.05	.01
☐ 259	Olden Polynice	.05	.02	.01
☐ 260	Danny Young	.05	.02	.01
☐ 261	Jud Buechler	.05	.02	.01
☐ 262	Jeff Grayer	.05	.02	.01
☐ 263	Bryon Houston	.05	.02	.01
☐ 264	Keith Jennings	.05	.02	.01
☐ 265	Ed Nealy	.05	.02	.01
☐ 266	Latrell Sprewell	2.00	.90	.25
☐ 267	Scott Brooks	.05	.02	.01
☐ 268	Matt Bullard	.05	.02	.01
☐ 269	Winston Garland	.05	.02	.01
☐ 270	Carl Herrera	.05	.02	.01
☐ 271	Robert Horry	.40	.18	.05
☐ 272	Tree Rollins	.05	.02	.01
☐ 273	Greg Dreiling	.05	.02	.01
☐ 274	Sean Green	.05	.02	.01
☐ 275	Sam Mitchell	.05	.02	.01
☐ 276	Pooh Richardson	.05	.02	.01
☐ 277	Malik Sealy	.15	.07	.02
☐ 278	Kenny Williams	.05	.02	.01
☐ 279	Mark Jackson	.05	.02	.01
☐ 280	Stanley Roberts	.05	.02	.01
☐ 281	Elmore Spencer	.05	.02	.01
☐ 282	Kiki Vandeweghe	.05	.02	.01
☐ 283	John S. Williams	.05	.02	.01
☐ 284	Randy Woods	.05	.02	.01
☐ 285	Alex Blackwell	.05	.02	.01
☐ 286	Duane Cooper	.05	.02	.01
☐ 287	James Edwards	.05	.02	.01
☐ 288	Jack Haley	.05	.02	.01
☐ 289	Anthony Peeler	.10	.05	.01
☐ 290	Keith Askins	.05	.02	.01
☐ 291	Matt Geiger	.05	.02	.01
☐ 292	Alec Kessler	.05	.02	.01
☐ 293	Harold Miner	.20	.09	.03
☐ 294	John Salley	.05	.02	.01
☐ 295	Anthony Avent	.05	.02	.01
☐ 296	Jon Barry	.08	.04	.01
☐ 297	Todd Day	.40	.18	.05
☐ 298	Blue Edwards	.05	.02	.01
☐ 299	Brad Lohaus	.05	.02	.01
☐ 300	Lee Mayberry	.10	.05	.01
☐ 301	Eric Murdock	.05	.02	.01
☐ 302	Dan Schayes	.05	.02	.01
☐ 303	Lance Blanks	.05	.02	.01
☐ 304	Christian Laettner	.60	.25	.08
☐ 305	Marlon Maxey	.05	.02	.01
☐ 306	Bob McCann	.05	.02	.01
☐ 307	Chuck Person	.08	.04	.01
☐ 308	Brad Sellers	.05	.02	.01
☐ 309	Chris Smith	.05	.02	.01
☐ 310	Gundars Vetra	.05	.02	.01
☐ 311	Micheal Williams	.05	.02	.01
☐ 312	Rafael Addison	.05	.02	.01
☐ 313	Chucky Brown	.05	.02	.01
☐ 314	Maurice Cheeks	.10	.05	.01

☐ 315	Tate George	.05	.02	.01
☐ 316	Rick Mahorn	.05	.02	.01
☐ 317	Rumeal Robinson	.05	.02	.01
☐ 318	Eric Anderson	.05	.02	.01
☐ 319	Rolando Blackman	.08	.04	.01
☐ 320	Tony Campbell	.05	.02	.01
☐ 321	Hubert Davis	.15	.07	.02
☐ 322	Doc Rivers	.05	.02	.01
☐ 323	Charles Smith	.05	.02	.01
☐ 324	Herb Williams	.05	.02	.01
☐ 325	Litterial Green	.05	.02	.01
☐ 326	Steve Kerr	.05	.02	.01
☐ 327	Greg Kite	.05	.02	.01
☐ 328	Shaquille O'Neal	8.00	3.60	1.00
☐ 329	Tom Tolbert	.05	.02	.01
☐ 330	Jeff Turner	.05	.02	.01
☐ 331	Greg Grant	.05	.02	.01
☐ 332	Jeff Hornacek	.08	.04	.01
☐ 333	Andrew Lang	.05	.02	.01
☐ 334	Tim Perry	.05	.02	.01
☐ 335	Clarence Weatherspoon	.60	.25	.08
☐ 336	Danny Ainge	.08	.04	.01
☐ 337	Charles Barkley	.60	.25	.08
☐ 338	Richard Dumas	.15	.07	.02
☐ 339	Frank Johnson	.05	.02	.01
☐ 340	Tim Kempton	.05	.02	.01
☐ 341	Oliver Miller	.25	.11	.03
☐ 342	Jerrod Mustaf	.05	.02	.01
☐ 343	Mario Elie	.05	.02	.01
☐ 344	Dave Johnson	.05	.02	.01
☐ 345	Tracy Murray	.05	.02	.01
☐ 346	Rod Strickland	.08	.04	.01
☐ 347	Randy Brown	.05	.02	.01
☐ 348	Pete Chilcutt	.05	.02	.01
☐ 349	Marty Conlon	.05	.02	.01
☐ 350	Jim Les	.05	.02	.01
☐ 351	Kurt Rambis	.05	.02	.01
☐ 352	Walt Williams	.60	.25	.08
☐ 353	Lloyd Daniels	.05	.02	.01
☐ 354	Vinny Del Negro	.05	.02	.01
☐ 355	Dale Ellis	.08	.04	.01
☐ 356	Avery Johnson	.05	.02	.01
☐ 357	Sam Mack	.05	.02	.01
☐ 358	J.R. Reid	.05	.02	.01
☐ 359	David Wood	.05	.02	.01
☐ 360	Vincent Askew	.05	.02	.01
☐ 361	Isaac Austin	.05	.02	.01
☐ 362	John Crotty	.05	.02	.01
☐ 363	Stephen Howard	.05	.02	.01
☐ 364	Jay Humphries	.05	.02	.01
☐ 365	Larry Krystkowiak	.05	.02	.01
☐ 366	Rex Chapman	.05	.02	.01
☐ 367	Tom Gugliotta	.50	.23	.06
☐ 368	Buck Johnson	.05	.02	.01
☐ 369	Charles Jones	.05	.02	.01
☐ 370	Don MacLean	.15	.07	.02
☐ 371	Doug Overton	.05	.02	.01
☐ 372	Brent Price	.05	.02	.01
☐ 373	Checklist 201-266	.05	.02	.01
☐ 374	Checklist 267-330	.05	.02	.01
☐ 375	Checklist 331-375	.05	.02	.01
☐ JS207	Pervis Ellison AU	15.00	6.75	1.90

(Certified Autograph)
Washington Bullets

☐ JS212	Duane Causwell AU	15.00	6.75	1.90

(Certified Autograph)
Sacramento Kings

☐ JS215	Stacey Augmon AU	40.00	18.00	5.00

(Certified Autograph)
Atlanta Hawks

☐ NNO	Jam Session Rank 1-10	2.00	.90	.25

David Robinson
Dikembe Mutombo
Otis Thorpe
Hakeem Olajuwon
Shawn Kemp
Charles Barkley
Pervis Ellison
Chris Morris
Brad Daugherty
Derrick Coleman

☐ NNO	Jam Session Rank 11-20	2.00	.90	.25

Tim Perry
Duane Causwell
Scottie Pippen
Robert Parish
Stacey Augmon
Michael Jordan
Karl Malone
John Williams
Horace Grant
Orlando Woolridge

1992-93 Ultra All-NBA

This set features 15 cards, one for each All-NBA first, second, and third-team player. The standard-size (2 1/2" by 3 1/2") cards were randomly inserted into approximately one out of every 14 first series foil packs. The fronts feature color action player photos which are full-bleed except at the bottom, where a gold foil stripe separates a marbleized diagonal bottom border. A crest showing which All-NBA team the player was on overlaps the border and picture. The player's name is gold-foil stamped at the bottom. The horizontal backs carry a cut-out player close-up and career highlights on a marbleized background. The cards are numbered on the back.

	MINT	NRMT	EXC
COMPLETE SET (15)	55.00	25.00	7.00
COMMON CARD (1-15)	.50	.23	.06
☐ 1 Karl Malone	2.50	1.15	.30
Utah Jazz			
☐ 2 Chris Mullin	1.00	.45	.13
Golden State Warriors			
☐ 3 David Robinson	5.00	2.30	.60
San Antonio Spurs			
☐ 4 Michael Jordan	30.00	13.50	3.80
Chicago Bulls			

☐ 5	Clyde Drexler	2.50	1.15	.30
	Portland Trail Blazers			
☐ 6	Scottie Pippen	2.50	1.15	.30
	Chicago Bulls			
☐ 7	Charles Barkley	5.00	2.30	.60
	Phoenix Suns			
☐ 8	Patrick Ewing	2.50	1.15	.30
	New York Knicks			
☐ 9	Tim Hardaway	1.00	.45	.13
	Golden State Warriors			
☐ 10	John Stockton	2.50	1.15	.30
	Utah Jazz			
☐ 11	Dennis Rodman	1.50	.65	.19
	Detroit Pistons			
☐ 12	Kevin Willis	.50	.23	.06
	Atlanta Hawks			
☐ 13	Brad Daugherty	.50	.23	.06
	Cleveland Cavaliers			
☐ 14	Mark Price	1.00	.45	.13
	Cleveland Cavaliers			
☐ 15	Kevin Johnson	1.25	.55	.16
	Phoenix Suns			

1992-93 Ultra
All-Rookies

Randomly inserted in second series foil packs at a reported rate of approximately one card per nine packs, this ten-card standard-size (2 1/2" by 3 1/2") set focuses on the 1992-93 class of outstanding rookies. A color action shot on the front has been cut out and superimposed on grid of identical close-up shots of the player, which resemble the effect produced by a wall of TV sets displaying the same image. The "All-Rookie" logo and the player's name are gold-foil stamped across the bottom of the picture. On the backs, a wheat-colored panel carrying a player profile overlays a second full-bleed color action photo. The cards are numbered in the lower left corner of the panel and arranged alphabetically.

		MINT	NRMT	EXC
COMPLETE SET (10)		30.00	13.50	3.80
COMMON CARD (1-10)		.50	.23	.06
☐ 1	LaPhonso Ellis	.75	.35	.09
	Denver Nuggets			
☐ 2	Tom Gugliotta	1.25	.55	.16
	Washington Bullets			
☐ 3	Robert Horry	2.00	.90	.25
	Houston Rockets			

☐ 4	Christian Laettner	1.50	.65	.19
	Minnesota Timberwolves			
☐ 5	Harold Miner	.50	.23	.06
	Miami Heat			
☐ 6	Alonzo Mourning	5.00	2.30	.60
	Charlotte Hornets			
☐ 7	Shaquille O'Neal	20.00	9.00	2.50
	Orlando Magic			
☐ 8	Latrell Sprewell	5.00	2.30	.60
	Golden State Warriors			
☐ 9	Clarence Weatherspoon	1.50	.65	.19
	Philadelphia 76ers			
☐ 10	Walt Williams	1.50	.65	.19
	Sacramento Kings			

1992-93 Ultra Award
Winners

This five-card standard size (2 1/2" by 3 1/2") Ultra Award Winners insert set spot lights the 1991-92 MVP, Rookie of the Year, Defensive Player of the Year, top "6th Man" and Most Improved Player. These cards were randomly inserted into first series packs at a rate of one card in every 42 packs according to information printed on the wrappers. Card fronts feature an action photo with the player's name and Award Winners logo at the bottom. Backs have career highlights and a photo.

		MINT	NRMT	EXC
COMPLETE SET (5)		50.00	23.00	6.25
COMMON CARD (1-5)		1.00	.45	.13
☐ 1	Michael Jordan	40.00	18.00	5.00
	Chicago Bulls			
☐ 2	David Robinson	6.00	2.70	.75
	San Antonio Spurs			
☐ 3	Larry Johnson	3.00	1.35	.40
	Charlotte Hornets			
☐ 4	Detlef Schrempf	2.00	.90	.25
	Indiana Pacers			
☐ 5	Pervis Ellison	1.00	.45	.13
	Washington Bullets			

1992-93 Ultra
Scottie Pippen

This 12-card "Career Highlights" set chronicles Scottie Pippen's rise to NBA stardom.

The cards were inserted at a rate of one card per 21 first series packs according to information printed on the wrappers. Pippen autographed more than 2,000 of these cards for random insertion in first series packs. These autograph cards have embossed Fleer logos for authenticity. Through a special mail-in offer only, two additional Pippen cards were made available to collectors who sent in ten wrappers and 1.00 for postage and handling. On the front, the standard-size (2 1/2" by 3 1/2") cards feature color action player photos with brownish-green marbleized borders. The player's name and the words "Career Highlights" are stamped in gold foil below the picture. On the same marbleized background, the backs carry a color head shot as well as biography and career summary. The cards are numbered on the back.

	MINT	NRMT	EXC
COMPLETE SET (10)	10.00	4.50	1.25
COMMON S.PIPPEN (1-10)	1.00	.45	.13
COMMON SEND-OFF (11-12)	1.00	.45	.13
☐ 1 Scottie Pippen (Dribbling, right index finger pointing down)	1.00	.45	.13
☐ 2 Scottie Pippen (Dribbling, Magnavox ad in background)	1.00	.45	.13
☐ 3 Scottie Pippen (Preparing to dunk)	1.00	.45	.13
☐ 4 Scottie Pippen (Dribbling, defender's hand reaching in)	1.00	.45	.13
☐ 5 Scottie Pippen (In air, ball in both hands, vs. Bucks)	1.00	.45	.13
☐ 6 Scottie Pippen (Driving toward basket, vs. Nuggets)	1.00	.45	.13
☐ 7 Scottie Pippen (Shooting over McDaniel of the Knicks)	1.00	.45	.13
☐ 8 Scottie Pippen (Dribbling, Laker cheerleader in background)	1.00	.45	.13
☐ 9 Scottie Pippen (Defending against McDaniel of the Knicks)	1.00	.45	.13
☐ 10 Scottie Pippen (Driving toward basket, vs. Nets)	1.00	.45	.13
☐ 11 Scottie Pippen (Defended by Rodman; ball in left hand)	1.00	.45	.13
☐ 12 Scottie Pippen (Dunking over Nugget player)	1.00	.45	.13
☐ AU Scottie Pippen (Certified autograph)	125.00	57.50	15.50

1992-93 Ultra Playmakers

Randomly inserted in second series foil packs at a reported rate of one card per 13 packs, this ten-card standard-size (2 1/2" by 3 1/2") set features the NBA's top point guards. The glossy color action photos on the fronts are full-bleed except at the bottom where a lavender stripe edges the picture. The "Playmaker" logo and the player's name are gold-foil stamped across the bottom of the picture. On the backs, a wheat-colored panel carrying a player profile overlays a second full-bleed color action photo. The cards are numbered in the lower left corner of the panel.

	MINT	NRMT	EXC
COMPLETE SET (10)	4.00	1.80	.50
COMMON CARD (1-10)	.25	.11	.03
☐ 1 Kenny Anderson New Jersey Nets	.75	.35	.09
☐ 2 Muggsy Bogues Charlotte Hornets	.50	.23	.06
☐ 3 Tim Hardaway Golden State Warriors	.50	.23	.06
☐ 4 Mark Jackson Los Angeles Clippers	.25	.11	.03
☐ 5 Kevin Johnson Phoenix Suns	.75	.35	.09
☐ 6 Mark Price Cleveland Cavaliers	.50	.23	.06
☐ 7 Terry Porter Portland Trail Blazers	.35	.16	.04
☐ 8 Scott Skiles Orlando Magic	.25	.11	.03
☐ 9 John Stockton Utah Jazz	1.50	.65	.19
☐ 10 Isiah Thomas Detroit Pistons	.75	.35	.09

1992-93 Ultra Rejectors

Randomly inserted in second series foil packs at a reported rate of one in 26, this five-card set showcases defensive big men who are aptly dubbed "Rejectors." The cards measure the standard size (2 1/2" by 3 1/2"). The glossy color action photos on the fronts are full-bleed except at the bottom where a gold stripe edges the picture. The player's name and the "Rejector" logo are gold-foil stamped across the bottom of the picture. On a black panel inside gold borders, the horizontal backs carry text describing the player's defensive accomplishments and a color close-up photo. The cards are numbered on the back.

	MINT	NRMT	EXC
COMPLETE SET (5)	20.00	9.00	2.50
COMMON CARD (1-5)	.75	.35	.09
☐ 1 Alonzo Mourning Charlotte Hornets	4.00	1.80	.50
☐ 2 Dikembe Mutombo Denver Nuggets	.75	.35	.09
☐ 3 Hakeem Olajuwon Houston Rockets	2.50	1.15	.30
☐ 4 Shaquille O'Neal Orlando Magic	15.00	6.75	1.90
☐ 5 David Robinson San Antonio Spurs	2.00	.90	.25

1993-94 Ultra

The complete 1993-94 Ultra basketball set consists of 375 standard-size (2 1/2" by 3 1/2") cards that were issued in series of

200 and 175 respectively. Cards were issued in 14 and 19-card packs. There are 36 packs per box. The glossy color action player photos on the fronts are full-bleed except at the bottom. The bottom of the front consists of player name, team name and a peach colored border. The horizontal backs feature a player photos against a basketball court background. The team logo and biographical information appear a pale peach bar, while the player's name and statistics are printed in team color-coded bars running across the card bottom. The cards are alphabetically arranged by team and are numbered alphabetically within teams: Atlanta Hawks (1-8/201-205), Boston Celtics (9-15/206-211), Charlotte Hornets (16-25/212-217), Chicago Bulls (26-34/218-224), Cleveland Cavaliers (35-42/225-229), Dallas Mavericks (43-48/230-235), Denver Nuggets (49-54/236-240), Detroit Pistons (55-62/241-246), Golden State Warriors (63-70/247-252), Houston Rockets (71-78/253-257), Indiana Pacers (79-85/258-264), Los Angeles Clippers (86-91/265-271), Los Angeles Lakers (92-97/272-278), Miami Heat (98-104/279-281), Milwaukee Bucks (105-112/282-286), Minnesota Timberwolves (113-117/287-293), New Jersey Nets (118-123/294-300), New York Knicks (124-132/301-303), Orlando Magic (133-138/304-308), Philadelphia 76ers (139-143/309-316), Phoenix Suns (144-152/317-321), Portland Trail Blazers (153-159/322-328), Sacramento Kings (160-166/329-335), San Antonio Spurs (167-174/336-341), Seattle Supersonics (175-183/342-346), Utah Jazz (184-191/347-351) and Washington Bullets (192-198/352-360). A USA Basketball sub-set contains cards 361-372. Ten second series wrappers and $1.50 could be redeemed for USA cards of Reggie Miller (M1), Shaquille O'Neal (M2) and team photo (M3). The offered was good through June 10, 1994. These cards are not considered part of the basic set.

	MINT	NRMT	EXC
COMPLETE SET (375)	30.00	13.50	3.80
COMPLETE SERIES 1 (200)	15.00	6.75	1.90
COMPLETE SERIES 2 (175)	15.00	6.75	1.90
COMMON CARD (1-375)	.05	.02	.01
☐ 1 Stacey Augmon	.08	.04	.01
☐ 2 Mookie Blaylock	.08	.04	.01
☐ 3 Doug Edwards	.08	.04	.01
☐ 4 Duane Ferrell	.05	.02	.01
☐ 5 Paul Graham	.05	.02	.01
☐ 6 Adam Keefe	.05	.02	.01
☐ 7 Dominique Wilkins	.15	.07	.02
☐ 8 Kevin Willis	.08	.04	.01
☐ 9 Alaa Abdelnaby	.05	.02	.01
☐ 10 Dee Brown	.08	.04	.01
☐ 11 Sherman Douglas	.05	.02	.01
☐ 12 Rick Fox	.05	.02	.01
☐ 13 Kevin Gamble	.05	.02	.01
☐ 14 Xavier McDaniel	.08	.04	.01
☐ 15 Robert Parish	.10	.05	.01
☐ 16 Muggsy Bogues	.10	.05	.01
☐ 17 Scott Burrell	.25	.11	.03

☐ 18	Dell Curry	.05	.02	.01	☐ 89	Stanley Roberts	.05	.02	.01
☐ 19	Kenny Gattison	.05	.02	.01	☐ 90	Loy Vaught	.08	.04	.01
☐ 20	Hersey Hawkins	.08	.04	.01	☐ 91	John Williams	.05	.02	.01
☐ 21	Eddie Johnson	.08	.04	.01	☐ 92	Sam Bowie	.05	.02	.01
☐ 22	Larry Johnson	.30	.14	.04	☐ 93	Doug Christie	.05	.02	.01
☐ 23	Alonzo Mourning	.60	.25	.08	☐ 94	Vlade Divac	.10	.05	.01
☐ 24	Johnny Newman	.05	.02	.01	☐ 95	George Lynch	.08	.04	.01
☐ 25	David Wingate	.05	.02	.01	☐ 96	Anthony Peeler	.05	.02	.01
☐ 26	B.J. Armstrong	.05	.02	.01	☐ 97	James Worthy	.10	.05	.01
☐ 27	Corie Blount	.05	.02	.01	☐ 98	Bimbo Coles	.05	.02	.01
☐ 28	Bill Cartwright	.05	.02	.01	☐ 99	Grant Long	.05	.02	.01
☐ 29	Horace Grant	.15	.07	.02	☐ 100	Harold Miner	.05	.02	.01
☐ 30	Michael Jordan	4.00	1.80	.50	☐ 101	Glen Rice	.10	.05	.01
☐ 31	Stacey King	.05	.02	.01	☐ 102	Rony Seikaly	.05	.02	.01
☐ 32	John Paxson	.05	.02	.01	☐ 103	Brian Shaw	.05	.02	.01
☐ 33	Will Perdue	.05	.02	.01	☐ 104	Steve Smith	.08	.04	.01
☐ 34	Scottie Pippen	.30	.14	.04	☐ 105	Anthony Avent	.05	.02	.01
☐ 35	Terrell Brandon	.05	.02	.01	☐ 106	Vin Baker	1.00	.45	.13
☐ 36	Brad Daugherty	.08	.04	.01	☐ 107	Frank Brickowski	.05	.02	.01
☐ 37	Danny Ferry	.05	.02	.01	☐ 108	Todd Day	.08	.04	.01
☐ 38	Chris Mills	.40	.18	.05	☐ 109	Blue Edwards	.05	.02	.01
☐ 39	Larry Nance	.08	.04	.01	☐ 110	Lee Mayberry	.05	.02	.01
☐ 40	Mark Price	.10	.05	.01	☐ 111	Eric Murdock	.05	.02	.01
☐ 41	Gerald Wilkins	.05	.02	.01	☐ 112	Orlando Woolridge	.05	.02	.01
☐ 42	John Williams	.08	.04	.01	☐ 113	Thurl Bailey	.05	.02	.01
☐ 43	Terry Davis	.05	.02	.01	☐ 114	Christian Laettner	.10	.05	.01
☐ 44	Derek Harper	.08	.04	.01	☐ 115	Chuck Person	.08	.04	.01
☐ 45	Donald Hodge	.05	.02	.01	☐ 116	Doug West	.05	.02	.01
☐ 46	Jim Jackson	.60	.25	.08	☐ 117	Micheal Williams	.05	.02	.01
☐ 47	Sean Rooks	.05	.02	.01	☐ 118	Kenny Anderson	.10	.05	.01
☐ 48	Doug Smith	.05	.02	.01	☐ 119	Derrick Coleman	.10	.05	.01
☐ 49	Mahmoud Abdul-Rauf...	.05	.02	.01	☐ 120	Rick Mahorn	.05	.02	.01
☐ 50	LaPhonso Ellis	.08	.04	.01	☐ 121	Chris Morris	.05	.02	.01
☐ 51	Mark Macon	.05	.02	.01	☐ 122	Rumeal Robinson	.05	.02	.01
☐ 52	Dikembe Mutombo	.25	.11	.03	☐ 123	Rex Walters	.08	.04	.01
☐ 53	Bryant Stith	.05	.02	.01	☐ 124	Greg Anthony	.05	.02	.01
☐ 54	Reggie Williams	.05	.02	.01	☐ 125	Rolando Blackman	.08	.04	.01
☐ 55	Mark Aguirre	.08	.04	.01	☐ 126	Hubert Davis	.05	.02	.01
☐ 56	Joe Dumars	.15	.07	.02	☐ 127	Patrick Ewing	.30	.14	.04
☐ 57	Bill Laimbeer	.08	.04	.01	☐ 128	Anthony Mason	.08	.04	.01
☐ 58	Terry Mills	.05	.02	.01	☐ 129	Charles Oakley	.08	.04	.01
☐ 59	Olden Polynice	.05	.02	.01	☐ 130	Doc Rivers	.05	.02	.01
☐ 60	Alvin Robertson	.05	.02	.01	☐ 131	Charles Smith	.05	.02	.01
☐ 61	Dennis Rodman	.10	.05	.01	☐ 132	John Starks	.08	.04	.01
☐ 62	Isiah Thomas	.15	.07	.02	☐ 133	Nick Anderson	.08	.04	.01
☐ 63	Victor Alexander	.05	.02	.01	☐ 134	Anthony Bowie	.05	.02	.01
☐ 64	Chris Gatling	.05	.02	.01	☐ 135	Shaquille O'Neal	2.50	1.15	.30
☐ 65	Tim Hardaway	.10	.05	.01	☐ 136	Dennis Scott	.05	.02	.01
☐ 66	Byron Houston	.05	.02	.01	☐ 137	Scott Skiles	.05	.02	.01
☐ 67	Sarunas Marciulionis	.05	.02	.01	☐ 138	Jeff Turner	.05	.02	.01
☐ 68	Chris Mullin	.10	.05	.01	☐ 139	Shawn Bradley	.40	.18	.05
☐ 69	Billy Owens	.08	.04	.01	☐ 140	Johnny Dawkins	.05	.02	.01
☐ 70	Latrell Sprewell	.60	.25	.08	☐ 141	Jeff Hornacek	.08	.04	.01
☐ 71	Matt Bullard	.05	.02	.01	☐ 142	Tim Perry	.05	.02	.01
☐ 72	Sam Cassell	.50	.23	.06	☐ 143	Clarence Weatherspoon	.10	.05	.01
☐ 73	Carl Herrera	.05	.02	.01	☐ 144	Danny Ainge	.08	.04	.01
☐ 74	Robert Horry	.10	.05	.01	☐ 145	Charles Barkley	.60	.25	.08
☐ 75	Vernon Maxwell	.05	.02	.01	☐ 146	Cedric Ceballos	.10	.05	.01
☐ 76	Hakeem Olajuwon	.75	.35	.09	☐ 147	Kevin Johnson	.15	.07	.02
☐ 77	Kenny Smith	.05	.02	.01	☐ 148	Negele Knight	.05	.02	.01
☐ 78	Otis Thorpe	.08	.04	.01	☐ 149	Malcolm Mackey	.05	.02	.01
☐ 79	Dale Davis	.08	.04	.01	☐ 150	Dan Majerle	.08	.04	.01
☐ 80	Vern Fleming	.05	.02	.01	☐ 151	Oliver Miller	.08	.04	.01
☐ 81	Reggie Miller	.30	.14	.04	☐ 152	Mark West	.05	.02	.01
☐ 82	Sam Mitchell	.05	.02	.01	☐ 153	Mark Bryant	.05	.02	.01
☐ 83	Pooh Richardson	.05	.02	.01	☐ 154	Clyde Drexler	.30	.14	.04
☐ 84	Detlef Schrempf	.10	.05	.01	☐ 155	Jerome Kersey	.05	.02	.01
☐ 85	Rik Smits	.10	.05	.01	☐ 156	Terry Porter	.08	.04	.01
☐ 86	Ron Harper	.08	.04	.01	☐ 157	Cliff Robinson	.10	.05	.01
☐ 87	Mark Jackson	.05	.02	.01	☐ 158	Rod Strickland	.08	.04	.01
☐ 88	Danny Manning	.10	.05	.01	☐ 159	Buck Williams	.08	.04	.01

☐ 160	Duane Causwell	.05	.02	.01	☐ 231	Lucious Harris	.10	.05	.01
☐ 161	Bobby Hurley	.20	.09	.03	☐ 232	Popeye Jones	.30	.14	.04
☐ 162	Mitch Richmond	.15	.07	.02	☐ 233	Tim Legler	.05	.02	.01
☐ 163	Lionel Simmons	.05	.02	.01	☐ 234	Fat Lever	.05	.02	.01
☐ 164	Wayman Tisdale	.08	.04	.01	☐ 235	Jamal Mashburn	2.00	.90	.25
☐ 165	Spud Webb	.08	.04	.01	☐ 236	Tom Hammonds	.05	.02	.01
☐ 166	Walt Williams	.10	.05	.01	☐ 237	Darnell Mee	.05	.02	.01
☐ 167	Willie Anderson	.05	.02	.01	☐ 238	Robert Pack	.05	.02	.01
☐ 168	Antoine Carr	.05	.02	.01	☐ 239	Rodney Rogers	.40	.18	.05
☐ 169	Lloyd Daniels	.05	.02	.01	☐ 240	Brian Williams	.05	.02	.01
☐ 170	Sean Elliott	.08	.04	.01	☐ 241	Greg Anderson	.05	.02	.01
☐ 171	Dale Ellis	.08	.04	.01	☐ 242	Sean Elliott	.08	.04	.01
☐ 172	Avery Johnson	.05	.02	.01	☐ 243	Allan Houston	.40	.18	.05
☐ 173	J.R. Reid	.05	.02	.01	☐ 244	Lindsey Hunter	.15	.07	.02
☐ 174	David Robinson	.60	.25	.08	☐ 245	Mark Macon	.05	.02	.01
☐ 175	Michael Cage	.05	.02	.01	☐ 246	David Wood	.05	.02	.01
☐ 176	Kendall Gill	.05	.02	.01	☐ 247	Jud Buechler	.05	.02	.01
☐ 177	Ervin Johnson	.10	.05	.01	☐ 248	Josh Grant	.05	.02	.01
☐ 178	Shawn Kemp	.60	.25	.08	☐ 249	Jeff Grayer	.05	.02	.01
☐ 179	Derrick McKey	.08	.04	.01	☐ 250	Keith Jennings	.05	.02	.01
☐ 180	Nate McMillan	.05	.02	.01	☐ 251	Avery Johnson	.05	.02	.01
☐ 181	Gary Payton	.10	.05	.01	☐ 252	Chris Webber	1.50	.65	.19
☐ 182	Sam Perkins	.08	.04	.01	☐ 253	Scott Brooks	.05	.02	.01
☐ 183	Ricky Pierce	.08	.04	.01	☐ 254	Sam Cassell	.05	.02	.01
☐ 184	David Benoit	.05	.02	.01	☐ 255	Mario Elie	.05	.02	.01
☐ 185	Tyrone Corbin	.05	.02	.01	☐ 256	Richard Petruska	.05	.02	.01
☐ 186	Mark Eaton	.05	.02	.01	☐ 257	Eric Riley	.05	.02	.01
☐ 187	Jay Humphries	.05	.02	.01	☐ 258	Antonio Davis	.10	.05	.01
☐ 188	Jeff Malone	.08	.04	.01	☐ 259	Scott Haskin	.05	.02	.01
☐ 189	Karl Malone	.30	.14	.04	☐ 260	Derrick McKey	.08	.04	.01
☐ 190	John Stockton	.30	.14	.04	☐ 261	Byron Scott	.08	.04	.01
☐ 191	Luther Wright	.05	.02	.01	☐ 262	Malik Sealy	.05	.02	.01
☐ 192	Michael Adams	.05	.02	.01	☐ 263	Kenny Williams	.05	.02	.01
☐ 193	Calbert Cheaney	.50	.23	.06	☐ 264	Haywoode Workman	.05	.02	.01
☐ 194	Pervis Ellison	.05	.02	.01	☐ 265	Mark Aguirre	.08	.04	.01
☐ 195	Tom Gugliotta	.10	.05	.01	☐ 266	Terry Dehere	.08	.04	.01
☐ 196	Buck Johnson	.05	.02	.01	☐ 267	Harold Ellis	.05	.02	.01
☐ 197	LaBradford Smith	.05	.02	.01	☐ 268	Gary Grant	.05	.02	.01
☐ 198	Larry Stewart	.05	.02	.01	☐ 269	Bob Martin	.05	.02	.01
☐ 199	Checklist	.05	.02	.01	☐ 270	Elmore Spencer	.05	.02	.01
☐ 200	Checklist	.05	.02	.01	☐ 271	Tom Tolbert	.05	.02	.01
☐ 201	Doug Edwards	.05	.02	.01	☐ 272	Sam Bowie	.05	.02	.01
☐ 202	Craig Ehlo	.05	.02	.01	☐ 273	Elden Campbell	.05	.02	.01
☐ 203	Jon Koncak	.05	.02	.01	☐ 274	Antonio Harvey	.08	.04	.01
☐ 204	Andrew Lang	.05	.02	.01	☐ 275	George Lynch	.05	.02	.01
☐ 205	Ennis Whatley	.05	.02	.01	☐ 276	Tony Smith	.05	.02	.01
☐ 206	Chris Corchiani	.05	.02	.01	☐ 277	Sedale Threatt	.05	.02	.01
☐ 207	Acie Earl	.05	.02	.01	☐ 278	Nick Van Exel	2.00	.90	.25
☐ 208	Jimmy Oliver	.05	.02	.01	☐ 279	Willie Burton	.05	.02	.01
☐ 209	Ed Pinckney	.05	.02	.01	☐ 280	Matt Geiger	.05	.02	.01
☐ 210	Dino Radja	.40	.18	.05	☐ 281	John Salley	.05	.02	.01
☐ 211	Matt Wenstrom	.05	.02	.01	☐ 282	Vin Baker	.50	.23	.06
☐ 212	Tony Bennett	.05	.02	.01	☐ 283	Jon Barry	.05	.02	.01
☐ 213	Scott Burrell	.05	.02	.01	☐ 284	Brad Lohaus	.05	.02	.01
☐ 214	LeRon Ellis	.05	.02	.01	☐ 285	Ken Norman	.05	.02	.01
☐ 215	Hersey Hawkins	.08	.04	.01	☐ 286	Derek Strong	.05	.02	.01
☐ 216	Eddie Johnson	.08	.04	.01	☐ 287	Mike Brown	.05	.02	.01
☐ 217	Rumeal Robinson	.05	.02	.01	☐ 288	Brian Davis	.05	.02	.01
☐ 218	Corie Blount	.05	.02	.01	☐ 289	Tellis Frank	.05	.02	.01
☐ 219	Dave Johnson	.05	.02	.01	☐ 290	Luc Longley	.05	.02	.01
☐ 220	Steve Kerr	.05	.02	.01	☐ 291	Marlon Maxey	.05	.02	.01
☐ 221	Toni Kukoc	.50	.23	.06	☐ 292	Isaiah Rider	.60	.25	.08
☐ 222	Pete Myers	.05	.02	.01	☐ 293	Chris Smith	.05	.02	.01
☐ 223	Bill Wennington	.05	.02	.01	☐ 294	P.J. Brown	.10	.05	.01
☐ 224	Scott Williams	.05	.02	.01	☐ 295	Kevin Edwards	.05	.02	.01
☐ 225	John Battle	.05	.02	.01	☐ 296	Armon Gilliam	.05	.02	.01
☐ 226	Tyrone Hill	.08	.04	.01	☐ 297	Johnny Newman	.05	.02	.01
☐ 227	Gerald Madkins	.05	.02	.01	☐ 298	Rex Walters	.05	.02	.01
☐ 228	Chris Mills	.05	.02	.01	☐ 299	David Wesley	.08	.04	.01
☐ 229	Bobby Phills	.05	.02	.01	☐ 300	Jayson Williams	.05	.02	.01
☐ 230	Greg Dreiling	.05	.02	.01	☐ 301	Anthony Bonner	.05	.02	.01

		MINT	NRMT	EXC
☐ 302	Derek Harper	.08	.04	.01
☐ 303	Herb Williams	.05	.02	.01
☐ 304	Litterial Green	.05	.02	.01
☐ 305	Anfernee Hardaway	4.00	1.80	.50
☐ 306	Greg Kite	.05	.02	.01
☐ 307	Larry Krystkowiak	.05	.02	.01
☐ 308	Keith Tower	.05	.02	.01
☐ 309	Dana Barros	.10	.05	.01
☐ 310	Shawn Bradley	.05	.02	.01
☐ 311	Greg Graham	.05	.02	.01
☐ 312	Sean Green	.05	.02	.01
☐ 313	Warren Kidd	.05	.02	.01
☐ 314	Eric Leckner	.05	.02	.01
☐ 315	Moses Malone	.15	.07	.02
☐ 316	Orlando Woolridge	.05	.02	.01
☐ 317	Duane Cooper	.05	.02	.01
☐ 318	Joe Courtney	.05	.02	.01
☐ 319	A.C. Green	.10	.05	.01
☐ 320	Frank Johnson	.05	.02	.01
☐ 321	Joe Kleine	.05	.02	.01
☐ 322	Chris Dudley	.05	.02	.01
☐ 323	Harvey Grant	.05	.02	.01
☐ 324	Jaren Jackson	.05	.02	.01
☐ 325	Tracy Murray	.05	.02	.01
☐ 326	James Robinson	.15	.07	.02
☐ 327	Reggie Smith	.05	.02	.01
☐ 328	Kevin Thompson	.05	.02	.01
☐ 329	Randy Brown	.05	.02	.01
☐ 330	Evers Burns	.05	.02	.01
☐ 331	Pete Chilcutt	.05	.02	.01
☐ 332	Bobby Hurley	.05	.02	.01
☐ 333	Mike Peplowski	.05	.02	.01
☐ 334	LaBradford Smith	.05	.02	.01
☐ 335	Trevor Wilson	.05	.02	.01
☐ 336	Terry Cummings	.08	.04	.01
☐ 337	Vinny Del Negro	.05	.02	.01
☐ 338	Sleepy Floyd	.05	.02	.01
☐ 339	Negele Knight	.05	.02	.01
☐ 340	Dennis Rodman	.20	.09	.03
☐ 341	Chris Whitney	.05	.02	.01
☐ 342	Vincent Askew	.05	.02	.01
☐ 343	Kendall Gill	.05	.02	.01
☐ 344	Ervin Johnson	.05	.02	.01
☐ 345	Chris King	.05	.02	.01
☐ 346	Detlef Schrempf	.10	.05	.01
☐ 347	Walter Bond	.05	.02	.01
☐ 348	Tom Chambers	.08	.04	.01
☐ 349	John Crotty	.05	.02	.01
☐ 350	Bryon Russell	.05	.02	.01
☐ 351	Felton Spencer	.05	.02	.01
☐ 352	Mitchell Butler	.05	.02	.01
☐ 353	Rex Chapman	.05	.02	.01
☐ 354	Calbert Cheaney	.05	.02	.01
☐ 355	Kevin Duckworth	.05	.02	.01
☐ 356	Don MacLean	.05	.02	.01
☐ 357	Gheorghe Muresan	.30	.14	.04
☐ 358	Doug Overton	.05	.02	.01
☐ 359	Brent Price	.05	.02	.01
☐ 360	Kenny Walker	.05	.02	.01
☐ 361	Derrick Coleman USA	.05	.02	.01
☐ 362	Joe Dumars USA	.08	.04	.01
☐ 363	Tim Hardaway USA	.05	.02	.01
☐ 364	Larry Johnson USA	.10	.05	.01
☐ 365	Shawn Kemp USA	.30	.14	.04
☐ 366	Dan Majerle USA	.05	.02	.01
☐ 367	Alonzo Mourning USA	.30	.14	.04
☐ 368	Mark Price USA	.05	.02	.01
☐ 369	Steve Smith USA	.05	.02	.01
☐ 370	Isiah Thomas USA	.08	.04	.01
☐ 371	Dominique Wilkins USA	.08	.04	.01
☐ 372	Don Nelson	.05	.02	.01

		MINT	NRMT	EXC
	Don Chaney			
☐ 373	Jamal Mashburn CL	.25	.11	.03
☐ 374	Checklist	.05	.02	.01
☐ 375	Checklist	.05	.02	.01
☐ M1	Reggie Miller USA	1.00	.45	.13
☐ M2	Shaquille O'Neal USA	5.00	2.30	.60
☐ M3	Team Checklist USA	2.00	.90	.25

1993-94 Ultra All-Defensive

Randomly inserted in 1 of 24 first series 19-card jumbo packs, this standard-size (2 1/2" by 3 1/2") 10-card set features members of the first (1-5) and second (6-10) All-NBA defensive teams. The design features a borderless front and color player action cutout set against a background of an enlarged and ghosted version of the same photo. The player's name appears in gold-foil lettering at the bottom. The back features a color player photo at the lower left, along with his career highlights set against the same ghosted photo background. The cards are numbered on the back as "X of 10."

		MINT	NRMT	EXC
COMPLETE SET (10)		175.00	80.00	22.00
COMMON CARD (1-10)		3.00	1.35	.40
☐ 1	Joe Dumars	5.00	2.30	.60
	Detroit Pistons			
☐ 2	Michael Jordan	125.00	57.50	15.50
	Chicago Bulls			
☐ 3	Hakeem Olajuwon	25.00	11.50	3.10
	Houston Rockets			
☐ 4	Scottie Pippen	10.00	4.50	1.25
	Chicago Bulls			
☐ 5	Dennis Rodman	6.00	2.70	.75
	Detroit Pistons			
☐ 6	Horace Grant	5.00	2.30	.60
	Chicago Bulls			
☐ 7	Dan Majerle	3.00	1.35	.40
	Phoenix Suns			
☐ 8	Larry Nance	3.00	1.35	.40
	Cleveland Cavaliers			
☐ 9	David Robinson	20.00	9.00	2.50
	San Antonio Spurs			
☐ 10	John Starks	3.00	1.35	.40
	New York Knicks			

1993-94 Ultra All-NBA

Randomly inserted in 14-card first series packs at a rate of approximately one in 16, this 14-card standard-size (2 1/2" by 3 1/2") set features one card for each All-NBA first (1-5), second (6-10) and third (11-14) team player from the 1992-93 season. Drazen Petrovic was named to the third team. Due to his death following the '92-93 season, a card was not produced. The fronts display full-bleed glossy color action photos with a series of three smaller photos along the left side. The player's name appears in gold-foil lettering at the lower right. The back carries a hardwood floor-design background with three small photos along the left side that progressively zoom in on the player. Career highlights appear alongside. The cards are numbered on the back as "X of 14."

	MINT	NRMT	EXC
COMPLETE SET (14)	50.00	23.00	6.25
COMMON CARD (1-14)	1.00	.45	.13
☐ 1 Charles Barkley Phoenix Suns	5.00	2.30	.60
☐ 2 Michael Jordan Chicago Bulls	30.00	13.50	3.80
☐ 3 Karl Malone Utah Jazz	2.50	1.15	.30
☐ 4 Hakeem Olajuwon Houston Rockets	6.00	2.70	.75
☐ 5 Mark Price Cleveland Cavaliers	1.00	.45	.13
☐ 6 Joe Dumars Detroit Pistons	1.25	.55	.16
☐ 7 Patrick Ewing New York Knicks	2.50	1.15	.30
☐ 8 Larry Johnson Charlotte Hornets	2.50	1.15	.30
☐ 9 John Stockton Utah Jazz	2.50	1.15	.30
☐ 10 Dominique Wilkins Atlanta Hawks	1.25	.55	.16
☐ 11 Derrick Coleman New Jersey Nets	1.00	.45	.13
☐ 12 Tim Hardaway Golden State Warriors	1.00	.45	.13
☐ 13 Scottie Pippen Chicago Bulls	2.50	1.15	.30
☐ 14 David Robinson San Antonio Spurs	5.00	2.30	.60

1993-94 Ultra All-Rookie Series

Randomly inserted in 14-card second series packs at an approximate rate of one in seven, this 15-card standard-size (2 1/2" by 3 1/2") set features some of the NBA's top draft picks of 1993-94. Each borderless front features a color action photo. The player's name appears in silver foil near the bottom. The horizontal borderless back carries a color player action shot on one side and career highlights on the other. The cards are numbered on the back as "X of 15."

	MINT	NRMT	EXC
COMPLETE SET (15)	50.00	23.00	6.25
COMMON CARD (1-15)	.75	.35	.09
☐ 1 Vin Baker Milwaukee Bucks	4.00	1.80	.50
☐ 2 Shawn Bradley Philadelphia 76ers	1.50	.65	.19
☐ 3 Calbert Cheaney Washington Bullets	2.00	.90	.25
☐ 4 Anfernee Hardaway Orlando Magic	15.00	6.75	1.90
☐ 5 Lindsey Hunter Detroit Pistons	.75	.35	.09
☐ 6 Bobby Hurley Sacramento Kings	1.00	.45	.13
☐ 7 Popeye Jones Dallas Mavericks	1.25	.55	.16
☐ 8 Toni Kukoc Chicago Bulls	2.00	.90	.25
☐ 9 Jamal Mashburn Dallas Mavericks	8.00	3.60	1.00
☐ 10 Chris Mills Cleveland Cavaliers	1.50	.65	.19
☐ 11 Dino Radja Boston Celtics	1.50	.65	.19
☐ 12 Isaiah Rider Minnesota Timberwolves	2.50	1.15	.30
☐ 13 Rodney Rogers Denver Nuggets	1.50	.65	.19
☐ 14 Nick Van Exel Los Angeles Lakers	8.00	3.60	1.00
☐ 15 Chris Webber Golden State Warriors	6.00	2.70	.75

1993-94 Ultra All-Rookie Team

Randomly inserted in series one 14-card packs at an approximate rate of one in 24, this five-card standard-size (2 1/2" by 3 1/2") set features the NBA's 1992-93 All-Rookie Team. Fronts feature borderless fronts with color player action cutouts breaking out of hardwood floor backgrounds. The player's name appears in gold-foil lettering at the bottom. The horizontal borderless back carries a color player cutout and career highlights on a hardwood floor background. The cards are numbered on the back as "X of 5."

	MINT	NRMT	EXC
COMPLETE SET (5)	15.00	6.75	1.90
COMMON CARD (1-5)	.50	.23	.06
☐ 1 LaPhonso Ellis Denver Nuggets	.50	.23	.06
☐ 2 Tom Gugliotta Washington Bullets (with Michael Jordan)	.75	.35	.09
☐ 3 Christian Laettner Minnesota Timberwolves	1.00	.45	.13
☐ 4 Alonzo Mourning Charlotte Hornets	2.50	1.15	.30
☐ 5 Shaquille O'Neal Orlando Magic	10.00	4.50	1.25

1993-94 Ultra Award Winners

Randomly inserted in first series 19-card jumbo packs at a rate of one in 36, this five-card standard-size (2 1/2" by 3 1/2") set features NBA award winners from the 1992-93 season. Borderless fronts feature color player action cutouts on metallic backgrounds. The player's name appears in silver-foil lettering at the bottom. The back carries a color player close-up and career highlights. The cards are numbered on the back as "X of 5."

	MINT	NRMT	EXC
COMPLETE SET (5)	30.00	13.50	3.80
COMMON CARD (1-5)	2.00	.90	.25
☐ 1 Mahmoud Abdul-Rauf Denver Nuggets	2.00	.90	.25
☐ 2 Charles Barkley Phoenix Suns	5.00	2.30	.60
☐ 3 Hakeem Olajuwon Houston Rockets	6.00	2.70	.75
☐ 4 Shaquille O'Neal Orlando Magic	20.00	9.00	2.50
☐ 5 Cliff Robinson Portland Trail Blazers	2.00	.90	.25

1993-94 Ultra Famous Nicknames

Randomly inserted into 14-card second series packs at a rate of one in five, this 15-card standard-size (2 1/2" by 3 1/2") set features popular nicknames of today's stars. Borderless fronts feature color action cutouts on hardwood-floor and basket-net backgrounds. The player's nickname appears in silver-foil lettering on the right. The borderless back carries a color player photo on one side. On the other, the shot's game background blends into a hardwood-floor background for the player's name in jumbo silver-foil lettering and his career highlights. The cards are numbered on the back as "X of 15."

	MINT	NRMT	EXC
COMPLETE SET (15)	60.00	27.00	7.50
COMMON CARD (1-15)	.50	.23	.06
☐ 1 Charles Barkley Sir Charles	3.00	1.35	.40

		MINT	NRMT	EXC
	Phoenix Suns			
☐ 2	Tyrone Bogues............... .50		.23	.06
	Muggsy			
	Charlotte Hornets			
☐ 3	Derrick Coleman .... .50		.23	.06
	D.C.			
	New Jersey Nets			
☐ 4	Clyde Drexler 1.50		.65	.19
	The Glide			
	Portland Trail Blazers			
☐ 5	Anfernee Hardaway 12.00		5.50	1.50
	Penny			
	Orlando Magic			
☐ 6	Larry Johnson................ 1.50		.65	.19
	L.J.			
	Charlotte Hornets			
☐ 7	Michael Jordan 20.00		9.00	2.50
	Air			
	Chicago Bulls			
☐ 8	Toni Kukoc 1.50		.65	.19
	The Pink Panther			
	Chicago Bulls			
☐ 9	Karl Malone................. 1.50		.65	.19
	The Mailman			
	Utah Jazz			
☐ 10	Harold Miner................ .50		.23	.06
	Baby Jordan			
	Miami Heat			
☐ 11	Alonzo Mourning 3.00		1.35	.40
	Zo			
	Charlotte Hornets			
☐ 12	Hakeem Olajuwon 4.00		1.80	.50
	The Dream			
	Houston Rockets			
☐ 13	Shaquille O'Neal........ 12.00		5.50	1.50
	Shaq			
	Orlando Magic			
☐ 14	David Robinson 3.00		1.35	.40
	The Admiral			
	San Antonio Spurs			
☐ 15	Dominique Wilkins .... .75		.35	.09
	Human Highlight Film			
	Atlanta Hawks			

1993-94 Ultra Inside/Outside

Randomly inserted in 14-card second series packs, this 10-card standard-size (2 1/2" by 3 1/2") set features on each borderless front a color player action cutout over a shot of a comet like basketball going through the basket, all on a black background. The player's name appears in gold

foil near the bottom. This design, but with a different action cutout, is mirrored somewhat on the borderless back, which also carries to the left of the player photo his career highlights within a ghosted box framed by a purple line. The cards are numbered on the back as "X of 10."

		MINT	NRMT	EXC
COMPLETE SET (10)		15.00	6.75	1.90
COMMON CARD (1-10)		.50	.23	.06
☐ 1	Patrick Ewing................... 1.00		.45	.13
	New York Knicks			
☐ 2	Jim Jackson................... 2.00		.90	.25
	Dallas Mavericks			
☐ 3	Larry Johnson................. 1.00		.45	.13
	Charlotte Hornets			
☐ 4	Michael Jordan 12.00		5.50	1.50
	Chicago Bulls			
☐ 5	Dan Majerle................... .50		.23	.06
	Phoenix Suns			
☐ 6	Hakeem Olajuwon 2.50		1.15	.30
	Houston Rockets			
☐ 7	Scottie Pippen............... 1.00		.45	.13
	Chicago Bulls			
☐ 8	Latrell Sprewell.............. 2.00		.90	.25
	Golden State Warriors			
☐ 9	John Starks................... .50		.23	.06
	New York Knicks			
☐ 10	Walt Williams................. .50		.23	.06
	Sacramento Kings			

1993-94 Ultra Jam City

Randomly inserted in 19-card second series jumbo packs at a rate of one in 37, this 9-card standard-size (2 1/2" by 3 1/2") set features borderless fronts with color player action cutouts on black and purple metallic cityscape backgrounds. The player's name appears in gold foil in a lower corner. The borderless back carries a color player action cutout on a non-metallic cityscape background otherwise similar to the front. The player's name and career highlights appear in a ghosted box to the left of the photo. The cards are numbered on the back as "X of 10."

	MINT	NRMT	EXC
COMPLETE SET (9)	130.00	57.50	16.50
COMMON CARD (1-9)	2.00	.90	.25

☐ 1	Charles Barkley .... Phoenix Suns	20.00	9.00	2.50
☐ 2	Derrick Coleman .... New Jersey Nets	4.00	1.80	.50
☐ 3	Clyde Drexler .... Portland Trail Blazers	10.00	4.50	1.25
☐ 4	Patrick Ewing .... New York Knicks	10.00	4.50	1.25
☐ 5	Shawn Kemp .... Seattle Supersonics	20.00	9.00	2.50
☐ 6	Harold Miner .... Miami Heat	2.00	.90	.25
☐ 7	Shaquille O'Neal .... Orlando Magic	75.00	34.00	9.50
☐ 8	David Robinson .... San Antonio Spurs	20.00	9.00	2.50
☐ 9	Dominique Wilkins .... Atlanta Hawks	5.00	2.30	.60

1993-94 Ultra Karl Malone

This ten-card set of Career Highlights spotlights Utah Jazz forward Karl Malone. The cards were randomly inserted in 14-card first series packs at a rate of approximately one in 16. The cards measure standard size (2 1/2" by 3 1/2"). The full-bleed color fronts have purple tinted ghosted backgrounds with Malone portrayed in normal color action and posed photos. Across the bottom edge is a marbleized border with the subset title "Career Highlights", above the lower border is a silver and black box containing Malone's name. The backs carry information about Malone within a purple tinted ghosted box that is superimposed over a color photo. The cards are numbered on the back. More than 2,000 autographed cards were randomly inserted in packs. These card have embossed Fleer logos for authenticity. An additional two cards (Nos.11 and 12) were available through a mail-in offer. Prior to June 10, 1994, collectors had to send 10 first series Ultra wrappers and $1.50 to receive the cards. The set is considered complete without these cards.

	MINT	NRMT	EXC
COMPLETE SET (10)	8.00	3.60	1.00
COMMON MALONE (1-10)	1.00	.45	.13
COMMON SEND-OFF (11-12) ..	2.00	.90	.25
☐ 1 Karl Malone .... Power Rig	1.00	.45	.13
☐ 2 Karl Malone .... Summerfield	1.00	.45	.13
☐ 3 Karl Malone .... Mailman-Born	1.00	.45	.13
☐ 4 Karl Malone .... Luck of the Draw	1.00	.45	.13
☐ 5 Karl Malone .... Double-Double	1.00	.45	.13
☐ 6 Karl Malone .... Dynamic Duo	1.00	.45	.13
☐ 7 Karl Malone .... Mt. Malone	1.00	.45	.13
☐ 8 Karl Malone .... Salt Lake Slammer	1.00	.45	.13
☐ 9 Karl Malone .... Overhead Delivery	1.00	.45	.13
☐ 10 Karl Malone .... Truckin'	1.00	.45	.13
☐ 11 Karl Malone .... Role Player	2.00	.90	.25
☐ 12 Karl Malone .... Rigged	2.00	.90	.25

1993-94 Ultra Power In The Key

Randomly inserted in 14-card second series packs at a rate of one in 37, this nine-card standard-size (2 1/2" by 3 1/2") features some of the NBA's top power players. Card fronts feature borderless color player action cutouts on multicolored metallic court illustration backgrounds. The player's name appears in gold-foil lettering at the lower right. The borderless horizontal back carries on its right side a color player close-up on a nonmetallic background otherwise similar to the front. The player's name and career highlights appear in a ghosted box to the left of the photo. The cards are numbered on the back as "X of 9."

	MINT	NRMT	EXC
COMPLETE SET (9)	90.00	40.00	11.50
COMMON CARD (1-9)	1.00	.45	.13

		MINT	NRMT	EXC
☐ 1	Larry Johnson	3.00	1.35	.40
	Charlotte Hornets			
☐ 2	Michael Jordan	40.00	18.00	5.00
	Chicago Bulls			
☐ 3	Karl Malone	3.00	1.35	.40
	Utah Jazz			
☐ 4	Oliver Miller	1.00	.45	.13
	Phoenix Suns			
☐ 5	Alonzo Mourning	6.00	2.70	.75
	Charlotte Hornets			
☐ 6	Hakeem Olajuwon	8.00	3.60	1.00
	Houston Rockets			
☐ 7	Shaquille O'Neal	25.00	11.50	3.10
	Orlando Magic			
☐ 8	Otis Thorpe	1.00	.45	.13
	Houston Rockets			
☐ 9	Chris Webber	10.00	4.50	1.25
	Golden State Warriors			

1993-94 Ultra Rebound Kings

Randomly inserted in 14-card second series packs at a rate of one in four, this 10-card standard-size (2 1/2" by 3 1/2") set features some of the NBA's top rebounders. Borderless fronts feature color player action shots on action backgrounds that blend from the actual action background at the bottom to a ghosted and color-screened player close-up at the top. The player's name appears vertically in gold foil on one side. The borderless horizontal back carries a color player cutout on one side and the player's name in gold foil and career highlights on the other, all on a ghosted and color-screened background. The cards are numbered on the back as "X of 10."

		MINT	NRMT	EXC
COMPLETE SET (10)		10.00	4.50	1.25
COMMON CARD (1-10)		.25	.11	.03
☐ 1	Charles Barkley	1.50	.65	.19
	Phoenix Suns			
☐ 2	Derrick Coleman	.35	.16	.04
	New Jersey Nets			
☐ 3	Shawn Kemp	1.50	.65	.19
	Seattle Supersonics			
☐ 4	Karl Malone	.75	.35	.09
	Utah Jazz			
☐ 5	Alonzo Mourning	1.50	.65	.19

			MINT	NRMT	EXC
		Charlotte Hornets			
☐ 6	Dikembe Mutombo		.60	.25	.08
	Denver Nuggets				
☐ 7	Charles Oakley		.25	.11	.03
	New York Knicks				
☐ 8	Hakeem Olajuwon		2.00	.90	.25
	Houston Rockets				
☐ 9	Shaquille O'Neal		6.00	2.70	.75
	Orlando Magic				
☐ 10	Dennis Rodman		.50	.23	.06
	San Antonio Spurs				

1993-94 Ultra Scoring Kings

Randomly inserted in first series hobby packs at a rate of one in 36, this 10-card standard-size (2 1/2" by 3 1/2") set features 10 of the NBA's top scorers. Card fronts feature color player action cutouts on borderless metallic backgrounds highlighted by lightning filaments. The player's name appears in silver-foil lettering in a lower corner. The horizontal back carries a color player close-up on the right, with the player's name appearing in silver-foil lettering at the upper left, followed below by career highlights, all on a dark borderless background again highlighted by lightning filaments. The cards are numbered on the back as "X of 10."

		MINT	NRMT	EXC
COMPLETE SET (10)		225.00	100.00	28.00
COMMON CARD (1-10)		5.00	2.30	.60
☐ 1	Charles Barkley	20.00	9.00	2.50
	Phoenix Suns			
☐ 2	Joe Dumars	5.00	2.30	.60
	Detroit Pistons			
☐ 3	Patrick Ewing	10.00	4.50	1.25
	New York Knicks			
☐ 4	Larry Johnson	10.00	4.50	1.25
	Charlotte Hornets			
☐ 5	Michael Jordan	125.00	57.50	15.50
	Chicago Bulls			
☐ 6	Karl Malone	10.00	4.50	1.25
	Utah Jazz			
☐ 7	Alonzo Mourning	20.00	9.00	2.50
	Charlotte Hornets			
☐ 8	Shaquille O'Neal	75.00	34.00	9.50
	Orlando Magic			

☐ 9	David Robinson	20.00	9.00	2.50
	San Antonio Spurs			
☐ 10	Dominique Wilkins.......	5.00	2.30	.60
	Atlanta Hawks			

	MINT	NRMT	EXC
COMPLETE SET (350)	40.00	18.00	5.00
COMPLETE SERIES 1 (200)...	20.00	9.00	2.50
COMPLETE SERIES 2 (150)...	20.00	9.00	2.50
COMMON CARD (1-350)	.10	.05	.01

1994-95 Ultra

The 350 standard-size (2 1/2" by 3 1/2") cards comprising the 1994-95 Ultra set were issued in two separate series of 200 and 150 cards each. Cards were distributed in 14-card ($1.99) and 17-card ($2.69) retail packs. Borderless fronts feature color player action shots. The player's name, team name, and position appear in vertical silver-foil lettering in an upper corner. The borderless back carries multiple player images, with the player's name and team logo appearing in gold foil, followed by biography and statistics near the bottom. The cards are numbered on the back, grouped alphabetically within teams, and checklisted below alphabetically according to teams as follows: Atlanta Hawks (1-7/201-206), Boston Celtics (8-16/207-211), Charlotte Hornets (17-24/212-215), Chicago Bulls (25-31/216-221), Cleveland Cavaliers (32-39/222-226), Dallas Mavericks (40-46/227-231), Denver Nuggets (47-54/232-235), Detroit Pistons (55-59/236-243), Golden State Warriors (60-64/244-251), Houston Rockets (65-71/252-255), Indiana Pacers (72-79/256-258), Los Angeles Clippers (80-83/259-269), Los Angeles Lakers (84-92/270-275), Miami Heat (93-101/276-281), Milwaukee Bucks (102-106/282-287), Minnesota Timberwolves (107-113/288-292), New Jersey Nets (114-121/293-297), New York Knicks (122-130/298-301), Orlando Magic (131-137/302-307), Philadelphia 76ers (138-144/308-313), Phoenix Suns (145-153/314-320), Portland Trail Blazers (154-163/321-323), Sacramento Kings (164-168/324-329), San Antonio Spurs (169-175/330-334), Seattle Supersonics (176-181/335-338), Utah Jazz (182-189/339-342), and Washington Bullets (190-197/343-348). Rookies include Grant Hill, Juwan Howard, Jason Kidd, Eddie Jones, and Glenn Robinson. There is an insert in every pack. Every 72nd pack is a Hot Pack that contains inserts only.

☐ 1	Stacey Augmon................	.12	.05	.02
☐ 2	Mookie Blaylock..............	.12	.05	.02
☐ 3	Craig Ehlo	.10	.05	.01
☐ 4	Adam Keefe.....................	.10	.05	.01
☐ 5	Andrew Lang....................	.10	.05	.01
☐ 6	Ken Norman.....................	.10	.05	.01
☐ 7	Kevin Willis	.12	.05	.02
☐ 8	Dee Brown	.12	.05	.02
☐ 9	Sherman Douglas............	.10	.05	.01
☐ 10	Acie Earl........................	.10	.05	.01
☐ 11	Pervis Ellison	.10	.05	.01
☐ 12	Rick Fox.........................	.10	.05	.01
☐ 13	Xavier McDaniel	.12	.05	.02
☐ 14	Eric Montross	.60	.25	.08
☐ 15	Dino Radja	.15	.07	.02
☐ 16	Dominique Wilkins...........	.20	.09	.03
☐ 17	Michael Adams	.10	.05	.01
☐ 18	Muggsy Bogues	.15	.07	.02
☐ 19	Dell Curry.......................	.10	.05	.01
☐ 20	Kenny Gattison	.10	.05	.01
☐ 21	Hersey Hawkins	.12	.05	.02
☐ 22	Larry Johnson.................	.30	.14	.04
☐ 23	Alonzo Mourning	.50	.23	.06
☐ 24	Robert Parish	.15	.07	.02
☐ 25	B.J. Armstrong	.10	.05	.01
☐ 26	Steve Kerr	.10	.05	.01
☐ 27	Toni Kukoc.....................	.15	.07	.02
☐ 28	Luc Longley	.10	.05	.01
☐ 29	Pete Myers.....................	.10	.05	.01
☐ 30	Will Perdue	.10	.05	.01
☐ 31	Scottie Pippen................	.40	.18	.05
☐ 32	Terrell Brandon	.10	.05	.01
☐ 33	Brad Daugherty	.12	.05	.02
☐ 34	Tyrone Hill	.12	.05	.02
☐ 35	Chris Mills......................	.15	.07	.02
☐ 36	Bobby Phills....................	.10	.05	.01
☐ 37	Mark Price	.15	.07	.02
☐ 38	Gerald Wilkins.................	.10	.05	.01
☐ 39	John Williams	.12	.05	.02
☐ 40	Terry Davis	.10	.05	.01
☐ 41	Jim Jackson....................	.50	.23	.06
☐ 42	Popeye Jones	.10	.05	.01
☐ 43	Jason Kidd	4.00	1.80	.50
☐ 44	Jamal Mashburn..............	.75	.35	.09
☐ 45	Sean Rooks	.10	.05	.01
☐ 46	Doug Smith	.10	.05	.01
☐ 47	Mahmoud Abdul-Rauf...	.12	.05	.02
☐ 48	LaPhonso Ellis	.10	.05	.01
☐ 49	Dikembe Mutombo	.25	.11	.03
☐ 50	Robert Pack	.10	.05	.01
☐ 51	Rodney Rogers	.15	.07	.02
☐ 52	Bryant Stith	.10	.05	.01
☐ 53	Brian Williams	.10	.05	.01
☐ 54	Reggie Williams	.10	.05	.01
☐ 55	Greg Anderson................	.10	.05	.01
☐ 56	Joe Dumars.....................	.20	.09	.03
☐ 57	Allan Houston	.15	.07	.02
☐ 58	Lindsey Hunter	.10	.05	.01
☐ 59	Terry Mills......................	.10	.05	.01
☐ 60	Tim Hardaway	.15	.07	.02
☐ 61	Chris Mullin....................	.15	.07	.02
☐ 62	Billy Owens	.12	.05	.02
☐ 63	Latrell Sprewell...............	.50	.23	.06
☐ 64	Chris Webber..................	.60	.25	.08

□ 65	Sam Cassell	.15	.07	.02
□ 66	Carl Herrera	.10	.05	.01
□ 67	Robert Horry	.15	.07	.02
□ 68	Vernon Maxwell	.10	.05	.01
□ 69	Hakeem Olajuwon	1.00	.45	.13
□ 70	Kenny Smith	.10	.05	.01
□ 71	Otis Thorpe	.12	.05	.02
□ 72	Antonio Davis	.10	.05	.01
□ 73	Dale Davis	.12	.05	.01
□ 74	Mark Jackson	.10	.05	.01
□ 75	Derrick McKey	.12	.05	.02
□ 76	Reggie Miller	.40	.18	.05
□ 77	Byron Scott	.12	.05	.02
□ 78	Rik Smits	.15	.07	.02
□ 79	Haywoode Workman	.10	.05	.01
□ 80	Gary Grant	.10	.05	.01
□ 81	Ron Harper	.12	.05	.02
□ 82	Elmore Spencer	.10	.05	.01
□ 83	Loy Vaught	.12	.05	.01
□ 84	Elden Campbell	.10	.05	.01
□ 85	Doug Christie	.10	.05	.01
□ 86	Vlade Divac	.15	.07	.02
□ 87	Eddie Jones	2.50	1.15	.30
□ 88	George Lynch	.10	.05	.01
□ 89	Anthony Peeler	.10	.05	.01
□ 90	Sedale Threatt	.10	.05	.01
□ 91	Nick Van Exel	.75	.35	.09
□ 92	James Worthy	.15	.07	.02
□ 93	Bimbo Coles	.10	.05	.01
□ 94	Matt Geiger	.10	.05	.01
□ 95	Grant Long	.10	.05	.01
□ 96	Harold Miner	.10	.05	.01
□ 97	Glen Rice	.15	.07	.02
□ 98	John Salley	.10	.05	.01
□ 99	Rony Seikaly	.10	.05	.01
□ 100	Brian Shaw	.10	.05	.01
□ 101	Steve Smith	.12	.05	.02
□ 102	Vin Baker	.40	.18	.05
□ 103	Jon Barry	.10	.05	.01
□ 104	Todd Day	.12	.05	.02
□ 105	Lee Mayberry	.10	.05	.01
□ 106	Eric Murdock	.10	.05	.01
□ 107	Thurl Bailey	.10	.05	.01
□ 108	Stacey King	.10	.05	.01
□ 109	Christian Laettner	.12	.05	.02
□ 110	Isaiah Rider	.25	.11	.03
□ 111	Chris Smith	.10	.05	.01
□ 112	Doug West	.10	.05	.01
□ 113	Micheal Williams	.10	.05	.01
□ 114	Kenny Anderson	.15	.07	.02
□ 115	Benoit Benjamin	.10	.05	.01
□ 116	P.J. Brown	.10	.05	.01
□ 117	Derrick Coleman	.15	.07	.02
□ 118	Yinka Dare	.12	.05	.01
□ 119	Kevin Edwards	.10	.05	.01
□ 120	Armon Gilliam	.10	.05	.01
□ 121	Chris Morris	.10	.05	.01
□ 122	Greg Anthony	.10	.05	.01
□ 123	Anthony Bonner	.10	.05	.01
□ 124	Hubert Davis	.10	.05	.01
□ 125	Patrick Ewing	.40	.18	.05
□ 126	Derek Harper	.12	.05	.02
□ 127	Anthony Mason	.12	.05	.02
□ 128	Charles Oakley	.12	.05	.02
□ 129	Doc Rivers	.10	.05	.01
□ 130	John Starks	.12	.05	.02
□ 131	Nick Anderson	.12	.05	.02
□ 132	Anthony Avent	.10	.05	.01
□ 133	Anthony Bowie	.10	.05	.01
□ 134	Anfernee Hardaway	1.50	.65	.19
□ 135	Shaquille O'Neal	2.00	.90	.25
□ 136	Dennis Scott	.10	.05	.01
□ 137	Jeff Turner	.10	.05	.01
□ 138	Dana Barros	.15	.07	.02
□ 139	Shawn Bradley	.15	.07	.02
□ 140	Greg Graham	.10	.05	.01
□ 141	Jeff Malone	.12	.05	.02
□ 142	Tim Perry	.10	.05	.01
□ 143	Clarence Weatherspoon	.15	.07	.02
□ 144	Scott Williams	.10	.05	.01
□ 145	Danny Ainge	.12	.05	.02
□ 146	Charles Barkley	.75	.35	.09
□ 147	Cedric Ceballos	.15	.07	.02
□ 148	A.C. Green	.15	.07	.02
□ 149	Frank Johnson	.10	.05	.01
□ 150	Kevin Johnson	.20	.09	.03
□ 151	Dan Majerle	.12	.05	.02
□ 152	Oliver Miller	.10	.05	.01
□ 153	Wesley Person	.75	.35	.09
□ 154	Mark Bryant	.10	.05	.01
□ 155	Clyde Drexler	.40	.18	.05
□ 156	Harvey Grant	.10	.05	.01
□ 157	Jerome Kersey	.10	.05	.01
□ 158	Tracy Murray	.10	.05	.01
□ 159	Terry Porter	.12	.05	.02
□ 160	Clifford Robinson	.12	.05	.02
□ 161	James Robinson	.10	.05	.01
□ 162	Rod Strickland	.12	.05	.02
□ 163	Buck Williams	.12	.05	.02
□ 164	Duane Causwell	.10	.05	.01
□ 165	Olden Polynice	.10	.05	.01
□ 166	Mitch Richmond	.20	.09	.03
□ 167	Lionel Simmons	.10	.05	.01
□ 168	Walt Williams	.12	.05	.02
□ 169	Willie Anderson	.10	.05	.01
□ 170	Terry Cummings	.12	.05	.02
□ 171	Sean Elliott	.12	.05	.02
□ 172	Avery Johnson	.10	.05	.01
□ 173	J.R. Reid	.10	.05	.01
□ 174	David Robinson	.75	.35	.09
□ 175	Dennis Rodman	.25	.11	.03
□ 176	Kendall Gill	.10	.05	.01
□ 177	Shawn Kemp	.75	.35	.09
□ 178	Nate McMillan	.10	.05	.01
□ 179	Gary Payton	.15	.07	.02
□ 180	Sam Perkins	.12	.05	.02
□ 181	Detlef Schrempf	.15	.07	.02
□ 182	David Benoit	.10	.05	.01
□ 183	Tyrone Corbin	.10	.05	.01
□ 184	Jeff Hornacek	.12	.05	.02
□ 185	Jay Humphries	.10	.05	.01
□ 186	Karl Malone	.40	.18	.05
□ 187	Bryon Russell	.10	.05	.01
□ 188	Felton Spencer	.10	.05	.01
□ 189	John Stockton	.40	.18	.05
□ 190	Mitchell Butler	.10	.05	.01
□ 191	Rex Chapman	.10	.05	.01
□ 192	Calbert Cheaney	.15	.07	.02
□ 193	Kevin Duckworth	.10	.05	.01
□ 194	Tom Gugliotta	.12	.05	.02
□ 195	Don MacLean	.10	.05	.01
□ 196	Gheorghe Muresan	.12	.05	.02
□ 197	Scott Skiles	.10	.05	.01
□ 198	Checklist	.10	.05	.01
□ 199	Checklist	.10	.05	.01
□ 200	Checklist	.10	.05	.01
□ 201	Tyrone Corbin	.10	.05	.01
□ 202	Doug Edwards	.10	.05	.01
□ 203	Jim Les	.10	.05	.01
□ 204	Grant Long	.10	.05	.01
□ 205	Ken Norman	.10	.05	.01
□ 206	Steve Smith	.12	.05	.02

☐ 207	Blue Edwards	.10	.05	.01
☐ 208	Greg Minor	.12	.05	.02
☐ 209	Eric Montross	.30	.14	.04
☐ 210	Derek Strong	.10	.05	.01
☐ 211	David Wesley	.10	.05	.01
☐ 212	Tony Bennett	.10	.05	.01
☐ 213	Scott Burrell	.10	.05	.01
☐ 214	Darrin Hancock	.10	.05	.01
☐ 215	Greg Sutton	.10	.05	.01
☐ 216	Corie Blount	.10	.05	.01
☐ 217	Jud Buechler	.10	.05	.01
☐ 218	Ron Harper	.12	.05	.02
☐ 219	Larry Krystkowiak	.10	.05	.01
☐ 220	Dickey Simpkins	.15	.07	.02
☐ 221	Bill Wennington	.10	.05	.01
☐ 222	Michael Cage	.10	.05	.01
☐ 223	Tony Campbell	.10	.05	.01
☐ 224	Steve Colter	.10	.05	.01
☐ 225	Greg Dreiling	.10	.05	.01
☐ 226	Danny Ferry	.10	.05	.01
☐ 227	Tony Dumas	.12	.05	.02
☐ 228	Lucious Harris	.10	.05	.01
☐ 229	Donald Hodge	.10	.05	.01
☐ 230	Jason Kidd	2.00	.90	.25
☐ 231	Lorenzo Williams	.10	.05	.01
☐ 232	Dale Ellis	.12	.05	.02
☐ 233	Tom Hammonds	.10	.05	.01
☐ 234	Jalen Rose	.75	.35	.09
☐ 235	Reggie Slater	.10	.05	.01
☐ 236	Rafael Addison	.10	.05	.01
☐ 237	Bill Curley	.20	.09	.03
☐ 238	Johnny Dawkins	.10	.05	.01
☐ 239	Grant Hill	6.00	2.70	.75
☐ 240	Eric Leckner	.10	.05	.01
☐ 241	Mark Macon	.10	.05	.01
☐ 242	Oliver Miller	.10	.05	.01
☐ 243	Mark West	.10	.05	.01
☐ 244	Victor Alexander	.10	.05	.01
☐ 245	Chris Gatling	.10	.05	.01
☐ 246	Tom Gugliotta	.12	.05	.02
☐ 247	Keith Jennings	.10	.05	.01
☐ 248	Ricky Pierce	.12	.05	.02
☐ 249	Carlos Rogers	.30	.14	.04
☐ 250	Clifford Rozier	.30	.14	.04
☐ 251	Rony Seikaly	.10	.05	.01
☐ 252	David Wood	.10	.05	.01
☐ 253	Tim Breaux	.10	.05	.01
☐ 254	Scott Brooks	.10	.05	.01
☐ 255	Zan Tabak	.10	.05	.01
☐ 256	Duane Ferrell	.10	.05	.01
☐ 257	Mark Jackson	.10	.05	.01
☐ 258	Sam Mitchell	.10	.05	.01
☐ 259	John Williams	.10	.05	.01
☐ 260	Terry Dehere	.10	.05	.01
☐ 261	Harold Ellis	.10	.05	.01
☐ 262	Matt Fish	.10	.05	.01
☐ 263	Tony Massenburg	.10	.05	.01
☐ 264	Lamond Murray	.60	.25	.08
☐ 265	Charles Outlaw	.10	.05	.01
☐ 266	Eric Piatkowski	.20	.09	.03
☐ 267	Pooh Richardson	.10	.05	.01
☐ 268	Malik Sealy	.10	.05	.01
☐ 269	Randy Woods	.10	.05	.01
☐ 270	Sam Bowie	.10	.05	.01
☐ 271	Cedric Ceballos	.15	.07	.02
☐ 272	Antonio Harvey	.10	.05	.01
☐ 273	Eddie Jones	1.25	.55	.16
☐ 274	Anthony Miller	.10	.05	.01
☐ 275	Tony Smith	.10	.05	.01
☐ 276	Ledell Eackles	.10	.05	.01
☐ 277	Kevin Gamble	.10	.05	.01
☐ 278	Brad Lohaus	.10	.05	.01
☐ 279	Billy Owens	.12	.05	.02
☐ 280	Khalid Reeves	.60	.25	.08
☐ 281	Kevin Willis	.12	.05	.02
☐ 282	Marty Conlon	.10	.05	.01
☐ 283	Alton Lister	.10	.05	.01
☐ 284	Eric Mobley	.20	.09	.03
☐ 285	Johnny Newman	.10	.05	.01
☐ 286	Ed Pinckney	.10	.05	.01
☐ 287	Glenn Robinson	4.00	1.80	.50
☐ 288	Howard Eisley	.10	.05	.01
☐ 289	Winston Garland	.10	.05	.01
☐ 290	Andres Guibert	.10	.05	.01
☐ 291	Donyell Marshall	.75	.35	.09
☐ 292	Sean Rooks	.10	.05	.01
☐ 293	Yinka Dare	.10	.05	.01
☐ 294	Sleepy Floyd	.10	.05	.01
☐ 295	Sean Higgins	.10	.05	.01
☐ 296	Rex Walters	.10	.05	.01
☐ 297	Jayson Williams	.10	.05	.01
☐ 298	Charles Smith	.10	.05	.01
☐ 299	Charlie Ward	.30	.14	.04
☐ 300	Herb Williams	.10	.05	.01
☐ 301	Monty Williams	.20	.09	.03
☐ 302	Horace Grant	.20	.09	.03
☐ 303	Geert Hammink	.10	.05	.01
☐ 304	Tree Rollins	.10	.05	.01
☐ 305	Donald Royal	.10	.05	.01
☐ 306	Brian Shaw	.10	.05	.01
☐ 307	Brooks Thompson	.12	.05	.02
☐ 308	Derrick Alston	.12	.05	.02
☐ 309	Willie Burton	.10	.05	.01
☐ 310	Jaren Jackson	.10	.05	.01
☐ 311	B.J. Tyler	.12	.05	.02
☐ 312	Scott Williams	.10	.05	.01
☐ 313	Sharone Wright	.50	.23	.06
☐ 314	Joe Kleine	.10	.05	.01
☐ 315	Danny Manning	.15	.07	.02
☐ 316	Elliot Perry	.10	.05	.01
☐ 317	Wesley Person	.40	.18	.05
☐ 318	Trevor Ruffin	.12	.05	.02
☐ 319	Dan Schayes	.10	.05	.01
☐ 320	Wayman Tisdale	.12	.05	.02
☐ 321	Chris Dudley	.10	.05	.01
☐ 322	James Edwards	.10	.05	.01
☐ 323	Alaa Abdelnaby	.10	.05	.01
☐ 324	Randy Brown	.10	.05	.01
☐ 325	Brian Grant	1.25	.55	.16
☐ 326	Bobby Hurley	.12	.05	.02
☐ 327	Michael Smith	.30	.14	.04
☐ 328	Henry Turner	.10	.05	.01
☐ 329	Trevor Wilson	.10	.05	.01
☐ 330	Vinny Del Negro	.10	.05	.01
☐ 331	Moses Malone	.20	.09	.03
☐ 332	Julius Nwosu	.10	.05	.01
☐ 333	Chuck Person	.12	.05	.02
☐ 334	Chris Whitney	.10	.05	.01
☐ 335	Vincent Askew	.10	.05	.01
☐ 336	Bill Cartwright	.10	.05	.01
☐ 337	Ervin Johnson	.10	.05	.01
☐ 338	Sarunas Marciulionis	.10	.05	.01
☐ 339	Antoine Carr	.10	.05	.01
☐ 340	Tom Chambers	.12	.05	.02
☐ 341	John Crotty	.10	.05	.01
☐ 342	Jamie Watson	.15	.07	.02
☐ 343	Juwan Howard	1.50	.65	.19
☐ 344	Jim McIlvaine	.10	.05	.01
☐ 345	Doug Overton	.10	.05	.01
☐ 346	Scott Skiles	.10	.05	.01
☐ 347	Anthony Tucker	.10	.05	.01
☐ 348	Chris Webber	.60	.25	.08

		MINT	NRMT	EXC
☐	349 Checklist	.10	.05	.01
☐	350 Checklist	.10	.05	.01

1994-95 Ultra All-NBA

Randomly inserted into approximately one in every three first series packs, cards from this 15-card set feature members of the All-NBA first (1-5), second (6-10), and third (11-15) teams. The fronts are laid out horizontally and have a color action photo and three photos that look like they were taken in a room with a black light. On the right side is the player's first name in white behind his last name in the color of his team. At the bottom in gold-foil are the words "ALL-NBA" and the corresponding team he made. On the backs are a color photo in front of the same photo with the black light look. Their is also player information and the cards are numbered "X of 15."

		MINT	NRMT	EXC
	COMPLETE SET (15)	15.00	6.75	1.90
	COMMON CARD (1-15)	.25	.11	.03
☐	1 Karl Malone	1.00	.45	.13
	Utah Jazz			
☐	2 Hakeem Olajuwon	.50	.23	.06
	Houston Rockets			
☐	3 Scottie Pippen	1.00	.45	.13
	Chicago Bulls			
☐	4 Latrell Sprewell	1.25	.55	.16
	Golden State Warriors			
☐	5 John Stockton	1.00	.45	.13
	Utah Jazz			
☐	6 Charles Barkley	2.00	.90	.25
	Phoenix Suns			
☐	7 Kevin Johnson	.50	.23	.06
	Phoenix Suns			
☐	8 Shawn Kemp	2.00	.90	.25
	Seattle Supersonics			
☐	9 Mitch Richmond	.50	.23	.06
	Sacramento Kings			
☐	10 David Robinson	2.00	.90	.25
	San Antonio Spurs			
☐	11 Derrick Coleman	.25	.11	.03
	New Jersey Nets			
☐	12 Shaquille O'Neal	5.00	2.30	.60
	Orlando Magic			
☐	13 Gary Payton	.25	.11	.03
	Seattle Supersonics			
☐	14 Mark Price	.25	.11	.03
	Cleveland Cavaliers			
☐	15 Dominique Wilkins	.50	.23	.06
	Boston Celtics			

1994-95 Ultra All-Rookie Team

Randomly inserted exclusively into first series jumbo packs at a rate of one in 36, cards from this 10-card set feature some of the top rookies from the 1993-94 season. Fronts feature a full-color action shot aside a bold, gold-foil All-Rookie logo with the player's name.

		MINT	NRMT	EXC
	COMPLETE SET (10)	175.00	80.00	22.00
	COMMON CARD (1-10)	4.00	1.80	.50
☐	1 Vin Baker	20.00	9.00	2.50
	Milwaukee Bucks			
☐	2 Anfernee Hardaway	80.00	36.00	10.00
	Orlando Magic			
☐	3 Jamal Mashburn	40.00	18.00	5.00
	Dallas Mavericks			
☐	4 Isaiah Rider	12.00	5.50	1.50
	Minnesota Timberwolves			
☐	5 Chris Webber	30.00	13.50	3.80
	Golden State Warriors			
☐	6 Shawn Bradley	8.00	3.60	1.00
	Philadelphia 76ers			
☐	7 Lindsey Hunter	4.00	1.80	.50
	Detroit Pistons			
☐	8 Toni Kukoc	10.00	4.50	1.25
	Chicago Bulls			
☐	9 Dino Radja	8.00	3.60	1.00
	Boston Celtics			
☐	10 Nick Van Exel	40.00	18.00	5.00
	Los Angeles Lakers			

1994-95 Ultra All-Rookies

Randomly inserted at a rate of one in every five second series packs, this 15-card stan-

dard-size set captures the best first-year players from the 1994-95 season. The fronts have a full-color photo with a hardwood floor background. The words "All-Rookie" and the player's name are on the left side in gold-foil. The backs a full-color photo with his name and a hardwood floor in the background. There is also player information and the cards are numbered "X of 15." The set is sequenced in alphabetical order.

	MINT	NRMT	EXC
COMPLETE SET (15)	30.00	13.50	3.80
COMMON CARD (1-15)	.40	.18	.05
☐ 1 Brian Grant	2.00	.90	.25
Sacramento Kings			
☐ 2 Grant Hill	10.00	4.50	1.25
Detroit Pistons			
☐ 3 Juwan Howard	2.50	1.15	.30
Washington Bullets			
☐ 4 Eddie Jones	4.00	1.80	.50
Los Angeles Lakers			
☐ 5 Jason Kidd	6.00	2.70	.75
Dallas Mavericks			
☐ 6 Donyell Marshall	1.25	.55	.16
Minnesota Timberwolves			
☐ 7 Eric Montross	1.00	.45	.13
Boston Celtics			
☐ 8 Lamond Murray	1.00	.45	.13
Los Angeles Clippers			
☐ 9 Wesley Person	1.25	.55	.16
Phoenix Suns			
☐ 10 Khalid Reeves	1.00	.45	.13
Miami Heat			
☐ 11 Glenn Robinson	6.00	2.70	.75
Milwaukee Bucks			
☐ 12 Carlos Rogers	.50	.23	.06
Golden State Warriors			
☐ 13 Jalen Rose	1.25	.55	.16
Denver Nuggets			
☐ 14 B.J. Tyler	.40	.18	.05
Philadelphia 76ers			
☐ 15 Sharone Wright	.75	.35	.09
Philadelphia 76ers			

1994-95 Ultra Award Winners

Randomly inserted into approximately one in every four first series packs, cards from

this four-card set feature players who won individual awards during the 1993-94 season. The fronts are laid out horizontally and have a color-action photo with the backgrounds having a black and white head shot with horizontal white lines across the card. At on of the bottom corners are the words "NBA Award Winner" with a basket-ball in gold-foil. The backs have a color photo from the chest up with a similar background to the front. There is also player information and the cards are numbered "X of 4." The set is sequenced in alphabetical order.

	MINT	NRMT	EXC
COMPLETE SET (4)	4.00	1.80	.50
COMMON CARD (1-4)	.25	.11	.03
☐ 1 Dell Curry	.25	.11	.03
Charlotte Hornets			
Sixth Man Award			
☐ 2 Don MacLean	.25	.11	.03
Washington Bullets			
Most Improved			
☐ 3 Hakeem Olajuwon	2.50	1.15	.30
Houston Rockets			
MVP and Defensive POY			
☐ 4 Chris Webber	1.50	.65	.19
Golden State Warriors			
Rookie of the Year			

1994-95 Ultra Defensive Gems

Randomly inserted at a rate of one in every 37 second-series packs, this 6-card standard-size set focuses on six NBA stars who play standout defense. The borderless fronts feature 100% etched-foil backgrounds. The player's name is located at the bottom while the words "Defensive Gems" surrounding a diamond are in the lower right. The backs are split between another player photo and some information about the player's defensive prowess. The cards are numbered in the lower left as "X" of 6. The set is sequenced in alphabetical order.

	MINT	NRMT	EXC
COMPLETE SET (6)	40.00	18.00	5.00
COMMON CARD (1-6)	3.00	1.35	.40
☐ 1 Mookie Blaylock	3.00	1.35	.40
Atlanta Hawks			
☐ 2 Hakeem Olajuwon	20.00	9.00	2.50
Houston Rockets			
☐ 3 Gary Payton	3.00	1.35	.40
Seattle Supersonics			
☐ 4 Scottie Pippen	8.00	3.60	1.00
Chicago Bulls			
☐ 5 David Robinson	15.00	6.75	1.90
San Antonio Spurs			
☐ 6 Latrell Sprewell	10.00	4.50	1.25
Golden State Warriors			

1994-95 Ultra Double Trouble

Randomly inserted into approximately one in every five first series packs, cards from this 10-card set feature a selection of multi-skilled NBA stars. The fronts feature two photos of the player in a split player design. The words "Double Trouble" and player's name are printed in silver foil on the bottom. The borderless backs are split between an explanation of the player's skills as well as a photo. The cards are numbered "X" of 10 in the lower left corner. The set is sequenced in alphabetical order.

	MINT	NRMT	EXC
COMPLETE SET (10)	15.00	6.75	1.90
COMMON CARD (1-10)	.50	.23	.06
☐ 1 Derrick Coleman	.50	.23	.06
New Jersey Nets			

☐ 2 Patrick Ewing	1.25	.55	.16
New York Knicks			
☐ 3 Anfernee Hardaway	5.00	2.30	.60
Orlando Magic			
☐ 4 Jamal Mashburn	2.50	1.15	.30
Dallas Mavericks			
☐ 5 Reggie Miller	1.25	.55	.16
Indiana Pacers			
☐ 6 Alonzo Mourning	1.50	.65	.19
Charlotte Hornets			
☐ 7 Scottie Pippen	1.25	.55	.16
Chicago Bulls			
☐ 8 David Robinson	2.50	1.15	.30
San Antonio Spurs			
☐ 9 Latrell Sprewell	1.50	.65	.19
Golden State Warriors			
☐ 10 John Stockton	1.25	.55	.16
Utah Jazz			

1994-95 Ultra Inside/Outside

Randomly inserted exclusively into one in every seven second series hobby packs, cards from this 10-card set focus on players who can score from anywhere on the court. The borderless fronts feature dual player photos against a gray background. The player's name is in the lower left corner while the words "Inside/Outside" are in the lower right corner. The backs describe the player's shooting ability and have a small photo as well. The cards are numbered in the lower right as "X" of 10. The set is sequenced in alphabetical order.

	MINT	NRMT	EXC
COMPLETE SET (10)	10.00	4.50	1.25
COMMON CARD (1-10)	.50	.23	.06
☐ 1 Sam Cassell	.75	.35	.09
Houston Rockets			
☐ 2 Cedric Ceballos	.75	.35	.09
Los Angeles Lakers			
☐ 3 Calbert Cheaney	.50	.23	.06
Washington Bullets			
☐ 4 Anfernee Hardaway	5.00	2.30	.60
Orlando Magic			
☐ 5 Jim Jackson	1.50	.65	.19
Dallas Mavericks			
☐ 6 Dan Majerle	.60	.25	.08

	MINT	NRMT	EXC
Phoenix Suns			
☐ 7 Robert Pack	.50	.23	.06
Denver Nuggets			
☐ 8 Scottie Pippen	1.25	.55	.16
Chicago Bulls			
☐ 9 Mitch Richmond	.60	.25	.08
Sacramento Kings			
☐ 10 Latrell Sprewell	1.50	.65	.19
Golden State Warriors			

1994-95 Ultra Jam City

Randomly inserted exclusively into one in every seven second series jumbo packs, cards from this 10-card standard size set spotlight ten well known dunkers. The borderless fronts feature color player action cutouts on a multi colored metallic cityscape background. The words "Jam City" and the player's name are printed in gold foil on the bottom of the card. The back features another cutout photo against a different skyscraper background with the player's name in the middle in gold foil. A brief blurb about the player is inset at the bottom. The cards are numbered "X" of 10 in the bottom right. The set is sequenced in alphabetical order.

	MINT	NRMT	EXC
COMPLETE SET (10)	80.00	36.00	10.00
COMMON CARD (1-10)	2.00	.90	.25
☐ 1 Vin Baker	5.00	2.30	.60
Milwaukee Bucks			
☐ 2 Grant Hill	25.00	11.50	3.10
Detroit Pistons			
☐ 3 Robert Horry	2.00	.90	.25
Houston Rockets			
☐ 4 Shawn Kemp	10.00	4.50	1.25
Seattle Supersonics			
☐ 5 Jamal Mashburn	10.00	4.50	1.25
Dallas Mavericks			
☐ 6 Alonzo Mourning	6.00	2.70	.75
Charlotte Hornets			
☐ 7 Dikembe Mutombo	3.00	1.35	.40
Denver Nuggets			
☐ 8 Shaquille O'Neal	25.00	11.50	3.10
Orlando Magic			

	MINT	NRMT	EXC
☐ 9 Glenn Robinson	15.00	6.75	1.90
Milwaukee Bucks			
☐ 10 Dominique Wilkins	2.50	1.15	.30
Boston Celtics			

1994-95 Ultra Power

Randomly inserted in all first series packs at an approximate rate of one in three, cards from this 10-card set feature a selection of the NBA's most powerful stars. This set features color player action cutouts set on a colorful and sparkly starburst background design. The player's name appears in vertical gold lettering in a lower corner. The colorful starburst design continues on the borderless horizontal back, which carries a color player head shot on one side, and career highlights on the other. The cards are numbered on the back as "X of 10." The set is sequenced in alphabetical order.

	MINT	NRMT	EXC
COMPLETE SET (10)	12.00	5.50	1.50
COMMON CARD (1-10)	.25	.11	.03
☐ 1 Charles Barkley	2.00	.90	.25
Phoenix Suns			
☐ 2 Derrick Coleman	.35	.16	.04
New Jersey Nets			
☐ 3 Larry Johnson	.75	.35	.09
Charlotte Hornets			
☐ 4 Shawn Kemp	2.00	.90	.25
Seattle Supersonics			
☐ 5 Karl Malone	1.00	.45	.13
Utah Jazz			
☐ 6 Dikembe Mutombo	.50	.23	.06
Denver Nuggets			
☐ 7 Charles Oakley	.25	.11	.03
New York Knicks			
☐ 8 Shaquille O'Neal	5.00	2.30	.60
Orlando Magic			
☐ 9 Dennis Rodman	.50	.23	.06
San Antonio Spurs			
☐ 10 Chris Webber	1.50	.65	.19
Golden State Warriors			

1994-95 Ultra Power In The Key

Randomly inserted exclusively into one in every seven second series hobby packs, cards from this 10-card set feature ten play ers who are effective playing near the basket. The front feature a player cutout against a multicolored basketball court design. The words "Power in the Key" are on either side, with the player's name directly underneath those words. The backs contain biographical information along with an inset photo of the player. The cards are numbered in the lower right as "X" of 10. The set is sequenced in alphabetical order.

	MINT	NRMT	EXC
COMPLETE SET (10)	25.00	11.50	3.10
COMMON CARD (1-10)	.75	.35	.09
☐ 1 Charles Barkley Phoenix Suns	4.00	1.80	.50
☐ 2 Patrick Ewing New York Knicks	2.00	.90	.25
☐ 3 Horace Grant Orlando Magic	1.00	.45	.13
☐ 4 Larry Johnson Charlotte Hornets	1.50	.65	.19
☐ 5 Karl Malone Utah Jazz	2.00	.90	.25
☐ 6 Hakeem Olajuwon Houston Rockets	5.00	2.30	.60
☐ 7 Shaquille O'Neal Orlando Magic	10.00	4.50	1.25
☐ 8 David Robinson San Antonio Spurs	4.00	1.80	.50
☐ 9 Chris Webber Washington Bullets	3.00	1.35	.40
☐ 10 Kevin Willis Miami Heat	.75	.35	.09

1994-95 Ultra Rebound Kings

Randomly inserted at a rate of one in every two second-series packs, cards from this 10-card set focus on league's top rebound-ers. The fronts have a color-action photo and a color picture of his head at the bot tom along with a gold-foil crown. The words "Rebound King" are at the top and side with rebound behind king at the top and vice-versa on the side, each card uses different colors for the words. The backs have a color photo with his name in gold-foil and information on why he is a top rebounder. The cards are numbered "X of 10." The set is sequenced in alphabetical order.

	MINT	NRMT	EXC
COMPLETE SET (10)	4.00	1.80	.50
COMMON CARD (1-10)	.25	.11	.03
☐ 1 Derrick Coleman New Jersey Nets	.25	.11	.03
☐ 2 A.C. Green Phoenix Suns	.25	.11	.03
☐ 3 Alonzo Mourning Charlotte Hornets	.50	.23	.06
☐ 4 Dikembe Mutombo Denver Nuggets	.35	.16	.04
☐ 5 Charles Oakley New York Knicks	.25	.11	.03
☐ 6 Hakeem Olajuwon Houston Rockets	1.00	.45	.13
☐ 7 Shaquille O'Neal Orlando Magic	2.00	.90	.25
☐ 8 David Robinson San Antonio Spurs	.75	.35	.09
☐ 9 Chris Webber Washington Bullets	.60	.25	.08
☐ 10 Kevin Willis Miami Heat	.25	.11	.03

1994-95 Ultra Scoring Kings

Randomly inserted exclusively into one in every 37 first series hobby packs, cards from this 10-card set feature a selection of perennial NBA scoring leaders. Fronts feature full-color player action shots cut out against 100% etched-foil backgrounds.

	MINT	NRMT	EXC
COMPLETE SET (10)	130.00	57.50	16.50
COMMON CARD (1-10)	5.00	2.30	.60
☐ 1 Charles Barkley	20.00	9.00	2.50
Phoenix Suns			
☐ 2 Patrick Ewing	10.00	4.50	1.25
New York Knicks			
☐ 3 Karl Malone	10.00	4.50	1.25
Utah Jazz			
☐ 4 Hakeem Olajuwon	25.00	11.50	3.10
Houston Rockets			
☐ 5 Shaquille O'Neal	50.00	23.00	6.25
Orlando Magic			
☐ 6 Scottie Pippen	10.00	4.50	1.25
Chicago Bulls			
☐ 7 Mitch Richmond	5.00	2.30	.60
Sacramento Kings			
☐ 8 David Robinson	20.00	9.00	2.50
San Antonio Spurs			
☐ 9 Latrell Sprewell	12.00	5.50	1.50
Golden State Warriors			
☐ 10 Dominique Wilkins	5.00	2.30	.60
Los Angeles Clippers			

1995-96 Ultra

Cards from this 200-card set comprise Fleer's 1995-96 Ultra series 1 set. Cards were issued in 12-card hobby and retail packs (SRP $2.49) in addition to 17-card pre-priced packs (SRP $2.99). Each 12-card pack contains two insert cards and one in every 72 packs contains nothing but

insert cards (referred to as a "Hot Pack"). Fleer upgraded the stock of the 1995-96 cards by making them 40% thicker than the previous year's Ultra release. The fronts have a full-color action photo with the player's name and team at the bottom in gold-foil. The backs have two color photos and one full black and white with statistics at the bottom. The basic issue cards are grouped alphabetically within teams and checklisted below alphabetically according to teams as follows: Atlanta Hawks (1-8), Boston Celtics (9-16), Charlotte Hornets (17-23), Chicago Bulls (24-28), Cleveland Cavaliers (29-35), Dallas Mavericks (36-43), Detroit Pistons (51-56), Golden State Warriors (57-64), Houston Rockets (65-71), Indiana Pacers (72-77), Los Angeles Clippers (78-84), Los Angeles Lakers (85-92), Miami Heat (93-99), Milwaukee Bucks (100-104), Minnesota Timberwolves (105-110), New Jersey Nets (111-115), New York Knicks (116-122), Orlando Magic (123-129), Philadelphia 76ers (130-137), Phoenix Suns (138-146), Portland Trail Blazers (147-154), Sacramento Kings (155-160), San Antonio Spurs (161-168), Seattle Supersonics (169-176), Toronto Raptors (177-181), Utah Jazz (182-187), Vancouver Grizzlies (188-190) and Washington Bullets (191-197).

	MINT	NRMT	EXC
COMPLETE SERIES 1 (200)	25.00	11.50	3.10
COMMON CARD (1-200)	.10	.05	.01
☐ 1 Stacey Augmon	.15	.07	.02
☐ 2 Mookie Blaylock	.15	.07	.02
☐ 3 Craig Ehlo	.10	.05	.01
☐ 4 Andrew Lang	.10	.05	.01
☐ 5 Grant Long	.10	.05	.01
☐ 6 Ken Norman	.10	.05	.01
☐ 7 Steve Smith	.15	.07	.02
☐ 8 Spud Webb	.10	.05	.01
☐ 9 Dee Brown	.15	.07	.02
☐ 10 Sherman Douglas	.10	.05	.01
☐ 11 Pervis Ellison	.10	.05	.01
☐ 12 Rick Fox	.10	.05	.01
☐ 13 Eric Montross	.20	.09	.03
☐ 14 Dino Radja	.20	.09	.03
☐ 15 David Wesley	.10	.05	.01
☐ 16 Dominique Wilkins	.25	.11	.03
☐ 17 Muggsy Bogues	.20	.09	.03
☐ 18 Scott Burrell	.10	.05	.01
☐ 19 Dell Curry	.10	.05	.01
☐ 20 Kendall Gill	.10	.05	.01
☐ 21 Larry Johnson	.30	.14	.04
☐ 22 Alonzo Mourning	.40	.18	.05
☐ 23 Robert Parish	.20	.09	.03
☐ 24 Ron Harper	.15	.07	.02
☐ 25 Michael Jordan	5.00	2.30	.60
☐ 26 Toni Kukoc	.15	.07	.02
☐ 27 Will Perdue	.10	.05	.01
☐ 28 Scottie Pippen	.40	.18	.05
☐ 29 Terrell Brandon	.10	.05	.01
☐ 30 Michael Cage	.10	.05	.01
☐ 31 Tyrone Hill	.15	.07	.02
☐ 32 Chris Mills	.15	.07	.02
☐ 33 Bobby Phills	.10	.05	.01
☐ 34 Mark Price	.20	.09	.03

☐ 35	John Williams	.15	.07	.02
☐ 36	Lucious Harris	.10	.05	.01
☐ 37	Jim Jackson	.40	.18	.05
☐ 38	Popeye Jones	.10	.05	.01
☐ 39	Jason Kidd	1.25	.55	.16
☐ 40	Jamal Mashburn	.50	.23	.06
☐ 41	George McCloud	.10	.05	.01
☐ 42	Roy Tarpley	.10	.05	.01
☐ 43	Lorenzo Williams	.10	.05	.01
☐ 44	Mahmoud Abdul-Rauf	.15	.07	.02
☐ 45	Dikembe Mutombo	.25	.11	.03
☐ 46	Robert Pack	.10	.05	.01
☐ 47	Jalen Rose	.25	.11	.03
☐ 48	Bryant Stith	.10	.05	.01
☐ 49	Brian Williams	.10	.05	.01
☐ 50	Reggie Williams	.10	.05	.01
☐ 51	Joe Dumars	.25	.11	.03
☐ 52	Grant Hill	2.00	.90	.25
☐ 53	Allan Houston	.15	.07	.02
☐ 54	Lindsey Hunter	.40	.18	.05
☐ 55	Terry Mills	.10	.05	.01
☐ 56	Mark West	.10	.05	.01
☐ 57	Chris Gatling	.10	.05	.01
☐ 58	Tim Hardaway	.20	.09	.03
☐ 59	Donyell Marshall	.25	.11	.03
☐ 60	Chris Mullin	.20	.09	.03
☐ 61	Carlos Rogers	.20	.09	.03
☐ 62	Clifford Rozier	.15	.07	.02
☐ 63	Rony Seikaly	.10	.05	.01
☐ 64	Latrell Sprewell	.40	.18	.05
☐ 65	Sam Cassell	.10	.05	.01
☐ 66	Clyde Drexler	.40	.18	.05
☐ 67	Mario Elie	.10	.05	.01
☐ 68	Carl Herrera	.10	.05	.01
☐ 69	Robert Horry	.20	.09	.03
☐ 70	Hakeem Olajuwon	1.00	.45	.13
☐ 71	Kenny Smith	.10	.05	.01
☐ 72	Antonio Davis	.10	.05	.01
☐ 73	Dale Davis	.15	.07	.02
☐ 74	Mark Jackson	.10	.05	.01
☐ 75	Derrick McKey	.15	.07	.02
☐ 76	Reggie Miller	.40	.18	.05
☐ 77	Rik Smits	.10	.05	.01
☐ 78	Terry Dehere	.10	.05	.01
☐ 79	Lamond Murray	.15	.07	.02
☐ 80	Charles Outlaw	.10	.05	.01
☐ 81	Pooh Richardson	.10	.05	.01
☐ 82	Rodney Rogers	.10	.05	.01
☐ 83	Malik Sealy	.10	.05	.01
☐ 84	Loy Vaught	.15	.07	.02
☐ 85	Sam Bowie	.10	.05	.01
☐ 86	Elden Campbell	.10	.05	.01
☐ 87	Cedric Ceballos	.20	.09	.03
☐ 88	Vlade Divac	.20	.09	.03
☐ 89	Eddie Jones	.75	.35	.09
☐ 90	Anthony Peeler	.10	.05	.01
☐ 91	Sedale Threatt	.10	.05	.01
☐ 92	Nick Van Exel	.50	.23	.06
☐ 93	Rex Chapman	.10	.05	.01
☐ 94	Bimbo Coles	.10	.05	.01
☐ 95	Matt Geiger	.10	.05	.01
☐ 96	Billy Owens	.15	.07	.02
☐ 97	Khalid Reeves	.20	.09	.03
☐ 98	Glen Rice	.20	.09	.03
☐ 99	Kevin Willis	.15	.07	.02
☐ 100	Vin Baker	.25	.11	.03
☐ 101	Marty Conlon	.10	.05	.01
☐ 102	Todd Day	.10	.05	.01
☐ 103	Eric Murdock	.10	.05	.01
☐ 104	Glenn Robinson	1.25	.55	.16
☐ 105	Winston Garland	.10	.05	.01
☐ 106	Tom Gugliotta	.15	.07	.02
☐ 107	Christian Laettner	.15	.07	.02
☐ 108	Isaiah Rider	.20	.09	.03
☐ 109	Sean Rooks	.10	.05	.01
☐ 110	Doug West	.10	.05	.01
☐ 111	Kenny Anderson	.20	.09	.03
☐ 112	P.J. Brown	.10	.05	.01
☐ 113	Derrick Coleman	.20	.09	.03
☐ 114	Armon Gilliam	.10	.05	.01
☐ 115	Chris Morris	.10	.05	.01
☐ 116	Anthony Bonner	.10	.05	.01
☐ 117	Patrick Ewing	.40	.18	.05
☐ 118	Derek Harper	.15	.07	.02
☐ 119	Anthony Mason	.15	.07	.02
☐ 120	Charles Oakley	.15	.07	.02
☐ 121	Charles Smith	.10	.05	.01
☐ 122	John Starks	.15	.07	.02
☐ 123	Nick Anderson	.15	.07	.02
☐ 124	Horace Grant	.25	.11	.03
☐ 125	Anfernee Hardaway	1.25	.55	.16
☐ 126	Shaquille O'Neal	2.00	.90	.25
☐ 127	Donald Royal	.10	.05	.01
☐ 128	Dennis Scott	.10	.05	.01
☐ 129	Brian Shaw	.10	.05	.01
☐ 130	Derrick Alston	.10	.05	.01
☐ 131	Dana Barros	.20	.09	.03
☐ 132	Shawn Bradley	.15	.07	.02
☐ 133	Willie Burton	.10	.05	.01
☐ 134	Jeff Malone	.15	.07	.02
☐ 135	Clarence Weatherspoon	.15	.07	.02
☐ 136	Scott Williams	.10	.05	.01
☐ 137	Sharone Wright	.15	.07	.02
☐ 138	Danny Ainge	.15	.07	.02
☐ 139	Charles Barkley	.75	.35	.09
☐ 140	A.C. Green	.20	.09	.03
☐ 141	Kevin Johnson	.25	.11	.03
☐ 142	Dan Majerle	.15	.07	.02
☐ 143	Danny Manning	.20	.09	.03
☐ 144	Elliot Perry	.10	.05	.01
☐ 145	Wesley Person	.25	.11	.03
☐ 146	Wayman Tisdale	.15	.07	.02
☐ 147	Chris Dudley	.10	.05	.01
☐ 148	Harvey Grant	.10	.05	.01
☐ 149	Aaron McKie	.15	.07	.02
☐ 150	Terry Porter	.15	.07	.02
☐ 151	Clifford Robinson	.15	.07	.02
☐ 152	Rod Strickland	.15	.07	.02
☐ 153	Otis Thorpe	.15	.07	.02
☐ 154	Buck Williams	.15	.07	.02
☐ 155	Brian Grant	.40	.18	.05
☐ 156	Bobby Hurley	.15	.07	.02
☐ 157	Olden Polynice	.10	.05	.01
☐ 158	Mitch Richmond	.25	.11	.03
☐ 159	Michael Smith	.15	.07	.02
☐ 160	Walt Williams	.15	.07	.02
☐ 161	Vinny Del Negro	.10	.05	.01
☐ 162	Sean Elliott	.10	.05	.01
☐ 163	Avery Johnson	.10	.05	.01
☐ 164	Chuck Person	.15	.07	.02
☐ 165	J.R. Reid	.10	.05	.01
☐ 166	Doc Rivers	.10	.05	.01
☐ 167	David Robinson	.75	.35	.09
☐ 168	Dennis Rodman	.25	.11	.03
☐ 169	Vincent Askew	.10	.05	.01
☐ 170	Hersey Hawkins	.15	.07	.02
☐ 171	Shawn Kemp	.75	.35	.09
☐ 172	Sarunas Marciulionis	.10	.05	.01
☐ 173	Nate McMillan	.10	.05	.01
☐ 174	Gary Payton	.20	.09	.03
☐ 175	Sam Perkins	.15	.07	.02
☐ 176	Detlef Schrempf	.20	.09	.03

		MINT	NRMT	EXC
☐ 177	B.J. Armstrong	.10	.05	.01
☐ 178	Jerome Kersey	.10	.05	.01
☐ 179	Tony Massenburg	.10	.05	.01
☐ 180	Oliver Miller	.10	.05	.01
☐ 181	John Salley	.10	.05	.01
☐ 182	David Benoit	.10	.05	.01
☐ 183	Antoine Carr	.10	.05	.01
☐ 184	Jeff Hornacek	.15	.07	.02
☐ 185	Karl Malone	.40	.18	.05
☐ 186	Felton Spencer	.10	.05	.01
☐ 187	John Stockton	.40	.18	.05
☐ 188	Greg Anthony	.10	.05	.01
☐ 189	Benoit Benjamin	.10	.05	.01
☐ 190	Byron Scott	.15	.07	.02
☐ 191	Calbert Cheaney	.15	.07	.02
☐ 192	Juwan Howard	.50	.23	.06
☐ 193	Don MacLean	.10	.05	.01
☐ 194	Gheorghe Muresan	.10	.05	.01
☐ 195	Doug Overton	.10	.05	.01
☐ 196	Scott Skiles	.10	.05	.01
☐ 197	Chris Webber	.40	.18	.05
☐ 198	Checklist (1-94)	.10	.05	.01
☐ 199	Checklist (95-190)	.10	.05	.01
☐ 200	Checklist (191-200)	.10	.05	.01

1991-92 Upper Deck

The 1991-92 set marks Upper Deck's debut in the basketball card industry. The set contains 500 cards, measuring the standard size (2 1/2" by 3 1/2"). The set was released in two series of 400 and 100 cards, respectively. High series cards are in relatively shorter supply because high series packs contained a mix of both high and low series cards. High series lockers contained seven 12-card packs of cards 1-500 and a special "Rookie Standouts" card. Both low and high series were offered in a 500-card factory set. The fronts feature glossy color player photos, bordered below and on the right by a hardwood basketball floor design. The player's name appears beneath the picture, while the team name is printed vertically alongside the picture. The backs display a second color player photo as well as biographical and statistical information. Special subsets featured include Draft Choices (1-21), Classic Confrontations (30-34), All-Rookie Team (35-39), All-Stars (49-72), and Team Checklists (73-99). The fronts feature glossy color player photos, bordered below and on the right by a hardwood basketball floor design. The player's name appears beneath the picture, while the team name is printed vertically alongside the picture. The backs display a second color player photo as well as biographical and statistical information. In addition to rookie and traded players, the high series includes the following topical subsets: Top Prospects (438-448), All-Star Skills (476-484), capturing players who participated in the slam dunk competition as well as the three-point shootout winner, Eastern All-Star Team (449, 451-462), and Western All-Star Team (450, 463-475). The cards are numbered on the back and checklisted below accordingly. Rookie Cards include Kenny Anderson, Stacey Augmon, Dale Davis, Larry Johnson, Terry Mills, Dikembe Mutombo, Billy Owens, Steve Smith, and John Starks.

	MINT	NRMT	EXC
COMPLETE SET (500)	20.00	9.00	2.50
COMPLETE FACT.SET (500)	20.00	9.00	2.50
COMPLETE SERIES 1 (400)	12.00	5.50	1.50
COMPLETE SERIES 2 (100)	8.00	3.60	1.00
COMMON CARD (1-400)	.05	.02	.01
COMMON CARD (401-500)	.10	.05	.01

☐ 1	Draft Checklist	.10	.05	.01
	(Stacey Augmon and Rodney Monroe)			
☐ 2	Larry Johnson UER	1.50	.65	.19
	Charlotte Hornets			
	(Career FG Percentage is .643, not .648)			
☐ 3	Dikembe Mutombo	1.25	.55	.16
	Denver Nuggets			
☐ 4	Steve Smith	.50	.23	.06
	Miami Heat			
☐ 5	Stacey Augmon	.50	.23	.06
	Atlanta Hawks			
☐ 6	Terrell Brandon	.30	.14	.04
	Cleveland Cavaliers			
☐ 7	Greg Anthony	.10	.05	.01
	New York Knicks			
☐ 8	Rich King	.05	.02	.01
	Seattle Supersonics			
☐ 9	Chris Gatling	.25	.11	.03
	Golden State Warriors			
☐ 10	Victor Alexander	.10	.05	.01
	Golden State Warriors			
☐ 11	John Turner	.05	.02	.01
	Houston Rockets			
☐ 12	Eric Murdock	.30	.14	.04
	Utah Jazz			
☐ 13	Mark Randall	.05	.02	.01
	Chicago Bulls			
☐ 14	Rodney Monroe	.05	.02	.01
	Atlanta Hawks			
☐ 15	Myron Brown	.05	.02	.01
	Minnesota Timberwolves			
☐ 16	Mike Iuzzolino	.05	.02	.01
	Dallas Mavericks			
☐ 17	Chris Corchiani	.05	.02	.01
	Orlando Magic			
☐ 18	Elliot Perry	.30	.14	.04
	Los Angeles Clippers			
☐ 19	Jimmy Oliver	.05	.02	.01

☐ 20	Doug Overton .... Cleveland Cavaliers Detroit Pistons	.05	.02	.01
☐ 21	Steve Hood UER .... Sacramento Kings (Card has NBA record, but he's a rookie)	.05	.02	.01
☐ 22	Michael Jordan .... Stay In School	1.00	.45	.13
☐ 23	Kevin Johnson .... Stay In School	.08	.04	.01
☐ 24	Kurk Lee .... New Jersey Nets	.05	.02	.01
☐ 25	Sean Higgins .... San Antonio Spurs	.05	.02	.01
☐ 26	Morlon Wiley .... Orlando Magic	.05	.02	.01
☐ 27	Derek Smith.................... Boston Celtics	.05	.02	.01
☐ 28	Kenny Payne .... Philadelphia 76ers	.05	.02	.01
☐ 29	Magic Johnson .... Assist Record	.30	.14	.04
☐ 30	Larry Bird CC .... and Chuck Person	.25	.11	.03
☐ 31	Karl Malone CC .... and Charles Barkley	.25	.11	.03
☐ 32	Kevin Johnson CC........... and John Stockton	.08	.04	.01
☐ 33	Hakeem Olajuwon CC..... and Patrick Ewing	.30	.14	.04
☐ 34	Magic Johnson CC........ and Michael Jordan	1.50	.65	.19
☐ 35	Derrick Coleman ART.... New Jersey Nets	.05	.02	.01
☐ 36	Lionel Simmons ART ..... Sacramento Kings	.05	.02	.01
☐ 37	Dee Brown ART .... Boston Celtics	.05	.02	.01
☐ 38	Dennis Scott ART............ Orlando Magic	.05	.02	.01
☐ 39	Kendall Gill ART .... Charlotte Hornets	.05	.02	.01
☐ 40	Winston Garland .... Los Angeles Clippers	.05	.02	.01
☐ 41	Danny Young .... Portland Trail Blazers	.05	.02	.01
☐ 42	Rick Mahorn .... Philadelphia 76ers	.05	.02	.01
☐ 43	Michael Adams .... Denver Nuggets	.05	.02	.01
☐ 44	Michael Jordan .... Chicago Bulls	4.00	1.80	.50
☐ 45	Magic Johnson .... Los Angeles Lakers	.60	.25	.08
☐ 46	Doc Rivers .... Atlanta Hawks	.05	.02	.01
☐ 47	Moses Malone .... Atlanta Hawks	.15	.07	.02
☐ 48	Michael Jordan .... All-Star Checklist	2.00	.90	.25
☐ 49	James Worthy AS .... Los Angeles Lakers	.05	.02	.01
☐ 50	Tim Hardaway AS .... Golden State Warriors	.05	.02	.01
☐ 51	Karl Malone AS .... Utah Jazz	.10	.05	.01
☐ 52	John Stockton AS .... Utah Jazz	.10	.05	.01
☐ 53	Clyde Drexler AS .... Portland Trail Blazers	.10	.05	.01
☐ 54	Terry Porter AS................ Portland Trail Blazers	.05	.02	.01
☐ 55	Kevin Duckworth AS .... Portland Trail Blazers	.05	.02	.01
☐ 56	Tom Chambers AS .... Phoenix Suns	.05	.02	.01
☐ 57	Magic Johnson AS........... Los Angeles Lakers	.30	.14	.04
☐ 58	David Robinson AS .... San Antonio Spurs	.40	.18	.05
☐ 59	Kevin Johnson AS............ Phoenix Suns	.08	.04	.01
☐ 60	Chris Mullin AS .... Golden State Warriors	.05	.02	.01
☐ 61	Joe Dumars AS................ Detroit Pistons	.08	.04	.01
☐ 62	Kevin McHale AS .... Boston Celtics	.05	.02	.01
☐ 63	Brad Daugherty AS .... Cleveland Cavaliers	.05	.02	.01
☐ 64	Alvin Robertson AS.......... Milwaukee Bucks	.05	.02	.01
☐ 65	Bernard King AS .... Washington Bullets	.05	.02	.01
☐ 66	Dominique Wilkins AS ... Atlanta Hawks	.08	.04	.01
☐ 67	Ricky Pierce AS .... Milwaukee Bucks	.05	.02	.01
☐ 68	Patrick Ewing AS .... New York Knicks	.10	.05	.01
☐ 69	Michael Jordan AS........... Chicago Bulls	2.00	.90	.25
☐ 70	Charles Barkley AS.......... Philadelphia 76ers	.30	.14	.04
☐ 71	Hersey Hawkins AS.......... Philadelphia 76ers	.05	.02	.01
☐ 72	Robert Parish AS .... Boston Celtics	.05	.02	.01
☐ 73	Alvin Robertson TC .... Milwaukee Bucks	.05	.02	.01
☐ 74	Bernard King TC .... Washington Bullets	.05	.02	.01
☐ 75	Michael Jordan TC........... Chicago Bulls	2.00	.90	.25
☐ 76	Brad Daugherty TC .... Cleveland Cavaliers	.05	.02	.01
☐ 77	Larry Bird TC .... Boston Celtics	.50	.23	.06
☐ 78	Ron Harper TC .... Los Angeles Clippers	.05	.02	.01
☐ 79	Dominique Wilkins TC .... Atlanta Hawks	.08	.04	.01
☐ 80	Rony Seikaly TC............... Miami Heat	.05	.02	.01
☐ 81	Rex Chapman TC .... Charlotte Hornets	.05	.02	.01
☐ 82	Mark Eaton TC .... Utah Jazz	.05	.02	.01
☐ 83	Lionel Simmons TC .... Sacramento Kings	.05	.02	.01
☐ 84	Gerald Wilkins TC .... New York Knicks	.05	.02	.01
☐ 85	James Worthy TC .... Los Angeles Lakers	.05	.02	.01
☐ 86	Scott Skiles TC................ Orlando Magic	.05	.02	.01
☐ 87	Rolando Blackman TC...... Dallas Mavericks	.05	.02	.01
☐ 88	Derrick Coleman TC .... New Jersey Nets	.05	.02	.01
☐ 89	Chris Jackson TC.............	.05	.02	.01

Denver Nuggets
☐ 90	Reggie Miller TC	.10	.05	.01

Indiana Pacers
| ☐ 91 | Isiah Thomas TC | .08 | .04 | .01 |

Detroit Pistons
| ☐ 92 | Hakeem Olajuwon TC | .40 | .18 | .05 |

Houston Rockets
| ☐ 93 | Hersey Hawkins TC | .05 | .02 | .01 |

Philadelphia 76ers
| ☐ 94 | David Robinson TC | .40 | .18 | .05 |

San Antonio Spurs
| ☐ 95 | Tom Chambers TC | .05 | .02 | .01 |

Phoenix Suns
| ☐ 96 | Shawn Kemp TC | .60 | .25 | .08 |

Seattle Supersonics
| ☐ 97 | Pooh Richardson TC | .05 | .02 | .01 |

Minnesota Timberwolves
| ☐ 98 | Clyde Drexler TC | .10 | .05 | .01 |

Portland Trail Blazers
| ☐ 99 | Chris Mullin TC | .05 | .02 | .01 |

Golden State Warriors
| ☐ 100 | Checklist 1-100 | .05 | .02 | .01 |
| ☐ 101 | John Shasky | .05 | .02 | .01 |

Dallas Mavericks
| ☐ 102 | Dana Barros | .10 | .05 | .01 |

Seattle Supersonics
| ☐ 103 | Stojko Vrankovic | .05 | .02 | .01 |

Boston Celtics
| ☐ 104 | Larry Drew | .05 | .02 | .01 |

Los Angeles Lakers
| ☐ 105 | Randy White | .05 | .02 | .01 |

Dallas Mavericks
| ☐ 106 | Dave Corzine | .05 | .02 | .01 |

Seattle Supersonics
| ☐ 107 | Joe Kleine | .05 | .02 | .01 |

Boston Celtics
| ☐ 108 | Lance Blanks | .05 | .02 | .01 |

Detroit Pistons
| ☐ 109 | Rodney McCray | .05 | .02 | .01 |

Dallas Mavericks
| ☐ 110 | Sedale Threatt | .05 | .02 | .01 |

Seattle Supersonics
| ☐ 111 | Ken Norman | .05 | .02 | .01 |

Los Angeles Clippers
| ☐ 112 | Rickey Green | .05 | .02 | .01 |

Philadelphia 76ers
| ☐ 113 | Andy Toolson | .05 | .02 | .01 |

Utah Jazz
| ☐ 114 | Bo Kimble | .05 | .02 | .01 |

Los Angeles Clippers
| ☐ 115 | Mark West | .05 | .02 | .01 |

Phoenix Suns
| ☐ 116 | Mark Eaton | .05 | .02 | .01 |

Utah Jazz
| ☐ 117 | John Paxson | .05 | .02 | .01 |

Chicago Bulls
| ☐ 118 | Mike Brown | .05 | .02 | .01 |

Utah Jazz
| ☐ 119 | Brian Oliver | .05 | .02 | .01 |

Philadelphia 76ers
| ☐ 120 | Will Perdue | .05 | .02 | .01 |

Chicago Bulls
| ☐ 121 | Michael Smith | .05 | .02 | .01 |

Boston Celtics
| ☐ 122 | Sherman Douglas | .05 | .02 | .01 |

Miami Heat
| ☐ 123 | Reggie Lewis | .10 | .05 | .01 |

Boston Celtics
| ☐ 124 | James Donaldson | .05 | .02 | .01 |

Dallas Mavericks
| ☐ 125 | Scottie Pippen | .30 | .14 | .04 |

Chicago Bulls
| ☐ 126 | Elden Campbell | .08 | .04 | .01 |

Los Angeles Lakers
| ☐ 127 | Michael Cage | .05 | .02 | .01 |

Seattle Supersonics
| ☐ 128 | Tony Smith | .05 | .02 | .01 |

Los Angeles Lakers
| ☐ 129 | Ed Pinckney | .05 | .02 | .01 |

Boston Celtics
| ☐ 130 | Keith Askins | .05 | .02 | .01 |

Miami Heat
| ☐ 131 | Darrell Griffith | .08 | .04 | .01 |

Utah Jazz
| ☐ 132 | Vinnie Johnson | .08 | .04 | .01 |

Detroit Pistons
| ☐ 133 | Ron Harper | .08 | .04 | .01 |

Los Angeles Clippers
| ☐ 134 | Andre Turner | .05 | .02 | .01 |

Philadelphia 76ers
| ☐ 135 | Jeff Hornacek | .08 | .04 | .01 |

Phoenix Suns
| ☐ 136 | John Stockton | .30 | .14 | .04 |

Utah Jazz
| ☐ 137 | Derek Harper | .08 | .04 | .01 |

Dallas Mavericks
| ☐ 138 | Loy Vaught | .08 | .04 | .01 |

Los Angeles Clippers
| ☐ 139 | Thurl Bailey | .05 | .02 | .01 |

Utah Jazz
| ☐ 140 | Olden Polynice | .05 | .02 | .01 |

Los Angeles Clippers
| ☐ 141 | Kevin Edwards | .05 | .02 | .01 |

Miami Heat
| ☐ 142 | Byron Scott | .08 | .04 | .01 |

Los Angeles Lakers
| ☐ 143 | Dee Brown | .10 | .05 | .01 |

Boston Celtics
| ☐ 144 | Sam Perkins | .08 | .04 | .01 |

Los Angeles Lakers
| ☐ 145 | Rony Seikaly | .05 | .02 | .01 |

Miami Heat
| ☐ 146 | James Worthy | .10 | .05 | .01 |

Los Angeles Lakers
| ☐ 147 | Glen Rice | .10 | .05 | .01 |

Miami Heat
| ☐ 148 | Craig Hodges | .05 | .02 | .01 |

Chicago Bulls
| ☐ 149 | Bimbo Coles | .05 | .02 | .01 |

Miami Heat
| ☐ 150 | Mychal Thompson | .08 | .04 | .01 |

Los Angeles Lakers
| ☐ 151 | Xavier McDaniel | .08 | .04 | .01 |

Phoenix Suns
| ☐ 152 | Roy Tarpley | .05 | .02 | .01 |

Dallas Mavericks
| ☐ 153 | Gary Payton | .10 | .05 | .01 |

Seattle Supersonics
| ☐ 154 | Rolando Blackman | .08 | .04 | .01 |

Dallas Mavericks
| ☐ 155 | Hersey Hawkins | .08 | .04 | .01 |

Philadelphia 76ers
| ☐ 156 | Ricky Pierce | .05 | .02 | .01 |

Seattle Supersonics
| ☐ 157 | Fat Lever | .05 | .02 | .01 |

Dallas Mavericks
| ☐ 158 | Andrew Lang | .05 | .02 | .01 |

Phoenix Suns
| ☐ 159 | Benoit Benjamin | .05 | .02 | .01 |

Seattle Supersonics
| ☐ 160 | Cedric Ceballos | .10 | .05 | .01 |

Phoenix Suns

☐ 161	Charles Smith Los Angeles Clippers	.05	.02	.01
☐ 162	Jeff Martin Los Angeles Clippers	.05	.02	.01
☐ 163	Robert Parish Boston Celtics	.10	.05	.01
☐ 164	Danny Manning Los Angeles Clippers	.10	.05	.01
☐ 165	Mark Aguirre Detroit Pistons	.08	.04	.01
☐ 166	Jeff Malone Utah Jazz	.08	.04	.01
☐ 167	Bill Laimbeer Detroit Pistons	.08	.04	.01
☐ 168	Willie Burton Miami Heat	.05	.02	.01
☐ 169	Dennis Hopson Chicago Bulls	.05	.02	.01
☐ 170	Kevin Gamble Boston Celtics	.05	.02	.01
☐ 171	Terry Teagle Los Angeles Lakers	.05	.02	.01
☐ 172	Dan Majerle Phoenix Suns	.08	.04	.01
☐ 173	Shawn Kemp Seattle Supersonics	1.25	.55	.16
☐ 174	Tom Chambers Phoenix Suns	.10	.05	.01
☐ 175	Vlade Divac Los Angeles Lakers	.10	.05	.01
☐ 176	Johnny Dawkins Philadelphia 76ers	.05	.02	.01
☐ 177	A.C. Green Los Angeles Lakers	.10	.05	.01
☐ 178	Manute Bol Philadelphia 76ers	.05	.02	.01
☐ 179	Terry Davis Miami Heat	.05	.02	.01
☐ 180	Ron Anderson Philadelphia 76ers	.05	.02	.01
☐ 181	Horace Grant Chicago Bulls	.15	.07	.02
☐ 182	Stacey King Chicago Bulls	.05	.02	.01
☐ 183	William Bedford Detroit Pistons	.05	.02	.01
☐ 184	B.J. Armstrong Chicago Bulls	.08	.04	.01
☐ 185	Dennis Rodman Detroit Pistons	.20	.09	.03
☐ 186	Nate McMillan Seattle Supersonics	.05	.02	.01
☐ 187	Cliff Levingston Chicago Bulls	.05	.02	.01
☐ 188	Quintin Dailey Seattle Supersonics	.05	.02	.01
☐ 189	Bill Cartwright Chicago Bulls	.05	.02	.01
☐ 190	John Salley Detroit Pistons	.05	.02	.01
☐ 191	Jayson Williams Philadelphia 76ers	.05	.02	.01
☐ 192	Grant Long Miami Heat	.05	.02	.01
☐ 193	Negele Knight Phoenix Suns	.05	.02	.01
☐ 194	Alec Kessler Miami Heat	.05	.02	.01
☐ 195	Gary Grant Los Angeles Clippers	.05	.02	.01
☐ 196	Billy Thompson	.05	.02	.01

	Miami Heat			
☐ 197	Delaney Rudd Utah Jazz	.05	.02	.01
☐ 198	Alan Ogg Miami Heat	.05	.02	.01
☐ 199	Blue Edwards Utah Jazz	.05	.02	.01
☐ 200	Checklist 101-200	.05	.02	.01
☐ 201	Mark Acres Orlando Magic	.05	.02	.01
☐ 202	Craig Ehlo Cleveland Cavaliers	.05	.02	.01
☐ 203	Anthony Cook Denver Nuggets	.05	.02	.01
☐ 204	Eric Leckner Charlotte Hornets	.05	.02	.01
☐ 205	Terry Catledge Orlando Magic	.05	.02	.01
☐ 206	Reggie Williams Denver Nuggets	.05	.02	.01
☐ 207	Greg Kite Orlando Magic	.05	.02	.01
☐ 208	Steve Kerr Cleveland Cavaliers	.05	.02	.01
☐ 209	Kenny Battle Denver Nuggets	.05	.02	.01
☐ 210	John Morton Cleveland Cavaliers	.05	.02	.01
☐ 211	Kenny Williams Indiana Pacers	.05	.02	.01
☐ 212	Mark Jackson New York Knicks	.05	.02	.01
☐ 213	Alaa Abdelnaby Portland Trail Blazers	.05	.02	.01
☐ 214	Rod Strickland San Antonio Spurs	.08	.04	.01
☐ 215	Micheal Williams Indiana Pacers	.05	.02	.01
☐ 216	Kevin Duckworth Portland Trail Blazers	.05	.02	.01
☐ 217	David Wingate San Antonio Spurs	.05	.02	.01
☐ 218	LaSalle Thompson Indiana Pacers	.05	.02	.01
☐ 219	John Starks New York Knicks	.40	.18	.05
☐ 220	Cliff Robinson Portland Trail Blazers	.10	.05	.01
☐ 221	Jeff Grayer Milwaukee Bucks	.05	.02	.01
☐ 222	Marcus Liberty Denver Nuggets	.05	.02	.01
☐ 223	Larry Nance Cleveland Cavaliers	.08	.04	.01
☐ 224	Michael Ansley Orlando Magic	.05	.02	.01
☐ 225	Kevin McHale Boston Celtics	.10	.05	.01
☐ 226	Scott Skiles Orlando Magic	.05	.02	.01
☐ 227	Darnell Valentine Cleveland Cavaliers	.05	.02	.01
☐ 228	Nick Anderson Orlando Magic	.10	.05	.01
☐ 229	Brad Davis Dallas Mavericks	.05	.02	.01
☐ 230	Gerald Paddio Cleveland Cavaliers	.05	.02	.01
☐ 231	Sam Bowie New Jersey Nets	.05	.02	.01
☐ 232	Sam Vincent	.05	.02	.01

Orlando Magic

☐ 233	George McCloud	.05	.02	.01
	Indiana Pacers			
☐ 234	Gerald Wilkins	.05	.02	.01
	New York Knicks			
☐ 235	Mookie Blaylock	.08	.04	.01
	New Jersey Nets			
☐ 236	Jon Koncak	.05	.02	.01
	Atlanta Hawks			
☐ 237	Danny Ferry	.05	.02	.01
	Cleveland Cavaliers			
☐ 238	Vern Fleming	.05	.02	.01
	Indiana Pacers			
☐ 239	Mark Price	.10	.05	.01
	Cleveland Cavaliers			
☐ 240	Sidney Moncrief	.10	.05	.01
	Atlanta Hawks			
☐ 241	Jay Humphries	.05	.02	.01
	Milwaukee Bucks			
☐ 242	Muggsy Bogues	.10	.05	.01
	Charlotte Hornets			
☐ 243	Tim Hardaway	.10	.05	.01
	Golden State Warriors			
☐ 244	Alvin Robertson	.05	.02	.01
	Milwaukee Bucks			
☐ 245	Chris Mullin	.10	.05	.01
	Golden State Warriors			
☐ 246	Pooh Richardson	.05	.02	.01
	Minnesota Timberwolves			
☐ 247	Winston Bennett	.05	.02	.01
	Cleveland Cavaliers			
☐ 248	Kelvin Upshaw	.05	.02	.01
	Dallas Mavericks			
☐ 249	John Williams	.08	.04	.01
	Cleveland Cavaliers			
☐ 250	Steve Alford	.05	.02	.01
	Dallas Mavericks			
☐ 251	Spud Webb	.08	.04	.01
	Atlanta Hawks			
☐ 252	Sleepy Floyd	.05	.02	.01
	Houston Rockets			
☐ 253	Chuck Person	.08	.04	.01
	Indiana Pacers			
☐ 254	Hakeem Olajuwon	.75	.35	.09
	Houston Rockets			
☐ 255	Dominique Wilkins	.15	.07	.02
	Atlanta Hawks			
☐ 256	Reggie Miller	.30	.14	.04
	Indiana Pacers			
☐ 257	Dennis Scott	.08	.04	.01
	Orlando Magic			
☐ 258	Charles Oakley	.08	.04	.01
	New York Knicks			
☐ 259	Sidney Green	.05	.02	.01
	San Antonio Spurs			
☐ 260	Detlef Schrempf	.10	.05	.01
	Indiana Pacers			
☐ 261	Rod Higgins	.05	.02	.01
	Golden State Warriors			
☐ 262	J.R. Reid	.05	.02	.01
	Charlotte Hornets			
☐ 263	Tyrone Hill	.10	.05	.01
	Golden State Warriors			
☐ 264	Reggie Theus	.08	.04	.01
	New Jersey Nets			
☐ 265	Mitch Richmond	.20	.09	.03
	Golden State Warriors			
☐ 266	Dale Ellis	.08	.04	.01
	Milwaukee Bucks			
☐ 267	Terry Cummings	.08	.04	.01
	San Antonio Spurs			

☐ 268	Johnny Newman	.05	.02	.01
	Charlotte Hornets			
☐ 269	Doug West	.05	.02	.01
	Minnesota Timberwolves			
☐ 270	Jim Petersen	.05	.02	.01
	Golden State Warriors			
☐ 271	Otis Thorpe	.08	.04	.01
	Houston Rockets			
☐ 272	John Williams	.05	.02	.01
	Washington Bullets			
☐ 273	Kennard Winchester	.05	.02	.01
	Houston Rockets			
☐ 274	Duane Ferrell	.05	.02	.01
	Atlanta Hawks			
☐ 275	Vernon Maxwell	.05	.02	.01
	Houston Rockets			
☐ 276	Kenny Smith	.05	.02	.01
	Houston Rockets			
☐ 277	Jerome Kersey	.05	.02	.01
	Portland Trail Blazers			
☐ 278	Kevin Willis	.08	.04	.01
	Atlanta Hawks			
☐ 279	Danny Ainge	.08	.04	.01
	Portland Trail Blazers			
☐ 280	Larry Smith	.05	.02	.01
	Houston Rockets			
☐ 281	Maurice Cheeks	.10	.05	.01
	New York Knicks			
☐ 282	Willie Anderson	.05	.02	.01
	San Antonio Spurs			
☐ 283	Tom Tolbert	.05	.02	.01
	Golden State Warriors			
☐ 284	Jerrod Mustaf	.05	.02	.01
	New York Knicks			
☐ 285	Randolph Keys	.05	.02	.01
	Charlotte Hornets			
☐ 286	Jerry Reynolds	.05	.02	.01
	Orlando Magic			
☐ 287	Sean Elliott	.10	.05	.01
	San Antonio Spurs			
☐ 288	Otis Smith	.05	.02	.01
	Orlando Magic			
☐ 289	Terry Mills	.40	.18	.05
	New Jersey Nets			
☐ 290	Kelly Tripucka	.05	.02	.01
	Charlotte Hornets			
☐ 291	Jon Sundvold	.05	.02	.01
	Miami Heat			
☐ 292	Rumeal Robinson	.05	.02	.01
	Atlanta Hawks			
☐ 293	Fred Roberts	.05	.02	.01
	Milwaukee Bucks			
☐ 294	Rik Smits	.10	.05	.01
	Indiana Pacers			
☐ 295	Jerome Lane	.05	.02	.01
	Denver Nuggets			
☐ 296	Dave Jamerson	.05	.02	.01
	Houston Rockets			
☐ 297	Joe Wolf	.05	.02	.01
	Denver Nuggets			
☐ 298	David Wood	.05	.02	.01
	Houston Rockets			
☐ 299	Todd Lichti	.05	.02	.01
	Denver Nuggets			
☐ 300	Checklist 201-300	.05	.02	.01
☐ 301	Randy Breuer	.05	.02	.01
	Minnesota Timberwolves			
☐ 302	Buck Johnson	.05	.02	.01
	Houston Rockets			
☐ 303	Scott Brooks	.05	.02	.01
	Minnesota Timberwolves			

☐ 304	Jeff Turner	.05	.02	.01
	Orlando Magic			
☐ 305	Felton Spencer	.05	.02	.01
	Minnesota Timberwolves			
☐ 306	Greg Dreiling	.05	.02	.01
	Indiana Pacers			
☐ 307	Gerald Glass	.05	.02	.01
	Minnesota Timberwolves			
☐ 308	Tony Brown	.05	.02	.01
	Utah Jazz			
☐ 309	Sam Mitchell	.05	.02	.01
	Minnesota Timberwolves			
☐ 310	Adrian Caldwell	.05	.02	.01
	Houston Rockets			
☐ 311	Chris Dudley	.05	.02	.01
	New Jersey Nets			
☐ 312	Blair Rasmussen	.05	.02	.01
	Denver Nuggets			
☐ 313	Antoine Carr	.05	.02	.01
	Sacramento Kings			
☐ 314	Greg Anderson	.05	.02	.01
	Denver Nuggets			
☐ 315	Drazen Petrovic	.08	.04	.01
	New Jersey Nets			
☐ 316	Alton Lister	.05	.02	.01
	Golden State Warriors			
☐ 317	Jack Haley	.05	.02	.01
	New Jersey Nets			
☐ 318	Bobby Hansen	.05	.02	.01
	Sacramento Kings			
☐ 319	Chris Jackson	.08	.04	.01
	Denver Nuggets			
☐ 320	Herb Williams	.05	.02	.01
	Dallas Mavericks			
☐ 321	Kendall Gill	.08	.04	.01
	Charlotte Hornets			
☐ 322	Tyrone Corbin	.05	.02	.01
	Minnesota Timberwolves			
☐ 323	Kiki Vandeweghe	.05	.02	.01
	New York Knicks			
☐ 324	David Robinson	.75	.35	.09
	San Antonio Spurs			
☐ 325	Rex Chapman	.05	.02	.01
	Charlotte Hornets			
☐ 326	Tony Campbell	.05	.02	.01
	Minnesota Timberwolves			
☐ 327	Dell Curry	.05	.02	.01
	Charlotte Hornets			
☐ 328	Charles Jones	.05	.02	.01
	Washington Bullets			
☐ 329	Kenny Gattison	.05	.02	.01
	Charlotte Hornets			
☐ 330	Haywoode Workman	.05	.02	.01
	Washington Bullets			
☐ 331	Travis Mays	.05	.02	.01
	Sacramento Kings			
☐ 332	Derrick Coleman	.10	.05	.01
	New Jersey Nets			
☐ 333	Isiah Thomas	.15	.07	.02
	Detroit Pistons			
☐ 334	Jud Buechler	.05	.02	.01
	New Jersey Nets			
☐ 335	Joe Dumars	.15	.07	.02
	Detroit Pistons			
☐ 336	Tate George	.05	.02	.01
	New Jersey Nets			
☐ 337	Mike Sanders	.05	.02	.01
	Indiana Pacers			
☐ 338	James Edwards	.05	.02	.01
	Detroit Pistons			
☐ 339	Chris Morris	.05	.02	.01
	New Jersey Nets			
☐ 340	Scott Hastings	.05	.02	.01
	Detroit Pistons			
☐ 341	Trent Tucker	.05	.02	.01
	New York Knicks			
☐ 342	Harvey Grant	.05	.02	.01
	Washington Bullets			
☐ 343	Patrick Ewing	.30	.14	.04
	New York Knicks			
☐ 344	Larry Bird	1.00	.45	.13
	Boston Celtics			
☐ 345	Charles Barkley	.60	.25	.08
	Philadelphia 76ers			
☐ 346	Brian Shaw	.05	.02	.01
	Boston Celtics			
☐ 347	Kenny Walker	.05	.02	.01
	New York Knicks			
☐ 348	Danny Schayes	.05	.02	.01
	Milwaukee Bucks			
☐ 349	Tom Hammonds	.05	.02	.01
	Washington Bullets			
☐ 350	Frank Brickowski	.05	.02	.01
	Milwaukee Bucks			
☐ 351	Terry Porter	.08	.04	.01
	Portland Trail Blazers			
☐ 352	Orlando Woolridge	.05	.02	.01
	Denver Nuggets			
☐ 353	Buck Williams	.08	.04	.01
	Portland Trail Blazers			
☐ 354	Sarunas Marciulionis	.05	.02	.01
	Golden State Warriors			
☐ 355	Karl Malone	.30	.14	.04
	Utah Jazz			
☐ 356	Kevin Johnson	.20	.09	.03
	Phoenix Suns			
☐ 357	Clyde Drexler	.30	.14	.04
	Portland Trail Blazers			
☐ 358	Duane Causwell	.05	.02	.01
	Sacramento Kings			
☐ 359	Paul Pressey	.05	.02	.01
	San Antonio Spurs			
☐ 360	Jim Les	.05	.02	.01
	Sacramento Kings			
☐ 361	Derrick McKey	.08	.04	.01
	Seattle Supersonics			
☐ 362	Scott Williams	.05	.02	.01
	Chicago Bulls			
☐ 363	Mark Alarie	.05	.02	.01
	Washington Bullets			
☐ 364	Brad Daugherty	.08	.04	.01
	Cleveland Cavaliers			
☐ 365	Bernard King	.10	.05	.01
	Washington Bullets			
☐ 366	Steve Henson	.05	.02	.01
	Milwaukee Bucks			
☐ 367	Darrell Walker	.05	.02	.01
	Washington Bullets			
☐ 368	Larry Krystkowiak	.05	.02	.01
	Milwaukee Bucks			
☐ 369	Henry James UER	.05	.02	.01
	Cleveland Cavaliers			
	(Scored 20 points vs.			
	Pistons, not Jazz)			
☐ 370	Jack Sikma	.08	.04	.01
	Milwaukee Bucks			
☐ 371	Eddie Johnson	.08	.04	.01
	Seattle Supersonics			
☐ 372	Wayman Tisdale	.08	.04	.01
	Sacramento Kings			
☐ 373	Joe Barry Carroll	.05	.02	.01
	Phoenix Suns			

☐ 374 David Greenwood San Antonio Spurs	.05	.02	.01
☐ 375 Lionel Simmons Sacramento Kings	.05	.02	.01
☐ 376 Dwayne Schintzius San Antonio Spurs	.05	.02	.01
☐ 377 Tod Murphy Minnesota Timberwolves	.05	.02	.01
☐ 378 Wayne Cooper Portland Trail Blazers	.05	.02	.01
☐ 379 Anthony Bonner Sacramento Kings	.05	.02	.01
☐ 380 Walter Davis Portland Trail Blazers	.10	.05	.01
☐ 381 Lester Conner Milwaukee Bucks	.05	.02	.01
☐ 382 Ledell Eackles Washington Bullets	.05	.02	.01
☐ 383 Brad Lohaus Milwaukee Bucks	.05	.02	.01
☐ 384 Derrick Gervin New Jersey Nets	.05	.02	.01
☐ 385 Pervis Ellison Washington Bullets	.05	.02	.01
☐ 386 Tim McCormick Atlanta Hawks	.05	.02	.01
☐ 387 A.J. English Washington Bullets	.05	.02	.01
☐ 388 John Battle Atlanta Hawks	.05	.02	.01
☐ 389 Roy Hinson New Jersey Nets	.05	.02	.01
☐ 390 Armon Gilliam Philadelphia 76ers	.05	.02	.01
☐ 391 Kurt Rambis Phoenix Suns	.05	.02	.01
☐ 392 Mark Bryant Portland Trail Blazers	.05	.02	.01
☐ 393 Chucky Brown Cleveland Cavaliers	.05	.02	.01
☐ 394 Avery Johnson San Antonio Spurs	.05	.02	.01
☐ 395 Rory Sparrow Sacramento Kings	.05	.02	.01
☐ 396 Mario Elie Golden State Warriors	.25	.11	.03
☐ 397 Ralph Sampson Sacramento Kings	.05	.02	.01
☐ 398 Mike Gminski Charlotte Hornets	.05	.02	.01
☐ 399 Bill Wennington Sacramento Kings	.05	.02	.01
☐ 400 Checklist 301-400	.05	.02	.01
☐ 401 David Wingate Washington Bullets	.10	.05	.01
☐ 402 Moses Malone Milwaukee Bucks	.30	.14	.04
☐ 403 Darrell Walker Detroit Pistons	.10	.05	.01
☐ 404 Antoine Carr San Antonio Spurs	.10	.05	.01
☐ 405 Charles Shackleford Philadelphia 76ers	.10	.05	.01
☐ 406 Orlando Woolridge Detroit Pistons	.10	.05	.01
☐ 407 Robert Pack Portland Trail Blazers	.10	.05	.01
☐ 408 Bobby Hansen Chicago Bulls	.10	.05	.01
☐ 409 Dale Davis Indiana Pacers	1.00	.45	.13
☐ 410 Vincent Askew Golden State Warriors	.10	.05	.01
☐ 411 Alexander Volkov Atlanta Hawks	.10	.05	.01
☐ 412 Dwayne Schintzius Sacramento Kings	.10	.05	.01
☐ 413 Tim Perry Phoenix Suns	.10	.05	.01
☐ 414 Tyrone Corbin Utah Jazz	.10	.05	.01
☐ 415 Pete Chilcutt Sacramento Kings	.10	.05	.01
☐ 416 James Edwards Los Angeles Clippers	.10	.05	.01
☐ 417 Jerrod Mustaf Phoenix Suns	.10	.05	.01
☐ 418 Thurl Bailey Minnesota Timberwolves	.10	.05	.01
☐ 419 Spud Webb Sacramento Kings	.15	.07	.02
☐ 420 Doc Rivers Los Angeles Clippers	.10	.05	.01
☐ 421 Sean Green Indiana Pacers	.10	.05	.01
☐ 422 Walter Davis Denver Nuggets	.20	.09	.03
☐ 423 Terry Davis Dallas Mavericks	.10	.05	.01
☐ 424 John Battle Cleveland Cavaliers	.10	.05	.01
☐ 425 Vinnie Johnson San Antonio Spurs	.15	.07	.02
☐ 426 Sherman Douglas Boston Celtics	.10	.05	.01
☐ 427 Kevin Brooks Denver Nuggets	.10	.05	.01
☐ 428 Greg Sutton San Antonio Spurs	.10	.05	.01
☐ 429 Rafael Addison New Jersey Nets	.10	.05	.01
☐ 430 Anthony Mason New York Knicks	1.00	.45	.13
☐ 431 Paul Graham Atlanta Hawks	.10	.05	.01
☐ 432 Anthony Frederick Charlotte Hornets	.10	.05	.01
☐ 433 Dennis Hopson Sacramento Kings	.10	.05	.01
☐ 434 Rory Sparrow Los Angeles Lakers	.10	.05	.01
☐ 435 Michael Adams Washington Bullets	.10	.05	.01
☐ 436 Kevin Lynch Charlotte Hornets	.10	.05	.01
☐ 437 Randy Brown Sacramento Kings	.10	.05	.01
☐ 438 NBA Top Prospects Checklist (Larry Johnson and Billy Owens)	.50	.23	.06
☐ 439 Stacey Augmon TP Atlanta Hawks	.40	.18	.05
☐ 440 Larry Stewart TP Washington Bullets	.10	.05	.01
☐ 441 Terrell Brandon TP Cleveland Cavaliers	.15	.07	.02
☐ 442 Billy Owens TP Golden State Warriors	1.00	.45	.13
☐ 443 Rick Fox TP Boston Celtics	.15	.07	.02
☐ 444 Kenny Anderson TP	1.50	.65	.19

New Jersey Nets
- ☐ 445 Larry Johnson TP . 1.25 .55 .16
  Charlotte Hornets
- ☐ 446 Dikembe Mutombo TP 1.00 .45 .13
  Denver Nuggets
- ☐ 447 Steve Smith TP .... .40 .18 .05
  Miami Heat
- ☐ 448 Greg Anthony TP .... .10 .05 .01
  New York Knicks
- ☐ 449 East All-Star .... .10 .05 .01
  Checklist
- ☐ 450 West All-Star .... .10 .05 .01
  Checklist
- ☐ 451 Isiah Thomas AS .... .25 .11 .03
  (Magic Johnson
  also shown)
- ☐ 452 Michael Jordan AS .... 4.00 1.80 .50
- ☐ 453 Scottie Pippen AS ..... .30 .14 .04
- ☐ 454 Charles Barkley AS ..... .60 .25 .08
- ☐ 455 Patrick Ewing AS .... .30 .14 .04
- ☐ 456 Michael Adams AS ...... .10 .05 .01
- ☐ 457 Dennis Rodman AS ..... .15 .07 .02
- ☐ 458 Reggie Lewis AS .... .10 .05 .01
- ☐ 459 Joe Dumars AS .... .15 .07 .02
- ☐ 460 Mark Price AS .... .10 .05 .01
- ☐ 461 Brad Daugherty AS ..... .10 .05 .01
- ☐ 462 Kevin Willis AS .... .10 .05 .01
- ☐ 463 Clyde Drexler AS .... .30 .14 .04
- ☐ 464 Magic Johnson AS ...... .60 .25 .08
- ☐ 465 Chris Mullin AS .... .10 .05 .01
- ☐ 466 Karl Malone AS .... .30 .14 .04
- ☐ 467 David Robinson AS ..... .75 .35 .09
- ☐ 468 Tim Hardaway AS .... .10 .05 .01
- ☐ 469 Jeff Hornacek AS .... .10 .05 .01
- ☐ 470 John Stockton AS .... .30 .14 .04
- ☐ 471 Dikembe Mutombo AS UER .50 .23 .06
  (Drafted in 1992,
  should be 1991)
- ☐ 472 Hakeem Olajuwon AS... .75 .35 .09
- ☐ 473 James Worthy AS .... .10 .05 .01
- ☐ 474 Otis Thorpe AS .... .10 .05 .01
- ☐ 475 Dan Majerle AS .... .10 .05 .01
- ☐ 476 Cedric Ceballos CL .... .10 .05 .01
  Phoenix Suns
  All-Star Skills
- ☐ 477 Nick Anderson SD .... .10 .05 .01
  Orlando Magic
- ☐ 478 Stacey Augmon SD ...... .10 .05 .01
  Atlanta Hawks
- ☐ 479 Cedric Ceballos SD ..... .10 .05 .01
  Phoenix Suns
- ☐ 480 Larry Johnson SD ...... .60 .25 .08
  Charlotte Hornets
- ☐ 481 Shawn Kemp SD .... 1.25 .55 .16
  Seattle Supersonics
- ☐ 482 John Starks SD .... .10 .05 .01
  New York Knicks
- ☐ 483 Doug West SD .... .10 .05 .01
  Minnesota Timberwolves
- ☐ 484 Craig Hodges .... .10 .05 .01
  Long Distance Shoot Out
- ☐ 485 LaBradford Smith .... .10 .05 .01
  Washington Bullets
- ☐ 486 Winston Garland .... .10 .05 .01
  Denver Nuggets
- ☐ 487 David Benoit .... .50 .23 .06
  Utah Jazz
- ☐ 488 John Bagley .... .10 .05 .01
  Boston Celtics
- ☐ 489 Mark Macon .... .10 .05 .01
  Denver Nuggets
- ☐ 490 Mitch Richmond .... .40 .18 .05
  Sacramento Kings
- ☐ 491 Luc Longley .... .20 .09 .03
  Minnesota Timberwolves
- ☐ 492 Sedale Threatt .... .10 .05 .01
  Los Angeles Lakers
- ☐ 493 Doug Smith .... .10 .05 .01
  Dallas Mavericks
- ☐ 494 Travis Mays .... .10 .05 .01
  Atlanta Hawks
- ☐ 495 Xavier McDaniel .... .13 .06 .02
  New York Knicks
- ☐ 496 Brian Shaw .... .10 .05 .01
  Miami Heat
- ☐ 497 Stanley Roberts .... .13 .06 .02
  Orlando Magic
- ☐ 498 Blair Rasmussen .... .10 .05 .01
  Atlanta Hawks
- ☐ 499 Brian Williams .... .15 .07 .02
  Orlando Magic
- ☐ 500 Checklist Card .... .10 .05 .01

1991-92 Upper Deck Award Winner Holograms

These holograms feature NBA statistical leaders in nine different categories. The first six holograms were random inserts in 1991-92 Upper Deck low series foil and jumbo packs, while the last three were inserted in high series foil and jumbo packs. The standard-size (2 1/2" by 3 1/2") holograms have the player's name and award received in the lower right corner on the front. The back has a color player photo and a summary of the player's performance. The cards are numbered on the back with an "AW" prefix before the number.

	MINT	NRMT	EXC
COMPLETE SET (9)	35.00	16.00	4.40
COMMON CARD (AW1-AW9)	.50	.23	.06
☐ AW1 Michael Jordan	15.00	6.75	1.90
Scoring Leader			
☐ AW2 Alvin Robertson	.50	.23	.06
Steals Leader			
☐ AW3 John Stockton	1.25	.55	.16

Assists Leader
- ☐ AW4 Michael Jordan....... 15.00 · 6.75 1.90
MVP
- ☐ AW5 Detlef Schrempf .... .60 .25 .08
Sixth Man
- ☐ AW6 David Robinson .... 3.00 1.35 .40
Rebounds Leader
- ☐ AW7 Derrick Coleman ...... 1.00 .45 .13
Rookie of the Year
- ☐ AW8 Hakeem Olajuwon .... 3.00 1.35 .40
Blocked Shots Leader
- ☐ AW9 Dennis Rodman .... .75 .35 .09
Defensive POY

1991-92 Upper Deck Rookie Standouts

Inserted one per jumbo and locker pack in both the low and high series, fronts of this standard-size (2 1/2" by 3 1/2") 40-card set feature color action player photos, bordered on the right and below by a hardwood basketball court and with the "'91-92 Rookie Standouts" emblem in the lower right corner. The back features a second color player photo and player profile.

	MINT	NRMT	EXC
COMPLETE SET (40)	20.00	9.00	2.50
COMPLETE SERIES 1 (20)	5.00	2.30	.60
COMPLETE SERIES 2 (20)	15.00	6.75	1.90
COMMON CARD (R1-R40)	.25	.11	.03

- ☐ R1 Gary Payton .... 1.25 .55 .16
Seattle Supersonics
- ☐ R2 Dennis Scott .... .60 .25 .08
Orlando Magic
- ☐ R3 Kendall Gill .... .50 .23 .06
Charlotte Hornets
- ☐ R4 Felton Spencer .... .25 .11 .03
Minnesota Timberwolves
- ☐ R5 Bo Kimble .... .25 .11 .03
Los Angeles Clippers
- ☐ R6 Willie Burton .... .25 .11 .03
Miami Heat
- ☐ R7 Tyrone Hill .... .75 .35 .09
Golden State Warriors
- ☐ R8 Loy Vaught .... .75 .35 .09
Los Angeles Clippers
- ☐ R9 Travis Mays .... .25 .11 .03
Sacramento Kings
- ☐ R10 Derrick Coleman .... 1.25 .55 .16
New Jersey Nets

- ☐ R11 Duane Causwell........... .25 .11 .03
Sacramento Kings
- ☐ R12 Dee Brown.................. .75 .35 .09
Boston Celtics
- ☐ R13 Gerald Glass .... .25 .11 .03
Minnesota Timberwolves
- ☐ R14 Jayson Williams .... .35 .16 .04
Philadelphia 76ers
- ☐ R15 Elden Campbell........... .75 .35 .09
Los Angeles Lakers
- ☐ R16 Negele Knight .... .25 .11 .03
Phoenix Suns
- ☐ R17 Chris Jackson............. .50 .23 .06
Denver Nuggets
- ☐ R18 Danny Ferry................ .35 .16 .04
Cleveland Cavaliers
- ☐ R19 Tony Smith .... .25 .11 .03
Los Angeles Lakers
- ☐ R20 Cedric Ceballos........... 1.50 .65 .19
Phoenix Suns
- ☐ R21 Victor Alexander.......... .35 .16 .04
Golden State Warriors
- ☐ R22 Terrell Brandon............ .75 .35 .09
Cleveland Cavaliers
- ☐ R23 Rick Fox .... .35 .16 .04
Boston Celtics
- ☐ R24 Stacey Augmon........... 1.25 .55 .16
Atlanta Hawks
- ☐ R25 Mark Macon .... .25 .11 .03
Denver Nuggets
- ☐ R26 Larry Johnson .... 4.00 1.80 .50
Charlotte Hornets
- ☐ R27 Paul Graham .... .25 .11 .03
Atlanta Hawks
- ☐ R28 Stanley Roberts UER ... .25 .11 .03
Orlando Magic
(Not the Magic's 1st
pick in 1991)
- ☐ R29 Dikembe Mutombo ...... 3.00 1.35 .40
Denver Nuggets
- ☐ R30 Robert Pack................ .25 .11 .03
Portland Trail Blazers
- ☐ R31 Doug Smith .... .25 .11 .03
Dallas Mavericks
- ☐ R32 Steve Smith .... 1.25 .55 .16
Miami Heat
- ☐ R33 Billy Owens .... 1.25 .55 .16
Golden State Warriors
- ☐ R34 David Benoit............... .60 .25 .08
Utah Jazz
- ☐ R35 Brian Williams .... .35 .16 .04
Orlando Magic
- ☐ R36 Kenny Anderson .... 2.00 .90 .25
New Jersey Nets
- ☐ R37 Greg Anthony .... .35 .16 .04
New York Knicks
- ☐ R38 Dale Davis .... 1.25 .55 .16
Indiana Pacers
- ☐ R39 Larry Stewart .... .25 .11 .03
Washington Bullets
- ☐ R40 Mike Iuzzolino .... .25 .11 .03
Dallas Mavericks

1991-92 Upper Deck Jerry West Heroes

This ten-card insert set was randomly inserted in Upper Deck's high series bas-

ketball foil packs. Also included in the packs were 2,500 checklist cards autographed by West. The fronts of the standard-size (2 1/2" by 3 1/2") cards capture memorable moments from his college and professional career. The player photos are cut out and superimposed over a jump ball circle on a hardwood basketball floor design. The card backs present commentary. The cards are numbered on the back.

	MINT	NRMT	EXC
COMPLETE SET (10)	10.00	4.50	1.25
COMMON J.WEST (1-9)	1.00	.45	.13
☐ 1 Jerry West 1959 NCAA Tournament MVP	1.00	.45	.13
☐ 2 Jerry West 1960 U.S. Team	1.00	.45	.13
☐ 3 Jerry West 1968-69 NBA Playoff MVP	1.00	.45	.13
☐ 4 Jerry West 1969-70 NBA Scoring Leader	1.00	.45	.13
☐ 5 Jerry West 1972 NBA World Championship	1.00	.45	.13
☐ 6 Jerry West 1973-74 25,000 Points	1.00	.45	.13
☐ 7 Jerry West 1979 Basketball Hall of Fame	1.00	.45	.13
☐ 8 Jerry West 1982 to the present Front Office Success	1.00	.45	.13
☐ 9 Jerry West Portrait Card	1.00	.45	.13
☐ AU Jerry West AU/2500 (Certified autograph)	175.00	80.00	22.00
☐ NNO Jerry West Cover/Title Card	2.00	.90	.25

1992-93 Upper Deck

The complete 1992-93 Upper Deck basketball set consists of 510 standard-size (2 1/2" by 3 1/2") cards issued in two series of 310 and 200 cards, respectively. High series cards are slightly tougher to find (compared to the low numbers) because high series packs contained a mix of high and low series cards. For both series, cards were issued in 15-card hobby and retail foil packs, 27-card locker packs and 27-card jumbo packs. No factory sets were produced by Upper Deck for this issue. Both series were also distributed through 27-card Locker packs. Card number 1A (available only in low series packs) is a "Trade Upper Deck" card that the collector could trade to Upper Deck for a Shaquille O'Neal mail-away trade card beginning on Jan. 1, 1993. The offer expired June 30, 1993. The fronts feature color action player photos with white borders. The team name is gold-foil stamped across the top of the picture. The border design at the bottom consists of a team colored stripe that shades from one team color to the other with diagonal stripes within the larger stripe that add texture. The entire design is edged in gold foil. The right end is off-set slightly by the Upper Deck logo. The backs show an action player photo that runs down the left side of the card. The right side displays statistics printed on a ghosted NBA logo. Topical subsets featured include NBA Draft (2-21), Team Checklists (35-61), and Scoring Threats (62-66). The set also includes two art cards (67-68) and one Stay in School card (69). The cards are numbered on the back. Subsets featured are Team Fact Cards (350-376), NBA East All-Star Game (421-433), NBA West All-Star Game (434-445), In Your Face (446-454), Top Prospects (455-482), NBA Game Faces (483-497), Scoring Threats (498-505), and Fanimation (506-510). The cards are numbered on the back. Rookie Cards include Doug Christie (second series SP), Richard Dumas, LaPhonso Ellis, Tom Gugliotta, Jim Jackson (second series SP), Christian Laettner, Harold Miner, Alonzo Mourning, Shaquille O'Neal, Latrell Sprewell, Clarence Weatherspoon and Walt Williams. A card commemorating the retirement of Larry Bird and Magic Johnson (SP1) and the 20,000th point scored by Dominique Wilkins and Michael Jordan (SP2) were first and second series inserts, respectively. There were inserted at a rate of one in 72 packs. The basic card numbers of Jordan (23), Magic (32) and Bird (33) represent their uniform numbers.

	MINT	NRMT	EXC
COMPLETE SET (514)	50.00	23.00	6.25
COMPLETE LO SERIES (311)	15.00	6.75	1.90
COMPLETE HI SERIES (203) .	40.00	18.00	5.00
COMMON CARD (1-310)	.05	.02	.01
COMMON CARD (311-510)	.05	.02	.01
☐ 1 Shaquille O'Neal SP	20.00	9.00	2.50
Orlando Magic			
NBA First Draft Pick			
☐ 1A 1992 NBA Draft Trade....	.50	.23	.06
Card SP			
☐ 1AX 1992 NBA Draft Trade .	.15	.07	.02
Card (Stamped)			
☐ 1B Shaquille O'Neal Trade	8.00	3.60	1.00
☐ 2 Alonzo Mourning	2.00	.90	.25
Charlotte Hornets			
☐ 3 Christian Laettner	.60	.25	.08
Minnesota Timberwolves			
☐ 4 LaPhonso Ellis	.30	.14	.04
Denver Nuggets			
☐ 5 Clarence Weatherspoon ..	.60	.25	.08
Philadelphia 76ers			
☐ 6 Adam Keefe	.15	.07	.02
Atlanta Hawks			
☐ 7 Robert Horry	.75	.35	.09
Houston Rockets			
☐ 8 Harold Miner	.20	.09	.03
Miami Heat			
☐ 9 Bryant Stith	.25	.11	.03
Denver Nuggets			
☐ 10 Malik Sealy	.15	.07	.02
Indiana Pacers			
☐ 11 Anthony Peeler	.15	.07	.02
Los Angeles Lakers			
☐ 12 Randy Woods	.05	.02	.01
Los Angeles Clippers			
☐ 13 Tracy Murray	.08	.04	.01
Portland Trail Blazers			
☐ 14 Tom Gugliotta	.50	.23	.06
Washington Bullets			
☐ 15 Hubert Davis	.15	.07	.02
New York Knicks			
☐ 16 Don MacLean	.15	.07	.02
Washington Bullets			
☐ 17 Lee Mayberry	.08	.04	.01
Milwaukee Bucks			
☐ 18 Corey Williams	.05	.02	.01
Chicago Bulls			
☐ 19 Sean Rooks	.08	.04	.01
Dallas Mavericks			
☐ 20 Todd Day	.40	.18	.05
Milwaukee Bucks			
☐ 21 NBA Draft Card CL	.10	.05	.01
Bryant Stith			
LaPhonso Ellis			
Denver Nuggets			
☐ 22 Jeff Hornacek	.08	.04	.01
Phoenix Suns			
☐ 23 Michael Jordan	4.00	1.80	.50
Chicago Bulls			
☐ 24 John Salley	.05	.02	.01
Detroit Pistons			
☐ 25 Andre Turner	.05	.02	.01
Washington Bullets			
☐ 26 Charles Barkley	.60	.25	.08
Philadelphia 76ers			
☐ 27 Anthony Frederick	.05	.02	.01
Charlotte Hornets			
☐ 28 Mario Elie	.05	.02	.01
Golden State Warriors			

	MINT	NRMT	EXC
☐ 29 Olden Polynice	.05	.02	.01
Los Angeles Clippers			
☐ 30 Rodney Monroe	.05	.02	.01
Atlanta Hawks			
☐ 31 Tim Perry	.05	.02	.01
Phoenix Suns			
☐ 32 Doug Christie SP	.20	.09	.03
Los Angeles Lakers			
☐ 32A Magic Johnson SP.....	1.25	.55	.16
Los Angeles Lakers			
☐ 33 Jim Jackson SP	10.00	4.50	1.25
Dallas Mavericks			
☐ 33A Larry Bird SP	2.00	.90	.25
Boston Celtics			
☐ 34 Randy White	.05	.02	.01
Dallas Mavericks			
☐ 35 Frank Brickowski TC	.05	.02	.01
Milwaukee Bucks			
☐ 36 Michael Adams TC	.05	.02	.01
Washington Bullets			
☐ 37 Scottie Pippen TC	.10	.05	.01
Chicago Bulls			
☐ 38 Mark Price TC	.05	.02	.01
Cleveland Cavaliers			
☐ 39 Robert Parish TC	.05	.02	.01
Boston Celtics			
☐ 40 Danny Manning TC	.05	.02	.01
Los Angeles Clippers			
☐ 41 Kevin Willis TC	.05	.02	.01
Atlanta Hawks			
☐ 42 Glen Rice TC	.05	.02	.01
Miami Heat			
☐ 43 Kendall Gill TC	.05	.02	.01
Charlotte Hornets			
☐ 44 Karl Malone TC	.10	.05	.01
Utah Jazz			
☐ 45 Mitch Richmond TC	.08	.04	.01
Sacramento Kings			
☐ 46 Patrick Ewing TC	.10	.05	.01
New York Knicks			
☐ 47 Sam Perkins TC	.05	.02	.01
Los Angeles Lakers			
☐ 48 Dennis Scott TC	.05	.02	.01
Orlando Magic			
☐ 49 Derek Harper TC	.05	.02	.01
Dallas Mavericks			
☐ 50 Drazen Petrovic TC	.05	.02	.01
New Jersey Nets			
☐ 51 Reggie Williams TC.........	.05	.02	.01
Denver Nuggets			
☐ 52 Rik Smits TC	.05	.02	.01
Indiana Pacers			
☐ 53 Joe Dumars TC	.08	.04	.01
Detroit Pistons			
☐ 54 Otis Thorpe TC	.05	.02	.01
Houston Rockets			
☐ 55 Johnny Dawkins TC	.05	.02	.01
Philadelphia 76ers			
☐ 56 Sean Elliott TC	.05	.02	.01
San Antonio Spurs			
☐ 57 Kevin Johnson TC	.08	.04	.01
Phoenix Suns			
☐ 58 Ricky Pierce TC	.05	.02	.01
Seattle Supersonics			
☐ 59 Doug West TC.................	.05	.02	.01
Minnesota Timberwolves			
☐ 60 Terry Porter TC	.05	.02	.01
Portland Trail Blazers			
☐ 61 Tim Hardaway TC............	.05	.02	.01
Golden State Warriors			
☐ 62 Michael Jordan ST	1.00	.45	.13

☐ 63	Kendall Gill ST	.10	.05	.01	Scottie Pippen Chicago Bulls
☐ 64	Tom Chambers ST	.05	.02	.01	Larry Johnson Charlotte Hornets
☐ 65	Tim Hardaway ST............	.05	.02	.01	Kevin Johnson Phoenix Suns
☐ 66	Karl Malone ST	.10	.05	.01	Chris Mullin Golden State Warriors
☐ 67	Michael Jordan MVP....	2.00	.90	.25	John Stockton Utah Jazz
☐ 68	Stacey Augmon..............	.05	.02	.01	Chicago Bulls
☐ 69	Bob Lanier	.10	.05	.01	Atlanta Hawks Six Million Point Man
☐ 70	Alaa Abdelnaby	.05	.02	.01	Stay in School
☐ 71	Andrew Lang...................	.05	.02	.01	Portland Trail Blazers
☐ 72	Larry Krystkowiak...........	.05	.02	.01	Phoenix Suns
☐ 73	Gerald Wilkins................	.05	.02	.01	Milwaukee Bucks
☐ 74	Rod Strickland	.08	.04	.01	New York Knicks
☐ 75	Danny Ainge	.08	.04	.01	San Antonio Spurs
☐ 76	Chris Corchiani...............	.05	.02	.01	Portland Trail Blazers
☐ 77	Jeff Grayer....................	.05	.02	.01	Orlando Magic
☐ 78	Eric Murdock	.05	.02	.01	Milwaukee Bucks
☐ 79	Rex Chapman	.05	.02	.01	Utah Jazz
☐ 80	LaBradford Smith	.05	.02	.01	Washington Bullets
☐ 81	Jay Humphries................	.05	.02	.01	Washington Bullets
☐ 82	David Robinson	.60	.25	.08	Milwaukee Bucks
☐ 83	William Bedford	.05	.02	.01	San Antonio Spurs
☐ 84	James Edwards...............	.05	.02	.01	Detroit Pistons
☐ 85	Dan Schayes...................	.05	.02	.01	Los Angeles Clippers
☐ 86	Lloyd Daniels	.05	.02	.01	Milwaukee Bucks
☐ 87	Blue Edwards.................	.05	.02	.01	San Antonio Spurs
☐ 88	Dale Ellis......................	.08	.04	.01	Utah Jazz
☐ 89	Rolando Blackman..........	.08	.04	.01	Milwaukee Bucks
☐ 90	Form Checklist 1	.25	.11	.03	Dallas Mavericks
☐ 91	Rik Smits	.10	.05	.01	Michael Jordan Chicago Bulls
☐ 92	Terry Davis	.05	.02	.01	Indiana Pacers
☐ 93	Bill Cartwright................	.05	.02	.01	Dallas Mavericks
☐ 94	Avery Johnson................	.05	.02	.01	Chicago Bulls
					Houston Rockets
☐ 95	Micheal Williams.............	.05	.02	.01	
☐ 96	Spud Webb.....................	.08	.04	.01	Indiana Pacers
☐ 97	Benoit Benjamin..............	.05	.02	.01	Sacramento Kings
☐ 98	Derek Harper...................	.08	.04	.01	Seattle Supersonics
☐ 99	Matt Bullard	.05	.02	.01	Dallas Mavericks
☐ 100A	Tyrone Corbin ERR....	1.00	.45	.13	Houston Rockets
☐ 100B	Tyrone Corbin COR....	.05	.02	.01	(Heat on front) Utah Jazz
☐ 101	Doc Rivers	.05	.02	.01	Utah Jazz
☐ 102	Tony Smith	.05	.02	.01	Los Angeles Clippers
☐ 103	Doug West.....................	.05	.02	.01	Los Angeles Lakers
☐ 104	Kevin Duckworth............	.05	.02	.01	Minnesota Timberwolves
☐ 105	Luc Longley	.05	.02	.01	Portland Trail Blazers
☐ 106	Antoine Carr...................	.05	.02	.01	Minnesota Timberwolves
☐ 107	Clifford Robinson..........	.10	.05	.01	San Antonio Spurs
☐ 108	Grant Long.....................	.05	.02	.01	Portland Trail Blazers
☐ 109	Terry Porter...................	.08	.04	.01	Miami Heat
☐ 110A	Steve Smith ERR	4.00	1.80	.50	Portland Trail Blazers
☐ 110B	Steve Smith COR.......	.10	.05	.01	(Jazz on front) Miami Heat
☐ 111	Brian Williams................	.05	.02	.01	Miami Heat
☐ 112	Karl Malone...................	.30	.14	.04	Orlando Magic
☐ 113	Reggie Williams.............	.05	.02	.01	Utah Jazz
☐ 114	Tom Chambers	.08	.04	.01	Denver Nuggets
☐ 115	Winston Garland............	.05	.02	.01	Phoenix Suns
☐ 116	John Stockton................	.30	.14	.04	Denver Nuggets
☐ 117	Chris Jackson	.08	.04	.01	Utah Jazz
☐ 118	Mike Brown....................	.05	.02	.01	Denver Nuggets
☐ 119	Kevin Johnson..............	.15	.07	.02	Utah Jazz
☐ 120	Reggie Lewis..................	.10	.05	.01	Phoenix Suns
☐ 121	Bimbo Coles	.05	.02	.01	Boston Celtics
☐ 122	Drazen Petrovic..............	.08	.04	.01	Miami Heat
☐ 123	Reggie Miller..................	.30	.14	.04	New Jersey Nets
☐ 124	Derrick Coleman	.10	.05	.01	Indiana Pacers
☐ 125	Chuck Person	.08	.04	.01	New Jersey Nets
☐ 126	Glen Rice	.10	.05	.01	Indiana Pacers
					Miami Heat

☐ 127	Kenny Anderson	.25	.11	.03
	New Jersey Nets			
☐ 128	Willie Burton	.05	.02	.01
	Miami Heat			
☐ 129	Chris Morris	.05	.02	.01
	New Jersey Nets			
☐ 130	Patrick Ewing	.30	.14	.04
	New York Knicks			
☐ 131	Sean Elliott	.08	.04	.01
	San Antonio Spurs			
☐ 132	Clyde Drexler	.30	.14	.04
	Portland Trail Blazers			
☐ 133	Scottie Pippen	.30	.14	.04
	Chicago Bulls			
☐ 134	Pooh Richardson	.05	.02	.01
	Minnesota Timberwolves			
☐ 135	Horace Grant	.15	.07	.02
	Chicago Bulls			
☐ 136	Hakeem Olajuwon	.75	.35	.09
	Houston Rockets			
☐ 137	John Paxson	.05	.02	.01
	Chicago Bulls			
☐ 138	Kendall Gill	.05	.02	.01
	Charlotte Hornets			
☐ 139	Michael Adams	.05	.02	.01
	Washington Bullets			
☐ 140	Otis Thorpe	.08	.04	.01
	Houston Rockets			
☐ 141	Dennis Scott	.05	.02	.01
	Orlando Magic			
☐ 142	Stacey Augmon	.10	.05	.01
	Atlanta Hawks			
☐ 143	Robert Pack	.05	.02	.01
	Portland Trail Blazers			
☐ 144	Kevin Willis	.08	.04	.01
	Atlanta Hawks			
☐ 145	Jerome Kersey	.05	.02	.01
	Portland Trail Blazers			
☐ 146	Paul Graham	.05	.02	.01
	Atlanta Hawks			
☐ 147	Stanley Roberts	.05	.02	.01
	Orlando Magic			
☐ 148	Dominique Wilkins	.15	.07	.02
	Atlanta Hawks			
☐ 149	Scott Skiles	.05	.02	.01
	Orlando Magic			
☐ 150	Rumeal Robinson	.05	.02	.01
	Atlanta Hawks			
☐ 151	Mookie Blaylock	.08	.04	.01
	New Jersey Nets			
☐ 152	Elden Campbell	.05	.02	.01
	Los Angeles Lakers			
☐ 153	Chris Dudley	.05	.02	.01
	New Jersey Nets			
☐ 154	Sedale Threatt	.05	.02	.01
	Los Angeles Lakers			
☐ 155	Tate George	.05	.02	.01
	New Jersey Nets			
☐ 156	James Worthy	.10	.05	.01
	Los Angeles Lakers			
☐ 157	B.J. Armstrong	.05	.02	.01
	Chicago Bulls			
☐ 158	Gary Payton	.10	.05	.01
	Seattle Supersonics			
☐ 159	Ledell Eackles	.05	.02	.01
	Washington Bullets			
☐ 160	Sam Perkins	.08	.04	.01
	Los Angeles Lakers			
☐ 161	Nick Anderson	.10	.05	.01
	Orlando Magic			
☐ 162	Mitch Richmond	.15	.07	.02
	Sacramento Kings			
☐ 163	Buck Williams	.08	.04	.01
	Portland Trail Blazers			
☐ 164	Blair Rasmussen	.05	.02	.01
	Atlanta Hawks			
☐ 165	Vern Fleming	.05	.02	.01
	Indiana Pacers			
☐ 166	Duane Ferrell	.05	.02	.01
	Atlanta Hawks			
☐ 167	George McCloud	.05	.02	.01
	Indiana Pacers			
☐ 168	Terry Cummings	.08	.04	.01
	San Antonio Spurs			
☐ 169	Detlef Schrempf	.10	.05	.01
	Indiana Pacers			
☐ 170	Willie Anderson	.05	.02	.01
	San Antonio Spurs			
☐ 171	Scott Williams	.05	.02	.01
	Chicago Bulls			
☐ 172	Vernon Maxwell	.05	.02	.01
	Houston Rockets			
☐ 173	Todd Lichti	.05	.02	.01
	Denver Nuggets			
☐ 174	David Benoit	.05	.02	.01
	Utah Jazz			
☐ 175	Marcus Liberty	.05	.02	.01
	Denver Nuggets			
☐ 176	Kenny Smith	.05	.02	.01
	Houston Rockets			
☐ 177	Dan Majerle	.08	.04	.01
	Phoenix Suns			
☐ 178	Jeff Malone	.08	.04	.01
	Utah Jazz			
☐ 179	Robert Parish	.10	.05	.01
	Boston Celtics			
☐ 180	Mark Eaton	.05	.02	.01
	Utah Jazz			
☐ 181	Rony Seikaly	.05	.02	.01
	Miami Heat			
☐ 182	Tony Campbell	.05	.02	.01
	Minnesota Timberwolves			
☐ 183	Kevin McHale	.10	.05	.01
	Boston Celtics			
☐ 184	Thurl Bailey	.05	.02	.01
	Minnesota Timberwolves			
☐ 185	Kevin Edwards	.05	.02	.01
	Miami Heat			
☐ 186	Gerald Glass	.05	.02	.01
	Minnesota Timberwolves			
☐ 187	Hersey Hawkins	.08	.04	.01
	Philadelphia 76ers			
☐ 188	Sam Mitchell	.05	.02	.01
	Minnesota Timberwolves			
☐ 189	Brian Shaw	.05	.02	.01
	Miami Heat			
☐ 190	Felton Spencer	.05	.02	.01
	Minnesota Timberwolves			
☐ 191	Mark Macon	.05	.02	.01
	Denver Nuggets			
☐ 192	Jerry Reynolds	.05	.02	.01
	Orlando Magic			
☐ 193	Dale Davis	.10	.05	.01
	Indiana Pacers			
☐ 194	Sleepy Floyd	.05	.02	.01
	Houston Rockets			
☐ 195	A.C. Green	.10	.05	.01
	Los Angeles Lakers			
☐ 196	Terry Catledge	.05	.02	.01
	Orlando Magic			
☐ 197	Byron Scott	.08	.04	.01
	Los Angeles Lakers			

☐ 198	Sam Bowie .05 .02 .01 New Jersey Nets				
☐ 199	Vlade Divac .10 .05 .01 Los Angeles Lakers				
☐ 200	Form Checklist 2 .25 .11 .03 Michael Jordan Chicago Bulls				
☐ 201	Brad Lohaus .05 .02 .01 Milwaukee Bucks				
☐ 202	Johnny Newman .05 .02 .01 Charlotte Hornets				
☐ 203	Gary Grant .05 .02 .01 Los Angeles Clippers				
☐ 204	Sidney Green .05 .02 .01 San Antonio Spurs				
☐ 205	Frank Brickowski .05 .02 .01 Milwaukee Bucks				
☐ 206	Anthony Bowie .05 .02 .01 Orlando Magic				
☐ 207	Duane Causwell .05 .02 .01 Sacramento Kings				
☐ 208	A.J. English .05 .02 .01 Washington Bullets				
☐ 209	Mark Aguirre .08 .04 .01 Detroit Pistons				
☐ 210	Jon Koncak .05 .02 .01 Atlanta Hawks				
☐ 211	Kevin Gamble .05 .02 .01 Boston Celtics				
☐ 212	Craig Ehlo .05 .02 .01 Cleveland Cavaliers				
☐ 213	Herb Williams .05 .02 .01 Dallas Mavericks				
☐ 214	Cedric Ceballos .10 .05 .01 Phoenix Suns				
☐ 215	Mark Jackson .05 .02 .01 New York Knicks				
☐ 216	John Bagley .05 .02 .01 Boston Celtics				
☐ 217	Ron Anderson .05 .02 .01 Philadelphia 76ers				
☐ 218	John Battle .05 .02 .01 Cleveland Cavaliers				
☐ 219	Kevin Lynch .05 .02 .01 Charlotte Hornets				
☐ 220	Donald Hodge .05 .02 .01 Dallas Mavericks				
☐ 221	Chris Gatling .05 .02 .01 Golden State Warriors				
☐ 222	Muggsy Bogues .10 .05 .01 Charlotte Hornets				
☐ 223	Bill Laimbeer .08 .04 .01 Detroit Pistons				
☐ 224	Anthony Bonner .05 .02 .01 Sacramento Kings				
☐ 225	Fred Roberts .05 .02 .01 Milwaukee Bucks				
☐ 226	Larry Stewart .05 .02 .01 Washington Bullets				
☐ 227	Darrell Walker .05 .02 .01 Detroit Pistons				
☐ 228	Larry Smith .05 .02 .01 Houston Rockets				
☐ 229	Billy Owens .10 .05 .01 Golden State Warriors				
☐ 230	Vinnie Johnson .08 .04 .01 San Antonio Spurs				
☐ 231	Johnny Dawkins .05 .02 .01 Philadelphia 76ers				
☐ 232	Rick Fox .05 .02 .01 Boston Celtics				

☐ 233 Travis Mays .05 .02 .01
Atlanta Hawks
☐ 234 Mark Price .10 .05 .01
Cleveland Cavaliers
☐ 235 Derrick McKey .10 .05 .01
Seattle Supersonics
☐ 236 Greg Anthony .05 .02 .01
New York Knicks
☐ 237 Doug Smith .05 .02 .01
Dallas Mavericks
☐ 238 Alec Kessler .05 .02 .01
Miami Heat
☐ 239 Anthony Mason .10 .05 .01
New York Knicks
☐ 240 Shawn Kemp .75 .35 .09
Seattle Supersonics
☐ 241 Jim Les .05 .02 .01
Sacramento Kings
☐ 242 Dennis Rodman .20 .09 .03
Detroit Pistons
☐ 243 Lionel Simmons .05 .02 .01
Sacramento Kings
☐ 244 Pervis Ellison .05 .02 .01
Washington Bullets
☐ 245 Terrell Brandon .08 .04 .01
Cleveland Cavaliers
☐ 246 Mark Bryant .05 .02 .01
Portland Trail Blazers
☐ 247 Brad Daugherty .08 .04 .01
Cleveland Cavaliers
☐ 248 Scott Brooks .05 .02 .01
Minnesota Timberwolves
☐ 249 Sarunas Marciulionis .05 .02 .01
Golden State Warriors
☐ 250 Danny Ferry .05 .02 .01
Cleveland Cavaliers
☐ 251 Loy Vaught .08 .04 .01
Los Angeles Clippers
☐ 252 Dee Brown .08 .04 .01
Boston Celtics
☐ 253 Alvin Robertson .05 .02 .01
Milwaukee Bucks
☐ 254 Charles Smith .05 .02 .01
Los Angeles Clippers
☐ 255 Dikembe Mutombo .40 .18 .05
Denver Nuggets
☐ 256 Greg Kite .05 .02 .01
Orlando Magic
☐ 257 Ed Pinckney .05 .02 .01
Boston Celtics
☐ 258 Ron Harper .08 .04 .01
Los Angeles Clippers
☐ 259 Elliot Perry .10 .05 .01
Charlotte Hornets
☐ 260 Rafael Addison .05 .02 .01
New Jersey Nets
☐ 261 Tim Hardaway .10 .05 .01
Golden State Warriors
☐ 262 Randy Brown .05 .02 .01
Sacramento Kings
☐ 263 Isiah Thomas .15 .07 .02
Detroit Pistons
☐ 264 Victor Alexander .05 .02 .01
Golden State Warriors
☐ 265 Wayman Tisdale .08 .04 .01
Sacramento Kings
☐ 266 Harvey Grant .05 .02 .01
Washington Bullets
☐ 267 Mike Iuzzolino .05 .02 .01
Dallas Mavericks
☐ 268 Joe Dumars .15 .07 .02

Detroit Pistons				
□ 269	Xavier McDaniel	.08	.04	.01
	New York Knicks			
□ 270	Jeff Sanders	.05	.02	.01
	Atlanta Hawks			
□ 271	Danny Manning	.10	.05	.01
	Los Angeles Clippers			
□ 272	Jayson Williams	.05	.02	.01
	Philadelphia 76ers			
□ 273	Ricky Pierce	.08	.04	.01
	Seattle Supersonics			
□ 274	Will Perdue	.05	.02	.01
	Chicago Bulls			
□ 275	Dana Barros	.10	.05	.01
	Seattle Supersonics			
□ 276	Randy Breuer	.05	.02	.01
	Minnesota Timberwolves			
□ 277	Manute Bol	.05	.02	.01
	Philadelphia 76ers			
□ 278	Negele Knight	.05	.02	.01
	Phoenix Suns			
□ 279	Rodney McCray	.05	.02	.01
	Dallas Mavericks			
□ 280	Greg Sutton	.05	.02	.01
	San Antonio Spurs			
□ 281	Larry Nance	.08	.04	.01
	Cleveland Cavaliers			
□ 282	John Starks	.10	.05	.01
	New York Knicks			
□ 283	Pete Chilcutt	.05	.02	.01
	Sacramento Kings			
□ 284	Kenny Gattison	.05	.02	.01
	Charlotte Hornets			
□ 285	Stacey King	.05	.02	.01
	Chicago Bulls			
□ 286	Bernard King	.10	.05	.01
	Washington Bullets			
□ 287	Larry Johnson	.50	.23	.06
	Charlotte Hornets			
□ 288	John Williams	.08	.04	.01
	Cleveland Cavaliers			
□ 289	Dell Curry	.05	.02	.01
	Charlotte Hornets			
□ 290	Orlando Woolridge	.05	.02	.01
	Detroit Pistons			
□ 291	Nate McMillan	.05	.02	.01
	Seattle Supersonics			
□ 292	Terry Mills	.08	.04	.01
	New Jersey Nets			
□ 293	Sherman Douglas	.05	.02	.01
	Boston Celtics			
□ 294	Charles Shackleford	.05	.02	.01
	Philadelphia 76ers			
□ 295	Ken Norman	.05	.02	.01
	Los Angeles Clippers			
□ 296	LaSalle Thompson	.05	.02	.01
	Indiana Pacers			
□ 297	Chris Mullin	.10	.05	.01
	Golden State Warriors			
□ 298	Eddie Johnson	.08	.04	.01
	Seattle Supersonics			
□ 299	Armon Gilliam	.05	.02	.01
	Philadelphia 76ers			
□ 300	Michael Cage	.05	.02	.01
	Seattle Supersonics			
□ 301	Moses Malone	.15	.07	.02
	Milwaukee Bucks			
□ 302	Charles Oakley	.08	.04	.01
	New York Knicks			
□ 303	David Wingate	.05	.02	.01
	Washington Bullets			
□ 304	Steve Kerr	.05	.02	.01
	Cleveland Cavaliers			
□ 305	Tyrone Hill	.08	.04	.01
	Golden State Warriors			
□ 306	Mark West	.05	.02	.01
	Phoenix Suns			
□ 307	Fat Lever	.05	.02	.01
	Dallas Mavericks			
□ 308	J.R. Reid	.05	.02	.01
	Charlotte Hornets			
□ 309	Ed Nealy	.05	.02	.01
	Phoenix Suns			
□ 310	Form Checklist 3	.25	.11	.03
	Michael Jordan			
	Chicago Bulls			
□ 311	Alaa Abdelnaby	.05	.02	.01
	Boston Celtics			
□ 312	Stacey Augmon	.10	.05	.01
	Atlanta Hawks			
□ 313	Anthony Avent	.05	.02	.01
	Milwaukee Bucks			
□ 314	Walter Bond	.05	.02	.01
	Dallas Mavericks			
□ 315	Byron Houston	.05	.02	.01
	Golden State Warriors			
□ 316	Rick Mahorn	.05	.02	.01
	New Jersey Nets			
□ 317	Sam Mitchell	.05	.02	.01
	Indiana Pacers			
□ 318	Mookie Blaylock	.08	.04	.01
	Atlanta Hawks			
□ 319	Lance Blanks	.05	.02	.01
	Minnesota Timberwolves			
□ 320	John Williams	.05	.02	.01
	Los Angeles Clippers			
□ 321	Rolando Blackman	.08	.04	.01
	New York Knicks			
□ 322	Danny Ainge	.08	.04	.01
	Phoenix Suns			
□ 323	Gerald Glass	.05	.02	.01
	Detroit Pistons			
□ 324	Robert Pack	.05	.02	.01
	Denver Nuggets			
□ 325	Oliver Miller	.25	.11	.03
	Phoenix Suns			
□ 326	Charles Smith	.05	.02	.01
	New York Knicks			
□ 327	Duane Ferrell	.05	.02	.01
	Atlanta Hawks			
□ 328	Pooh Richardson	.05	.02	.01
	Indiana Pacers			
□ 329	Scott Brooks	.05	.02	.01
	Houston Rockets			
□ 330	Walt Williams	.60	.25	.08
	Sacramento Kings			
□ 331	Andrew Lang	.05	.02	.01
	Philadelphia 76ers			
□ 332	Eric Murdock	.05	.02	.01
	Milwaukee Bucks			
□ 333	Vinny Del Negro	.05	.02	.01
	San Antonio Spurs			
□ 334	Charles Barkley	.60	.25	.08
	Phoenix Suns			
□ 335	James Edwards	.05	.02	.01
	Los Angeles Lakers			
□ 336	Xavier McDaniel	.08	.04	.01
	Boston Celtics			
□ 337	Paul Graham	.05	.02	.01
	Atlanta Hawks			
□ 338	David Wingate	.05	.02	.01
	Charlotte Hornets			

☐ 339 Richard Dumas .... .15 Phoenix Suns	.07	.02
☐ 340 Jay Humphries .... .05 Utah Jazz	.02	.01
☐ 341 Mark Jackson .... .05 Los Angeles Clippers	.02	.01
☐ 342 John Salley .... .05 Miami Heat	.02	.01
☐ 343 Jon Koncak .... .05 Atlanta Hawks	.02	.01
☐ 344 Rodney McCray .... .05 Chicago Bulls	.02	.01
☐ 345 Chuck Person .... .08 Minnesota Timberwolves	.04	.01
☐ 346 Mario Elie .... .05 Portland Trail Blazers	.02	.01
☐ 347 Frank Johnson .... .05 Phoenix Suns	.02	.01
☐ 348 Rumeal Robinson .... .05 New Jersey Nets	.02	.01
☐ 349 Terry Mills .... .08 Detroit Pistons	.04	.01
☐ 350 Kevin Willis TFC .... .05 Atlanta Hawks	.02	.01
☐ 351 Dee Brown TFC .... .05 Boston Celtics	.02	.01
☐ 352 Muggsy Bogues TFC .... .05 Charlotte Hornets	.02	.01
☐ 353 B.J. Armstrong TFC ..... .05 Chicago Bulls	.02	.01
☐ 354 Larry Nance TFC .... .05 Cleveland Cavaliers	.02	.01
☐ 355 Doug Smith TFC........... .05 Dallas Mavericks	.02	.01
☐ 356 Robert Pack TFC .... .05 Denver Nuggets	.02	.01
☐ 357 Joe Dumars TFC .... .08 Detroit Pistons	.04	.01
☐ 358 Sarunas Marciulionis TFC .05 Golden State Warriors	.02	.01
☐ 359 Kenny Smith TFC .... .05 Houston Rockets	.02	.01
☐ 360 Pooh Richardson TFC .. .05 Indiana Pacers	.02	.01
☐ 361 Mark Jackson TFC .... .05 Los Angeles Clippers	.02	.01
☐ 362 Sedale Threatt TFC...... .05 Los Angeles Lakers	.02	.01
☐ 363 Grant Long TFC............ .05 Miami Heat	.02	.01
☐ 364 Eric Murdock TFC .... .05 Milwaukee Bucks	.02	.01
☐ 365 Doug West TFC .... .05 Minnesota Timberwolves	.02	.01
☐ 366 Kenny Anderson TFC ... .05 New Jersey Nets	.02	.01
☐ 367 Anthony Mason TFC..... .05 New York Knicks	.02	.01
☐ 368 Nick Anderson TFC ...... .05 Orlando Magic	.02	.01
☐ 369 Jeff Hornacek TFC........ .05 Philadelphia 76ers	.02	.01
☐ 370 Dan Majerle TFC.......... .05 Phoenix Suns	.02	.01
☐ 371 Clifford Robinson TFC.. .05 Portland Trail Blazers	.02	.01
☐ 372 Lionel Simmons TFC..... .05 Sacramento Kings	.02	.01
☐ 373 Dale Ellis TFC .... .05 San Antonio Spurs	.02	.01
☐ 374 Gary Payton TFC .... .05 Seattle Supersonics	.02	.01
☐ 375 David Benoit TFC .... .05 Utah Jazz	.02	.01
☐ 376 Harvey Grant TFC........ .05 Washington Bullets	.02	.01
☐ 377 Buck Johnson .... .05 Washington Bullets	.02	.01
☐ 378 Brian Howard .... .05 Dallas Mavericks	.02	.01
☐ 379 Travis Mays .... .05 Atlanta Hawks	.02	.01
☐ 380 Jud Buechler............... .05 Golden State Warriors	.02	.01
☐ 381 Matt Geiger .... .05 Miami Heat	.02	.01
☐ 382 Bob McCann .... .05 Minnesota Timberwolves	.02	.01
☐ 383 Cedric Ceballos .... .10 Phoenix Suns	.05	.01
☐ 384 Rod Strickland .... .08 Portland Trail Blazers	.04	.01
☐ 385 Kiki Vandeweghe.......... .05 Los Angeles Clippers	.02	.01
☐ 386 Latrell Sprewell .... 2.00 Golden State Warriors	.90	.25
☐ 387 Larry Krystkowiak .... .05 Utah Jazz	.02	.01
☐ 388 Dale Ellis .... .08 San Antonio Spurs	.04	.01
☐ 389 Trent Tucker .... .05 Chicago Bulls	.02	.01
☐ 390 Negele Knight .... .05 Phoenix Suns	.02	.01
☐ 391 Stanley Roberts .... .05 Los Angeles Clippers	.02	.01
☐ 392 Tony Campbell .... .05 New York Knicks	.02	.01
☐ 393 Tim Perry .... .05 Philadelphia 76ers	.02	.01
☐ 394 Doug Overton .... .05 Washington Bullets	.02	.01
☐ 395 Dan Majerle .... .08 Phoenix Suns	.04	.01
☐ 396 Duane Cooper .... .05 Los Angeles Lakers	.02	.01
☐ 397 Kevin Willis .... .08 Atlanta Hawks	.04	.01
☐ 398 Micheal Williams .... .05 Minnesota Timberwolves	.02	.01
☐ 399 Avery Johnson .... .05 San Antonio Spurs	.02	.01
☐ 400 Dominique Wilkins....... .15 Atlanta Hawks	.07	.02
☐ 401 Chris Smith .... .05 Minnesota Timberwolves	.02	.01
☐ 402 Blair Rasmussen .... .05 Atlanta Hawks	.02	.01
☐ 403 Jeff Hornacek .... .08 Philadelphia 76ers	.04	.01
☐ 404 Blue Edwards............... .05 Milwaukee Bucks	.02	.01
☐ 405 Olden Polynice............. .05 Detroit Pistons	.02	.01
☐ 406 Jeff Grayer .... .05 Golden State Warriors	.02	.01
☐ 407 Tony Bennett............... .05 Charlotte Hornets	.02	.01
☐ 408 Don MacLean............... .05 Washington Bullets	.02	.01
☐ 409 Tom Chambers .... .10 Phoenix Suns	.05	.01

☐ 410	Keith Jennings .... .05 Golden State Warriors	.02	.01
☐ 411	Gerald Wilkins .... .05 Cleveland Cavaliers	.02	.01
☐ 412	Kennard Winchester .. .05 Houston Rockets	.02	.01
☐ 413	Doc Rivers .... .05 New York Knicks	.02	.01
☐ 414	Brent Price.................. .05 Washington Bullets	.02	.01
☐ 415	Mark West .... .05 Phoenix Suns	.02	.01
☐ 416	J.R. Reid .... .05 San Antonio Spurs	.02	.01
☐ 417	Jon Barry .... .08 Milwaukee Bucks	.04	.01
☐ 418	Kevin Johnson .... .15 Phoenix Suns	.07	.02
☐ 419	Form Checklist.......... .25 (Michael Jordan)	.11	.03
☐ 420	Form Checklist.............. .25 (Michael Jordan)	.11	.03
☐ 421	John Stockton............. .10 Karl Malone NBA All-Star Game Checklist	.05	.01
☐ 422	Scottie Pippen AS .... .10	.05	.01
☐ 423	Larry Johnson AS .... .25	.11	.03
☐ 424	Shaquille O'Neal AS ... 2.50	1.15	.30
☐ 425	Michael Jordan AS 2.00	.90	.25
☐ 426	Isiah Thomas AS.......... .08	.04	.01
☐ 427	Brad Daugherty AS ...... .05	.02	.01
☐ 428	Joe Dumars AS............ .08	.04	.01
☐ 429	Patrick Ewing AS .... .10	.05	.01
☐ 430	Larry Nance AS............ .05	.02	.01
☐ 431	Mark Price AS .... .05	.02	.01
☐ 432	Detlef Schrempf AS ...... .05	.02	.01
☐ 433	Dominique Wilkins AS . .08	.04	.01
☐ 434	Karl Malone AS .... .10	.05	.01
☐ 435	Charles Barkley AS....... .30	.14	.04
☐ 436	David Robinson AS .... .30	.14	.04
☐ 437	John Stockton AS .... .10	.05	.01
☐ 438	Clyde Drexler AS .... .10	.05	.01
☐ 439	Sean Elliott AS .... .05	.02	.01
☐ 440	Tim Hardaway AS .... .05	.02	.01
☐ 441	Shawn Kemp AS............ .40	.18	.05
☐ 442	Dan Majerle AS .... .05	.02	.01
☐ 443	Danny Manning AS .... .05	.02	.01
☐ 444	Hakeem Olajuwon AS.... .40	.18	.05
☐ 445	Terry Porter AS............. .05	.02	.01
☐ 446	Harold Miner FACE........ .05 Miami Heat	.02	.01
☐ 447	David Benoit FACE .... .05 Utah Jazz	.02	.01
☐ 448	Cedric Ceballos FACE... .05 Phoenix Suns	.02	.01
☐ 449	Chris Jackson FACE..... .05 Denver Nuggets	.02	.01
☐ 450	Tim Perry FACE............. .05 Philadelphia 76ers	.02	.01
☐ 451	Kenny Smith FACE........ .05 Houston Rockets	.02	.01
☐ 452	Clarence Weatherspoon .20 FACE Philadelphia 76ers	.09	.03
☐ 453A	Michael Jordan .... 100.00 FACE ERR (Slam Dunk Champ in 1985 and 1990) Chicago Bulls	45.00	12.50
☐ 453B	Michael Jordan FACE 2.00 COR (Slam Dunk Champ	.90	.25

	in 1987 and 1988) Chicago Bulls		
☐ 454A	Dominique Wilkins .. 8.00 FACE ERR (Slam Dunk Champ in 1987 and 1988) Atlanta Hawks	3.60	1.00
☐ 454B	Dominique Wilkins .... .15 FACE COR (Slam Dunk Champ in 1985 and 1990) Atlanta Hawks	.07	.02
☐ 455	Anthony Peeler .... .05 Duane Cooper CL Los Angeles Lakers	.02	.01
☐ 456	Adam Keefe TP .... .05 Atlanta Hawks	.02	.01
☐ 457	Alonzo Mourning TP...... .60 Charlotte Hornets	.25	.08
☐ 458	Jim Jackson TP .... 1.25 Dallas Mavericks	.55	.16
☐ 459	Sean Rooks TP .... .05 Dallas Mavericks	.02	.01
☐ 460	LaPhonso Ellis TP......... .08 Denver Nuggets	.04	.01
☐ 461	Bryant Stith TP............. .05 Denver Nuggets	.02	.01
☐ 462	Byron Houston TP .... .05 Golden State Warriors	.02	.01
☐ 463	Latrell Sprewell TP......... .60 Golden State Warriors	.25	.08
☐ 464	Robert Horry TP............. .25 Houston Rockets	.11	.03
☐ 465	Malik Sealy TP .... .05 Indiana Pacers	.02	.01
☐ 466	Doug Christie TP .... .05 Los Angeles Lakers	.02	.01
☐ 467	Duane Cooper TP .... .05 Los Angeles Lakers	.02	.01
☐ 468	Anthony Peeler TP .... .05 Los Angeles Lakers	.02	.01
☐ 469	Harold Miner TP............. .05 Miami Heat	.02	.01
☐ 470	Todd Day TP .... .08 Milwaukee Bucks	.04	.01
☐ 471	Lee Mayberry TP .... .05 Milwaukee Bucks	.02	.01
☐ 472	Christian Laettner TP ... .20 Minnesota Timberwolves	.09	.03
☐ 473	Hubert Davis TP............. .05 New York Knicks	.02	.01
☐ 474	Shaquille O'Neal TP ... 2.50 Orlando Magic	1.15	.30
☐ 475	Clarence Weatherspoon TP .20 Philadelphia 76ers	.09	.03
☐ 476	Richard Dumas TP......... .05 Phoenix Suns	.02	.01
☐ 477	Oliver Miller TP .... .05 Phoenix Suns	.02	.01
☐ 478	Tracy Murray TP .... .05 Portland Trail Blazers	.02	.01
☐ 479	Walt Williams TP .... .20 Sacramento Kings	.09	.03
☐ 480	Lloyd Daniels TP............ .05 San Antonio Spurs	.02	.01
☐ 481	Tom Gugliotta TP .... .10 Washington Bullets	.05	.01
☐ 482	Brent Price TP................ .05 Washington Bullets	.02	.01
☐ 483	Mark Aguirre GF............ .05 Detroit Pistons	.02	.01
☐ 484	Frank Brickowski GF .... .05 Milwaukee Bucks	.02	.01

☐ 485 Derrick Coleman GF..... .05 New Jersey Nets		.02	.01
☐ 486 Clyde Drexler GF........... .10 Portland Trail Blazers		.05	.01
☐ 487 Harvey Grant GF............ .05 Washington Bullets		.02	.01
☐ 488 Michael Jordan GF... 2.00 Chicago Bulls		.90	.25
☐ 489 Karl Malone GF .... .10 Utah Jazz		.05	.01
☐ 490 Xavier McDaniel GF...... .05 Boston Celtics		.02	.01
☐ 491 Drazen Petrovic GF ...... .05 New Jersey Nets		.02	.01
☐ 492 John Starks GF............. .05 New York Knicks		.02	.01
☐ 493 Robert Parish GF .... .05 Boston Celtics		.02	.01
☐ 494 Christian Laettner GF.... .20 Minnesota Timberwolves		.09	.03
☐ 495 Ron Harper GF............. .05 Los Angeles Clippers		.02	.01
☐ 496 David Robinson GF...... .30 San Antonio Spurs		.14	.04
☐ 497 John Salley GF............. .05 Miami Heat		.02	.01
☐ 498 Brad Daugherty ST....... .05 Mark Price Cleveland Cavaliers		.02	.01
☐ 499 Dikembe Mutombo ST.. .08 Chris Jackson Denver Nuggets		.04	.01
☐ 500 Isiah Thomas ST........... .08 Joe Dumars Detroit Pistons		.04	.01
☐ 501 Hakeem Olajuwon......... .10 Otis Thorpe ST Houston Rockets		.05	.01
☐ 502 Derrick Coleman ST...... .05 Drazen Petrovic New Jersey Nets		.02	.01
☐ 503 Terry Porter ST .... .08 Clyde Drexler Portland Trail Blazers		.04	.01
☐ 504 Lionel Simmons ST ...... .05 Mitch Richmond Sacramento Kings		.02	.01
☐ 505 David Robinson ST....... .10 Sean Elliott San Antonio Spurs		.05	.01
☐ 506 Michael Jordan FAN... 2.00 Chicago Bulls		.90	.25
☐ 507 Larry Bird FAN .... .50 Boston Celtics		.23	.06
☐ 508 Karl Malone FAN .... .10 Utah Jazz		.05	.01
☐ 509 Dikembe Mutombo FAN .20 Denver Nuggets		.09	.03
☐ 510 Bird/Jordan FAN .... 1.00 SP1 Bird/Magic Retirement 3.00 Larry Bird Magic Johnson		.45 1.35	.13 .40
☐ SP2 20,000 Points............. 8.00 Dominique Wilkins Atlanta Hawks (Nov. 6, 1992) Michael Jordan Chicago Bulls (Jan. 8, 1993)		3.60	1.00

1992-93 Upper Deck All-Division

Inserted one per second series red or gray jumbo pack, this 20-card set consists of Upper Deck's selection of the top five players in each of the NBA's four divisions. There is a special logo representing each division. The cards are arranged according to division as follows: Atlantic (1-5), Central (6-10), Midwest (11-15), and Pacific (16-20). These standard size (2 1/2" by 3 1/2") cards are numbered with an "AD" prefix. The fronts feature full-bleed, color, action player photos. A black and tan color-coded bar outlined with gold foil carries the player's name and position. These cards can be distinguished by an All-Division Team icon in the lower left corner above the player's name. The backs display career highlights against a light blue panel. A U.S. map shows the player's division. The cards are numbered on the back.

	MINT	NRMT	EXC
COMPLETE SET (20)	25.00	11.50	3.10
COMMON CARD (AD1-AD20) ..	.25	.11	.03
☐ AD1 Shaquille O'Neal.......	12.00	5.50	1.50
☐ AD2 Derrick Coleman...........	.35	.16	.04
☐ AD3 Glen Rice	.35	.16	.04
☐ AD4 Reggie Lewis...............	.25	.11	.03
☐ AD5 Kenny Anderson...........	.35	.16	.04
☐ AD6 Brad Daugherty	.25	.11	.03
☐ AD7 Dominique Wilkins.......	.50	.23	.06
☐ AD8 Larry Johnson.............	.75	.35	.09
☐ AD9 Michael Jordan........	10.00	4.50	1.25
☐ AD10 Mark Price.................	.35	.16	.04
☐ AD11 David Robinson.......	1.50	.65	.19
☐ AD12 Karl Malone.............	.75	.35	.09
☐ AD13 Sean Elliott..............	.25	.11	.03

Under AD2: New Jersey Nets
Under AD3: Miami Heat
Under AD4: Boston Celtics
Under AD5: New Jersey Nets
Under AD6: Cleveland Cavaliers
Under AD7: Atlanta Hawks
Under AD8: Charlotte Hornets
Under AD9: Chicago Bulls
Under AD10: Cleveland Cavaliers
Under AD11: San Antonio Spurs
Under AD12: Utah Jazz

	MINT	NRMT	EXC
San Antonio Spurs			
☐ AD14 John Stockton	.75	.35	.09
Utah Jazz			
☐ AD15 Derek Harper	.25	.11	.03
Dallas Mavericks			
☐ AD16 Kevin Duckworth	.25	.11	.03
Portland Trail Blazers			
☐ AD17 Chris Mullin	.35	.16	.04
Golden State Warriors			
☐ AD18 Charles Barkley	1.50	.65	.19
Phoenix Suns			
☐ AD19 Tim Hardaway	.35	.16	.04
Golden State Warriors			
☐ AD20 Clyde Drexler	.75	.35	.09
Portland Trail Blazers			

1992-93 Upper Deck All-NBA

This ten-card set featuring the 1991-92 All-NBA team was issued one per 27-card low series Locker pack. Each plastic locker box contained four specially wrapped. The cards measure the standard size (2 1/2" by 3 1/2"). The fronts feature full-bleed color action player photos with black bottom borders. The player's name is foil-stamped in the border, and the words "All-NBA Team" are foil-stamped at the top. Gold and silver foil stamping are used to designate the First (1-5) and Second Teams (6-10) respectively. The backs carry a close-up player photo and career summary. The cards are numbered on the back with an "AN" prefix.

	MINT	NRMT	EXC
COMPLETE SET (10)	80.00	36.00	10.00
COMMON CARD (AN1-AN10)	2.00	.90	.25
☐ AN1 Michael Jordan	50.00	23.00	6.25
Chicago Bulls			
☐ AN2 Clyde Drexler	4.00	1.80	.50
Portland Trail Blazers			
☐ AN3 David Robinson	8.00	3.60	1.00
San Antonio Spurs			
☐ AN4 Karl Malone	4.00	1.80	.50
Utah Jazz			
☐ AN5 Chris Mullin	2.00	.90	.25
Golden State Warriors			
☐ AN6 John Stockton	4.00	1.80	.50

	MINT	NRMT	EXC
Utah Jazz			
☐ AN7 Tim Hardaway	2.00	.90	.25
Golden State Warriors			
☐ AN8 Patrick Ewing	4.00	1.80	.50
New York Knicks			
☐ AN9 Scottie Pippen	4.00	1.80	.50
Chicago Bulls			
☐ AN10 Charles Barkley	8.00	3.60	1.00
Philadelphia 76ers			

1992-93 Upper Deck All-Rookies

Randomly inserted in low series 15-card retail foil packs at a reported rate of one card for every nine packs, this ten-card subset features the top first-year players for the 1991-92 season. Card numbers 1-5 present the first team and card numbers 6-10 the second team. The cards measure the standard size (2 1/2" by 3 1/2"). The cards are numbered with an "AR" prefix. The fronts feature full-bleed, color, action player photos. A gold and red bottom border design carries the player's name, position, the number team (first or second), and an NBA All-Rookie Team icon. The backs carry player profiles. The cards are numbered on the back.

	MINT	NRMT	EXC
COMPLETE SET (10)	8.00	3.60	1.00
COMMON CARD (AR1-AR10)	.50	.23	.06
☐ AR1 Larry Johnson	3.00	1.35	.40
Charlotte Hornets			
☐ AR2 Dikembe Mutombo	2.50	1.15	.30
Denver Nuggets			
☐ AR3 Billy Owens	1.00	.45	.13
Golden State Warriors			
☐ AR4 Steve Smith	1.00	.45	.13
Miami Heat			
☐ AR5 Stacey Augmon	1.00	.45	.13
Atlanta Hawks			
☐ AR6 Rick Fox	.50	.23	.06
Boston Celtics			
☐ AR7 Terrell Brandon	.75	.35	.09
Cleveland Cavaliers			
☐ AR8 Larry Stewart	.50	.23	.06
Washington Bullets			
☐ AR9 Stanley Roberts	.50	.23	.06

Orlando Magic
☐ AR10 Mark Macon .... .50 .23 .06
Denver Nuggets

1992-93 Upper Deck Award Winner Holograms

The 1992-93 Upper Deck Award Winner Holograms set features nine holograms depicting league leaders in various statistical categories. The set also honors 1991-92 award winners such as top Sixth Man, Rookie of the Year, Defensive Player of the Year and Most Valuable Player. Card numbers 1-6 were randomly inserted in all forms of low series packs while card numbers 7-9 were included in all forms of high series packs. The card numbers have an "AW" prefix. The fronts feature holographic cutout images of the player against a game-action photo of the player. The player's name and award are displayed at the bottom. The backs carry vertical, color player photos. A light blue plaque-style panel contains information about the player and the award won. The cards are numbered on the back.

	MINT	NRMT	EXC
COMPLETE SET (9)	35.00	16.00	4.40
COMPLETE LO SERIES (6)	20.00	9.00	2.50
COMPLETE HI SERIES (3)	18.00	8.00	2.30
COMMON CARD (AW1-AW9)	.50	.23	.06

☐ AW1 Michael Jordan........ 15.00 6.75 1.90
Chicago Bulls
Scoring
☐ AW2 John Stockton .... 1.25 .55 .16
Utah Jazz
Steals
☐ AW3 Dennis Rodman.......... .75 .35 .09
Detroit Pistons
Rebounds
☐ AW4 Detlef Schrempf .... .50 .23 .06
Indiana Pacers
Sixth Man
☐ AW5 Larry Johnson .... 1.25 .55 .16
Charlotte Hornets

Rookie of the Year
☐ AW6 David Robinson........ 2.50 1.15 .30
San Antonio Spurs
Blocked Shots
☐ AW7 David Robinson........ 2.50 1.15 .30
San Antonio Spurs
Def. Player of Year
☐ AW8 John Stockton .... 1.25 .55 .16
Utah Jazz
Assists
☐ AW9 Michael Jordan........ 15.00 6.75 1.90
Chicago Bulls
Most Valuable Player

1992-93 Upper Deck Larry Bird Heroes

Randomly inserted into all forms of high series packs, this ten-card set chronicles the career of Larry Bird from his college days at Indiana State University to pro stardom with the Boston Celtics. The cards measure the standard size (2 1/2" by 3 1/2"). The color action player photos on the fronts are bordered on the left and bottom by black borders that carry the card subtitle and "Basketball Heroes, Larry Bird" respectively. On a background shading from white to green, brief summaries of Bird's career are presented on a center panel. The cards are numbered on the back in continuation of the Upper Deck Basketball Heroes.

	MINT	NRMT	EXC
COMPLETE SET (10)	10.00	4.50	1.25
COMMON BIRD (19-27)	1.00	.45	.13

☐ 19 Larry Bird..................... 1.00 .45 .13
1979 College Player
of the Year
☐ 20 Larry Bird..................... 1.00 .45 .13
1979-80 Rookie of
the Year
☐ 21 Larry Bird..................... 1.00 .45 .13
1980-92 12-Time
NBA All-Star
☐ 22 Larry Bird..................... 1.00 .45 .13
1981-86 Three NBA
Championships
☐ 23 Larry Bird..................... 1.00 .45 .13

	MINT	NRMT	EXC
1984-86 3-Time NBA MVP			
☐ 24 Larry Bird	1.00	.45	.13
1986-88 3-Point King			
☐ 25 Larry Bird	1.00	.45	.13
1990 20,000 Points			
☐ 26 Larry Bird	1.00	.45	.13
Larry Legend			
☐ 27 Larry Bird	1.00	.45	.13
(Portrait by Alan Studt)			
☐ NNO Larry Bird	3.00	1.35	.40
Title/Header Card			

1992-93 Upper Deck Wilt Chamberlain Heroes

Randomly inserted in all forms of low series packs, this ten-card set honors Wilt Chamberlain by highlighting various points in his career. The cards are standard size (2 1/2" by 3 1/2"). Circular photos on the fronts depict Wilt from college, to the Globetrotter's to pro basketball. Information on the back corresponds to the portion of his career that is represented on front.

	MINT	NRMT	EXC
COMPLETE SET (10)	5.00	2.30	.60
COMMON CHAMBERLAIN (10-18)	.50	.23	.06
☐ 10 1956-58 College Star	.50	.23	.06
☐ 11 1958-59 Harlem Globetrotter	.50	.23	.06
☐ 12 1960 NBA ROY	.50	.23	.06
☐ 13 1962 100-Point Game	.50	.23	.06
☐ 14 1960-68 Four-time NBA MVP	.50	.23	.06
☐ 15 1960-66 Seven consecutive scoring titles	.50	.23	.06
☐ 16 1971-72 30,000-Point Plateau	.50	.23	.06
☐ 17 1978 Basketball HOF	.50	.23	.06
☐ 18 Basketball Heroes CL	.50	.23	.06
☐ NNO Basketball Heroes (Header card)	1.50	.65	.19

1992-93 Upper Deck 15000 Point Club

Randomly inserted in 15-card high series hobby packs at a reported rate of one card per nine packs, this 20-card set spotlights then-active NBA players who had scored more than 15,000 points in their career. The fronts feature full-bleed color action player photos accented at the top and bottom by team color-coded stripes carrying the phrase "15,000 Point Club" and the player's name respectively. A gold 15,000-Point club logo at the lower left corner carries the season the player joined this elite club. The backs display a small player photo and year-by-year scoring totals. The cards are numbered on the back. These standard size (2 1/2" by 3 1/2") cards are numbered with an "PC" prefix.

	MINT	NRMT	EXC
COMPLETE SET (20)	120.00	55.00	15.00
COMMON CARD (PC1-PC20)	1.50	.65	.19
☐ PC1 Dominique Wilkins Atlanta Hawks	4.00	1.80	.50
☐ PC2 Kevin McHale Boston Celtics	3.00	1.35	.40
☐ PC3 Robert Parish Boston Celtics	3.00	1.35	.40
☐ PC4 Michael Jordan Chicago Bulls	100.00	45.00	12.50
☐ PC5 Isiah Thomas Detroit Pistons	4.00	1.80	.50
☐ PC6 Mark Aguirre Detroit Pistons	1.50	.65	.19
☐ PC7 Kiki Vandeweghe Los Angeles Clippers	1.50	.65	.19
☐ PC8 James Worthy Los Angeles Lakers	3.00	1.35	.40
☐ PC9 Rolando Blackman New York Knicks	1.50	.65	.19
☐ PC10 Moses Malone Milwaukee Bucks	4.00	1.80	.50
☐ PC11 Charles Barkley Phoenix Suns	15.00	6.75	1.90
☐ PC12 Tom Chambers Phoenix Suns	1.50	.65	.19
☐ PC13 Clyde Drexler Portland Trail Blazers	8.00	3.60	1.00
☐ PC14 Terry Cummings San Antonio Spurs	1.50	.65	.19

	MINT	NRMT	EXC
☐ PC15 Eddie Johnson	1.50	.65	.19
Seattle Supersonics			
☐ PC16 Karl Malone	8.00	3.60	1.00
Utah Jazz			
☐ PC17 Bernard King	3.00	1.35	.40
Washington Bullets			
☐ PC18 Larry Nance	1.50	.65	.19
Cleveland Cavaliers			
☐ PC19 Jeff Malone	1.50	.65	.19
Utah Jazz			
☐ PC20 Hakeem Olajuwon	20.00	9.00	2.50
Houston Rockets			

1992-93 Upper Deck Foreign Exchange

Inserted one card per pack in second series 4-pack locker boxes, this ten-card set showcases foreign born players who are stars in the NBA. Each card uses the colors of the flag from the player's homeland as well as a "Foreign Exchange" logo. These standard size (2 1/2" by 3 1/2") cards are numbered with an "FE" prefix. The fronts carry full-bleed, color, action player photos. The player's name, position, and place of birth appear in border stripes at the bottom. The backs display either an action or close-up player photo on a pale beige panel along with a player profile. A small representation of the player's home flag appears at the lower right corner of the picture. The cards are numbered on the back and arranged alphabetically.

	MINT	NRMT	EXC
COMPLETE SET (10)	25.00	11.50	3.10
COMMON CARD (FE1-FE10)	1.00	.45	.13
☐ FE1 Manute Bol	1.00	.45	.13
Philadelphia 76ers			
☐ FE2 Vlade Divac	2.00	.90	.25
Los Angeles Lakers			
☐ FE3 Patrick Ewing	5.00	2.30	.60
New York Knicks			
☐ FE4 Sarunas Marciulionis	1.00	.45	.13
Golden State Warriors			
☐ FE5 Dikembe Mutombo	4.00	1.80	.50
Denver Nuggets			
☐ FE6 Hakeem Olajuwon	12.00	5.50	1.50
Houston Rockets			
☐ FE7 Drazen Petrovic	1.50	.65	.19
New Jersey Nets			
☐ FE8 Detlef Schrempf	2.00	.90	.25
Indiana Pacers			
☐ FE9 Rik Smits	2.00	.90	.25
Indiana Pacers			
☐ FE10 Dominique Wilkins	2.50	1.15	.30
Atlanta Hawks			

1992-93 Upper Deck Rookie Standouts

Randomly inserted in high series retail and high series red jumbo packs at a reported rate of one card per nine packs, this 20-card set honors top rookies who have made the most impact during the 1992-93 NBA season. These standard size (2 1/2" by 3 1/2") cards are numbered on the back with an "RS" prefix. The fronts feature full-bleed, color, action player photos. The player's name and position appear in a teal stripe across the bottom. A "Rookie Standouts" icon overlaps the stripe and the picture at the lower right corner. The backs have a vertical action photo and career highlights within a gold box. A red banner over a gold basketball icon accent the top of the box. The cards are numbered on the back.

	MINT	NRMT	EXC
COMPLETE SET (20)	25.00	11.50	3.10
COMMON CARD (RS1-RS20)	.25	.11	.03
☐ RS1 Adam Keefe	.25	.11	.03
Atlanta Hawks			
☐ RS2 Alonzo Mourning	4.00	1.80	.50
Charlotte Hornets			
☐ RS3 Sean Rooks	.25	.11	.03
Dallas Mavericks			
☐ RS4 LaPhonso Ellis	.50	.23	.06
Denver Nuggets			
☐ RS5 Latrell Sprewell	4.00	1.80	.50
Golden State Warriors			
☐ RS6 Robert Horry	1.50	.65	.19
Houston Rockets			
☐ RS7 Malik Sealy	.50	.23	.06
Indiana Pacers			
☐ RS8 Anthony Peeler	.25	.11	.03
Los Angeles Lakers			

		MINT	NRMT	EXC
☐ RS9	Harold Miner	.50	.23	.06
	Miami Heat			
☐ RS10	Anthony Avent	.25	.11	.03
	Milwaukee Bucks			
☐ RS11	Todd Day	.75	.35	.09
	Milwaukee Bucks			
☐ RS12	Lee Mayberry	.25	.11	.03
	Milwaukee Bucks			
☐ RS13	Christian Laettner	1.25	.55	.16
	Minnesota Timberwolves			
☐ RS14	Hubert Davis	.25	.11	.03
	New York Knicks			
☐ RS15	Shaquille O'Neal	15.00	6.75	1.90
	Orlando Magic			
☐ RS16	Clarence Weatherspoon	1.25	.55	.16
	Philadelphia 76ers			
☐ RS17	Richard Dumas	.50	.23	.06
	Phoenix Suns			
☐ RS18	Walt Williams	1.25	.55	.16
	Sacramento Kings			
☐ RS19	Lloyd Daniels	.25	.11	.03
	San Antonio Spurs			
☐ RS20	Tom Gugliotta	1.00	.45	.13
	Washington Bullets			

1992-93 Upper Deck Team MVPs

This 28-card set honors a top player from each NBA team. One "Team MVP" card was inserted into each 1992-93 Upper Deck low series 27-card jumbo pack. Card fronts feature a photo that takes up most of the front. The only other feature on front is the player's name within a bottom border. Backs contain a photo with highlights. These standard size (2 1/2" by 3 1/2") cards are numbered on the back with a "TM" prefix.

	MINT	NRMT	EXC
COMPLETE SET (28)	110.00	50.00	14.00
COMMON CARD (TM1-TM28)	.75	.35	.09
☐ TM1 Checklist Card	50.00	23.00	6.25
Michael Jordan			
Chicago Bulls			
☐ TM2 Dominique Wilkins	2.50	1.15	.30
Atlanta Hawks			
☐ TM3 Reggie Lewis	1.00	.45	.13
Boston Celtics			

☐ TM4 Kendall Gill	.75	.35	.09
Charlotte Hornets			
☐ TM5 Michael Jordan	60.00	27.00	7.50
Chicago Bulls			
☐ TM6 Brad Daugherty	1.00	.45	.13
Cleveland Cavaliers			
☐ TM7 Derek Harper	1.00	.35	.09
Dallas Mavericks			
☐ TM8 Dikembe Mutombo	4.00	1.80	.50
Denver Nuggets			
☐ TM9 Isiah Thomas	2.50	1.15	.30
Detroit Pistons			
☐ TM10 Chris Mullin	1.50	.65	.19
Golden State Warriors			
☐ TM11 Hakeem Olajuwon	12.00	5.50	1.50
Houston Rockets			
☐ TM12 Reggie Miller	5.00	2.30	.60
Indiana Pacers			
☐ TM13 Ron Harper	1.00	.45	.13
Los Angeles Clippers			
☐ TM14 James Worthy	1.50	.65	.19
Los Angeles Lakers			
☐ TM15 Rony Seikaly	.75	.35	.09
Miami Heat			
☐ TM16 Alvin Robertson	.75	.35	.09
Milwaukee Bucks			
☐ TM17 Pooh Richardson	.75	.35	.09
Minnesota Timberwolves			
☐ TM18 Derrick Coleman	1.50	.65	.19
New Jersey Nets			
☐ TM19 Patrick Ewing	5.00	2.30	.60
New York Knicks			
☐ TM20 Scott Skiles	.75	.35	.09
Orlando Magic			
☐ TM21 Hersey Hawkins	1.00	.35	.09
Philadelphia 76ers			
☐ TM22 Kevin Johnson	2.50	1.15	.30
Phoenix Suns			
☐ TM23 Clyde Drexler	5.00	2.30	.60
Portland Trail Blazers			
☐ TM24 Mitch Richmond	2.50	1.15	.30
Sacramento Kings			
☐ TM25 David Robinson	10.00	4.50	1.25
San Antonio Spurs			
☐ TM26 Ricky Pierce	1.00	.45	.13
Seattle Supersonics			
☐ TM27 John Stockton	5.00	2.30	.60
Utah Jazz			
☐ TM28 Pervis Ellison	.75	.35	.09
Washington Bullets			

1992-93 Upper Deck Jerry West Selects

Randomly inserted in 15-card low series hobby packs at a reported rate of one card per nine packs, this 20-card set pays tribute to Jerry West's selection of NBA players who are the most dominant (or projected to be) in ten different basketball skills. The cards measure the standard size (2 1/2" by 3 1/2") and feature color action player photos bordered on the right edge by a white stripe containing the player's name. Two stripes border the bottom of the cards, a black stripe containing a gold foil facsimile

autograph of Jerry West and the word *"Select,"* and a gradated team-colored stripe. This second stripe contains the player's specific achievement. The backs show a smaller color action shot of the player above a pale gray panel containing comments by West. The right edge of the card has a 1/2" white border containing the player's name. A small cut-out action image of Jerry West appears at the lower right corner. Card numbers 1-10 feature his present selections for best in ten different categories while card numbers 11-20 are his future selections. The cards are numbered on the back with a *"JW"* prefix. The set includes four cards of Michael Jordan.

	MINT	NRMT	EXC
COMPLETE SET (20)	100.00	45.00	12.50
COMMON CARD (JW1~JW20)	1.00	.45	.13
☐ JW1 Michael Jordan Chicago Bulls Best Shooter	20.00	9.00	2.50
☐ JW2 Dennis Rodman Detroit Pistons Best Rebounder	2.50	1.15	.30
☐ JW3 David Robinson San Antonio Spurs Best Shot Blocker	8.00	3.60	1.00
☐ JW4 Michael Jordan Chicago Bulls Best Defender	20.00	9.00	2.50
☐ JW5 Magic Johnson Los Angeles Lakers Best Point Guard	4.00	1.80	.50
☐ JW6 Detlef Schrempf Indiana Pacers Best Sixth Man	2.00	.90	.25
☐ JW7 Magic Johnson Los Angeles Lakers Most Inspirational Player	4.00	1.80	.50
☐ JW8 Michael Jordan Chicago Bulls Best All-Around Player	20.00	9.00	2.50
☐ JW9 Michael Jordan Chicago Bulls Best Clutch Player	20.00	9.00	2.50
☐ JW10 Magic Johnson Los Angeles Lakers Best Court Leader	4.00	1.80	.50
☐ JW11 Glen Rice Miami Heat Best Shooter	2.00	.90	.25
☐ JW12 Dikembe Mutombo Denver Nuggets Best Rebounder	3.00	1.35	.40
☐ JW13 Dikembe Mutombo Denver Nuggets Best Shot Blocker	3.00	1.35	.40
☐ JW14 Stacey Augmon Atlanta Hawks Best Defender	1.00	.45	.13
☐ JW15 Tim Hardaway Golden State Warriors Best Point Guard	2.00	.90	.25
☐ JW16 Shawn Kemp Seattle Supersonics Best Sixth Man	10.00	4.50	1.25
☐ JW17 Danny Manning Los Angeles Clippers Most Inspirational Player	2.00	.90	.25
☐ JW18 Larry Johnson Charlotte Hornets Best All-Around Player	4.00	1.80	.50
☐ JW19 Reggie Lewis Boston Celtics Best Clutch Player	2.00	.90	.25
☐ JW20 Tim Hardaway Golden State Warriors Best Court Leader	2.00	.90	.25

1993-94 Upper Deck

This 510-card standard-size (2 1/2" by 3 1/2") UV-coated set was issued in two series of 255. The cards were issued in 12-card hobby and retail packs (36 per box), 22-card green and blue retail jumbo packs (first series only), 22-card red and purple retail jumbo packs (second series only) and 22-card hobby locker packs for both series. Card fronts feature glossy color player action photos on the fronts. The left and bottom borders (team colors) contain the team and player's name respectively. The backs feature another color action player photo at the top. At bottom, player stats are shaded in team colors. Topical subsets featured are the following: Season Leaders (166-177), NBA Playoffs Highlights (178-197), NBA Finals Highlights (198-209), Schedules (210-236), Signature Moves (237-251), Executive Board (421-435), Breakaway Threats (436-455), Game Images (456-465), Skylights (467-480), Top Prospects (482-497) and McDonald's Open (498-507). The cards are numbered on the back. The SP3 card was inserted randomly in all forms of first series packaging with the SP4 in the second series. Both cards were inserted at a rate of 1 in 72 packs. Rookie Cards include Vin Baker, Shawn Bradley, Sam Cassell, Calbert Cheaney, Anfernee Hardaway, Lindsey Hunter, Bobby Hurley, Toni Kukoc, Jamal Mashburn, Dino Rajda, Isaiah Rider, Nick Van Exel and Chris Webber.

	MINT	NRMT	EXC
COMPLETE SET (510)	30.00	13.50	3.80
COMPLETE SERIES 1 (255)	15.00	6.75	1.90
COMPLETE SERIES 2 (255)	15.00	6.75	1.90
COMMON CARD (1-510)	.05	.02	.01

☐ 1 Muggsy Bogues Charlotte Hornets	.10	.05	.01
☐ 2 Kenny Anderson New Jersey Nets	.10	.05	.01
☐ 3 Dell Curry Charlotte Hornets	.05	.02	.01
☐ 4 Charles Smith New York Knicks	.05	.02	.01
☐ 5 Chuck Person Minnesota Timberwolves	.08	.04	.01
☐ 6 Chucky Brown New Jersey Nets	.05	.02	.01
☐ 7 Kevin Johnson Phoenix Suns	.15	.07	.02
☐ 8 Winston Garland Houston Rockets	.05	.02	.01
☐ 9 John Salley Miami Heat	.05	.02	.01
☐ 10 Dale Ellis San Antonio Spurs	.08	.04	.01
☐ 11 Otis Thorpe Houston Rockets	.08	.04	.01
☐ 12 John Stockton Utah Jazz	.30	.14	.04
☐ 13 Kendall Gill Charlotte Hornets	.05	.02	.01
☐ 14 Randy White Dallas Mavericks	.05	.02	.01
☐ 15 Mark Jackson Los Angeles Clippers	.05	.02	.01
☐ 16 Vlade Divac Los Angeles Lakers	.10	.05	.01
☐ 17 Scott Skiles Miami Heat	.05	.02	.01
☐ 18 Xavier McDaniel Boston Celtics	.08	.04	.01
☐ 19 Jeff Hornacek Philadelphia 76ers	.08	.04	.01
☐ 20 Stanley Roberts Los Angeles Clippers	.05	.02	.01
☐ 21 Harold Miner Miami Heat	.05	.02	.01
☐ 22 Terrell Brandon Cleveland Cavaliers	.05	.02	.01
☐ 23 Michael Jordan Chicago Bulls	4.00	1.80	.50
☐ 24 Jim Jackson Dallas Mavericks	.60	.25	.08
☐ 25 Keith Askins Miami Heat	.05	.02	.01
☐ 26 Corey Williams Chicago Bulls	.05	.02	.01
☐ 27 David Benoit Utah Jazz	.05	.02	.01
☐ 28 Charles Oakley New York Knicks	.08	.04	.01
☐ 29 Michael Adams Washington Bullets	.05	.02	.01
☐ 30 Clarence Weatherspoon Philadelphia 76ers	.10	.05	.01
☐ 31 Jon Koncak Atlanta Hawks	.05	.02	.01
☐ 32 Gerald Wilkins Cleveland Cavaliers	.05	.02	.01
☐ 33 Anthony Bowie Orlando Magic	.05	.02	.01
☐ 34 Willie Burton Miami Heat	.05	.02	.01
☐ 35 Stacey Augmon Atlanta Hawks	.08	.04	.01
☐ 36 Doc Rivers New York Knicks	.05	.02	.01
☐ 37 Luc Longley Minnesota Timberwolves	.05	.02	.01
☐ 38 Dee Brown Boston Celtics	.08	.04	.01
☐ 39 Litterial Green Orlando Magic	.05	.02	.01
☐ 40 Dan Majerle Phoenix Suns	.08	.04	.01
☐ 41 Doug West Minnesota Timberwolves	.05	.02	.01
☐ 42 Joe Dumars Detroit Pistons	.15	.07	.02
☐ 43 Dennis Scott Orlando Magic	.05	.02	.01
☐ 44 Mahmoud Abdul-Rauf Denver Nuggets (formerly Chris Jackson)	.05	.02	.01
☐ 45 Mark Eaton Utah Jazz	.05	.02	.01
☐ 46 Danny Ferry Cleveland Cavaliers	.05	.02	.01
☐ 47 Kenny Smith Houston Rockets	.05	.02	.01
☐ 48 Ron Harper Los Angeles Clippers	.08	.04	.01
☐ 49 Adam Keefe Atlanta Hawks	.05	.02	.01
☐ 50 David Robinson San Antonio Spurs	.60	.25	.08
☐ 51 John Starks New York Knicks	.08	.04	.01
☐ 52 Jeff Malone Utah Jazz	.08	.04	.01
☐ 53 Vern Fleming Indiana Pacers	.05	.02	.01
☐ 54 Olden Polynice Los Angeles Clippers	.05	.02	.01
☐ 55 Dikembe Mutombo Denver Nuggets	.25	.11	.03
☐ 56 Chris Morris New Jersey Nets	.05	.02	.01
☐ 57 Paul Graham Atlanta Hawks	.05	.02	.01
☐ 58 Richard Dumas Phoenix Suns	.08	.04	.01
☐ 59 J.R. Reid San Antonio Spurs	.05	.02	.01
☐ 60 Brad Daugherty Cleveland Cavaliers	.08	.04	.01
☐ 61 Blue Edwards Milwaukee Bucks	.05	.02	.01
☐ 62 Mark Macon Denver Nuggets	.05	.02	.01

☐ 63	Latrell Sprewell .... Golden State Warriors	.60	.25	.08
☐ 64	Mitch Richmond .... Sacramento Kings	.15	.07	.02
☐ 65	David Wingate .... Charlotte Hornets	.05	.02	.01
☐ 66	LaSalle Thompson .... Indiana Pacers	.05	.02	.01
☐ 67	Sedale Threatt .... Los Angeles Lakers	.05	.02	.01
☐ 68	Larry Krystkowiak .... Utah Jazz	.05	.02	.01
☐ 69	John Paxson .... Chicago Bulls	.05	.02	.01
☐ 70	Frank Brickowski .... Milwaukee Bucks	.05	.02	.01
☐ 71	Duane Causwell .... Sacramento Kings	.05	.02	.01
☐ 72	Fred Roberts .... Milwaukee Bucks	.05	.02	.01
☐ 73	Rod Strickland .... Portland Trail Blazers	.08	.04	.01
☐ 74	Willie Anderson .... San Antonio Spurs	.05	.02	.01
☐ 75	Thurl Bailey .... Utah Jazz	.05	.02	.01
☐ 76	Ricky Pierce .... Seattle Supersonics	.08	.04	.01
☐ 77	Todd Day .... Milwaukee Bucks	.08	.04	.01
☐ 78	Hot Rod Williams .... Cleveland Cavaliers	.05	.02	.01
☐ 79	Danny Ainge .... Phoenix Suns	.08	.04	.01
☐ 80	Mark West .... Phoenix Suns	.05	.02	.01
☐ 81	Marcus Liberty .... Denver Nuggets	.05	.02	.01
☐ 82	Keith Jennings .... Golden State Warriors	.05	.02	.01
☐ 83	Derrick Coleman .... New Jersey Nets	.10	.05	.01
☐ 84	Larry Stewart .... Washington Bullets	.05	.02	.01
☐ 85	Tracy Murray .... Portland Trail Blazers	.05	.02	.01
☐ 86	Robert Horry .... Houston Rockets	.10	.05	.01
☐ 87	Derek Harper .... Dallas Mavericks	.08	.04	.01
☐ 88	Scott Hastings .... Denver Nuggets	.05	.02	.01
☐ 89	Sam Perkins .... Seattle Supersonics	.08	.04	.01
☐ 90	Clyde Drexler .... Seattle Supersonics	.30	.14	.04
☐ 91	Brent Price .... Washington Bullets	.05	.02	.01
☐ 92	Chris Mullin .... Golden State Warriors	.10	.05	.01
☐ 93	Rafael Addison .... New Jersey Nets	.05	.02	.01
☐ 94	Tyrone Corbin .... Minnesota Timberwolves	.05	.02	.01
☐ 95	Sarunas Marciulionis ..... Golden State Warriors	.05	.02	.01
☐ 96	Antoine Carr .... San Antonio Spurs	.05	.02	.01
☐ 97	Tony Bennett .... Charlotte Hornets	.05	.02	.01
☐ 98	Sam Mitchell .... Indiana Pacers	.05	.02	.01
☐ 99	Lionel Simmons .... Sacramento Kings	.05	.02	.01
☐ 100	Tim Perry .... Phoenix Suns	.05	.02	.01
☐ 101	Horace Grant .... Chicago Bulls	.15	.07	.02
☐ 102	Tom Hammonds .... Denver Nuggets	.05	.02	.01
☐ 103	Walter Bond .... Dallas Mavericks	.05	.02	.01
☐ 104	Detlef Schrempf .... Indiana Pacers	.10	.05	.01
☐ 105	Terry Porter .... Portland Trail Blazers	.08	.04	.01
☐ 106	Dan Schayes .... Milwaukee Bucks	.05	.02	.01
☐ 107	Rumeal Robinson .... New Jersey Nets	.05	.02	.01
☐ 108	Gerald Glass .... Detroit Pistons	.05	.02	.01
☐ 109	Mike Gminski .... Charlotte Hornets	.05	.02	.01
☐ 110	Terry Mills .... Detroit Pistons	.05	.02	.01
☐ 111	Loy Vaught .... Los Angeles Clippers	.08	.04	.01
☐ 112	Jim Les .... Sacramento Kings	.05	.02	.01
☐ 113	Byron Houston .... Golden State Warriors	.05	.02	.01
☐ 114	Randy Brown .... Sacramento Kings	.05	.02	.01
☐ 115	Anthony Avent .... Milwaukee Bucks	.05	.02	.01
☐ 116	Donald Hodge .... Dallas Mavericks	.05	.02	.01
☐ 117	Kevin Willis .... Atlanta Hawks	.08	.04	.01
☐ 118	Robert Pack .... Denver Nuggets	.05	.02	.01
☐ 119	Dale Davis .... Indiana Pacers	.08	.04	.01
☐ 120	Grant Long .... Miami Heat	.05	.02	.01
☐ 121	Anthony Bonner .... Sacramento Kings	.05	.02	.01
☐ 122	Chris Smith .... Minnesota Timberwolves	.05	.02	.01
☐ 123	Elden Campbell .... Los Angeles Lakers	.05	.02	.01
☐ 124	Cliff Robinson .... Portland Trail Blazers	.10	.05	.01
☐ 125	Sherman Douglas .... Boston Celtics	.05	.02	.01
☐ 126	Alvin Robertson .... Milwaukee Bucks	.05	.02	.01
☐ 127	Rolando Blackman .... New York Knicks	.08	.04	.01
☐ 128	Malik Sealy .... Indiana Pacers	.05	.02	.01
☐ 129	Ed Pinckney .... Boston Celtics	.05	.02	.01
☐ 130	Anthony Peeler .... Los Angeles Lakers	.05	.02	.01
☐ 131	Scott Brooks .... Houston Rockets	.05	.02	.01
☐ 132	Rik Smits .... Indiana Pacers	.10	.05	.01
☐ 133	Derrick McKey .... Seattle Supersonics	.08	.04	.01

☐ 134	Alaa Abdelnaby	.05	.02	.01
	Boston Celtics			
☐ 135	Rex Chapman	.05	.02	.01
	Washington Bullets			
☐ 136	Tony Campbell	.05	.02	.01
	New York Knicks			
☐ 137	John Williams	.05	.02	.01
	Los Angeles Clippers			
☐ 138	Vincent Askew	.05	.02	.01
	Seattle Supersonics			
☐ 139	LaBradford Smith	.05	.02	.01
	Washington Bullets			
☐ 140	Vinny Del Negro	.05	.02	.01
	San Antonio Spurs			
☐ 141	Darrell Walker	.05	.02	.01
	Chicago Bulls			
☐ 142	James Worthy	.10	.05	.01
	Los Angeles Lakers			
☐ 143	Jeff Turner	.05	.02	.01
	Orlando Magic			
☐ 144	Duane Ferrell	.05	.02	.01
	Atlanta Hawks			
☐ 145	Larry Smith	.05	.02	.01
	Houston Rockets			
☐ 146	Eddie Johnson	.08	.04	.01
	Seattle Supersonics			
☐ 147	Chris Gatling	.05	.02	.01
	Golden State Warriors			
☐ 148	Buck Williams	.08	.04	.01
	Portland Trail Blazers			
☐ 149	Donald Royal	.05	.02	.01
	Orlando Magic			
☐ 150	Dino Radja	.40	.18	.05
	Boston Celtics			
☐ 151	Johnny Dawkins	.05	.02	.01
	Philadelphia 76ers			
☐ 152	Tim Legler	.05	.02	.01
	Dallas Mavericks			
☐ 153	Bill Laimbeer	.08	.04	.01
	Detroit Pistons			
☐ 154	Glen Rice	.10	.05	.01
	Miami Heat			
☐ 155	Bill Cartwright	.05	.02	.01
	Chicago Bulls			
☐ 156	Luther Wright	.05	.02	.01
	Utah Jazz			
☐ 157	Rex Walters	.08	.04	.01
	New Jersey Nets			
☐ 158	Doug Edwards	.08	.04	.01
	Atlanta Hawks			
☐ 159	George Lynch	.08	.04	.01
	Los Angeles Lakers			
☐ 160	Chris Mills	.40	.18	.05
	Cleveland Cavaliers			
☐ 161	Sam Cassell	.50	.23	.06
	Houston Rockets			
☐ 162	Nick Van Exel	2.00	.90	.25
	Los Angeles Lakers			
☐ 163	Shawn Bradley	.40	.18	.05
	Philadelphia 76ers			
☐ 164	Calbert Cheaney	.50	.23	.06
	Washington Bullets			
☐ 165	Corie Blount	.05	.02	.01
	Chicago Bulls			
☐ 166	Michael Jordan SL	2.00	.90	.25
	Chicago Bulls Scoring			
☐ 167	Dennis Rodman SL	.08	.04	.01
	Detroit Pistons Rebounds			
☐ 168	John Stockton SL	.10	.05	.01
	Utah Jazz Assists			
☐ 169	B.J. Armstrong SL	.05	.02	.01
	Chicago Bulls 3-pt. field goals			
☐ 170	Hakeem Olajuwon SL	.40	.18	.05
	Houston Rockets Blocked shots			
☐ 171	Michael Jordan SL	2.00	.90	.25
	Chicago Bulls Steals			
☐ 172	Cedric Ceballos SL	.05	.02	.01
	Phoenix Suns Field goal percentage			
☐ 173	Mark Price SL	.05	.02	.01
	Cleveland Cavaliers Free-throw percentage			
☐ 174	Charles Barkley SL	.30	.14	.04
	Phoenix Suns MVP			
☐ 175	Clifford Robinson SL	.05	.02	.01
	Portland Trail Blazers Sixth man			
☐ 176	Hakeem Olajuwon SL	.40	.18	.05
	Houston Rockets Defensive player			
☐ 177	Shaquille O'Neal SL	1.25	.55	.16
	Orlando Magic ROY			
☐ 178	R.Miller/C.Oakley PO	.08	.04	.01
☐ 179	1st Round: Hornets 3,	.05	.02	.01
	Celtics 1 PH Rick Fox Kenny Gattison			
☐ 180	1st Round: Bulls 3,	1.00	.45	.13
	Hawks 0 PH Michael Jordan Stacey Augmon			
☐ 181	1st Round: Cavs 3,	.05	.02	.01
	Nets 2 PH Brad Daugherty			
☐ 182	1st Round: Suns 3,	.05	.02	.01
	Lakers 2 PH Byron Scott Oliver Miller			
☐ 183	D.Robinson/S.Elliott PO	.10	.05	.01
☐ 184	1st Round: Rockets 3,	.05	.02	.01
	Clippers 2 PH Kenny Smith Mark Jackson			
☐ 185	1st Round: Sonics	.05	.02	.01
	3, Jazz 2 PH Eddie Johnson			
☐ 186	A.Mason/P.Ewing	.10	.05	.01
	A.Mourning PO			
☐ 187	East Semis: Bulls 4,	1.00	.45	.13
	Cavaliers 0 PH Michael Jordan Gerald Wilkins			
☐ 188	West Semis: Suns 4,	.05	.02	.01
	Spurs 2 PH Oliver Miller			
☐ 189	West Semis: Sonics 4,	.05	.02	.01
	Rockets 3 PH Sam Perkins Hakeem Olajuwon			
☐ 190	East Finals: Bulls 4,	.05	.02	.01
	Knicks 2 PH Bill Cartwright			
☐ 191	K.Johnson PO	.10	.05	.01
☐ 192	Majerle hits record	.05	.02	.01

	eight treys PH Dan Majerle			
☐ 193	Jordan scores 54 points PH Michael Jordan Charles Oakley John Starks	2.00	.90	.25
☐ 194	L.Johnson/M.Bogues PO	.08	.04	.01
☐ 195	Miller ties Playoffs free-throw mark PH Reggie Miller	.10	.05	.01
☐ 196	Bulls and Knicks renew rivalry PH John Starks Scottie Pippen	.08	.04	.01
☐ 197	C.Barkley PO	.10	.05	.01
☐ 198	Michael Jordan G1 Game One Finals	2.00	.90	.25
☐ 199	Scottie Pippen G2 Game Two Finals	.10	.05	.01
☐ 200	Kevin Johnson G3 Game Three Finals	.08	.04	.01
☐ 201	Michael Jordan G4 Game Four Finals	2.00	.90	.25
☐ 202	Richard Dumas G5 Game Five Finals	.05	.02	.01
☐ 203	Horace Grant G6 Game Six Finals	.08	.04	.01
☐ 204	Michael Jordan 1993 Finals MVP	2.00	.90	.25
☐ 205	S.Pippen/C.Barkley FIN	.10	.05	.01
☐ 206	John Paxson Hits 3 for title	.05	.02	.01
☐ 207	B.J. Armstrong Finals records	.05	.02	.01
☐ 208	1992-93 Bulls Road to 1993 Finals	.10	.05	.01
☐ 209	1992-93 Suns Road to 1993 Finals	.10	.05	.01
☐ 210	Atlanta Hawks Sked	.05	.02	.01
☐ 211	Boston Celtics Sked	.05	.02	.01
☐ 212	Charlotte Hornets Sked	.05	.02	.01
☐ 213	Chicago Bulls Sked (Michael Jordan)	.75	.35	.09
☐ 214	Cleveland Cavaliers Sked (Mark Price)	.05	.02	.01
☐ 215	Dallas Mavericks Sked (Jim Jackson and Sean Rooks)	.15	.07	.02
☐ 216	Denver Nuggets Sked	.05	.02	.01
☐ 217	Detroit Pistons Sked (Isiah Thomas)	.08	.04	.01
☐ 218	Golden State Warriors Sked	.05	.02	.01
☐ 219	Houston Rockets Sked (Hakeem Olajuwon)	.20	.09	.03
☐ 220	Indiana Pacers Sked (Rik Smits)	.05	.02	.01
☐ 221	L.A. Clippers Sked	.05	.02	.01
☐ 222	L.A. Lakers Sked	.05	.02	.01
☐ 223	Miami Heat Sked	.05	.02	.01
☐ 224	Milwaukee Bucks Sked	.05	.02	.01
☐ 225	Minnesota Timberwolves Sked	.05	.02	.01
☐ 226	New Jersey Nets Sked	.05	.02	.01
☐ 227	New York Knicks Sked	.05	.02	.01
☐ 228	Orlando Magic Sked (Shaquille O'Neal)	.60	.25	.08
☐ 229	Philadelphia 76ers Sked (Hersey Hawkins)	.05	.02	.01
☐ 230	Phoenix Suns Sked	.15	.07	.02
	(Charles Barkley)			
☐ 231	Portland Trail Blazers Sked (Jerome Kersey and Terry Porter)	.05	.02	.01
☐ 232	Sacramento Kings Sked	.05	.02	.01
☐ 233	San Antonio Spurs Sked (David Robinson)	.15	.07	.02
☐ 234	G.Payon/S.Kemp SKED	.15	.07	.02
☐ 235	Utah Jazz Sked	.05	.02	.01
☐ 236	Washington Bullets Sked (Michael Adams)	.05	.02	.01
☐ 237	Michael Jordan Chicago Bulls	2.00	.90	.25
☐ 238	Clyde Drexler SM Portland Trail Blazers	.10	.05	.01
☐ 239	Tim Hardaway SM Golden State Warriors	.05	.02	.01
☐ 240	Dominique Wilkins SM Atlanta Hawks	.08	.04	.01
☐ 241	Brad Daugherty SM Cleveland Cavaliers	.05	.02	.01
☐ 242	Chris Mullin SM Golden State Warriors	.05	.02	.01
☐ 243	Kenny Anderson SM New Jersey Nets	.05	.02	.01
☐ 244	Patrick Ewing SM New York Knicks	.10	.05	.01
☐ 245	Isiah Thomas SM Detroit Pistons	.08	.04	.01
☐ 246	Dikembe Mutombo SM Denver Nuggets	.08	.04	.01
☐ 247	Danny Manning SM Los Angeles Clippers	.05	.02	.01
☐ 248	David Robinson SM San Antonio Spurs	.30	.14	.04
☐ 249	Karl Malone SM Utah Jazz	.10	.05	.01
☐ 250	James Worthy SM Los Angeles Lakers	.05	.02	.01
☐ 251	Shawn Kemp SM Seattle Supersonics	.30	.14	.04
☐ 252	Checklist 1-64	.05	.02	.01
☐ 253	Checklist 65-128	.05	.02	.01
☐ 254	Checklist 129-192	.05	.02	.01
☐ 255	Checklist 193-255	.05	.02	.01
☐ 256	Patrick Ewing New York Knicks	.30	.14	.04
☐ 257	B.J. Armstrong Chicago Bulls	.05	.02	.01
☐ 258	Oliver Miller Phoenix Suns	.08	.04	.01
☐ 259	Jud Buechler Golden State Warriors	.05	.02	.01
☐ 260	Pooh Richardson Indiana Pacers	.05	.02	.01
☐ 261	Victor Alexander Golden State Warriors	.05	.02	.01
☐ 262	Kevin Gamble Boston Celtics	.05	.02	.01
☐ 263	Doug Smith Dallas Mavericks	.05	.02	.01
☐ 264	Isiah Thomas Detroit Pistons	.15	.07	.02
☐ 265	Doug Christie Los Angeles Lakers	.05	.02	.01
☐ 266	Mark Bryant Portland Trail Blazers	.05	.02	.01
☐ 267	Lloyd Daniels San Antonio Spurs	.05	.02	.01
☐ 268	Micheal Williams Minnesota Timberwolves	.05	.02	.01

☐ 269	Nick Anderson	.08	.04	.01
	Orlando Magic			
☐ 270	Tom Gugliotta	.10	.05	.01
	Washington Bullets			
☐ 271	Kenny Gattison	.05	.02	.01
	Charlotte Hornets			
☐ 272	Vernon Maxwell	.05	.02	.01
	Houston Rockets			
☐ 273	Terry Cummings	.08	.04	.01
	San Antonio Spurs			
☐ 274	Karl Malone	.30	.14	.04
	Utah Jazz			
☐ 275	Rick Fox	.05	.02	.01
	Boston Celtics			
☐ 276	Matt Bullard	.05	.02	.01
	Houston Rockets			
☐ 277	Johnny Newman	.05	.02	.01
	Charlotte Hornets			
☐ 278	Mark Price	.10	.05	.01
	Cleveland Cavaliers			
☐ 279	Mookie Blaylock	.08	.04	.01
	Atlanta Hawks			
☐ 280	Charles Barkley	.60	.25	.08
	Phoenix Suns			
☐ 281	Larry Nance	.08	.04	.01
	Cleveland Cavaliers			
☐ 282	Walt Williams	.10	.05	.01
	Sacramento Kings			
☐ 283	Brian Shaw	.05	.02	.01
	Miami Heat			
☐ 284	Robert Parish	.10	.05	.01
	Boston Celtics			
☐ 285	Pervis Ellison	.05	.02	.01
	Washington Bullets			
☐ 286	Spud Webb	.08	.04	.01
	Sacramento Kings			
☐ 287	Hakeem Olajuwon	.75	.35	.09
	Houston Rockets			
☐ 288	Jerome Kersey	.05	.02	.01
	Portland Trail Blazers			
☐ 289	Carl Herrera	.05	.02	.01
	Houston Rockets			
☐ 290	Dominique Wilkins	.15	.07	.02
	Atlanta Hawks			
☐ 291	Billy Owens	.08	.04	.01
	Golden State Warriors			
☐ 292	Greg Anthony	.05	.02	.01
	New York Knicks			
☐ 293	Nate McMillan	.05	.02	.01
	Seattle Supersonics			
☐ 294	Christian Laettner	.10	.05	.01
	Minnesota Timberwolves			
☐ 295	Gary Payton	.10	.05	.01
	Seattle Supersonics			
☐ 296	Steve Smith	.08	.04	.01
	Miami Heat			
☐ 297	Anthony Mason	.08	.04	.01
	New York Knicks			
☐ 298	Sean Rooks	.05	.02	.01
	Dallas Mavericks			
☐ 299	Toni Kukoc	.50	.23	.06
	Chicago Bulls			
☐ 300	Shaquille O'Neal	2.50	1.15	.30
	Orlando Magic			
☐ 301	Jay Humphries	.05	.02	.01
	Utah Jazz			
☐ 302	Sleepy Floyd	.05	.02	.01
	San Antonio Spurs			
☐ 303	Bimbo Coles	.05	.02	.01
	Miami Heat			
☐ 304	John Battle	.05	.02	.01
	Atlanta Hawks			
☐ 305	Shawn Kemp	.60	.25	.08
	Seattle Supersonics			
☐ 306	Scott Williams	.05	.02	.01
	Chicago Bulls			
☐ 307	Wayman Tisdale	.08	.04	.01
	Sacramento Kings			
☐ 308	Rony Seikaly	.05	.02	.01
	Miami Heat			
☐ 309	Reggie Miller	.30	.14	.04
	Indiana Pacers			
☐ 310	Scottie Pippen	.30	.14	.04
	Chicago Bulls			
☐ 311	Chris Webber	1.50	.65	.19
	Golden State Warriors			
☐ 312	Trevor Wilson	.05	.02	.01
	Los Angeles Lakers			
☐ 313	Derek Strong	.05	.02	.01
	Milwaukee Bucks			
☐ 314	Bobby Hurley	.20	.09	.03
	Sacramento Kings			
☐ 315	Herb Williams	.05	.02	.01
	New York Knicks			
☐ 316	Rex Walters	.05	.02	.01
	New Jersey Nets			
☐ 317	Doug Edwards	.05	.02	.01
	Atlanta Hawks			
☐ 318	Ken Williams	.05	.02	.01
	Indiana Pacers			
☐ 319	Jon Barry	.05	.02	.01
	Milwaukee Bucks			
☐ 320	Joe Courtney	.05	.02	.01
	Phoenix Suns			
☐ 321	Ervin Johnson	.10	.05	.01
	Seattle Supersonics			
☐ 322	Sam Cassell	.05	.02	.01
	Houston Rockets			
☐ 323	Tim Hardaway	.10	.05	.01
	Golden State Warriors			
☐ 324	Ed Stokes	.05	.02	.01
	Miami Heat			
☐ 325	Steve Kerr	.05	.02	.01
	Chicago Bulls			
☐ 326	Doug Overton	.05	.02	.01
	Washington Bullets			
☐ 327	Reggie Williams	.05	.02	.01
	Portland Trail Blazers			
☐ 328	Avery Johnson	.05	.02	.01
	Golden State Warriors			
☐ 329	Stacey King	.05	.02	.01
	Chicago Bulls			
☐ 330	Vin Baker	1.00	.45	.13
	Milwaukee Bucks			
☐ 331	Greg Kite	.05	.02	.01
	Orlando Magic			
☐ 332	Michael Cage	.05	.02	.01
	Seattle Supersonics			
☐ 333	Alonzo Mourning	.60	.25	.08
	Charlotte Hornets			
☐ 334	Acie Earl	.05	.02	.01
	Boston Celtics			
☐ 335	Terry Dehere	.08	.04	.01
	Los Angeles Clippers			
☐ 336	Negele Knight	.05	.02	.01
	San Antonio Spurs			
☐ 337	Gerald Madkins	.05	.02	.01
	Cleveland Cavaliers			
☐ 338	Lindsey Hunter	.15	.07	.02
	Detroit Pistons			
☐ 339	Luther Wright	.05	.02	.01
	Utah Jazz			

☐ 340	Mike Peplowski	.05	.02	.01
	Sacramento Kings			
☐ 341	Gerald Paddio	.20	.09	.03
	Indiana Pacers			
☐ 342	Danny Manning	.10	.05	.01
	Los Angeles Clippers			
☐ 343	Chris Mills	.05	.02	.01
	Cleveland Cavaliers			
☐ 344	Kevin Lynch	.05	.02	.01
	Charlotte Hornets			
☐ 345	Shawn Bradley	.05	.02	.01
	Philadelphia 76ers			
☐ 346	Evers Burns	.05	.02	.01
	Sacramento Kings			
☐ 347	Rodney Rogers	.40	.18	.05
	Denver Nuggets			
☐ 348	Cedric Ceballos	.10	.05	.01
	Phoenix Suns			
☐ 349	Warren Kidd	.05	.02	.01
	Philadelphia 76ers			
☐ 350	Darnell Mee	.05	.02	.01
	Denver Nuggets			
☐ 351	Matt Geiger	.05	.02	.01
	Miami Heat			
☐ 352	Jamal Mashburn	2.00	.90	.25
	Dallas Mavericks			
☐ 353	Antonio Davis	.10	.05	.01
	Indiana Pacers			
☐ 354	Calbert Cheaney	.05	.02	.01
	Washington Bullets			
☐ 355	George Lynch	.05	.02	.01
	Los Angeles Lakers			
☐ 356	Derrick McKey	.08	.04	.01
	Indiana Pacers			
☐ 357	Jerry Reynolds	.05	.02	.01
	Orlando Magic			
☐ 358	Don MacLean	.05	.02	.01
	Washington Bullets			
☐ 359	Scott Haskin	.05	.02	.01
	Indiana Pacers			
☐ 360	Malcolm Mackey	.05	.02	.01
	Phoenix Suns			
☐ 361	Isaiah Rider	.60	.25	.08
	Minnesota Timberwolves			
☐ 362	Detlef Schrempf	.10	.05	.01
	Seattle Supersonics			
☐ 363	Josh Grant	.05	.02	.01
	Golden State Warriors			
☐ 364	Richard Petruska	.05	.02	.01
	Houston Rockets			
☐ 365	Larry Johnson	.30	.14	.04
	Charlotte Hornets			
☐ 366	Felton Spencer	.05	.02	.01
	Utah Jazz			
☐ 367	Ken Norman	.05	.02	.01
	Milwaukee Bucks			
☐ 368	Anthony Cook	.05	.02	.01
	Orlando Magic			
☐ 369	James Robinson	.15	.07	.02
	Portland Trail Blazers			
☐ 370	Kevin Duckworth	.05	.02	.01
	Washington Bullets			
☐ 371	Chris Whitney	.05	.02	.01
	San Antonio Spurs			
☐ 372	Moses Malone	.15	.07	.02
	Philadelphia 76ers			
☐ 373	Nick Van Exel	1.00	.45	.13
	Los Angeles Lakers			
☐ 374	Scott Burrell	.25	.11	.03
	Charlotte Hornets			
☐ 375	Harvey Grant	.05	.02	.01
	Portland Trail Blazers			
☐ 376	Benoit Benjamin	.05	.02	.01
	New Jersey Nets			
☐ 377	Henry James	.05	.02	.01
	Los Angeles Clippers			
☐ 378	Craig Ehlo	.05	.02	.01
	Atlanta Hawks			
☐ 379	Ennis Whatley	.05	.02	.01
	Atlanta Hawks			
☐ 380	Sean Green	.05	.02	.01
	Philadelphia 76ers			
☐ 381	Eric Murdock	.05	.02	.01
	Milwaukee Bucks			
☐ 382	Anfernee Hardaway	4.00	1.80	.50
	Orlando Magic			
☐ 383	Gheorghe Muresan	.30	.14	.04
	Washington Bullets			
☐ 384	Kendall Gill	.05	.02	.01
	Seattle Supersonics			
☐ 385	David Wood	.05	.02	.01
	Detroit Pistons			
☐ 386	Mario Elie	.05	.02	.01
	Houston Rockets			
☐ 387	Chris Corchiani	.05	.02	.01
	Boston Celtics			
☐ 388	Greg Graham	.05	.02	.01
	Philadelphia 76ers			
☐ 389	Hersey Hawkins	.08	.04	.01
	Charlotte Hornets			
☐ 390	Mark Aguirre	.08	.04	.01
	Los Angeles Clippers			
☐ 391	LaPhonso Ellis	.08	.04	.01
	Denver Nuggets			
☐ 392	Anthony Bonner	.05	.02	.01
	New York Knicks			
☐ 393	Lucious Harris	.10	.05	.01
	Dallas Mavericks			
☐ 394	Andrew Lang	.05	.02	.01
	Atlanta Hawks			
☐ 395	Chris Dudley	.05	.02	.01
	Portland Trail Blazers			
☐ 396	Dennis Rodman	.20	.09	.03
	San Antonio Spurs			
☐ 397	Larry Krystkowiak	.05	.02	.01
	Orlando Magic			
☐ 398	A.C. Green	.10	.05	.01
	Phoenix Suns			
☐ 399	Eddie Johnson	.08	.04	.01
	Charlotte Hornets			
☐ 400	Kevin Edwards	.05	.02	.01
	New Jersey Nets			
☐ 401	Tyrone Hill	.08	.04	.01
	Cleveland Cavaliers			
☐ 402	Greg Anderson	.05	.02	.01
	Detroit Pistons			
☐ 403	P.J. Brown	.10	.05	.01
	New Jersey Nets			
☐ 404	Dana Barros	.10	.05	.01
	Philadelphia 76ers			
☐ 405	Allan Houston	.40	.18	.05
	Detroit Pistons			
☐ 406	Mike Brown	.05	.02	.01
	Minnesota Timberwolves			
☐ 407	Lee Mayberry	.05	.02	.01
	Milwaukee Bucks			
☐ 408	Fat Lever	.05	.02	.01
	Dallas Mavericks			
☐ 409	Tony Smith	.05	.02	.01
	Los Angeles Lakers			
☐ 410	Tom Chambers	.08	.04	.01
	Utah Jazz			

☐ 411	Manute Bol .... .05 Miami Heat	.02	.01
☐ 412	Joe Kleine .... .05 Phoenix Suns	.02	.01
☐ 413	Bryant Stith .... .05 Denver Nuggets	.02	.01
☐ 414	Eric Riley .... .05 Houston Rockets	.02	.01
☐ 415	JoJo English .... .05 Chicago Bulls	.02	.01
☐ 416	Sean Elliott .... .08 Detroit Pistons	.04	.01
☐ 417	Sam Bowie .... .05 Los Angeles Lakers	.02	.01
☐ 418	Armon Gilliam .... .05 New Jersey Nets	.02	.01
☐ 419	Brian Williams .... .05 Denver Nuggets	.02	.01
☐ 420	Popeye Jones .... .30 Dallas Mavericks	.14	.04
☐ 421	Dennis Rodman EB ...... .08 San Antonio Spurs	.04	.01
☐ 422	Karl Malone EB .... .10 Utah Jazz	.05	.01
☐ 423	Tom Gugliotta EB .... .05 Washington Bullets	.02	.01
☐ 424	Kevin Willis EB .... .05 Atlanta Hawks	.02	.01
☐ 425	Hakeem Olajuwon EB ... .40 Houston Rockets	.18	.05
☐ 426	Charles Oakley EB .... .05 New York Knicks	.02	.01
☐ 427	Clarence Weatherspoon EB .05 Philadelphia 76ers	.02	.01
☐ 428	Derrick Coleman EB ..... .05 New Jersey Nets	.02	.01
☐ 429	Buck Williams EB .... .05 Portland Trail Blazers	.02	.01
☐ 430	Christian Laettner EB ... .05 Minnesota Timberwolves	.02	.01
☐ 431	Dikembe Mutombo EB . .08 Denver Nuggets	.04	.01
☐ 432	Rony Seikaly EB .... .05 Miami Heat	.02	.01
☐ 433	Brad Daugherty EB....... .05 Cleveland Cavaliers	.02	.01
☐ 434	Horace Grant EB .... .08 Chicago Bulls	.04	.01
☐ 435	Larry Johnson EB .... .10 Charlotte Hornets	.05	.01
☐ 436	Dee Brown BT .... .05 Boston Celtics	.02	.01
☐ 437	Muggsy Bogues BT....... .05 Charlotte Hornets	.02	.01
☐ 438	Michael Jordan BT ...... 2.00 Chicago Bulls	.90	.25
☐ 439	Tim Hardaway BT.......... .05 Golden State Warriors	.02	.01
☐ 440	Micheal Williams BT ..... .05 Minnesota Timberwolves	.02	.01
☐ 441	Gary Payton BT............. .05 Seattle Supersonics	.02	.01
☐ 442	Mookie Blaylock BT ...... .05 Atlanta Hawks	.02	.01
☐ 443	Doc Rivers BT............... .05 New York Knicks	.02	.01
☐ 444	Kenny Smith BT............ .05 Houston Rockets	.02	.01
☐ 445	John Stockton BT .... .10 Utah Jazz	.05	.01
☐ 446	Alvin Robertson BT ...... .05 Detroit Pistons	.02	.01
☐ 447	Mark Jackson BT .... .05 Los Angeles Clippers	.02	.01
☐ 448	Kenny Anderson BT...... .05 New Jersey Nets	.02	.01
☐ 449	Scottie Pippen BT .... .10 Chicago Bulls	.05	.01
☐ 450	Isiah Thomas BT............ .08 Detroit Pistons	.04	.01
☐ 451	Mark Price BT .... .05 Cleveland Cavaliers	.02	.01
☐ 452	Latrell Sprewell BT........ .30 Golden State Warriors	.14	.04
☐ 453	Sedale Threatt BT.......... .05 Los Angeles Lakers	.02	.01
☐ 454	Nick Anderson BT .... .05 Orlando Magic	.02	.01
☐ 455	Rod Strickland BT .... .05 Portland Trail Blazers	.02	.01
☐ 456	Oliver Miller GI .... .05 Phoenix Suns	.02	.01
☐ 457	J.Worthy/V.Divac GI ..... .05 Los Angeles Lakers	.02	.01
☐ 458	Robert Horry GI .... .05 Houston Rockets	.02	.01
☐ 459	Rockets Shoot-Around GI .05 Dallas Mavericks	.02	.01
☐ 460	Rooks/Jackson/Legler GI .15 Dallas Mavericks	.07	.02
☐ 461	Mitch Richmond GI......... .08 Sacramento Kings	.04	.01
☐ 462	Chris Morris GI .... .05 New Jersey Nets	.02	.01
☐ 463	M.Jackson/G.Grant GI.. .05 Los Angeles Clippers	.02	.01
☐ 464	David Robinson GI......... .30 San Antonio Spurs	.14	.04
☐ 465	Danny Ainge GI............. .05 Phoenix Suns	.02	.01
☐ 466	Michael Jordan SL...... 2.00 Chicago Bulls	.90	.25
☐ 467	Dominique Wilkins SL . .08 Atlanta Hawks	.04	.01
☐ 468	Alonzo Mourning SL...... .30 Charlotte Hornets	.14	.04
☐ 469	Shaquille O'Neal SL ... 1.25 Orlando Magic	.55	.16
☐ 470	Tim Hardaway SL........... .05 Golden State Warriors	.02	.01
☐ 471	Patrick Ewing SL........... .10 New York Knicks	.05	.01
☐ 472	Kevin Johnson SL .... .08 Phoenix Suns	.04	.01
☐ 473	Clyde Drexler SL .... .10 Portland Trail Blazers	.05	.01
☐ 474	David Robinson SL .... .30 San Antonio Spurs	.14	.04
☐ 475	Shawn Kemp SL .... .30 Seattle Supersonics	.14	.04
☐ 476	Dee Brown SL................ .05 Boston Celtics	.02	.01
☐ 477	Jim Jackson SL .... .30 Dallas Mavericks	.14	.04
☐ 478	John Stockton SL .... .10 Utah Jazz	.05	.01
☐ 479	Robert Horry SL............. .05 Houston Rockets	.02	.01
☐ 480	Glen Rice SL .... .05 Miami Heat	.02	.01
☐ 481	Micheal Williams SIS.... .05 Minnesota Timberwolves	.02	.01
☐ 482	G.Lynch/T.Dehere CL.... .05	.02	.01

☐	483	Chris Webber TP .... Golden State Warriors	.60	.25 .08
☐	484	Anfernee Hardaway TP Orlando Magic	1.50	.65 .19
☐	485	Shawn Bradley TP .... Philadelphia 76ers	.10	.05 .01
☐	486	Jamal Mashburn TP ..... Dallas Mavericks	.75	.35 .09
☐	487	Calbert Cheaney TP .... Washington Bullets	.10	.05 .01
☐	488	Isaiah Rider TP .... Minnesota Timberwolves	.25	.11 .03
☐	489	Bobby Hurley TP .... Sacramento Kings	.08	.04 .01
☐	490	Vin Baker TP .... Milwaukee Bucks	.40	.18 .05
☐	491	Rodney Rogers TP .... Denver Nuggets	.10	.05 .01
☐	492	Lindsey Hunter TP .... Detroit Pistons	.05	.02 .01
☐	493	Allan Houston TP .... Detroit Pistons	.10	.05 .01
☐	494	Terry Dehere TP .... Los Angeles Clippers	.05	.02 .01
☐	495	George Lynch TP .... Los Angeles Lakers	.05	.02 .01
☐	496	Scott Burrell TP .... Charlotte Hornets	.08	.04 .01
☐	497	Rex Walters TP .... New Jersey Nets	.75	.35 .09
☐	498	Charles Barkley MO ..... Phoenix Suns	.30	.14 .04
☐	499	A.C. Green MO .... Phoenix Suns	.05	.02 .01
☐	500	Dan Majerle MO .... Phoenix Suns	.05	.02 .01
☐	501	Jerrod Mustaf MO .... Phoenix Suns	.05	.02 .01
☐	502	Kevin Johnson MO .... Phoenix Suns	.08	.04 .01
☐	503	Negele Knight MO .... Phoenix Suns	.05	.02 .01
☐	504	Danny Ainge MO .... Phoenix Suns	.05	.02 .01
☐	505	Oliver Miller MO .... Phoenix Suns	.05	.02 .01
☐	506	Joe Courtney MO .... Phoenix Suns	.05	.02 .01
☐	507	Checklist	.05	.02 .01
☐	508	Checklist	.05	.02 .01
☐	509	Checklist	.05	.02 .01
☐	510	Checklist	.05	.02 .01
☐	SP3	Michael Jordan .... Chicago Bulls Wilt Chamberlain	8.00	3.60 1.00
☐	SP4	Chicago Bulls' Third .. NBA Championship	8.00	3.60 1.00

1993-94 Upper Deck All-NBA

Inserted one per blue and green first series retail 22-card jumbo packs, this 15-card set spotlights All-NBA first, second and third teams. Measuring the standard size (3 1/2" by 2 1/2"), the cards feature a borderless

front with a color action photo set against a game-crowd background. The player's name appears in a red vertical stripe along the right side. The All NBA Team appears in a blue vertical stripe along the right side. The back features a color action photo along the left side with player's statistics along the right side.

	MINT	NRMT	EXC
COMPLETE SET (15)	15.00	6.75	1.90
COMMON CARD (AN1-AN15)	.25	.11	.03
☐ AN1 Charles Barkley .... Phoenix Suns	1.50	.65	.19
☐ AN2 Karl Malone .... Utah Jazz	.75	.35	.09
☐ AN3 Hakeem Olajuwon .... Houston Rockets	2.00	.90	.25
☐ AN4 Michael Jordan .... Chicago Bulls	10.00	4.50	1.25
☐ AN5 Mark Price .... Cleveland Cavaliers	.25	.11	.03
☐ AN6 Dominique Wilkins ...... Atlanta Hawks	.40	.18	.05
☐ AN7 Larry Johnson .... Charlotte Hornets	.75	.35	.09
☐ AN8 Patrick Ewing .... New York Knicks	.75	.35	.09
☐ AN9 John Stockton .... Utah Jazz	.75	.35	.09
☐ AN10 Joe Dumars .... Detroit Pistons	.40	.18	.05
☐ AN11 Scottie Pippen .... Chicago Bulls	.75	.35	.09
☐ AN12 Derrick Coleman .... New Jersey Nets	.25	.11	.03
☐ AN13 David Robinson .... San Antonio Spurs	1.50	.65	.19
☐ AN14 Tim Hardaway .... Golden State Warriors	.25	.11	.03
☐ AN15 Michael Jordan CL ...... Chicago Bulls	5.00	2.30	.60

1993-94 Upper Deck All-Rookies

Randomly inserted in first series 12-card retail packs at a rate of one in 30, this 10-card standard-size (2 1/2" by 3 1/2") set features the NBA All-Rookie first (1-5) and second (6-10) teams from 1992-93. The cards feature color game-action player pho-

tos on their fronts. They are borderless, except at the top, where a red stripe edges the cards of the first team and a blue one edges those of the second. The player's name appears in white lettering within a red or blue stripe near the bottom. The back carries a color player action photo on the left and career highlights on the right.

	MINT	NRMT	EXC
COMPLETE SET (10)	50.00	23.00	6.25
COMMON CARD (AR1-AR10)	1.00	.45	.13
☐ AR1 Shaquille O'Neal...... Orlando Magic	30.00	13.50	3.80
☐ AR2 Alonzo Mourning....... Charlotte Hornets	8.00	3.60	1.00
☐ AR3 Christian Laettner..... Minnesota Timberwolves	2.50	1.15	.30
☐ AR4 Tom Gugliotta .... Washington Bullets	2.00	.90	.25
☐ AR5 LaPhonso Ellis .... Denver Nuggets	2.00	.90	.25
☐ AR6 Walt Williams .... Sacramento Kings	2.50	1.15	.30
☐ AR7 Robert Horry .... Houston Rockets	3.00	1.35	.40
☐ AR8 Latrell Sprewell .... Golden State Warriors	8.00	3.60	1.00
☐ AR9 Clarence Weatherspoon Philadelphia 76ers	2.50	1.15	.30
☐ AR10 Richard Dumas .... Phoenix Suns	1.00	.45	.13

1993-94 Upper Deck Flight Team

Michael Jordan selected the league's best dunkers for this 20-card insert set. The cards are randomly inserted in first series 12-card hobby packs at a rate of one in 30. The standard-size (2 1/2" by 3 1/2") cards feature on their fronts full-bleed color action player photos. The words "Michael Jordan's Flight Team" appear in ghosted block lettering over the background. The player's name is gold-foil stamped at the bottom, with the Flight Team insignia displayed immediately above carrying his team's city name and the his uniform number. On a background consisting of blue sky and clouds, the back carries a color player action cutout and an evaluative quote by Jordan.

	MINT	NRMT	EXC
COMPLETE SET (20)	100.00	45.00	12.50
COMMON CARD (FT1-FT20)....	1.50	.65	.19
☐ FT1 Stacey Augmon.......... Atlanta Hawks	1.50	.65	.19
☐ FT2 Charles Barkley .... Phoenix Suns	12.00	5.50	1.50
☐ FT3 David Benoit............... Utah Jazz	1.50	.65	.19
☐ FT4 Dee Brown .... Boston Celtics	1.50	.65	.19
☐ FT5 Cedric Ceballos .... Phoenix Suns	2.50	1.15	.30
☐ FT6 Derrick Coleman .... New Jersey Nets	2.50	1.15	.30
☐ FT7 Clyde Drexler............. Portland Trail Blazers	6.00	2.70	.75
☐ FT8 Sean Elliott............... San Antonio Spurs	1.50	.65	.19
☐ FT9 LaPhonso Ellis .... Denver Nuggets	1.50	.65	.19
☐ FT10 Kendall Gill............... Charlotte Hornets	1.50	.65	.19
☐ FT11 Larry Johnson.......... Charlotte Hornets	6.00	2.70	.75
☐ FT12 Shawn Kemp.......... Seattle Supersonics	12.00	5.50	1.50
☐ FT13 Karl Malone............. Utah Jazz	6.00	2.70	.75
☐ FT14 Harold Miner............ Miami Heat	1.50	.65	.19
☐ FT15 Alonzo Mourning...... Charlotte Hornets	12.00	5.50	1.50
☐ FT16 Shaquille O'Neal..... Orlando Magic	50.00	23.00	6.25
☐ FT17 Scottie Pippen.......... Chicago Bulls	6.00	2.70	.75
☐ FT18 Clarence Weatherspoon Philadelphia 76ers	4.00	1.80	.50
☐ FT19 Spud Webb.............. Sacramento Kings	1.50	.65	.19
☐ FT20 Dominique Wilkins.... Atlanta Hawks	3.00	1.35	.40

1993-94 Upper Deck Future Heroes

Inserted one per first series locker pack, this set continues Upper Deck's year-by-

year basketball Heroes program. Unlike previous sets devoted to individual players, the 1993-94 set features a selection of young phenoms destined to be stars. This 10-card standard-size (2 1/2" by 3 1/2") set features color player action shots on its fronts. The photos are bordered on the left and bottom by gray and team color-coded stripes. The player's name and position appear in white lettering in the color-coded stripe at the bottom. An embossed silver-foil basketball appears at the lower left. The white back carries the player's career highlights. The cards are numbered on the back as "X of 36."

appears in white lettering within the photo's "torn" lower right corner. The back carries the same quote at the upper right, within a shot of a locker that has a print of the front's action shot taped to the door. Another player photo and more personal player quotes round out the back.

		MINT	NRMT	EXC
COMPLETE SET (10)		50.00	23.00	6.25
COMMON CARD (28-36)		1.00	.45	.13
☐ 28	Derrick Coleman New Jersey Nets	1.50	.65	.19
☐ 29	LaPhonso Ellis Denver Nuggets	1.00	.45	.13
☐ 30	Jim Jackson Dallas Mavericks	6.00	2.70	.75
☐ 31	Larry Johnson Charlotte Hornets	3.00	1.35	.40
☐ 32	Shawn Kemp Seattle Supersonics	6.00	2.70	.75
☐ 33	Christian Laettner Minnesota Timberwolves	1.50	.65	.19
☐ 34	Alonzo Mourning Charlotte Hornets	6.00	2.70	.75
☐ 35	Shaquille O'Neal Orlando Magic	25.00	11.50	3.10
☐ 36	Walt Williams Sacramento Kings	1.50	.65	.19
☐ NNO	Checklist Card LaPhonso Ellis Christian Laettner	1.00	.45	.13

		MINT	NRMT	EXC
COMPLETE SET (15)		110.00	50.00	14.00
COMMON CARD (LT1-LT15)		1.00	.45	.13
☐ LT1	Michael Jordan Chicago Bulls	50.00	23.00	6.25
☐ LT2	Stacey Augmon Atlanta Hawks	1.00	.45	.13
☐ LT3	Shaquille O'Neal Orlando Magic	30.00	13.50	3.80
☐ LT4	Alonzo Mourning Charlotte Hornets	8.00	3.60	1.00
☐ LT5	Harold Miner Miami Heat	1.00	.45	.13
☐ LT6	Clarence Weatherspoon Philadelphia 76ers	2.50	1.15	.30
☐ LT7	Derrick Coleman New Jersey Nets	2.00	.90	.25
☐ LT8	Charles Barkley Phoenix Suns	8.00	3.60	1.00
☐ LT9	David Robinson San Antonio Spurs	8.00	3.60	1.00
☐ LT10	Chuck Person Minnesota Timberwolves	1.00	.45	.13
☐ LT11	Karl Malone Utah Jazz	4.00	1.80	.50
☐ LT12	Muggsy Bogues Charlotte Hornets	2.00	.90	.25
☐ LT13	Latrell Sprewell Golden State Warriors	8.00	3.60	1.00
☐ LT14	John Starks New York Knicks	1.00	.45	.13
☐ LT15	Jim Jackson Dallas Mavericks	8.00	3.60	1.00

1993-94 Upper Deck Locker Talk

Inserted one per Series II locker pack, this 15-card standard-size (2 1/2" by 3 1/2") set features color player action photos on their fronts. The player's name appears in white lettering within the gold stripe that edges the left side. A personal player quote

1993-94 Upper Deck Mr. June

Randomly inserted in series two 12-card hobby packs at a rate of one in 30, this 10-card standard-size (2 1/2" by 3 1/2") set focuses on Michael Jordan's performance while leading his team to three consecutive NBA Championships. The front features a

color action shot of Michael Jordan with his name, accomplishment, and year thereof printed in the team-colored (Chicago Bulls) stripe at bottom. The back features a color action photo at the upper right with a description of his accomplishments printed alongside and below.

	MINT	NRMT	EXC
COMPLETE SET (10)	250.00	115.00	31.00
COMMON JORDAN (1-10)	25.00	11.50	3.10
☐ MJ1 Michael Jordan ...... Jordan's a Steal	25.00	11.50	3.10
☐ MJ2 Michael Jordan ...... M.J.'s High Five	25.00	11.50	3.10
☐ MJ3 Michael Jordan ...... 1991 NBA Finals MVP	25.00	11.50	3.10
☐ MJ4 Michael Jordan ...... 35 Points in One Half	25.00	11.50	3.10
☐ MJ5 Michael Jordan ...... Three-Points King	25.00	11.50	3.10
☐ MJ6 Michael Jordan ...... Back-To-Back Finals MVP	25.00	11.50	3.10
☐ MJ7 Michael Jordan ...... 55-Point Game	25.00	11.50	3.10
☐ MJ8 Michael Jordan ...... Record Scoring Average	25.00	11.50	3.10
☐ MJ9 Michael Jordan ...... Jordan's Three-Peat	25.00	11.50	3.10
☐ MJ10 Checklist	25.00	11.50	3.10

1993-94 Upper Deck Rookie Exchange Silver

This 10-card standard-size (2 1/2" by 3 1/2") set features the top ten players from

the 1993 NBA Draft. The set could only be obtained by mail in exchange for the Silver Trade card that was randomly inserted in first series 12-card packs at a rate of one in 72. The Silver Exchange expiration date was 12/31/93. The borderless front features a color player action photo with the his name printed in white lettering within a red stripe near the bottom. The word "Exchange" runs vertically along the left side in silver-foil lettering. The white and gray back carries a color player photo at the upper left and career highlights and statistics alongside and below. The cards are numbered on the back with an "RE" prefix.

	MINT	NRMT	EXC
COMPLETE SET (10)	10.00	4.50	1.25
COMMON CARD (RE1-RE10)	.25	.11	.03
☐ RE1 Chris Webber .... Golden State Warriors	2.00	.90	.25
☐ RE2 Shawn Bradley .... Philadelphia 76ers	.50	.23	.06
☐ RE3 Anfernee Hardaway ... Orlando Magic	5.00	2.30	.60
☐ RE4 Jamal Mashburn........ Dallas Mavericks	2.50	1.15	.30
☐ RE5 Isaiah Rider.................. Minnesota Timberwolves	.75	.35	.09
☐ RE6 Calbert Cheaney .... Washington Bullets	.60	.25	.08
☐ RE7 Bobby Hurley................ Sacramento Kings	.25	.11	.03
☐ RE8 Vin Baker.................. Milwaukee Bucks	1.25	.55	.16
☐ RE9 Rodney Rogers............ Denver Nuggets	.50	.23	.06
☐ RE10 Lindsey Hunter............ Detroit Pistons	.25	.11	.03
☐ TC2 Redeemed Silver Trade	.25	.11	.03
☐ TC2 Unredeemed Silver Trade	.10	.05	.01

1993-94 Upper Deck Rookie Exchange Gold

This 10-card standard-size (2 1/2" by 3 1/2") set features the top ten players from the 1993 NBA Draft. The set could only be *obtained by mail in exchange for the Gold Trade Card that was randomly inserted (one in 288) in 12-card first series packs. The Gold Trade expiration date was 12/31/93. The cards are identical to the basic "Rookie Exchange" inserts except for the word "Exchange" on the card front, which is featured in gold-foil instead of silver. Please refer to the multiplier listed below for card values.*

	MINT	NRMT	EXC
COMPLETE SET (10)	20.00	9.00	2.50
COMMON CARD (RE1-RE10)	1.00	.45	.13
*GOLD CARDS: 2X VALUE OF SILVER			
☐ TC1 Redeemed Gold Trade	.50	.23	.06
☐ TC1 Unredeemed Gold Trade	2.00	.90	.25

1993-94 Upper Deck Rookie Standouts

Randomly inserted at a rate of one in 30 second series 12-card retail packs and inserted one per second series 22-card purple jumbo pack, this 20-card standard-size (2 1/2" by 3 1/2") set showcases the top rookies of the 1993-94 NBA season. The borderless front features a color player action photo with his name printed in a gold-foil banner beneath the silver-foil set logo in a lower corner. The gray back carries a color player photo on one side and career highlights on the other.

	MINT	NRMT	EXC
COMPLETE SET (20)	50.00	23.00	6.25
COMMON CARD (RS1-RS20)	.50	.23	.06
☐ RS1 Chris Webber	8.00	3.60	1.00
Golden State Warriors			
☐ RS2 Bobby Hurley	1.00	.45	.13
Sacramento Kings			
☐ RS3 Isaiah Rider	3.00	1.35	.40
Minnesota Timberwolves			
☐ RS4 Terry Dehere	.50	.23	.06
Los Angeles Clippers			
☐ RS5 Toni Kukoc	2.50	1.15	.30
Chicago Bulls			
☐ RS6 Shawn Bradley	2.00	.90	.25
Philadelphia 76ers			

☐ RS7 Allan Houston	2.00	.90	.25
Detroit Pistons			
☐ RS8 Chris Mills	2.00	.90	.25
Cleveland Cavaliers			
☐ RS9 Jamal Mashburn	10.00	4.50	1.25
Dallas Mavericks			
☐ RS10 Acie Earl	.50	.23	.06
Boston Celtics			
☐ RS11 George Lynch	.50	.23	.06
Los Angeles Lakers			
☐ RS12 Scott Burrell	1.25	.55	.16
Charlotte Hornets			
☐ RS13 Calbert Cheaney	2.50	1.15	.30
Washington Bullets			
☐ RS14 Lindsey Hunter	.50	.23	.06
Detroit Pistons			
☐ RS15 Nick Van Exel	10.00	4.50	1.25
Los Angeles Lakers			
☐ RS16 Rex Walters	.50	.23	.06
New Jersey Nets			
☐ RS17 Anfernee Hardaway	20.00	9.00	2.50
Orlando Magic			
☐ RS18 Sam Cassell	2.50	1.15	.30
Houston Rockets			
☐ RS19 Vin Baker	5.00	2.30	.60
Milwaukee Bucks			
☐ RS20 Rodney Rogers	2.00	.90	.25
Denver Nuggets			

1993-94 Upper Deck Team MVPs

Cards from this 27-card standard size (3 1/2" by 2 1/2") set were issued one per second series red and purple 22-card jumbo packs. The set highlights one key "Team MVP" from each of the 27 NBA teams. The white- and prismatic team-colored foil-bordered front features a color player action shot, with the player's name printed vertically in the foil border at the upper right. The horizontal back is bordered in white and a team color and carries a color action shot on the left with career highlights appearing in a gray panel alongside on the right.

	MINT	NRMT	EXC
COMPLETE SET (27)	20.00	9.00	2.50
COMMON CARD (TM1-TM27)	.25	.11	.03

☐ TM1	Dominique Wilkins......	.40	.18	.05
	Atlanta Hawks			
☐ TM2	Robert Parish..............	.25	.11	.03
	Boston Celtics			
☐ TM3	Larry Johnson	.75	.35	.09
	Charlotte Hornets			
☐ TM4	Scottie Pippen	.75	.35	.09
	Chicago Bulls			
☐ TM5	Mark Price.................	.25	.11	.03
	Cleveland Cavaliers			
☐ TM6	Jim Jackson................	1.50	.65	.19
	Dallas Mavericks			
☐ TM7	Mahmoud Abdul-Rauf	.25	.11	.03
	Denver Nuggets			
☐ TM8	Joe Dumars	.40	.18	.05
	Detroit Pistons			
☐ TM9	Chris Mullin	.25	.11	.03
	Golden State Warriors			
☐ TM10	Hakeem Olajuwon ...	2.00	.90	.25
	Houston Rockets			
☐ TM11	Reggie Miller	.75	.35	.09
	Indiana Pacers			
☐ TM12	Danny Manning	.25	.11	.03
	Los Angeles Clippers			
☐ TM13	James Worthy	.25	.11	.03
	Los Angeles Lakers			
☐ TM14	Glen Rice	.25	.11	.03
	Miami Heat			
☐ TM15	Blue Edwards............	.25	.11	.03
	Milwaukee Bucks			
☐ TM16	Christian Laettner	.25	.11	.03
	Minnesota Timberwolves			
☐ TM17	Derrick Coleman	.25	.11	.03
	New Jersey Nets			
☐ TM18	Patrick Ewing	.75	.35	.09
	New York Knicks			
☐ TM19	Shaquille O'Neal	6.00	2.70	.75
	Orlando Magic			
☐ TM20	Clarence Weatherspoon	.40	.18	.05
	Philadelphia 76ers			
☐ TM21	Charles Barkley..........	1.50	.65	.19
	Phoenix Suns			
☐ TM22	Clyde Drexler	.75	.35	.09
	Portland Trail Blazers			
☐ TM23	Mitch Richmond	.40	.18	.05
	Sacramento Kings			
☐ TM24	David Robinson	1.50	.65	.19
	San Antonio Spurs			
☐ TM25	Shawn Kemp	1.50	.65	.19
	Seattle Supersonics			
☐ TM26	John Stockton	.75	.35	.09
	Utah Jazz			
☐ TM27	Tom Gugliotta............	.25	.11	.03
	Washington Bullets			

every 11 first series 22-card locker packs. The standard-size (2 1/2" by 3 1/2") horizontal hologram cards feature one color player action cutout and two hologram action shots on their fronts. Each of the three images show the player performing three different skills (scoring, rebounding, passing or blocking) necessary to achieve a triple-double. The words "Triple Double" appear vertically on the left. The player's name appears at the upper right of the hologram. The horizontal back displays another color player action shot on the left, with a story of the player's triple-double feat on the right. The player's name appears in a team-colored bar at the bottom.

	MINT	NRMT	EXC
COMPLETE SET (10)	25.00	11.50	3.10
COMMON CARD (TD1-TD10)	.50	.23	.06

☐ TD1	Charles Barkley..........	3.00	1.35	.40
	Phoenix Suns			
☐ TD2	Michael Jordan..........	20.00	9.00	2.50
	Chicago Bulls			
☐ TD3	Scottie Pippen	1.50	.65	.19
	Chicago Bulls			
☐ TD4	Detlef Schrempf	.75	.35	.09
	Indiana Pacers			
☐ TD5	Mark Jackson	.50	.23	.06
	Los Angeles Clippers			
☐ TD6	Kenny Anderson	.75	.35	.09
	New Jersey Nets			
☐ TD7	Larry Johnson	1.50	.65	.19
	Charlotte Hornets			
☐ TD8	Dikembe Mutombo	1.25	.55	.16
	Denver Nuggets			
☐ TD9	Rumeal Robinson	.50	.23	.06
	New Jersey Nets			
☐ TD10	Micheal Williams	.50	.23	.06
	Minnesota Timberwolves			

1993-94 Upper Deck Triple Double

This 10-card set features the NBA leaders in triple-doubles from the 1992-93 season. Cards were randomly inserted at a rate of 1 in 20 first series 12-card hobby and retail packs, 1 in 20 first series 22-card blue jumbo packs, one per first series 22-card green jumbo pack and approximately 1 in

1993-94 Upper Deck Pro View

This 110-card standard-size (2 1/2" by 3 1/2") set was distributed in 5-card packs (48 per box) that included 3-D glasses with which to see the 3-D effect. Fronts feature white-bordered color player action shots, with the player's name appearing within a vertical ghosted strip on the left. The back

carries a color player action shot on the left, with career highlights horizontally printed alongside on the right. The set closes with the following subsets: 3-D Playground Legends (71-79), 3-D Rookie (80-88) and 3-D Jams (89-108). The cards are numbered on the back.

	MINT	NRMT	EXC
COMPLETE SET (110)	25.00	11.50	3.10
COMMON CARD (1-110)	.05	.02	.01

		MINT	NRMT	EXC
☐ 1	Karl Malone	.30	.14	.04
	Utah Jazz			
☐ 2	Chuck Person	.08	.04	.01
	Minnesota Timberwolves			
☐ 3	Latrell Sprewell	.60	.25	.08
	Golden State Warriors			
☐ 4	Dominique Wilkins	.15	.07	.02
	Atlanta Hawks			
☐ 5	Reggie Miller	.30	.14	.04
	Indiana Pacers			
☐ 6	Vlade Divac	.10	.05	.01
	Los Angeles Lakers			
☐ 7	Otis Thorpe	.08	.04	.01
	Houston Rockets			
☐ 8	Patrick Ewing	.30	.14	.04
	New York Knicks			
☐ 9	Ron Harper	.08	.04	.01
	Los Angeles Clippers			
☐ 10	Brad Daugherty	.08	.04	.01
	Cleveland Cavaliers			
☐ 11	Robert Parish	.10	.05	.01
	Boston Celtics			
☐ 12	Glen Rice	.08	.04	.01
	Miami Heat			
☐ 13	Kevin Johnson	.15	.07	.02
	Phoenix Suns			
☐ 14	Christian Laettner	.08	.04	.01
	Minnesota Timberwolves			
☐ 15	Ricky Pierce	.05	.02	.01
	Seattle Supersonics			
☐ 16	Joe Dumars	.15	.07	.02
	Detroit Pistons			
☐ 17	James Worthy	.10	.05	.01
	Los Angeles Lakers			
☐ 18	John Stockton	.30	.14	.04
	Utah Jazz			
☐ 19	Robert Horry	.10	.05	.01
	Houston Rockets			
☐ 20	John Starks	.08	.04	.01
	New York Knicks			
☐ 21	Danny Manning	.08	.04	.01
	Los Angeles Clippers			
☐ 22	Alonzo Mourning	.60	.25	.08
	Charlotte Hornets			
☐ 23	Michael Jordan	4.00	1.80	.50
	Chicago Bulls			
☐ 24	Hakeem Olajuwon	.75	.35	.09
	Houston Rockets			
☐ 25	Scott Skiles	.05	.02	.01
	Orlando Magic			
☐ 26	Stacey Augmon	.08	.04	.01
	Atlanta Hawks			
☐ 27	Mitch Richmond	.15	.07	.02
	Sacramento Kings			
☐ 28	Derrick Coleman	.08	.04	.01
	New Jersey Nets			
☐ 29	Jeff Malone	.08	.04	.01
	Utah Jazz			
☐ 30	Larry Johnson	.30	.14	.04
	Charlotte Hornets			
☐ 31	Sam Perkins	.08	.04	.01
	Seattle Supersonics			
☐ 32	Shaquille O'Neal	2.50	1.15	.30
	Orlando Magic			
☐ 33	Walt Williams	.10	.05	.01
	Sacramento Kings			
☐ 34	Doug West	.05	.02	.01
	Minnesota Timberwolves			
☐ 35	Mark Price	.10	.05	.01
	Cleveland Cavaliers			
☐ 36	Rony Seikaly	.05	.02	.01
	Miami Heat			
☐ 37	Michael Adams	.05	.02	.01
	Washington Bullets			
☐ 38	Anthony Peeler	.05	.02	.01
	Los Angeles Lakers			
☐ 39	Larry Nance	.05	.02	.01
	Cleveland Cavaliers			
☐ 40	Shawn Kemp	.60	.25	.08
	Seattle Supersonics			
☐ 41	Terry Porter	.08	.04	.01
	Portland Trail Blazers			
☐ 42	Dan Majerle	.05	.02	.01
	Phoenix Suns			
☐ 43	Dennis Rodman	.20	.09	.03
	San Antonio Spurs			
☐ 44	Isiah Thomas	.15	.07	.02
	Detroit Pistons			
☐ 45	Spud Webb	.08	.04	.01
	Sacramento Kings			
☐ 46	Pooh Richardson	.05	.02	.01
	Indiana Pacers			
☐ 47	Tim Hardaway	.10	.05	.01
	Golden State Warriors			
☐ 48	Derek Harper	.08	.04	.01
	Dallas Mavericks			
☐ 49	Pervis Ellison	.05	.02	.01
	Washington Bullets			
☐ 50	Xavier McDaniel	.05	.02	.01
	Boston Celtics			
☐ 51	Jeff Hornacek	.08	.04	.01
	Philadelphia 76ers			
☐ 52	Ken Norman	.05	.02	.01
	Milwaukee Bucks			
☐ 53	LaPhonso Ellis	.05	.02	.01
	Denver Nuggets			
☐ 54	Charles Barkley	.60	.25	.08
	Phoenix Suns			
☐ 55	Tom Gugliotta	.10	.05	.01
	Washington Bullets			
☐ 56	Clifford Robinson	.10	.05	.01
	Portland Trail Blazers			
☐ 57	Mark Jackson	.05	.02	.01
	Los Angeles Clippers			
☐ 58	Mahmoud Abdul-Rauf	.05	.02	.01
	Denver Nuggets			
☐ 59	Todd Day	.08	.04	.01

☐ 60	Kenny Anderson	.10	.05	.01
	New Jersey Nets			
☐ 61	Jim Jackson	.60	.25	.08
	Dallas Mavericks			
☐ 62	Chris Mullin	.10	.05	.01
	Golden State Warriors			
☐ 63	Scottie Pippen	.30	.14	.04
	Chicago Bulls			
☐ 64	Dikembe Mutombo	.25	.11	.03
	Denver Nuggets			
☐ 65	Sean Elliott	.05	.02	.01
	Detroit Pistons			
☐ 66	Clarence Weatherspoon	.10	.05	.01
	Philadelphia 76ers			
☐ 67	Chris Morris	.05	.02	.01
	New Jersey Nets			
☐ 68	Clyde Drexler	.30	.14	.04
	Portland Trail Blazers			
☐ 69	Dennis Scott	.05	.02	.01
	Orlando Magic			
☐ 70	David Robinson	.60	.25	.08
	San Antonio Spurs			
☐ 71	Larry Johnson PL	.10	.05	.01
	Charlotte Hornets			
☐ 72	Chris Webber PL	.60	.25	.08
	Golden State Warriors			
☐ 73	Alonzo Mourning PL	.30	.14	.04
	Charlotte Hornets			
☐ 74	Lloyd Daniels PL	.05	.02	.01
	San Antonio Spurs			
☐ 75	Derrick Coleman PL	.05	.02	.01
	New Jersey Nets			
☐ 76	Tim Hardaway PL	.05	.02	.01
	Golden State Warriors			
☐ 77	Isiah Thomas PL	.08	.04	.01
	Detroit Pistons			
☐ 78	Chris Mullin PL	.05	.02	.01
	Golden State Warriors			
☐ 79	Shaquille O'Neal PL	1.25	.55	.16
	Orlando Magic			
☐ 80	Shawn Bradley	.40	.18	.05
	Philadelphia 76ers			
☐ 81	Chris Webber	1.50	.65	.19
	Golden State Warriors			
☐ 82	Jamal Mashburn	2.00	.90	.25
	Dallas Mavericks			
☐ 83	Anfernee Hardaway	4.00	1.80	.50
	Orlando Magic			
☐ 84	Calbert Cheaney	.50	.23	.06
	Washington Bullets			
☐ 85	Vin Baker	1.00	.45	.13
	Milwaukee Bucks			
☐ 86	Isaiah Rider	.60	.25	.08
	Minnesota Timberwolves			
☐ 87	Lindsey Hunter	.15	.07	.02
	Detroit Pistons			
☐ 88	Bobby Hurley	.20	.09	.03
	Sacramento Kings			
☐ 89	Dominique Wilkins 3DJ	.08	.04	.01
	Atlanta Hawks			
☐ 90	Charles Barkley 3DJ	.30	.14	.04
	Phoenix Suns			
☐ 91	Michael Jordan 3DJ	2.00	.90	.25
	Chicago Bulls			
☐ 92	Derrick Coleman 3DJ	.05	.02	.01
	New Jersey Nets			
☐ 93	Scottie Pippen 3DJ	.10	.05	.01
	Chicago Bulls			
☐ 94	Karl Malone 3DJ	.10	.05	.01
	Utah Jazz			

☐ 95	Larry Johnson 3DJ	.10	.05	.01
	Charlotte Hornets			
☐ 96	Cedric Ceballos 3DJ	.05	.02	.01
	Phoenix Suns			
☐ 97	David Robinson 3DJ	.30	.14	.04
	San Antonio Spurs			
☐ 98	Patrick Ewing 3DJ	.10	.05	.01
	New York Knicks			
☐ 99	Clarence Weatherspoon 3DJ	.05	.02	.01
	Philadelphia 76ers			
☐ 100	Alonzo Mourning 3DJ	.30	.14	.04
	Charlotte Hornets			
☐ 101	Stacey Augmon 3DJ	.05	.02	.01
	Atlanta Hawks			
☐ 102	Shaquille O'Neal 3DJ	1.25	.55	.16
	Orlando Magic			
☐ 103	Clyde Drexler 3DJ	.10	.05	.01
	Portland Trail Blazers			
☐ 104	Shawn Kemp 3DJ	.30	.14	.04
	Seattle Supersonics			
☐ 105	Harold Miner 3DJ	.05	.02	.01
	Miami Heat			
☐ 106	Chris Webber 3DJ	.60	.25	.08
	Golden State Warriors			
☐ 107	Dikembe Mutombo 3DJ	.08	.04	.01
	Denver Nuggets			
☐ 108	Doug West 3DJ	.05	.02	.01
	Minnesota Timberwolves			
☐ 109	Checklist 1	.25	.11	.03
	Michael Jordan			
☐ 110	Checklist 2	.25	.11	.03
	Michael Jordan			

1993-94
Upper Deck SE

This 225-card standard size (2 1/2" by 3 1/2") set was distributed in 12-card hobby East, hobby West, retail and 10-card magazine retail packs. There are 36 packs per box. Card fronts feature color player action shots that are borderless, except on the left, where a strip carries the player's name in gold foil along with his position and a vertically distorted black-and-white version of the action shot. The player's team name appears in vertical gold-foil lettering near the right edge. The back carries a color player action photo, with his name, position, and brief biography appearing in stripes across the top. Statistics and career high-

lights are displayed horizontally in a ghosted panel on the left. The set closes with the following topical subsets: NBA All-Star Weekend Highlights (181-198) and Team Headlines (199-225). The cards are numbered on the back. Two Michael Jordan insert cards are a Kilroy card (JK1) and a retirement tribute card (MJR1). These were inserted at a rate of 1 in 72 packs.

	MINT	NRMT	EXC
COMPLETE SET (225)	15.00	6.75	1.90
COMMON CARD (1-225)	.05	.02	.01

		MINT	NRMT	EXC
☐ 1	Scottie Pippen	.30	.14	.04
	Chicago Bulls			
☐ 2	Todd Day	.08	.04	.01
	Milwaukee Bucks			
☐ 3	Detlef Schrempf	.10	.05	.01
	Seattle Supersonics			
☐ 4	Chris Webber	1.50	.65	.19
	Golden State Warriors			
☐ 5	Michael Adams	.05	.02	.01
	Washington Bullets			
☐ 6	Loy Vaught	.08	.04	.01
	Los Angeles Clippers			
☐ 7	Doug West	.05	.02	.01
	Minnesota Timberwolves			
☐ 8	A.C. Green	.10	.05	.01
	Phoenix Suns			
☐ 9	Anthony Mason	.08	.04	.01
	New York Knicks			
☐ 10	Clyde Drexler	.30	.14	.04
	Portland Trail Blazers			
☐ 11	Popeye Jones	.30	.14	.04
	Dallas Mavericks			
☐ 12	Vlade Divac	.10	.05	.01
	Los Angeles Lakers			
☐ 13	Armon Gilliam	.05	.02	.01
	New Jersey Nets			
☐ 14	Hersey Hawkins	.08	.04	.01
	Charlotte Hornets			
☐ 15	Dennis Scott	.05	.02	.01
	Orlando Magic			
☐ 16	Bimbo Coles	.05	.02	.01
	Miami Heat			
☐ 17	Blue Edwards	.05	.02	.01
	Milwaukee Bucks			
☐ 18	Negele Knight	.05	.02	.01
	San Antonio Spurs			
☐ 19	Dale Davis	.05	.02	.01
	Indiana Pacers			
☐ 20	Isiah Thomas	.15	.07	.02
	Detroit Pistons			
☐ 21	Latrell Sprewell	.60	.25	.08
	Golden State Warriors			
☐ 22	Kenny Smith	.05	.02	.01
	Houston Rockets			
☐ 23	Bryant Stith	.05	.02	.01
	Denver Nuggets			
☐ 24	Terry Porter	.08	.04	.01
	Portland Trail Blazers			
☐ 25	Spud Webb	.08	.04	.01
	Sacramento Kings			
☐ 26	John Battle	.05	.02	.01
	Cleveland Cavaliers			
☐ 27	Jeff Malone	.08	.04	.01
	Philadelphia 76ers			
☐ 28	Olden Polynice	.05	.02	.01
	Sacramento Kings			
☐ 29	Kevin Willis	.08	.04	.01
	Atlanta Hawks			
☐ 30	Robert Parish	.10	.05	.01
	Boston Celtics			
☐ 31	Kevin Johnson	.15	.07	.02
	Phoenix Suns			
☐ 32	Shaquille O'Neal	2.50	1.15	.30
	Orlando Magic			
☐ 33	Willie Anderson	.05	.02	.01
	San Antonio Spurs			
☐ 34	Micheal Williams	.05	.02	.01
	Minnesota Timberwolves			
☐ 35	Steve Smith	.08	.04	.01
	Miami Heat			
☐ 36	Rik Smits	.10	.05	.01
	Indiana Pacers			
☐ 37	Pete Myers	.05	.02	.01
	Chicago Bulls			
☐ 38	Oliver Miller	.08	.04	.01
	Phoenix Suns			
☐ 39	Eddie Johnson	.08	.04	.01
	Charlotte Hornets			
☐ 40	Calbert Cheaney	.50	.23	.06
	Washington Bullets			
☐ 41	Vernon Maxwell	.05	.02	.01
	Houston Rockets			
☐ 42	James Worthy	.10	.05	.01
	Los Angeles Lakers			
☐ 43	Dino Radja	.40	.18	.05
	Boston Celtics			
☐ 44	Derrick Coleman	.10	.05	.01
	New Jersey Nets			
☐ 45	Reggie Williams	.05	.02	.01
	Denver Nuggets			
☐ 46	Dale Ellis	.08	.04	.01
	San Antonio Spurs			
☐ 47	Clifford Robinson	.10	.05	.01
	Portland Trail Blazers			
☐ 48	Doug Christie	.05	.02	.01
	Los Angeles Lakers			
☐ 49	Ricky Pierce	.08	.04	.01
	Seattle Supersonics			
☐ 50	Sean Elliott	.08	.04	.01
	Detroit Pistons			
☐ 51	Anfernee Hardaway	4.00	1.80	.50
	Orlando Magic			
☐ 52	Dana Barros	.10	.05	.01
	Philadelphia 76ers			
☐ 53	Reggie Miller	.30	.14	.04
	Indiana Pacers			
☐ 54	Brian Williams	.05	.02	.01
	Denver Nuggets			
☐ 55	Otis Thorpe	.08	.04	.01
	Houston Rockets			
☐ 56	Jerome Kersey	.05	.02	.01
	Portland Trail Blazers			
☐ 57	Larry Johnson	.30	.14	.04
	Charlotte Hornets			
☐ 58	Rex Chapman	.05	.02	.01
	Washington Bullets			
☐ 59	Kevin Edwards	.05	.02	.01
	New Jersey Nets			
☐ 60	Nate McMillan	.05	.02	.01
	Seattle Supersonics			
☐ 61	Chris Mullin	.10	.05	.01
	Golden State Warriors			
☐ 62	Bill Cartwright	.05	.02	.01
	Chicago Bulls			
☐ 63	Dennis Rodman	.20	.09	.03
	San Antonio Spurs			
☐ 64	Pooh Richardson	.05	.02	.01
	Indiana Pacers			

☐ 65	Tyrone Hill .... Cleveland Cavaliers	.05	.02	.01
☐ 66	Scott Brooks .... Houston Rockets	.05	.02	.01
☐ 67	Brad Daugherty .... Cleveland Cavaliers	.08	.04	.01
☐ 68	Joe Dumars .... Detroit Pistons	.15	.07	.02
☐ 69	Vin Baker .... Milwaukee Bucks	1.00	.45	.13
☐ 70	Rod Strickland .... Portland Trail Blazers	.08	.04	.01
☐ 71	Tom Chambers .... Utah Jazz	.08	.04	.01
☐ 72	Charles Oakley .... New York Knicks	.08	.04	.01
☐ 73	Craig Ehlo .... Atlanta Hawks	.05	.02	.01
☐ 74	LaPhonso Ellis .... Denver Nuggets	.08	.04	.01
☐ 75	Kevin Gamble .... Boston Celtics	.05	.02	.01
☐ 76	Shawn Bradley .... Philadelphia 76ers	.40	.18	.05
☐ 77	Kendall Gill .... Seattle Supersonics	.05	.02	.01
☐ 78	Hakeem Olajuwon .... Houston Rockets	.75	.35	.09
☐ 79	Nick Anderson .... Orlando Magic	.08	.04	.01
☐ 80	Anthony Peeler .... Los Angeles Lakers	.05	.02	.01
☐ 81	Wayman Tisdale .... Sacramento Kings	.08	.04	.01
☐ 82	Danny Manning .... Los Angeles Clippers	.10	.05	.01
☐ 83	John Starks .... New York Knicks	.08	.04	.01
☐ 84	Jeff Hornacek .... Utah Jazz	.08	.04	.01
☐ 85	Victor Alexander .... Golden State Warriors	.05	.02	.01
☐ 86	Mitch Richmond .... Sacramento Kings	.15	.07	.02
☐ 87	Mookie Blaylock .... Atlanta Hawks	.08	.04	.01
☐ 88	Harvey Grant .... Portland Trail Blazers	.05	.02	.01
☐ 89	Doug Smith .... Dallas Mavericks	.05	.02	.01
☐ 90	John Stockton .... Utah Jazz	.30	.14	.04
☐ 91	Charles Barkley .... Phoenix Suns	.60	.25	.08
☐ 92	Gerald Wilkins .... Cleveland Cavaliers	.05	.02	.01
☐ 93	Mario Elie .... Houston Rockets	.05	.02	.01
☐ 94	Ken Norman .... Milwaukee Bucks	.05	.02	.01
☐ 95	B.J. Armstrong .... Chicago Bulls	.05	.02	.01
☐ 96	John Williams .... Cleveland Cavaliers	.08	.04	.01
☐ 97	Rony Seikaly .... Miami Heat	.05	.02	.01
☐ 98	Sean Rooks .... Dallas Mavericks	.05	.02	.01
☐ 99	Shawn Kemp .... Seattle Supersonics	.60	.25	.08
☐ 100	Danny Ainge	.08	.04	.01
☐ 101	Terry Mills .... Phoenix Suns	.05	.02	.01
☐ 102	Doc Rivers .... Detroit Pistons	.05	.02	.01
☐ 103	Chuck Person .... New York Knicks	.08	.04	.01
☐ 104	Sam Cassell .... Minnesota Timberwolves	.50	.23	.06
☐ 105	Kevin Duckworth .... Houston Rockets	.05	.02	.01
☐ 106	Dan Majerle .... Washington Bullets	.08	.04	.01
☐ 107	Mark Jackson .... Phoenix Suns	.05	.02	.01
☐ 108	Steve Kerr .... Los Angeles Clippers	.05	.02	.01
☐ 109	Sam Perkins .... Chicago Bulls	.08	.04	.01
☐ 110	Clarence Weatherspoon ..... Seattle Supersonics	.10	.05	.01
☐ 111	Felton Spencer .... Philadelphia 76ers	.05	.02	.01
☐ 112	Greg Anthony .... Utah Jazz	.05	.02	.01
☐ 113	Pete Chilcutt .... New York Knicks	.05	.02	.01
☐ 114	Malik Sealy .... Sacramento Kings	.05	.02	.01
☐ 115	Horace Grant .... Indiana Pacers	.15	.07	.02
☐ 116	Chris Morris .... Chicago Bulls	.05	.02	.01
☐ 117	Xavier McDaniel .... New Jersey Nets	.08	.04	.01
☐ 118	Lionel Simmons .... Boston Celtics	.05	.02	.01
☐ 119	Dell Curry .... Sacramento Kings	.05	.02	.01
☐ 120	Moses Malone .... Charlotte Hornets	.15	.07	.02
☐ 121	Lindsey Hunter .... Philadelphia 76ers	.15	.07	.02
☐ 122	Buck Williams .... Detroit Pistons	.08	.04	.01
☐ 123	Mahmoud Abdul-Rauf .. Portland Trail Blazers	.05	.02	.01
☐ 124	Rumeal Robinson .... Denver Nuggets	.05	.02	.01
☐ 125	Chris Mills .... Charlotte Hornets	.40	.18	.05
☐ 126	Scott Skiles .... Cleveland Cavaliers	.05	.02	.01
☐ 127	Derrick McKey .... Orlando Magic	.08	.04	.01
☐ 128	Avery Johnson .... Indiana Pacers	.05	.02	.01
☐ 129	Harold Miner .... Golden State Warriors	.05	.02	.01
☐ 130	Frank Brickowski .... Miami Heat	.05	.02	.01
☐ 131	Gary Payton .... Charlotte Hornets	.10	.05	.01
☐ 132	Don MacLean .... Seattle Supersonics	.05	.02	.01
☐ 133	Thurl Bailey .... Washington Bullets	.05	.02	.01
☐ 134	Nick Van Exel .... Minnesota Timberwolves	2.00	.90	.25
☐ 135	Matt Geiger .... Los Angeles Lakers	.05	.02	.01
	Miami Heat			

☐ 136 Stacey Augmon	.08	.04	.01
Atlanta Hawks			
☐ 137 Sedale Threatt	.05	.02	.01
Los Angeles Lakers			
☐ 138 Patrick Ewing	.30	.14	.04
New York Knicks			
☐ 139 Tyrone Corbin	.05	.02	.01
Utah Jazz			
☐ 140 Jim Jackson	.60	.25	.08
Dallas Mavericks			
☐ 141 Christian Laettner	.10	.05	.01
Minnesota Timberwolves			
☐ 142 Robert Horry	.10	.05	.01
Houston Rockets			
☐ 143 J.R. Reid	.05	.02	.01
San Antonio Spurs			
☐ 144 Eric Murdock	.05	.02	.01
Milwaukee Bucks			
☐ 145 Alonzo Mourning	.60	.25	.08
Charlotte Hornets			
☐ 146 Sherman Douglas	.05	.02	.01
Boston Celtics			
☐ 147 Tom Gugliotta	.10	.05	.01
Washington Bullets			
☐ 148 Glen Rice	.10	.05	.01
Miami Heat			
☐ 149 Mark Price	.10	.05	.01
Cleveland Cavaliers			
☐ 150 Dikembe Mutombo	.25	.11	.03
Denver Nuggets			
☐ 151 Derek Harper	.08	.04	.01
New York Knicks			
☐ 152 Karl Malone	.30	.14	.04
Utah Jazz			
☐ 153 Byron Scott	.08	.04	.01
Indiana Pacers			
☐ 154 Reggie Jordan	.05	.02	.01
Los Angeles Lakers			
☐ 155 Dominique Wilkins	.15	.07	.02
Atlanta Hawks			
☐ 156 Bobby Hurley	.20	.09	.03
Sacramento Kings			
☐ 157 Ron Harper	.08	.04	.01
Los Angeles Clippers			
☐ 158 Bryon Russell	.05	.02	.01
Utah Jazz			
☐ 159 Frank Johnson	.05	.02	.01
Phoenix Suns			
☐ 160 Toni Kukoc	.50	.23	.06
Chicago Bulls			
☐ 161 Lloyd Daniels	.05	.02	.01
San Antonio Spurs			
☐ 162 Jeff Turner	.05	.02	.01
Orlando Magic			
☐ 163 Muggsy Bogues	.05	.02	.01
Charlotte Hornets			
☐ 164 Chris Gatling	.05	.02	.01
Golden State Warriors			
☐ 165 Kenny Anderson	.10	.05	.01
New Jersey Nets			
☐ 166 Elmore Spencer	.05	.02	.01
Los Angeles Clippers			
☐ 167 Jamal Mashburn	2.00	.90	.25
Dallas Mavericks			
☐ 168 Tim Perry	.05	.02	.01
Philadelphia 76ers			
☐ 169 Antonio Davis	.10	.05	.01
Indiana Pacers			
☐ 170 Isaiah Rider	.60	.25	.08
Minnesota Timberwolves			
☐ 171 Dee Brown	.08	.04	.01
Boston Celtics			
☐ 172 Walt Williams	.10	.05	.01
Sacramento Kings			
☐ 173 Elden Campbell	.05	.02	.01
Los Angeles Lakers			
☐ 174 Benoit Benjamin	.05	.02	.01
New Jersey Nets			
☐ 175 Billy Owens	.08	.04	.01
Golden State Warriors			
☐ 176 Andrew Lang	.05	.02	.01
Atlanta Hawks			
☐ 177 David Robinson	.60	.25	.08
San Antonio Spurs			
☐ 178 Checklist 1	.05	.02	.01
☐ 179 Checklist 2	.05	.02	.01
☐ 180 Checklist 3	.05	.02	.01
☐ 181 Shawn Bradley AS	.10	.05	.01
Philadelphia 76ers			
☐ 182 Calbert Cheaney AS	.10	.05	.01
Washington Bullets			
☐ 183 Toni Kukoc AS	.10	.05	.01
Chicago Bulls			
☐ 184 Popeye Jones AS	.08	.04	.01
Dallas Mavericks			
☐ 185 Lindsey Hunter AS	.05	.02	.01
Detroit Pistons			
☐ 186 Chris Webber AS	.60	.25	.08
Golden State Warriors			
☐ 187 Bryon Russell AS	.05	.02	.01
Utah Jazz			
☐ 188 Anfernee Hardaway AS	1.50	.65	.19
Orlando Magic			
☐ 189 Nick Van Exel AS	.75	.35	.09
Los Angeles Lakers			
☐ 190 P.J. Brown AS	.10	.05	.01
New Jersey Nets			
☐ 191 Isaiah Rider AS	.25	.11	.03
Minnesota Timberwolves			
☐ 192 Chris Mills AS	.10	.05	.01
Cleveland Cavaliers			
☐ 193 Antonio Davis AS	.10	.05	.01
Indiana Pacers			
☐ 194 Jamal Mashburn AS	.75	.35	.09
Dallas Mavericks			
☐ 195 Dino Radja AS	.10	.05	.01
Boston Celtics			
☐ 196 Sam Cassell AS	.10	.05	.01
Houston Rockets			
☐ 197 Isaiah Rider ASW	.25	.11	.03
Minnesota Timberwolves			
☐ 198 Mark Price ASW	.05	.02	.01
Cleveland Cavaliers			
☐ 199 Stacey Augmon HDL	.05	.02	.01
Atlanta Hawks			
☐ 200 Celtics Team HDL	.05	.02	.01
Boston Celtics			
☐ 201 Eddie Johnson HDL	.05	.02	.01
Charlotte Hornets			
☐ 202 Scottie Pippen HDL	.10	.05	.01
Chicago Bulls			
☐ 203 Brad Daugherty HDL	.05	.02	.01
Cleveland Cavaliers			
☐ 204 Jamal Mashburn HDL	.50	.23	.06
Dallas Mavericks			
☐ 205 Dikembe Mutombo HDL	.08	.04	.01
Oliver Miller HDL			
Denver Nuggets			
☐ 206 Lindsey Hunter HDL	.05	.02	.01
Detroit Pistons			
☐ 207 Chris Webber HDL	.40	.18	.05
Golden State Warriors			

☐ 208	Rockets Team HDL ...... Houston Rockets	.05	.02	.01
☐ 209	Derrick McKey HDL ..... Indiana Pacers	.05	.02	.01
☐ 210	Danny Manning HDL .05 Los Angeles Clippers	.05	.02	.01
☐ 211	Doug Christie HDL ...... .05 Los Angeles Lakers	.05	.02	.01
☐ 212	Glen Rice HDL .... Miami Heat	.05	.02	.01
☐ 213	Todd Day HDL .... Ken Norman HDL Vin Baker HDL Jon Barry HDL Milwaukee Bucks	.05	.02	.01
☐ 214	Isaiah Rider HDL........... .15 Minnesota Timberwolves	.15	.07	.02
☐ 215	Kenny Anderson HDL.... New Jersey Nets	.05	.02	.01
☐ 216	Patrick Ewing HDL .... New York Knicks	.10	.05	.01
☐ 217	Anfernee Hardaway HDL Orlando Magic	1.00	.45	.13
☐ 218	Moses Malone HDL ..... Philadelphia 76ers	.08	.04	.01
☐ 219	Kevin Johnson HDL ..... Phoenix Suns	.08	.04	.01
☐ 220	Clifford Robinson HDL. .05 Portland Trail Blazers	.05	.02	.01
☐ 221	Wayman Tisdale HDL.... Sacramento Kings	.05	.02	.01
☐ 222	David Robinson HDL .... San Antonio Spurs	.30	.14	.04
☐ 223	Sonics Team HDL .... Seattle Supersonics	.05	.02	.01
☐ 224	John Stockton HDL....... Utah Jazz	.10	.05	.01
☐ 225	Don MacLean HDL........ Washington Bullets	.05	.02	.01
☐ JK1	Johnny Kilroy.............. 5.00	5.00	2.30	.60
☐ MJR1	Michael Jordan ...... 12.00 Retirement Card	12.00	5.50	1.50

1993-94
Upper Deck SE
Electric Court

This 225-card set parallels that of the 1993-94 Upper Deck SE. The only difference in design is an "Electric Court" logo that appears on the fronts. These cards were distributed one per 12-card hobby East, hobby West and retail pack and two per 10-card magazine pack. Please refer to the multipliers provided below (coupled with the prices of the corresponding regular issue cards) to ascertain values.

	MINT	NRMT	EXC
COMPLETE SET (225)	60.00	27.00	7.50
COMMON CARD (1-225)	.15	.07	.02
*STARS: 1.5X to 3X BASIC CARDS..			
*ROOKIES: 1X to 2X BASIC CARDS.			

1993-94
Upper Deck SE
Electric Gold

Randomly inserted in hobby East, hobby West and retail packs at a rate of one in 36, this is a parallel set to '93-94 Upper Deck SE. The Electric Gold set name appears in gold foil lettering near the bottom. Only the top few cards in the set are individually priced below. Please refer to the multipliers listed below (coupled with the prices of the corresponding regular issue cards) to ascertain values.

	MINT	NRMT	EXC
COMPLETE SET (225)	600.00	275.00	75.00
COMMON CARD (1-225)	2.00	.90	.25
*STARS: 25X to 40X BASIC CARDS.			
*ROOKIES: 12X to 20X BASIC CARDS			

☐ 4	Chris Webber.............. Golden State Warriors	30.00	13.50	3.80
☐ 21	Latrell Sprewell .... Golden State Warriors	25.00	11.50	3.10
☐ 32	Shaquille O'Neal....... Orlando Magic	100.00	45.00	12.50
☐ 51	Anfernee Hardaway .... Orlando Magic	75.00	34.00	9.50
☐ 78	Hakeem Olajuwon ...... Houston Rockets	30.00	13.50	3.80
☐ 91	Charles Barkley .... Phoenix Suns	25.00	11.50	3.10
☐ 99	Shawn Kemp..............	25.00	11.50	3.10

		MINT	NRMT	EXC
	Seattle Supersonics			
☐ 134	Nick Van Exel	40.00	18.00	5.00
	Los Angeles Lakers			
☐ 140	Jim Jackson	25.00	11.50	3.10
	Dallas Mavericks			
☐ 145	Alonzo Mourning	25.00	11.50	3.10
	Charlotte Hornets			
☐ 167	Jamal Mashburn	40.00	18.00	5.00
	Dallas Mavericks			
☐ 177	David Robinson	25.00	11.50	3.10
	San Antonio Spurs			
☐ 188	Anfernee Hardaway AS	30.00	13.50	3.80
	Orlando Magic			

1993-94
Upper Deck SE
Behind the Glass

Randomly inserted in 12-card retail packs at a rate of one in 30, cards from this 15-card standard-size (2 1/2" by 3 1/2") set capture some of the NBA's best dunkers from the unique camera angle behind the backboard glass. A gold-foil "Behind the Glass Trade Card" was randomly inserted in retail and hobby packs at a rate of one in 360. The collector could redeem the card for the complete 15-card "Behind the Glass" set. The redemption deadline was August 31, 1994. The borderless front features a color player action shot on a gold metallic finish. The player's name and position appear vertically along the right side. The back features a color player action shot on the right side with career highlights appearing alongside on the left.

		MINT	NRMT	EXC
COMPLETE SET (15)		50.00	23.00	6.25
COMMON CARD (G1-G15)		.75	.35	.09
☐ G1	Shawn Kemp	5.00	2.30	.60
	Seattle Supersonics			
☐ G2	Patrick Ewing	2.50	1.15	.30
	New York Knicks			
☐ G3	Dikembe Mutombo	2.00	.90	.25
	Denver Nuggets			
☐ G4	Charles Barkley	5.00	2.30	.60
	Phoenix Suns			
☐ G5	Hakeem Olajuwon	6.00	2.70	.75
	Houston Rockets			
☐ G6	Larry Johnson	2.50	1.15	.30
	Charlotte Hornets			
☐ G7	Chris Webber	8.00	3.60	1.00
	Golden State Warriors			
☐ G8	John Starks	.75	.35	.09
	New York Knicks			
☐ G9	Kevin Willis	.75	.35	.09
	Atlanta Hawks			
☐ G10	Scottie Pippen	2.50	1.15	.30
	Chicago Bulls			
☐ G11	Michael Jordan	30.00	13.50	3.80
	Chicago Bulls			
☐ G12	Alonzo Mourning	5.00	2.30	.60
	Charlotte Hornets			
☐ G13	Shaquille O'Neal	20.00	9.00	2.50
	Orlando Magic			
☐ G14	Shawn Bradley	2.00	.90	.25
	Philadelphia 76ers			
☐ G15	Ron Harper	.75	.35	.09
	Los Angeles Clippers			
☐ NNO	Behind the Glass Trade Card	1.50	.65	.19
☐ NNO	Redeemed BHG Trade	.25	.11	.03

1993-94
Upper Deck SE
Die Cut All-Stars

In these two 15-card insert sets, Upper Deck saluted a selection of current and potential future all-stars. The cards were available in East hobby and West hobby packs at a rate of one in 30 packs. Hobby dealers in the East received cases containing players from the Eastern conference, while hobby dealers in the West received cases containing players from the Western conference. Measuring the standard-size (2 1/2" by 3 1/2"), these die-cut cards were inserted in hobby packs only. This unique card design features a partial gold-foil border at the top only. Centered is a color player action photo. The player's name and team appear in red vertical lettering along the left side. The back features brief statistics.

	MINT	NRMT	EXC
COMPLETE SET (30)	900.00	400.00	115.00
COMPLETE EAST SET (15)..	425.00	190.00	52.50
COMPLETE WEST SET (15)..	475.00	210.00	60.00
COMMON EAST (E1-E15)	10.00	4.50	1.25
COMMON WEST (W1-W15) ..	10.00	4.50	1.25

		MINT	NRMT	EXC
☐ E1	Dominique Wilkins..... Atlanta Hawks	12.00	5.50	1.50
☐ E2	Alonzo Mourning........ Charlotte Hornets	50.00	23.00	6.25
☐ E3	B.J. Armstrong......... Chicago Bulls	10.00	4.50	1.25
☐ E4	Scottie Pippen............ Chicago Bulls	25.00	11.50	3.10
☐ E5	Mark Price .... Cleveland Cavaliers	10.00	4.50	1.25
☐ E6	Isiah Thomas .... Detroit Pistons	12.00	5.50	1.50
☐ E7	Harold Miner.............. Miami Heat	10.00	4.50	1.25
☐ E8	Vin Baker .... Milwaukee Bucks	35.00	16.00	4.40
☐ E9	Kenny Anderson......... New Jersey Nets	10.00	4.50	1.25
☐ E10	Derrick Coleman .... New Jersey Nets	10.00	4.50	1.25
☐ E11	Patrick Ewing .... New York Knicks	25.00	11.50	3.10
☐ E12	Anfernee Hardaway ... Orlando Magic	160.00	70.00	20.00
☐ E13	Shaquille O'Neal........ Orlando Magic	175.00	80.00	22.00
☐ E14	Shawn Bradley.......... Philadelphia 76ers	15.00	6.75	1.90
☐ E15	Calbert Cheaney........ Washington Bullets	20.00	9.00	2.50
☐ W1	Jim Jackson .... Dallas Mavericks	50.00	23.00	6.25
☐ W2	Jamal Mashburn......... Dallas Mavericks	75.00	34.00	9.50
☐ W3	Dikembe Mutombo ..... Denver Nuggets	20.00	9.00	2.50
☐ W4	Latrell Sprewell.......... Golden State Warriors	50.00	23.00	6.25
☐ W5	Chris Webber............. Golden State Warriors	60.00	27.00	7.50
☐ W6	Hakeem Olajuwon...... Houston Rockets	60.00	27.00	7.50
☐ W7	Danny Manning .... Los Angeles Clippers	10.00	4.50	1.25
☐ W8	Nick Van Exel............ Los Angeles Lakers	75.00	34.00	9.50
☐ W9	Isaiah Rider .... Minnesota Timberwolves	25.00	11.50	3.10
☐ W10	Charles Barkley.......... Phoenix Suns	50.00	23.00	6.25
☐ W11	Clyde Drexler .... Portland Trail Blazers	30.00	13.50	3.80
☐ W12	Mitch Richmond ..... Sacramento Kings	12.00	5.50	1.50
☐ W13	David Robinson .... San Antonio Spurs	50.00	23.00	6.25
☐ W14	Shawn Kemp............. Seattle Supersonics	50.00	23.00	6.25
☐ W15	Karl Malone .... Utah Jazz	25.00	11.50	3.10

1993-94
Upper Deck SE
USA Trade

This 24-card set was only available by exchanging the Upper Deck SE USA Trade card (random insert at one in 360 packs) before August 31, 1994. The set previewed the USA Basketball set that was released in the summer of 1994. The cards depict the 12 players selected by USA Basketball for "Dream Team II" plus Tim Hardaway, who was originally selected to the team was unable to participate due to injury, and 11 from the original Dream Team. Measuring the standard size (2 1/2" by 3 1/2"), each card features a borderless color player action shot on its front. The player's name and position appear in white lettering within red and blue stripes near the bottom. The words "Exchange Set" in vertical gold-foil lettering and the gold-foil Upper Deck logo appear at the upper left. On a background of the American flag, the back carries a posed color shot of the player in his USA uniform and career highlights. The cards are numbered on the back with a "USA" prefix.

	MINT	NRMT	EXC
COMPLETE SET (24)	50.00	23.00	6.25
COMMON CARD (1-24)	.50	.23	.06

		MINT	NRMT	EXC
☐ 1	Charles Barkley..............	4.00	1.80	.50
☐ 2	Larry Bird......................	6.00	2.70	.75
☐ 3	Clyde Drexler.................	2.00	.90	.25
☐ 4	Patrick Ewing.................	2.00	.90	.25
☐ 5	Michael Jordan	25.00	11.50	3.10
☐ 6	Christian Laettner...........	.75	.35	.09
☐ 7	Karl Malone	2.00	.90	.25
☐ 8	Chris Mullin	.75	.35	.09
☐ 9	Scottie Pippen................	2.00	.90	.25
☐ 10	David Robinson	4.00	1.80	.50
☐ 11	John Stockton................	2.00	.90	.25
☐ 12	Dominique Wilkins..........	1.00	.45	.13
☐ 13	Isiah Thomas	1.00	.45	.13
☐ 14	Dan Majerle...................	.50	.23	.06
☐ 15	Steve Smith...................	.50	.23	.06
☐ 16	Alonzo Mourning............	4.00	1.80	.50
☐ 17	Shawn Kemp..................	4.00	1.80	.50
☐ 18	Larry Johnson................	2.00	.90	.25
☐ 19	Tim Hardaway................	.75	.35	.09
☐ 20	Joe Dumars...................	1.00	.45	.13

		MINT	NRMT	EXC
☐ 21	Mark Price	.75	.35	.09
☐ 22	Derrick Coleman	.75	.35	.09
☐ 23	Reggie Miller	2.00	.90	.25
☐ 24	Shaquille O'Neal	15.00	6.75	1.90
☐ NNO	Exp. USA Trade Card	1.50	.65	.19
☐ NNO	Red. USA Trade Card	.25	.11	.03

1994 Upper Deck USA

These 90 standard-size (2 1/2" by 3 1/2") cards honor the '94 Team USA players. Cards were distributed in 10-card packs. Each foil box contained 36 packs. The borderless fronts feature color posed and action player shots. The player's name and position appear in red, white, and blue bars near the bottom. The card's subtitle appears vertically in gold-foil lettering near the left edge, information for which appears on the back. The cards are numbered on the back.

		MINT	NRMT	EXC
COMPLETE SET (90)		10.00	4.50	1.25
COMMON CARD (1-90)		.05	.02	.01
☐ 1	Derrick Coleman Player Quotebook	.05	.02	.01
☐ 2	Derrick Coleman DC 1 Draft Choice	.05	.02	.01
☐ 3	Derrick Coleman 1991 Rookie of the Year	.05	.02	.01
☐ 4	Derrick Coleman 1994 All-Star Game	.05	.02	.01
☐ 5	Derrick Coleman The Jordan Report	.05	.02	.01
☐ 6	Derrick Coleman Career Statistics	.05	.02	.01
☐ 7	Joe Dumars Player Quotebook	.10	.05	.01
☐ 8	Joe Dumars 1986 All-Rookie Team	.10	.05	.01
☐ 9	Joe Dumars 1989 NBA Finals MVP	.10	.05	.01
☐ 10	Joe Dumars 4-Time All-Star	.10	.05	.01
☐ 11	Joe Dumars The Jordan Report	.10	.05	.01
☐ 12	Joe Dumars Career Statistics	.10	.05	.01

		MINT	NRMT	EXC
☐ 13	Tim Hardaway Player Quotebook	.05	.02	.01
☐ 14	Tim Hardaway 1990 NBA All-Rookie Team	.05	.02	.01
☐ 15	Tim Hardaway Run TMC	.05	.02	.01
☐ 16	Tim Hardaway 3-Time All-Star	.05	.02	.01
☐ 17	Tim Hardaway The Jordan Report	.05	.02	.01
☐ 18	Tim Hardaway Career Statistics	.05	.02	.01
☐ 19	Larry Johnson Player Quotebook	.15	.07	.02
☐ 20	Larry Johnson Franchise Player	.15	.07	.02
☐ 21	Larry Johnson 1992 Rookie Of The Year	.15	.07	.02
☐ 22	Larry Johnson 2-Time All-Star	.15	.07	.02
☐ 23	Larry Johnson The Jordan Report	.15	.07	.02
☐ 24	Larry Johnson Career Statistics	.15	.07	.02
☐ 25	Shawn Kemp Player Quotebook	.40	.18	.05
☐ 26	Shawn Kemp 19-Year-Old Rookie	.40	.18	.05
☐ 27	Shawn Kemp 2-Time NBA All-Star	.40	.18	.05
☐ 28	Shawn Kemp Reign Man	.40	.18	.05
☐ 29	Shawn Kemp The Jordan Report	.40	.18	.05
☐ 30	Shawn Kemp Career Statistics	.40	.18	.05
☐ 31	Dan Majerle Player Quotebook	.05	.02	.01
☐ 32	Dan Majerle 1988 USAB	.05	.02	.01
☐ 33	Dan Majerle 3-Time NBA All-Star	.05	.02	.01
☐ 34	Dan Majerle 3-Point King	.05	.02	.01
☐ 35	Dan Majerle The Jordan Report	.05	.02	.01
☐ 36	Dan Majerle Career Statistics	.05	.02	.01
☐ 37	Reggie Miller Player Quotebook	.20	.09	.03
☐ 38	Reggie Miller Miller Bloodlines	.20	.09	.03
☐ 39	Reggie Miller 1990 NBA All-Star	.20	.09	.03
☐ 40	Reggie Miller 57-Point Game	.20	.09	.03
☐ 41	Reggie Miller The Jordan Report	.20	.09	.03
☐ 42	Reggie Miller Career Statistics	.20	.09	.03
☐ 43	Alonzo Mourning Player Quotebook	.25	.11	.03
☐ 44	Alonzo Mourning 1990 World Championships	.25	.11	.03
☐ 45	Alonzo Mourning 1994 NBA All-Star	.25	.11	.03
☐ 46	Alonzo Mourning Zo-man's Land	.25	.11	.03
☐ 47	Alonzo Mourning The Jordan Report	.25	.11	.03
☐ 48	Alonzo Mourning	.25	.11	.03

Career Statistics		
☐ 49 Shaquille O'Neal........... 1.00	.45	.13
Player Quotebook		
☐ 50 Shaquille O'Neal........... 1.00	.45	.13
1993 Rookie of The Year		
☐ 51 Shaquille O'Neal........... 1.00	.45	.13
Time NBA All-Star		
☐ 52 Shaquille O'Neal........... 1.00	.45	.13
Shaqmania		
☐ 53 Shaquille O'Neal........... 1.00	.45	.13
The Jordan Report		
☐ 54 Shaquille O'Neal........... 1.00	.45	.13
Career Statistics		
☐ 55 Mark Price .... .05	.02	.01
Player Quotebook		
☐ 56 Mark Price .... .05	.02	.01
1983 Pan American Games		
☐ 57 Mark Price .... .05	.02	.01
4-Time NBA All-Star		
☐ 58 Mark Price .... .05	.02	.01
On The Mark		
☐ 59 Mark Price .... .05	.02	.01
The Jordan Report		
☐ 60 Mark Price .... .05	.02	.01
Career Statistics		
☐ 61 Steve Smith .... .05	.02	.01
Player Quotebook		
☐ 62 Steve Smith .... .05	.02	.01
Turning Up The Heat		
☐ 63 Steve Smith .... .05	.02	.01
1992 NBA All-Rookie Team		
☐ 64 Steve Smith .... .05	.02	.01
Playground Legend		
☐ 65 Steve Smith .... .05	.02	.01
The Jordan Report		
☐ 66 Steve Smith .... .05	.02	.01
Career Statistics		
☐ 67 Isiah Thomas .... .10	.05	.01
Player Quotebook		
☐ 68 Isiah Thomas .... .10	.05	.01
1980 USAB		
☐ 69 Isiah Thomas .... .10	.05	.01
1990 NBA Finals MVP		
☐ 70 Isiah Thomas .... .10	.05	.01
2-Time All-Star MVP		
☐ 71 Isiah Thomas .... .10	.05	.01
The Jordan Report		
☐ 72 Isiah Thomas .... .10	.05	.01
Career Statistics		
☐ 73 Dominique Wilkins........ .10	.05	.01
Player Quotebook		
☐ 74 Dominique Wilkins........ .10	.05	.01
1986 Scoring Champion		
☐ 75 Dominique Wilkins........ .10	.05	.01
8-Time NBA All-Star		
☐ 76 Dominique Wilkins........ .10	.05	.01
57-Point Games		
☐ 77 Dominique Wilkins........ .10	.05	.01
The Jordan Report		
☐ 78 Dominique Wilkins........ .10	.05	.01
Career Statistics		
☐ 79 Jennifer Azzi .... .05	.02	.01
USAB Women		
☐ 80 Daedra Charles .... .05	.02	.01
USAB Women		
☐ 81 Lisa Leslie .... .10	.05	.01
USAB Women		
☐ 82 Katrina McClain .... .05	.02	.01
USAB Women		
☐ 83 Dawn Staley .... .10	.05	.01
USAB Women		

☐ 84 Sheryl Swoopes........... .10	.05	.01
USAB Women		
☐ 85 Michael Jordan........... 4.00	1.80	.50
USAB Greats		
Chicago Bulls		
☐ 86 Larry Bird .... .75	.35	.09
USAB Greats		
Boston Celtics		
☐ 87 Jerry West .... .75	.35	.09
USAB Greats		
Los Angeles Lakers		
☐ 88 Adrian Dantley .... .05	.02	.01
USAB Greats		
☐ 89 Cheryl Miller .... .25	.11	.03
USAB Greats		
☐ 90 Henry Iba CO .... .10	.05	.01
USAB Greats		
☐ CK1 Checklist 1.............. .50	.23	.06
☐ CK2 Checklist 2.............. .50	.23	.06

1994
Upper Deck USA
Gold Medal

Inserted one per '94 Upper Deck USA pack, these gold cards are identical to the regular issues except for the Upper Deck Gold Medal logos appearing on the fronts. The cards are numbered on the back. Please refer to the multiplier provided below (coupled with the prices of the corresponding regular issue cards) to ascertain value.

	MINT	NRMT	EXC
COMPLETE SET (90)	25.00	11.50	3.10
COMMON CARD (1-90)	.15	.07	.02
*STARS: 1.25X TO 2.5X BASIC CARDS			

1994
Upper Deck USA
Chalk Talk

Randomly inserted in Upper Deck USA packs at a rate of one in 35, the Chalk Talk

set consists of 14 cards. Card fronts include a small hologram of Don Nelson who is also quoted on the back in reference to the player on the card. The card fronts are full-bleed on one side with a gray border on the other that contains the player's name. In addition to Nelson's quote, a small photo of him and a larger photo of the player appear on the back.

	MINT	NRMT	EXC
COMPLETE SET (14)	60.00	27.00	7.50
COMMON CARD (CT1-CT14)...	1.50	.65	.19
☐ CT1 Derrick Coleman .... New Jersey Nets	2.00	.90	.25
☐ CT2 Joe Dumars .... Detroit Pistons	3.00	1.35	.40
☐ CT3 Tim Hardaway............ Golden State Warriors	2.00	.90	.25
☐ CT4 Larry Johnson .... Charlotte Hornets	5.00	2.30	.60
☐ CT5 Shawn Kemp .... Seattle Supersonics	12.00	5.50	1.50
☐ CT6 Dan Majerle .... Phoenix Suns	1.50	.65	.19
☐ CT7 Reggie Miller .... Indiana Pacers	6.00	2.70	.75
☐ CT8 Alonzo Mourning .... Charlotte Hornets	8.00	3.60	1.00
☐ CT9 Shaquille O'Neal .... Orlando Magic	30.00	13.50	3.80
☐ CT10 Mark Price .... Cleveland Cavaliers	2.00	.90	.25
☐ CT11 Steve Smith .... Miami Heat	1.50	.65	.19
☐ CT12 Isiah Thomas .... Detroit Pistons	3.00	1.35	.40
☐ CT13 Dominique Wilkins .. Atlanta Hawks	3.00	1.35	.40
☐ CT14 Kevin Johnson.......... Phoenix Suns	3.00	1.35	.40

1994
Upper Deck USA
Follow Your Dreams

Randomly inserted at a rate of one in 14 packs, these 42 standard-size (2 1/2" by 3 1/2") game-prize cards feature borderless color player action shots on front. The cards

are broken into three 14-card sets that are distinguished by categories: assists, rebounds and scoring. The category appears on gold foil stamping on the front that appears in on one side along with the player's name. The back carries the rules for playing the game. Briefly, each game card depicts one of the 14 players from the '94 USA Dream Team. Each card also designates the player as either a "Top Scorer," "Top Rebounder," or "Top Assists." The player that led Dream Team II in either of these categories could have that specific card redeemed by the collector for a 14-card set of that category. Kevin Johnson's Assists card and Shaquille O'Neal's Rebounds and Scoring cards qualify as the three exchange cards. The redemption deadline for the three cards was November 30, 1994. All exchange cards are equally valued to the cards priced below.

	MINT	NRMT	EXC
COMP.ASSISTS SET (14)	20.00	9.00	2.50
COMP.REBOUNDS SET (14)..	20.00	9.00	2.50
COMP.SCORING SET (14)	20.00	9.00	2.50
COMMON CARD (1-14)	.50	.23	.06
*EXCHANGE CARDS: EQUAL VALUE			
☐ 1 Derrick Coleman .... New Jersey Nets	.75	.35	.09
☐ 2 Joe Dumars .... Detroit Pistons	1.00	.45	.13
☐ 3 Tim Hardaway................ Golden State Warriors	.75	.35	.09
☐ 4 Kevin Johnson............... Phoenix Suns	1.00	.45	.13
☐ 5 Larry Johnson .... Charlotte Hornets	1.50	.65	.19
☐ 6 Shawn Kemp .... Seattle Supersonics	4.00	1.80	.50
☐ 7 Dan Majerle.................... Phoenix Suns	.50	.23	.06
☐ 8 Reggie Miller.................. Indiana Pacers	2.00	.90	.25
☐ 9 Alonzo Mourning .... Charlotte Hornets	2.50	1.15	.30
☐ 10 Shaquille O'Neal........ Orlando Magic	10.00	4.50	1.25
☐ 11 Mark Price .... Cleveland Cavaliers	.75	.35	.09
☐ 12 Steve Smith .... Miami Heat	.50	.23	.06
☐ 13 Isiah Thomas .... Detroit Pistons	1.00	.45	.13
☐ 14 Dominique Wilkins....... Atlanta Hawks	1.00	.45	.13

1994
Upper Deck USA
Jordan's Highlights

Topical subsets featured are All-Rookie Team (1-10), All-NBA (11-25), USA Basketball (167-180), Draft Analysis (181-198), and Then and Now (352-360).

	MINT	NRMT	EXC
COMPLETE SET (360)	50.00	23.00	6.25
COMPLETE SERIES 1 (180)	30.00	13.50	3.80
COMPLETE SERIES 2 (180)	20.00	9.00	2.50
COMMON CARD (1-360)	.10	.05	.01

Randomly inserted at a rate of one in 35 packs, the five-card standard size (2 1/2" by 3 1/2") set features action photos of Michael Jordan representing the United States during international play. A facsimile autograph in gold foil lettering appears near the bottom. On back, the American flag is used as a backdrop to highlights and statistics that pertains to action on the front. The cards are numbered with a "JH" prefix.

	MINT	NRMT	EXC
COMPLETE SET (5)	75.00	50.00	14.00
COMMON JORDAN (JH1-JH5)	20.00	11.50	3.10
☐ JH1 Michael Jordan Chicago Bulls 1992 Summer Games	20.00	11.50	3.10
☐ JH2 Michael Jordan Chicago Bulls 1992 Tournament of the Americas	20.00	11.50	3.10
☐ JH3 Michael Jordan Chicago Bulls 1984 Summer Games	20.00	11.50	3.10
☐ JH4 Michael Jordan Chicago Bulls 1983 World University Games	20.00	11.50	3.10
☐ JH5 Michael Jordan Chicago Bulls International Games	20.00	11.50	3.10

1994-95 Upper Deck

The 1994-95 Upper Deck basketball set consists of 360 standard-size cards, released in two separate 180-card series. Cards were primarily distributed in 12-card packs, each of which carried a suggested retail price of $1.99. Fronts feature full-color action photos with player's name and team running in color-coded bars along the side.

	MINT	NRMT	EXC
☐ 1 Chris Webber ART Golden State Warriors	.30	.14	.04
☐ 2 Anfernee Hardaway ART Orlando Magic	.75	.35	.09
☐ 3 Vin Baker ART Milwaukee Bucks	.15	.07	.02
☐ 4 Jamal Mashburn ART Dallas Mavericks	.40	.18	.05
☐ 5 Isaiah Rider ART Minnesota Timberwolves	.12	.05	.02
☐ 6 Dino Radja ART Boston Celtics	.10	.05	.01
☐ 7 Nick Van Exel ART Los Angeles Lakers	.40	.18	.05
☐ 8 Shawn Bradley ART Philadelphia 76ers	.10	.05	.01
☐ 9 Toni Kukoc ART Chicago Bulls	.10	.05	.01
☐ 10 Lindsey Hunter ART Detroit Pistons	.10	.05	.01
☐ 11 Scottie Pippen AN Chicago Bulls	.15	.07	.02
☐ 12 Karl Malone AN Utah Jazz	.15	.07	.02
☐ 13 Hakeem Olajuwon AN Houston Rockets	.50	.23	.06
☐ 14 John Stockton AN Utah Jazz	.15	.07	.02
☐ 15 Latrell Sprewell AN Golden State Warriors	.25	.11	.03
☐ 16 Shawn Kemp AN Seattle Supersonics	.40	.18	.05
☐ 17 Charles Barkley AN Phoenix Suns	.40	.18	.05
☐ 18 David Robinson AN San Antonio Spurs	.40	.18	.05
☐ 19 Mitch Richmond AN Sacramento Kings	.12	.05	.02
☐ 20 Kevin Johnson AN Phoenix Suns	.12	.05	.02
☐ 21 Derrick Coleman AN New Jersey Nets	.10	.05	.01
☐ 22 Dominique Wilkins AN Los Angeles Clippers	.12	.05	.02
☐ 23 Shaquille O'Neal AN Orlando Magic	1.00	.45	.13

□	#	Player	Team			
□	24	Mark Price AN	Cleveland Cavaliers	.10	.05	.01
□	25	Gary Payton AN	Seattle Supersonics	.10	.05	.01
□	26	Dan Majerle	Phoenix Suns	.10	.05	.01
□	27	Vernon Maxwell	Houston Rockets	.10	.05	.01
□	28	Matt Geiger	Miami Heat	.10	.05	.01
□	29	Jeff Turner	Orlando Magic	.10	.05	.01
□	30	Vinny Del Negro	San Antonio Spurs	.10	.05	.01
□	31	B.J. Armstrong	Chicago Bulls	.10	.05	.01
□	32	Chris Gatling	Golden State Warriors	.10	.05	.01
□	33	Tony Smith	Los Angeles Lakers	.10	.05	.01
□	34	Doug West	Minnesota Timberwolves	.10	.05	.01
□	35	Clyde Drexler	Portland Trail Blazers	.40	.18	.05
□	36	Keith Jennings	Golden State Warriors	.10	.05	.01
□	37	Steve Smith	Miami Heat	.12	.05	.02
□	38	Kendall Gill	Seattle Supersonics	.10	.05	.01
□	39	Bob Martin	Los Angeles Clippers	.10	.05	.01
□	40	Calbert Cheaney	Washington Bullets	.15	.07	.02
□	41	Terrell Brandon	Cleveland Cavaliers	.10	.05	.01
□	42	Pete Chilcutt	Detroit Pistons	.10	.05	.01
□	43	Avery Johnson	San Antonio Spurs	.10	.05	.01
□	44	Tom Gugliotta	Washington Bullets	.12	.05	.02
□	45	LaBradford Smith	Sacramento Kings	.10	.05	.01
□	46	Sedale Threatt	Los Angeles Lakers	.10	.05	.01
□	47	Chris Smith	Minnesota Timberwolves	.10	.05	.01
□	48	Kevin Edwards	New Jersey Nets	.10	.05	.01
□	49	Lucious Harris	Dallas Mavericks	.10	.05	.01
□	50	Tim Perry	Philadelphia 76ers	.10	.05	.01
□	51	Lloyd Daniels	San Antonio Spurs	.10	.05	.01
□	52	Dee Brown	Boston Celtics	.12	.05	.02
□	53	Sean Elliott	San Antonio Spurs	.12	.05	.02
□	54	Tim Hardaway	Golden State Warriors	.15	.07	.02
□	55	Christian Laettner	Minnesota Timberwolves	.12	.05	.02
□	56	Charles Outlaw	Los Angeles Clippers	.10	.05	.01
□	57	Kevin Johnson	Phoenix Suns	.20	.09	.03
□	58	Duane Ferrell	Atlanta Hawks	.10	.05	.01
□	59	Jo Jo English	Chicago Bulls	.10	.05	.01
□	60	Stanley Roberts	Los Angeles Clippers	.10	.05	.01
□	61	Kevin Willis	Atlanta Hawks	.12	.05	.02
□	62	Dana Barros	Philadelphia 76ers	.15	.07	.02
□	63	Gheorghe Muresan	Washington Bullets	.12	.05	.02
□	64	Vern Fleming	Indiana Pacers	.10	.05	.01
□	65	Anthony Peeler	Los Angeles Lakers	.10	.05	.01
□	66	Negele Knight	San Antonio Spurs	.10	.05	.01
□	67	Harold Ellis	Los Angeles Clippers	.10	.05	.01
□	68	Vincent Askew	Seattle Supersonics	.10	.05	.01
□	69	Ennis Whatley	Atlanta Hawks	.10	.05	.01
□	70	Elden Campbell	Los Angeles Lakers	.10	.05	.01
□	71	Sherman Douglas	Boston Celtics	.10	.05	.01
□	72	Luc Longley	Chicago Bulls	.10	.05	.01
□	73	Lorenzo Williams	Dallas Mavericks	.10	.05	.01
□	74	Jay Humphries	Utah Jazz	.10	.05	.01
□	75	Chris King	Seattle Supersonics	.10	.05	.01
□	76	Tyrone Corbin	Utah Jazz	.10	.05	.01
□	77	Bobby Hurley	Sacramento Kings	.12	.05	.02
□	78	Dell Curry	Charlotte Hornets	.10	.05	.01
□	79	Dino Radja	Boston Celtics	.15	.07	.02
□	80	A.C. Green	Phoenix Suns	.15	.07	.02
□	81	Craig Ehlo	Atlanta Hawks	.10	.05	.01
□	82	Gary Payton	Seattle Supersonics	.15	.07	.02
□	83	Sleepy Floyd	San Antonio Spurs	.10	.05	.01
□	84	Rodney Rogers	Denver Nuggets	.15	.07	.02
□	85	Brian Shaw	Miami Heat	.10	.05	.01
□	86	Kevin Gamble	Boston Celtics	.10	.05	.01
□	87	John Stockton	Utah Jazz	.40	.18	.05
□	88	Hersey Hawkins	Charlotte Hornets	.12	.05	.02
□	89	Johnny Newman	New Jersey Nets	.10	.05	.01
□	90	Larry Johnson	Charlotte Hornets	.30	.14	.04
□	91	Robert Pack	Denver Nuggets	.10	.05	.01
□	92	Willie Burton	Miami Heat	.10	.05	.01
□	93	Bobby Phills	Cleveland Cavaliers	.10	.05	.01
□	94	David Benoit	Utah Jazz	.10	.05	.01

☐ 95 Harold Miner	.10	.05	.01
Miami Heat			
☐ 96 David Robinson	.75	.35	.09
San Antonio Spurs			
☐ 97 Nate McMillan	.10	.05	.01
Seattle Supersonics			
☐ 98 Chris Mills	.15	.07	.02
Cleveland Cavaliers			
☐ 99 Hubert Davis	.10	.05	.01
New York Knicks			
☐ 100 Shaquille O'Neal	2.00	.90	.25
Orlando Magic			
☐ 101 Loy Vaught	.12	.05	.02
Los Angeles Clippers			
☐ 102 Kenny Smith	.10	.05	.01
Houston Rockets			
☐ 103 Terry Dehere	.12	.05	.02
Los Angeles Clippers			
☐ 104 Carl Herrera	.10	.05	.01
Houston Rockets			
☐ 105 LaPhonso Ellis	.10	.05	.01
Denver Nuggets			
☐ 106 Armon Gilliam	.10	.05	.01
New Jersey Nets			
☐ 107 Greg Graham	.10	.05	.01
Philadelphia 76ers			
☐ 108 Eric Murdock	.10	.05	.01
Milwaukee Bucks			
☐ 109 Ron Harper	.12	.05	.02
Los Angeles Clippers			
☐ 110 Andrew Lang	.10	.05	.01
Atlanta Hawks			
☐ 111 Johnny Dawkins	.10	.05	.01
Philadelphia 76ers			
☐ 112 David Wingate	.10	.05	.01
Charlotte Hornets			
☐ 113 Tom Hammonds	.10	.05	.01
Denver Nuggets			
☐ 114 Brad Daugherty	.12	.05	.02
Cleveland Cavaliers			
☐ 115 Charles Smith	.10	.05	.01
New York Knicks			
☐ 116 Dale Ellis	.12	.05	.02
San Antonio Spurs			
☐ 117 Bryant Stith	.10	.05	.01
Denver Nuggets			
☐ 118 Lindsey Hunter	.10	.05	.01
Detroit Pistons			
☐ 119 Patrick Ewing	.40	.18	.05
New York Knicks			
☐ 120 Kenny Anderson	.15	.07	.02
New Jersey Nets			
☐ 121 Charles Barkley	.75	.35	.09
Phoenix Suns			
☐ 122 Harvey Grant	.10	.05	.01
Portland Trail Blazers			
☐ 123 Anthony Bowie	.10	.05	.01
Orlando Magic			
☐ 124 Shawn Kemp	.75	.35	.09
Seattle Supersonics			
☐ 125 Lee Mayberry	.10	.05	.01
Milwaukee Bucks			
☐ 126 Reggie Miller	.40	.18	.05
Indiana Pacers			
☐ 127 Scottie Pippen	.40	.18	.05
Chicago Bulls			
☐ 128 Spud Webb	.12	.05	.02
Sacramento Kings			
☐ 129 Antonio Davis	.10	.05	.01
Indiana Pacers			
☐ 130 Greg Anderson	.10	.05	.01
Detroit Pistons			
☐ 131 Jim Jackson	.50	.23	.06
Dallas Mavericks			
☐ 132 Dikembe Mutombo	.25	.11	.03
Denver Nuggets			
☐ 133 Terry Porter	.12	.05	.02
Portland Trail Blazers			
☐ 134 Mario Elie	.10	.05	.01
Houston Rockets			
☐ 135 Vlade Divac	.15	.07	.02
Los Angeles Lakers			
☐ 136 Robert Horry	.15	.07	.02
Houston Rockets			
☐ 137 Popeye Jones	.10	.05	.01
Dallas Mavericks			
☐ 138 Brad Lohaus	.10	.05	.01
Milwaukee Bucks			
☐ 139 Anthony Bonner	.10	.05	.01
New York Knicks			
☐ 140 Doug Christie	.10	.05	.01
Los Angeles Lakers			
☐ 141 Rony Seikaly	.10	.05	.01
Miami Heat			
☐ 142 Allan Houston	.15	.07	.02
Detroit Pistons			
☐ 143 Tyrone Hill	.12	.05	.02
Cleveland Cavaliers			
☐ 144 Latrell Sprewell	.50	.23	.06
Golden State Warriors			
☐ 145 Andres Guibert	.10	.05	.01
Minnesota Timberwolves			
☐ 146 Dominique Wilkins	.20	.09	.03
Boston Celtics			
☐ 147 Jon Barry	.10	.05	.01
Milwaukee Bucks			
☐ 148 Tracy Murray	.10	.05	.01
Portland Trail Blazers			
☐ 149 Mike Peplowski	.10	.05	.01
Sacramento Kings			
☐ 150 Mike Brown	.10	.05	.01
Minnesota Timberwolves			
☐ 151 Cedric Ceballos	.15	.07	.02
Los Angeles Lakers			
☐ 152 Stacey King	.10	.05	.01
Minnesota Timberwolves			
☐ 153 Trevor Wilson	.10	.05	.01
Sacramento Kings			
☐ 154 Anthony Avent	.10	.05	.01
Orlando Magic			
☐ 155 Horace Grant	.20	.09	.03
Orlando Magic			
☐ 156 Bill Curley	.20	.09	.03
Detroit Pistons			
☐ 157 Grant Hill	6.00	2.70	.75
Detroit Pistons			
☐ 158 Charlie Ward	.30	.14	.04
New York Knicks			
☐ 159 Jalen Rose	.75	.35	.09
Denver Nuggets			
☐ 160 Jason Kidd	4.00	1.80	.50
Dallas Mavericks			
☐ 161 Yinka Dare	.12	.05	.02
New Jersey Nets			
☐ 162 Eric Montross	.60	.25	.08
Boston Celtics			
☐ 163 Donyell Marshall	.75	.35	.09
Minnesota Timberwolves			
☐ 164 Tony Dumas	.12	.05	.02
Dallas Mavericks			
☐ 165 Wesley Person	.75	.35	.09
Phoenix Suns			

☐ 166	Eddie Jones .... 2.50 Los Angeles Lakers	1.15	.30
☐ 167	Tim Hardaway USA .... .10 Golden State Warriors	.05	.01
☐ 168	Isiah Thomas USA .... .12 Detroit Pistons	.05	.02
☐ 169	Joe Dumars USA .... .12 Detroit Pistons	.05	.02
☐ 170	Mark Price USA .... .10 Cleveland Cavaliers	.05	.01
☐ 171	Derrick Coleman USA .. .10 New Jersey Nets	.05	.01
☐ 172	Shawn Kemp USA......... .40 Seattle Supersonics	.18	.05
☐ 173	Steve Smith USA .... .10 Miami Heat	.05	.01
☐ 174	Dan Majerle USA.......... .10 Phoenix Suns	.05	.01
☐ 175	Reggie Miller USA........ .15 Indiana Pacers	.07	.02
☐ 176	Kevin Johnson USA ...... .12 Phoenix Suns	.05	.02
☐ 177	Dominique Wilkins USA .12 Boston Celtics	.05	.02
☐ 178	Shaquille O'Neal USA. 1.00 Orlando Magic	.45	.13
☐ 179	Alonzo Mourning USA . .25 Charlotte Hornets	.11	.03
☐ 180	Larry Johnson USA....... .15 Charlotte Hornets	.07	.02
☐ 181	Brian Grant DA............. .50 Sacramento Kings	.23	.06
☐ 182	Darrin Hancock DA ...... .10 Charlotte Hornets	.05	.01
☐ 183	Grant Hill DA............... 2.50 Detroit Pistons	1.15	.30
☐ 184	Jalen Rose DA .... .30 Denver Nuggets	.14	.04
☐ 185	Lamond Murray DA ..... .25 Los Angeles Clippers	.11	.03
☐ 186	Jason Kidd DA .... 1.50 Dallas Mavericks	.65	.19
☐ 187	Donyell Marshall DA .... .30 Minnesota Timberwolves	.14	.04
☐ 188	Eddie Jones DA........... 1.00 Los Angeles Lakers	.45	.13
☐ 189	Eric Montross DA......... .25 Boston Celtics	.11	.03
☐ 190	Khalid Reeves DA......... .25 Miami Heat	.11	.03
☐ 191	Sharone Wright DA....... .15 Philadelphia 76ers	.07	.02
☐ 192	Wesley Person DA .... .30 Phoenix Suns	.14	.04
☐ 193	Glenn Robinson DA .... 1.50 Milwaukee Bucks	.65	.19
☐ 194	Carlos Rogers DA .... .12 Golden State Warriors	.05	.02
☐ 195	Aaron McKie DA............ .12 Portland Trail Blazers	.05	.02
☐ 196	Juwan Howard DA........ .60 Washington Bullets	.25	.08
☐ 197	Charlie Ward DA .... .12 New York Knicks	.05	.02
☐ 198	Brooks Thompson DA.. .12 Orlando Magic	.05	.02
☐ 199	Tony Massenburg .... .10 Los Angeles Clippers	.05	.01
☐ 200	James Robinson .... .10 Portland Trail Blazers	.05	.01
☐ 201	Dickey Simpkins .... .20 Chicago Bulls	.09	.03
☐ 202	Johnny Dawkins .... .10 Detroit Pistons	.05	.01
☐ 203	Joe Kleine .... .10 Phoenix Suns	.05	.01
☐ 204	Bill Wennington .... .10 Chicago Bulls	.05	.01
☐ 205	Sean Higgins .... .10 New Jersey Nets	.05	.01
☐ 206	Larry Krystkowiak .... .10 Chicago Bulls	.05	.01
☐ 207	Winston Garland .... .10 Minnesota Timberwolves	.05	.01
☐ 208	Muggsy Bogues .... .15 Charlotte Hornets	.07	.02
☐ 209	Charles Oakley .... .12 New York Knicks	.05	.02
☐ 210	Vin Baker .... .40 Milwaukee Bucks	.18	.05
☐ 211	Malik Sealy .... .10 Los Angeles Clippers	.05	.01
☐ 212	Willie Anderson............. .10 San Antonio Spurs	.05	.01
☐ 213	Dale Davis.................... .12 Indiana Pacers	.05	.02
☐ 214	Grant Long .... .10 Atlanta Hawks	.05	.01
☐ 215	Danny Ainge .... .12 Phoenix Suns	.05	.02
☐ 216	Toni Kukoc................... .15 Chicago Bulls	.07	.02
☐ 217	Doug Smith................... .10 Dallas Mavericks	.05	.01
☐ 218	Danny Manning .... .15 Phoenix Suns	.07	.02
☐ 219	Otis Thorpe.................. .12 Houston Rockets	.05	.02
☐ 220	Mark Price .... .15 Cleveland Cavaliers	.07	.02
☐ 221	Victor Alexander........... .10 Golden State Warriors	.05	.01
☐ 222	Brent Price .... .10 Washington Bullets	.05	.01
☐ 223	Howard Eisley .... .10 Minnesota Timberwolves	.05	.01
☐ 224	Chris Mullin .... .15 Golden State Warriors	.07	.02
☐ 225	Nick Van Exel............... .75 Los Angeles Lakers	.35	.09
☐ 226	Xavier McDaniel............ .12 Boston Celtics	.05	.02
☐ 227	Khalid Reeves .... .60 Miami Heat	.25	.08
☐ 228	Anfernee Hardaway .... 1.50 Orlando Magic	.65	.19
☐ 229	B.J. Tyler...................... .12 Philadelphia 76ers	.05	.02
☐ 230	Elmore Spencer .... .10 Los Angeles Clippers	.05	.01
☐ 231	Rick Fox....................... .10 Boston Celtics	.05	.01
☐ 232	Alonzo Mourning .... .50 Charlotte Hornets	.23	.06
☐ 233	Hakeem Olajuwon .... 1.00 Houston Rockets	.45	.13
☐ 234	Blue Edwards................ .10 Boston Celtics	.05	.01
☐ 235	P.J. Brown.................... .10 New Jersey Nets	.05	.01
☐ 236	Ron Harper .... .12 Chicago Bulls	.05	.02

☐ 237	Isaiah Rider	.25	.11	.03
	Minnesota Timberwolves			
☐ 238	Eric Mobley	.20	.09	.03
	Milwaukee Bucks			
☐ 239	Brian Williams	.10	.05	.01
	Denver Nuggets			
☐ 240	Eric Piatkowski	.20	.09	.03
	Los Angeles Clippers			
☐ 241	Karl Malone	.40	.18	.05
	Utah Jazz			
☐ 242	Wayman Tisdale	.12	.05	.02
	Phoenix Suns			
☐ 243	Sarunas Marciulionis	.10	.05	.01
	Seattle Supersonics			
☐ 244	Sean Rooks	.10	.05	.01
	Minnesota Timberwolves			
☐ 245	Ricky Pierce	.12	.05	.02
	Golden State Warriors			
☐ 246	Don MacLean	.10	.05	.01
	Washington Bullets			
☐ 247	Aaron McKie	.30	.14	.04
	Portland Trail Blazers			
☐ 248	Kenny Gattison	.10	.05	.01
	Charlotte Hornets			
☐ 249	Derek Harper	.10	.05	.01
	New York Knicks			
☐ 250	Michael Smith	.30	.14	.04
	Sacramento Kings			
☐ 251	John Williams	.12	.05	.02
	Cleveland Cavaliers			
☐ 252	Pooh Richardson	.10	.05	.01
	Los Angeles Clippers			
☐ 253	Sergei Bazarevich	.10	.05	.01
	Atlanta Hawks			
☐ 254	Brian Grant	1.25	.55	.16
	Sacramento Kings			
☐ 255	Ed Pinckney	.10	.05	.01
	Milwaukee Bucks			
☐ 256	Ken Norman	.10	.05	.01
	Atlanta Hawks			
☐ 257	Marty Conlon	.10	.05	.01
	Milwaukee Bucks			
☐ 258	Matt Fish	.10	.05	.01
	Los Angeles Clippers			
☐ 259	Darrin Hancock	.10	.05	.01
	Charlotte Hornets			
☐ 260	Mahmoud Abdul-Rauf.	.12	.05	.02
	Denver Nuggets			
☐ 261	Roy Tarpley	.10	.05	.01
	Dallas Mavericks			
☐ 262	Chris Morris	.10	.05	.01
	New Jersey Nets			
☐ 263	Sharone Wright	.50	.23	.06
	Philadelphia 76ers			
☐ 264	Jamal Mashburn	.75	.35	.09
	Dallas Mavericks			
☐ 265	John Starks	.12	.05	.02
	New York Knicks			
☐ 266	Rod Strickland	.12	.05	.02
	Portland Trail Blazers			
☐ 267	Adam Keefe	.10	.05	.01
	Utah Jazz			
☐ 268	Scott Burrell	.10	.05	.01
	Charlotte Hornets			
☐ 269	Eric Riley	.10	.05	.01
	Houston Rockets			
☐ 270	Sam Perkins	.12	.05	.02
	Seattle Supersonics			
☐ 271	Stacey Augmon	.12	.05	.02
	Atlanta Hawks			
☐ 272	Kevin Willis	.12	.05	.02

	Miami Heat			
☐ 273	Lamond Murray	.60	.25	.08
	Los Angeles Clippers			
☐ 274	Derrick Coleman	.15	.07	.02
	New Jersey Nets			
☐ 275	Scott Skiles	.10	.05	.01
	Washington Bullets			
☐ 276	Buck Williams	.12	.05	.02
	Portland Trail Blazers			
☐ 277	Sam Cassell	.15	.07	.02
	Houston Rockets			
☐ 278	Rik Smits	.15	.07	.02
	Indiana Pacers			
☐ 279	Dennis Rodman	.25	.11	.03
	San Antonio Spurs			
☐ 280	Olden Polynice	.10	.05	.01
	Sacramento Kings			
☐ 281	Glenn Robinson	4.00	1.80	.50
	Milwaukee Bucks			
☐ 282	Clarence Weatherspoon	.15	.07	.02
	Philadelphia 76ers			
☐ 283	Monty Williams	.20	.09	.03
	New York Knicks			
☐ 284	Terry Mills	.10	.05	.01
	Detroit Pistons			
☐ 285	Oliver Miller	.10	.05	.01
	Detroit Pistons			
☐ 286	Dennis Scott	.10	.05	.01
	Orlando Magic			
☐ 287	Micheal Williams	.10	.05	.01
	Minnesota Timberwolves			
☐ 288	Moses Malone	.20	.09	.03
	San Antonio Spurs			
☐ 289	Donald Royal	.10	.05	.01
	Orlando Magic			
☐ 290	Mark Jackson	.10	.05	.01
	Indiana Pacers			
☐ 291	Walt Williams	.12	.05	.02
	Sacramento Kings			
☐ 292	Bimbo Coles	.10	.05	.01
	Miami Heat			
☐ 293	Derrick Alston	.12	.05	.02
	Philadelphia 76ers			
☐ 294	Scott Williams	.10	.05	.01
	Philadelphia 76ers			
☐ 295	Acie Earl	.10	.05	.01
	Boston Celtics			
☐ 296	Jeff Hornacek	.12	.05	.02
	Utah Jazz			
☐ 297	Kevin Duckworth	.10	.05	.01
	Washington Bullets			
☐ 298	Dontonio Wingfield	.15	.07	.02
	Seattle Supersonics			
☐ 299	Danny Ferry	.10	.05	.01
	Cleveland Cavaliers			
☐ 300	Mark West	.10	.05	.01
	Detroit Pistons			
☐ 301	Jayson Williams	.10	.05	.01
	New Jersey Nets			
☐ 302	David Wesley	.10	.05	.01
	Boston Celtics			
☐ 303	Jim McIlvaine	.10	.05	.01
	Washington Bullets			
☐ 304	Michael Adams	.10	.05	.01
	Charlotte Hornets			
☐ 305	Greg Minor	.12	.05	.02
	Boston Celtics			
☐ 306	Jeff Malone	.12	.05	.02
	Philadelphia 76ers			
☐ 307	Pervis Ellison	.10	.05	.01
	Boston Celtics			

☐ 308	Clifford Rozier	.30	.14	.04
	Golden State Warriors			
☐ 309	Billy Owens	.12	.05	.02
	Miami Heat			
☐ 310	Duane Causwell	.10	.05	.01
	Sacramento Kings			
☐ 311	Rex Chapman	.10	.05	.01
	Washington Bullets			
☐ 312	Detlef Schrempf	.15	.07	.02
	Seattle Supersonics			
☐ 313	Mitch Richmond	.20	.09	.03
	Sacramento Kings			
☐ 314	Carlos Rogers	.30	.14	.04
	Golden State Warriors			
☐ 315	Byron Scott	.12	.05	.02
	Indiana Pacers			
☐ 316	Dwayne Morton	.10	.05	.01
	Golden State Warriors			
☐ 317	Bill Cartwright	.10	.05	.01
	Seattle Supersonics			
☐ 318	J.R. Reid	.10	.05	.01
	San Antonio Spurs			
☐ 319	Derrick McKey	.12	.05	.02
	Indiana Pacers			
☐ 320	Jamie Watson	.20	.09	.03
	Utah Jazz			
☐ 321	Mookie Blaylock	.12	.05	.02
	Atlanta Hawks			
☐ 322	Chris Webber	.60	.25	.08
	Washington Bullets			
☐ 323	Joe Dumars	.20	.09	.03
	Detroit Pistons			
☐ 324	Shawn Bradley	.15	.07	.02
	Philadelphia 76ers			
☐ 325	Chuck Person	.12	.05	.02
	San Antonio Spurs			
☐ 326	Haywoode Workman	.10	.05	.01
	Indiana Pacers			
☐ 327	Benoit Benjamin	.10	.05	.01
	New Jersey Nets			
☐ 328	Will Perdue	.10	.05	.01
	Chicago Bulls			
☐ 329	Sam Mitchell	.10	.05	.01
	Indiana Pacers			
☐ 330	George Lynch	.10	.05	.01
	Los Angeles Lakers			
☐ 331	Juwan Howard	1.50	.65	.19
	Washington Bullets			
☐ 332	Robert Parish	.15	.07	.02
	Charlotte Hornets			
☐ 333	Glen Rice	.15	.07	.02
	Miami Heat			
☐ 334	Michael Cage	.10	.05	.01
	Cleveland Cavaliers			
☐ 335	Brooks Thompson	.10	.05	.01
	Orlando Magic			
☐ 336	Rony Seikaly	.10	.05	.01
	Golden State Warriors			
☐ 337	Steve Kerr	.10	.05	.01
	Chicago Bulls			
☐ 338	Anthony Miller	.10	.05	.01
	Los Angeles Lakers			
☐ 339	Nick Anderson	.12	.05	.02
	Orlando Magic			
☐ 340	Clifford Robinson	.10	.05	.02
	Portland Trail Blazers			
☐ 341	Todd Day	.12	.05	.02
	Milwaukee Bucks			
☐ 342	Jon Koncak	.10	.05	.01
	Atlanta Hawks			
☐ 343	Felton Spencer	.10	.05	.01
	Utah Jazz			
☐ 344	Willie Burton	.10	.05	.01
	Philadelphia 76ers			
☐ 345	Ledell Eackles	.10	.05	.01
	Miami Heat			
☐ 346	Anthony Mason	.12	.05	.02
	New York Knicks			
☐ 347	Derek Strong	.10	.05	.01
	Boston Celtics			
☐ 348	Reggie Williams	.10	.05	.01
	Denver Nuggets			
☐ 349	Johnny Newman	.10	.05	.01
	Milwaukee Bucks			
☐ 350	Terry Cummings	.12	.05	.02
	San Antonio Spurs			
☐ 351	Anthony Tucker	.10	.05	.01
	Washington Bullets			
☐ 352	Junior Bridgeman TN	.10	.05	.01
☐ 353	Jerry West TN	.50	.23	.06
☐ 354	Harvey Catchings TN	.10	.05	.01
☐ 355	John Lucas TN	.10	.05	.01
☐ 356	Bill Bradley TN	.25	.11	.03
☐ 357	Bill Walton TN	.25	.11	.03
☐ 358	Don Nelson TN	.10	.05	.01
☐ 359	Michael Jordan TN	2.50	1.15	.30
☐ 360	Tom(Satch) Sanders TN	.10	.05	.01

1994-95 Upper Deck Draft Trade

This set was available exclusively by redeeming the Upper Deck Draft Trade card before the June 30th, 1995 deadline. Draft Trade cards were randomly seeded into one in every 240 first series Upper Deck packs. The first ten players selected in the 1994 NBA Draft are featured within this set. The fronts feature the words NBA Draft Lottery Picks 1994 on the top of the card with the player vertically identified on the front left. The NBA draft logo is in the lower left corner. All of this surrounds a playerr cutout photo against a shaded background. The backs contain player information as well as a player photo. The cards are numbered with a D prefix in the upper left corner.

	MINT	NRMT	EXC
COMPLETE SET (10)	25.00	11.50	3.10
COMMON CARD (D1-D10)	1.00	.45	.13

			MINT	NRMT	EXC
☐	D1	Glenn Robinson	6.00	2.70	.75
		Milwaukee Bucks			
☐	D2	Jason Kidd	6.00	2.70	.75
		Dallas Mavericks			
☐	D3	Grant Hill	10.00	4.50	1.25
		Detroit Pistons			
☐	D4	Donyell Marshall	1.25	.55	.16
		Minnesota Timberwolves			
☐	D5	Juwan Howard	2.50	1.15	.30
		Washington Bullets			
☐	D6	Sharone Wright	1.00	.45	.13
		Philadelphia 76ers			
☐	D7	Lamond Murray	1.00	.45	.13
		Los Angeles Clippers			
☐	D8	Brian Grant	2.00	.90	.25
		Sacramento Kings			
☐	D9	Eric Montross	1.00	.45	.13
		Boston Celtics			
☐	D10	Eddie Jones	4.00	1.80	.50
		Los Angeles Lakers			
☐	NNO	Draft Trade Card	1.50	.65	.19

1994-95 Upper Deck Jordan He's Back

One of these cards was inserted in each second-series retail rack pack; the set celebrates Michael Jordan's return to the NBA. The set is composed of various Upper Deck Jordan cards from the past several years. The cards are distinguished by the "He's Back March 19, 1995" slogan gold-foil stamped on the fronts. The cards are numbered the same as the original cards, therefore the set is skip-numbered.

	MINT	NRMT	EXC
COMPLETE SET (9)	15.00	6.75	1.90
COMMON CARD	2.00	.90	.25
☐ 23 Michael Jordan	2.00	.90	.25
(92-93 Upper Deck)			
☐ 23 Michael Jordan	2.00	.90	.25
(93-94 Upper Deck)			
☐ 41 Michael Jordan	2.00	.90	.25
(94-95 SP Championship)			
☐ 44 Michael Jordan	2.00	.90	.25
(91-92 Upper Deck)			
☐ 204 Michael Jordan	2.00	.90	.25
(93-94 Upper Deck)			
☐ 237 Michael Jordan	2.00	.90	.25

	MINT	NRMT	EXC
(93-94 Upper Deck)			
☐ 402 Michael Jordan	2.00	.90	.25
(94-95 Collector's Choice)			
☐ 425 Michael Jordan	2.00	.90	.25
(92-93 Upper Deck)			
☐ 453 Michael Jordan	2.00	.90	.25
(92-93 Upper Deck)			

1994-95 Upper Deck Jordan Heroes

Randomly inserted in 12-card first series hobby and retail packs at a rate of one in 30, these 10 (nine numbered cards and one unnumbered header card) standard-size (2 1/2" by 3 1/2") cards spotlight Michael Jordan's outstanding career. The fronts feature color action shots of Jordan from different stages in his career. His name appears in gold-foil lettering in the bottom margin and also as a facsimile autograph in gold foil in the upper margin. The card's subtitle appears in vertical gold-foil lettering in the left margin. The right side is full-bleed. The back carries a color action shot of Jordan on a ghosted background. A small color action shot appears at the lower left. Career highlights appear in a colored panel set off to one side. The cards are numbered on the back 37-45, a continuation of previous Heroes sets of Jerry West, Wilt Chamberlain, Larry Bird, and Future Heroes.

	MINT	NRMT	EXC
COMPLETE SET (10)	150.00	80.00	22.00
COMMON JORDAN (37-45)	20.00	9.00	2.50
☐ 37 Michael Jordan	20.00	9.00	2.50
1985 NBA Rookie of the Year			
☐ 38 Michael Jordan	20.00	9.00	2.50
1986 63-Point Game			
☐ 39 Michael Jordan	20.00	9.00	2.50
1987-88 Air Raid			
☐ 40 Michael Jordan	20.00	9.00	2.50
1988			
☐ 41 Michael Jordan	20.00	9.00	2.50
1985-93 9-Time NBA All-Star			
☐ 42 Michael Jordan	20.00	9.00	2.50
1984			

		MINT	NRMT	EXC
☐ 43	Michael Jordan	20.00	9.00	2.50
	1991-93 MJOs Highlight Zone			
☐ 44	Michael Jordan	20.00	9.00	2.50
	1984-93 Rare Air			
☐ 45	Checklist	20.00	9.00	2.50
☐ NNO	Header Card	20.00	9.00	2.50

1994-95 Upper Deck Predictor Award Winners

Randomly inserted exclusively into one in every 25 first and second series hobby packs, cards from this 40-card set are sub-divided into All-Star MVP (H1-H10), Defensive Player of the Year (H11-H20), MVP (H21-H30) and ROY (H31-H40) sub-sets. If the featured player placed first or second in his respective category, the card was redeemable before the June 30th, 1995 deadline for a special Predictors exchange set (of which mailing was delayed until late October, 1995). Winner cards have been designated below with a "W1"(good for a 20-card exchange set) or "W2" (good for a 10-card exchange set) listing. The fronts feature the player photo for most of the card. The award that the card is good for is vertically on the left side of the card. The player's name, team and position is in the lower right corner and is printed in white. The backs of the card contain contest information. The cards are numbered with an "H" prefix.

	MINT	NRMT	EXC
COMPLETE SET (40)	140.00	65.00	17.50
COMPLETE SERIES 1 (20)	60.00	27.00	7.50
COMPLETE SERIES 2 (20)	80.00	36.00	10.00
COMMON AS MVP (H1-H10)	1.00	.45	.13
COMMON DEF POY (H11-H20)	.75	.35	.09
COMMON MVP (H21-H30)	.75	.35	.09
COMMON ROY (H31-H40)	.75	.35	.09

			MINT	NRMT	EXC
☐ H1	Charles Barkley		5.00	2.30	.60
	Phoenix Suns				
☐ H2	Hakeem Olajuwon		6.00	2.70	.75
	Houston Rockets				
☐ H3	Shaquille O'Neal		12.00	5.50	1.50
	Orlando Magic				
☐ H4	Scottie Pippen		2.50	1.15	.30
	Chicago Bulls				
☐ H5	David Robinson		5.00	2.30	.60
	San Antonio Spurs				
☐ H6	Shawn Kemp W2		6.00	2.70	.75
	Seattle Supersonics				
☐ H7	Alonzo Mourning		3.00	1.35	.40
	Charlotte Hornets				
☐ H8	Larry Johnson		2.00	.90	.25
	Charlotte Hornets				
☐ H9	Patrick Ewing		2.50	1.15	.30
	New York Knicks				
☐ H10	AS-MVP Wild Card W1		1.00	.45	.13
☐ H11	Hakeem Olajuwon		6.00	2.70	.75
	Houston Rockets				
☐ H12	Dikembe Mutombo W1		2.00	.90	.25
	Denver Nuggets				
☐ H13	Nate McMillan		.75	.35	.09
	Seattle Supersonics				
☐ H14	Dennis Rodman		1.50	.65	.19
	San Antonio Spurs				
☐ H15	Shaquille O'Neal		3.00	1.35	.40
	Orlando Magic				
☐ H16	Patrick Ewing		2.50	1.15	.30
	New York Knicks				
☐ H17	Charles Barkley		5.00	2.30	.60
	Phoenix Suns				
☐ H18	David Robinson		5.00	2.30	.60
	San Antonio Spurs				
☐ H19	John Stockton		2.50	1.15	.30
	Utah Jazz				
☐ H20	DEF-POY Wild Card W2		1.00	.45	.13
☐ H21	Shaquille O'Neal W2		15.00	6.75	1.90
	Orlando Magic				
☐ H22	Hakeem Olajuwon		6.00	2.70	.75
	Houston Rockets				
☐ H23	David Robinson W1		6.00	2.70	.75
	San Antonio Spurs				
☐ H24	Scottie Pippen		2.50	1.15	.30
	Chicago Bulls				
☐ H25	Alonzo Mourning		3.00	1.35	.40
	Charlotte Hornets				
☐ H26	Shawn Kemp		5.00	2.30	.60
	Seattle Supersonics				
☐ H27	Charles Barkley		5.00	2.30	.60
	Phoenix Suns				
☐ H28	Patrick Ewing		2.50	1.15	.30
	New York Knicks				
☐ H29	Larry Johnson		2.00	.90	.25
	Charlotte Hornets				
☐ H30	MVP Wild Card W2		.75	.35	.09
☐ H31	Jason Kidd W1		10.00	4.50	1.25
	Dallas Mavericks				
☐ H32	Grant Hill W1		15.00	6.75	1.90
	Detroit Pistons				
☐ H33	Glenn Robinson		8.00	3.60	1.00
	Milwaukee Bucks				
☐ H34	Eddie Jones		5.00	2.30	.60
	Los Angeles Lakers				
☐ H35	Donyell Marshall		1.50	.65	.19
	Minnesota Timberwolves				
☐ H36	Eric Montross		1.25	.55	.16
	Boston Celtics				
☐ H37	Sharone Wright		1.00	.45	.13
	Philadelphia 76ers				
☐ H38	Juwan Howard		3.00	1.35	.40
	Washington Bullets				
☐ H39	Carlos Rogers		1.00	.45	.13
	Golden State Warriors				
☐ H40	ROY Wild Card W1		1.00	.45	.13

1994-95 Upper Deck Predictor League Leaders

Randomly inserted exclusively into one in every 25 first and second series retail packs, cards from this 40-card set are sub-divided into Scoring (R1-R10), Assists (R11-R20), Rebounds (R21-R30) and Blocks (R31-R40) subsets. If the featured player placed first or second in his respective category, the card was redeemable before the June 30th, 1995 deadline for a special Predictors exchange set (of which mailing was delayed until late October, 1995). Winner cards have been designated below with a "W1"(good for a 20-card exchange set) or "W2"(good for a 10-card exchange set) listing. Card design is identical to the Predictor Award Winners inserts.

	MINT	NRMT	EXC
COMPLETE SET (40)	110.00	50.00	14.00
COMPLETE SERIES 1 (20)	50.00	23.00	6.25
COMPLETE SERIES 2 (20)	60.00	27.00	7.50
COMMON SCORERS (R1-R10)	.75	.35	.09
COMMON ASSISTS (R11-R20)	.75	.35	.09
COMMON REBOUNDS (R21-R30)	.75	.35	.09
COMMON BLOCKS (R31-R40)	.75	.35	.09
☐ R1 David Robinson	5.00	2.30	.60
San Antonio Spurs			
☐ R2 Shaquille O'Neal W1	15.00	6.75	1.90
Orlando Magic			
☐ R3 Hakeem Olajuwon W2	8.00	3.60	1.00
Houston Rockets			
☐ R4 Scottie Pippen	2.50	1.15	.30
Chicago Bulls			
☐ R5 Chris Webber	4.00	1.80	.50
Golden State Warriors			
☐ R6 Karl Malone	2.50	1.15	.30
Utah Jazz			
☐ R7 Patrick Ewing	2.50	1.15	.30
New York Knicks			
☐ R8 Mitch Richmond	1.25	.55	.16
Sacramento Kings			
☐ R9 Charles Barkley	5.00	2.30	.60
Phoenix Suns			
☐ R10 Scorers Wild Card	.75	.35	.09
☐ R11 John Stockton W1	3.00	1.35	.40
Utah Jazz			
☐ R12 Mookie Blaylock	.75	.35	.09
Atlanta Hawks			
☐ R13 Kenny Anderson W2	1.25	.55	.16
New Jersey Nets			
☐ R14 Kevin Johnson	1.25	.55	.16
Phoenix Suns			
☐ R15 Muggsy Bogues	.75	.35	.09
Charlotte Hornets			
☐ R16 Tim Hardaway	.75	.35	.09
Golden State Warriors			
☐ R17 Anfernee Hardaway	10.00	4.50	1.25
Orlando Magic			
☐ R18 Rod Strickland	.75	.35	.09
Portland Trail Blazers			
☐ R19 Sherman Douglas	.75	.35	.09
Boston Celtics			
☐ R20 Assists Wild Card	.75	.35	.09
☐ R21 Shaquille O'Neal	12.00	5.50	1.50
Orlando Magic			
☐ R22 Hakeem Olajuwon	6.00	2.70	.75
Houston Rockets			
☐ R23 Dennis Rodman W1	2.00	.90	.25
San Antonio Spurs			
☐ R24 Dikembe Mutombo W2	2.00	.90	.25
Denver Nuggets			
☐ R25 Karl Malone	2.50	1.15	.30
Utah Jazz			
☐ R26 Kevin Willis	.75	.35	.09
Atlanta Hawks			
☐ R27 Chris Webber	4.00	1.80	.50
Golden State Warriors			
☐ R28 Alonzo Mourning	3.00	1.35	.40
Charlotte Hornets			
☐ R29 Derrick Coleman	.75	.35	.09
New Jersey Nets			
☐ R30 Rebounds Wild Card	.75	.35	.09
☐ R31 Dikembe Mutombo WIN1	2.00	.90	.25
Denver Nuggets			
☐ R32 Hakeem Olajuwon WIN2	8.00	3.60	1.00
Houston Rockets			
☐ R33 David Robinson	5.00	2.30	.60
San Antonio Spurs			
☐ R34 Shawn Bradley	.75	.35	.09
Philadelphia 76ers			
☐ R35 Shaquille O'Neal	12.00	5.50	1.50
Orlando Magic			
☐ R36 Patrick Ewing	2.50	1.15	.30
New York Knicks			
☐ R37 Alonzo Mourning	3.00	1.35	.40
Charlotte Hornets			
☐ R38 Shawn Kemp	5.00	2.30	.60
Seattle Supersonics			
☐ R39 Derrick Coleman	.75	.35	.09
New Jersey Nets			
☐ R40 Blocks Wild Card	.75	.35	.09

1994-95 Upper Deck Rookie Standouts

Randomly inserted into one in every 30 second series pack, cards from this 20-card set feature a selection of the top rookies from the 1994-95 season. The borderless fronts feature a color photo in the middle. The words "Rookie Standouts" are in gold foil in the bottom left corner. The hard to read player's names are in the upper left corner. The backs have player information and are numbered with a RS

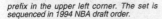

prefix in the upper left corner. The set is sequenced in 1994 NBA draft order.

	MINT	NRMT	EXC
COMPLETE SET (20)	120.00	55.00	15.00
COMMON CARD (RS1-RS20)..	1.00	.45	.13
☐ RS1 Glenn Robinson ...... Milwaukee Bucks	20.00	9.00	2.50
☐ RS2 Jason Kidd .... Dallas Mavericks	20.00	9.00	2.50
☐ RS3 Grant Hill .... Detroit Pistons	35.00	16.00	4.40
☐ RS4 Donyell Marshall ...... Minnesota Timberwolves	4.00	1.80	.50
☐ RS5 Juwan Howard .... Washington Bullets	8.00	3.60	1.00
☐ RS6 Sharone Wright......... Philadelphia 76ers	2.50	1.15	.30
☐ RS7 Lamond Murray .... Los Angeles Clippers	3.00	1.35	.40
☐ RS8 Brian Grant .... Sacramento Kings	6.00	2.70	.75
☐ RS9 Eric Montross .... Boston Celtics	3.00	1.35	.40
☐ RS10 Eddie Jones .... Los Angeles Lakers	12.00	5.50	1.50
☐ RS11 Carlos Rogers .... Golden State Warriors	1.50	.65	.19
☐ RS12 Khalid Reeves......... Miami Heat	3.00	1.35	.40
☐ RS13 Jalen Rose .... Denver Nuggets	4.00	1.80	.50
☐ RS14 Michael Smith .... Sacramento Kings	1.50	.65	.19
☐ RS15 Eric Piatkowski........ Los Angeles Clippers	1.00	.45	.13
☐ RS16 Clifford Rozier .... Golden State Warriors	1.50	.65	.19
☐ RS17 Aaron McKie............ Portland Trail Blazers	1.50	.65	.19
☐ RS18 Eric Mobley .... Milwaukee Bucks	1.00	.45	.13
☐ RS19 Bill Curley................ Detroit Pistons	1.00	.45	.13
☐ RS20 Wesley Person .... Phoenix Suns	4.00	1.80	.50

1994-95 Upper Deck Slam Dunk Stars

Randomly inserted into one in every 30 second series packs, cards from this 20-

card set feature Upper Deck spokesperson Shawn Kemp's selections of the top dunkers. The fronts feature the words "Kemp Slam Dunk Stars" as well as a sculpture of Kemp in gold foil on the left. The rest of the card is dedicated to a photo of the player dunking. The back has Kemp's opinion of each player. There is also a small inset photo of Kemp as well as a cutout of the featured player. The set is sequenced in alphabetical order.

	MINT	NRMT	EXC
COMPLETE SET (20)	150.00	70.00	19.00
COMMON CARD (S1-S20)....	1.50	.65	.19
☐ S1 Vin Baker .... Milwaukee Bucks	6.00	2.70	.75
☐ S2 Charles Barkley............ Phoenix Suns	12.00	5.50	1.50
☐ S3 Derrick Coleman .... New Jersey Nets	2.50	1.15	.30
☐ S4 Clyde Drexler............... Portland Trail Blazers	6.00	2.70	.75
☐ S5 LaPhonso Ellis .... Denver Nuggets	1.50	.65	.19
☐ S6 Larry Johnson .... Charlotte Hornets	5.00	2.30	.60
☐ S7 Shawn Kemp .... Seattle Supersonics	12.00	5.50	1.50
☐ S8 Donyell Marshall .... Minnesota Timberwolves	4.00	1.80	.50
☐ S9 Jamal Mashburn........... Dallas Mavericks	12.00	5.50	1.50
☐ S10 Gheorghe Muresan .... Washington Bullets	2.50	1.15	.30
☐ S11 Alonzo Mourning .... Charlotte Hornets	8.00	3.60	1.00
☐ S12 Shaquille O'Neal ...... Orlando Magic	35.00	16.00	4.40
☐ S13 Hakeem Olajuwon ..... Houston Rockets	15.00	6.75	1.90
☐ S14 Scottie Pippen .... Chicago Bulls	6.00	2.70	.75
☐ S15 Isiah Rider .... Minnesota Timberwolves	4.00	1.80	.50
☐ S16 David Robinson .... San Antonio Spurs	12.00	5.50	1.50
☐ S17 Clarence Weatherspoon	1.50	.65	.19
Philadelphia 76ers			
☐ S18 Chris Webber .... Golden State Warriors	10.00	4.50	1.25
☐ S19 Dominique Wilkins .... Boston Celtics	3.00	1.35	.40
☐ S20 Rik Smits .... Indiana Pacers	2.50	1.15	.30

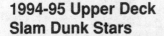

1994-95 Upper Deck Special Edition

Inserted one per pack into both first and second series 12-card packs and four per second series rack pack, cards from this 180-card set (issued in two separate 90-card series) are comprised of a wide selection of the top stars and prospects in the NBA. Fronts feature full-color player action shots against silver-foil backgrounds. The players are categorized by team name as follows: Atlanta Hawks (1-3, 91, 93-94), Boston Celtics (4-6, 95-97), Charlotte Hornets (5-7, 98-100), Chicago Bulls (10-12, 101-103), Cleveland Cavaliers (13-15, 104-106), Dallas Mavericks (16-19, 107-109, 116), Denver Nuggets (20-23, 110-112), Detroit Pistons (24-26, 113-115), Golden State Warriors (27-30, 117-121), Houston Rockets (31-34, 122-124), Indiana Pacers (35-37, 125-127), Los Angeles Clippers (38-40, 128-130, 134), Los Angeles Lakers (41-44, 131-133), Miami Heat (45-48, 135-137), Milwaukee Bucks (49-51, 138-140), Minnesota Timberwolves (52-54, 141-143), New Jersey Nets (55-57, 144-146), New York Knicks (58-62, 148-150), Orlando Magic (63-65, 151-154), Philadelphia 76ers (66-68, 147, 155-157), Phoenix Suns (69-71, 158-161), Portland Trail Blazers (72-74, 162-164), Sacramento Kings (75-77, 165-167, 174), San Antonio Spurs (78-81, 168-170), Seattle Supersonics (82-84, 171-173), Utah Jazz (85-87, 175-177), Washington Bullets (88-90, 92, 178-180). Cards are numbered with an SE prefix on back.

	MINT	NRMT	EXC
COMPLETE SET (180)	50.00	23.00	6.25
COMPLETE SERIES 1 (90)	12.00	5.50	1.50
COMPLETE SERIES 2 (90)	40.00	18.00	5.00
COMMON CARD (1-180)	.15	.07	.02

☐ 1	Stacey Augmon	.20	.09	.03
☐ 2	Kevin Willis	.20	.09	.03
☐ 3	Mookie Blaylock	.20	.09	.03
☐ 4	Rick Fox	.15	.07	.02
☐ 5	Xavier McDaniel	.15	.07	.02
☐ 6	Dee Brown	.20	.09	.03
☐ 7	Muggsy Bogues	.30	.14	.04
☐ 8	Kenny Gattison	.15	.07	.02
☐ 9	Alonzo Mourning	1.00	.45	.13
☐ 10	B.J. Armstrong	.15	.07	.02
☐ 11	Bill Cartwright	.15	.07	.02
☐ 12	Toni Kukoc	.30	.14	.04
☐ 13	Mark Price	.30	.14	.04
☐ 14	Gerald Wilkins	.15	.07	.02
☐ 15	John Williams	.20	.09	.03
☐ 16	Jamal Mashburn	1.50	.65	.19
☐ 17	Sean Rooks	.15	.07	.02
☐ 18	Doug Smith	.15	.07	.02
☐ 19	Jim Jackson	1.00	.45	.13
☐ 20	Mahmoud Abdul-Rauf	.20	.09	.03
☐ 21	Rodney Rogers	.30	.14	.04
☐ 22	Reggie Williams	.15	.07	.02
☐ 23	LaPhonso Ellis	.15	.07	.02
☐ 24	Allan Houston	.30	.14	.04
☐ 25	Terry Mills	.15	.07	.02
☐ 26	Joe Dumars	.40	.18	.05
☐ 27	Chris Mullin	.30	.14	.04
☐ 28	Billy Owens	.20	.09	.03
☐ 29	Latrell Sprewell	1.00	.45	.13
☐ 30	Chris Webber	1.25	.55	.16
☐ 31	Sam Cassell	.30	.14	.04
☐ 32	Vernon Maxwell	.15	.07	.02
☐ 33	Hakeem Olajuwon	2.00	.90	.25
☐ 34	Otis Thorpe	.20	.09	.03
☐ 35	Rik Smits	.30	.14	.04
☐ 36	Derrick McKey	.20	.09	.03
☐ 37	Haywood Workman	.15	.07	.02
☐ 38	Charles Outlaw	.15	.07	.02
☐ 39	Elmore Spencer	.15	.07	.02
☐ 40	Loy Vaught	.20	.09	.03
☐ 41	George Lynch	.15	.07	.02
☐ 42	Nick Van Exel	1.50	.65	.19
☐ 43	James Worthy	.30	.14	.04
☐ 44	Elden Campbell	.15	.07	.02
☐ 45	Grant Long	.15	.07	.02
☐ 46	Harold Miner	.15	.07	.02
☐ 47	Glen Rice	.30	.14	.04
☐ 48	Steve Smith	.20	.09	.03
☐ 49	Todd Day	.15	.07	.02
☐ 50	Eric Murdock	.15	.07	.02
☐ 51	Vin Baker	.75	.35	.09
☐ 52	Christian Laettner	.20	.09	.03
☐ 53	Isaiah Rider	.50	.23	.06
☐ 54	Micheal Williams	.15	.07	.02
☐ 55	Benoit Benjamin	.15	.07	.02
☐ 56	Derrick Coleman	.30	.14	.04
☐ 57	Chris Morris	.15	.07	.02
☐ 58	Charles Smith	.15	.07	.02
☐ 59	Greg Anthony	.15	.07	.02
☐ 60	Doc Rivers	.15	.07	.02
☐ 61	Derek Harper	.20	.09	.03
☐ 62	John Starks	.20	.09	.03
☐ 63	Anfernee Hardaway	3.00	1.35	.40
☐ 64	Dennis Scott	.15	.07	.02
☐ 65	Nick Anderson	.20	.09	.03
☐ 66	Shawn Bradley	.30	.14	.04
☐ 67	Clarence Weatherspoon	.30	.14	.04
☐ 68	Jeff Malone	.15	.07	.02
☐ 69	Cedric Ceballos	.30	.14	.04
☐ 70	Kevin Johnson	.40	.18	.05
☐ 71	Oliver Miller	.15	.07	.02
☐ 72	Clifford Robinson	.20	.09	.03
☐ 73	Rod Strickland	.20	.09	.03
☐ 74	Buck Williams	.20	.09	.03
☐ 75	Mitch Richmond	.40	.18	.05
☐ 76	Walt Williams	.20	.09	.03
☐ 77	Lionel Simmons	.15	.07	.02
☐ 78	Willie Anderson	.15	.07	.02
☐ 79	Terry Cummings	.20	.09	.03
☐ 80	J.R. Reid	.15	.07	.02

☐ 81	Dennis Rodman	.60	.25	.08
☐ 82	Kendall Gill	.15	.07	.02
☐ 83	Sam Perkins	.20	.09	.03
☐ 84	Detlef Schrempf	.30	.14	.04
☐ 85	Jeff Hornacek	.20	.09	.03
☐ 86	Karl Malone	.75	.35	.09
☐ 87	Felton Spencer	.15	.07	.02
☐ 88	Calbert Cheaney	.30	.14	.04
☐ 89	Don MacLean	.15	.07	.02
☐ 90	Brent Price	.15	.07	.02
☐ 91	Tyrone Corbin	.15	.07	.02
☐ 92	Rex Chapman	.15	.07	.02
☐ 93	Ken Norman	.15	.07	.02
☐ 94	Steve Smith	.20	.09	.03
☐ 95	Eric Montross	1.00	.45	.13
☐ 96	Dino Radja	.30	.14	.04
☐ 97	Dominique Wilkins	.40	.18	.05
☐ 98	Scott Burrell	.15	.07	.02
☐ 99	Hersey Hawkins	.20	.09	.03
☐ 100	Larry Johnson	.60	.25	.08
☐ 101	Ron Harper	.20	.09	.03
☐ 102	Scottie Pippen	.75	.35	.09
☐ 103	Dickey Simpkins	.30	.14	.04
☐ 104	Tyrone Hill	.20	.09	.03
☐ 105	Chris Mills	.30	.14	.04
☐ 106	Bobby Phills	.15	.07	.02
☐ 107	Lorenzo Williams	.15	.07	.02
☐ 108	Popeye Jones	.15	.07	.02
☐ 109	Jason Kidd	6.00	2.70	.75
☐ 110	Dikembe Mutombo	.50	.23	.06
☐ 111	Robert Pack	.15	.07	.02
☐ 112	Jalen Rose	1.25	.55	.16
☐ 113	Bill Curley	.30	.14	.04
☐ 114	Grant Hill	10.00	4.50	1.25
☐ 115	Lindsey Hunter	.15	.07	.02
☐ 116	Roy Tarpley	.15	.07	.02
☐ 117	Tim Hardaway	.30	.14	.04
☐ 118	Ricky Pierce	.20	.09	.03
☐ 119	Carlos Rogers	.40	.18	.05
☐ 120	Clifford Rozier	.40	.18	.05
☐ 121	Rony Seikaly	.15	.07	.02
☐ 122	Mario Elie	.15	.07	.02
☐ 123	Robert Horry	.30	.14	.04
☐ 124	Kenny Smith	.15	.07	.02
☐ 125	Antonio Davis	.15	.07	.02
☐ 126	Dale Davis	.20	.09	.03
☐ 127	Reggie Miller	.75	.35	.09
☐ 128	Lamond Murray	1.00	.45	.13
☐ 129	Eric Piatkowski	.30	.14	.04
☐ 130	Pooh Richardson	.15	.07	.02
☐ 131	Cedric Ceballos	.30	.14	.04
☐ 132	Vlade Divac	.30	.14	.04
☐ 133	Eddie Jones	4.00	1.80	.50
☐ 134	Mark Jackson	.15	.07	.02
☐ 135	Matt Geiger	.15	.07	.02
☐ 136	Khalid Reeves	1.00	.45	.13
☐ 137	Kevin Willis	.20	.09	.03
☐ 138	Lee Mayberry	.15	.07	.02
☐ 139	Eric Mobley	.15	.07	.02
☐ 140	Glenn Robinson	6.00	2.70	.75
☐ 141	Doug West	.15	.07	.02
☐ 142	Donyell Marshall	1.25	.55	.16
☐ 143	Chris Smith	.15	.07	.02
☐ 144	Kenny Anderson	.30	.14	.04
☐ 145	Chris Morris	.15	.07	.02
☐ 146	Armon Gilliam	.15	.07	.02
☐ 147	Dana Barros	.30	.14	.04
☐ 148	Patrick Ewing	.75	.35	.09
☐ 149	Charles Oakley	.20	.09	.03
☐ 150	Charlie Ward	.30	.14	.04
☐ 151	Horace Grant	.40	.18	.05

☐ 152	Shaquille O'Neal	4.00	1.80	.50
☐ 153	Brian Shaw	.15	.07	.02
☐ 154	Brooks Thompson	.30	.14	.04
☐ 155	B.J. Tyler	.20	.09	.03
☐ 156	Scott Williams	.15	.07	.02
☐ 157	Sharone Wright	.75	.35	.09
☐ 158	Charles Barkley	1.50	.65	.19
☐ 159	Dan Majerle	.20	.09	.03
☐ 160	Danny Manning	.30	.14	.04
☐ 161	Wesley Person	1.25	.55	.16
☐ 162	Clyde Drexler	.75	.35	.09
☐ 163	Harvey Grant	.15	.07	.02
☐ 164	Terry Porter	.20	.09	.03
☐ 165	Brian Grant	2.00	.90	.25
☐ 166	Bobby Hurley	.20	.09	.03
☐ 167	Olden Polynice	.15	.07	.02
☐ 168	Sean Elliott	.20	.09	.03
☐ 169	Chuck Person	.20	.09	.03
☐ 170	David Robinson	1.50	.65	.19
☐ 171	Shawn Kemp	1.50	.65	.19
☐ 172	Nate McMillan	.15	.07	.02
☐ 173	Gary Payton	.30	.14	.04
☐ 174	Michael Smith	.40	.18	.05
☐ 175	David Benoit	.15	.07	.02
☐ 176	Jay Humphries	.15	.07	.02
☐ 177	John Stockton	.75	.35	.09
☐ 178	Juwan Howard	2.50	1.15	.30
☐ 179	Chris Webber	1.25	.55	.16
☐ 180	Scott Skiles	.15	.07	.02

1994-95 Upper Deck Special Edition Gold

Randomly inserted at the rate of one per 35 first and second series packs, these 180 standard-size (2 1/2" by 3 1/2") cards are similar in design to their regular Special Edition counterparts, except that their fronts are gold foil instead of silver foil, and their backs have a gold-hued background for the area that carries the team logo. Only the top few cards from the set are individually priced below. Please refer to the multipliers provided below (coupled with the prices for the corresponding basic Special Edition inserts) to ascertain value for unlisted cards. Cards are numbered with an SE prefix on back.

	MINT	NRMT	EXC
COMPLETE SET (180)	550.00	250.00	70.00
COMPLETE SERIES 1 (90)	175.00	80.00	22.00
COMPLETE SERIES 2 (90)	375.00	170.00	47.50
COMMON CARD (1-180)	1.25	.55	.16
*STARS: 5X to 10X BASIC CARDS			
*ROOKIES: 2X to 4X BASIC CARDS			

		MINT	NRMT	EXC
☐ 16	Jamal Mashburn	15.00	6.75	1.90
☐ 33	Hakeem Olajuwon	20.00	9.00	2.50
☐ 42	Nick Van Exel	15.00	6.75	1.90
☐ 63	Anfernee Hardaway	30.00	13.50	3.80
☐ 109	Jason Kidd	25.00	11.50	3.10
☐ 114	Grant Hill	40.00	18.00	5.00
☐ 133	Eddie Jones	15.00	6.75	1.90
☐ 140	Glenn Robinson	25.00	11.50	3.10
☐ 152	Shaquille O'Neal	40.00	18.00	5.00
☐ 158	Charles Barkley	15.00	6.75	1.90
☐ 171	David Robinson	15.00	6.75	1.90
☐ 171	Shawn Kemp	15.00	6.75	1.90

1994-95 Upper Deck Special Edition Jumbos

One of these twenty-seven different over-sized Special Edition Jumbo cards was inserted into each Upper Deck second series hobby box. The cards parallel their corresponding basic Special Edition inserts except for their size and numbering.

	MINT	NRMT	EXC
COMPLETE SET (27)	50.00	23.00	6.25
COMMON CARD (1-27)	1.00	.45	.13

		MINT	NRMT	EXC
☐ 1	Steve Smith	1.00	.45	.13
	Atlanta Hawks			
☐ 2	Dominique Wilkins	1.50	.65	.19
	Boston Celtics			
☐ 3	Larry Johnson	2.50	1.15	.30
	Charlotte Hornets			
☐ 4	Scottie Pippen	3.00	1.35	.40
	Chicago Bulls			
☐ 5	Chris Mills	1.00	.45	.13
	Cleveland Cavaliers			
☐ 6	Jason Kidd	10.00	4.50	1.25
	Dallas Mavericks			
☐ 7	Jalen Rose	2.00	.90	.25
	Denver Nuggets			
☐ 8	Lindsey Hunter	1.00	.45	.13
	Detroit Pistons			
☐ 9	Tim Hardaway	1.00	.45	.13
	Golden State Warriors			
☐ 10	Kenny Smith	1.00	.45	.13
	Houston Rockets			
☐ 11	Mark Jackson	1.00	.45	.13
	Indiana Pacers			
☐ 12	Lamond Murray	1.50	.65	.19
	Los Angeles Clippers			
☐ 13	Cedric Ceballos	1.00	.45	.13
	Los Angeles Lakers			
☐ 14	Kevin Willis	1.00	.45	.13
	Miami Heat			
☐ 15	Glenn Robinson	10.00	4.50	1.25
	Milwaukee Bucks			
☐ 16	Doug West	1.00	.45	.13
	Minnesota Timberwolves			
☐ 17	Kenny Anderson	1.25	.55	.16
	New Jersey Nets			
☐ 18	Patrick Ewing	3.00	1.35	.40
	New York Knicks			
☐ 19	Horace Grant	1.50	.65	.19
	Orlando Magic			
☐ 20	Sharone Wright	1.25	.55	.16
	Philadelphia 76ers			
☐ 21	Charles Barkley	6.00	2.70	.75
	Phoenix Suns			
☐ 22	Clyde Drexler	3.00	1.35	.40
	Portland Trail Blazers			
☐ 23	Brian Grant	3.00	1.35	.40
	Sacramento Kings			
☐ 24	Sean Elliott	1.00	.45	.13
	San Antonio Spurs			
☐ 25	Shawn Kemp	6.00	2.70	.75
	Seattle Supersonics			
☐ 26	John Stockton	3.00	1.35	.40
	Utah Jazz			
☐ 27	Juwan Howard	4.00	1.80	.50
	Washington Bullets			

1991 Classic Draft Picks

Larry Johnson

This 50-card set of basketball draft picks was produced by Classic Games, Inc. and features 48 players picked in the first two rounds of the 1991 NBA draft. A total of 450,000 sets were issued, and each set is accompanied by a letter of limited edition.

The cards were only available for sale in these factory-sealed complete sets with no wax product being produced. The cards measure the standard size (2 1/2" by 3 1/2"). The fronts feature a glossy color action photo of each player. The backs have statistics and biographical information. Special cards included in the set are a commemorative number one draft choice card of Larry Johnson and a "One-on-One" card of Billy Owens slam-dunking over Johnson.

	MINT	NRMT	EXC
COMPLETE SET (50)	4.00	1.80	.50
COMMON CARD (1-50)	.04	.02	.01
☐ 1 Larry Johnson	1.50	.65	.19
UNLV			
☐ 2 Billy Owens	.50	.23	.06
Syracuse			
☐ 3 Dikembe Mutombo	.75	.35	.09
Georgetown			
☐ 4 Mark Macon	.04	.02	.01
Temple			
☐ 5 Brian Williams	.15	.07	.02
Arizona			
☐ 6 Terrell Brandon	.15	.07	.02
Oregon			
☐ 7 Greg Anthony	.25	.11	.03
UNLV			
☐ 8 Dale Davis	.40	.18	.05
Clemson			
☐ 9 Anthony Avent	.04	.02	.01
Seton Hall			
☐ 10 Chris Gatling	.20	.09	.03
Old Dominion			
☐ 11 Victor Alexander	.15	.07	.02
Iowa State			
☐ 12 Kevin Brooks	.04	.02	.01
Southwest Louisiana			
☐ 13 Eric Murdock	.25	.11	.03
Providence			
☐ 14 LeRon Ellis	.04	.02	.01
Syracuse			
☐ 15 Stanley Roberts	.15	.07	.02
LSU			
☐ 16 Rick Fox	.15	.07	.02
North Carolina			
☐ 17 Pete Chilcutt	.15	.07	.02
North Carolina			
☐ 18 Kevin Lynch	.04	.02	.01
Minnesota			
☐ 19 George Ackles	.04	.02	.01
UNLV			
☐ 20 Rodney Monroe	.04	.02	.01
North Carolina State			
☐ 21 Randy Brown	.04	.02	.01
New Mexico State			
☐ 22 Chad Gallagher	.04	.02	.01
Creighton			
☐ 23 Donald Hodge	.04	.02	.01
Temple			
☐ 24 Myron Brown	.04	.02	.01
Slippery Rock			
☐ 25 Mike Iuzzolino	.04	.02	.01
St. Francis			
☐ 26 Chris Corchiani	.04	.02	.01
North Carolina State			
☐ 27 Elliot Perry UER	.30	.14	.04
Memphis State			
☐ 28 Joe Wylie	.04	.02	.01

Miami (FL)			
☐ 29 Jimmy Oliver	.04	.02	.01
Purdue			
☐ 30 Doug Overton	.04	.02	.01
LaSalle			
☐ 31 Sean Green	.04	.02	.01
Iona			
☐ 32 Steve Hood	.04	.02	.01
James Madison			
☐ 33 Lamont Strothers	.04	.02	.01
Chris. Newport			
☐ 34 Alvaro Teheran	.04	.02	.01
Houston			
☐ 35 Bobby Phills	.25	.11	.03
Southern			
☐ 36 Richard Dumas	.15	.07	.02
DNP (Spain/Okla.St.)			
☐ 37 Keith Hughes	.04	.02	.01
Rutgers			
☐ 38 Isaac Austin	.04	.02	.01
Arizona State			
☐ 39 Greg Sutton	.04	.02	.01
Oral Roberts			
☐ 40 Joey Wright	.04	.02	.01
Texas			
☐ 41 Anthony Jones	.04	.02	.01
Oral Roberts			
☐ 42 Von McDade	.04	.02	.01
Milwaukee/Wisconsin			
☐ 43 Marcus Kennedy	.04	.02	.01
E. Michigan			
☐ 44 Larry Johnson	.50	.23	.06
UNLV Top Pick			
☐ 45 Larry Johnson and	.30	.14	.04
Billy Owens			
UNLV and Syracuse			
☐ 46 Anderson Hunt	.04	.02	.01
UNLV			
☐ 47 Darrin Chancellor	.04	.02	.01
S. Mississippi			
☐ 48 Damon Lopez	.04	.02	.01
Fordham			
☐ 49 Thomas Jordan	.04	.02	.01
DNP (Spain/Okla.St.)			
☐ 50 Tony Farmer	.04	.02	.01
Nebraska			

1991 Classic Four-Sport

This 230-card multi-sport set includes all 200 draft picks players from the four Classic Draft Picks sets (football, baseball,

basketball, and hockey), plus an additional 30 draft picks not previously found in these other sets. The standard-size (2 1/2" by 3 1/2") cards display new color player photos, with blue-gray marbled borders. The "1991 Classic Draft Picks" emblem appears as a wine-colored wax seal. The full color card backs present biographical information and statistics. Appended to the 230-card set is a special ten-card bonus subset, with nine silver bordered cards and a tenth "Gold Card" featuring Raghib "Rocket" Ismail. A five-card Ismail subset is also to be found within the nine silver bordered cards. A final special subset within the 230 cards consists of five cards highlighting the publicized one-on-one game between Billy Owens and Larry Johnson. As an additional incentive to collectors, Classic randomly inserted over 60,000 autographed cards into the 15-card foil packs; it is claimed that each case should contain two or more autographed cards. The autographed cards feature 61 different players, approximately two-thirds of whom were hockey players. The production run for the English version was 25,000 cases, and a bilingual version of the set was also produced at 20 percent of the English production. The French versions are valued the same as the English cards. The major subdivisions of set are according to sport: hockey (2-50), baseball (51-101), football (102-148), and basketball (149-202). The cards are numbered on the back and checklisted below accordingly.

	MINT	NRMT	EXC
COMPLETE SET (230)	12.00	5.50	1.50
COMMON CARD (1-230)	.05	.02	.01

		MINT	NRMT	EXC
☐ 1	Future Stars	1.00	.45	.13
	Larry Johnson			
	Brien Taylor			
	Russell Maryland			
	Eric Lindros			
☐ 2	Pat Falloon	.25	.11	.03
☐ 3	Scott Niedermayer	.40	.18	.05
☐ 4	Scott Lachance	.12	.05	.02
☐ 5	Peter Forsberg	1.50	.65	.19
☐ 6	Alex Stojanov	.05	.02	.01
☐ 7	Richard Matvichuk	.05	.02	.01
☐ 8	Patrick Poulin	.15	.07	.02
☐ 9	Martin Lapointe	.15	.07	.02
☐ 10	Tyler Wright	.05	.02	.01
☐ 11	Philippe Boucher	.05	.02	.01
☐ 12	Pat Peake	.15	.07	.02
☐ 13	Markus Naslund	.05	.02	.01
☐ 14	Brent Bilodeau	.05	.02	.01
☐ 15	Glen Murray	.05	.02	.01
☐ 16	Niklas Sundblad	.05	.02	.01
☐ 17	Martin Rucinsky	.05	.02	.01
☐ 18	Trevor Halverson	.05	.02	.01
☐ 19	Dean McAmmond	.05	.02	.01
☐ 20	Ray Whitney	.20	.09	.03
☐ 21	Rene Corbet	.05	.02	.01
☐ 22	Eric Lavigne	.05	.02	.01
☐ 23	Zigmund Palffy	.20	.09	.03
☐ 24	Steve Staios	.05	.02	.01
☐ 25	Jim Campbell	.05	.02	.01
☐ 26	Jassen Cullimore	.05	.02	.01
☐ 27	Martin Hamrlik	.05	.02	.01
☐ 28	Jamie Pushor	.05	.02	.01
☐ 29	Donevan Hextall	.05	.02	.01
☐ 30	Andrew Verner	.05	.02	.01
☐ 31	Jason Dawe	.05	.02	.01
☐ 32	Jeff Nelson	.05	.02	.01
☐ 33	Darcy Werenka	.05	.02	.01
☐ 34	Jozef Stumpel	.05	.02	.01
☐ 35	Francois Groleau	.05	.02	.01
☐ 36	Guy Leveque	.05	.02	.01
☐ 37	Jamie Matthews	.05	.02	.01
☐ 38	Dody Wood	.05	.02	.01
☐ 39	Yanic Perreault	.05	.02	.01
☐ 40	Jamie McLennan	.20	.09	.03
☐ 41	Yanick Dupre UER	.05	.02	.01
	(Yanic misspelled on both sides)			
☐ 42	Sandy McCarthy	.05	.02	.01
☐ 43	Chris Osgood	.30	.14	.04
☐ 44	Fredrik Lindquist	.05	.02	.01
☐ 45	Jason Young	.05	.02	.01
☐ 46	Steve Konowalchuk	.05	.02	.01
☐ 47	Michael Nylander UER	.12	.05	.02
☐ 48	Shane Peacock	.05	.02	.01
☐ 49	Yves Sarault	.05	.02	.01
☐ 50	Marcel Cousineau	.05	.02	.01
☐ 51	Brien Taylor	.20	.09	.03
☐ 52	Mike Kelly	.05	.02	.01
☐ 53	David McCarty	.05	.02	.01
☐ 54	Dmitri Young	.20	.09	.03
☐ 55	Joe Vitiello	.20	.09	.03
☐ 56	Mark Smith	.05	.02	.01
☐ 57	Tyler Green	.15	.07	.02
☐ 58	Shawn Estes UER	.05	.02	.01
	(Reversed negative)			
☐ 59	Doug Glanville	.05	.02	.01
☐ 60	Manny Ramirez	1.50	.65	.19
☐ 61	Cliff Floyd	.40	.18	.05
☐ 62	Tyrone Hill	.05	.02	.01
☐ 63	Eduardo Perez	.05	.02	.01
☐ 64	Al Shirley	.10	.05	.01
☐ 65	Benji Gil	.30	.14	.04
☐ 66	Calvin Reese	.30	.14	.04
☐ 67	Allen Watson	.05	.02	.01
☐ 68	Brian Barber	.10	.05	.01
☐ 69	Aaron Sele	.30	.14	.04
☐ 70	Jon Farrell UER	.05	.02	.01
☐ 71	Scott Ruffcorn	.05	.02	.01
☐ 72	Brent Gates	.15	.07	.02
☐ 73	Scott Stahoviak	.05	.02	.01
☐ 74	Tom McKinnon	.05	.02	.01
☐ 75	Shawn Livsey	.05	.02	.01
☐ 76	Jason Pruitt	.05	.02	.01
☐ 77	Greg Anthony	.05	.02	.01
	(Baseball)			
☐ 78	Justin Thompson	.10	.05	.01
☐ 79	Steve Whitaker	.05	.02	.01
☐ 80	Jorge Fabregas	.05	.02	.01
☐ 81	Jeff Ware	.05	.02	.01
☐ 82	Bobby Jones	.30	.14	.04
☐ 83	J.J. Johnson	.05	.02	.01
☐ 84	Mike Rossiter	.05	.02	.01
☐ 85	Dan Cholowsky	.05	.02	.01
☐ 86	Jimmy Gonzalez	.05	.02	.01
☐ 87	Trever Miller UER	.05	.02	.01
☐ 88	Scott Hatteberg	.05	.02	.01
☐ 89	Mike Groppuso	.05	.02	.01
☐ 90	Ryan Long	.05	.02	.01
☐ 91	Eddie Williams	.05	.02	.01
☐ 92	Mike Durant	.05	.02	.01
☐ 93	Buck McNabb	.05	.02	.01
☐ 94	Jimmy Lewis	.05	.02	.01

☐ 95	Eddie Ramos	.05	.02	.01
☐ 96	Terry Horn	.05	.02	.01
☐ 97	Jon Barnes	.05	.02	.01
☐ 98	Shawn Curran	.05	.02	.01
☐ 99	Tommy Adams	.05	.02	.01
☐ 100	Trevor Mallory	.05	.02	.01
☐ 101	Frankie Rodriguez	.20	.09	.03
☐ 102	Raghib(Rocket) Ismail	.30	.14	.04
☐ 103	Russell Maryland	.30	.14	.04
☐ 104	Eric Turner	.30	.14	.04
☐ 105	Bruce Pickens	.05	.02	.01
☐ 106	Mike Croel	.20	.09	.03
☐ 107	Todd Lyght	.10	.05	.01
☐ 108	Eric Swann	.25	.11	.03
☐ 109	Antone Davis	.05	.02	.01
☐ 110	Stanley Richard ("Sheriff")	.20	.09	.03
☐ 111	Pat Harlow	.05	.02	.01
☐ 112	Alvin Harper	.30	.14	.04
☐ 113	Mike Pritchard	.30	.14	.04
☐ 114	Leonard Russell	.20	.09	.03
☐ 115	Dan McGwire	.05	.02	.01
☐ 116	Bobby Wilson	.05	.02	.01
☐ 117	Vinnie Clark	.05	.02	.01
☐ 118	Kelvin Pritchett	.05	.02	.01
☐ 119	Harvey Williams	.25	.11	.03
☐ 120	Stan Thomas	.05	.02	.01
☐ 121	Randal Hill	.20	.09	.03
☐ 122	Todd Marinovich	.05	.02	.01
☐ 123	Henry Jones	.10	.05	.01
☐ 124	Mike Dumas	.05	.02	.01
☐ 125	Ed King	.05	.02	.01
☐ 126	Reggie Johnson	.05	.02	.01
☐ 127	Roman Phifer	.10	.05	.01
☐ 128	Mike Jones	.05	.02	.01
☐ 129	Brett Favre	1.25	.55	.16
☐ 130	Browning Nagle	.05	.02	.01
☐ 131	Esera Tuaolo	.05	.02	.01
☐ 132	George Thornton	.05	.02	.01
☐ 133	Dixon Edwards	.05	.02	.01
☐ 134	Darryl Lewis UER	.05	.02	.01
☐ 135	Eric Bieniemy	.10	.05	.01
☐ 136	Shane Curry	.05	.02	.01
☐ 137	Jerome Henderson	.05	.02	.01
☐ 138	Wesley Carroll	.05	.02	.01
☐ 139	Nick Bell	.05	.02	.01
☐ 140	John Flannery	.05	.02	.01
☐ 141	Ricky Watters	.50	.23	.06
☐ 142	Jeff Graham	.30	.14	.04
☐ 143	Eric Moten	.05	.02	.01
☐ 144	Jesse Campbell	.05	.02	.01
☐ 145	Chris Zorich	.30	.14	.04
☐ 146	Doug Thomas	.05	.02	.01
☐ 147	Phil Hansen	.05	.02	.01
☐ 148	Reggie Barrett	.05	.02	.01
☐ 149	Larry Johnson	1.25	.55	.16
☐ 150	Billy Owens	.40	.18	.05
☐ 151	Dikembe Mutombo	.60	.25	.08
☐ 152	Mark Macon	.05	.02	.01
☐ 153	Brian Williams	.10	.05	.01
☐ 154	Terrell Brandon	.10	.05	.01
☐ 155	Greg Anthony (Basketball)	.05	.02	.01
☐ 156	Dale Davis	.30	.14	.04
☐ 157	Anthony Avent	.05	.02	.01
☐ 158	Chris Gatling	.10	.05	.01
☐ 159	Victor Alexander	.10	.05	.01
☐ 160	Kevin Brooks	.05	.02	.01
☐ 161	Eric Murdock	.20	.09	.03
☐ 162	LeRon Ellis	.05	.02	.01
☐ 163	Stanley Roberts	.10	.05	.01
☐ 164	Rick Fox	.10	.05	.01
☐ 165	Pete Chilcutt	.10	.05	.01
☐ 166	Kevin Lynch	.05	.02	.01
☐ 167	George Ackles	.05	.02	.01
☐ 168	Rodney Monroe	.05	.02	.01
☐ 169	Randy Brown	.05	.02	.01
☐ 170	Chad Gallagher	.05	.02	.01
☐ 171	Donald Hodge	.05	.02	.01
☐ 172	Myron Brown	.05	.02	.01
☐ 173	Mike Iuzzolino	.05	.02	.01
☐ 174	Chris Corchiani	.05	.02	.01
☐ 175	Elliot Perry UER	.25	.11	.03
☐ 176	Joe Wylie	.05	.02	.01
☐ 177	Jimmy Oliver	.05	.02	.01
☐ 178	Doug Overton	.05	.02	.01
☐ 179	Sean Green	.05	.02	.01
☐ 180	Steve Hood	.05	.02	.01
☐ 181	Lamont Strothers	.05	.02	.01
☐ 182	Alvaro Teheran	.05	.02	.01
☐ 183	Bobby Phills	.20	.09	.03
☐ 184	Richard Dumas	.10	.05	.01
☐ 185	Keith Hughes	.05	.02	.01
☐ 186	Isaac Austin	.05	.02	.01
☐ 187	Greg Sutton	.05	.02	.01
☐ 188	Joey Wright	.05	.02	.01
☐ 189	Anthony Jones	.05	.02	.01
☐ 190	Von McDade	.05	.02	.01
☐ 191	Marcus Kennedy	.05	.02	.01
☐ 192	Larry Johnson (Number One Pick)	.40	.18	.05
☐ 193	Classic One on One II	.15	.07	.02
☐ 194	Anderson Hunt	.05	.02	.01
☐ 195	Darrin Chancellor	.05	.02	.01
☐ 196	Damon Lopez	.05	.02	.01
☐ 197	Thomas Jordan	.05	.02	.01
☐ 198	Tony Farmer	.05	.02	.01
☐ 199	Billy Owens (Number Three Pick)	.10	.05	.01
☐ 200	Owens Takes 4-3 Lead (Billy Owens)	.15	.07	.02
☐ 201	Johnson Slams for 6-6 Tie (Larry Johnson)	.15	.07	.02
☐ 202	Score Tied with :49 Left	.15	.07	.02
☐ 203	Gary Brown	1.00	.45	.13
☐ 204	Rob Carpenter	.05	.02	.01
☐ 205	Ricky Ervins	.10	.05	.01
☐ 206	Donald Hollas	.05	.02	.01
☐ 207	Greg Lewis	.05	.02	.01
☐ 208	Darren Lewis	.05	.02	.01
☐ 209	Anthony Morgan	.20	.09	.03
☐ 210	Chris Smith	.05	.02	.01
☐ 211	Perry Carter	.05	.02	.01
☐ 212	Melvin Cheatum	.05	.02	.01
☐ 213	Jerome Harmon	.05	.02	.01
☐ 214	Keith(Mr.) Jennings	.05	.02	.01
☐ 215	Brian Shorter	.05	.02	.01
☐ 216	Dexter Davis	.05	.02	.01
☐ 217	Ed McCaffrey	.10	.05	.01
☐ 218	Joey Hamilton	.25	.11	.03
☐ 219	Marc Kroon	.10	.05	.01
☐ 220	Moe Gardner	.05	.02	.01
☐ 221	Jon Vaughn	.05	.02	.01
☐ 222	Lawrence Dawsey	.15	.07	.02
☐ 223	Michael Stonebreaker	.05	.02	.01
☐ 224	Shawn Moore	.05	.02	.01
☐ 225	Shawn Green	.30	.14	.04
☐ 226	Scott Pisciotta	.05	.02	.01
☐ 227	Checklist 1	.05	.02	.01
☐ 228	Checklist 2	.05	.02	.01

☐ 229 Checklist 3	.05	.02	.01
☐ 230 Checklist 4	.05	.02	.01

1991 Classic Four-Sport Autographs

The 1991 Classic Draft Collection Autograph set consists of 61 standard-size (2 1/2" by 3 1/2") cards. They were randomly inserted throughout the foil packs. Listed after the player's name is how many cards were autographed by that player. An "A" suffix after the card number is used here for convenience.

	MINT	NRMT	EXC
COMPLETE SET (61)	1000.00	450.00	125.00
COMMON AUTOGRAPH	10.00	4.50	1.25

☐ 2A Pat Falloon/1100	30.00	13.50	3.80
☐ 3A S.Niedermayer/1250	40.00	18.00	5.00
☐ 4A Scott Lachance/1100	15.00	6.75	1.90
☐ 6A Alek Stojanov/950	10.00	4.50	1.25
☐ 8A Patrick Poulin/1100	15.00	6.75	1.90
☐ 10A Tyler Wright/950	10.00	4.50	1.25
☐ 11A Philippe Boucher/1150	10.00	4.50	1.25
☐ 12A Pat Peake/1100	20.00	9.00	2.50
☐ 14A Brent Bilodeau/1000	10.00	4.50	1.25
☐ 15A Glen Murray/1100	10.00	4.50	1.25
☐ 16A Niklas Sundblad/900	10.00	4.50	1.25
☐ 17A Martin Rucinsky/1100	15.00	6.75	1.90
☐ 18A Trevor Halverson/1100	10.00	4.50	1.25
☐ 19A Dean McAmmond/1100	10.00	4.50	1.25
☐ 20A Ray Whitney/2600	15.00	6.75	1.90
☐ 21A Rene Corbet/950	10.00	4.50	1.25
☐ 22A Eric Lavigne/1100	10.00	4.50	1.25
☐ 24A Steve Staios/1100	10.00	4.50	1.25
☐ 25A Jim Campbell/1100	10.00	4.50	1.25
☐ 26A Jassen Cullimore/1000	10.00	4.50	1.25
☐ 28A Jamie Pushor/1050	10.00	4.50	1.25
☐ 29A Donevan Hextall/1100	10.00	4.50	1.25
☐ 30A Andrew Verner/1200	10.00	4.50	1.25
☐ 31A Jason Dawe/950	10.00	4.50	1.25
☐ 32A Jeff Nelson/1100	10.00	4.50	1.25
☐ 33A Darcy Werenka/1150	10.00	4.50	1.25
☐ 35A Francois Groleau/1150	10.00	4.50	1.25
☐ 36A Guy Leveque/1150	10.00	4.50	1.25
☐ 37A Jamie Matthews/1100	10.00	4.50	1.25
☐ 38A Dody Wood/1050	10.00	4.50	1.25

☐ 39A Yanic Perreault/1100	15.00	6.75	1.90
☐ 40A Jamie McLennan/1100	15.00	6.75	1.90
☐ 41A Yanick Dupre/1050	10.00	4.50	1.25
☐ 42A Sandy McCarthy/1150	10.00	4.50	1.25
☐ 43A Chris Osgood/1100	25.00	11.50	3.10
☐ 44A Fredr.Lindquist/1100	10.00	4.50	1.25
☐ 45A Jason Young/1200	10.00	4.50	1.25
☐ 46A S.Konowalchuk/1350	10.00	4.50	1.25
☐ 47A Michael Nylander/1100	15.00	6.75	1.90
☐ 48A Shane Peacock/1150	10.00	4.50	1.25
☐ 49A Yves Sarault/1150	10.00	4.50	1.25
☐ 50A Marcel Cousineau/1100	10.00	4.50	1.25
☐ 51A Brien Taylor/2600	20.00	9.00	2.50
☐ 52A Mike Kelly/2600	15.00	6.75	1.90
☐ 53A David McCarty/2450	10.00	4.50	1.25
☐ 54A Dmitri Young/2600	20.00	9.00	2.50
☐ 55A Joe Vitiello/1900	15.00	6.75	1.90
☐ 56A Mark Smith/1700	10.00	4.50	1.25
☐ 58A Shawn Estes/2000	10.00	4.50	1.25
☐ 59A Doug Glanville/2000	10.00	4.50	1.25
☐ 61A Cliff Floyd/2000	40.00	18.00	5.00
☐ 62A Tyrone Hill/1000	10.00	4.50	1.25
☐ 63A Eduardo Perez/950	10.00	4.50	1.25
☐ 101A F.Rodriguez/1450	40.00	18.00	5.00
☐ 102A Rocket Ismail/2000	40.00	18.00	5.00
☐ 103A Russell Maryland/1000	25.00	11.50	3.10
☐ 150A Billy Owens/2500	30.00	13.50	3.80
☐ 151A Dikembe Mutombo/1000	60.00	27.00	7.50
☐ 153A Brian Williams/1500	15.00	6.75	1.90
☐ 163A Stanley Roberts/2000	15.00	6.75	1.90
☐ 218A Joey Hamilton/2000	30.00	13.50	3.80

1991 Classic Four-Sport LPs

Cards from this ten-card bonus subset were randomly inserted in 1991 Classic Draft Picks Collection foil packs. The cards are distinguished from the regular issue in that nine of them have a silver inner border while one has a gold inner border. A five-card Ismail subset is also to be found within the nine silver-bordered cards. The "1991 Classic Draft Picks" emblem appears as a wine-colored wax seal at the upper left corner. The horizontally oriented backs carry brief comments superimposed over a dusted version of Classic's wax seal emblem. The cards are numbered on the back.

	MINT	NRMT	EXC
COMPLETE SET (10)	25.00	11.50	3.10
COMMON CARD (LP6-LP10)...	1.50	.65	.19
☐ LP1 Rocket Lands In..........	2.00	.90	.25
Canada			
☐ LP2 Rocket Surveys...........	2.00	.90	.25
The Future			
☐ LP3 Rocket Launch............	2.00	.90	.25
☐ LP4 Track Star.................	2.00	.90	.25
(Rocket Ismail)			
☐ LP5 Rocket Knows Classic	2.00	.90	.25
☐ LP6 Johnson's Guns..........	5.00	2.30	.60
(Larry Johnson)			
☐ LP7 Brien Taylor..............	1.50	.65	.19
☐ LP8 Classic Gold Card SP.	8.00	3.60	1.00
☐ LP9 The Final Shot...........	4.00	1.80	.50
(Larry Johnson			
and Billy Owens)			
☐ LP10 Russell Maryland.....	1.50	.65	.19
(Number One Pick)			

		MINT	NRMT	EXC
	Maryland			
☐ 5	Christian Laettner	12.00	5.50	1.50
	Duke			

1992 Classic Draft

1992 Classic BK Previews

These Classic Basketball Draft Picks preview cards were randomly inserted in the 1992 Classic Football Draft Picks 15-card foil packs. Only 10,000 of each card were produced. The standard-size cards (2 1/2" by 3 1/2") cards feature on the front glossy color action player photos enclosed by white borders. The Classic logo, player's name, and position appear in a silver stripe beneath the picture. The backs read repeatedly "For Promotional Purposes Only" as well as bearing an advertisement and the Classic logo. The cards are numbered on the back.

	MINT	NRMT	EXC
COMPLETE SET (5)	150.00	70.00	19.00
COMMON CARD (1-5)	8.00	3.60	1.00
☐ 1 Shaquille O'Neal..........	100.00	45.00	12.50
LSU			
☐ 2 Alonzo Mourning	40.00	18.00	5.00
Georgetown			
☐ 3 Don MacLean..............	8.00	3.60	1.00
UCLA			
☐ 4 Walt Williams...............	10.00	4.50	1.25

The 1992 Classic Basketball Draft Picks set contains 100 standard-size (2 1/2" by 3 1/2") cards, including all 54 drafted players. The set features the first nationally distributed 1992 trading card of NBA first overall pick Shaquille O'Neal as well as the only draft cards of second pick Alonzo Mourning and fourth pick Jimmy Jackson. The set also includes a Flashback (95-98) subset. The fronts feature glossy color action photos bordered in white. The player's name appears in a silver stripe beneath the picture, which intersects the Classic logo at the lower left corner. The backs have a second color player photo and present biographical information, complete college statistics, and a scouting report. The cards are numbered on the back. Cards 61-100 were only available in 15-card foil packs as the blister sets contained only cards 1-60. The production run was reportedly 28,000 ten-box cases and 125,000 60-card factory blister sets.

	MINT	NRMT	EXC
COMPLETE BLISTER SET (61)	15.00	6.75	1.90
COMPLETE FOIL SET (100) ...	15.00	6.75	1.90
COMMON CARD (1-100)	.05	.02	.01
☐ 1 Shaquille O'Neal............	5.00	2.30	.60
LSU			
☐ 2 Walt Williams.................	.50	.23	.06
Maryland			
☐ 3 Lee Mayberry.................	.15	.07	.02
Arkansas			
☐ 4 Tony Bennett.................	.05	.02	.01
Wisconsin (Green Bay)			
☐ 5 Litterial Green................	.05	.02	.01
Georgia			
☐ 6 Chris Smith...................	.15	.07	.02
Connecticut			
☐ 7 Henry Williams	.05	.02	.01
NC (Charlotte)			
☐ 8 Terrell Lowery...............	.05	.02	.01
Loyola			
☐ 9 Radenko Dobras	.05	.02	.01

☐ 10 Curtis Blair	.05	.02	.01
South Florida			
☐ 11 Randy Woods	.05	.02	.01
Richmond			
☐ 12 Todd Day	.40	.18	.05
La Salle			
☐ 13 Anthony Peeler	.15	.07	.02
Arkansas			
☐ 14 Darin Archbold	.05	.02	.01
Missouri			
☐ 15 Benford Williams	.05	.02	.01
Butler			
☐ 16 Terrence Lewis	.05	.02	.01
Texas			
☐ 17 James McCoy	.05	.02	.01
Washington State			
☐ 18 Damon Patterson	.05	.02	.01
Massachusetts			
☐ 19 Bryant Stith	.30	.14	.04
Oklahoma			
☐ 20 Doug Christie	.15	.07	.02
Virginia			
☐ 21 Latrell Sprewell	1.25	.55	.16
Pepperdine			
☐ 22 Hubert Davis	.15	.07	.02
Alabama			
☐ 23 David Booth	.05	.02	.01
North Carolina			
☐ 24 David Johnson	.05	.02	.01
DePaul			
☐ 25 Jon Barry	.15	.07	.02
Syracuse			
☐ 26 Everick Sullivan	.05	.02	.01
Georgia Tech			
☐ 27 Brian Davis	.05	.02	.01
Louisville			
☐ 28 Clarence Weatherspoon	.75	.35	.09
Duke			
☐ 29 Malik Sealy	.30	.14	.04
Southern Mississippi			
☐ 30 Matt Geiger	.15	.07	.02
St. John's			
☐ 31 Jimmy Jackson	2.00	.90	.25
Georgia Tech			
☐ 32 Matt Steigenga	.05	.02	.01
Ohio State			
☐ 33 Robert Horry	1.00	.45	.13
Michigan State			
☐ 34 Marlon Maxey	.05	.02	.01
Alabama			
☐ 35 Reggie Slater	.05	.02	.01
UTEP			
☐ 36 Lucius Davis	.05	.02	.01
Wyoming			
☐ 37 Chris King	.05	.02	.01
UC Santa Barbara			
☐ 38 Dexter Cambridge	.05	.02	.01
Wake Forest			
☐ 39 Alonzo Jamison	.05	.02	.01
Texas			
☐ 40 Anthony Tucker	.05	.02	.01
Kansas			
☐ 41 Tracy Murray	.15	.07	.02
Wake Forest			
☐ 42 Vernel Singleton	.05	.02	.01
UCLA			
☐ 43 Christian Laettner	.60	.25	.08
LSU			
☐ 44 Don MacLean	.40	.18	.05
Duke			
UCLA			

☐ 45 Adam Keefe	.15	.07	.02
Stanford			
☐ 46 Tom Gugliotta	.75	.35	.09
North Carolina State			
☐ 47 LaPhonso Ellis	.25	.11	.03
Notre Dame			
☐ 48 Byron Houston	.05	.02	.01
Oklahoma			
☐ 49 Oliver Miller	.20	.09	.03
Arkansas			
☐ 50 Ron "Popeye" Jones	.20	.09	.03
Murray State			
☐ 51 P.J. Brown	.15	.07	.02
Louisiana Tech			
☐ 52 Eric Anderson	.05	.02	.01
Indiana			
☐ 53 Darren Morningstar	.05	.02	.01
Pittsburgh			
☐ 54 Isaiah Morris	.05	.02	.01
Arkansas			
☐ 55 Stephen Howard	.05	.02	.01
DePaul			
☐ 56 Reggie Smith	.05	.02	.01
TCU			
☐ 57 Elmore Spencer	.15	.07	.02
UNLV			
☐ 58 Sean Rooks	.15	.07	.02
Arizona			
☐ 59 Robert Werdann	.05	.02	.01
St. John's			
☐ 60 Alonzo Mourning	2.00	.90	.25
Georgetown			
☐ 61 Steve Rogers	.05	.02	.01
Alabama State			
☐ 62 Tim Burroughs	.05	.02	.01
Jacksonville			
☐ 63 Ed Book	.05	.02	.01
Canisius			
☐ 64 Herb Jones	.05	.02	.01
Cincinnati			
☐ 65 Mik Kilgore	.05	.02	.01
Temple			
☐ 66 Ken Leeks	.05	.02	.01
Central Florida			
☐ 67 Sam Mack	.05	.02	.01
Houston			
☐ 68 Sean Miller	.05	.02	.01
Pittsburgh			
☐ 69 Craig Upchurch	.05	.02	.01
Houston			
☐ 70 Van Usher	.05	.02	.01
Tennessee Tech			
☐ 71 Corey Williams	.05	.02	.01
Oklahoma State			
☐ 72 Duane Cooper	.05	.02	.01
USC			
☐ 73 Brett Roberts	.05	.02	.01
Morehead State			
☐ 74 Elmer Bennett	.05	.02	.01
Notre Dame			
☐ 75 Brent Price	.05	.02	.01
Oklahoma			
☐ 76 Daimon Sweet	.05	.02	.01
Notre Dame			
☐ 77 Darrick Martin	.05	.02	.01
UCLA			
☐ 78 Gerald Madkins	.05	.02	.01
UCLA			
☐ 79 Jo Jo English	.05	.02	.01
South Carolina			
☐ 80 Alex Blackwell	.05	.02	.01

	Monmouth			
☐ 81	Anthony Dade	.05	.02	.01
	Louisiana Tech			
☐ 82	Matt Fish	.05	.02	.01
	NC (Wilmington)			
☐ 83	Byron Tucker	.05	.02	.01
	George Mason			
☐ 84	Harold Miner	.20	.09	.03
	USC			
☐ 85	Greg Dennis	.05	.02	.01
	East Tennessee State			
☐ 86	Jeff Roulston	.05	.02	.01
	South Carolina			
☐ 87	Keir Rogers	.05	.02	.01
	Loyola (Illinois)			
☐ 88	Billy Law	.05	.02	.01
	Colorado			
☐ 89	Geoff Lear	.05	.02	.01
	Pepperdine			
☐ 90	Lambert Shell	.05	.02	.01
	Bridgeport			
☐ 91	Elbert Rogers	.05	.02	.01
	Alabama (Birmingham)			
☐ 92	Ron Ellis	.05	.02	.01
	Louisiana Tech			
☐ 93	Predrag Danilovic	.05	.02	.01
☐ 94	Calvin Talford	.05	.02	.01
	East Tennessee State			
☐ 95	Stacey Augmon	.15	.07	.02
	UNLV			
	Flashback 1			
☐ 96	Steve Smith	.15	.07	.02
	Michigan State			
	Flashback 2			
☐ 97	Billy Owens	.15	.07	.02
	Syracuse			
	Flashback 3			
☐ 98	Dikembe Mutombo	.15	.07	.02
	Georgetown			
	Flashback 4			
☐ 99	Checklist 1-50	.05	.02	.01
☐ 100	Checklist 51-100	.05	.02	.01
☐ NNO	Christian Laettner BC	1.25	.55	.16
	(Bonus Card found			
	only in blister sets)			

1992 Classic Draft Gold

This 101-card set features all 54 drafted players and measures the standard size (2

1/2" by 3 1/2"). Only 8,500 sequentially numbered sets were produced, and each set was packaged in a walnut display case. Each set included an individually numbered Shaquille O'Neal autograph card. The fronts feature action color player photos with white borders. The player's name and position are gold foil stamped in a black border stripe at the bottom. The Classic Draft Picks Gold logo overlaps the stripe and the photo at the lower left corner. The white background on the backs displays a vertical action color picture and a scouting report, while the player's name (in a gold stripe), biography, and statistics appear horizontally. The cards are numbered on the back. Gold star cards are valued at three to six times the corresponding value of the regular card.

	MINT	NRMT	EXC
COMPLETE FACT. SET (101)	250.00	115.00	31.00
COMMON CARD (1-100)	.30	.14	.04
☐ AU Shaquille O'Neal AU	175.00	80.00	22.00
LSU			
(Certified autograph,			
one of 8500)			

1992 Classic Draft LPs

This ten-card set, subtitled "Top Ten Pick", features the top ten picks of the 1992 NBA Draft. These standard size (2 1/2" by 3 1/2") cards were randomly inserted in 1992 Classic Draft Picks 15-card foil packs. The fronts feature glossy color action photos enclosed by white borders. The player's name appears in a silver foil stripe beneath the picture, which intersects the Classic logo at the lower left corner. The production figures "1 of 56,000" and the "Top Ten Pick" emblem at the card top are also silver foil. The horizontally oriented backs have a silver background and feature a second color player photo and player profile. The cards are numbered on the back with an "LP" (limited print) prefix. An 8 1/2" by 11" version of Alonzo Mourning is known to exist.

	MINT	NRMT	EXC
COMPLETE SET (10)	80.00	36.00	10.00
COMMON CARD (LP1-LP10)	1.00	.45	.13

	MINT	NRMT	EXC
☐ LP1 Shaquille O'Neal LSU	40.00	18.00	5.00
☐ LP2 Alonzo Mourning Georgetown	16.00	7.25	2.00
☐ LP3 Christian Laettner Duke	5.00	2.30	.60
☐ LP4 Jimmy Jackson Ohio State	16.00	7.25	2.00
☐ LP5 LaPhonso Ellis Notre Dame	2.00	.90	.25
☐ LP6 Tom Gugliotta North Carolina State	6.00	2.70	.75
☐ LP7 Walt Williams Maryland	4.00	1.80	.50
☐ LP8 Todd Day Arkansas	3.50	1.55	.45
☐ LP9 Clarence Weatherspoon Southern Mississippi	6.00	2.70	.75
☐ LP10 Adam Keefe Stanford	1.00	.45	.13

☐ BC1 Doug Christie Pepperdine	.50	.23	.06
☐ BC2 Billy Owens FLB Syracuse	.50	.23	.06
☐ BC3 Latrell Sprewell Alabama	2.50	1.15	.30
☐ BC4 Stacey Augmon FLB UNLV	.50	.23	.06
☐ BC5 Steve Smith FLB Michigan State	.50	.23	.06
☐ BC6 Jon Barry Georgia Tech	.50	.23	.06
☐ BC7 Christian Laettner Duke	1.25	.55	.16
☐ BC8 Jimmy Jackson Ohio State	4.00	1.80	.50
☐ BC9 Tracy Murray UCLA	.50	.23	.06
☐ BC10 Walt Williams Maryland	1.00	.45	.13
☐ BC11 Todd Day Arkansas	.75	.35	.09
☐ BC12 Dave Johnson Syracuse	.30	.14	.04
☐ BC13 Byron Houston Oklahoma State	.30	.14	.04
☐ BC14 Robert Horry Alabama	2.00	.90	.25
☐ BC15 Harold Miner USC	.50	.23	.06
☐ BC16 Bryant Stith Virginia	.60	.25	.08
☐ BC17 Malik Sealy St. John's	.60	.25	.08
☐ BC18 Randy Woods La Salle	.30	.14	.04
☐ BC19 Anthony Peeler Missouri	.50	.23	.06
☐ BC20 Lee Mayberry Arkansas	.50	.23	.06

1992 Classic Draft Magicians

Inserted one per jumbo pack, this 20-card standard-size (2 1/2" by 3 1/2") set features white-bordered color action shots on the fronts. Each card displays the player's name in blue lettering inside a silver foil stripe at the bottom of the photo, with the player's position appearing just beneath inside a black bar, and the Classic logo atop the foil to the left. The silver foil Magician logo in the top right rounds out the front. The backs have narrow-cropped color action photos on their right sides and silver stripes down the left with the player's name. Scouting reports and horizontally oriented biography and stats appear between. Cards 2, 4 and 5 have "'91 Flashback" printed in white across the tops of the fronts. The cards are numbered on the back with a "BC" prefix.

	MINT	NRMT	EXC
COMPLETE SET (20)	14.00	6.25	1.75
COMMON CARD (BC1-BC20)	.30	.14	.04

1992 Classic Four-Sport Previews

These five preview cards were randomly inserted in baseball and hockey draft picks foil packs. According to the backs, just 10,000 of each card were produced. The *cards measure the standard size (2 1/2" by 3 1/2"). The fronts display the full-bleed glossy color player photos. At the upper right corner, the word "Preview" surmounts the Classic logo. This logo overlays a black stripe that runs down the left side and features the player's name and position. The gray backs have the word "Preview" in red lettering at the top and are accented by short purple diagonal stripes on each side. Between the stripes are a congratulations and an advertisement. The cards are numbered on the back with a "CC" prefix.*

	MINT	NRMT	EXC
COMPLETE SET (5)	75.00	34.00	9.50
COMMON CARD (CC1-CC5)	1.50	.65	.19
☐ CC1 Shaquille O'Neal	50.00	23.00	6.25
☐ CC2 Desmond Howard	2.50	1.15	.30
☐ CC3 Roman Hamrlik	3.00	1.35	.40
☐ CC4 Phil Nevin	1.50	.65	.19
☐ CC5 Alonzo Mourning	25.00	11.50	3.10

1992 Classic Four-Sport

The 1992 Classic Draft Picks Collection consists of 325 standard-size (2 1/2" by 3 1/2") cards, featuring the top picks from football, basketball, baseball, and hockey drafts. Only 40,000 12-box foil cases were produced. Randomly inserted in the 12-card packs were over 100,000 autograph cards from over 50 of the top draft picks from basketball, football, baseball, and hockey, including cards autographed by Shaquille O'Neal, Desmond Howard, Roman Hamrlik, and Phil Nevin. Also inserted in the packs were "Instant Win Giveaway Cards" that entitled the collector to the 500,000.00 sports memorabilia giveaway that Classic offered in this contest. Finally a 25-card limited print, foil-stamped insert set, which included the special "Future Superstars" card and the "King and His Heir" card, was randomly collated into the packs; only 46,080 of each LP card was produced.

	MINT	NRMT	EXC
COMPLETE SET (325)	18.00	8.00	2.30
COMMON CARD (1-325)	.05	.02	.01
☐ 1 Shaquille O'Neal	4.00	1.80	.50
☐ 2 Walt Williams	.40	.18	.05
☐ 3 Lee Mayberry	.10	.05	.01
☐ 4 Tony Bennett	.05	.02	.01
☐ 5 Litterial Green	.05	.02	.01
☐ 6 Chris Smith	.10	.05	.01
☐ 7 Henry Williams	.05	.02	.01
☐ 8 Terrell Lowery	.05	.02	.01
☐ 9 Curtis Blair	.05	.02	.01
☐ 10 Randy Woods	.05	.02	.01
☐ 11 Todd Day	.10	.05	.01
☐ 12 Anthony Peeler	.10	.05	.01
☐ 13 Darin Archbold	.05	.02	.01
☐ 14 Benford Williams	.05	.02	.01
☐ 15 Damon Patterson	.05	.02	.01
☐ 16 Bryant Stith	.20	.09	.03
☐ 17 Doug Christie	.10	.05	.01
☐ 18 Latrell Sprewell	.75	.35	.09
☐ 19 Hubert Davis	.25	.11	.03
☐ 20 David Booth	.05	.02	.01
☐ 21 Dave Johnson	.05	.02	.01
☐ 22 Jon Barry	.10	.05	.01
☐ 23 Everick Sullivan	.05	.02	.01
☐ 24 Brian Davis	.05	.02	.01
☐ 25 Clarence Weatherspoon	.60	.25	.08
☐ 26 Malik Sealy	.20	.09	.03
☐ 27 Matt Geiger	.10	.05	.01
☐ 28 Jimmy Jackson	1.50	.65	.19
☐ 29 Matt Steigenga	.05	.02	.01
☐ 30 Robert Horry	.90	.40	.11
☐ 31 Marlon Maxey	.05	.02	.01
☐ 32 Chris King	.05	.02	.01
☐ 33 Dexter Cambridge	.05	.02	.01
☐ 34 Alonzo Jamison	.05	.02	.01
☐ 35 Anthony Tucker	.05	.02	.01
☐ 36 Tracy Murray	.10	.05	.01
☐ 37 Vernel Singleton	.05	.02	.01
☐ 38 Christian Laettner	.50	.23	.06
☐ 39 Don MacLean	.30	.14	.04
☐ 40 Adam Keefe	.10	.05	.01
☐ 41 Tom Gugliotta	.60	.25	.08
☐ 42 LaPhonso Ellis	.15	.07	.02
☐ 43 Byron Houston	.05	.02	.01
☐ 44 Oliver Miller	.10	.05	.01
☐ 45 Ron(Popeye) Jones	.20	.09	.03
☐ 46 P.J. Brown	.10	.05	.01
☐ 47 Eric Anderson	.05	.02	.01
☐ 48 Darren Morningstar	.05	.02	.01
☐ 49 Isaiah Morris	.05	.02	.01
☐ 50 Stephen Howard	.05	.02	.01
☐ 51 Elmore Spencer	.10	.05	.01
☐ 52 Sean Rooks	.10	.05	.01
☐ 53 Robert Werdann	.05	.02	.01
☐ 54 Alonzo Mourning	1.50	.65	.19
☐ 55 Steve Rogers	.05	.02	.01
☐ 56 Tim Burroughs	.05	.02	.01
☐ 57 Herb Jones	.05	.02	.01
☐ 58 Sean Miller	.05	.02	.01
☐ 59 Corey Williams	.05	.02	.01
☐ 60 Duane Cooper	.05	.02	.01
☐ 61 Brett Roberts	.05	.02	.01
☐ 62 Elmer Bennett	.05	.02	.01
☐ 63 Brent Price	.05	.02	.01
☐ 64 Daimon Sweet	.05	.02	.01
☐ 65 Darrick Martin	.05	.02	.01
☐ 66 Gerald Madkins	.05	.02	.01
☐ 67 Jo Jo English	.05	.02	.01

☐ 68 Matt Fish	.05	.02	.01
☐ 69 Harold Minor	.15	.07	.02
☐ 70 Greg Dennis	.05	.02	.01
☐ 71 Jeff Roulston	.05	.02	.01
☐ 72 Keir Rogers	.05	.02	.01
☐ 73 Geoff Lear	.05	.02	.01
☐ 74 Ron Ellis	.05	.02	.01
☐ 75 Predrag Danilovic	.05	.02	.01
☐ 76 Desmond Howard	.40	.18	.05
☐ 77 David Klingler	.10	.05	.01
☐ 78 Quentin Coryatt	.40	.18	.05
☐ 79 Bill Johnson	.05	.02	.01
☐ 80 Eugene Chung	.05	.02	.01
☐ 81 Derek Brown	.05	.02	.01
☐ 82 Carl Pickens	1.00	.45	.13
☐ 83 Chris Mims	.10	.05	.01
☐ 84 Charles Davenport	.05	.02	.01
☐ 85 Ray Roberts	.05	.02	.01
☐ 86 Chuck Smith	.05	.02	.01
☐ 87 Tony Smith RB	.05	.02	.01
☐ 88 Ken Swilling	.05	.02	.01
☐ 89 Greg Skrepenak	.05	.02	.01
☐ 90 Phillipi Sparks	.05	.02	.01
☐ 91 Alonzo Spellman	.10	.05	.01
☐ 92 Bernard Dafney	.05	.02	.01
☐ 93 Edgar Bennett	1.00	.45	.13
☐ 94 Shane Dronett	.10	.05	.01
☐ 95 Jeremy Lincoln	.05	.02	.01
☐ 96 Dion Lambert	.05	.02	.01
☐ 97 Siran Stacy	.05	.02	.01
☐ 98 Tony Sacca	.05	.02	.01
☐ 99 Sean Lumpkin	.05	.02	.01
☐ 100 Tommy Vardell	.10	.05	.01
☐ 101 Keith Hamilton	.05	.02	.01
☐ 102 Sean Gilbert	.60	.25	.08
☐ 103 Casey Weldon	.10	.05	.01
☐ 104 Marc Boutte	.05	.02	.01
☐ 105 Arthur Marshall	.05	.02	.01
☐ 106 Santana Dotson	.10	.05	.01
☐ 107 Ronnie West	.05	.02	.01
☐ 108 Mike Pawlawski	.05	.02	.01
☐ 109 Dale Carter	.10	.05	.01
☐ 110 Carlos Snow	.05	.02	.01
☐ 111 Mark D'Onofrio	.05	.02	.01
☐ 112 Matt Blundin	.05	.02	.01
☐ 113 Patrick Rowe	.05	.02	.01
☐ 114 Joel Steed	.05	.02	.01
☐ 115 Erick Anderson	.05	.02	.01
☐ 116 Rodney Culver	.05	.02	.01
☐ 117 Chris Hakel	.05	.02	.01
☐ 118 Kevin Smith	.25	.11	.03
☐ 119 Robert Brooks	.50	.23	.06
☐ 120 Bucky Richardson	.05	.02	.01
☐ 121 Steve Israel	.05	.02	.01
☐ 122 Marco Coleman	.50	.23	.06
☐ 123 Johnny Mitchell	.40	.18	.05
☐ 124 Scottie Graham	.10	.05	.01
☐ 125 Keith Goganious	.05	.02	.01
☐ 126 Tommy Maddox	.05	.02	.01
☐ 127 Terrell Buckley	.05	.02	.01
☐ 128 Dana Hall	.05	.02	.01
☐ 129 Ty Detmer	.20	.09	.03
☐ 130 Darryl Williams	.05	.02	.01
☐ 131 Jason Hanson	.25	.11	.03
☐ 132 Leon Searcy	.05	.02	.01
☐ 133 Will Furrer	.05	.02	.01
☐ 134 Darren Woodson	.30	.14	.04
☐ 135 Corey Widmer	.05	.02	.01
☐ 136 Larry Tharpe	.05	.02	.01
☐ 137 Lance Olberding	.05	.02	.01
☐ 138 Stacey Dillard	.05	.02	.01
☐ 139 Anthony Hamlet	.05	.02	.01
☐ 140 Mike Evans	.05	.02	.01
☐ 141 Chester McGlockton	.10	.05	.01
☐ 142 Marquez Pope	.10	.05	.01
☐ 143 Tyrone Legette	.05	.02	.01
☐ 144 Derrick Moore	.20	.09	.03
☐ 145 Calvin Holmes	.05	.02	.01
☐ 146 Eddie Robinson Jr.	.05	.02	.01
☐ 147 Robert Jones	.10	.05	.01
☐ 148 Ricardo McDonald	.05	.02	.01
☐ 149 Howard Dinkins	.05	.02	.01
☐ 150 Todd Collins	.05	.02	.01
☐ 151 Roman Hamrlik	.20	.09	.03
☐ 152 Alexei Yashin	.75	.35	.09
☐ 153 Mike Rathje	.05	.02	.01
☐ 154 Darius Kasparaitis	.12	.05	.02
☐ 155 Cory Stillman	.05	.02	.01
☐ 156 Robert Petrovicky	.05	.02	.01
☐ 157 Andrei Nazarov	.12	.05	.02
☐ 158 Jason Bowen	.05	.02	.01
☐ 159 Jason Smith	.05	.02	.01
☐ 160 David Wilkie	.05	.02	.01
☐ 161 Curtis Bowen	.12	.05	.02
☐ 162 Grant Marshall	.05	.02	.01
☐ 163 Valeri Bure	.20	.09	.03
☐ 164 Jeff Shantz	.05	.02	.01
☐ 165 Justin Hocking	.05	.02	.01
☐ 166 Mike Peca	.05	.02	.01
☐ 167 Marc Hussey	.05	.02	.01
☐ 168 Sandy Allan	.05	.02	.01
☐ 169 Kirk Maltby	.05	.02	.01
☐ 170 Cale Hulse	.05	.02	.01
☐ 171 Sylvain Cloutier	.05	.02	.01
☐ 172 Martin Gendron	.05	.02	.01
☐ 173 Kevin Smyth	.05	.02	.01
☐ 174 Jason McBain	.05	.02	.01
☐ 175 Lee J. Leslie	.05	.02	.01
☐ 176 Ralph Intranuovo	.05	.02	.01
☐ 177 Martin Reichel	.05	.02	.01
☐ 178 Stefan Ustorf	.12	.05	.02
☐ 179 Jarkko Varvio	.05	.02	.01
☐ 180 Martin Straka	.20	.09	.03
☐ 181 Libor Polasek	.05	.02	.01
☐ 182 Jozef Cierny	.05	.02	.01
☐ 183 Sergei Krivokrasov	.15	.07	.02
☐ 184 Sergei Gonchar	.12	.05	.02
☐ 185 Boris Mironov	.12	.05	.02
☐ 186 Denis Metyluk	.05	.02	.01
☐ 187 Sergei Klimovich	.05	.02	.01
☐ 188 Sergei Brylin	.05	.02	.01
☐ 189 Andrei Nikolishin	.12	.05	.02
☐ 190 Alexander Cherbayev	.05	.02	.01
☐ 191 Vitali Tomilin	.05	.02	.01
☐ 192 Sandy Moger	.05	.02	.01
☐ 193 Darrin Madeley	.05	.02	.01
☐ 194 Denny Felsner	.05	.02	.01
☐ 195 Dwayne Norris	.05	.02	.01
☐ 196 Joby Messier	.05	.02	.01
☐ 197 Michael Stewart	.05	.02	.01
☐ 198 Scott Thomas	.05	.02	.01
☐ 199 Daniel Laperriere	.05	.02	.01
☐ 200 Martin Lacroix	.05	.02	.01
☐ 201 Scott LaGrand	.05	.02	.01
☐ 202 Scott Pellerin	.05	.02	.01
☐ 203 Jean-Yves Roy	.05	.02	.01
☐ 204 Rob Gaudreau	.05	.02	.01
☐ 205 Jeff McLean	.05	.02	.01
☐ 206 Dallas Drake	.05	.02	.01
☐ 207 Doug Zmolek	.05	.02	.01
☐ 208 Duane Derksen	.05	.02	.01
☐ 209 Jim Cummins	.05	.02	.01

☐ 210 Lonnie Loach	.05	.02	.01
☐ 211 Rob Zamuner	.05	.02	.01
☐ 212 Brad Werenka	.12	.05	.02
☐ 213 Brent Grieve	.05	.02	.01
☐ 214 Sean Hill	.05	.02	.01
☐ 215 Peter Ciavaglia	.05	.02	.01
☐ 216 Jason Ruff	.05	.02	.01
☐ 217 Shawn McCosh	.05	.02	.01
☐ 218 Dave Tretowicz	.05	.02	.01
☐ 219 Mike Vukonich	.05	.02	.01
☐ 220 Kevin Wortman	.05	.02	.01
☐ 221 Jason Muzzatti	.12	.05	.02
☐ 222 Dmitri Kvartalnov	.05	.02	.01
☐ 223 Ray Whitney	.05	.02	.01
☐ 224 Manon Rheaume	5.00	2.30	.60
☐ 225 Viktor Kozlov	.40	.18	.05
☐ 226 Phil Nevin	.05	.02	.01
☐ 227 Paul Shuey	.05	.02	.01
☐ 228 B.J. Wallace	.05	.02	.01
☐ 229 Jeffrey Hammonds	.25	.11	.03
☐ 230 Chad Mottola	.10	.05	.01
☐ 231 Derek Jeter	1.00	.45	.13
☐ 232 Michael Tucker	.30	.14	.04
☐ 233 Derek Wallace	.05	.02	.01
☐ 234 Kenny Felder	.05	.02	.01
☐ 235 Chad McConnell	.05	.02	.01
☐ 236 Sean Lowe	.05	.02	.01
☐ 237 Ricky Greene	.05	.02	.01
☐ 238 Chris Roberts	.05	.02	.01
☐ 239 Shannon Stewart	.25	.11	.03
☐ 240 Benji Grigsby	.05	.02	.01
☐ 241 Jamie Arnold	.05	.02	.01
☐ 242 Rick Helling	.05	.02	.01
☐ 243 Jason Kendall	.40	.18	.05
☐ 244 Todd Steverson	.05	.02	.01
☐ 245 Dan Serafini	.10	.05	.01
☐ 246 Jeff Schmidt	.05	.02	.01
☐ 247 Sherard Clinkscales	.05	.02	.01
☐ 248 Ryan Luzinski	.05	.02	.01
☐ 249 Shon Walker	.10	.05	.01
☐ 250 Brandon Cromer	.05	.02	.01
☐ 251 Dave Landaker	.05	.02	.01
☐ 252 Michael Mathews	.05	.02	.01
☐ 253 Brian Sackinsky	.05	.02	.01
☐ 254 Jon Lieber	.10	.05	.01
☐ 255 Jim Rosenbohm	.05	.02	.01
☐ 256 DeShawn Warren	.05	.02	.01
☐ 257 Mike Buddie	.10	.05	.01
☐ 258 Chris Smith	.05	.02	.01
☐ 259 Dwain Bostic	.05	.02	.01
☐ 260 Bobby Hughes	.05	.02	.01
☐ 261 Rick Magdellano	.05	.02	.01
☐ 262 Bob Wolcott	.15	.07	.02
☐ 263 Mike Gulan	.05	.02	.01
☐ 264 Yuri Sanchez	.05	.02	.01
☐ 265 Tony Sheffield	.05	.02	.01
☐ 266 Dan Melendez	.05	.02	.01
☐ 267 Jason Giambi	.10	.05	.01
☐ 268 Ritchie Moody	.05	.02	.01
☐ 269 Trey Beamon	.60	.25	.08
☐ 270 Tim Crabtree	.05	.02	.01
☐ 271 Chad Roper	.05	.02	.01
☐ 272 Mark Thompson	.05	.02	.01
☐ 273 Marquis Riley	.05	.02	.01
☐ 274 Tom Knauss	.05	.02	.01
☐ 275 Chris Holt	.05	.02	.01
☐ 276 Jonathan Nunnally	.10	.05	.01
☐ 277 Everett Stull	.05	.02	.01
☐ 278 Billy Owens	.05	.02	.01
☐ 279 Todd Etler	.05	.02	.01
☐ 280 Benji Simonton	.05	.02	.01

☐ 281 Dwight Maness	.05	.02	.01
☐ 282 Chris Eddy	.05	.02	.01
☐ 283 Brant Brown	.05	.02	.01
☐ 284 Kurt Ehmann	.05	.02	.01
☐ 285 Chris Widger	.05	.02	.01
☐ 286 Steve Montgomery	.05	.02	.01
☐ 287 Chris Gomez	.20	.09	.03
☐ 288 Jared Baker	.05	.02	.01
☐ 289 Doug Hecker	.05	.02	.01
☐ 290 David Spykstra	.05	.02	.01
☐ 291 Scott Miller	.05	.02	.01
☐ 292 Carey Paige	.05	.02	.01
☐ 293 Dave Manning	.05	.02	.01
☐ 294 James Keefe	.05	.02	.01
☐ 295 Levon Largusa	.05	.02	.01
☐ 296 Roger Bailey	.05	.02	.01
☐ 297 Rich Ireland	.05	.02	.01
☐ 298 Matt Williams	.05	.02	.01
☐ 299 Scott Gentile	.05	.02	.01
☐ 300 Hut Smith	.05	.02	.01
☐ 301 Dave Brown	.50	.23	.06
☐ 302 Bobby Bonds Jr.	.05	.02	.01
☐ 303 Reggie Smith	.05	.02	.01
☐ 304 Preston Wilson	.25	.11	.03
☐ 305 John Burke	.05	.02	.01
☐ 306 Rodney Henderson	.05	.02	.01
☐ 307 Pete Janicki	.05	.02	.01
☐ 308 Brien Taylor FLB	.05	.02	.01
☐ 309 Mike Kelly FLB	.05	.02	.01
☐ 310 Rocket Ismail FLB	.10	.05	.01
☐ 311 Billy Owens FLB	.10	.05	.01
☐ 312 Dikembe Mutombo FLB	.10	.05	.01
☐ 313 Ty Detmer and Desmond Howard	.10	.05	.01
☐ 314 Jim Pittsley	.20	.09	.03
☐ 315 Christian Laettner JWA	.20	.09	.03
☐ 316 Harold Miner JWA	.05	.02	.01
☐ 317 Jimmy Jackson JWA	.75	.35	.09
☐ 318 Shaquille O'Neal JWA	2.00	.90	.25
☐ 319 Alonzo Mourning JWA	.75	.35	.09
☐ 320 Checklist 1	.05	.02	.01
☐ 321 Checklist 2	.05	.02	.01
☐ 322 Checklist 3	.05	.02	.01
☐ 323 Checklist 4	.05	.02	.01
☐ 324 Checklist 5	.05	.02	.01
☐ 325 Checklist 6	.05	.02	.01

1992 Classic Four-Sport Gold

This 326-card set features all 325 cards of the regular set plus an additional "Future

Superstars" autographed card. The cards measure the standard size (2 1/2" by 3 1/2"). Only 9,500 sequentially numbered sets were produced, and each set was packaged in a walnut display case. The cards are numbered on the back. Gold star cards are valued at three to six times the corresponding value of the regular card.

	MINT	NRMT	EXC
COMPLETE FACT. SET (326)	160.00	70.00	20.00
COMMON CARD (1-325)	.40	.18	.05

	MINT	NRMT	EXC
☐ AU Future Superstars AU	75.00	34.00	9.50
Phil Nevin			
Shaquille O'Neal			
Desmond Howard			
Roman Hamrlik			
(Certified autograph,			
one of 9500)			

1992 Classic Four-Sport Autographs

The 1992 Classic Draft Collection Autograph set consists of 54 standard-size (2 1/2" by 3 1/2") cards. They were randomly inserted throughout the foil packs. Listed after the player's name is how many cards were autographed by that player. An "A" suffix after the card number is used here for convenience. Jan Caloun and Jan Vopat were not included in the regular set and hence are unnumbered.

	MINT	NRMT	EXC
COMPLETE SET (54)	2800.00	1250.00	350.00
COMMON AUTOGRAPH	10.00	4.50	1.25

		MINT	NRMT	EXC
☐	1A Shaquille O'Neal/150	1800.00	800.00	230.00
☐	2A Walt Williams/2550	25.00	11.50	3.10
☐	3A Lee Mayberry/2575	15.00	6.75	1.90
☐	11A Todd Day/1575	15.00	6.75	1.90
☐	25A C.Weatherspoon/1575	40.00	18.00	5.00
☐	26A Malik Sealy/1575	15.00	6.75	1.90
☐	28A Jimmy Jackson/1575	80.00	36.00	10.00
☐	36A Tracy Murray/1450	15.00	6.75	1.90
☐	38A C.Laettner/725	45.00	20.00	5.75
☐	39A Don MacLean/2575	20.00	9.00	2.50
☐	40A Adam Keefe/1575	10.00	4.50	1.25
☐	54A Alonzo Mourning/975	160.00	70.00	20.00

		MINT	NRMT	EXC
☐	69A Harold Miner/1475	20.00	9.00	2.50
☐	76A Desmond Howard/975	40.00	18.00	5.00
☐	77A David Klingler/1125	15.00	6.75	1.90
☐	78A Quentin Coryatt/3500	20.00	9.00	2.50
☐	82A Carl Pickens/1475	50.00	23.00	6.25
☐	87A Tony Smith/3450	10.00	4.50	1.25
☐	97A Siran Stacy/4325	10.00	4.50	1.25
☐	98A Tony Sacca/1575	10.00	4.50	1.25
☐	103A Casey Weldon/4350	10.00	4.50	1.25
☐	112A Matt Blundin/1575	10.00	4.50	1.25
☐	127A Terrell Buckley/1475	15.00	6.75	1.90
☐	129A Ty Detmer/1475	20.00	9.00	2.50
☐	144A Derrick Moore/1575	15.00	6.75	1.90
☐	151A Roman Hamrlik/1550	15.00	6.75	1.90
☐	153A Mike Rathje/2075	10.00	4.50	1.25
☐	155A Cory Stillman/2125	10.00	4.50	1.25
☐	158A Jason Bowen/2075	10.00	4.50	1.25
☐	159A Jason Smith/2075	10.00	4.50	1.25
☐	165A Justin Hocking/2075	10.00	4.50	1.25
☐	170A Cale Hulse/1850	10.00	4.50	1.25
☐	181A Libor Polasek/1950	10.00	4.50	1.25
☐	185A Boris Mironov/2075	15.00	6.75	1.90
☐	192A Sandy Moger/1075	10.00	4.50	1.25
☐	195A Dwayne Norris/1075	10.00	4.50	1.25
☐	196A Joby Messier/1075	10.00	4.50	1.25
☐	207A Doug Zmolek/1075	10.00	4.50	1.25
☐	226A Phil Nevin/1475	15.00	6.75	1.90
☐	227A Paul Shuey/4050	10.00	4.50	1.25
☐	229A Jeffrey Hammonds/2950	30.00	13.50	3.80
☐	231A Derek Jeter/1125	75.00	34.00	9.50
☐	233A Derek Wallace/1475	10.00	4.50	1.25
☐	241A Jamie Arnold/1575	10.00	4.50	1.25
☐	242A Rick Helling/2875	10.00	4.50	1.25
☐	245A Dan Serafini/1475	15.00	6.75	1.90
☐	248A Ryan Luzinski/1575	10.00	4.50	1.25
☐	253A Brian Sackinsky/1575	10.00	4.50	1.25
☐	259A Dwain Bostic/2075	10.00	4.50	1.25
☐	290A David Spykstra/1575	10.00	4.50	1.25
☐	301A Dave Brown/1575	25.00	11.50	3.10
☐	307A Pete Janicki/1875	10.00	4.50	1.25
☐	NNO Jan Caloun/1975	10.00	4.50	1.25
☐	NNO Jan Vopat/1775	10.00	4.50	1.25

1992 Classic Four-Sport BCs

Randomly inserted in Classic Draft Picks Collection jumbo packs, these 20 bonus cards measure the standard size (2 1/2" by 3 1/2"). The fronts feature full-bleed glossy color action player photos. A silver foil strip

runs down the card face near the left edge and carries the player's name and position. On a silver panel edged by a dark gray stripe, the backs carry statistics, biography, and career summary; a color player photo running down the right edge rounds out the back. The cards are numbered on the dark gray stripe and arranged according to sport as follows: basketball (1-6), hockey (7-12), football (13-17), and baseball (18-20). A randomly inserted Future Superstars card has a picture of all four players on its front, shot against a horizon with dark clouds and lightning; the back indicates that just 10,000 of these cards were produced.

action player photos on the fronts. A vertical gold foil stripe runs down each card face near the left edge and carries the player's name and position. Parallel to the stripe, "One of 46,080" appears in gold foil characters. The backs carry a brief biography in a silver panel edged on the left by a dark green stripe that contains the player's name and position. A color player photo along the right edge completes the back. The sports represented are football (1-7, 16), basketball (8-14), baseball (17-21), and hockey (22-25). The cards are numbered on the back with an "LP" prefix.

	MINT	NRMT	EXC
COMPLETE SET (20)	20.00	9.00	2.50
COMMON CARD (BC1-BC20)	.40	.18	.05
☐ BC1 Alonzo Mourning........ Georgetown	3.00	1.35	.40
☐ BC2 Christian Laettner ...... Duke	1.00	.45	.13
☐ BC3 Jim Jackson .... Ohio State	3.00	1.35	.40
☐ BC4 Tom Gugliotta............ North Carolina State	1.25	.55	.16
☐ BC5 Walt Williams .... Maryland	.60	.25	.08
☐ BC6 Harold Miner .... USC	.60	.25	.08
☐ BC7 Roman Hamrlik	.60	.25	.08
☐ BC8 Valeri Bure...............	.75	.35	.09
☐ BC9 Dallas Drake	.40	.18	.05
☐ BC10 Dmitri Kvartalnov......	.40	.18	.05
☐ BC11 Manon Rheaume	10.00	4.50	1.25
☐ BC12 Viktor Kozlov...........	.40	.18	.05
☐ BC13 Desmond Howard...... Michigan	.75	.35	.09
☐ BC14 David Klingler.......... Houston	.40	.18	.05
☐ BC15 Terrell Buckley......... Florida State	.40	.18	.05
☐ BC16 Quentin Coryatt........ Texas A and M	.75	.35	.09
☐ BC17 Carl Pickens .... Tennessee	2.00	.90	.25
☐ BC18 Phil Nevin .... Cal State Fullerton	.40	.18	.05
☐ BC19 Jeffrey Hammonds.... Stanford	.75	.35	.09
☐ BC20 Michael Tucker......... Longwood	.75	.35	.09
☐ FS1 Future Superstars .... Phil Nevin Shaquille O'Neal Desmond Howard Roman Hamrlik	40.00	18.00	5.00

1992 Classic Four-Sport LPs

Randomly inserted in foil packs, this 25-card standard-size (2 1/2" by 3 1/2") limited print set features full-bleed glossy color

	MINT	NRMT	EXC
COMPLETE SET (25)	90.00	40.00	11.50
COMMON CARD (LP1-LP25)....	.50	.23	.06
☐ LP1 Desmond Howard......	1.50	.65	.19
☐ LP2 David Klingler...........	.50	.23	.06
☐ LP3 Tommy Maddox	.50	.23	.06
☐ LP4 Casey Weldon...........	.50	.23	.06
☐ LP5 Tony Smith RB	.50	.23	.06
☐ LP6 Terrell Buckley..........	.50	.23	.06
☐ LP7 Carl Pickens	4.00	1.80	.50
☐ LP8 Shaquille O'Neal	35.00	16.00	4.40
☐ LP9 Jimmy Jackson..........	10.00	4.50	1.25
☐ LP10 Alonzo Mourning	10.00	4.50	1.25
☐ LP11 Christian Laettner	4.00	1.80	.50
☐ LP12 Harold Miner	1.50	.65	.19
☐ LP13 Todd Day	1.00	.45	.13
☐ LP14 The King and .... His Heir Kareem Abdul-Jabbar Shaquille O'Neal	15.00	6.75	1.90
☐ LP15 Future Superstars.. Phil Nevin Shaquille O'Neal Roman Hamrlik Desmond Howard	15.00	6.75	1.90
☐ LP16 Classic Quarterbacks . Matt Blundin David Klingler Tommy Maddox Mike Pawlawski Tony Sacca Casey Weldon	.50	.23	.06
☐ LP17 Phil Nevin	.50	.23	.06
☐ LP18 Jeffrey Hammonds ..	2.00	.90	.25
☐ LP19 Paul Shuey	.50	.23	.06
☐ LP20 Ryan Luzinski UER	.50	.23	.06
☐ LP21 Brien Taylor	.50	.23	.06
☐ LP22 Roman Hamrlik	2.00	.90	.25
☐ LP23 Mike Rathje.............	.50	.23	.06
☐ LP24 Valeri Bure..............	4.00	1.80	.50
☐ LP25 Alexei Yashin	6.00	2.70	.75

1993 Classic Draft Previews

These basketball cards were randomly inserted in 1993 Classic Football Draft Picks foil packs as well as 1993 Classic NFL Pro Line Collection packs. Reportedly 17,500 of each card were produced and randomly inserted an average of two cards per case, evenly distributed through both products. The cards measure the standard size (2 1/2" by 3 1/2"). The fronts feature color player action shots with simulated pinewood borders. The player's name and position appear in a colored stripe at the bottom of the photo. The red-bordered back carries a basketball icon and the number of cards produced. The cards are unnumbered and are checklisted below in alphabetical order.

	MINT	NRMT	EXC
COMPLETE SET (4)	70.00	32.00	8.75
COMMON CARD (BK1-BK4)	10.00	4.50	1.25
☐ BK1 Anfernee Hardaway Memphis State	15.00	6.75	1.90
☐ BK2 Allan Houston UER (Misspelled Alan) Tennessee	25.00	11.50	3.10
☐ BK3 Jamal Mashburn Kentucky	30.00	13.50	3.80
☐ BK4 Chris Webber Michigan	10.00	4.50	1.25

1993 Classic Draft Picks

The 1993 Classic Draft Picks set consists of 110 standard-size (2 1/2" by 3 1/2") cards. Randomly inserted throughout the foil packs were the following subsets: ten limited-print, foil-stamped cards, five Hockey Draft Picks preview cards, three superhero cards, and a five-card visually interlocking set of clear acetate cards. The production run was limited to 32,500 ten-box cases. The fronts feature color action

player photos with simulated pinewood borders. The player's name and position, along with the 1993 Classic Draft Picks logo, appears in a white bar across the base of each picture. The simulated pinewood design continues on the horizontal back. The player's name appears at the top in an ellipse that is of a lighter-colored simulated pinewood. Stats are displayed in a lighter-colored rectangle at the bottom. A narrow-cropped pinewood-bordered player color action shot along the left side rounds out the card. The cards are numbered on the back.

	MINT	NRMT	EXC
COMPLETE SET (110)	7.00	3.10	.85
COMMON CARD (1-110)	.05	.02	.01
☐ 1 Chris Webber Michigan	1.00	.45	.13
☐ 2 Anfernee Hardaway Memphis State	2.00	.90	.25
☐ 3 Jamal Mashburn Kentucky	1.50	.65	.19
☐ 4 J.R. Rider UNLV	.75	.35	.09
☐ 5 Vin Baker Hartford	.75	.35	.09
☐ 6 Rodney Rogers Wake Forest	.60	.25	.08
☐ 7 Lindsey Hunter Jackson State	.25	.11	.03
☐ 8 Allan Houston Tennessee	.60	.25	.08
☐ 9 George Lynch North Carolina	.15	.07	.02
☐ 10 Toni Kukoc (Croatia)	.75	.35	.09
☐ 11 Ashraf Amaya Southern Illinois	.05	.02	.01
☐ 12 Mark Bell Western Kentucky	.05	.02	.01
☐ 13 John Best Tennessee Tech	.05	.02	.01
☐ 14 Corie Blount Cincinnati	.05	.02	.01
☐ 15 Dexter Boney UNLV	.05	.02	.01
☐ 16 Tim Brooks Tennessee (Chattanooga)	.05	.02	.01
☐ 17 James Bryson Villanova	.05	.02	.01
☐ 18 Evers Burns Maryland	.05	.02	.01
☐ 19 Scott Burrell Connecticut	.30	.14	.04

☐ 20 Sam Cassell .75 .35 .09			
Florida State			
☐ 21 Derrick Chandler .05 .02 .01			
Nebraska			
☐ 22 Sam Crawford .05 .02 .01			
New Mexico State			
☐ 23 Ron Curry .05 .02 .01			
Marquette			
☐ 24 William Davis .05 .02 .01			
James Madison			
☐ 25 Rodney Dobard .05 .02 .01			
Florida State			
☐ 26 Tony Dunkin .05 .02 .01			
Coastal Carolina			
☐ 27 Spencer Dunkley .05 .02 .01			
Delaware			
☐ 28 Bill Edwards .05 .02 .01			
Wright State			
☐ 29 Bryan Edwards .05 .02 .01			
James Madison			
☐ 30 Doug Edwards .05 .02 .01			
Florida State			
☐ 31 Chuck Evans .05 .02 .01			
Mississippi State			
☐ 32 Terry Evans .05 .02 .01			
Oklahoma			
☐ 33 Will Flemons .05 .02 .01			
Texas Tech			
☐ 34 Alphonso Ford .05 .02 .01			
Miss. Valley State			
☐ 35 Brian Gilgeous .05 .02 .01			
American			
☐ 36 Josh Grant .05 .02 .01			
Utah			
(Guarded by Shawn Bradley)			
☐ 37 Evric Gray .05 .02 .01			
UNLV			
☐ 38 Geert Hammink .05 .02 .01			
LSU			
☐ 39 Lucious Harris .15 .07 .02			
Long Beach State			
☐ 40 Joe Harvell .05 .02 .01			
Mississippi			
☐ 41 Antonio Harvey .05 .02 .01			
Pfeiffer College			
☐ 42 Scott Haskin .05 .02 .01			
Oregon State			
☐ 43 Brian Hendrick .05 .02 .01			
California			
☐ 44 Sascha Hupmann .05 .02 .01			
Evansville			
☐ 45 Stanley Jackson .05 .02 .01			
Alabama (Birmingham)			
☐ 46 Ervin Johnson .05 .02 .01			
New Orleans			
☐ 47 Adonis Jordan .05 .02 .01			
Kansas			
☐ 48 Warren Kidd .05 .02 .01			
Middle Tennessee State			
☐ 49 Malcolm Mackey .05 .02 .01			
Georgia Tech			
☐ 50 Rich Manning .05 .02 .01			
Washington			
☐ 51 Chris McNeal .05 .02 .01			
Pittsburgh			
☐ 52 Conrad McRae .05 .02 .01			
Syracuse			
☐ 53 Lance Miller .05 .02 .01			
Villanova			
☐ 54 Chris Mills .40 .18 .05			
Arizona			

☐ 55 Matt Nover .05 .02 .01			
Indiana			
☐ 56 Charles(Bo) Outlaw .05 .02 .01			
Houston			
☐ 57 Eric Pauley .05 .02 .01			
Kansas			
☐ 58 Mike Peplowski .05 .02 .01			
Michigan State			
☐ 59 Stacey Poole .05 .02 .01			
Florida			
☐ 60 Anthony Reed .05 .02 .01			
Tulane			
☐ 61 Eric Riley .05 .02 .01			
Michigan			
☐ 62 Darrin Robinson .05 .02 .01			
Sacred Heart			
☐ 63 Jackie Robinson .05 .02 .01			
So. Carolina State			
☐ 64 James Robinson .20 .09 .03			
Alabama			
☐ 65 Bryon Russell .15 .07 .02			
Long Beach State			
☐ 66 Brent Scott .05 .02 .01			
Rice			
☐ 67 Bennie Seltzer .05 .02 .01			
Washington State			
☐ 68 Ed Stokes .05 .02 .01			
Arizona			
☐ 69 Antoine Stoudamire .05 .02 .01			
Oregon			
☐ 70 Dirk Surles .05 .02 .01			
George Washington			
☐ 71 Justus Thigpen .05 .02 .01			
Iowa State			
☐ 72 Kevin Thompson .05 .02 .01			
North Carolina State			
☐ 73 Ray Thompson .05 .02 .01			
Oral Roberts			
☐ 74 Gary Trost .05 .02 .01			
Brigham Young			
☐ 75 Nick Van Exel 1.00 .45 .13			
Cincinnati			
☐ 76 Jerry Walker .05 .02 .01			
Seton Hall			
☐ 77 Rex Walters .05 .02 .01			
Kansas			
☐ 78 Leonard White .05 .02 .01			
Southern			
☐ 79 Chris Whitney .05 .02 .01			
Clemson			
☐ 80 Steve Worthy .05 .02 .01			
Rutgers			
☐ 81 Alex Wright .05 .02 .01			
Central State			
☐ 82 Luther Wright .05 .02 .01			
Seton Hall			
☐ 83 Mark Buford .05 .02 .01			
Miss. Valley State			
☐ 84 Keith Bullock .05 .02 .01			
Manhattan			
☐ 85 Mitchell Butler .15 .07 .02			
UCLA			
☐ 86 Brian Clifford .05 .02 .01			
Niagara			
☐ 87 Terry Dehere .25 .11 .03			
Seton Hall			
☐ 88 Acie Earl .15 .07 .02			
Iowa			
☐ 89 Greg Graham .05 .02 .01			
Indiana			
☐ 90 Angelo Hamilton .05 .02 .01			

			MINT	NRMT	EXC
☐ 91	Thomas Hill	Oklahoma	.05	.02	.01
		Duke			
☐ 92	Alex Holcombe		.05	.02	.01
		Baylor			
☐ 93	Khari Jaxon		.05	.02	.01
		New Mexico			
☐ 94	Darnell Mee		.05	.02	.01
		Western Kentucky			
☐ 95	Sherron Mills		.05	.02	.01
		Virginia Commonwealth			
☐ 96	Gheorge Muresan		.25	.11	.03
		(Romania)			
☐ 97	Marcelo Nicola		.05	.02	.01
		UTEP			
☐ 98	Julius Nwosu		.05	.02	.01
		Liberty			
☐ 99	Richard Petruska		.05	.02	.01
		UCLA			
☐ 100	Bryan Sallier		.05	.02	.01
		Oklahoma			
☐ 101	Harper Williams		.05	.02	.01
		Massachusetts			
☐ 102	Ike Williams		.05	.02	.01
		New Mexico			
☐ 103	Byron Wilson		.05	.02	.01
		Utah			
☐ 104	Shaquille O'Neal FLB		.60	.25	.08
		LSU			
☐ 105	Alonzo Mourning FLB		.30	.14	.04
		Georgetown			
☐ 106	Christian Laettner FLB		.15	.07	.02
		Duke			
☐ 107	Jimmy Jackson FLB		.30	.14	.04
		Ohio State			
☐ 108	Harold Miner FLB		.05	.02	.01
		USC			
☐ 109	Checklist 1		.05	.02	.01
☐ 110	Checklist 2		.05	.02	.01

1993 Classic Draft Gold

This parallel set to the regular '93 Classic also features one Mashburn and one Webber autograph card included per '93 Classic Gold set. Both players each signed 9500 cards. Except for the gold-foil highlights, the standard-size (2 1/2" by 3 1/2") cards are identical to their regular '93 Classic counterparts. The cards are numbered on the back. Gold stars are valued at three to six times the corresponding value of the regular card.

	MINT	NRMT	EXC
COMPLETE FACT. SET (112)	80.00	36.00	10.00
COMMON CARD (1-110)	.25	.11	.03
☐ AU Jamal Mashburn AU	30.00	13.50	3.80
Kentucky			
(Certified autograph,			
one of 9500)			
☐ AU Chris Webber AU	20.00	9.00	2.50
Michigan			
(Certified autograph,			
one of 9500)			

1993 Classic Draft Acetate Stars

These five acetate cards were randomly inserted in foil packs. By visually interlocking these cards, the collector created a "Draft Stars" panoramic image featuring Webber, Hardaway, Mashburn, Rider, and Rogers. These visually interlocking clear plastic acetate cards were inserted on an average of three per ten-box case of 1993 Classic Basketball Draft Picks. The cards are unnumbered and checklisted below in alphabetical order.

	MINT	NRMT	EXC
COMPLETE SET (5)	35.00	16.00	4.40
COMMON CARD (AD1-AD5)	5.00	2.30	.60
☐ AD1 Anfernee Hardaway	16.00	7.25	2.00
Memphis St.			
☐ AD2 Jamal Mashburn	14.00	6.25	1.75
Kentucky			
☐ AD3 J.R. Rider	6.00	2.70	.75
UNLV			
☐ AD4 Rodney Rogers	5.00	2.30	.60
Wake Forest			
☐ AD5 Chris Webber	8.00	3.60	1.00
Michigan			

1993 Classic Draft Chromium Stars

Inserted one per jumbo pack, these 20 standard-size (2 1/2" by 3 1/2") cards fea-

ture on their metallic fronts borderless color player action shots. The player's name and position appear within the silver bar near the bottom. The horizontal simulated pinewood back carries a narrow-cropped color player action shot on the left. The player's name and biography appear at the top, followed below by a congratulatory message and statistics. The cards are numbered on the back with a "DS" prefix.

	MINT	NRMT	EXC
COMPLETE SET (20)	20.00	9.00	2.50
COMMON CARD (DS21-DS40)	.40	.18	.05
☐ DS21 Vin Baker	1.50	.65	.19
Hartford			
☐ DS22 Terry Dehere	.40	.18	.05
Seton Hall			
☐ DS23 Sam Cassell	1.50	.65	.19
Florida State			
☐ DS24 Doug Edwards	.40	.18	.05
Florida State			
☐ DS25 Greg Graham	.40	.18	.05
Indiana			
☐ DS26 Scott Haskin	.40	.18	.05
Oregon State			
☐ DS27 Allan Houston	1.25	.55	.16
Tennessee			
☐ DS28 Toni Kukoc	1.50	.65	.19
Benetton			
☐ DS29 George Lynch	.40	.18	.05
North Carolina			
☐ DS30 Jamal Mashburn	3.00	1.35	.40
Kentucky			
☐ DS31 Harold Miner	.40	.18	.05
Miami Heat			
☐ DS32 Rex Walters	.40	.18	.05
Kansas			
☐ DS33 James Robinson	.40	.18	.05
Alabama			
☐ DS34 Rodney Rogers	1.25	.55	.16
Wake Forrest			
☐ DS35 Luther Wright	.40	.18	.05
Seton Hall			
☐ DS36 Alonzo Mourning	1.25	.55	.16
Charlotte Hornets			
☐ DS37 Anfernee Hardaway	4.00	1.80	.50
Memphis State			
☐ DS38 Isaiah Rider	1.50	.65	.19
UNLV			
☐ DS39 Lindsey Hunter	.50	.23	.06
Jackson State			
☐ DS40 Chris Webber	2.00	.90	.25
Michigan			

1993 Classic Draft Illustrated

Drawn by artist Craig Hamilton, these three cards display images of basketball superstars and they were reportedly inserted on an average of three per ten-box case. Measuring the standard-size (2 1/2" by 3 1/2"), the fronts feature full-bleed artistic portraits of exaggerated action scenes. The player's name and position appear in a white bar across the bottom, and 1993 Classic Draft Picks logo overlays the bar. On a background consisting of a ghosted blow-up of the front portrait, the backs have a narrowly-cropped color player picture and a player profile. The production figures ("1 of 39,000") round out the back. The cards are numbered on the back with an "SS" prefix.

	MINT	NRMT	EXC
COMPLETE SET (3)	20.00	9.00	2.50
COMMON CARD (SS1-SS3)	5.00	2.30	.60
☐ SS1 Chris Webber	6.00	2.70	.75
Michigan			
☐ SS2 Jamal Mashburn	10.00	4.50	1.25
Kentucky			
☐ SS3 Anfernee Hardaway	12.00	5.50	1.50
Memphis St.			

1993 Classic Draft LPs

These ten standard-size (2 1/2" by 3 1/2") cards were randomly inserted on an average of two per box of 1993 Classic Basketball Draft Picks. The fronts feature full-bleed color action player photos. The player's name and position appear in a holographic bar at the bottom, with the production run figures ("1 of 74,500") in holographic lettering immediately above. Also the 1993 Classic Draft Picks logo overlays the holographic bar. On a woodgrain-textured silver background, the horizontal backs carry a narrowly-cropped color player picture on the left and a player profile on the right. The player's name appears in a silver foil oval at the top. The cards are numbered on the back with an "LP" prefix.

	MINT	NRMT	EXC
COMPLETE SET (10)	35.00	16.00	4.40
COMMON CARD (LP1-LP10)	1.50	.65	.19
☐ LP1 Chris Webber Michigan	5.00	2.30	.60
☐ LP2 Anfernee Hardaway Memphis St.	10.00	4.50	1.25
☐ LP3 Jamal Mashburn Kentucky	8.00	3.60	1.00
☐ LP4 J.R. Rider UNLV	3.00	1.35	.40
☐ LP5 Vin Baker Hartford	3.00	1.35	.40
☐ LP6 Rodney Rogers Wake Forest	2.00	.90	.25
☐ LP7 Lindsey Hunter Jackson St.	1.50	.65	.19
☐ LP8 Toni Kukoc Italy	3.00	1.35	.40
☐ LP9 Shaquille O'Neal FLB LSU	6.00	2.70	.75
☐ LP10 Alonzo Mourning FLB Georgetown	2.00	.90	.25

1993 Classic Draft Special Bonus

Issued one per jumbo sheet, these 20 standard-size (2 1/2" by 3 1/2") cards feature on their fronts borderless color player action shots. The player's name and position appear within the gold-foil bar near the bottom. The horizontal simulated pinewood back carries a narrow-cropped color player action shot on the left. The player's name and biography appear at the top, followed below by a scouting report and statistics. The cards are numbered on the back with an "SB" prefix.

	MINT	NRMT	EXC
COMPLETE SET (20)	20.00	9.00	2.50
COMMON CARD (SB1-SB20)	.40	.18	.05

☐ SB1 Chris Webber Michigan	2.00	.90	.25
☐ SB2 Anfernee Hardaway Memphis State	4.00	1.80	.50
☐ SB3 Jamal Mashburn Kentucky	3.00	1.35	.40
☐ SB4 Isaiah Rider UNLV	1.50	.65	.19
☐ SB5 Rodney Rogers Wake Forrest	1.25	.55	.16
☐ SB6 Vin Baker Hartford	1.50	.65	.19
☐ SB7 Lindsey Hunter Jackson State	.50	.23	.06
☐ SB8 Allan Houston Tennessee	1.25	.55	.16
☐ SB9 Toni Kukoc Benetton	1.50	.65	.19
☐ SB10 Acie Earl Iowa	.50	.23	.06
☐ SB11 George Lynch North Carolina	.50	.23	.06
☐ SB12 Terry Dehere Seton Hall	.50	.23	.06
☐ SB13 Rex Walters Kansas	.40	.18	.05
☐ SB14 Harold Miner Miami Heat	.50	.23	.06
☐ SB15 Scott Haskin Oregon State	.40	.18	.05
☐ SB16 Doug Edwards Florida State	.40	.18	.05
☐ SB17 Greg Graham Indiana	.40	.18	.05
☐ SB18 Christian Laettner Minnesota Timberwolves	.50	.23	.06
☐ SB19 Alonzo Mourning Charlotte Hornets	1.25	.55	.16
☐ SB20 Shaquille O'Neal Orlando Magic	3.00	1.35	.40
☐ NNO Chris Webber Special Michigan	6.00	2.70	.75

1993 Classic Four-Sport Previews

Issued as unnumbered inserts in '93 Classic hockey packs, these five cards measure the standard size (2 1/2" by 3 1/2"). The fronts are similar in design to regular 1993 Classic Four-Sport cards. The backs carry a congratulatory message. The cards are unnumbered and checklisted below in alphabetical order.

	MINT	NRMT	EXC
COMPLETE SET (5)	40.00	18.00	5.00
COMMON CARD (CC1-CC5)	4.00	1.80	.50
☐ CC1 Alexandre Daigle	7.00	3.10	.85
☐ CC2 Jeff Granger	4.00	1.80	.50
☐ CC3 Rick Mirer	12.00	5.50	1.50
☐ CC4 Chris Webber	20.00	9.00	2.50
☐ CC5 Toni Kukoc	8.00	3.60	1.00

1993 Classic Four-Sport

The 1993 Classic Four-Sport Draft Pick Collection set consists of 325 standard-size (2 1/2" by 3 1/2") cards of the top 1993 draft picks from football, basketball, baseball, and hockey. Just 49,500 sequentially numbered 12-box cases were produced. Randomly inserted throughout the foil packs were a 15-card Tri-Card subset, a 25-card LP subset, a 12-card Acetate subset, and over 30,000 autograph cards. The borderless fronts feature color player action shots, with the player's name appearing vertically in green and gold-foil lettering within a ghosted strip near the right edge. The gold-foil Classic Four-Sport logo rests at the lower right. The back carries a narrow-cropped color player action shot on the right, and player statistics, biography, and career highlights on the left within a gray lithic background. The set includes two topical subsets: John R. Wooden Award (310-314) and All-Rookie Basketball Team (315-319). The cards are numbered on the back.

	MINT	NRMT	EXC
COMPLETE SET (325)	12.00	5.50	1.50
COMMON CARD (1-325)	.05	.02	.01

		MINT	NRMT	EXC
☐ 1	Chris Webber	.75	.35	.09
☐ 2	Anfernee Hardaway	1.50	.65	.19
☐ 3	Jamal Mashburn	1.25	.55	.16
☐ 4	Isaiah Rider	.60	.25	.08
☐ 5	Vin Baker	.60	.25	.08
☐ 6	Rodney Rogers	.50	.23	.06
☐ 7	Lindsey Hunter	.20	.09	.03
☐ 8	Allan Houston	.50	.23	.06
☐ 9	George Lynch	.05	.02	.01
☐ 10	Toni Kukoc	.50	.23	.06
☐ 11	Ashraf Amaya	.05	.02	.01
☐ 12	Mark Bell	.05	.02	.01
☐ 13	Corie Blount	.05	.02	.01
☐ 14	Dexter Boney	.05	.02	.01
☐ 15	Tim Brooks	.05	.02	.01
☐ 16	James Bryson	.05	.02	.01
☐ 17	Evers Burns	.05	.02	.01
☐ 18	Scott Burrell	.20	.09	.03
☐ 19	Sam Cassell	.50	.23	.06
☐ 20	Sam Crawford	.05	.02	.01
☐ 21	Ron Curry	.05	.02	.01
☐ 22	William Davis	.05	.02	.01
☐ 23	Rodney Dobard	.05	.02	.01
☐ 24	Tony Dunkin	.05	.02	.01
☐ 25	Spencer Dunkley	.05	.02	.01
☐ 26	Bryan Edwards	.05	.02	.01
☐ 27	Doug Edwards	.08	.04	.01
☐ 28	Chuck Evans	.05	.02	.01
☐ 29	Terry Evans	.05	.02	.01
☐ 30	Will Flemons	.05	.02	.01
☐ 31	Alphonso Ford	.05	.02	.01
☐ 32	Josh Grant	.05	.02	.01
☐ 33	Eric Gray	.05	.02	.01
☐ 34	Geert Hammink	.05	.02	.01
☐ 35	Joe Harvell	.05	.02	.01
☐ 36	Scott Haskin	.05	.02	.01
☐ 37	Brian Hendrick	.05	.02	.01
☐ 38	Sascha Hupmann	.05	.02	.01
☐ 39	Stanley Jackson	.05	.02	.01
☐ 40	Ervin Johnson	.10	.05	.01
☐ 41	Adonis Jordan	.05	.02	.01
☐ 42	Malcolm Mackey	.05	.02	.01
☐ 43	Rich Manning	.05	.02	.01
☐ 44	Chris McNeal	.05	.02	.01
☐ 45	Conrad McRae	.05	.02	.01
☐ 46	Lance Miller	.05	.02	.01
☐ 47	Chris Mills	.30	.14	.04
☐ 48	Matt Nover	.05	.02	.01
☐ 49	Charles(Bo) Outlaw	.05	.02	.01
☐ 50	Eric Pauley	.05	.02	.01
☐ 51	Mike Peplowski	.05	.02	.01
☐ 52	Stacey Poole	.05	.02	.01
☐ 53	Anthony Reed	.05	.02	.01
☐ 54	Eric Riley	.05	.02	.01
☐ 55	Darrin Robinson	.05	.02	.01
☐ 56	James Robinson	.10	.05	.01
☐ 57	Bryon Russell	.10	.05	.01
☐ 58	Brent Scott	.05	.02	.01
☐ 59	Bennie Sellzer	.05	.02	.01
☐ 60	Ed Stokes	.05	.02	.01
☐ 61	Antoine Stoudamire	.05	.02	.01
☐ 62	Dirkk Surles	.05	.02	.01
☐ 63	Justus Thigpen	.05	.02	.01
☐ 64	Kevin Thompson	.05	.02	.01
☐ 65	Ray Thompson	.05	.02	.01
☐ 66	Gary Trost	.05	.02	.01
☐ 67	Nick Van Exel	.75	.35	.09
☐ 68	Jerry Walker	.05	.02	.01
☐ 69	Rex Walters	.08	.04	.01
☐ 70	Chris Whitney	.05	.02	.01
☐ 71	Steve Worthy	.05	.02	.01
☐ 72	Luther Wright	.05	.02	.01
☐ 73	Mark Buford	.05	.02	.01
☐ 74	Mitchell Butler	.10	.05	.01
☐ 75	Brian Clifford	.05	.02	.01
☐ 76	Terry Dehere	.20	.09	.03
☐ 77	Acie Earl	.08	.04	.01
☐ 78	Greg Graham	.08	.04	.01
☐ 79	Angelo Hamilton	.05	.02	.01
☐ 80	Thomas Hill	.05	.02	.01
☐ 81	Khari Jaxon	.05	.02	.01
☐ 82	Darnell Mee	.05	.02	.01
☐ 83	Sherron Mills	.05	.02	.01
☐ 84	Gheorghe Muresan	.20	.09	.03
☐ 85	Eddie Rivera	.05	.02	.01
☐ 86	Richard Petruska	.05	.02	.01
☐ 87	Bryan Sallier	.05	.02	.01
☐ 88	Harper Williams	.05	.02	.01
☐ 89	Ike Williams	.05	.02	.01
☐ 90	Byron Wilson	.05	.02	.01
☐ 91	Drew Bledsoe	1.75	.80	.22
☐ 92	Rick Mirer	.75	.35	.09
☐ 93	Garrison Hearst	.50	.23	.06

☐	94	Marvin Jones	.05	.02	.01	☐	165	Reggie Givens	.05	.02	.01

	#	Name					#	Name			
☐	94	Marvin Jones	.05	.02	.01	☐	165	Reggie Givens	.05	.02	.01
☐	95	John Copeland	.05	.02	.01	☐	166	Travis Hill	.05	.02	.01
☐	96	Eric Curry	.05	.02	.01	☐	167	Rich McKenzie	.05	.02	.01
☐	97	Curtis Conway	.50	.23	.06	☐	168	Darrin Smith	.10	.05	.01
☐	98	Willie Roaf	.25	.11	.03	☐	169	Steve Tovar	.05	.02	.01
☐	99	Lincoln Kennedy	.05	.02	.01	☐	170	Patrick Bates	.05	.02	.01
☐	100	Jerome Bettis	.50	.23	.06	☐	171	Dan Footman	.05	.02	.01
☐	101	Mike Compton	.05	.02	.01	☐	172	Ryan McNeil	.05	.02	.01
☐	102	John Gerak	.05	.02	.01	☐	173	Danan Hughes	.05	.02	.01
☐	103	Will Shields	.05	.02	.01	☐	174	Mark Brunell	.15	.07	.02
☐	104	Ben Coleman	.05	.02	.01	☐	175	Ron Moore	.20	.09	.03
☐	105	Ernest Dye	.05	.02	.01	☐	176	Antonio London	.05	.02	.01
☐	106	Lester Holmes	.05	.02	.01	☐	177	Steve Everitt	.05	.02	.01
☐	107	Brad Hopkins	.05	.02	.01	☐	178	Wayne Simmons	.05	.02	.01
☐	108	Everett Lindsay	.05	.02	.01	☐	179	Robert Smith	.30	.14	.04
☐	109	Todd Rucci	.05	.02	.01	☐	180	Dana Stubblefield	.25	.11	.03
☐	110	Lance Gunn	.05	.02	.01	☐	181	George Teague	.05	.02	.01
☐	111	Elvis Grbac	.10	.05	.01	☐	182	Carl Simpson	.05	.02	.01
☐	112	Shane Matthews	.05	.02	.01	☐	183	Billy Joe Hobert	.05	.02	.01
☐	113	Rudy Harris	.05	.02	.01	☐	184	Gino Torretta	.10	.05	.01
☐	114	Richie Anderson	.05	.02	.01	☐	185	Alexandre Daigle	.50	.23	.06
☐	115	Derek Brown	.25	.11	.03	☐	186	Chris Pronger	.25	.11	.03
☐	116	Roger Harper	.05	.02	.01	☐	187	Chris Gratton	.25	.11	.03
☐	117	Terry Kirby	.30	.14	.04	☐	188	Paul Kariya	.75	.35	.09
☐	118	Natrone Means	1.25	.55	.16	☐	189	Rob Niedermayer	.30	.14	.04
☐	119	Glyn Milburn	.30	.14	.04	☐	190	Viktor Kozlov	.25	.11	.03
☐	120	Adrian Murrell	.10	.05	.01	☐	191	Jason Arnott	.60	.25	.08
☐	121	Lorenzo Neal	.20	.09	.03	☐	192	Niklas Sundstrom	.20	.09	.03
☐	122	Roosevelt Potts	.25	.11	.03	☐	193	Todd Harvey	.20	.09	.03
☐	123	Kevin Williams WR	.60	.25	.08	☐	194	Jocelyn Thibault	.20	.09	.03
☐	124	Fred Baxter	.05	.02	.01	☐	195	Kenny Jonsson	.40	.18	.05
☐	125	Troy Drayton	.20	.09	.03	☐	196	Denis Pederson	.12	.05	.02
☐	126	Chris Gedney	.05	.02	.01	☐	197	Adam Deadmarsh	.20	.09	.03
☐	127	Irv Smith	.10	.05	.01	☐	198	Mats Lindgren	.20	.09	.03
☐	128	Olanda Truitt	.05	.02	.01	☐	199	Nick Stadjuhar	.05	.02	.01
☐	129	Victor Bailey	.20	.09	.03	☐	200	Jason Allison	.20	.09	.03
☐	130	Horace Copeland	.10	.05	.01	☐	201	Jesper Mattsson	.12	.05	.02
☐	131	Ron Dickerson Jr.	.05	.02	.01	☐	202	Saku Koivu	.60	.25	.08
☐	132	Willie Harris	.05	.02	.01	☐	203	Anders Eriksson	.05	.02	.01
☐	133	Tyrone Hughes	.10	.05	.01	☐	204	Todd Bertuzzi	.12	.05	.02
☐	134	Qadry Ismail	.30	.14	.04	☐	205	Eric Lecompte	.05	.02	.01
☐	135	Reggie Brooks	.10	.05	.01	☐	206	Nikolai Tsulygin	.05	.02	.01
☐	136	Sean LaChapelle	.05	.02	.01	☐	207	Janne Niinimaa	.05	.02	.01
☐	137	O.J. McDuffie	.60	.25	.08	☐	208	Maxim Bets	.05	.02	.01
☐	138	Henny Shedd	.05	.02	.01	☐	209	Rory Fitzpatrick	.05	.02	.01
☐	139	Brian Stablein	.05	.02	.01	☐	210	Eric Manlow	.05	.02	.01
☐	140	Lamar Thomas	.05	.02	.01	☐	211	David Roche	.05	.02	.01
☐	141	Kevin Williams RB	.05	.02	.01	☐	212	Vladimir Chebaturkin	.05	.02	.01
☐	142	Othello Henderson	.05	.02	.01	☐	213	Bill McCauley	.05	.02	.01
☐	143	Kevin Henry	.05	.02	.01	☐	214	Chad Lang	.05	.02	.01
☐	144	Todd Kelly	.05	.02	.01	☐	215	Cosmo DuPaul	.05	.02	.01
☐	145	Devon McDonald	.05	.02	.01	☐	216	Bob Wren	.05	.02	.01
☐	146	Michael Strahan	.05	.02	.01	☐	217	Chris Simon	.05	.02	.01
☐	147	Dan Williams	.05	.02	.01	☐	218	Ryan Brown	.05	.02	.01
☐	148	Gilbert Brown	.05	.02	.01	☐	219	Mikhail Shtalenkov	.15	.07	.02
☐	149	Mark Caesar	.05	.02	.01	☐	220	Vladimir Krechin	.05	.02	.01
☐	150	John Parrella	.05	.02	.01	☐	221	Jason Saal	.05	.02	.01
☐	151	Leonard Renfro	.05	.02	.01	☐	222	Dion Darling	.05	.02	.01
☐	152	Coleman Rudolph	.05	.02	.01	☐	223	Chris Helleher	.05	.02	.01
☐	153	Ronnie Bradford	.05	.02	.01	☐	224	Antti Aalto	.05	.02	.01
☐	154	Tom Carter	.10	.05	.01	☐	225	Alain Nasreddine	.05	.02	.01
☐	155	Deon Figures	.20	.09	.03	☐	226	Paul Vincent	.05	.02	.01
☐	156	Derrick Frazier	.05	.02	.01	☐	227	Manny Legace	.05	.02	.01
☐	157	Darrien Gordon	.05	.02	.01	☐	228	Igor Chibirev	.05	.02	.01
☐	158	Carlton Gray	.05	.02	.01	☐	229	Tom Noble	.05	.02	.01
☐	159	Adrian Hardy	.05	.02	.01	☐	230	Mike Bales	.05	.02	.01
☐	160	Mike Reid	.05	.02	.01	☐	231	Jozef Cierny	.05	.02	.01
☐	161	Thomas Smith	.05	.02	.01	☐	232	Ivan Droppa	.05	.02	.01
☐	162	Robert O'Neal	.05	.02	.01	☐	233	Anatoli Fedotov	.05	.02	.01
☐	163	Chad Brown	.10	.05	.01	☐	234	Martin Gendron	.05	.02	.01
☐	164	Demetrius DuBose	.05	.02	.01	☐	235	Daniel Guerard	.05	.02	.01

☐ 236 Corey Hirsch	.15	.07	.02
☐ 237 Steven King	.05	.02	.01
☐ 238 Sergei Krivokrasov	.12	.05	.02
☐ 239 Darrin Madeley	.05	.02	.01
☐ 240 Grant Marshall	.05	.02	.01
☐ 241 Sandy McCarthy	.05	.02	.01
☐ 242 Bill McDougall	.05	.02	.01
☐ 243 Dean Melanson	.05	.02	.01
☐ 244 Roman Oksiuta	.05	.02	.01
☐ 245 Robert Petrovicky	.05	.02	.01
☐ 246 Mike Rathje	.05	.02	.01
☐ 247 Eldon Reddick	.05	.02	.01
☐ 248 Andrei Trefilov	.05	.02	.01
☐ 249 Jiri Slegr	.05	.02	.01
☐ 250 Leonid Toropchenko	.05	.02	.01
☐ 251 Dody Wood	.05	.02	.01
☐ 252 Kevin Paden	.05	.02	.01
☐ 253 Manon Rheaume	2.00	.90	.25
☐ 254 Cammi Granato	.75	.35	.09
☐ 255 Patrick Charboneau	.05	.02	.01
☐ 256 Curtis Bowen	.05	.02	.01
☐ 257 Kevin Brown	.05	.02	.01
☐ 258 Valeri Bure	.25	.11	.03
☐ 259 Janne Laukkanen	.12	.05	.02
☐ 260 Alex Rodriguez	1.25	.55	.16
☐ 261 Darren Dreifort	.05	.02	.01
☐ 262 Matt Brunson	.05	.02	.01
☐ 263 Matt Drews	.40	.18	.05
☐ 264 Wayne Gomes	.10	.05	.01
☐ 265 Jeff Granger	.05	.02	.01
☐ 266 Steve Soderstrom	.15	.07	.02
☐ 267 Brooks Kieschnick	.75	.35	.09
☐ 268 Daron Kirkreit	.05	.02	.01
☐ 269 Billy Wagner	.50	.23	.06
☐ 270 Alan Benes	.50	.23	.06
☐ 271 Scott Christman	.05	.02	.01
☐ 272 Willie Adams	.05	.02	.01
☐ 273 Jermaine Allensworth	.20	.09	.03
☐ 274 Jason Baker	.05	.02	.01
☐ 275 Brian Banks	.05	.02	.01
☐ 276 Marc Barcelo	.25	.11	.03
☐ 277 Jeff D'Amico IF	.10	.05	.01
(Redmond High;			
see also card 306)			
☐ 278 Todd Dunn	.05	.02	.01
☐ 279 Dan Ehler	.05	.02	.01
☐ 280 Tony Fuduric	.05	.02	.01
☐ 281 Ryan Hancock	.05	.02	.01
☐ 282 Vee Hightower	.05	.02	.01
☐ 283 Andre King	.05	.02	.01
(See also card 288A)			
☐ 284 Brett King	.05	.02	.01
☐ 285 Derrek Lee	.60	.25	.08
☐ 286 Andrew Lorraine	.05	.02	.01
☐ 287 Eric Ludwick	.05	.02	.01
☐ 288A Ryan McGuire ERR	.05	.02	.01
(Card misnumbered 283;			
should be 288)			
☐ 288B Ryan McGuire COR	.10	.05	.01
(In jumbo packs)			
☐ 289 Anthony Medrano	.05	.02	.01
☐ 290 Joel Moore	.05	.02	.01
☐ 291 Dan Perkins	.05	.02	.01
☐ 292 Kevin Pickford	.05	.02	.01
☐ 293 Jon Ratliff	.05	.02	.01
☐ 294 Bryan Rekar	.10	.05	.01
☐ 295 Andy Rice	.05	.02	.01
☐ 296 Carl Schutz	.05	.02	.01
☐ 297 Chris Singleton	.05	.02	.01
☐ 298 Cameron Smith	.05	.02	.01
☐ 299 Marc Valdes	.10	.05	.01

☐ 300 Joe Wagner	.05	.02	.01
☐ 301 John Wasdin	.50	.23	.06
☐ 302 Pat Watkins	.50	.23	.06
☐ 303 Dax Winslett	.10	.05	.01
☐ 304 Jamey Wright	.30	.14	.04
☐ 305 Kelly Wunsch	.15	.07	.02
☐ 306A Jeff D'Amico P ERR	.15	.07	.02
(Northeast High;			
card misnumbered 277,			
should be 306)			
☐ 306B Jeff D'Amico P COR	.25	.11	.03
(In jumbo packs)			
☐ 307 Brian Anderson	.25	.11	.03
☐ 308 Trot Nixon	.50	.23	.06
☐ 309 Kirk Presley	.30	.14	.04
☐ 310 John R. Wooden	.15	.07	.02
☐ 311 Chris Webber JWA	.30	.14	.04
☐ 312 Jamal Mashburn JWA	.40	.18	.05
☐ 313 Anfernee Hardaway JWA	.50	.23	.06
☐ 314 Terry Dehere JWA	.05	.02	.01
☐ 315 Shaquille O'Neal ART	.60	.25	.08
☐ 316 Alonzo Mourning ART	.30	.14	.04
☐ 317 Christian Laettner ART	.10	.05	.01
☐ 318 Jimmy Jackson ART	.30	.14	.04
☐ 319 Harold Miner ART	.05	.02	.01
☐ 320 Checklist 1	.05	.02	.01
☐ 321 Checklist 2	.05	.02	.01
☐ 322 Checklist 3	.05	.02	.01
☐ 323 Checklist 4	.05	.02	.01
☐ 324 Checklist 5	.05	.02	.01
☐ 325 Checklist 6	.05	.02	.01
☐ NNO Jamal Mashburn	2.50	1.15	.30
Draft Star Mail-In			

1993 Classic Four-Sport Gold

This parallel issue to the '93 Classic Four-Sport set consists of the 325 Gold versions of the regular set, plus four player autograph cards that were inserted into each factory gold set. Each of the four players autographed 3900 cards. Aside from the special gold-foil highlights (such as the ghosted stripe carrying the player's name being offset by gold-foil lines) the cards are identical to the regular '93 Classic Four-Sport cards. The cards are numbered on the back. Gold stars are valued at three to six times the corresponding value of the regular card.

	MINT	NRMT	EXC
COMPLETE FACT. SET (329)	250.00	115.00	31.00
COMMON CARD (1-325)	.40	.18	.05

		MINT	NRMT	EXC
☐	AU1 Jerome Bettis AU	30.00	13.50	3.80
☐	AU2 Chris Gratton AU	20.00	9.00	2.50
☐	AU3 Alonzo Mourning AU	40.00	18.00	5.00
☐	AU4 Alex Rodriguez AU	50.00	23.00	6.25

1993 Classic Four-Sport Acetates

Randomly inserted throughout the 1993 Classic Four-Sport foil packs, this 12-card standard-size (2 1/2" by 3 1/2") acetate set features on its fronts clear-bordered color player action cutouts set on basketball, football, baseball, or hockey stick backgrounds. The back carries the player's name at the lower left, with career highlights appearing above. The cards are unnumbered but carry letter designations. They are checklisted below in the order that spells '93 Rookie Class.

	MINT	NRMT	EXC
COMPLETE SET (12)	40.00	18.00	5.00
COMMON CARD (1-12)	2.00	.90	.25

		MINT	NRMT	EXC
☐	1 Chris Webber	4.00	1.80	.50
☐	2 Anfernee Hardaway	8.00	3.60	1.00
☐	3 Jamal Mashburn	7.00	3.10	.85
☐	4 Isaiah Rider	3.00	1.35	.40
☐	5 Toni Kukoc	3.00	1.35	.40
☐	6 Drew Bledsoe	8.00	3.60	1.00
☐	7 Rick Mirer	4.00	1.80	.50
☐	8 Garrison Hearst	3.00	1.35	.40
☐	9 Alex Rodriguez	7.00	3.10	.85
☐	10 Jeff Granger	2.00	.90	.25
☐	11 Alexandre Daigle	2.50	1.15	.30
☐	12 Chris Pronger	2.00	.90	.25

1993 Classic Four-Sport Autographs

Randomly inserted in '93 Classic Four-Sport packs, these 26 standard-size (2 1/2"

by 3 1/2") cards feature on their fronts borderless color player action shots. Within a ghosted stripe near the right edge, the player's first name appears in vertical gold-foil lettering and his last name in vertical green-colored lettering. The player's autograph appears in blue ink across the card face. A fraction representing the card's production number over the number of cards produced appears in blue ink at the lower left. The back carries a congratulatory message. The cards are listed below by their corresponding regular card numbers, except for Jennings and Klippenstein, which are shown as unnumbered cards (NNO) at the end of the checklist, since they are not in the regular set. The number of cards each player signed is shown beneath the card listing. The Rider card may have been autopenned.

	MINT	NRMT	EXC
COMPLETE SET (26)	2700.00	1200.00	350.00
COMMON AUTOGRAPH	10.00	4.50	1.25

		MINT	NRMT	EXC
☐	1A Chris Webber AU/550	225.00	100.00	28.00
☐	3A Jamal Mashburn AU/800	175.00	80.00	22.00
☐	4A Isaiah Rider AU/4100	30.00	13.50	3.80
☐	6A Rodney Rogers AU/4000	25.00	11.50	3.10
☐	7A Acie Earl AU/550	20.00	9.00	2.50
☐	91A Drew Bledsoe AU/275	350.00	160.00	45.00
☐	92A Rick Mirer AU/375	150.00	70.00	19.00
☐	93A Garrison Hearst AU/650	40.00	18.00	5.00
☐	94A Marvin Jones AU/3650	10.00	4.50	1.25
☐	184A Gino Torretta AU/3200	15.00	6.75	1.90
☐	189A Rob Niedermayer AU/4500	15.00	6.75	1.90
☐	196A Denis Pederson AU/2050	15.00	6.75	1.90
☐	197A Adam Deadmarsh AU/4250	15.00	6.75	1.90
☐	218A Ryan Brown AU/900	10.00	4.50	1.25
☐	222A Dion Darling AU/1500	10.00	4.50	1.25
☐	253A Manon Rheaume AU/1250	150.00	70.00	19.00

		MINT	NRMT	EXC
☐ 260A	Alex Rodriguez AU/4300	50.00	23.00	6.25
☐ 261A	Darren Dreifort AU/3875	10.00	4.50	1.25
☐ 265A	Jeff Granger AU/150	80.00	36.00	10.00
☐ 267A	Brooks Kieschnick AU/450	100.00	45.00	12.50
☐ 268A	Daron Kirkreit AU/275	40.00	18.00	5.00
☐ 310A	John Wooden AU/150	375.00	170.00	47.50
☐ 315A	Shaquille O'Neal AU/500	450.00	200.00	57.50
☐ 316A	Alonzo Mourning AU/400	250.00	115.00	31.00
☐ NNO	Jason Jennings AU/1475	10.00	4.50	1.25
☐ NNO	Wade Klippenstein AU/800	10.00	4.50	1.25

☐ DS46	Rodney Rogers	.60	.25	.08
☐ DS47	Chris Mills	.50	.23	.06
☐ DS48	Drew Bledsoe	3.00	1.35	.40
☐ DS49	Rick Mirer	1.25	.55	.16
☐ DS50	Garrison Hearst	.75	.35	.09
☐ DS51	Jerome Bettis	1.00	.45	.13
☐ DS52	Terry Kirby	.50	.23	.06
☐ DS53	Glyn Milburn	.75	.35	.09
☐ DS54	Reggie Brooks	.30	.14	.04
☐ DS55	Alex Rodriguez	2.50	1.15	.30
☐ DS56	Brooks Kieschnick	1.25	.55	.16
☐ DS57	Jeff Granger	.30	.14	.04
☐ DS58	Alexandre Daigle	.75	.35	.09
☐ DS59	Chris Pronger	.30	.14	.04
☐ DS60	Chris Gratton	.30	.14	.04

1993 Classic Four-Sport Chromium Draft

Inserted one per jumbo pack, these 20 standard-size (2 1/2" by 3 1/2") cards feature color player action cutouts on their borderless metallic fronts. The player's name, along with the production number (1 of 80,000), appear vertically in gold foil at the lower left. The back carries a narrow-cropped color player action shot on the right. The player's biography and career highlights appear on the left, within a gray lithic background. The cards are numbered on the back with a "DS" prefix.

	MINT	NRMT	EXC
COMPLETE SET (20)	18.00	8.00	2.30
COMMON CARD (DS41-DS60)	.30	.14	.04

		MINT	NRMT	EXC
☐ DS41	Chris Webber	1.50	.65	.19
☐ DS42	Anfernee Hardaway	3.00	1.35	.40
☐ DS43	Jamal Mashburn	2.50	1.15	.30
☐ DS44	Isaiah Rider	.75	.35	.09
☐ DS45	Toni Kukoc	.75	.35	.09

1993 Classic Four-Sport LPs

Randomly inserted throughout the 1993 Classic Four-Sport foil packs, this 25-card standard-size (2 1/2" by 3 1/2") set features the hottest draft pick players in 1993. The borderless fronts feature color player action shots. The player's name appears vertically at the lower left. The production number (1 of 63,400) appears in gold foil at the lower right. The back carries a narrow-cropped color player action shot on the right. The player's career highlights appear on the left, within a gray lithic background. The cards are numbered on the back with an "LP" prefix.

	MINT	NRMT	EXC
COMPLETE SET (25)	45.00	20.00	5.75
COMMON CARD (LP1-LP25)	.75	.35	.09

		MINT	NRMT	EXC
☐ LP1	Four-in-One Card Chris Webber Drew Bledsoe Alex Rodriguez Alexandre Daigle	4.00	1.80	.50
☐ LP2	Chris Webber	4.00	1.80	.50
☐ LP3	Anfernee Hardaway	8.00	3.60	1.00
☐ LP4	Jamal Mashburn	6.00	2.70	.75
☐ LP5	Isaiah Rider	2.00	.90	.25
☐ LP6	Shaquille O'Neal	4.00	1.80	.50

		MINT	NRMT	EXC
☐	LP7 Toni Kukoc	2.00	.90	.25
☐	LP8 Rodney Rogers	1.50	.65	.19
☐	LP9 Lindsey Hunter	1.25	.55	.16
☐	LP10 Drew Bledsoe	8.00	3.60	1.00
☐	LP11 Rick Mirer	3.50	1.55	.45
☐	LP12 Garrison Hearst	3.00	1.35	.40
☐	LP13 Jerome Bettis	3.00	1.35	.40
☐	LP14 Marvin Jones	.75	.35	.09
☐	LP15 Terry Kirby	1.25	.55	.16
☐	LP16 Glyn Milburn	2.00	.90	.25
☐	LP17 Reggie Brooks	.75	.35	.09
☐	LP18 Alex Rodriguez	7.00	3.10	.85
☐	LP19 Darren Dreifort	.75	.35	.09
☐	LP20 Jeff Granger	.75	.35	.09
☐	LP21 Brooks Kieschnick	3.00	1.35	.40
☐	LP22 Alexandre Daigle	2.00	.90	.25
☐	LP23 Chris Pronger	.75	.35	.09
☐	LP24 Chris Gratton	.75	.35	.09
☐	LP25 Paul Kariya	3.50	1.55	.45

1993 Classic Four-Sport LP Jumbos

Random inserts in hobby boxes, these five oversized cards measure approximately 3 1/2" by 5" and feature on their fronts borderless color player action shots. Within a ghosted stripe near the right edge, the player's first name appears in vertical gold-foil lettering and his last name in vertical green-colored lettering. The back carries a narrow-cropped color player action shot on the right. The player's name, statistics, biography, and career highlights, along with the card's production number out of 8,000 produced, appear on a gray lithic background to the left. The cards are numbered on the back as "X of 5."

	MINT	NRMT	EXC
COMPLETE SET (5)	35.00	16.00	4.40
COMMON CARD (1-5)	3.50	1.55	.45
☐ 1 Drew Bledsoe	10.00	4.50	1.25
☐ 2 Alexandre Daigle	3.50	1.55	.45
☐ 3 Alex Rodriguez	10.00	4.50	1.25
☐ 4 Chris Webber	6.00	2.70	.75
☐ 5 Four in One	6.00	2.70	.75

1993 Classic Four-Sport Power Pick Bonus

Issued one per jumbo sheet, these 20 standard-size (2 1/2" by 3 1/2") cards feature on their borderless fronts color player action shots, the backgrounds for which are faded to black-and-white. The player's name and the sets production number (1 of 80,000) appear in green-foil cursive lettering near the bottom. On a gray lithic background, the back carries a color player action cutout on the right, with the player's biography and career highlights appearing alongside the left. The cards are numbered on the back with a "PP" prefix.

	MINT	NRMT	EXC
COMPLETE SET (20)	18.00	8.00	2.30
COMMON CARD (PP1-PP20)	.30	.14	.04
☐ PP1 Chris Webber	1.50	.65	.19
☐ PP2 Anfernee Hardaway	3.00	1.35	.40
☐ PP3 Jamal Mashburn	2.50	1.15	.30
☐ PP4 Isaiah Rider	.75	.35	.09
☐ PP5 Toni Kukoc	.75	.35	.09
☐ PP6 Rodney Rogers	.60	.25	.08
☐ PP7 Chris Mills	.50	.23	.06
☐ PP8 Drew Bledsoe	3.00	1.35	.40
☐ PP9 Rick Mirer	1.25	.55	.16
☐ PP10 Garrison Hearst	.75	.35	.09
☐ PP11 Jerome Bettis	1.00	.45	.13
☐ PP12 Terry Kirby	.50	.23	.06
☐ PP13 Glyn Milburn	.75	.35	.09
☐ PP14 Reggie Brooks	.30	.14	.04
☐ PP15 Alex Rodriguez	2.50	1.15	.30
☐ PP16 Brooks Kieschnick	1.25	.55	.16
☐ PP17 Jeff Granger	.30	.14	.04
☐ PP18 Alexandre Daigle	.75	.35	.09
☐ PP19 Chris Pronger	.30	.14	.04
☐ PP20 Chris Gratton	.30	.14	.04
☐ NNO Four in One Special	6.00	2.70	.75

1993 Classic Four-Sport Tri-Cards

Randomly inserted throughout the 1993 Classic Four-Sport foil packs, this set fea-

tures five standard-size (2 1/2" by 3 1/2")
cards with three players on each card separated by perforations. The horizontal fronts
feature three separate color player action
shots, with each player's name appearing
in green and gold-foil lettering at the bottom
of his strip. The back carries three color
player head shots on the left, stacked one
upon the other. To the right of each head
shot is the player's name and biography
within a gray lithic background. The cards
are numbered on the back with a "TC" prefix.

	MINT	NRMT	EXC
COMPLETE SET (5)	32.00	14.50	4.00
COMMON PANEL (TC1-TC5) ...	4.00	1.80	.50

		MINT	NRMT	EXC
☐ TC1	Anfernee Hardaway..	10.00	4.50	1.25
	TC6 Shaquile O'Neal			
	TC11 Chris Webber			
☐ TC2	Drew Bledsoe............	8.00	3.60	1.00
	TC7 Rick Mirer			
	TC12 Garrison Hearst			
☐ TC3	Jeff Granger...............	6.00	2.70	.75
	TC8 Brooks Kieschnick			
	TC13 Alex Rodriquez			
☐ TC4	Alexandre Daigle........	4.00	1.80	.50
	TC9 Chris Pronger			
	TC14 Chris Gratton			
☐ TC5	Drew Bledsoe	13.00	5.75	1.65
	TC10 Chris Webber			
	TC15 Alex Rodriquez			

1993 Classic McDonald's Four-Sport

Classic has produced this 35-card four-
sport set for a promotion at McDonald's
restaurants in central and southeastern
Pennsylvania, southern New Jersey,
Delaware, and central Florida. Measuring
the standard size (2 1/2" by 3 1/2"), the
cards were distributed in five-card packs. A
five-card "limited production" subset was
randomly inserted throughout these packs.
The promotion also featured instant win
cards awarding 2,000 pieces of auto-

graphed Score Board memorabilia. An
autographed Chris Webber card was also
randomly inserted in the packs on a limited
basis. The fronts feature full-bleed action
photos except on the right side, where a
dark gray stripe carries the player's name
and position in gold foil lettering. Between a
dark gray stripe and a narrowly-cropped
player photo, the backs have gray panel
displaying biography and career summary.
The set is arranged according to sports as
follows: football (1-10), baseball (11, 26,
31-35), hockey (12-20), and basketball (21-
25, 27-30). The cards are numbered on the
back in the upper left, and the McDonald's
trademark is gold foil stamped toward the
bottom.

		MINT	NRMT	EXC
COMPLETE SET (35)		10.00	4.00	1.00
COMMON CARD (1-35)		.05	.02	.00

☐		MINT	NRMT	EXC
☐ 1	Troy Aikman	1.00	.40	.10
☐ 2	Drew Bledsoe.................	1.50	.50	.12
☐ 3	Eric Curry	.25	.10	.02
☐ 4	Garrison Hearst.............	.25	.12	.03
☐ 5	Lester Holmes	.10	.04	.01
☐ 6	Marvin Jones	.20	.08	.02
☐ 7	O.J. McDuffie	.60	.24	.06
☐ 8	Rick Mirer	1.25	.50	.12
☐ 9	Leonard Renfro..............	.10	.04	.01
☐ 10	Jerry Rice	.30	.12	.03
☐ 11	Darren Daulton	.15	.06	.01
☐ 12	Vyacheslav Butsayev.....	.10	.04	.01
☐ 13	Kevin Dineen	.15	.06	.01
☐ 14	Andre Faust	.10	.04	.01
☐ 15	Roman Hamrlik..............	.15	.06	.01
☐ 16	Mark Recchi	.15	.06	.01
☐ 17	Manon Rheaume............	2.00	.80	.20
☐ 18	Dominic Roussel............	.30	.12	.03
☐ 19	Teemu Selanne	.50	.20	.05
☐ 20	Tommy Soderstrom........	.15	.06	.01
☐ 21	Anfernee Hardaway........	1.50	.60	.15
☐ 22	Jimmy Jackson..............	.50	.20	.05
☐ 23	Christian Laettner	.25	.10	.02
☐ 24	Jamal Mashburn............	.90	.36	.09
☐ 25	Harold Miner.................	.08	.03	.01
☐ 26	Bull and Baby Bull........	.08	.03	.01
	Greg Luzinski			
	Ryan Luzinski			
☐ 27	Alonzo Mourning	1.00	.40	.10
☐ 28	Shaquille O'Neal............	1.50	.60	.15
☐ 29	Clarence Weatherspoon..	.30	.12	.03
☐ 30	Chris Webber	2.00	.80	.20
☐ 31	Chad McConnell............	.15	.06	.01
☐ 32	Phil Nevin	.25	.12	.03
☐ 33	Paul Shuey....................	.15	.06	.01

	MINT	NRMT	EXC
☐ 34 Derek Wallace	.08	.03	.01
☐ 35 Trench Warfare Leonard Renfro Lester Holmes	.05	.02	.00

1993 Classic McDonald's Four-Sport LPs

Measuring the standard size (2 1/2" by 3 1/2"), these five limited production cards were randomly inserted in 1993 Classic McDonald's five-card packs. Chris Webber, the number one pick in the NBA draft, autographed 1,250 of his cards. The front features a glossy color player action photo that is borderless except for the gold foil band on the right edge, which contains the player's name and position. Printed vertically, and parallel and next to the gold foil band, "1 of 16,750" appears in gold foil. The Classic Four Sport logo appears in the upper right. The back has a narrow-cropped color player action photo along the right edge, a dark green band along the left edge that contains the player's name in gold foil, and brief highlights of the player's career printed in the middle silver panel. The McDonald's logo is gold-foil stamped at the bottom. The cards are numbered on the back in gold foil with an "LP" prefix.

	MINT	NRMT	EXC
COMPLETE SET (5)	30.00	12.00	3.00
COMMON CARD (LP1-LP5)	1.00	.40	.10
☐ LP1 Darren Daulton	2.00	.80	.20
☐ LP2 Trench Warfare Leonard Renfro Lester Holmes	1.00	.40	.10
☐ LP3 Alonzo Mourning	8.00	3.25	.80
☐ LP4 Manon Rheaume	20.00	8.00	2.00
☐ LP5 Steve Young	3.00	1.20	.30
☐ NNO Chris Webber AU/1250	175.00	70.00	18.00
(Certified autograph)			

1993 Classic Futures

These 100 cards measure approximately 2 1/2" by 4 3/4" and feature on their fronts color player action shots with backgrounds that have been thrown out of focus. The card has white borders at the top and bottom. The player's name and position appear in gold-foil lettering within the bottom white margin. The same border design is duplicated on the back, which carries a narrow-cropped color player action shot on the left, and biography, career highlights and statistics on the right. The cards are numbered on the back.

	MINT	NRMT	EXC
COMPLETE SET (100)	12.00	5.50	1.50
COMMON CARD (1-100)	.10	.05	.01
☐ 1 Chris Webber Michigan	1.50	.65	.19
☐ 2 Bill Edwards Wright State	.10	.05	.01
☐ 3 Anfernee Hardaway Memphis State	3.00	1.35	.40
☐ 4 Bryan Edwards James Madison	.10	.05	.01
☐ 5 Jamal Mashburn Kentucky	2.00	.90	.25
☐ 6 Doug Edwards Florida State	.20	.09	.03
☐ 7 Isaiah Rider UNLV	1.00	.45	.13
☐ 8 Chuck Evans Mississippi State	.10	.05	.01
☐ 9 Vin Baker Hartford	1.00	.45	.13
☐ 10 Terry Evans Oklahoma	.10	.05	.01
☐ 11 Rodney Rogers Wake Forest	.90	.40	.11
☐ 12 Will Flemons Texas Tech	.10	.05	.01
☐ 13 Lindsey Hunter Jackson State	.40	.18	.05
☐ 14 Alphonso Ford	.10	.05	.01

☐ 15	Allan Houston Mississippi Valley Tennessee	.90	.40	.11
☐ 16	Josh Grant Utah	.10	.05	.01
☐ 17	George Lynch North Carolina	.10	.05	.01
☐ 18	Evric Gray UNLV	.10	.05	.01
☐ 19	Toni Kukoc Benetton	1.00	.45	.13
☐ 20	Geert Hammink LSU	.10	.05	.01
☐ 21	Ashraf Amaya Southern Illinois	.10	.05	.01
☐ 22	Lucious Harris Long Beach State	.20	.09	.03
☐ 23	Mark Bell Western Kentucky	.10	.05	.01
☐ 24	Joe Harvell Mississippi	.10	.05	.01
☐ 25	Corie Blount Cincinnati	.10	.05	.01
☐ 26	Antonio Harvey Pfeiffer	.10	.05	.01
☐ 27	Dexter Bonoy UNLV	.10	.05	.01
☐ 28	Scott Haskin Oregon State	.10	.05	.01
☐ 29	Tim Brooks Tennessee Chattanooga	.10	.05	.01
☐ 30	Brian Hendrick California	.10	.05	.01
☐ 31	James Bryson Villanova	.10	.05	.01
☐ 32	Sascha Hupmann Evansville	.10	.05	.01
☐ 33	Evers Burns Maryland	.10	.05	.01
☐ 34	Stanley Jackson UAB	.10	.05	.01
☐ 35	Scott Burrell Connecticut	.50	.23	.06
☐ 36	Ervin Johnson New Orleans	.20	.09	.03
☐ 37	Sam Cassell Florida State	1.00	.45	.13
☐ 38	Adonis Jordan Kansas	.10	.05	.01
☐ 39	Sam Crawford New Mexico State	.10	.05	.01
☐ 40	Warren Kidd Mid Tennessee State	.10	.05	.01
☐ 41	Ron Curry Marquette	.10	.05	.01
☐ 42	Malcolm Mackey Georgia Tech	.10	.05	.01
☐ 43	William Davis James Madison	.10	.05	.01
☐ 44	Rich Manning Washington	.10	.05	.01
☐ 45	Rodney Dobard Florida State	.10	.05	.01
☐ 46	Chris McNeal Pittsburgh	.10	.05	.01
☐ 47	Tony Dunkin Coastal Carolina	.10	.05	.01
☐ 48	Conrad McRae Syracuse	.10	.05	.01
☐ 49	Spencer Dunkley Delaware	.10	.05	.01
☐ 50	Lance Miller Villanova	.10	.05	.01
☐ 51	Chris Mills Arizona	.60	.25	.08
☐ 52	Chris Whitney Clemson	.10	.05	.01
☐ 53	Matt Nover Indiana	.10	.05	.01
☐ 54	Steve Worthy Rutgers	.10	.05	.01
☐ 55	Charles(Bo) Outlaw Houston	.10	.05	.01
☐ 56	Luther Wright Seton Hall	.10	.05	.01
☐ 57	Eric Pauley Kansas	.10	.05	.01
☐ 58	Mark Buford Mississippi Valley	.10	.05	.01
☐ 59	Mike Peplowski Michigan State	.10	.05	.01
☐ 60	Mitchell Butler UCLA	.20	.09	.03
☐ 61	Stacey Poole Florida	.10	.05	.01
☐ 62	Brian Clifford Niagara	.10	.05	.01
☐ 63	Anthony Reed Tulane	.10	.05	.01
☐ 64	Terry Dehere Seton Hall	.40	.18	.05
☐ 65	Eric Riley Michigan	.10	.05	.01
☐ 66	Acie Earl Iowa	.20	.09	.03
☐ 67	Darrin Robinson Sacred Heart	.10	.05	.01
☐ 68	Greg Graham Indiana	.10	.05	.01
☐ 69	James Robinson Alabama	.20	.09	.03
☐ 70	Angelo Hamilton Oklahoma	.10	.05	.01
☐ 71	Bryon Russell Long Beach State	.20	.09	.03
☐ 72	Thomas Hill Duke	.10	.05	.01
☐ 73	Brent Scott Rice	.10	.05	.01
☐ 74	Khari Jaxon New Mexico	.10	.05	.01
☐ 75	Bennie Seltzer Washington State	.10	.05	.01
☐ 76	Darnell Mee Western Kentucky	.10	.05	.01
☐ 77	Ed Stokes Arizona	.10	.05	.01
☐ 78	Sherron Mills VCU	.10	.05	.01
☐ 79	Antoine Stoudamire Oregon	.10	.05	.01
☐ 80	Gheorghe Muresan Pau Orthez	.40	.18	.05
☐ 81	Dirkk Surles George Washington	.10	.05	.01
☐ 82	Eddie Vivera UTEP	.10	.05	.01
☐ 83	Justus Thigpen Iowa State	.10	.05	.01
☐ 84	Julius Nwosu Liberty	.10	.05	.01
☐ 85	Kevin Thompson	.10	.05	.01

North Carolina State

		MINT	NRMT	EXC
☐ 86	Richard Petruska .... .10 UCLA		.05	.01
☐ 87	Ray Thompson .... .10 Oral Roberts		.05	.01
☐ 88	Bryan Sallier .... .10 Oklahoma		.05	.01
☐ 89	Gary Trost .... .10 BYU		.05	.01
☐ 90	Harper Williams .... .10 Massachusetts		.05	.01
☐ 91	Nick Van Exel .... 1.50 Cincinnati		.65	.19
☐ 92	Ike Williams .... .10 New Mexico		.05	.01
☐ 93	Jerry Walker .... .10 Seton Hall		.05	.01
☐ 94	Bryon Wilson .... .10 Utah		.05	.01
☐ 95	Rex Walters .... .20 Kansas		.09	.03
☐ 96	Alex Holcombe............... .10 Baylor		.05	.01
☐ 97	Leonard White .... .10 Southern		.05	.01
☐ 98	Alex Wright .... .10 Central Oklahoma		.05	.01
☐ 99	Checklist 1-50............... .10		.05	.01
☐ 100	Checklist 51-100........... .10		.05	.01
☐ NNO	Shaquille O'Neal ..... 60.00 Acetate		27.00	7.50

	MINT	NRMT	EXC
COMPLETE SET (5)	25.00	11.50	3.10
COMMON CARD (LP1-LP5).....	3.00	1.35	.40
☐ LP1 Chris Webber.............	4.00	1.80	.50
Michigan			
☐ LP2 Anfernee Hardaway....	9.00	4.00	1.15
Memphis State			
☐ LP3 Jamal Mashburn........	7.00	3.10	.85
Kentucky			
☐ LP4 Isaiah Rider	3.00	1.35	.40
UNLV			
☐ LP5 Toni Kukoc................	3.00	1.35	.40
Benneton			

1993 Classic Futures Team

1993 Classic Futures LPs

This 1993 Classic Futures Limited Edition five-card set had a production of 29,500. The cards measure approximately 2 1/2" by 4 3/4". The fronts contain full-bleed color action player photos. The player's name is printed in bold lettering within a wide white bar across the lower edge. The white backs have the number of cards produced prominently displayed across the top of the card. Below is biography, career summary and statistics. The player's name is printed at the bottom. The cards are unnumbered and checklisted below in draft order.

Randomly inserted in packs, these five cards measure approximately 2 1/2" by 4 3/4" and feature on their fronts elliptical color player action shots set on white backgrounds. The player's name and position appear in gold-foil lettering at the bottom. The back carries a color player action shot at the top and career highlights at the bottom. The cards are numbered on the back with a "CFT" prefix.

	MINT	NRMT	EXC
COMPLETE SET (5)	30.00	13.50	3.80
COMMON CARD (CFT1-CFT5) .	4.00	1.80	.50
☐ 1 Chris Webber..................	5.00	2.30	.60
Michigan			
☐ 2 Anfernee Hardaway......	10.00	4.50	1.25
Memphis State			
☐ 3 Jamal Mashburn	8.00	3.60	1.00
Kentucky			
☐ 4 Isaiah Rider....................	4.00	1.80	.50
UNLV			
☐ 5 Toni Kukoc.....................	4.00	1.80	.50
Benneton			

1994 Classic Previews

Randomly inserted in 1994 Classic football and ProLine football packs, these five standard-size (2 1/2" by 3 1/2") cards feature color player action shots on their borderless fronts. The player's name and position appear in a black bar near the bottom. The back carries a congratulatory message. The complete set was also available using a redemption card. This offer expired Oct. 1, 1994.

	MINT	NRMT	EXC
COMPLETE SET (5)	55.00	25.00	7.00
COMMON CARD (1-5)	4.00	1.80	.50
☐ BP1 Eric Montross	8.00	3.60	1.00
North Carolina			
☐ BP2 Jason Kidd	25.00	11.50	3.10
California			
☐ BP3 Yinka Dare	4.00	1.80	.50
George Washington			
☐ BP4 Glenn Robinson	25.00	11.50	3.10
Purdue			
☐ BP5 Clifford Rozier	5.00	2.30	.60
Louisville			

1994 Classic Draft

These 105 standard-size (2 1/2" by 3 1/2") cards feature borderless color player action shots on their fronts. The player's name

and position appear within a black bar near the bottom. The back carries another borderless color player action shot, which is gradually ghosted toward the bottom. The player's name and position appear at the top; statistics and career highlights appear near the bottom. Dick Vitale's facsimile autograph at the lower right rounds out the card. The cards are numbered on the back.

	MINT	NRMT	EXC
COMPLETE SET (105)	10.00	4.50	1.25
COMMON CARD (1-105)	.05	.02	.01
☐ 1 Glenn Robinson	2.00	.90	.25
Purdue			
☐ 2 Jason Kidd	2.00	.90	.25
California			
☐ 3 Charlie Ward	.20	.09	.03
Florida State			
☐ 4 Grant Hill	2.50	1.15	.30
Duke			
☐ 5 Juwan Howard	.75	.35	.09
Michigan			
☐ 6 Eric Montross	.50	.23	.06
North Carolina			
☐ 7 Carlos Rogers	.30	.14	.04
Tennessee State			
☐ 8 Wesley Person	.50	.23	.06
Auburn			
☐ 9 Anthony Miller	.05	.02	.01
Michigan State			
☐ 10 Dwayne Morton	.05	.02	.01
Louisville			
☐ 11 Chris Mills ART	.05	.02	.01
Cleveland Cavaliers			
☐ 12 Jamal Mashburn ART	.15	.07	.02
Dallas Mavericks			
☐ 13 Chris Webber ART	.05	.02	.01
Golden State Warriors			
☐ 14 Anfernee Hardaway ART	.20	.09	.03
Golden State Warriors			
☐ 15 Isaiah Rider ART	.05	.02	.01
Minnesota Timberwolves			
☐ 16 Billy McCaffrey	.05	.02	.01
Vanderbilt			
☐ 17 Steve Woodberry	.05	.02	.01
Kansas			
☐ 18 Damon Bailey	.20	.09	.03
Indiana			
☐ 19 Deon Thomas	.05	.02	.01
Illinois			
☐ 20 Dontonio Wingfield	.05	.02	.01
Cincinnati			
☐ 21 Albert Burditt	.05	.02	.01
Texas			
☐ 22 Aaron McKie	.15	.07	.02
Temple			
☐ 23 Steve Smith	.05	.02	.01
Arizona State			
☐ 24 Tony Dumas	.15	.07	.02
Missouri-K.C.			
☐ 25 Adrian Autry	.05	.02	.01
Syracuse			
☐ 26 Monty Williams	.05	.02	.01
Notre Dame			
☐ 27 Askia Jones	.05	.02	.01
Kansas State			
☐ 28 Howard Eisley	.05	.02	.01
Boston College			
☐ 29 Brian Grant	.75	.35	.09

	Xavier			
☐ 30	Eddie Jones	1.00	.45	.13
	Temple			
☐ 31	Dickey Simpkins	.20	.09	.03
	Providence			
☐ 32	Michael Smith	.30	.14	.04
	Providence			
☐ 33	Clifford Rozier	.25	.11	.03
	Louisville			
☐ 34	Travis Ford	.05	.02	.01
	Kentucky			
☐ 35	Jervaughn Scales	.05	.02	.01
	Southern			
☐ 36	Tracy Webster	.05	.02	.01
	Wisconsin			
☐ 37	Brooks Thompson	.05	.02	.01
	Oklahoma State			
☐ 38	Jim McIlvaine	.05	.02	.01
	Marquette			
☐ 39	Eric Piatkowski	.15	.07	.02
	Nebraska			
☐ 40	Arturas Karnishovas	.05	.02	.01
	Seton Hall			
☐ 41	Rodney Dent	.05	.02	.01
	Kentucky			
☐ 42	Robert Shannon	.05	.02	.01
	UAB			
☐ 43	Derrick Phelps	.05	.02	.01
	North Carolina			
☐ 44	Brian Reese	.05	.02	.01
	North Carolina			
☐ 45	Kevin Salvadori	.05	.02	.01
	North Carolina			
☐ 46	Shon Tarver	.05	.02	.01
	UCLA			
☐ 47	Anthony Goldwire	.05	.02	.01
	Houston			
☐ 48	Jamie Watson	.05	.02	.01
	South Carolina			
☐ 49	Damon Key	.05	.02	.01
	Marquette			
☐ 50	Kevin Rankin	.05	.02	.01
	Northwestern			
☐ 51	Khalid Reeves	.50	.23	.06
	Arizona			
☐ 52	Doremus Benneman	.05	.02	.01
	Siena			
☐ 53	Sharone Wright	.50	.23	.06
	Clemson			
☐ 54	Melvin Simon	.05	.02	.01
	New Orleans			
☐ 55	Andrei Fetisov	.05	.02	.01
	Forum Valladolid			
☐ 56	Barry Brown	.05	.02	.01
	Jacksonville			
☐ 57	B.J. Tyler	.15	.07	.02
	Texas			
☐ 58	Lawrence Funderburke	.05	.02	.01
	Ohio State			
☐ 59	Darrin Hancock	.05	.02	.01
	Kansas			
☐ 60	Gaylon Nickerson	.05	.02	.01
	NW Oklahoma			
☐ 61	Jeff Webster	.05	.02	.01
	Oklahoma			
☐ 62	Derrick Alston	.05	.02	.01
	Duquesne			
☐ 63	Kendrick Warren	.05	.02	.01
	VCU			
☐ 64	Yinka Dare	.05	.02	.01
	G. Washington			
☐ 65	Shawnelle Scott	.05	.02	.01
	St. John's			
☐ 66	Patrick Ewing CEN	.05	.02	.01
	New York Knicks			
☐ 67	Dikembe Mutombo CEN	.05	.02	.01
	Denver Nuggets			
☐ 68	Alonzo Mourning CEN	.15	.07	.02
	Charlotte Hornets			
☐ 69	Shaquille O'Neal CEN	.25	.11	.03
	Orlando Magic			
☐ 70	Hakeem Olajuwon CEN	.05	.02	.01
	Houston Rockets			
☐ 71	Thomas Hamilton	.05	.02	.01
	MLK High School			
☐ 72	Joey Brown	.05	.02	.01
	Georgetown			
☐ 73	Voshon Lenard	.15	.07	.02
	Minnesota			
☐ 74	Donyell Marshall	.75	.35	.09
	Connecticut			
☐ 75	Abdul Fox	.05	.02	.01
	Rhode Island			
☐ 76	Checklist	.05	.02	.01
☐ 77	Checklist	.05	.02	.01
☐ 78	Jalen Rose	.50	.23	.06
	Michigan			
☐ 79	Trevor Ruffin	.05	.02	.01
	Hawaii			
☐ 80	Sam Mitchell	.05	.02	.01
	Cleveland State			
☐ 81	Dick Vitale ANN	.30	.14	.04
☐ 82	Charlie Ward 2-Sport	.20	.09	.03
	Florida State			
☐ 83	Cornell Parker	.05	.02	.01
	Virginia			
☐ 84	Clayton Ritter	.05	.02	.01
	James Madison			
☐ 85	Carl Ray Harris	.05	.02	.01
	Fresno State			
☐ 86	Randy Blocker	.05	.02	.01
	Northern Iowa			
☐ 87	Chuck Graham	.05	.02	.01
	Florida State			
☐ 88	Greg Minor	.25	.11	.03
	Louisville			
☐ 89	Bill Curley	.05	.02	.01
	Boston College			
☐ 90	Harry Moore	.05	.02	.01
	St. Bonaventure			
☐ 91	Melvin Booker	.05	.02	.01
	Missouri			
☐ 92	Gary Collier	.05	.02	.01
	Tulsa			
☐ 93	Myron Walker	.05	.02	.01
	Robert Morris			
☐ 94	Jamie Brandon	.05	.02	.01
	LSU			
☐ 95	Eric Mobley	.05	.02	.01
	Pittsburgh			
☐ 96	Byron Starks	.05	.02	.01
	SW Louisiana			
☐ 97	Antonio Lang	.05	.02	.01
	Duke			
☐ 98	Jevon Crudup	.05	.02	.01
	Missouri			
☐ 99	Robert Churchwell	.05	.02	.01
	Georgetown			
☐ 100	Aaron Swinson	.05	.02	.01
	Auburn			
☐ 101	Glenn Robinson COMIC	1.50	.65	.19
	Purdue			

		MINT	NRMT	EXC
☐ 102	Jason Kidd COMIC..... California	1.50	.65	.19
☐ 103	Juwan Howard COMIC. Michigan	.60	.25	.08
☐ 104	Charlie Ward COMIC.... Florida State	.20	.09	.03
☐ 105	Eric Montross COMIC.... North Carolina	.40	.18	.05
☐ NNO	Shaquille O'Neal ... AU/500	400.00	180.00	50.00
☐ NNO	Shaquille O'Neal ..... (Chrome)	25.00	11.50	3.10

1994 Classic Draft Gold

Inserted one per '94 Classic pack, the 105 standard-size (2 1/2" by 3 1/2") cards of this parallel set feature borderless color player action shots on their fronts. The player's name and position are stamped within a gold-foil bar near the bottom. The back carries another borderless color player action shot, which is gradually ghosted toward the bottom. The player's name and position appear at the top; statistics and career highlights appear near the bottom. Dick Vitale's facsimile autograph at the lower right rounds out the card. The cards are numbered on the back. Gold stars are valued at two to four times the price of the regular issue corresponding card.

	MINT	NRMT	EXC
COMPLETE SET (105)	40.00	18.00	5.00
COMMON CARD (1-105)	.15	.07	.02
*STARS: 2X TO 4X BASIC CARDS....			

1994 Classic Printer's Proofs

Randomly inserted in hobby boxes, this 105-card set parallels the 1994 Classic series. The cards are distinguished by the "Printer's Proofs" logo on their fronts.

	MINT	NRMT	EXC
COMPLETE SET (105)	400.00	180.00	50.00
COMMON CARD (1-105)	2.00	.90	.25
*STARS: 20X TO 40X BASIC CARDS			

1994 Classic BCs

Inserted one per jumbo pack, these 25 standard-size (2 1/2" by 3 1/2") cards feature borderless color player action shots on their metallic fronts. The player's name and position appear within a black bar at the lower right. The back carries another borderless color action shot, with the player's biography appearing at the lower right within a ghosted triangle. The cards are numbered on the back with a "BC" prefix.

		MINT	NRMT	EXC
COMPLETE SET (25)		15.00	6.75	1.90
COMMON CARD (BC1-BC25)		.25	.11	.03
☐ BC1	Glenn Robinson.......... Purdue	4.00	1.80	.50
☐ BC2	Jason Kidd .... California	4.00	1.80	.50
☐ BC3	Grant Hill .... Duke	5.00	2.30	.60
☐ BC4	Donyell Marshall.......... Connecticut	1.50	.65	.19
☐ BC5	Juwan Howard .... Michigan	1.50	.65	.19
☐ BC6	Sharone Wright.......... Clemson	1.00	.45	.13
☐ BC7	Brian Grant................ Xavier	1.50	.65	.19
☐ BC8	Eric Montross.............	1.00	.45	.13

		MINT	NRMT	EXC
	North Carolina			
☐ BC9	Eddie Jones	2.00	.90	.25
	Temple			
☐ BC10	Carlos Rogers	.60	.25	.08
	Tennessee State			
☐ BC11	Khalid Reeves	1.00	.45	.13
	Arizona			
☐ BC12	Jalen Rose	1.00	.45	.13
	Michigan			
☐ BC13	Yinka Dare	.25	.11	.03
	George Washington			
☐ BC14	Eric Piatkowski	.25	.11	.03
	Nebraska			
☐ BC15	Clifford Rozier	.50	.23	.06
	Louisville			
☐ BC16	Aaron McKie	.25	.11	.03
	Temple			
☐ BC17	Eric Mobley	.25	.11	.03
	Pittsburgh			
☐ BC18	Tony Dumas	.25	.11	.03
	Missouri-KC			
☐ BC19	B.J. Tyler	.25	.11	.03
	Texas			
☐ BC20	Dickey Simpkins	.40	.18	.05
	Providence			
☐ BC21	Bill Curley	.25	.11	.03
	Boston College			
☐ BC22	Wesley Person	1.00	.45	.13
	Auburn			
☐ BC23	Monty Williams	.25	.11	.03
	Notre Dame			
☐ BC24	Greg Minor	.25	.11	.03
	Louisville			
☐ BC25	Charlie Ward	.40	.18	.05
	Florida State			
☐ NNO	Jason Kidd Chrome	20.00	9.00	2.50

1994 Classic Game Cards

Inserted one per jumbo pack, these cards were redeemable for a gold sheet. The cards feature the expression "game card" in red letters down the left side of the front while the rest of the card displays the player's photo and in the bottom right part are the players' name and who drafted them. The back features instructions on how to play and scratch off your cards for the gold sheet prize.

	MINT	NRMT	EXC
COMPLETE SET (5)	7.00	3.10	.85
COMMON CARD (GC1-GC5)	.75	.35	.09
*PRIZE BOX SCRATCHED: HALF VALUE			
☐ GC1 Glenn Robinson	2.50	1.15	.30
☐ GC2 Jason Kidd	2.50	1.15	.30
☐ GC3 Juwan Howard	1.25	.55	.16
☐ GC4 Donyell Marshall	1.25	.55	.16
☐ GC5 Sharone Wright	.75	.35	.09

1994 Classic Picks *

Randomly inserted in packs, this 25-card standard-size set features on its fronts color action player cutouts superimposed on a metallized background. The player's name appears on the bottom, while the words "Classic Pick" are printed at the top. On a ghosted background, the backs carry a small color player portrait, along with a short biography and a player profile. The football picks (1-5) were found in the football draft picks packs; the basketball picks (6-10) were in the basketball draft pick packs; the hockey picks (11-15) were in the hockey draft pick packs while the four-sport picks (16-25) were in four-sport packs.

	MINT	NRMT	EXC
COMPLETE SET (25)	175.00	77.50	21.25
COMMON CARD (1-25)	5.00	2.30	.60
☐ 1 Heath Shuler	12.00	5.50	1.50
☐ 2 Trent Dilfer	7.00	3.10	.85
☐ 3 Johnnie Morton	4.00	1.80	.50
☐ 4 David Palmer	4.00	1.80	.50
☐ 5 Marshall Faulk	25.00	11.50	3.10
☐ 6 Glenn Robinson	12.00	5.50	1.50
☐ 7 Jason Kidd	12.00	5.50	1.50
☐ 8 Grant Hill	18.00	8.00	2.30
☐ 9 Eric Montross	5.00	2.30	.60
☐ 10 Juwan Howard	6.00	2.70	.75
☐ 11 Ed Jovanovski	7.00	3.10	.85
☐ 12 Oleg Tverdovsky	5.00	2.30	.60
☐ 13 Radek Bonk	6.00	2.70	.75
☐ 14 Jason Allison	4.00	1.80	.50
☐ 15 Manon Rheaume	15.00	6.75	1.90
☐ 16 Paul Wilson	9.00	4.00	1.15
☐ 17 Ben Grieve	10.00	4.50	1.25
☐ 18 Trey Moore	4.00	1.80	.50
☐ 19 Nomar Garciaparra	5.00	2.30	.60

		MINT	NRMT	EXC
☐ 20	Doug Million	5.00	2.30	.60
☐ 21	Dan Wilkinson	4.00	1.80	.50
☐ 22	Willie McGinest	4.00	1.80	.50
☐ 23	Khalid Reeves	7.00	3.10	.85
☐ 24	Grant Hill	18.00	8.00	2.30
☐ 25	Ethan Moreau	5.00	2.30	.60

1994 Classic Phone Cards

1994 Classic Basketball Jumbo is the first Classic trading card product to include Sprint PrePaid Foncards. Randomly inserted at a rate of one in every seven 12-card jumbo packs, each Sprint card provides $2.00 worth of Sprint long distance service. The packs were sold at selected Walmart, Bookland, Sam's and other major retailers. The potential usage of these cards expired on June 30, 1995. The fronts feature a full-color player photo along with the Sprint logo in the upper left corner and the Scoreboard logo in the upper right corner. The bottom of the card features in red lettering the amount the card is worth along with the player's name. The horizontal back features information on how to use the card. The phone cards are unnumbered and checklisted below in alphabetical order.

		MINT	NRMT	EXC
	COMPLETE SET (6)	40.00	18.00	5.00
	COMMON CARD (1-6)	2.50	1.15	.30
	*PIN NUMBER REVEALED: HALF VAUEL			
☐ 1	Yinka Dare	2.50	1.15	.30
☐ 2	Jason Kidd	16.00	7.25	2.00
☐ 3	Donyell Marshall	7.00	3.10	.85
☐ 4	Eric Montross	6.00	2.70	.75
☐ 5	Glenn Robinson	16.00	7.25	2.00
☐ 6	Jalen Rose	6.00	2.70	.75

1994 Classic ROY Sweepstakes

Randomly inserted in foil and jumbo packs, these 20 standard-size (2 1/2" by 3 1/2")

cards feature color action player cutouts on a borderless basketball background. A silhouette of a player appears to the left. The player's name appears within a gold-foil stripe near the bottom. Also in gold foil is the number of cards produced, 6,225. The card of the player selected Rookie of the Year was redeemable for an uncut Vitale's PTPers set sheet. The cards are numbered on the back with an "ROY" prefix.

		MINT	NRMT	EXC
	COMPLETE SET (20)	150.00	70.00	19.00
	COMMON CARD (ROY1-ROY20)	2.00	.90	.25
☐ 1	Glenn Robinson Purdue	25.00	11.50	3.10
☐ 2	Jason Kidd California	30.00	13.50	3.80
☐ 3	Grant Hill Duke	40.00	18.00	5.00
☐ 4	Sharone Wright Clemson	8.00	3.60	1.00
☐ 5	Juwan Howard Michigan	12.00	5.50	1.50
☐ 6	Monty Williams Notre Dame	2.00	.90	.25
☐ 7	Khalid Reeves Arizona	8.00	3.60	1.00
☐ 8	Eddie Jones Temple	14.00	6.25	1.75
☐ 9	Clifford Rozier Louisville	5.00	2.30	.60
☐ 10	Aaron McKie Temple	2.00	.90	.25
☐ 11	Eric Montross North Carolina	8.00	3.60	1.00
☐ 12	Askia Jones Kansas State	2.00	.90	.25
☐ 13	Yinka Dare George Washington	2.00	.90	.25
☐ 14	Dontonio Wingfield Cincinnati	2.00	.90	.25
☐ 15	Carlos Rogers Tennessee State	6.00	2.70	.75
☐ 16	Eric Piatkowski Nebraska	2.00	.90	.25
☐ 17	Charlie Ward Florida State	4.00	1.80	.50
☐ 18	Deon Thomas Illinois	2.00	.90	.25
☐ 19	Dickey Simpkins Providence	4.00	1.80	.50
☐ 20	Field Card/Vitale	5.00	2.30	.60

1994 Classic Vitale's PTPers

Randomly inserted in packs, these 15 standard-size (2 1/2" by 3 1/2") cards feature on their borderless metallic fronts color player action cutouts set on multicolored backgrounds. The player's name appears within a colored stripe across the bottom. The back carries a color player action shot on the right and career highlights on a yellow panel on the left. A color cutout of Dick Vitale and his facsimile autograph at the bottom round out the card. The cards are numbered on the back with a "PTP" prefix.

	MINT	NRMT	EXC
COMPLETE SET (15)	60.00	27.00	7.50
COMMON CARD (PTP1-PTP15)	1.75	.80	.22
☐ 1 Glenn Robinson Purdue	12.00	5.50	1.50
☐ 2 Jason Kidd California	12.00	5.50	1.50
☐ 3 Grant Hill Duke	15.00	6.75	1.90
☐ 4 Sharone Wright Clemson	6.00	2.70	.75
☐ 5 Juwan Howard Michigan	8.00	3.60	1.00
☐ 6 Billy McCaffrey Vanderbilt	1.75	.80	.22
☐ 7 Khalid Reeves Arizona	5.00	2.30	.60
☐ 8 Eddie Jones Temple	9.00	4.00	1.15
☐ 9 Clifford Rozier Louisville	2.50	1.15	.30
☐ 10 Charlie Ward Florida State	2.50	1.15	.30
☐ 11 Eric Montross North Carolina	6.00	2.70	.75
☐ 12 Wesley Person Auburn	5.00	2.30	.60
☐ 13 Yinka Dare G. Washington	1.75	.80	.22
☐ 14 Dontonio Wingfield Cincinnati	1.75	.80	.22
☐ 15 Carlos Rogers Tennessee State	3.00	1.35	.40

1994 Classic Four-Sport Previews

Randomly inserted in 1994-95 Classic hockey foil packs at a rate of three per case, these five standard-size preview cards show the design of the 1994-95 Classic Four-Sport series. The full-bleed color action photos are gold-foil stamped with the "4-Sport Preview" emblem and the player's name. The backs feature another full-bleed closeup photo, with biography and statistics displayed on a ghosted panel.

	MINT	NRMT	EXC
COMPLETE SET (5)	70.00	32.00	8.75
COMMON CARD (P1-P5)	6.00	2.70	.75
☐ P1 Jeff O'Neill	6.00	2.70	.75
☐ P2 Marshall Faulk	25.00	11.50	3.10
☐ P3 Grant Hill	25.00	11.50	3.10
☐ P4 Jason Kidd	20.00	9.00	2.50
☐ P5 Ben Grieve	14.00	6.25	1.75

1994 Classic Four-Sport

Featuring top rookies from basketball, baseball, football and hockey, the 1994 Classic Four-Sport set consists of 200 standard-size cards. No more than 25,000 cases were produced. Over 100 players

signed 100,000 cards that were randomly inserted four per case. Collectors who found one of 100 Glenn Robinson Instant Winner Cards received a complete Classic Four-Sport autographed card set. Also inserted on an average of one in every five cases were 4,695 hand-numbered 4-in-1 cards featuring all four #1 picks. Classic's wrapper redemption program offered four levels of participation: 1) bronze-collect 20 wrappers and receive a 4-card Classic Player of the Year set, featuring Grant Hill, Shaquille O'Neal, Emmitt Smith, and Steve Young; 2) silver-collect 30 wrappers and receive the Classic Player of the Year set and a random autograph card; 3) gold-collect 144 wrappers and receive the Classic Player of the Year set and an autograph card by Muhammad Ali; and 4) platinum-collect 216 wrappers and receive the Classic Player of the Year set plus an autograph card by Shaquille O'Neal. The fronts feature full-bleed color action player photos. The player's name is gold-foil stamped across the bottom of the picture. The backs display a full-bleed color player close-up, with player information displayed on a ghosted panel. The cards are numbered on the back and checklisted below by sport as follows: basketball (1-50), football (51-114), hockey (115-160), baseball (161-188), and Wooden Award Contenders (189-197).

		MINT	NRMT	EXC
	COMPLETE SET (200)	12.00	5.50	1.50
	COMMON CARD (1-200)	.05	.02	.01
☐ 1	Glenn Robinson	1.25	.55	.16
☐ 2	Jason Kidd	1.25	.55	.16
☐ 3	Grant Hill	1.75	.80	.22
☐ 4	Donyell Marshall	.50	.23	.06
☐ 5	Juwan Howard	.50	.23	.06
☐ 6	Sharone Wright	.40	.18	.05
☐ 7	Billy McCaffrey	.05	.02	.01
☐ 8	Brian Grant	.50	.23	.06
☐ 9	Eric Montross	.40	.18	.05
☐ 10	Eddie Jones	.75	.35	.09
☐ 11	Carlos Rogers	.20	.09	.03
☐ 12	Khalid Reeves	.35	.16	.04
☐ 13	Jalen Rose	.35	.16	.04
☐ 14	Yinka Dare	.05	.02	.01
☐ 15	Eric Piatkowski	.10	.05	.01
☐ 16	Clifford Rozier	.15	.07	.02
☐ 17	Aaron McKie	.10	.05	.01
☐ 18	Eric Mobley	.05	.02	.01
☐ 19	Tony Dumas	.05	.02	.01
☐ 20	B.J. Tyler	.10	.05	.01
☐ 21	Dickey Simpkins	.12	.05	.02
☐ 22	Bill Curley	.05	.02	.01
☐ 23	Wesley Person	.35	.16	.04
☐ 24	Monty Williams	.05	.02	.01
☐ 25	Greg Minor	.15	.07	.02
☐ 26	Charlie Ward	.15	.07	.02
☐ 27	Brooks Thompson	.05	.02	.01
☐ 28	Deon Thomas	.05	.02	.01
☐ 29	Antonio Lang	.05	.02	.01
☐ 30	Howard Eisley	.05	.02	.01
☐ 31	Rodney Dent	.05	.02	.01
☐ 32	Jim McIlvaine	.05	.02	.01
☐ 33	Derrick Alston	.05	.02	.01
☐ 34	Gaylon Nickerson	.05	.02	.01
☐ 35	Michael Smith	.20	.09	.03
☐ 36	Andrei Fetisov	.05	.02	.01
☐ 37	Dontonio Wingfield	.05	.02	.01
☐ 38	Darrin Hancock	.05	.02	.01
☐ 39	Anthony Miller	.05	.02	.01
☐ 40	Jeff Webster	.05	.02	.01
☐ 41	Arturas Karnishovas	.05	.02	.01
☐ 42	Gary Collier	.05	.02	.01
☐ 43	Shawnelle Scott	.05	.02	.01
☐ 44	Damon Bailey	.15	.07	.02
☐ 45	Dwayne Morton	.05	.02	.01
☐ 46	Jamie Watson	.05	.02	.01
☐ 47	Jevon Crudup	.05	.02	.01
☐ 48	Melvin Booker	.05	.02	.01
☐ 49	Brian Reese	.05	.02	.01
☐ 50	Lawrence Funderburke	.05	.02	.01
☐ 51	Dan Wilkinson	.12	.05	.02
☐ 52	Marshall Faulk	1.75	.80	.22
☐ 53	Heath Shuler	.75	.35	.09
☐ 54	Willie McGinest	.12	.05	.02
☐ 55	Trev Alberts	.10	.05	.01
☐ 56	Trent Dilfer	.50	.23	.06
☐ 57	Bryant Young	.25	.11	.03
☐ 58	Sam Adams	.05	.02	.01
☐ 59	Antonio Langham	.20	.09	.03
☐ 60	Jamir Miller	.05	.02	.01
☐ 61	John Thierry	.05	.02	.01
☐ 62	Aaron Glenn	.10	.05	.01
☐ 63	Joe Johnson	.05	.02	.01
☐ 64	Bernard Williams	.05	.02	.01
☐ 65	Wayne Gandy	.05	.02	.01
☐ 66	Aaron Taylor	.05	.02	.01
☐ 67	Charles Johnson	.25	.11	.03
☐ 68	Dewayne Washington	.05	.02	.01
☐ 69	Todd Steussie	.05	.02	.01
☐ 70	Tim Bowens	.20	.09	.03
☐ 71	Johnnie Morton	.15	.07	.02
☐ 72	Rob Fredrickson	.15	.07	.02
☐ 73	Shante Carver	.10	.05	.01
☐ 74	Thomas Lewis	.05	.02	.01
☐ 75	Calvin Jones	.05	.02	.01
☐ 76	Henry Ford	.05	.02	.01
☐ 77	Jeff Burris	.15	.07	.02
☐ 78	William Floyd	.40	.18	.05
☐ 79	Derrick Alexander	.25	.11	.03
☐ 80	Darnay Scott	.30	.14	.04
☐ 81	Tre Johnson	.05	.02	.01
☐ 82	Eric Mahlum	.05	.02	.01
☐ 83	Errict Rhett	1.00	.45	.13
☐ 84	Kevin Lee	.05	.02	.01
☐ 85	Andre Coleman	.15	.07	.02
☐ 86	Corey Sawyer	.05	.02	.01
☐ 87	Chuck Levy	.05	.02	.01
☐ 88	Greg Hill	.30	.14	.04
☐ 89	David Palmer	.15	.07	.02
☐ 90	Ryan Yarborough	.05	.02	.01
☐ 91	Charlie Garner	.25	.11	.03
☐ 92	Mario Bates	.25	.11	.03
☐ 93	Bert Emanuel	.20	.09	.03
☐ 94	Thomas Randolph	.05	.02	.01
☐ 95	Bucky Brooks	.05	.02	.01
☐ 96	Rob Waldrop	.05	.02	.01
☐ 97	Charlie Ward	.10	.05	.01
☐ 98	Winfred Tubbs	.05	.02	.01
☐ 99	James Folston	.05	.02	.01
☐ 100	Kevin Mitchell	.05	.02	.01
☐ 101	Aubrey Beavers	.10	.05	.01
☐ 102	Fernando Smith	.05	.02	.01
☐ 103	Jim Miller	.10	.05	.01
☐ 104	Byron Morris	.60	.25	.08
☐ 105	Donnell Bennett	.05	.02	.01

☐ 106	Jason Sehorn	.05	.02	.01
☐ 107	Glenn Foley	.05	.02	.01
☐ 108	Lonnie Johnson	.05	.02	.01
☐ 109	Tyrone Drakeford	.05	.02	.01
☐ 110	Vaughn Parker	.05	.02	.01
☐ 111	Doug Nussmeier	.05	.02	.01
☐ 112	Perry Klein	.05	.02	.01
☐ 113	Jason Gildon	.05	.02	.01
☐ 114	Lake Dawson	.30	.14	.04
☐ 115A	Ed Jovanovski	.40	.18	.05
☐ 115B	Ed Jovanovski COR	.50	.23	.06
☐ 116	Oleg Tverdovsky	.25	.11	.03
☐ 117	Radek Bonk	.20	.09	.03
☐ 118	Jason Bonsignore	.12	.05	.02
☐ 119	Jeff O'Neill	.25	.11	.03
☐ 120	Ryan Smyth	.15	.07	.02
☐ 121	Jamie Storr	.35	.16	.04
☐ 122	Jason Wiemer	.15	.07	.02
☐ 123	Evgeni Ryabchikov	.05	.02	.01
☐ 124	Nolan Baumgartner	.12	.05	.02
☐ 125	Jeff Friesen	.60	.25	.08
☐ 126	Wade Belak	.05	.02	.01
☐ 127	Maxim Bets	.05	.02	.01
☐ 128	Ethan Moreau	.12	.05	.02
☐ 129	Alexander Kharlamov	.12	.05	.02
☐ 130	Eric Fichaud	.30	.14	.04
☐ 131	Wayne Primeau	.15	.07	.02
☐ 132	Brad Brown	.05	.02	.01
☐ 133	Chris Dingman	.05	.02	.01
☐ 134	Craig Darby	.05	.02	.01
☐ 135	Darby Hendrickson	.05	.02	.01
☐ 136	Yan Golubovsky	.05	.02	.01
☐ 137	Chris Wells	.05	.02	.01
☐ 138	Vadim Sharifijanov	.05	.02	.01
☐ 139	Dan Cloutier	.15	.07	.02
☐ 140	Todd Marchant	.05	.02	.01
☐ 141	David Roberts	.05	.02	.01
☐ 142	Brian Rolston	.05	.02	.01
☐ 143	Garth Snow	.05	.02	.01
☐ 144	Cory Stillman	.05	.02	.01
☐ 145	Chad Penney	.05	.02	.01
☐ 146	Jeff Nelson	.05	.02	.01
☐ 147	Michael Stewart	.05	.02	.01
☐ 148	Mike Dunham	.05	.02	.01
☐ 149	Joe Frederick	.05	.02	.01
☐ 150	Mark DeSantis	.05	.02	.01
☐ 151	David Cooper	.05	.02	.01
☐ 152	Andrei Buschan	.05	.02	.01
☐ 153	Mike Greenlay	.05	.02	.01
☐ 154	Geoff Sarjeant	.05	.02	.01
☐ 155	Pauli Jaks	.05	.02	.01
☐ 156	Greg Andrusak	.05	.02	.01
☐ 157	Denis Metlyuk	.05	.02	.01
☐ 158	Mike Fountain	.05	.02	.01
☐ 159	Brent Gretzky	.12	.05	.02
☐ 160	Jason Allison	.15	.07	.02
☐ 161	Paul Wilson	.60	.25	.08
☐ 162	Ben Grieve	1.00	.45	.13
☐ 163	Doug Million	.25	.11	.03
☐ 164	C.J. Nitkowski	.20	.09	.03
☐ 165	Tommy Davis	.40	.18	.05
☐ 166	Dustin Hermanson	.20	.09	.03
☐ 167	Travis Miller	.15	.07	.02
☐ 168	McKay Christiansen	.12	.05	.02
☐ 169	Victor Rodriguez	.15	.07	.02
☐ 170	Jacob Cruz	.40	.18	.05
☐ 171	Rick Heiserman	.10	.05	.01
☐ 172	Mark Farris	.15	.07	.02
☐ 173	Nomar Garciaparra	.20	.09	.03
☐ 174	Paul Konerko	.30	.14	.04
☐ 175	Trey Moore	.05	.02	.01

☐ 176	Brian Stephenson	.05	.02	.01
☐ 177	Matt Smith	.15	.07	.02
☐ 178	Kevin Brown	.25	.11	.03
☐ 179	Cade Gaspar	.12	.05	.02
☐ 180	Bret Wagner	.20	.09	.03
☐ 181	Mike Thurman	.12	.05	.02
☐ 182	Doug Webb	.05	.02	.01
☐ 183	Ryan Nye	.20	.09	.03
☐ 184	Brian Buchanan	.15	.07	.02
☐ 185	Scott Elarton	.30	.14	.04
☐ 186	Mark Johnson	.15	.07	.02
☐ 187	Jacob Shumate	.15	.07	.02
☐ 188	Kevin Witt	.20	.09	.03
☐ 189	Glenn Robinson JWA	.50	.23	.06
☐ 190	Jason Kidd JWA	.50	.23	.06
☐ 191	Grant Hill JWA	.75	.35	.09
☐ 192	Donyell Marshall JWA	.25	.11	.03
☐ 193	Eric Montross JWA	.20	.09	.03
☐ 194	Khalid Reeves JWA	.05	.02	.01
☐ 195	Jalen Rose JWA	.20	.09	.03
☐ 196	Clifford Rozier JWA	.05	.02	.01
☐ 197	Damon Bailey JWA	.05	.02	.01
☐ 198	Checklist 1	.05	.02	.01
☐ 199	Checklist 2	.05	.02	.01
☐ 200	Checklist 3	.05	.02	.01
☐ FO1	4-in-1	40.00	18.00	5.00

Glenn Robinson
Dan Wilkinson
Paul Wilson
Ed Jovanovski
Number One Draft Picks

1994 Classic Four-Sport Gold

Featuring top rookies from basketball, baseball, football and hockey, the 1994 Classic Four-Sport gold set consists of 200 standard-size cards. The fronts feature full-bleed color action player photos. The player's name and the Classic Four-Sport logo is on the right side of the picture along with the information that this is a gold card. The backs display a full-bleed color player close-up, with player information displayed on a ghosted panel. The cards are numbered on the back and checklisted below by sport as follows: basketball (1-50), football (51-114), hockey (115-160), baseball (161-188), and Wooden Award Contenders (189-197). Grant Hill's card (#191) is an uncorrected error with Mark Johnson's name.

	MINT	NRMT	EXC
COMPLETE SET (200)	50.00	23.00	6.25
COMMON CARD (1-200)	.15	.07	.02
*STARS: 2X TO 4X BASIC CARDS....			

1994 Classic Four-Sport Printer's Proofs

Featuring top rookies from basketball, baseball, football and hockey, the 1994 Classic Four-Sport printer's proof set consists of 200 standard-size cards. The fronts feature full-bleed color action player photos. The information that this is a printer's proof card is directly above the player's name. Both the printer's proof logo and the name of the player are in red. The backs carry a full-bleed color player close-up, with player information displayed on a ghosted panel. The cards are numbered on the back and checklisted below by sport as follows: basketball (1-50), football (51-114), hockey (115-160), baseball (161-188), and Wooden Award Contenders (189-197).

	MINT	NRMT	EXC
COMPLETE SET (200)	600.00	275.00	75.00
COMMON CARD (1-200)	2.00	.90	.25
*STARS: 30X TO 50X BASIC CARDS			

1994 Classic Four-Sport Autographs

This 82-card standard-size set features players from the 1994 Classic Four-Sport set who autographed cards within the set. The fronts feature full-bleed color action player photos. The player's name is gold-foil stamped across the bottom of the picture. The backs have a congratulatory message about receiving an autographed card. Though the cards are unnumbered, we have assigned them the same number as their four-sport regular issue counterpart.

	MINT	NRMT	EXC
COMPLETE SET (82)	1200.00	550.00	150.00
COMMON AUTOGRAPH	10.00	4.50	1.25
☐ 1A Glenn Robinson AU/1000	110.00	50.00	14.00
☐ 2A Jason Kidd AU/1300	90.00	40.00	11.50
☐ 5A Juwan Howard AU/940	40.00	18.00	5.00
☐ 9A Eric Montross AU/1000	30.00	13.50	3.80
☐ 11A Carlos Rogers AU/660	20.00	9.00	2.50
☐ 13A Jalen Rose AU/970	30.00	13.50	3.80
☐ 15A Eric Piatkowski AU/1090	15.00	6.75	1.90
☐ 16A Clifford Rozier AU/900	15.00	6.75	1.90
☐ 22A Bill Curley AU/1120	15.00	6.75	1.90
☐ 23A Wesley Person AU/1000	30.00	13.50	3.80
☐ 24A Monty Williams AU/1100	15.00	6.75	1.90
☐ 28A Deon Thomas AU/1090	10.00	4.50	1.25
☐ 30A Howard Eisley AU/970	10.00	4.50	1.25
☐ 32A Jim McIlvaine AU/965	10.00	4.50	1.25
☐ 33A Derrick Alston AU/1050	10.00	4.50	1.25
☐ 36A Andrei Fetisov AU/1080	10.00	4.50	1.25
☐ 39A Anthony Miller AU/1000	10.00	4.50	1.25
☐ 40A Jeff Webster AU/1070	10.00	4.50	1.25
☐ 41A Arturas Karnishovas AU/980	10.00	4.50	1.25
☐ 42A Gary Collier AU/1000	10.00	4.50	1.25
☐ 44A Damon Bailey AU/1050	20.00	9.00	2.50
☐ 45A Dwayne Morton AU/1000	10.00	4.50	1.25
☐ 46A Jamie Watson AU/1080	15.00	6.75	1.90
☐ 47A Jevon Crudup AU/1180	10.00	4.50	1.25
☐ 49A Brian Reese AU/960	10.00	4.50	1.25
☐ 53A Heath Shuler AU/1330	60.00	27.00	7.50
☐ 55A Trev Alberts AU/2520	10.00	4.50	1.25
☐ 56A Trent Dilfer AU/1495	30.00	13.50	3.80
☐ 81A Tre Johnson AU/1000	10.00	4.50	1.25
☐ 82A Eric Mahlum AU/1090	10.00	4.50	1.25
☐ 90A Ryan Yarborough AU/1020	10.00	4.50	1.25
☐ 93A Bert Emanuel/1100	20.00	9.00	2.50
☐ 96A Rob Waldrop	10.00	4.50	1.25

	AU/1095			
☐ 97A	Charlie Ward	20.00	9.00	2.50
	AU/1520			
☐ 99A	James Folston	10.00	4.50	1.25
	AU/1100			
☐ 100A	Kevin Mitchell	10.00	4.50	1.25
	AU/1090			
☐ 103A	Jim Miller	10.00	4.50	1.25
	AU/1030			
☐ 108A	Lonnie Johnson	10.00	4.50	1.25
	AU/1050			
☐ 110A	Vaughn Parker	10.00	4.50	1.25
	AU/750			
☐ 115A	Ed Jovanovski	40.00	18.00	5.00
	AU/1180			
☐ 119A	Jeff O'Neill	25.00	11.50	3.10
	AU/3000			
☐ 124A	Nolan Baumgartner	15.00	6.75	1.90
	AU/2900			
☐ 134A	Craig Darby	10.00	4.50	1.25
	AU/2990			
☐ 139A	Dan Cloutier	10.00	4.50	1.25
	AU/2980			
☐ 140A	Todd Marchant	10.00	4.50	1.25
	AU/3100			
☐ 143A	Garth Snow	10.00	4.50	1.25
	AU/3050			
☐ 144A	Cory Stillman	10.00	4.50	1.25
	AU/3000			
☐ 148A	Mike Dunham	10.00	4.50	1.25
	AU/2960			
☐ 149A	Joe Frederick	10.00	4.50	1.25
	AU/3000			
☐ 150A	Mark DeSantis	10.00	4.50	1.25
	AU/3000			
☐ 154A	Geoff Sarjeant	10.00	4.50	1.25
	AU/3000			
☐ 156A	Greg Andrusak	10.00	4.50	1.25
	AU/2970			
☐ 157A	Denis Metlyuk	10.00	4.50	1.25
	AU/2960			
☐ 158A	Mike Fountain	10.00	4.50	1.25
	AU/3000			
☐ 161A	Paul Wilson	30.00	13.50	3.80
	AU/2400			
☐ 162A	Ben Grieve	35.00	16.00	4.40
	AU/2500			
☐ 163A	Doug Million	20.00	9.00	2.50
	AU/1020			
☐ 164A	C.J. Nitkowski	20.00	9.00	2.50
	AU/970			
☐ 165A	Tommy Davis	15.00	6.75	1.90
	AU/960			
☐ 166A	Dustin Hermanson	20.00	9.00	2.50
	AU/1020			
☐ 167A	Travis Miller	20.00	9.00	2.50
	AU/760			
☐ 169A	Victor Rodriguez	15.00	6.75	1.90
	AU/1000			
☐ 170A	Jacob Cruz	15.00	6.75	1.90
	AU/990			
☐ 171A	Rick Heiserman	10.00	4.50	1.25
	AU/600			
☐ 172A	Mark Farris	15.00	6.75	1.90
	AU/1020			
☐ 173A	Nomar Garciaparra	20.00	9.00	2.50
	AU/1020			
☐ 174A	Paul Konerko	30.00	13.50	3.80
	AU/970			
☐ 176A	Brian Stephenson	10.00	4.50	1.25
	AU/1100			

☐ 177A	Matt Smith	15.00	6.75	1.90
	AU/1090			
☐ 178A	Kevin Brown	15.00	6.75	1.90
	AU/1090			
☐ 179A	Cade Gaspar	15.00	6.75	1.90
	AU/1090			
☐ 180A	Bret Wagner	20.00	9.00	2.50
	AU/970			
☐ 181A	Mike Thurman	15.00	6.75	1.90
	AU/990			
☐ 182A	Doug Webb	10.00	4.50	1.25
	AU/1000			
☐ 183A	Ryan Nye	15.00	6.75	1.90
	AU/1015			
☐ 184A	Brian Buchanan	15.00	6.75	1.90
	AU/950			
☐ 186A	Mark Johnson	20.00	9.00	2.50
	AU/1000			
☐ 187A	Jacob Shumate	15.00	6.75	1.90
	AU/980			
☐ 188A	Kevin Witt	15.00	6.75	1.90
	AU/970			

1994 Classic Four-Sport BCs

This 20-card bonus set was randomly inserted one per '94 Classic Four-Sport jumbo packs. The fronts feature full color player photos. The backs carry biographical and statistical information about the player.

		MINT	NRMT	EXC
COMPLETE SET (20)		20.00	9.00	2.50
COMMON CARD (BC1-BC20)		.25	.11	.03
☐ BC1	Marshall Faulk	3.50	1.55	.45
☐ BC2	Heath Shuler	1.50	.65	.19
☐ BC3	Antonio Langham	.40	.18	.05
☐ BC4	Derrick Alexander	.50	.23	.06
☐ BC5	Byron Bam Morris	1.25	.55	.16
☐ BC6	Glenn Robinson	2.50	1.15	.30
☐ BC7	Jason Kidd	2.50	1.15	.30
☐ BC8	Grant Hill	3.50	1.55	.45
☐ BC9	Jalen Rose	.75	.35	.09
☐ BC10	Donyell Marshall	1.00	.45	.13
☐ BC11	Juwan Howard	1.00	.45	.13
☐ BC12	Khalid Reeves	.75	.35	.09
☐ BC13	Paul Wilson	1.25	.55	.16
☐ BC14	Ben Grieve	1.50	.65	.19
☐ BC15	Doug Million	.50	.23	.06
☐ BC16	Nomar Garciaparra	.40	.18	.05
☐ BC17	Ed Jovanovski	1.00	.45	.13
☐ BC18	Radek Bonk	.50	.23	.06
☐ BC19	Jeff O'Neill	.60	.25	.08
☐ BC20	Ethan Moreau	.35	.16	.04

1994 Classic Four-Sport High Voltage

This 20-card sequentially-numbered set measures the standard-size and features

the top draft picks. The cards are printed on holographic foil board with a striking design. 2,995 of each even-numbered card and 5,495 of each odd-numbered cards were produced. The cards were inserted on an average of 3 per case. The fronts feature the players against a background of lightning while the backs feature a biography on the left side of the card. The right side shows more lightning and the player's photo.

	MINT	NRMT	EXC
COMPLETE SET (20)	300.00	135.00	38.00
COMMON CARD (HV1-HV20)	8.00	3.60	1.00

		MINT	NRMT	EXC
☐	HV1 Dan Wilkinson	8.00	3.60	1.00
☐	HV2 Glenn Robinson	50.00	23.00	6.25
☐	HV3 Paul Wilson	25.00	11.50	3.10
☐	HV4 Ed Jovanovski	25.00	11.50	3.10
☐	HV5 Marshall Faulk	40.00	18.00	5.00
☐	HV6 Jason Kidd	50.00	23.00	6.25
☐	HV7 Ben Grieve	30.00	13.50	3.80
☐	HV8 Oleg Tverdovsky	20.00	9.00	2.50
☐	HV9 Heath Shuler	20.00	9.00	2.50
☐	HV10 Grant Hill	60.00	27.00	7.50
☐	HV11 Dustin Hermanson	10.00	4.50	1.25
☐	HV12 Radek Bonk	18.00	8.00	2.30
☐	HV13 Trent Dilfer	12.00	5.50	1.50
☐	HV14 Donyell Marshall	20.00	9.00	2.50
☐	HV15 Doug Million	10.00	4.50	1.25
☐	HV16 Jason Bonsignore	15.00	6.75	1.90
☐	HV17 Willie McGinest	8.00	3.60	1.00
☐	HV18 Juwan Howard	20.00	9.00	2.50
☐	HV19 Jeff O'Neill	8.00	3.60	1.00
☐	HV20 Nomar Garciaparra	18.00	8.00	2.30

1994 Classic Four-Sport Phone Cards

This set of 8 phone cards was randomly inserted in four-sport packs. Printed on hard plastic, each card measures 2 1/8" by 3 3/8" and has rounded corners. The fronts display full-bleed color action photos, with the value (1.00, 2.00, 3.00, 4.00 or 5.00) and the player's name printed vertically in red along the right edge. The horizontal backs carry instructions for use of the cards. The cards are unnumbered and checklisted below in alphabetical order. The 3.00 and 5.00 cards were inserted into

retail packs. The values listed below are for 1.00 cards; the 2.00 cards are worth 1X-2X more, the 3.00 cards are worth 2X-4X more, the 4.00 cards are worth 3X-6X more and the 5.00 cards 4X-8x more.

	MINT	NRMT	EXC
COMPLETE SET (8)	55.00	25.00	7.00
COMMON CARD (1-8)	2.50	1.15	.30
*PIN NUMBER REVEALED: HALF VALUE			

		MINT	NRMT	EXC
☐	1 Trent Dilfer	2.50	1.15	.30
☐	2 Marshall Faulk	16.00	7.25	2.00
☐	3 Ben Grieve	8.00	3.60	1.00
☐	4 Ed Jovanovski	5.00	2.30	.60
☐	5 Jason Kidd	12.00	5.50	1.50
☐	6 Jeff O'Neill	2.50	1.15	.30
☐	7 Glenn Robinson	12.00	5.50	1.50
☐	8 Paul Wilson	2.50	1.15	.30

1994 Classic Four-Sport Shaq-Fu Tip Cards

Inserted one in every 18 packs, this 25-card standard-size set features hints and secret clues to play Shaq-Fu, an exciting new video game for Super Nintendo and Sega systems. The fronts feature the title on the left side along with a computerized photo showing on the right 3/4 of the card. The backs are divided between a computer photo on the left side and a description of what the photo means on the right side of the card. The cards are numbered on the back and checklisted below as follows: Character Profiles (SF1-SF12), Special Moves (SF13-SF24), and Secret Tip (SF25). The cards are also licensed throught Electronic Arts and Dolphine Software International.

	MINT	NRMT	EXC
COMPLETE SET (25)	20.00	9.00	2.50
COMMON CARD (SF1-SF25)	1.00	.45	.13
☐ SF1 Shaq	1.00	.45	.13
☐ SF2 Kaori	1.00	.45	.13
☐ SF3 Voodoo	1.00	.45	.13
☐ SF4 Rajah	1.00	.45	.13
☐ SF5 Mephis	1.00	.45	.13
☐ SF6 Beast	1.00	.45	.13
☐ SF7 Sett Ra	1.00	.45	.13
☐ SF8 Nezu	1.00	.45	.13
☐ SF9 Leotsu	1.00	.45	.13
☐ SF10 Colonel X	1.00	.45	.13
☐ SF11 Aurok	1.00	.45	.13
☐ SF12 Diesel	1.00	.45	.13
☐ SF13 Shaq-uriken	1.00	.45	.13
☐ SF14 Teleport Kirk	1.00	.45	.13
☐ SF15 Voodoo Doll Stab	1.00	.45	.13
☐ SF16 Sword Toss	1.00	.45	.13
☐ SF17 Summon Lightning	1.00	.45	.13
☐ SF18 Auto Three Hit Combo	1.00	.45	.13
☐ SF19 Earth Rap Attack	1.00	.45	.13
☐ SF20 Eno Bomb	1.00	.45	.13
☐ SF21 Thunder Kai	1.00	.45	.13
☐ SF22 Micro Missile	1.00	.45	.13
☐ SF23 Eruption Fist	1.00	.45	.13
☐ SF24 Knuckle Dash	1.00	.45	.13
☐ SF25 Secret Guy in the Jungle	1.00	.45	.13

1994 Classic Four-Sport Tri-Cards

Inserted one in every three cases, this 5-card standard-size set features three top running backs, linebackers, hockey centers, pitchers and basketball guards and compares their individual skills. Every card is sequentially-numbered out of 2,695. The horizontal fronts feature the three players equally while the backs gives a brief biography of why the three players are grouped together.

	MINT	NRMT	EXC
COMPLETE SET (5)	55.00	25.00	7.00
COMMON CARD (TC1-TC5)	6.00	2.70	.75
☐ TC1 Marshall Faulk Calvin Jones Errict Rhett	22.00	10.00	2.80
☐ TC2 Willie McGinest Trev Alberts Jamir Miller	6.00	2.70	.75
☐ TC3 Jalen Rose Jason Kidd Khalid Reeves	15.00	6.75	1.90
☐ TC4 Radek Bonk Chris Wells Jeff O'Neill	10.00	4.50	1.25
☐ TC5 Paul Wilson Doug Million Cade Gaspar	10.00	4.50	1.25

1994 Classic Images *

These 150 standard-size (2 1/2" by 3 1/2") cards feature on their borderless fronts color player action shots with backgrounds that have been thrown out of focus. The player's name and position appear in gold-foil lettering within a black strip near the bottom. The gold-foil Classic Images logo appears in an upper corner. The back carries a narrow-cropped color player action shot on the right. On the white background to the left, career highlights, biography and statistics are displayed. Just 6,500 of each card were produced. The cards are numbered on the back. The set closes with Classic Headlines (128-147) and checklists (148-150). A redemption card inserted one per case entitled the collector to one set of basketball draft preview cards.

	MINT	NRMT	EXC
COMPLETE SET (150)	15.00	6.75	1.90
COMMON CARD (1-150)	.05	.02	.01
☐ 1 Drew Bledsoe	1.75	.80	.22
☐ 2 Chris Webber	1.00	.45	.13

3	Alex Rodriguez	1.50	.65	.19
4	Alexandre Daigle	.50	.23	.06
5	Rick Mirer	.75	.35	.09
6	Anfernee Hardaway	2.00	.90	.25
7	Jeff D'Amico P	.20	.09	.03
8	Chris Pronger	.25	.11	.03
9	Robert Smith	.30	.14	.04
10	Sherron Mills	.05	.02	.01
11	Alan Benes	.50	.23	.06
12	Warren Kidd	.05	.02	.01
13	Bryon Russell	.10	.05	.01
14	Mike Peplowski	.05	.02	.01
15	Jeff Granger	.05	.02	.01
16	Jim Montgomery	.05	.02	.01
17	Todd Marchant	.05	.02	.01
18	Doug Edwards	.05	.02	.01
19	Daron Kirkreit	.05	.02	.01
20	Mike Dunham	.05	.02	.01
21	Garth Snow	.20	.09	.03
22	Darnell Mee	.05	.02	.01
23	Billy Wagner	.50	.23	.06
24	Barry Richter	.05	.02	.01
25	Lincoln Kennedy	.05	.02	.01
26	Jerome Bettis	.50	.23	.06
27	Corie Blount	.05	.02	.01
28	Matt Martin	.05	.02	.01
29	Deon Figures	.20	.09	.03
30	Rob Niedermayer	.25	.11	.03
31	Brian Anderson	.20	.09	.03
32	Jesse Belanger	.05	.02	.01
33	George Teague	.05	.02	.01
34	Chris Schwab	.25	.11	.03
35	Peter Ferraro	.25	.11	.03
36	Shaquille O'Neal Rap	1.00	.45	.13
37	Matt Brunson	.05	.02	.01
38	Ted Drury	.05	.02	.01
39	Glyn Milburn	.30	.14	.04
40	George Lynch	.10	.05	.01
41	Gheorghe Muresan	.20	.09	.03
42	Kirk Presley	.25	.11	.03
43	Derek Plante	.20	.09	.03
44	Gino Torretta	.10	.05	.01
45	Roger Harper	.05	.02	.01
46	Jim Campbell	.05	.02	.01
47	Chris Carpenter	.20	.09	.03
48	Victor Bailey	.20	.09	.03
49	Kelly Wunsch	.15	.07	.02
50	Isaiah Rider	.60	.25	.08
51	Jon Ratliff	.05	.02	.01
52	Wayne Gomes	.10	.05	.01
53	Thomas Smith	.05	.02	.01
54	Trot Nixon	.40	.18	.05
55	Andre King	.05	.02	.01
56	Chris Osgood	.25	.11	.03
57	Reggie Brooks	.10	.05	.01
58	Ron Moore	.20	.09	.03
59	Vin Baker	.50	.25	.08
60	Rodney Rogers	.50	.23	.06
61	Dan Footman	.05	.02	.01
62	Jason Arnott	.75	.35	.09
63	Darren Dreifort	.05	.02	.01
64	Tom Carter	.10	.05	.01
65	Qadry Ismail	.30	.14	.04
66	Josh Grant	.05	.02	.01
67	Luther Wright	.05	.02	.01
68	Allan Houston	.60	.25	.08
69	Brooks Kieschnick	.75	.35	.09
70	Marvin Jones	.05	.02	.01
71	Garrison Hearst	.50	.23	.06
72	John Copeland	.05	.02	.01
73	Darrien Gordon	.05	.02	.01
74	Jocelyn Thibault	.25	.11	.03
75	Lindsey Hunter	.20	.09	.03
76	Scott Burrell	.20	.09	.03
77	Torii Hunter	.20	.09	.03
78	Chad Brown	.10	.05	.01
79	Sam Cassell	.60	.25	.08
80	Steve Soderstrom	.15	.07	.02
81	Jimmy Jackson	.40	.18	.05
82	Irv Smith	.10	.05	.01
83	Troy Drayton	.20	.09	.03
84	Chris Mills	.30	.14	.04
85	Derek Lee	.60	.25	.08
86	Chris Gratton	.25	.11	.03
87	Carlton Gray	.05	.02	.01
88	Billy Joe Hobert	.05	.02	.01
89	Acie Earl	.10	.05	.01
90	Terry Dehere	.20	.09	.03
91	Carl Simpson	.05	.02	.01
92	Mike Rathje	.05	.02	.01
93	Jay Powell	.05	.02	.01
94	James Robinson	.10	.05	.01
95	Roosevelt Potts	.25	.11	.03
96	Jamal Mashburn	1.00	.45	.13
97	Derek Brown RB	.15	.07	.02
98	Ed Stokes	.05	.02	.01
99	Ervin Johnson	.05	.02	.01
100	Nick Van Exel	.75	.35	.09
101	Martin Brodeur	.50	.23	.06
102	Curtis Conway	.50	.23	.06
103	Lamar Thomas	.05	.02	.01
104	Willie Roaf	.25	.11	.03
105	Matt Drews	.40	.18	.05
106	Paul Kariya	1.00	.45	.13
107	Eric Curry	.05	.02	.01
108	Todd Kelly	.05	.02	.01
109	Rex Walters	.05	.02	.01
110	Chris Whitney	.05	.02	.01
111	Manon Rheaume	2.00	.90	.25
112	Alonzo Mourning	.50	.23	.06
113	Lucious Harris	.10	.05	.01
114	Horace Copeland	.05	.02	.01
115	Scott Christman	.05	.02	.01
116	Terry Kirby	.30	.14	.04
117	Demetrius DuBose	.05	.02	.01
118	Will Shields	.05	.02	.01
119	Natrone Means	1.25	.55	.16
120	O.J. McDuffie	.60	.25	.08
121	Felix Potvin	.60	.25	.08
122	Dino Radja	.40	.18	.05
123	Harold Miner	.10	.05	.01
124	Greg Graham	.05	.02	.01
125	Alexei Yashin	.50	.23	.06
126	Kevin Williams WR	.60	.25	.08
127	Lorenzo Neal	.15	.07	.02
128	Shaquille O'Neal BW	.30	.14	.04
129	Drew Bledsoe BW	.75	.35	.09
130	Alexei Yashin BW	.20	.09	.03
131	Kirk Presley BW	.20	.09	.03
132	Chris Webber BW	.30	.14	.04
133	Rick Mirer BW	.35	.16	.04
134	Anfernee Hardaway BW	.60	.25	.08
135	Chris Pronger BW	.05	.02	.01
136	Alonzo Mourning BW	.20	.09	.03
137	Jerome Bettis BW	.25	.11	.03
138	Chris Gratton BW	.05	.02	.01
139	Trot Nixon BW	.20	.09	.03
140	Terry Kirby BW	.10	.05	.01
141	Jamal Mashburn BW	.40	.18	.05
142	Jason Arnott BW	.30	.14	.04
143	Alex Rodriguez BW	.60	.25	.08
144	Derek Brown RB BW	.05	.02	.01

		MINT	NRMT	EXC
☐	145 Isaiah Rider BW	.25	.11	.03
☐	146 Harold Miner BW	.05	.02	.01
☐	147 Manon Rheaume BW	2.50	1.15	.30
☐	148 Checklist 1	.05	.02	.01
☐	149 Checklist 2	.05	.02	.01
☐	150 Checklist 3	.05	.02	.01
☐	NNO BK Preview Redemption Card Expired	3.00	1.35	.40

1994 Classic Images Acetates *

Randomly inserted in 1994 Classic Images packs (four per case; 6,500 of each), these four standard-size (2 1/2" by 3 1/2") clear acetate cards feature color player action cutouts on their fronts. The player's name appears in vertical lettering within a black bar at the upper right. The back carries a ghosted action cutout, which also utilizes the reverse image of the front's cutout. The player's name appears in vertical lettering within a black bar at the upper left. Career highlights appear over the ghosted panel at the bottom. The cards are numbered on the back.

		MINT	NRMT	EXC
	COMPLETE SET (4)	35.00	16.00	4.40
	COMMON CARD (1-4)	7.00	3.10	.85
☐	1 Chris Webber	12.00	5.50	1.50
☐	2 Jerome Bettis	7.00	3.10	.85
☐	3 Steve Young	10.00	4.50	1.25
☐	4 Hakeem Olajuwon	10.00	4.50	1.25

1994 Classic Images Chrome *

Randomly inserted in 1994 Classic Images packs, these 20 limited print (9,750 of each) cards measure the standard size (2 1/2" by 3 1/2") and feature color player action shots on their borderless metallic fronts. The player's name appears in gold-colored let-

tering at the top. The set logo rests at the bottom of the card, and is also displayed behind the player. The back carries the player's name in the white margin at the top, followed below by an action close-up and career highlights on a white background. The cards are numbered on the back with a "CC" prefix.

		MINT	NRMT	EXC
	COMPLETE SET (20)	110.00	50.00	14.00
	COMP. UNCUT SHEET	125.00	57.50	15.50
	COMMON CARD (CC1-CC20)	3.00	1.35	.40
☐	CC1 Chris Webber	6.00	2.70	.75
☐	CC2 Anfernee Hardaway	12.00	5.50	1.50
☐	CC3 Jimmy Jackson	6.00	2.70	.75
☐	CC4 Nick Van Exel	6.00	2.70	.75
☐	CC5 Jamal Mashburn	10.00	4.50	1.25
☐	CC6 Isaiah Rider	5.00	2.30	.60
☐	CC7 Drew Bledsoe	18.00	8.00	2.30
☐	CC8 Jerome Bettis	6.00	2.70	.75
☐	CC9 Terry Kirby	4.00	1.80	.50
☐	CC10 Dana Stubblefield	3.00	1.35	.40
☐	CC11 Rick Mirer	7.00	3.10	.85
☐	CC12 Cammi Granato	5.00	2.30	.60
☐	CC13 Alexei Yashin	4.00	1.80	.50
☐	CC14 Alexandre Daigle	4.00	1.80	.50
☐	CC15 Manon Rheaume	16.00	7.25	2.00
☐	CC16 Radek Bonk	7.00	3.10	.85
☐	CC17 Alex Rodriguez	15.00	6.75	1.90
☐	CC18 Kirk Presley	4.00	1.80	.50
☐	CC19 Trot Nixon	4.00	1.80	.50
☐	CC20 Brooks Kieschnick	6.00	2.70	.75

1994 Classic Images Marshall Faulk

Randomly inserted in 1994 Classic Images packs (three per case; 3,250 each), these *six standard-size (2 1/2" by 3 1/2") cards feature color player action shots on their fronts. The photos are borderless, except at a lower corner, where a blue triangular area carries the player's position. The player's name an team helmet appears in the other corner. The back carries a borderless color player action shot that is ghosted, except for the area around the player's head. Career highlights appear below. The cards are numbered on the back with an "M" prefix. Card M5 was redeemable for a Classic Images Chrome sheet until 10/1/94.*

	MINT	NRMT	EXC
COMPLETE SET (6)	60.00	27.00	7.50
COMMON FAULK (M1-M6)	8.00	3.60	1.00
☐ M1 Tampa Bay Buccaneers	8.00	3.60	1.00
☐ M2 Cincinnati Bengals	8.00	3.60	1.00
☐ M3 Chicago Bears	8.00	3.60	1.00
☐ M4 New England Patriots	8.00	3.60	1.00
☐ M5 Indianapolis Colts	20.00	9.00	2.50
☐ M6 Field Card	8.00	3.60	1.00

1994 Classic Images Sudden Impact *

Inserted one per '94 Classic Images pack, these 20 gold foil-board cards measure the standard-size (2 1/2" by 3 1/2"). The gold metallic fronts feature borderless color player action shots on backgrounds that have been thrown out of focus. The player's name and position appear in vertical lettering within a black strip across the card near the right edge. The back carries a color player action shot at the top, followed below by career highlights on a white panel. The player's name appears in vertical black lettering within a ghosted action strip at the left edge. The cards are numbered on the back with an "SI" prefix.

	MINT	NRMT	EXC
COMPLETE SET (20)	12.00	5.50	1.50
COMMON CARD (1-20)	.10	.05	.01
☐ SI1 Carlos Delgado	.50	.23	.06
☐ SI2 Vin Baker	.60	.25	.08

☐ SI3 Derek Jeter	1.00	.45	.13
☐ SI4 Alex Rodriguez	1.50	.65	.19
☐ SI5 Alexandre Daigle	.50	.23	.06
☐ SI6 Rob Niedermayer	.30	.14	.04
☐ SI7 Jocelyn Thibault	.10	.05	.01
☐ SI8 Derek Plante	.20	.09	.03
☐ SI9 Shaquille O'Neal	1.00	.45	.13
☐ SI10 Alonzo Mourning	.50	.23	.06
☐ SI11 Harold Miner	.10	.05	.01
☐ SI12 Chris Webber	.75	.35	.09
☐ SI13 Anfernee Hardaway	1.50	.65	.19
☐ SI14 Jamal Mashburn	1.00	.45	.13
☐ SI15 Drew Bledsoe	2.00	.90	.25
☐ SI16 Rick Mirer	.75	.35	.09
☐ SI17 Derek Brown RB	.25	.11	.03
☐ SI18 Ron Moore	.25	.11	.03
☐ SI19 Jerome Bettis	.50	.23	.06
☐ SI20 Dino Radja	.50	.23	.06

1994-95 Classic Assets *

Produced by Classic, the 1994 Assets set features stars from basketball, hockey, football, baseball, and auto racing. The set was released in two series of 50 cards each. 1,994 cases were produced of each series. This standard-sized card set features a player photo with his name in silver letters on the lower left corner and the Assets logo on the upper right. The back has a color photo on the left side along with a biography on the right side of the card. A Sprint phone card is randomly inserted in each 5-card pack.

	MINT	NRMT	EXC
COMPLETE SET (100)	20.00	9.00	2.50
COMPLETE SET SERIES 1 (50)	10.00	4.50	1.25
COMPLETE SET SERIES 2 (50)	10.00	4.50	1.25
COMMON CARD (1-50)	.10	.05	.01
COMMON CARD (51-100)	.10	.05	.01
☐ 1 Shaquille O'Neal	1.00	.45	.13
☐ 2 Hakeem Olajuwon	.50	.23	.06
☐ 3 Troy Aikman	.60	.25	.08
☐ 4 Nolan Ryan	1.25	.55	.16
☐ 5 Dale Earnhardt	1.25	.55	.16
☐ 6 Glenn Robinson	1.50	.65	.19
☐ 7 Marshall Faulk	1.50	.65	.19

☐ 8 Ed Jovanovski	.40	.18	.05
☐ 9 Drew Bledsoe	1.25	.55	.16
☐ 10 Alonzo Mourning	.30	.14	.04
☐ 11 Steve Young	.60	.25	.08
☐ 12 Dan Wilkinson	.10	.05	.01
☐ 13 Paul Wilson	.60	.25	.08
☐ 14 Jason Kidd	1.50	.65	.19
☐ 15 Charlie Garner	.25	.11	.03
☐ 16 Derrick Alexander	.30	.14	.04
☐ 17 Donyell Marshall	.50	.23	.06
☐ 18 Ben Grieve	1.00	.45	.13
☐ 19 Eric Montross	.30	.14	.04
☐ 20 Radek Bonk	.20	.09	.03
☐ 21 Manon Rheaume	1.50	.65	.19
☐ 22 Jalen Rose	.30	.14	.04
☐ 23 Antonio Langham	.20	.09	.03
☐ 24 Greg Hill	.30	.14	.04
☐ 25 Marshall Faulk	.25	.11	.03
Checklist #1			
☐ 26 Shaquille O'Neal	1.00	.45	.13
☐ 27 Hakeem Olajuwon	.50	.23	.06
☐ 28 Troy Aikman	.60	.25	.08
☐ 29 Nolan Ryan	1.25	.55	.16
☐ 30 Dale Earnhardt	1.25	.55	.16
☐ 31 Glenn Robinson	1.50	.65	.19
☐ 32 Marshall Faulk	1.50	.65	.19
☐ 33 Ed Jovanovski	.40	.18	.05
☐ 34 Drew Bledsoe	1.25	.55	.16
☐ 35 Alonzo Mourning	.30	.14	.04
☐ 36 Steve Young	.60	.25	.08
☐ 37 Dan Wilkinson	.10	.05	.01
☐ 38 Paul Wilson	.60	.25	.08
☐ 39 Jason Kidd	1.50	.65	.19
☐ 40 Charlie Garner	.25	.11	.03
☐ 41 Derrick Alexander	.30	.14	.04
☐ 42 Donyell Marshall	.50	.23	.06
☐ 43 Ben Grieve	1.00	.45	.13
☐ 44 Eric Montross	.30	.14	.04
☐ 45 Radek Bonk	.20	.09	.03
☐ 46 Manon Rheaume	1.50	.65	.19
☐ 47 Jalen Rose	.30	.14	.04
☐ 48 Antonio Langham	.20	.09	.03
☐ 49 Greg Hill	.30	.14	.04
☐ 50 Glenn Robinson	.25	.11	.03
Checklist #2			
☐ 51 Dikembe Mutombo	.15	.07	.02
☐ 52 Rashaan Salaam	1.00	.45	.13
☐ 53 Anfernee Hardaway	.60	.25	.08
☐ 54 Isaiah Rider	.30	.14	.04
☐ 55 Emmitt Smith	1.00	.45	.13
☐ 56 Juwan Howard	.50	.23	.06
☐ 57 Jeff O'Neill	.25	.11	.03
☐ 58 Jamal Mashburn	.50	.23	.06
☐ 59 Byron Morris	.60	.25	.08
☐ 60 Petr Sykora	.75	.35	.09
☐ 61 Errict Rhett	1.00	.45	.13
☐ 62 Eric Fichaud	.40	.18	.05
☐ 63 Heath Shuler	.60	.25	.08
☐ 64 Doug Million	.25	.11	.03
☐ 65 Barry Bonds	.50	.23	.06
☐ 66 William Floyd	.40	.18	.05
☐ 67 Willie McGinest	.15	.07	.02
☐ 68 Jeff Gordon	1.25	.55	.16
☐ 69 Eddie Jones	.75	.35	.09
☐ 70 Steve McNair	.75	.35	.09
☐ 71 Ki-Jana Carter	.75	.35	.09
☐ 72 Manon Rheaume	1.50	.65	.19
☐ 73 Shaquille O'Neal	1.00	.45	.13
☐ 74 Drew Bledsoe	1.00	.45	.13
☐ 75 Checklist	.25	.11	.03
☐ 76 Dikembe Mutombo	.15	.07	.02

☐ 77 Rashaan Salaam	1.00	.45	.13
☐ 78 Anfernee Hardaway	.60	.25	.08
☐ 79 Isaiah Rider	.30	.14	.04
☐ 80 Emmitt Smith	1.00	.45	.13
☐ 81 Juwan Howard	.60	.25	.08
☐ 82 Jeff O'Neill	.25	.11	.03
☐ 83 Jamal Mashburn	.50	.23	.06
☐ 84 Byron Bam Morris	.60	.25	.08
☐ 85 Petr Sykora	.75	.35	.09
☐ 86 Errict Rhett	1.00	.45	.13
☐ 87 Eric Fichaud	.40	.18	.05
☐ 88 Heath Shuler	.60	.25	.08
☐ 89 Doug Million	.25	.11	.03
☐ 90 Barry Bonds	.50	.23	.06
☐ 91 William Floyd	.40	.18	.05
☐ 92 Willie McGinest	.15	.07	.02
☐ 93 Jeff Gordon	1.25	.55	.16
☐ 94 Eddie Jones	.75	.35	.09
☐ 95 Steve McNair	.75	.35	.09
☐ 96 Ki-Jana Carter	.75	.35	.09
☐ 97 Manon Rheaume	1.50	.65	.19
☐ 98 Shaquille O'Neal	1.00	.45	.13
☐ 99 Drew Bledsoe	1.25	.55	.16
☐ 100 Checklist	.25	.11	.03

1994-95 Classic Assets Silver Signature *

This 48-card standard-size set was randomly inserted at a rate of four per box. The cards are identical to the first twenty-four cards in the each series, except that these show a silver facsimile autograph on their fronts. The first 24 cards correspond to cards 1-24 in the first series while the second 24 cards correspond to cards 51-74 in the second series.

	MINT	NRMT	EXC
COMPLETE SET (48)	120.00	55.00	15.00
COMP. SET SERIES 1 (24)	60.00	27.00	7.50
COMP. SET SERIES 2 (24)	60.00	27.00	7.50
COMMON SIGNATURE (1-24)	.50	.23	.06
COMMON SIGNATURE (51-74)	.50	.23	.06
*STARS: 3X TO 6X BASIC CARDS			

1994-95 Classic Assets Die Cuts *

This 25-card standard-size set was randomly inserted into packs. DC1-10 were included in series 1 while DC11-25 were included in series 2 packs. These cards feature the player on the card and the ability to separate the player's photo. The back contains information about the player on the section of the card that is separable. The cards are numbered in the upper left corner.

	MINT	NRMT	EXC
COMPLETE SET (25)	185.00	85.00	23.00
COMPLETE SET SERIES 1 (10)	85.00	38.00	10.50
COMPLETE SET SERIES 2 (15)	100.00	45.00	12.50
COMMON CARD (DC1-DC10)..	4.00	1.80	.50
COMMON CARD (DC11-DC25)	4.00	1.80	.50
☐ DC1 Shaquille O'Neal......	15.00	6.75	1.90
☐ DC2 Hakeem Olajuwon	4.00	1.80	.50
☐ DC3 Troy Aikman	7.00	3.10	.85
☐ DC4 Nolan Ryan	15.00	6.75	1.90
☐ DC5 Dale Earnhardt	15.00	6.75	1.90
☐ DC6 Glenn Robinson	15.00	6.75	1.90
☐ DC7 Marshall Faulk.........	15.00	6.75	1.90
☐ DC8 Steve Young............	7.00	3.10	.85
☐ DC9 Ed Jovanovski	5.00	2.30	.60
☐ DC10 Manon Rheaume.....	15.00	6.75	1.90
☐ DC11 Grant Hill...............	18.00	8.00	2.30
☐ DC12 Jason Kidd.............	15.00	6.75	1.90
☐ DC13 Eddie Jones............	9.00	4.00	1.15
☐ DC14 Heath Shuler..........	7.00	3.10	.85
☐ DC15 Nomar Garciaparra..	4.00	1.80	.50
☐ DC16 Byron Bam Morris...	5.00	2.30	.60
☐ DC17 Barry Bonds...........	4.00	1.80	.50
☐ DC18 Paul Wilson............	7.00	3.10	.85
☐ DC19 Jeff Gordon............	15.00	6.75	1.90
☐ DC20 Isaiah Rider............	4.00	1.80	.50
☐ DC21 Steve McNair..........	8.00	3.60	1.00
☐ DC22 Donyell Marshall	7.00	3.10	.85
☐ DC23 Errict Rhett.............	9.00	4.00	1.15
☐ DC24 Eric Fichaud...........	6.00	2.70	.75
☐ DC25 Emmitt Smith.........	10.00	4.50	1.25

1994-95 Classic Assets Phone Cards One Minute/$2

Measuring 2" by 3 1/4", these cards have rounded corners and were randomly inserted into packs. Cards 1-24 were in first series packs while 25-48 were included with second series packs. The front features the player's photo and on the side is how long the card is good for. The Assets logo is in the bottom left corner. The back gives instructions on how to use the phone card.

	MINT	NRMT	EXC
COMPLETE SET (48)	150.00	70.00	19.00
COMPLETE SET SERIES 1 (24)	80.00	36.00	10.00
COMPLETE SET SERIES 2 (24)	70.00	32.00	8.75
COMMON CARD (1-24)	1.50	.65	.19
COMMON CARD (25-48)	1.50	.65	.19
*PIN NUMBER REVEALED: HALF VALUE			
☐ 1 Troy Aikman	5.00	2.30	.60
☐ 2 Derrick Alexander	2.00	.90	.25
☐ 3 Drew Bledsoe...............	10.00	4.50	1.25
☐ 4 Radek Bonk.................	1.50	.65	.19
☐ 5 Dale Earnhardt.............	8.00	3.60	1.00
☐ 6 Marshall Faulk.............	10.00	4.50	1.25
☐ 7 Charlie Garner.............	1.75	.80	.22
☐ 8 Ben Grieve	5.00	2.30	.60
☐ 9 Greg Hill....................	2.00	.90	.25
☐ 10 Ed Jovanovski............	2.50	1.15	.30
☐ 11 Jason Kidd.................	6.00	2.70	.75
☐ 12 Antonio Langham	1.50	.65	.19
☐ 13 Donyell Marshall	2.50	1.15	.30
☐ 14 Eric Montross	2.00	.90	.25
☐ 15 Alonzo Mourning	2.00	.90	.25
☐ 16 Hakeem Olajuwon.......	3.00	1.35	.40
☐ 17 Shaquille O'Neal.........	5.00	2.30	.60
☐ 18 Manon Rheaume.........	5.00	2.30	.60
☐ 19 Glenn Robinson..........	6.00	2.70	.75
☐ 20 Jalen Rose.................	1.50	.65	.19
☐ 21 Nolan Ryan	10.00	4.50	1.25
☐ 22 Dan Wilkinson............	1.50	.65	.19
☐ 23 Paul Wilson................	3.00	1.35	.40
☐ 24 Steve Young...............	5.00	2.30	.60
☐ 25 Drew Bledsoe.............	10.00	4.50	1.25
☐ 26 Barry Bonds...............	2.50	1.15	.30
☐ 27 Ki-Jana Carter............	4.00	1.80	.50

		MINT	NRMT	EXC
☐	28 Eric Fichaud	2.00	.90	.25
☐	29 William Floyd	2.50	1.15	.30
☐	30 Jeff Gordon	8.00	3.60	1.00
☐	31 Anfernee Hardaway	3.00	1.35	.40
☐	32 Juwan Howard	2.50	1.15	.30
☐	33 Eddie Jones	4.00	1.80	.50
☐	34 Jamal Mashburn	2.50	1.15	.30
☐	35 Willie McGinest	1.50	.65	.19
☐	36 Steve McNair	5.00	2.30	.60
☐	37 Doug Million	2.00	.90	.25
☐	38 Byron Bam Morris	3.00	1.35	.40
☐	39 Dikembe Mutombo	1.50	.65	.19
☐	40 Shaquille O'Neal	4.00	1.80	.50
☐	41 Jeff O'Neill	2.00	.90	.25
☐	42 Manon Rheaume	5.00	2.30	.60
☐	43 Errict Rhett	5.00	2.30	.60
☐	44 Isaiah Rider	2.00	.90	.25
☐	45 Rashaan Salaam	5.00	2.30	.60
☐	46 Heath Shuler	3.00	1.35	.40
☐	47 Emmitt Smith	6.00	2.70	.75
☐	48 Petr Sykora	3.00	1.35	.40

1994-95 Classic Assets Phone Cards $25

These rounded corner cards measuring 2" by 3 1/4" were randomly inserted into first series packs. The front features the player's photo, with "Twenty-five Dollars" written in cursive script along the left edge. In the bottom left corner is the Classic Assets logo. The back gives instructions on how to use the phone card. These cards are listed in alphabetical order. Two combo cards were available to dealers at the rate of 1 per every six second-series boxes ordered.

		MINT	NRMT	EXC
COMPLETE SET (5)		350.00	160.00	45.00
COMMON CARD (1-5)		70.00	32.00	8.75
*PIN NUMBER REVEALED: HALF VALUE				
☐	1 Dale Earnhardt	80.00	36.00	10.00
☐	2 Marshall Faulk	80.00	36.00	10.00
☐	3 Shaquille O'Neal	80.00	36.00	10.00
☐	4 Manon Rheaume	80.00	36.00	10.00
☐	5 Glenn Robinson	70.00	32.00	8.75
☐	NNO Troy Aikman Steve Young	60.00	27.00	7.50
☐	NNO Shaquille O'Neal Glenn Robinson	60.00	27.00	7.50

1994-95 Classic Assets Phone Cards $5

These cards measure 2" by 3 1/4", have rounded corners and were randomly inserted into packs. Cards 1-5 were inserted into first series packs while 6-15 were in second series packs. The front features the player's photo, with "Five Dollars" written in cursive script along the left edge. In the bottom left corner is the Assets logo. The back gives instructions on how to use the phone card.

		MINT	NRMT	EXC
COMPLETE SET (15)		225.00	100.00	28.00
COMPLETE SET SERIES 1 (5)		75.00	34.00	9.50
COMPLETE SET SERIES 2 (10)		150.00	70.00	19.00
COMMON CARD (1-5)		10.00	4.50	1.25
COMMON CARD (6-15)		10.00	4.50	1.25
*PIN NUMBER REVEALED: HALF VALUE				
☐	1 Troy Aikman	12.00	5.50	1.50
☐	2 Drew Bledsoe	30.00	13.50	3.80
☐	3 Jason Kidd	20.00	9.00	2.50
☐	4 Hakeem Olajuwon	10.00	4.50	1.25
☐	5 Nolan Ryan	30.00	13.50	3.80
☐	6 Drew Bledsoe	30.00	13.50	3.80
☐	7 Barry Bonds	10.00	4.50	1.25
☐	8 Ki-Jana Carter	15.00	6.75	1.90
☐	9 Jeff Gordon	25.00	11.50	3.10
☐	10 Jason Kidd	20.00	9.00	2.50
☐	11 Byron Bam Morris	10.00	4.50	1.25
☐	12 Rashaan Salaam	20.00	9.00	2.50
☐	13 Emmitt Smith	20.00	9.00	2.50
☐	14 Manon Rheaume	20.00	9.00	2.50
☐	15 Glenn Robinson	20.00	9.00	2.50

1994-95 Classic Assets Phone Cards $50

These cards, which measure 2" by 3 1/4", have rounded corners and were included in second series packs. The front features the player's photo, with "Fifty Dollars" written in cursive script along the left edge. In the bottom left corner is the Assets logo. The back gives instructions on how to use the phone card.

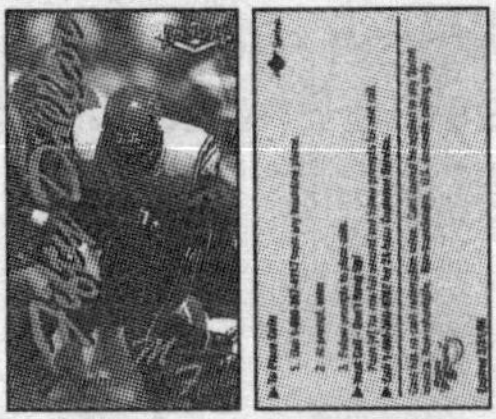

	MINT	NRMT	EXC
COMPLETE SET (5)	500.00	230.00	65.00
COMMON CARD (1-5)	100.00	45.00	12.50

*PIN NUMBER REVEALED: HALF VALUE

	MINT	NRMT	EXC
☐ 1 Marshall Faulk	125.00	57.50	15.50
☐ 2 Anfernee Hardaway	100.00	45.00	12.50
☐ 3 Shaquille O'Neal	125.00	57.50	15.50
☐ 4 Emmitt Smith	125.00	57.50	15.50
☐ 5 Steve Young	100.00	45.00	12.50

1994-95 Classic Assets Phone Cards $100

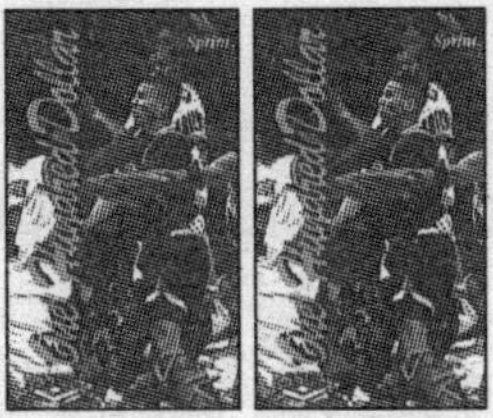

These 2" by 3 1/4" rounded corner cards were randomly inserted into packs. These cards were placed into series 1 packs. The front features the player's photo, with "One Hundred Dollars" written in cursive script along the left edge. The Assets logo is in the bottom left corner. The back gives instructions on how to use the phone card. These cards are listed in alphabetical order.

	MINT	NRMT	EXC
COMPLETE SET (5)	900.00	400.00	115.00
COMMON CARD (1-5)	150.00	70.00	19.00

*PIN NUMBER REVEALED: HALF VALUE

	MINT	NRMT	EXC
☐ 1 Troy Aikman	160.00	70.00	20.00
☐ 2 Drew Bledsoe	250.00	115.00	31.00
☐ 3 Jason Kidd	200.00	90.00	25.00
☐ 4 Hakeem Olajuwon	150.00	70.00	19.00
☐ 5 Nolan Ryan	250.00	115.00	31.00

1994-95 Classic Assets Phone Cards $200

These rounded corner cards were randomly inserted into second series packs and measure 2" by 3 1/4". The front features the player's photo, with "Two Hundred Dollars" written in cursive script along the left edge. In the bottom left corner is the Assets logo. The back gives instructions on how to use the phone card. These cards are arranged in alphabetical order.

	MINT	NRMT	EXC
COMPLETE SET (5)	1200.00	550.00	150.00
COMMON CARD (1-5)	250.00	115.00	31.00

*PIN NUMBER REVEALED: HALF VALUE

	MINT	NRMT	EXC
☐ 1 Drew Bledsoe	350.00	160.00	45.00
☐ 2 Barry Bonds	250.00	115.00	31.00
☐ 3 Ki-Jana Carter	250.00	115.00	31.00
☐ 4 Jason Kidd	300.00	135.00	38.00
☐ 5 Rashaan Salaam	250.00	115.00	31.00

1994-95 Classic Assets Phone Cards $1000

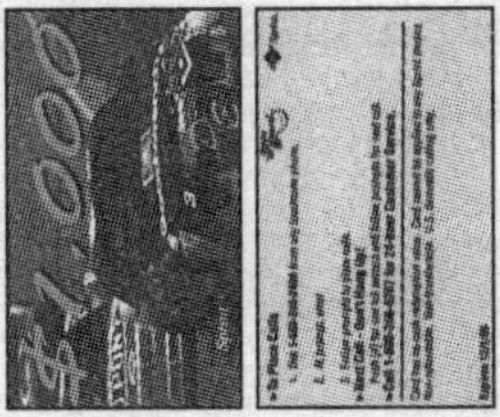

Measuring 2" by 3 1/4", these rounded-corner cards were randomly inserted in first-series packs. The fronts feature color player photos, with "One Thousand Dollars" in cursive script along the left edge. The backs give instructions on how to use the phone cards. The cards expired December 1, 1995.

	MINT	NRMT	EXC
COMPLETE SET (5)	8000.00	3600.00	1000.00
COMMON CARD (1-5)	1500.00	700.00	190.00

*PIN NUMBER REVEALED: HALF VALUE

	MINT	NRMT	EXC
☐ 1 Dale Earnhardt	1800.00	800.00	230.00
☐ 2 Marshall Faulk	1800.00	800.00	230.00

		MINT	NRMT	EXC
☐ 3	Shaquille O'Neal	1800.00	800.00	230.00
☐ 4	Manon Rheaume	1800.00	800.00	230.00
☐ 5	Glenn Robinson	1500.00	700.00	190.00

1994-95 Classic Assets Phone Cards $2000

These rounded-corner cards measuring 2" by 3 1/4" were randomly inserted into second series packs. Just four of each of these cards were produced. The front features the player's photo, with "Two Thousand Dollars" written in cursive script along the left edge. In the bottom left corner is the Assets logo. The back gives instructions on how to use the phone card. The cards are unnumbered and checklisted below in alphabetical order.

		MINT	NRMT	EXC
COMPLETE SET (5)		11000.00	5000.00	1400.00
COMMON CARD (1-5)		2400.00	1100.00	300.00
*PIN NUMBER REVEALED: HALF VALUE				

		MINT	NRMT	EXC
☐ 1	Marshall Faulk	2700.00	1200.00	350.00
☐ 2	Shaquille O'Neal	2700.00	1200.00	350.00
☐ 3	Manon Rheaume	2700.00	1200.00	350.00
☐ 4	Emmitt Smith	2700.00	1200.00	350.00
☐ 5	Steve Young	2400.00	1100.00	300.00

1995 Classic Assets Gold *

This 50-card set measures the standard size. The fronts feature borderless player action phots with the player's name printed in gold at the bottom. The backs carry a portrait of the player with his name, career highlights, and statistics. The cards are numbered on the back.

		MINT	NRMT	EXC
COMPLETE SET (50)		20.00	9.00	2.50
COMMON CARD (1-50)		.20	.09	.03

		MINT	NRMT	EXC
☐ 1	Dale Earnhardt	1.50	.65	.19
☐ 2	Jeff O'Neill	.40	.18	.05
☐ 3	Jeff Friesen	1.00	.45	.13
☐ 4	Aki-Petteri Berg	.75	.35	.09
☐ 5	Todd Marchant	.20	.09	.03
☐ 6	Blaine Lacher	1.25	.55	.16
☐ 7	Petr Sykora	.75	.35	.09
☐ 8	David Oliver	.30	.14	.04
☐ 9	Manon Rheaume	1.50	.65	.19
☐ 10	Ed Jovanovski	.50	.23	.06
☐ 11	Nolan Ryan	1.50	.65	.19
☐ 12	Barry Bonds	.60	.25	.08
☐ 13	Ben Grieve	1.25	.55	.16
☐ 14	Dustin Hermanson	.25	.11	.03

☐ 15	Rashaan Salaam	1.25	.55	.16
☐ 16	Kyle Brady	.40	.18	.05
☐ 17	J.J. Stokes	1.25	.55	.16
☐ 18	James Stewart	.40	.18	.05
☐ 19	Michael Westbrook	1.00	.45	.13
☐ 20	Ki-Jana Carter	1.00	.45	.13
☐ 21	Steve McNair	1.00	.45	.13
☐ 22	Kerry Collins	1.00	.45	.13
☐ 23	Byron Bam Morris	.75	.35	.09
☐ 24	Errict Rhett	1.25	.55	.16
☐ 25	William Floyd	.50	.23	.06
☐ 26	Drew Bledsoe	1.50	.65	.19
☐ 27	Marshall Faulk	2.50	1.15	.30
☐ 28	Troy Aikman	.75	.35	.09
☐ 29	Steve Young	.75	.35	.09
☐ 30	Trent Dilfer	.60	.25	.08
☐ 31	Emmitt Smith	1.50	.65	.19
☐ 32	Rasheed Wallace	.75	.35	.09
☐ 33	Corliss Williamson	.50	.23	.06
☐ 34	Tyrus Edney	.40	.18	.05
☐ 35	Ed O'Bannon	1.25	.55	.16
☐ 36	Damon Stoudamire	.60	.25	.08
☐ 37	Eddie Jones	1.00	.45	.13
☐ 38	Khalid Reeves	.50	.23	.06
☐ 39	Jason Kidd	2.00	.90	.25
☐ 40	Glenn Robinson	2.00	.90	.25
☐ 41	Juwan Howard	.60	.25	.08
☐ 42	Jamal Mashburn	.60	.25	.08
☐ 43	Shaquille O'Neal	1.25	.55	.16
☐ 44	Alonzo Mourning	.40	.18	.05
☐ 45	Donyell Marshall	.60	.25	.08
☐ 46	Jalen Rose	.40	.18	.05
☐ 47	Wesley Person	.50	.23	.06
☐ 48	Grant Hill	2.50	1.15	.30
☐ 49	Rasheed Wallace CL	.30	.14	.04
☐ 50	Ki-Jana Carter CL	.50	.23	.06

1995 Classic Assets Gold Printer's Proofs

This 50-card set measures the standard size. The fronts feature borderless player action phots with the player's name printed in gold at the bottom. The words "Printer's Proof" is printed in red across the front. The backs carry a portrait of the player with his name, career highlights, and statistics. The cards are numbered on the back.

		MINT	NRMT	EXC
COMPLETE SET (50)		500.00	230.00	65.00
COMMON CARD (1-50)		4.00	1.80	.50
*STARS: 15X TO 30X BASIC CARDS				

1995 Classic Assets Gold Silver Signatures

This 50-card set measures the standard size. The fronts feature borderless player

1995 Classic Assets $2 Gold Phone Cards

action phots with the player's name printed in gold at the bottom. Each card has two facsimile silver signatures across the front. The backs carry a portrait of the player with his name, career highlights, and statistics. The cards are number on the back.

	MINT	NRMT	EXC
COMPLETE SET (50)	120.00	55.00	15.00
COMMON CARD (1-50)	1.00	.45	.13
*STARS: 3X TO 6X BASIC CARDS			

1995 Classic Assets Gold Die Cuts Silver

Theis 20-card set was randomly inserted in packs at a rate of one in 18. The fronts feature a borderless player color action photo with a diamond-shaped top and the player's action taking place in front of the card name. The backs carry the card name, player's name and career highlights. The cards are numbered on the backs. Gold versions are valued up to three times the values below. They were inserted at a rate of one in 72 packs.

	MINT	NRMT	EXC
COMPLETE SET (20)	200.00	90.00	25.00
COMMON CARD (SDC1-SDC20)	8.00	3.60	1.00

		MINT	NRMT	EXC
☐	SDC1 Ben Grieve	8.00	3.60	1.00
☐	SDC2 Shaquille O'Neal	12.00	5.50	1.50
☐	SDC3 Kyle Brady	8.00	3.60	1.00
☐	SDC4 Glenn Robinson	10.00	4.50	1.25
☐	SDC5 Marshall Faulk	14.00	6.25	1.75
☐	SDC6 Grant Hill	16.00	7.25	2.00
☐	SDC7 Rasheed Wallace	12.00	5.50	1.50
☐	SDC8 Ed O'Bannon	14.00	6.25	1.75
☐	SDC9 Barry Bonds	8.00	3.60	1.00
☐	SDC10 Dale Earnhardt	12.00	5.50	1.50
☐	SDC11 Ki-Jana Carter	10.00	4.50	1.25
☐	SDC12 Rashaan Salaam	12.00	5.50	1.50
☐	SDC13 Manon Rheaume	12.00	5.50	1.50
☐	SDC14 Jason Kidd	10.00	4.50	1.25
☐	SDC15 Emmitt Smith	14.00	6.25	1.75
☐	SDC16 Drew Bledsoe	18.00	8.00	2.30
☐	SDC17 Kerry Collins	10.00	4.50	1.25
☐	SDC18 Nolan Ryan	12.00	5.50	1.50
☐	SDC19 Michael Westbrook	12.00	5.50	1.50
☐	SDC20 Heath Shuler	8.00	3.60	1.00

This 47-card set was randomly inserted in packs and measures 2 1/8" by 3 3/8". The fronts feature color action player photos with the player's name below. The $2 calling value is printed vertically down the left. The backs carry the instructions on how to use the cards which expire on 7/31/96. The cards are unnumbered.

	MINT	NRMT	EXC
COMPLETE SET (47)	200.00	90.00	25.00
COMMON CARD (1-47)	2.00	.90	.25
*PIN NUMBER REVEALED: HALF VALUE			

		MINT	NRMT	EXC
☐	1 Dale Earnhardt	8.00	3.60	1.00
☐	2 Jeff O'Neill	3.00	1.35	.40
☐	3 Jeff Friesen	5.00	2.30	.60
☐	4 Aki-Petteri Berg	4.00	1.80	.50
☐	5 Todd Marchant	2.00	.90	.25
☐	6 Blaine Lacher	6.00	2.70	.75
☐	7 Petr Sykora	4.00	1.80	.50
☐	8 David Oliver	2.50	1.15	.30
☐	9 Manon Rheaume	7.00	3.10	.85
☐	10 Ed Jovanovski	3.00	1.35	.40
☐	11 Nolan Ryan	10.00	4.50	1.25
☐	12 Barry Bonds	3.00	1.35	.40
☐	13 Ben Grieve	6.00	2.70	.75
☐	14 Dustin Hermanson	2.50	1.15	.30
☐	15 Rashaan Salaam	6.00	2.70	.75
☐	16 Kyle Brady	3.00	1.35	.40
☐	17 J.J. Stokes	6.00	2.70	.75
☐	18 James Stewart	3.00	1.35	.40
☐	19 Michael Westbrook	5.00	2.30	.60
☐	20 Ki-Jana Carter	5.00	2.30	.60
☐	21 Steve McNair	4.00	1.80	.50
☐	22 Kerry Collins	4.00	1.80	.50
☐	23 Byron Bam Morris	3.50	1.55	.45
☐	24 Errict Rhett	6.00	2.70	.75
☐	25 William Floyd	3.00	1.35	.40
☐	26 Drew Bledsoe	12.00	5.50	1.50
☐	27 Marshall Faulk	12.00	5.50	1.50
☐	28 Troy Aikman	6.00	2.70	.75
☐	29 Steve Young	6.00	2.70	.75
☐	30 Trent Dilfer	3.50	1.55	.45
☐	31 Emmitt Smith	8.00	3.60	1.00
☐	32 Rasheed Wallace	4.00	1.80	.50
☐	33 Corliss Williamson	3.50	1.55	.45

			MINT	NRMT	EXC
☐	34	Tyrus Edney	3.00	1.35	.40
☐	35	Ed O'Bannon	6.00	2.70	.75
☐	36	Damon Stoudamire	3.00	1.35	.40
☐	37	Eddie Jones	5.00	2.30	.60
☐	38	Khalid Reeves	3.00	1.35	.40
☐	39	Jason Kidd	7.00	3.10	.85
☐	40	Glenn Robinson	7.00	3.10	.85
☐	41	Juwan Howard	3.00	1.35	.40
☐	42	Jamal Mashburn	3.00	1.35	.40
☐	43	Shaquille O'Neal	6.00	2.70	.75
☐	44	Alonzo Mourning	2.50	1.15	.30
☐	45	Donyell Marshall	3.00	1.35	.40
☐	46	Jalen Rose	2.50	1.15	.30
☐	47	Wesley Person	3.00	1.35	.40

1995 Classic Assets $5 Gold Phone Cards

This 16-card set measures 2 1/8" by 3 3/8" and was randomly inserted in packs. The fronts feature color action player photos with the player's name below. The $5 calling value is printed vertically down the left. The backs carry the instructions on how to use the cards which expire on 7/31/96. The cards are unnumbered. The Microlined versions are inserted at a rate of one in 18 packs versus one in six packs for the basic $5 card.

			MINT	NRMT	EXC
	COMPLETE SET (16)		275.00	125.00	34.00
	COMMON CARD (1-16)		10.00	4.50	1.25
	*PIN NUMBER REVEALED: HALF VALUE				
☐	1	Drew Bledsoe	30.00	13.50	3.80
☐	2	Marshall Faulk	30.00	13.50	3.80
☐	3	Manon Rheaume	20.00	9.00	2.50
☐	4	Nolan Ryan	30.00	13.50	3.80
☐	5	Emmitt Smith	25.00	11.50	3.10
☐	6	J.J. Stokes	15.00	6.75	1.90
☐	7	Damon Stoudamire	10.00	4.50	1.25
☐	8	Michael Westbrook	14.00	6.25	1.75
☐	9	Troy Aikman	15.00	6.75	1.90
☐	10	Barry Bonds	10.00	4.50	1.25
☐	11	Ki-Jana Carter	15.00	6.75	1.90
☐	12	Dale Earnhardt	25.00	11.50	3.10
☐	13	Jason Kidd	25.00	11.50	3.10
☐	14	Ed O'Bannon	20.00	9.00	2.50

			MINT	NRMT	EXC
☐	15	Shaquille O'Neal	25.00	11.50	3.10
☐	16	Glenn Robinson	25.00	11.50	3.10

1995 Classic Assets $25 Gold Phone Cards

This 5-card set measures 2 1/8" by 3 3/8" and was randomly inserted in packs. The fronts feature color action player photos of two different players with the player's name in gold below each photo. The $25 calling value is printed vertically in gold separating the two players. The backs carry the instructions on how to use the cards which expire on 7/31/96. The cards are unnumbered.

			MINT	NRMT	EXC
	COMPLETE SET (5)		350.00	160.00	45.00
	COMMON CARD (1-5)		70.00	32.00	8.75
	*PIN NUMBER REVEALED: HALF VALUE				
☐	1	M.Faulk/K.Carter	100.00	45.00	12.50
☐	2	S.McNair/K.Collins	80.00	36.00	10.00
☐	3	G.Robinson/R.Wallace	70.00	32.00	8.75
☐	4	N.Ryan/B.Bonds	100.00	45.00	12.50
☐	5	C.Williamson/E.O'Bannon	90.00	40.00	11.50

1995 Classic Images Previews *

Randomly inserted one per 24 packs in second-series '94-95 Assets packs, this 5-

card standard-size was issued to promote the Classic Images series. Just 5,000 of each card were produced. The fronts display the player's photo showcased against a metallic background. The backs are devoted on the left side to the player's identification and a note saying you have received a limited edition preview card. The right side of the reverse has a full-color photo of the player and the card is numbered at the upper right corner.

	MINT	NRMT	EXC
COMPLETE SET (5)	60.00	27.00	7.50
COMMON CARD (IP1-IP5)	15.00	6.75	1.90
☐ IP1 Grant Hill	20.00	9.00	2.50
☐ IP2 Shaquille O'Neal	18.00	8.00	2.30
☐ IP3 Marshall Faulk	20.00	9.00	2.50
☐ IP4 Manon Rheaume	15.00	6.75	1.90
☐ IP5 Emmitt Smith	20.00	9.00	2.50

1995 Classic Images *

Printed on 18-point micro-lined foil board, the 1995 Classic Images set consists of 120 standard-size cards, featuring the top draft picks from the four major sports. Classic produced 1,995 sequentially-numbered 16-box hobby cases. This series also features one "Hot Box" in every four cases; each pack in it included at least one card from live insert sets, plus the special Clear Excitement chase cards not found anywhere else, for a total of 24 inserts per Hot Box. The set subdivides according to sport as follows: basketball (1-37), football (38-75), baseball (76-93), and hockey (94-120).

	MINT	NRMT	EXC
COMPLETE SET (120)	30.00	13.50	3.80
COMMON CARD (1-120)	.10	.05	.01
☐ 1 Glenn Robinson	2.50	1.15	.30
☐ 2 Jason Kidd	2.50	1.15	.30
☐ 3 Grant Hill	3.50	1.55	.45
☐ 4 Donyell Marshall	1.00	.45	.13
☐ 5 Juwan Howard	1.00	.45	.13
☐ 6 Sharone Wright	.75	.35	.09
☐ 7 Brian Grant	1.00	.45	.13
☐ 8 Eric Montross	.75	.35	.09
☐ 9 Eddie Jones	1.50	.65	.19
☐ 10 Carlos Rogers	.40	.18	.05
☐ 11 Khalid Reeves	.75	.35	.09
☐ 12 Jalen Rose	.75	.35	.09
☐ 13 Yinka Dare	.10	.05	.01
☐ 14 Eric Piatkowski	.20	.09	.03
☐ 15 Clifford Rozier	.30	.14	.04
☐ 16 Aaron McKie	.10	.05	.01
☐ 17 Eric Mobley	.10	.05	.01
☐ 18 B.J. Tyler	.20	.09	.03
☐ 19 Dickey Simpkins	.25	.11	.03
☐ 20 Bill Curley	.10	.05	.01
☐ 21 Wesley Person	.75	.35	.09
☐ 22 Monty Williams	.30	.14	.04
☐ 23 Antonio Lang	.10	.05	.01
☐ 24 Darrin Hancock	.10	.05	.01
☐ 25 Michael Smith	.40	.18	.05
☐ 26 Rodney Dent	.10	.05	.01
☐ 27 Charlie Ward	.25	.11	.03
☐ 28 Jim McIlvaine	.10	.05	.01
☐ 29 Brooks Thompson	.10	.05	.01
☐ 30 Gaylon Nickerson	.10	.05	.01
☐ 31 Jamie Watson	.10	.05	.01
☐ 32 Damon Bailey	.30	.14	.04
☐ 33 Dontonio Wingfield	.10	.05	.01
☐ 34 Trevor Ruffin	.10	.05	.01
☐ 35 Greg Minor	.30	.14	.04
☐ 36 Dwayne Morton	.10	.05	.01
☐ 37 Shaquille O'Neal	1.25	.55	.16
☐ 38 Dan Wilkinson	.25	.11	.03
☐ 39 Marshall Faulk	3.50	1.55	.45
☐ 40 Heath Shuler	1.25	.55	.16
☐ 41 Willie McGinest	.25	.11	.03
☐ 42 Trev Alberts	.20	.09	.03
☐ 43 Trent Dilfer	1.00	.45	.13
☐ 44 Bryant Young	.50	.23	.06
☐ 45 Sam Adams	.10	.05	.01
☐ 46 Antonio Langham	.40	.18	.05
☐ 47 Jamir Miller	.10	.05	.01
☐ 48 Aaron Glenn	.10	.05	.01
☐ 49 Bernard Williams	.10	.05	.01
☐ 50 Charles Johnson	.50	.23	.06
☐ 51 Dewayne Washington	.10	.05	.01
☐ 52 Tim Bowens	.40	.18	.05
☐ 53 Johnnie Morton	.30	.14	.04
☐ 54 Rob Fredrickson	.30	.14	.04
☐ 55 Shante Carver	.20	.09	.03
☐ 56 Henry Ford	.10	.05	.01
☐ 57 Jeff Burris	.30	.14	.04
☐ 58 William Floyd	.75	.35	.09
☐ 59 Derrick Alexander	.50	.23	.06
☐ 60 Darnay Scott	.60	.25	.08
☐ 61 Errict Rhett	2.00	.90	.25
☐ 62 Greg Hill	.60	.25	.08
☐ 63 David Palmer	.25	.11	.03
☐ 64 Charlie Garner	.50	.23	.06
☐ 65 Mario Bates	.50	.23	.06
☐ 66 Bert Emanuel	.40	.18	.05
☐ 67 Thomas Randolph	.10	.05	.01
☐ 68 Aubrey Beavers	.20	.09	.03
☐ 69 Byron Bam Morris	1.25	.55	.16
☐ 70 Lake Dawson	.50	.23	.06
☐ 71 Todd Steussie	.10	.05	.01
☐ 72 Aaron Taylor	.10	.05	.01
☐ 73 Corey Sawyer	.10	.05	.01
☐ 74 Kevin Mitchell	.10	.05	.01
☐ 75 Emmitt Smith	1.50	.65	.19
☐ 76 Paul Wilson	1.25	.55	.16
☐ 77 Ben Grieve	2.00	.90	.25
☐ 78 Doug Million	.40	.18	.05
☐ 79 Bret Wagner	.40	.18	.05
☐ 80 Dustin Hermanson	.40	.18	.05

☐ 81	Doug Webb	.10	.05	.01
☐ 82	Brian Stephenson	.10	.05	.01
☐ 83	Doug Webb	.75	.35	.09
☐ 84	Cade Gaspar	.25	.11	.03
☐ 85	Nomar Garciaparra	.40	.18	.05
☐ 86	Mike Thurman	.25	.11	.03
☐ 87	Brian Buchanan	.30	.14	.04
☐ 88	Mark Johnson	.30	.14	.04
☐ 89	Jacob Shumate	.30	.14	.04
☐ 90	Kevin Witt	.40	.18	.05
☐ 91	Victor Rodriguez	.30	.14	.04
☐ 92	Trey Moore	.10	.05	.01
☐ 93	Barry Bonds	.75	.35	.09
☐ 94	Ed Jovanovski	1.00	.45	.13
☐ 95	Oleg Tverdovsky	.50	.23	.06
☐ 96	Radek Bonk	.40	.18	.05
☐ 97	Jason Bonsignore	.25	.11	.03
☐ 98	Jeff O'Neill	.40	.18	.05
☐ 99	Ryan Smyth	.30	.14	.04
☐ 100	Jamie Storr	.75	.35	.09
☐ 101	Jason Wiemer	.30	.14	.04
☐ 102	Nolan Baumgarner	.25	.11	.03
☐ 103	Jeff Friesen	1.00	.45	.13
☐ 104	Wade Belak	.10	.05	.01
☐ 105	Ethan Moreau	.25	.11	.03
☐ 106	Alexander Kharlamov	.25	.11	.03
☐ 107	Eric Fichaud	.60	.25	.08
☐ 108	Wayne Primeau	.10	.05	.01
☐ 109	Brad Brown	.10	.05	.01
☐ 110	Chris Dingman	.10	.05	.01
☐ 111	Chris Wells	.25	.11	.03
☐ 112	Vadim Sharifjanov	.25	.11	.03
☐ 113	Dan Cloutier	.25	.11	.03
☐ 114	Jason Allison	.25	.11	.03
☐ 115	Todd Marchant	.25	.11	.03
☐ 116	Brent Gretzky	.25	.11	.03
☐ 117	Petr Sykora	.75	.35	.09
☐ 118	Manon Rheaume	2.00	.90	.25
☐ 119	Checklist	1.00	.45	.13
☐ 120	Checklist	1.00	.45	.13
☐ NNO	Basketball Redemption Card	100.00	45.00	12.50

cards with the prefix "C" were found in retail hot boxes. The cards are numbered out of 300.

	MINT	NRMT	EXC
COMPLETE SET (10)	1350.00	600.00	170.00
COMPLETE SET HOBBY (5).	650.00	300.00	80.00
COMPLETE SET RETAIL (5).	700.00	325.00	90.00
COMMON CARD (C1-C5)	140.00	65.00	17.50
COMMON CARD (E1-E5)	100.00	45.00	12.50
☐ C1 Shaquille O'Neal	160.00	70.00	20.00
☐ C2 Emmitt Smith	160.00	70.00	20.00
☐ C3 Troy Aikman	140.00	65.00	17.50
☐ C4 Steve Young	140.00	65.00	17.50
☐ C5 Nolan Ryan	180.00	80.00	23.00
☐ E1 Grant Hill	160.00	70.00	20.00
☐ E2 Marshall Faulk	160.00	70.00	20.00
☐ E3 Drew Bledsoe	200.00	90.00	25.00
☐ E4 Hakeem Olajuwon	100.00	45.00	12.50
☐ E5 Manon Rheaume	100.00	45.00	12.50

1995 Classic Images
Classic
Performances

Randomly inserted in hobby boxes at a rate of one in every 12 packs, this 20-card standard-size set relives great moments from the careers of 20 top athletes. Each card is numbered out of 4,495. The fronts feature the player against a gold background. The back contains on the left side a description of the great moment and on the right side a color player photo.

	MINT	NRMT	EXC
COMPLETE SET (20)	250.00	115.00	31.00
COMMON CARD (CP1-CP20) ..	6.00	2.70	.75
☐ CP1 Glenn Robinson	25.00	11.50	3.10
☐ CP2 Grant Hill	35.00	16.00	4.40
☐ CP3 Jason Kidd	25.00	11.50	3.10
☐ CP4 Juwan Howard	8.00	3.60	1.00
☐ CP5 Shaquille O'Neal	18.00	8.00	2.30
☐ CP6 Alonzo Mourning	7.00	3.10	.85
☐ CP7 Jamal Mashburn	8.00	3.60	1.00
☐ CP8 Steve Young	10.00	4.50	1.25
☐ CP9 Marshall Faulk	30.00	13.50	3.80

1995 Classic Images
Clear Excitement *

Randomly inserted at a rate of one in every 24 packs, these two 5-card acetate sets each feature five of the greatest athletes of our time. Cards with the prefix "E" were inserted in hobby hot boxes, while

		MINT	NRMT	EXC
☐ CP10	Derrick Alexander	6.00	2.70	.75
☐ CP11	William Floyd	7.00	3.10	.85
☐ CP12	Errict Rhett	18.00	8.00	2.30
☐ CP13	Byron Bam Morris	12.00	5.50	1.50
☐ CP14	Heath Shuler	15.00	6.75	1.90
☐ CP15	Emmitt Smith	16.00	7.25	2.00
☐ CP16	Paul Wilson	8.00	3.60	1.00
☐ CP17	Barry Bonds	6.00	2.70	.75
☐ CP18	Nolan Ryan	15.00	6.75	1.90
☐ CP19	Ed Jovanovski	7.00	3.10	.85
☐ CP20	Eric Fichaud	6.00	2.70	.75

1995 Classic Images NFL Draft Challenge

Randomly inserted in hobby and retail boxes at a rate of one in every 24 packs, this 25-card standard-size set previews the next generation of NFL superstars. Five players are featured in four different uniforms and a field card. Just 3,195 of each card were produced. Collectors who received a player in the uniform of the team that drafted him could redeem the card, along with 15 wrappers, for a 5-card acetate set. Each incorrect card, along with 10 wrappers, could be redeemed for one corresponding correct acetate card. Finally, the first 200 collectors who submitted all five cards featuring the players in the uniform of the team that drafted them, plus 20 wrappers, received a 5-card autographed set of these future gridiron greats. After 200 sets were redeemed, collectors received one acetate set for each correct card. The redemption program ran until October 31, 1995. In the listing below, each player's highest-price card features him in the uniform of the team that drafted him.

	MINT	NRMT	EXC
COMPLETE SET (25)	250.00	115.00	31.00
COMMON SALAAM (DC1-DC5)	10.00	4.50	1.25
COMMON CARTER (DC6-DC10)	8.00	3.60	1.00
COMMON WALSH (DC11-DC15)	6.00	2.70	.75
COMMON MCNAIR (DC16-DC20)	8.00	3.60	1.00
COMMON COLLINS (DC21-DC25)	8.00	3.60	1.00

		MINT	NRMT	EXC
☐ DC1	Rashaan Salaam	10.00	4.50	1.25
☐ DC2	Rashaan Salaam	10.00	4.50	1.25
☐ DC3	Rashaan Salaam	30.00	13.50	3.80
☐ DC4	Rashaan Salaam	10.00	4.50	1.25
☐ DC5	Rashaan Salaam	10.00	4.50	1.25
☐ DC6	Ki-Jana Carter	8.00	3.60	1.00
☐ DC7	Ki-Jana Carter	8.00	3.60	1.00
☐ DC8	Ki-Jana Carter	8.00	3.60	1.00
☐ DC9	Ki-Jana Carter	25.00	11.50	3.10
☐ DC10	Ki-Jana Carter	8.00	3.60	1.00
☐ DC11	John Walsh	6.00	2.70	.75
☐ DC12	John Walsh	6.00	2.70	.75
☐ DC13	John Walsh	6.00	2.70	.75
☐ DC14	John Walsh	6.00	2.70	.75
☐ DC15	John Walsh	20.00	9.00	2.50
☐ DC16	Steve McNair	8.00	3.60	1.00
☐ DC17	Steve McNair	8.00	3.60	1.00
☐ DC18	Steve McNair	25.00	11.50	3.10
☐ DC19	Steve McNair	8.00	3.60	1.00
☐ DC20	Steve McNair	8.00	3.60	1.00
☐ DC21	Kerry Collins	8.00	3.60	1.00
☐ DC22	Kerry Collins	8.00	3.60	1.00
☐ DC23	Kerry Collins	8.00	3.60	1.00
☐ DC24	Kerry Collins	8.00	3.60	1.00
☐ DC25	Kerry Collins	25.00	11.50	3.10

1995 Classic Images Flashbacks

These 10 standard-size cards were randomly inserted into retail boxes at a rate of 1 per 24 packs. The fronts display color action photos, while the backs carry a second photo and player information.

	MINT	NRMT	EXC
COMPLETE SET (10)	140.00	65.00	17.50
COMMON CARD (TF1-TF10)	4.00	1.80	.50

		MINT	NRMT	EXC
☐ TF1	Glenn Robinson Purdue	30.00	13.50	3.80
☐ TF2	Jason Kidd California	30.00	13.50	3.80
☐ TF3	Grant Hill Duke	35.00	16.00	4.40
☐ TF4	Donyell Marshall Connecticut	8.00	3.60	1.00
☐ TF5	Jamal Mashburn Kentucky	8.00	3.60	1.00
☐ TF6	Eric Montross North Carolina	7.00	3.10	.85
☐ TF7	Eddie Jones	14.00	6.25	1.75

	Temple			
☐ TF8	Alonzo Mourning	7.00	3.10	.85
	Georgetown			
☐ TF9	Jalen Rose	4.00	1.80	.50
	Michigan			
☐ TF10	Shaquille O'Neal	20.00	9.00	2.50
	LSU			

1995 Classic Images NFL Update

Randomly inserted in both hobby and retail at a rate of one in every 24 packs, this 10-card standard-size set provides up-to-date statistics on the hottest players in the 1994 Classic NFL Images series. The front has a player photo in the same style as the regular 1994 Classic Images cards. The back features a black-and-white player photo along with his 1994 and career statistics.

	MINT	NRMT	EXC
COMPLETE SET (10)	150.00	70.00	19.00
COMMON CARD (126-135)	4.00	1.80	.50

☐ 126	Emmitt Smith	30.00	13.50	3.80
☐ 127	Troy Aikman	12.00	5.50	1.50
☐ 128	Steve Young	12.00	5.50	1.50
☐ 129	Deion Sanders	10.00	4.50	1.25
☐ 130	Ben Coates	5.00	2.30	.60
☐ 131	Natrone Means	15.00	6.75	1.90
☐ 132	Drew Bledsoe	35.00	16.00	4.40
☐ 133	Cris Carter	4.00	1.80	.50
☐ 134	Marshall Faulk	25.00	11.50	3.10
☐ 135	Errict Rhett	15.00	6.75	1.90

1995 Classic Rookies Previews

This 5-card set measures the standard size. Both a hobby and retail set were produced and inserted at a rate of one per box in both the 1995 Classic Assets Gold and 1995 NFL ProLine boxes. The fronts feature borderless color action player photos with the player's name below. The hobby version has a aqua printer's proof logo while the retail version carries a silver foil signature across the bottom above the player's name. The backs show another player action photo with the player's name, position, biographical information, and career statistics. Sponsors' logos are below. The cards are numbered on the back with prefixes of RP for the retail version and HP for the hobby version.

	MINT	NRMT	EXC
COMPLETE SET (5)	35.00	16.00	4.40
COMMON CARD (1-5)	6.00	2.70	.75

☐ 1	Ed O'Bannon	10.00	4.50	1.25
☐ 2	Corliss Williamson	6.00	2.70	.75
☐ 3	Joe Smith	12.00	5.50	1.50
☐ 4	Rasheed Wallace	8.00	3.60	1.00
☐ 5	Damon Stoudamire	6.00	2.70	.75

1995 Classic Rookies

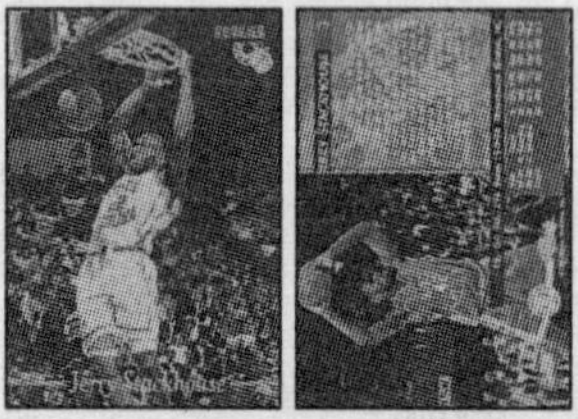

This 120-card set measures the standard size. The fronts feature a borderless color action player photo with the player's name across the bottom. The backs carry a color action player shot on the left with the player's name, career highlights, biographical information, and statistics on the right. Sponsors' logos are below. The cards are numbered on the back.

	MINT	NRMT	EXC
COMPLETE SET (120)	15.00	6.75	1.90
COMMON CARD (1-120)	.05	.02	.01
☐ 1 Joe Smith	1.50	.65	.19
☐ 2 Antonio McDyess	1.00	.45	.13
☐ 3 Jerry Stackhouse	2.00	.90	.25
☐ 4 Rasheed Wallace	1.00	.45	.13
☐ 5 Kevin Garnett	1.00	.45	.13
☐ 6 Damon Stoudamire	.75	.35	.09
☐ 7 Shawn Respert	.75	.35	.09
☐ 8 Ed O'Bannon	1.25	.55	.16
☐ 9 Kurt Thomas	.75	.35	.09
☐ 10 Gary Trent	.75	.35	.09
☐ 11 Cherokee Parks	.75	.35	.09
☐ 12 Corliss Williamson	.75	.35	.09
☐ 13 Eric Williams	.60	.25	.08
☐ 14 Brent Barry	.50	.23	.06
☐ 15 Bob Sura	.60	.25	.08
☐ 16 Theo Ratliff	.50	.23	.06
☐ 17 Randolph Childress	.75	.35	.09
☐ 18 Jason Caffey	.50	.23	.06
☐ 19 Michael Finley	.50	.23	.06
☐ 20 George Zidek	.40	.18	.05
☐ 21 Travis Best	.50	.23	.06
☐ 22 Loren Meyer	.40	.18	.05
☐ 23 David Vaughn	.40	.18	.05
☐ 24 Sherrell Ford	.40	.18	.05
☐ 25 Mario Bennett	.40	.18	.05
☐ 26 Greg Ostertag	.30	.14	.04
☐ 27 Cory Alexander	.30	.14	.04
☐ 28 Lou Roe	.40	.18	.05
☐ 29 Dragan Tarlac	.25	.11	.03
☐ 30 Terrence Rencher	.30	.14	.04
☐ 31 Junior Burrough	.30	.14	.04
☐ 32 Andrew DeClercq	.30	.14	.04
☐ 33 Jimmy King	.25	.11	.03
☐ 34 Lawrence Moten	.25	.11	.03
☐ 35 Frankie King	.25	.11	.03
☐ 36 Rashard Griffith	.15	.07	.02
☐ 37 Donny Marshall	.40	.18	.05
☐ 38 Julius Michalik	.05	.02	.01
☐ 39 Erik Meek	.20	.09	.03
☐ 40 Donnie Boyce	.20	.09	.03
☐ 41 Eric Snow	.20	.09	.03
☐ 42 Anthony Pelle	.20	.09	.03
☐ 43 Troy Brown	.15	.07	.02
☐ 44 George Banks	.15	.07	.02
☐ 45 Tyus Edney	.30	.14	.04
☐ 46 Mark Davis	.15	.07	.02
☐ 47 Jerome Allen	.15	.07	.02
☐ 48 Fred Holberg	.15	.07	.02
☐ 49 Constantin Popa	.15	.07	.02
☐ 50 Erwin Claggett	.05	.02	.01
☐ 51 Michael McDonald	.15	.07	.02
☐ 52 Andre Riddick	.05	.02	.01
☐ 53 Cuonzo Martin	.15	.07	.02
☐ 54 Don Reid	.15	.07	.02
☐ 55 James Forrest	.05	.02	.01
☐ 56 Glen Whisby	.05	.02	.01
☐ 57 Dwight Stewart	.05	.02	.01
☐ 58 Jamal Faulkner	.05	.02	.01
☐ 59 Tom Kleinschmidt	.05	.02	.01
☐ 60 Donald Williams	.05	.02	.01
☐ 61 Dan Cross	.05	.02	.01
☐ 62 Rick Brunson	.05	.02	.01
☐ 63 Corey Beck	.15	.07	.02
☐ 64 Lance Hughes	.05	.02	.01
☐ 65 Bernard Blunt	.05	.02	.01
☐ 66 Clint McDaniel	.05	.02	.01
☐ 67 John Amaechi	.05	.02	.01
☐ 68 Lorenzo Orr	.05	.02	.01
☐ 69 Randy Rutherford	.15	.07	.02
☐ 70 Ray Jackson	.15	.07	.02
☐ 71 Reggie Jackson	.05	.02	.01
☐ 72 Russell Larson	.05	.02	.01
☐ 73 Carlin Warley	.05	.02	.01
☐ 74 James Scott	.05	.02	.01
☐ 75 Roderick Anderson	.05	.02	.01
☐ 76 Antoine Gillespie	.05	.02	.01
☐ 77 Gerard King	.05	.02	.01
☐ 78 Petey Sessoms	.05	.02	.01
☐ 79 Steve Payne	.05	.02	.01
☐ 80 William Gates	.25	.11	.03
☐ 81 Arthur Agee	.25	.11	.03
☐ 82 Rebecca Lobo	.50	.23	.06
☐ 83 Devin Gray	.05	.02	.01
☐ 84 Scotty Thurman	.15	.07	.02
☐ 85 Matt Maloney	.05	.02	.01
☐ 86 Michael Evans	.05	.02	.01
☐ 87 LaZelle Durden	.05	.02	.01
☐ 88 Ronnie McMahan	.05	.02	.01
☐ 89 Ed O'Bannon AW	.60	.25	.08
☐ 90 Mario Bennett AW	.20	.09	.03
☐ 91 Randolph Childress AW	.40	.18	.05
☐ 92 Rasheed Wallace AW	.50	.23	.06
☐ 93 Lawrence Moten AW	.12	.05	.02
☐ 94 Shawn Respert AW	.40	.18	.05
☐ 95 Lou Roe AW	.20	.09	.03
☐ 96 Damon Stoudamire AW	.40	.18	.05
☐ 97 Gary Trent AW	.40	.18	.05
☐ 98 Corliss Williamson AW	.40	.18	.05
☐ 99 Jerry Stackhouse AW	1.00	.45	.13
☐ 100 Glenn Robinson AR	.50	.23	.06
☐ 101 Jason Kidd AR	.50	.23	.06
☐ 102 Juwan Howard AR	.25	.11	.03
☐ 103 Brian Grant AR	.20	.09	.03
☐ 104 Eddie Jones AR	.25	.11	.03
☐ 105 Shaquille O'Neal CA	.25	.11	.03
☐ 106 Dikembe Mutombo CA	.05	.02	.01
☐ 107 Alonzo Mourning CA	.12	.05	.02
☐ 108 Hakeem Olajuwon CA	.15	.07	.02
☐ 109 Cherokee Parks SS	.40	.18	.05
☐ 110 Corliss Williamson SS	.40	.18	.05
☐ 111 Shawn Respert SS	.40	.18	.05
☐ 112 Bob Sura SS	.30	.14	.04
☐ 113 Michael Finley SS	.25	.11	.03
☐ 114 Greg Ostertag SS	.15	.07	.02
☐ 115 Lou Roe SS	.20	.09	.03
☐ 116 Loren Meyer SS	.20	.09	.03
☐ 117 Mario Bennett SS	.20	.09	.03
☐ 118 Cuonzo Martin	.05	.02	.01
☐ 119 Joe Smith CL	.40	.18	.05
☐ 120 Jerry Stackhouse CL	.50	.23	.06

1995 Classic Rookies Printer's Proofs

Inserted at a rate of 1 per 18 packs, these 120 standard size cards are the same as the Classic Rookies but with the words "Printer's Proof 1 of 949" across the front. The fronts feature a borderless color action player photo with the player's name across the bottom The backs carry a color action player shot on the left with the player's

name, career highlights, biographical information, and statistics on the right. Sponsors' logos are below. The cards are numbered on the back.

	MINT	NRMT	EXC
COMPLETE SET (120)	350.00	160.00	45.00
COMMON CARD (1-120)	1.25	.55	.16

1995 Classic Rookies Silver

Inserted one per '95 Classic Rookies pack, these 120 standard-size cards are similar to the Classic Rookies but with a metallic sheen. The fronts feature a borderless color action player photo with the player's name across the bottom. The backs carry a color action player shot on the left with the player's name, career highlights, biographical information, and statistics on the right. Sponsors' logos are below. The cards are numbered on the back.

	MINT	NRMT	EXC
COMPLETE SET (120)	45.00	20.00	5.75
COMMON CARD (1-120)	.10	.05	.01

1995 Classic Rookies Center Stage

Randomly inserted in hobby packs, this 10-card set captures outstanding college play

ers. The fronts display a color action cut out on a metallic background. Each card is hand-numbered out of 1,750 produced. The backs have a second color photo and a player profile.

	MINT	NRMT	EXC
COMPLETE SET (20)	120.00	55.00	15.00
COMMON CARD (CS1-CS10)	8.00	3.60	1.00
☐ CS1 Joe Smith	20.00	9.00	2.50
☐ CS2 Antonio McDyess	12.00	5.50	1.50
☐ CS3 Rasheed Wallace	12.00	5.50	1.50
☐ CS4 Kevin Garnett	12.00	5.50	1.50
☐ CS5 Damon Stoudamire	8.00	3.60	1.00
☐ CS6 Ed O'Bannon	14.00	6.25	1.75
☐ CS7 Gary Trent	10.00	4.50	1.25
☐ CS8 Corliss Williamson	10.00	4.50	1.25
☐ CS9 Jerry Stackhouse	25.00	11.50	3.10
☐ CS10 Randolph Childress	10.00	4.50	1.25

1995 Classic Rookies Clear Cuts

The first five cards were randomly inserted in hobby "Hot Boxes," while the second five were included in retail "Hot Boxes." These cards have a color player action cutouts superposed on a colored transparent stock that is die cut along the right edge. The backs have the mirror image of the fronts.

	MINT	NRMT	EXC
COMPLETE SET (10)	750.00	350.00	95.00
COMPLETE SET HOBBY (5)	425.00	190.00	52.50
COMPLETE SET RETAIL (5)	325.00	145.00	40.00
COMMON CARD (CCH1-CCH5)	60.00	27.00	7.50
COMMON CARD (CCR1-CCR5)	60.00	27.00	7.50

☐ CCH1	Shaquille O'Neal..	150.00	70.00	19.00
☐ CCH2	Joe Smith............	150.00	70.00	19.00
☐ CCH3	Rasheed Wallace..	100.00	45.00	12.50
☐ CCH4	Kevin Garnett	100.00	45.00	12.50
☐ CCH5	Corliss Williamson	60.00	27.00	7.50
☐ CCR1	Jason Kidd...........	125.00	57.50	15.50
☐ CCR2	Ed O'Bannon.......	125.00	57.50	15.50
☐ CCR3	Antonio McDyess	100.00	45.00	12.50
☐ CCR4	Damon Stoudamire	60.00	27.00	7.50
☐ CCR5	Shawn Respert......	60.00	27.00	7.50

1995 Classic Rookies ProLine Previews $2 Phone Cards

These phone cards were random inserts in hobby packs. Measuring 2 1/8" by 3 3/8", they are printed on plastic stock and have rounded corners. The fronts display full-bleed color action shots, while the backs carry how-to-use instructions.

	MINT	NRMT	EXC
COMPLETE SET (4)	50.00	23.00	6.25
COMMON CARD (1-4)	10.00	4.50	1.25
☐ 1 Troy Aikman	12.00	5.50	1.50
☐ 2 Drew Bledsoe................	20.00	9.00	2.50
☐ 3 Ki-Jana Carter	10.00	4.50	1.25
☐ 4 Marshall Faulk...............	20.00	9.00	2.50

1995 Classic Rookies ProLine Previews $5 Phone Cards

These phone cards were random inserts in hobby packs. Measuring 2 1/8" by 3 3/8",

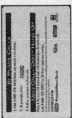

they are printed on plastic stock and have rounded corners. The fronts display full-bleed color action shots, while the backs carry how-to-use instructions.

	MINT	NRMT	EXC
COMPLETE SET (4)	110.00	50.00	14.00
COMMON CARD (1-4)	20.00	9.00	2.50
☐ 1 Troy Aikman	25.00	11.50	3.10
☐ 2 Drew Bledsoe................	40.00	18.00	5.00
☐ 3 Ki-Jana Carter	20.00	9.00	2.50
☐ 4 Marshall Faulk...............	40.00	18.00	5.00

1995 Classic Rookies Rookie of the Year Redemption

Inserted at a rate of 1 per 72 packs, these 20 standard-size cards feature a borderless color player action photo with the player's name above "Rookie of the Year" in gold on the left. The backs carry the player's name and instructions on how to participate in the redemption program. A checklist is listed below the instructions.

	MINT	NRMT	EXC
COMPLETE SET (20)	170.00	75.00	21.00
COMMON CARD (1-20)	5.00	2.30	.60

		MINT	NRMT	EXC
☐ 1	Joe Smith	20.00	9.00	2.50
☐ 2	Rasheed Wallace	12.00	5.50	1.50
☐ 3	Ed O'Bannon	14.00	6.25	1.75
☐ 4	Antonio McDyess	12.00	5.50	1.50
☐ 5	Shawn Respert	8.00	3.60	1.00
☐ 6	Mario Bennett	6.00	2.70	.75
☐ 7	Jerry Stackhouse	25.00	11.50	3.10
☐ 8	Cherokee Parks	8.00	3.60	1.00
☐ 9	Damon Stoudamire	6.00	2.70	.75
☐ 10	Kurt Thomas	8.00	3.60	1.00
☐ 11	Randolph Childress	6.00	2.70	.75
☐ 12	Brent Barry	6.00	2.70	.75
☐ 13	Corliss Williamson	8.00	3.60	1.00
☐ 14	Gary Trent	8.00	3.60	1.00
☐ 15	Bob Sura	6.00	2.70	.75
☐ 16	David Vaughn	6.00	2.70	.75
☐ 17	Michael Finley	6.00	2.70	.75
☐ 18	Rashard Griffith	5.00	2.30	.60
☐ 19	Lou Roe	6.00	2.70	.75
☐ 20	Field Card	5.00	2.30	.60

		MINT	NRMT	EXC
☐ S14	David Vaughn	3.00	1.35	.40
☐ S15	Mario Bennett	3.00	1.35	.40
☐ S16	Greg Ostertag	2.00	.90	.25
☐ S17	Bob Sura	5.00	2.30	.60
☐ S18	Lou Roe	3.00	1.35	.40
☐ S19	Tyus Edney	2.00	.90	.25
☐ S20	Jimmy King	2.00	.90	.25

1991 Courtside Draft Pix

1995 Classic Rookies Showtime

Each of these 20 cards was randomly inserted in retail packs. On a metallic background with color streaks radiating from a row of stage lights, the fronts display a color action player cutout. On a similar design, the backs have a player profile at top and a second color photo at the bottom.

The 1991 Courtside Draft Pix basketball set consists of 45 cards measuring the standard size (2 1/2" by 3 1/2"). All 198,000 sets produced are numbered and distributed as complete sets in their own custom boxes each accompanied by a certificate with a unique serial number. It has also been reported that 30,000 autographed cards were randomly inserted in the 9,900 cases. The card front features a color action player photo. The design of the card fronts features a color rectangle (either pearlized red, blue, or green) on a pearlized white background, with two border stripes in the same color intersecting at the upper right corner. The player's name appears at the upper right corner of the card face, with the words "Courtside 1991" at the bottom. The backs reflect the color on the fronts and present stats (biographical), college record (year by year statistics), and player profile. The cards are numbered on the back. The unnumbered Larry Johnson sendaway card is not included in the complete set price below. The autographed cards are valued at 25 to 50 times the prices listed below. Promo versions of all cards in the set are known to exist; they bear a circle-shaped disclaimer reading "Sample Not For Sale" on their back. Single promo cards were given out at the 1991 San Francisco Labor Day show. These promo versions are valued at four times the regualr issue values.

	MINT	NRMT	EXC
COMPLETE SET (20)	90.00	40.00	11.50
COMMON CARD (S1-S20)	2.00	.90	.25
☐ S1 Joe Smith	12.00	5.50	1.50
☐ S2 Antonio McDyess	8.00	3.60	1.00
☐ S3 Rasheed Wallace	8.00	3.60	1.00
☐ S4 Kevin Garnett	8.00	3.60	1.00
☐ S5 Shawn Respert	6.00	2.70	.75
☐ S6 Kurt Thomas	6.00	2.70	.75
☐ S7 Gary Trent	6.00	2.70	.75
☐ S8 Cherokee Parks	6.00	2.70	.75
☐ S9 Eric Williams	5.00	2.30	.60
☐ S10 Jerry Stackhouse	15.00	6.75	1.90
☐ S11 Travis Best	4.00	1.80	.50
☐ S12 Michael Finley	4.00	1.80	.50
☐ S13 George Zidek	3.00	1.35	.40

	MINT	NRMT	EXC
COMP. SEALED SET (45)	4.00	1.80	.50
COMMON CARD (1-45)	.04	.02	.01
COMMON NBA CARD	.10	.05	.01
COMMON AUTOGRAPH	10.00	4.50	1.25

☐ 1 Larry Johnson .... .40 .18 .05
First Draft Pick
UNLV
☐ 2 George Ackles .... .04 .02 .01
UNLV
☐ 3 Kenny Anderson .... .75 .35 .09
Georgia Tech
☐ 4 Greg Anthony .... .25 .11 .03
UNLV
☐ 5 Anthony Avent .... .04 .02 .01
Seton Hall
☐ 6 Terrell Brandon .... .25 .11 .03
Oregon
☐ 7 Kevin Brooks .... .04 .02 .01
Southwestern Louisiana
☐ 8 Marc Brown .... .04 .02 .01
Siena
☐ 9 Myron Brown .... .04 .02 .01
Slippery Rock
☐ 10 Randy Brown .... .04 .02 .01
New Mexico State
☐ 11 Darrin Chancellor .... .04 .02 .01
Southern Mississippi
☐ 12 Pete Chilcutt .... .10 .05 .01
North Carolina
☐ 13 Chris Corchiani .... .04 .02 .01
North Carolina State
☐ 14 John Crotty .... .04 .02 .01
Virginia
☐ 15 Dale Davis .... .40 .18 .05
Clemson
☐ 16 Marty Dow .... .04 .02 .01
San Diego State
☐ 17 Richard Dumas .... .10 .05 .01
Oklahoma State
☐ 18 LeRon Ellis .... .04 .02 .01
Syracuse
☐ 19 Tony Farmer .... .04 .02 .01
Nebraska
☐ 20 Roy Fisher .... .04 .02 .01
California
☐ 21 Rick Fox .... .10 .05 .01
North Carolina
☐ 22 Chad Gallagher .... .04 .02 .01
Creighton
☐ 23 Chris Gatling .... .20 .09 .03
Old Dominion
☐ 24 Sean Green .... .04 .02 .01
Iona
☐ 25 Reggie Hanson .... .04 .02 .01
Kentucky
☐ 26 Donald Hodge .... .04 .02 .01
Temple
☐ 27 Steve Hood .... .04 .02 .01
James Madison
☐ 28 Keith Hughes .... .04 .02 .01
Rutgers
☐ 29 Mike Iuzzolino .... .04 .02 .01
St.Francis
☐ 30 Keith Jennings .... .04 .02 .01
East Tenn. State
☐ 31 Larry Johnson .... 1.50 .65 .19
UNLV
☐ 32 Treg Lee .... .04 .02 .01
Ohio State
☐ 33 Cedric Lewis .... .04 .02 .01
Maryland
☐ 34 Kevin Lynch .... .04 .02 .01
Minnesota
☐ 35 Mark Macon .... .04 .02 .01
Temple

☐ 36 Jason Matthews .... .04 .02 .01
Pittsburgh
☐ 37 Eric Murdock .... .25 .11 .03
Providence
☐ 38 Jimmy Oliver .... .04 .02 .01
Purdue
☐ 39 Doug Overton .... .04 .02 .01
LaSalle
☐ 40 Elliot Perry .... .30 .14 .04
Memphis State
☐ 41 Brian Shorter .... .04 .02 .01
Pittsburgh
☐ 42 Alvaro Teheran .... .04 .02 .01
Houston
☐ 43 Joey Wright .... .04 .02 .01
Texas
☐ 44 Joe Wylie .... .04 .02 .01
Miami (FL)
☐ 45 Larry Johnson .... .40 .18 .05
Collegiate Player
of the Year
☐ NNO Larry Johnson SP ..... 4.00 1.80 .50
(Sendaway)

1991 Front Row Italian/English 100

The 1991 Front Row Italian/English Basketball Draft Pick set contains 100 cards measuring standard size (2 1/2" by 3 1/2"). Each factory set comes with an official certificate of authenticity that bears a unique serial number. This set is distinguished from the American version by length (100 instead of 50 cards), different production quantities (30,000 factory sets and 3,000 wax cases), and a red stripe on the card front. The front design features glossy color action player photos with white borders. The player's name appears in a red stripe beneath the picture. The backs have different smaller color photos (upper right corner) as well as biography, college statistics, and achievements superimposed on a gray background with an orange basketball. The set also includes a second (career highlights) card of some players (39-43), a subset devoted to Larry Johnson (44-49), and two "Retrospect" cards (96-97). The cards are numbered on the back.

500 / 1991 Front Row Italian/English 100

		MINT	NRMT	EXC
	COMPLETE SET (100)	5.00	2.00	.50
	COMMON CARD (1-50)	.04	.02	.00
	COMMON CARD (51-100)	.04	.02	.00
☐ 1	Larry Johnson UNLV	1.50	.60	.15
☐ 2	Kenny Anderson Georgia Tech	.75	.30	.07
☐ 3	Rick Fox North Carolina	.40	.12	.03
☐ 4	Pete Chilcutt North Carolina	.15	.06	.01
☐ 5	George Ackles UNLV	.07	.03	.01
☐ 6	Mark Macon Temple	.10	.04	.01
☐ 7	Greg Anthony UNLV	.15	.06	.01
☐ 8	Mike Iuzzolino St. Francis	.07	.03	.01
☐ 9	Anthony Avent Seton Hall	.15	.06	.01
☐ 10	Terrell Brandon Oregon	.20	.08	.02
☐ 11	Kevin Brooks SW Louisiana	.07	.03	.01
☐ 12	Myron Brown Slippery Rock	.07	.03	.01
☐ 13	Chris Corchiani North Carolina State	.10	.04	.01
☐ 14	Chris Gatling Old Dominion	.15	.06	.01
☐ 15	Marcus Kennedy Eastern Michigan	.04	.02	.00
☐ 16	Eric Murdock Providence	.35	.14	.03
☐ 17	Tony Farmer Nebraska	.04	.02	.00
☐ 18	Keith Hughes Rutgers	.04	.02	.00
☐ 19	Kevin Lynch Minnesota	.07	.03	.01
☐ 20	Chad Gallagher Creighton	.04	.02	.00
☐ 21	Darrin Chancellor Southern Mississippi	.04	.02	.00
☐ 22	Jimmy Oliver Purdue	.04	.02	.00
☐ 23	Von McDade Wisconsin-Milwaukee	.04	.02	.00
☐ 24	Donald Hodge Temple	.07	.03	.01
☐ 25	Randy Brown New Mexico State	.10	.04	.01
☐ 26	Doug Overton LaSalle	.10	.04	.01
☐ 27	LeRon Ellis Syracuse	.10	.04	.01
☐ 28	Sean Green Iona	.07	.03	.01
☐ 29	Elliot Perry Memphis State	.07	.03	.01
☐ 30	Richard Dumas Oklahoma State	.10	.04	.01
☐ 31	Dale Davis Clemson	.40	.16	.04
☐ 32	Lamont Strothers Christopher Newport	.07	.03	.01
☐ 33	Steve Hood James Madison	.04	.02	.00
☐ 34	Joey Wright Texas	.04	.02	.00
☐ 35	Patrick Eddie Mississippi	.04	.02	.00
☐ 36	Joe Wylie Miami	.04	.02	.00
☐ 37	Bobby Phills Southern	.15	.06	.01
☐ 38	Alvaro Teheran Houston	.04	.02	.00
☐ 39	Dale Davis Career Highlights	.20	.08	.02
☐ 40	Rick Fox Career Highlights	.15	.06	.01
☐ 41	Terrell Brandon Career Highlights	.10	.04	.01
☐ 42	Greg Anthony Career Highlights	.07	.03	.01
☐ 43	Mark Macon Career Highlights	.07	.03	.01
☐ 44	Larry Johnson Career Highlights	.40	.20	.05
☐ 45	Larry Johnson First in the Nation	.40	.20	.05
☐ 46	Larry Johnson Power	.40	.20	.05
☐ 47	Larry Johnson A Class Act	.40	.20	.05
☐ 48	Larry Johnson Flashback	.40	.20	.05
☐ 49	Larry Johnson Up Close and Personal	.40	.20	.05
☐ 50A	Bonus Card	.50	.20	.05
☐ 50B	Marty Conlon Providence	.10	.04	.01
☐ 51	Mike Goodson Pittsburgh	.04	.02	.00
☐ 52	Drexel Deveaux Tampa	.04	.02	.00
☐ 53	Sean Muto St. John's	.04	.02	.00
☐ 54	Keith Owens UCLA	.04	.02	.00
☐ 55	Joao Viana Nassuna	.04	.02	.00
☐ 56	Chancellor Nichols James Madison	.04	.02	.00
☐ 57	Charles Thomas Eastern Michigan	.04	.02	.00
☐ 58	Carl Thomas Eastern Michigan	.04	.02	.00
☐ 59	Anthony Blakley Panhandle State	.04	.02	.00
☐ 60	Demetrius Calip Michigan	.04	.02	.00
☐ 61	Dale Turnquist Bethel College	.04	.02	.00
☐ 62	Carlos Funchess Northeast Louisiana	.04	.02	.00
☐ 63	Tharon Mayes Florida State	.04	.02	.00
☐ 64	Andy Kennedy Alabama - Birmingham	.04	.02	.00
☐ 65	Oliver Taylor Seton Hall	.04	.02	.00
☐ 66	David Benoit Alabama	.20	.08	.02
☐ 67	Gary Waites Alabama	.04	.02	.00
☐ 68	Corey Crowder Kentucky Wesleyan	.04	.02	.00

			MINT	NRMT	EXC
☐	69	Sydney Grider Southwestern Louisiana	.04	.02	.00
☐	70	Derek Strong Xavier	.07	.03	.01
☐	71	Larry Stewart Coppin State	.10	.04	.01
☐	72	Matt Roe Maryland	.04	.02	.00
☐	73	Cedric Lewis Maryland	.04	.02	.00
☐	74	Anthony Houston St. Mary's	.04	.02	.00
☐	75	Steve Bardo Illinois	.04	.02	.00
☐	76	Marc Brown Siena	.04	.02	.00
☐	77	Michael Cutright McNeese State	.04	.02	.00
☐	78	Emanuel Davis Deleware State	.04	.02	.00
☐	79	Paris McCurdy Ball State	.04	.02	.00
☐	80	Jackie Jones Oklahoma State	.04	.02	.00
☐	81	Mark Peterson Rutgers	.04	.02	.00
☐	82	Clifford Scales Nebraska	.04	.02	.00
☐	83	Robert Pack USC	.25	.10	.02
☐	84	Doug Lee Purdue	.04	.02	.00
☐	85	Cameron Burns Mississippi State	.04	.02	.00
☐	86	Tom Copa Marquette	.04	.02	.00
☐	87	Clinton Venable Bowling Green State	.04	.02	.00
☐	88	Ken Redfield Michigan State	.04	.02	.00
☐	89	Melvin Newbern Minnesota	.04	.02	.00
☐	90	Darren Henrie David Lipscomb	.04	.02	.00
☐	91	Chris Harris Illinois (Chicago)	.04	.02	.00
☐	92	John Crotty Virginia	.10	.04	.01
☐	93	Paul Graham Ohio	.10	.04	.01
☐	94	Stevie Thompson Syracuse	.04	.02	.00
☐	95	Clifford Martin Idaho	.04	.02	.00
☐	96	Brian Shaw UC Santa Barbara	.07	.03	.01
☐	97	Danny Ferry Duke	.07	.03	.01
☐	98	Doug Loescher	.04	.02	.00
☐	99	Checklist	.04	.02	.00
☐	100	Bonus Card	.50	.20	.05

1991 Front Row Update

Comprising of 50 standard size cards, the update version is a continuation (51-100) of

the 50-card Draft Pick set. The checklist to the Draft Pick is identical (with identical values) tot he first 50 cards of the Italian/Englisg 100 version. Each set was accompanied by a certificate of authenticity that bears a unique serial number, with the production run reported to be 50,000 sets. The fronts feature glossy color action player photos enclosed by white borders. A basketball backboard and rim with the words "Update 92" appears in the lower left corner, with the player's name and position in a dark green stripe beneath the picture. On a gray background with an orange basketball, the backs carry biography, color close-up photo, statistics, and achievements. The cards are numbered on the back. Gold versions of the cards are valued at three times the values below; silver versions of the cards are valued at two times the values below.

			MINT	NRMT	EXC
		COMPLETE SET (50)	3.00	1.35	.40
		COMMON CARD (51-100)	.04	.02	.01
		COMMON NBA CARD	.10	.05	.01
		*GOLD: 3X VALUE			
		*SILVER: 2X VALUE			
☐	51	Billy Owens Syracuse	.50	.23	.06
☐	52	Dikembe Mutombo Georgetown	.75	.35	.09
☐	53	Steve Smith Michigan State	.50	.23	.06
☐	54	Luc Longley New Mexico	.10	.05	.01
☐	55	Doug Smith Missouri	.04	.02	.01
☐	56	Stacey Augmon UNLV	.40	.18	.05
☐	57	Brian Williams Arizona	.10	.05	.01
☐	58	Stanley Roberts LSU	.10	.05	.01
☐	59	Rodney Monroe North Carolina State	.04	.02	.01
☐	60	Isaac Austin Arizona State	.04	.02	.01
☐	61	Rich King Nebraska	.04	.02	.01
☐	62	Victor Alexander Iowa State	.10	.05	.01
☐	63	LaBradford Smith Louisville	.04	.02	.01
☐	64	Greg Sutton Oklahoma City	.04	.02	.01

		MINT	NRMT	EXC
☐ 65	John Turner .... .04	.02	.01
	Phillips		
☐ 66	Joao Viana .... .04	.02	.01
	Nassuna		
☐ 67	Charles Thomas .... .04	.02	.01
	Eastern Michigan		
☐ 68	Carl Thomas .... .04	.02	.01
	Eastern Michigan		
☐ 69	Tharon Mayes .... .04	.02	.01
	Florida State		
☐ 70	David Benoit .... .20	.09	.03
	Alabama		
☐ 71	Corey Crowder .... .04	.02	.01
	Kentucky Wesleyan		
☐ 72	Larry Stewart .... .04	.02	.01
	Coppin State		
☐ 73	Steve Bardo .... .04	.02	.01
	Illinois		
☐ 74	Paris McCurdy .... .04	.02	.01
	Ball State		
☐ 75	Robert Pack .... .30	.14	.04
	USC		
☐ 76	Doug Lee .... .04	.02	.01
	Purdue		
☐ 77	Tom Copa .... .04	.02	.01
	Marquette		
☐ 78	Keith Owens .... .04	.02	.01
	UCLA		
☐ 79	Mike Goodson .... .04	.02	.01
	Pittsburgh		
☐ 80	John Crotty .... .04	.02	.01
	Virginia		
☐ 81	Sean Muto .... .04	.02	.01
	St. John's		
☐ 82	Chancellor Nichols .... .04	.02	.01
	James Madison		
☐ 83	Stevie Thompson .... .04	.02	.01
	Syracuse		
☐ 84	Demetrius Calip .... .04	.02	.01
	Michigan		
☐ 85	Clifford Martin .... .04	.02	.01
	Idaho		
☐ 86	Andy Kennedy .... .04	.02	.01
	Alabama (Birmingham)		
☐ 87	Oliver Taylor .... .04	.02	.01
	Seton Hall		
☐ 88	Gary Waites .... .04	.02	.01
	Alabama		
☐ 89	Matt Roe .... .04	.02	.01
	Maryland		
☐ 90	Cedric Lewis .... .04	.02	.01
	Maryland		
☐ 91	Emanuel Davis .... .04	.02	.01
	Deleware State		
☐ 92	Jackie Jones .... .04	.02	.01
	Oklahoma		
☐ 93	Clifford Scales............... .04	.02	.01
	Nebraska		
☐ 94	Cameron Burns.............. .04	.02	.01
	Mississippi State		
☐ 95	Clinton Venable.............. .04	.02	.01
	Bowling Green		
☐ 96	Ken Redfield .... .04	.02	.01
	Michigan State		
☐ 97	Melvin Newbern .... .04	.02	.01
	Minnesota		
☐ 98	Chris Harris................... .04	.02	.01
	Illinois (Chicago)		
☐ 99	Bonus Card .... .04	.02	.01
☐ 100	Checklist...................... .04	.02	.01

1991-92 Front Row Premier

The 1991-92 Front Row Premier set contains 120 standard-size (2 1/2" by 3 1/2") cards. No factory sets were made, and the production run was limited to 2,500 waxbox cases, with 360 cards per box. The set included five bonus cards (86, 88, 90, 91, 93) that were redeemable through a mail-in offer for unnamed player cards. Moreover, limited edition cards as well as gold, silver, and autographed cards were randomly inserted in the wax packs. The glossy color player photos on the fronts are enclosed by borders with different shades of white and blue. The player's name appears in a silver stripe beneath the picture. The backs have biography, statistics, and achievements superimposed on an orange basketball icon. The cards are numbered on the back.

		MINT	NRMT	EXC
COMPLETE SET (120)		8.00	3.25	.80
COMMON CARD (1-120)		.04	.02	.00
☐ 1	Rich King .... .10	.04	.01
	Nebraska		
☐ 2	Kenny Anderson .... .75	.30	.07
	Georgia Tech		
☐ 3	Billy Owens ACC .... .15	.06	.01
	Syracuse		
☐ 4	Ken Redfield .... .04	.02	.00
	Michigan State		
☐ 5	Robert Pack .... .25	.10	.02
	USC		
☐ 6	Clinton Venable .... .04	.02	.00
	Bowling Green		
☐ 7	Tom Copa .... .04	.02	.00
	Marquette		
☐ 8	Rick Fox HL .... .10	.04	.01
	North Carolina		
☐ 9	Cameron Burns............... .04	.02	.00
	Mississippi State		
☐ 10	Doug Lee .... .04	.02	.00
	Purdue		
☐ 11	LaBradford Smith .... .07	.03	.01
	Louisville		
☐ 12	Clifford Scales................ .04	.02	.00
	Nebraska		
☐ 13	Mark Peterson .... .04	.02	.00
	Rutgers		
☐ 14	Jackie Jones .... .04	.02	.00

☐ 15	Paris McCurdy .... Oklahoma Ball State	.04	.02	.00
☐ 16	Dikembe Mutombo ACC. Georgetown	.25	.10	.02
☐ 17	Emanuel Davis .... Delaware State	.04	.02	.00
☐ 18	Michael Cutright .... McNeese State	.04	.02	.00
☐ 19	Marc Brown .... Siena	.04	.02	.00
☐ 20	Steve Bardo .... Illinois	.04	.02	.00
☐ 21	John Turner .... Phillips	.04	.02	.00
☐ 22	Anthony Houston .... St. Mary's	.04	.02	.00
☐ 23	Cedric Lewis .... Maryland	.04	.02	.00
☐ 24	Matt Roe .... Maryland	.04	.02	.00
☐ 25	Larry Stewart .... Coppin State	.10	.04	.01
☐ 26	Derek Strong .... Xavier	.07	.03	.01
☐ 27	Sydney Grider .... Southwestern Louisiana	.04	.02	.00
☐ 28	Corey Crowder .... Kentucky Wesleyan	.04	.02	.00
☐ 29	Gary Waites .... Alabama	.04	.02	.00
☐ 30	David Benoit .... Alabama	.20	.08	.02
☐ 31	Larry Johnson ACC .... UNLV	.40	.16	.04
☐ 32	Oliver Taylor UER .... Seton Hall (Chris Corchiani's name on back)	.04	.02	.00
☐ 33	Andy Kennedy .... Alabama-Birmingham	.04	.02	.00
☐ 34	Tharon Mayes .... Florida State	.04	.02	.00
☐ 35	Carlos Funchess .... Northeast Louisiana	.04	.02	.00
☐ 36	Dale Turnquist .... Bethel	.04	.02	.00
☐ 37	Luc Longley .... New Mexico	.20	.08	.02
☐ 38	Demetrius Calip .... Michigan	.04	.02	.00
☐ 39	Anthony Blakley .... Panhandle State	.04	.02	.00
☐ 40	Carl Thomas .... Eastern Michigan	.04	.02	.00
☐ 41	Charles Thomas .... Eastern Michigan	.04	.02	.00
☐ 42	Chancellor Nichols .... James Madison	.04	.02	.00
☐ 43	Joao Viana .... Nassuna	.04	.02	.00
☐ 44	Keith Owens .... UCLA	.04	.02	.00
☐ 45	Sean Muto .... St. Johns	.04	.02	.00
☐ 46	Drexel Deveaux .... Tampa	.04	.02	.00
☐ 47	Stacey Augmon ACC .... UNLV	.15	.06	.01
☐ 48	Mike Goodson .... Pittsburgh	.04	.02	.00
☐ 49	Marty Conlon .... Providence	.07	.03	.01
☐ 50	Mark Macon .... Temple	.10	.04	.01
☐ 51	Greg Anthony .... UNLV	.15	.06	.01
☐ 52	Dale Davis .... Clemson	.40	.16	.04
☐ 53	Isaac Austin .... Arizona State	.04	.02	.00
☐ 54	Alvaro Teheran .... Houston	.04	.02	.00
☐ 55	Bobby Phills .... Southern	.15	.06	.01
☐ 56	Joe Wylie .... Miami	.04	.02	.00
☐ 57	Patrick Eddie .... Mississippi	.04	.02	.00
☐ 58	Joey Wright .... Texas	.04	.02	.00
☐ 59	Steve Hood .... James Maidson	.04	.02	.00
☐ 60	Lamont Strothers .... Christopher Newport	.07	.03	.01
☐ 61	Victor Alexander .... Iowa State	.15	.06	.01
☐ 62	Richard Dumas .... Oklahoma State	.10	.04	.01
☐ 63	Elliot Perry .... Memphis State	.07	.03	.01
☐ 64	Sean Green .... Iona	.07	.03	.01
☐ 65	Rick Fox .... North Carolina	.40	.12	.03
☐ 66	LeRon Ellis .... Syracuse	.10	.04	.01
☐ 67	Doug Overton .... LaSalle	.10	.04	.01
☐ 68	Randy Brown .... New Mexico State	.10	.04	.01
☐ 69	Donald Hodge .... Temple	.07	.03	.01
☐ 70	Von McDade .... Wisconsin-Milwaukee	.04	.02	.00
☐ 71	Greg Sutton .... Oral Roberts	.04	.02	.00
☐ 72	Jimmy Oliver .... Purdue	.04	.02	.00
☐ 73	Terrell Brandon HL .... Oregon	.10	.04	.01
☐ 74	Darrin Chancellor .... Southern Mississippi	.04	.02	.00
☐ 75	Chad Gallagher .... Creighton	.04	.02	.00
☐ 76	Kevin Lynch .... Minnesota	.07	.03	.01
☐ 77	Keith Hughes .... Rutgers	.04	.02	.00
☐ 78	Tony Farmer .... Nebraska	.04	.02	.00
☐ 79	Eric Murdock .... Providence	.35	.14	.03
☐ 80	Marcus Kennedy .... Eastern Michigan	.04	.02	.00
☐ 81	Larry Johnson .... UNLV	1.50	.60	.15
☐ 82	Stacey Augmon .... UNLV	.50	.20	.05
☐ 83	Dikembe Mutombo .... Georgetown	.75	.30	.07
☐ 84	Steve Smith	.60	.20	.05

☐ 85	Billy Owens UER .... Michigan State Syracuse	.50	.20	.05
☐ 86	Bonus Card 1 .... Stanley Roberts LSU	.15	.06	.01
☐ 87	Brian Shaw .... UC Santa Barbara	.07	.03	.01
☐ 88	Bonus Card 2 .... Rodney Monroe North Carolina State	.15	.06	.01
☐ 89	LaBradford Smith HL ..... Louisville	.07	.03	.01
☐ 90	Bonus Card 3 .... Mark Randall Kansas	.15	.06	.01
☐ 91	Bonus Card 4 .... Brian Williams Arizona	.15	.06	.01
☐ 92	Danny Ferry FLB .... Duke	.07	.03	.01
☐ 93	Bonus Card 5 .... Shawn Vandiver Colorado	.15	.06	.01
☐ 94	Doug Smith HL .... Missouri	.07	.03	.01
☐ 95	Luc Longley HL .... New Mexico	.10	.04	.01
☐ 96	Billy Owens HL .... Syracuse	.15	.06	.01
☐ 97	Steve Smith HL .... Michigan State	.20	.06	.01
☐ 98	Dikembe Mutombo HL .... Georgetown	.25	.10	.02
☐ 99	Stacey Augmon HL .... UNLV	.15	.06	.01
☐ 100	Larry Johnson HL .... UNLV	.40	.16	.04
☐ 101	Chris Gatling .... Old Dominion	.15	.06	.01
☐ 102	Chris Corchiani .... North Carolina State	.10	.04	.01
☐ 103	Myron Brown .... Slippery Rock	.07	.03	.01
☐ 104	Kevin Brooks .... Southwestern Louisiana	.07	.03	.01
☐ 105	Anthony Avent .... Seton Hall	.15	.06	.01
☐ 106	Steve Smith ACC .... Michigan State	.20	.06	.01
☐ 107	Mike Iuzzolino .... Saint Francis	.07	.03	.01
☐ 108	George Ackles .... UNLV	.07	.03	.01
☐ 109	Melvin Newbern .... Minnesota	.04	.02	.00
☐ 110	Robert Pack HL .... USC	.10	.04	.01
☐ 111	Darren Henrie .... David Lipscomb	.04	.02	.00
☐ 112	Chris Harris .... Illinois-Chicago	.04	.02	.00
☐ 113	John Crotty .... Virginia	.10	.04	.01
☐ 114	Terrell Brandon .... Oregon	.20	.08	.02
☐ 115	Paul Graham .... Ohio	.10	.04	.01
☐ 116	Stevie Thompson .... Syracuse	.04	.02	.00
☐ 117	Clifford Martin	.04	.02	.00

☐ 118	Doug Smith .... Idaho Missouri	.15	.06	.01
☐ 119	Pete Chilcutt .... North Carolina	.15	.06	.01
☐ 120	Checklist Card	.07	.03	.01

1992 Front Row Draft Picks

The 1992 Front Row Draft Picks basketball set consists of 100 standard-size (2 1/2" by 3 1/2") cards. The set was sold in a card-board box, and the back panel carries the set serial number and total production run (150,000). The fronts feature color action player photos. Teal borders shading from dark to light surround the pictures. A gra-dated orange vertical bar containing the player's name is superimposed over one side of the photo. The Front Row Draft Picks logo appears below it. The miniature representation of the team mascot appears in the lower left corner. The horizontal backs display biography, collegiate statis-tics, and career highlights on a teal back-ground with white borders. An orange bar similar to the one on the front runs down the right edge and contains the words "Draft Picks '92". Four cards (90, 92, 96, and 99) have player photos instead of text on their backs. The cards are numbered on the back. Gold versions of the cards are valued at four times the values below; silver versions of the cards are valued at two times the values below.

	MINT	NRMT	EXC
COMPLETE SET (100)	8.00	3.60	1.00
COMMON CARD (1-100)	.04	.02	.01
COMMON NBA CARD	.10	.05	.01
*GOLD: 4X VALUE			
*SILVER: 2X VALUE			

☐ 1	Eric Anderson .... Indiana	.04	.02	.01
☐ 2	Darin Archbold .... Butler	.04	.02	.01
☐ 3	Woody Austin .... Purdue	.04	.02	.01
☐ 4	Mark Baker	.10	.05	.01

Ohio State				
☐ 5 Jon Barry	.04	.02	.01	
Georgia Tech				
☐ 6 Elmer Bennett	.04	.02	.01	
Notre Dame				
☐ 7 Tony Bennett	.04	.02	.01	
Wisconsin-Green Bay				
☐ 8 Alex Blackwell	.04	.02	.01	
Monmouth				
☐ 9 Curtis Blair	.04	.02	.01	
Richmond				
☐ 10 Ed Book	.04	.02	.01	
Canisius				
☐ 11 Marques Bragg	.04	.02	.01	
Providence				
☐ 12 P.J. Brown	.10	.05	.01	
Louisiana Tech				
☐ 13 Anthony Buford	.04	.02	.01	
Cincinnati				
☐ 14 Dexter Cambridge	.04	.02	.01	
Texas				
☐ 15 Brian Davis	.04	.02	.01	
Duke				
☐ 16 Lucius Davis	.04	.02	.01	
UC Santa Barbara				
☐ 17 Todd Day	.40	.18	.05	
Arkansas				
☐ 18 Greg Dennis	.04	.02	.01	
East Tennessee State				
☐ 19 Radenko Dobras	.04	.02	.01	
South Florida				
☐ 20 Harold Ellis	.04	.02	.01	
Morehouse				
☐ 21 Chris King	.04	.02	.01	
Wake Forest				
☐ 22 Jo Jo English	.04	.02	.01	
South Carolina				
☐ 23 Deron Feldhaus	.04	.02	.01	
Kentucky				
☐ 24 Matt Geiger	.10	.05	.01	
Georgia Tech				
☐ 25 Lewis Geter	.04	.02	.01	
Ohio University				
☐ 26 George Gilmore	.04	.02	.01	
Chaminade				
☐ 27 Litterial Green	.04	.02	.01	
Georgia				
☐ 28 Tom Gugliotta	.75	.35	.09	
North Carolina State				
☐ 29 Jim Havrilla	.04	.02	.01	
Western Michigan				
☐ 30 Robert Horry	1.00	.45	.13	
Alabama				
☐ 31 Stephen Howard	.04	.02	.01	
DePaul				
☐ 32 Alonzo Jamison	.04	.02	.01	
Kansas				
☐ 33 David Johnson	.04	.02	.01	
Syracuse				
☐ 34 Herb Jones	.04	.02	.01	
Cincinnati				
☐ 35 Popeye Jones	.20	.09	.03	
Murray State				
☐ 36 Adam Keefe	.10	.05	.01	
Stanford				
☐ 37 Dan Cyrulik	.04	.02	.01	
Connecticut				
☐ 38 Ken Leeks	.04	.02	.01	
Central Florida				
☐ 39 Ricardo Leonard	.04	.02	.01	
Old Dominion				

☐ 40 Gerald Madkins	.04	.02	.01	
UCLA				
☐ 41 Eric Manuel	.04	.02	.01	
Oklahoma City				
☐ 42 Marlon Maxey	.04	.02	.01	
UTEP				
☐ 43 Jim McCoy	.04	.02	.01	
Massachusetts				
☐ 44 Oliver Miller	.15	.07	.02	
Arkansas				
☐ 45 Sean Miller	.04	.02	.01	
Pittsburgh				
☐ 46 Darren Morningstar	.04	.02	.01	
Pittsburgh				
☐ 47 Isaiah Morris	.04	.02	.01	
Arkansas				
☐ 48 James Moses	.04	.02	.01	
Iowa				
☐ 49 Doug Christie	.10	.05	.01	
Pepperdine				
☐ 50 Damon Patterson	.04	.02	.01	
Oklahoma				
☐ 51 John Pelphrey	.04	.02	.01	
Kentucky				
☐ 52 Brent Price	.04	.02	.01	
Oklahoma				
☐ 53 Brett Roberts	.04	.02	.01	
Morehead State				
☐ 54 Steve Rogers	.04	.02	.01	
Alabama State				
☐ 55 Sean Rooks	.10	.05	.01	
Arizona				
☐ 56 Malik Sealy	.30	.14	.04	
St. John's				
☐ 57 Tom Schurfranz	.04	.02	.01	
Bellarmine Kentucky				
☐ 58 David Scott	.04	.02	.01	
Miami (Ohio)				
☐ 59 Rod Sellers	.04	.02	.01	
Connecticut				
☐ 60 Vernel Singleton	.04	.02	.01	
LSU				
☐ 61 Reggie Slater	.04	.02	.01	
Wyoming				
☐ 62 Elmore Spencer	.10	.05	.01	
UNLV				
☐ 63 Chris Smith	.10	.05	.01	
Connecticut				
☐ 64 Latrell Sprewell	1.25	.55	.16	
Alabama				
☐ 65 Matt Steigenga	.04	.02	.01	
Michigan State				
☐ 66 Bryant Stith	.30	.14	.04	
Virginia				
☐ 67 Daimon Sweet	.04	.02	.01	
Notre Dame				
☐ 68 Craig Upchurch	.04	.02	.01	
Houston				
☐ 69 Van Usher	.04	.02	.01	
Tennessee Tech				
☐ 70 Tony Watts	.04	.02	.01	
Mississippi State				
☐ 71 Clarence Weatherspoon	.75	.35	.09	
Southern Mississippi				
☐ 72 Robert Werdann	.04	.02	.01	
St. John's				
☐ 73 Benford Williams	.04	.02	.01	
Texas				
☐ 74 Corey Williams	.04	.02	.01	
Oklahoma State				
☐ 75 Henry Williams	.04	.02	.01	

UNC-Charlotte

			MINT	NRMT	EXC
☐ 76	Tim Burroughs	.04	.02	.01	
	Jacksonville Florida				
☐ 77	Erik Wilson	.04	.02	.01	
	Virginia Tech				
☐ 78	Randy Woods	.04	.02	.01	
	LaSalle				
☐ 79	Kendall Youngblood	.04	.02	.01	
	Utah State				
☐ 80	Terry Boyd	.04	.02	.01	
	Western Carolina				
☐ 81	Tracy Murray	.10	.05	.01	
	UCLA				
☐ 82	Reggie Smith	.04	.02	.01	
	Texas Christian				
☐ 83	Lee Mayberry	.10	.05	.01	
	Arkansas				
☐ 84	Matt Fish	.04	.02	.01	
	UNC Wilmington				
☐ 85	Hubert Davis	.10	.05	.01	
	North Carolina				
☐ 86	Duane Cooper	.04	.02	.01	
	USC				
☐ 87	Anthony Peeler	.10	.05	.01	
	Missouri				
☐ 88	Harold Miner	.20	.09	.03	
	USC				
☐ 89	Harold Miner	.04	.02	.01	
	"Miner on Dunking"				
	USC				
☐ 90	Harold Miner	.04	.02	.01	
	(Action on both sides)				
	USC				
☐ 91	Christian Laettner	.60	.25	.08	
	Duke				
☐ 92	Christian Laettner	.20	.09	.03	
	(Action shot on				
	front, portrait on back)				
	Duke				
☐ 93	Christian Laettner	.20	.09	.03	
	and Brian Davis				
	Duke				
	"A Devilish Duo"				
☐ 94	Walt Williams	.50	.23	.06	
	Maryland				
☐ 95	Walt Williams	.15	.07	.02	
	"ACC Terror"				
	Maryland				
☐ 96	Walt Williams	.15	.07	.02	
	(Action shot on				
	front, portrait on back)				
	Maryland				
☐ 97	LaPhonso Ellis	.25	.11	.03	
	Notre Dame				
☐ 98	LaPhonso Ellis	.10	.05	.01	
	"The Ellis File"				
	Notre Dame				
☐ 99	Laphonso Ellis	.10	.05	.01	
	(Action shot on				
	front, portrait on back)				
	Notre Dame				
☐ 100	Checklist 1-100	.04	.02	.01	

1992 Front Row Dream Picks

The 1992 Front Row Dream Picks basketball set contains 100 cards measuring the

standard size (2 1/2" by 3 1/2"). The set
features five cards each of the top ten players who signed with Front Row from the
1991 NBA Draft and five cards of the top
ten from the 1992 draft. The fronts display
color action player photos bordered in purple. The player's name appears above the
picture in a yellow bar accented by a red
shadow border. The Front Row logo
appears at the lower right corner in an
orange diagonal stripe. The backs are pre-
dominantly yellow and present career summary and highlights. The words "Dream
Picks" appear in an orange diagonal stripe
on the back. The fifth card of each five-card
set has a second color player photo on its
back. The cards are numbered on the back.
Gold versions of the cards are valued at
three times the values below; silver versions of the cards are valued at two times
the values below.

			MINT	NRMT	EXC
COMPLETE SET (100)		8.00	3.25	.80	
COMMON CARD (1-100)		.04	.02	.00	
☐ 1	Larry Johnson	.50	.20	.05	
	UNLV				
	College Stats				
☐ 2	Larry Johnson	.40	.16	.04	
	Career Highlights				
☐ 3	Larry Johnson	.40	.16	.04	
	NBA All-Rookie Team				
☐ 4	Larry Johnson	.40	.16	.04	
	NBA Rookie of the Year				
☐ 5	Larry Johnson	.40	.16	.04	
☐ 6	Dikembe Mutombo	.20	.08	.02	
	Georgetown				
	College Stats				
☐ 7	Dikembe Mutombo	.20	.08	.02	
	Career Highlights				
☐ 8	Dikembe Mutombo	.20	.08	.02	
	NBA All-Rookie Team				
☐ 9	Dikembe Mutombo	.20	.08	.02	
	NBA All-Star				
☐ 10	Dikembe Mutombo	.20	.08	.02	
☐ 11	Stacey Augmon	.12	.05	.01	
	UNLV				
	College Stats				
☐ 12	Stacey Augmon	.12	.05	.01	
	Career Highlights				
☐ 13	Stacey Augmon	.12	.05	.01	
	NBA All-Rookie Team				
☐ 14	Stacey Augmon	.12	.05	.01	
	Defensive Specialist				
☐ 15	Stacey Augmon	.12	.05	.01	
☐ 16	Billy Owens	.12	.05	.01	

	Syracuse			
	College Stats			
☐ 17	Billy Owens	.12	.05	.01
	Career Highlights			
☐ 18	Billy Owens	.12	.05	.01
	NBA All-Rookie Team			
☐ 19	Billy Owens	.12	.05	.01
	A Proven Winner			
☐ 20	Billy Owens	.12	.05	.01
☐ 21	Clarence Weatherspoon	.30	.12	.03
	Southern Miss.			
	College Stats			
☐ 22	Clarence Weatherspoon	.30	.12	.03
	Career Highlights			
☐ 23	Clarence Weatherspoon	.30	.12	.03
	NBA Scouting Report			
☐ 24	Clarence Weatherspoon	.30	.12	.03
	Flexible Golden Eagle			
☐ 25	Clarence Weatherspoon	.30	.12	.03
☐ 26	Steve Smith	.15	.05	.01
	Michigan State			
	College Stats			
☐ 27	Steve Smith	.15	.05	.01
	Career Highlights			
☐ 28	Steve Smith	.15	.05	.01
	NBA All-Rookie Team			
☐ 29	Steve Smith	.15	.05	.01
	Withstanding the Heat			
☐ 30	Steve Smith	.15	.05	.01
☐ 31	Larry Stewart	.04	.02	.00
	Coppin State			
	College Stats			
☐ 32	Larry Stewart	.04	.02	.00
	Career Highlights			
☐ 33	Larry Stewart	.04	.02	.00
	NBA All-Rookie Team			
☐ 34	Larry Stewart	.04	.02	.00
	Against the Odds			
☐ 35	Larry Stewart	.04	.02	.00
☐ 36	Rick Fox	.07	.03	.01
	North Carolina			
	College Stats			
☐ 37	Rick Fox	.07	.03	.01
	Career Highlights			
☐ 38	Rick Fox	.07	.03	.01
	NBA All-Rookie Team			
☐ 39	Rick Fox	.07	.03	.01
	Divine Intervention			
☐ 40	Rick Fox	.07	.03	.01
☐ 41	Christian Laettner	.20	.08	.02
	Duke			
	College Stats			
☐ 42	Christian Laettner	.20	.08	.02
	Career Highlights			
☐ 43	Christian Laettner	.20	.08	.02
	NBA Scouting Report			
☐ 44	Christian Laettner	.20	.08	.02
	Championship Season			
☐ 45	Christian Laettner	.20	.08	.02
☐ 46	Bryant Stith	.07	.03	.01
	Virginia			
	College Stats			
☐ 47	Bryant Stith	.07	.03	.01
	Career Highlights			
☐ 48	Bryant Stith	.07	.03	.01
	NBA Scouting Report			
☐ 49	Bryant Stith	.07	.03	.01
	A Change in Perspective			
☐ 50	Bryant Stith	.07	.03	.01
☐ 51	Harold Miner	.12	.05	.01
	USC			

	College Stats			
☐ 52	Harold Miner	.12	.05	.01
	Career Highlights			
☐ 53	Harold Miner	.12	.05	.01
	NBA Scouting Report			
☐ 54	Harold Miner	1.00	.40	.10
	An Encounter With Michael			
☐ 55	Harold Miner	.12	.05	.01
☐ 56	Mark Macon	.04	.02	.00
	Temple			
	College Stats			
☐ 57	Mark Macon	.04	.02	.00
	Career Highlights			
☐ 58	Mark Macon	.04	.02	.00
	NBA All-Rookie Team			
☐ 59	Mark Macon	.04	.02	.00
	Stealing the Show			
☐ 60	Mark Macon	.04	.02	.00
☐ 61	Adam Keefe	.04	.02	.00
	Stanford			
	College Stats			
☐ 62	Adam Keefe	.04	.02	.00
	Career Highlights			
☐ 63	Adam Keefe	.04	.02	.00
	NBA Scouting Report			
☐ 64	Adam Keefe	.04	.02	.00
	Premier Big Man			
☐ 65	Adam Keefe	.04	.02	.00
☐ 66	Tom Gugliotta	.25	.10	.02
	North Carolina State			
	College Stats			
☐ 67	Tom Gugliotta	.25	.10	.02
	Career Highlights			
☐ 68	Tom Gugliotta	.25	.10	.02
	NBA Scouting Report			
☐ 69	Tom Gugliotta	.25	.10	.02
	Most Improved			
☐ 70	Tom Gugliotta	.25	.10	.02
☐ 71	Todd Day	.10	.04	.01
	Arkansas			
	College Stats			
☐ 72	Todd Day	.10	.04	.01
	Career Highlights			
☐ 73	Todd Day	.10	.04	.01
	NBA Scouting Report			
☐ 74	Todd Day	.10	.04	.01
	One Bright Day			
☐ 75	Todd Day	.10	.04	.01
☐ 76	Walt Williams	.10	.04	.01
	Maryland			
	College Stats			
☐ 77	Walt Williams	.10	.04	.01
	Career Highlights			
☐ 78	Walt Williams	.10	.04	.01
	NBA Scouting Report			
☐ 79	Walt Williams	.10	.04	.01
	Nation's Longest Streaks			
☐ 80	Walt Williams	.10	.04	.01
☐ 81	Malik Sealy	.07	.03	.01
	St. Johns			
	College Stats			
☐ 82	Malik Sealy	.07	.03	.01
	Career Highlights			
☐ 83	Malik Sealy	.07	.03	.01
	NBA Scouting Report			
☐ 84	Malik Sealy	.07	.03	.01
	Malik Wear			
☐ 85	Malik Sealy	.07	.03	.01
☐ 86	Stanley Roberts	.07	.03	.01
	LSU			
	College Stats			

☐ 87	Stanley Roberts	.07	.03	.01
	Career Highlights			
☐ 88	Stanley Roberts	.07	.03	.01
	NBA All-Rookie Team			
☐ 89	Stanley Roberts	.07	.03	.01
	The Spanish League			
☐ 90	Stanley Roberts	.07	.03	.01
☐ 91	LaPhonso Ellis	.30	.12	.03
	Notre Dame College Stats			
☐ 92	LaPhonso Ellis	.30	.12	.03
	Career Highlights			
☐ 93	LaPhonso Ellis	.30	.12	.03
	NBA Scouting Report			
☐ 94	LaPhonso Ellis	.30	.12	.03
	Dream Come True			
☐ 95	LaPhonso Ellis	.30	.12	.03
☐ 96	Terrell Brandon	.07	.03	.01
	Oregon College Stats			
☐ 97	Terrell Brandon	.07	.03	.01
	Career Highlights			
☐ 98	Terrell Brandon	.07	.03	.01
	NBA All-Rookie Team			
☐ 99	Terrell Brandon	.07	.03	.01
	Quickest in the League			
☐ 100	Terrell Brandon	.07	.03	.01

1994 Pacific Prism Draft

This 72-card standard-size (2 1/2" by 3 1/2") set was licensed by Classic Games and produced by Pacific. Just 3,999 individually-numbered cases were produced. Among the rookie players are top NBA stars: Anfernee Hardaway (21, 69), Jamal Mashburn (31, 70), Harold Miner (35), Isaiah Rider (49), Alonzo Mourning (40, 71), and Dikembe Mutombo (41, 72). The cards were available in both silver and gold prism foil and were printed on 18-point card stock with UV coating on both sides. The fronts display a player action cutout on a prism foil background. The player's name and the Pacific logo appear in a bar toward the bottom. On a background displaying colorful rays of light emanating from a central point, the horizontal back carries a color player photo, biography, and player profile. The cards are numbered on the back and arranged alphabetically.

		MINT	NRMT	EXC
	COMPLETE SET (74)	60.00	27.00	7.50
	COMP. MAJERLE SET	7.00	3.10	.85
	COMMON CARD (1-72)	.50	.23	.06
☐ 1	Derrick Alston	.50	.23	.06
	Duquesne			
☐ 2	Adrian Autry	.50	.23	.06
	Syracuse			
☐ 3	Damon Bailey	1.25	.55	.16
	Indiana			
☐ 4	Melvin Booker	.50	.23	.06
	Missouri			
☐ 5	Joey Brown	.50	.23	.06
	Georgetown			
☐ 6	Albert Burditt	.50	.23	.06
	Texas			
☐ 7	Robert Churchwell	.50	.23	.06
	Georgetown			
☐ 8	Gary Collier	.50	.23	.06
	Tulsa			
☐ 9	Jevon Crudup	.50	.23	.06
	Missouri			
☐ 10	Bill Curley	.50	.23	.06
	Boston			
☐ 11	Yinka Dare	.50	.23	.06
	George Washington			
☐ 12	Rodney Dent	.50	.23	.06
	Kentucky			
☐ 13	Tony Dumas	.75	.35	.09
	Missouri-Kansas City			
☐ 14	Howard Eisley	.50	.23	.06
	Boston			
☐ 15	Travis Ford	.50	.23	.06
	Kentucky			
☐ 16	Lawrence Funderburke	.50	.23	.06
	Ohio			
☐ 17	Anthony Goldwire	.50	.23	.06
	Houston			
☐ 18	Chuck Graham	.50	.23	.06
	Florida State			
☐ 19	Brian Grant	4.00	1.80	.50
	Xavier			
☐ 20	Darrin Hancock	.50	.23	.06
	France/Kansas			
☐ 21	Anfernee Hardaway	2.50	1.15	.30
	Orlando Magic			
☐ 22	Carl Ray Harris	.50	.23	.06
	Fresno State			
☐ 23	Grant Hill	15.00	6.75	1.90
	Duke			
☐ 24	Askia Jones	.50	.23	.06
	Kansas State			
☐ 25	Eddie Jones	6.00	2.70	.75
	Temple			
☐ 26	Arturas Karnishovas	.50	.23	.06
	Seton Hall			
☐ 27	Damon Key	.50	.23	.06
	Marquette			
☐ 28	Jason Kidd	12.00	5.50	1.50
	California			
☐ 29	Antonio Lang	.50	.23	.06
	Duke			
☐ 30	Donyell Marshall	4.00	1.80	.50
	Connecticut			
☐ 31	Jamal Mashburn	2.00	.90	.25
	Dallas Mavericks			
☐ 32	Billy McCaffrey	.50	.23	.06
	Vanderbilt			
☐ 33	Jim McIlvaine	.50	.23	.06
	Marquette			

☐ 34	Aaron McKie .... Temple	.50	.23	.06
☐ 35	Harold Miner .... Miami Heat	.50	.23	.06
☐ 36	Greg Minor .... Louisville	1.50	.65	.19
☐ 37	Eric Mobley .... Pittsburgh	.50	.23	.06
☐ 38	Eric Montross .... North Carolina	3.00	1.35	.40
☐ 39	Dwayne Morton .... Louisville	.50	.23	.06
☐ 40	Alonzo Mourning .... Charlotte Hornets	1.75	.80	.22
☐ 41	Dikembe Mutombo .... Denver Nuggets	1.25	.55	.16
☐ 42	Gaylon Nickerson .... N.W. Oklahoma	.50	.23	.06
☐ 43	Wesley Person .... Auburn	3.00	1.35	.40
☐ 44	Derrick Phelps .... North Carolina	.50	.23	.06
☐ 45	Eric Piatkowski .... Nebraska	.75	.35	.09
☐ 46	Kevin Rankin .... Northwestern	.50	.23	.06
☐ 47	Brian Reese .... North Carolina	.50	.23	.06
☐ 48	Khalid Reeves .... Arizona	3.00	1.35	.40
☐ 49	Isaiah Rider .... Minnesota Timberwolves	1.25	.55	.16
☐ 50	Glenn Robinson .... Purdue	12.00	5.50	1.50
☐ 51	Carlos Rogers .... Tennessee	2.00	.90	.25
☐ 52	Jalen Rose .... Michigan	3.00	1.35	.40
☐ 53	Clifford Rozier .... Louisville	1.50	.65	.19
☐ 54	Kevin Salvadori .... North Carolina	.50	.23	.06
☐ 55	Jervaughn Scales .... Southern	.50	.23	.06
☐ 56	Shawnelle Scott .... St. John's	.50	.23	.06
☐ 57	Dickey Simpkins .... Providence	1.00	.45	.13
☐ 58	Michael Smith .... Providence	2.00	.90	.25
☐ 59	Shon Tarver .... UCLA	.50	.23	.06
☐ 60	Deon Thomas .... Illinois	.50	.23	.06
☐ 61	Brooks Thompson .... Oklahoma	.50	.23	.06
☐ 62	B.J. Tyler .... Texas	.75	.35	.09
☐ 63	Charlie Ward .... Florida	1.25	.55	.16
☐ 64	Jamie Watson .... South Carolina	.50	.23	.06
☐ 65	Jeff Webster .... Oklahoma	.50	.23	.06
☐ 66	Monty Williams .... Notre Dame	.50	.23	.06
☐ 67	Dontonio Wingfield .... Cincinnati	.50	.23	.06
☐ 68	Steve Woodberry .... Kansas	.50	.23	.06
☐ 69	Anfernee Hardaway	2.50	1.15	.30
	Orlando Magic			
☐ 70	Jamal Mashburn .... Dallas Mavericks	2.00	.90	.25
☐ 71	Alonzo Mourning .... Charlotte Hornets	1.75	.80	.22
☐ 72	Dikembe Mutombo .... Denver Nuggets	1.25	.55	.16
☐ NNO	Pacific Logo	.25	.11	.03

1994 Pacific Prisms Gold

This 72-card standard-size set was inserted at a rate of two per box. The cards were printed on 18-point card stock with UV coating on both sides. The fronts display a player action cutout on a prism foil background. The player's name and the Pacific logo appear in a bar toward the bottom. On a background displaying colorful rays of light emanating from a central point, the horizontal back carries a color player photo, biography, and player profile. The cards are numbered on the back and arranged alphabetically.

	MINT	NRMT	EXC
COMPLETE SET (72)	300.00	135.00	38.00
COMMON CARD (1-72)	2.50	1.15	.30

*STARS: 2.5X TO 5X BASIC CARDS.

1995 SR Draft Day

This 50-card set measures the standard size. The fronts carry a borderless color player action photo with the player's name and a player's silhouette is printed in gold in a faded black stripe at the bottom. The backs carry three small additional action player photos with the player's name, position, biographical information, career highlights, college attended, and statistics.

	MINT	NRMT	EXC
COMPLETE SET (50)	10.00	4.50	1.25
COMMON CARD (1-50)	.10	.05	.01
☐ 1 Donny Marshall	.40	.18	.05
☐ 2 Mario Bennett	.40	.18	.05
☐ 3 Dan Cross	.10	.05	.01
☐ 4 Devin Gray	.10	.05	.01
☐ 5 Dwight Stewart	.10	.05	.01
☐ 6 Jerome Allen	.15	.07	.02
☐ 7 Travis Best	.50	.23	.06
☐ 8 Tyus Edney	.30	.14	.04
☐ 9 Mark Davis	.15	.07	.02
☐ 10 Michael Finley	.50	.23	.06
☐ 11 Gary Trent	.75	.35	.09
☐ 12 Julius Michalik	.10	.05	.01
☐ 13 Clint McDaniel	.10	.05	.01
☐ 14 Sherell Ford	.40	.18	.05
☐ 15 Junior Burrough	.30	.14	.04
☐ 16 Bryan Collins	.10	.05	.01
☐ 17 Andrew DeClercq	.30	.14	.04
☐ 18 Glen Whisby	.10	.05	.01
☐ 19 Terrance Rencher	.30	.14	.04
☐ 20 Eric Snow	.20	.09	.03
☐ 21 Alan Henderson	.60	.25	.08
☐ 22 Bob Sura	.60	.25	.08
☐ 23 James Forrest	.10	.05	.01
☐ 24 Jimmy King	.25	.11	.03
☐ 25 Scotty Thurman	.15	.07	.02
☐ 26 Matt Maloney	.10	.05	.01
☐ 27 Paul O'Liney	.10	.05	.01
☐ 28 Lazelle Durden	.10	.05	.01
☐ 29 Eric Williams	.60	.25	.08
☐ 30 Tom Kleinschmidt	.10	.05	.01
☐ 31 Cory Alexander	.40	.18	.05
☐ 32 James Scott	.10	.05	.01
☐ 33 Michael McDonald	.15	.07	.02
☐ 34 Randy Rutherford	.15	.07	.02
☐ 35 Donald Williams	.15	.07	.02
☐ 36 Kurt Thomas	.75	.35	.09
☐ 37 Loren Meyer	.40	.18	.05
☐ 38 Donnie Boyce	.20	.09	.03
☐ 39 Michael Hawkins	.10	.05	.01
☐ 40 Lou Roe	.40	.18	.05
☐ 41 Larry Skyes	.10	.05	.01
☐ 42 Cuonzo Martin	.15	.07	.02
☐ 43 Jason Caffey	.50	.23	.06
☐ 44 Scott Highmark	.10	.05	.01
☐ 45 Lawrence Moten	.25	.11	.03
☐ 46 Anthony Pelle	.20	.09	.03
☐ 47 Randolph Childress	.75	.35	.09
☐ 48 Ray Jackson	.15	.07	.02
☐ 49 Corey Beck	.15	.07	.02
☐ 50 Fred Hoiberg	.15	.07	.02
☐ NNO Checklist Card	.10	.05	.01

1995 SR Draft Day Signatures

Inserted one per '95 Signature Rookies Draft Day pack, these 50 standard-size cards are the same as 1995 Draft Day only with the player's signature on the front. All 50 players in the set signed 7750 cards.

	MINT	NRMT	EXC
COMPLETE SET (50)	250.00	115.00	31.00
COMMON CARD (1-50)	3.00	1.35	.40
☐ 1 Donny Marshall	8.00	3.60	1.00
☐ 2 Mario Bennett	8.00	3.60	1.00
☐ 3 Dan Cross	3.00	1.35	.40
☐ 4 Devin Gray	3.00	1.35	.40
☐ 5 Dwight Stewart	3.00	1.35	.40
☐ 6 Jerome Allen	4.00	1.80	.50
☐ 7 Travis Best	10.00	4.50	1.25
☐ 8 Tyus Edney	7.00	3.10	.85
☐ 9 Mark Davis	4.00	1.80	.50
☐ 10 Michael Finley	10.00	4.50	1.25
☐ 11 Gary Trent	15.00	6.75	1.90
☐ 12 Julius Michalik	3.00	1.35	.40
☐ 13 Clint McDaniel	3.00	1.35	.40
☐ 14 Sherell Ford	8.00	3.60	1.00
☐ 15 Junior Burrough	7.00	3.10	.85
☐ 16 Bryan Collins	3.00	1.35	.40
☐ 17 Andrew DeClercq	7.00	3.10	.85
☐ 18 Glen Whisby	3.00	1.35	.40
☐ 19 Terrance Rencher	7.00	3.10	.85
☐ 20 Eric Snow	5.00	2.30	.60
☐ 21 Alan Henderson	12.00	5.50	1.50
☐ 22 Bob Sura	12.00	5.50	1.50
☐ 23 James Forrest	3.00	1.35	.40
☐ 24 Jimmy King	6.00	2.70	.75
☐ 25 Scotty Thurman	4.00	1.80	.50
☐ 26 Matt Maloney	3.00	1.35	.40
☐ 27 Paul O'Liney	3.00	1.35	.40
☐ 28 Lazelle Durden	3.00	1.35	.40
☐ 29 Eric Williams	12.00	5.50	1.50
☐ 30 Tom Kleinschmidt	3.00	1.35	.40
☐ 31 Cory Alexander	8.00	3.60	1.00
☐ 32 James Scott	3.00	1.35	.40
☐ 33 Michael McDonald	4.00	1.80	.50
☐ 34 Randy Rutherford	4.00	1.80	.50
☐ 35 Donald Williams	4.00	1.80	.50
☐ 36 Kurt Thomas	15.00	6.75	1.90
☐ 37 Loren Meyer	8.00	3.60	1.00
☐ 38 Donnie Boyce	5.00	2.30	.60
☐ 39 Michael Hawkins	3.00	1.35	.40
☐ 40 Lou Roe	8.00	3.60	1.00

		MINT	NRMT	EXC
☐ 41	Larry Skyes	3.00	1.35	.40
☐ 42	Cuonzo Martin	4.00	1.80	.50
☐ 43	Jason Caffey	10.00	4.50	1.25
☐ 44	Scott Highmark	3.00	1.35	.40
☐ 45	Lawrence Moten	6.00	2.70	.75
☐ 46	Anthony Pelle	5.00	2.30	.60
☐ 47	Randolph Childress	14.00	6.25	1.75
☐ 48	Ray Jackson	4.00	1.80	.50
☐ 49	Corey Beck	4.00	1.80	.50
☐ 50	Fred Hoiberg	4.00	1.80	.50

1995 SR Draft Day Kareem Abdul Jabbar

Inserted at a rate of one per 87 packs, these 5 standard-size cards consist of different action portraits of Kareem Abdul Jabbar on the front. All the cards have a black stripe down the left side with his name printed in gold. The backs carry his different career highlights and collegiate stats printed over another color action photo.

		MINT	NRMT	EXC
COMPLETE SET (5)		40.00	18.00	5.00
COMMON KAREEM (K1-K5)		8.00	3.60	1.00
COMP. SIGNED SET (5)		600.00	275.00	75.00
☐ K1	Kareem Abdul Jabbar	8.00	3.60	1.00
☐ K2	Kareem Abdul Jabbar	8.00	3.60	1.00
☐ K3	Kareem Abdul Jabbar	8.00	3.60	1.00
☐ K4	Kareem Abdul Jabbar	8.00	3.60	1.00
☐ K5	Kareem Abdul Jabbar	8.00	3.60	1.00

1995 SR Draft Day Draft Gems

Randomly inserted at a rate of 1 per 22 packs, these 10 standard-size cards consist of five player's with two cards each. The fronts feature two different color player action photos. The larger background one

is faded while the smaller foreground one is bright. The player's last name is in big gold letters above the bottom of a thin red "L" on the left with his first name printed in red above it. The backs carry the player's name, biographical information, career highlights, statistics, and college printed over a faded player action photo with part of the photo brightly displayed inside a diamond-shaped frame.

		MINT	NRMT	EXC
COMPLETE SET (10)		50.00	23.00	6.25
COMMON CARD (DG1-DG10)		3.00	1.35	.40
☐ DG1	Jerry Stackhouse	10.00	4.50	1.25
☐ DG2	Jerry Stackhouse	10.00	4.50	1.25
☐ DG3	Antonio McDyess	5.00	2.30	.60
☐ DG4	Antonio McDyess	5.00	2.30	.60
☐ DG5	Cherokee Parks	3.00	1.35	.40
☐ DG6	Cherokee Parks	3.00	1.35	.40
☐ DG7	Joe Smith	8.00	3.60	1.00
☐ DG8	Joe Smith	8.00	3.60	1.00
☐ DG9	Rasheed Wallace	5.00	2.30	.60
☐ DG10	Rasheed Wallace	5.00	2.30	.60

1995 SR Draft Day Draft Gems Signatures

Inserted at a rate of 1 per 87 packs, these 10 cards are the same as the 1995 Draft Day Draft Gems cards except for the player's signature on the front. The cards are numbered on the back.

		MINT	NRMT	EXC
COMPLETE SET (10)		650.00	300.00	80.00
COMMON CARD (DG1-DG10)		40.00	18.00	5.00
☐ DG1	Jerry Stackhouse	125.00	57.50	15.50
☐ DG2	Jerry Stackhouse	125.00	57.50	15.50
☐ DG3	Antonio McDyess	60.00	27.00	7.50
☐ DG4	Antonio McDyess	60.00	27.00	7.50
☐ DG5	Cherokee Parks	40.00	18.00	5.00
☐ DG6	Cherokee Parks	40.00	18.00	5.00
☐ DG7	Joe Smith	100.00	45.00	12.50
☐ DG8	Joe Smith	100.00	45.00	12.50
☐ DG9	Rasheed Wallace	60.00	27.00	7.50
☐ DG10	Rasheed Wallace	60.00	27.00	7.50

		MINT	NRMT	EXC
☐ NNO	Kevin Garnett	100.00	45.00	12.50
☐ AU1	K. Garnett AU/260	100.00	45.00	12.50

1995 SR Draft Day Reflections

Inserted at a rate of 1 per 18 packs, these 5 cards measure the standard size. The fronts feature borderless player action photos with the player's name and a player silhouette printed in gold in a vertical black stripe on the left. The backs carry the player's name, college, biographical information, career highlights and statistics along with another action player photo and a narrowly-cropped version of the front photo.

		MINT	NRMT	EXC
COMPLETE SET (5)		8.00	3.60	1.00
COMMON CARD (R1-R5)		1.25	.55	.16
☐ R1	Brian Grant	1.50	.65	.19
☐ R2	Wesley Person	1.25	.55	.16
☐ R3	Eric Montross	1.25	.55	.16
☐ R4	Juwan Howard	1.50	.65	.19
☐ R5	Eddie Jones	2.50	1.15	.30

1995 SR Draft Day Reflections Signatures

Inserted at a rate of 1 per 346 packs, these 5 cards are the same as the 1995 Draft Day Reflections only with the player's signature on the front.

		MINT	NRMT	EXC
COMPLETE SET (5)		500.00	230.00	65.00
COMMON CARD (R1-R5)		80.00	36.00	10.00
☐ R1	Brian Grant	100.00	45.00	12.50
☐ R2	Wesley Person	80.00	36.00	10.00
☐ R3	Eric Montross	90.00	40.00	11.50
☐ R4	Juwan Howard	125.00	57.50	15.50
☐ R5	Eddie Jones	160.00	70.00	20.00

1995 SR Draft Day Show Stoppers

Inserted at a rate of 1 per 3 packs, these 25 cards measure the standard size. The set consists of five cards each of five different players. The fronts feature color action player photos with a border resembling a roll of film. The player's name is printed in gold in a black bar at the bottom with a gold player silhouette. The backs carry another color action photo, the player's name, position, biographical information, career highlights, college, and statistics over a background of game action.

		MINT	NRMT	EXC
COMPLETE SET (25)		35.00	16.00	4.40
COMMON REEVES (B1-B5)		2.00	.90	.25
COMMON WILLIAMSON (C1-C5)		1.50	.65	.19
COMMON STOUDAMIRE (D1-D5)		1.50	.65	.19
COMMON O'BANNON (E1-E5)		2.50	1.15	.30
COMMON RESPERT (S1-S5)		1.50	.65	.19
☐ B1	Bryant Reeves	2.00	.90	.25
☐ B2	Bryant Reeves	2.00	.90	.25
☐ B3	Bryant Reeves	2.00	.90	.25
☐ B4	Bryant Reeves	2.00	.90	.25
☐ B5	Bryant Reeves	2.00	.90	.25
☐ C1	Corliss Williamson	1.50	.65	.19
☐ C2	Corliss Williamson	1.50	.65	.19
☐ C3	Corliss Williamson	1.50	.65	.19
☐ C4	Corliss Williamson	1.50	.65	.19
☐ C5	Corliss Williamson	1.50	.65	.19
☐ D1	Damon Stoudamire	1.50	.65	.19
☐ D2	Damon Stoudamire	1.50	.65	.19
☐ D3	Damon Stoudamire	1.50	.65	.19
☐ D4	Damon Stoudamire	1.50	.65	.19
☐ D5	Damon Stoudamire	1.50	.65	.19
☐ E1	Ed O'Bannon	2.50	1.15	.30
☐ E2	Ed O'Bannon	2.50	1.15	.30
☐ E3	Ed O'Bannon	2.50	1.15	.30
☐ E4	Ed O'Bannon	2.50	1.15	.30
☐ E5	Ed O'Bannon	2.50	1.15	.30
☐ S1	Shawn Respert	1.50	.65	.19
☐ S2	Shawn Respert	1.50	.65	.19
☐ S3	Shawn Respert	1.50	.65	.19
☐ S4	Shawn Respert	1.50	.65	.19
☐ S5	Shawn Respert	1.50	.65	.19

1995 SR Draft Day Show Stoppers Signatures

Inserted at a rate of 1 per 18 packs, these 25 cards are the same as the Draft Day Show Stoppers except for the player's signature on the front.

	MINT	NRMT	EXC
COMPLETE SET (25)	500.00	230.00	65.00
COMMON REEVES (B1-B5)	25.00	11.50	3.10
COMMON WILLIAMSON (C1-C5)	20.00	9.00	2.50
COMMON STOUDAMIRE (D1-D5)	20.00	9.00	2.50
COMMON O'BANNON (E1-E5)	35.00	16.00	4.40
COMMON RESPERT (S1-S5)	20.00	9.00	2.50
☐ B1 Bryant Reeves	25.00	11.50	3.10
☐ B2 Bryant Reeves	25.00	11.50	3.10
☐ B3 Bryant Reeves	25.00	11.50	3.10
☐ B4 Bryant Reeves	25.00	11.50	3.10
☐ B5 Bryant Reeves	25.00	11.50	3.10
☐ C1 Corliss Williamson	20.00	9.00	2.50
☐ C2 Corliss Williamson	20.00	9.00	2.50
☐ C3 Corliss Williamson	20.00	9.00	2.50
☐ C4 Corliss Williamson	20.00	9.00	2.50
☐ C5 Corliss Williamson	20.00	9.00	2.50
☐ D1 Damon Stoudamire	20.00	9.00	2.50
☐ D2 Damon Stoudamire	20.00	9.00	2.50
☐ D3 Damon Stoudamire	20.00	9.00	2.50
☐ D4 Damon Stoudamire	20.00	9.00	2.50
☐ D5 Damon Stoudamire	20.00	9.00	2.50
☐ E1 Ed O'Bannon	35.00	16.00	4.40
☐ E2 Ed O'Bannon	35.00	16.00	4.40
☐ E3 Ed O'Bannon	35.00	16.00	4.40
☐ E4 Ed O'Bannon	35.00	16.00	4.40
☐ E5 Ed O'Bannon	35.00	16.00	4.40
☐ S1 Shawn Respert	20.00	9.00	2.50
☐ S2 Shawn Respert	20.00	9.00	2.50
☐ S3 Shawn Respert	20.00	9.00	2.50
☐ S4 Shawn Respert	20.00	9.00	2.50
☐ S5 Shawn Respert	20.00	9.00	2.50

1995 SR Draft Day Swat Team

Inserted at a rate of 1 per 3 packs, these 5 cards measure the standard size. The

fronts feature borderless color action player photos. The player's name is printed in green above gold sunbeams in the lower right. The backs carry the player's name, position, biographical information, college, career highlights, and statistics.

	MINT	NRMT	EXC
COMPLETE SET (5)	7.00	3.10	.85
COMMON CARD (ST1-ST5)	.75	.35	.09
☐ ST1 Tony Maroney	.75	.35	.09
☐ ST2 Greg Ostertag	1.50	.65	.19
☐ ST3 George Zidek	2.00	.90	.25
☐ ST4 Constantin Popa	.75	.35	.09
☐ ST5 Theo Ratliff	2.00	.90	.25

1995 SR Draft Day Swat Team Signatures

Inserted at a rate of 1 per 18 packs, these 5 cards are identical to the regular Draft Day Swat Team with the exception of the player's autograph and number of signed cards across the front above the player's name.

	MINT	NRMT	EXC
COMPLETE SET (5)	40.00	18.00	5.00
COMMON CARD (ST1-ST5)	6.00	2.70	.75
☐ ST1 Tony Maroney	6.00	2.70	.75
☐ ST2 Greg Ostertag	10.00	4.50	1.25
☐ ST3 George Zidek	12.00	5.50	1.50
☐ ST4 Constantin Popa	6.00	2.70	.75
☐ ST5 Theo Ratliff	12.00	5.50	1.50

1994 SR Gold Standard *

This multi-sport set consists of 100 standard-size cards. The fronts feature color action players photos with a circular gold

foil seal at the upper left corner. The player's name appears on a diagonal black stripe edged by yellow. The horizontal backs carry a narrowly-cropped closeup photo and, on a ghosted panel, biography and player profile. The set is subdivided according to sport as follows: basketball (1-25), football (26-50), baseball (51-75), and hockey (76-100).

	MINT	NRMT	EXC
COMPLETE SET (100)	10.00	4.50	1.25
COMMON CARD (1-100)	.05	.02	.01
COMMON PROSPECT	.15	.07	.02
☐ 1 Derrick Alston	.05	.02	.01
☐ 2 Damon Bailey	.25	.11	.03
☐ 3 Bill Curley	.05	.02	.01
☐ 4 Yinka Dare	.05	.02	.01
☐ 5 Rodney Dent	.05	.02	.01
☐ 6 Brian Grant	.60	.25	.08
☐ 7 Juwan Howard	.60	.25	.08
☐ 8 Askia Jones	.05	.02	.01
☐ 9 Eddie Jones	1.00	.45	.13
☐ 10 Donyell Marshall	.60	.25	.08
☐ 11 Aaron McKie	.05	.02	.01
☐ 12 Greg Minor	.20	.09	.03
☐ 13 Eric Montross	.50	.23	.06
☐ 14 Wesley Person	.50	.23	.06
☐ 15 Eric Piatkowski	.15	.07	.02
☐ 16 Jalen Rose	.50	.23	.06
☐ 17 Clifford Rozier	.25	.11	.03
☐ 18 Dickey Simpkins	.20	.09	.03
☐ 19 Deon Thomas	.05	.02	.01
☐ 20 Brooks Thompson	.05	.02	.01
☐ 21 B.J. Tyler	.15	.07	.02
☐ 22 Charlie Ward	.20	.09	.03
☐ 23 Monty Williams	.05	.02	.01
☐ 24 Dontonio Wingfield	.05	.02	.01
☐ 25 Sharone Wright	.50	.23	.06
☐ 26 Sam Adams	.05	.02	.01
☐ 27 Trev Alberts	.15	.07	.02
☐ 28 Derrick Alexander	.50	.23	.06
☐ 29 Mitch Berger	.05	.02	.01
☐ 30 Tim Bowens	.30	.14	.04
☐ 31 Jeff Burris	.25	.11	.03
☐ 32 Shante Carver	.15	.07	.02
☐ 33 Lake Dawson	.50	.23	.06
☐ 34 Marshall Faulk	3.00	1.35	.40
☐ 35 Glenn Foley	.05	.02	.01
☐ 36 Rob Fredrickson	.25	.11	.03
☐ 37 Wayne Gandy	.05	.02	.01
☐ 38 Charles Johnson	.50	.23	.06
☐ 39 Tre Johnson	.05	.02	.01
☐ 40 Perry Klein	.05	.02	.01
☐ 41 Antonio Langham	.30	.14	.04
☐ 42 Eric Mahlum	.05	.02	.01
☐ 43 Willie McGinest	.20	.09	.03
☐ 44 Jamir Miller	.05	.02	.01
☐ 45 Byron Bam Morris	1.00	.45	.13
☐ 46 Errict Rhett	1.50	.65	.19
☐ 47 John Thierry	.05	.02	.01
☐ 48 DeWayne Washington	.05	.02	.01
☐ 49 Dan Wilkinson	.20	.09	.03
☐ 50 Bernard Williams	.05	.02	.01
☐ 51 Josh Booty	.50	.23	.06
☐ 52 Roger Cedeno	.50	.23	.06
☐ 53 Cliff Floyd	.15	.07	.02
☐ 54 Ben Grieve	2.50	1.15	.30
☐ 55 Joey Hamilton	.25	.11	.03
☐ 56 Todd Hollandsworth	.40	.18	.05
☐ 57 Brian Hunter	.50	.23	.06
☐ 58 Charles Johnson	.30	.14	.04
☐ 59 Brooks Kieschnick	1.25	.55	.16
☐ 60 Mike Kelly	.05	.02	.01
☐ 61 Ray McDavid	.05	.02	.01
☐ 62 Kurt Miller	.05	.02	.01
☐ 63 James Mouton	.05	.02	.01
☐ 64 Phil Nevin	.05	.02	.01
☐ 65 Alex Ochoa	.25	.11	.03
☐ 66 Herbert Perry	.15	.07	.02
☐ 67 Kirk Presley	.50	.23	.06
☐ 68 Bill Pulsipher	.50	.23	.06
☐ 69 Scott Ruffcorn	.05	.02	.01
☐ 70 Paul Shuey	.05	.02	.01
☐ 71 Michael Tucker	.30	.14	.04
☐ 72 Terrell Wade	.50	.23	.06
☐ 73 Gabe White	.05	.02	.01
☐ 74 Paul Wilson	1.00	.45	.13
☐ 75 Dmitri Young	.25	.11	.03
☐ 76 Nolan Baumgartner	.20	.09	.03
☐ 77 Wade Belak	.05	.02	.01
☐ 78 Radek Bonk	.40	.18	.05
☐ 79 Brad Brown	.05	.02	.01
☐ 80 Dan Cloutier	.25	.11	.03
☐ 81 Johan Davidsson	.05	.02	.01
☐ 82 Yannick Dube	.05	.02	.01
☐ 83 Eric Fichaud	.50	.23	.06
☐ 84 Johann Finnstrom	.05	.02	.01
☐ 85 Edvin Frylen	.05	.02	.01
☐ 86 Patrik Juhlin	.15	.07	.02
☐ 87 Valeri Karpov	.30	.14	.04
☐ 88 Nikolai Khabibulin	.05	.02	.01
☐ 89 Mattias Ohlund	.05	.02	.01
☐ 90 Jason Podollan	.05	.02	.01
☐ 91 Vadim Sharifijanov	.20	.09	.03
☐ 92 Ryan Smyth	.25	.11	.03
☐ 93 Dimitri Tabarin	.05	.02	.01
☐ 94 Nikolai Tsulygin	.05	.02	.01
☐ 95 Stefan Ustorf	.05	.02	.01
☐ 96 Paul Vincent	.05	.02	.01
☐ 97 Roman Vopat	.05	.02	.01
☐ 98 Rhett Warrener	.05	.02	.01
☐ 99 Vitali Yachmenov	.15	.07	.02
☐ 100 Vadim Yepenchinstev	.05	.02	.01

1994 SR Gold Standard Hall of Fame Signatures*

Inserted at a rate of one per box, this 24-card set is identical to the standard set except for the signatures inscribed across the front and the expression "Hall of Fame" gold-foil stamped at the upper left. Each card is numbered out of 2500. The collector could obtain unsigned versions by mailing in a redemption card that was randomly inserted in packs. These redemption cards are valued at 1/10 the value of the signed cards. The cards are numbered with HOF prefix.

	MINT	NRMT	EXC
COMPLETE SET (24)	300.00	135.00	38.00
COMMON SIGNATURE (1-24)	10.00	4.50	1.25

		MINT	NRMT	EXC
☐ 1	Nate Archibald	10.00	4.50	1.25
☐ 2	Rick Barry	15.00	6.75	1.90
☐ 3	Mike Bossy	15.00	6.75	1.90
☐ 4	Bob Cousy	20.00	9.00	2.50
☐ 5	Dave Cowens	15.00	6.75	1.90
☐ 6	Dave DeBusschere	12.00	5.50	1.50
☐ 7	Tony Esposito	18.00	8.00	2.30
☐ 8	Walt Frazier	15.00	6.75	1.90
☐ 9	Otto Graham	15.00	6.75	1.90
☐ 10	Jack Ham	12.00	5.50	1.50
☐ 11	Connie Hawkins	12.00	5.50	1.50
☐ 12	Elvin Hayes	15.00	6.75	1.90
☐ 13	Paul Hornung	20.00	9.00	2.50
☐ 14	Sam Huff	15.00	6.75	1.90
☐ 15	Jim Hunter	10.00	4.50	1.25
☐ 16	Bob Lilly	15.00	6.75	1.90
☐ 17	Don Maynard	10.00	4.50	1.25
☐ 18	Ray Nitschke	15.00	6.75	1.90
☐ 19	Bob Pettit	15.00	6.75	1.90
☐ 20	Willie Stargell	12.00	5.50	1.50
☐ 21	Y.A. Tittle	15.00	6.75	1.90
☐ 22	Bill Walton	15.00	6.75	1.90
☐ 23	Paul Warfield	12.00	5.50	1.50
☐ 24	Randy White	15.00	6.75	1.90

		MINT	NRMT	EXC
	Boston Celtics			
☐ L3	Nolan Ryan	4.00	1.80	.50
	Texas Rangers			
☐ L4	"Pee Wee" Reese	1.00	.45	.13
	Brooklyn Dodgers			
☐ L5	Brian Leetch	.75	.35	.09
	New York Rangers			

1994 SR Gold Standard Signatures *

Randomly inserted in foil packs, this 20-card set measures the standard-size. The fronts display full-bleed color player photos. A facsimile autograph, the "Gold Standard" seal, and another emblem are gold-foil stamped on the fronts. Also a diagonal line carrying the player's name (also in gold foil) is edged by gold foil stripes. On the left side, the horizontal backs show a narrowly-cropped closeup of the front photo. The remainder of the backs carry biography, statistics, and player profile, all on a ghosted background. In addition to card number, each back carries a serial number.

1994 SR Gold Standard Legends *

This five-card standard size set was randomly inserted into packs. This set has great athletes past and presents from all sports. The fronts have the word "Legends" on the top and the player's name on the bottom printed in silver ink against a black background. Meanwhile, the player's photo is shown against a gold background. The backs contains the player's photo on the left quarter with a biography about that player on the remainder of the card.

	MINT	NRMT	EXC
COMPLETE SET (5)	8.00	3.60	1.00
COMMON CARD (L1-L5)	.75	.35	.09

		MINT	NRMT	EXC
☐ L1	Isiah Thomas	.75	.35	.09
	Detroit Pistons			
☐ L2	Larry Bird	3.00	1.35	.40

	MINT	NRMT	EXC
COMPLETE SET (20)	10.00	4.50	1.25
COMMON SIGNATURE (GS1-GS20)	.15	.07	.02

		MINT	NRMT	EXC
☐ GS1	Marshall Faulk	3.50	1.55	.45
	Indianapolis Colts			
☐ GS2	Josh Booty	1.00	.45	.13
	Florida Marlins			
☐ GS3	Radek Bonk	.50	.23	.06
	Ottawa Senators			
☐ GS4	Nolan Baumgartner	.15	.07	.02
	Washington Capitals			
☐ GS5	Sam Adams	.15	.07	.02
	Seattle Seahawks			
☐ GS6	Brooks Kieschnick	1.50	.65	.19
	Chicago Cubs			
☐ GS7	Valeri Karpov	.40	.18	.05
	Anaheim Mighty Ducks			
☐ GS8	Charles Johnson	.40	.18	.05
	Florida Marlins			
☐ GS9	Juwan Howard	.75	.35	.09
	Washington Bullets			

☐ GS10 Cliff Floyd	.15	.07	.02
Montreal Expos			
☐ GS11 James Mouton	.15	.07	.02
Houston Astros			
☐ GS12 Eric Montross	.60	.25	.08
Boston Celtics			
☐ GS13 Willie McGinest	.15	.07	.02
New England Patriots			
☐ GS14 Donyell Marshall	.75	.35	.09
Minnesota Timberwolves			
☐ GS15 Perry Klein	.15	.07	.02
Atlanta Falcons			
☐ GS16 Sharone Wright	.60	.25	.08
Philadelphia 76ers			
☐ GS17 Dan Wilkinson	.15	.07	.02
Cincinnati Bengals			
☐ GS18 Ryan Smyth	.30	.14	.04
Edmonton Oilers			
☐ GS19 Clifford Rozier	.30	.14	.04
Golden State Warriors			
☐ GS20 Jalen Rose	.60	.25	.08
Denver Nuggets			

1995 SR Kromax

1,995 8-box cases were produced, and every box contained one randomly inserted autographed card of a First Round Pick, a Super Acrylium player, or a Flash From the Past star. The packs were designed to have a suggested retail price of $5. Insert sets include Flash from the Past available one in every six packs, Super Acrylium which were inserted in the ratio of one every 12 packs, and First Rounders which were available one every 19 packs. There were no more than 10,000 Super Acrylium and 2,500 First Rounders and Flash from the Past of each player made. Each box of Kro-max included one autograph from one of the three insert sets. One group of players autographed 1,050 each of their cards (Dumas, Montross, Person, Rose, and Rozier). A second group autographed 2,100 each of their cards (Curley, Dare, Grant, Jones, Jones, McKie, Piatkowski, Williams, and Wright). The front features the player's name on the left side and the Kromax logo across the bottom of the card. Most of the card is used for the player's photo in a game action shot; the other players in the photo are ghosted to give them a cartoon-like effect. The backs contain biographical

information, a player profile, and career collegiate statistics. Members received one of 1,995 uncut sheets, featuring cards 1-40 and accompanied by a certificate of authenticity.

	MINT	NRMT	EXC
COMPLETE SET (50)	25.00	11.50	3.10
COMMON CARD (1-50)	.15	.07	.02

		MINT	NRMT	EXC
☐ 1	Donyell Marshall	2.00	.90	.25
☐ 2	Juwan Howard	2.00	.90	.25
☐ 3	Sharone Wright	1.50	.65	.19
☐ 4	Brian Grant	2.00	.90	.25
☐ 5	Eric Montross	1.50	.65	.19
☐ 6	Eddie Jones	3.00	1.35	.40
☐ 7	Jalen Rose	1.50	.65	.19
☐ 8	Yinka Dare	.15	.07	.02
☐ 9	Eric Piatkowski	.30	.14	.04
☐ 10	Clifford Rozier	.75	.35	.09
☐ 11	Aaron McKie	.15	.07	.02
☐ 12	Eric Mobley	.15	.07	.02
☐ 13	Tony Dumas	.30	.14	.04
☐ 14	B.J. Tyler	.30	.14	.04
☐ 15	Dickey Simpkins	.60	.25	.08
☐ 16	Bill Curley	.15	.07	.02
☐ 17	Wesley Person	1.50	.65	.19
☐ 18	Monty Williams	.15	.07	.02
☐ 19	Greg Minor	.75	.35	.09
☐ 20	Charlie Ward	.60	.25	.08
☐ 21	Brooks Thompson	.15	.07	.02
☐ 22	Deon Thomas	.15	.07	.02
☐ 23	Howard Eisley	.30	.14	.04
☐ 24	Rodney Dent	.15	.07	.02
☐ 25	Jim McIlvaine	.15	.07	.02
☐ 26	Derrick Alston	.15	.07	.02
☐ 27	Gaylon Nickerson	.15	.07	.02
☐ 28	Michael Smith	.90	.40	.11
☐ 29	Andre Fetisov	.15	.07	.02
☐ 30	Dontonio Wingfield	.15	.07	.02
☐ 31	Anthony Miller	.15	.07	.02
☐ 32	Jeff Webster	.15	.07	.02
☐ 33	Shawnelle Scott	.15	.07	.02
☐ 34	Damon Bailey	.60	.25	.08
☐ 35	Jevon Crudup	.15	.07	.02
☐ 36	Lawrence Funderburke	.15	.07	.02
☐ 37	Anthony Goldwire	.15	.07	.02
☐ 38	Adrian Autry	.15	.07	.02
☐ 39	Doremus Bennerman	.15	.07	.02
☐ 40	Melvin Booker	.15	.07	.02
☐ 41	Dwayne Fontana	.15	.07	.02
☐ 42	Travis Ford	.15	.07	.02
☐ 43	Kenny Harris	.15	.07	.02
☐ 44	Askia Jones	.15	.07	.02
☐ 45	Jason Kidd	6.00	2.70	.75
☐ 46	Bill McCaffrey	.15	.07	.02
☐ 47	Kevin Rankin	.15	.07	.02
☐ 48	Melvin Simon	.15	.07	.02
☐ 49	Glenn Robinson	6.00	2.70	.75
☐ 50	Kendrick Warren	.15	.07	.02

1995 SR Kromax Signatures

Thirteen players signed cards for Signature Rookies for inserts in Kromax boxes. The cards are listed below in alphabetical order by player's last name.

	MINT	NRMT	EXC
COMPLETE SET (13)	200.00	90.00	25.00
COMMON SIGNATURE (1-13)	10.00	4.50	1.25
☐ 1 Bill Curley 2100	10.00	4.50	1.25
☐ 2 Yinka Dare 2100	10.00	4.50	1.25
☐ 3 Tony Dumas 1050	10.00	4.50	1.25
☐ 4 Brian Grant 2100	30.00	13.50	3.80
☐ 5 Eddie Jones 2100	35.00	16.00	4.40
☐ 6 Aaron McKie 2100	10.00	4.50	1.25
☐ 7 Eric Montross 1050	30.00	13.50	3.80
☐ 8 Wesley Person 1050	30.00	13.50	3.80
☐ 9 Eric Piatkowski 2100	10.00	4.50	1.25
☐ 10 Jalen Rose 1050	30.00	13.50	3.80
☐ 11 Clifford Rozier 1050	15.00	6.75	1.90
☐ 12 Monty Williams 2100	10.00	4.50	1.25
☐ 13 Sharone Wright 2100	25.00	11.50	3.10

1995 SR Kromax First Rounders

This 10-card standard-size set is one of three different insert sets that were randomly seeded in 7-card packs. The fronts give the information about the print amounts on the left side of the card. The First Rounder title is at the lower left corner while the player's name is on the bottom in very bright colors. The player's photo is projected in front of a wave effect. 2,500 of each card were produced.

	MINT	NRMT	EXC
COMPLETE SET (10)	50.00	23.00	6.25
COMMON CARD (FR1-FR10)	1.50	.65	.19
☐ FR1 Donyell Marshall	8.00	3.60	1.00
☐ FR2 Juwan Howard	8.00	3.60	1.00
☐ FR3 Sharone Wright	7.00	3.10	.85
☐ FR4 Brian Grant	8.00	3.60	1.00
☐ FR5 Eric Montross	7.00	3.10	.85
☐ FR6 Eddie Jones	12.00	5.50	1.50
☐ FR7 Jalen Rose	7.00	3.10	.85
☐ FR8 Yinka Dare	1.50	.65	.19
☐ FR9 B.J. Tyler	1.50	.65	.19
☐ FR10 Charlie Ward	2.50	1.15	.30

1995 SR Kromax Flash From The Past

This 10-card standard-size set is one of three different insert sets that were randomly seeded in 7-card packs. All the players signed 1,050 of their cards, except for Abdul-Jabbar (1,550), Bird (100), and Thomas (100). The fronts feature former NBA greats in air-brushed uniforms and the identification of the player under his photo. The information about the print total is on the left side of the card. The backs contain a brief biography about the player pictured and on the bottom the front photo is cropped so the face of the player is shown again.

	MINT	NRMT	EXC
COMPLETE SET (10)	25.00	11.50	3.10
COMMON CARD (FP1-FP10)	1.50	.65	.19
☐ FP1 Bob Cousy	3.00	1.35	.40
☐ FP2 Larry Bird	6.00	2.70	.75
☐ FP3 Walt Frazier	3.00	1.35	.40
☐ FP4 Rick Barry	3.00	1.35	.40
☐ FP5 Isiah Thomas	2.00	.90	.25
☐ FP6 Tiny Archibald	1.50	.65	.19
☐ FP7 Dave DeBusschere	1.50	.65	.19
☐ FP8 Dave Cowens	2.00	.90	.25
☐ FP9 Elvin Hayes	3.00	1.35	.40
☐ FP10 Kareem Abdul-Jabbar	3.00	1.35	.40

1995 SR Kromax Flash From The Past Signatures

All the players signed 1,050 of their cards, except for Abdul-Jabbar (1,550), Bird (100), and Thomas (100). There were 9,100 cards signed in total. The fronts feature former NBA greats in air-brushed uniforms, with the identification of the player under his photo. The information about the print total is on the left side of the card. The backs contain a brief biography about the player pictured and on the bottom the front photo is cropped so that the face of the player is shown again.

	MINT	NRMT	EXC
COMPLETE SET (10)	1200.00	550.00	150.00
COMMON SIGNATURE (FP1-FP10)	35.00	16.00	4.40

		MINT	NRMT	EXC
☐ FP1	Bob Cousy 1050	70.00	32.00	8.75
☐ FP2	Larry Bird 100	750.00	350.00	95.00
☐ FP3	Walt Frazier 1050	70.00	32.00	8.75
☐ FP4	Rick Barry 1050	70.00	32.00	8.75
☐ FP5	Isiah Thomas 100	250.00	115.00	31.00
☐ FP6	Tiny Archibald 1050	35.00	16.00	4.40
☐ FP7	Dave DeBusschere 1050	35.00	16.00	4.40
☐ FP8	Dave Cowens 1050	40.00	18.00	5.00
☐ FP9	Elvin Hayes 1050	70.00	32.00	8.75
☐ FP10	K. Abdul-Jabbar 1550	80.00	36.00	10.00

1990 Star Pics

This premier edition showcases sixty of college basketball's top pro prospects. The cards were issued exclusively in complete factory set boxes distributed by hobby dealers. The cards measure the standard size (2 1/2" by 3 1/2"). The front features a color action player photo, with the player shown in his college uniform. A white border separates the picture from the surrounding "basketball" background. The player's name appears in an aqua box at the bottom. The back has a head shot of the player in the upper left corner and the card number in a red star in the upper right corner. On a tan-colored basketball court design, the back presents biography, accomplishments, and a mini-scouting report that assesses a player's strengths and weaknesses. The more limited "Medallion" edition (supposedly only 25,000 Medallion sets were produced, each with its own serial number) is valued at approximately two times the prices listed below. The Medallion cards are distinguished by their more glossy feel and gold metallic print. The Medallion sets did not contain any random autographed cards inserted. The autographed cards are valued at 40 to 75 times the prices listed below.

	MINT	NRMT	EXC
COMP. SEALED SET (70)	8.00	3.60	1.00
COMMON CARD (1-70)	.05	.02	.01
COMMON AUTOGRAPH	15.00	6.75	1.90

		MINT	NRMT	EXC
☐ 1	Checklist Card	.05	.02	.01
☐ 2	David Robinson (Mr. Robinson)	2.00	.90	.25
☐ 3	Antonio Davis UTEP	.60	.25	.08
☐ 4	Steve Bardo Illinois	.05	.02	.01
☐ 5	Jayson Williams St. John's	.15	.07	.02
☐ 6	Alaa Abdelnaby Duke	.05	.02	.01
☐ 7	Trevor Wilson UCLA	.05	.02	.01
☐ 8	Dee Brown Jacksonville	1.00	.45	.13
☐ 9	Dennis Scott Georgia Tech	.75	.35	.09
☐ 10	Danny Ferry (Flashback)	.15	.07	.02
☐ 11	Stevie Thompson Syracuse	.05	.02	.01
☐ 12	Anthony Bonner St. Louis	.05	.02	.01
☐ 13	Keith Robinson Notre Dame	.05	.02	.01
☐ 14	Sean Higgins Michigan	.05	.02	.01
☐ 15	Bo Kimble Loyola Marymount	.05	.02	.01
☐ 16	David Jamerson Ohio University	.05	.02	.01
☐ 17	Anthony Pullard McNeese State	.05	.02	.01
☐ 18	Phil Henderson Duke	.05	.02	.01
☐ 19	Mike Mitchell Colorado State	.05	.02	.01
☐ 20	Vanderbilt Team	.05	.02	.01
☐ 21	Gary Payton Oregon State	1.75	.80	.22
☐ 22	Tony Massenburg Maryland	.15	.07	.02
☐ 23	Cedric Ceballos Cal State-Fullerton	1.75	.80	.22
☐ 24	Dwayne Schintzius Florida	.15	.07	.02
☐ 25	Bimbo Coles Virginia Tech	.50	.23	.06
☐ 26	Scott Williams North Carolina	.15	.07	.02
☐ 27	Willie Burton Minnesota	.60	.25	.08
☐ 28	Tate George U Conn	.05	.02	.01
☐ 29	Mark Stevenson Duquesne	.05	.02	.01
☐ 30	UNLV Team	1.00	.45	.13
☐ 31	Earl Wise Tennessee Tech	.05	.02	.01
☐ 32	Alec Kessler Georgia	.05	.02	.01
☐ 33	Les Jepsen Iowa	.05	.02	.01
☐ 34	Boo Harvey St. John's	.05	.02	.01
☐ 35	Elden Campbell	.60	.25	.08

	Clemson			
☐ 36	Jud Buechler	.05	.02	.01
	Arizona			
☐ 37	Loy Vaught	.75	.35	.09
	Michigan			
☐ 38	Tyrone Hill	.75	.35	.09
	Xavier			
☐ 39	Toni Kukoc	2.00	.90	.25
	Jugoplastika			
☐ 40	Jim Calhoun CO	.15	.07	.02
	U Conn			
☐ 41	Felton Spencer	.25	.11	.03
	Louisville			
☐ 42	Dan Godfread	.05	.02	.01
	Evansville			
☐ 43	Derrick Coleman	1.50	.65	.19
	Syracuse			
☐ 44	Terry Mills	.75	.35	.09
	Michigan			
☐ 45	Kendall Gill	.75	.35	.09
	Illinois			
☐ 46	A.J. English	.05	.02	.01
	Virginia Union			
☐ 47	Duane Causwell	.15	.07	.02
	Temple			
☐ 48	Jerrod Mustaf	.05	.02	.01
	Maryland			
☐ 49	Alan Ogg	.05	.02	.01
	Alabama Birmingham			
☐ 50	Pervis Ellison	.30	.14	.04
	(Flashback)			
☐ 51	Matt Bullard	.15	.07	.02
	Iowa			
☐ 52	Melvin Newbern	.05	.02	.01
	Minnesota			
☐ 53	Marcus Liberty	.05	.02	.01
	Ilinois			
☐ 54	Walter Palmer	.05	.02	.01
	Dartmouth			
☐ 55	Negele Knight	.15	.07	.02
	Dayton			
☐ 56	Steve Henson	.05	.02	.01
	Kansas State			
☐ 57	Greg Foster	.05	.02	.01
	UTEP			
☐ 58	Brian Oliver	.05	.02	.01
	Georgia Tech			
☐ 59	Travis Mays	.05	.02	.01
	Texas			
☐ 60	All-Rookie Team	.60	.25	.08
☐ 61	Steve Scheffler	.05	.02	.01
	Purdue			
☐ 62	Chris Jackson	.75	.35	.09
	LSU			
☐ 63	Derek Strong	.15	.07	.02
	Xavier			
☐ 64	David Butler	.05	.02	.01
	UNLV			
☐ 65	Kevin Pritchard	.05	.02	.01
	Kansas			
☐ 66	Lionel Simmons	.40	.18	.05
	LaSalle			
☐ 67	Gerald Glass	.05	.02	.01
	Mississippi			
☐ 68	Tony Harris	.05	.02	.01
	New Orleans			
☐ 69	Lance Blanks	.05	.02	.01
	Texas			
☐ 70	Draft Overview	.05	.02	.01
☐ O	Medallion special card	1.00	.45	.13
	(Only available as part			

of Medallion set;
numbered 0)

1991 Star Pics

This 73-card set was produced by Star Pics, subtitled "Pro Prospects," and features 45 of the 54 players picked in the 1991 NBA draft. The cards were issued exclusively in complete factory set boxes distributed by hobby dealers. The cards measure the standard size (2 1/2" by 3 1/2"). The front features a color action photo of player in his college uniform. This picture overlays a black background with a basketball partially in view. The back has a color head shot of the player in the upper left corner and an orange border. On a two color jersey background, the back presents biographical information, accomplishments, and a mini scouting report assessing the player's strengths and weaknesses. The cards are numbered on the back. The Medallion version of this set is tougher to find than that of the previous year and is valued at triple the prices listed below. The Medallion sets again did not contain any random autographed cards inserted. The autographed cards are valued at 20 to 40 times the prices listed below for draft picks; 150 to 250 times for flashback players.

	MINT	NRMT	EXC
COMP. SEALED SET (73)	5.00	2.30	.60
COMMON CARD (1-72)	.04	.02	.01
COMMON AUTOGRAPH	8.00	3.60	1.00

☐ 1	Draft Overview	.04	.02	.01
☐ 2	Derrick Coleman	.30	.14	.04
	Flashback			
☐ 3	Treg Lee	.04	.02	.01
	Ohio State			
☐ 4	Rich King	.04	.02	.01
	Nebraska			
☐ 5	Kenny Anderson	.75	.35	.09
	Georgia Tech			
☐ 6	John Crotty	.04	.02	.01
	Virginia			
☐ 7	Mark Randall	.04	.02	.01
	Kansas			
☐ 8	Kevin Brooks	.04	.02	.01
	Southwestern Lousiana			

☐ 9 Lamont Strothers .... Christopher Newport	.04	.02	.01
☐ 10 Tim Hardaway .... Flashback	.20	.09	.03
☐ 11 Eric Murdock .... Providence	.25	.11	.03
☐ 12 Melvin Cheatum .... Alabama	.04	.02	.01
☐ 13 Pete Chilcutt .... North Carolina	.04	.02	.01
☐ 14 Zan Tabak .... Jugoplastika	.04	.02	.01
☐ 15 Greg Anthony .... UNLV	.04	.02	.01
☐ 16 George Ackles .... UNLV	.04	.02	.01
☐ 17 Stacey Augmon .... UNLV	.40	.18	.05
☐ 18 Larry Johnson .... UNLV	1.50	.65	.19
☐ 19 Alvaro Teheran .... Houston	.04	.02	.01
☐ 20 Reggie Miller .... Flashback	.25	.11	.03
☐ 21 Steve Smith .... Michigan State	.50	.23	.06
☐ 22 Sean Green .... Iona	.04	.02	.01
☐ 23 Johnny Pittman .... Oklahoma State	.04	.02	.01
☐ 24 Anthony Avent .... Seton Hall	.04	.02	.01
☐ 25 Chris Gatling .... Old Dominion	.20	.09	.03
☐ 26 Mark Macon .... Temple	.04	.02	.01
☐ 27 Joey Wright .... Texas	.04	.02	.01
☐ 28 Von McDade .... Wisconsin (Milwaukee)	.04	.02	.01
☐ 29 Bobby Phills .... Southern U	.25	.11	.03
☐ 30 Larry Fleisher .... HOF and Lawyer (In Memoriam)	.04	.02	.01
☐ 31 Luc Longley .... New Mexico	.04	.02	.01
☐ 32 Jean Derouillere .... Kansas State	.04	.02	.01
☐ 33 Doug Smith .... Missouri	.04	.02	.01
☐ 34 Chad Gallagher .... Creighton	.04	.02	.01
☐ 35 Marty Dow .... San Diego State	.04	.02	.01
☐ 36 Tony Farmer .... Nebraska	.04	.02	.01
☐ 37 John Taft .... Marshall	.04	.02	.01
☐ 38 Reggie Hanson .... Kentucky	.04	.02	.01
☐ 39 Terrell Brandon .... Oregon	.04	.02	.01
☐ 40 Dee Brown .... Flashback	.04	.02	.01
☐ 41 Doug Overton .... La Salle	.04	.02	.01
☐ 42 Joe Wylie .... Miami	.04	.02	.01
☐ 43 Myron Brown .... Slippery Rock	.04	.02	.01

☐ 44 Steve Hood .... James Madison	.04	.02	.01
☐ 45 Randy Brown .... New Mexico State	.04	.02	.01
☐ 46 Chris Corchiani .... NC State	.04	.02	.01
☐ 47 Kevin Lynch .... Minnesota	.04	.02	.01
☐ 48 Donald Hodge .... Temple	.04	.02	.01
☐ 49 LaBradford Smith .... Louisville	.04	.02	.01
☐ 50 Shawn Kemp .... Flashback	.30	.14	.04
☐ 51 Brian Shorter .... Pittsburgh	.04	.02	.01
☐ 52 Gary Waites .... Alabama	.04	.02	.01
☐ 53 Mike Iuzzolino .... St. Francis	.04	.02	.01
☐ 54 LeRon Ellis .... Syracuse	.04	.02	.01
☐ 55 Perry Carter .... Ohio State	.04	.02	.01
☐ 56 Keith Hughes .... Rutgers	.04	.02	.01
☐ 57 John Turner .... Phillips University	.04	.02	.01
☐ 58 Marcus Kennedy .... Eastern Michigan	.04	.02	.01
☐ 59 Randy Ayers CO .... Ohio State	.04	.02	.01
☐ 60 All-Rookie Team	.30	.14	.04
☐ 61 Jackie Jones .... Oklahoma	.04	.02	.01
☐ 62 Shaun Vandiver .... Colorado	.04	.02	.01
☐ 63 Dale Davis .... Clemson	.40	.18	.05
☐ 64 Jimmy Oliver .... Purdue	.04	.02	.01
☐ 65 Elliot Perry .... Memphis State	.30	.14	.04
☐ 66 Jerome Harmon .... Louisville	.04	.02	.01
☐ 67 Darrin Chancellor .... Southern Mississippi	.04	.02	.01
☐ 68 Roy Fisher .... California (Berkeley)	.04	.02	.01
☐ 69 Rick Fox .... North Carolina	.04	.02	.01
☐ 70 Kenny Anderson .... Special Second Card	.30	.14	.04
☐ 71 Richard Dumas .... Oklahoma State	.04	.02	.01
☐ 72 Checklist Card	.04	.02	.01
☐ NNO Salute/American Flag ..	.07	.03	.01

1992 Star Pics

The 1992 Star Pics Pro Prospects Basketball HotPics set contains 90 cards measuring the standard size (2 1/2" by 3 1/2"). The set includes 47 of the 54 players selected in the 1992 NBA Draft as well as some free agents who had a chance to make NBA rosters. Special cards featured

in the set include eight StarStats (10, 31, 36, 43, 74, 78, 81, 89), five Flashbacks (30, 40, 50, 60, 70), three Kid cards (33, 68, 83), and two coaches cards (5, 15). Each nine-card foil StarPak included one "Jump At The Chance" game card, with which collectors could win various prizes. The fronts display color action player photos with white borders. The player's position and name are printed vertically in the right border, with the latter in a colored stripe. The Star Pics logo in the lower right corner rounds out the card face. The backs present accomplishments, strengths, weaknesses, and biographical information. A close-up photo appears at the lower right corner inside the Star Pics logo. The cards are numbered on the back. The unnumbered Bonus card of Steve Smith features a full-bleed color illustration by artist Rip Evans. The autographed cards are valued at 25 to 50 times the prices listed below for draft picks; 100 to 150 times for flashback players.

	MINT	NRMT	EXC
COMPLETE SET (90)	8.00	3.60	1.00
COMMON CARD (1-90)	.04	.02	.01
COMMON AUTOGRAPH	8.00	3.60	1.00
☐ 1 Draft Overview	.04	.02	.01
☐ 2 Bryant Stith	.30	.14	.04
Virginia			
☐ 3 Reggie Smith	.04	.02	.01
Texas Christian			
☐ 4 Todd Day	.40	.18	.05
Arkansas			
☐ 5 Bobby Knight CO	.20	.09	.03
Indiana			
☐ 6 Darren Morningstar	.04	.02	.01
Pittsburgh			
☐ 7 Clarence Weatherspoon	.75	.35	.09
Southern Mississippi			
☐ 8 Matt Geiger	.10	.05	.01
Georgia Tech			
☐ 9 Marlon Maxey	.04	.02	.01
Texas El Paso			
☐ 10 Christian Laettner SS	.20	.09	.03
Duke			
☐ 11 Tony Bennett	.04	.02	.01
Wisconsin (Green Bay)			
☐ 12 Sean Rooks	.10	.05	.01
Arizona			
☐ 13 Tom Gugliotta	.75	.35	.09
North Carolina State			
☐ 14 Chris King	.04	.02	.01
Wake Forest			
☐ 15 Mike Krzyzewski CO	.25	.11	.03
Duke			
☐ 16 Sam Mack	.04	.02	.01
Houston			
☐ 17 Matt Fish	.04	.02	.01
NC (Wilmington)			
☐ 18 Brian Davis	.04	.02	.01
Duke			
☐ 19 Oliver Miller	.15	.07	.02
Arkansas			
☐ 20 Daimon Sweet	.04	.02	.01
Notre Dame			
☐ 21 Eric Anderson	.04	.02	.01
Indiana			
☐ 22 Henry Williams	.04	.02	.01
NC (Charlotte)			
☐ 23 David Johnson	.04	.02	.01
Syracuse			
☐ 24 Duane Cooper	.04	.02	.01
USC			
☐ 25 Lucius Davis	.04	.02	.01
UC Santa Barbara			
☐ 26 Matt Steigenga	.04	.02	.01
Michigan State			
☐ 27 Robert Horry	1.00	.45	.13
Alabama			
☐ 28 Brent Price	.04	.02	.01
Oklahoma			
☐ 29 Chris Smith	.10	.05	.01
Connecticut			
☐ 30 Vlade Divac FLB	.10	.05	.01
☐ 31 Adam Keefe SS	.04	.02	.01
Stanford			
☐ 32 Christian Laettner	.60	.25	.08
Duke			
☐ 33 LaPhonso Ellis	.10	.05	.01
Notre Dame			
Kid Card			
☐ 34 Alex Blackwell	.04	.02	.01
Monmouth			
☐ 35 Popeye Jones	.20	.09	.03
Murray State			
☐ 36 Walt Williams SS	.10	.05	.01
Maryland			
☐ 37 Radenko Dobras	.04	.02	.01
South Florida			
☐ 38 Latrell Sprewell	1.25	.55	.16
Alabama			
☐ 39 Isaiah Morris	.04	.02	.01
Arkansas			
☐ 40 Horace Grant FLB	.10	.05	.01
☐ 41 Craig Upchurch	.04	.02	.01
Houston			
☐ 42 Alonzo Jamison	.04	.02	.01
Kansas			
☐ 43 Bryant Stith SS	.15	.07	.02
Virginia			
☐ 44 Jon Barry	.10	.05	.01
Georgia Tech			
☐ 45 Litterial Green	.04	.02	.01
Georgia			
☐ 46 Malik Sealy	.30	.14	.04
St. John's			
☐ 47 Anthony Peeler	.10	.05	.01
Missouri			
☐ 48 Dexter Cambridge	.04	.02	.01
Texas			
☐ 49 Eric Manuel	.04	.02	.01
Oklahoma City			
☐ 50 Kendall Gill FLB	.04	.02	.01
☐ 51 Hubert Davis	.10	.05	.01

North Carolina

☐ 52	Steve Rogers Alabama State	.04	.02	.01
☐ 53	Byron Houston Oklahoma State	.04	.02	.01
☐ 54	Randy Woods LaSalle	.04	.02	.01
☐ 55	Elmer Bennett Notre Dame	.04	.02	.01
☐ 56	Smokey McCovery Oklahoma City	.04	.02	.01
☐ 57	George Gilmore Chaminade	.04	.02	.01
☐ 58	Predrag Danilovic Belgrade	.04	.02	.01
☐ 59	John Pelphrey Kentucky	.04	.02	.01
☐ 60	Dan Majerle FLB Central Michigan	.04	.02	.01
☐ 61	Elmore Spencer UNLV	.10	.05	.01
☐ 62	Calvin Talford East Tennessee State	.04	.02	.01
☐ 63	David Booth DePaul	.04	.02	.01
☐ 64	Herb Jones Cincinnati	.04	.02	.01
☐ 65	Benford Williams Texas	.04	.02	.01
☐ 66	Greg Dennis East Tennessee State	.04	.02	.01
☐ 67	James McCoy Massachusetts	.04	.02	.01
☐ 68	Clarence Weatherspoon Southern Mississippi Kid Card	.25	.11	.03
☐ 69	LaPhonso Ellis Notre Dame	.25	.11	.03
☐ 70	Sarun.Marciulionis FLB	.04	.02	.01
☐ 71	Walt Williams Maryland	.50	.23	.06
☐ 72	Lee Mayberry Arkansas	.10	.05	.01
☐ 73	Doug Christie Pepperdine	.10	.05	.01
☐ 74	Jon Barry SS Georgia Tech	.04	.02	.01
☐ 75	Adam Keefe Stanford	.10	.05	.01
☐ 76	Robert Werdann St. John's	.04	.02	.01
☐ 77	P.J. Brown Louisiana Tech	.10	.05	.01
☐ 78	Tom Gugliotta SS North Carolina State	.25	.11	.03
☐ 79	Terrell Lowery Loyola Marymount	.04	.02	.01
☐ 80	Tracy Murray UCLA	.10	.05	.01
☐ 81	Clar.Weatherspoon SS Southern Mississippi	.25	.11	.03
☐ 82	Melvin Robinson St. Louis	.04	.02	.01
☐ 83	Todd Day Arkansas Kid Card	.10	.05	.01
☐ 84	Harold Miner USC	.20	.09	.03
☐ 85	Tim Burroughs Jacksonville	.04	.02	.01
☐ 86	Damon Patterson	.04	.02	.01

Oklahoma

☐ 87	Corey Williams Oklahoma State	.04	.02	.01
☐ 88	Harold Ellis Morehouse College	.04	.02	.01
☐ 89	LaPhonso Ellis SS Notre Dame	.10	.05	.01
☐ 90	Checklist	.04	.02	.01
☐ NNO	Steve Smith Art Miami Heat	2.50	1.15	.30

1995 Superior Pix

Formerly known as Superior Rookies, this Pro Basketball Draft Pix set consists of 80 standard-size cards. This set was released as a sub-license of Classic. Just 2,995 numbered cases were produced, with 12 boxes per case. Two authentic autographs were inserted in each box; players auto-graphing include Shaquille O'Neal (200), Glenn Robinson (1,500), Jason Kidd (1,500), Dikembe Mutombo (1,000), Alonzo Mourning (1,000), and Jamal Mashburn (1,000). Each case included one auto-graphed card of Robinson or Kidd, as well as one of Mutombo, Mourning or Mashburn. The 8-card packs consist of 7 regular cards and one of 30 1st-round chrome cards (1-26, 74-77). The fronts feature full-bleed color action photos, except on the left and bottom where pebble-grain stripes edge the pictures and have the player's name. The backs carry a small color player close-up in the upper left corner, a small black-and-white player action shot in the lower right, as well as biography and player profile.

	MINT	NRMT	EXC
COMPLETE SET (80)	12.00	5.50	1.50
COMMON CARD (1-80)	.05	.02	.01

☐ 1	Glenn Robinson Purdue	2.00	.90	.25
☐ 2	Jason Kidd California	2.00	.90	.25
☐ 3	Grant Hill Duke	2.50	1.15	.30
☐ 4	Donyell Marshall Connecticut	.75	.35	.09
☐ 5	Juwan Howard Michigan	.75	.35	.09

☐	#	Player / Team			
☐	6	Sharone Wright, Clemson	.50	.23	.06
☐	7	Brian Grant, Xavier	.75	.35	.09
☐	8	Eric Montross, North Carolina	.50	.23	.06
☐	9	Eddie Jones, Temple	1.00	.45	.13
☐	10	Carlos Rogers, Tennessee State	.30	.14	.04
☐	11	Khalid Reeves, Arizona	.50	.23	.06
☐	12	Jalen Rose, Michigan	.50	.23	.06
☐	13	Yinka Dare, George Washington	.05	.02	.01
☐	14	Eric Piatkowski, Nebraska	.15	.07	.02
☐	15	Clifford Rozier, Louisville	.25	.11	.03
☐	16	Aaron McKie, Temple	.05	.02	.01
☐	17	Eric Mobley, Pittsburgh	.05	.02	.01
☐	18	Tony Dumas, Missouri-KC	.15	.07	.02
☐	19	B.J. Tyler, Texas	.15	.07	.02
☐	20	Dickey Simpkins, Providence	.20	.09	.03
☐	21	Bill Curley, Boston College	.05	.02	.01
☐	22	Wesley Person, Auburn	.50	.23	.06
☐	23	Monty Williams, Notre Dame	.05	.02	.01
☐	24	Greg Minor, Louisville	.25	.11	.03
☐	25	Charlie Ward, Florida State	.20	.09	.03
☐	26	Brooks Thompson, Oklahoma State	.05	.02	.01
☐	27	Sam Mitchell, Cleveland State	.05	.02	.01
☐	28	Deon Thomas, Illinois	.05	.02	.01
☐	29	Antonio Lang, Duke	.05	.02	.01
☐	30	Howard Eisley, Boston College	.05	.02	.01
☐	31	Jamie Watson, South Carolina	.05	.02	.01
☐	32	Jim McIlvaine, Marquette	.05	.02	.01
☐	33	Jervaughn Scales, Southern	.05	.02	.01
☐	34	Kendrick Warren, VCU	.05	.02	.01
☐	35	Melvin Simon, New Orleans	.05	.02	.01
☐	36	Albert Burditt, Texas	.05	.02	.01
☐	37	Robert Shannon, UAB	.05	.02	.01
☐	38	Kevin Rankin, Northwestern	.05	.02	.01
☐	39	Byron Starks, SW Louisiana	.05	.02	.01
☐	40	Askia Jones, Kansas State	.05	.02	.01
☐	41	Harry Moore	.05	.02	.01
☐	42	Abdul Fox, St. Bonaventure Rhode Island	.05	.02	.01
☐	43	Doremus Bennerman, Siena	.05	.02	.01
☐	44	Adrian Autry, Syracuse	.05	.02	.01
☐	45	Myron Walker, Robert Morris	.05	.02	.01
☐	46	Shawnelle Scott, St. John's	.05	.02	.01
☐	47	Tracy Webster, Wisconsin	.05	.02	.01
☐	48	Billy McCaffrey, Vanderbilt	.05	.02	.01
☐	49	Arturas Karnishovas, Seton Hall	.05	.02	.01
☐	50	Dwayne Morton, Louisville	.05	.02	.01
☐	51	Anthony Miller, Michigan State	.05	.02	.01
☐	52	Damon Bailey, Indiana	.20	.09	.03
☐	53	Lawrence Funderburke, Ohio State	.05	.02	.01
☐	54	Darrin Hancock, Kansas	.05	.02	.01
☐	55	Jeff Webster, Oklahoma	.05	.02	.01
☐	56	Jevon Crudup, Missouri	.05	.02	.01
☐	57	Robert Churchwell, Georgetown	.05	.02	.01
☐	58	Damon Key, Marquette	.05	.02	.01
☐	59	Chuck Graham, Florida State	.05	.02	.01
☐	60	Jamie Brandon, LSU	.05	.02	.01
☐	61	Travis Ford, Kentucky	.05	.02	.01
☐	62	Derrick Phelps, North Carolina	.05	.02	.01
☐	63	Stevin Smith, Arizona State	.05	.02	.01
☐	64	Brian Reese, North Carolina	.05	.02	.01
☐	65	Kevin Salvadori, North Carolina	.05	.02	.01
☐	66	Steve Woodberry, Kansas	.05	.02	.01
☐	67	Shon Tarver, UCLA	.05	.02	.01
☐	68	Joey Brown, Georgetown	.05	.02	.01
☐	69	Melvin Booker, Missouri	.05	.02	.01
☐	70	Carl Ray Harris, Fresno State	.05	.02	.01
☐	71	Gaylon Nickerson, NW Oklahoma	.05	.02	.01
☐	72	Trevor Ruffin, Hawaii	.05	.02	.01
☐	73	Anthony Goldwire, Houston	.05	.02	.01
☐	74	Shaquille O'Neal, LSU	.25	.11	.03
☐	75	Dikembe Mutombo, Georgetown	.05	.02	.01
☐	76	Alonzo Mourning, Georgetown	.15	.07	.02

		MINT	NRMT	EXC
☐ 77	Jamal Mashburn Kentucky	.15	.07	.02
☐ 78	Glenn Robinson Purdue	2.00	.90	.25
☐ 79	Grant Hill Duke	2.50	1.15	.30
☐ 80	Checklist	.05	.02	.01

1995 Superior Pix Autographs

Formerly known as Superior Rookies, this Pro Basketball Draft Pix Autograph set consists of 38 standard-size cards. Key players who autographed cards include Shaquille O'Neal (200), Glenn Robinson (1,500), Jason Kidd (1,500), Dikembe Mutombo (1,000), Alonzo Mourning (1,000), and Jamal Mashburn (1,000). The fronts feature full-bleed color action photos, except on the left and bottom where pebble-grain stripes edge the pictures and have the player's name. The signature is on the player's photo with the serial number on the bottom of the card. The backs carry a small color player close-up in the upper left corner, and a small black-and-white player action shot in the lower right, along with player biography and profile.

		MINT	NRMT	EXC
COMPLETE SET (38)		1500.00	700.00	190.00
COMMON AUTOGRAPH (1-38)		8.00	3.60	1.00
☐ 1	Glenn Robinson AU/1500	70.00	32.00	8.75
☐ 2	Jason Kidd AU/1500	70.00	32.00	8.75
☐ 3	Juwan Howard AU/1250	25.00	11.50	3.10
☐ 4	Sharone Wright AU/2500	20.00	9.00	2.50
☐ 5	Brian Grant AU/3000	30.00	13.50	3.80
☐ 6	Eric Montross AU/2500	20.00	9.00	2.50
☐ 7	Eddie Jones AU/3000	30.00	13.50	3.80
☐ 8	Yinka Dare AU/2000	8.00	3.60	1.00
☐ 9	Eric Piatkowksi AU/2500	10.00	4.50	1.25
☐ 10	Clifford Rozier AU/2500	10.00	4.50	1.25
☐ 11	Aaron McKie AU/3500	8.00	3.60	1.00
☐ 12	Eric Mobley AU/3000	20.00	9.00	2.50
☐ 13	Tony Dumas AU/3000	10.00	4.50	1.25
☐ 14	B.J. Tyler AU/3000	12.00	5.50	1.50
☐ 15	Dickey Simpkins AU/2000	15.00	6.75	1.90
☐ 16	Bill Curley AU/3000	8.00	3.60	1.00
☐ 17	Wesley Person AU/3500	20.00	9.00	2.50
☐ 18	Monty Williams AU/2500	10.00	4.50	1.25
☐ 19	Greg Minor AU/2500	12.00	5.50	1.50
☐ 20	Charlie Ward AU/2500	15.00	6.75	1.90
☐ 21	Brooks Thompson AU/2000	8.00	3.60	1.00
☐ 22	Deon Thomas AU/2700	8.00	3.60	1.00
☐ 23	Howard Eisley AU/2500	8.00	3.60	1.00
☐ 24	Jim McIlvaine AU/2600	8.00	3.60	1.00
☐ 25	Askia Jones AU/3600	8.00	3.60	1.00
☐ 26	Harry Moore AU/3000	8.00	3.60	1.00
☐ 27	Adrian Autry AU/2500	8.00	3.60	1.00
☐ 28	Shawnelle Scott AU/4000	8.00	3.60	1.00
☐ 29	Damon Bailey AU/2500	10.00	4.50	1.25
☐ 30	Darrin Hancock AU/3000	8.00	3.60	1.00
☐ 31	Jeff Webster AU/1250	8.00	3.60	1.00
☐ 32	Robert Churchwell AU/3000	8.00	3.60	1.00
☐ 33	Travis Ford AU/3000	8.00	3.60	1.00
☐ 34	Joey Brown AU/3000	8.00	3.60	1.00
☐ 35	Shaquille O'Neal AU/200	1000.00	450.00	125.00
☐ 36	Dikembe Mutombo AU/1000	50.00	23.00	6.25
☐ 37	Alonzo Mourning AU/1000	125.00	57.50	15.50
☐ 38	Jamal Mashburn AU/1000	150.00	70.00	19.00

1995 Superior Pix Chrome

These cards were inserted one per pack. These standard-sized cards feature the

player in their collegiate uniform. Every player in this insert set was a first round draft pick in the NBA draft. There was one chrome gold card in each box. The fronts feature the player in action against a basketball background. The backs says 1st round pick against a basketball background.

	MINT	NRMT	EXC
COMPLETE SET (30)	25.00	11.50	3.10
COMMON CARD (1-30)	.15	.07	.02
GOLD VERSIONS: 2X to 3X BASIC CARDS			
1 Glenn Robinson Purdue	4.00	1.80	.50
2 Jason Kidd California	4.00	1.80	.50
3 Grant Hill Duke	5.00	2.30	.60
4 Donyell Marshall Connecticut	1.50	.65	.19
5 Juwan Howard Michigan	1.50	.65	.19
6 Sharone Wright Clemson	1.00	.45	.13
7 Brian Grant Xavier	1.50	.65	.19
8 Eric Montross North Carolina	1.00	.45	.13
9 Eddie Jones Temple	2.50	1.15	.30
10 Carlos Rogers Tennessee State	.60	.25	.08
11 Khalid Reeves Arizona	1.00	.45	.13
12 Jalen Rose Michigan	1.00	.45	.13
13 Yinka Dare George Washington	.15	.07	.02
14 Eric Piatkowski Nebraska	.15	.07	.02
15 Clifford Rozier Louisville	.50	.23	.06
16 Aaron McKie Temple	.15	.07	.02
17 Eric Mobley Pittsburgh	.15	.07	.02
18 Tony Dumas Missouri-KC	.15	.07	.02
19 B.J. Tyler Texas	.15	.07	.02
20 Dickey Simpkins Providence	.40	.18	.05
21 Bill Curley Boston College	.15	.07	.02
22 Wesley Person	1.00	.45	.13
Auburn			
23 Monty Williams Notre Dame	.15	.07	.02
24 Greg Minor Louisville	.50	.23	.06
25 Charlie Ward Florida State	.40	.18	.05
26 Brooks Thompson Oklahoma State	.15	.07	.02
27 Dikembe Mutombo Georgetown	.15	.07	.02
28 Alonzo Mourning Georgetown	.60	.25	.08
29 Jamal Mashburn Kentucky	.75	.35	.09
30 Shaquille O'Neal LSU	1.50	.65	.19

1995 Superior Pix Instant Impact

This 10-card standard-size chrome set was inserted at a rate of one in every nine packs. The front features the players in a box for most of the left hand side of the card. Just above the photo is the player's name. The words "Instant Impact" are at the lower right corner. The backs feature a larger version of the front photo on the left side of the card.

	MINT	NRMT	EXC
COMPLETE SET (10)	40.00	18.00	5.00
COMMON CARD (10)	1.50	.65	.19
1 Shaquille O'Neal LSU	8.00	3.60	1.00
2 Glenn Robinson Purdue	8.00	3.60	1.00
3 Jason Kidd California	8.00	3.60	1.00
4 Grant Hill Duke	10.00	4.50	1.25
5 Dikembe Mutombo Georgetown	1.50	.65	.19
6 Alonzo Mourning Georgetown	3.00	1.35	.40
7 Jamal Mashburn Kentucky	4.00	1.80	.50
8 Juwan Howard Michigan	4.00	1.80	.50
9 Brian Grant Xavier	4.00	1.80	.50

☐ 10 Wesley Person.......... 4.00 1.80 .50
　　　Auburn

1995 Superior Pix Lottery Pick

This 10-card standard-size set was inserted at a rate of one in every 36 packs. The cards are made of clear plastic. The fronts feature the player in their college uniform with the Superior Pix logo in the upper left hand corner and the player's name on the bottom left corner of the card. Since the card is made of clear plastic, the back allows one to see what is on the front from a reverse angle.

	MINT	NRMT	EXC
COMPLETE SET (10)	70.00	32.00	8.75
COMMON CARD (1-10)	2.00	.90	.25
☐ 1 Glenn Robinson .... Purdue	15.00	6.75	1.90
☐ 2 Jason Kidd .... California	15.00	6.75	1.90
☐ 3 Grant Hill .... Duke	18.00	8.00	2.30
☐ 4 Donyell Marshall .... Connecticut	5.00	2.30	.60
☐ 5 Juwan Howard .... Michigan	5.00	2.30	.60
☐ 6 Sharone Wright .... Clemson	4.00	1.80	.50
☐ 7 Brian Grant .... Xavier	5.00	2.30	.60
☐ 8 Eric Montross .... North Carolina	5.00	2.30	.60
☐ 9 Eddie Jones .... Temple	7.00	3.10	.85
☐ 10 Carlos Rogers .... Tennessee State	2.00	.90	.25

1994 Tetrad Previews *

Randomly inserted in Signature Rookies Football packs, these seven standard-size

(2 1/2" by 3 1/2") cards feature borderless color player action shots on their fronts. The player's name and position appear in gold-foil lettering near the bottom. The words "Promo, 1 of 10,000" appear in vertical gold-foil lettering within a simulated marble column near the left edge. On a ghosted background drawing of a Greek temple, the back carries the player's name, position, team, height and weight, and career highlights. The cards of this multisport set are numbered on the back with a "T" prefix.

	MINT	NRMT	EXC
COMPLETE SET (7)	18.00	8.00	2.30
COMMON CARD (T1-T6) ..	1.25	.55	.16
☐ T1 Eric Montross	3.00	1.35	.40
☐ T2 Tim Taylor	1.25	.55	.16
☐ T3 Jeff Granger	1.25	.55	.16
☐ T4 Roger Cedeno	3.50	1.55	.45
☐ T5 Charlie Ward	1.50	.65	.19
☐ T6 O.J. Simpson	10.00	4.50	1.25
☐ NNO Header Card............	10.00	4.50	1.25

1994 Tetrad *

These 120 standard-size (2 1/2" by 3 1/2") cards feature borderless color player action shots on their fronts. The player's name appears in gold-foil lettering near the bottom. The words "1 of 45,000" appear in vertical gold-foil lettering within a simulated marble column near the left edge. On a ghosted background drawing of a Greek temple, the back carries the player's name, position, team, height and weight, and

career highlights. The cards of this four-sport set are numbered on the back in Roman numerals and organized as follows: Football (1-40), Basketball (41-83), Baseball (84-103), and Hockey (104-118).

	MINT	NRMT	EXC
COMPLETE SET (120)	12.00	5.50	1.50
COMMON CARD (1-118)	.05	.02	.01

		MINT	NRMT	EXC
☐ 1	Jay Walker	.05	.02	.01
☐ 2	Ricky Brady	.05	.02	.01
☐ 3	Paul Duckworth	.05	.02	.01
☐ 4	Jim Flanigan	.05	.02	.01
☐ 5	Brice Adams	.05	.02	.01
☐ 6	William Floyd	.60	.25	.08
☐ 7	Charlie Garner	.40	.18	.05
☐ 8	Pete Bercich	.05	.02	.01
☐ 9	Frank Harvey	.05	.02	.01
☐ 10	Willie Clark	.05	.02	.01
☐ 11	Bernard Williams	.05	.02	.01
☐ 12	Kurt Haws	.05	.02	.01
☐ 13	Dennis Collier	.05	.02	.01
☐ 14	Filmel Johnson	.05	.02	.01
☐ 15	Zane Beehn	.05	.02	.01
☐ 16	Johnnie Morton	.30	.14	.04
☐ 17	Lonnie Johnson	.05	.02	.01
☐ 18	Jay Kearney	.05	.02	.01
☐ 19	Steve Shine	.05	.02	.01
☐ 20	Dexter Nottage	.05	.02	.01
☐ 21	Ervin Collier	.05	.02	.01
☐ 22	Dorsey Levens	.15	.07	.02
☐ 23	Kevin Knox	.05	.02	.01
☐ 24	Doug Nussmeier	.05	.02	.01
☐ 25	Bill Schroeder	.05	.02	.01
☐ 26	Winfred Tubbs	.05	.02	.01
☐ 27	Rodney Harrison	.05	.02	.01
☐ 28	Rob Waldrop	.05	.02	.01
☐ 29	Mike Davis	.05	.02	.01
☐ 30	John Burke	.05	.02	.01
☐ 31	Allen Aldridge	.05	.02	.01
☐ 32	Kevin Mitchell	.05	.02	.01
☐ 33	Greg Hill	.50	.23	.06
☐ 34	Ernest Jones	.05	.02	.01
☐ 35	Kevin Mawae	.05	.02	.01
☐ 36	John Covington	.05	.02	.01
☐ 37	Mike Wells	.05	.02	.01
☐ 38	Thomas Lewis	.05	.02	.01
☐ 39	Chad Bratzke	.05	.02	.01
☐ 40	Darren Studstill	.05	.02	.01
☐ 41	Derrick Alston	.05	.02	.01
☐ 42	Adrian Autry	.05	.02	.01
☐ 43	Damon Bailey	.25	.11	.03
☐ 44	Doremus Bennerman	.05	.02	.01
☐ 45	Melvin Booker	.05	.02	.01
☐ 46	Jevon Crudup	.05	.02	.01
☐ 47	Yinka Dare	.05	.02	.01
☐ 48	Rodney Dent	.05	.02	.01
☐ 49	Tony Dumas	.15	.07	.02
☐ 50	Dwayne Fontana	.05	.02	.01
☐ 51	Travis Ford	.05	.02	.01
☐ 52	Lawrence Funderburke	.05	.02	.01
☐ 53	Anthony Goldwire	.05	.02	.01
☐ 54	Brian Grant	.75	.35	.09
☐ 55	Kenny Harris	.05	.02	.01
☐ 56	Juwan Howard UER (Misspelled Juwon)	.75	.35	.09
☐ 57	Askia Jones	.05	.02	.01
☐ 58	Eddie Jones	1.00	.45	.13
☐ 59	Arturas Karnishovas	.05	.02	.01
☐ 60	Donyell Marshall	.75	.35	.09
☐ 61	Billy McCaffrey	.05	.02	.01
☐ 62	Jim McIlvaine	.05	.02	.01
☐ 63	Aaron McKie	.05	.02	.01
☐ 64	Greg Minor	.25	.11	.03
☐ 65	Eric Mobley	.05	.02	.01
☐ 66	Eric Montross	.50	.23	.06
☐ 67	Gaylon Nickerson	.05	.02	.01
☐ 68	Wesley Person	.50	.23	.06
☐ 69	Eric Piatkowski	.15	.07	.02
☐ 70	Kevin Rankin	.05	.02	.01
☐ 71	Shawnelle Scott	.05	.02	.01
☐ 72	Melvin Simon	.05	.02	.01
☐ 73	Dickey Simpkins	.20	.09	.03
☐ 74	Michael Smith	.30	.14	.04
☐ 75	Stevin Smith	.05	.02	.01
☐ 76	Deon Thomas	.05	.02	.01
☐ 77	Brooks Thompson	.05	.02	.01
☐ 78	B.J. Tyler	.15	.07	.02
☐ 79	Kendrick Warren	.05	.02	.01
☐ 80	Jeff Webster	.05	.02	.01
☐ 81	Monty Williams	.05	.02	.01
☐ 82	Dontonio Wingfield	.05	.02	.01
☐ 83	Sharone Wright	.60	.25	.08
☐ 84	Edgardo Alfonzo	.50	.23	.06
☐ 85	David Bell	.05	.02	.01
☐ 86	Chris Carpenter	.20	.09	.03
☐ 87	Roger Cedeno	.50	.23	.06
☐ 88	Phil Geisler	.05	.02	.01
☐ 89	Curtis Goodwin	.25	.11	.03
☐ 90	Jeff Granger	.05	.02	.01
☐ 91	Brian L. Hunter	.50	.23	.06
☐ 92	Adam Hyzdu	.05	.02	.01
☐ 93	Scott Klingenbeck	.05	.02	.01
☐ 94	Derrek Lee	.60	.25	.08
☐ 95	Calvin Murray	.05	.02	.01
☐ 96	Roberto Petagine	.15	.07	.02
☐ 97	Bill Pulsipher	.50	.23	.06
☐ 98	Marquis Riley	.05	.02	.01
☐ 99	Frankie Rodriguez	.20	.09	.03
☐ 100	Scott Ruffcorn	.05	.02	.01
☐ 101	Roger Salkeld	.05	.02	.01
☐ 102	Marc Valdes	.15	.07	.02
☐ 103	Ernie Young	.05	.02	.01
☐ 104	Sven Butenschon	.05	.02	.01
☐ 105	Dan Cloutier	.25	.11	.03
☐ 106	Pat Jablonski	.05	.02	.01
☐ 107	Valeri Karpov	.30	.14	.04
☐ 108	Nikolai Khabibulin	.25	.11	.03
☐ 109	Sergei Klimentiev	.05	.02	.01
☐ 110	Krzysztof Oliwa	.05	.02	.01
☐ 111	Dmitri Riabykh	.05	.02	.01
☐ 112	Ryan Risidore	.05	.02	.01
☐ 113	Shawn Rivers	.05	.02	.01
☐ 114	Vadim Sharifijanov	.05	.02	.01
☐ 115	Mika Stromberg	.05	.02	.01
☐ 116	Tim Taylor	.05	.02	.01
☐ 117	Vitali Yachmeneu	.05	.02	.01
☐ 118	Wendell Young	.05	.02	.01
☐ NNO	Checklist	.05	.02	.01
☐ NNO	Checklist	.05	.02	.01

1994 Tetrad Signatures *

Inserted one card (or trade coupon) per pack, these 120 standard-size (2 1/2" by 3

1/2") autographed cards comprise a parallel set to the regular '94 Tetrad set. Aside from the autographs and each card's numbering out of 7,750 produced, they are identical in design to their regular issue counterparts. The cards of this four-sport set are numbered on the back in Roman numerals and organized as follows: Football (1-40), Basketball (41-83), Baseball (84-103), and Hockey (104-118).

	MINT	NRMT	EXC
COMPLETE SET (118)	450.00	200.00	57.50
COMMON SIGNATURE (1-118)	2.50	1.15	.30

		MINT	NRMT	EXC
☐	1 Jay Walker	2.50	1.15	.30
☐	2 Ricky Brady	2.50	1.15	.30
☐	3 Paul Duckworth	2.50	1.15	.30
☐	4 Jim Flanigan	2.50	1.15	.30
☐	5 Brice Adams	2.50	1.15	.30
☐	6 William Floyd	12.00	5.50	1.50
☐	7 Charlie Garner	8.00	3.60	1.00
☐	8 Pete Bercich	2.50	1.15	.30
☐	9 Frank Harvey	2.50	1.15	.30
☐	10 Willie Clark	2.50	1.15	.30
☐	11 Bernard Williams	2.50	1.15	.30
☐	12 Kurt Haws	2.50	1.15	.30
☐	13 Dennis Collier	2.50	1.15	.30
☐	14 Filmel Johnson	2.50	1.15	.30
☐	15 Zane Beehn	2.50	1.15	.30
☐	16 Johnnie Morton	7.00	3.10	.85
☐	17 Lonnie Johnson	2.50	1.15	.30
☐	18 Jay Kearney	2.50	1.15	.30
☐	19 Steve Shine	2.50	1.15	.30
☐	20 Dexter Nottage	2.50	1.15	.30
☐	21 Ervin Collier	2.50	1.15	.30
☐	22 Dorsey Levens	4.00	1.80	.50
☐	23 Kevin Knox	2.50	1.15	.30
☐	24 Doug Nussmeier	2.50	1.15	.30
☐	25 Bill Schroeder	2.50	1.15	.30
☐	26 Winfred Tubbs	2.50	1.15	.30
☐	27 Rodney Harrison	2.50	1.15	.30
☐	28 Rob Waldrop	2.50	1.15	.30
☐	29 Mike Davis	2.50	1.15	.30
☐	30 John Burke	2.50	1.15	.30
☐	31 Allen Aldridge	2.50	1.15	.30
☐	32 Kevin Mitchell	2.50	1.15	.30
☐	33 Greg Hill	10.00	4.50	1.25
☐	34 Ernest Jones	2.50	1.15	.30
☐	35 Kevin Mawae	2.50	1.15	.30
☐	36 John Covington	2.50	1.15	.30
☐	37 Mike Wells	2.50	1.15	.30
☐	38 Thomas Lewis	2.50	1.15	.30
☐	39 Chad Bratzke	2.50	1.15	.30
☐	40 Darren Studstill	2.50	1.15	.30
☐	41 Derrick Alston	2.50	1.15	.30
☐	42 Adrian Autry	2.50	1.15	.30
☐	43 Damon Bailey	8.00	3.60	1.00
☐	44 Doremus Bennerman	2.50	1.15	.30
☐	45 Melvin Booker	2.50	1.15	.30
☐	46 Jevon Crudup	2.50	1.15	.30
☐	47 Yinka Dare	2.50	1.15	.30
☐	48 Rodney Dent	2.50	1.15	.30
☐	49 Tony Dumas	4.00	1.80	.50
☐	50 Dwayne Fontana	2.50	1.15	.30
☐	51 Travis Ford	2.50	1.15	.30
☐	52 Lawrence Funderburke	2.50	1.15	.30
☐	53 Anthony Goldwire	2.50	1.15	.30
☐	54 Brian Grant	16.00	7.25	2.00
☐	55 Kenny Harris	2.50	1.15	.30
☐	56 Juwan Howard UER	16.00	7.25	2.00
	(Misspelled Juwon)			
☐	57 Askia Jones	2.50	1.15	.30
☐	58 Eddie Jones	18.00	8.00	2.30
☐	59 Arturas Karnishovas	2.50	1.15	.30
☐	60 Donyell Marshall	16.00	7.25	2.00
☐	61 Billy McCaffrey	2.50	1.15	.30
☐	62 Jim McIlvaine	2.50	1.15	.30
☐	63 Aaron McKie	2.50	1.15	.30
☐	64 Greg Minor	8.00	3.60	1.00
☐	65 Eric Mobley	2.50	1.15	.30
☐	66 Eric Montross	14.00	6.25	1.75
☐	67 Gaylon Nickerson	2.50	1.15	.30
☐	68 Wesley Person	12.00	5.50	1.50
☐	69 Eric Piatkowski	4.00	1.80	.50
☐	70 Kevin Rankin	2.50	1.15	.30
☐	71 Shawnelle Scott	2.50	1.15	.30
☐	72 Melvin Simon	2.50	1.15	.30
☐	73 Dickey Simpkins	5.00	2.30	.60
☐	74 Michael Smith	8.00	3.60	1.00
☐	75 Stevin Smith	2.50	1.15	.30
☐	76 Deon Thomas	2.50	1.15	.30
☐	77 Brooks Thompson	2.50	1.15	.30
☐	78 B.J. Tyler	4.00	1.80	.50
☐	79 Kendrick Warren	2.50	1.15	.30
☐	80 Jeff Webster	2.50	1.15	.30
☐	81 Monty Williams	2.50	1.15	.30
☐	82 Dontonio Wingfield	2.50	1.15	.30
☐	83 Sharone Wright	14.00	6.25	1.75
☐	84 Edgardo Alfonzo	12.00	5.50	1.50
☐	85 David Bell	4.00	1.80	.50
☐	86 Chris Carpenter	5.00	2.30	.60
☐	87 Roger Cedeno	12.00	5.50	1.50
☐	88 Phil Geisler	2.50	1.15	.30
☐	89 Curtis Goodwin	8.00	3.60	1.00
☐	90 Jeff Granger	2.50	1.15	.30
☐	91 Brian L. Hunter	13.00	5.75	1.65
☐	92 Adam Hyzdu	2.50	1.15	.30
☐	93 Scott Klingenbeck	2.50	1.15	.30
☐	94 Derrek Lee	13.00	5.75	1.65
☐	95 Calvin Murray	2.50	1.15	.30
☐	96 Roberto Petagine	4.00	1.80	.50
☐	97 Bill Pulsipher	14.00	6.25	1.75
☐	98 Marquis Riley	2.50	1.15	.30
☐	99 Frankie Rodriguez	6.00	2.70	.75
☐	100 Scott Ruffcorn	2.50	1.15	.30
☐	101 Roger Salkeld	2.50	1.15	.30
☐	102 Marc Valdes	4.00	1.80	.50
☐	103 Ernie Young	2.50	1.15	.30
☐	104 Sven Butenschon	2.50	1.15	.30
☐	105 Dan Cloutier	7.00	3.10	.85
☐	106 Pat Jablonski	2.50	1.15	.30
☐	107 Valeri Karpov	8.00	3.60	1.00
☐	108 Nikolai Khabibulin	7.00	3.10	.85
☐	109 Sergei Klimentiev	2.50	1.15	.30
☐	110 Krzysztof Oliwa	2.50	1.15	.30
☐	111 Dmitri Riabykin	2.50	1.15	.30
☐	112 Ryan Risidore	2.50	1.15	.30

		MINT	NRMT	EXC
☐ 113	Shawn Rivers............	2.50	1.15	.30
☐ 114	Vadim Sharifjanov......	2.50	1.15	.30
☐ 115	Mika Stromberg........	2.50	1.15	.30
☐ 116	Tim Taylor...............	2.50	1.15	.30
☐ 117	Vitali Yachmeneu......	2.50	1.15	.30
☐ 118	Wendell Young..........	2.50	1.15	.30

	MINT	NRMT	EXC
COMPLETE SET (2)	250.00	115.00	31.00
COM. SIGNATURE (AU1-AU2)	100.00	45.00	12.50

		MINT	NRMT	EXC
☐ AU1	Charles Johnson ... BB/275	150.00	70.00	19.00
☐ AU2	Glenn/Monty Williams/275	100.00	45.00	12.50

1994 Tetrad Flip Cards *

Randomly inserted in packs, these five standard-size (2 1/2" by 3 1/2") two-player cards feature a borderless color action shot of one player per side. The player's name appears in gold-foil lettering near the bottom. The words "1 of 7,500" appear in vertical gold-foil lettering within a simulated marble column near the left edge. The cards are numbered on both sides.

	MINT	NRMT	EXC
COMPLETE SET (5)	45.00	20.00	5.75
COMMON CARD (1-5)	5.00	2.30	.60

		MINT	NRMT	EXC
☐ 1	Charles Johnson BB..... Charles Johnson FB	10.00	4.50	1.25
☐ 2	Tony Dorsett.................. Gale Sayers	8.00	3.60	1.00
☐ 3	Charlie Ward BK........ Charlie Ward FB	5.00	2.30	.60
☐ 4	Juwan Howard UER ..... (Misspelled Juwon) Jalen Rose	15.00	6.75	1.90
☐ 5	Glenn Williams UER....... (Misspelled Glen) Monty Williams	5.00	2.30	.60

1994 Tetrad Flip Cards Signatures *

Randomly inserted in packs, this two-card set features two-player cards with a borderless color action shot of one player per side. The player's name appears in gold-foil lettering near the bottom. Each card is autographed. The cards are numbered on both sides.

1994 Tetrad Titans *

Randomly inserted in packs, these 12 standard-size (2 1/2" by 3 1/2") cards feature borderless color player action shots on their fronts. The player's name appears in gold-foil lettering near the bottom. The words "1 of 10,000" appear in vertical gold-foil lettering within a simulated marble column near the left edge. On a ghosted background drawing of a Greek temple, the back carries the player's name, position, team, height and weight, and career highlights. The cards of this multisport set are numbered on the back in Roman numerals.

	MINT	NRMT	EXC
COMPLETE SET (12)	50.00	23.00	6.25
COMMON CARD (119-130)	3.00	1.35	.40

		MINT	NRMT	EXC
☐ 119	Bobby Allison..............	5.00	2.30	.60
☐ 120	Larry Bird...................	12.00	5.50	1.50
☐ 121	Larry Holmes..............	6.00	2.70	.75
☐ 122	Bobby Hull.................	5.00	2.30	.60
☐ 123	Dan Jansen................	3.00	1.35	.40
☐ 124	Bruce Jenner..............	3.00	1.35	.40
☐ 125	Tony Meola.................	3.00	1.35	.40
☐ 126	Shannon Miller............	3.00	1.35	.40
☐ 127	Frank Shorter.............	3.00	1.35	.40
☐ 128	Picabo Street..............	4.00	1.80	.50
☐ 129	O.J. Simpson UER ...... (Misnumbered T6)	10.00	4.50	1.25
☐ 130	Isiah Thomas UER ...... (Misspelled Isaiah)	6.00	2.70	.75

1994 Tetrad Titans Signatures *

Randomly inserted in packs, these 12 standard-size (2 1/2" by 3 1/2") autographed

cards comprise a parallel set to the regular 1994 Tetrad Titans set. Aside from the autographs and each card's numbering out of 1,050 produced (except the 2,500 signed O.J. cards), they are identical in design to their regular issue counterparts. The cards of this multisport set are numbered on the back in Roman numerals.

		MINT	NRMT	EXC
	COMPLETE SET (12)	850.00	375.00	105.00
	COMMON SIGNATURE	25.00	11.50	3.10
☐ 119	Bobby Allison............	50.00	23.00	6.25
☐ 120	Larry Bird................	175.00	80.00	22.00
☐ 121	Larry Holmes............	60.00	27.00	7.50
☐ 122	Bobby Hull..............	50.00	23.00	6.25
☐ 123	Dan Jansen..............	30.00	13.50	3.80
☐ 124	Bruce Jenner............	30.00	13.50	3.80
☐ 125	Tony Meola..............	30.00	13.50	3.80
☐ 126	Shannon Miller	30.00	13.50	3.80
☐ 127	Frank Shorter	25.00	11.50	3.10
☐ 128	Picabo Street	40.00	18.00	5.00
☐ 129	O.J. Simpson	350.00	160.00	45.00
	(2500 autographed)			
☐ 130	Isiah Thomas UER ...	60.00	27.00	7.50
	(Misspelled Isaiah)			

1994 Tetrad
Top Prospects *

Randomly inserted in packs, these four standard-size (2 1/2" by 3 1/2") cards feature borderless color player action shots on their fronts. The player's name appears in gold-foil lettering near the bottom. The words "1 of 20,000" appear in vertical gold-

foil lettering within a simulated marble column near the left edge. On a ghosted background drawing of a Greek temple, the back carries the player's name, biography, statistics, and career highlights. The cards of this multisport set are numbered on the back in Roman numerals.

		MINT	NRMT	EXC
	COMPLETE SET (4)	8.00	3.60	1.00
	COMMON CARD (131-134)	1.25	.55	.16
☐ 131	Charlie Ward............	1.50	.65	.19
☐ 132	Willie McGinest........	1.50	.65	.19
☐ 133	Shante Carver	1.25	.55	.16
☐ 134	Paul Wilson..............	3.00	1.35	.40

1994 Tetrad Top
Prospects
Signatures *

This four-card standard size set was randomly inserted in packs. The fronts feature borderless color player action shots with the player's name in gold-foil lettering near the bottom. The cards are autographed on the fronts. The backs carry the player's name, biography, statistics, and career highlights on a ghosted background drawing of a Greek temple. The cards are numbered on the back in Roman numerals.

		MINT	NRMT	EXC
	COMPLETE SET (4)	60.00	27.00	7.50
	COMMON SIGNATURE	7.00	3.10	.85
☐ 131A	Charlie Ward..........	20.00	9.00	2.50
☐ 132A	Willie McGinest.......	9.00	4.00	1.15
☐ 133A	Shante Carver	7.00	3.10	.85
☐ 134A	Paul Wilson	30.00	13.50	3.80

1991-92 Wild Card
Promos

These two standard-size (2 1/2" by 3 1/2") cards were issued to preview the design of

1991-92 Wild Card basketball issue. Two versions of each card were produced; one was marked with and given out at the 1991 San Francisco Sports Card Expo, while the other version (without the San Francisco Sports Expo emblem) was given to dealers and also available as a random insert in Wild Card College Football foil packs. The color action player photos on the fronts are black-bordered, and colored numbers are displayed in the black border above and to the right of the picture. The backs carry a color headshot, biography, and statistics. The cards are numbered on the back with a "P" prefix. The San Francisco give-away cards are arguably less than valuable than the harder-to-obtain football foil pack insert versions.

	MINT	NRMT	EXC
COMPLETE SET (2)	12.00	5.00	1.20
COMMON CARD (P1-P2)	5.00	2.00	.50
☐ P1 Larry Johnson UNLV	8.00	3.25	.80
☐ P2 Kenny Anderson Georgia Tech	5.00	2.00	.50

1991-92 Wild Card

The Wild Card Collegiate Basketball set contains 120 cards measuring the standard size (2 1/2" by 3 1/2"). One out of every 100 cards is "Wild", with a numbered stripe to indicate how many cards it can be redeemed for. There are 5, 10, 20, 50, 100, and 1,000 denominations, with the highest numbers the scarcest. Whatever the number, the card can be redeemed for that number of regular cards of the same player, after paying a redemption fee of 4.95 per order. The front design features glossy color action player photos on a black card face, with an orange frame around the picture and different color numbers in the top and right borders. The backs have different shades of purple and a color head shot, biography, and statistics. The cards are numbered on the back. At the San Francisco Card Expo (Aug. 30 to Sept. 2, 1991), promo cards of Kenny Anderson and Larry Johnson were given away. These

cards are identical to those inserted in 1991 Wild Card Collegiate football packs, except that they have the San Francisco Expo logo at the lower left corner on the back.

	MINT	NRMT	EXC
SET W/SURPRISE CARDS (120)	7.00	3.10	.85
COMMON CARD (1-120)	.04	.02	.01
☐ 1 Larry Johnson First NBA Draft Pick	.40	.18	.05
☐ 2 LeRon Ellis Syracuse	.04	.02	.01
☐ 3 Alvaro Teheran Houston	.04	.02	.01
☐ 4 Eric Murdock Providence	.25	.11	.03
☐ 5A Surprise Card 1	.04	.02	.01
☐ 5B Dikembe Mutombo Georgetown	.75	.35	.09
☐ 6 Anthony Avent Seton Hall	.04	.02	.01
☐ 7 Isiah Thomas Indiana	.20	.09	.03
☐ 8 Abdul Shamsid-Deen Providence	.04	.02	.01
☐ 9 Linton Townes James Madison	.04	.02	.01
☐ 10 Joe Wylie Miami	.04	.02	.01
☐ 11 Cozell McQueen North Carolina State	.04	.02	.01
☐ 12 David Benoit Alabama	.20	.09	.03
☐ 13 Chris Mullin St. John's	.15	.07	.02
☐ 14 Dale Davis Clemson	.40	.18	.05
☐ 15 Patrick Ewing Georgetown	.25	.11	.03
☐ 16 Greg Anthony UNLV	.10	.05	.01
☐ 17 Robert Pack USC	.30	.14	.04
☐ 18 Phil Zevenbergen Washington	.04	.02	.01
☐ 19 Rick Fox North Carolina	.10	.05	.01
☐ 20 Chris Corchiani North Carolina State	.04	.02	.01
☐ 21 Elliot Perry Memphis State	.30	.14	.04
☐ 22 Kevin Brooks SW Louisiana	.04	.02	.01
☐ 23 Mark Macon Temple	.04	.02	.01
☐ 24 Larry Johnson UNLV	1.50	.65	.19
☐ 25 George Ackles UNLV	.04	.02	.01
☐ 26A Surprise Card 5	.04	.02	.01
☐ 26B Christian Laettner (Promo) Duke	.10	.05	.01
☐ 27 Andy Fields Cheyney State	.04	.02	.01
☐ 28 Kevin Lynch Minnesota	.04	.02	.01
☐ 29 Graylin Warner SW Louisiana	.04	.02	.01
☐ 30 James Bullock	.04	.02	.01

	Purdue			
☐ 31	Steve Bucknall	.04	.02	.01
	North Carolina			
☐ 32	Carl Thomas	.04	.02	.01
	Eastern Michigan			
☐ 33	Doug Overton	.04	.02	.01
	La Salle			
☐ 34	Brian Shorter	.04	.02	.01
	Pittsburgh			
☐ 35	Chad Gallagher	.04	.02	.01
	Creighton			
☐ 36	Antonio Davis	.10	.05	.01
	Texas-El Paso			
☐ 37	Sean Green	.04	.02	.01
	Iona			
☐ 38	Randy Brown	.04	.02	.01
	New Mexico State			
☐ 39	Richard Dumas	.10	.05	.01
	Oklahoma State			
☐ 40	Terrell Brandon	.25	.11	.03
	Oregon			
☐ 41	Marty Embry	.04	.02	.01
	DePaul			
☐ 42	Ronald Coleman	.04	.02	.01
	USC			
☐ 43	King Rice	.04	.02	.01
	North Carolina			
☐ 44	Perry Carter	.04	.02	.01
	Ohio State			
☐ 45	Andrew Gaze	.04	.02	.01
☐ 46A	Surprise Card 2	.04	.02	.01
☐ 46B	Billy Owens	.50	.23	.06
	Syracuse			
☐ 47A	Surprise Card 3	.04	.02	.01
	UNLV			
☐ 47B	Stacey Augmon	.40	.18	.05
	Seton Hall			
☐ 48	Jimmy Oliver	.04	.02	.01
	Purdue			
☐ 49	Treg Lee	.04	.02	.01
	Ohio State			
☐ 50	Ricky Winslow	.04	.02	.01
	Houston			
☐ 51	Danny Vranes	.04	.02	.01
	Utah			
☐ 52	Jay Murphy	.04	.02	.01
	Boston College			
☐ 53	Adrian Dantley	.10	.05	.01
	Notre Dame			
☐ 54	Joe Arlauckas	.04	.02	.01
	Niagara University			
☐ 55	Moses Scurry	.04	.02	.01
	UNLV			
☐ 56	Andy Toolson	.04	.02	.01
	Brigham Young			
☐ 57	Ramon Rivas	.04	.02	.01
	Temple			
☐ 58	Charles Davis	.04	.02	.01
	Vanderbilt			
☐ 59	Butch Wade	.04	.02	.01
	Michigan			
☐ 60	John Pinone	.04	.02	.01
	Villanova			
☐ 61	Bill Wennington	.04	.02	.01
	St. John's			
☐ 62	Walter Berry	.04	.02	.01
	St. John's			
☐ 63	Terry Dozier	.04	.02	.01
	South Carolina			
☐ 64	Mitchell Anderson	.04	.02	.01
	Bradley			
☐ 65	Pace Mannion	.04	.02	.01
	Utah			
☐ 66	Pete Myers	.04	.02	.01
	Little Rock			
☐ 67	Eddie Lee Wilkins	.04	.02	.01
	Gardner Webb			
☐ 68	Mark Hughes	.04	.02	.01
	Michigan			
☐ 69	Darryl Dawkins	.10	.05	.01
	(No College)			
☐ 70	Jay Vincent	.04	.02	.01
	Michigan State			
☐ 71	Doug Lee	.04	.02	.01
	Purdue			
☐ 72	Russ Schoene	.04	.02	.01
	Tennessee-Chattanooga			
☐ 73	Tim Kempton	.04	.02	.01
	Notre Dame			
☐ 74	Earl Cureton	.04	.02	.01
	Detroit			
☐ 75	Terence Stansbury	.04	.02	.01
	Temple			
☐ 76	Frank Kornet	.04	.02	.01
	Vanderbilt			
☐ 77	Bob McAdoo	.10	.05	.01
	North Carolina			
☐ 78	Haywoode Workman	.04	.02	.01
	Oral Roberts			
☐ 79	Vinny Del Negro	.04	.02	.01
	North Carolina State			
☐ 80	Harold Pressley	.04	.02	.01
	Villanova			
☐ 81	Robert Smith	.04	.02	.01
	UNLV			
☐ 82	Adrian Caldwell	.04	.02	.01
	Lamar			
☐ 83	Scottie Pippen	.25	.11	.03
	Central Arkansas			
☐ 84	John Stockton	.20	.09	.03
	Gonzaga			
☐ 85	Elwayne Campbell	.04	.02	.01
	Henderson State			
☐ 86	Chris Gatling	.20	.09	.03
	Old Dominion			
☐ 87	Cedric Henderson	.04	.02	.01
	Georgia			
☐ 88	Mike Iuzzolino	.04	.02	.01
	St. Francis			
☐ 89	Fennis Dembo	.04	.02	.01
	Wyoming			
☐ 90	Darnell Valentine	.04	.02	.01
	Kansas			
☐ 91	Michael Brooks	.04	.02	.01
	LaSalle			
☐ 92	Marty Conlon	.04	.02	.01
	Providence			
☐ 93	Lamont Strothers	.04	.02	.01
	Christopher Newport			
☐ 94	Donald Hodge	.04	.02	.01
	Temple			
☐ 95	Pete Chilcutt	.04	.02	.01
	North Carolina			
☐ 96	Kenny Anderson ERR	.75	.35	.09
	(1990-87 stats)			
	Georgia Tech			
☐ 96B	Kenny Anderson COR	.75	.35	.09
	(1990-91 stats)			
	Georgia Tech			
☐ 97	Ian Lockhart	.04	.02	.01
	Tennessee			
☐ 98A	Surprise Card 4	.04	.02	.01

		MINT	NRMT	EXC
☐ 98B	Steve Smith .... Michigan State	.50	.23	.06
☐ 99	Larry Lawrence .... Dartmouth	.04	.02	.01
☐ 100	Jerome Mincy .... Alabama-Birmingham	.04	.02	.01
☐ 101	Ben Coleman .... Maryland	.04	.02	.01
☐ 102	Tom Copa .... Marquette	.04	.02	.01
☐ 103	Demetrius Calip .... Michigan	.04	.02	.01
☐ 104	Myron Brown .... Slippery Rock	.04	.02	.01
☐ 105	Derrick Pope .... Montana	.04	.02	.01
☐ 106	Kelvin Upshaw .... Utah	.04	.02	.01
☐ 107	Andrew Moten .... Florida	.04	.02	.01
☐ 108	Terry Tyler .... Detroit	.04	.02	.01
☐ 109	Kevin Magee .... Cal-Irvine	.04	.02	.01
☐ 110	Tharon Mayes .... Florida State	.04	.02	.01
☐ 111	Perry McDonald .... Georgetown	.04	.02	.01
☐ 112	Jose Ortiz .... Oregon State	.04	.02	.01
☐ 113	Rick Mahorn .... Hampton	.04	.02	.01
☐ 114	David Butler .... UNLV	.04	.02	.01
☐ 115	Carl Herrera .... Houston	.10	.05	.01
☐ 116	Darrell Mickens .... Houston	.04	.02	.01
☐ 117	Steve Bardo .... Illinois	.04	.02	.01
☐ 118	Checklist 1	.04	.02	.01
☐ 119	Checklist 2	.04	.02	.01
☐ 120	Checklist 3	.04	.02	.01

1/2"). The front design features glossy color action player photos on a black card face, with an orange frame around the picture and different color numbers in the top and right borders. The "Red Hot Rookies" emblem in the lower left corner rounds out the card face. The backs have a color close-up photo, biography, and complete college statistics. The cards are numbered on the back.

		MINT	NRMT	EXC
COMPLETE SET (10)		25.00	11.50	3.10
COMMON CARD (1-10)		.50	.23	.06
☐ 1	Dikembe Mutombo .... Georgetown	5.00	2.30	.60
☐ 2	Larry Johnson .... UNLV	10.00	4.50	1.25
☐ 3	Steve Smith .... Michigan State	3.00	1.35	.40
☐ 4	Billy Owens .... Syracuse	3.00	1.35	.40
☐ 5	Mark Macon .... Temple	.50	.23	.06
☐ 6	Stacey Augmon UER ...... UNLV	2.50	1.15	.30
☐ 7	Victor Alexander .... Iowa State	.50	.23	.06
☐ 8	Mike Iuzzolino .... St. Francis	.50	.23	.06
☐ 9	Rick Fox .... North Carolina	.50	.23	.06
☐ 10	Terrell Brandon UER .... Oregon (Name misspelled Terrel on card front)	1.00	.45	.13

1991-92 Wild Card Red Hot Rookies

These cards were randomly packed in the Collegiate Basketball foil cases, and they included denomination cards. The cards measure the standard size (2 1/2" by 3

1991-92 Wild Card Redemption Prototypes

This six-card standard-size (2 1/2" by 3 1/2") set was intended to preview the forth-coming Wild Card basketball set. By sending in a surprise card from the 1991-92 Wild Card Collegiate set, the collector received a cello pack consisting of a replacement card and two redemption proto-type cards. The fronts feature color action player photos with white borders and colored numbers suspended in the top and right borders. The backs feature a color headshot, biography, and statistics. The cards are numbered on the back with a "P" prefix.

	MINT	NRMT	EXC
COMPLETE SET (6)	2.00	.80	.20
COMMON CARD (P1-P6)	.12	.05	.01
☐ P1 LaPhonso Ellis Notre Dame	.90	.36	.09
☐ P2 Adam Keefe Stanford	.12	.05	.01
☐ P3 Robert Horry Alabama	.90	.36	.09
☐ P4 Bryant Stith Virginia	.50	.20	.05
☐ P5 Christian Laettner Duke	.60	.24	.06
☐ P6 Malik Sealy St. John's	.15	.06	.01

1995 Ted Williams

The 1994 Ted Williams Draft Pick set consists of 90 standard-size cards, featuring key 1994 draft picks and second-year standouts. 2,999 cases were produced. This set was issued as a sub-license of Classic. These cards were sold in 8-card packs, and each 24-pack box contained either one signature card or a hot pack, which had all inserts. The fronts feature the player's last name in the middle left with the Ted Williams logo in the upper left corner and a silhouette of a basketball player in the lower left side of the card. The backs feature biographical information along with collegiate statistics and a player profile. The first eighty cards are arranged in alphabetical order. The set closes with a Flashback (80-88) subset and checklist cards (89-90).

	MINT	NRMT	EXC
COMPLETE SET (90)	10.00	4.50	1.25
COMMON CARD (1-90)	.05	.02	.01
☐ 1 Derrick Alston Duquesne	.05	.02	.01
☐ 2 Adrian Autry	.05	.02	.01

Syracuse			
☐ 3 Damon Bailey Indiana	.20	.09	.03
☐ 4 Doremus Bennerman Siena	.05	.02	.01
☐ 5 Randy Blocker Northern Iowa	.05	.02	.01
☐ 6 Melvin Booker Missouri	.05	.02	.01
☐ 7 Jamie Brandon LSU	.05	.02	.01
☐ 8 Barry Brown UER Jacksonville (Joey Brown pictured on card)	.05	.02	.01
☐ 9 Joey Brown UER Georgetown (Barry Brown pictured on card)	.05	.02	.01
☐ 10 Albert Burditt Texas	.05	.02	.01
☐ 11 Robert Churchwell Georgetown	.05	.02	.01
☐ 12 Gary Collier Tulsa	.05	.02	.01
☐ 13 Jevon Crudup Missouri	.05	.02	.01
☐ 14 Bill Curley Boston College	.05	.02	.01
☐ 15 Yinka Dare George Washignton	.05	.02	.01
☐ 16 Rodney Dent Kentucky	.05	.02	.01
☐ 17 Tony Dumas Missouri-Kansas City	.15	.07	.02
☐ 18 Howard Eisley Boston College	.15	.07	.02
☐ 19 Andrei Fetisov Forum Valladolid	.05	.02	.01
☐ 20 Travis Ford Kentucky	.05	.02	.01
☐ 21 Abdul Fox Rhode Island	.05	.02	.01
☐ 22 Lawrence Funderburke Ohio State	.05	.02	.01
☐ 23 Anthony Goldwire Houston	.05	.02	.01
☐ 24 Chuck Graham Florida State	.05	.02	.01
☐ 25 Brian Grant Xavier	.75	.35	.09
☐ 26 Thomas Hamilton Martin Luther King Jr. High School--Chicago	.05	.02	.01
☐ 27 Darrin Hancock Kansas	.05	.02	.01
☐ 28 Carl Ray Harris Fresno State	.05	.02	.01
☐ 29 Askia Jones Kansas State	.05	.02	.01
☐ 30 Eddie Jones Temple	1.00	.45	.13
☐ 31 Arturas Karnishovas Seton Hall	.05	.02	.01
☐ 32 Damon Key Marquette	.05	.02	.01
☐ 33 Jason Kidd California	2.00	.90	.25
☐ 34 Antonio Lang Duke	.05	.02	.01
☐ 35 Donyell Marshall	.75	.35	.09

	Connecticut		
☐ 36	Bill McCaffrey .05	.02	.01
	Vanderbilt		
☐ 37	Jim McIlvaine .05	.02	.01
	Marquette		
☐ 38	Aaron McKie .15	.07	.02
	Temple		
☐ 39	Anthony Miller .05	.02	.01
	Michigan State		
☐ 40	Greg Minor .25	.11	.03
	Louisville		
☐ 41	Eric Mobley .05	.02	.01
	Pittsburgh		
☐ 42	Eric Montross .50	.23	.06
	North Carolina		
☐ 43	Harry Moore .05	.02	.01
	St. Bonaventure		
☐ 44	Dwayne Morton .05	.02	.01
	Louisville		
☐ 45	Gaylon Nickerson .05	.02	.01
	Northwestern Oklahoma		
☐ 46	Cornell Parker .05	.02	.01
	Virginia		
☐ 47	Wesley Person .50	.23	.06
	Auburn		
☐ 48	Derrick Phelps .05	.02	.01
	North Carolina		
☐ 49	Eric Piatkowski .15	.07	.02
	Nebraska		
☐ 50	Kevin Rankin .05	.02	.01
	Northwestern		
☐ 51	Brian Reese .05	.02	.01
	North Carolina		
☐ 52	Khalid Reeves .50	.23	.06
	Arizona		
☐ 53	Clayton Ritter .05	.02	.01
	James Madison		
☐ 54	Carlos Rogers .30	.14	.04
	Tennessee State		
☐ 55	Jalen Rose .50	.23	.06
	Michigan		
☐ 56	Clifford Rozier .25	.11	.03
	Louisville		
☐ 57	Kevin Salvadori .05	.02	.01
	North Carolina		
☐ 58	Jervaughn Scales .05	.02	.01
	Southern		
☐ 59	Shawnelle Scott .05	.02	.01
	St. John's		
☐ 60	Robert Shannon .05	.02	.01
	Alabam-Birmingham		
☐ 61	Melvin Simon .05	.02	.01
	New Orleans		
☐ 62	Dickey Simpkins .20	.09	.03
	Providence		
☐ 63	Michael Smith .30	.14	.04
	Providence		
☐ 64	Stevin Smith .05	.02	.01
	Arizona State		
☐ 65	Byron Starks .05	.02	.01
	Southwestern Louisiana		
☐ 66	Aaron Swinson .05	.02	.01
	Auburn		
☐ 67	Shon Tarver .05	.02	.01
	UCLA		
☐ 68	Deon Thomas .05	.02	.01
	Illinois		
☐ 69	Brooks Thompson .05	.02	.01
	Oklahoma State		
☐ 70	B.J. Tyler .15	.07	.02
	Texas		

☐ 71	Myron Walker .05	.02	.01
	Robert Morris		
☐ 72	Charlie Ward .20	.09	.03
	Florida State		
☐ 73	Kendrick Warren .05	.02	.01
	Virginia Commonwealth		
☐ 74	Jamie Watson .05	.02	.01
	South Carolina		
☐ 75	Jeff Webster .05	.02	.01
	Oklahoma		
☐ 76	Tracy Webster .05	.02	.01
	Wisconsin		
☐ 77	Monty Williams .05	.02	.01
	Notre Dame		
☐ 78	Dontonio Wingfield .05	.02	.01
	Cincinnati		
☐ 79	Steve Woodberry .05	.02	.01
	Kansas		
☐ 80	Charles Barkley FB .40	.18	.05
	Auburn		
☐ 81	Larry Bird FB .50	.23	.06
	Indiana State		
☐ 82	Anfernee Hardaway FB .30	.14	.04
	Memphis State		
☐ 83	Jamal Mashburn FB .25	.11	.03
	Kentucky		
☐ 84	Chris Mills FB .05	.02	.01
	Arizona		
☐ 85	Harold Miner FB .05	.02	.01
	USC		
☐ 86	Alonzo Mourning FB .20	.09	.03
	Georgetown		
☐ 87	Dikembe Mutombo FB .05	.02	.01
	Georgetown		
☐ 88	Rodney Rogers FB .05	.02	.01
	Wake Forest		
☐ 89	Checklist (1-45) .05	.02	.01
☐ 90	Checklist (46-90) .05	.02	.01

1995 Ted Williams Kareem Abdul Jabbar

These 9 standard-size cards were randomly inserted at a rate of one in every sixteen mass retail packs. The fronts feature full-bleed color action photos, with the player's name in a stripe across the bottom. On a cloudy sky background, the backs describe various highlights from his career. The

cards are numbered in small gold letters directly under the player's name.

	MINT	NRMT	EXC
COMPLETE SET (9)	18.00	8.00	2.30
COMMON KAREEM (KAJ1-KAJ9)	2.00	.90	.25
☐ KAJ1 A Legend is Born	2.00	.90	.25
☐ KAJ2 Hot Prospect	2.00	.90	.25
☐ KAJ3 Milwaukee's Best	2.00	.90	.25
☐ KAJ4 On to Los Angeles	2.00	.90	.25
☐ KAJ5 The Greatest Ever?	2.00	.90	.25
☐ KAJ6 Number 33	2.00	.90	.25
☐ KAJ7 Life After Basketball	2.00	.90	.25
☐ KAJ8 Hello Hollywood!	2.00	.90	.25
☐ KAJ9 Checklist	2.00	.90	.25

1995 Ted Williams Constellation

Randomly inserted in foil packs, this 9-card standard-size set consists of cards from the main set as well as the insert sets. Each card sports the distinctive design of the card series to which it belongs. They differ only in their consecutive numbering C1-C9 on the back.

	MINT	NRMT	EXC
COMPLETE SET (9)	25.00	11.50	3.10
COMMON CARD (C1-C9)	2.00	.90	.25
☐ C1 Kareem Abdul-Jabbar	3.00	1.35	.40
☐ C2 Charles Barkley	2.50	1.15	.30
☐ C3 Larry Bird	6.00	2.70	.75
☐ C4 Anfernee Hardaway	2.00	.90	.25
☐ C5 Juwan Howard	2.50	1.15	.30
☐ C6 Jason Kidd	5.00	2.30	.60
☐ C7 George Mikan	2.00	.90	.25
☐ C8 Alonzo Mourning	2.00	.90	.25
☐ C9 Glenn Robinson	5.00	2.30	.60

1995 Ted Williams Co-op

This 9-card standard-size set was randomly inserted at a rate of one in every twelve

packs. This set spotlights both NBA superstars (active and retired) and rookies. The fronts feature the player highlighted against a dotted background. The player's name is on the left side of the card. The Ted Williams logo is in the upper left corner while the Classic logo is in the upper right corner. The back carries biography and a player photo.

	MINT	NRMT	EXC
COMPLETE SET (9)	18.00	8.00	2.30
COMMON CARD (CO1-CO9)	1.00	.45	.13
☐ CO1 Charles Barkley	2.50	1.15	.30
☐ CO2 Larry Bird	4.00	1.80	.50
☐ CO3 Anfernee Hardaway	1.50	.65	.19
☐ CO4 Grant Hill	5.00	2.30	.60
☐ CO5 Jason Kidd	4.00	1.80	.50
☐ CO6 Pete Maravich	1.50	.65	.19
☐ CO7 Alonzo Mourning	1.00	.45	.13
☐ CO8 Glenn Robinson	4.00	1.80	.50
☐ CO9 Checklist	1.00	.45	.13

1995 Ted Williams Eclipse

Randomly inserted at a rate of one in every twelve packs, this 9-card standard-size set features NBA legends. The cards show the players in air-brushed professional uniforms with the word "Eclipse" in large red letters on the bottom and the player's name immediately below. The backs carry biographical information. The cards are unnumbered and checklisted below in alphabetical order.

	MINT	NRMT	EXC
COMPLETE SET (9)	12.00	5.50	1.50
COMMON CARD (EC1-EC9)	1.00	.45	.13
☐ EC1 Rick Barry	1.50	.65	.19
☐ EC2 Larry Bird	3.00	1.35	.40
☐ EC3 Bob Pettit	1.50	.65	.19
☐ EC4 Hal Greer	1.00	.45	.13
☐ EC5 Kareem Abdul-Jabbar	1.50	.65	.19
☐ EC6 Pete Maravich	1.50	.65	.19
☐ EC7 George Mikan	2.00	.90	.25
☐ EC8 Dolph Schayes	1.00	.45	.13
☐ EC9 Checklist	1.00	.45	.13

1995 Ted Williams Gallery

This nine-card standard-size set was randomly inserted at a rate of one in every sixteen packs. The fronts feature a drawing of each player, with both a head-and-shoulder and an action drawing of each player. In the bottom left corner are the words "The Gallery." The backs provide biographical information about the player as well as a blurb about the player in the professional ranks. The cards are numbered in the upper left corner and sequentially numbered at the bottom middle.

	MINT	NRMT	EXC
COMPLETE SET (9)	20.00	9.00	2.50
COMMON CARD (G1-G9)	1.50	.65	.19
☐ G1 Charles Barkley	4.00	1.80	.50
☐ G2 Larry Bird	6.00	2.70	.75
☐ G3 Kareem Abdul-Jabbar	3.00	1.35	.40
☐ G4 Walt Frazier	2.00	.90	.25
☐ G5 Anfernee Hardaway	3.00	1.35	.40
☐ G6 Jamal Mashburn	2.50	1.15	.30
☐ G7 Alonzo Mourning	2.00	.90	.25
☐ G8 Dikembe Mutombo	1.50	.65	.19
☐ G9 Checklist	1.50	.65	.19

1995 Ted Williams Hardwood Legends

This 9-card standard-size set of retired basketball greats as selected by Larry Bird was

randomly inserted at a rate of one in every eight regional hobby packs. This set features outstanding duos from New York (1-2), Golden State (3-4), Chicago (5-6), and Boston (7-8). The fronts feature the player in action in airbrushed uniforms while the backs feature biographical information as well as a informational blurb about the player.

	MINT	NRMT	EXC
COMPLETE SET (9)	6.00	2.70	.75
COMMON CARD (HL1-HL9)	.60	.25	.08
☐ HL1 Walt Frazier	1.00	.45	.13
☐ HL2 Dave DeBusschere	.75	.35	.09
☐ HL3 Rick Barry	1.00	.45	.13
☐ HL4 Nate Thurmond	.60	.25	.08
☐ HL5 Artis Gilmore	.60	.25	.08
☐ HL6 Norm Van Lier	.60	.25	.08
☐ HL7 Bill Sharman	.75	.35	.09
☐ HL8 Jo Jo White	.60	.25	.08
☐ HL9 Checklist	.60	.25	.08

1995 Ted Williams Royal Court

This 9-card standard-size set was randomly inserted into packs at a rate of one in every twelve packs. This set features some of Charles Barkley's favorite players. The fronts contains a full-color action photo of the player with the Ted Williams Logo in the upper left corner, the player's name in yellow lettering down the left side and a Royal Court of Charles logo in the bottom right corner. The backs present biography and

on the right side a sword with the name of the player printed on it.

	MINT	NRMT	EXC
COMPLETE SET (9)	10.00	4.50	1.25
COMMON CARD (RC1-RC9)	.60	.25	.08
☐ RC1 Anfernee Hardaway ...	1.50	.65	.19
☐ RC2 Harold Miner	.60	.25	.08
☐ RC3 Jason Kidd	5.00	2.30	.60
☐ RC4 Donyell Marshall	2.00	.90	.25
☐ RC5 Jamal Mashburn	1.25	.55	.16
☐ RC6 Juwan Howard	2.50	1.15	.30
☐ RC7 Alonzo Mourning	1.00	.45	.13
☐ RC8 Aaron Swinson	.60	.25	.08
☐ RC9 Checklist	.60	.25	.08

Williams logo while the What's Up logo is in the lower left corner of the card. The name of the player is printed in white in the bottom right corner of the card.

1995 Ted Williams What's Up

This 12-card standard-size set was randomly inserted at a rate of one in every twelve packs. This set featured some of the star attractions of the 94-5 NBA Rookie Class. The fronts feature a full-bleed player photo. In the upper left corner is the Ted

	MINT	NRMT	EXC
COMPLETE SET (9)	10.00	4.50	1.25
COMMON CARD (WU1-WU9)	.75	.35	.09
☐ WU1 Brian Grant	2.00	.90	.25
☐ WU2 Eric Montross	1.50	.65	.19
☐ WU3 Jason Kidd	4.00	1.80	.50
☐ WU4 Anthony Miller	.75	.35	.09
☐ WU5 Khalid Reeves	1.25	.55	.16
☐ WU6 Carlos Rogers	.90	.40	.11
☐ WU7 Jalen Rose	1.25	.55	.16
☐ WU8 Charlie Ward	.75	.35	.09
☐ WU9 Checklist	.75	.35	.09

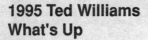

Acknowledgments

A great deal of diligence, hard work, and dedicated effort went into this year's volume. The high standards to which we hold ourselves, however, could not have been met without the expert input and generous amount of time contributed by many people. Our sincere thanks are extended to each and every one of you.

Each year we refine the process of developing the most accurate and up-to-date information for this book. I believe this year's Price Guide is our best yet. Thanks again to all of the contributors nationwide (listed below) as well as our staff here in Dallas.

Those who have worked closely with us on this and many other books, have again proven themselves invaluable in every aspect of producing this book: Rich Altman, Randy Archer, Mike Aronstein, Jerry Bell, Chris Benjamin, Mike Blaisdell, Bill Bossert (Mid-Atlantic Coin Exchange), Classic (Ken Goldin and Mark Pokedoff), Todd Crosner (California Sportscard Exchange), Bud Darland, Bill and Diane Dodge, Rick Donohoo, Willie Erving, Fleer/SkyBox International (Doug Drotman and Ted Taylor), Gervise Ford, Steve Freedman, Larry and Jeff Fritsch, Jim Galusha, Dick Gariepy, Dick Gilkeson, Mike and Howard Gordon, Sally Grace, George Grauer, John Greenwald, Wayne Grove, Bill Haber, George Henn, Mike Hersh, John Inouye, Steven L. Judd, Edward J. Kabala, Judy and Norman Kay, Robert Levin (The Star Company), Lew Lipset, Dave Lucey, Paul Marchant, Brian Marcy (Scottsdale Baseball Cards), Dr. John McCue, Mike Mosier (Columbia City Collectibles Co.), Clark Muldavin, B.A. Murry, Pacific Trading Cards (Mike Cramer and Bob Wilke), Earl N. Petersen (U.S.A. Coins), Pinnacle (Laurie Goldberg), Jack Pollard, Jonathan Pullano, Tom Reid, Henry M. Reizes, Gavin Riley, Alan Rosen (Mr. Mint), Rotman Productions, John Rumierz, San Diego Sport Collectibles (Bill Goepner and Nacho Arredondo), Kevin Savage (Sports Gallery), Mike Schechter (MSA), Dan Sherlock, Bill Shonscheck, Glen J. Sidler, John Spalding, Spanky's, Nigel Spill (Oldies and Goodies), Sports Collectors Store (Pat Quinn and Don Steinbach), Frank Steele, Murvin Sterling, Dan Stickney, Steve Taft, Ed Taylor, Lee Temanson, Topps (Marty Appel, Sy Berger and Melissa Rosen), Upper Deck (Rich Bradley), Bill Vizas, Bill Wesslund (Portland Sports Card Co.), Jim Woods, Kit Young, Robert Zanze, and Bill Zimpleman.

Many other individuals have provided price input, illustrative material, checklist verifications, errata, and/or background information. At the risk of inadvertently overlooking or omitting these many contributors, we should like to personally thank Joseph A. Abram, Jerry Adamic, Tom Akins, Anthony Amada Jr., Dennis Anderson, Ellis Anmuth, Toni Axtell, Darryl B. Baker, Earle Baldwin, Baseball Cards Plus, Baseball Hobby News (Frank and Vivian Barning), William E. Baxendale, Bay State Cards (Lenny DeAngelico), John Beaman, Glen Beram (Lakeside National Cards, Inc.), Philip Berg, Carl Bergstrom, Beulah Sports, Brian Bigelow (Candl), Walter Bird, Theodore Bodnar, Keith and Ryan Bonner, Gary Boyd, Dan Brandenburg, Briggs Sportscards, Fritz Brogan, Douglas J. Brown (Doug's Dugout), George and Donald Brown, Jason Brown, Dan Bruner (The Card King), Bob Bubnick, Buckhead Baseball Cards (Marc Spector), Terry L. Bunt, Virgil Burns, California Card Co., David Cadelina, Mark Cantin, Danny Cariseo, Cee Tim's Cards, N. Garrett Chan (The Greatest Moment), Dwight Chapin, Philip L. Chapman, Manfred Chiu, Judy Chung (The Sportsman's Gallery), Michael Chung, Shane Cohen (Grand Slam), Barry Colla, Collectors Edge, Matt Collett, Jose E. Conde, H. William Cook, Joe Court, Steve Crane, Rob Croft,

Robert Curtis, Herb Dallas Jr., David Diehl, Byron Dittamore, Bill Dodson, Cliff Dolgins, Discount Dorothy, Robin Doty, Eagle Collectibles, Ed Emmitt, Mark Enger, Tom England, Michael Estreicher, Karen Eudaley, Gary Farbstein, L.V. Fischer (The Collectors Den), G.E. Forst, Steve Foster, Mark Franke, Doug French, Rob Gagnon, Steve Galletta, Tony Galovich, Ron Gerencher, Michael R. Gionet, Steve Gold (AU Sports), Jeff Goldstein, Mark Goodman, Arthur Goyette, Gary W. Graber (Minden Games), David Grauf (Cards for the Connoisseur), Don Guilbert, Hall's Nostalgia, Monty Hamilton, Wynn Hansen, Lenny Helicher, Bill Henderson, Jerry and Etta Hersh, Clay Hill, Alisa Hills, H.L.T. and T. Sports (Harold and Todd Nelkin), Will Ho, Russell Hoffman, Home Plate of Provo (Ken Edick), Chris Hooper, James R. Hopper III, Keith Hora, Gene Horvath, Steve Johnson, Barbara-Lee Jordan, James Jordan (Squeeze Play), Jay and Mary Kasper, Alan Kaye, Koinz and Kardz, George Koziol, Roger Krafve, Thomas Kunnecke, Tim Landis, William Langley, Ted Larkins (The Card Clubhouse), Dan Lavin, John Law, Stephen M. Lawson, Henry Lee, Irv Lerner, Howie Levy, Scott Lewandowski, Kendall Loyd (Orlando Sportscards South), Brian Luther, Jim Macie, Ben Macre, Jack Maiden, Larry Marks, Robert Matonis, Jack Mayes, Mike McDonald (Sports Page), Brad McNail (ACCI Sports Cards), James McNaughton, Patrick Menasche, Blake Meyer, Deron Milligan, Pat Mills, Ronald Moermond, J.L. Montgomery Inc. (Colorado Cards), William Moorhead, Joe Morano, Michael Moretto, Brian Morris, John G. Most, Jeff Mowers, Randy Munn, Michael J. Nadeau, Dr. Richard Neel, Robert Neff, No Gum Just Cards, Lon J. Normandin, Efrain Ochoa, John O'Hara, G. Michael Oyster, Russ Palmer, Ed Parkin (Home Front), Clay Pasternack, Bill Pekarik (Pastime Hobbies), Daren Pelletier, Richard Pellizzer, G.N. Perkins (Illini Sportscards), Michael Petruso, Tom Pfirrmann, Wesley Philpott, Roger Porter, Adam Price, Lee Prince (Time Out Sports Shop), Randy Ramuglia, Richard H. Ranck, Phil Regli, David Renshaw, Rocky Mountain Sports Cards, Chuck Roethel, Terry Sack, Joe Sak, Dale A. Sakamoto, Jennifer Salems, Garret Salomon, Ron Sanders, Ray Sandlin, Bob Santos, Guy Scebat, Nathan Schank, Jason Schubert, Sebring Sports, Steven Senft, Rob Shilt, Greg Sholes (Hall of Fame Sportscards), Ryan Shrimplin, Darrin Silverman, Tom Skinner, Ron Smith, Steve Smith (Sports Memories, Inc.), David Snider, Bob Snyder, Carl Specht, Sports Legends, Paul M. Stefani, Allen Stengel (Perfect Image), Cary Stephenson, Arnold Stern, Rao Tadikonda, George Tahinos, Mark Tanaka (Front Row), Chad Taniguchi, Chris Tateosian, Paul S. Taylor, Steve Taylor, Harold Teller, Nick Teresi, Bud Tompkins (Minnesota Connection), Felix F. Torres (Ponce Card & Memorabilia), Huy Tran, Jeffrey K. Tsai, Peter Tsang, Carlo Tulloch, University Trading Cards (Mike Livingston), Mark Velger (Trade Mark SportsCards), Steve Verkman (Baseball Cards & Sports Memorabilia), Adam Wandy, Howard Weissman, Adam B. Weldaz, Richard West, Paul Wetterau, Brian Wilkie, Ali Raza Williams, Jeff Williams, Mark Williams, Opry Winston, Matt Winters, John L. Witcher, Mike Woods (The Dugout), World Series Cards (Neil Armstrong), Scot York, Zards Cards, Dean Zindler, and Adam Zuwerink.

Every year we make active solicitations for expert input. We are particularly appreciative of the help (however extensive or cursory) provided for this volume. We receive many inquiries, comments and questions regarding material within this book. In fact, each and every one is read and digested. Time constraints, however, prevent us from personally replying. But keep sharing your knowledge. Your letters and input are part of the "big picture" of hobby information we can pass along to readers of our books and magazines. Even though we cannot respond to each letter, you are making significant contributions to the hobby through your interest and comments.

The effort to continually refine and improve this book also involves a growing number of people and types of expertise on our home team. Our company boasts a substantial Technical Services team, which strengthens our ability to provide comprehensive analysis of the marketplace. Technical Services capably handled numerous technical details and provided able assistance in the preparation of this edition.

Our basketball analysts played a major part in compiling this year's book, travelling thousands of miles during the past year to attend sports card shows and visit card shops around the United States and Canada. The Beckett basketball specialists are Theo Chen (Assistant Manager, Hobby Information), Mike Jaspersen (Product Information Coordinator) and Grant Sandground (Assistant Manager, Pricing Analysis). Their baseline analysis and careful proofreading were key contributions to the accuracy of this annual.

Grant Sandground's coordination of input as *Beckett Basketball Monthly* title analyst helped immeasurably, as did Rich Klein's encyclopedic knowledge and meticulous attention to detail. Tom Layberger also contributed many hours of painstaking analysis in his specialist role and was assisted by Randy Barning.

The effort was led by Director of Technical Services Jay Johnson. He was ably assisted by the rest of the Price Guide analysts: Pat Blandford, Ben Ecklar, Eddie Kelly, Allan Muir and Dave Sliepka. Also contributing to Technical Services functions were Gabriel Rangel, Steve Smith and Rob Springs.

The price gathering and analytical talents of this fine group of hobbyists have helped make our Beckett team stronger, while making this guide and its companion monthly Price Guide more widely recognized as the hobby's most reliable and relied upon sources of pricing information.

Scott Layton, assistant manager of Database Production, was a key person in the organization of both technological and people resources for the book. He set up initial schedules and ensured that all deadlines were met, while looking for all the fine points to improve our process and presentation throughout the cycle. He was ably assisted by Jeany Finch and Beverly Mills, who entered new sets, ensured the proper administration of our contributor Price Guide surveys and performed various other tasks.

The Information Services department, ably headed by Mark Harwell, again played a crucial role in technology. Rich Olivieri spent countless hours programming, testing and implementing it to simplify the handling of thousands of prices that must be checked and updated for each section.

In the Production department, Paul Kerutis supervised the formatting and card illustration of the price guide. He was ably assisted by Rob Barry, Belinda Cross and Mary Gonzalez-Davis. Lisa O'Neill was responsible for formatting the introductory material.

Loretta Gibbs spent tireless hours on the phone attending to the wishes of our dealer advertisers. Once the ad specifications were delivered to our offices, Dawn Ciaccio used her computer skills to turn raw copy into attractive display advertisements.

In the years since this guide debuted, Beckett Publications has grown beyond any rational expectation. A great many talented and hard working individuals have been instrumental in this growth and success. Our whole team is to be congratulated for what we together have accomplished. Our Beckett Publications team is led by Vice Presidents Jeff Amano, Joe Galindo and Fred Reed, Director of Finance Claire Backus, Directors Mark Harwell and Jay Johnson, and Senior Managers Beth Harwell, Pepper Hastings and Reed Poole. They are ably assisted by Dana Alecknavage, Theresa Anderson, Jeff Anthony, Kelly Atkins, Kaye Ball, Airey Baringer, Barbara Barry, James R. Beane, Therese Bellar, Louise Bird, Cathryn Black, Amy Brougher, Bob Brown, Chris Calandro, Randall Calvert, Emily Camp, Mary Campana, Susan Catka, Jud Chappell, Albert Chavez, Cindy Cockroft, Laura Corley, Randy Cummings, Patrick Cunningham, Marlon DePaula, Marcelo Gomez DeSouza, Gail Docekal, Paulo Egusquiza, Eric Evans, Craig Ferris, Gean Paul Figari, Jeany Finch, Kim Ford, Gayle Gasperin, Rosanna Gonzalez-Olaechea, Jeff Greer, Mary Gregory, Jenifer Grellhesl, Julie Grove, Leslie Harris, Joanna Hayden, Chris Hellem, Tracy Hinton, E.J. Hradek, Julia Jernigan, Wendy Kizer, Rudy Klancnik, Frances Knight, Jane Ann Layton, Sara Leeman, Benedito Leme, Lori Lindsey, Stanley Lira, Lisa Lujan, Sara Maneval, Louis Marroquin, Mike McAllister, Omar Mediano, Lisa McQuilkin Monaghan, Sherry Monday, Rob Moore, Mila Morante, Daniel Moscoso Jr., Mike Moss, Randy Mosty, Hugh Murphy, Shawn Murphy, Steve Naughton, Stacy Olivieri, Mike Pagel, Wendy Pallugna, Laura Patterson, Mike Payne, Diego Picon, Tim Polzer, Fran Poole, Bob Richardson, Tina Riojas, Susan Sainz, Gary Santaniello, Elaine Simmons, Judi Smalling, Sheri Smith, Jeff Stanton, Margaret Steele, Marcia Stoesz, Doree Tate, Jim Tereschuk, Lawrence Treachler, Carol Weaver, Steve Wilson and Mark Zeske. The whole Beckett Publications team has my thanks for jobs well done. Thank you, everyone.

I also thank my family, especially my wife, Patti, and our daughters, Christina, Rebecca, and Melissa, for putting up with me again.

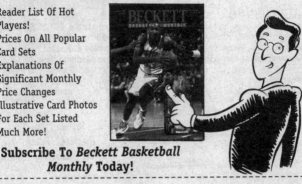